T0324141

Routledge Handbook of Cultural Sociology

The thoroughly revised and updated second edition of the *Routledge Handbook of Cultural Sociology* provides an unparalleled overview of sociological and related scholarship on the complex relations of culture to social structures and everyday life. With 70 essays written by scholars from around the world, the book brings diverse approaches into dialogue, charting new pathways for understanding culture in our global era.

Short, accessible chapters by contributing authors address classic questions, emergent issues, and new scholarship on topics ranging from cultural and social theory to politics and the state, social stratification, identity, community, aesthetics, and social and cultural movements. In addition, contributors explore developments central to the constitution and reproduction of culture, such as power, technology, and the organization of work.

This handbook is essential reading for undergraduate and postgraduate students interested in a wide range of subfields within sociology, as well as cultural studies, media and communication, and postcolonial theory.

Laura Grindstaff is Professor of Sociology at the University of California, Davis, and a faculty affiliate in Gender Studies, Performance Studies, and Cultural Studies. Her research and teaching focus on the cultural dimensions of sex/gender, race, and class inequality, with a particular emphasis on American media and popular culture. She is the author of *The Money Shot: Trash, Class, and the Making of TV Talk Shows* as well as numerous articles and essays on aspects of popular culture ranging from sports and cheerleading to reality TV and social media.

Ming-Cheng M. Lo is Professor of Sociology at the University of California, Davis. Lo's research focuses on culture, illness experiences, and civic engagement. She is the author of *Doctors within Borders: Profession, Ethnicity, and Modernity in Colonial Taiwan* (University of California Press, 2002; Japanese edition, 2014). A recent series of articles addresses the roles of cultural capital and non-dominant cultural resources in health, healthcare, and environmental justice activism.

John R. Hall is Research Professor of Sociology at the University of California, Santa Cruz and Davis. His published works include *Apocalypse: From Antiquity to the Empire of Modernity* (Polity, 2009), *Visual Worlds* (Routledge, 2005, with co-editors), *Sociology on Culture* (Routledge, 2003, with co-authors), and *Cultures of Inquiry* (Cambridge University Press, 1999).

Routledge International Handbooks

For more information about this series, please visit: www.routledge.com/
Routledge-International-Handbooks/book-series/RIHAND

Routledge Handbook of Cultural Sociology

Second Edition

Edited by Laura Grindstaff,
Ming-Cheng M. Lo, and John R. Hall

Routledge
Taylor & Francis Group

LONDON AND NEW YORK

Second edition published 2019
by Routledge
2 Park Square, Milton Park, Abingdon, Oxon, OX14 4RN

and by Routledge
605 Third Avenue, New York, NY 10017

First issued in paperback 2020

Routledge is an imprint of the Taylor & Francis Group, an informa business

First edition published by Routledge 2010

British Library Cataloguing-in-Publication Data
A catalogue record for this book is available from the British Library

Library of Congress Cataloging-in-Publication Data
Names: Grindstaff, Laura, editor. | Lo, Ming-cheng Miriam, editor. | Hall, John R., editor.
Title: Routledge handbook of cultural sociology / edited by Laura Grindstaff, Ming-Cheng Lo, John R. Hall. Other titles: Handbook of cultural sociology.
Description: Second edition. | Abingdon, Oxon ; New York, NY : Routledge, 2019. | Series: Routledge international handbooks | Earlier edition published as: Handbook of cultural sociology. | Includes bibliographical references.
Identifiers: LCCN 2018029465 | ISBN 9781138288621 (hardback) | ISBN 9781315267784 (ebook)
Subjects: LCSH: Culture.
Classification: LCC HM621 .H344 2019 | DDC 306—dc23
LC record available at https://lccn.loc.gov/2018029465

Typeset in Bembo
by Apex CoVantage, LLC

ISBN 13: 978-0-367-73284-4 (pbk)
ISBN 13: 978-1-138-28862-1 (hbk)

Contents

Contents

Contents

Contributors

Jeffrey C. Alexander is the Lillian Chavenson Saden Professor of Sociology at Yale University, founder and co-director of Yale's Center for Cultural Sociology, and co-editor of the *American Journal of Cultural Sociology*. Among his recent publications are *The Drama of Social Life* (2017), *The Dark Side of Modernity* (2013), *Trauma: A Social Theory* (2012), and *The Performance of Politics: Obama's Victory and the Democratic Struggle for Power* (2010). With Carlo Tognato, he edited *The Civil Sphere in Latin America* (2018).

Victoria D. Alexander (AB, Princeton; AM, PhD, Stanford) is Senior Lecturer of Arts Management at Goldsmiths, University of London. Her research falls in the intersection of sociologies of the arts, visual culture, organizations, and culture. She has studied art museums, arts policy, sociology of the arts, neighborhoods, and visual sociology. Her books include *Sociology of the Arts*; *Museums and Money*; *Art and the State* (co-authored); and *Art and the Challenge of Markets* (co-edited).

Sarah S. Amsler is Associate Professor in Education in the School of Education at the University of Nottingham. She has recently published *The Education of Radical Democracy* and a number of papers on the politics of knowledge and education in anti-capitalist and autonomous social movements. She is currently working on projects about "learning and organizing hope," pedagogies of critical anticipation, and the role of onto-epistemic learning in radical social transformation.

Lucas Azambuja is a graduate student of sociology at Stony Brook University. He is currently working toward his dissertation on elites, the state, and democratic transition in Brazil and Portugal.

Zeke Baker received his PhD in sociology at the University of California, Davis. His dissertation investigates the relationship between climate knowledge and government in the US from the late eighteenth century until recent decades. He also studies the use of climate information among water managers and national security experts in the US. Recent articles include "Climate State" (in *Social Studies of Science*), "Meteorological Frontiers" (in *Social Science History*) and "Climate Information?" (in *Environmental Sociology*).

Marshall Battani is Professor of Sociology at Grand Valley State University, Michigan. His primary research interests are in photography, aesthetics, and social theory. His publications include "Photography's Decline into Modernism" (2005), "Aura, Self, and Aesthetic Experience" (2011), and "Atrocity Aesthetics" (2011). His current work uses Weberian ideal typologies in analyzing emerging aesthetics of terrorism.

Zygmunt Bauman was Emeritus Professor of Sociology, University of Leeds, when he died on January 9, 2017. His last books include *Living on Borrowed Times* (2009), *44 Letters from the Liquid Modern World* (2010), and *Retrotopia* (2017).

Peter Beilharz is Research Professor of Culture and Society at Curtin University, Western Australia. Recent publications include *The Martin Presence* and *Thinking the Antipodes*, both published in 2014. He is working on books of essays on Marx, on Gramsci, and on a farewell book for Zygmunt Bauman.

Tony Bennett is Research Professor in Social and Cultural Theory in the Institute for Culture and Society at Western Sydney University. He is a member of the Australian Academy of the Humanities and of the Academy of the Social Sciences in the UK. His recent publications include *Making Culture, Changing Society* (2013) and *Museums, Power, Knowledge* (2018). He is currently working on the political history of habit and its role in the governance of conduct.

Rodney Benson is Professor in the Department of Media, Culture, and Communication, and an affiliated faculty member in the Department of Sociology, both at New York University. He is the author of *Shaping Immigration News: A French-American Comparison* (Cambridge, 2013) and has published widely on social theories of media, sociology of news, public media, and comparative media systems. His current research examines logics of media ownership, drawing on fieldwork in Sweden, France, and the United States.

Claudio E. Benzecry is Associate Professor of Communication Studies at Northwestern University. His book *The Opera Fanatic* (University of Chicago Press, 2011) received the Mary Douglas Award for best book in the Sociology of Culture, and honorable mention for the ASA Distinguished Book award. He is the co-editor of *Social Theory Now* (University of Chicago Press, 2017) and is currently completing a manuscript on embodied knowledge, creativity, and globalization based on an ethnography of the work of designing and developing shoes for the US market.

Denise D. Bielby is Distinguished Professor of Sociology at the University of California, Santa Barbara, and affiliated faculty in the Department of Film and Media Studies. She is the author of *Global TV: Exporting Television and Culture in the World Market* with C. Lee Harrington, and *Brokerage and Production in the American and French Entertainment Industries: Invisible Hands in Cultural Markets* with Violaine Roussel. She publishes widely on the culture industries of film and television.

Francesca Bray is Emerita Professor of Social Anthropology at the University of Edinburgh and Past President of the Society for the History of Technology. Her research seeks to challenge the Eurocentric assumptions of much global history of science and technology. Publications include *Technology, Gender and History in Late Imperial China: Great Divergences Reconsidered* (2013) and *Rice: Global Networks and New Histories* (2015); current research includes a collaborative project on Moving Crops and the Scales of History.

Matthew J. Chandler is a Post-Doctoral Research Fellow with the Interdisciplinary Center for Network Science and Applications at the University of Notre Dame. His current research engages multiple aspects of relational dynamics, ranging from the evolution of interpersonal communication networks to contentious political transitions. His most recent publication,

"Civil Resistance Mechanisms and Disrupted Democratization: The Ambiguous Outcomes of Unarmed Insurrections in Egypt," appears in *Peace and Change* vol. 43, no. 1 (2018).

Elizabeth Cherry is Associate Professor of Sociology at Manhattanville College in Purchase, New York, where she conducts research on human-animal relationships, social movements, culture, and environmental sociology. She is the author of *Culture and Activism: Animal Rights in France and the United States* (Routledge, 2016). Her new book, tentatively titled *For the Birds: Protecting Wildlife through the Naturalist Gaze*, explores birding as an environmental hobby and conservation practice.

Maxine Leeds Craig is Professor of Sociology at the University of California, Davis, and a faculty affiliate in Performance Studies and Cultural Studies. She is the author of *Sorry I Don't Dance: Why Men Refuse to Move* (Oxford University Press, 2014) and *Ain't I a Beauty Queen? Black Women, Beauty, and the Politics of Race* (Oxford University Press, 2002). She is Past Chair of the Body and Embodiment Section of the American Sociological Association.

Jon Cruz is Associate Professor of Sociology at the University of California, Santa Barbara. He is author of *Culture on the Margins: The Black Spiritual and the Rise of American Cultural Interpretation*, co-editor of *Viewing, Reading, Listening: Audiences and Cultural Reception*, and recently finished serving as the US-based editor with the *European Journal of Cultural Studies*. His current research traces how the conflicts stemming from the digital turn in music impact additional cultural domains and institutions.

Nina Eliasoph is Professor of Sociology at the University of Southern California and author of numerous scholarly and non-scholarly essays and articles, as well as three books: *Avoiding Politics* (1998), *Making Volunteers* (2011), and a primer for high school and college students, *The Politics of Volunteering* (2012). She is currently working on defining a newly prevalent type of organization, the "empowerment project," locating its universe of members, and identifying its typical dilemmas.

Yến Lê Espiritu is Distinguished Professor and former Chair of the Department of Ethnic Studies at the University of California, San Diego. An award-winning author, she has published widely on Asian American panethnicity, gender and migration, and US colonialism and wars in Asia. Her most recent book is *Body Counts: The Vietnam War and Militarized Refuge(es)* (University of California Press, 2014). She is also a founding member of the Critical Refugee Studies Collective.

Donald Fels is a visual artist and has been making art about trade since the 1980s. A Fulbright Fellow to Italy and a Fulbright Senior Research Scholar to India, Fels continues to theorize about and make visible the relationship between the exchange of goods, ideas, and culture around the world. He lectures at the University of Washington. Visit: www.artisthinker.com.

Gary Alan Fine is James E. Johnson Professor of Sociology at Northwestern University. He is an ethnographer, social theorist, social psychologist, and sociologist of culture. His most recent book is *Talking Art: The Culture of Practice and Practice of Culture in MFA Education* (2018). He recently published *Players and Pawns: How Chess Builds Community and Culture* (2015). His current ethnography is a study of Senior Citizen Activists.

Alexandre Frenette is Assistant Professor of Sociology and Associate Director of the Curb Center at Vanderbilt University. Using the music industry as his case study, Frenette is currently working on a monograph about the challenges and the promise of internships as part of higher education. His writings on creative workers and the intern economy have won awards from the Society for the Study of Social Problems as well as the Labor and Employment Relations Association.

Joshua Gamson is Professor of Sociology and Academic Assistant Dean at the University of San Francisco. He is the author of *Claims to Fame: Celebrity in Contemporary America* (1994); *Freaks Talk Back: Tabloid Talk Shows and Sexual Nonconformity* (1998); *The Fabulous Sylvester* (2005); and *Modern Families: Stories of Extraordinary Journeys to Kinship* (2015), along with numerous scholarly articles on social movements, sexualities, and contemporary culture.

David Gartman is Professor Emeritus of Sociology at the University of South Alabama. His most recent book is *Culture, Class, and Critical Theory: Between Bourdieu and the Frankfurt School* (2013). He is currently working on a book on the built environment of the Great Depression.

Amin Ghaziani is Associate Professor of Sociology and Canada Research Chair in Sexuality and Urban Studies at the University of British Columbia. His research addresses the cultural, political, and spatial expressions of sexuality. He is author or co-editor of *A Decade of HAART* (Oxford), *The Dividends of Dissent* (Chicago), *There Goes the Gayborhood?* (Princeton), *Sex Cultures* (Polity), and *Imagining Queer Methods* (NYU).

Andreas Glaeser is Professor of Sociology at the University of Chicago. He is the author of *Political Epistemics: The Secret Police, the Opposition, and the End of East German Socialism* (Chicago 2011). His main research interests lie in political knowledge making practices, political imaginaries, critical social ontologies, and hermeneutic approaches to the study of social life.

Daniel P. S. Goh is Associate Professor of Sociology at the National University of Singapore. His research focuses on state formation, nationalism and multiculturalism, religion, and Asian urbanisms. His recent publications include the edited volumes, *Worlding Multiculturalisms: The Politics of Inter-Asian Dwelling* (2015) and *Precarious Belongings: Affect and Nationalism in Asia* (2017).

Jeffrey C. Goldfarb is the Michael E. Gellert Professor of Sociology at the New School for Social Research. He is the editor of *Public Seminar*. His work focuses on the sociology of media, culture and politics. Recent publications include *Reinventing Political Culture: The Power Of Culture Versus The Culture Of Power* (Polity Press 2011; Polish edition 2012) and *The Politics of Small Things: The Power of the Powerless in Dark Times* (University of Chicago Press, 2006; Korean and Polish editions 2011).

Mary-Jo DelVecchio Good, a comparative sociologist and medical anthropologist, is Professor of Global Health and Social Medicine, Harvard Medical School, Harvard University. She studies the culture of medicine in the United States and globally, with a focus on medicine's modernist projects. Her publications include *American Medicine: The Quest for Competence*; *Postcolonial Disorders; Shattering Culture: American Medicine Responds to Cultural Diversity*; and *A Reader in Medical Anthropology: Theoretical Trajectories, Emergent Realities*. She co-edited *Culture, Medicine and Psychiatry* (1986–2004).

Philip Gorski is Professor of Sociology and Religious Studies at Yale University. His most recent book is *American Covenant: A History of Civil Religion from the Puritans to the Present* (2017). He is currently writing a book on social ontology.

Contributors

Kevin Fox Gotham is Associate Dean in the School of Liberal Arts (SLA) and Professor of Sociology at Tulane University. He has research interests in real estate and mortgage markets, the political economy of tourism, and post-disaster redevelopment. He has authored four books and over 100 peer-reviewed articles and book chapters on housing policy, racial segregation, urban redevelopment, and tourism.

David Grazian is Associate Professor of Sociology and Communication and Faculty Director of Urban Studies at the University of Pennsylvania. He is an urban ethnographer who investigates places of popular culture and entertainment in cities. He is the author is *Blue Chicago: The Search for Authenticity in Urban Blues Clubs* (2003), *On the Make: The Hustle of Urban Nightlife* (2008), *American Zoo: A Sociological Safari* (2015), and *Mix It Up: Popular Culture, Mass Media, and Society* (2nd ed., 2017).

Laura Grindstaff is Professor of Sociology at the University of California, Davis, and a faculty affiliate in Gender Studies, Performance Studies, and Cultural Studies. Her research and teaching focus on the cultural dimensions of sex/gender, race, and class inequality, with a particular emphasis on American media and popular culture. She is the author of *The Money Shot: Trash, Class, and the Making of TV Talk Shows*, as well as numerous articles and essays on aspects of popular culture ranging from sports and cheerleading to reality TV and social media.

Harini Dilma Gunasekera is currently a student at The Pennsylvania State University pursuing a Bachelor of Arts in Sociology. Although this is her first publication, she is studying to one day become a lawyer and is interested in specializing in Business and/or Immigration.

Yifat Gutman is Senior Lecturer of Sociology at Ben-Gurion University, Israel. Among her recent publications are "Memory Activism: Reimagining the Past for the Future in Israel-Palestine" (Vanderbilt University Press, 2017) and the co-edited volume "Memory and the Future: Transnational Politics, Ethics and Society" (Palgrave Macmillan, 2010).

John R. Hall is Research Professor of Sociology at the University of California, Santa Cruz and Davis. His published works include *Apocalypse: From Antiquity to the Empire of Modernity* (Polity, 2009), *Visual Worlds* (Routledge, 2005, with co-editors), *Sociology on Culture* (Routledge, 2003, with co-authors), and *Cultures of Inquiry* (Cambridge University Press, 1999).

Karen Bettez Halnon died at the age of 55 on January 21, 2018. Karen studied contemporary manifestations of carnival culture in the US, including heavy metal, 420 marijuana smoker culture, stigma experiences, and the phenomenon known as "Poor Chic." In her work, including her 2013 book *The Consumption of Inequality: Weapons of Mass Distraction* (Palgrave Macmillan), she explored multiple modalities of stratification, including segregation, gentrification, objectification, and stigmatization. She devoted 18 years of her life to teaching, research, and service at Pennsylvania State University, first as Assistant and then as Associate Professor.

Gary G. Hamilton is Professor Emeritus of Sociology and of International Studies at the University of Washington. He specializes in historical/comparative sociology, economic and organizational sociology, and Asian societies. He is an author of numerous articles and books, including most recently *The Market Makers: How Retailers Are Changing the Global Economy* (2010, co-edited with Misha Petrovic and Benjamin Senaur) and *Making Money: How Taiwanese Industrialists Embraced the Global Economy* (2017, co-authored with Cheng-Shu Kao).

Martin Hand is Associate Professor of Sociology at Queen's University, Kingston, Canada. His publications include *Big Data?* (co-edited, 2014), *Ubiquitous Photography* (2012), *Making Digital Cultures* (2008), *The Design of Everyday Life* (co-authored, 2007), plus articles and essays about visual culture, digitization, technology, and consumption. He is currently conducting research into the mediatization of time.

Seth Hannah is a full-time Lecturer in Sociology in the Department of Social Sciences at California State Polytechnic University in San Luis Obispo. He is a co-editor and contributing author of *Shattering Culture: American Medicine Responds to Cultural Diversity*. He is currently working on a research project comparing how healthcare providers in the United States, Canada, and Switzerland respond to the "hyperdiversity" of their patient populations.

Nancy Weiss Hanrahan, Associate Professor of Sociology at George Mason University, is the author of *Difference in Time: A Critical Theory of Culture* and co-editor of *The Blackwell Companion to the Sociology of Culture*. Her current book project explores the impact of digitization on the aesthetic experience of music and critically examines the meanings of "democracy" that have attended public discourse about music throughout US history, including in the present digital era.

Ben Highmore is Professor of Cultural Studies at the University of Sussex. His most recent books are *The Art of Brutalism: Rescuing Hope from Catastrophe in 1950s Britain* (Yale University Press) and *Cultural Feelings: Mood, Mediation, and Cultural Politics* (Routledge), both published in 2017. Previous books include *The Great Indoors: At Home in the Modern British House* (Profile Books 2014) and *Ordinary Lives: Studies in the Everyday* (Routledge 2011).

Ronald N. Jacobs is Professor of Sociology at the University at Albany, State University of New York. His research focuses on culture, media, and public life. Among his recent publications are *The Space of Opinion* (2011) and "Journalism After Trump" (2017). He is co-editor of the *American Journal of Cultural Sociology*.

Elihu Katz has served as Distinguished Trustee Professor of Communication at the Annenberg School of the University of Pennsylvania, Professor of Sociology and Communication at the Hebrew University of Jerusalem, and Director of the Israel Institute of Applied Social Research. His most recent book is *Echoes of Gabriel Tarde: What We Know Better or Different 100 Years Later* (with Christopher Ali and Joohan Kim). He holds honorary degrees from nine universities and is winner of the McLuhan Prize of Canadian UNESCO, the Israel Prize, and the Ogburn Career Award of the American Sociological Association.

Rebecca Chiyoko King-O'Riain is Senior Lecturer in the Department of Sociology at Maynooth University with research interests in globalization, emotions and technology; racial/ethnic beauty pageants (*Pure Beauty* [University of Minnesota Press]); critical race theory; qualitative methods; interracial marriage and multiracial people (*Global Mixed Race* [New York University Press]). Her current research explores globalized interpersonal and interactive forms of bodily culture through skin altering practices in Asia and Europe, beauty pageants, and Asian popular culture (Korean and Japanese dramas).

Pei-Chia Lan is Distinguished Professor of Sociology and the Director of Global Asia Research Center at National Taiwan University. Her research interest centers on social inequalities in everyday life under the influence of migration and globalization. Her major publications include *Global Cinderellas: Migrant Domestics and Newly Rich Employers in Taiwan* (Duke 2006, ASA Sex and Gender Book Award) and *Raising Global Families: Parenting, Immigration, and Class in Taiwan and the US* (Stanford 2018).

Robin Leidner is Associate Professor of Sociology at the University of Pennsylvania whose scholarship focuses on the sociology of work and of gender. She is the author of *Fast Food, Fast Talk: Service Work and the Routinization of Everyday Life*. Her current research is on work and identity in theater.

Paul Lichterman is currently Professor of Sociology and Religion and Director of Ethnography of Public Life at the University of Southern California. Among his recent publications are *Elusive Togetherness* (2005) and "Civic Action" (co-authored with Nina Eliasoph), in *American Journal of Sociology*, November 2014. He is currently working on a book titled *How Civic Action Works*, based on ethnographic, archival and network survey research on housing advocacy in Los Angeles.

Omar Lizardo is Leroy Nieman term chair Professor of Sociology at the University of California Los Angeles. He holds a PhD from the University of Arizona. His research deals with various topics at the intersection of cultural sociology, stratification, social theory, and theory of action. He has published widely in the sociology of taste, culture and networks, and processes of distinction and symbolic exclusion via cultural consumption.

Ming-Cheng M. Lo is Professor of Sociology at the University of California, Davis. Lo's research focuses on culture, illness experiences, and civic engagement. She is the author of *Doctors within Borders: Profession, Ethnicity, and Modernity in Colonial Taiwan* (University of California Press 2002; Japanese edition, 2014). A recent series of articles addresses the roles of cultural capital and non-dominant cultural resources in health, healthcare, and environmental justice activism.

Kevin McElmurry is Associate Professor of Sociology at Indiana University Northwest. His research is focused on music, moral community, and religious practice. He is currently working on a book based on ethnographic work looking at media production practices in contemporary Protestant megachurches.

Scott McQuire is Professor of Media and Communications in the School of Culture and Communication at the University of Melbourne, Australia. He is one of the founders of the Research Unit for Public Cultures, which fosters interdisciplinary research at the nexus of digital media, art, urbanism, and social theory. His books include *The Media City: Media, Architecture and Urban Space* (Sage/TC&S 2008) and *Geomedia: Networked Cities and the Future of Public Space* (Polity, 2016).

Joshua Meyrowitz is Professor Emeritus of Communication at the University of New Hampshire, where he has won the Lindberg Award for Outstanding Scholar-Teacher in the College of Liberal Arts. He is the author of the award-winning *No Sense of Place: The Impact of Electronic Media on Social Behavior* (Oxford University Press) and over 100 articles on media and society that have appeared in scholarly journals and anthologies, as well as in general-interest magazines and newspapers.

Murray Milner Jr. is Senior Fellow at the Institute for Advanced Studies in Culture and Professor Emeritus of Sociology at the University of Virginia. His most recent books are *Elites: A General Model* (2015) and *Freaks, Geeks, and Cool Kids: Teenagers in an Era of Consumerism, Standardized Tests and Social Media* (2nd ed., 2016). He is currently working on a book on sociological theology.

Ann Mische is Associate Professor of Sociology and Peace Studies at the University of Notre Dame. Mische's book, *Partisan Publics: Communication and Contention Across Brazilian Youth Activist Networks* (Princeton 2008), examines civic networks and political communication in Brazilian youth politics during 20 years of democratic restructuring. Currently, she is researching the role of futures thinking and scenario methods in social and political reform efforts related to democracy, development, peace building and climate change.

John W. Mohr is Professor of Sociology at the University of California, Santa Barbara. His work focuses especially on meaning systems and their measurement. He is co-editor of *Matters of Culture* (2004, with Roger Friedland), co-editor of a special issue of *Theory & Society* on measuring culture (with Amin Ghaziani, 2012), and author of widely cited articles concerned with the use of formal models and big data in cultural analysis, the history of the welfare state, and the racial politics of affirmative action.

Chandra Mukerji is Distinguished Professor Emerita at the University of California, San Diego. She is author of *Impossible Engineering*, which won the ASA Distinguished Book Award; *Territorial Ambitions and the Gardens of Versailles*, which won the book prize from the culture section of the ASA; and a recent book, *Modernity Reimagined*. She is currently writing a book on cultural imaginaries and state power.

Mary Jo Neitz is Professor Emerita in Women's and Gender Studies at the University of Missouri. Her research is at the intersection of religion and gender. She is a co-author of *Sociology on Culture* (2003). She is currently working ethnography of small-town churches focusing on the ways women make a spaces for themselves through the work that they do – through both paid labor and unpaid labor.

Jeffrey K. Olick is William R. Kenan Jr. Professor of Sociology and History and Chair of the Sociology Department at the University of Virginia. His most recent book is *The Sins of the Fathers: Germany, Memory, Method* (Chicago 2016).

Jackie Orr is Associate Professor of Sociology at Syracuse University. She teaches, writes, and performs at the crossroads of critical technoscience studies, the politics of bodies, and the poetics of knowledge. She is the author of *Panic Diaries: A Genealogy of Panic Disorder* (Duke 2006). Her most recent work, "Slow Disaster at the Digital Edge," stages the everyday catastrophe of deep time in petro-capitalist cultures, and has been performed at the University of Chicago, Goldsmiths, Stanford, and the Rhode Island School of Design.

Eileen M. Otis is Associate Professor of Sociology at the University of Oregon. She is the author of the award-winning book *Markets and Bodies: Women, Service Work and the Making of Inequality in China* (Stanford 2011). Her research has been published in the *American Sociological Review, Politics and Society*, and *American Behavioral Scientist*, among other journals. She is currently working on a book about Walmart retail workers in China.

Contributors

Orlando Patterson, a historical and cultural sociologist, is John Cowles Professor of Sociology at Harvard University. His empirical works include the comparative study of ethno-racial inequality, slavery and other forms of domination, as well as the culture and practice of freedom, democracy, and movements toward equality. He is the author of numerous papers and books, including Slavery and Social Death, Freedom in the Making of Western Culture, and Rituals of Blood: Consequences of Slavery in Two American Centuries, and editor of The Cultural Matrix: Understanding Black Youth.

Francesca Polletta is Professor of Sociology at the University of California, Irvine. She is the author of *Freedom Is an Endless Meeting: Democracy in American Social Movements* (University of Chicago, 2002), *It Was Like a Fever: Storytelling in Protest and Politics* (University of Chicago, 2006), and editor, with Jeff Goodwin and James M. Jasper, of *Passionate Politics: Emotions and Social Movements* (University of Chicago, 2001). She is currently working on a manuscript on how imagined relationships shape moral action.

Mark Poster was Emeritus Professor in the Film and Media Studies Department and the History Department at the University of California, Irvine, when he died on October 10, 2012. His numerous publications include *Information Please: Culture and Politics in a Digital Age* (2006), *What's the Matter with the Internet?: A Critical Theory of Cyberspace* (2001), and *The Information Subject (Critical Voices in Art, Theory and Culture)* (2001).

Nick Prior is Professor of Cultural Sociology at the University of Edinburgh. He has published widely in the fields of popular music studies and music sociology and is author of *Popular Music, Digital Technology and Society* (Sage, 2018). He is co-editor of the journal *Cultural Sociology*, an amateur electronic musician, and currently working on his next monograph, *Assembling Virtual Idols: Music, Mediation and Miku* (Bloomsbury).

Craig M. Rawlings is Assistant Professor of Sociology at Duke University. His research interests are in social networks and how social structure shapes individual and collective emotions, beliefs, and understandings

Victoria Reyes is Assistant Professor of Sociology at the University of California, Riverside. She studies the relationship between culture and global inequality. Her most recent work will appear in *Social Forces* (forthcoming) and *Ethnography* (forthcoming), and her book manuscript examines Subic Bay, Philippines as an example of what she calls "global borderlands" – semi-autonomous, foreign-controlled places of international exchange like overseas military bases and special economic zones.

Fernando Domínguez Rubio (PhD Sociology, University of Cambridge, 2008) is Assistant Professor of Communication at the University of California, San Diego. His research focuses on the different practices, materials, and infrastructures through which forms of subjectivity and objectivity are produced. He is the co-editor of *The Politics of Knowledge* (Routledge 2012) and is currently working on a manuscript based on ethnography of the Museum of Modern Art (MoMA).

Hiro Saito is Assistant Professor of Sociology at Singapore Management University. His research examines how interactions between government and citizens shape public policy. He is the author of *The History Problem: The Politics of War Commemoration in East Asia* and currently completing a book manuscript on democracy in post-Fukushima Japan.

Barry Schwartz, Professor Emeritus of Sociology, University of Georgia, is author of numerous articles, chapters, and books on collective memory, including work on American history and American presidents. Schwartz's research also addresses collective memory issues in Europe, the Middle East, and Asia. Employing a theoretical lens developed in earlier studies, Schwartz's recent work includes memories of the historical Jesus and their transmission among first-century Christian communities.

Giuseppe Sciortino teaches sociology at the Università di Trento, Italy. He is a faculty fellow of the Center for Cultural Sociology at Yale. Among his recent publications are *Great Minds: Encounters with Social Theory* (2011, with Gianfranco Poggi) and *Solidarity, Justice and Incorporation* (2015, with Peter Kivisto).

Susan S. Silbey is Leon and Anne Goldberg Professor of Sociology and Anthropology at Massachusetts Institute of Technology. Her works include *The Common Place of Law: Stories from Everyday Life* (1998), "After Legal Consciousness" (2005), "Taming Prometheus: Talking of Safety and Culture" (2009), "Governing the Gap: Forging Safe Science through Relational Regulation" (2011), and "Governing inside the Organization: Interpreting Regulation and Compliance" (2014). She is working on a book exploring the persistent regulatory challenges in long chains of distributed labor.

Philip Smith is Professor of Sociology at Yale University. His most recent book is *Climate Change as Social Drama* (2015, co-authored with Nicolas Howe). With a focus on performance and representation in the public sphere this work illustrates a Strong Program approach to environmental issues. His next volume will be a comprehensive history of Durkheimian thought from the beginning until today.

Ann Swidler is Professor of the Graduate School at the University of California, Berkeley. Her most recent book (with Susan Cotts Watkins) is *A Fraught Embrace: The Romance and Reality of AIDS Altruism in Africa* (Princeton 2017). Currently she is studying churches and chieftaincies in Africa and global health governance, in order to understand how culture shapes institutional capacities.

Iddo Tavory is Associate Professor of Sociology at NYU. A sociologist of culture and an interactionist, his two books to date are *Abductive Analysis* (with Stefan Timmermans) and *Summoned*. He is currently working on an ethnography of knowledge production in an advertising agency in New York, and co-authoring a book on pro bono work and notions of worth in the advertising world.

Steven J. Tepper is a sociologist and Professor of Arts, Media and Engineering at the Herberger Institute for Design and the Arts at Arizona State University, where he also serves as dean. He studies the intersections of arts, culture, and public life, focusing on social change and cultural conflict, creative work and identity, and changes in cultural participation. He is author of *Not Here, Not Now, Not That: Protest Over Art and Culture in America*.

Bryan S. Turner is Professor of the Sociology of Religion at the Australian Catholic University (Melbourne); Honorary Professor of Sociology Potsdam University, Germany; and Emeritus Professor of Sociology, Graduate Center, City University of New York USA; and a Fellow of the Edward Cadbury Centre University of Birmingham. He was the recipient of the Max Planck Award 2015. His recent publication is *The Wiley-Blackwell Encyclopedia of Social Theory* in 2018.

Contributors

Robin Wagner-Pacifici is University in Exile Professor of Sociology at the New School. She is the author of *The Art of Surrender: Decomposing Sovereignty at Conflict's End*, *Theorizing the Standoff: Contingency in Action*, *Discourse and Destruction: The City of Philadelphia vs MOVE*, *The Moro Morality Play: Terrorism as Social Drama*, and most recently, *What is an Event?* A collaboration with John W. Mohr and Ronald L. Breiger analyzing national security language has generated several publications.

Suzanna Danuta Walters is Professor of Sociology and Director of the Women's, Gender, and Sexuality Program at Northeastern University, where she is also the editor of *Signs: Journal of Women in Culture and Society*. She is the author of numerous books and articles, including *Material Girls: Making Sense of Feminist Cultural Theory*, *All the Rage: The Story of Gay Visibility in America*, and *The Tolerance Trap: How God, Genes, and Good Intentions Are Sabotaging Gay Equality*.

Frederick F. Wherry is Professor of Sociology at Princeton and faculty associate at the Princeton Institute of International and Regional Studies. He serves as the 2018 president of the Social Science History Association and has chaired both the Economic Sociology Section of the American Sociological Association and the Consumers and Consumption Section. His most recent publication is *Money Talks: Explaining How Money Really* Works (2017), co-edited with Nina Bandelj and Viviana Zelizer.

Michel Wieviorka is Professor at the École des Hautes Études en Sciences Sociales and President of the Fondation Maison des Sciences de l'Homme, is past president of the International Sociological Association, a member of the Scientific Council of the European Research Council, and editor of *SOCIO*. His research focuses on social movements, democracy, multiculturalism, and on violence and racism. Books include *The Making of Terrorism*, and, with Craig Calhoun, *Manifeste pour les sciences sociales*.

Nicholas Hoover Wilson is Assistant Professor of Sociology at Stony Brook University. His work focuses on how culture, state formation, and imperial administration intersect, and has been published in the *American Journal of Sociology, Political Power and Social Theory*, and *Sociological Research*, and is forthcoming in the *European Journal of Sociology*. His current work examines the connection between empire and corruption and maps the research practices of historical social science.

Daniel Winchester is Assistant Professor of Sociology at Purdue University. His interest areas include culture, religion, subjectivity, and social theory. His research on religious conversion has been published in journals such as *Social Forces, Theory and Society*, and the *Journal for the Scientific Study of Religion*, and he received the ASA Culture Section's Clifford Geertz Award for Best Article in 2017. He is currently conducting research for a new project on contemporary evangelical missionary culture.

David Wright is Associate Professor in the Centre for Cultural and Media Policy Studies at the University of Warwick. His research interests are in taste, popular culture, the cultural industries, and cultural policy, and he is the author of *Understanding Cultural Taste* (Palgrave, 2015). He was a member of a team of researchers that conducted an inquiry into British tastes, published as *Culture, Class, Distinction* (Routledge, 2009).

Xiaohong Xu is Assistant Professor of Sociology at Lingnan University in Hong Kong. He has previously taught at National University of Singapore. His recent publications include articles appearing in *Critical Historical Studies* (2017) and *American Sociological Review* (2013) that provides cultural-sociological analysis of political movements in modern China. He is currently working on a book manuscript on the Chinese Cultural Revolution, a quantitative analysis of revolutionary state-building, and a project on the social and political implications of the rise of China's high-tech innovations.

Alford A. Young Jr. is Arthur F. Thurnau Professor of Sociology, Afroamerican and African Studies, and Public Policy (by courtesy) at the University of Michigan. His central research focus has been on how low-income African American men construct understandings of various aspects of social reality. He has also studied how African America scholars conceive of the social utility of scholarship and the teaching experiences of higher education faculty in response to diversity, equity, and inclusion agendas.

Geneviève Zubrzycki is Professor of Sociology and Director of the Weiser Center for Europe and Eurasia at the University of Michigan. She is the author of *The Crosses of Auschwitz: Nationalism and Religion in Post-Communist Poland* (2006), *Beheading the Saint: Nationalism, Religion and Secularism in Quebec* (2016), and the editor of *National Matters: Materiality, Culture, and Nationalism* (2017). She is currently writing a book on nationalism and symbolic boundaries through a study of philo-Semitism in contemporary Poland.

Acknowledgments

Producing a book is rarely a solitary process, and some books are more collaborative in nature than others. This second edition of the *Routledge Handbook of Cultural Sociology* is a case in point. With 70 chapters, 80 contributors, and three editors, it bears the imprint of many hands, hearts, and minds. As editors, we feel fortunate to have worked with so many good people on this volume, especially since its form – falling somewhere between a conventional handbook and an encyclopedia – is somewhat unorthodox. For the engagement, patience, and good humor of our authors, we are grateful. Others we want to thank include student researcher Allison Brooke, who formatted the chapters; Alison Claffey and Diana Ciobotea, who coordinated the project at Routledge, and Autumn Spalding, who served as project manager for copy-editing and proofing. We continue to be indebted to Gerhard Boomgaarden, Routledge's senior sociology commissioning editor, without whom neither edition of the *Handbook* would exist. As with the first edition, Gerhard gave great encouragement and timely counsel, and he respected our intellectual vision of how this version should evolve. Finally, we editors acknowledge one another for the contributions each has made. None of us would have wanted to undertake this work alone, and we all feel that the *Handbook* is stronger for our collaboration. In this edition, Laura spearheaded the logistics and acted as the liaison to Routledge, but, as with the original, all three of us participated equally in discussions that defined the project and carried it forward, we each worked as "lead" editor with approximately one third of the contributors, and we shared in the editorial review of all the chapters. In short, editing was very much a collective effort and we supported each other along the way. We sincerely hope this effort has produced a body of scholarship that will engage and enrich readers for many years to come.

Introduction
Culture, lifeworlds, and globalization

Laura Grindstaff, Ming-Cheng M. Lo, and John R. Hall

Webs of significance

Let's start with a bit of culture. In 2013, the Oxford English Dictionary (OED) selected "selfie" as the word of the year. A press release characterized the decision as unanimous and said that the word's usage in mainstream media had increased 17,000 percent in just one year. Defined by the OED as "a photographic self-portrait, especially one taken with a smartphone or webcam and shared via social media," the selfie is a ubiquitous global phenomenon, most common on platforms such as Facebook, Instagram, and Snapchat. Young people are particularly active in taking and sharing selfies, with girls and young women participating at much higher rates than boys and young men (Syme 2015).

Sociologists might understand selfies as a vehicle for inserting the autobiographical into the social; with roots tracing back to self-portraiture, selfies draw upon and reproduce a set of aesthetic and cultural codes for instantiating particular forms of subjectivity. A feminist perspective might further suggest that participating in selfie culture puts girls, and young people generally, in conversation about matters both personal and political – identity, sexuality, visibility, and social exclusion/marginalization. As blogger Rachel Syme (2015) argues, selfie politics are attention politics: "it is all about who gets to be seen, who gets to occupy the visual field." For Syme, the corresponding rise of "selfie-shaming" helps to reinforce the point, as detractors typically psychologize selfie-taking as narcissistic and vulgar (too much, too often, too sexual). Like most cultural phenomena, from art museums to reality television, selfies are polyvalent, bearing a range of different and sometimes contradictory meanings (see Grindstaff 2008).

The rise of selfie culture is coincident with more weighty cultural developments and contradictions. The recent upsurge in nationalist/populist movements – not only in Europe and the US, but also the Philippines, India, Turkey, and Russia – counters the historic decline in nationalism since World War II. Natural disasters of unprecedented frequency and strength sweep the globe, even as climate change is dismissed as a political hoax. Rising levels of income inequality, partly generated by globalization, produce class resentments locally, often expressed in cultural rather than economic terms. In the US, the culture wars – by which we mean, quite simply, the struggle over public meaning – have resurfaced with a vengeance in tandem with post-truth discourse ("post-truth" was the OED's 2016 word of the year). The aim of cultural sociology is

1

not to adjudicate social facts but to help us make sense of ironies and contradictions as social, economic, and political forces touch down and find expression in "lifeworlds" – the everyday worlds of people's lived experience. Analyzing lifeworlds is a thoroughly cultural matter. As anthropologist Clifford Geertz once wrote, people are animals "suspended in webs of significance" that they themselves spin (1973:5).

Of course, how people spin webs of significance is complex and historically variable; the cultural and the social are mutually implicated. Following any single strand of cultural analysis is likely to quickly open out into a broad set of lifeworldly considerations: of personal relationships, kinship and community, work and leisure, social institutions and their cultural bases, technological change, transnational differences, and global diffusion, to name but a few. The ways in which the social and cultural intersect and mutually constitute one another routinely connect lifeworlds to broader global currents and processes. A specifically cultural sociology, as we editors envision it, takes up the challenge of understanding these analytic relationships. Optimally, cultural sociology is sociology tout court.

A brief history of cultural sociology

Sociology is itself cultural, and triply so. First, the discipline has always involved cultural acts of social reflexivity, influenced in part by Enlightenment dreams confronting the possibilities and hard realities of the Industrial Revolution. Second, culture as an analytic issue can be found at the center of much classical and post-classical sociology – for example, in Marx, Durkheim, Weber, Simmel, Veblen, Gramsci, Pareto, Mannheim, Horkheimer, Adorno, and Parsons. Third, although the nineteenth-century *Methodenstreit* (conflict over methods) in the social sciences will persist, one contention in that debate is beyond doubt: cultural meanings are fundamental to the organization of the social and how the social unfolds (Hall 1999:10–11, 45–6). As the chair of the American Sociological Association's Culture section noted in 2017 concerning the importance of culture, "We seem to have convinced most of our colleagues from other specialty areas. And besides, any glance at the newspaper or the television drives this point home on a daily basis" (Jacobs 2017:2).

Despite the now widely acknowledged importance of culture, however, controversy about it has divided the discipline of sociology virtually from the beginning. The antinomies evident during the high-modern epoch of sociology following World War II and the rapid eclipse of that epoch in the 1960s and 1970s are revealing. A broad range of sociologists interested in social structure – including both positivists and Marxists – when they discussed culture at all (typically by reference to ideas and values), dismissed it as ephemeral and lacking any robust role in social causation. Marxists were most emphatic, identifying an ideal "superstructure" as little more than a reflection of the material "base" of the society – constituted in the forces and relations that organize production.

Differences between positivist and structural Marxist theories already suggest that the high moment of modernist sociology was not all of a piece. Yet even sociological approaches sympathetic to cultural analysis sometimes had a dialectical tendency to undermine any project of cultural sociology. Thus, Durkheim's analysis of the transition from organic to mechanical solidarity might be read as a lament about the erosion of shared communitarian meanings binding people to the social order, and modern theorists of secularization made arguments about the declining importance of religion for public life, which left the status of Talcott Parsons's idea of cultural values as an overarching societal subsystem in doubt. Nor did the waning of the high-modernist epoch of sociology eliminate antipathy to cultural analysis. Perhaps the most daring expression of a disinterested view was offered by Theda Skocpol, who in *States and Social Revolutions* acknowledged that her hypotheses gave "short shrift" to any importance of revolutionary ideology in accounting for success of revolutions (1979:114).

Those who would chart the emergence of cultural sociology could find stirrings long before Skocpol wrote her pithy dismissal. In the conventional division of academic labor before World War II, culture – whether understood as systems of ideas, meanings, and practices, or as material tools and products of human action – remained largely the purview of anthropologists. After World War II through 1970, things changed, as a perusal of sociological abstracts will show. Sociologists in Europe and North and South America were at work exploring the earlier theories of Thorstein Veblen, framing a sociology of comparative literature, studying issues of cultural relativity, and considering art, theater, radio, popular music, and the "jam session," as well as cultural aspects of individual consciousness, mass society, social and religious conflict, and even violence and terror.

From the 1970s onward, differentiation of subfields – stratification, social movements, family, and so on – took place across the entire discipline of sociology. Following this pattern, the sociology of culture emerged as a distinct enterprise in the 1970s and 1980s. It initially centered on questions about popular culture and high culture – largely refracted in relation to conventional modern tropes of culture (in a holistic sense), subcultures, and countercultures as relatively coherent societal phenomena – and increasingly focused on issues of the production of culture. But a puzzle remains. The big surprise was not that the sociology of culture, like other specialties, became a recognizable and increasingly robust subfield, but that cultural issues began to permeate virtually all subfields of sociology, such that today, people conventionally and rightly talk about a "cultural sociology" – that is, a general sociology that is cultural on every front, in every subdiscipline. How is it that cultural sociology has become so important so widely? Both sociohistorical and intellectual shifts help explain this development.

The sociohistorical shifts certainly include the broad transformation from a society organized along industrial lines to a society centrally ordered through a postindustrial logic. This shift created conditions in which leisure gained in importance relative to work, yielding an increased valuation to self-expression through cultural choices and practices, thus stimulating sociological interest in the (often "popular") culture of everyday life.

Paralleling the socioeconomic shift, beginning in the late 1950s and more concertedly in the 1960s, eruptions of diverse, often broad-based social and countercultural movements challenged the previously conventional assumption that "culture" was something singular or universal. Both the anti-Vietnam War movement and civil-rights movements in the US and radical movements in Europe (France in 1968, for example) shifted away from strictly class-based issues. Moreover, emergent "new," non-class-based social movements (e.g., concerned with gender, ethnicity, lifestyle, the environment) often focused not only on the pursuit of political objectives but also on the construction of new cultural identities. The disruptions brought by such movements, including countermovements (e.g., of religious fundamentalism), unveiled the "arbitrary" and socially constructed character of previously conventional and taken-for-granted institutionalized cultural patterns. Both feeding upon and turbocharging such developments were the subsequent rise of the internet and the relentless mediatization of the social, lately appropriated for deployment of new forms of agitprop and agendas of delegitimation (see, e.g., contributors to Mast and Alexander 2017 and Dodd, Lamont, and Savage 2017). Such developments now give a fresh and disturbing significance to Geertz's point cited earlier, about the suspension of social life within cultural webs of significance. In short, under postindustrial, postmodern, and increasingly hypermediatized conditions, cultural objects, practices, and processes have become ever more central to how the social works. Across sociology as an empirical discipline, these shifts rightly have inspired increased attention to culture as an object of analysis.

As for intellectual developments, they subtend the chapters in this handbook. In brief, a sociology that could be mapped fairly completely 50 years ago in relation to structural-functionalism, systems theory, quantitative empiricism, symbolic interactionism, and radical critique underwent an efflorescence that opened it up to wider intellectual currents. The consequences in sociology of what broadly may be called the "cultural turn" were forged by appropriations of diverse approaches and thinkers – hermeneutics (e.g., Clifford Geertz, Paul Ricoeur), semiotics and symbolic structuralism (Ferdinand de Saussure, Claude Lévi-Strauss), phenomenology and social constructionism (Peter Berger and colleagues, and Dorothy Smith, all drawing on Alfred Schutz), poststructuralism (philosophically, Jacques Derrida; epistemologically and in a way that advanced a program of substantive analysis, Michel Foucault), feminist theory and analysis (Judith Butler, Donna Haraway, bell hooks), and postcolonial theory (Frantz Fanon, Edward Said, and, in a somewhat different vein, W.E.B. Du Bois).

These currents and their interminglings challenged structural, functional, and positivist sociologies, and the end of the Cold War spelled the end of any robust Marxist intellectual project. Because intellectual upheavals occurred with near simultaneity across the human sciences, the importance of interdisciplinarity cannot be overstated: the cultural turn was both a cause and consequence of increasing dialogue across the social sciences and humanities – among cultural sociology, cultural history, cultural anthropology, and cultural studies, and even, if less visibly, economics and political science.

Certain key developments carried inquiry along the cultural turn. One was what Lawrence Stone (1979) called a "revival of narrative." Along with narrative came cultural history, itself something of a successor to the social history that in the 1950s and 1960s had begun to supplant grand metanarrative and political history. Amplifying this development, the cultural turn in the corridors of literary criticism and the humanities more generally encompassed a turn toward history, in the so-called new historicism championed by Stephen Greenblatt, and a turn toward social theory, in which Pierre Bourdieu gained a considerable following. The border crossings and poachings in all directions have proceeded apace ever since.

Given that the anthropological enterprise was fundamentally cultural from the beginning, the cultural turn there might seem a non-event. But just as empirical observation and structural analysis replaced armchair philosophizing during the early days of the discipline, feminist and postmodern critiques of objectivity challenged the modernist goal of theorizing case studies in relation to general social processes. Attention to the politics of meaning and representation, coupled with political critiques of asymmetrical power relations and exploitation of research subjects, has ushered in a more thoroughly "cultural" cultural anthropology, one increasingly concerned with the symbolic and ideological dimensions of both "objects" of inquiry and categories and modes of analysis. Similar concerns have informed the rise and development of cultural studies. From the emergence in the 1960s of the Birmingham School in Britain to current trends in postcolonial and queer scholarship both in the US and elsewhere, there has been an increasing recognition that social life is thoroughly constituted by language, subjectivity, and power.

This very brief account of the emergence of cultural sociology in relation to disciplines and interdisciplinarity can only serve as a placeholder marking complex developments detailed in the handbook's chapters that follow. Nevertheless, the overall development is already clear: a fundamental shift has underwritten the dramatic emergence of cultural sociology. "Culture" can no longer be seen as a coherent system aligned (functionally or not) with a counterpart social system; instead it is to be found in the myriad symbolic and material dimensions of life that attain what coherence they might have through the invocations and practices of the social actors who develop or encounter them. Both intellectual ferment and the ways culture is being appropriated across the globe to break down and (re)organize the social order warrant a criti-cally engaged cultural sociology that permeates every topic and issue of sociological analysis. A cultural sociology elaborated in this way, by connecting culture directly, intimately, and per-vasively to the social, can help diverse scholars and the general public to engage and shape the world around us. Yet given both the current "crisis of history" (Steinmetz 2017) and the cultural lag of sociology as a discipline in many ways still mired in twentieth-century understandings of the social (see Beck 2016), the project of cultural sociology beckons us anew, and urgently so.

The "Broad Program," lifeworlds, and globalization

Scholars often associate the turn from a "sociology of culture" to a "cultural sociology" with the "strong program" championed by Jeffrey Alexander and his colleagues. Although the Strong Program is important (and the subject of discussion in the present volume), the many scholars who embrace this turn have sometimes formulated other analytic agendas and pursued diverse topics and questions subject to sociocultural analysis in the study of work, emotions, the state, social movements – in short, in all manner of social phenomena.

This handbook is thus based on a central thesis: cultural sociology encompasses more than any single program and it is important precisely for its breadth. A "Broad Program" is necessary to constitute the field in a way that encourages controversy, debate, and research, and that speaks to scholars engaged in cultural analysis more widely. This Broad Program fulfills the agenda discussed earlier – connecting lifeworlds and globalization.

Fundamentally, a cultural sociology ought to be grounded in the analysis of everyday social life. As Georg Simmel recognized a century ago – and Charles Tilly (1984) reminded us more recently – "society" is not a thing. Instead, the social consists of networked relationships that develop through face-to-face and mediated interactions. All people live in the lifeworld – or, more accurately, in lifeworlds (plural) – where we enact our lives socially, episodically, in rela-tion to other people. Taken seriously, this point has two implications. First, whatever the ways in which culture exists outside lifeworlds (an important topic in itself), culture that has any specifically sociological bearing would have to come into play within lifeworlds, that is, where "society" happens. Second, given the diversity of social phenomena that manifest in lifeworlds (work, leisure activities, bureaucracy, religion, markets, war, social movements, and so on), Sim-mel's (and our) concept of the social warrants the shift we have already described, to a cultural sociology concerned with all sites, processes, and meaningful activities of social life.

In itself, this broad tack does not settle the complex questions concerning (presumably myriad) relationships between cultural materials and lifeworldly manifestations. Nor does it presume lifeworlds that are increasingly subordinated to "colonization" by a system (as Haber-mas [1981] 1987 argued). Rather, a cultural analysis suggests that lifeworlds, insofar as they are subject to systems of institutionalized practices, reflexively produce – through rules, laws, codes, and conventions of various sorts – whatever systematicity emerges (Hall 2009:127–8). In the Broad Program, and in the chapters in this handbook, coming to understand the interdepend-ent relationships between cultural practices, material culture, lifeworlds, and institutionalized systematicity is a priority.

To consider fully how culture "happens" in lifeworlds, we must come to terms with the Eurocentric biases inherent in Western sociology. European economic, cultural, and political modernities developed in part through colonial expansions. Yet sociology has largely failed to adequately consider how colonial relationships have shaped its theorizations (Connell 1997; Lo 2002; Steinmetz 2007). An especially relevant case in point here is Alfred Schutz and Thomas Luckmann's essentialized theorization of structures of *the* lifeworld (1973), which failed to account for differences among lifeworlds (Hall 1977). More generally, earlier sociologists and anthropologists often unabashedly assumed the European self to be superior to non-European others, attributing differences to the persistence of fading "tradition," thereby justifying their refusal to take other viewpoints seriously. However, European intellectual canonization as a process masked such racist overtones by largely disengaging scholarship from discussions of Europe's relationships with the colonies (Connell 1997). Western theorizations of the lifeworld in effect bracketed these difficult considerations (for an exception, see Berger, Berger, and Kellner 1973).

Similarly, the later Habermasian conceptualization of the public sphere, although preferable to many alternative, explicitly oppressive theorizations, remains oblivious to the political significance of the "hidden transcripts" (Scott 1990) embedded in its conceptual framing. Habermas sees a nation-state's public sphere – at its most democratic – as approximating an "ideal speech community" in which all arguments are evaluated rationally, on their merits, with participants' status differences temporarily bracketed. No doubt Habermas's framework can yield important insights about how and where public discourse falls short in nation-states with essentially democratic institutions. But focusing solely on this ideal speech community would largely exclude analysis of how most colonial and postcolonial subjects have articulated their sufferings and protests. In these contexts, what can be said in public is typically closely policed, regardless of its "merit" on a rational basis.

From above, colonial subjects might appear to be silent (or silenced) in the public sphere, but from below, it is clear that they have actively produced "hidden transcripts" – jokes, songs, and stories with double meanings – circulated "off the grid," in ethnic bars or slave quarters, for example (Scott 1990). The Habermasian model envisions a stronger democracy when all subjects can participate in the institutionalized public sphere, making rational arguments without fear of reprisal. Viewed from below, this vision rings hollow: it asks that people in communities whose own narratives and identities have been forged almost entirely through "hidden transcripts" abandon their familiar cultural language – or, alternatively, that they place trust in public institutions established by their oppressors and "translate" narratives from their language into rational arguments as defined by those oppressors (Lo and Fan 2010). To conceptualize the public sphere in a way that excludes consideration of hidden transcripts risks perpetuating a Western-centric perspective on emancipation, agency, and rationality itself.

Some four decades of feminist and postcolonial scholarship have pointed to the previously obscured Western biases in sociological theory. Yet challenges remain. Chakrabarty poses the poignant question, "why can we [third world historians] not return the gaze?" (2000:29). Why do non-Western scholars seem to have little option but to conceptualize their societies in theoretical terms generated by Europeans? To pursue the alternative – in Chakrabarty's vivid image, to "provincialize Europe" – does not require embracing cultural relativism. Rather, the task is to reveal the intricate connections, not only historically but also conceptually, between the multiple expressions of the "modern" and multiple expressions of the "traditional" (Eisenstadt 1999; Adams, Clemens, and Orloff 2005).

The West, however dominant it may be, does not define the only or even the primary reference point in non-Western social lives. Recent scholarship offers a more nuanced picture of Western/non-Western social formations by attending on the one hand to global processes – sometimes of institutional isomorphism, sometimes not – and on the other, to local developments. Recent studies on music ("world" music), visual culture (anime), the media (Bollywood), medical care (acupuncture), and many other topics explore the rise of non-Western centers of global cultural influence. This scholarship debunks the assumption that the West is the default center of forces of globalization.

Under multicentric conditions, sociologists need to ask new questions about cultural processes in relation to (increasingly globalized) lifeworlds. For instance, with the rise of China as a global power, cultural globalization can no longer be adequately explained as the spread of European modernity or Western imperialism. But it would also be an oversimplification to view China's increasing global influence and visibility as evidence of "returning the gaze" or provincializing Europe. Instead, cultural sociologists are challenged to historicize the China-centered worldview that had existed in China long before the consolidation of European hegemony, and to analyze its continued hegemony, in part shaped by ongoing interactions with Western- or American-centered perspectives.

Underlying these important issues is a fundamental question that we must confront: what comes after "provincializing Europe?" To be sure, we endorse the call that sociologists in the West need to engage with multiple non-Western gazes. In the present handbook, we have responded to this call by seeking participation from diverse contributors, especially those based outside the West, as well as Western scholars whose works are in conversation with non-Western perspectives and cultural phenomena. At the same time, global approaches to cultural analysis are raising new questions about how to position scholarship, both politically and academically, in lifeworlds where the West is being actively provincialized.

These questions are as broad and multifaceted as they are important. And they prompt an additional, related challenge: how to make sense of the increasing contestation over meaning that comes with the dispersal and recalibration of power. The currents of globalization produce countercurrents of anti-globalization; the diffusion of hegemonic discourses generates claims about post-truths and alternative facts. Ironically, the dramatic intensification of the culture wars in recent years has put deconstructionists and other critical scholars (including cultural sociologists) in the position of defending "truth." Historically, critical scholars have emphasized the destabilization of meaning, categories, objectivity, and so forth as a way of critiquing the conflation of "truth" with the perspectives and experiences of the powerful; this critique has allowed competing truths to emerge from the perspectives and experiences of marginal and subaltern communities.

Now, just as the "hidden transcripts" of such communities are becoming increasingly visible and institutionalized, their "weapons of the weak" are being appropriated by people who have benefited (if only marginally) from the very hegemony being challenged. Ultra-nationalists, white supremacists, and climate-change deniers, for example, imply that meaning is socially constructed when they seek to provincialize the truth claims produced by scientific research and other forms of knowledge associated with "liberal" institutions. Does respecting marginalized perspectives, then, grant legitimacy to the attempts of such groups to relativize truth?

Now more than ever, we must attend to the social construction of lies, in relation to what McVeigh (2004) calls "structured ignorance." As sociologists are well aware, saying that there are "two sides" to issues such as slavery, the Holocaust, or the plight of Japanese "comfort" women is to lose sight of the fact that one side is grounded in documented patterns of lived oppression, whereas the other side is the product of strategic framing divorced from comparable standards of evidence. The job of social constructionists is not simply to insist that meaning is socially constructed but to analyze the different standards of evidence and narrative structures subtending the construction process itself, because it is the process that produces the various outcomes that people designate as truth, lies, ignorance, and so forth. With this in mind, we look forward to ongoing dialogue about global approaches to cultural analysis that, among other things, shed light on how meaning-making in lifeworlds is, in often radically different ways, grounded in lived experience as well as in denials of such experience.

Opening the handbook

The overarching principle for the second edition of the *Routledge Handbook of Cultural Sociology* continues to be the central importance of understanding lifeworlds in a global context. This emphasis brings to the fore a variety of analytic issues about the relation of culture to social phenomena ranging from the gendering of service work to the ethics of consumption to the politics of art and popular culture, and much more. As in the first edition (Hall, Grindstaff, and Lo 2010), rather than commissioning fewer, longer handbook chapters, we have followed the Broad Program by commissioning a larger number of somewhat shorter chapters, thereby increasing the range of substantive topics and participating authors. A number of the chapters, especially ones addressing recent cultural developments or where notable new scholarship has appeared, are thoroughly revised from what was originally published. Some chapters are new to this edition, and some chapters from the first edition do not appear here, so we encourage readers to consult that earlier volume as well. Our aim in both editions – by bringing together established scholars with emerging ones, by encouraging thematic connection and dialogue across chapters, and by acknowledging the importance of regional and international diversity to both cultural practice and cultural analysis – is to widen the sociological conversation about why and how culture matters around the world. We hope that the handbook exemplifies the vitality and scope of discussion that we seek to encourage.

Our effort to facilitate this discussion – revealed most obviously in our choice of topics and authors but also in our organization of the sections and their relations to one another – reflects many editorial discussions about how to structure the handbook. Because the chapters discuss a wide array of overlapping phenomena, there is no single "appropriate" ordering; indeed, the chapters might have been displayed in a hyperlinked sphere of networked connections. But given that the chapters exist in book form, with its sequence of pages, we have organized the chapters in a series of 10 thematic sections. Readers may fruitfully construct their own links across topics. The handbook begins with sections concerning general programmatic, theoretical, and methodological topics, and then turns to issues of aesthetics, ethics, legitimacy, and culture and stratification. From these basic concerns, the section topics shift to groups, identities, and performances, and the making and using of culture. Subsequent sections include chapters focused on work and professions, political culture, and globalization per se. The handbook concludes with a series of discussions of movements, memory, and change. In all cases, we asked authors to anchor their discussions in previous scholarship without pursuing comprehensive reviews, and to take stock of emergent issues of importance. We also encouraged them to engage with scholarship that either analyzes issues or has origins outside the West, and, for all scholarship, to bring comparative cases and global processes into consideration where appropriate. The resulting handbook, with its diverse short chapters, blurs genres: organized like a conventional handbook, it nevertheless covers topics in a way more encyclopedic.

Sociological discussions have by now moved well beyond arguments about whether culture is derivative or autonomous – by insisting upon more complex, contradictory formulations in which culture is both the medium of everyday lived experience and the scaffolding on which institutions and social orders emerge, cohere, and change – both within nation-states and globally. The authors contributing to the handbook address many different social manifestations with cultural aspects – including discourses, identities, practices, material objects, institutions, systems, and beliefs and values. Although this complexity makes the range of cultural sociology somewhat unwieldy, it also invites interdisciplinary cross-fertilization and disperses cultural authority. We do not presume to speak for our authors, but, for our part, we believe that this Broad Program of cultural sociology, connecting lifeworlds and globality, is the ever more urgent basis on which both sociology and cultural analysis more generally can best proceed in the twenty-first century.

References

Adams, Julia, Elisabeth Clemens, and Ann Orloff. 2005. "Introduction: Social Theory, Modernity, and the Three Waves of Historical Sociology." Pp. 1–72 in *Remaking Modernity*, edited by J. Adams, E. Clemens, and A. Orloff. Durham, NC: Duke University Press.

Beck, Ulrich. 2016. *The Metamorphosis of the World: How Climate Change is Transforming Our Concept of the World*. Cambridge: Polity Press.

Berger, Peter L., Brigitte Berger, and Hansfried Kellner. 1973. *The Homeless Mind: Modernization and Consciousness*. New York: Random House.

Chakrabarty, D. 2000. Provincializing Europe: Postcolonial Thought and Historical Difference. New Delhi: Oxford University Press.

Connell, R.W. 1997. "Why is Classical Theory Classical?" *American Journal of Sociology* 102(6):1511–57.

Dodd, Nigel, Michèle Lamont, and Mike Savage, eds. 2017. Special Issue: The Trump/Brexit Moment: Causes and Consequences. *British Journal of Sociology* 68(S1):S1–S280.

Eisenstadt, S.N. 1999. "Multiple Modernities in an Age of Globalization." *Canadian Journal of Sociology* 24(2):283–95.

Geertz, Clifford. 1973. *The Interpretation of Cultures*. New York: Basic.

Grindstaff, Laura. 2008. "Culture and Popular Culture: A Case for Sociology." *The Annals of the American Academy of Political and Social Science 619* (September): 206-222.

Habermas, Jürgen. [1981] 1987. *The Theory of Communicative Action*. Vol. 2, *Lifeworld and System*. Boston: Beacon Press.

Hall, John R. 1977. "Alfred Schutz, His Critics, and Applied Phenomenology." *Cultural Hermeneutics* 4(3):265–74.

———. 1999. *Cultures of Inquiry: From Epistemology to Discourse in Sociohistorical Research*. Cambridge: Cambridge University Press.

———. 2009. *Apocalypse: From Antiquity to the Empire of Modernity*. Cambridge: Polity Press.

Hall, John R., Laura Grindstaff, and Ming-Cheng M. Lo, eds. 2010. *Handbook of Cultural Sociology*. London: Routledge.

Jacobs, Ron. 2017. "Letter From the Chair." *Section Culture* 29(3):1–3.

Lo, Ming-Cheng M. 2002. *Doctors within Borders: Profession, Ethnicity, and Modernity in Colonial Taiwan*. Berkeley: University of California Press.

Lo, Ming-Cheng M., and Yun Fan. 2010. "Hybrid Cultural Codes in Nonwestern Civil Society: Images of Women in Taiwan and Hong Kong." *Sociological Theory* 28(2):167–92.

Mast, Jason L., and Jeffrey C. Alexander, eds. 2017. Special issue on the 2016 US Election. *American Journal of Cultural Sociology* 5(3).

McVeigh, Rory. 2004. "Structured Ignorance and Organized Racism in the United States." *Social Forces* 82(3):895–936.

Oxford English Dictionary (online version). Retrieved September 29, 2017 (https://en.oxforddictionaries.com/word-of-the-year/word-of-the-year-2013).

Schutz, Alfred, and Thomas Luckmann. 1973. *Structures of the Lifeworld*. Evanston, IL: Northwestern University Press.

Scott, James. 1990. *Domination and the Arts of Resistance: Hidden Transcripts*. New Haven, CT: Yale University Press.

Skocpol, Theda. 1979. *States and Social Revolutions*. Cambridge: Cambridge University Press.

Steinmetz, George. 2007. *The Devil's Handwriting: Precoloniality and the German Colonial State in Qingdao, Samoa, and Southwest Africa*. Chicago: University of Chicago Press.

———. 2017. "The Crisis of History and the History of Crisis: Sociology as a 'crisis science.'" *Trajectories*, Newsletter of the ASA Comparative and Historical Section 29(1):1–5.

Stone, Lawrence. 1979. "The Revival of Narrative: Reflections on a New Old History." *Past & Present* 85(November):3–24.

Syme, Rachel. 2015. "Selfie: The Revolutionary Potential of Your Own Face, in Seven Chapters." Retrieved September 29, 2017 (https://medium.com/matter/selfie-fe945dcba6b0).

Tilly, Charles. 1984. *Big Structures, Large Processes, Huge Comparisons*. New York: Russell Sage Foundation.

Part I
Sociological programs of cultural analysis

The Strong Program in cultural sociology

Meaning first

Jeffrey C. Alexander and Philip Smith

Introduction

The contours of the Strong Program were publicly announced some years ago in a polemic that underwent several iterations (Alexander 1996; Alexander and Smith 1998, 2001, 2010). However, its origins go back further. In the late 1980s a small research group at the University of California, Los Angeles (UCLA) attempted to bring deep meanings into sociological analysis in a non-reductionist way. We are now some 30 years from those cult-like origins in evening meetings at studio apartments scattered over greater Los Angeles. Today the Strong Program is a recognized, institutionally sustained global force.

But just what is the Strong Program? To our reading it remains the most controversial, least apologetic, and least ambiguous advocate of the cultural turn in sociology. It asserts that every aspect of social life, even those that appear purely coercive like torture, war, or imprisonment (Binder 2013; Smith 2005, 2008a, 2008b) or technocratic and instrumental like central banking policy (Tognato 2012) has a meaningful dimension. The role of the sociologist is to grasp these meanings, to interpret them, to understand their force, and to see how they can be considered as "causes" that shape policy, outcomes, opinions, technologies, actions, politics, preferences, consumption, gestures, and expressions. The Strong Program insists these meanings cannot be traced back or reduced to origins in power or social structure. Rather they exist in autonomous and patterned ways as culture structures that circulate through social life: they are codes, narratives, myths, icons, or other non-material collective representations. For the Strong Program, these meanings are also "hot" and laden with affect. They mark things out as sacred or profane and hence are far more potent than the "cold" schemas or pragmatic "toolkits" that are at the analytic center of many rival, mainstream, and less threatening approaches. The Strong Program is revolutionary, not just additive. Although it believes that social life is multidimensional (in addition to meaning, there are also power, reason, materiality, and organization), it does not hold meaning to be just another factor to be thrown into the explanatory mixing bowl. Like Emile Durkheim in his *Elementary Forms of Religious Life*, we insist that the deepest foundations of social life are ideal, not material. No meaning, no society.

The Strong Program is also unique relative to its immediate competition in having a big picture vision of our social world today. It proclaims that modernity is not really "modern," never fully "rational." Ideas about the sacred, ritualistic politics, narratives of salvation, collective emotions, and iconic attractions still shape social life at every level from the interpersonal to the macro-historical. Yet the Strong Program is more than simply a provocation, or manifesto, or worldview. It is also a research program, along with a set of transposable modules – models, methods, and conceptual tools – that taken separately or together allow interpretation and explanation of the social world. With these, it has relentlessly made the case for a switch from the "sociology of culture" toward a truly "cultural sociology."

Origins

For a long time American sociology resisted the cultural turn upon which the Strong Program has built. Yet in the mid-1980s, things started to change. The initial gestures were hesitant. Like a swimming lesson where the students stay in the shallow end, people wanted to talk about meaning but were unwilling to trust an elusive medium. They made certain their toes could still touch power, interests, and class, and all the other tiles at the bottom of the pool – hence the growing influence during this period of the three big "weak programs" we identified and called out in the initial Strong Program chapter. Although the water wings and rubber rings were initially useful, such aids as Foucault, Bourdieu, and the Birmingham School were eventually debilitating.

During this same period, there emerged from within American sociology influential middle-range nods to meaning that similarly revealed the uncertainties of this early phase: John Meyer's neo-institutionalism, Ann Swidler's toolkit theory, David Snow's "framing" concept, and the work of Pete Peterson, Wendy Griswold, and others on the production of culture. Yet we do not wish to make the Strong Program the only white knight in our tale. Key figures such as Viviana Zelizer, Robin Wagner-Pacifici, Barry Schwartz, Michele Lamont, and Eviatar Zerubavel also pioneered. As early as 1987, John R. Hall's book on Jonestown was subtitled with the words "cultural history" (Hall 1987). However, only the Strong Program had the qualities of a "program," movement, or collective enterprise. By picking fights with weak programs (Sherwood, Smith, and Alexander 1993) and by calling out reductionist accounts as inadequate (Alexander, Sherwood, and Smith 1993), it was also the most visibly combative force in American cultural sociology.

Today the Strong Program grows in power and influence. One indicator is that it has global reach, with self-defined associates and/or partner centers in such places as Japan, Korea, China, Colombia, Hong Kong, Italy, Germany, Sweden, Israel, the Czech Republic, Russia, South Africa, and Australia. The creation of the Yale Center for Cultural Sociology (CCS) in 2003 offered a symbolic home for this worldwide intellectual movement, hosting visitors and sponsoring conferences. The depth and range of scholarship has also improved as second-generation Strong Programmers move into midcareer. Google Scholar has a "cultural sociology" label; at the time of writing, Strong Program affiliates make up six of the 30 most cited profiles under that tag. Consider also the case of monographs. Earlier versions of the present chapter tended to circle around book-length investigations by Alexander, Eyerman, Jacobs, Ku, and Smith, and to cite shorter articles by our students. The past five years have seen the pool of Strong Program monographs dramatically expand. We now have access to long-awaited books by Binder, Howe, Jaworsky, Kane, Mast, McCormick, Osbaldiston, Reed, Riley, Tognato, West, and Woods that explicitly deploy and deepen our paradigms (see references). In another indicator of success, the Strong Program has become a point of reference for other scholarship. The Strong Program set up its stall in opposition to weak programs; today, we can enjoy the irony that others define themselves in contrast to us. For example, in their introduction, the editors of this volume identify a "Broad Program" that is more inclusive of diverse intellectual orientations. Gary Alan Fine (2010) promoted a "puny program" that contrasts with the Strong Program in giving more attention to pragmatics and interpersonal contexts. Strong Program scholars have gained disciplinary centrality and gatekeeping power, founding and editing the *American Journal of Cultural Sociology* and the Palgrave Macmillan Series on Cultural Sociology. Although such enterprises are not exclusively Strong Program in brand, the pursuit of meanings and meaning-centered explanation is a requirement for entry. We are also deeply concerned with an effort to systematically explain the world around us. From the Strong Program perspective, too much cultural work is theory of theory, history of theory, "compare and contrast scholars and concepts," pseudo-theory, intervention, and normative theory, or impressionistic "readings" of meaning without long-term empirical investigation. By contrast, the Strong Program draws upon and reconstructs theory so as to engage in sociological explanation.

Achievements

Doing cultural sociology is not as easy as it sometimes looks. Indeed, the late arrival of the cultural turn in sociology undoubtedly reflected the problem of translating resources from literary theory, theater studies, aesthetics, philosophy, and anthropology into tractable idea-sets for explaining contemporary (and historical) social life. This translation is necessary in order to move beyond the impressionist hit-or-miss schools of esoteric interpretation. Indeed, we see the emergence and refinement of a range of middle-level resources over the past three decades as perhaps the single most important contribution of the Strong Program. These research programs, paradigms in the Mertonian sense, are set out below.

Collective conscience, civil society, and the mass media

Durkheim wrote many years ago about the collective conscience of a society. The idea is intuitively appealing, but also somewhat amorphous and plagued by metaphor. Drawing from Habermas's ideas about the public sphere and rejecting his pessimistic conclusions as well as the notion that deliberation is "rational," the Strong Program has argued since the late 1980s that we can see the collective conscience at work in a "civil sphere" (Alexander 2006). This is a place where the diffuse moral authority and pressure of public opinion is concretized and where the social evaluation of actors and policies is made possible. With the civil sphere in mind, there can be a concerted effort to explore public and observable speech acts through which claims are made, both in political and social movement arenas and in the mass media (Alexander and Jacobs 1998; Sherwood 1994). Recent work has explored issues of access and symbolic power in this process (Jacobs and Townsley 2011). Moving away from an early reliance on quality journalism, political speeches, news conferences, and opinion leaders, scholarship has expanded its methodological repertoire to include civil debate among ordinary people. This is possible due to the rise of new media environments that facilitate direct citizen-to-citizen exchange. Examples include enthusiast threads deliberating racism in video games (McKernan 2015), town-based internet forums on local immigration (Jaworsky 2016), and posts in response to environmental news items in the mainstream media (Smith and Howe 2015).

Binary oppositions and the discourse of civil society

Binary opposition, of course, was a staple of semiotic structuralism from Jacobson to Lévi-Strauss, Barthes, and Sahlins. A major step by the Strong Program pioneers of the 1980s was to understand public sphere talk as shaped by strong binary logics. Emerging out of Alexander's Watergate research, we published studies about the "discourse of civil society" that offered a new way of reading politics (e.g., Alexander and Smith 1993; Smith 1991). Not only debate and public thinking but political action itself was shown to be organized around the codes through which sacred and profane motivations, relations, and institutions were defined and applied in processes of typification. Strong Program scholars have confirmed their distribution throughout liberal democracies (e.g., Smith 2005 for the UK, Spain, and France) and in pro-democracy movements in less tolerant places (Baiocchi 2006 for Brazil; Ku 2001 for China). In addition, there have been efforts to explore illiberal codes (fascism, authoritarianism, communism) and their relationship to civil discourse (Baiocchi 2006; Edles 1998; Smith 1996b). Finally, the investigation of the binary opposition has by no means been restricted to political arenas. Strong Program members have identified diverse, context-flexible binaries at work in more local institutional settings and lifeworld domains. The early computer was coded by commentators as bringing salvation or doom (Alexander 1992); concert performers are seen by their audiences as deeply musical or as robotic and shallow (McCormick 2015); in the men's movement, masculinity can be read as regressive and hegemonic or as sensitive and reformed (Magnuson 2008); and places like a remote Afro-Ecuadorian valley (Jijon 2013), an Australian beach resort (Osbaldiston 2012), or an American small town (Kidder 2018) are perceived as authentic and life-enhancing in a binary that contrasts them with the anomic, soul-destroying, and corrupt city.

Narrative and genre

Analyzing binary oppositions is a critical intellectual tool, but its use does not exhaust the culture structures that we should be trying to detect in a post-Geertzian theoretical world. More is needed to capture fully the nuance and hermeneutic specificity of particular settings and struggles. Draft papers written by our members toward the end of the Cold War and during the buildup to the Gulf War developed a model of narrative process in civil society (e.g., Sherwood 1994). The Strong Program argues that narratives, just like binary codes, circulate and are contested in the collective conscience/civil sphere, and in this process can shape history. The political crises of Watergate and Irangate, for example, are similar in that each involved an intensive deployment of the discourse of civil society, yet each also featured divergent efforts at storytelling and narrative accounting.

Realizing that cognition is tied to storytelling, Strong Program members have developed two approaches to narrative. One is more inductive and historically embedded, even if it employs general theory or language of plot and character en passant. Thus, Alexander (2002) demonstrates that the Holocaust was initially seen as a war crime and only later renarrated as universal evil. Eyerman (2001) traces continuous conflict in African American history between more optimistic and progressive narrations of slavery and more pessimistic and tragic ones. In multiple case studies with very different aims West (2015) and Howe (2016) both show how the nation, locale, history, memory, and the sacred are intimately connected through collective narrative work. The other approach is ontological and Aristotelian, identifying the inner logic of culture structures. This approach has produced a more systematic and robust model of narrative process. Jacobs (2000) and Smith (2005) first employed Northrop Frye's theories of literary genre to show how powers of action, plot trajectories toward a happy society or its collapse, and imputed motivations vary systematically over a gamut of genre types (romance, tragedy, comedy, irony). These play out in predictable ways in struggles over legitimacy, authority, and reconciliation. Such models open the way toward a less idiographic mode of narrative inquiry, making a more systematic comparative cultural sociology possible. Tracking genres against outcomes, for example, Smith (2005) explains decisions in four nations as they encountered the same foreign policy crises. And Jacobs (2000) is able to predict the kinds of narrative that will accompany successful civic repair in a time of racial crisis. Likewise, divergent attitudes toward climate change are embedded in narrative projections of possible futures (Smith and Howe 2015). This structural narrative model remains one of our most persuasive generalizable tools.

Performance

A major problem of text-based approaches to culture is that agency tends to be squeezed out of the frame. The Strong Program has responded to this challenge by conceptualizing cultural pragmatics, thus building upon a general understanding, derived from Aristotle, Victor Turner, and others, that political and social life is deeply dramatic. The turn toward performance was foreshadowed in earlier studies, such as that of Edles (1998) on the democratic transition in Spain, Jacobs (2000) on civic crisis in Los Angeles, and Smith (1996a) in his account of the eighteenth-century public execution. More recently, these intuitions have been formalized and thickened by drawing on the philosophy of performativity, drama theory in the humanities, and the new discipline of performance studies; and also through careful alignments with other bodies of theory on the nature of social power (Reed 2013). The "cultural pragmatics" that emerged in the early 2000s (Alexander, Giesen, and Mast 2006) provided a repertoire of transposable concepts – fusion/defusion/refusion, scripts and background representations, means of symbolic production, mise-en-scène, hermeneutical power – and showed how they could be employed in various settings to explain social dynamics. What separates this approach from Goffmanian dramaturgy is not only its macro orientation but its insistence that performances are oriented by and toward deep culture structures and myths, not only situational contingencies and interpersonal interaction norms. This model has been especially effective for case study investigations of politics such as the reputational travails of Bill Clinton (Mast 2012), various acts of political violence (Eyerman 2008), the pivotal role of the Truth and Reconciliation Commission in South Africa (Goodman 2009), or anti-colonial land struggles in Ireland (Kane 2011). It also has also been turned back onto the arts themselves (Eyerman and McCormick 2006), even explaining how musicians communicate with audiences (McCormick 2015). Ideas about performativity also have enabled the return of a more Geertzian spirit of interpretation, allowing aesthetic play and historical locality (e.g., Trondman 2008) to balance the structuralism that emanated from earlier, more text-based Strong Program writings.

Cultural trauma

The most problem-oriented paradigm of the Strong Program has focused on episodes of social trauma and their cultural reinterpretations (Alexander et al. 2004). The focus here is not on individual psychological process. Moreover, the approach takes aim at lay theories that view collective responses as rational or irrational adaptation. The spotlight, instead, is on meaning-work, how it orients painful experiences, constructs new collective identities, defines moral responsibilities, and channels the course of future actions and events. Cultural trauma makes binaries about polluted others, even as it shapes narratives about past, present, and future confrontations between perpetrators and victims (Giesen 2004). These cultural processes are propelled by the ideal and material interests of carrier groups, powerfully mediated by the institutional fields in which they unfold, and significantly affected by existing distributions of vertical resources. So far, this trauma model has framed Strong Program investigations into war, genocide, mass murder, slavery, political assassination, child abuse, and postcolonialism (for a recent example and a literature review, see Woods 2016). The intellectual schema is very transposable. Reconfiguring their ongoing work on collective memory or social crisis in terms of the trauma paradigm, scholars throughout the world have found pathways for more systematic explanation.

Iconicity

A major challenge for cultural sociology lies in coming to terms with the non-discursive and non-verbal elements of social life. How do we explain the fact that an iPhone is "cool" or that material vinyl records (Bartmanski and Woodward 2015) inspire a cult-like enthusiasm that a digital MP3 download cannot? Building from an initial discussion of iconic consciousness in the appreciation of artworks (Alexander 2008), the Strong Program has most recently begun challenging the materialist vision of commodity fetishism more comprehensively, offering in its place a truly multidimensional vision of social materiality (see Alexander, Bartmanski, and Giesen 2013). We illuminate how sensuous aesthetic surfaces remain powerful and how they are often experienced as seamlessly intertwined with the diverse social meanings and circulating background scripts that establish the moral, social, and intellectual biographies of objects. Our ongoing work builds on both semiotics and studies of material culture, exploring the multifold, often mysterious attraction of things. It draws from systematic earlier Strong Program surveys of both visual culture (Emmison and Smith 2000) and material culture (Woodward 2007), as well as case studies that captured the iconic dimension of such corporal punishment technologies as the guillotine and electric chair (Smith 2008a). Rather than turning to museums, monuments, artworks, and the spectacular, this paradigm seems increasingly concerned with the sacral aura that inspires consumption and adheres to apparently mundane objects (Alexander 1992; Woodward 2007; Bartmanski and Woodward 2015). Most recently it has branched out to consider iconic and somatic aspects of embodiment (Champagne 2016).

Critiques and challenges

As the outspoken carrier of the cultural turn in sociology, the Strong Program has inevitably become subject to critique, increasingly so as its theorizing has so markedly extended into the middle range. There are three substantial literature clusters. First, Strong Program scholars have engaged in auto-critique as they attempt to refine the paradigms or add new resources. Dmitry Kurakin (2015) has suggested that the Strong Program wrongly equates the sacred and profane with good and bad, whereas in Durkheim's original formulation the sacred was a volatile, ambiguous force of terrifying instability and ambivalence. In a related vein, Alexander Riley (2010) retraces the genealogy of the "left sacred" or "impure sacred" and insists on its centrality for twentieth-century cultural theory. Smith (2014) argues that existing deployments of the Mary Douglas model of pollution have become routinized and complacent. He urges the Strong Program to give more attention to neglected but somewhat parallel concepts and experiences such as the uncanny. Madigan (2016) asserts that Strong Program models of genre and narrative are misleading, returning to Frye and Aristotle to propose a more elegant, simplified model. Smith and Howe (2015) also refine earlier Strong Program understandings of narrative. Following Hegel, they emphasize character and choice in contemporary understandings of tragedy, contrasting these with the stress on caprice and fate in the Aristotelian model. At the level of metatheory, Isaac Reed (2011) has provided a comprehensive justification for interpretation as explanation. Confronting recent challenges to the very idea of a cultural sociology, Reed significantly upgrades Alexander's earlier 1980s work on the logics of social action, showing how every sociological explanation references meanings that are both internal (reasons, motivations) and external (cultural and social structures) to agents.

A second body of critique comes from fellow travelers. Often the Strong Program polemic is combined with a weak program or with another paradigm. The complaint here is the relatively mild one that the Strong Program can provide only a partial explanation and that it requires a supplement. For example, Shai Dromi (2016) uses Strong Program theories about the role of the sacred to account for the rise of the International Red Cross from origins in Swiss Calvinism. However, he also makes use of Bourdieusian "fields" to account for the subsequent institutionalization of transnational humanitarianism. Likewise, Marco Santoro and Marco Solaroli (2016) insist that the Strong Program and Bourdieu make an attractive pairing of theoretical approaches, each compensating for the excesses and omissions of the other. Matthew Norton (2014) explores the role of ritual and cultural classification in the regulation and control of piracy in the seventeenth and eighteenth centuries, melding this analysis with more Weberian explanatory logics on militarism, empire, and the rise of the early modern state. Such work makes it harder today to draw a clear boundary around the Strong Program's membership or output. Especially where younger scholars are concerned – including those who are students of the authors of this chapter – the Strong Program can become one source of influence to be combined with others in a more additive than (our trademark) combative manner.

Critics from the outside, even when sympathetic, are less forgiving. They generally focus on idealism, an accusation that goes with the territory. This plaint has several dimensions: (1) we have an overly optimistic view of human nature; (2) we neglect strategic action by elites; (3) we fail to see that civil society is weak (Cutler 2006); (4) we ignore the situational interactions of concrete actors and groups in favor of a meta-discourse that goes about its business in a transcendental quasi-Hegelian, neo-Lévi-Straussian way (Battani, Hall, and Powers 1997; Fine, Harrington, and Segre 2008; Morris 2007); (5) we have little to say about the material/power bases of inequality that connect culture back to such foundations (Antonio 2007; Garland 2009; Gartman 2007; McLennan 2004, 2005); and (6) we are anti-scientific, espousing a culturalist and anti-positivist relativism where interpretation replaces explanation (Boudon 2007; Steensland 2009) – or, more charitably, we cannot explain why some meanings and performances stick and others do not (Emirbayer 2004; Kurasawa 2004).

Even as such critics ignore our carefully worded caveats about power, interests, resources, and strategy, they point to real issues of balance, emphasis, and relative neglect. Although there is not space here to mount a protracted defense against these charges, we would maintain that pretty much every Strong Program exploration has been about struggles over meaning, not consensus. Indeed, power itself has become the object of intense scrutiny (Norton 2014; Reed 2013): as something that energizes and directs, even as it is channeled by, cultural perceptions of geopolitical threat (Smith 2005); as something that attempts to deploy meaning as it goes about the task of controlling deviance or motivating armed men (Smith 2008b); as something that is augmented and challenged by the deft performance of ideology and "character" or what Aristotle called "ethos" (Mast 2012; Smith and Howe 2015); and as the cultural outcome of ferociously aggressive political struggles (Jacobs 2000; Alexander 2009).

Two barbs against the Strong Program have been particularly productive. The argument that we are Hegelians has alerted us to the problems of text-based research. Whereas the early work of the program was more desk-driven and media-focused, the younger generation has largely taken a different tack. It has generated more ethnographic and interview-based studies, tracing the interaction between symbolic structures and interaction at the local, concrete, more empirically observable levels that are the normal stuff of American qualitative sociology (e.g., see references for work by Jaworsky, Jijon, Kidder, Magnuson, McCormick, Osbaldiston, and West).

The second useful critique has come from those who have conjured the specter of indeterminacy (Emirbayer 2004; Kurasawa 2004). Strong Program arguments typically explain outcomes by pointing to the rise and fall of cultural patterns, or to successful and failed performances, or to seductive or faulty iconicity. An apocalyptic narrative dogged Saddam Hussein in 1992; unable to shake this off, the "new Hitler" was driven out of Kuwait (Smith 2005). Mast (2012) tracks the major failures of Clinton's presidency to his "slick Willy" shadow. Edles (1998) links the successful post-Franco Spanish democracy to the emergence of three powerful sets of new representations. And Jacobs (2000) accounts for civil renewal in Los Angeles with reference to an ascendant Romantic genre. But just why does one cultural structure succeed and another fail? What makes a meaning "stick"? It would seem there is always another Russian doll as we look for an answer by "going micro," another black box to be opened as we scan yet more institutions and contexts for a resolution.

The truth is that the Strong Program has chosen a bed of nails. We have repeatedly avoided the easy choice of referring the triumph of one meaning system or another back to something that seems more concrete (power, a network, an institution, a gatekeeper), insisting instead that culture has its own autonomous structures (Kane 1992) and that there can be cultural factors behind cultural outcomes. If the Strong Program is to retain a belief in the relative autonomy of meaning, then we must recognize a moment of contingency that escapes crude explanatory ambitions. Combining this reality with disciplinary norms that focus on the observable and testable is an ongoing challenge (Reed 2011).

Despite these critiques and ripostes – indeed because of them – the Strong Program is a progressive research program in the Lakatosian sense: it is theoretically and empirically cumulative, even as it innovates, revises, and expands. The conditions are more propitious than ever for explaining outcomes with culture – if not exclusively with it, then never without reference to it. At the end of the day, this is what the Strong Program is all about.

References

Alexander, J. 1992. "The Promise of a Cultural Sociology." Pp. 293–323 in *Theory of Culture*, edited by R. Munch and N. Smelser. Berkeley: University of California Press.

_____. 1996. "Cultural Sociology or Sociology of Culture?" *Culture* 10(3–4):1–5.

_____. 2002. "On the Social Construction of Moral Universals." *European Journal of Social Theory* 5(1):5–86.

_____. 2006. *The Civil Sphere*. Oxford: Oxford University Press.

_____. 2008. "Iconic Experience in Art and Life." *Theory, Culture and Society* 25:3.

_____. 2009. "The Democratic Struggle for Power." *Journal of Power* 2:65–88.

Alexander, J., D. Bartmanski, and B. Giesen, eds. 2013. *Iconic Power*. London: Palgrave Macmillan.

Alexander, J., B. Giesen, R. Eyerman, N. Smelser, P. Stzompka. 2004. *Cultural Trauma*. Berkeley: University of California Press.

Alexander, J., B. Giesen, and J. Mast, eds. 2006. *Social Performance: Symbolic Action, Cultural Pragmatics and Ritual*. Cambridge: Cambridge University Press.

Alexander, J., and R. Jacobs. 1998. "Mass Communication, Ritual, and Civil Society." Pp. 23–41 in *Media, Ritual, and Identity*, edited by T. Liebes and J. Curran. London: Routledge.

Alexander, J., S. Sherwood, and P. Smith. 1993. "Risking Enchantment." *Culture* 4(4):10–14.

Alexander, J., and P. Smith. 1993. "The Discourse of American Civil Society." *Theory and Society* 22(2):151–207.

_____. 1998. "Sociologie culturelle ou sociologie de la culture? Un programme fort pour donner à sociologie son second souffle." *Sociologie et Sociétés* 30(1):107–16.

_____. 2001. "The Strong Program in Cultural Sociology: Elements of a Structural Hermeneutics." Pp. 135–50 in *Handbook of Sociological Theory*, edited by J. Turner. New York: Springer.

_____. 2010. "The Strong Program: Origins, Achievements and Prospects." Pp. 13–24 in *Handbook of Cultural Sociology*, edited by J. Hall, L. Grindstaff, and M. Lo. New York: Routledge.

Antonio, R.J. 2007. "Locating 'The Civil Sphere.'" *Sociological Quarterly* 48(4):601–14.

Baiocchi, G. 2006. "The Civilizing Force of Social Movements." *Sociological Theory* 24(4):285–311.

Bartmanski, D., and I. Woodward. 2015. *Vinyl*. London: Bloomsbury.

Battani, M., R. Hall, and D. Powers. 1997. "Culture's Structures." *Theory and Society* 26:781–812.

Binder, W. 2013. *Abu Ghraib und die Folgen*. Bielefeld: Transcript Verlag.

Boudon, R. 2007. "Nouveau Durkheim? Vrai Durkheim?" *Durkheimian Studies* 12(1):137–48.

Champagne, A.M. 2016. "*The Iconicity of the Breast*." Manuscript.

Cutler, J. 2006. "War Cultures and Culture Wars." *Contexts* 5(3):52–4.

Dromi, S. 2016. "For Good and Country." *Sociological Review Monographs* 64:79–97.

Edles, L. 1998. *Symbol and Ritual in the New Spain*. Cambridge: Cambridge University Press.

Emirbayer, M. 2004. "The Alexander School of Cultural Sociology." *Thesis Eleven* 79(1):5–15.

Emmison, M., and P. Smith. 2000. *Researching the Visual*. London: Sage.

Eyerman, R. 2001. *Cultural Trauma: Slavery and the Formation of African-American Identity*. Cambridge: Cambridge University Press.

_____. 2008. *The Assassination of Theo Van Gogh*. Durham, NC: Duke University Press.

Eyerman, R., and L. McCormick, eds. 2006. *Myth, Meaning and Performance*. Boulder, CO: Paradigm Press.

Fine, G.A. 2010. "The Sociology of the Local." *Sociological Theory* 28(4):355–76.

Fine, G.A., B. Harrington, and S. Segre. 2008. "Tiny Publics and Group Practice." *Sociologica* 1:1–6.

Garland, D. 2009. "A Culturalist Theory of Punishment?" *Punishment and Society* 11(2):259–68.

Gartman, D. 2007. "The Strength of Weak Programs." *Theory and Society* 36(5):381–413.

Giesen, B. 2004. *Triumph and Trauma*. Boulder, CO: Paradigm Press.

Goodman, T. 2009. *Staging Solidarity: Truth and Reconciliation in the new South Africa*. Boulder, CO: Paradigm Press.

Hall, J.R. 1987. *Gone from the Promised Land*. New York: Transaction.

Howe, N. 2016. *Landscapes of the Secular*. Chicago: University of Chicago Press.

Jacobs, R. 2000. *Race, Media and the Crisis of Civil Society*. Cambridge: Cambridge University Press.

Jacobs, R. and E. Townsley. 2011. *The Space of Opinion*. New York: Oxford University Press.

Jaworsky, B.N. 2016. *The Boundaries of Belonging*. New York: Palgrave Macmillan.

Jijon, I. 2013. "The Glocalization of Time and Space." *International Sociology* 28(4):373–90.

Kane, A. 1992. "Cultural Analysis in Historical Sociology." *Sociological Theory* 9(1):53–69.

_____. 2011. *Constructing Irish National Identity*. New York. Palgrave Macmillan.

Kidder, J. 2018. "Civil and Uncivil Places." *American Journal of Cultural Sociology* 6(1):161–188

Ku, A. 2001. "The Public Up Against the State." *Theory, Culture and Society* 18(1):121–44.

Kurakin, D. 2015. "Reassembling the Ambiguity of the Sacred." *Journal of Classical Sociology* 15(4):377–95.

Kurasawa, F. 2004. "Alexander and the Cultural Refounding of American Sociology." *Thesis Eleven* 79(1):53–64.

Madigan, T. 2016. "*Farewell to Genre*." Manuscript.

Magnuson, E. 2008. *Changing Men, Transforming Culture*. Boulder, CO: Paradigm.

Mast, J. 2012. *The Performative Presidency*. Cambridge: Cambridge University Press.

McCormick, L. 2015. *Performing Civility*. Cambridge: Cambridge University Press.

McKernan, B. 2015. "The Meaning of a Game." *American Journal of Cultural Sociology* 3(2):224–53.

McLennan, G. 2004. "Rationalizing Musicality." *Thesis Eleven* 79(1):75–86.

_____. 2005. "The New American Cultural Sociology: An Appraisal." *Theory, Culture and Society* 22(6):1–18.

Morris, A. 2007. "Naked Power and 'The Civil Sphere.'" *Sociological Quarterly* 48(4):615–28.

Norton, M. 2014. "Classification and Coercion." *American Journal of Sociology* 119(6):1537–75.

Osbaldiston, N. 2012. *Seeking Authenticity in Place, Culture, and the Self*. New York: Palgrave Macmillan.

Reed, I. 2011. *Interpretation and Social Knowledge*. Chicago: University of Chicago Press.

_____. 2013. "Power: Relational, Discursive and Performative." *Sociological Theory* 31(3): 193–218.

Riley, A. 2010. *Godless Intellectuals*. New York: Berghahn Books.

Santoro, M. and M. Solaroli. 2016. "Contesting Culture: Bourdieu and the Strong Program in Cultural Sociology." Pp. 49–76 in *Routledge International Handbook of the Sociology of the Arts and Culture*, edited by M. Savage and L. Hanquinet. London: Routledge.

Sherwood, S. 1994. "Narrating the Social." *Journal of Narrative and Life History* 4(1–2):69–88.

Sherwood, S., P. Smith, and J. Alexander. 1993. "The British are Coming . . . Again! The Hidden Agenda of 'Cultural Studies.'" *Contemporary Sociology* 22(2):370–75.

Smith, P. 1991. "Codes and Conflict." *Theory and Society* 20(3):101–38.

_____. 1996a. "Executing Executions." *Theory and Society* 25(2):235–61.

_____. 1996b. "Barbarism and Civility in the Discourses of Fascism, Communism and Democracy." Pp. 115–37 in *Real Civil Societies*, edited by J. Alexander. London: Sage.

_____. 2005. *Why War?* Chicago: University of Chicago Press.

_____. 2008a. *Punishment and Culture*. Chicago: University of Chicago Press.

_____. 2008b. "Meaning and Military Power." *Journal of Power* 1:275–93.

_____. 2014. "Of 'near pollution' and Non-linear Cultural Effects." *American Journal of Cultural Sociology* 2(3):329–47.

Smith, P., and N. Howe. 2015. *Climate Change as Social Drama*. Cambridge: Cambridge University Press.

Steensland, B. 2009. "Restricted and Elaborated Modes in the Cultural Analysis of Politics." *Sociological Forum* 24(4):926–34.

Tognato, C. 2012. *Central Bank Independence*. New York: Palgrave Macmillan.

Trondman, M. 2008. "To Locate in the Tenor of Their Setting the Sources of Their Spell." *Cultural Sociology* 2(2):201–21.

West, B. 2015. *Re-enchanting Nationalisms*. New York: Springer-Verlag.

Woods, E. 2016. *A Cultural Sociology of Anglican Missions and the Indian Residential Schools in Canada*. London: Palgrave Macmillan.

Woodward, I. 2007. *Understanding Material Culture*. London: Sage.

2

"Culture studies" and the culture complex

Tony Bennett

Introduction

In *Reassembling the Social*, Bruno Latour argues that culture "does not act surreptitiously behind the actor's back" but is "manufactured at specific places and institutions, be it the messy offices of the top floor of Marshal Sahlins's house on the Chicago campus or the thick Area Files kept in the Pitts River [*sic*] museum in Oxford" (2005:175). He goes on to characterize this close attention to the sites where things are made as a distinguishing trait of science studies. In doing so, he counterposes these concerns to those of "sociologists of the social" who aim to bring to light hidden structures – of language or ideologies, for example – to account for social actions in ways that social actors themselves are unaware of. Such approaches pass over the more mundane and material processes of making culture that Latour highlights. In what follows, I explore the implications of Latour's approach for the analysis of the relations between culture and the social. I suggest that science studies and actor-network theory (ANT) provide useful models for the development of forms of cultural analysis – which, analogically, I shall call "culture studies" – capable of illuminating how culture operates as a historically distinctive set of assemblages (the "culture complex" of my title), which act on the social in a variety of ways. I then relate these concerns to those of Foucauldian governmentality theory to suggest how the analysis of culture might best be approached when viewed as part of a field of government. Finally, I consider the implications of these approaches for the development of a properly historical approach to the tasks of cultural analysis. (In addressing these issues, I draw on Bennett 2007a and 2007b. Bennett 2013 develops these arguments in more detail.)

Culture studies

To look to Latour for guidance in analyzing the relations between culture and the social might seem quixotic given his opposition to the two-house collective dividing the assembly of things (nature) from the assembly of humans (society) that he attributes to early modern science and political thought (Latour 1993). For the concern to distinguish culture from the social as a subdivision within the assembly of humans is a further aspect of the "modern settlement" that Latour has worked so assiduously to unsettle. Latour makes this clear in *Politics of Nature*, where he suggests that we put aside the ideas of culture, nature, and society to focus instead on the processes through which humans and non-humans are assembled into collectives whose constitution is always simultaneously natural, social, cultural, and technical. Yet Latour also qualifies this position by arguing that although the division between nature and society as incommensurable realms has no valid epistemological foundations, it has real historical force if understood as referring not to "domains of reality" but to "a quite specific form of public organization" (Latour 2004:53).

Similarly, in *Reassembling the Social*, Latour is less iconoclastic in relation to the concept of the social than in many of his earlier formulations. The central difficulty, he argues, lies not in the concept of the social, if this is thought of as a stabilized bundle of connections between human and non-human actants that might be mobilized to account for some other phenomenon – the connections between the middle classes, works of art, and the organization of class distinctions, for example (Latour 2005:40). Rather, problems arise when the social is thought of as a specific kind of material, as if there were a distinctive kind of "social stuff" that can be distinguished from other "non-social" phenomena and then invoked, in the form of an encompassing social context or social structure, as an explanatory ground in relation to the latter (Latour 2005:1–4). In place of this conception of the social, Latour recommends that it be thought of as an assemblage of diverse components brought together via a work of connection performed by a diverse set of agents. John Law's formulations point in a similar direction, interpreting the social as the outcome of varied processes of translation through which different "bits and pieces" of the socio-material world are brought into association with one another in the context of relationally configured networks of people and things (Law 1994:102–05).

Although it is not a move that either Latour or Law makes, a similar case can be made for seeing culture not as made up of a distinctive kind of "cultural stuff" (representations, say) but as a provisional assemblage of all kinds of "bits and pieces" that are fashioned into durable networks whose interactions produce culture as a distinctive public organization of people and things. We can see, too, how the historical emergence of culture as a result of the production of new assemblages of human and non-human actors through which its differentiation from the social and the economy was enacted might be accounted for in a similar fashion. Before pursuing this line of inquiry further, however, I want to consider some more general aspects of science studies and actor-network theory for the light they throw on both the work that goes into the making of culture and the distinctive kind of work that culture, in turn, performs. I shall focus on three issues here.

The first concerns ANT's focus on the "*relational materiality*" constituted by different assemblages of human and non-human actors, in which what matters is how the elements of such assemblages work together to order and perform the social (Law 1999:4). Such practices of social ordering are, as Law (1994) puts it elsewhere, "*materially heterogeneous*," made up of bits and pieces of talk, architecture, bodies, texts, machines, and so forth, all of which interact to construct and perform the social. This relational materialism has much in common with the accounts of discursive or ideological articulation that have played such a significant role in cultural studies. In both cases, the identity and effectivity of elements derive not from their intrinsic properties but from the networks of relations in which they are installed. The main difference between these two positions – one which, in my view, should be counted in ANT's favor – concerns the expanded, and more convincingly materialist, field of analysis that results from ANT's incorporation of non-human actors into the networks that go to make up and perform the social. This approach has several advantages over the view associated with the "cultural turn" – that social relations are essentially cultural in form because they are informed by linguistic or meta-linguistic articulations of social meanings, positions, and identities. For it makes possible a non-tautological account of the constitution of culture, understood as a distinctive public organization of things and people that is distinguished from the social rather than merged with it. When those whom Latour characterizes as "sociologists of the social" try to account for the durability of social ties, Latour argues, they typically appeal to the role of social norms and values, thus engaging in the "tautology of social ties made out of social ties" (Latour 2005:70). A good deal of work in cultural studies proceeds similarly by defining culture as a meaning-making system that makes meanings. This is avoidable in an approach that focuses on culture as an assemblage of heterogeneous elements whose "culturalness" derives from, rather than precedes, their assembly.

I take my second point from Andrew Pickering's characterization of the adjacent field of practice studies as amounting to a *"social theory of the visible"* (Pickering 2001:164) that does not look for any deeper or hidden structures beneath the "the visible and specific intertwinings of the human and the nonhuman" (Pickering 2001:167). This commitment to the analysis of natural/cultural/social/technical networks and assemblages as consisting only of visible surfaces, a single-planed set of wholly observable events, actions, and processes with no hidden, deep, or invisible structures or levels, stands in contradistinction to the dualistic ontologies of the social that still characterize those versions of the cultural turn that have most influenced the development of cultural sociology. Such ontologies provide the basis for ANT's opposition to the language of "cultural constructivism": the very notion that culture constructs the social is at odds with ANT's focus on the complex entanglements of people and things in the intersecting networks through which the social is performed without any prior distinction between what might be allocated to culture and what to society. By locating intellectual work on a single-planed reality, this position also questions intellectual practices that aim to organize their own authority and distinctive forms of political intervention by claiming insight into another set of hidden or invisible processes and realities that are held to take place behind the backs of other actors. It construes intellectuals not as seers but as mobilizers and transformers, reshaping relations between things and people by the production of new entities and their mobilization in the context of the material-semiotic networks through which the social is made and performed.

Third, there is a strong focus in science and practice studies on the specific settings – most notably laboratories – in which scientific work is conducted, and on the transformations (purifications, reductions, translations, etc.) to which scientific practice subjects the materials it works with so as to produce new entities in the field of knowledge. This comprises an exemplary materialism in the attention it pays to the material settings and instruments through which such entities are made and mobilized. There is a good deal of common ground here between ANT and those readings of Foucault's concept of discourse which – somewhat against the authority of Foucault's own texts – stress its material and institutional properties (Sawyer 2002). But there is also a difference to the extent that ANT places a greater emphasis on analyzing the processes through which things are put together to comprise those ordering strategies that Foucauldian analysis calls discursive but whose formation – the processes of their making and remaking – it tends to occlude (Law 1994:18–26). This opens up the space for a productive interchange between ANT and Foucauldian theory in its potential to add a denser materiality to Foucault's insistence on the need for an "ascending analysis of power" that would

> begin with its infinitesimal mechanisms, which have their own history, their own trajectory, their own techniques and tactics, and then look at how these mechanisms of power, which have their solidity and, in a sense, their own technology, have been and are invested, colonized, used, infected, transformed, displaced, extended, and so on by increasingly general mechanisms and forms of overall domination.
>
> *(Foucault 2003:30)*

In a similar vein, Latour argues that "power, like society, is the final result of a process and not a reservoir, a stock or a capital that will automatically provide an explanation. Power and domination have to be made up, composed" (Latour 2005:64). The task that this enjoins analytically is one of tracing the networks of associations through which particular forms of power are assembled, aiming for as dense a description as possible of the capacities and affordances that are folded into and accumulate within those assemblages.

The implication is that we should consider how distinctive kinds of cultural power are organized through the operations of cultural assemblages – museums, libraries, broadcasting, art galleries, heritage sites – which, as components of the "culture complex," articulate a distinctive organization of the relations between persons, things, techniques, and texts, and bring these to bear on the social through the changes in conduct they seek to effect.

The culture complex and the analytics of government

I turn now to the implications of setting these concerns within the perspective of governmentality theory. Yet here, too, we need to probe whether there is any place in Foucault's account of governmentality for a set of concerns focused specifically on culture. The term is not one Foucault used except casually: it is not a part of the system of concepts he used to lay out the field of governmental practices or of the techniques he proposed for their analysis. And a number of governmentality theorists have been wary of the concept. Nikolas Rose has expressed his doubts as to whether "the amorphous domain of culture" has any specific analytical purchase (Rose 1998:24), while Mitchell Dean has lodged his reservations concerning the thesis of "culture governance" associated with the role attributed to self-reflexive forms of individualization in relation to the agendas of neoliberalism (Dean 2007). Both cautions are justified: Rose's because the logic of the cultural turn, in interpreting culture as comprising the mechanisms of meaning-making that form a component of all practices, extends its reach at the price of depriving it of an analytical domain of its own; and Dean's because such accounts of individualization fail to specify the historically specific mechanisms through which its effects are produced.

Yet there is now a considerable body of work applying the analytics of government to a wide range of cultural practices and institutions. In referring to the "analytics of government" here, I draw on the terms proposed by Mitchell Dean in summarizing the perspective of governmentality:

> Government is any more or less calculated and rational activity, undertaken by a multiplicity of authorities and agencies, employing a variety of techniques and forms of knowledge, that seeks to shape conduct by working through our desires, aspirations, interests, and beliefs, for definite but shifting ends and with a diverse set of relatively unpredictable consequences, effects, and outcomes.
>
> *(Dean 1999:11)*

Interpreted in this light, there is no shortage of studies examining how cultural practices and institutions are implicated in the processes through which this governmental concern with "the conduct of conduct" is organized. There is now a good deal of historical work focused on the roles played by the development of a new complex of cultural institutions – public libraries, exhibitions, museums, archives, art galleries, and so forth – in the context of eighteenth- and nineteenth-century programs of liberal government (Bennett 1995, 1998, 2004; Joyce 2003; Bennett, Dodsworth, and Joyce 2007; Otter 2008). This, as Foucault elaborates it, refers to arts of governing which make the freedom and autonomy of individuals aspects of the very mechanisms of government – making them the means by and through which government works – by, for example, cultivating specific practices of the self through which individuals become responsible for managing their own conduct (Foucault 2007:353). The relations between the development of literary education and popular schooling, and indeed the development of popular schooling more generally, have been examined from a similar perspective (Hunter 1988; Donald 1992; Watkins 2012). There is also a growing literature concerned with the role of broadcasting – and of its varied genres, from soap operas, through lifestyle programs, and reality TV – as a cultural technology of liberal government (Miller 1998, 2007; Ouellete and Hay 2008), with a number of collections addressing a range of popular media and cultural practices (Dillon and Valentine 2002; Bratich, Packer, and McCarthy 2003; Grieveson and Wasson 2008). The governmental role of arts and cultural policies has also been addressed (Yudice 2003; Belfiore and Bennett 2008). And there is, finally, a considerable literature on the role of culture in colonial forms of governmentality (Mitchell 1989; Pels and Salemink 2000; Dirks 2001; Stoler 2002; Bennett, Dibley, and Harrison, 2014; Bennett et al. 2017).

What is less clear is how these different concerns might add up to a distinctive account of culture. I shall broach this question from two angles. The first derives from Foucault's account of governmental power as the result of a process that, in the West, "has led to the development of a series of specific governmental apparatuses (*appareils*) on the one hand, [and, on the other] to the development of a series of knowledges (*savoirs*)" (Foucault 2007:108). I take two things from this definition. The first concerns the relations between culture and adjacent fields of government. If culture is to occupy a distinctive place within an analytics of government, it is necessary to identify it in terms of a distinctive set of knowledges connected to a specific set of governmental apparatuses, with these working together in ways that establish distinctive techniques of intervention into the conduct of conduct. The second is that these ensembles of knowledges and apparatuses should bring together persons, things, and techniques – ways of doing and making – that give rise to historically distinctive forms of power and modes of its exercise.

My contention, then, is that a distinctive field of cultural government has been shaped into being via the deployment of the modern cultural disciplines (literature, aesthetics, art history, folk studies, drama, heritage studies, cultural sociology, and cultural and media studies) in the apparatuses of the culture complex (museums, libraries, cinema, broadcasting, universities, schools, heritage sites, etc.) as distinctive technologies that connect particular ways of doing and making – particular regimes of cultural practice – to regularized ways of acting on the social to bring about calculated changes in conduct related to particular rationalities of government. This is not to suggest an absolute separation between cultural and other fields of government. We can, for example, see how the culture complex and the psy-complex overlap in the use of psychology alongside program-making expertise in the forms of cultural governance associated with reality TV (Ouellete and Hay 2008). Nor is it to suggest that the culture complex operates on one side of a historical dike that separates it entirely from earlier forms of power. The scripts of many museums are clearly a mix of sovereign and governmental forms of power while many contemporary cultural disciplines and apparatuses are still marked by their relations to earlier forms of pastoral power (Bennett 2014). However, these qualifications do not affect our capacity to distinguish the relations between the culture complex and the cultural disciplines as a distinctive ensemble of power relations and practices.

Analysis of the culture complex involves paying close attention to the assembly, to paraphrase Law, of those "*materially heterogeneous*" networks, made up of bits and pieces of talk, architecture, bodies, texts, machines, and so forth, which interact to construct and perform "culture" and to organize its relations to "the economy," "the social," and "the political." The issues at stake here can be illustrated by reviewing the history of *Bildung*. Reinhart Koselleck has identified three main ways in which *Bildung*, as a practice of self-formation, was connected to social and political programs: first, its role in training the new corpus of experts, administrators, scientists, and so forth who formed the nucleus of the bureaucratic state; second, its role in the internal forms of socialization through which the bourgeoisie – in marriage, in social life, in clubs, and at home – secured a specific identity for itself; and, third, its political mobilization in programs of public education (2002:172–73). However, Koselleck offers little sense of what this work of connecting *Bildung* to public pedagogy amounted to or of the material processes that it involved. Yet it clearly entailed both the deletion of earlier networks and the organization of new ones, work in which new cultural knowledges (of art history and archeology, for example) were centrally implicated (Marchand 1996). The articulation of *Bildung* as a program of public education involved a new ensemble of institutions (public libraries, concert halls, museums and art galleries, and exhibitions) that organized new networks of relations between human and non-human actors through the new publics they brought together with new assemblages of things, texts, and instruments in specially contrived architectural spaces. As Patrick Joyce (2003) shows, these spaces were themselves parts of new forms of socio-spatial ordering associated with the moral economy of the liberal city in which *Bildung* was hardwired into the material environment. The material economy of the nineteenth-century city of culture thus depended not only on a new partitioning of urban space but on the severance of the nexus of the relations between people and things that had been inscribed in the quite different institutional nexus of the spa city and its practices (Borsay 1989).

This material economy of culture depended equally on the relocation of varied objects from their previous location in private settings (aristocratic and royal households) and, in thus being detached from earlier purely decorative functions or from their role in the spectacularization of power, on their acquiring new properties that enabled them to be refunctioned for new purposes. The deployment of aesthetic discourses in art museums transformed works of art into resources for developing a new in-depth interiority on the part of the subject. This opened up an inner space within which a developmental relationship of the kind required by *Bildung* could be constructed (see, for example, Belting 2001; Bennett 2005). But, as Maiken Umbach (2009) shows, the relationship between new forms of design and the restructuring of the bourgeois household also proved critical in reassembling the home as a space for the fashioning of new forms of interiority.

Historicizing culture

Here, then, are the rudiments of an account of the processes of assembling culture as a distinctive historical formation that is made up of specific networks of relations between human and non-human actors, one which acts on the social in varied ways to bring about changes of conduct or new forms of social interaction. Its modes of engagement with the social, however, are not with a set of realities and processes that are somehow prior to those through which culture is assembled; they are rather forms of engagement with realities and processes of similar kinds, made up of similar kinds of stuff, whose differentiation from one another (the economy, the social, culture) is sectoral rather than substantive. For the materials from which they are assembled are all of a piece ontologically speaking: they are made up of the same kind of heterogeneous elements. Where they differ is in the forms of public organization into which they have been assembled, and it is with this that "culture studies" should concern itself.

There is no question in all of this of looking to develop an account of culture as an anthropological constant that operates in the same way in all kinds of societies. The remit of the program outlined earlier is limited to the forms of cultural assemblage that are associated with the development of secular forms of cultural knowledge, the institutions in which these are set to work, and the ways in which their operations – viewed in the light of the parallel development of the social and economic sciences – are related to the simultaneous assembly of the social and the economy as different public organizations of people and things (Mitchell 1989, 2002). This is not to suggest a distinction of a fundamental kind between modern and premodern knowledge formations and the manner of their functioning. David Turnbull has thus interpreted medieval cathedrals as knowledge spaces that, like laboratories, brought together specific resources, skills, and labor in operating as "powerful loci of social transformation" (Turnbull 2000:67), and he makes the same case for the knowledge assemblages of indigenous peoples. The distinctiveness of the ways of interrogating the relations between culture and the social that I am proposing thus consists in the focus on the operations of, and the interactions between, historically new forms of cultural and social knowledge in the context of the public differentiation of culture, the social, and the economy that is both their outcome and – so long as these differentiations remain durable – their condition.

Foucault comments usefully on these issues in his lecture series on *The Birth of Biopolitics*, which he begins with a methodological reflection on the status of so-called universals in the social and historical sciences. His method, he says, is not to start from the supposition that there are universals – the state, society, sovereign, subjects, and madness are the examples he gives – and to then put these "through the grinder of history" (Foucault 2008:3) to examine the varied forms in which they are inflected. Rather, starting out from the opposite assumption that these supposed universals do not exist, the task of historical analysis becomes one of showing how, in the case of madness, for example, the conjunction of a set of practices and its coordination with a regime of truth could make something that did not exist before become something – a something that is made by the "set of practices, real practices, which established it and thus imperiously marks it out in reality" (Foucault 2003: 19).

And, in his earlier series of lectures on *Security, Territory, Population*, Foucault provides a clue regarding the implications of this move for a non-universalist approach to culture in his comments on the changing orientation to population associated with the historical transition from sovereignty to security. In the former, it is primarily the size of the population that matters, as a source and symbol of sovereign power, a resource for the royal troops, and as a means of populating the towns and keeping their markets going. The primary aim of government in this context is to ensure that the population is obedient and animated by zeal in service of the sovereign. This requires an apparatus that will ensure that the population will work properly (labor laws), in the right place (immigration), and on the right objects. The transition to a regime based on the principle of security brings along a new conception of population according to which government is no longer primarily concerned with the formal or juridical adjudication of the rights and wills of subjects of the sovereign. Instead it is informed by the more general connections between security and liberalism according to which government seeks to direct things by allowing them to go their own way. Population then appears in a new form, as something that is to be managed on the basis of its immanent properties. There are, Foucault argues, two different ways in which these immanent properties of population are constituted as new surfaces for the exercise of governmental power. The first, borrowing from the biological sciences, links the notion of population to that of species as something that is shaped by the conditions of life provided by a distinctive milieu. The second points toward the public: that is, "the population seen under the aspect of its opinions, ways of doing things, forms of behavior, customs, fears, prejudices, and requirements; it is what one gets a hold on through education, campaigns, and convictions." Putting these two together, Foucault continues:

> The population is therefore everything that extends from biological rootedness through the species up to the surface that gives one a hold provided by the public. From the species to

the public; we have here a whole field of new realities in the sense that they are the pertinent elements for mechanisms of power, the pertinent space within which and regarding which one must act.

(Foucault 2007:75)

And it is in relation to this space that culture, understood as a set of new knowledges and technologies, is progressively assembled, producing its own new realities as a means of intervening in and acting on conduct.

References

Belfiore, Eleonora, and Oliver Bennett. 2008. *The Social Impact of the Arts: An Intellectual History*. Houndmills: Palgrave Macmillan.

Belting, Hans. 2001. *The Invisible Masterpiece*. London: Reaktion Books.

Bennett, Tony. 1995. *The Birth of the Museum*. London: Routledge.

———. 1998. *Culture: A Reformer's Science*. Sydney: Allen and Unwin; London: Sage.

———. 2004. *Pasts Beyond Memory: Evolution, Museums, Colonialism*. London: Routledge.

———. 2005. "Civic Laboratories: Museums, Cultural Objecthood, and the Governance of the Social." *Cultural Studies* 19(5):521–47.

———. 2007a. "Making Culture, Changing Society: The Perspective of Culture Studies." *Cultural Studies* 21(4–5):610–29.

———. 2007b. "The Work of Culture." *Journal of Cultural Sociology* 1(1):31–48.

———. 2013. *Making Culture, Changing Society*. London: Routledge.

———. 2014. "Museums, Nations, Empires, Religions." Pp. 66–86 in *National Museums and Nation-building in Europe 1750–2010*, edited by P. Aronsson. London: Routledge.

Bennett, Tony, Fiona Cameron, Nélia Dias, Ben Dibley, Rodney Harrison, Ira Jacknis, and Conal McCarthy. 2017. *Collecting, Ordering, Governing: Anthropology, Museums and Liberal Government*. Durham, NC: Duke University Press.

Bennett, Tony, Ben Dibley, and Rodney Harrison. 2014. "Introduction: Anthropology, Collecting and Colonial Governmentalities." *History and Anthropology* 25(2):137–49.

Bennett, Tony, Francis Dodsworth, and Patrick Joyce. 2007. "Introduction: Liberalisms, Government, Culture." *Cultural Studies* 21(4–5):525–48.

Borsay, Peter. 1989. *The English Urban Renaissance: Culture and Society in the English Provincial Town, 1660–1770*. Oxford: Clarendon Press.

Bratich, Jack Z., Jeremy Packer, and Cameron McCarthy, eds. 2003. *Foucault, Cultural Studies and Governmentality*. New York: State University of New York Press.

Dean, Mitchell. 1999. *Governmentality: Power and Rule in Modern Society*. London: Sage.

———. 2007. *Governing Societies*. Maidenhead, UK: Open University Press.

Dillon, Mick, and Jeremy Valentine. 2002. "Culture and Governance." *Cultural Values: Journal for Cultural Research* 6(1–2):5–9.

Dirks, Nicholas B. 2001. *Castes of Mind: Colonialism and the Making of Modern India*. Princeton, NJ: Princeton University Press.

Donald, James. 1992. *Sentimental Education: Schooling, Popular Culture and the Regulation of Liberty*. London: Verso.

Foucault, Michel. 2003. *Society Must Be Defended: Lectures at the College de France, 1975–76*. New York: Picador.

———. 2007. *Security, Territory, Population: Lectures at the Collège de France, 1977–1978*. London: Palgrave Macmillan.

———. 2008. *The Birth of Biopolitics: Lectures at the Collège de France, 1978–9*. London: Palgrave Macmillan.

Grieveson, Lee and Haidee Wasson, eds. 2008. *Inventing Film Studies*. Durham, NC: Duke University Press.

Hunter, Ian. 1988. *Culture and Government: The Emergence of Literary Education*. London: Macmillan.

Joyce, Patrick. 2003. *The Rule of Freedom: Liberalism and the Modern City*. London: Verso.

Koselleck, Reinhart. 2002. *The Practice of Conceptual History: Timing History, Spacing Concepts*. Stanford, CA: Stanford University Press.

Latour, B. 1993. *We Have Never Been Modern*. Cambridge, MA: Harvard University Press.

———. 2004. *Politics of Nature: How to Bring the Sciences into Democracy*. Cambridge, MA: Harvard University Press.

———. 2005. *Reassembling the Social: An Introduction to Actor-Network-Theory*. Oxford: Oxford University Press.

Law, J. 1994. *Organising Modernity*. Oxford: Blackwell.

———. 1999. "After ANT: Complexity, Naming and Topology." Pp. 1–14 in *Actor Network Theory and After*, edited by J. Law and J. Hassard. Oxford: Blackwell/The Sociological Review.

Marchand, Suzanne L. 1996. *Down from Olympus: Archaeology and Philhellenism in Germany, 1759–1970*. Princeton, NJ: Princeton University Press.

Miller, Toby. 1998. *Technologies of Truth: Cultural Citizenship and the Popular Media*. Minneapolis: University of Minnesota Press.

———. 2007. *Cultural Citizenship: Cosmopolitanism, Consumerism, and Television in a Neoliberal Age*. Philadelphia, PA: Temple University Press.

Mitchell, Timothy. 1989. *Colonising Egypt*. Cambridge: Cambridge University Press.

———. 2002. *Rule of Experts: Egypt, Techno-Politics, Modernity*. Berkeley: University of California Press.

Otter, Chris. 2008. *The Victorian Eye: A Political History of Light and Vision in Britain, 1800–1910*. Chicago: University of Chicago Press.

Ouellete, Laurie and James Hay. 2008. *Better Living through Reality TV*. Oxford: Blackwell.

Pels, Peter and Oscar Salemink, eds. 2000. *Colonial Subjects: Essays on the practical history of anthropology*. Ann Arbor: University of Michigan Press.

Pickering, Andrew. 2001. "Practice and Posthumanism: Social Theory and a History of Agency." Pp. 163–74 in *The Practice Turn in Contemporary Theory*, edited by T. Schatzki, K. Knorr Cetina, and E. von Savigny. London: Routledge.

Rose, Nikolas. 1998. *Inventing Our Selves: Psychology, Power and Personhood*. Cambridge: Cambridge University Press.

Sawyer, R. Keith. 2002. "A Discourse on Discourse: An Archaeological History of an Intellectual Concept." *Cultural Studies* 16(3):433–56.

Stoler, Ann Laura. 2002. *Carnal Knowledge and Imperial Power: Race and the Intimate in Colonial Rule*. Berkeley: University of California Press.

Turnbull, David. 2000. *Masons, Tricksters and Cartographers: Comparative Studies in the Sociology of Scientific and Indigenous Knowledge*. Amsterdam: Harwood Academic.

Umbach, Maiken. 2009. *German Cities and Bourgeois Modernism, 1890–1924*. Oxford: Oxford University Press.

Watkins, Megan. 2012. *Discipline and Learn: Bodies, Pedagogy and Writing*. Rotterdam: Sense.

Yudice, George. 2003. *The Expediency of Culture: Uses of Culture in the Global Era*. Durham, NC: Duke University Press.

3

Sociologies of culture and cultural studies

Reflections on inceptions and futures

Jon Cruz

Installations

The *sociology of culture, cultural studies, cultural sociology*, and *cultural analysis* are critical analytical developments that have achieved an important place in sociology and kindred fields. These developments have now had at least a half century to build in breadth and depth, and this chapter explores their significance and lasting effects in light of some key transformations that took place during the second half of the twentieth century.

The post-war years were permeated with Cold War worries that a far more tragic form of war – nuclear – could occur (Mills 1961; Nutall 1968). While a political culture that stressed anti-communism induced political quietism and conformity, powerful social and economic changes heralded new public problems that could not be silenced or ignored. The period saw an expanding middle class that complemented the explosion of consumer goods. New levels of mass consumption offered release from earlier restrictions based on depression and wartime limitations, but the celebration of the cornucopia of material abundance was challenged by the long-simmering problems of racial inequality and a Civil Rights Movement that called critical attention to racism, political disenfranchisement, poverty, and civic as well as state-tolerated repression. A new socio-demographic – the teenager – came into being and with it a new youth culture.

In Western societies, particularly in the US, the expansion of the "culture industries" produced new relationships among cultural forms as well as between and among producers and consumers. Older media forms were absorbed and overlaid by new ones. Radio, already well established, continued to flood the sonic sphere with news and music – commercially underwritten. Cinema and radio competed with the innovation of television, which merged audio-visual symbolic production made for the private home. Popular literature, particularly paperback books and magazines, proliferated. Popular music assimilated older genres (drawing from the abundance from Tin-Pan Alley, country music, jazz, and rhythm and blues), and yielded "rock 'n' roll" – a hybrid constellation that drew from white working-class country music and the music of black Americans rooted in blues, gospel, jazz, and rhythm and blues. At the same time that US society was steeped in the mores of anti-miscegenation, the popular cultural sphere, especially the realm of music, encouraged aesthetic miscegenation. Although such developments and the social tensions they refract had their precursors – after all, this period is well into cultural modernity – the popular forms were novel as were their production processes, content, circuits of dissemination, and their consumers, audiences, and publics.

It is in this context that social critics and social scientists began to take stock of the cultural landscape. Rosenberg and White's edited book, *Mass Culture: The Popular Arts in America* (1957), and Whannel and Hall's *The Popular Arts* (1965) captured the attempt to account for the rapidly shifting terrain. These titles are noteworthy; they belied an older ideology clashing and commingling with the new, and they signaled the early crossing of traditional boundaries between elite and popular culture. Consider the terminology: "culture," "arts," "mass," and "popular" all joined in proximity, reconceptualizing relationships among cultural forms. In the older view, "popular arts" was an oxymoron and though it persisted, it was also in full challenge. Borders between "high" and "popular" were becoming increasingly porous and gatekeepers were relentlessly shrill as a result, but there was no reversing what was being culturally released. In this early scholarship was a new sensibility; innovation, expansion, and proliferation within the cultural sphere – propelled by technological change and rapid commodification – warranted serious attention. The juncture was variously theorized as transformations in "taste" (Gans 1974; Peterson and Kern 1996), as a tighter grip of market ideology (Marcuse 1968), and a condition conducive to new expressivities (Denisoff 1972).

An invigorated sociology of culture and cultural studies thus emerged, with older views adapted, recombined, and carried forward with burgeoning variations. Having changed rapidly, the cultural sphere had to be comprehended, fathomed, and charted. The context demanded new accounting and an accounting of the new. In this fecund milieu, older classical social theory was newly tested, but it, too, hosted new (and for some, unwelcomed) mergers and paradigms. Marxism, with an established view of culture as a reflection or epiphenomena of the economic realm, was resynthesized in dialogic engagement with Weberian, Durkheimian, Freudian, and linguistic-semiotic theories. Let us recall that when Marx published the first volume of *Das Kapital* in 1867, systems of communication meant *railroads*, the *telegraph*, and the materiality of discrete and tangible *print*. But in the post-WWII social formation, an explosion had taken place within mass communication and the systems of symbolic (and thus social, political, cultural, and ideological) production. It was no longer easy to transpose the lessons of the nineteenth-century political economy as a way to account for the economic and cultural conditions that had emerged by the mid-twentieth century. In highly industrialized Germany, Italy, and Japan, populist authoritarianism flummoxed the earlier notion that advanced proletarianization would yield an inexorable myth-busting revolutionary historical subject. Mass culture, mass communications, new demographics, and new social movements presented a more complex set of cultural developments that linked older concerns of alienation and exploitation to new problems involving mass consumption but also increased social fragmentation. Marx never got to witness the rise of the Disney Corporation, but we can read Adorno and Horkheimer (1947) for an approximation of what his assessment might have been. Mass culture, the immensely productive technologies and apparatuses that enabled it, and its thorough enmeshment in society challenged the ideals of rational, participatory, and critically engaged *publics* (Habermas [1962] 1989). These new formations were not as class transparent as they arguably were in earlier stages of industrial capitalism. The social and cultural sphere, in tandem with the economy, had generated an entirely new cultural terrain with which theories had to contend.

Marxism was complemented by – but was also pushed from – the cultural side by critical dialogue with a sociology of culture that drew from Weber and Durkheim. Weber's thesis in *The Protestant Ethic and the Spirit of Capitalism* ([1904–1905] 1958) did not displace the Marxian view of alienated labor as foundational to modern capitalism; it did, however, argue that capitalism could also have roots in a cultural-religious crisis. Durkheimian sociology was enlisted to endorse the notion of a functionalist normative order, systems maintenance, and the progressive institutionalization of civil society (Parsons 1949; Bellah1967). The symbolic roots of domination took on a different accent charted in the passage from Saussure to Lévi-Strauss (culture worked like language), and then brought back into conversation with Marxism in the writings of Barthes and Althusser, both of whom grasped a functionalist *"solidarity as dominant ideology"* paradigm. The emphasis shifted not just to people's consent to be ruled but to the operations of cultural repression backed by recourse to system-generated violence (Saussure [1916] 1959; Barthes [1957] 1972; Lévi-Strauss 1963; Althusser 1971; Foucault 1977). The functionalism drawn from Durkheim was thus recast as a form of social reproduction rooted in a dominant culture. These interventions illuminate something fundamental in the development of social theory: an incessant, historically engaged, unfolding conversation of interpretive assessments and analytical arguments, schisms, and compromises.

A more contemporary challenge springs from arguments of a "Strong Program" that has *finally* been achieved, which pivots on the proposition of *cultural autonomy* (Alexander and Smith 2001). Upon close examination, the idea of "cultural autonomy" is a split concept: there is the posited idea of an underlying, ahistorical, transcendent domain of culture, but one evident through its modes of enactment and manifestation. In other words, the autonomy of culture is constantly subjected to the modes of its articulation and forms of expressivity. Indeed, the forms that make it discernable are the evidence for it's a priori essence. This raises many questions. Curious cases abound.

If an ahistoricist autonomous culture is pre-given, for example, why would a society move rapidly from one taken-for-granted and widely accepted division of labor to another, necessitating a thorough recalibration of gender ideology? This is what happened in the wake of World War II in the US, when the men who filled the vast majority of stable, relatively high-wage manufacturing jobs were called into the armed services and women replaced them in the factories (the so-called Rosie the Riveter program). If there were an underlying culture that was so autonomous, how could something as deeply systemic and structural as the gendered division of labor be altered so quickly? Or one could ask why the Germany we knew at the beginning of the twentieth century – renowned for its intellectual freedom and creativity – became in just a few decades a military state engaged in a racialized pogrom that killed millions of innocent people? And what do we make of the Black Lives Matter movement, a spontaneous (albeit long-simmering) eruption of anger that mobilized thousands of bodies across space and place to protest the killing of unarmed black men and boys by police? The movement was not the product of (although it was eventually embraced by) formal organizations and institutions; rather, it arose out of the emotion/affect generated by images captured on cell phones circulating online. If culture is autonomous, how do its modes of articulation prompt individuals and groups to spiral and veer toward major collective action so swiftly? The notion of "autonomous culture" appears to beg the question: it is always "there." But what is *that* that is "there"? The autonomous culture proposition requires a constant trail of evidence to function as *operational definitions* – culture is there because it is being *symbolized, expressed, refracted, enacted,* and so forth.

The problem continues to challenge functionalist and structural theorizing, their Marxian, Durkheimian, and Weberian inflections, and their more modern extensions and elaborations that move toward specificities involving new complexities of class, race, sexuality, gender, and other shifting identity formations not easily reducible to a priori categorical enclosures. Bourdieusian cultural sociology (which is an exceptionally good example of how modern social and cultural theory draws itself out of deep *conversation* with, and *assimilating/accommodating appropriations* of, many earlier theoretical perspectives) gets at the hierarchies and pluralities of a culture by discerning the matrices and positions that govern *fields, habituses, dispositions,* and *practices.* But fields are not forever fixed; they develop over time. Like habituses, dispositions, and practices, they may rise, and then unravel – which makes the weighty currency metaphor of *capital* in Bourdieusian theory problematic when subjected to historical perspective (cf. Somers 2005). We are left with historical problems: Where do these configurations come from? How do they work? What keeps them operative? Why do they unravel, loose efficacy, and give way to reinvention? When are substantive changes the result of distinct people and their actions? When might change be induced by technological innovation? When does it result from well-positioned organizations or corporations making decisions that become socially altering? When is change the result of natural – and, these days, man-made – calamity? The problem lies in explaining how some cultural formations and not others interrogate, challenge, upend, and transform the meanings of social life. Cultural autonomy thus appears not so much an entity unto itself but rather a social plasticity capable of vast permutations and combinations. A point, then, to remember: theories were never – and are never – stand-alone ideational moments in themselves. They absorb and challenge antecedents, and are, in turn, challenged by ensuing views. Horizons in flux invariably host cross-fertilization. This statement may seem banal. But cross-fertilization is something to argue for, as it is an argument against theoretical closures, standpoints, and convictions that appear as struggles over intellectual property rights.

The narcissism of small differences – or who's got the best goods?

The points raised thus far may appear as obvious rehash. But this is purposive. I want to revisit the problem of grasping culture by coming through a back door: the mid-twentieth century changes came with a watershed of theorizing culture. It was a socio-historical situation that could not be ignored. It is the very juncture that set us up. And yet, much of cultural theorizing has moved forward by assimilating the conditions that generated the very problems that we now define as "cultural." Profiles – the care given to grasp culture(s) in transformation – emerge. When we enter into the rich and vast realm of social theorizing, and its applications in the sociology of culture and cultural studies appearing after the 1970s, several observations crystalize. By the early 1980s, the American Sociological Association's "Culture Section" was one of the fast-growing sections in the discipline and it remains vibrant today. The interest corresponds to the cultural transformations noted earlier, which demanded critical responses. One notable development was a growing tension over "culture" as a term, which appeared as competitive struggles over intellectual property. The telltale sign was how the term fractured into pluralized appropriations – the *sociology of culture, cultural sociology, cultural studies,* and *cultural analysis* – signaling different inflections, adoptions, and identifications. The "sociology of culture" and "cultural sociology" came to be associated with sociologists working in departments of sociology while "cultural studies" became identified with the work and legacy of scholars affiliated with the Centre for Contemporary Cultural Studies in the UK in the 1970s (also known as the Birmingham School). Terms carry identifications and investments; they are seldom happenstance. In the last three decades of the twentieth century such terms were pushed more toward entrenched standpoints reflecting theoretical divisions, as conflicts over the modes of theoretical appropriation, over preferred *theorists,* and in some cases over "schools" of thought emerged (cf. Hall 1978, 1980; Long 1997; Bonnell and Hunt 1999). Particularly critical positions were taken by Sherwood, Smith, and Alexander (1993) and Alexander and Smith (2001), who viewed much of cultural theory and case-based examples as "weak" from the perspective of the "Strong Program" grounded in assumptions of *cultural autonomy.* British cultural studies was especially problematic (see Cruz 2012). I note the singling out of the Birmingham School by the advocates of a "Strong Program" because the posture represents something of an ideal type in comparative theorizing, with cultural studies occupying the negative, other pole.

Yet when the various standpoints are explored more fully, and when we get beyond the trench-like arm wrestling over intellectual property, the surface scuffles give way to deeper continuities, cross-referential terms, framing similarities, kindred questions, and shared concerns. Likenesses – at first obscured by intellectual dislikes – are discernable among purportedly different and incommensurate theories and approaches in the *sociologies* (from here on I use the plural term) of culture and cultural studies. This recalls a phrase used by Freud: the "narcissism of small differences." Freud attempted to get at how conflict may result not from vast differences between people and their dispositions but rather from the compressions and intimacies among individuals who are so very similar that a premium develops in seeking exaggerated difference (cf. Freud [1930] 1962). Bourdieu reiterates the principle (though with no attribution to Freud): "social identity lies in difference, and difference is asserted against what is closest, which represents the greatest threat" (Bourdieu 1984:479). We might even reach back to Durkheim: under population expansion, increased pressure is put upon older forms of like-minded solidarity which has to accommodate more potential variations. Durkheim referred to the rise of "moral density" as the result of material and psychic expansion. The solution was for social systems to allow for *differentiation* and *individuation*. When we look at the longer arc of the sociologies of culture and cultural studies as they arise and proliferate in the second half of the twentieth century, we see something similar: the narcissism of minor differences yields "theoretical density," and resulting boundaries and enclosures within a relatively small number of people who are members of a vast academic world – and who are, to paraphrase Bourdieu, a *dominated fraction within a dominant class* (weep now; then let's move on).

When one reads astute overviews of cultural analyses, with detailed literature reviews and careful comparisons and contrasts, the descriptive terrain appears diverse and sprawling. But if we shift the foci to consider the historical juncture as intellectual terrain, we see that distinctions and firmly stated standpoints have continuities and similarities, even as they remain capable of hosting (in the closer look) the nuance and variation noted. Shared and overlapping questions, similarities of social terrain, and historically bounded contexts reveal key, consistent frames. Concerns with prerequisite premises and causes, observations, cases, questions, and practices seem to coagulate around familiar problems: How do socially situated and embedded individuals, groups, classes, and more complex combinatorial formations involving ideological dispositions act in ways that appear to order their inherited and immediate worlds? What are the extant dynamics – histories, systems, social structures, and ideologies – that presumably shape social inheritances? How do people (in distinct contexts) come to assimilate pre-existing symbols, practices, ideologies, rituals, and scripts, and to what extent do they adopt and adapt to them, or alter them, or feel compelled to interrogate them, and transform them to fit different needs – or, in some cases, antagonistically reject them in lieu of different needs? How are people "set up" by social and cultural conditions? When do they act in ways that reset such conditions, thus transforming what has been bequeathed to them? How are the domains of immediate, discrete, everyday life the result of entrenched cultural histories and social structures? When do such inheritances lose efficacy? These are rather generic questions, but they span a great range of social and cultural theorizing. When dialing back the lens, the continuity, consistency, and similarity is remarkable – regardless of the appearance of emphatic and at times vociferous declaration of difference.

An excursion in to the *manifest* differences yet *latent* similarities can be useful (I am thinking of Merton's lesson [Merton 1957]). Cultural studies is often flagged by American sociologists for its lack of canonical orientation. Yet if we look at a seminal study by Raymond Williams, one of the key founders of British cultural studies, and compare him to Max Weber, we begin to see important similarities that are elided in the divisive boundary work between sociology and cultural studies. Weber's *The Protestant Ethic and the Spirit of Capitalism* ([1904–1905] 1958) is the classic study of the cultural-religious crisis that helped install modern capitalism; Weber complicated rather than debunked Marx's proclivity to reduce the cultural sphere to class dynamics via the labor theory of value. He pours over the *textual* track record (or what Foucauldians and Deconstructionists later would call the *discursive forms*) of theological anguish and its shifting standpoints, tracing how early Protestantism worked its place in and against the rise of modern acquisitiveness and capital accumulation. It is a long hike from Luther and Calvin, who held profound disdain for worldly possessions, to a contemporary Christian conservative embrace of republican virtue and corporatist trust, conflating market freedoms with religious freedoms. The Marx-Weber synthesis would become a crucial strand of social and cultural theory, weaving into Lukacs's seminal *History and Class Consciousness* ([1923] 1999) and winding its way into important critical perspectives launched by members of the Frankfurt School.

Williams's *Culture and Society* (1958) is an intellectually rich study of the formation of the ideologies that emerge constitutively with the development of the English state and modern capitalism. Williams explores the historical arc and trajectory of how key ideas (*industry, democracy, class, art*, and *culture*) were forged in tandem with the rise of capitalist modernity and the installation of corresponding dominant ideologies. He exemplifies the application of what Weber called *elective affinities* – how historical processes invariably entail individuals and groups constantly putting together inherited "ideas" with contemporary "interests." His work informs cultural studies, yet it also has much in common with Weber's sociology of culture. Both scholars carry out something familiar – key individuals, writings, and theoretical confrontations are viewed through the lens of their textual production, with their dispositions carefully linked to the transformations that intersect language, arguments, and ideologies, thus grounding historically what eventually became the dominant forms of social, economic, political, and cultural life. In comparison with Weber, Williams is arguably much more *canonically* in tandem with *founding* problems in sociology than perhaps many more recent sociologists of culture – who come of age embracing the study of culture shaped by technically refined methodologies that arguably *really get at* culture.

To note another parallel: Weber's theorizing does not settle for a singular causal force, condition, or formation. In this regard he is ontologically different than Marx or Durkheim. Weber argued that societies are knitted together by multiple rationalities (*traditional-oriented, value-oriented, goal-oriented*, and *emotional-oriented*). Each of these is present, but their relationship and combination differ according to historical specificity, and they tend to produce their own forms of political legitimacy. The *quality of the mix* thus gives the society its cultural feel, meaning, and horizons of sentiment, sensibility, and experience. Yet horizons of meaning may register differently among individuals, groups, classes, and identity formations – since such domains of lived experience will likely have different relationships to the cultural mix of rationalities (e.g., a society at one point may appear settled in traditional Catholicism but be challenged by the value-oriented insurgency of Protestantism). Weber held a wild card: traditional-oriented, value-oriented, or goal-oriented rationalities could fail; they could run out of steam, lose control, or fumble in ways that undermined their legitimacy. When such failures reached a crisis, *emotional rationality* could present itself as the crisis-engendered default. And it is in such circumstances that the emotionally charged forces of *charismatic* impulse could rise as irruptive force and offer urgent solution. In this regard it is instructive to note how Williams travels similar theoretical terrain, though with much less elaboration. Elsewhere Williams (1977) sketches multiple impulses in society: *traditional, residual, emergent, dominant*, and *oppositional*. Like Weber, these are co-present sensibilities; the similarities and the historical fluidity they signal are formidable.

Jon Cruz

The preceding excursion is admittedly selective, but my purpose is to highlight the obvious likeness, overlap, and continuity that can be extrapolated among the various interests, motivations, concerns, and typologies of problems that intersect the sociologies of culture and cultural studies. This is evident despite the intellectual orientations that, over time, are associated with standpoints that occupy different sides of presumed chasms. Other examples could be considered, such as the kindred relationship between the critical ethnographic studies of the Chicago School in the US and the ethnographic work central to British cultural studies, or the Chicago School tradition of reframing questions of "deviant behavior" and the focus of Birmingham School scholars on subcultures and youth cultures (Cruz 2012).

Our juncture – our challenge

Writing in the mid-1920s, Karl Mannheim ([1929] 1936) noted that subjectivities and personalities as well as social systems intersect, shaped by grids that are vertical (hierarchically stratified and organized with power) and horizontal (the spread and sprawl of societal configurations over spatial patterns). However, vertical or horizontal systems can undergo major change; older, power-based, stratified systems of authority and control can unravel; established relationships (within communities, among institutions, etc.) can be destabilized; anxieties can abound (to this we must add rapid developments that degrade the quality of life and escalate human suffering). Such changes may offer new opportunities to escape (or expand access to) the effects of power for some groups. When both vertical and horizontal systems undergo unraveling, the sense of crisis, erosion, indeterminacy, instability, doubt, and insecurity constitute serious problems that churn without clear solutions. This was the world for Mannheim in Germany in the 1920s. It was a juncture of tremendous upheaval, a condition that pulled the complexity of society into focus: things hitherto obscured were revealed. Such a juncture was ripe for a new mode of social and cultural theory he called the "sociology of knowledge."

In the spirit of Mannheim's challenge, what kind of knowledge lies ahead for the study of culture? An invigorated interest in the cultural sphere took hold in the second half of the twentieth century; it has fired the remarkable expansion we now associate with sociologies of culture and cultural studies. But our juncture now is equally critical. Our world is morphing and changing rapidly such that we cannot spell out for our students what their lives will be like even a few years from now. The digital turn has transformed much – from ways of packaging knowledge to the reconstitution of experience through personalized use of "social" media. Institutions that once governed news and information are undergoing rapid transformation – some are waning, some are disappearing, and others are reconfiguring their place; cultural and symbolic goods, once material possessions (think music), are displaced by momentary *access-experience*; mass protests coagulate through "tweets" that transcend formative face-to-face conditions; identities take on qualities facilitated by temporal and spatial mobilities; and subcultures (whose meanings stem from relatively contained notions of mid-nineteenth-century folk culture) are now traversed by technologies that allow identification with distant subjects. The promise of technocultural innovations expands democratic impulses yet also inspires nefarious hijacking, surveillance, and manipulation – actions carried out along the spectrum from isolated individuals to corporations to the largest nation-states.

The challenges that installed our sociologies of culture and cultural studies over the past half decade have now metastasized into forms that outstrip yesteryear's orientations. Which theories will continue to have traction? Which will be necessarily modified? What theories beg to be born? And which veins of the sociologies of culture and cultural studies will remain woefully disconnected from the massive transformations that now unfold? Answers are illusive.

The juncture we are in today, like that of the mid-twentieth century, presents us with a cultural sphere arguably shifting the very terrain we inhabit. We should ask the question posed long ago by Robert Lynd (1939): "*knowledge for what?*" The tedious narcissism of small differences will not generate the kind of new, critical understandings demanded by the present and what lies beyond. Instead we need *trans-theoretical* and *trans-methodological* dialogue – to generate vibrant, relevant, and critical knowledge of what the cultural sphere is coming to be. . . .

References

Adorno, Theodore, and Max Horkheimer. 1947. *Dialectic of Enlightenment*, trans. John Cumming. New York: Continuum.

Alexander, Jeffrey, and Philip Smith. 2001. "The Strong Program in Cultural Theory: Elements of a Structural Hermeneutics." Pp. 135–50 in *Handbook of Sociological Theory*, edited by J. Turner. New York: Springer.

Althusser, Louis. 1971. "Ideology and Ideological State Apparatuses (Notes Toward an Investigation)." In *Lenin and Philosophy and Other Essays*. New York: Monthly Review Press.

Barthes, Roland. [1957] 1972. *Mythologies*. New York: Farrar, Straus and Giroux.

Bellah, Robert N. 1967. "Civil Religion in America." *Daedalus, Journal of the American Academy of Arts and Sciences* 96(1):1–21.

Bonnell, Victoria E., and Lynn Hunt, eds. 1999. *Beyond the Cultural Turn: New Directions in the Study of Society and Culture*. Berkeley: University of California Press.

Bourdieu, Pierre. 1984. *Distinction: A Social Critique of the Judgment of Taste*. Cambridge, MA: Harvard University Press.

Cruz, Jon D. 2012. "Cultural Studies and Social Movements: A Crucial Nexus in the American Case." *European Journal of Cultural Studies* 15(3):254–301.

Denisoff, R. Serge. 1972 *The Sounds of Social Change: Studies in Popular Culture*. New York: Rand McNally.

Foucault, Michel. 1977. *Discipline and Punish*, trans. Alan Sheridan. New York: Pantheon Books.

Freud, Sigmund. [1930] 1962. *Civilization and its Discontents*. New York: W.W. Norton.

Gans, Herbert J. 1974. *Popular Culture and High Culture: An Analysis and Evaluation of Taste*. New York: Basic Books.

Habermas, Jürgen. [1962] 1989. *The Structural Transformation of the Pubic Sphere*, trans. Thomas Burger. Cambridge, MA: Massachusetts Institute of Technology.

Hall, Stuart. 1978. "Culture, the Media, and the 'Ideological Effect.'" Pp. 315–48 in *Mass Communication and Society*, edited by J. Curran, M. Gurevitch, and J. Woollacott. Beverly Hills: Sage.

———. 1980. "Cultural Studies: 'Two Paradigms.'" *Media, Culture and Society* 2(1):57–72.

Lévi-Strauss, Claude. 1963. *Structural Anthropology*. New York: Basic Books.

Long, Elizabeth. 1997. *From Sociology to Cultural Studies*. London: Wiley-Blackwell.

Lukács, G. [1923] 1999. *History and Class Consciousness: Studies in Marxist Dialectics*. Cambridge, MA: MIT Press.

Lynd, Robert. 1939. *Knowledge For What? The Place of Social Science in American Culture*. Princeton, NJ: Princeton University Press.

Mannheim, Karl. [1929] 1936. *Ideology and Utopia: An Introduction to the Sociology of Knowledge*, trans. L. Wirth and E. Shils. New York: Harcourt, Brace & World.

Marcuse, Herbert. 1968. *One-Dimensional Man: Studies in the Ideology of Advanced Industrial Society*. Boston: Beacon Press.

Merton, Robert K. 1957. "Manifest and Latent Functions." Pp. 60–9 in *Social Theory and Social Structure*. Glencoe, IL: Free Press.

Mills, C. Wright. 1961. *The Causes of World War Three*. New York: Ballantine.

Nutall, Jeff. 1968. *Bomb Culture*. London: MacGibbon & Kee.

Parsons, Talcott. 1949. *Essays in Sociological Theory*. New York: The Free Press.

Peterson, Richard A., and Roger M. Kern. 1996. "Changing Highbrow Taste: From Snob to Omnivore." *American Sociological Review* 61(5):900–7.

Rosenberg, Bernard, and David Manning White, eds. 1957. *Mass Culture: The Popular Arts in America*. Glencoe, IL: The Free Press.

Saussure, Ferdinand. [1916] 1959. *Course in General Linguistics*, trans. Wade Bask. New York: Philosophical Library.

Sherwood, Steven, Philip Smith, and Jeffrey C. Alexander. 1993. "The British Are Coming." *Contemporary Sociology* 22(2):370–5.

Somers, Margaret R. 2005. "Beware Trojan Horses Bearing Social Capital: How Privatization Turned *Solidarity* into a Bowling Team." Pp. 233–74 in *The Politics of Method in the Human Sciences: Positivism and its Epistemological Others*, edited by G. Steinmetz. Durham, NC: Duke University Press.

Weber, Max. [1904–1905] 1958. *The Protestant Ethic and the Spirit of Capitalism*. New York: Charles Scribner's Sons.

Whannel, Paddy, and Stuart Hall. 1965. *The Popular Arts*. New York: Pantheon.

Williams, Raymond. 1958. *Culture and Society 1780–1950*. New York: Doubleday Anchor.

———. 1977. *Marxism and Literature*. Oxford: Oxford University Press.

4

Lost in translation

Feminist cultural/media studies in the new millennium

Suzanna Danuta Walters

Introduction

For roughly 20 years – from the mid-1970s to the mid-1990s – feminist media scholarship was both prodigious and pioneering. Many – myself included – have written about the (non-linear, overlapping) and heady shifts in this scholarship from a largely quantitative "images of women" approach through the many challenges and revisions wrought by psychoanalytic film theory, spectatorship studies, audience work, theories of the gaze, institutional and political-economic framings, and beyond. Many of these histories frame the trajectory of the field through disciplinary logics, as humanities-based film studies debated/contested the more social-science-oriented TV studies, or through logics produced through theoretical allegiances (psychoanalytic work vs. social-structural) or, yet again, logics derived from the specificity of the medium itself (film, television, advertising). My entrée into the field was the more overarching frame of cultural studies, which cuts across disciplinary logics, genres, and media. For many of us, this was indeed the main draw of Birmingham-style cultural studies – its deep and wide range, its connections to activism, especially in its feminist incarnations, and its refusal to be cornered in by the demands of allegiances other than that of critical, political analysis. Formed in the post-1960s milieu of new social movements and institutional re-evaluations, cultural studies couldn't afford the Marxist *longue durée* of avoidance; the barbarians were through the gate too quickly and the borders were too porous to begin with.

Cultural studies questions seemed tailor made for the new identity politics, focusing on the intricacies and variabilities of cultural resistance while continuing to reckon with the (older?) problems of commodification and cultural hegemony. Feminist cultural theorists seemed particularly astute. After moving quickly from the "images of women" approach that posited an "already there" meaning – filled with stereotype or rich with latent possibility – they produced some of the most challenging and explosive analyses to come out of the media/cultural studies tradition. From brazen inquiries into the pleasures of romance, to nuanced evidence of counter-reading in female fan culture, to sustained critiques of the persistence of masculinist ideologies in even the most avowedly progressive images, feminist media criticism took male critics to task for their blithe refusal to reckon with sexual difference and offering up treatise after treatise that exposed the vexed intransigence of patriarchy while at the same time trumpeting the ever-present (or so we believed) possibilities of subversive readings and hidden feminist imagery (see Hanmer 2014; Summers and Miller 2014).

Questions of visibility were at the heart of early feminist concerns. For many a marginalized group, to simply be seen – to be part of the panorama of cultural vision – was at least part of the battle. But for all the complexities of cultural analysis, we often seemed to wind down to the conclusion "more and better." More people of color less confined to limited and narrow roles. More women, less stereotypically depicted. A reasonable goal perhaps, but one that ran up against both right-wing resistance and cultural studies innovations. Who is to say what better is? One person's feisty feminist warrior princess is another's sexualized bimbo. One person's subversive mainstreaming is another's shallow assimilation. Surely the decisive and transformative innovations of spectatorship theory problematized the "more and better" approach and made it increasingly difficult to make overly broad statements about the certain meaning of images or cultural moments (see Stacey 1994; Williams 2008; Block 2010; Chaudhuri 2014; Reinhard and Olson 2016). Feminist cultural critics have always been wary of marking visibility as the easy sign of liberatory imaginings. The very theorizing of the "male gaze" (Mulvey 1975) explicitly argued that vision was not all it was cracked up to be and that, sometimes, being seen was itself the act of violation, the imprimatur of power. In later years, of course, the theory of the gaze itself came under increased scrutiny (for its assumption of only heterosexual desire, for its insistence that identification was at the heart of viewing pleasure, and for so much else!), and thus pushed even further against the futuristic promises of visibility politics (see esp. Taylor 2014).

For gay theorists and activists, visibility always seemed to hold out more promise (see Gross 2001; Walters 2001, 2014; Schiappa 2008; Streitmatter 2009; Jacobs 2014; Goldmark 2015). Plagued by ugly stereotypes or crude indifference, we were the terrifying "others" of Hollywood's darkest fears – preying perverts, stealthy spies, simpering aesthetes, ridiculous glam boys, sinister prison matrons, troubled youth. It was either some such portrayal or the despair of invisibility. If they could only see us in all our normal glory, in all our proud sameness, society would slowly shift. If we could only just edge out from behind the thick curtain of invisibility, we would emerge into the bright sunshine of acceptance. But, just like the singular (white, hetero) spectator was revealed as a fantasy, this too fell into disrepute as both queer theory and transnational feminism challenged the politics of visibility and recognition. Concerns with visibility have not wholly disappeared but have surely receded, or at the very least been reformatted to fit the new era of spectacularized identities.

New sites, old challenges

So if not visibility, if not more and better, if not accurate and true, then what is the (new) subject/object of feminist media criticism? This is an historic moment, characterized by any number of political and intellectual shifts – including but not limited to the rise of a global media culture and the persistence of national forms; the increasing diversity of media forms and venues, including web and new media locations; the rise of new genres and the persistence of old ones; and the various posts (post-9/11 security states, putative postfeminism and its critics, postcolonialism). In an interesting essay that examines the much-debated phenomenon of postfeminism, Angela McRobbie situates the early 1990s as a crucial period in the academy for feminism and, specifically, for feminist cultural studies. Indeed, she articulates a kind of convergence where feminist self-criticism meets "popular feminism" via the work of postcolonial feminists, theorists such as Judith Butler, and the emergence of the body, subjectivity, and performance as key feminist tropes (McRobbie 2004:256; see also Lumby 2011; Press 2011; Gill 2016). Recent work has provocatively focused on how some attenuated, troubled, complicated versions of feminism come to circulate through popular culture, particularly in network television (see Kalogeropoulos Householder and Trier-Bieniek 2016; Patterson 2016). Much remains to be done in this vein, however, as we need to pay more detailed attention to the mechanisms by which attenuated and desultory versions of feminism actually help demonize the more robust versions theorized and practiced around the world. The biggest challenge, I think, has been to reckon with the ways in which new genres and new media forms – from "reality TV" to narrowcasting, the internet, and media interactivity – "speak" gender and gendered identities and politics in perhaps new and troublesome ways. These new genres and forms may not have produced new feminist methodologies but they have perhaps forged new emphases. For example, following wider recent trends in feminist theory, newer work often construes gender more broadly, asking less how "women" are represented in any given film or TV show and more how a wide variety of gendered identities are invoked, produced, hailed, and so forth (see Scanlon and Lewis 2016). Work on representations of trans-subjectivities has been particularly fruitful, in part because the questions raised (about the relationship between gender and sexuality, about authenticity and the body, about fluidity and constraint) more easily avoid the pitfalls of "positive/negative" media theories and narrowly textual and small-scale approaches (see Dhaenens and Van Bauwel 2012).

Indeed, one real appeal of transcultural scholarship – like diasporic scholarship – is, for me, methodological: the broadness of scope and vision is almost forced by the site of analysis. Feminist scholars who work in television have been most challenged. While film as a medium has surely changed (with the rise of digital technology, the dominance of the blockbuster, the retreat of independent filmmaking and distribution, the increasing focus on international markets and nonpublic distribution sites, etc.), television has undergone dramatic revision in the years since feminists starting mining that particular vein – including but not limited to the rise of multichannel cable and satellite technologies, increasing commercialization, deregulation, and media concentration, the growth of new digital technologies and platforms, and internet convergence, all of which have transformed what TV "is" and how we experience it (see Spigel 2005). Alongside other structural shifts, including the YouTube phenomenon and similar forms of do-it-yourself (DIY) entertainment, these changes have not only required a necessary retooling of feminist scholarship but have provoked a more fundamental rethinking about the "site" of popular representations when the more public forms have receded or at least significantly dispersed (see Gurr 2015; Mattoon D'Amore 2016). Reality TV – particularly the genres that emphasize the makeover – has proved to be a particularly fertile ground for these debates and feminist scholarship more generally. This should be no surprise, as these genres both target women as audiences and invoke them as subjects. The rise of reality TV may not have provoked substantially innovative theories or methodologies for feminist cultural studies, but it has forced a series of critical questions, including how to reckon with the increasingly direct address of consumerism and commodification and how to signify bodily autonomy and ethics in an era of triumphant plasticity (see Ouellette and Hay 2008; Heyes and Jones 2009; Weber 2009; Sender 2012; Smit 2014; Steinhoff 2015).

Another issue that remains current for feminist cultural theorists – indeed, one hopes it never disappears! – is that of pleasure. If critical cultural studies (and in particular post-Birmingham feminist work) reclaimed filmic and other pleasure from the dour Frankfurt School critics and orthodox feminists alike, then how has the renewed emphasis on the (hidden, dirty, bad) pleasures of popular culture altered the field? The pleasure question cuts through the new sites, and many critics

> long to move outside the conceptual trap of 'guilty media pleasures' to develop a new
> third-wave feminist media theory that builds on the work of such innovative thinkers as bell

hooks and Tania Modleski but works toward a less restrictive paradigm than the subversion/ containment model that at times leads down a dead-end path.

(Johnson 2007:292)

Of course, we always want to be able to capture the complexity – the sometimes simultaneous expression of exhilarating liberation and teeth-gnashing containment – that characterizes high-end cultural artifacts of the early twenty-first century. We want to get past or get over or get beyond the either/or options of violation or liberation. Nonetheless, figuring out how to do this successfully is difficult at best. Too often, attempts to mediate between binaries (results) in a "little bit of victimization" and "little bit of empowerment" formulation, rendering the analysis very limp indeed, like Donny and Marie trying to merge country and rock aesthetics ("she's a little bit country, I'm a little bit rock 'n' roll") in their witless eponymous TV variety show of the late 1970s. Are there no more hegemonic forms in a culture of such dispersal? And has the emphasis on contestation and unevenness allowed us the illusion of a diversity that may exist only in our fantasies? What difference does difference make when it is attached at the hip to all the unhip machinery of neoliberal dominance? Feminist cultural/media studies not only responds and shifts in relation to structural changes in media formations and innovations in media criticism, but – perhaps more importantly – also is deeply enmeshed in and responsive to larger shifts and currents in feminist theorizing writ large. Two of the most profound and thoroughgoing strands in feminist theorizing in recent years – transnational feminism and sexuality and queer studies – have enormously impacted both the objects of feminist cultural work and the analytic tropes used in the interpretation of those objects (see Gopinath 2011; Usher 2014).

Importantly, the new transnational feminist cultural work is not narrowly anthropological in tenor. Rather, it addresses circulations of representation as they weave in and out of national locales, engaged by multiple constituencies in complicated ways. Thus, there has been an important shift not only in the presumptive "Westernness" of cultural forces but in the understanding of the uneven ways in which people experience popular culture – mediated by all the identities we already obsess about but also sometimes cutting across national/racial/sexual boundaries in ways that surprise and ignite. The most compelling renditions of this have come, I believe, from scholars working around questions of diaspora and borderlands, particularly when those questions are inflected with queer subjectivities (see esp. Hegde 2011). I think particularly here of work that examines how "feminine" identities slip precariously across borders in ways that show both their marked particularity and, simultaneously, their embeddedness in dominant ideological frames – for example in the scholarship of Gayatri Gopinath (2005) and Angharad Valdivia (2011), who both engage with the movement of an eclectic and varied set of cultural texts, including Bollywood musicals and the complex icons of Latinidad.

Queer studies and its mellower twin, sexuality studies, has provided the second major challenge to feminist theorizing and, therefore, to feminist cultural/media studies as well. It would be a mistake, however, to characterize these challenges on a simple linear timeline; to do so perpetuates a tendency to set up a truncated (and simply inaccurate) history of feminist theorizing that starts out with the (dumpy) big, bad, white, middle-class, hetero essentialists and ends up in the funky garden of de-lite with the happy-go-lucky queer Asian/black/Latina sophisticates. Indeed, both transnational and queer cultural scholarship (and, by the way, US black feminism) came on the (feminist cultural) scene early on. This is not to deny institutional resistances and continuous willful omissions, but rather to insist that we "break up" this romantic history, which always posits a transcendent true love that rescues the poorly matched lovers from years of desultory fumblings. Queer and diasporic emphases have been – for a quite a while – substantive if not equal players on the feminist cultural studies field. So when gay, and later queer, theorists joined the cultural studies stew (or emerged as a distinct voice – we were, of course there from the outset), the project of cultural studies began to move even farther away from "representations of" and to hone in on the productiveness of popular images. Gayness, straightness, femininity, masculinity, ethnic, and racial categorizations became understood as essentially "fictive" categories that assumed a scary realness when produced in and through popular images and discourses (see esp. Waters 2016). The vaunted authenticity of marginalized sexual identities necessarily gave way to analyses of fraught and deeply split subjectivities, at least in the world of cultural theory. Indeed, some of the most fruitful work in recent years has been located in the intersection of these interests, for example in analyses that examine the production of gendered and sexed subjectivities across and through national borders (see Maira 2002; McCann and Seung-kyung 2013).

Maybe bigger is better?

So where is feminist cultural/media studies now? Is Lynn Rakow right when she wonders if

> feminist scholars [have] said all there is to say about the media? Is our work done? Do we now know enough about gender, representation, and technology to spend our time filling in details by looking at specific texts and specific audiences?
>
> *(Rakow 2001:41)*

I wonder if we have returned (with new eyes perhaps) to some of the old questions that emerged from second-wave feminist work. I think here specifically of how the current focus on the body (the queer body, the mutilated body, the abject body, the diasporic body, the changeable body, etc.) has emerged as a key trope in recent feminist cultural criticism (see McRobbie 2009; Ford 2016; Herson 2016). Where once the body was seen as a simple template upon which patriarchy worked its objectifying magic, now the body becomes a site of complex negotiations and contestations. Particularly in queer, trans, and diasporic analyses, the body becomes not merely (only?) a location of enacted violence and control, but a more fluid space of potential and possibility. From musings on transnational makeover genres to discussions on the ("native") female body as signifier of a dangerous modernity, feminist cultural critics have reinvigorated discussions of the body in feminist theory (see McLaughlin and Carter 2014; Loreck 2016; Munt 2016). But I do wonder if we have gone a bit too far here, if in imagining the plasticity of body politics we have avoided a continuing engagement with issues of commodification and objectification. For surely these are not transcended realities or simply the tired detritus of old (essentialist) theories of bodily wholeness and integrity. Women's bodies – transnationally – still serve far too often as the place to vent rage, to assert nationhood, to claim territory, to use with impunity (see Ince 2017). Just as cultural transgression and stolen pleasures may not imply transformation or challenge, neither does bodily plasticity and variability necessarily signal anything other than just that.

As Mary Ann Doane (2004:1231) rightly notes in relation to film studies, we abjure the large questions at our peril: the "logic of the local and its corresponding suspicion of abstraction . . . risks an aphasia of theory in which nothing can be said." This might be too strong a statement, but divisions in the field are often less about the content of particular analyses than about territorial debates regarding the appropriate purview of feminist cultural work. The result is that, paradoxically, both too much and too little are claimed – too much, in the sense of making grand claims for small cultural moments, and too little, in the sense of refusing all generalities in the quest for local verifications. Like many critics who claim some origin story with British cultural studies, I still see enormous value in what may be called a synthetic approach (or, rather, a contextual and intertextual one; see Lotz and Ross 2007; Braudy and Cohen 2009; Hollinger 2012). We may refer to it by any number of names (the one that seems most accurate, albeit awkward, is something like a "feminist social history of culture") but it has undoubtedly produced some very productive work in recent years, not only in reclaiming all the lost women filmmakers, videographers, spectators, and so forth but in creatively integrating two of the central frames of early, Birmingham-style cultural studies – the social and the historical – and infusing them with a deep sense of political immediacy (see Gill 2007; Tasker and Negra 2007; Scharff and Gill 2010; Mendes 2015).

Perhaps I am too pessimistic about the present, put off by narrowness as much as by misplaced hubris. Another way to understand this current moment is not as a lost girl in search of a paradigm but rather as the triumph of a sort of earnest eclecticism where traditional frameworks of cultural analysis have responded fruitfully and creatively to the challenges of postcolonial theory, critical race studies, queer studies, and other newer forms. True enough. But for all the talk of hybridity, contested readings, uneven patterns of cultural hegemony, and other assorted tropes of the current moment, have we lost sight of large, impinging (and yes, multifaceted) forms of masculinist domination? I like a resistant reading as much as the next girl, and god knows I have my share of guilty pleasures, but so what? Wouldn't it be the case that the world would be quite different if all this supposed variability in media meaning were actually feminist? How do we account for the relationship between the truism that popular culture is a space of gender contestation and against-the-grain pleasures and the truism that damaging conceptions of (in this case) gender continue to rule the day, even as they morph and become, sometimes, more nuanced? Has the pluralization (femininities, masculinities) perhaps disenabled theorists to speak more broadly about hegemonic forms? For while it is true that pop culture provides a variety of gendered representations for us to consume/contest/engage, it is equally true that it does not provide an endless variety. The question of how these pleasures, these resistances, these mis/readings translate seems to have receded as cultural studies becomes at once more sophisticated and less sublime. Rest assured, I'm not invoking "translate" to imply a glib sense of political action (I watch *Orange is the New Black* and I want to smash the prison industrial complex!), but rather to provoke a sense of mattering, rendering, deciphering, decoding. In any good translation, there is a process of evaluation and adjudication: I choose this word over another possibility, this phrase expresses most pungently the passionate tone of the speaker, this intonation and not another. A compelling translation does not merely follow the intricacies of the language but locates that moment of utterance in larger contexts of culture, intention, identities of interlocutors, and history.

Although this synthetic approach certainly shouldn't and doesn't trump others, it has faded in prominence in recent years and does – particularly in these perilous times – need to find a way home again, if only because synthetic frameworks often ask questions that are left unaddressed in more modest work. Perhaps what I am bemoaning here is that true interdisciplinarity in feminist cultural studies still seems so elusive a goal. When you think of the pioneering work of a Mulvey or a Radway or a Brunsdon or a de Lauretis or any number of other scholars, you understand (and, yes, miss) their paradigm-shifting capacities. This reinvigoration of the synthetic can and should be just that: a reinvigoration. For if much of that earlier "grand theory" conveniently overlooked its own moorings, no such narrowness of vision need characterize a feminist "grand theory" for the twenty-first century.

Acknowledgments

Thanks particularly to Nick Clarkson and Jack Gronau for their able assistance in preparing this chapter.

References

Block, Marcelline. 2010. *Situating the Feminist Gaze and Spectatorship in Postwar Cinema*. Cambridge: Cambridge University Press.

Braudy, Leo, and Marshall Cohen. 2009. *Film Theory and Criticism: Introductory Readings*. New York: Oxford University Press.

Chaudhuri, Shohini. 2014. *Cinema of the Dark Side: Atrocity and the Ethics of Film Spectatorship*. Edinburgh: Edinburgh University Press.

Dhaenens, Frederick, and Sofie Van Bauwel. 2012. "The Good, the Bad or the Queer: Articulations of Queer Resistance in *The Wire*." *Sexualities* 15(5–6):702–17.

Doane, Mary Ann. 2004. "Aesthetics and Politics." *Signs: Journal of Women in Culture and Society* 30(1):1229–35.

Ford, Jessica. 2016. "The 'smart' Body Politics of Lena Dunham's Girls." *Feminist Media Studies* 16(6):1029–42.

Gill, Rosalind. 2007. *Gender and the Media*. Cambridge: Polity Press.

———. 2016. "Post-postfeminism?: New Feminist Visibilities in Postfeminist Times." *Feminist Media Studies* 16(4):610–30.

Goldmark, Matthew. 2015. "National Drag: The Language of Inclusion in RuPaul's Drag Race." *GLQ: A Journal of Lesbian and Gay Studies* 21(4):501–20.

Gopinath, Gayatri. 2005. "Bollywood Spectacles: Queer Diasporic Critique in the Aftermath of 9/11." *Social Text* 23(3–4 84–85):157–69.

———. 2011. "Foreword: Queer Diasporic Interventions." *Textual Practice* 25(4):635–38.

Gross, Larry. 2001. *Invisibility: Lesbians, Gay Men and the Media in America*. New York: Columbia University Press.

Gurr, Barbara, ed. 2015. *Race, Gender, and Sexuality in Post-Apocalyptic TV and Film*. New York: Palgrave Macmillan.

Hanmer, Rosalind. 2014. "Xenasubtexttalk." *Feminist Media Studies* 14(4):608–22.

Hegde, Radha S. 2011. *Circuits of Visibility Gender and Transnational Media Cultures*. New York: NYU Press.

Herson, Kellie. 2016. "Transgression, Embodiment, and Gendered Madness: Reading Homeland and Enlightened through Critical Disability Theory." *Feminist Media Studies* 16(6):1000–13.

Heyes, Cressida J., and Meredith Jones, eds. 2009. *Cosmetic Surgery: A Feminist Primer*. New York: Ashgate.

Hollinger, Karen. 2012. *Feminist Film Studies*. New York: Routledge.

Ince, Kate. 2017. *Thinking Cinema Series*. Vol. 5, *The Body and the Screen: Female Subjectivities in Contemporary Women's Cinema*. London: Bloomsbury Academic.

Jacobs, Jason. 2014. "Raising Gays: On Glee, Queer Kids, and the Limits of the Family." *GLQ: A Journal of Lesbian and Gay Studies* 20(3):319–52.

Johnson, Merri Lisa. 2007. "Gangster Feminism: The Feminist Cultural Work of HBO's The Sopranos." *Feminist Studies* 33(2):269–96.

Kalogeropoulos Householder, April, and Adrienne Trier-Bieniek, eds. 2016. *Feminist Perspectives on Orange Is the New Black: Thirteen Critical Essays*. Jefferson, NC: McFarland.

Loreck, Janice. 2016. *Violent Women in Contemporary Cinema*. New York: Palgrave Macmillan.

Lotz, Amanda D., and Sharon Marie Ross. 2007. "Bridging Media-specific Approaches." *Feminist Media Studies* 4(2):185–202. Lumby, Catharine. 2011. "Past the Post in Feminist Media Studies." *Feminist Media Studies* 11(1):95–100.

Maira, Sunaina. 2002. *Desis in the House: Indian-American Youth Culture in New York City*. Philadelphia, PA: Temple University Press.

Mattoon D'Amore, Laura, ed. 2016. *Smart Chicks on Screen: Representing Women's Intellect in Film and Television*. New York: Rowman & Littlefield.

McCann, Carole, and Seung-kyung Kim, eds. 2013. *Feminist Theory Reader: Local and Global Perspectives*. 3rd ed. New York: Routledge.

McLaughlin, Lisa, and Cynthia Carter, eds. 2014. *Current Perspectives in Feminist Media Studies*. London: Routledge.

McRobbie, Angela. 2004. "Post-feminism and Popular Culture." *Feminist Media Studies* 4(3):255–64.

———. 2009. *The Aftermath of Feminism: Gender, Culture and Social Change*. London: SAGE.

Mendes, Kaitlynn. 2015. *SlutWalk: Feminism, Activism and Media*. 2015. New York: Palgrave Macmillan.

Mulvey, Laura. 1975. "Visual Pleasure and Narrative Cinema." *Screen* 16(3):6–18.

Munt, Sally. 2016. "Argumentum ad misericordiam – The Critical Intimacies of Victimhood." *Feminist Media Studies* 17(6):1–18.

Ouellette, Laurie, and James Hay. 2008. "Makeover Television, Governmentality and the Good Citizen." *Continuum* 22(4):471–84.

Patterson, Eleanor. 2016. "The Golden Girls Live: Residual Television Texts, Participatory Culture, and Queering TV Heritage through Drag." *Feminist Media Studies* 16(5):1–14.

Press, Andrea L. 2011. "Feminism and Media in the Post-feminist Era: What to Make of the 'feminist' in Feminist Media Studies." *Feminist Media Studies* 11(1):107–13.

Rakow, Lynn. 2001. "Feminists, Media, Freed Speech." *Feminist Media Studies* 1(1):41–4.

Reinhard, CarrieLynn, and Christopher J. Olson, eds. 2016. *Making Sense of Cinema: Empirical Studies into Film Spectators and Spectatorship*. London: Bloomsbury Academic.

Scanlon, Julie, and Ruth Lewis. 2016. "Whose Sexuality is it Anyway? Women's Experiences of Viewing Lesbians on Screen." *Feminist Media Studies* 16(5):1–17.

Scharff, Cindy M., and Rosalind Gill. 2010. *New Femininities: Post-feminism, Neoliberalism and Subjectivity*. London: Palgrave Macmillan.

Schiappa, Edward. 2008. *Beyond Representational Correctness: Rethinking Criticism of Popular Media*. New York: State University of New York Press.

Sender, Katherine. 2012. *The Makeover: Reality Television and Reflexive Audiences*. New York: NYU Press.

Smit, Alexia. 2014. "Care, Shame, and Intimacy: Reconsidering the Pleasures of Plastic Surgery Reality Television." *Camera Obscura* 29(2 86):59–83.

Spigel, Lynn. 2005. "TV's Next Season?" *Cinema Journal* 45(1):83–90.

Stacey, Jackie. 1994. *Star Gazing: Hollywood Cinema and Female Spectatorship*. New York: Routledge.

Steinhoff, Heike. 2015. *Transforming Bodies: Makeovers and Monstrosities in American Culture*. New York: Palgrave Macmillan.

Streitmatter, Rodger. 2009. *From Perverts to Fab Five: The Media's Changing Depiction of Gay Men and Lesbians*. New York: Routledge.

Summers, Alicia, and Monica K. Miller. 2014. "From Damsels in Distress to Sexy Superheroes." *Feminist Media Studies* 14(6):1028–40.

Tasker, Yvonne, and Diane Negra, eds. 2007. *Interrogating Postfeminism: Gender and the Politics of Popular Culture*. Durham, NC: Duke University Press.

Taylor, Jessica. 2014. "Romance and the Female Gaze Obscuring Gendered Violence in The Twilight Saga." *Feminist Media Studies* 14(3):388–402.

Usher, Nikki. 2014. "Anderson Cooper and Jodie Foster: The Glass Closet and Gay Visibility in the Media." *QED: A Journal in GLBTQ Worldmaking* 1(1):193–98.

Valdivia, Angharad. 2011. The Gendered Face of Latinidad: Global Circulation of Hybridity." In *Circuits of Visibility, Gender and Transnational Media Culture*, edited by R. Hedge. New York: New York University Press.

Walters, Suzanna Danuta. 2001. *All the Rage: The Story of Gay Visibility in America*. Chicago: University of Chicago Press.

———. 2014. *The Tolerance Trap: How God, Genes, and Good Intentions Are Sabotaging Gay Equality*. New York: New York University Press.

Waters, M., ed. 2016. *Women on Screen: Feminism and Femininity in Visual Culture*. 2nd ed. New York: Palgrave, Macmillan.

Weber, Brenda R. 2009. *Makeover TV: Selfhood, Citizenship, and Celebrity*. Durham, NC: Duke University Press.

Williams, Linda. 2008. *Screening Sex*. Durham, NC: Duke University Press.

5

The cultural turn

Language, globalization, and media

Mark Poster

Introduction

In *The Cultural Contradictions of Capitalism*, Daniel Bell (1984) as early as 1976 discerned a new importance to culture as a social question, placing it high in the category of dangers, threats, and disruptive forces. Bell noticed recent changes in culture that implied a departure from the individualism of the rational self that grounded the culture of modernity since the Enlightenment. Youth were moving away from the modern figure of the individual as autonomous and centered toward avenues that Bell perceived only dimly but nonetheless did not like. Culture for him had become a general social problem. Others soon followed his lead in decrying the drift from rationality that was widespread and growing, notably Christopher Lasch in *The Culture of Narcissism* (Lasch 1979). The question of culture was thereby considerably raised in stature on the agenda of sociology, given the prominence of Bell as a leading social theorist. I believe Bell got it right in his perception of a deep change in culture but perhaps not for the reasons he gave, nor for the negative value he placed on the phenomenon. Surely the great theorists who founded sociology – Max Weber, Auguste Comte, Emile Durkheim – all considered culture as central to their domain of inquiry. Yet Bell was on to something new and distinct from the earlier theorists. I cannot trace in detail these changes in the discipline of sociology as they pertain to the question of culture, however important this project may be. Instead I will focus on three large trends that I believe have, in distinct but interrelated ways, altered at least for the time being and probably well into the future, the way sociologists consider the question of culture. The three trends I shall discuss are the linguistic turn, globalization, and new media.

The first trend is theoretical and refers to what is often called "the linguistic turn" in philosophy. I argue this is best understood, from the standpoint of sociology, as a "cultural turn" since it conceives the individual as constituted by language, implying a new understanding of the cultural figure of the individual in society. (Fredric Jameson [1998] titles a collection of essays with this term but does not define it or discuss it.) The second trend is globalization. Here the persistent and massive crossing of cultures disrupts the sense of the local, the stability of any one culture. Finally, the rise and spread of new media, a third trend, transforms both the process of the cultural constitution of the self in language, as in the first trend, and the character and dynamics of globalization of the second trend. New media, I shall contend, position the individual in relation to information machines, altering the long-standing relation of humans to objects in the world.

In the social sciences, culture is often regarded as the body of meanings embraced by individuals in a given society. More broadly, the term is often distinguished from "nature" and understood as the sum of practices through which humans build their societies or worlds. The Oxford English Dictionary, for instance, gives this as one of its definitions of the noun culture: "The distinctive ideas, customs, social behavior, products, or way of life of a particular society, people, or period." In a more restricted sense, culture often refers to refinement of taste or to the fine arts or to farming practices. In the discipline of sociology the term has been deployed in numerous ways and on countless objects of study, in far too many varieties for me to enumerate or analyze in this short paper. For my purposes I shall highlight one point: culture has become a chief problem for sociologists increasingly since the latter part of the twentieth century, continuing with ever more intensity in the current century. In the earlier period, say from the eighteenth to the mid-twentieth century, culture in Western societies was mainly naturalized under the sign of human rationality. The study of society did not focus sharply on culture because it was assumed to be a universal aspect of humanity, grounded in individual reason. After the discovery of reason as the essence of man by the *philosophes* in the eighteenth century, the question of culture was subordinated to more pressing issues. These were chiefly the formation of democratic nation-states and the development of industrial economies, two phenomena that preoccupied students of society until well into the twentieth century.

After World War II the assumed universality of culture came into question, especially in France, but more widely in the West, and finally in the rest of the world as well. Certainly the collapse of European empires contributed greatly to a new uncertainty about the naturalness of Western culture and its unquestioned supremacy, but the atrocities of the war – Nazi exterminations and the devastation of the American atom bombs dropped on Japan – also were part of the picture. If American science and the "rational" organization of German institutions were so deeply flawed, how could one argue for the universality of Western culture? Indeed, was not Western culture itself open for and in need of a thoroughgoing examination and critique?

Many intellectual currents contributed to this critique but the most comprehensive and convincing of them was no doubt the movement that came to be known, especially in the United States, as poststructuralism, and sometimes called, especially in sociology, postmodernism (although I prefer the former term). Poststructuralism began in France and quickly spread to the United States and later more widely around the world. Its leading thinkers included Jacques Derrida, Michel Foucault, Jean-François Lyotard, Gilles Deleuze, Jacques Lacan, Louis Althusser, Pierre Bourdieu, Jean Baudrillard, and Michel de Certeau – a list that could be extended. These poststructuralists, whatever their sometimes considerable differences, developed an analysis of culture in which the rational, autonomous individual of the West was understood not as a value to be treasured, defended, and justified but as a problem, a question to be pursued to define its limitations, restrictions, and confusions. In this way a path might be opened to construct a superior and less constraining vision of possible future cultural formations. Poststructuralists deepened and extended the insight of Ferdinand de Saussure (1959), that language is not simply a tool to be deployed by a fully conscious individual but that, on the contrary, to a considerable extent, language constructs the individual. There was thus conceptualized a form of *unconsciousness* pervading the individual as he or she engaged in language practices.

For the discipline of sociology, poststructuralist arguments concerning the relation of language to the cultural construction of individuals opened a new project, a new manner of understanding and investigating cultural formations, and a new way of theorizing culture in relation to society. In Britain, this task was quickly taken up by Stuart Hall, a sociologist at the Birmingham

School of Cultural Studies (Hall 1996); in France by Michel de Certeau and Pierre Bourdieu; and in the United States by Larry Grossberg and many others (see Jacobs and Hanrahan 2005 for a comprehensive interrogation of the question of culture for sociologists).

The poststructuralist concept of the cultural construction of the individual enables sociologists to avoid imposing Western notions of individualism, assuming their universality, and projecting them throughout global cultures. For many groups are disadvantaged by Western precepts – women, ethnic minorities, working classes, children, and of course the non-Western world. Armed with a poststructuralist sense of the construction of individuals through languages and practices, sociologists study the historical formation of Western individuals as well as the formation of cultural groups outside the aegis of Western society. Although it is true that the pioneers of sociology such as Max Weber (1958) experimented with cultural analysis, they often fell into universalizing positions in part because of the absence of language theory in their work.

The second trend urging a repositioning of the problem of culture is globalization. Exchanges between cultures, even long-distance trade, characterize human society as far back as scholars have been able to determine. As transport and communications systems improved, such encounters only increased. In the wake of World War II, along with the ensuing overthrow of Western imperialist states, and finally with the emergence of neoliberal demands for unrestricted global trade in the 1980s, the process of globalization expanded exponentially. As late as the 1990s some economists cautiously pointed to the relative low percentages of global trade compared with intranational movements of goods (Carnoy 1993). But by the turn of the new century no one convincingly denied the prominence of an economically interconnected world. From the integration of major stock markets to the industrialization of Asian economies, from the instantaneous communication of news events by satellites circling the Earth to the startling unification of oil markets, globalization was recognized as a permanent and rapidly increasing feature of human society. At the economic level, globalization applied not only to commodity markets but to labor markets as well. Workers in one sector of national production now competed with others around the planet.

Economic globalization, whatever its benefits, also produced numerous discontents and resistances (Sassen 1998). Political responses to economic globalization have been and continue to be complex and in many ways unprecedented. From attacks on McDonald's outlets to the Seattle protests of 1999 against the meeting of the World Trade Organization, to the worldwide opposition movements against the Bush administration's war in Iraq in February 2003, globalization has not been greeted warmly by all groups. As a suggestion for further research, despite the often nationalist aspirations of some of these movements, one might find in the protests an emerging form of planetary political culture. Although it is tempting to understand contemporary globalization as yet another example of Western imperialism – and certainly George W. Bush's rhetoric about bringing democracy to Iraq lent itself to this interpretation – I find it too simple to reduce economic globalization to a new form of Western domination. If one limits oneself to that perspective, one would have to explain the eagerness of some nations especially in Asia to enter the global economy. Al-Qaeda and China arguably form two opposite poles on a continuum of responses to Western aspects of globalization. The former presents an absolute resistance (although, when it suits their purposes, al-Qaeda adopts Western originating technologies like the internet and the video camera); the latter constitutes a creative adaptation of Western economic practices, attuned to Chinese ways of doing things.

At the cultural level, globalization propelled images, sounds, and texts around the globe. Before the twentieth century, European colonialism as well as regional movements of groups established contacts and encounters between peoples of different cultures (Pratt 1992). In new spaces created in ports, border towns, and elsewhere, cultures confronted one another in face-to-face encounters, most often with unequal resources and disastrous results. Humans seemingly had great difficulty cognitively and emotionally when confronted by others, by those whose appearance, beliefs, languages, and practices were strange and incomprehensible. With more recent globalizing trends these mixings multiplied enormously, perhaps to the point that the coherence of individual cultures became no longer possible. In the late twentieth and early twenty-first centuries, transcultural encounters extended beyond face-to-face contacts to include flows of images, texts, and sounds in numerous media forms (Morely and Robins 1995; Castells 1996; Soares 1996). Sociologists would now have to account for culture not only at the level of individual societies but also at that of cultural contacts and exchanges, at the level of transnational national cultural phenomena, international cultural phenomena, and global cultural flows.

The third trend of a new sociology of culture – the globalization of media – follows perhaps from economic globalization. Texts, sounds, and images now flow across the globe with an unprecedented intensity and density. Trillions of bytes of information circulate continuously if unequally to every corner of the planet, with a full one sixth of the human population using the internet, not to speak of television broadcasts and film audiences. Manuel Castells refers quite appropriately to this phenomenon as "the Internet Galaxy" (Castells 2001). It no longer comes as a surprise that instantaneous reception of news and other forms of information are an everyday occurrence. What may be less understood is that scientific knowledge, like the genome project, also is part of this global flow and indeed, as Eugene Thacker (2005) argues, is essential to the success of genome research. The circulation of genome data, he argues, is an essential condition for its development and use. In his words, "the processes of globalization form a core component of biological knowledge and practice" (Thacker 2005:xvii). From financial markets to peer-to-peer file sharing, from scientific research to social networking, from online gaming to consumer buying, the global aspect of culture is now and increasingly so an integral part of human culture.

The chief challenge for the sociology of culture that takes the global flows of information into account is to theorize and analyze the specificity of different media forms in the process. At the same time, the relation of local cultures to the new media is also of critical importance. Compared with analogue broadcast media like print, television, radio, and film, the internet certainly provides an entirely different relation of the consumer/user to the producer. The online receiver is also at once a sender, the consumer a producer, the audience is an author. What is more, the user/consumer is attached to an information machine in new ways. The human and the machine are integrated as an assemblage or ensemble so that the old Western individual no longer is configured as a "subject" over against a relatively inert "object." Further, the internet is the first medium of cultural exchange that consistently violates political borders. The posts that the nation-state established – paper mail, export control of books, magazines, film, and television programming – are bypassed to a great extent by the global network of computers.

Although new media introduce new cultural configurations, in good part as a consequence of their material structure, they also interact with social phenomena that are not per se new media. Two aspects of the relation of new media to culture that I shall discuss, however briefly, are the nation-state and the corporation and adaptations of new media by non-Western cultures. First, the institutions that predate the internet, especially the nation-state and the industrial economy, appropriate the new media and attempt to shape it in their own image. China notoriously censors websites, for example, attempting to retrofit the internet to state control of cultural dissemination. Corporations attempt to control the reproduction of cultural content, from software to music, film, and television. These actions form one end of a continuum of response by older institutions. A second level of adaptation of new media to older ways of doing things is cultural. Anthropologists have studied how some cultures extend existing practices and attitudes to the internet (Miller and Slater 2000). The innovative features of networked computing are in this case minimized. Older cultural patterns are simply brought to the internet, evaporating the opportunity for new patterns while reinforcing existing values.

Another and very distinct way that new media are adapted at the cultural level is one that makes fewer compromises with pre-digital worlds. Here the users throw themselves into the new domain, attempting to explore the differences it affords from analogue cultures. Massively multiplayer online gaming, creating websites, engaging in peer-to-peer exchanges of content, artist experiments with digital culture, and so forth are not simply substitutions for pre-existing behaviors (such as Skype for the telephone) but innovations in basic conditions of culture. Of course these individuals and groups remain participants in their local cultures and are by no means born anew in their exploration of new media. Yet, especially the younger generation around the world is less socialized into analogue media forms than older generations and is perhaps more open to experimenting with new media.

These three large trends in the relation between global media and culture, as well as countless variations between them, open the salient political question of their resolution: which model will prevail? Will the internet become a mere extension of older social and cultural forms? Or will its innovative features emerge in relief, becoming the basis of new cultural configurations, in the context of wider aspects of globalization? Perhaps as a consequence in part of global media, "man" as Foucault says will disappear. Or perhaps as Freud says at the conclusion of *Civilization and Its Discontents*, some new, unforeseen and unforeseeable cultural form will arise in conjunction with global media, completely altering our sense of what is possible. The tasks are truly daunting for the sociology of culture in accounting for the impact of new media while at the same time giving due recognition of the multiple contexts of their dissemination.

One issue that, if pursued, might lead to some clarification of the question of a sociology of culture is that of media and self-constitution, and this is my main concern in this chapter. Although the relations between the three trends affecting culture (the linguistic turn, globalization, and new media) might be studied in detail and are already being looked at to be sure, my interest lies elsewhere. I mean the problematic developed with especial force by Michel Foucault throughout his works: the need to place the Western figure of the individual in question, in particular, in historical question. Unless we understand how the self in the West is constituted by discourses and practices, we inevitably naturalize and universalize that self and consequently approach the context of globalization and multiple cultures with serious handicaps, blindness, and misrecognition of the others, of those with significantly different cultural figures. Of course this problem holds not only for the Western figure of the self but for all cultures. Yet the Western individual is the cultural form that accompanied the spread of Western power across the globe over the past half millennium and is therefore especially implicated in the issue. If this problematic is accepted as pertinent, then one can focus on the role of media in the complex processes of self-constitution. One can move to this question without any sort of ontological privileging of media, any reliance on media determinism, but simply with the recognition that information machines have been and continue to be positioned in relation to human beings in such manner that their imbrication is undeniable (McLuhan 1964). Man and machine are now and surely will continue to be joined at the hip, so to speak. Their relations are essential to a sociology of culture (Latour 1979).

The next step in the argument is to explore the question of media specificity: how are information machines implicated differently in the question of self-constitution? Do typewriters (Kittler 1986), print machinery (Johns 1998), telegraph (Carey 1989), telephone (Marvin 1988), film (Crary 1992), radio (Brecht 1979–1980), television (Dienst 1994), and the internet (Poster 2006) create the same or different cultural forms (i.e., space/time configurations, imaginary registries, body/mind relations)? How do these media interact with other everyday practices, with ethnicity, age, gender, and sexual preference? How do they interact in different national and regional cultures? How do they interact in different historic epochs? Without detailed analyses of these issues, the sociology of culture cannot contribute much to an understanding of our global, postmodern condition. Nor can it contribute much to a clarification of the important political matters that confront us. It is time then to take information machines – media – seriously into account in a developing and changing sociology of culture.

Acknowledgments

It is with a real sense of loss to cultural sociology that we note the death of Mark Poster on October 10, 2012. In tribute to his many contributions, this chapter is reprinted as it appeared in the first (2009) edition of the *Routledge Handbook of Cultural Sociology*

—the Editors.

References

Bell, Daniel. 1984. *The Cultural Contradictions of Capitalism, and Beyond Mechanization: Work and Technology in a Postindustrial Age*. Cambridge: MIT Press.

Brecht, Bertolt. 1979–1980. "On Radio." *Screen* 20(3–4):19.

Carey, James. 1989. *Communication as Culture: Essays on Media and Society*. New York: Routledge.

Carnoy, Martin and Manuel Castells, Stephen Cohen, and Fernando-Henrique Cardoso. 1993. *The New Global Economy in the Information Age*. University Park: Pennsylvania State University Press.

Castells, Manuel. 1996. *The Rise of the Network Society*. Cambridge, MA: Blackwell.

———. 2001. *The Internet Galaxy: Reflections on the Internet, Business, and Society*. New York: Oxford University Press.

Crary, Jonathan. 1992. *Techniques of the Observer: On Vision and Modernity in the Nineteenth Century*. Cambridge: MIT Press.

Dienst, Richard. 1994. *Still Life in Real Time: Theory After Television*. Durham, NC: Duke University Press.

Hall, Stuart. 1996. "The Question of Cultural Identity." Pp. 595–634 in *Modernity: An Introduction to Modern Societies*, edited by S. Hall, D. Held, D. Hubert, and K. Thompson. London: Blackwell.

Jacobs, Mark, and Nancy Weiss Hanrahan, eds. 2005. *The Blackwell Companion to the Sociology of Culture*. London: Blackwell.

Jameson, Fredric. 1998. *The Cultural Turn: Selected Writings on the Postmodern, 1983–1998*. New York: Verso.

Johns, Adrian. 1998. *The Nature of the Book: Print and Knowledge in the Making*. Chicago: University of Chicago Press.

Kittler, Friedrich A. 1986. *Grammophon, Film, Typewriter*. Berlin: Brinkmann & Bose.

Lasch, Christopher. 1979. *The Culture of Narcissism: American Life in An Age of Diminishing Expectations*. New York: Norton.

Latour, Bruno. 1979. *Laboratory Life: The Social Construction of Scientific Facts*. Beverly Hills, CA: Sage.

Marvin, Carolyn. 1988. *When Old Technologies Were New: Thinking About Electric Communication in the Late Nineteenth Century*. New York: Oxford.

McLuhan, Marshall. 1964. *Understanding Media: The Extensions of Man*. New York: McGraw-Hill.

Miller, Daniel, and Don Slater. 2000. *The Internet: An Ethnographic Approach*. New York: Berg.

Morely, David, and Kevin Robins. 1995. *Spaces of Identity: Global Media, Electronic Landscapes and Cultural Boundaries*. New York: Routledge.

Poster, Mark. 2006. *Information Please: Culture and Politics in the Age of Digital Machines*. Durham, NC: Duke University Press.

Pratt, Mary Louise. 1992. *Imperial Eyes: Travel Writing and Transculturation*. New York: Routledge.

Sassen, Saskia. 1998. *Globalization and Its Discontents*. New York: New Press.

Saussure, Ferdinand de. 1959. *Course in General Linguistics*. New York: Philosophical Library.

Soares, Luiz, ed. 1996. *Cultural Pluralism, Identity, and Globalization*. Rio de Janeiro: Conjunto Universitário Candido Mendes.

Thacker, Eugene. 2005. *The Global Genome: Biotechnology, Politics, and Culture*. Cambridge: MIT Press.

Weber, Max. 1958. *The Protestant Ethic and the Spirit of Capitalism*. New York: Macmillan.

6

Cultures of colonialism

Nicholas Hoover Wilson and Lucas Azambuja

Introduction

Sociology is interested in empires again – those expansionist political organizations that dominated the world at least until 1945, and whose legacy continues to shape contemporary political and social dynamics in the early twenty-first century (Tilly 1997:2). This interest is emphatically a *renewal*, for while classical sociology is often taught as a scholarly attempt to grapple with European modernization, in fact a rich literature emerged in the nineteenth century on empires and imperialism only to be ignored and even suppressed by the middle of the twentieth century (Go 2013; Steinmetz 2013).

However, while scholars have returned to studying empires, they have done so in new ways. Some important touchstones of this renewed interest within sociology have focused on long-standing areas of interest in the study of empires, like international relations, structural organization, and political economy (Eisenstadt 1963; Wallerstein 1974), but one of the central threads of interest has concerned the self-understandings of colonizer and colonized, the set of cultural tools they used to (mis)understand one another, and how both of these cultural phenomena related to material, symbolic, and institutional practices. This concern with the cultures of colonialism and empire came in the context of two larger changes that have occurred both within and outside the field of sociology. Within the discipline, beginning in the 1980s many subfields – including those typically focused on social structures – increasingly began to focus on questions of meaning and significance (Bonnell and Hunt 1999; Adams et al. 2005; Sewell 2005). Beyond sociology, history and the humanities – and particularly the school of "subaltern studies" emerging from India (Go 2016) – have been deeply influenced by the rise of postcolonial theory, which also centralizes questions of how general knowledge and situated meanings intersect. More specifically, a broad literature now suggests two things: first, that there was a deep relationship between the categories that colonizers used to understand subject populations and the way those categories were resisted and shaped by those populations; and second, that the categories and the marks of struggle that they bear continue to shape both postcolonial social relations and the outlook of the social sciences as a whole today.

In this chapter, we suggest that focusing on culture and colonialism continues to be productive and fruitful. We begin by clarifying what we mean when we say "colonialism." Next, we survey key recent scholarly interventions and controversies in the field, emphasizing their congruence around the effects of imperial cultural frameworks and the creation of institutional spaces predicated on the "rule of colonial difference." We close by suggesting four avenues for further work that span empirical and theoretical concerns.

What is "colonialism"?

To begin, we need to unwind our central term of discussion: colonialism. Although in the following sections we use the terms interchangeably for the sake of linguistic variety, both "colonialism" and "empire" reflect long and varied intellectual genealogies, stretching from Marxian political economy to poststructuralism. Yet before even developing a definition of colonialism, it is first necessary to define empire. At base, empires are large, composite political formations with central powers that, to varying degrees of effectiveness, exercise political control over subordinate groups, societies, or peoples (Tilly 1997; Go 2009). In contrast to the (idealized) modern nation-state, empires work through "political control imposed by some political societies over the effective sovereignty of other political societies" (Doyle 1986:19), and use a variety of tactics to draw societies into vast "imperial formations" (Go 2009). These tactics can range from explicit, formal sovereign control that amounts to the annexation and liquidation of a polity's existing political structures, to much less formal practices such as creating a network of subsidiary military alliances or coercing a polity into making economic concessions like opening its markets to imperial commodities.

Along this continuum, then, "colonialism" counts as explicit territorial control and administration in which one central power exercises effective sovereignty over a subordinated, populated, and substantial territorial space (Steinmetz 2005:28). Among scholars, this definition of colonialism is almost as notable for what it excludes as what it includes. The logic of territorial "subordination" excludes many processes familiar to modern states, such as the extension of citizenship rights, or other legal guarantees of formal equality (Doyle 1986; Tilly 1997). Likewise, the definition excludes much of the legacy of Marxian discussion of "empire" and "imperialism," wherein control is often exerted economically without the markers of formal sovereignty (see Hobson [1902] 1965; Lenin [1916] 1999; Gallagher and Robinson 1953). This definition also excludes concepts of "empire" and "imperialism" that make it coterminous with the operation of postindustrial capitalism and the imposition of an abstract world-culture (Hardt and Negri 2000). Of course, these dimensions of "empire" are not unimportant; rather, each has such a distinct intersection with "culture" that fully elaborating them would be a subject in its own right!

Important recent work

To speak of *cultures* of colonialism is to make a basic point: empires are, at heart, engines of difference. In one sense, this simply means that since empires are expansionist political organizations, they bring themselves into (often violent) contact with other societies over time. Indeed, it is hard to imagine the complexion of the modern world absent the violent expansions of Eurasian marcher empires such as the Mongols (Darwin 2009; Burbank and Cooper 2010:93–115), or the incorporation and expropriation of the Americas by European powers (Elliott 2006). Yet empires handled this violent social contact very differently over time, and they employed a wide variety of meanings, social practices, and moral judgments to establish social boundaries in light of that contact (Lamont and Molnar 2002). For instance, while ancient empires could express chauvinism to the point of dismissing the humanity of other peoples – after all, the word "barbarian" stems from the Greek word for "non-Greek speaker" – they typically dominated the elites of other societies while leaving the texture of everyday social life largely intact. As Michael Mann argues, ancient empires typically demanded the "compulsory cooperation" of conquered military elites, yet "as long as tribute, tax, or labor was provided, subject cultures would be left largely untouched" (1986:143–45). There were important exceptions to this policy, especially with the rise of evangelical religions such as Islam and Christianity, where empire meant both the conquest of territory and the conversion of souls. But even here the story is more complex than simple, violent assimilation; the imperial expansion of religion often produced counter-protests concerning the savagery and cruelty of conversion, and actual religious practices that emerged could mix elements of colonizer and colonized religions, and even when representing a "pure" imperial form, the imperial power's faith could be professed with dubious enthusiasm. The notoriously harsh and violent conversion practices of Spanish missionaries in Latin America produced strong internal countercurrents (Stamatov 2013:45–72); the Mughal empire practiced an explicitly syncretic blend of Islam and Hinduism (Wink 2012:86–106); and, as Deringil (2000:548) describes the religious expectations of the Ottomans, "for the ruling elite, conversion to Islam was simply a way to qualify for a certain station in life: that of the ruling class . . . sincerity of the conversion did not unduly occupy [them]." As Karen Barkey neatly summarizes (2008:21), empires certainly created or managed cultural markers, such as ethnicity, legal status, religion, and geographical origin, to differentiate their populations, and hence governed wide-ranging networks of diverse populations. Yet these markers themselves relied on outward conformity (rather than a "deep" connection with one's inner identity), and could be ambiguous and subject to negotiation.

Such relatively flexible cultures of colonialism did not persist into the modern era, which is usually dated from the late eighteenth century. Instead, as (mainly) European powers expanded their territorial reach across the globe, they coupled enlightenment theories of social progress with the explicit articulation of social and racial differences, and they deployed liberal and scientific discourses to justify rigid social hierarchies separating colonizer and colonized, and sometimes even violent subjugation. Thus, instead of maintaining and brokering a flexible set of cultural boundaries, modern colonialists began to obsess about fixing and marking the boundaries of difference in ways that also empowered colonial officials as expert judges of the "true" nature of subject populations (on the relationship between culture and expert judgments, see Camic and Gross 2001; Eyal and Buchholz 2010; Glaeser 2011). Thus, in his magisterial *The Devil's Handwriting*, George Steinmetz shows how three different German colonies defined "native policies," the logic of governing colonial populations, in terms of an "ethnographic capital," or the knowledge officials claimed to have about their subjects. As Steinmetz notes, the goal of native policy was above all

> [T]o arrest the mobility of the colonized within this slippery cultural space [where colonizers met colonized populations], to put an end to the maddening oscillation between local and European signifying systems . . . [and] to identify a uniform cultural essence beneath the shimmering surface of indigenous practice and to restrict the colonized to this unitary identity.
>
> *(Steinmetz 2007:43)*

Thus, whereas premodern empires had admitted a fluid interplay among many different possible kinds of difference – be it based on religion, language, geography, law, or economic class – modern empires tended to bundle these markers together and to insist, first, that they reflected natural, essential characteristics of colonizer and colonized, and second, that they be used to permanently separate the two. In service of this goal, modern colonial states engaged in wide-ranging practices. They regulated the physical space of colonial territory, carefully separating "settled" and "unsettled" communities from one another while also attempting to demarcate religious, gender, and racial distinctions (Wyrtzen 2015), even as, in some exceptional circumstances, such as Japanese imperialism in Korea, these distinctions could emphasize cultural similarity between colonizer and colonized in the face of Western influence! (Chae 2013:404). Imperial states likewise carefully regulated intimate, domestic, and sexual relations between colonizers and colonial subjects, even as these boundaries were repeatedly transgressed (Stoler 2002). As Cohn (1996) has shown, they also resituated a variety of "traditional" indigenous political and legal practices, appropriating them as tools of hierarchical colonial control. Remarkably, such techniques of social control and differentiation parallel the activities of contemporary non-imperial states, and there is a line of scholarship that argues they were first developed in colonial settings before being imported to the metropole (Mitchell 1988).

If empires attempted to fix the boundaries between colonizer and colonized as they became modern, they also experienced increasingly intense conflict among the officials, settlers, missionaries, and adventurers who actually carried out their policies. Any imperial policy or edict ran through reciprocal "chains of empire" (Go 2000) stretching back and forth from the colony to metropole, and the various stakeholders concerning any imperial practices together constituted a social field that was itself the site of intense competition among perspectives on the "best" mode of colonialism (Steinmetz 2007; Comaroff 1997). These colonial fields typically excluded all but the most elite and culturally assimilated indigenous voices, but they nonetheless had powerful consequences; instead of simply "reflecting" the underlying nature of indigenous social structure, cultural lenses powerfully "refracted" the observation of those societies by the colonial administration. Indeed, these lenses differed so dramatically that they explain sharp variations in colonial government policy in the same districts (Wilson 2011). And even colonial metropoles were shaped by their relationship to and image of colonies. Magubane (2004:8), for instance, documents how early twentieth-century English discourses on capitalism, poverty, and citizenship were shaped by gendered and racialized depictions of colonized South Africans, and Hall (2002) and Kumar (2003) have both stressed how the very notion of an "English" or "British" identity was forged in contrast to colonized subjects throughout the world.

Of course, while colonial states may have attempted to enforce their rigid conceptions of difference, and monopolize the means of violence and coercion, these efforts were always challenged, and sometimes even undermined, by the resistance of colonized populations. The definition of "resistance" has been hotly debated, not least because the term implies a binary: it fails to capture the ambiguity, tension, and dynamism that characterized interactions between colonizer and colonized, where the "lines that divided engagement from appropriation, deflection from denial, and desire from discipline" could not be easily drawn (Cooper and Stoler 1997:6). Nonetheless, taken as an expansive category containing the strategies and tactics utilized by colonized populations to withstand, oppose, and defy colonial rule, resistance to colonial rule was "an irreducible sociological fact in colonialism" (Goh 2013:469). At one extreme, anti-colonial resistance has been seen as a necessarily violent, spontaneous response to the basic psychic violence imposed by colonial categories (Fanon 1967, 1963). But since Fanon, most scholars have emphasized that most resistance to colonial rule was not to be found in the occasional open revolt, insurrection, or protest, but in its "everyday forms." Resistance, in this sense, could mean quiet evasion of colonial edicts, recalcitrance, deliberate foot-dragging, and disguised ideological insubordination through irony, humor, and coded messages obscure to colonial agents (Scott 1987). It could also mean deliberately ceding certain domains of colonial life, such as public discourse, to colonial control while carefully guarding others, such as the private or domestic sphere (Chatterjee 1993). Or it could mean a simple refusal to accept colonial "renderings of the world" and "claims to superhuman status" (Magubane 2004:8). Thus, behind anti-colonial mass movements and rebellion stood an "autonomous undercurrent of subaltern thoughts and practices" that could work against the colonial state, yet escaped its institutional power (Goh 2013:469).

Whatever form anti-colonial resistance took, it has been seen as a determining factor in the creation of colonial policy, as "the code-switching abilities of the colonized and their resistance to being defined by the outsider" increasingly led colonial officials to obsess over stabilizing the "essential" qualities of indigenous cultures and subjectivities (Steinmetz 2007:41). And as anti-colonial resistance took on more directly threatening forms, decisions by colonial officials to either suppress or co-opt such challenges created the possibility of political crises over native policy, thereby "interfering" with the rationalities of colonial governance and state formation (Goh 2013). In mounting these challenges, indigenous populations both rejected and appropriated colonial discourses, ideologies, and institutions to articulate their demands and ultimately work toward the dissolution of colonial power itself (Cooper 1997). The anti-colonial resistance was by no means monolithic, as Fanon was keenly aware, and sometimes even resulted in direct conflicts among the colonized over divergent conceptions of citizenship, nationhood, class, and solidarity (Cooper 1997), as, for instance, the bitter history of sectarian conflict in postcolonial British India attests (e.g., Seal 1968; Pandey 1999). Yet as Mann (2012:56) suggests, through their deployment of enlightenment and liberal ideologies, empires were unwittingly "creating their own gravediggers," because the "contrast between these ideologies and the real-world exploitation and racism of the empires was jarring, and conducive to resistance."

It is in the contrast between the universalizing claims made by empires and their sordid practices that we find what distinguishes a specifically *imperial* mode of control, as opposed to the activity of any government power: to maintain the tissue-thin legitimacy of their rule, colonizers use the "rule of colonial difference" (Chatterjee 1993) to reproduce the purported inferiority of subject populations. Put differently, while imperial powers and their subject territories are often (yet not always) characterized by vast differences in economic and military power, a key aspect of modern empires is that they organize and justify their rule – both to themselves and others – by repeatedly establishing and perpetuating hierarchical divisions among the populations that they govern (Cooper 2005; Barkey 2008). But even as empires may claim that such differences are essential and unchanging, they are always subject to struggle and renewal; indeed, Cooper (2005:23) goes so far as to call the relationship between categorization and resistance the *politics* of colonial difference, suggesting that "all empires, in one way or another, had to articulate difference with incorporation."

Another dimension of recent work on cultures of colonialism takes Cooper's notion of the politics of colonial difference to a radical conclusion, asking how the theoretical perspectives and methodological techniques of contemporary social science are structured by, or even implicated in, the legacies of empire. This scholarship has two roots: first, a set of literary criticism that stresses how the imagination of European scholars stereotyped, "orientalized," exoticized, and silenced subject populations over the course of modern colonialism (Said 1978; Spivak 1988); and second, the long-running engagement by a variety of "subaltern" scholars with the Hegelian, universalistic assumptions that undergird much Marxian and liberal engagement with empire and economic development (Guha 1997; Chakrabarty 2000). Within sociology, this perspective emphasizes how imperialism shaped the discipline's early history, particularly as a source of data, funding, and employment (Go 2013). By the mid-twentieth century, however, this history was forgotten, as American social scientists tended to focus on postcolonial populations as "a mass of interchangeable potential customers, as junior Americans in the making" (Steinmetz 2005:302). Also, the mainstream of sociology and adjacent disciplines began to narrow their analytic view to the data and problems produced within national-states themselves, hence taking the postcolonial nation-state for granted as a starting point for research (Wimmer and Schiller 2002). Today, the recovery of this history is seen as a crucial aspect of critical sociology, stressing how the universalism inherent in categories such as "gender," "ethnicity," "citizenship," or even "progress" subtly reproduce imperial differentiation (Connell 1997; cf. Collins 1997).

To provide a road map for the field, we have identified four dimensions of important recent work on the cultures of colonialism, each emphasizing the sense that empires are, above all, engines of difference. One dimension emphasizes that ancient empires created sometimes radical cultural contact by their expansionistic incorporation of other societies, yet managed the resulting difference in syncretic and flexible ways. A second dimension stresses how, in the age of modern empires, this differentiation ossified, and was placed into much stricter hierarchies along racial, ethnic, and religious lines. Third, others have sought to show (1) how these processes shaped debates within colonial administrations over where exactly the essence of colonial difference lay, (2) how these debates influenced both colonial policy and metropolitan politics, and (3) how colonized people resisted these categories. Finally, a radical scholarship has criticized the practice of contemporary social science itself, pointing out that the data, methods, and concepts it uses are all implicated in the history and legacies of empire.

Promising future directions

While salutary scholarship on the cultures of colonialism has already pointed to fruitful areas of research, there are three directions that, in our view, deserve further examination.

One avenue for further work is to evaluate the explanatory role that culture plays in colonialism. While contemporary work on colonialism has firmly established colonial fields as stratified by different visions of the nature of subjected societies, more work needs to be done to connect the dynamics of these spaces to other sociological outcomes of interest. Did, for example, alternative French visions of the nature of Moroccan society entail different visions of economic activity? (Wyrtzen 2015). How did the internal dynamics of competition *within* colonial fields interface with wider patterns of inter-imperial, international, and global competition? (Go 2011). And how did efforts at controlling colonial agents drive large-scale economic change? (Erikson 2014). Answering questions like these invites researchers to more clearly state their causal claims and assumptions about the role that culture plays in colonialism (Mahoney and Rueschemeyer 2003:23–4).

Second, there is a stark empirical contrast between ancient and early-modern cultures of colonialism and those of modern imperialism. Yet it is not always clear how and why the transition occurred between a flexible mode of colonial cultures that blended different modes of control together, and, the more familiar mode that relied on emphatic differentiation of colonizer from colonized. Some have suggested that this transition occurred sometime in the "enigmatic" eighteenth century (Adams 2005) and accompanied large-scale crises of colonial control (Wezel and Ruef 2017). Yet other recent work has traced the "rule of colonial difference" back to medieval Europe (Chatterjee 2012). In our view, it is less productive to treat this transition as a world-historical shift in the nature of all empires (thus reproducing a binary, epochal division between modernity and its antecedents) than it is to see the shift as a specific cultural change, shaped by identifiable forces, that took place in particular times as Barkey (2008) has so effectively demonstrated. This conceptual approach enables novel comparisons and also suggests interesting theoretical questions. Did, for example, the same forces drive the emergence of universalistic imperial cultures in non-European empires at different times in history? And if such forces are removed or attenuated, does modern colonial culture "decay" back into flexible, syncretic forms of domination?

Finally, as work on cultures of colonialism continues, postcolonialism's empirical and methodological challenges will continue to loom large. One area of controversy concerns the theoretical and empirical scope of the claims implied in a postcolonial perspective. If universalistic, hierarchical, and categorical logics so common in twentieth-century social science are indeed handmaids of empire, then do they have any place in scholarship today, and if so, what?

Chibber (2013), for instance, has argued that capitalist development does indeed universalize the logic of politics and economics in both the "East" and the "West," thus negating the need to "provincialize" European perspectives, and privileging the analysis of political economy over the meanings and scope of its accompanying categories (see Warren 2016 for a collection of responses to Chibber). Likewise, if the goal of postcolonial theory is to unwind the universalisms entailed in "Enlightenment" thought, modern cultures of colonialism, and social theory, the basis for criticism itself and the sources of analytical leverage can at times seem obscure. Connell (2007) has suggested that these issues can be overcome through the incorporation of the often-overlooked works and substantive analyses of scholars from the Global South. In our view, such acts of analytic incorporation challenge both the mainstream and postcolonial views of the cultures of colonialism: for postcolonial perspectives, the challenge is to balance the particularity of indigenous experiences of colonialism with the analytical and critical leverage that can accompany (carefully used) general categories; mainstream studies of the cultures of colonialism, meanwhile, would do well to confront how seemingly general analytic categories often occlude and exclude empirically critical dimensions of the experience of living with, under, and against empire. Happily, promising examples of this reconciliation have been produced, for instance, in Magubane's emphasis in her work on the relative weight of both material relations and "discursive structures" (2004:11), Chatterjee's concrete genealogy of the "rule of colonial difference" (2012), and Chakrabarty's (2011) emphasis on the universalization undertaken by concrete imperial agents.

Taken together, these three avenues of further work on the cultures of colonialism revolve around a common theme: the concrete, empirical study of actually existing imperial structures and colonized populations, with the goal of specifying the processes, relationships, practices, and meanings that determined one of world history's most important, and enduring, phenomena.

References

Adams, Julia. 2005. *The Familial State*. Ithaca, NY: Cornell University Press.

Adams, Julia, Elisabeth S. Clemens, and Ann Shola Orloff. 2005. "Introduction: Social Theory, Modernity, and the Three Waves of Historical Sociology." Pp. 1–72 in *Remaking Modernity: Politics, History, and Sociology*, edited by J. Adams, E.S. Clemens, and A.S. Orloff. Durham, NC: Duke University Press.

Barkey, Karen. 2008. *Empire of Difference*. New York: Cambridge University Press.

Bonnell, Victoria, and Lynn Hunt. 1999. *Beyond the Cultural Turn*. Berkeley: University of California Press.

Burbank, Jane, and Frederick Cooper. 2010. *Empires in World History*. Princeton, NJ: Princeton University Press.

Camic, Charles, and Neil Gross. 2001. "The New Sociology of Ideas." Pp. 236–49 in *Blackwell Companion to Sociology*, edited by J.R. Blau. Malden, MA: Blackwell.

Chae, Ou-Byung. 2013. "Japanese Colonial Structure in Korea in Comparative Perspective." Pp. 396–414 in *Sociology and Empire*, edited by G. Steinmetz. Durham, NC: Duke University Press.

Chakrabarty, Dipesh. 2000. *Provincializing Europe*. Princeton, NJ: Princeton University Press.

Chakrabarty, Dipesh. 2011. "The Muddle of Modernity." *American Historical Review* 116(3):663–75.

Chatterjee, Partha. 1993. *The Nation and Its Fragments*. Princeton, NJ: Princeton University Press.

———. 2012. *The Black Hole of Empire*. Princeton, NJ: Princeton University Press.

Chibber, Vivek. 2013. *Postcolonial Theory and the Specter of Capital*. New York: Verso.

Cohn, Bernard S. 1996. *Colonialism and its Forms of Knowledge*. Princeton, NJ: Princeton University Press.

Collins, Randall. 1997. "A Sociological Guilt Trip: Comment on Connell." *American Journal of Sociology* 102(6):1558–64.

Comaroff, John L. 1997. "Images of Empire, Contests of Conscience." Pp. 163–97 in *Tensions of Empire: Colonial Cultures in a Bourgeois World*, edited by F. Cooper and A.L. Stoler. Berkeley: University of California Press.

Connell, Raewyn. 1997. "Why is Classical Theory Classical?" *American Journal of Sociology* 102(6):1511–57.

Connell, Raewyn. 2007. *Southern Theory: South Science and the Global Dynamics of Knowledge*. Cambridge: Polity Press.

Cooper, Frederick. 1997. "The Dialectics of Decolonization: Nationalism and Labor Movements in Postwar French Africa." Pp. 406–35 in *Tensions of Empire: Colonial Cultures in a Bourgeois World*, edited by F. Cooper and A.L. Stoler. Berkeley: University of California Press.

Cooper, Fredrick. 2005. *Colonialism in Question*. Berkeley: University of California Press.

Cooper, Frederick, and Ann Laura Stoler. 1997. "Between Metropole and Colony: Rethinking a Research Agenda." Pp. 1–58 in *Tensions of Empire: Colonial Cultures in a Bourgeois World*, edited by F. Cooper and A.L. Stoler. Berkeley: University of California Press.

Darwin, John. 2009. *After Tamerlane*. London: Penguin.

Deringil, Selim. 2000. "'There is No Compulsion in Religion': On Conversion and Apostasy in the Late Ottoman Empire: 1839–1856." *Comparative Studies in Society and History* 42(3):547–75.

Doyle, Michael W. 1986. *Empires*. Ithaca, NY: Cornell University Press.

Eisenstadt, Shmuel. 1963. *The Political Systems of Empires*. London: Free Press Glencoe.

Elliott, John Huxtable. 2006. *Empires of the Atlantic World*. New Haven, CT: Yale University Press.

Erikson, Emily. 2014. *Between Monopoly and Free Trade*. Princeton, NJ: Princeton University Press.

Eyal, Gil, and Larissa Buchholz. 2010. "From the Sociology of Intellectuals to the Sociology of Interventions." *Annual Review of Sociology* 36:117–37.

Fanon, Frantz. 1963. *The Wretched of the Earth*. New York: Grove Press.

Fanon, Frantz. 1967. *Black Skin, White Masks*. New York: Grove Press.

Gallagher, John, and Ronald Robinson. 1953. "The Imperialism of Free Trade." *The Economic History Review* 6(1):1–15

Glaeser, Andreas. 2011. *Political Epistemics*. Chicago: University of Chicago Press.

Go, Julian. 2000. "Chains of Empire, Projects of State: Political Education and U.S. Colonial Rule in Puerto Rico and the Philippines." *Comparative Studies in Society and History* 42(2):333–62

———. 2009. "The 'New' Sociology of Empire and Colonialism." *Sociology Compass* 3(5):775–88.

———. 2011. *Patterns of Empire*. New York: Cambridge University Press.

———. 2013. "Sociology's Imperial Unconscious: The Emergence of American Sociology in the Context of Empire." Pp. 1–52 in *Sociology and Empire*, edited by G. Steinmetz. Durham, NC: Duke University Press.

———. 2016. *Postcolonial Thought and Social Theory*. New York: Oxford University Press.

Goh, Daniel P.S. 2013. "Resistance and the Contradictory Rationalities of State Formation in British Malaya and the American Philippines." Pp. 465–88 in *Sociology and Empire*, edited by G. Steinmetz. Durham, NC: Duke University Press.

Guha, Ranajit. 1997. *Dominance Without Hegemony*. Cambridge, MA: Harvard University Press.

Hall, Catherine. 2002. *Civilizing Subjects*. Chicago: University of Chicago Press.

Hardt, Michael, and Antonio Negri. 2000. *Empire*. Cambridge, MA: Harvard University Press.

Hobson, John A. [1902] 1965. *Imperialism: A Study*. Ann Arbor: University of Michigan Press.

Kumar, Krishan. 2003. *The Making of English National Identity*. Cambridge, UK: Cambridge University Press.

Lamont, Michèle, and Virág Molnár. 2002. "The Study of Boundaries in the Social Sciences." *Annual Review of Sociology* 28(1):167–95.

Lenin, Vladimir. [1916] 1999. *Imperialism: The Highest Stage of Capitalism*. Sydney: Resistance Books.

Magubane, Zine. 2004. *Bringing the Empire Home*. Chicago: University of Chicago Press.

Mahoney, James, and Dietrich Rueschemeyer. 2003. "Comparative Historical Analysis: Achievements and Agendas" Pp. 3–40 in *Comparative Historical Analysis in the Social Sciences*, edited by J. Mahoney, and D. Rueschemeyer. New York: Cambridge University Press.

Mann, Michael. 1986. *The Sources of Social Power.* Vol. 1, *A History of Power from the Beginning to AD 1760*. New York: Cambridge University Press.

———. 2012. *The Sources of Social Power.* Vol. 3, *Global Empires and Revolution, 1890–1945*. New York: Cambridge University Press.

Mitchell, Timothy. 1988. *Colonising Egypt*. New York: Cambridge University Press.

Pandey, Gyanendra. 1999. "Can A Muslim be an Indian?" *Comparative Studies in Society and History* 41(4):608–29.

Said, Edward. 1978. *Orientalism*. New York: Pantheon Books.

Scott, James C. 1987. *Weapons of the Weak*. New Haven, CT: Yale University Press.

Seal, Anil. 1968. *The Emergence of Indian Nationalism*. Cambridge: Cambridge University Press.

Sewell, William H., Jr. 2005. *Logics of History: Social Theory and Social Transformation*. Chicago: University of Chicago Press.

Spivak, Gayatri Chakravorty. 1988. "Can the Subaltern Speak." Pp. 271–313 in *Marxism and the Interpretation of Culture*, edited by C. Nelson and L. Grossberg. London: Macmillan.

Stamatov, Peter. 2013. *The Origins of Global Humanitarianism: Religion, Empires, and Advocacy*. New York: Cambridge University Press.

Steinmetz, George. 2005. "Scientific Authority and the Transition to Post-Fordism: The Plausibility of Positivism in U.S. Sociology since 1945." Pp. 275–323 in *The Politics of Method in the Human Sciences*, edited by G. Steinmetz. Durham, NC: Duke University Press.

———. 2007. *The Devil's Handwriting: Precolonial Ethnography and the German Colonial State in Qingdao, Samoa, and Southwest Africa*. Chicago: University of Chicago Press.

———. 2013. "Major Contributions to Sociological Theory and Research on Empire, 1830s–Present." Pp. 1–52 in *Sociology and Empire: The Imperial Entanglements of a Discipline*, edited by G. Steinmetz. Durham, NC: Duke University Press.

Stoler, Ann Laura. 2002. *Carnal Knowledge and Imperial Power: Race and the Intimate in Colonial Rule*. Berkeley: University of California Press.

Tilly, Charles. 1997. "How Empires End." Pp. 1–11 in *After Empire: Multiethnic Societies and Nation-Building*, edited by K. Barkey and M. von Hagen. Boulder, CO: Westview Press.

Wallerstein, Immanuel 1974. *The Modern World-System*. New York: Academic Press.

Warren, Rosie, ed. 2016. *The Debate on Postcolonial Theory and the Specter of Capital*. New York: Verso.

Wezel, Filippo Carlo, and Martin Ruef. 2017. "Agents with Principles: The Control of Labor in the Dutch East India Company, 1700 to 1796." *American Sociological Review* 82(5):1009–36.

Wilson, Nicholas H. 2011. "From Reflection to Refraction: State Administration in British India, circa 1770–1855." *American Journal of Sociology* 116(5):1437–77

Wimmer, Andreas, and Nina Glick Schiller 2002. "Methodological Nationalism and Beyond: Nation-State Building, Migration and the Social Sciences." *Global Networks* 2:301–34.

Wink, André. 2012. *Akbar*. London: Oneworld.

Wyrtzen, Jonathan. 2015. *Making Morocco*. Ithaca, NY: Cornell University Press.

7

Critique and possibility in cultural sociology

Nancy Weiss Hanrahan and Sarah S. Amsler

Orienting cultural sociology in a "post-critical" society

Critique and judgment were once regarded as the distinguishing features of an emancipatory social science, yet their role in the study of culture has become particularly contested in recent years. The growth of identity-based politics and the proliferation of new social movements in the 1970s and 1980s, and the accompanying cultural turn within social theory, highlighted the analytical and ethical limitations of the authoritative knowledge claims that have conventionally been associated with critique. Recognition of cultural difference, now widely regarded as crucial for advancing claims for social equality and analyzing many aspects of social life, challenged universal conceptions of human freedom, including those that had been the basis of earlier generations of critical theory. The crisis and collapse of Soviet socialism during this period seemed only to mirror an exhaustion with Marxist conceptions of domination and liberation that had been underpinnings of both normative social critique and struggles for social justice. Developments in cultural sociology opened up the field to a rich exploration of cultural practices across a wide range of social and cultural groups, many of which were not previously recognized as "legitimate" in themselves or legitimate as subjects of cultural study. This "democratization" of both the culture concept and its analysis seemed to favor interpretive over critical methodologies. Indeed, by the end of the twentieth century, there was a strong "discourse of suspicion" in the field toward any normative claims that linked culture specifically to the expansion or denial of human freedom, beyond the basic theoretical observation that in practice it may do both (Reed 2007:12).

However, while cultural sociologists may have become disenchanted with critical theory, culture itself is not "post-critical." On the contrary, culture has always been an "arena of intense political controversy" (Benhabib 2002:1). As new social movements and identity politics emerged during this period, critiques of culture and cultures of critique formed around struggles for recognition and human rights, localized practices such as veiling, the symbolic mediation of terrorism and the political force of narrative about a geopolitical "clash of civilizations" (Buck-Morss 2003; Calhoun, Price, and Timmer 2002; Eisenstein 2004; Fraser and Honneth 2003). Within the Global North, social critics also expressed concern that the autonomy of culture was being increasingly weakened through the commercialization of artistic production in a "new cultural environment" which, despite the claims of democratization, is shaped by the economic and political centralization of cultural production as much as by the postmodern disarticulation of social meaning (Bourdieu 2003; Kellner 2002; Wolf 2007).

More recently, social critics have turned their attention to the right-wing populist attack on cultural difference that blames migration, immigration, or more generally "others" for the economic immiseration brought about through neoliberal policies (Abromeit 2016; Smith 2014). In addition to its impact on the migration debate in Europe, the renewed focus on cultural difference as a political problematic shaped the 2016 US presidential election and has become a focal point of the protest against its outcome. The destruction of spaces of cultural meaning and practice – such as the ancient city of Palmyra overtaken by ISIS, or the sacred ground of the Standing Rock Sioux Tribe despoiled by the Dakota Access Pipeline – have also sparked critical reaction. These material attempts to render forms of culture mute contribute to what Santos (2014) describes as "epistemicide" – the eradication of knowledge of subordinated culture that connects us to the past and can either keep alive or bring into being other possible (counter-hegemonic) meanings and forms of life. A similar concern has animated the critique of the neoliberal university, seeing in its turn toward utilitarianism a devaluation of the cultural traditions of humanistic knowledge and critical inquiry that can open up spaces of alternative thought and practice (Amsler 2011, 2014).

The tension between a widespread disavowal of critique in cultural sociology and the persistence of critical judgment in cultural life thus raises several questions for sociologists. Can, and should, normative judgment be an integral part of a fully articulated approach to culture, one that values in equal measure the interpretation of meaning, its normative evaluation, and its relation to action in the social world? Does sociology best fulfill its "democratic imperative" (Reed 2007:12) by renouncing critical theories of culture, or can the normative practices of critique and judgment be reconceptualized and renewed to further democratic goals of dialogue, interpretation, and an empathetic "ethic of engagement" with others? (Kompridis 2005, 2006; see also Allen 2008, 2016). Cultural sociologists have answered these questions in part by highlighting the analytical and ethical dangers of deterministic modes of critique that preclude dialogue and close down interpretive and learning processes. However, concluding that critical theories of culture inherently do just this leaves little scope for exploring how and why specifically normative analysis is important for making sense of the complex relationship between culture and politics, on the one hand, and for orienting our action with others in the world, on the other.

Here, we offer an alternative perspective: that critical theory – including, and indeed particularly that within the Frankfurt School tradition – offers important insights for combining deep interpretations of meaning-making practices, which are essential for cultural understanding, with their normative evaluation, which is a necessary element of critical participation in political life. First, rather than essentializing critique as elitist and interpretation as democratic, critical theory demands that we continually problematize how particular forms of knowledge – including critique, judgment, and imagination – are legitimized or marginalized in practice. It thereby opens up new lines of inquiry into the role of critique as a socially and historically situated cultural practice. Second, although critical theorists regard "autonomous culture" as a potential space of freedom and possibility in that cultural forms exhibit modes of rationality that are neither fully instrumental nor entirely governed by social steering mechanisms, they also argue that cultural autonomy must be understood as a problematic category rather than a social fact. In other words, while it may be possible to "uncouple culture from social structure" for analytical purposes and recognize the specific role of cultural practices in shaping actions and institutions (Alexander and Smith 2004:14), we cannot overlook their relationship to the political and economic logics that also shape conditions for meaning-making and expressive action. Finally, in contrast with deterministic approaches to critique, a critical theoretical mode of critique challenges positivist epistemologies in which knowledge is created in order to arrive at a single, absolute, empirical truth. It points to the limitations of claims to "total" knowledge, suggesting the difficulty of developing rich understandings of cultural action without attending to other modes of understanding such as aesthetics, affect, and imagination.

Although these insights are developed in various ways throughout much feminist, postcolonial, and poststructuralist forms of critical theory, their clear articulation within the Frankfurt School tradition – some of which prefigures the later developments – makes this body of work an important point of reference for contemporary cultural sociologists. Before examining what critical theory has to offer, however, it is important to discuss its current status within cultural sociology and to explain how critique has come to be interpreted as antithetical to culture, rather than as a cultural practice in its own right.

Situating the "cultural turn" in the sociology of culture

Introducing the "Strong Program" in American cultural sociology, Jeffrey Alexander and Philip Smith argued that the study of culture had reached a new stage of professional maturity, overcoming the inadequacies of its critical predecessors (2004). The emergence of post-critical theories appeared to mark the beginning of a new intellectual era – one in which we could divest ourselves of the romanticism and reductionism of "weaker" traditions of cultural study and embrace the complexity, ambiguity, and autonomous power of culture itself. Within this perspective, normative approaches to culture were often interpreted as both intellectually and politically regressive. Frankfurt School critical theory came to play a "traditional role in cultural studies . . . as a kind of negative or naive moment" that "has to be overcome for cultural studies to properly exist at all" (Nealon and Irr 2002:3; see also Kellner 2002; Szeman 2002). However, the narrative of progress from reductionist approaches in the sociology of culture to the more intellectually and ethically advanced "structural hermeneutics" of cultural sociology was itself rooted in judgments about the nature of social scientific truth and the imagination of alternative possibilities. In other words, it was rooted in critical practices. The rhetorical devices deployed to structure this story, particularly the boundary drawn between descriptions of authentic cultural practice and normative judgments that impose objective meaning onto subjective experience, indicate that critical judgment remains central to the analysis of culture itself.

Although the turn away from critical theory in the sociology of culture defies any simple explanation, it was rooted in a number of intersecting social and intellectual developments. By the 1970s, it became clear that neither critical theory nor the traditional sociology of culture, as they had been institutionalized, offered adequate conceptual tools for understanding how individuals experience, communicate, and negotiate the cultural resources that orient their being in the world. Although both critical theorists and cultural sociologists offered competent explanations of how culture is implicated in or used as an instrument of social domination, their work was rarely employed to develop analyses of culture as a separate space or practice of autonomy and possibility (Goldfarb 2005). On the one hand, critical theorists were called upon by social movements to reflect on the viability of critique as a mode of action-oriented reflection and to develop theoretical approaches that could explain the emergence of new forms of cultural struggle. On the other, sociologists of culture began to distance themselves from conceptions of culture that were grounded either in aesthetic discourse and hence considered abstract and elitist, or theories of "the culture industry," which were deemed economically reductionist and deterministic.

However, neither project seemed capable of reconciling the perceived antimony between particular or subjective experience and general or objective truth without subordinating one to the other in epistemologically or even politically violent ways (for a detailed introduction to the concept of "violent epistemology," see Titchiner 2016). Critique, which is always grounded in a normative claim to *some sort of* truth beyond individual self-understanding or culturally sanctioned knowledge, hence came to be regarded as inherently constraining, reifying, and anti-democratic. For in contexts where truth claims are equated with determinate judgments or total representations of objective reality, both truth and judgment are anti-critical insofar as they foreclose rather than open up possibilities for autonomous thought and action. Regarding criticality as a hopelessly flawed epistemological project, cultural sociologists therefore turned toward the "thick description" of phenomena based on ethnographic research and the descriptive reconstruction of social performance and meaning-making practices.

But can critique justifiably be abandoned as a dismissive and exclusive practice that is both intellectually and morally suspect? Authoritative claims to universal or hegemonic truth are antithetical to democratic deliberation, but making judgments is vital for cultural action, critical thought, and sociological analysis. We argue that the exercise of judgment, in which individuals participate in producing and deliberating claims to truth (or, as Adorno once argued, "act as subjects in the truth") is in itself a cultural practice (1967:244). The question is therefore not how critique and judgment can be transcended or replaced but how they can be conceptualized and practiced in ways that advance cultural freedom.

The autonomy of culture as problematic

One way of answering this question is to examine how and why critique has been traditionally linked to concepts of freedom and cultural autonomy in critical theory. Given the importance of the autonomy of culture within cultural sociology, it is interesting that the Frankfurt School, for whom autonomy was a pressing social and epistemological problem, has been virtually written out of the Strong Program's history of the field (see, for example, Alexander 1990; Alexander and Smith 1993, 2004). References to the Frankfurt School's work tend to be oblique rather than specific, lumped together with "Marxist" or "Leftist" analyses that reduce culture to its hidden material interests. Critical theory is presented as proceeding through "demystification" and "denunciation," through methods of ideology critique that are conducted from "on high" and deny the autonomy of culture (Eliasoph 2007; Lichterman 2005, 2007; Reed and Alexander 2007).

However, this characterization of critical theory is itself reductive, as the Frankfurt School theorists wrote prolifically about the dangers of reductionism and absolutism in cultural critique. They also drew on a variety of strands of Marxist analysis, such as theories of critique as a confrontation between norm and reality, as well as Kant's notion of critique as reasoned reflection on the conditions of rational knowledge, judgment, and action. Theodor Adorno specifically argued against the "barbarism" of reducing culture to its material interests, and for the need to proceed dialectically between transcendent and immanent positions when conducting cultural critique (1967:32). He did so because autonomy, which he defined as human freedom, enables "the single existential judgment" on which the whole project of critique depends (Horkheimer 1972:227; see also Brunkhorst 1995:82). The autonomy of culture is neither theoretically affirmed nor denied, but conceptualized as a possibility – one whose nature and existence must be investigated, disclosed, or determined through critical analysis.

Links between the autonomy of culture and critique are present throughout classical critical theory. Through interdisciplinary social research on the "great transformation" from liberal to monopoly capitalism, from democratic to authoritarian states, and from bourgeois to mass culture – in short, on the "transition to the world of the administered life" – critical theorists aimed to analyze forms of social domination that threatened individual autonomy and reflective forms of thought (Horkheimer and Adorno 1997:ix). Culture entered these analyses both as an instrument of domination (through the distortion of language and cultural symbols as well as the manipulation of communication media that made the mass mobilizations of fascism possible), and as a relatively autonomous domain of thought and action. Art in particular held promise in that its specifically aesthetic forms and conventions embodied a non-instrumental kind of rationality that could open space for reflection and allow both the articulation of utopian projects and the transcendent critique of social conditions.

The autonomy of culture in critical theory was therefore not a matter of disciplinary disposition that preceded analysis, but precisely a matter to be determined through the analysis of specific cultural configurations as against their historical possibilities and future potentials. Most importantly, because art and culture were implicated in both the reality of social domination and the possibility of eventual human freedom, distinguishing between these possibilities and making judgments about culture were crucial. For the Frankfurt School, judgment was therefore both a political imperative and a moment of autonomous culture itself. Yet what was clearly conceived as an act of subjective freedom, however contradictory and difficult to achieve, has come to be read as elitism or even domination.

Understanding critique as cultural practice

An alternative perspective can be obtained by conceptualizing critique as a complex and situated cultural practice. This perspective opens space for examining: how different forms of critique may open or close down dialogue; whether critique functions to "demystify" or "disclose," evaluate or judge; whether it is practiced as common sense or a specialized skill; and under what conditions critique recognizes or excludes and alienates others. To address these questions, we can explore how critical theorists distinguish between critique and truth-claiming, and the different ethics of engagement that these practices require.

These issues are explicitly addressed in what has become the Frankfurt School's emblematic and ironically most criticized text, *Dialectic of Enlightenment* (1997), originally published in 1944. Critical theories of culture have often been criticized for taking a "god's-eye view" of culture and proceeding at an abstract "level of theorising that does not address or attempt to document the *actual* mechanisms" of cultural mediation in social life (DeNora 2003:40, 2005:149). However, it is in *Dialectic of Enlightenment* that Horkheimer and Adorno inveighed most strongly against the very types of truth-claims and social scientific knowledge that they are accused of producing. Their analysis marked a turn away from authoritative social science and its positivistic methods of inquiry, which the authors believed had become implicated in the "total administration" of human beings. The book is also a sustained reflection on the contradictions of Enlightenment thought itself – in particular, that its potential for critical self-reflection remains a necessary condition for human freedom at the same time that its instrumentality undermines that very possibility.

As an alternative, the authors proceeded mimetically in the opening essays of *Dialectic of Enlightenment*, employing forms of presentation that challenged dominant expectations of scientific reason and mastery. Rather than undertaking a "positivistic search for information" about the nature of culture in their society, they used hermeneutic and metaphorical methods to evoke and persuade readers to consider alternative representations of the social world (Horkheimer and Adorno 1997:x; Honneth 2007:59). As Bernstein has argued, their aim was less to tell a truth than to raise questions about culture "from the perspective of its relation to the possibilities for social transformation" (1991:2). In this light, the question "remains open as to the kind of truth claims it can actually uphold" (Honneth 2007:61). Far from being a factual description of social reality, therefore, the text may be read as a "world-disclosing critique" of dominant interpretations of it (Honneth 2007).

This understanding of critical theory is significant, for the argument within cultural sociology that critique is anti-democratic is based largely on the assumption that it stakes a claim, not only to *the* truth, but to a *superior* truth, and in particular one not recognized by or accessible to ordinary social actors. But this is not the assumption underlying *Dialectic of Enlightenment*, which, while engaging in unmasking and demystification, does not presume that there is a final and absolute truth that can simply be "uncovered." Indeed, the authors argued, "the proposition that truth is the whole turns out to be identical with its contrary, namely, that in each case it exists only as a part" (Horkheimer and Adorno 1997:244). Writing at a time when the authoritarian manipulation of truth was being used to justify highly rationalized forms of anti-Semitism, political conformity, and mass mobilization, critical theorists had purposes beyond unmasking the ideological underpinnings of fascist propaganda. They also aimed to open up spaces for autonomous critical thought, and did so by producing alternative interpretations of society that made it necessary for others to actively judge the merit and value of competing claims to truth (Horkheimer and Adorno 1997:244).

Certainly there is a tension here between, on the one hand, opening space for autonomous thought and action by inviting others to participate in critical reflection about culture, and on the other, critical theory's self-understanding as a specialized practice able to produce unique insights and to reveal instances of domination otherwise obscured. Horkheimer and Adorno clearly struggled with this problem and the tension between the different strands of critique is not fully resolved in the text. Similarly, the precise relationship between critique and description is sometimes undeveloped, and in a later edition of the book the authors made explicit references to the "reality of the times" and social changes that required the reconsideration of their central arguments. Yet their intention as dialecticians was to reveal, however imperfectly, a world or possible worlds that were not yet recognized in the facts – a world understood not through the observation of its particular temporal appearance, but through critical reflection on its actual and potential constellations of thought, emotion, relationships, imagination, values, and judgments.

From "world-disclosing" to intimate and cooperative critique

Some theorists have recently developed this line of reasoning to conceptualize critique as something other than as the establishment of scientific or political truths, and to renew the cultural tradition of critical theory. Nikolas Kompridis, for example, argues that neither the establishment of empirical truth nor the accomplishment of rational or pragmatic consensus can be the goal of any form of critique that is oriented toward "re-opening the future" and disclosing possibilities for democratic life (2011:256). "Knowledge is not primarily what is at issue," he writes. "What *is* at issue is the disclosure and realization of possibilities for going on with our practice more reflectively, cooperatively enlarging the space of freedom as we cooperatively enlarge the space of possibility" (Kompridis 2006:170). Toward this end, Kompridis suggests that critique may be an "intimate" rather than alienating encounter when it is deliberately oriented toward learning with other people with whom we speak. Thus, rather than a "world-disclosing critique" that proceeds through critical reflection to illuminate possible worlds behind the "facts" of existing social conditions, this "reflective disclosure of possibility" emerges through encounter with others and is oriented toward future practice. In an ideal relationship of intimate critique, Kompridis suggests, the aim "is not just the critical transformation of the object of critique, but also of the subjectivity of the critic" (2006:175).

In another reconstruction of the tradition, Amy Allen (2016) brings Frankfurt School theorists into dialogue with Michel Foucault's historical "problematization" and postcolonial and decolonial critiques of modernity to suggest that traditional formulations of normative critique in European critical theory should be decolonized to reveal their historical contingency. Her work responds to concerns that the normative foundations of critique articulated by Eurocentric critical theorists, such as "freedom, autonomy, reflexivity, inclusiveness and equality" (Allen 2016:27), are not only insufficient for confronting globalized capitalism but inappropriate so long as they depend upon a "particular reading of reality that . . . did not include colonialism as a system of oppression" in any serious way (Santos 2014:40). This is both epistemologically and strategically problematic, as while these modes of critique were historically developed in the Global North, some of "the most innovative and effective transformative left practices of recent decades . . . have been occurring in the Global South" (ibid.). Rather than abandoning the normative foundations of Eurocentric critique or assuming that critical potential is exhausted in the North, however, Allen argues that the future of critique lies in bringing these traditions into "reciprocal elucidation" with others (borrowing a term from James Tully) and making it non-identical with itself. In doing so, we might "unlearn" our particular epistemological commitments and open the "possibility that there may well be some future in which our own normative commitments and ways of thinking and ordering things will have been transcended" (Allen 2016:205). She thus offers a radicalized concept of critique as "the wholly immanent and fragmentary practices of opening up lines of fragility and fracture in the social world" – cracks which can be inhabited in new, not-yet knowable ways (ibid.:201).

These alternative notions of critique point to the diverse contributions that critical theory can make to a sociology which, in addition to understanding how cultural meaning is constituted in everyday practice, is also capable of explaining how it is implicated in the defense and expansion of human freedom. Critical theory also has particular importance for explaining how and why respect for cultural difference and the practice of normative understanding can be articulated in new forms of critique. In contrast to arguments that democratic critique is impossible across cultural boundaries, these forms of cooperative, radically reflexive, intimate, and possibility-disclosing critique in fact require and invite radical differences that disrupt the horizons of sedimented cultural sensibilities and, in the spirit of (un)learning, contribute to their transformation (Kompridis 2006:145, 246).

Conclusion

Throughout this chapter, we have argued that this normative interpretation of the "democratic imperative" is a valuable element of any democratically oriented and critical sociology of culture. Indeed, it is particularly important for any project that engages complex cultural meanings, practices, and controversies in an era marked by the neoliberal challenge to democracy (Brown 2015). The autonomy of culture was a central problematic for the Frankfurt School critical theorists, who believed that it was always possible and everywhere threatened. They developed their methods of critique as analytical strategies for assessing its possibility, and understood reflective judgment as one form of resistance to its closing down. Though the terms of their analysis were generated in response to particular social and historical conditions, the problem of cultural freedom remains urgent today. As long as it is possible for spaces of cultural memory and practice to be destroyed, for cultural difference to be treated as a threat to democracy, and for universities to become agencies of bureaucratic management and the training of entrepreneurial selves – in other words, to the extent that the autonomy of culture remains a political problematic – critique must remain a central theoretical method for cultural sociology.

Hence, in political and intellectual contexts that are "inhospitable to the practice of critique" (Kompridis 2005:326), sociologists have a vital role to play in developing normative approaches to analysis that open up spaces for the reflective, intimate, and critical interpretation of culture. One of our main tasks is to work out how culture mediates judgment and how judgment mediates meaning. Another is to critically evaluate our own practices of knowledge production in light of those more open, imaginative and reflective possibilities. However, a critical theory of culture need not aim to *establish* the truth of these meanings and practices. It need not understand them in an illusory "pure" form or explain their causal roles as mechanisms for social change. Instead, as *Dialectic of Enlightenment* so compellingly illustrates, and as new critical theorists suggest, by disclosing how social life, and cultural sociology itself, could be otherwise, we might open up moments of autonomy in which the possibilities of culture can be critically evaluated and enlarged.

References

Abromeit, J. 2016. "Critical Theory and the Persistence of Right-Wing Populism." *Logos* 15(2–3). Retrieved October 26, 2017 (http://logosjournal.com/2016/abromeit/).

Adorno, T. 1967. "Cultural Criticism and Society." Pp. 17–34 in *Prisms*. Cambridge, MA: MIT Press.

Alexander, J. 1990. "Analytic Debates." Pp. 1–30 in *Culture and Society: Contemporary Debates*, edited by J. Alexander and S. Seidman. Cambridge: Cambridge University Press.

Alexander, J., and P. Smith. 1993. "The Discourse of American Civil Society: A New Proposal for Cultural Studies." *Theory and Society* 22(2):151–207.

———. 2004. "The Strong Program in Cultural Sociology: Elements of a Structural Hermeneutics." Pp. 11–26 in *The Meanings of Social Life: A Cultural Sociology*, edited by J. Alexander. New York: Oxford University Press.

Allen, A. 2008. *The Politics of Our Selves: Power, Autonomy and Gender in Contemporary Critical Theory*. New York: Columbia University Press.

———. 2016. *The End of Progress: Decolonizing the Normative Foundations of Critical Theory*. New York: Columbia University Press.

Amsler, S. 2011. "Beyond All Reason: Spaces of Hope in the Struggle for England's Universities." *Representations* 116(1):62–87.

———. 2014. "For Feminist Consciousness in the Academy." *Politics and Culture*. Retrieved October 26, 2017 (https://politicsandculture.org/2014/03/09/for-feminist-consciousness-in-the-academy/).

Benhabib, S. 2002. *The Claims of Culture: Equality and Diversity in the Global Era*. Princeton, NJ: Princeton University Press.

Bernstein, J.M. 1991. "Introduction." Pp. 1–27 in *Theodor W. Adorno The Culture Industry: Selected Essays on Mass Culture*, edited by J.M. Bernstein. London: Routledge.

Bourdieu, P. 2003. *Firing Back: Against the Tyranny of the Market 2*. New York: New Press.

Brown, W. 2015. *Undoing the Demos: Neoliberalism's Stealth Revolution*. Cambridge, MA: MIT Press.

Brunkhorst, H. 1995. "Dialectical Positivism of Happiness: Horkheimer's Materialist Deconstruction of Philosophy." Pp. 67–98 in *On Max Horkheimer: New Perspectives*, edited by S. Benhabib, W. Bonss, and J. McCole. Cambridge, MA: MIT Press.

Buck-Morss, S. 2003. *Thinking Past Terror: Islam and Critical Theory on the Left*. London: Verso.

Calhoun, C., P. Price, and A. Timmer, eds. 2002. *Understanding September 11*. New York: New Press.

DeNora, T. 2003. *After Adorno: Rethinking Music Sociology*. Cambridge: Cambridge University Press.

———. 2005. "Music and Social Experience." Pp. 147–59 in *The Blackwell Companion to the Sociology of Culture*, edited by M. Jacobs and N. Hanrahan. Malden, MA: Blackwell.

Eisenstein, Z. 2004. *Against Empire: Feminisms, Racism and the West*. London: Zed Books.

Eliasoph, N. 2007. "Beyond the Politics of Denunciation: Cultural Sociology as the 'Sociology for the Meantime.'" Pp. 55–100 in *Culture, Society, and Democracy: The Interpretive Approach*, edited by I. Reed and J. Alexander. Boulder, CO: Paradigm.

Fraser, N., and A. Honneth. 2003. *Redistribution or Recognition? A Political – Philosophical Exchange*. London: Verso.

Goldfarb, J. 2005. "Dialogue, Culture, Critique: The Sociology of Culture and the New Sociological Imagination." *International Journal of Politics, Culture, and Society* 18(3–4):281–92.

Honneth, A. 2007. *Disrespect: The Normative Foundations of Critical Theory*. Cambridge: Polity Press.

Horkheimer, M. 1972. "Traditional and Critical Theory." In *Critical Theory: Selected Essays*. New York: Continuum.

Horkheimer, M., and T.W. Adorno. 1997. *Dialectic of Enlightenment*. New York: Continuum.

Kellner, D. 2002. "The Frankfurt School and British Cultural Studies: The Missed Articulation." Pp. 31–58 in *Rethinking the Frankfurt School: Alternative Legacies of Cultural Critique*, edited by J.T. Nealon and C. Irr. New York: SUNY Press.

Kompridis, N. 2005. "Disclosing Possibility: The Past and Future of Critical Theory." *International Journal of Philosophical Studies* 13(3):325–51.

———. 2006. *Critique and Disclosure: Critical Theory between Past and Future*. Cambridge, MA: MIT Press.

———. 2011. "Receptivity, possibility, and democratic politics." *Ethics and Global Politics* 4(4):255–72. (www.tandfonline.com/doi/full/10.3402/egp.v4i4.14829).

Lichterman, P. 2005. "Civic Culture at the Grass Roots." Pp. 383–97 in *The Blackwell Companion to the Sociology of Culture*, edited by M. Jacobs and N. Hanrahan. Malden, MA: Blackwell.

———. 2007. "Invitation to a Practical Cultural Sociology." Pp. 19–53 in *Culture, Society, and Democracy: The Interpretive Approach*, edited by I. Reed and J. Alexander. Boulder, CO: Paradigm.

Nealon, J., and C. Irr, eds. 2002. *Rethinking the Frankfurt School: Alternative Legacies of Cultural Critique*. New York: SUNY Press.

Reed, I. 2007. "Cultural Sociology and the Democratic Imperative." Pp. 1–18 in *Culture, Society, and Democracy: The Interpretive Approach*, edited by I. Reed and J. Alexander. Boulder, CO: Paradigm.

Reed, I., and J. Alexander, eds. 2007. *Culture, Society, and Democracy: The Interpretive Approach*. Boulder, CO: Paradigm.

Santos, B.D.S. 2014. *Epistemologies of the South: Justice against Epistemicide*. Boulder, CO: Paradigm Press.

Smith, R.C. 2014. "Insecure Britain: On the Anti-Immigrant Narrative, the Rise of UKIP and the Unquestionableness of Capitalism." *Heathwood Press*. Retrieved October 26, 2017 (www.heathwoodpress.com/insecure-britain-anti-immigrant-narrative-rise-ukip-unquestionableness-capitalism/).

Szeman, I. 2002. "The Limits of Culture: The Frankfurt School and/for Cultural Studies." Pp. 59–79 in *Rethinking the Frankfurt School: Alternative Legacies of Cultural Critique*, edited by J. Nealon and C. Irr. New York: SUNY Press.

Titchiner, B. 2016. "The Epistemology of Violence: Understanding the Root Causes of Violence and 'Non-Conducive' Social Circumstances in Schooling, with a Case Study from Brazil." Doctoral thesis, School of Education, University of East Anglia.

Wolf, N. 2007. *The End of America: Letter of Warning to a Young Patriot*. White River Junction, VT: Chelsea Green.

Part II
The place of "culture" in sociological analysis

8

What is "the relative autonomy of culture"?

Jeffrey K. Olick

Introduction

A central shibboleth of the new cultural sociology that began to emerge in the 1970s and 1980s has been the term "the relative autonomy of culture." With it, advocates want to indicate at a minimum that we think culture is an important, sometimes even the most important, topic for sociological analysis. The problem is that "the relative autonomy of culture" often fails to specify anything beyond a general allegiance to "cultural" perspectives in sociology: the term, and its casual uses, do not specify what culture is supposedly autonomous from (the two major possibilities are structure and agency, though these clearly refer to distinct arguments in the philosophy of the social sciences; Hays 1994); "relative," moreover, is hardly a robust descriptor.

The term "relative autonomy," of course, has a long history in social thought. A wide variety of writers, including Durkheim, Lukacs, Sartre, and Elias have employed it (Kilminster 1991:xxvii). Most famous is its use by Althusser and his followers, particularly Poulantzas, to reject economic reductionism in Marxist state theory. In cultural sociology, specifically, its most intentional and elaborated use was in a foundational essay by Jeffrey Alexander (1990) on culture and society. There and elsewhere in Alexander's so-called Strong Program for cultural sociology (Alexander and Smith 2003; see also Alexander and Smith, this volume), "the relative autonomy of culture" has a more precise purpose than simply serving as an emblem for those interested in meaning and interpretation who see themselves on the humanistic side of sociology. "The relative autonomy of culture," in Alexander's use, indicates a meta-theoretical argument about the role of culture in sociological analysis, one that insists on avoiding what Parsons, following Whitehead, called "the fallacy of misplaced concreteness." "The relative autonomy of culture" is thus an imprecise substitute for what is better described as "*analytical* autonomy," which implies that meaning and interpretation are important in particular ways.

In this chapter, I outline this "autonomist" position, focusing on the arguments of Jeffrey Alexander (1990, 1995) and Margaret Archer (1988) – though to be sure there are differences between these authors, and with others, like William Sewell (1992) or Nicos Mouzelis (1995), who also advance autonomist positions. Autonomists, I show, are concerned with avoiding not only the classical reduction of culture to other factors, but also the treatment of culture as a concrete force rather than as an analytical dimension. In fighting the fallacy of misplaced concreteness (often referred to as the "concrete autonomy" argument), however, the autonomist position can lead to a misreading of a different position, what I call "constitutive" theory, represented most prominently by Norbert Elias, Anthony Giddens, and Pierre Bourdieu, among others (e.g., Zygmunt Bauman). In contrast to the "autonomist" position, "constitutivists" reject the analytical distinction between culture and structure in favor of an approach that highlights mutual constitution over analytical autonomy (on Bourdieu in particular, see Vandenberghe 1999). Because analytical autonomists are mainly concerned with distinguishing analytical autonomy from concrete autonomy, however, they mischaracterize constitutivists merely as failed autonomists and thus do not take on the constitutive argument in its own terms (see also Decoteau 2016). But constitutivists are not bad analytical autonomists: for better or worse, they reject analytical autonomy intentionally in favor of different meta-theoretical commitments.

The autonomist position

As with most issues in contemporary sociological theory, the question of cultural autonomy makes important reference to Max Weber. In contrast to reductionist arguments, particularly the Marxist materialist one, Weber argued in *The Protestant Ethic* that ideas can act as "switchmen," changing the course laid down by the dynamics of interest. This argument, however, is not quite the same as the one Weber made when he distinguished material and ideal interests. The former argument can be read as an example of what Anne Kane (1991), in a seminal article on the autonomy of culture, calls "concrete autonomy" – ideas as determinative forces; the latter, in contrast, signals a more profound epistemological dualism between material and ideal.

The contemporary "analytical autonomy" argument, however, owes its origins more directly to Parsons than to Weber, or at least to Parsons's interpellation of Weber's dichotomous approach in a less historical direction. As John Hall (1999:108) puts it, "Parsons sought to displace (1) a broadly qualitative and historical-comparative case-oriented approach . . . in favor of (2) a more abstract analytic approach focused on describing *variable elements* of action." How so? In the concluding chapter of his first major work, *The Structure of Social Action*, Parsons ([1937] 1968) identified four basic epistemological stances, including (1) *utilitarianism*, which reifies its analytical frame (rational self-interest); (2) *radical positivism*, which denies any analytical frame, claiming only to generalize on the basis of empirical induction; and (3) *idealism*, which allows for frames of reference, but does not accept that they are general and transcend a particular situation. A fourth frame, Parsons associates with Weber – the belief that scientific concepts are merely "useful fictions"; "ideal types," for Parsons, are the prime example.

Although Parsons acknowledges "an element of truth" in this fourth, Weberian approach, he seeks to develop a fifth position, what he calls "analytical realism." Ideal types, he argued, must not be understood merely as useful fictions; they are as real as the empirical world they are used to describe. "Analytical realism" depends on Parsons's assertion – which as numerous commentators (e.g., Bershady 1973) note is close to that of Immanuel Kant – that we must distinguish between analytical and concrete aspects of reality. For Parsons ([1937] 1968:730), the concepts of science are analytical, and hence "correspond, not to concrete phenomena, but to elements in them which are analytically separable from other elements." For example, we may be able to concretely dissect out the brain of an individual, but the distinction between mind and body is only an analytical one. Such analytical distinctions are essential to science, and particularly appropriate to the social sciences, which must take into account the ideal element, lest they treat their objects as machines and hence cease to be social sciences at all.

Parsons made clear, however, that analytical categories are to be distinguished from "emergent properties." For Weber, normative patterns (e.g., the Protestant ethic) must be understood to emerge from the accumulated actions of individuals; they are thus concrete emergences. For Parsons, in contrast, norms are an analytic element of action systems. When Parsons refers to "normative order" or to the "integrative powers of culture," norms or culture are thus not concrete elements but analytical dimensions. For Parsons, then, all explanations must be multi-dimensional, which is different from merely saying they must take into account emergence. To miss this is to succumb to the fallacy of misplaced concreteness.

Not every analytical autonomist, to be sure, has come to that position through a critical reading of Parsons. But Jeffrey Alexander quite explicitly points out the flaw in Parsons's conceptualization of culture in developing his autonomist position: despite Parsons's emphasis on the analytical autonomy of culture and structure (conditions and norms, in his language), Parsons was in practice most interested in the concrete institutionalization of culture as values. In Alexander's view, however, Parsons's approach commits the sin of "internalized reduction," failing to fulfill the promise of his putatively multidimensional theory. And indeed, multidimensionalism is the overriding principle of Alexander's analytical-autonomy position. As Kane (1991:54) has put it, "analytical autonomy ... posits the complete and independent structure of culture; it is conceptualized through the theoretical, artificial separation of culture from other social structures, conditions, and action." The basic principle of the analytical-autonomy position is thus to overcome the elision of concrete and analytical autonomy: not only do ideas act as switchmen, ideal interests are always present, as part of an autonomous analytical dimension, even in the most material circumstances.

If "relative autonomy" refers to "analytical autonomy," then, it is a very poor choice of terms indeed, for "autonomy of culture" is not meant in the sense that Althusser and his followers meant "autonomy of the state." The state is a concrete agency with buildings, resources, personnel, and so forth. The analytical autonomy of culture, however, corresponds better to the distinction between, for instance, the political and economic aspects of a negotiation, which are not reducible to the presence of a politician and a banker. In Althusserian state theory, relative autonomy refers explicitly and clearly to concrete autonomy. Perhaps this is one reason why the new culturalists have carefully sought to distinguish their position from the fallacy of misplaced concreteness, which leads to the treatment of culture as emergent rather than as analytically autonomous. This urgency to reject concrete autonomy, however, leads analytical autonomists to misunderstand the argument of those who reject the durable status of such analytical distinctions, namely those I call "constitutivists."

Autonomy versus constitution

Bourdieu

The work of Pierre Bourdieu is perhaps the most prominent invocation of constitutivism in recent discussions of theory in the US. Bourdieu constructs his position as a response to what he sees as two failed sociological projects – structuralism (mainly Lévi-Straussian structural anthropology) and "subjectivism" (under which he includes phenomenology, existentialism, symbolic interactionism, and rational-choice theory). The problem with structuralism, according to Bourdieu, is that it reifies structure; structuralists claim to grasp structures clairvoyantly rather than through their appearance in human behavior. This position, Bourdieu argues, creates a false dichotomy between structure and agency by positing an existence for structures that is completely external to individuals and that reduces agents to mere automatons. In contrast, subjectivism ignores structuring processes, locating each interaction or decision in an immediate unstructured context. Subjectivists are thus unable to explain regularity and the reproduction over generations of the categories that agents draw on to "construct" social relations.

Bourdieu's response is that structures are not "real," but exist only in the regularities of human behavior. Similarly, agency is not the product of an unstructured subjectivity but of a structured set of dispositions, the "habitus." "Habitus" is difficult to pin down because, consistent with Bourdieu's critique of idealism, he is reluctant to specify concepts once and for all. Nevertheless, Bourdieu develops the notion of habitus as a method for grasping the inseparability of culture, structure, and agency. For Bourdieu, habitus gives expression to the dialectical relation between subjectivity and objectivity. The shared dispositions of the habitus generate certain groupings of attitudes and behavior: actors are "naturally" – by virtue of the habitus – oriented to what is conventionally called structure without consciously orienting themselves in this manner.

But habitus alone does not ensure the reproduction of structuring processes. The concept of "field" designates a vast number of hierarchically structured arenas of social life. "A field," Bourdieu writes, "may be defined as a network, or a configuration, of objective relations between positions." Furthermore,

> In a highly differentiated society, the social cosmos is made up of a number of such relatively autonomous social microcosms, i.e., spaces of objective relations that are the site of a logic and a necessity that are specific and irreducible to those that regulate other fields.
>
> *(Bourdieu and Wacquant 1992:97)*

Insofar as a field is a place of struggle, its very nature and its rules of operation are always either reproduced or changed, and thus cannot be taken for granted as fixed. Indeed, the struggle is not just about the internal structure of the field, but over the very boundaries of the field and its relations to other fields. Bourdieu's formulation thus suggests that institutions are produced by the struggles that go on within them, and that the relations among fields are always potentially fluid.

There are, however, two major points of criticism, points that Alexander addresses powerfully. Despite the fluidity of Bourdieu's field concept, he seems to bring a hierarchical ordering in through the back door: Bourdieu "discovers" empirically that the most important condition for the development of the habitus is the distance from economic necessity. But then he seems to generalize this empirical "discovery" into an a priori condition: habitus, he writes (Bourdieu 1984:170), is "necessity internalized and converted into a disposition that generates meaningful practices and meaning-given perceptions." Furthermore,

> Without ever being totally coordinated . . . the dispositions and the situations which combine synchronically to constitute a determinate conjuncture are never wholly independent, since they are engendered by the objective structures, that is, in the last analysis, by the economic bases of the social formation.
>
> *(Bourdieu 1977:83)*

This assertion that economic structures are the main determinants of habitus, many critics have charged, compromises Bourdieu's claim that dimensions of the social world are mutually constitutive. If constitution is mutual, then a single dimension (economic structure) must not be treated as primary and determining. This is Parsons's problem of internalized reduction redux.

Alexander's critique

Alexander's (1995) response to Bourdieu is thus shaped not by the claim that Bourdieu is insufficiently constitutive, but that he is too constitutive, that he sees the habitus as the site of non-rational, practical consciousness but wants to show that apparently non-economic realms of life are the objects of calculation. For Bourdieu, the habitus is the location of strategic action. According to Alexander, this leads Bourdieu to conflate economy and culture. The habitus must not only structure action, it must explain why people tend to act in such a way that, against their "interests," reproduces inequalities in various fields – "the regularities immanent in the objective condition of the production of their generative principle" (Bourdieu 1977:78). In order to explain these regularities without falling back into a mechanistic model, Bourdieu insists that instead of following rules, agents as knowing subjects are capable of deploying strategies. According to Alexander, the result is a theoretical paradox. On the one hand, Bourdieu shows that structural analysis of cultural codes is inadequate to understanding action, since people possess varying degrees of mastery of these codes or ability to improvise within them. On the other hand, the habitus conceived as practical consciousness means repeated recourse to norms and habits, that is, to non-rational sources of motivation. According to Alexander, Bourdieu cannot have it both ways:

> Internalized, normative order and rational action are like oil and water; they can be placed beside one another but they cannot mix. If actors are simply calculating creatures, the objects of their calculation may certainly be norms; if so, then these same norms cannot form the character (habitus) of these calculating agents as well.
>
> *(Alexander 1995:155)*

Thus, Alexander argues that Bourdieu has conflated dimensions of the social world. The cultural dimension of action, which allows people to exercise agency through interpretation, has been reduced to strategy, unconscious or not, which is at root an economic dimension.

Whereas Alexander sees this conflation as endemic to the constitutive project, however, it is also possible to see it as a particular problem of Bourdieu's that derives from his commitment to explaining reproduction rather than transformation of structures. Alexander's main concern is that distinctions between dimensions be preserved. However, Bourdieu's conflationary problems might also be solved by conceptually eliminating the problem of balance between structure and agency – in Bourdieu, unbalanced in favor of structure – by eliminating the conceptual distinction between structure and agency. But before I explore such a possibility, it will be useful to examine Giddens's version of constitutive theory, which has the opposite weakness from Bourdieu's overbalancing in favor of agency. By examining Margaret Archer's response to Giddens, we will gain an even clearer understanding of what the autonomist position entails.

Giddens

In the context of Anglo-American sociological theory, and independently of Bourdieu, Anthony Giddens developed his own version of constitutive theory. "Structuration theory," as Giddens conceives it, is an attempt to resolve the foundational Western sociological dualism between action and system. In contrast to Parsons's theory, dependent on internalization of norms, Giddens seeks to conceptualize the process whereby knowledgeable actors interact to produce and reproduce the systematicity of social relations. Into this "mutual constitution" of structure and agency, to avoid the interactionist pitfall of seeing all actors as equal in interaction, Giddens adds a broad concept of power.

Following Kilminster (1990), I offer the following two quotations as summarizing the core of structuration theory:

> All structural properties of social systems . . . are the medium and outcome of the contingently accomplished activities of situated actors. The reflexive monitoring of action in

situations of co-presence is the main anchoring feature of social integration, but both the conditions and the outcomes of situated interaction stretch far beyond those situations as such. The mechanisms of "stretching" are variable but in modern societies tend to involve reflexive monitoring itself.

(Giddens 1984:195)

Power is not, as such, an obstacle to freedom or emancipation but is their very medium. . . . The existence of power presumes structures of domination whereby power that "flows smoothly" in processes of social reproduction (and is, as it were, "unseen") operates.

(Giddens 1984:257)

Giddens's point is thus to replace dualism with "duality," seeing neither structure (system) nor agency apart from the other. Structures, in this account, have only a "virtual existence." They are instantiated in action, and are perpetuated as "memory traces." This ontological observation is necessary, according to Giddens, to avoid reifying structures as entities when they are only immanent orderings. Action instantiates and perpetuates structure.

Giddens's intention, however, is to do away with what he sees as the ontological reifications inhering in dualistic theory. Dualism, for Giddens, is the assertion that agency and institutional structure are conceivable apart from one another. In contrast, he agrees that institutionalized practices and relations – more fluid and open categories – are where order is to be found. Sociology should study social practices and relations, not institutions and agents.

Archer's critique

"Institutions," in Giddens's account, as Margaret Archer (1995:95) critiques it, "are never something concrete to which we can point but are essentially processual; ever in a fluid process of becoming and never in a (temporarily or temporary) fixed state of being, because all structural properties and all actions are always potentially transformable." In her statement of an analytical autonomy position, Archer (1988) therefore characterizes structuration theory as a variety of "central conflationism," which can be read as a pejorative characterization of "constitutivism." Its hallmark, she argues, is to insist on the mutual constitution of structure and agency, thus precluding examination of their interplay. In contrast, Archer insists "that the two [structure and agency, individual and society] have to be related rather than conflated" (Archer 1995:6). The crux of Archer's argument is that central conflationism denies either structure and culture independent *causal* power. "Conversely social realism accentuates the importance of emergent properties at the levels of both agency and structure, but considers these as proper to the strata in question and therefore distinct from each other and irreducible to one another" (Archer 1995:14).

Archer's assertion of analytical autonomy allows her to reintroduce separate temporal horizons for structure and agency – an independence denied by central conflation:

Properties and powers of some strata are anterior to those of others; they have relative autonomy; such autonomous properties exert independent causal influences in their own right and it is the identification of these causal powers at work which validates their existence, for they may indeed be non-observables.

(Archer 1995:14)

Structuration, she argues, does not allow for this kind of analytical and temporal disentanglement. The crux of Archer's critique is her assertion that "by enjoining the examination of a single process in the present tense, issues surrounding the relative independence, causal influence, and temporal precedence of the components have been eliminated at a stroke" (Archer 1995:93). Two questions thus arise: what is left unexplainable by mutual constitution? And why should we believe that the components are indeed separate, analytically or otherwise?

According to Archer, mutual constitution means that, despite an awareness of the unintended consequences of action, there are no emergent properties of the system that can vary independently of action. Moreover, "elisionists" (her term for constitutivists) "deliberately turn their backs upon any autonomous features which could pertain independently to either structure or agency. Otherwise such features could be investigated separately" (Archer 1995:97). According to Giddens, structures have only a virtual existence, instantiated in action. For Archer, this means that structure exists only in people's heads; Giddens's account thus cannot explain structures that exist outside people's heads (e.g., knowledge contained in libraries).

A second unacceptable implication of mutual constitution for Archer is that seeing structure as having only virtual existence requires consigning its structuring influence to the moment of instantiation. This means, for Archer, that it is impossible to explain the persistence of structures that collectivities do not want. From the agency side, this approach is problematic as well: agents are denied autonomous properties and independent influences. In contrast, Archer asserts the value of emergent structural properties on the one hand and psychological and biological aspects of agency that are socially unmediated on the other. Duality of structure, according to Archer's critique, decenters the subject because it implies that "human beings only become people, as opposed to organisms, through drawing upon structural properties to generate social practices" (Archer 1995:101). Central conflationism, Archer argues, thus deprives both elements – structure and agency – of their "relative autonomy."

To defend the relative autonomy of the self from the social agent, Archer appeals first to Kant's "Transcendental Unity of Apperception," which she follows Kant in arguing stands as an a priori condition for the ordering of experience. The metaphysical nature of her musings becomes most clear when Archer connects analytical autonomy and religious faith:

> [W]hilst no spiritual experience (of itself) is auto-veridical, neither is it automatically a candidate for being explained away sociologically. After all, sociology can never be robust enough to substantiate and sustain the faith of the atheist. But what is at issue here is not verification or falsification ... but rather the possibility of authentic inner experience.
>
> *(Archer 1995:292–93)*

My point in noting this connection in Archer's work is that, taken to its logical conclusions, analytical autonomy seems to imply some sort of metaphysics, more often a manifest belief not in God but in a priori concepts.

The view from the other side: Kilminster on Giddens

Before concluding, let us examine the situation from the constitutivist side, based on Richard Kilminster's (1990) detailed critique of Giddens. In contrast to Archer, he argues that Giddens is insufficiently developmental and remains wedded to a solipsistic, aprioristic conception of agency. In other words, Giddens is not too constitutive, he is not constitutive enough! According to Kilminster, Giddens fails to appreciate the ways in which dualistic concepts have developed historically. Giddens's solution thus takes part in the same aprioristic logic that brought about the problem in the first place. In part, this is due to his discontinuist understanding of modernity as a world apart from other patterns of social organization, and of sociology as an enterprise distinctly formed to analyze that unique constellation. According to Kilminster, there is no historical, genetic device in Giddens's theory, and "lacking a dynamic principle, he can only logically assess the cognitive value of the perspectives and schools [that comprise his theoretical synthesis], which he treats as comparable and equipollent" (Kilminster 1990:108). As a result Giddens's ahistoricism leads him to preserve a solipsistic, aprioristic conception of agency: "despite his attempt to transcend the individual/society dichotomy by the duality of agency and structure, the ghost of the old dualism haunts the theory because his point of departure is action theory, which carries dualism at its core" (Kilminster (1990:98).

As Kilminster argues, Giddens responds on the one hand to the functionalist conception of the actor as a "cultural dope" and on the other hand to the structuralist understanding of the actor as constructed by discourses. He is centrally concerned with articulating a concept of the actor as knowledgeable, possessing capacities for both discursive self-reflexivity and practical consciousness. His actors are individuals acting knowledgeably and intentionally, bounded by both the unconscious and by institutions. Giddens thus "ascribes vaunting power to human agency, including that of generating apparently social-structural properties, which are all said to be instantiated by action" (Kilminster 1990:118).

By theorizing structures as only virtual, and thus internal to the individual, Giddens makes it possible to analyze structures only through a process of methodological bracketing or an *Epoché* of agency. According to Kilminster (1990:102), this "recommendation for methodological bracketing seems to embody a liberalistic timidity about the possibility of representing and theorizing social wholes, lest this procedure erases [*sic*] individuals." For Kilminster (1990:101), the image of the actor in structuration theory thus "articulates, with an implicit normative stress, the dominant self-experience and public code of behavior of highly self-controlled individuals in advanced industrial societies." Kilminster's alternative has two constituent elements: to show how this kind of individual came to develop in the first place, and to reconceptualize the understanding of relations among people.

In sum, Kilminster faults Giddens not for being conflationary, as Archer does, but for having an insufficient grasp on interdependence, one that brings a self-contained rationalistic agent in through the back door. Kilminster (1990:98) thus agrees with Archer that Giddens is unable to grasp the properties of far-flung structures:

> the interacting individuals in conditions of co-presence can only be visualized as connected to other individuals who are not present by using metaphors such as stretching of social practices (time-space distanciation) or by reference to their lateral properties or to the channeling of time-space paths of individuals in system integration.

But unlike Archer, Kilminster does not claim that Giddens insufficiently separates agent (and agency's constitutive elements) and structure, but that he separates them too much:

> There is no conceptual grasp of the perspective from which [individuals] are regarded by others in the total social web, nor of their combined relatedness. . . . Giddens thus fails to grasp interdependence as a much more multileveled, complex, and relational structure. . . . In analyzing such multidimensional functional nexuses, one can show how the nature of bonds between individuals and groups changes over time as part of wider societal changes.
> *(Kilminster 1990:121)*

Kilminster's solution, inspired by theorists like Norbert Elias, is to see structural and agentic dimensions as historically, rather than philosophically, emergent. From the perspective of analytical autonomy, this move appears to be a return to concrete autonomy, albeit one that emerges over a long course of history rather than within a situation.

Conclusion

I have argued that Alexander rightly critiques Bourdieu's constitutivism for tending to over-emphasize an economistic determination. Alexander's response, however, is not to encourage a reconstruction of more faithful constitutive procedures but to use Bourdieu's errors as a basis on which to justify the analytical autonomist approach. Alexander's approach can be appreciated if we remember the positions he is trying to avoid. He is not arguing principally against constitutivism but against concrete autonomy (realism). In his much cited introductory essay on culture and society, for instance, Alexander (1990:5) writes,

> Parsons's insistence on the analytical autonomy of cultural, social, and psychological systems promises a way out of the mechanistic-subjectivistic dichotomy without giving up on either side. There is a place for culture, but it is only a relatively autonomous sphere.

then warns,

> The promise of this solution can be neutralized if the separation between these levels is taken in a concrete rather than an analytical way. By concretizing the social system as independent of culture, functionalism raises significant problems for an interpretive, culturally sensitive position.

Elsewhere, Alexander refutes the concrete solution to the culture-agency problem as well, arguing that giving action pride of place may refute theories that give too much weight to the internal relations of symbolic elements, but that as a result:

> [C]ulture is reduced to a resource, a tool kit whose symbol supply is so elastic that the limits it imposes become largely irrelevant. The problem with such an approach is that it asks us to choose between cultural system and action. Such a choice can be avoided if an analytic rather than concrete approach to the action-environment relation is taken.
>
> *(Alexander 1988:329)*

In his critique of Bourdieu, Alexander thus seems to gloss over the elaborate relational and constitutive argument. He is not wrong about Bourdieu's faults, but his solution – which is to make an analytical distinction, surely the product of a long process of development and possible only at a particular point in history – is clearly Kantian, treating, that is, an historical development as an a priori distinction. In this way, Alexander does not seem to have engaged with the main point of Bourdieu's work, which is not accidentally constitutive, but intentionally anti-Kantian. Archer is much clearer about her enemy. Nonetheless, she refutes Giddens's constitutivism not by engaging with it, but by using Giddens's inconsistent application of constitutivism to dismiss constitutivism in general. Where Alexander dismissed Bourdieu's constitutivism because Bourdieu overemphasized structure, Archer dismisses Giddens's constitutivism because Giddens overemphasized agency.

By counterposing Kilminster's constitutivist critique of Giddens's residual solipsism, dualism, and apriorism, perhaps we finally can inaugurate a clear debate between a consistent autonomist and a consistent constitutivist position, a debate that is not well served by vague assertions about "the relative autonomy of culture."

Jeffrey K. Olick

Acknowledgments

The author is grateful to Matthew Morrison for comments on an earlier draft, and to Victoria Johnson for relevant discussions many years ago about the ideas expressed in this chapter. This acknowledgment is not meant to imply that they agree with what I have written!

References

Alexander, Jeffrey C. 1988. *Action and Its Environments.* New York: Columbia University Press.

———. 1990. "Analytical Debates: Understanding the Relative Autonomy of Culture." Pp. 1–30 in *Culture and Society: Contemporary Debates*, edited by J.C. Alexander and S. Seidman. Cambridge: Cambridge University Press.

———. 1995. "The Reality of Reduction: The Failed Synthesis of Pierre Bourdieu." Pp. 128–217 in *Fin de Siecle Social Theory: Relativism, Reduction, and the Problem of Reason.* London: Verso.

Alexander, Jeffrey C., and Philip Smith. 2003. "The Strong Program in Cultural Sociology: Elements of a Structural Hermeneutics." Pp. 11–26 in *The Meanings of Social Life: A Cultural Sociology*, edited by J.C. Alexander. Oxford: Oxford University Press.

Archer, Margaret S. 1988. *Culture and Agency: The Place of Culture in Social Theory.* Cambridge: Cambridge University Press.

———. 1995. *Realist Social Theory: The Morphogenetic Approach.* Cambridge: Cambridge University Press.

Bershady, Harold. 1973. *Ideology and Social Knowledge.* Oxford: Basil Blackwell.

Bourdieu, Pierre. 1977. *Outline of a Theory of Practice*, trans. Richard Nice. Cambridge: Cambridge University Press.

———. 1984. *Distinction: A Social Critique of the Judgment of Taste*, trans. Richard Nice. Cambridge, MA: Harvard University Press.

Bourdieu, Pierre, and Loic J.D. Wacquant. 1992. *An Invitation to Reflexive Sociology.* Chicago: University of Chicago Press.

Decoteau, Claire Laurier. 2016. "The Reflexive *Habitus*: Critical Realist and Bourdieusian Social Action." *European Journal of Social Theory* 19(3):303–21.

Giddens, Anthony. 1984. *The Constitution of Society: Outline of the Theory of Structuration.* Berkeley: University of California Press.

Hall, John. 1999. *Cultures of Inquiry: From Epistemology to Discourse in Sociohistorical Research.* Cambridge: Cambridge University Press.

Hays, Sharon. 1994. "Structure and Agency and the Sticky Problem of Culture." *Sociological Theory* 12(1):57–92.

Kane, Anne. 1991. "Cultural Analysis in Historical Sociology: The Analytic and Concrete Forms of the Autonomy of Culture." *Sociological Theory* 9(1):53–69.

Kilminster, Richard. 1990. "Structuration Theory as a World-View." Pp. 74–115 in *Giddens' Theory of Structuration: A Critical Appreciation*, edited by C. Bryant and D. Jary. London: Routledge.

———. 1991. "Editorial Introduction." Pp. vii–xxv in *The Symbol Theory*, edited by R. Kilminster. London: Sage.

Mouzelis, Nicos. 1995. *Sociological Theory: What Went Wrong?* London: Routledge.

Parsons, Talcott. [1937] 1968. *The Structure of Social Action.* Glencoe, IL: The Free Press.

Sewell, William, Jr. 1992. "A Theory of Structure: Duality, Agency, and Transformation." *American Journal of Sociology* 98(1):1–29.

Vandenberghe, Frédéric. 1999. "The Real is the Relational: An Epistemological Analysis of Pierre Bourdieu's Genetic Structuralism." *Sociological Theory* 17(1):32–67.

9

Formal models of culture

John W. Mohr and Craig M. Rawlings

Introduction

Since the earliest days of the discipline, sociologists have typically studied culture, by which we mean the more aesthetically or meaningfully constituted components of social life, with qualitative methodologies – close readings, ethnographies, interviews, introspective and participatory methods, semiotic decodings, and interpretations of archival, psychoanalytic, or media data. Presumably this approach reflects the affinity between subjective experiences of art and language and the social meanings of objects. Yet, almost since the beginning, social scientists have also used quantitative methodologies to analyze culture. Sometimes they have sought to interpret meanings. At other times researchers have used pre-existing cultural metrics precisely because they require little interpretation. This chapter focuses on how these more quantitative efforts have been conducted and what kinds of studies have resulted. We begin by defining a formal model of culture. We then offer a brief history of how American sociologists have used formal approaches to study culture over the last century. We conclude by describing some of the new methods, theories, and projects currently being developed to generate formal models of culture in the digital age.

A formal model of culture

What is a formal model of culture? Although others use the term differently, we focus on research projects where cultural information has been gathered (or simulated), compiled into a dataset, and transformed into a representational model of the phenomena under investigation. More specifically, for us, a formal model is

> a reduced form representation of a larger, more complexly ordered system of information. . . [that] depends on some specifiable process for reducing this larger complexity . . . achieved by an agreed on set of analytic practices (hence, a transformation toward greater simplicity based on an elaborated theory of pattern reduction).
>
> *(Mohr and Rawlings 2012:72)*

We focus on data analysis because doing so brings a different type of materiality to cultural studies, one in which embodiment affects the construction of formal models in a social field (Bourdieu 2004). Although we appreciate the virtues of reflexivity, we understand data analysis to be an inherently social process, from the institutional logics and systems of power that govern conceptualizing of data to organizational practices that order its gathering, storage, and retrieval, to the limited rhetorical palettes through which it must be presented in order to count as legitimate knowledge within a dominant logic of truth. We nonetheless maintain our criteria for a formal model, defined as the product of a dataset and an analysis, because we see this couplet as capturing the essence of scientific practice. Here we find common cause with those who would embrace critical realism in social science (Gorski 2004). Our own formulation is that:

> data analysis creates what, following Ricoeur (1973), we think of as a second order externalization (and thus, as with Ricoeur, we see this as a kind of materialization function) by taking our theories about the world, giving them material form (as data, however hobbled), interacting with them, (however roughly, through analysis), and, then interpreting them, (however heroically through a reading of signs).
>
> *(Mohr and Rawlings 2012:73)*

By focusing on formal analysis of collected data, we draw attention to the special class of models that operate through logical or mathematical reductions of information. The distinction between qualitative and quantitative is murky here, but deliberately so. We want to include formal modes of qualitative work like that pioneered by Charles Ragin (1987), who applied Boolean set theory to analyze qualitative distinctions in historical-comparative research. We also would include another powerful type of formal modeling of communicative content – datasets from interviews that have been coded in qualitative software programs such as Atlas TI.

However, to focus on the virtues of formalization, we exclude from our conception of formal models those cultural analyses that work only at the level of interpretation, impression, intuition, or close reading because we see these as involving a different style of sociological understanding, albeit one that is tightly coupled with formal modeling and fully essential to understanding culture. One virtue of formalization is that its "materialization function" provides a way to test theories in the material world. Formal models are also more replicable and more likely to be incorporated into a social technology employed by others. Thus, Bourdieu observes,

> the "art" of the scientist is indeed separated from the "art" of the artist by two major differences: on the one hand, the importance of the formalized knowledge which is mastered in the practical state, owing in particular to formalization and formularization, and, on the other hand, the role of the instruments, which, as Bachelard put it, is formalized knowledge turned into things.
>
> *(Bourdieu 2004:40)*

Given these parameters of formal models, how can they be employed in the analysis of cultural phenomena?

A brief history of culture modeling in American sociology, 1900–2017

In the case of American sociology there have been significant changes in both how culture is understood and in how it has been modeled. Pragmatically, we divide the history of American sociology into six periods. In each period we describe some of the ways that formal models were used to study culture. We pay special attention to two different types of culture models, those with explicitly hermeneutic goals versus those without them.

Period 1: pre-formal phase (through 1920)

From the origins of American sociology through the 1920s, quantitative methodologies were quite primitive. Two streams of formal modeling of culture by proto-sociologists are relevant. Both come from the world of social reform, site of much of the early roots of American sociology (Ross 1991). First, professionalizing social workers developed standardized procedures for gathering sociological information. Notably, Mary Richmond, Director of the Charity Organization Department at the Russell Sage Foundation, developed elaborate arguments about the logic of inference that social workers should use when conducting a social diagnosis, which she defined as "the attempt to make as exact a definition as possible of the situation and personality of a human being in some social need" (1917:357). Her book is filled with pages of questionnaires. But Richmond drew on the medical profession as her model, and her systematizing efforts tended toward abstract taxonomies of social pathologies and of the diagnostic skills needed to assess them.

A second important initiative was the Pittsburgh survey of 1907, followed by more than 2,500 similar endeavors over the next two decades. The Pittsburgh project was inspired by W.E.B. Du Bois's (1899) study of the Philadelphia black community, Jane Addams's studies of immigrant neighborhoods around Chicago's Hull House, and Charles Booth's studies of the London working class. With funding from the Russell Sage Foundation, the project had 74 field staff compiling information about social and cultural processes in order "to provide an inventory and an overview of the state of the city, for which the investigators were omnivorous in their methods of data collection" (Converse [1987] 2009:24). The data collection procedures were rough-hewn by modern standards. Data came in the form of a schedule that "in the hands of the social surveyors was an instrument for making observations *or* for conducting interviews with respondents, or a mixture of both" (Converse [1987] 2009:34). But these procedures reflected an appreciation for the importance of qualitative distinctions. The checklist for clothing included check-off categories for "spotted ... dusty ... torn ... worn ... patched ... mussed ... wrinkled." They also borrowed from social work's methodologies by collecting "case-history interviews, which were gathered and then counted and compared among some dimensions, thus providing a 'case-mounting' that represented a merger of the case study and statistical methods" (Converse 1987: 34).

However, as Bulmer noted, "the Survey used quantitative data in more of an exploratory and descriptive than analytic way" (1996:18). He continued,

> It was as if there was an intuitive sense of the value of collecting extensive data about individuals in the population being studied, without the necessary knowledge either about sampling or how to handle the data once collected other than to compute simple counts of characteristics and then treat respondents on a case-by-case basis.
>
> *(Bulmer 1996:26)*

In short, although researchers were beginning to make measurements about cultural matters, the concept of culture itself was undeveloped, as were the understanding of formal data analysis and the extent to which such methods could improve validity or generalizability.

Period 2: the formalist turn (1920–1940)

Around the end of World War I there was a shift toward a more modern scientific program (Ross 1991; Platt 1996). Among a variety of factors, a key influence was the spread of modern survey research technologies in the late 1920s and early 1930s. For the first time, surveys gave sociologists a flexible, adaptable, convenient tool for creating quantitative models of most anything. There were three critical developments – statistical innovations in sampling theory, the rise of election and public opinion polling organizations, and the invention of attitude scaling. Sampling theory meant that it was possible, at relatively low cost, to ask a question to a reasonable number of respondents with some degree of confidence that results could be extrapolated to a larger population. This method broke social scientists' long-standing dependence on the state for statistical information about the polity (Lazarsfeld 1961).

The invention of attitude measurement provided a way to systematically measure culture. W. I. Thomas is generally credited with first sociologically conceptualizing attitudes in his work with Znaniecki (1918) on *The Polish Peasant in Europe and America*. Attitudes conveyed the sense of a deep structure of meanings and orientations that had direct consequences for action in the world. In 1925, both Floyd Allport and Emory Bogardus published independent approaches to constructing "attitude scales." Later developments by Thurstone, Likert, and others produced rapid advances in using surveys to measure subjective experiences, including cultural orientations, values, systems of meanings and beliefs, and subjective understandings of social situations (Converse [1987] 2009). During this period, both interpretative and explanatory models of culture became abundant and they underwent rapid innovation, development, and diffusion.

Period 3: the institutionalization of formalist program (1940–1960)

World War II was relatively short, but its impact on the social sciences was profound. Sociologists employed in the war effort mixed with scientists from other disciplines, a situation that promoted interdisciplinary borrowing of methods, procedures, and theories. In one important development, large teams of coders were put to work analyzing newspapers and other public communications to gather intelligence and assess enemy propaganda. Harold Lasswell directed a staff at the US Library of Congress, where they created new methods for reading large textual corpora, especially foreign newspapers, to extract critical bits of information along with statistical measures of reliability. These were some of the first modern protocols for what sociologists call content analysis (Lasswell et al. 1949).

Other scholars advanced social survey research. Samuel Stouffer and his team (1949) surveyed over a half million American soldiers during the war, asking a wide range of attitude questions about unit solidarity, the legitimacy of authority, social integration, and so forth. Projects like this were catalysts for the subsequent development and legitimation of survey methodologies in sociology. Paul Lazarsfeld was a pivotal proponent of formalization in sociology during these years. As director of Columbia University's Bureau for Applied Social Research, he promoted research projects, mentored others, and developed the theoretical foundations for a quantitatively based formalist sociology. His writings addressed practical problems such as how to conceptualize and operationalize variables, how to link indicators to concepts, how to use crosstabulations to assess causality, and how to measure latent structures. Importantly, Lazarsfeld sees no clear distinction between qualitative and quantitative methodologies. He and his colleagues moved easily between these two styles of research. In this era, American sociologists drew on both survey and content analysis methodologies while developing new ways to model culture.

Period 4: fragmentation (1960–1980)

The 1950s ascendance of a formalist research project in American sociology co-occurred with the flowering of Talcott Parsons's theories. By the early 1960s, the legitimacy of that theoretical framework was being strongly questioned. In its place came the stirrings of what we call the "fragmentation period." Robert Merton's program of middle-range theorizing provided some intellectual cover as sociologists turned away from grand theory, toward grounded methods and practices. This was true of both qualitative and quantitative scholars. For example, Harold Garfinkel developed a rigorously grounded interpretative sociology, influencing many projects including modern conversation analysis. On the quantitative side, sociologists began applying multivariate analyses in new ways, developing more sophisticated models of institutional life, perhaps most famously, Blau and Duncan's (1967) study of intergenerational stratification systems.

This period was something of a dead zone for formal models of culture by American sociologists (although there were exceptions, such as the models of organizational fields by Warren, Rose, and Bergunder 1974). One reason was that the concept itself had been hollowed out. Under structural-functionalism, culture – operationalized as measures of values and norms – was a system-level construct, describing societies as a whole. With the demise of Parsonian system theory, grand theory waned, and culture lost its previous theoretical place. Communities of qualitative researchers worked some on culture, but quantitative scholars were focused on middle-range projects, many of which were anti-cultural. Research programs like resource dependency theory, exchange theory, and social network theory, for example, turned their backs on questions of culture. In cognate fields – psychology, anthropology, political science, and linguistics – researchers made major advances in the formal analysis of culture and meaning during these years. However, in American sociology, qualitative and quantitative scholars went their separate ways and culture became less an object of formal investigation.

Period 5: the cultural turn (1980–2010)

The late 1970s and early 1980s saw the return of culture as an object for widespread study in sociology. The work of qualitative sociologists, anthropologists, critical theorists, structuralists, poststructuralists, and cognitive psychologists all pointed to the need to incorporate cultural factors more fully into sociological explanation. An early study of the popular music industry was out in front of this trend. Focusing on industry changes in the record industry, such as concentration of ownership, Peterson and Berger (1975) developed models to explain variations in the kinds of songs that became hits. They thereby launched an important tradition for analyzing culture – the production of culture perspective.

Subsequently, music and musical tastes became a major focus in the formal modeling of culture. Abbott and Forrest (1986) studied sequences in dance steps to trace the history of Morris dancing. Cerulo (1988) studied the musical logics of national anthems. Modeling them as relational code systems, she showed that these code signatures could be predicted by key social variables such as a nation's position within the world political-economic system, and its relationships to neighboring countries, one or another specific colonial power, and a cohort of other nations. Dowd (1992) used similar methods to analyze popular songs sampled from 1955 to 1988. He measured each song's length, melodic form, tempo, melodic ornamentation, and chordal structure in order to produce models to explain market success. Ten years later Dowd and colleagues (2002) modeled musical content by tracking which pieces by which composers were played by what orchestras across some 86,000 orchestral performances. Over time, the formal study of musical fields became well established, with contemporary work exploring, for example, the duality between rap musicians sampling one another's work and the status network within their field (Lena and Pachucki 2013).

In the same period, organizational sociology saw the rise of the New Institutionalists, who highlighted the effects of cultural processes on organizational fields. Early studies by institutionalists used measures of homogenization to demonstrate cultural effects (e.g., Powell and DiMaggio 1991). Over time, very sophisticated models of culture emerged – especially in studies of categories, classifications, typifications, and logics – and came to be incorporated into mainstream organizational science (e.g., Podolny 1993; Zuckerman 1999; Pólos, Hannan, and Carroll 2002; Hsu and Hannan 2005). Some of this work focused on a more interpretive orientation to studies of texts. Ruef (1999) used text data to map out niche structures within the healthcare field, and Rawlings and Bourgeois (2004) did the same for higher education.

Building on the ideas of Pierre Bourdieu, Paul DiMaggio brought formal models of culture into the heart of American stratification theory. Using a factor analysis of survey data, he showed that American high school students used cultural capital (measured as appreciation, and experience with elite culture) to achieve school success (DiMaggio 1982). A long line of research followed, including a thread leading to contemporary studies, showing that culture is a key resource for constructing social networks (Lizardo 2006; Vaisey and Lizardo 2010). Social movement scholars also turned to measuring cultural meanings. Snow and Benford (1988) started by borrowing from Erving Goffman's idea of "framing" to build formal measures of ideologies and political narratives that helped to explain the success and failure of social movement mobilizations. Subsequently, the use of textual data to analyze frames developed into a very sophisticated component of the social movements research program (Earl et al. 2004).

Harrison White was one of the most important proponents of the cultural turn in formal models. A long-time leader in social network analysis, by the early 1990s White had come to see interpretative analyses of meaning as a necessity for formal sociology. In *Identity and Control*, White (1992) laid out a new research agenda that treated social life as a series of dually linked social and cultural network structures, which White called net-doms. White's work consolidated an important trend – the move by sociologists to exploit a potential affinity between semiotic theories of meaning and relational methodologies of network science. This consolidation helped open up new types of formal models of texts, institutions, and cultural forms. Thus, Carley (1994) employed network mapping to analyze the linkages of concepts in science fiction novels. Mohr (1994) used block modeling to map otherwise implicit taxonomies linking identities and practices used by social-control organizations in New York City during the Progressive era. Bearman and Stovel (2000) used network models to analyze the narrative flows in the life stories of successful Nazis. Smith (2007) applied these methods to compare and contrast narratives of their shared history from the perspectives of two ethnic communities living alongside the Yugoslavian/Italian border. And Fuhse (2009) has continued to push on this front, thinking through how meaningful narratives are embedded within and ultimately constitutive of social structures.

Another development came with the application of dual-logic network methods to the study of culture. These models analyze relational linkages between two different orders of social life (Breiger 1974). Bourdieu (1984) highlighted these kinds of models of culture with his use of correspondence-analysis maps to analyze the duality of economic and cultural logics in French society. The anthropologist Thomas Schweizer (1993) extended Bourdieu's models of duality by using Galois lattices to map out articulations linking the status order of a Tahitian community with the cultural value of their material possessions. Mohr and Duquenne (1997) used the method to map the duality of institutional practices and cultural identities in Progressive era poverty organizations. Wiley and Martin (1999) used lattices to analyze the dual structure ordering political belief systems. Mische and Pattison (2000) used lattices to model the dualities linking political ideologies with the membership histories of Brazilian youth activists. Breiger (2000) modeled the dual logic of power and precedent at the US Supreme Court. And Gibson (2003) modeled the duality between rules and action sequences in natural conversations.

In short, participating in the cultural turn, sociologists employed formal models of culture all across the discipline. Innovative research designs took on the empirical study of categories, frames, logics, niches, and network models of culture. And, in contrast to earlier periods, models began to highlight the power of culture as a constitutive social force, rather than (as had previously been the analytic default) a phenomenon shaped by other social forces (Mohr and Rawlings 2012).

Period 6: formal models of culture in an era of big data (2010 and after)

As information becomes digitized and social life becomes increasingly saturated by digital media, the development of formal models of culture has now emerged as a central area of research. The engineering of the internet yielded many new technological possibilities for modeling culture. Early on, computer scientists led the way. A few humanists and social science pioneers came along early in this century, and over the last decade an increasing number of social scientists and digital humanists have begun to work on digital media, and they are quickly bringing emergent computational technologies back to their home disciplines (Evans and Aceves 2016).

Work in the digital humanities has exploded. The rapid digitization of the world's bibliographic corpus has opened up stunning new opportunities. Humanists who have long focused on the interpretation of texts are now finding themselves with completely new research agendas. Moretti (2013) has called this an era of "distant reading," to distinguish it from the traditional humanist methodology of "close reading." He is a good example. Along with colleagues at the Stanford Literary Lab, Moretti has produced a wide range of new cultural models that link large textual corpora to problems in literary theory. Many other scholars are at work on similarly path-breaking projects (see Liu 2012; Wagner-Pacifici, Mohr, and Breiger 2015).

Social scientists have also taken advantage of the increasingly large stocks of digital information. Michel et al. (2011) examined a digital corpus of over five million books published over the last four centuries, describing the changing patterns of highly frequent n-grams (word-combinations) as a way to trace dynamic patterns in cultural history. Others have used latent Dirichlet allocation (LDA) models of document topic sets to quickly carve through large textual corpora in relation to a wide range of research questions (Mohr and Bogdanov 2013). DiMaggio, Naga, and Blei (2013) analyzed 8,000 newspaper articles published from 1986 to 1997 to explain changing dynamics in public support of the arts. Bonilla and Grimmer (2013) studied 51,000 news stories sampled just after the George W. Bush administration had implemented color-coded terror-alert levels. These models were used to assess the impacts of the alerts on public opinion regarding other matters, such as support for Bush administration policies. Fligstein, Brundage, and Schultz (2014) used topic models to analyze the meeting transcripts of the Federal Reserve's Federal Open Market Committee, showing how its members systematically misinterpreted signals of the emerging financial crisis.

These are just some of the new computational tools being used by scholars to model culture. Others include use sentiment analysis, natural-language processing, and machine learning. For example, McFarland, Jurafsky, and Rawlings (2013) have mined a large corpus of recorded and transcribed events of "speed dating" to reveal that the felt chemistry of romantic bonds emerges through gendered rituals. Lazer et al. (2009), Bail (2014), Wagner-Pacifici et al. (2015), and Evans and Aceves (2016) provide useful overviews. In brief, in this most recent period, formal models of culture have taken off and the field is poised for new waves of creativity.

Conclusion

We have traced the lineages of formal models of culture here by focusing on the history of American sociology. Similar stories could be told in other disciplines and other national milieus. We also described the emergence of new tools for modeling culture that have spread from the computational to the social sciences as social life itself becomes increasingly digitized. As we move forward on this new research agenda, we believe that cultural sociology will be well served by continuing to explore the ways in which formalism and hermeneutics can usefully complement one another.

References

Abbott, A., and J. Forrest. 1986. "Optimal Matching Methods for Historical Sequences." *Journal of Interdisciplinary History* 16(3):471–94.

Bail, Christopher A. 2014. "The Cultural Environment: Measuring Culture with Big Data." *Theory and Society* 43(3–4):465–82.

Bearman, P. S., and K. Stovel. 2000. "Becoming a Nazi: A Model for Narrative Networks." *Poetics* 27(2–3):69–90.

Blau, P., and O.D. Duncan. 1967. *The American Occupational Structure*. New York: John Wiley & Sons.

Bonilla, T., and J. Grimmer, J. 2013). "Elevated Threat Levels and Decreased Expectations: How Democracy Handles Terrorist Threats." *Poetics* 41(6):650–69.

Bourdieu, P. 1984. *Distinction: A Social Critique of the Judgment of Taste*. Cambridge, MA: Harvard University Press.

———. 2004. *Science of Science and Reflexivity*. Chicago: University of Chicago Press.

Breiger, R.L. 1974. "The Duality of Persons and Groups." *Social Forces* 53(2):181–90.

———. 2000. "A Tool Kit for Practice Theory." *Poetics* 27:91–115.

Bulmer, M. 1996. "The Social Survey Movement and Early Twentieth Century Sociological Methodology." Pp. 15–34 in *Pittsburgh Surveyed: Social Science and Social Reform in the Early Twentieth Century*, edited by M. Greenwald and M. Anderson. Pittsburgh, PA: University of Pittsburgh Press.

Carley, K.M. 1994. "Extracting Culture through Textual Analysis." *Poetics* 22:291–312.

Cerulo, K. 1988. "Analyzing Cultural Products: A New Method of Measurement." *Social Science Research* 17(4):317–52.

Converse, J.M. [1987] 2009. *Survey Research in the United States: Roots and Emergence 1890–1960*. New Brunswick, NJ: Transaction.

DiMaggio, P.J. 1982. "Cultural Capital and School Success: The Impact of Status Culture Participation on the Grades of U.S. High School Students." *American Sociological Review* 47(2):189–201.

DiMaggio, Paul, Manish Naga, and David Blei. 2013. "Exploiting Affinities between Topic Modeling and the Sociological Perspective on Culture: Application to Newspaper Coverage of U.S. Government Arts Funding." *Poetics* 41(6):570–606.

Dowd, T.J. 1992. "The Musical Structure and Social Context of Number One Songs, 1955 to 1988: An Exploratory Analysis." Pp. 130–57 in *Vocabularies of Public Life: Empirical Essays in Symbolic Structure*, edited by R. Wuthnow. London: Routledge.

Dowd, T.J., K. Liddle, K. Lupo, and A. Borden. 2002. "Organizing the Musical Canon: The Repertoires of Major U.S. Symphony Orchestras, 1842 to 1969." *Poetics* 30(1–2):35–61.

Du Bois, W.E.B. 1899. *The Philadelphia Negro*. Philadelphia: University of Pennsylvania Press.

Earl, J., A. Martin, J.D. McCarthy, and S.A. Soule. 2004. "The Use of Newspaper Data in the Study of Collective Action." *Annual Review of Sociology* 30:65–80.

Evans, J.A., and P. Aceves. 2016. "Machine Translation: Mining Text for Social Theory." *Annual Review of Sociology* 42:21–50.

Fligstein, N., J.S. Brundage, and M. Schultz. 2014. "Why the Federal Reserve Failed to see the Financial Crisis of 2008: The Role of 'Macroeconomics' as a Sense making and Cultural Frame." IRLE Working Paper No. 111–14.

Fuhse, J. 2009. "The Meaning Structure of Social Networks." *Sociological Theory* 27(1):51–73.

Gibson, D.R. 2003. "Participation Shifts: Order and Differentiation in Group Conversation." *Social Forces* 81(4):1335–80.

Gorski, P. 2004. "The Poverty of Deductivism: A Constructive Realist Model of Sociological Explanation." *Sociological Methodology* 34(1):1–33.

Hsu, Greta, and Michael T. Hannan. 2005. "Identities, Genres, and Organizational Forms." *Organization Science* 16(5):474–90.

Lasswell, Harold, and Nathan Leites and Associates. 1949. *Language of Politics: Studies in Quantitative Semantics*. New York: George W. Stewart.

Lazarsfeld, Paul. 1961. "Notes on the History of Quantification in Sociology – Trends, Sources and Problems." Pp. 147–203 in *Quantification: A History of the Meaning of Measurement*, edited by H. Woolf. Indianapolis, IN: Bobbs-Merrill.

Lazer, David, Alex Pentland, Lada Adamic, Sinan Aral, Albert-Laszlo Barabasi, Devon Brewer, Nicholas Christakis, Noshir Contractor, James Fowler, Myron Gutmann, Tony Jebara, Gary King, Michael Macy, Deb Roy, and Marshall Van Alstyne. 2009. "Computational Social Science." *Science* 323(5915): 721–23.

Lena, J.C., and M.C. Pachucki. 2013. "The Sincerest Form of Flattery: Innovation Repetition, and Status in an Art Movement." *Poetics* 41(3):236–64.

Liu, Alan. 2012. "The State of the Digital Humanities: A Report and a Critique." *Arts and Humanities in Higher Education* 11(1–2):8–41.

Lizardo, O. 2006. "How Cultural Tastes Shape Personal Networks." *American Sociological Review* 71: 778–807

McFarland, Daniel, Dan Jurafsky, and Craig Rawlings. 2013. "Making the Connection: Social Bonding in Courtship Situations." *American Journal of Sociology* 118(6):1596–649.

Michel, J.B., Y.K. Shen, A.P. Aiden, A. Veres, and M.K. Gray. 2011. "Quantitative Analysis of Culture Using Millions of Digitized Books." *Science* 331(6014):176–82.

Mische, A., and P. Pattison. 2000. "Composing a Civic Arena: Publics, Projects, and Social Settings." *Poetics* 27:163–94.

Mohr, J.W. 1994. "Soldiers, Mothers, Tramps and Others: Discourse Roles in the 1907 New York City Charity Directory." *Poetics* 22:327–57.

Mohr, J.W., and Petko Bogdanov. 2013. "Topic Models: What They Are and Why They Matter." *Poetics* 41(6):545–69.

Mohr, J.W., and V. Duquenne. 1997. "The Duality of Culture and Practice: Poverty Relief in New York City, 1888–1917." *Theory and Society* 26(2/3):305–56.

Mohr, J.W., and C. M. Rawlings. 2012. "Four Ways to Measure Culture: Social Science, Hermeneutics, and the Cultural Turn." Pp. 70–113 in *The Oxford Handbook of Cultural Sociology*, edited by J. Alexander, R. Jacobs, and P. Smith. Oxford: Oxford University Press.

Moretti, Franco. 2013. *Distant Reading*. London: Verso.

Peterson, R.A., and D.G. Berger. 1975. "Cycles in Symbol Production: The Case of Popular Music." *American Sociological Review* 40(2):158–73.

Platt, J. 1996. *A History of Sociological Research Methods in America: 1920–1960*. Cambridge: Cambridge University Press.

Podolny, Joel M. 1993. "A Status-Based Model of Market Competition." *American Journal of Sociology* 98(4):829–72.

Pólos, László, Michael T. Hannan, and Glenn R. Carroll. 2002. "Foundations of a Theory of Social Forms." *Industrial and Corporate Change* 11(1):85–115.

Powell, W.W., and Paul J. DiMaggio. 1991. *The New institutionalism in Organizational Science*. Chicago: University of Chicago Press.

Ragin, Charles. 1987. *The Comparative Method: Moving Beyond Qualitative and Quantitative Strategies*. Berkeley: University of California Press.

Rawlings, C.M., and M.D. Bourgeois. 2004. "The Complexity of Institutional Niches: Credentials and Organizational Differentiation in a Field of U.S. Higher Education." *Poetics* 32:411–37.

Richmond, M. 1917. *Social Diagnosis*. New York: Russell Sage Foundation.

Ricoeur, P. 1973. "The Model of a Text: Meaningful Action Considered as a Text." *New Literary History* 5(1): 91–117.

Ross, D. 1991. *The Origins of American Social Science*. New York: Cambridge University Press.

Ruef, M. 1999. "Social Ontology and the Dynamics of Organizational Forms: Creating Market Actors in the Healthcare Field, 1966–1994." *Social Forces* 77(4):1403–32.

Schweizer, T. 1993. "The Dual Ordering of Actors and Possessions." *Current Anthropology* 34(4):469–83.

Smith, T. 2007. "Narrative Boundaries and the Dynamics of Ethnic Conflict and Conciliation." *Poetics* 35(1):22–46.

Snow, D.A., and R.D. Benford. 1988. "Ideology, Frame Resonance, and Participant Mobilization." Pp. 197–217 in *From Structure to Action: Social Movement Participation Across Cultures*, edited by B. Klandermans, H. Kriesi, and S. Tarrow. Greenwich, CN: JAI Press.

Stouffer, S., E.A. Suchman, L.C. DeVinney, S.A. Star, and R.M. Williams Jr. 1949. *Studies in Social Psychology in World War II: The American Soldier*. Vol. 1, *Adjustment During Army Life*. Princeton, NJ: Princeton University Press.

Thomas, W.I., with F. Znaniecki. 1918. *The Polish Peasant in Europe and America*. Chicago: University of Chicago Press.

Vaisey, S., and O. Lizardo. 2010. "Can Cultural Worldviews Influence Network Composition?" *Social Forces* 88(4):1595–618.

Wagner-Pacifici, R., J. Mohr, and R.L. Breiger. 2015. "Ontologies, Methodologies and New Uses of Big Data in the Social and Cultural Sciences." *Big Data and Society* 2(2):1–11.

Warren, R.L., S.M. Rose, and A.F. Bergunder. 1974. *The Structure of Urban Reform*. Lexington, MA: Lexington Books.

White, H.C. 1992. *Identity and Control*. Princeton, NJ: Princeton University Press.

Wiley, J., and J.L. Martin. 1999. "Algebraic Representations of Beliefs and Attitudes: Partial Order Models for Item Responses." *Sociological Methodology* 29(1):113–46.

Zuckerman, Ezra W. 1999. "The Categorical Imperative: Securities Analysts and the Legitimacy Discount." *American Journal of Sociology* 104(5):1398–438.

10

Three propositions toward a cultural sociology of climate change

Zeke Baker

Introduction

"What does culture have to do with climate change? Everything." Thus opens the program to a 2013 art exhibition and festival titled "Climate is Culture," hosted in Toronto, Canada, by the Cape Farewell Foundation. "We need a cultural shift in our ambition, behavior and values," the directors declare, and so "Cape Farewell engages and inspires our greatest creative and visionary minds to... [envision] and help create the non-carbon society we must all aspire to." Contemporary social commentary, certainly not limited to Cape Farewell, frequently invokes "culture" as a central component of policy and social (in)action concerning global warming, often construing the climate change issue as a "culture war" (Hoffman 2012). Yet there exists no organized cultural sociology of climate and climate change. This situation is problematic not only because of how sociologists might intervene in moments of "culture war," but more fundamentally because what "climate" means varies considerably among scholars of culture, and sociological theories of culture have had little import for studying climate change. This chapter therefore outlines a cultural approach to a sociology of climate (and climate change). Unlike most approaches to climate change, it takes culture – not scientific projections, political economy, or policy goals – as the starting point for analysis. In other words, I wager that we can understand climate-society relations best when we take culture as constitutive of that relationship, rather than a "variable" affecting a technical outcome of concern.

To begin, this chapter explains why cultural sociologists have rarely engaged issues of climate. I then advance three propositions toward establishing a cultural sociology of climate, illustrated by examples drawn from others' and my own research. Each proposition opens up areas for cultural-sociological inquiry and for refining existing problematics within cultural sociology. First, climate is not reducible to a physical system "out there," and the effects, trajectories, and interpretations of climate(s) are constitutively intertwined through cultural processes. In other words, the effects of weather are legible through cultural refraction, such that relationships between climate and society rest on context-specific interpretive practices. Second, to understand contemporary climate change, we must historicize "climate," "culture," and the vexing term "civilization" as fundamentally related and embattled categories – both historically and in our era, tied especially to dynamics of symbolic power. Third, modern climate science and policies remain culturally embedded, and the cultural authority around "adaptation" strategies and climate futures is a critical site of contemporary cultural politics.

Whither "climate" in cultural sociology?

As Bruno Latour (1993), Noel Castree (2001), and others have demonstrated, a dualism between "nature" and "culture" underlays both the modern *episteme* and conventional sociological analysis. Sociologies of culture, therefore, have historically held a reasoned ambivalence toward the whole set of problems long associated with "nature." Nature and its representations through scientific spokespersons are alleged to exist in a separate domain, walled off from concerns of cultural sociologists.

The history of the human sciences helps explain boundaries between cultural interpretation and naturalistic explanation, particularly of environmental-social dynamics. On the one hand, as human sciences developed within colonial contexts, "culture" was employed to explain differential trajectories of societies in ways that valorized particular "civilized" engagements with nature over "uncivilized" ones. As I shall discuss in detail, the modern category of "climate" is significantly wrapped up in this history insofar as climate dynamics allegedly helped explain human difference and cultural development. Broadly speaking, by aligning the study of nature, especially climate, with that of culture, early ethnological and social scientific inquiry largely settled on validating social hierarchies as a matter of natural-climatic laws or historical socio-evolutionary patterns. Of course, such a climate-culture trajectory naturalized social reality and hence became increasingly problematic for subsequent social scientists.

On the other hand, yet as a result, sociologists until quite recently came to oppose environmental "determinism" by situating the domain of culture squarely on the axes of values, symbols, language, and representations. Outside of human geography and physical anthropology, social science approaches to culture therefore took up elements of nature mostly as symbols for meaning-making practices about the social. This lineage extends at least from Emile Durkheim's analysis of social order in *The Elementary Forms of Religious Life* to cultural anthropologists including Branislow Malinowski (1948) and later Mary Douglas (1966) and Clifford Geertz (1973). Insofar as this lineage of scholars engaged the imbrication of natural and social orders, it did so largely in order to demonstrate that cultural codes signify the natural world through myth, discourse, and classificatory practices that construct it as a mirror, totem, or expression of social life. Natural order, in other words, was woven into broader, social "webs of significance." However, these moves left climate as at most a static backdrop to a sociocultural drama.

Even through the "cultural turn," cultural sociology maintained such an orientation to nature, especially when taking up objects of inquiry associated with a broadly modern/postmodern epoch, with its post-materialist values (Inglehart 1997) and other cultural dynamics associated with "postindustrial" society. To the extent that nature and "the environment" mattered in this trajectory, concern for it arose variously from a reflexively modern or "risk" society via a synthesis of romantic subjectivity, the devastating effects of instrumental domination, and the simulacra of spectacular capitalism. By and large, however, what we might label the society-culture question, most recently in the "Strong Program" heralded by Jeffrey Alexander, trumped the *climate*-culture question that had preoccupied much theoretical debate about cultural dynamics well into the twentieth century, for example, in the human geographer Ellsworth Huntington's ([1915] 1924) landmark text, *Civilization and Climate*.

The intellectual contexts for cultural sociology roughly span the same period during which climate science emerged, beginning in the 1960s, and gaining strength in subsequent decades. However, the trajectories were separate: climate and climate change as scientific issues remained remote from the interests of cultural sociologists. Thus the complaint of "environmental" sociologists – who have engaged the issue of climate change most resolutely since the 1990s – reflected the original program of the "New Ecological Paradigm." Associated initially with Catton and Dunlap (1978), this paradigm claimed that sociology writ large, especially structural-functionalism but also cultural analysis under the auspices of postmodernism, had proceeded, in Raymond Murphy's (1995) terms, "as if nature did not matter." Although "constructivist" analyses of climate change have emerged sporadically within environmental sociology (Rosa and Dietz 1998; Hannigan 1995; Yearley 2009), central analytic approaches to the issue have been and remain political-economic (Clark and York 2005), socio-ecological (Dunlap and Brulle 2015), or related to socio-political mobilization (McCright and Dunlap 2011).

Culture, caught between "constructivism" and realism or ecological materialism, therefore holds an ambiguous position within environmental sociology, a situation reflected by the general absence of cultural analysis in the recent "Task Force on Sociology and Global Climate Change," published through the American Sociological Association (Dunlap and Brulle 2015). There, culture is either reduced to "public opinion" (Shwom et al. 2015:278) or considered as "a driving force of consumption and decision-making," often captive to "intentional efforts to shape culture by those in power" (Rosa et al. 2015:44). Such an approach, especially concerned with how consumer culture drives climate change through a "treadmill of consumption" (ibid.), is undoubtedly important, yet it does not investigate the wider analytical significance of culture, which roughly defines cultural sociology both in the Strong Program and more broadly. The following three propositions therefore chart possible paths into the hinterlands between cultural sociology and the developing sociology of climate change.

Proposition 1: cultural refractions – climate is more than a physical system

Cultural sociologists have long rejected propositions holding that physical or economic conditions determine or define social life. This rejection needs to be reaffirmed in developing ways that sociologists conceptualize climate and climate change. An initial and basic proposition is that climate cannot be taken as simply the physical system "out there" that appears in statistical accounts or in climate change scenario projections. Physical phenomena of the atmosphere, land, and water are, first and foremost, experienced in their capricious immediacy. The impacts and effects of weather are, moreover, perceived and interpreted in culturally refracted ways. Like Howard Becker's marijuana users, who rely on one another to evaluate the experience of "being high," experiences of weather are conditional on meaningful social context. As a basic example, consider the 2016 standoff at Standing Rock, during which Sioux tribal leaders, members, and other activists braved frigid temperatures (and water cannons) in protest against the Dakota Access Pipeline for transporting crude oil. Participants claimed the weather was dangerous but also provided a means for movement solidarity by organizing the division of labor at the encampment, by synthesizing traditional teepee shelters and imported goods, and by rejecting police discourse that the bitter cold could be used as a "scare tactic" (Gaffen and Scheyder 2016). Weather, as this example highlights, is experienced through cultural forms, in this case, solidarity through the material culture of shelter, warmth, and collective resistance.

Compared to "the weather" as a phenomenon of the existential moment, climate is more difficult to pin down as an experienced reality, often involving more layers of interpretation and abstraction. As Mike Hulme (2015:3) suggests, "the idea of climate" provides a way of "navigating between the human experience of a constantly changing atmosphere and its attendant insecurities, and the need to live with a sense of stability and regularity." Thus, like weather effects and events, "climate" is a matter of experience, knowledge, and interpretation in collective life. This circumstance yields important entry points for cultural sociologists. A major question is how communities or groups perceive and interpret environmental changes, and how these interpretations either express related (even global) patterns, or otherwise reorganize cultural life at various scales. Methodological developments like multisite ethnography (Marcus 1995) notwithstanding, anthropologists addressing this question focus primarily on specific (often indigenous) communities. Krupnik and Jolly (2002), for example, trace how Arctic natives interpret local, dramatic sea-ice changes through a combination of inherited traditions and the tools of climate scientists (see also Crate and Nuttal 2009; Barnes and Dove 2015).

The cultural sociology of media, cultural consumption, and everyday life remains incompletely developed in research relevant to climate change, especially in comparative contexts. Such work might take inspiration from the "ethnoclimatologies" (Orlove, Chiang, and Cane 2002) described by anthropologists. A variety of questions emerge. How do mobile individuals who circulate through privileged environments experience changes in the manicured climates of offices, homes, cars, foreign vacation sites, and idealized or vicarious media experiences? And how might their experiences compare to experiences of sea-level rise in the case of many small-island societies? To what extent can cultural sociologists speak of or conceptualize "global climate change" while not erasing such cultural contexts and the various mediations of climatic experience? More important, how does social inequality manifest disparate capacities to impose climatic order on cultural life, at one extreme by modifying weather to fit cultural norms like "room temperature" or at the other extreme by adapting to severe ecological disruptions like sea-level rise that challenge cultural survival? (Garrett 2010; Weir, Dovey, and Orcherton 2016; Willette, Norgaard, and Reed 2016). In direct contrast to political and policy discourses organized around mitigation at the international level and reflected in a science until recently devoted almost exclusively to the global climate system, cultural scholars have a lot to add by beginning with a conceptualization of climate change on the ground and in the lifeworld, recognizing the multiple, uneven layers of climatic meaning and experience.

Proposition 2: climate, culture, civilization – historicize embattled categories

Climate change is not controversial simply as a result of misinformation or "denialist" propaganda, even if challenges to widespread scientific consensus are indeed remarkable. By tracing climate historically, we can see that it is a power-laden and embattled category from the start. That we may inhabit "the Anthropocene," during which human-caused climate changes mark a new era for the Earth and humanity, should not tempt us to abandon historical analysis. Yet scholars have thus far embarked on diverse and disconnected historical forays into issues of culture and climate, and cultural sociologists unfortunately have not weighed in. Historical sociology is in part focused on understanding the terms by which present knowledge, politics, and movements have formed and developed, and through counterfactual analysis or critique, to offer up possible alternative explanations or paths. As John Walton (2001) has argued, history is constitutively both event and narrative, and historical analysis is itself an intervention into the narrative about particular events or developments. Here lies a fruitful entry point for historical-cultural sociologies of climate.

Let us start by noting that rather fuzzy concepts of culture have been employed in recent historical studies. Anderson, Maasch, and Sandweiss (2007:3) frame an impressive collection of physical-anthropological studies into "climate and culture change" by stating, "to understand the consequences of sustained higher than average temperatures, we believe that changes in climate and culture that occurred during the Mid-Holocene warm period [c. 7000–3000 BCE] are the best case that we can explore in detail." By labeling "culture" as the totality of human organization within environmental constraints, such constraints reductively equate culture with temperature in radically different periods, namely the Mid-Holocene and today. In this view, temperature is a driver of culture. More nuanced, Behringer (2010) performs a cultural history of the Little Ice Age (c. 1500–1850 CE). For this period of variable but extreme cooling, he shows how witchcraft trials, winter landscape painting, and demonological theologies in northern Europe reflected a broad "allegory of collapse" that made meaningful the suffering associated with winter storms, failed harvests, and associated social unrest and moral anxieties (2010:141). Behringer considers the period "a trial run of global warming" insofar as paleoclimatic and cultural dynamics can be traced together (2010:vii). For all that histories such as this provide in accounting for climate-culture relations, however, they often fail to problematize the modern category of "climate" itself. On this point sociological approaches are critical to understanding climatic patterns that are notable in terms not only of physical changes but of the cultures through which such climates are known and engaged.

In modern historical development, roughly since the mid-seventeenth century, "climate" emerged as a way for scientists, explorers, and travelers to make sense of human, social, and natural difference. In particular, Enlightenment natural and political histories developed neo-Hippocratic theories of climate that allegedly helped to explain "culture," "civilization," and their degree of attainment among various groups (on "civilization" and "culture" but *not* climate, see Williams 1983:57–60, 87–93; Bauman 1985; Mazlish 2005). Thus, English natural philosopher James Dunbar argued in 1780, "hot" tropical climates engendered societies that were "cultivated slowly, and with inferior ardor," whereas climates "more pernicious in nature" (in his analysis, Northern Europe) made up for natural deficiencies with "the resources of industry and invention" (Dunbar 1780: 209–10). Over time, Dunbar claimed, civilizing land and political order rendered his native English climate more temperate, productive, healthy, and superior.

Through the nineteenth century, a strongly civilizational logic undergirded the scientific development and cultural salience of "climate." Notably, climate provided a means for organizing historical and future social trajectories in a time of grave meteorological uncertainties – for instance among migrants and settlers – and of imperial ambitions among colonial and national states (Duncan 2007; Golinski 2008). The intellectual stakes of recovering such a history of climate are high. If global warming threatens us, who, as Oreskes and Conway (2014:ix) provoke, are the "children of Enlightenment" facing the possible "collapse of Western civilization," climate, civilization, and culture remain embattled, related categories. The unmet challenge is to perform a thoroughly historicized sociology of contemporary climates by piecing together the events and narratives that have constituted "climate" and "civilization" over time.

Proposition 3: cultural authority – climate futures are a site of struggle

Like meteorological sciences in the eighteenth century, climate knowledge, whether among climate modelers, "adaptation" policy experts, or communities around the world, remains culturally embedded. Also, as in previous periods, cultural authority asserted for climate knowledge remains unevenly distributed across social, geographic, and cultural contexts. Yet sociologists have yet to address climate knowledge as a domain of credibility struggles and, more broadly, the accumulation and exercise of symbolic power. That in 2012 Donald Trump might proclaim global warming a hoax perpetrated by China baffled observers, but it raises a fundamental question: how do scientists' (and their critics') representations of global, regional, and local climates come to count as legitimate knowledge and thereby form a basis of social action and power?

By treating science as cultural production, scholars associated with science and technology studies (STS; Demeritt 2001; Edwards 2010; Shackley and Wynne 1996; Yearley 2009) have shown how climate science is constituted as an assemblage of different kinds of experts, data, and technologies, as well as different modes of knowing, measuring, and experiencing the world. As Steven Epstein (2008) has suggested, scholars working in cultural sociology might benefit from engaging STS work on issues of scientific-cultural production, especially regarding climate change. Some work in this vein has emerged. For example, Demeritt (2001) and Hulme (2014) show how a specifically technocratic worldview has developed among climate scientists who work "upstream" from climate politics, as they settle controversies surrounding climate modeling and present findings to scientific and policy audiences. To follow up on this line of inquiry and without either dismissing or endorsing the findings of climate scientists, cultural scholars might reflexively engage proposed capacities to "stabilize" the global climate through policy, and technological, intervention. How are such managerial visions, along with other imaginaries of climate-society equilibrium (or collapse), accomplished?

Beyond the epistemic communities of scientists, how climate change knowledge institutes climate futures casts into relief the assumptions of policymakers and experts, on the one hand, and the lived experiences within communities on the other, and the two increasingly interact in terms of a paradigm of "climate adaptation." Embedded within this paradigm is a cultural politics over "adaptation" itself. In a dynamic, uncertain world, the struggles concern *who* gets to say what is happening or will happen and how people should or will respond. Will it be scientists, national security experts, insurance forecasters, energy technologists, or vulnerable populations (who are also internally stratified)? These questions suggest that climate impacts and futures are settled through symbolic power and cultural negotiation, not "adaptation" as such. However, we know little about such culturally infused processes. One possible approach is to follow the lead of Marcus Taylor (2014), who rejects "adaptation" as an analytic framework and instead examines cases of what he calls "relational vulnerability" in which climate impacts are shaped by historical and ongoing socio-ecological marginalization that is in fact perpetuated by formal "adaptation" policies.

Taylor and other political ecologists (Davis 2015; Leach and Mearns 1996) have published a number of case studies of what Michael Goldman (2004) labeled the "eco-governmentality" often reflected in narratives of environmental change. Sociological concepts – especially Bourdieu's concepts of cultural and symbolic capital in relation to state and market logics, but also those of valuation (Lamont 2012) and place-based identities (Gieryn 2000) – could be deployed to yield a deeper understanding of how climate policies reflect, extend, or resist existing cultural dynamics of power. For example, in ongoing research by myself and colleagues among water managers during California's recent severe drought, questions of "adaptation" to a changing hydrology highlight cultural conflicts over the meanings of water, climate, and the future (Baker et al. 2018). For the state of California, climate change is a set of parameters that must enter into engineering, policy, and capital-investment decisions in order to reduce uncertainties that interfere with water-supply planning and economic growth. Constructing water and climate as meaningful categories for "adaptation" in this way conflicts with some Indian tribes who, living on ancestral lands in historically diverted and polluted watersheds, view state strategies not as adaptive, but as compounding long-standing threats against traditional subsistence fishing and other cultural practices. Here, and I submit elsewhere, the meaning and content of "resiliency" and "adaptation," like the basic categories of climate and weather addressed previously, is an important question for analysts of cultural politics.

Cultural authority over the future has always proved especially contentious. As with Francis Bacon's seventeenth-century vision of philosophical "priests of nature" in the *New Atlantis*, or with Max Weber's early twentieth-century distinction between priestly authority and prophetic revelations, so with recent claims by James Hansen and colleagues (2016) that multiple-meter, catastrophic sea-level rise may occur within the next century. In each of these moments, taking hold of the future is an inevitably political enterprise. The temporal axis of cultural representation and power is a final aspect of climate change to which cultural sociologists might productively orient themselves. How are temporal frames for action achieved? Emerging work (Hall 2016; Hjerpe and Linner 2009; Skrimshire 2010) asks especially how utopian (or dystopian) representations of future scenarios are structured by present social relations in ways that animate conflicting worldviews. Others show how futures are generated within the epistemic cultures of science (Edwards 2010; Luke 2015) – which as Hansen et al.'s (2016) rejection of the moderate sea-level-rise projections of the Intergovernmental Panel on Climate Change shows, are by no means unitary. Analyses of such futures, however, have yet to sufficiently follow these future-constructions through society. To do so, we must ask, how are the production, circulation, and application of conflictual futures and their effects connected in the contemporary? As I have already indicated with respect to the issues of "adaptation" and the variable interpretations of weather and climate, this question can be addressed in various historical periods and existing contexts. Yet "following" climate in this way likely will entail transgressing topical and disciplinary terrains upon which both existing climate change scholarship and cultural sociology have thus far proceeded.

Conclusion

Embroiled in the 1950s national revolutionary movements in Africa, Frantz Fanon (1959:245) declared that "culture is not left in cold storage during the conflict." By this he meant that it is necessary to study culture to understand the interplay of tumultuous conditions and the inner life of people, and only on this basis is it possible to make legible intellectual interventions and political alternatives. Lacking the gift of divination, we can still reasonably assume that social conflict will increasingly organize around climate change, whether between political parties, between competitors for climate-impacted resources, or between ways of life and capacities to legitimately speak for people's experiences, environments, and their futures. In order to approach these issues from disciplined points of strength, this chapter brought together three propositions that can help to organize cultural-sociological research and, to extend Fanon's metaphor, help to pull the cultural analysis of climate out of cold storage. We began with a cultural conception of existential experience and, by extension, of the meanings and interpretations of "climate" itself. Conceptual and empirical specification regarding climate and culture, I showed, requires greater historical work insofar as modern climate knowledge and interpretations have a cultural history that sociologists have yet to appreciate. Thus contextualized and situated, climate knowledge, interpretation, and collective experience – wherever we find them – emerge as loci of struggle, negotiation, and conflict. Building on these initiatives, we can pry open how credibility is assigned or lost, how symbolic power is exercised, and how constructions of and struggles over the future proceed in the contemporary. Climate change as culture – in meanings and practices – runs much deeper than we have understood so far. Thus, the future of climate change will be shaped in part by whether and how we reflexively come to terms with its cultural instantiations.

References

Anderson, David, Kirk Maasch, and Daniel Sandweiss, eds. 2007. *Climate Change and Cultural Dynamics: A Global Perspective on Mid-Holocene Transitions*. New York: Elsevier.

Baker, Zeke, Julia Ekstrom, and Louise Bedsworth. 2018. "Climate Information? Embedding Climate Futures within Temporalities of California Water Management." *Environmental Sociology*. DOI: 10.1080/23251042.2018.1455123.

Barnes, Jessica, and Michael R. Dove, eds. 2015. *Climate Cultures: Anthropological Perspectives on Climate Change*. New Haven, CT: Yale University Press.

Bauman, Zygmunt. 1985. "On the Origins of Civilisation: A Historical Note." *Theory, Culture & Society* 2(3):7–14.

Behringer, Wolfgang. 2010. *A Cultural History of Climate*. Malden, MA: Polity Press.

Castree, Noel. 2001. "Socializing Nature." Pp. 1–21 in *Social Nature: Theory, Politics, Practice*, edited by N. Castree and B. Braun. Malden, MA: Blackwell.

Catton, William R., and Riley E. Dunlap. 1978. "Environmental Sociology: A New Paradigm." *American Sociologist* 13:41–9.

Clark, Brett, and Richard York. 2005. "Carbon Metabolism: Global Capitalism, Climate Change, and the Biospheric Rift." *Theory and Society* 34:391–428.

Crate, Susan A., and Mark Nuttal. 2009. *Anthropology and Climate Change: From Encounters to Actions*. Walnut Creek, CA: Left Coast Press.

Davis, Diana K. 2015. *The Arid Lands: History, Power, Knowledge*. Cambridge, MA: MIT Press.

Demeritt, David. 2001. "The Construction of Global Warming and the Politics of Science." *Annals of the Association of American Geographers* 91(2):307–37.

Douglas, Mary. 1966. *Purity and Danger: An Analysis of Concepts of Pollution and Taboo*. London: Routledge.

Dunbar, James. 1780. *Essays on the History of Mankind in Rude and Cultivated Ages*. London: Strahan.

Duncan, James S. 2007. *In the Shadows of the Tropics: Climate, Race and Biopower in Nineteenth Century Ceylon*. Hampshire, UK: Ashgate.

Dunlap, Riley E., and Robert J. Brulle, eds. 2015. *Climate Change and Society: Sociological Perspectives*. New York: Oxford University Press.

Edwards, Paul N. 2010. *A Vast Machine: Computer Models, Climate Data, and the Politics of Global Warming*. Cambridge, MA: MIT Press.

Epstein, Steven. 2008. "Culture and Science/Technology: Rethinking Knowledge, Power, Materiality, and Nature." *Annals of the American Academy of Political and Social Science* 619:165–82.

Fanon, Frantz. 1959. "On National Culture." Pp. 206–48 in *The Wretched of the Earth*. New York: Grove Press.

Gaffen, David, and Ernest Scheyder. 2016. "Dakota Access Pipeline Protesters Hunker Down For Winter At Standing Rock," *Huffington Post*, December 3. (www.huffingtonpost.com/entry/dakota-access-pipeline-standing-rock_us_58432f81e4b09e21702ef519).

Garrett, Bradley L. 2010. "Drowned Memories: The Submerged Places of the Winnemem Wintu." *Archaeologies* 6:346–71.

Geertz, Clifford. 1973. *The Interpretation of Cultures*. New York: Basic Books.

Gieryn, Thomas. 2000. "A Space for Place in Sociology." *Annual Review of Sociology* 26(1):463–96.

Goldman, Michael. 2004. "Eco-governmentality and Other Transnational Practices of a 'Green' World Bank." Pp. 166–92 in *Liberation Ecologies: Environment, Development, Social Movements*, edited by R. Peet and M. Watts. New York: Routledge.

Golinski, Jan. 2008. "American Climate and the Civilization of Nature." Pp. 153–74 in *Science and Empire in the Atlantic World*, edited by J. Delbourgo and N. Dew. New York: Routledge.

Hall, John R. 2016. "Social Futures of Global Climate Change: A Structural Phenomenology." *American Journal of Cultural Sociology* 4(1):1–45.

Hannigan, James. 1995. *Environmental Sociology: A Social Constructionist Approach*. New York: Routledge.

Hansen, James, et al. 2016. "Ice Melt, Sea Level Rise and Superstorms: Evidence from Paleoclimate Data, Climate Modeling, and Modern Observations that 2C Global Warming Could be Dangerous." *Atmospheric Chemistry and Physics* 16:3761–12.

Hjerpe, Mattias, and Bjorn-Ola Linner. 2009. "Utopian and Dystopian Thought in Climate Change Science and Policy." *Futures* 41:234–45.

Hoffman, Andrew J. 2012. "Climate Change as Culture War." *Stanford Social Innovation Review*. (https://ssir.org/articles/entry/climate_science_as_culture_war).

Hulme, Mike. 2014. *Can Science Fix Climate Change?: A Case Against Climate Engineering*. Malden, MA: Polity Press.

———. 2015. "Climate and its Changes: A Cultural Appraisal." *Geo: Geography and Environment* 2(1):1–11.

Huntington, Ellsworth. [1915] 1924. *Civilization and Climate.* New Haven, CT: Yale University Press.

Inglehart, Ronald. 1997. *Modernization and Postmodernization: Cultural, Economic, and Political Change in 43 Societies.* Princeton, NJ: Princeton University Press.

Krupnik, Igor, and Dyanna Jolly, eds. 2002. *The Earth is Faster Now: Indigenous Observations of Arctic Environmental Change.* Fairbanks: Arctic Research Consortium.

Lamont, Michèle. 2012. "Toward a Comparative Sociology of Valuation and Evaluation." *Annual Review of Sociology* 38(1):201–21.

Latour, Bruno. 1993. *We Have Never Been Modern.* Cambridge, MA: Harvard University Press.

Leach, Melissa, and Robin Mearns, eds. 1996. *The Lie of the Land: Challenging Received Wisdom on the African Environment.* Portsmouth, NH: Heinemann.

Luke, Timothy. 2015. "The Climate Change Imaginary." *Current Sociology* 63(2):280–96.

Malinowski, Bronislaw. 1948. *Magic, Science and Religion and Other Essays.* Glencoe, IL: The Free Press.

Marcus, George E. 1995. "Ethnography in/of the World System: The Emergence of Multi-sited Ethnography." *Annual Review of Anthropology* 24:95–117.

Mazlish, Bruce. 2005. *Civilization and its Contents.* Stanford, CA: Stanford University Press.

McCright, Aaron M., and Riley E. Dunlap. 2011. "The Politicization of Climate Change and Polarization in the American Public's Views of Global Warming, 2001–2010." *Sociological Quarterly* 52(2):155–94.

Murphy, Raymond. 1995. "Sociology as if Nature did not Matter: An Ecological Critique." *British Journal of Sociology* 46(4):688–707.

Oreskes, Naomi, and Erik M. Conway. 2014. *The Collapse of Western Civilization: A View from the Future.* New York: Columbia University Press.

Orlove, Susan B., John C. Chiang, and Mark A. Cane. 2002. "Ethnoclimatology in the Andes." *American Scientist* 90:428–35.

Rosa, Eugene A., and Thomas Dietz. 1998. "Climate Change and Society: Speculation, Construction, and Scientific Investigation." *International Sociology* 13(4):421–55.

Rosa, Eugene A., Thomas K. Rudel, Richard York, Andrew K. Jorgenson, and Thomas Dietz. 2015. "The Human (Anthropogenic) Driving Forces of Climate Change." Pp. 32–60 in *Climate Change and Society: Sociological Perspectives*, edited by R.E. Dunlap and R.J. Brulle. New York: Oxford University Press.

Shackley, Simon, and Brian Wynne. 1996. "Representing Uncertainty in Global Climate Change Science and Policy: Boundary-ordering Devices and Authority." *Science, Technology, & Human Values* 21(3):275–302.

Shwom, Rachel L., Aaron M. McCright, and Steven R. Brechin, with Riley E. Dunlap, Sandra T. Marquart-Pyatt, and Lawrence C. Hamilton. 2015. "Public Opinion on Climate Change." Pp. 269–99 in *Climate Change and Society: Sociological Perspectives*, edited by R.E. Dunlap and R.J. Brulle. New York: Oxford University Press.

Skrimshire, Stefan, ed. 2010. *Future Ethics: Climate Change and Apocalyptic Imagination.* New York: Continuum.

Taylor, Marcus. 2014. *A Political Ecology of Climate Change Adaptation: Livelihoods, Agrarian Change, and the Conflicts of Development.* New York: Routledge.

Walton, John. 2001. *Storied Land: Community and Memory in Monterey.* Berkeley: University of California Press.

Weir, Tony, Liz Dovey, and Dan Orcherton. 2016. "Social and Cultural Issues Raised by Climate Change in Pacific Island Countries: An Overview." *Regional Environmental Change* 16:1–12.

Willette, Mirranda, Kari Norgaard, and Ron Reed. 2016. "You Got to Have Fish: Families, Environmental Decline and Cultural Reproduction." *Families, Relationships and Societies* 5(3):375–93.

Williams, Raymond. 1983. *Keywords: A Vocabulary of Culture and Society.* New York: Oxford University Press.

Yearley, Steven. 2009. "Sociology and Climate Change after Kyoto: What Roles for Social Science in Understanding Climate Change?" *Current Sociology* 57(3):389–405.

11

The sociological experience of cultural objects

Robin Wagner-Pacifici

Introduction

How do cultural sociologists experience their objects of analysis? Does it even matter if they do come to know and experience them? Isn't it more the point that they understand how these objects operate in the social world, how they come to be produced, assessed, valued, and exchanged by individuals and organizations? Although the category of culture includes a vast array of objects, values, ideas, and relationships, I want to focus in this chapter on aesthetic objects, objects like novels and paintings and photographs, in order to identify the types of cultural-sociological knowledge of them available to analysts, as well as to consider the stakes in such knowing.

The chapter makes a case for cultural sociologists knowing their objects from the inside-out as well as from the outside-in. Further, I will want to assert that it is only by gaining access to the operations and logics of the inner workings of cultural objects that any cultural sociology can begin to track the meanings and resonance of these objects in the social contexts in which they appear. And finally, I claim that such knowledge of aesthetic objects actually provides insight into the ways that these objects model social reality in their own turn. Human experience of art affects human experience of the world. This chapter is thus written in much the same spirit as John Dewey when he wrote, in his book *Art as Experience*, "Aesthetic experience is always more than aesthetic. In it a body of matters and meanings, not in themselves aesthetic, become aesthetic as they enter into an ordered rhythmic movement towards consummation. The material itself is widely human" (1934:248). Human materials require a human science.

Thus, adhering to the conception of such thinkers as Wilhelm Dilthey that sociology is a "human science" (2002:92), with *interpretation* its signature modality, any analysis of the ways that cultural sociologists can know (or refrain from knowing) their objects of analysis must clarify what "knowing" means. When approaching a painting, for example, does the sociologist examine the painting's style, its participation in a particular school of rendering, its internal composition, its allegorical allusions? Or, alternatively, does the sociologist look around the painting – at its placement in a frame and a museum, as an object of exchange garnering a certain sum of money, as produced by way of patron's commissions, as extolled or decried as excellent or repugnant by critics and publics? If the interpretive role of the sociologist is highlighted, questions of style, composition, representational dynamics, and aesthetic genealogy will be paramount in the sociological analysis. Such emphasis does not mean that the social, economic, or political context in which the work appears is irrelevant. Rather, it means that such contextual concerns cannot substitute for an analysis of the object itself.

Diffidence toward an experiential approach to cultural objects, including, importantly, aesthetic objects, has diverse motives. On the one hand, "production of culture" proponents are particularly interested in social uptake or rejection of cultural objects and they thus "focus on how the symbolic elements of culture are shaped by the systems within which they are created, distributed, evaluated, taught, and preserved" (Peterson and Anand 2004:1). Studies developed within this framework focus on the contexts of culture and on cultural change, especially rapid change: "Such rapid change exposes the constituent elements comprising a field of symbolic production composed of six facets. These include technology, law and regulation, industry structure, organization structure, occupational career, and market" (Peterson and Anand 2004:1). It is certainly possible to track all of these facets without ever coming into direct contact with the produced objects themselves. And indeed, production-of-culture proponents do not tend to engage with the produced objects in their analyses. Such avoidance points to yet another reason why some (critical) sociologists of culture eschew experience of the cultural objects at the heart of their studies. These scholars tend to reason that the objects are variable stand-ins for the ideologies (e.g., of class or gender) whose business they do. French sociologist Antoine Hennion takes aim at this critical sociological approach to cultural objects, an approach exemplified by Pierre Bourdieu. Hennion contends,

> Direct contact with things, uncertainty of sensations, methods, and techniques used to become sensitive to, and to feel the feeling of, the object being sought – in the sociology of culture, these moments and gestures of taste are either neglected or are directly denounced as rituals whose principal function is less to make amateurs "feel," than to make them "believe."

> *(2007:98)*

For Hennion, by contrast, the pragmatic, sensual modalities by which amateurs *attach themselves* to the cultural objects of their worlds is of great and complex significance for understanding human relationships to that world and to each other.

On the other hand, many cultural sociologists, including Hennion, advocate a more intimate knowledge of the objects under investigation: some term this approach "endogenous explanation" (Kaufman 2004:335). And the more Durkheimian of these approaches "ask not why a specific genre of art appears at a particular time and place but what the signs and symbols embedded in that genre say about that time and place" (Kaufman 2004:337). Whether analysis moves in the more phenomenological direction of Hennion or the more semiotic direction of the Durkheimian approaches, it highlights the direct experience of and with cultural objects. This chapter will push on such intimate knowledge to consider not only how aesthetic objects reflect or refract their times and places, but also to explore how they themselves act to temporalize and shape the very worlds in which they appear. The chapter manages this task by way of a consideration of several (not mutually exclusive) choices confronting cultural sociologists – preoccupation with content or preoccupation with context; coming in close or keeping a distance from the objects of analysis; utilizing methods and theories developed primarily in the humanities or those developed primarily in the social and natural sciences. Resolutions of these choices can signal the diverse responses to appeals to either highlight or bracket the experience of the objects confronting cultural sociologists.

Arts and humanities as models

When cultural sociologists understand their discipline as fundamentally a "human science," they inevitably invoke approaches to cultural objects forged in the arts and humanities. Such approaches assume the intrinsically hermeneutic dimension to all social research. Art historian Blake Stimson refers, for example, to the "affective grip given by the sensory experience of vision itself" (Hall, Stimson, and Becker 2005:2) lying at the junction of aesthetics and projects of cultural and historical sociology concerned with visuality. But the affective grip of an object or of the perception of the object must necessarily prompt the movement from inside to outside, one in which, I argue, the hermeneutic approach and the semiotic approach can actually join forces. How does this movement manifest itself?

Clearly, sociologists and humanists have divergent interests, questions, and methodologies (of course, there are divergences within sociology and within the humanities). And these divergences make explicit crossovers or borrowings somewhat rare and epistemologically problematic. These rare, apparently hybrid forms of scholarship reconfigure aspects of our endeavor in significant ways. Do we even recognize them? Thinking about the ways that the social sciences and the humanities both coincide and diverge around apparently similar objects and topics involves thinking quite specifically about our choice of methods and objects. In the humanities, we find the methods of hermeneutics, semiotics, structuralism, deconstructionism, and the new historicism, and we find objects like paintings, sculptures, monuments, icons, novels, folktales, poems, and so forth. There are exceptions, of course. Some humanists use quantitative or network forms of analysis. Some humanists analyze medical or business texts rather than novels or poems (for example, see the work of Mary Poovey [1998, 2008] on double-entry bookkeeping and on genres of the credit economy of nineteenth-century Britain). Sometimes, the methods and objects of social scientific and humanistic analysis appear to be identical. But a fundamental difference seems perduring: sociologists have different resting places, different states of satisfaction that their interests have been addressed, their questions answered. Sociological questions normally involve examining the relationships between what is going on in the work of art or cultural object and the world that generates and hosts (or resists) that work. Sometimes the differences between sociological questions and those in the arts and humanities are very subtle – they hinge on what is foregrounded, what is marginal, what is the main issue, and what is parenthetical. Given these differences within apparent similarity, what would it mean concretely to argue that sociologists need a *feeling for the text or the image* in the same ways that most literary theorists or art historians embrace?

Most cultural sociologists do not demonstrate a feeling for the text or image, regardless of what their actual experience of them may be. How and where do we find paintings, sculptures, or novels in sociology writing? This should be recognized as a fundamentally different question from that asking where we find the careers, networks, and social milieus of painters, sculptors, and writers in sociological studies – which we do in the work of Harrison and Cynthia White (1965), Natalie Heinich (1996), Howard Becker (1982), Pierre Bourdieu (1993), and Diana Crane (1987), among others. Some sociologists actually *feature* these cultural/artistic objects in their work (as opposed to featuring the worlds around the objects and their producers): Robert Witkin's (1997) article about Manet's painting *Olympia*; Emanuel Schegloff's (1998) article about body torque in which he features and briefly analyzes Titian's "Venus with the Organ Player"; Wendy Griswold's (1987) cultural methodology article, in which she addresses the issue of genre via the Nigerian novel; Luc Boltanski's (1999) explorations of the sentimental novel and the writings of the Marquis de Sade; Chandra Mukerji's (1997) gorgeous intellectual foray into the gardens of Versailles; Andrew Abbott's (2007) appreciation of the lyric moment in sociological writing; Jeff Alexander's (2008) appreciation of Giacometti's sculptures in his analysis of icons; and my own coming to terms with the tensions in Diego Velazquez's painting *The Surrender of Breda* (Wagner-Pacifici 2005).

In spite of such examples, there is a paucity of direct-contact scholarship among cultural sociologists. This paucity is noted by Robert Witkin (1997:103) when he assesses a general desire to "distance sociological inquiry from direct contact with art objects themselves." Such practiced indifference to the objects of attention and consumption – objects powerful enough to move people to tears, awe, or anger – must be taken a little more seriously. Could there be some unconscious fear of contamination or enthrallment if the sociologist comes too close to the work's aura? The word "aura" evokes the name of Walter Benjamin, of course. And Benjamin seemed singularly able to walk this line, particularly in his evocative and moving analysis of Paul Klee's painting "The Angel of History" and his elegy for the disappearance of the storyteller (Benjamin 1969).

A recent exception to this aesthetic diffidence is represented by Jeffrey Alexander's and others' recent work on the iconicity of art objects (Alexander 2008; Alexander, Bartmanski, and Giesen 2012). By addressing their iconic status and powers, these scholars are able to constitute a trading zone between the domains and distinctions of the social sciences and those of the humanities. It is a zone where the analyst has a hybrid sensibility that matches the resonance of the objects: "Esoteric aesthetic objects become iconic by drawing us into the heart of the world . . . In the course of everyday life, we are drawn into the experience of meaning and emotionality by surface forms" (Alexander 2008:6). Surface forms are thus anything but superficial in their resonance and consequentiality.

One useful way to get beyond disciplinarily conventional habits of thinking about this social science/humanities fault line or their mutual blind spots is by highlighting analyses that go against their given disciplinary grains. Two exemplars stand out here: one is that of Franco Moretti, a social-scientific-oriented literary theorist, and the other is Andrew Abbott, who, in some recent work on what he calls lyrical sociology, demonstrates a humanistic orientation to sociology.

Among other sociologically inclined works, Moretti completed a study in which he claimed to reveal the deep structure of the social geographies of cities in nineteenth-century novels (statistically calculating where, for example, characters of particular social classes do and do not travel within these cities and where they do and do not encounter characters of other social classes; Moretti 1987). To do this he needed to encompass literally hundreds of novels (and maps) in his study's methodology. The idea of iconic novels or a feeling for the text becomes irrelevant, and maybe a distraction in this framework. More recently, Moretti wrote three essays considering different abstract models for literary history: graphs, maps, and (genealogical) trees (Moretti 2005). In this most recent book of essays, the rural space and spatial patterns of villagers going out for walks in British and German "village novels" map the sociological transformations consequent upon nineteenth-century rural class struggles and industrialization, "where a perceptual system centered in the isolated village is replaced by an abstract network of roads" (Moretti 2005:84). Moretti asks:

> What do literary maps do. . . . First, they are a good way to prepare a text for analysis. You choose a unit – walks, lawsuits, luxury goods, whatever – find its occurrences, place them in space . . . or in other words: you reduce the text to a few elements, and abstract them, and construct a new, artificial object.
>
> *(Moretti 2005:84)*

This kind of analysis requires an abstracting and generalizing view from afar, one that seems to preclude a close, hermeneutic approach.

Moving in the opposite direction is Andrew Abbott's article "Against Narrative: A Preface to Lyrical Sociology." Abbott appeals to the ability of certain works of sociological writing to recreate an "experience of social discovery," an experience that, unlike classical narrative forms of ethnography and other genres, "should not be the telling of a story but rather the use of a single image to communicate a mood, an emotional sense of social reality" (2007:73). The key elements of a lyrical sociology are engagement, personal location (of the observer/analyst), and a moment of time (rather than a process that occurs over time and that has an outcome). Whereas language is the medium for writing lyrical sociology, language seems to give way to images, or congeries of images. Causality and transformation over time gives way to states of being. Among other examples, Abbott refers to Michael Mayerfeld Bell's (1994) book, *Childerley*, in which the ringing of the church bells in the provincial village that Bell details in his book sociologically resonate in precisely the manner Abbott describes as "lyrical."

These two writers, Moretti and Abbott, are cognizant of the costs and benefits of coming in close or backing away when observing and analyzing cultural, aesthetic objects. A key issue here concerns the preoccupation with fundamental epistemological categories of time and place. Moretti assumes a readership of literary critics and scholars who begin with their experiences of (many) of the novels he analyzes – and he wants to pull them back in order to gaze about the social and political territories they map. Abbott assumes a readership of sociologists who begin with knowledge of social structures, institutions, and social movements – and he wants to pull them in close in order to catch moments of revelation or transformation that cultural objects identify and refract. Cultural sociologists may feel flummoxed in the face of such opposed vantage points and methodologies. How might they deal with the multiplicity of meanings of cultural objects? Ought they be forced to choose? I would argue for alternations of approach that are contingent on the nature of the questions posed. Cultural sociologists can actually sustain *alternating* visions – those of revelation at the level of social structure and those of revelation at the level of being in time – as they work to transform discussions of revelation into analyses of social and political meaning, and, often, power. On this point, Blake Stimson refers to Walter Benjamin's claim that "the deep formation of 'political tendency' . . . reveals itself only in the fissures of art history (and in works of art)" (Hall et al., 2005:7). Thus it behooves us to head directly toward those fissures.

Art models reality: the case for images

The next step in cultivating an experiential cultural sociology involves assessing if, and how, art *models* social reality, rather than simply refracts it. Here, the claim is that one's perception of the world is changed by familiarity with stylized and aesthetic renderings of it. Visual art offers a particular cultural-sociological opportunity. We perceive and shape the world through the images of it that we absorb. Art may be understood to offer itself as a tool for sociological analysis of social life, as sociological data, and as a cultural process that participates in the shaping of worldviews. How might this work?

In 1973, Paul Ricoeur published an article in the journal *New Literary History* that would serve as a touchstone for all hermeneutically inclined social scientists. It was titled "The Model of the Text: Meaningful Action Considered as a Text." In it, Ricoeur raised the questions: "To what extent may we consider the notion of text as a good paradigm for the so-called object of the social sciences? And to what extent may we use the methodology of text-interpretation as a paradigm for interpretation in general in the field of the social sciences?" (Ricoeur 1973:91). In this chapter, the questions are similar, but the paradigmatic model is that of the artistic image rather than the text. And rather than text-interpretation or hermeneutics, I want to raise the question of the use of a new iconology (sometimes termed "image science" or the "pictorial turn") as a model for cultural-sociological investigation. What then, might it mean to propose that the image is a good paradigm for the object of social sciences, to paraphrase Ricoeur? Surely images function and communicate differently than texts. They may thus provide us with a different purchase on social life, on power relations, on institutions than the purchase we attained via imagining social life as a text.

Images and texts are rather different creatures, with different carrying capacities. Texts are invested in the temporality of diachrony, and thus manage action and transformation. Images can present inaction, inasmuch as they capture a moment in time. In fact, social life itself is as replete with inaction, pauses, frozen moments, and temporary congealings as it is with action, progress, and change. Although social scientists have been rightly preoccupied with getting an analytical handle on the dynamism of action and interaction, they have not been sufficiently concerned to understand the embodiments and informings of objects or revealed moments (or what I'm calling here inaction) that may have their own meanings and power, somewhat along the lines suggested by Abbott. We might even begin to ask what it would mean to see scenes of social life *as* works of art (in ways that neither trivialize nor reify them, but rather acknowledge their resonance)? If we turn to art as a model for analysis in the sociology of culture, it is partly for its usefulness in getting at precisely those moments of inaction – moments that are critical and revelatory. But we cannot use images as models if we do not know how to read images.

There are several issues involved in developing this vantage point, and most of them have to do with finding the tools to discern the ways that art models life. Just as Ricoeur had to detail the hermeneutic strategies of textual analysis, we would have to detail the iconological strategies of pictorial analysis. But I want to make clear at the outset that such tools are not restricted to analysis of figurative art only – abstract art can also be approached as a model for cultural sociology. What tools have been developed to grasp these elements?

Semiotics, in the manner of Roland Barthes (1972) and others, can begin to illuminate the social and cultural meanings of images, by taking into account the structure of their internal relations – the figure and the background, the high and the low, the central and the peripheral, the dark and the light. But that is only the beginning. Scholars such as W.J.T. Mitchell (1994, 2005a, 2005b), Theo van Leeuwen and Carey Jewitt (2001), and Hans Belting (2005) have pushed further with iconologies that aim to grasp the social lives in and of images.

Some of the most pressing issues involve (1) the art-historical traditions brought to bear on singular creations, (2) the position, vision, and involvement of the spectator, and (3) the ability of the artistic object to both absorb aspects of the outer world and to attach itself to (or, in a more aggressive idiom, impose itself on) that outer world. This involves, but is not restricted to, issues of the image-object's generalizability.

We have seen that pictures, unlike texts, present a scene "all at once." In theory, a spectator can take in an artistic image in a moment. In contrast to texts, which are fatally dependent on language's linearity (and thus a kind of implicit transformational syntax of cause and effect), images can appear outside of time, or capturing one moment of time. For example, history paintings anchor and orient their spectators with their vanishing points, their spatial simultaneity, and their frames. They also claim a particular trans-temporal purchase on a transformational historical moment. Alternatively, maps orient viewing subjects in terms of sovereign centers, routes of exchange, and boundaries. Specific pictorial genres are thus variably capable of representing and conjuring the world.

The spectator/witness/analyst is always an important figure in these new iconologies. Here questions of proximity, involvement, and familiarity are key. In terms of the interactions among spectators and art objects, the worlds in the pictures and the world outside the frame, art historian Michael Fried (2007) has highlighted the critical moment of realist painting, what he calls the moment of the "magic of absorption" at the end of the sixteenth century (such painters as Caravaggio are key here), when painters represented figures literally absorbed in their own activities. Such paintings actually worked to deny the presence of any beholder outside the composed scene, including the spectator of the painting. They did so "in the first place by depicting personages [in the paintings] wholly absorbed in what they are doing, thinking, and feeling, and in multifigure paintings, by binding those figures together in a single, unified composition – to establish the ontological fiction that the beholder does not exist. Only if this was accomplished could the actual beholder be stopped and held before the canvas" (Fried 2007:500). Why does the spectator need to be ignored in order to be transfixed? Because only then do we know that the subjects in the painting (and by extension, in life itself) are not "acting" for the benefit of the spectator. Fried quotes Wittgenstein: "Nothing could be more remarkable than seeing someone who thinks himself unobserved engaged in some quite simple everyday activity....We should be seeing life itself" (Fried 2007:517). Such a scene caught up in its own autonomy captivates and, paradoxically, frees the spectator while convincing him or her of its "reality" or "near-reality." Thus it functions as what Fried calls the "near-documentary mode," as true of contemporary photographs as it is of these realist paintings. Of course, the next, sociological, step might be to move from an apprehension of such nearly real scenes in artistic renderings to an enhanced apprehension of the really real scenes of everyday life – now refamiliarized by their resemblance to the nearly real. If social scenes constitute our data – visible and tangible compositions and configurations of figures in space – our knowledge of artistic compositions and configurations is reflexively deployed to illuminate the stakes and the meanings of these scenes. But then, by analogy, do we sociologists need to be ignored in order to be able to see life itself? Issues of proximity and involvement remain key: how close up should we get to examine a scene, what distance brings most of a scene's elements and relationships to light? How singular is the scene, how generalizable? Are we as equipped to capture its stillness as we are to capture its dynamism (its origins, its exchanges, its trajectory)? Can we recognize the structure of relations that take shape? These are questions for sociology to take to heart as modes of inquiry incorporating images and scenes are brought forward by ethnographers and sociologists of culture, among others.

As points of reflexivity, artistic images certainly do act as models of and models for social relations. But, as I hope I am conveying, they do a lot more than that. The relations presented within the artistic image may even absorb, contain, and displace the inchoate, sometimes violent, energy of actual social life. This may be particularly true for violent actions. Here, art can model relations of a more pacific nature, rendering hierarchy, charisma, and loyalty visible, among other things, appearing to put contentious matters to rest (but always temporarily). The inaction or stillness of images is potent here in that it provides a pause or break in action that needs such an outlet to desist. Of course, images can also carry forward the programs of violence. This is another reason it is so important to have the tools to interrogate them. Images are migratory. They inhabit one medium after another. Think of the pervasive, circulating, and disturbing images of Abu Ghraib. One of these images, in particular, that of the "Hooded Man," made to stand balancing on a wooden box,

> has become iconic for the American war on terror because it condenses . . . unspeakable scenarios [from the narrative of the life of Christ, to the Crusades] into an eloquent form whose simplicity and directness makes it ideal for duplication and repetition.
>
> *(Mitchell 2005b:305)*

Thus, part of thinking about art as a model for sociological analysis involves confronting the anxiety about images and their power, the alleged iconoclasm of a culture invested in discourse, suspicious of images. In the end, fear of or disdain for cultural texts or cultural images is simply not an option for cultural sociologists.

It behooves cultural sociologists to pause and consider the opportunities presented by prolonged direct contact with the objects they analyze. Theories and methods originating in the humanities and the early hermeneutically inclined social sciences provide several avenues of approach to objects that both live in the world and reshape that world in their own turn.

References

Abbott, Andrew. 2007. "Against Narrative: A Preface to Lyrical Sociology." *Sociological Theory* 25(1):67–99.

Alexander, Jeffrey C. 2008. "Iconic Experience in Art and Life: Beginning with Giacometti's 'Standing Woman.'" *Theory, Culture and Society* 25(5):1–19.

Alexander, Jeffrey C., Dominik Bartmanski, and Bernhard Giesen, eds. 2012. *Iconic Power: Materiality and Meaning in Social Life.* London: Palgrave Macmillan Press.

Barthes, Roland. 1972. *Mythologies*, selected and trans. Annette Lavers. New York: Hill and Wang.

Becker, Howard Saul. 1982. *Art Worlds.* Berkeley: University of California Press.

Bell, Michael Mayerfeld. 1994. *Childerley: Nature and Morality in a Country Village*, Illustrated by Christian Potter Drury. Chicago: University of Chicago Press.

Belting, Hans. 2005. "Image, Medium, Body: A New Approach to Iconology." *Critical Inquiry* 31(2):302–19.

Benjamin, Walter. 1969. *Illuminations*, edited and with an introduction by Hannah Arendt, trans. Harry Zohn. New York: Schocken Books.

Boltanski, Luc. 1999. *Distant Suffering: Morality, Media, and Politics*, trans. Graham Burchell. New York: Cambridge University Press.

Bourdieu, Pierre. 1993. *The Field of Cultural Production: Essays on Art and Literature*, edited and with an introduction by Randal Johnson. New York: Columbia University Press.

Crane, Diana. 1987. *The Transformation of the Avant-garde: The New York Art World, 1940–1985.* Chicago: University of Chicago Press.

Dewey, John. 1934. *Art as Experience.* New York: Minton, Balch.

Dilthey, Wilhelm. 2002. *The Formation of the Historical World in the Human Sciences*, edited and with an introduction by Rudolf A. Makkreel and Frithjof Rodi. Princeton, NJ: Princeton University Press.

Fried, Michael. 2007. "Jeff Wall, Wittgenstein, and the Everyday." *Critical Inquiry* 33(3):495–526.

Griswold, Wendy. 1987. "A Methodological Framework for the Sociology of Culture." *Sociological Methodology* 17:1–35.

Hall, John R., Blake Stimson, and Lisa Tamaris Becker, eds. 2005. *Visual Worlds.* London: Routledge.

Heinich, Natalie. 1996. *The Glory of Van Gogh An Anthropology of Admiration.* Princeton, NJ: Princeton University Press.

Hennion, Antoine. 2007. "Those Things That Hold Us Together." *Cultural Sociology* 1(1):97–114.

Kaufman, Jason. 2004. "Endogenous Explanation in the Sociology of Culture." *Annual Review of Sociology* 30:335–57.

Mitchell, W.J. Thomas. 1994. *Picture Theory: Essays on Verbal and Visual Representation.* Chicago: University of Chicago Press.

———. 2005a. *What do Pictures Want? The Lives and Loves of Images.* Chicago: University of Chicago Press.

———. 2005b. "The Unspeakable and the Unimaginable: Word and Image in a Time of Terror." *English Literary History* 72(2):291–308.

Moretti, Franco. 1987. *The Way of the World: The Bildungsroman in European Culture.* London: Verso.

———. 2005. *Graphs, Maps, Trees: Abstract Models for a Literary History.* London: Verso.

Mukerji, Chandra. 1997. *Territorial Ambitions and the Gardens of Versailles.* New York: Cambridge University Press.

Peterson, Richard, and N. Anand. 2004. "The Production of Culture Perspective." *Annual Review of Sociology* 30:311–34.

Poovey, Mary. 1998. *A History of the Modern Fact: Problems of Knowledge in the Sciences of Wealth and Society.* Chicago: University of Chicago Press.

———. 2008. *Genres of the Credit Economy: Mediating Value in Eighteenth- and Nineteenth-century Britain*. Chicago: University of Chicago Press.

Ricoeur, Paul. 1973. "The Model of the Text: Meaningful Action Considered as a Text." *New Literary History* 5(1):91–117.

Schegloff, Emanuel. 1998. "Notes on Body Torque." *Social Research* 65(3):535–96.

Van Leeuwen, Theo, and Carey Jewitt, eds. 2001. *Handbook of Visual Analysis*. London: Sage.

Wagner-Pacifici, Robin. 2005. *The Art of Surrender: Decomposing Sovereignty at Conflict's End*. Chicago: University of Chicago Press.

White, Harrison C., and Cynthia A. White. 1965. *Canvases and Careers; Institutional Change in the French Painting World*. New York: Wiley.

Witkin, Robert W. 1997. "Constructing a Sociology for an Icon of Aesthetic Modernity: Olympia Revisited." *Sociological Theory* 15(2):101–25.

12

It goes without saying

Imagination, inarticulacy, and materiality in political culture

Chandra Mukerji

Introduction

C. Wright Mills was vividly aware of the power and importance of political imagination to modern selves. Sociological imagination (Mills 1959) was for him a source of empowerment for ordinary people. It allowed them to see themselves autobiographically – as historical actors both shaped by and shaping history. By understanding themselves as part of historical patterns of power, "ordinary men," as he called them, could develop their political identities and gain a sense of personal agency. Mills was clear that this made sociology, particularly historical sociology, extremely important. He was less clear why *imagination* was crucial to the political empowerment of modern individuals. Free imagination, he argued, was good for sociologists, allowing them to see beyond normal preconceptions about social life. But he did not really explain how these preconceptions were formed or worked on "ordinary men." Mills argued that rationalization and mass society were the threats to modern individuals, not the colonization of imagination. So in the end, he underestimated the importance of imagination as an important element of social thought and way of understanding relations of power and patterns of history.

This chapter explores the role of imagination in modern life and thought – particularly historical imagination – by analyzing cultural imaginaries of history and destiny embedded in things. These imaginaries affect people who hardly notice them, constraining their views of historical possibilities. Works of art and engineering have been historically used by states to embody and convey state power and collective historical possibility (Schwartz 2000; Spillman 1997; Falasca-Zamponi 1997; Berezin 1997; Harrison and Johnson 2009; Mukerji 2009, 2010; Zanker 1988). These works colonize cultural imagination with transcendental dreams of historical trajectories that leave little room for dreams of small changes.

The political imaginaries of ordinary people – the ones creating the sense of personal impotence and political irrelevance that Mills thinks plague modern life – are products of spaces of power that define the context of social action (Lefebvre 1991; Harvey 2001, 2004; Alexander, Bartmanski, and Giesen 2012). Dreams of collective transcendence are embedded in the architecture and decorations of schools, public offices, state infrastructure, and monuments, as well as in films and posters, offering citizens political imaginaries of extraordinary achievement fulfilling destiny (Schwartz 2000; Spillman 1997; Falasca-Zamponi 1997; Berezin 1997). They provide members of the collectivity a reason to belong to the polity, but they also describe heroic action far from everyday experience. So they can diminish the individual's sense of worth and agency while promoting collective dreams of power.

I contend that the sociological imagination is powerful in precisely the way Mills suggests because it counters the sense of history and destiny at the heart of state political imaginaries. Such imaginaries are felt and acted upon unselfconsciously, but they also alienate people from other forms of political action. They are fluid and adaptable so they are hard to pin down, even as they colonize the imagination. Sociology cannot replace these dreams with truth because they are too slippery and abstract, but sociology provides means of imagining how power flows differently through everyday practices. So, sociology can help people develop a sense of historical efficacy outside of dominant political imaginaries, giving dignity to ordinary lives.

Cultural imaginaries are vague but useful orienting devices for social improvisation, suggesting what is possible or preferable for people to do. They are ordinary and ubiquitous parts of social life, and mostly not political. As Holland et al. (1998) argue, people decide what to do next in relation to what they imagine is possible to do or what others might do. They take the role of the "other," as Mead (1964) suggests, by developing rough conceptions of social roles and scenarios (rather than sure knowledge) to engage in forms of collective life. The social roles that people enter into are not "real" in themselves, but rather imagined versions of what people do or can do that individuals make real by acting on them (Thomas 1951; Burke and Gusfield 1989). Cultural imaginaries are scaffolded with tools and environments that reflect and further them. People design contexts for social action that not only constrain the outcomes, but also point to possibilities.

Political imaginaries are much like the cultural imaginaries of everyday life, but they are more consciously promoted and invested in things. They are orienting fictions that have a distinctive role in shaping collective life at the level of history.

Imagination and discourse are both important to political life, and particularly to defining the contexts of social action. But they work differently. Discourse serves the kinds of politics so well described by Charles Tilly (Tilly 2003; Tilly and Tarrow 2015); political debates are contentious, articulate, and combative. Discourse works at the level of everyday life (Foucault 1966). Commonsense reasoning, according to Deleuze (1994), is a product of discourse – an expression of categorical commitments that fit shared language practices. In contrast, political imagination provides bases for collective identities, as Benedict Anderson (1983) has shown for nation-states. Political imaginaries are powerful not only because they are coordinating (as social imaginaries are in general), but also because (being outside language) they lie beyond debate, so their logics are hard to question, and they can obscure practices of power by replacing them with fictions.

Imagination is powerful because sometimes what people imagine exceeds or violates discursive common sense, allowing people to see beyond the confines of commonsense political discourse (Polanyi 1966; Mukerji 2014). And political imagination can also enter discourse through the articulation of dreams. The sociological imagination, in bringing alternative visions of power and history to people, gives them tools for thinking beyond the political cultures promoted by states both in discourse and political imaginaries.

Part of the discomfort of modern life comes from the disparities between political imaginaries and the habitus of ordinary people (Bourdieu 1984). Both are cultural imaginaries invested in things that work at the level of imagination, but only political imaginaries work at the level of history. Members of social classes see themselves in each other, and in the tastes and practices they imagine they share. They recognize possibilities for their own lives in what they see others doing, and in this way, they produce social class distinctions as a logic of action (Lizardo 2004). But the resulting social worlds are made to seem enduring and ahistorical products of coordinating practices (Becker 1982). So ordinary people do not often learn historical reasoning from their families, but rather from states (Vygotski and Cole 1978). They thus have few ways to imagine history as lying in their own hands and emerging from their everyday lifeworlds. Political imaginaries promoted by states elevate the polity by presenting it as a product of superhuman forces and exceptional individuals, and in doing so, limit the extent to which people think they can make a difference at the historical level. So, political imaginaries alienate people from history, creating a habitus that discourages political engagement.

The interplay of discourse and cultural imaginaries is of sociological interest to those want to understand in how culture works, and particularly the role of imagination in culture. It is a way to understand connections between the imaginaries explored in the production of culture and the cultural imaginaries working at the level of history (Anderson 1983; Harrison and Johnson 2009).

I will focus here on the built environment or spaces that are culturally and politically meaningful. Lefebvre (1991) and Harvey (2001, 2004) both point to the power of places to shape political consciousness, immersing people in political assumptions in the conduct of daily life. In sociological terms, built environments form a political habitus not constrained by class (Alexander et al. 2012). Discourse is important in the development of the political logics invested in things, but the things are more politically powerful because they stand outside political debate where what they embody "goes without saying." So cultural imaginaries of modern built environments produce unselfconscious forms of governmentality (Joyce 2003).

To show how political imaginaries are constructed and work, I will turn to the cultural program of the French state in the seventeenth century that was dedicated to associating France with Rome (Perrault 1688; Goldstein 2008). This dream of imperial history and destiny was used to turn the "Sun King" into an extraordinarily powerful monarch and France into a powerful state both quickly and with little conflict (Mukerji 2012, 2017). And through architecture, this dream was used to create political habitus in which Roman revival seemed normal.

The French Royal Academy of Architecture

I focus here on the Royal Academy of Architecture (*Académie royale d'architecture*) and its role in building the political imaginary of French inheritance from Rome. It was established toward the end of the reign of Louis XIV and determined how to derive French architecture from classical precedents. It created a political taste culture beyond debate and designed a habitus for dreaming about collective identity in imperial terms.

Members of the Academy never considered the deep political issue of whether France was indeed heir to Rome. Instead, they spoke of creating monuments in France equal to the monuments from Rome. The point was to celebrate superhuman achievement in war, art, science, and so forth and to place France in a genealogy of greatness with roots in Rome and a future in empire.

The architects of the Academy were first charged with inventing a classical tradition for France to inherit, and replacing the architectural traditions of the French building trades (Hobsbawm and Ranger 1983; cf. Turnbull 2000; Mukerji 2012). According to the Academy's director, Blondel (1675:preface), academicians assembled "one day of each week to confer and communicate their knowledge ... [and] undo the abuses of ignorance and the presumptions that Workers have introduced, [returning French architecture to] its natural beauties and graces that were made so commendable among the Ancients." And as the director and professor of the Academy, Blondel developed a curriculum for young architects, providing guidelines for following in the footsteps of the ancients (1675).

Members of the Royal Academy of Architecture were all called *architectes du roi*, but there were two ranks of members. The architects of the first rank had the status of academicians and were charged with debating principles and practices every week. Members of the second rank only rarely took part in these discussions (Lemonnier 1913:tome III, x). The students of the Academy served as a kind of third estate trained to obey their superiors. The elite members of the Academy mainly used discourse, then, to address the imperial ambitions of Louis XIV. But this gave them the last word on good taste and control of a hierarchy of architects.

The debates

To realize their charge of "restoring the ancient illustriousness of architecture" (Blondel 1675:tome I, preface), members of the Academy dutifully studied and debated the *Ten Books on Architecture* by Vitruvius (1673) – the touchstone of classical architectural design, construction, and structural engineering. They also read Renaissance commentators on Vitruvius and ancient architecture more generally, such as Andrea Palladio, Giacomo Barozzi de Vignola, and Vincenzo Scamozzi. In their meetings, they sometimes discussed lectures and writings by members, too, mainly the course material by Blondel, but also work by Philibert de l'Orme, Philippe La Hire, and Antoine Desgodets or Desgodetz. They tried to understand what accounted for the greatness of classical architecture, and how to reproduce ancient beauty (Blondel 1675:tomes I, II, and III, preface).

The proceedings of the Academy help to reveal the power and limits of discourse in shaping culture. The participants developed a shared vocabulary for thinking about architectural aesthetics that shaped what could be said and done. The terms of the debates did not change over decades even as members died and were replaced. Henry Lemonnier in compiling the proceedings apologized,

> Parts of the proceedings are repetitive, and we have had to limit censoring this in the notes to recover in this way the continuity of the academic theories during the first forty years of the institution which, by the way, does not signify that it changed later.
>
> *(Lemonnier 1913:tome III, xii)*

The academicians in their weekly meetings in 1697 (to take one year as an example) mostly debated Blondel's course on architecture – the basis for the lessons to the students of the Academy (Lemonnier1913:tome III, viii). Each week they turned to the next section of the course and discussed it in detail, even though the issues had been the same in earlier conferences (Lemonnier 1913:tome III, 1–5; Blondel 1675:tome I, preface). The point of the practice was to establish or reaffirm principles for French classicism (Lemonnier 1913:tome III, xxiv; Blondel 1675:tome I, preface).

The *Cours d'Architecture* by Blondel began with the basic elements of classical architecture: the column, the pedestal, the entablature (upper structure supported by columns), and the facade (1675:tome I, 5). Each of these features was discussed in more depth in the second volume of the *Cours* with "books" devoted to columns, pedestals, entablatures, architraves, friezes, cornices, pediments, and pilasters, balustrades, and so forth. The *Cours* subdivided each of these books into sections. So for example, the book on columns had a chapter on the origin of columns and the different orders of architecture. The second chapter discussed the height of columns. The third addressed the thickness of columns. The fourth described the shapes columns needed to take to seem straight to viewers. The fifth presented a method of computing the shape of columns to produce this illusion. The sixth treated the different forms of columns (smooth, fluted, etc.).

The seventh focused on the bases on which columns were built, and the eighth addressed their capitals (Blondel 1675:tomes II and III, table of contents). The discourse set the terms of debate, which excluded architectural features that did not reference the ancients.

Blondel's course used the power of discourse to shape architectural aesthetics and practice. Students who learned to speak in these terms were recognized as architects. Anyone crossing the discursive boundaries of the Academy risked being called a builder rather than an architect. So the meetings of the academicians not only created a community of linguistic practice, but used the power of discourse to distinguish artists from artisans, gentlemen from workers (Mukerji 2014). The result was that architects made France heir to Rome, using categories for describing classical architecture that sustained this imaginary.

The measures

The *Cours d'Architecture* by Blondel (1675) was a work of mathematics as well as classification, approaching aesthetics through proportions as well as discourse. Blondel described himself on the title page of the book as a member of the French Royal Academy of Science, then Conseiller Lecteur et Professeur du Roy in mathematics, and only then as Professeur et Directeur de l'Academie Royale d'Architecture. He also went on to characterizes himself as *Mareschal de Camp* in the king's army, and mathematics instructor to *M. le Dauphin*, heir to the throne.

Each of these offices pointed to the importance of mathematics to Blondel's approach to architecture and the Academy. He wanted to create a science of architectural aesthetics, measuring proportions because what made classical architecture so inspiring could never be captured in words. Mathematical relations were important to the ancients themselves. Roman members of the building trades used relational or proportional rather than absolute measures, and Vitruvius used proportions to discuss aesthetics. So mathematical studies of buildings were treated as means of building semiotic chains from Rome to France, piercing the silence of classical ruins by extralinguistic means (Perrault and McEwen 1993; Picon 1988).

On the political level, Blondel's ability to teach mathematics (to the dauphin) brought him to the attention of the king, who appointed him as professor of the Academy as well as its director. Blondel's interest in military architecture drew him to pedagogical uses of mathematics as well. The French military had long relied on measures to teach architecture and engineering. The military engineers who designed fortifications and rebuilt them during sieges gained experience by going to war, but they were also often killed in battle. So they made measures of what worked, and left these records for followers. In this way, mathematics was used as a substitute for experience, codifying what engineers learned about constructing fortresses or conducting sieges (Mukerji 2006).

But measurements had their own limits. They posed problems of accuracy that were just as troubling as the limits of language. For example, Desgodetz, one of the first students of the Academy, went to Rome to measure buildings there over two years, publishing a book from his studies in 1682. *Les Monuments antiques de Rome dessinés et measurés très exactement* displayed in illustrations measures of roughly 25 temples, many triumphal arches, and so forth with descriptive summaries of the buildings. (Lemonnier 1913:tome III, xviii; Desgodetz 1682).

Desgodetz's work was celebrated for its fine measures of even the smallest details of classical buildings, but his book's publication also led to questions about the accuracy of his work. Was Desgodetz inventing proportions or finding them? Given the doubts, the Academy asked the director of the academy in Rome to let Oppenordt, a student of the school, verify the measures. Proportions were not the buildings themselves but representations of them, and their limitations came up for debate (Lemonnier 1913:tome III, xix). They did not really escape discourse.

Monuments and imagination

Words and measures were effective means for capturing some qualities of classical architecture, but they could not in themselves link France to Rome. This required creating a built environment linked to Rome. The best way to start the process, according to members of the Royal Academy, was to use classical precedents to erect monuments to glorify France under Louis XIV. Monuments like triumphal arches could span the divide between the living and the dead by semiotic means, using measures of proportions. Blondel had already championed the simplicity of the arch that he felt allowed it to speak across the ages. So the classical revival orchestrated by the Academy began with arches.

Colbert asked Blondel to develop a plan to rebuild and modernize Paris, which meant making the city a habitus of Roman revival. Blondel wanted to open up the city by taking down its walls, and opening up new plazas, but most of all, he wanted to replace the doors of the city with triumphal arches as iconic "likenesses," in Peirce's terms, of arches in Rome, using mathematically codified mimetic properties (Peirce 1955:106–9; Colapietro and Olshewsky 1996:187).

One of these new doors to Paris was the Porte Saint-Denis, which Blondel erected in 1672–1674. It was set at the intersection of a busy road and garden constructed where the city wall and moat had been. It was a landmark for visitors entering the city, and for its inhabitants, an icon of the new Paris set in an open space at the edge of the very crowded city. As they took their promenades, Parisians were supposed see and learn to appreciate the new tastes of the New Rome (Gerbino 2010:73–84; cf. Turner 2012). The parks where the walls had been were characterized by formal *allées* of trees like those found in classical gardens, repeating the theme of classical revival, and creating a habitus of political possibility in imitation of Rome (Berger 1994:74–83; Gerbino 2010:73–84)

The Porte Saint-Denis was modeled on the arch of Titus in Rome and celebrated French military prowess. A frieze on one side of the arch depicted the French army's passage of the Rhine; its counterpart on the reverse side depicted the capture of a Dutch city. Below the friezes, trumpets and laurels were raised for the victors, symbols of spiritual blessing and success in battle, and above them were the words *Ludovico Magno* (to Louis the Great). Two obelisks on the front of the arch were strewn with flags, weapons, and armor – tributes to soldiers who died in battle. The Porte Saint-Denis in both its classical form and military decorations linked French power to that of the Roman Empire (Berger 1994:74–83; Gerbino 2010:73–84).

The Porte Saint-Denis did not argue that Louis XIV was an imperial leader. The imperial dream was silently invested in this arch and other echoes of Rome across the city. Paris was filled with silent testimonials to the Roman revival in France, making it a political habitus where dreams of history and destiny seemed to be coming true.

And this imaginary was subsequently built upon, becoming such a taken-for-granted and orienting dream in French politics that it survived the French Revolution and animated the imperial strivings of the Napoleonic Era.

The association of France with Rome permanently defined the cultural context in which French politics was played out as the Pantheon, Madeleine, National Assembly, Arc de Triomphe, and the buildings and fountains of the Place de la Concorde spread neo-classical and beaux-arts echoes of Rome through Paris. Classical inheritance was kept alive in structures that made sense of France as a state and gave dignity to anyone associated with it.

Orienting fictions

The material demonstrations of classical inheritance bring us back to C.W. Mills and the sociological imagination (1959). Why did he see ordinary people suffering from a lack of historical imagination? And why did he think that a sociological imagination would help? I think he recognized the depersonalization of modern life that detached ordinary people from history, but he did not appreciate how built environments could colonize historical imaginaries, repressing political agency and creating forms of political despair.

The sociological imagination is a good means for querying the silent political habitus of things established by states that has silently and relentlessly eroded the ability of people to dream of change, because it addresses dreams of possibility in a different way than states. It points to the power of everyday practices, and pushes back against a vision of power as necessarily superhuman. As Mills suggested, sociological imagination can give people a sense of history and possibility at the level of everyday life, so they can conceive of how to live more happily and what they can do to improve public life.

Paying attention to imaginaries invested in things and distinguishing them from discourse provides a productive methodology for doing many forms of cultural sociology. It provides a means of studying the material environment in which social life takes place, linking forms of thought to the forms of things. This approach to materiality would be useful, for example, in studies of collective memory and memorials, allowing analysts to trace the interplay of discourse and imaginaries in the development of national political identities through stories and things (see Saito, this volume). Looking at the role of cultural imaginaries versus discourse also provides a way to disentangle different levels of "meaning" in the conduct of everyday life since people engage in both articulated (discursive) and inarticulate (embodied) forms of action, but sociologists rarely trace their different dynamics. Distinguishing between imaginaries and discourses could also be important to cognitive studies of culture, providing a way to think about the work of the visual cortex and language areas of the brain, and could raise questions about distributed processes of cognition in cultural forms of thought. Looking at imaginaries and discourse in things also should be useful to sociologists reinventing a production-of-culture approach to the sociology of art. Experimentation in the arts, according to Deleuze (1986), provides a way to move beyond discourse through material practices, following logics of practice that evade discursive logics. Thinking about the discursive and inarticulate qualities of the built environment also provides a way to understand the workings of the habitus, where living in social spaces shapes consciousness without articulation. Finally, paying attention to imagination allows us to understand in new terms the improvised forms of social activity that are at the heart of social life, and that prevent cultures of cognition from becoming iron cages of cultural constraint on thought. States and other institutions may have the material means to colonize consciousness with things, but they do not control imaginaries that slip beyond discourse in silent practices.

Acknowledgments

Thanks to the Center for Advanced Study in the Behavioral Sciences and the University of California Humanities Research Institute for funding in support of this project. And thanks to Alvaro Santana-Acuna and Terra Eggink for their invaluable help with the research.

References

Alexander, J., D. Bartmanski, and B. Giesen. 2012. *Iconic Power: Materiality and Meaning in Social Life*. New York: Palgrave Macmillan.
Anderson, B.R. 1983. *Imagined Communities: Reflections on the Origin and Spread of Nationalism*. London: Verso.
Becker, Howard S. 1982. *Art Worlds*. Berkeley: University of California Press.
Berezin, Mabel. 1997. *Making the Fascist Self*. Ithaca, NY: Cornell University Press.

Berger, R.W. 1994. *A Royal Passion: Louis XIV as Patron of Architecture.* Cambridge: Cambridge University Press.

Blondel, F. and Académie Royale D'architecture (France). 1675. *Cours d'architecture enseigné dans l'Academie royale d'architecture.* Paris: De l'imprimerie de Lambert Roulland.

Bourdieu, P. 1984. *Distinction: A Social Critique of the Judgement of Taste.* London: Routledge & Kegan Paul.

Burke, Kenneth, and Joseph Gusfield. 1989. *Symbols and Society.* Chicago: University of Chicago Press.

Colapietro, V.M., and T.M. Olshewsky. 1996. *Peirce's Doctrine of Signs: Theory, Applications, and Connections.* New York: Mouton de Gruyter.

Deleuze, Gilles. 1986. *Cinema 1: The Movement Image.* London: Athlone Press.

———. 1994. *Difference and Repetition.* New York: Columbia University Press.

Desgodetz, Antoine. 1682. *Les monuments antiques de Rome dessinés et measurés très exactement.* Paris: Chez Jean Baptiste Coignard.

Falasca-Zamponi, Simonetta. 1997. *Fascist Spectacle.* Berkeley: University of California Press.

Foucault, Michel. 1966. *Order of Things.* New York: Vintage.

Gerbino, A. 2010. *François Blondel: Architecture, Erudition, and the Scientific Revolution.* London: Routledge.

Goldstein, C. 2008. *Vaux and Versailles: The Appropriations, Erasures, and Accidents that Made Modern France.* Philadelphia: University of Pennsylvania Press.

Harrison, C.E., and A. Johnson, eds. 2009. *Osiris.* Vol. 24, *National Identity: The Role of Science and Technology.* Chicago: University of Chicago Press.

Harvey, David 2001. *Spaces of Capital: Towards a Critical Geography.* New York: Routledge.

———. 2004. *Paris: Capital of Modernity.* New York: Routledge.

Hobsbawm, Eric, and Terence Ranger. 1983. *The Invention of Tradition.* Cambridge: Cambridge University Press.

Holland, D.C., W. Lachicotte, D. Skinner, and C. Cain. 1998. *Identity and Agency in Cultural Worlds.* Cambridge, MA: Harvard University Press.

Joyce, Patrick. 2003. *Rule of Freedom.* London: Verso.

Lefebvre, Henri. 1991. *The Production of Space,* trans. Donald Nicholson-Smith. Cambridge, MA: Blackwell.

Lemonnier, Henry. 1913. *Procès-Verbaux de l'Académie Royale d'Architecture, 1697–1711,* Tome III. Paris: Édouard Champion.

Lizardo, O. 2004. "The Cognitive Origins of Bourdieu's Habitus." *Journal for the Theory of Social Behavior* 34(4):375–401.

Mead, George Herbert. 1964. *On Social Psychology-Selected Papers.* Chicago: University of Chicago Press.

Mills, C. Wright. 1959. *The Sociological Imagination.* New York: Oxford University Press.

Mukerji, C. 2006. "Tacit Knowledge and Classical Technique in 17th-Century France: Hydraulic Cement as a Living Practice Among Masons and Military Engineers." *Technology and Culture* 47(4):713–33.

———. 2009. "The New Rome: Infrastructure and National Identity on the Canal du Midi." Pp. 15–32 in *National Identity: the Role of Science and Technology,* edited by C.E. Harrison and A. Johnson. Chicago: University of Chicago Press.

———. 2010. "The Territorial State as a Figured World of Power: Strategics, Logistics and Impersonal Rule." *Sociological Theory* 28:402–25.

———. 2012. "Space and Political Pedagogy at the Gardens of Versailles." *Public Culture* 24(3):515–40.

———. 2014. "The Cultural Power of Tacit Knowledge: Inarticulacy and Bourdieu's Habitus." *American Journal of Cultural Sociology* 2(3):348–75.

———. 2017. "Artisans and the Construction of the French State: The Political Role of the Louvre's Workshops." Pp. 21–36 in *National Matters: Materiality, Culture, Nationalism,* edited by G. Zubrzycki. Stanford, CA: Stanford University Press.

Peirce, C.S. 1955. *Philosophical Writings of Peirce.* New York: Dover.

Perrault, C. 1688. *Parallèle des Anciens et des Modernes . . . Texte imprimée A.* Paris: chez Jean Baptiste Coignard.

Perrault, C., and I.K. McEwen. 1993. *Ordonnance For the Five Kinds of Columns After the Method of the Ancients.* Santa Monica, CA: Getty Center for the History of Art and the Humanities, Distributed by University of Chicago Press.

Picon, Antoine. 1988. *Claude Perrault, 1613–1688, ou, la curiosité d'un classique.*

Polanyi, Michel. 1966. *The Tacit Dimension*. Chicago: University of Chicago Press.

Schwartz, B. 2000. *Abraham Lincoln and the Forge of National Memory*. Chicago: University of Chicago Press.

Spillman, Lyn. 1997. *Nation and Commemoration*. New York: Cambridge University Press.

Thomas, W.I. 1951. *Social Behavior and Personality*, edited by E. Volkart. New York: Social Science Research Council.

Tilly, Charles. 2003. *The Politics of Collective Violence*. Cambridge: Cambridge University Press.

Tilly, Charles, and Sidney Tarrow. 2015. *Contentious Politics*. New York: Oxford University Press.

Turnbull, David. 2000. *Masons, Tricksters and Cartographers: Makers of Knowledge and Space*. Amsterdam and Abingdon: Harwood Academic & Marston.

Turner, Fred. 2012. "The Family of Man and the Politics of Attention in Cold War America." *Public Culture* 24(1):55–84.

Vitruvius, P. 1673. *Les dix livres d'architecture de Vitruve, corrigez et tradvits nouvellement en françois, avec des notes et des figures*, trans. C. Perrault. Paris: J.B. Coignard.

Vygotski, L.S., and M. Cole, eds. 1978. *Mind in Society: The Development of Higher Psychological Processes*. Cambridge, MA: Harvard University Press.

Zanker, P. 1988. *The Power of Images in the Age of Augustus*. Ann Arbor: University of Michigan Press.

13

The mechanisms of cultural reproduction
Explaining the puzzle of persistence

Orlando Patterson

Introduction

One of the most challenging problems in the sociology of culture has been steadfastly neglected by the discipline – the puzzle of persistence. This may in part be explained by the discipline's preoccupation with change, its understandable disdain for cultural determinism, the well-based suspicion of essentialism, and the laudable need to acknowledge the role of meaning-making and agency in cultural analysis. These are all concerns that reflect the errors of an earlier generation of scholars, but they are erroneously associated with the question of cultural reproduction and persistence. Whatever the reasons, it is unfortunate that an understanding of the most fundamental feature of culture – that it is the prime source of the predictability and stability without which human society is impossible – is now largely left to other disciplines such as psychology (Nisbett and Cohen 1996), evolutionary studies (Boyd and Richerson 2005), cognitive anthropology (Cole 1996), and even economics (Barro and McCleary 2006)

It is not my objective to underplay the role of change in understanding culture. Indeed, my approach is processual and I see change as an inherent aspect of all cultural activity. The problem is to understand how persistence is possible in the face of such dynamism, and to account for the mechanisms that allow for this reconciliation.

A perdurantist view of cultural processes

Before examining how culture is persistently reproduced, one must first be clear about what it is. Culture is the production, reproduction, and transmission of relatively stable informational processes and knowledge structures and their public representations that are variously distributed in groups or social networks. The information is declarative and procedural, pertaining to ideas, beliefs, values, skills, and routinized practices as well as information about the transmission process. The transmission occurs both between and within generations; moreover, processes are shared unevenly, may be spread across non-localized groups, and may not be integrated. Finally, in pragmatic terms, culture as constituted knowledge depends on activation in social practices that are in part shaped by context (Patterson 2014).

Cultural processes allow for incremental changes that result from transmission errors and unwitting or deliberate alterations by learners. A perdurantist approach resolves the apparent paradox of how something can change incrementally – and over the long run quite substantially – yet maintain its identity. As philosopher Sally Haslanger (2003:318) explains, the persisting object does not undergo alteration by "gaining" or "losing" properties; instead, it changes like a lighted candle. That is,

> contradiction is avoided by modifying the proper subject condition: the persisting thing (the composite) is not the proper subject of the properties "gained" and "lost" (the stages are), but the proper subjects of the properties are at least parts of the persisting thing.
>
> *(Haslanger 2003:318)*

Lévi-Strauss's (1963) treatment of a myth as the totality of all pre-existing and current versions is a classic example of this approach.

Culture is both internalized and externally represented in social relations, material structures, symbolic media, and other artifacts (Sperber 1996:34). Although all structured behaviors and artifacts have a cultural dimension, many areas of culture – calculus, jazz, cricket, Hamlet – are delinked from their originating structures and can be limitlessly reproduced in varied contexts. A critical feature of all stable cultural processes is that their identities are collectively imputed, regardless of criterial properties – this being true of what W. V. Quine calls "time-extended objects."

There is a substantial literature on reproduction in sociology, but nearly all of it is devoted to the problem of structural and organizational stability rather than cultural reproduction (e.g., DiMaggio and Powell 1983). Social reproduction, which will not concern us here, refers to the means by which structural features of a society – class, gender, race, segregation, and other patterns of differentiation and organization – are maintained (see Hall, Neitz, and Battani 2003:1–15). When cultural reproduction is considered, most sociologists view it as social learning or socialization via family, schooling, and peers. Bourdieu, the most widely cited sociologist on the subject, is typical. His habitus concept does double duty, directly explaining cultural reproduction, which in turn explains "the reproduction of structures" (Bourdieu 1973:71). Adopting an earlier view of social learning, circa 1950–1975 (see Schonpflug 2009:11–14), Bourdieu does not explore the mechanisms of the reproductive process itself except to refer to an "internal law" by which external necessities are "constantly exerted" (1990:278).

To deepen the analysis of reproduction, here, I identify seven broad mechanisms: enculturating, institutional, structural, frequency-dependent, communication-based, reinterpretive, and embedded.

The mechanisms of persistence

Enculturation or social learning

This is the most familiar mechanism of cultural reproduction. Often referred to as socialization, it is transmission through social learning and imitation both within and between generations. Beyond this, we need to know why only some processes persist, while others change or disappear, and to identify what agents are more likely, and others less likely, to transfer different kinds of cultural processes.

In their classic work, Cavalli-Sforza and his associates tackle the problem by modeling "who transmits what to whom, the number of transmitters per receiver, their ages and other relations between them" (Cavalli-Sforza et al. 1982:19–20). There can be many-to-one transmissions (for example, a class or caste's influence on the naïve recipient), or one-to-many (such as a teacher's transmission to a class), and one-to-one or one-to-few transmissions (the last of which generate moderate rates of cultural change). The other distinction is that between vertical (parents and children), oblique (between non-parental adults and children), and horizontal (between peers). The authors argue that the rate of cultural reproduction (measured in terms of the rate of trait frequencies and variations over time), as well as the content of reproduction, will depend on the interaction of transmission ratio and direction, along with additional mediating factors such as age and transmitter-recipient gender differences. They find that certain kinds of transmissions tend to be trait-specific; for example, among Americans, political and religious attitudes and sports preferences are strongly vertically transmitted, which largely explains their stability. Mothers and fathers account for the transmission of different cultural processes and, significantly, there is little interaction effect (Cavalli-Sforza et al. 1982:218).

Researchers have specified the precise psychological processes involved in transmission processes. In a review of psychological studies of socialization, Putallaz et al. conclude that the "enabling materials of transmission" include primarily:

> [T]he proximity between caretaker and offspring, the quality of the emotional and interactional bond between them, the quality of the caretaker's life-long social relationship experiences, the translation of these experiences into schematized forms (such as memories), the presence of conflict among significant interaction partners in the family context, and the gender of both caretaker and child.
>
> *(Putallaz et al. 1998:417–18)*

Studies have also documented the intergenerational transmission of parenting strategies (e.g., Chen and Kaplan 2001). This research shows, unexpectedly, that familial socioeconomic status fails to predict the parenting strategies of adult children. It has also been shown that intergenerational transmission is bidirectional, although the degree to which children influence parents varies with context (Kuczynski 2003); parent-offspring cultural similarity is strong only in some domains (Schonpflug and Bilz 2009:212–39); and the degree of corroboration varies with class, region, immigrant status, the motivation of parents, and sibling position (Trommsdorff 2009).

Institutional reproduction: hegemonic and counter-hegemonic

Cultural institutions – ranging from simple salutations to complex formal rites – can be defined as routinized processes that have become normative. The main force of reproduction and persistence is simply the fact that the process in question has become a part of the taken-for-granted, normative social world. They are part of the shared definition of a reality that is experienced as objectively and externally real. Hence "each actor fundamentally perceives and describes social reality by enacting it and, in this way transmits it to other actors in the social system" (Zucker 1977:728). A general principle is that the more institutionalized and complex a routine or belief, then the less the reliance on childhood socialization or internalization, which, indeed, may not even be possible where the process is confined to adulthood and involves complex practices. Institutions are not strictly learned; they are enacted or performed. Their meanings may be accessible to only a few specialists. Thus, for over a thousand years, the single most important institutional rite in the Western world, the Catholic mass, was conducted in a language that 95 percent of participants did not understand.

How exactly do values and practices become institutionalized? "The key to institutionalizing a value," Stinchcombe (1968:108–12) wrote, "is to concentrate power in the hands of those who believe in that value." Succeeding generations of power holders foster institutional self-reproduction "by selection, socialization, and controlling conditions of incumbency and hero worship." The powerful select those who share their values and other cultural preferences, and they control the processes of socialization. They also act as ego-ideals, as role models for ambitious younger persons, ensuring that the cultural processes they favor will be disproportionately imitated and re-enacted. And by arranging the institutional conditions under which later generations come to power, they ensure that independent forces will keep potential deviants in line with their values. Power-backed beliefs and values also have a much greater chance of being popularly adopted, due to general admiration for the powerful and their proponents' greater access to communicative channels.

Stinchcombe's is a well-argued theory of hegemony. However, it neglects the subaltern origins and replication of values and knowledge structures (Spivak 1988). Though lacking legal, economic, and political power, some individuals are still able to exercise considerable influence and sometimes charismatic authority in the production and reproduction of subaltern cultures. African American religious history provides a clear example of how a dominated group is able to not only resist cultural hegemony but also appropriate and transform the dominant creed to match their own likings and interests (Genovese 1976; Raboteau 1978). Levine (1970:part 6) documents the powerful role of charismatic counter-heroes – Stagalee, John Henry – in the rise of African American folk and modern culture. In the extreme, the subaltern can turn the tables on elites and greatly influence the cultural beliefs and practices of dominant groups, best illustrated by the outsized influence of African Americans on contemporary American popular culture. The same holds for Jamaica, where dance hall culture, Rastafarianism, creole speech, and other areas of the previously denigrated Afro-Jamaican lifestyle now dominate popular culture (Thomas 2004).

Structural reproduction

Here a persisting structural condition continuously recreates the cultural pattern in question even in the absence of cultural institutionalization. In America the intergenerational transmission of impoverished contexts, in which blacks live in the same ghetto environment for generations, results not only in greatly reduced life chances (Sharkey 2008) but also in persisting patterns of violence and victimization and impaired cognitive and educational functioning (Sampson, Raudenbush, and Earls 1997; Sampson, Sharkey, and Raudenbush 2008), as well as distinct speech communities (Labov and Harris 1986). In Jamaica, as elsewhere, chronic unemployment and extremely low wages often lead to a persistent pattern of seeming disdain for work, preference for hustling, and, especially in rural areas, a response to marginal increases in wages with less work (Patterson 1975).

The non-institutionalized nature of many such cultural outcomes is evinced by their erosion in the face of changed structural environments. Thus Jamaicans recruited to work as farm laborers in America are noted for their work ethic. And the long tradition of prostitution in pre-revolutionary Havana disappeared for 30 years right after the revolution, then promptly returned after 1991 with the reemergence of economic insecurity during the *periodo especial* following the collapse of Soviet aid (Clancy 2002).

The culture of honor in Mediterranean societies and the US South is perhaps the best-studied case of a long-term continuity of this kind. In the honorific cultural process, individuals (especially men) are extremely sensitive to real or perceived insults, and are inclined to react violently toward such perceptions. The culture is accompanied by a strong sense of shame, especially when people are unable to defend their honor. Scholars have found this cultural process primarily in herding or agri-pastoral societies, large-scale slave systems, conditions where centralized authority and law enforcement are weak, and especially where these conditions reinforce each other (Peristiany 1966; Wyatt-Brown 1982; Patterson 1982a:77–101; Patterson 1984; Nisbett and Cohen 1996). The persistence of the process in modern Greece is one of the most durable cultural traditions on record, with scholars finding clear parallels between the tradition today and Homeric times 27 centuries ago (Walcot 1996). In the Deep South of the US, a durable honor culture accounts for, among other things, the region's much higher rate of violent crime (Nisbett and Cohen 1996).

An important aspect of the structural mechanism is that after a sustained period of reproduction, a given process may well become institutionalized and reproduced by both means in a pattern of mutual reinforcement, or independently of the structural context that originally generated it. Thus Sampson et al. (2008) has found the persistence of neighborhood-induced reading impairment long after affected individuals have left the neighborhoods that generated it. And Nisbett has demonstrated in psychological experiments that students of Southern background living in the North are far more inclined to react honorifically to perceived threats to their manhood (Nisbett and Cohen 1996:53). It is possible that a similar shift in the mechanism of reproduction from the structural to the institutional may have occurred in the honorific violence of inner-city African American youth (Courtwright 1996:225–46; Papachristos 2009) and in the familial patterns of poor Jamaicans (Patterson 1982b).

Frequency-dependent reproduction

Frequency-dependent reproduction occurs when individuals *disproportionately* select a variant of a cultural process either because it is the most or the least frequent. Take Lieberson's (2003) study of naming practices among Americans and Europeans. Since the second half of the nineteenth century there have been two striking changes in Western naming practices – a growing turnover and diversity in names given children and a significant, though less pronounced, shift in the concentration of names. For centuries up to the early nineteenth century, half of all boys and girls were given one of the three most popular names, whereas today the most popular names are given to only a small minority of the population. This change cannot be explained by structural forces such as urbanization and growing ethnic diversity, nor by the rate of name turnover. Instead, Lieberson shows that the most likely explanation is "popularity as taste." Here a distribution of name choices occurs largely on the basis of their relative popularity, with some people choosing names mainly because they are popular, others because they are unpopular, and still others making choices in between. The result is a distinctive distribution in the reproduction of names that is consistent with the dynamics of frequency-dependent choices. Lieberson has suggested that this pattern characterizes the reproduction of other kinds of tastes such as music, the arts, and political ideas.

Path-dependent processes constitute yet another form of this mechanism. Sometimes, after originating in a specific period from a set of often quite adventitious initiating conditions, transmitted cultural practices become "locked in." The favorite, although disputed, example is the QWERTY keyboard layout. The process is maintained, once established, by mechanisms characterized by what economist Paul David (2005) calls "local positive feedback mechanisms," meaning factors such as sunk costs, the reluctance to learn new techniques, and coordination effects derived from aligning one's actions with others (Arthur 1994:112–13). However, as critics note, these factors are not peculiar to path-dependent processes. Frequency-dependent selection would seem to be the critical factor (called bandwagon and reinforcing expectations in the path-dependent literature). It is when people begin to disproportionately choose a process based on its frequency (initially in conjunction with sunk- and learning-cost considerations) that it becomes locked in and, once locked in, frequency dependence alone explains its persistence, trumping other factors. In a compelling series of web-based experiments, Salganik and Watts (2009) have attempted to explain the winner-take-all puzzle of cultural markets, wherein books, songs, and movies that are only marginally different, and often judged to be inferior by experts, unpredictably outsell competing products by orders of magnitude. Hits emerge as the dynamic collective outcome of a path-dependent process driven by social influence and conformist individual behavior. After an initial chance lead, they get locked into a "cumulative advantage" in which success breeds success due to the "observation learning" of fans engaging in frequency-dependent decision-making.

Communication-based reproduction

In some cases, the reproduction of culture is a direct result of the dynamics of communication itself and entails emergent population-level consequences of individual interactions.

The "common ground" approach of Lyons and Kashima (2001:374) explores how "information circulated through communication channels contributes to the information environment of individual members, influencing the availability of information to confirm or disconfirm cultural knowledge." They focus on the tendency of communicated knowledge to converge toward shared understanding. The basic idea is that when people communicate, they are more interested in confirming their own established beliefs, values, and worldview than in accurately passing on what was communicated to them. Shared knowledge becomes "common ground," rather than a simple repository, which each person in the communicative chain believes others possess, and which they all use to make sense of new information. As a result, ambiguity and incoherence are minimized, creating an inherent tendency in information transmission toward weeding out messages that are inconsistent with established beliefs. Cultural stereotypes are typical of such processes: in an experiment simulating a serial communicative process, Lyons and Kashima show how a story about an Australian football player converged toward the common-ground stereotype about footballers despite inconsistent versions transmitted in the early stages of the communicative chain.

The French anthropologist Dan Sperber (1996) draws analogously from virology to theorize an epidemiology of representation. Durable cultural processes, he argues, are "contagious." Populations are inhabited by vast numbers of mental representations, only some of which become public and enduring. This happens when a particular process becomes an "attractor" that provides the least costly way of achieving a given goal. Reproduction is not simple imitation, but rather, one form of cultural production. Communication is a recognition of what one interprets the other person to mean, in the process creating one's own meaning in terms of what is most relevant to the person and the broader cultural context (Sperber 1996:53). Micro variation achieves macro stability by movement toward attractors. "In the logical space of possible versions of a tale," he writes of the reproduction of the Red Riding Hood folktale, "some versions have a better form: that is, a form seen as being without either missing or superfluous parts, easier to remember, and more attractive" (Sperber 1996:106).

What is largely metaphor for Sperber becomes a literal social epidemiology in the empirically grounded network studies of Christakis and Fowler (2009). They have shown that behaviors such as smoking, overeating, drinking, expressing happiness, and voting are reproduced or spread through networks in remarkably patterned ways. They go far beyond the traditional emphasis on the structural component of networks (how people are connected) to large-scale empirical explorations of contagion (of what flows between the nodes), arguing that people shape and are shaped by their networks, that ideas, norms, behaviors, and even emotional states flow through chains of friends and acquaintances in hyperdyadic spreads of up to three degrees of influence (friends of friends of friends), and that these networks and contagions have emergent properties unknown to the individuals involved (Christakis and Fowler 2009:24–25, 31, 116–17). Not only have they powerfully demonstrated what the European sociologists, Paul Willis (2004) and Dan Sperber (1996) could only surmise from their ethnographies – that the production and reproduction of cultural processes are intimately related – but they have given new life to the role of the superorganic in cultural systems, an idea that reaches all the way back to Emile Durkheim through Alfred Kroeber and Leslie White (see Chase 2006:47–9).

Reinterpretation

Reinterpretation is the often-covert persistence or adoption of a cultural process through the representation of its meaning or practice in terms of another, established process. The mechanism, once widely recognized and studied by anthropologists after its identification and definitive analysis by Melville Herskovits (e.g., 1949:553–60), was abandoned or viewed with hostility in the late twentieth century (Matory 2005:ch. 7). The classic case of reinterpretation is the identification of African deities with Catholic saints in the creolization process underlying the formation of black Atlantic religions such as Voudon, Santeria, and Condomble (e.g., Brandon 1997). However, the reinterpretive mechanism is found in all cultures, sometimes under other names, such as Brammen's (1992) description of "recontextualization." Native Americans, like West Africans and European pagans before them, used this mechanism as a way of retaining and camouflaging some of their traditions, and the Alaskan Tlingits did so as well when they secretly incorporated potlatch practices into Russian Orthodox and Protestant ceremonies (Nagel 1996:201).

Reinterpretation can operate both as a mechanism of change and persistence, accommodation and contestation, and domination and counter-domination, depending on the perspective of the agents involved, the context in which the interpretation takes place, and whether the issue is temporal connections in a single culture or lateral connections between different cultures. In the middle of the fourth century, Christian church leaders reinterpreted the practices around the winter solstice as the birthday of the Christian Son of God rather than the annual rebirth of the sun (Nissenbaum 1997). From the Christian perspective, this was a rather devious exercise in cultural reproduction; to the European pagans it was an effort at hegemony. In due course it became less and less clear which side had reinterpretively co-opted the other, so much so that eventually the American Puritans abolished Christmas as a heathen custom, admitting that the pagans had won!

Recently, reinterpretation has been rediscovered. Hatch (2004:199–201) reprises Herskovits's concepts of focus and reinterpretation in her analysis of organizational culture. Anthropologist De Sardan (2005:ch. 9) characterizes development in third world countries as a cultural contest between the powerful and the marginalized, in which the new cultural package is "systematically disarticulated," selectively adopted, and often appropriated to ends that subvert the goals of the developer. He calls this "innovation as reinterpretation." Human rights scholars and advocates who seek to improve the status of women in patriarchal societies have also rediscovered the value of "cultural reinterpretation," in this case seeking "to provide cultural 'ground' for the acceptance of women's rights by reinterpreting traditional gender ideologies that have been used to legitimate male domination and discrimination against women" (Bell, Nathan, and Peleg 2000:180).

Sometimes what the mechanism of reinterpretation reproduces is a group's belief in its own identity and continuity, its sense of a living past that informs the present and leads into the future. Such reinterpretation may draw on a wide range of traditions from other groups, and even invent new processes. A famous case is the ghost-dance movement of Native Americans during the last decades of the nineteenth century, which reaffirmed a sense of continuity with Native Americans' past, however imagined. As Smoak shows (2008), the movement was as much about innovation as persistence, a dynamic expression of an emerging pan-Indian identity that integrated reinterpreted aspects of Christianity and traditional beliefs in a fierce struggle against Euro-American cultural hegemony.

Embedded reproduction

Finally, consider the most covert of all the means of cultural reproduction. Cultural embedding is the mechanism by which a process survives through its insertion into the core of a dominant institution. Here, I discuss only the most remarkable, though least apparent, form of this mechanism, *embedded introjection*. This occurs when a cultural pattern persists by shifting from an overt, secular belief to an inner, spiritual one, in which form it can remain, mainly dormant, for centuries. At any time, however, a reverse introjection or projection may occur, in which the pattern is projected back into the secular, outer world. This, in brief, is the history of Western freedom from its introjection by Paul of Tarsus into the creedal core of the infant Christian religion during the first century of the modern era until its projective breakout during the sixteenth and seventeenth centuries.

I have shown elsewhere (Patterson 1991:316–44; cf. Martin 1990) that early Pauline Christianity took over the Roman secular notions of freedom (*libertas*) as liberation from slavery and as the exercise of absolute power, and made them the religion's core doctrine. In his Letter to the Galatians, Paul reconceived sin as a kind of inner slavery and Christ's salvific crucifixion as the price paid to redeem mankind from spiritual thralldom (the Christian word *redemption* being derived from the Latin, *redemptio* which literally means to purchase someone out of slavery). Also, the Augustan imperial notion of freedom as absolute power was reconceived by Paul as the spiritual freedom that came with surrender (Paul wrote "enslavement") to the absolute power and freedom of God.

From the beginning, Church leaders were fully aware of the explosive secular potential of Christianity's core doctrine and so worked hard to prevent its projection back into the secular world. When the doctrine became hegemonic following the conversion of Constantine in 312, the concealment took more elaborate form – in the tight and complex organizational structure of the Church, the careful screening and education of priests, and the use of an increasingly alien language, Latin, for the Mass. For the majority of European peasants, the introjection was only partly successful (Patterson 2007). In the late Middle Ages and early modern Europe, we see the full projection back into the secular world of the Christian doctrine of freedom. As Ernst Kantorowicz (1957) has shown, nearly all political thought during the late Middle Ages and early-modern Europe were simply secularized Christology.

Conclusion

The mechanisms identified here are not mutually exclusive. Indeed, we often find two or more interacting in the reproduction of cultural processes. Thus introjection involves reinterpretation, and in hegemonic persistence, the powerful establish structures that reinforce the replication of favored values. Also, cultural processes reproduced structurally can sometimes become institutionalized. In the very long run, a similar tendency toward institutionalization characterizes many path-dependent reproductions.

It has not been my objective to underplay the role of socio-cultural change. Rather, I contend, the problem of cultural reproduction and persistence should be of equal importance for at least two reasons. First, social and cultural change may be accompanied and powerfully influenced by deep underlying continuities. Thus radical changes in the turnover of American names have been accompanied by shifting but far more stable patterns of name concentration and even greater stability in the distribution of frequency-dependent preferences, and volatility in criminal behavior and speech patterns are outward manifestations of deep-seated continuities in patterns of racial segregation. Second, we need to study continuity because a deep understanding of change itself is not possible without knowledge of the processes of persistence against which it is measured and can only be properly understood.

References

Arthur, W.B. 1994. *Increasing Returns and Path Dependence in the Economy.* Ann Arbor: University of Michigan Press.

Barro, Robert, and R.M. McCleary. 2006. "Religion and economy." *Journal of Economic Perspectives* 20(2):49–72.

Bell, Lydia S., Andrew Nathan, and Ilan Peleg. 2000. *Negotiating Culture and Human Rights.* New York: Columbia University Press.

Bourdieu, Pierre. 1973. "Cultural Reproduction and Social Reproduction." Pp. 71–112 in *Knowledge, Education and Cultural Change*, edited by R. Brown. London: Tavistock.

———. 1990. *The Logic of Practice.* Stanford, CA: Stanford University Press.

Boyd, Robert, and Peter Richerson. 2005. *The Origins and Evolution of Cultures.* New York: Oxford University Press.

Brammen, M.Y. 1992. "Bwana Mickey: Constructing Cultural Consumption at Tokyo Disneyland." Pp. 216–64 in *Re-made in Japan*, edited by J.J. Tobin. New Haven, CT: Yale University Press.

Brandon, George. 1997. *Santeria from Africa to the New World.* Bloomington: Indiana University Press.

Cavalli-Sforza, L.L., M.V. Feldman, K.H. Chen, and S.M. Dornbusch. 1982. "Theory and Observation in Cultural Transmission." *Science* 218(1):19–27.

Chase, Philip. 2006. *The Emergence of Culture.* New York: Springer.

Chen, Zeng-Yin, and Howard Kaplan. 2001. "Intergenerational Transmission of Constructive Parenting." *Journal of Marriage and Family* 63(1):17–31.

Christakis, N., and J. Fowler. 2009. *Connected: The Surprising Power of Our Social Networks and How They Shape Our Lives.* New York: Little, Brown.

Clancy, Michael. 2002. "The Globalization of Sex Tourism and Cuba." *Studies in Comparative International Development* 36(4):63–88.

Cole, M. 1996. *Cross-Cultural Psychology.* Cambridge, MA: Harvard University Press.

Courtwright, David T. 1996. *Violent Land: Single Men and Social Disorder from the Frontier to the Inner City.* Cambridge, MA: Harvard University Press.

David, Paul A. 2005. "Path Dependence, its Critics, and the Quest for Historical Economics." Working Paper. Stanford, CA: Stanford University Department of Economics.

De Sardan, Jean-Pierre Olivier. 2005. *Anthropology and Development: Understanding Contemporary Social Change.* London: Zed Books.

DiMaggio, Paul, and W. Powell. 1983. "The Iron Cage Revisited: Institutional Isomorphism and Collective Rationality in Organizational Fields." *American Sociological Review* 48(2):147–60.

Genovese, Eugene 1976. *Roll, Jordan, Roll.* New York: Vintage.

Hall, John R., Mary Jo Neitz, and Marshall Battani. 2003. *Sociology on Culture.* London: Routledge.

Haslanger, Sally. 2003. "Persistence Through Time." Pp. 315–54 in *Oxford Handbook of Metaphysics*, edited by M. Loux and D. Zimmerman. Oxford: Oxford University Press.

Hatch, Mary Jo. 2004. "Dynamics of Organizational Culture." Pp. 190–211 in *Handbook of Organizational Change and Innovation*, edited by M.S. Poole and A.H. Van de Ven. Oxford: Oxford University Press.

Herskovits, M.J. 1949. *Man and His Works*. New York: Knopf.

Kantorowicz, Ernst. 1957. *The King's Two Bodies: A Study in Medieval Political Theology*. Princeton, NJ: Princeton University Press.

Kuczynski, L. 2003. "Beyond Directionality: Bilateral Conceptual Frameworks for Understanding Dynamics in Parent-child Relations." Pp. 1–24 in *Handbook of Dynamics in Parent-Child Relations*, edited by L. Kuczynski. Newbury Park, CA: Sage.

Labov, W., and W. Harris. 1986. "De Facto Segregation of Black and White Vernaculars." Pp. 1–24 in *Diversity and Diachrony*, edited by D. Sankoff. Philadelphia: John Benjamins.

Levine, Lawrence. 1970. *Black Culture and Black Consciousness: Afro-American Folk Thought from Slavery to Freedom*. Oxford: Oxford University Press.

Lévi-Strauss, Claude. 1963. *Structural Anthropology*. New York: Basic Books.

Lieberson, Stanley. 2003. "Popularity as Taste: An Application to the Naming Process." *Onoma* 38:235–76.

Lyons, Anthony, and Yoshihisa Kashima. 2001. "The Reproduction of Culture: Communication Processes Tend to Maintain Cultural Stereotypes." *Social Cognition* 19(3):372–94.

Martin, Dale B. 1990. *Slavery as Salvation: The Metaphor of Slavery in Pauline Christianity*. New Haven, CT: Yale University Press.

Matory, J. Leonard. 2005. *Black Atlantic Religion*. Princeton, NJ: Princeton University Press.

Nagel, Joane. 1996. *American Indian Ethnic Renewal: Red Power and the Resurgence of Identity and Culture*. Oxford: Oxford University Press.

Nisbett, Richard, and Dov Cohen. 1996. *Culture of Honor: The Psychology of Violence in the South*. Boulder, CO: Westview Press.

Nissenbaum, Stephen. 1997. *The Battle for Christmas*. New York: Vintage.

Papachristos, A. 2009. "Murder by Structure: Dominance Relations and the Social Structure of Gang Homicide." *American Journal of Sociology* 115(1):74–128.

Patterson, Orlando. 1975. *The Condition of the Low-Income Population in the Kingston Metropolitan Area* (Government Report). Kingston, Jamaica: Office of the Prime Minister.

———. 1982a. *Slavery and Social Death*. Cambridge, MA: Harvard University Press.

———. 1982b. "Persistence, Continuity, and Change in the Jamaican Working Class Family." *Journal of Family History* 7(2):135–61.

———. 1984. "The Code of Honor in the Old South." *Reviews in American History* 12:24–30.

———. 1991. *Freedom: Freedom in the Making of Western Culture*. New York: Basic.

———. 2007. "The Ancient and Medieval Origins of Modern Freedom." Pp. 31–66 in *The Problem of Evil*, edited by S. Mintz and J. Stauffer. Amherst: University of Massachusetts Press.

———. 2014. "Making Sense of Culture." *Annual Review of Sociology* 40:1–30.

Peristiany, J.G. 1966. *Honor and Shame: The Values of Mediterranean Society*. Chicago: University of Chicago Press.

Putallaz, Martha, Philip Costanzo, C.L. Grimes, and D.M. Sherman. 1998. "Intergenerational Continuities and their Influences on Children's Social Development." *Social Development* 7(3):389–427.

Raboteau, Albert. 1978. *Slave Religion*. Oxford: Oxford University Press.

Salganik, Matthew, and Duncan Watts. 2009. "Web-based Experiments for the Study of Collective Social Dynamics in Cultural Markets." *Topics in Cognitive Science* 1(3):439–68.

Sampson, R., S. Raudenbush, and F. Earls. 1997. "Neighborhoods and Violent Crime: A Multilevel Study of Collective Efficacy." *Science* 227(5328):918–24.

Sampson, R., P. Sharkey, and S. Raudenbush. 2008. "Durable Effects of Concentrated Disadvantage on Verbal Ability among African-American Children." *Proceedings of the National Academy of Sciences* 105(3):845–53.

Schonpflug, Ute. 2009. "Theory and Research in Cultural Transmission: A Short History." Pp. 9–30 in *Cultural Transmission*, edited by U. Schonpflug. Cambridge: Cambridge University Press.

Schonpflug, U., and L. Bilz. 2009. "The Transmission Process: Mechanisms and Context." Pp. 212–39 in *Cultural Transmission*, edited by U. Schonpflug. Cambridge: Cambridge University Press.

Sharkey, Patrick. 2008. "The Intergenerational Transmission of Context." *American Journal of Sociology* 113(4):931–69.

Smoak, Gregory E. 2008. *Ghost Dances and Identity: Prophetic Religion and American Indian Ethnogenesis in the Nineteenth Century*. Berkeley: University of California Press.

Sperber, Dan. 1996. *Explaining Culture: A Naturalistic Approach*. Oxford: Blackwell.

Spivak, Gayatri. 1988. "Can the Subaltern Speak?" Pp. 271–313 in *Marxism and the Interpretation of Culture*, edited by C. Nelson and L. Grossberg. Urbana: University of Illinois Press.

Stinchcombe, Arthur. 1968. *Constructing Social Theories*. Chicago: University of Chicago Press.

Thomas, Deborah. 2004. *Modern Blackness*. Durham, NC: Duke University Press.

Trommsdorff, Gisela. 2009. "Intergenerational Relations and Cultural Transmission." Pp. 120–60 in *Cultural Transmission*, edited by U. Schonpflug. Cambridge: Cambridge University Press.

Walcot, Peter. 1996. "Continuity and Tradition: The Persistence of Greek Values." *Greece and Rome* 43(2):169–77.

Willis, Paul. 2004. "Cultural Production and Theories of Reproduction." Pp. 178–202 in *Culture: Critical Concepts in Sociology*, edited by C. Jenks. London: Routledge.

Wyatt-Brown, Bertram. 1982. *Southern Honor: Ethics and Behavior in the Old South*. Oxford: Oxford University Press.

Zucker, Lynne. 1977. "The Role of Institutionalization in Cultural Persistence." *American Sociological Review* 42(5):726–43.

Part III
Aesthetics, ethics, and cultural legitimacy

14

Cultural traumas

Giuseppe Sciortino

Introduction

Shit happens. This basic truth about the human condition has gained much traction in popular culture: it appears in 11 million web pages, it has its own emoji, and it is currently enshrined in around 3,000 items sold by Amazon.com (mostly T-shirts and coffee mugs but also bumper stickers and, unsurprisingly, diapers). Not bad for a phrase that, according to Wikipedia, was unknown before 1964 and had never appeared in print before 1983.

"Shit happens" expresses a realistic acceptance of the well-known fact that bad things happen to good people. Its mundane anti-theodicy conveys the modern idea of evil as an external, impersonal fact. Those who forget (or underestimate) it do so at their peril. We use "shit happens" to advise people to play safe and to acknowledge ironically that shit happens to everybody.

The aphorism's popularity, however, has some clear limitations. No civilized member of modern society would email a "shit happens" emoji to the victim of a hate crime. If "shit happens" were used as a social commentary on the Holocaust, slavery, the gulags, or the bombing of Aleppo, it would raise outrage. These events are perceived as sharply and clearly distinguished from those covered by the maxim. They are experienced, and presented to all kind of audiences, as undeserved, unjust, and inflicted upon a collectivity that could not prevent it. They carry with them a strong expectation of sympathy: those who do not feel it are deemed insensitive. The sympathy aroused is not fatalistic. It is meant to mobilize indignation and action.

Still, even dreadful events are usually perceived as objective and self-evident facts. We believe that the sympathy for the victims – as well as the indignation for the action of the perpetrators and the inaction of bystanders – should derive automatically from the features of the events themselves: the severity of the wounds inflicted, the scale of the sufferings, the weight of their consequences for the lives of survivors. Their meaning should be uncontroversial and it should command a predictable response. Once reporters, international organizations, and researchers have established that such crimes have indeed occurred, once they have measured and documented them, once mass graves have been dug and bullets identified, these horrors will become crimes judged in tribunals, motivations for political reforms, torts for which damages will have to be claimed and awarded, sufferance to be diagnosed and therapeutically treated.

Albeit morally commendable, such rational, progressive distinction between ironic acknowledgment of private misfortunes and tragic indignation for collective horrors provides a poor description of social reality. Grisly crimes often fail to reach enough public attention and outrage to command inclusion in the special category. Activities that were once commended as noble, humanitarian efforts – such as those of missionaries among colonized natives – may be considered, only a few decades later, fundamental violations of human dignity (Woods 2016). Wounded victims may sometimes prefer to deal with their sorrows in private, avoiding public commemoration. Conversely, victims of what was once considered an individual misfortune – consider the cases of abused children or patients – may successfully establish their pain as a collective wound with social consequences (Degloma 2009). The boundary between the two classes of events turns out to be ambiguous, unstable, and – what is worse – selective.

To describe and explain the processes through which horrendous events come (or fail) to be perceived as fundamental threats to social identities has been at the center of several scholarly efforts. Some ways of defining the problem have paid attention to the psychological and social consequences of objectively defined events. Drawing mostly from the psychoanalytic tradition, scholars in the humanities have explored how the experience of such events shapes, often unconsciously, the memories and actions of victims, perpetrators, as well as others (Caruth 1995; LaCapra 2013; Andermahr 2015). Social psychologists have highlighted how memories of atrocious events often evolve into a set of pervasive narratives of collective victimhood. Such narratives make the conflict among the reciprocally victimized groups "intractable," resistant to de-escalation (Bar-Tal 2007; Bar-Tal et al. 2009).

In cultural sociology, a group of scholars has developed in the last two decades an ambitious research perspective on what they have called "cultural traumas" or "trauma dramas" (hereinafter CTP). Drawing on the resources made available by collective memory research (see Saito, this volume) and the "Strong Program" in cultural sociology (see Alexander and Smith, this volume), CTP scholars have criticized any factualist treatment of evil. They have argued, on the contrary, that even extreme forms of suffering become traumatic only if they are interpreted and made meaningful to an audience in terms of wider symbolic structures (Alexander et al. 2004; Eyerman, Alexander, and Breese 2011). Even to acknowledge that evil and suffering have occurred is never only a cognitive operation. Many are the documented cases of collective wounds. Few are the dreadful events that transubstantiate into socially shared and emotionally charged referents demanding narration. Only when the transubstantiation happens does collective suffering become emotionally and intellectually significant for members of a collectivity that have never actually experienced it (and for the subsequent generations). Only under such conditions does the recollection of horrendous events and private suffering become a cultural trauma, a break in the continuity of collective identities (with a public claim to recognition and respect).

The main tenet of the CTP is that any social trauma is the outcome of a process of signification and narration. The meaning of the events, and the associated feeling (or lack thereof) of solidarity with the victims and of indignation toward the perpetrators, is never a direct consequence of the actual suffering. It is a cultural achievement. It requires establishing a story that successfully defines the nature of the victims and the extraordinary guilt of perpetrators. Such a story must have the capacity to demonstrate that the narrated suffering has wider meaning, commanding enough emotional and moral energy to trigger some form of vicarious traumatization among members of the collectivity who never experienced the suffering, and even among those who do not belong to the victimized group.

Analyzing the features of the trauma process, trauma scholars have advanced a second, equally controversial claim: the transformation of collective suffering in social trauma is never determined by power alone. When scholars and activists are confronted with the selectivity of the trauma process, when they must recognize that many hideous events fail to command the sympathy they deserve, they often react by adopting the Humpty Dumpty philosophy of history: to determine why certain events trigger indignation while others are considered unfortunate collateral damage is simply a question of power – that is all (Carroll [1871] 2014:364). In the CTP, however, the success of collective memories is never only the outcome of political expediency, nor does it reflect simply the strength of group interests. CTP scholars do not deny that money, political power, and social prestige offer sizeable advantages in the trauma process. They claim, however, that these can never be the only ingredients of the recipe. Trauma claims establish themselves, or fail to, not only on the basis of their capacity to mobilize money and power, but also depending on the quality of the narration itself and the performative skills of its proponents and adversaries.

What's in a definition: establishing cultural trauma as a phenomenon

"Trauma" is currently a popular word. In the vast corpus of texts and journals collected by Google, the word "trauma" has grown in the period 1940–2008 (the last year for which data are available) from 0.0004 percent to 0.0016 percent of the affordances. Such growing popularity, one of many examples of the contemporary psychologization of life, no doubt reflects the heightened sensitivity to human frailty that is part and parcel of the modern cult of the individual. The first effort of CTP scholars, unsurprisingly, has been to define their topic in a way that avoids any psychologizing. They have done so on two fronts. From one side, they have criticized the psychological definition of trauma as objectivist, defined as an external event that inflicts a deep wound to one or more individuals. On the other side, they have claimed that cultural trauma is not an aggregate of individual traumas, but a distinct phenomenon with its own dynamic development.

Jeffrey C. Alexander provided the classical definition of "cultural trauma" in his seminal 2004 chapter on the topic. He stated that

> cultural trauma occurs when members of a collectivity feel they have been subjected to a horrendous event that leaves indelible marks upon their group consciousness, marking their memories forever and changing their future identity in fundamental and irrevocable ways.
>
> *(Alexander 2004:1)*

A related definition is offered, in the very same book, by Neil J. Smelser:

> a memory accepted and publicly given credence by a relevant membership group and evoking an event or situation which is a) laden with negative affect; b) represented as indelible; and c) regarded as threatening a society's existence or violating one or more of its fundamental cultural presuppositions.
>
> *(Smelser 2004:44)*

Both definitions, present themselves as empirically descriptive of a class of phenomena, although with different emphasis. Their carefully phrased wordings, however, were also meant to radically challenge existing scholarship on the subject on at least three counts.

The first, most obvious challenge is that the definition of cultural trauma is focused on collectivities, not individuals (the latter, in fact, appear in it only as members of the former). Cultural traumas have a strong psychological dimension, revealed by the choice of the verb "feel" and by the fact that the mobilization of affect is a necessary dimension of the trauma process (Smelser 2004). CTP scholars, however, claim that social traumas are not generated by individual experiences of evil. On the contrary, it is the existence of a socially shared process of signification that allows individuals to give form to their personal suffering as part of a larger and compelling cultural pattern of societal significance. Neither remembrance nor claim-making is an individual pursuit. Ron Eyerman's seminal work on the memory of slavery in the US is a good example (Eyerman 2001). Slavery is obviously a traumatic experience, and Eyerman stresses its long-lasting consequences on actual behavioral patterns. At the same time, however, he documents how the claim that the historical experience of slavery is the basis of a collective, unified identity – something able to transcend all other cleavages within the emerging African American community – appeared only after the Civil War, when slavery had been abolished. Such collective memory was established by a broad network of intellectuals and professionals who had not been slaves themselves. The construction of this collective memory, and its use as the dominant frame to interpret African Americans' collective experience of US society, was a creative act. It required overcoming the feeling of shame for the degradation endured by ancestors, as well as the resistance of the many people convinced that it was time to forget and "move on." It required forging a narrative that could challenge the dominant view of slaves as hapless persons who had been "liberated" by magnanimous Northern whites, making them instead part of a heroic tale of resistance. However, their narrative achievement was not fixed once and for all. Subsequent generations would reconstruct the narrative, each in its own terms, thus reproducing the feeling of a common past. Although significant within the boundaries of the African American community for most of its history, such collective memory in recent decades has also acquired a wider audience, and a more universal meaning (Eyerman 2001).

The second novelty is a radical break with any naturalistic understanding of trauma as an objective fact. Here the CTP militates not only against the widespread modern tendency to treat evil cognitively – the "shit happens" attitude – but also against the widespread view that questioning the self-evident, factual, nature of evil is both an offense to the victims and a possible apology for the perpetrators. In a world where even those who deny the Holocaust or Soviet crimes are increasingly outspoken, to deny the facticity of evil may easily be construed as an irresponsible attitude. Still, Alexander is adamant in dismantling what he calls the "naturalistic fallacy," the tendency to attribute cultural traumas to actual events and to evaluate the events only in terms of truth criteria (Alexander 2004). Alexander does not deny the obvious importance of historical research and forensic science. His point is rather that narrations, not actual events, are the stuff of which cultural traumas are made. In order to become socially shared, events are to be believed and represented. They need names, contexts, attributions of guilt and presumptions of innocence, heroes and villains. They need symbolic anchors and powerful analogies. The representation of the harmful events requires a specific form of cultural imagination that selects, shapes, and condenses any element of actual experience. To acknowledge this cultural imagination does not imply an "anything goes" attitude. An example will suffice. The early editors of the diaries of Anne Frank chose to downplay in their selections the specific Jewish considerations in her writing, while highlighting her adolescent tribulations. Doing so, they facilitated identification with her tragic fate by non-Jewish readers. Anne Frank became the symbol of a shared wounded humanity. Does their editing imply that her diaries are fabrications? Should schoolchildren be instructed to read only the complete critical edition? It is surely not what any CTP scholar would even consider. The CTP rather sees such an editorial choice as one of many examples of strategic practices that help constitute trauma performances (Alexander 2013). An even more critical exemplar is provided by Ivana Spasic's study of the role played by the 1389 battle of Kosovo in contemporary Serbian debates: strongly felt (and fateful) collective traumas may be quite weak in terms of historical accuracy (Spasic 2011). Should we proclaim such traumas false and forget about them? The anti-naturalist orientation of the CTP is precisely a way to escape the easy debunking mode that still dominates intellectual debates on collective identities (Woods and Debs 2013). CTP scholars want to focus explicitly on the creative dimension implied in any process of collective representation. Historical or forensic research may trigger or feed such efforts at representation – and (hopefully) contribute to weakening its most paranoid variants – but they can never completely replace the autonomy of the socio-emotional process of signification.

The third challenge is thoroughly intertwined with the previous two. CTP scholars criticize attempts, best exemplified by Kai Erikson's cutting-edge work, to provide an account of collective trauma that minimizes the cultural dimension in favor of a strictly social-organizational analysis (Erikson 1976, 1994). In Erikson's work, collective trauma is above all a social trauma, an external blow that shatters the established form of social organization, destroying the bonds between individuals, places, and community. Social destruction long outlasts the individual traumas experienced by the original participants (Erikson 1976). The nature of the blow is critical for Erikson: his main thesis is that natural disasters are increasingly displaced by disasters caused by human action or by human negligence. Whereas the former helped to strengthen social cohesion against a cruel environment, the latter cause further destruction of communitarian bonds among the victims and between them and the wider society. CTP scholars, on the contrary, argue that establishing the nature and causes of the tragic events is not defined by the events themselves but is, rather, the most pressing task of any trauma narrative. The distinction between natural and man-made disasters is discursively constituted and often a matter of contention (Debs 2013; Eyerman 2015). The semantic structures of trauma narratives are analytically independent of social organization.

The cultural trauma process

The core of the CTP is the analysis of the symbolic processes through which suffering – real or perceived – is inscribed with compelling meaning. Following Turner's dramaturgical model, most CTP scholars refer to such process as a "trauma drama." Attempts at establishing such dramatic processes are usually highly contested, with a variety of actors competing both to establish their own narrative and to raise attention of an already taxed audience.

In the seminal works of the CTP, the trauma-drama model was introduced in a rather rudimentary way. In Alexander's original chapter, there are just a few pages highlighting a set of elements of any trauma process (Alexander 2004). The first is a *claim*, made on behalf of a group, that some fundamental injury has occurred. Such claim is advanced by a special kind of *carrier group*, a group or network of agents who have, besides both material and ideal stakes in the process, at least some capacity to produce and circulate meaning in the civil sphere. These carrier groups articulate their claim addressing a wider *audience*, a universe of potential listeners rhetorically described as homogeneous and well-intended, but in reality, often socially fragmented and distracted. The main aim for the carrier group is to project its claim onto the audience – composed by putative members of the victimized groups, sometimes by wider social sectors or even a society – triggering a process of vicarious traumatization. To do so, they must provide a narrative, charged with emotional energy, that addresses at least four issues: the nature of the pain, the nature of the victim, the similarities between the victim and the audience that facilitate identification, and the allocation of responsibility to perpetrators. Finally, there is the *situation*, the set of material, institutional, and symbolic structures that enable and constrain the given trauma process. The successful combination of these elements will determine if, and when, a given claim will become a master narrative, capable of sealing a given interpretation of the event in collective memory.

This rudimentary model has subsequently been expended and refined, as part of the development of a systematic theory of social performance (Alexander, Giesen, and Mast 2006). Trauma dramas have been investigated as performances intended to achieve effective refusion of representation, affect, and widely shared cultural scripts. Such theoretical developments have been matched by a rich wave of case studies. Some of them have highlighted the importance of the frequent "latency phase," in which the events – already felt as traumatic by individuals and groups – still lack any publicly accepted standing. Politically repressed memories in the memory of the Katyn massacres in Communist Poland, for example, may be preserved only in local, family-rooted circles, to be mobilized later, when the context allows (Bartmanski and Eyerman 2011). Others may be represented and memorialized in popular culture, which – given the lower entry barriers – more easily incorporate controversial memories and counternarratives (Hashimoto 2015). Still others may turn out to be traumatic not because of their novelty, but rather because they reproduce an offensive continuity of treatment at a time when the expectation of the group has been changing (Onwuachi-Willig 2016).

A second line of development has revised the list of potential actors performing the drama. Studies have acknowledged that trauma narratives are constructed and circulated by a variety of actors, well beyond the boundaries of movement intellectuals (Degloma 2009). Also, dominant groups, organizations, and even states may promote trauma dramas of their own, backed by well-staged performances, as a way to boost the legitimacy of their actions (Zhukova 2016) and to indict the desired culpable ones (Gao 2015).

The development of CTP research also has brought to light an emerging aspect of the contextual situation of trauma dramas, something that may be defined – paralleling the realist notion of political opportunity structures – as a *cultural opportunity structure*. In a way unappreciated in earlier studies, groups putting forward their claims usually have to enter a fairly crowded arena. There is no scarcity of groups having rightful claims to having been traumatized, and there are competing claims concerning the boundaries of traumatized groups and their proper places in the wider society. Most intractable conflicts are actually characterized precisely by a plurality of groups claiming their suffering is more significant than that of others (Noor et al. 2012).

The interactional interdependence among a plurality of competing trauma dramas is still only vaguely understood (Rothberg 2011). An important step toward such understanding has been made by studies that have stressed how the chances of being heard are contingent upon the fit between a specific grievance and wider and more established narratives. For example, the many horrendous events experienced by the German population during World War II were not, as is widely believed, repressed or silenced. They were, however, effectively marginalized by the compelling pressure to interpret them within the overall frame of a "perpetrator trauma," the guilt of a country that had inflicted endless suffering on millions of innocents. Germans experienced horrendous events that would not, and could not, become cultural traumas in their own right, precisely because they were – and are – shadowed by the foundational memory of the Holocaust (Heins and Langenohl 2011). It is enough to compare Germany with Japan, another defeated nation with a record of heinous war crimes, to realize how dominant discursive configurations sometimes have strongly shaped the possibilities of establishing trauma narratives at various levels of significance (Hashimoto 2015).

Any given cultural opportunity structure also can have a transnational dimension, particularly evident in the adoption by carrier groups across very different locales of scripts and stage props aimed at strengthening analogies with more established and universalized traumas. An example is S-21, the infamous site of the Khmer Rouge security branch, now known as the Tuol Sleng

Genocide museum. The museum, which has played an important role in establishing the traumatic status of the Khmer Rouge massacres, was established in 1980 by local and Vietnamese experts who had visited several Holocaust sites in Eastern Europe and had been trained by their curators in the proper ways of presenting the evidence (Chandler 2000).

Does it matter? The consequence of trauma narratives

CTP scholars claim that trauma dramas are largely independent of both individual experience and historical events. They also claim, consistent with the broader aims of the Strong Program of cultural sociology, that meaning-making exerts an independent causal role in social life. The ways that traumas are constituted and narrated constrains the memories of a variety of collective groups, shaping how they react to challenges and opportunities. What are the consequences for a collectivity of successfully establishing a cultural trauma?

At the origins of the CTP program, a main reason to be interested in cultural traumas was the possibility that its experience could promote an expansion of solidarity within groups and a breakdown of barriers among them. Although the CTP has always been a sociological endeavor, the fact that successful cultural traumas may define the meaning of suffering in a way that allows individuals to share the suffering of others and assume some significant moral responsibility for it was undoubtedly part of its appeal (Alexander 2013:6). Alexander's seminal essay on the meaning of the Holocaust is exemplary in this regard. He chronicled how the mass murder of European Jews was originally coded as just one of many instances of Nazi barbaric atrocities. The acceptance of the Holocaust as a stand-alone trauma played a role in weakening both popular and institutional anti-Semitism in the United States, but only as part of the general, progressive, narrative of the immediate post-war period. Over time, however, its symbolization gradually shifted. The Holocaust became a moral universal, a lesson for all human beings about the nature and ubiquity of evil. In this new form, the Holocaust was capable of traveling well beyond Jewish memories and identities, indeed, well beyond the memory of Nazi evil, marking the memory of many generations and triggering wave after wave of strongly emotional identification and morally compelled actions. By now, the Holocaust has changed the world, contributing to a universalization, albeit uneven and incomplete, of moral and political responsibility (Alexander 2002). Not by chance, in the first edited collection on cultural trauma, all the case studies revealed some form of inclusionary, universalizing logic (Alexander et al. 2004). Cultural trauma could modify understandings about our dangerous world without resurrecting any naïve faith in progress.

In subsequent studies, inclusionary processes of trauma specification have been explored in more detail. A significant study is Tognato's analysis of kidnapping by the Revolutionary Armed Forces of Colombia (FARC or *Fuerzas Armadas Revolucionarias de Colombia*), documenting how – in highly fragmented societies – universalizing tendencies may fail to gain ground, defeated by the lure of competing adversarial interpretations (Tognato 2011). Other studies of traumas have produced a sober assessment of an equally important alternative: a successful cultural trauma may be achieved through a *particularizing* frame, one that defines the identity of the group in an exclusive way. Within such a frame, the trauma becomes an occasion for self-pity as well as a justification for pre-emptive self-defense and reduction of any expectation concerning moral responsibility toward outsiders. A few years after having established a convincing case for the universalizing process of the Holocaust, Alexander explored with equal detail the particularizing role played by Holocaust narratives in Israel (Alexander and Dromi 2011). This sober analysis inevitably triggers a question about which factors, including narrative styles and semiotic structures, may be influential in determining a given outcome or in producing narrative shifts.

Conclusion

CTP scholars have succeeded, in a remarkably short span of time, in establishing a consistent research program about a key feature of contemporary collective life. Through a wealth of (mostly) case studies, CTP scholars have argued in favor of a cultural approach to collective evil, based on radically anti-objectivist premises. Looking for an alternative to both psychological and power-centered explanations of collective memories, they have gradually improved a performative model intended to explain how claims about collective victimhood are constituted, promoted, defeated, transmitted, and fought over. They have also argued that the ways in which such traumas are interpreted and remembered have serious consequences – sometimes benign, sometimes paving the way for intractable conflicts – for the actual life of contemporary society. The CTP is a program of cultural sociology with a certain cumulative development. Over time, the original framework has been enriched and tested on an increasingly diverse set of case studies. As it reaches its maturity, the CTP will face the important challenge of going beyond case studies and toward more systematic comparative research.

References

Alexander, J.C. 2002. "On the Social Construction of Moral Universals: The 'Holocaust' From War Crime to Trauma Drama." *European Journal of Social Theory* 5(1):5–85.

———. 2004. "Toward a Theory of Cultural Trauma." Pp. 1–30 in *Cultural Trauma and Collective Identity*, edited by J.C. Alexander, R. Eyerman, B. Giesen, J.N. Smelsen, and P. Sztompka. Berkeley: University of California Press.

———. 2013. *Trauma: A Social Theory*. New York: John Wiley & Sons.

Alexander, J.C., and S. Dromi. 2011. "Trauma Construction and Moral Restriction: The Ambiguity of the Holocaust for Israel." Pp. 107–32 in *Narrating Trauma*, edited by R. Eyerman, J.C. Alexander, and E.B. Breese. Boulder: Paradigm.

Alexander, J.C., R. Eyerman, B. Giesen, J.N. Smelsen, and P. Sztompka, eds. 2004. *Cultural Trauma and Collective Identity*. Berkeley: University of California Press.

Alexander, J.C., B. Giesen, and J. Mast, eds. 2006. *Social Performance: Symbolic Action, Cultural Pragmatics, and Ritual*. Cambridge: Cambridge University Press.

Andermahr, S. 2015. "Decolonizing Trauma Studies." *Humanities* 4:500–05.

Bar-Tal, D. 2007. "Sociopsychological Foundations of Intractable Conflicts." *American Behavioral Scientist* 50(11):1430–53.

Bar-Tal, D., L. Chernyak-Hai, N. Schori, and A. Gundar. 2009. "A Sense of Self-perceived Collective Victimhood in Intractable Conflicts." *International Review of the Red Cross* 91(874):229–58.

Bartmanski, D., and R. Eyerman. 2011. "The Worst was Silence: The Unfinished Drama of the Katyn Massacre." Pp. 237–66 in *Narrating Trauma*, edited by R. Eyerman, J.C. Alexander, and E.B. Breese. Boulder: Paradigm.

Carroll, L. [1871] 2014. *Through the Looking-Glass, and What Alice Found There*. Oxford: Oxford University Press.

Caruth, C. 1995. *Trauma: Explorations in Memory*. Baltimore, MD: Johns Hopkins University Press.

Chandler, D. 2000. *Voices from S-21: Terror and History in Pol Pot's Secret Prison*. Berkeley: University of California Press.

Debs, M. 2013. "The Suffering of Symbols: Giotto Frescoes and the Cultural Trauma of Objects." *Cultural Sociology* 7(4):479–94.

Degloma, T. 2009. "Expanding Trauma through Space and Time." *Social Psychology Quarterly* 72(2):105–22.

Erikson, K.T. 1976. *Everything In Its Path*. New York: Simon and Schuster.

———. 1994. *A New Species of Trouble: Explorations in Disaster, Trauma, and Community*. New York: W.W. Norton.

Eyerman, R. 2001. *Cultural Trauma: Slavery and the Formation of African American Identity.* Cambridge: Cambridge University Press.

———. 2015. *Is this America?: Katrina as Cultural Trauma.* Austin: University of Texas Press.

Eyerman, R., J.C. Alexander, and E.B. Breese, eds. 2011. *Narrating Trauma: On the Impact of Collective Suffering.* Boulder: Paradigm.

Gao, R. 2015. "The Paradoxes of Solidarity: Cultural Trauma and Collective Identity in Mao's China." *Society: Chinese Journal of Sociology/Shehui* 35(3):108–34.

Hashimoto, A. 2015. *The Long Defeat: Cultural Trauma, Memory, and Identity in Japan.* Oxford: Oxford University Press.

Heins, V., and A. Langenohl. 2011. "A Fire That Doesn't Burn? The Allied Bombing of Germany and the Cultural Politics of Trauma." Pp. 3–26 in *Narrating Trauma*, edited by R. Eyerman, J.C. Alexander, and E.B. Breese. Boulder: Paradigm.

LaCapra, D. 2013. *Writing History, Writing Trauma.* Baltimore, MD: Johns Hopkins University Press.

Noor, M., N. Shnabel, S. Halabi, and A. Nadler. 2012. "When Suffering Begets Suffering." *Personality and Social Psychology Review* 16(4):351–74.

Onwuachi-Willig, A. 2016. "The Trauma of the Routine." *Sociological Theory* 34(4):335–57.

Rothberg, M. 2011. "From Gaza to Warsaw: Mapping Multidirectional Memory." *Criticism* 53(4):523–48.

Smelser, N.J. 2004. "Psychological Trauma and Cultural Trauma." Pp. 31–59 in *Cultural Trauma and Collective Identity*, edited by J.C. Alexander, R. Eyerman, B. Giesen, J.N. Smelsen, and P. Sztompka. Berkeley: University of California Press.

Spasic, I. 2011. "The Trauma of Kosovo in Serbian National Narratives." Pp. 81–106 in *Narrating Trauma*, edited by R. Eyerman, J.C. Alexander, and E.B. Breese. Boulder: Paradigm.

Tognato, C. 2011. "Extending Cultural Trauma Across Cultural Divides: On Kidnapping and Solidarity in Colombia." Pp. 191–212 in *Narrating Trauma*, edited by R. Eyerman, J.C. Alexander, and E.B. Breese. Boulder: Paradigm.

Woods, E.T. 2016. *A Cultural Sociology of Anglican Mission and the Indian Residential Schools in Canada.* London: Palgrave Macmillan.

Woods, E.T., and M. Debs. 2013. "Towards a Cultural Sociology of Nations and Nationalism." *Nations and Nationalism* 19(4):607–14.

Zhukova, E. 2016. "Trauma Management: Chernobyl in Belarus and Ukraine." *British Journal of Sociology* 67(2):195–215.

15

Modern and postmodern

Peter Beilharz

Introduction

What is the modern, and the postmodern? And why does this matter? What was this controversy about? For it was a controversy, and like others, it may have generated more heat than enlightenment. Postmodern versus modern was the key debate in social theory from the 1980s on. In retrospect, it might be seen as a symptom of significant transformations within modernity itself. Likely, it represented the anxiety of our age in that moment, and the need to name it. In an even larger proliferation of ways, we now mostly call this anxiety "globalization," though even the heat has gone out of that, too. What originally concerned us as globalization was loss, which now sometimes has been turned into the hope of "gain," that even the wretched of the poorer parts of the earth will cheer up if they drink up. What was the fuss about?

There was a sense, among intellectuals, anyway, that our world was changing, that there was a sea change, that the old modern ways would no longer do, that if we were still modern, we should choose no longer to be. There was a sense of restlessness, of the need to begin anew. Yet this restlessness is itself also the very spirit of modernity, of the unrelenting search for the new.

The controversy over the idea of the postmodern was clearly about naming, about naming our worlds, and ourselves, and performing this act negatively, against the image of the post-World War II boom, Fordism, suburbia, the one-dimensional society of abundance that grew into the 1960s and kept growing thereafter. Whether the postmodern itself is in any way responsible for this or not, the anxiety has in the meantime often turned into celebration, skepticism into indifference, as the progress-narrative of modernity is enthusiastically embraced throughout the world, not least in China and India. The political category of BRICS (Brazil, Russia, India, China, and South Africa) conceals the fact that it is China and India that are the really revolutionary actors when it comes to modernity today, even if Brazil and South Africa also have serious claims to modernity. The UK after Brexit and the United States under Trump are both bruised or damaged modernities, seeking repair through some kind of protectionism. Here, it is as though those who pioneered Fordism now want it back, or at least miss the advantages of the post-war political economy of Keynesianism. The most conspicuous dynamo of modernity, meanwhile, is China, building cities like Faust out of nothing and nowhere. The permanent revolution of modernity is alive and well, and living in China. What this signals is that the idea of modernization still remains moot. The notion of progress through growth and development has somehow survived unscathed even though the ecological scene has darkened considerably over the last few decades. Meanwhile, the semantics of modernity and modernism, kindred yet not identical, also still survive to extend the conceptual confusion.

Conventionally, modernity is understood as a philosophical or sociological term referring to the idea that we moderns make ourselves, that societies self-constitute their forms, structures, institutions, and relationships. We make our worlds, large and small. And if we do not like the results, we believe we can remake them. Even if we fall easily back on reassurances about evil and human nature, we know that we can do better, that our social arrangements are at least in principle open. Anticipated by humanism, championed by the leading thinkers of the Enlightenment, modernity has been viewed as coming historically closer to us with the Age of Revolutions – Industrial, French, American. Modernity came to mean industrialization, though modernization also means more than that, and modernization theory often presumes that industrialization brings all the other advantages of liberal-democratic development with it (not so).

Modernity also has its dark sides, as we shall see further. Many citizens of the planet are systematically deprived of its material gains through the dialectics of masters and slaves. More, their invisible labors hold the shiny world up. Modernity, to modify Walter Benjamin, is always given to rest on barbarism. It is carried by an underside, whether organized more by capital or by the state, as social engineering par excellence – totalitarianism, colonialism, the favelas of Brazil, or the townships of South Africa.

What, then, is modernism, and where does it live? Modernism is everywhere, as design, architecture, as international style, brutalism, and the fantasy forms that we associate with the work of Frank Gehry (but if you want to see the future of Fantasyland, look at the skyline of Shanghai!). Modernism historically is less often identified as the culture of modernity than as the aesthetic movement that became especially visible around World War I and mainstreamed with more prominence into the 1960s. Associated in writing with Woolf and Joyce; in architecture with Corbusier, international style, and functionalism; in art with Picasso and Dada, modernism has a whole series of later correlates in industry, reflecting standardization and sleek design, from aerodynamic cars to flying refrigerators. Its leading protagonist was not Henry Ford, but Harley Earl, Alfred Sloan's designer at General Motors. Its high point can be best seen in an artist like Warhol, whose work merges avant-garde and mass consumption of repetitive icons. Coca-Cola rules (Gideon 1948; Conrad 1998; Gay 2008), as does Americanism, although the end of the American century and the rise of megacities in Asia and Latin America are now challenging this older hegemony. In itself, this is nothing new. As Trotsky observed a century ago in reference to futurism, modernist cultural energies often peaked in places also characterized by uneven development, such as Russia and the early Soviet Union, and Italy as it first slid into fascism. Modernist aesthetic sensibilities often coincide with modernization, but they are not only caused by modernity. Culture can work in mysterious ways.

The postmodern is usually identified as a reaction against modernism rather than modernity. In architecture, for example, functionalism was replaced by novelty, folly, dual-coding, ornament, and pastiche (Jencks 1996). However, these features might also be viewed as playfully (or earnestly) modernist: Gehry rather than Mies van der Rohe. The postmodern involves an aspect of "up yours!," which results in the wider claim that "anything goes!" Semantically, the postmodern might then be identified as the critical rejection of tradition rather than of modernity; but then there are also earlier movements based on the rejection of modernity, such as romanticism, that complicate all this reception and controversy.

The postmodern also coincides with a Western sense of "being after"; there are many posts, including postindustrialism, postcapitalism, postsocialism, postnationalism, poststructuralism, and postcolonialism. The idea of the critique of progress might more precisely be called post-Enlightenment. But this then begs the question of whether any of us can step out of modernity, especially in the West. To reject the modern may be impossible, not least because modernity is always anyway a mixed form, itself necessarily combining cultures of past, present, and future. And it is always changing. Modernity might be what Habermas called the unfulfilled project because it is unfulfillable: we are always carrying different traditions, some chosen, some inherited (Habermas 1989). Or as Bruno Latour put it, in a different register, we simply never have been thoroughly modern at all (Latour 1993). "Modernity" always necessarily includes the "pre-modern," and the postmodern cannot escape either of these.

Central to all of this, finally, is the idea of the decline or exhaustion of the West. If we do not progress, we decline, or else we are doomed to repetition. Each of the three scenarios is plausible. At best, we understand the world better but no longer claim to know how to better it. Yet the new still continues; innovation and creation persist. The postmodern is – or was – not only a refiguration of romanticism reacting against its own projection of modernity as hard-headed Enlightenment, but it was partly that (Beilharz 1994, 2005; Murphy and Roberts 2004).

This much by way of introduction. In order better to map the controversy, we need to enter the labyrinth of some of its key arguments and sensibilities, here, by visiting the views of some of its more eloquent and central interlocutors: Jean-François Lyotard, Ferenc Fehér and Agnes Heller, Zygmunt Bauman, Fredric Jameson, and David Harvey. In another setting, our authorities might be from elsewhere: from the Global South, as in Mignolo or Canclini, Mbembe or Chakrabarty, or in another setting again, the key motif might be that of alternative modernities, guided by sociologists like Arnason and Wagner. The authorities we use here are European, or Western, but they are also – importantly in the case of Heller and Bauman – Eastern, more precisely East European. For modernities are not only Western, and they are not always shiny.

Where did it all begin, now that the postmodern is supposedly history? Is the postmodern indeed passé, history, or have we just grown weary of that particular debate or set of language games? Whatever the case, we need a text. Lyotard's *Postmodern Condition: A Report on Knowledge* (1984) is as good a place to start as any. The original French edition, commissioned by the Canadian Conseil des Universités de Quebec, was published in 1979 and translated into English in 1984. With the passing of time, its purpose and substance have been forgotten, for it was a report on knowledge and society, explicitly on the knowledge society. Its most famous claim was that the grand narrative of modernity was no longer viable. In this, Lyotard's was another installment in the long history of the critique of Enlightenment. The postmodern era, or attitude, signaled the contemporary incredulity toward metanarrative. Lyotard's target was the kind of project associated with Jürgen Habermas. In Lyotard's gaze, the defense of Enlightenment became the advocacy of Reason and Totalization. Habermas here was the Devil. The critique thus broadly echoed Foucault's critique of Enlightenment as totalitarian. What was overlooked, in its more generalized reception, was the substantive engagement of the book with the question of the status of knowledge in computerized societies. In retrospect, this particular work of Lyotard really extended McLuhan and anticipated the work of Manuel Castells more than that of Foucault. The distinction between modern and postmodern was more like that between traditional and critical theory articulated in the 1940s by Horkheimer. Claims to truth led to totalitarianism; there would henceforth only be little or personal claims to truth. In a fragmented world, truth would also be fragmented.

Lyotard's missile at least implied a clear periodization: modern was then, passé, postmodern now, even if the detail of his case occasionally indicated otherwise. Ferenc Fehér and Agnes Heller put a distinct interpretation upon this separation. As they wrote in *The Postmodern Political Condition* – for Lyotard's title brought echoes – postmodernity is neither a historical period nor a cultural or political trend with well-delineated characteristics. Rather, postmodernity may be understood as the private, collective time and space within the wider time and space of modernity, inhabited by those who have problems with and queries addressed to modernity, who want to take it to task, and by those who make an inventory of modernity's achievements as well as its unresolved dilemmas. Those who have chosen to dwell in postmodernity nevertheless live among moderns as well as premoderns. For the very foundation of postmodernity consists of viewing the world as a plurality of heterogenous spaces and temporalities. Postmodernity can only define itself within this plurality, against these heterogeneous others (Fehér and Heller 1988:1).

The issue opened up, or named, so to say, by Lyotard, had become a space or field, and the postmodern was by this move more fully to be contemplated as a way of thinking about the present. For postmoderns, anything goes. For Fehér and Heller, this told against Europe, and not only against modernity or tradition. Europe risked becoming a museum. The profound sense was one of "being after" – after history, after the modern, after Europe (Fehér and Heller 1988:2–3). The postmodern in this optic was therefore profoundly aesthetic and cultural, but it had other coordinates as well. Politically, it was often self-styled as the avant-garde, but that stylization itself exuded a strong modernist resonance. As Fehér and Heller had argued earlier, modernity was characterized by three logics, often operating in tension – capitalism, industrialization, and democracy (Fehér and Heller 1983). Technology, science, and economy were also crucial (Heller 1999). The postmodern was not narrowly cultural, or to be read in culturalist terms alone, except in the broader sense that everything is culturally constituted. Postmodernity, in every regard, was parasitic on these dilemmas and achievements of modernity. Its culture fed back off high-modern forms and then rebelled against some in particular, as say against uniform international style in architecture. But its politics could also look plainly romantic, Dada, in your face, the antimodern reacting against modernism within modernity itself.

For Fehér and Heller, then, the postmodern matters because of its impact on the lifeworld: it is a kind of counterculture in modernity. Zygmunt Bauman has also been given to the image of the counterculture, though historically he associates this with socialism as a current within modernity (Bauman 1976; Beilharz 2000, 2009). Bauman's most significant early intervention on the postmodern was *Legislators and Interpreters: On Modernity, Post-Modernity, and Intellectuals* (1987). It is the last term that is most telling here, for Bauman initially viewed the postmodern as an intellectual rather than popular ambit. The title also indicates the shift: the transition from legislators to interpreters as the dominant ideal type of intellectual coincides with the shift of intellectual focus from government to hermeneutics, from control to interpretation, from the avant-garde to the critic, or as Bauman frames it, from gardeners back to gamekeepers. Bauman's book therefore includes the critique of modernity as a social engineering project, where the postmodern offers the implicit promise of something gentler. Modern intellectuals desire to control cultural matters, taste, morality: they are the secular priests, *les philosophes*. The postmodern heralds the promise of what comes after. Is this progress, for Bauman? The answer is both positive and yet somehow non-committal, wait and see. Bauman already indicates his reservations regarding the seductive and regressive powers of postmodern culture, which after all is mediated by consumerism. He indicates his own deep ambivalence about the postmodern phenomenon by closing *Legislators and Interpreters* with two conclusions, one modern, one postmodern; one, so to say, with Habermas, one with Rorty; one with judgment, one with relativism.

Bauman's *Legislators and Interpreters* is also a shadow critique of communism, specifically of Bolshevism as Enlightenment (Beilharz 2000). For modernity and modernism are not only Western European or American forms; every place has its own modernity, from Melbourne to Montevideo, and Soviet-type societies also have a modern story to tell (Smith 1997, 2007).

Indeed, the Soviets and Nazis in some ways outperform all others at high modernity, where the state drives developmental patterns of destruction to the brink of extinction. And this should give us pause, for we need to face the abyss. We need to look not only into the dark side of the shiny face of modernity in Manhattan or Paris, to recognize the faces of the others who make these modern or postmodern cities work, who clean them and stock their shelves while we sleep safely. We also need, with Heller and Bauman, to look into the dark side of those modernities in Nazi Germany and in Soviet-type societies, those that were never democratic but decidedly modern in their will to power, their will to industrialize and develop at all human and natural costs. And we will need also to give countenance to the idea that even such abhorrent regimes as apartheid were also clearly modern in their technologies and racialized utopian projects. Apartheid, like Stalinism and Nazism, was a built form, a geographic and architectural project.

After Bauman, we can no longer avoid the hinge that connects modernity and the Holocaust. Yet the collapse of the Soviet Union also compels us to face the possibility that modernity can exist after modernism, ergo, as postmodern. Bauman's later writings, after 1989, open up onto the multiplicity of postmodern forms. In *Intimations of Postmodernity*, the postmodern is viewed as the mixing of styles and genres, or as a state of mind. It is self-critical, or critical at least, but at the same time, "anything goes." Yet the postmodern also offers the possibility of re-enchantment. The postmodern might also be global, or postnational; yet in these possibilities it nevertheless constitutes a development of modernity (Bauman 1992:65, 187). As most critics in the field agree, the postmodern also corresponds with a series of other "afters," "ends," or posts – postindustrial, postcapitalist, later, posttraditional. Yet it remains, for Bauman, primarily an intellectual phenomenon: it throws light on intellectuals, and also on ethics. Thus, his subsequent works include *Postmodern Ethics* (1994) and *Postmodernity and Its Discontents* (1997), and across these the inflection shifts, as the emancipatory promise of the postmodern disappears into the shopping malls. Freedom becomes a consumer good. The postmodern mind is tolerant, but then again, everything goes, including poverty and exploitation. Surplus tolerance leads to shared indifference.

For Bauman, as a sociologist, the postmodern is an inescapable phenomenon: whether it is superficial or deep, it is a presence, and therefore begs for interpretation. Nevertheless, Bauman makes his preference clear when he distinguishes between two different projects – a postmodern sociology and a sociology of postmodernity (Bauman 1989). Bauman is a lifelong critic of modernity and postmodernity, not a celebrant of its forms or practices. Yet at the same time we are all part of these phenomena. Something like a sense of postmodern fatigue perhaps eventually leads Bauman to coin a new term, "liquid modernity," this in contrast to the high, solid modernism of the post-war period. The analytical tension suggested by the postmodern nevertheless remains.

Two further approaches bring together culture and political economy, in exhaustive Western scope: these are the work of Fred Jameson and of David Harvey, both of whom reinstall Marx as a central figure for the postmodern, which just goes to show how modern we still are.

Jameson's central work here is *Postmodernism, or, The Cultural Logic of Late Capitalism* (1991), built upon his pioneering *New Left Review* essay of 1984. The table of contents of the book indicates the ambition of the survey: it covers culture, ideology, video, architecture, sentences, space, theory, economy, and film. Jameson's broad sensibilities are in sympathy with others scanned here: it is safest to grasp the concept of the postmodern as an attempt to think the present historically in an age that has forgotten how to think historically (Jameson 1991:ix), that is to say, as a present of the present which has forgotten pasts and is blind to the possibility of other futures, or utopias. High commodification, here, is timeless: everything can be exchanged for everything else, as in Marx's critique, which means that at a certain level of abstraction everything becomes leveled, qualitatively indistinguishable. Thus, Jameson does seek to periodize the modern and postmodern, but only notionally, in terms of correspondences. He summons the idea of late capitalism, via the thinkers of the Frankfurt School and the Belgian Trotskyist Ernest Mandel, to argue this centrality of periodization. "Late," here, works with "post"; "post" is primarily aesthetic, but late capitalism involves the expansion of the aesthetic and visual. Van Gogh, Magritte, and Corbusier are central actors in this story, but especially Warhol, where standardization includes the aesthetic commodity – image and not only the old commodity – form. Post-functional architecture, notoriously Portman's Westin Bonaventure Hotel in Los Angeles, offers fully playful and willful expressions of this wave. As Jameson puts it in conclusion, the postmodern is primarily based in visual culture, wired for sound (1991:299). Yet this cultural revolution is also homogenized and always "new." This is the acme of modernization's attack on nature (Jameson 1991:310–11).

David Harvey works in a similar register to Jameson, even if the entry point is in political economy rather than culture. The title of Harvey's study, like that of Fehér and Heller, echoes back to Lyotard: Harvey's variation is *The Condition of Postmodernity* (1989). Harvey begins with the sense of sea change in political economy from around 1972. The new capitalism brings with it postmodern culture and a further wave of the space-time compression that Marx used to characterize capitalism's ongoing revolutions. The organizational focus in Harvey's work is the city, here, the postmodern city. Where Jameson tends to feature L.A., Harvey's city at this point is Baltimore. His frame of reference is also Marxian, but it is less flavored by the Frankfurt School and more given to the frame provided by Marshall Berman in *All That Is Solid Melts Into Air* (1984). From Baudelaire to Berman, this frame centers on aesthetics but also on the revolution in everyday life – the experience of modernity and modernism on the street. Like Jameson, Harvey views the postmodern as the latest wave of the modernization process, which he connects to Schumpeter's idea of creative destruction, the emphasis here more heavily on noun than adjective (Harvey 1989:106). The result is influenced by Berman, but considerably less celebrative of the dizzying success of modernism or what follows. Rather than euphoria on the street, the core of modernism for Harvey is Fordism in factory and home (1989:ch. 8). Fordism develops as a total way of life, based on mass production, mass consumption, and standardization. What follows is "flexible accumulation" and postmodern culture. Culture and economy, aesthetic and technological form, here combine into one.

So what's new in all this? Little, and yet so much. This is the world anticipated more than a century ago by Marx, Weber, and Simmel, where time accelerates and space contracts, where the world ossifies, culture becomes hard as soon as it emerges, and yet it also seems that all that is solid melts into air. We no longer have a sense of foundations from which to work or to judge, and yet we go on: we rely on a daily sense that everyday life is a matter of business, or busyness, as usual. Marx, Weber, and Simmel are all rediscovered or reinvented in the postmodern debate; this may be its most positive effect for the traditions of classical social theory. Durkheim, in turn, is called out again as we reconsider the extent to which (postmodern) cultures make or remake (modern) society or economy. More broadly, in terms of a sociology of everyday life or of cultural sociology in general, the great impact of the postmodern is to force the reconsideration of the root term and the broader horizons of modernity itself.

Even if the idea of the postmodern now falls into disuse, its function as a thought experiment has been to challenge moderns to reconsider the very idea of being modern at all. Even if the postmodern moves were often petulant, their results have been productive. To be postmodern, we need to embrace modernity in all its difference, diversity, and ambivalence. To be post, we first of all need to be modern. If there is nothing outside or beyond modernity, there are evidently different ways of being modern, more industrial or not, more democratic or less. The process of self-reflection and critique continues.

Peter Beilharz

References

Bauman, Z. 1976. *Socialism: The Active Utopia*. London: Allen and Unwin.

———. 1987. *Legislators and Interpreters: On Modernity, Post-modernity and Intellectuals*. Oxford: Polity Press.

———. 1989. "Sociological Responses to Postmodernity." *Thesis Eleven* 23:35–63.

———. 1992. *Intimations of Postmodernity*. London: Routledge.

———. 1994. *Postmodern Ethics*. Oxford: Polity Press.

———. 1997. *Postmodernity and its Discontents*. Oxford: Polity Press.

Beilharz, P. 1994. *Postmodern Socialism: Romanticism, City and State*. Melbourne: Melbourne University Press.

———. 2000. *Zygmunt Bauman: Dialectic of Modernity*. London: Sage.

———. 2005. "Postmodern Socialism Revisited." In *Confronting Globalization*, edited by P. Hayden and C. Ojeili. London: Palgrave Macmillan.

———. 2009. *Socialism and Modernity*. Minneapolis: University of Minnesota Press.

Berman, M. 1984. *All That is Solid Melts into Air*. New York: Simon and Schuster.

Conrad, P. 1998. *Modern Times, Modern Places*. London: Thames & Hudson.

Fehér, F. and A. Heller. 1983. "Class, Democracy, Modernity." *Theory and Society* 12:211–44.

———. 1988. *The Postmodern Political Condition*. Cambridge: Polity Press.

Gay, P. 2008. *Modernism: The Lure of Heresy from Baudelaire to Beckett and Beyond*. New York: Norton.

Gideon, S. 1948. *Mechanization Takes Command*. New York: Oxford University Press.

Habermas, J. 1989. *The Philosophical Discourse of Modernity*. Cambridge: Polity Press.

Harvey, D. 1989. *The Condition of Postmodernity*. Oxford: Blackwell.

Heller, A. 1999. *A Theory of Modernity*. Oxford: Blackwell.

Jameson, F. 1991. *Postmodernism, or, the Cultural Logic of Late Capitalism*. London: Verso.

Jencks, C. 1996. *What is Postmodernism?* London: Academy.

Latour, B. 1993. *We Have Never Been Modern*. Cambridge, MA: Harvard University Press.

Lyotard, J.F. 1984. *The Postmodern Condition: A Report on Knowledge*. Minneapolis: University of Minnesota Press.

Murphy, P. and D. Roberts. 2004. *Dialectic of Romanticism*. New York: Continuum.

Smith, B. 1997. *Modernism's History*. New Haven, CT: Yale University Press.

———. 2007. *The Formalesque*. Melbourne: Macmillan.

16

Social aesthetics

Ben Highmore

Introduction

In his book *The Comfort of Things* the cultural anthropologist Daniel Miller presents 30 portraits of individuals and their relationship to the things they possess (and, as he will suggest, possess them). He writes:

> There is an overall logic to the pattern of these relationships to both persons and things, for which I use the term "aesthetic." By choosing this term I don't mean anything technical or artistic, and certainly nothing pretentious. It simply helps convey something of the overall desire for harmony, order and balance that may be discerned in certain cases – and also dissonance, contradiction and irony in others.
>
> *(Miller 2008:5)*

Miller wants to use the term "aesthetic" to describe his informants' intimate material worlds, but as soon as he does so, he energetically distances himself from the connotations of artiness and connoisseurship that often accompanies the term "aesthetic." The story I tell here about aesthetics will need to do its share of distancing too, and although such pedantic positioning may appear overly fussy, it is a necessary result of the history of aesthetics in intellectual thought.

But why does Miller choose the term "aesthetic"? What would be wrong with "style" or "lifestyle" to describe the pattern of our relations with the world of things? My guess is that, for Miller, "lifestyle" has become too easily associated with a one-dimensional critique of consumer capitalism, where material culture is merely a way of showcasing status and prestige. Aesthetics on the other hand suggests sensual contact with things; bodies perceiving themselves and other bodies; a world thick with emotion and sentiment. This gives the term "aesthetic" a lively visceral sense, distinct from the stifling snobbery of aesthetes. It is this corporeal sense of the term, addressed to sensual perception and registering emotional intensities, that will make it useful to the sociologically informed study of culture. For social aesthetics, matter matters, and rationality and reason have to play second fiddle to sensation, affect, and perception. But before I offer examples of the productivity of social aesthetics, it is worth addressing the historical roots of the term "aesthetics" and the various paths this term has taken.

Historical roots and routes

From the mid-eighteenth century the term "aesthetics" wavers between a limited conception concerned with beauty, taste, and art and an extended view more concerned with the everyday perception of the sensual, phenomenal world. If the former is driven by a desire to judge and appreciate, the latter is oriented to more general descriptive exploration. Writing in 1750, Alexander Baumgarten, who is usually acknowledged as coining the term "aesthetics," describes it as the "science of sensual cognition" (Baumgarten cited in Hammermeister 2002:7). From the start, aesthetics poses a problem: if we typically use the term "cognition" to describe our dealings in the ideational world of thoughts and concepts, should we talk about "cognition" when we are dealing with the world of emotions and sensations? Baumgarten's insistence on the word cognition here is in keeping with his overall intention. For Baumgarten, our sensual "knowledge" of the world is neither to be trusted nor to be championed: "impressions received from the senses, fantasies, emotional disturbances, etc. are unworthy of philosophers and beneath the scope of their consideration" (Baumgarten [1998] 1750:490). In this, he sets the tone for numerous accounts of aesthetic knowledge, recognizing that the world we live in is experienced sensually and passionately but that this sensual engagement is often "base" and creaturely. The aesthetic task is not simply to explore the sensual realm but to transform it, to rescue it from its mere sensual form and to set it on a par with the higher purpose of reason. And it is here that poetry, theater, novels, sculptures, or painting can work their magic – by transcending ordinary life and realizing the beauty of order and sensitive taste.

The sociological potential of aesthetics (its potential to attend to the full range of sensual experience) was effectively quashed by an overriding concern among philosophers and social commentators (from the mid- to late eighteenth century onwards) to concentrate on polite sensitivity and the categories of the beautiful and sublime. Other forms of sensual experience – for instance, finding something unnerving, or being confused and anxious, or enjoying the comfort and familiarity of things, or finding something contemptible, and so on – simply got left out of the picture. While the business of tasteful discrimination continued into the twentieth century, it was by then more obviously in conflict with a social paradox: on the one hand, philosophical attention to taste had sought to establish immutable laws for beauty; on the other hand, commercial culture and commodity exchange were also in the business of producing taste and had to establish beauty as something profoundly mutable in order to generate endless cycles of new commodities. As Jean Epstein wrote, "One talks of the eternal canons of beauty when two successive catalogues of the Bon Marché [a Parisian department store] confound this drivel" (Epstein cited in Marcus 2007:2).

The understanding of aesthetics as a form of art theory or as a labyrinthine discussion of "the beautiful" and "the sublime," have been challenged by a much more generous understanding of what might count for aesthetic study. In 1884, in his essay "What Is an Emotion?," the philosopher and psychologist William James described "the aesthetic sphere of the mind" as the mind's "longings, pleasures and pains, and its emotions" (James 1884:188). Such a perspective connects to Baumgarten's original meaning for the term, but without the desire to rescue this sphere from our creaturely habits and desires. For James, the aesthetic sphere is the arena of our most visceral forms of life, our most insistently human domains; the task is not to transcend it but to explore it as our empirical reality. Here James reconnects us to a moment prior to Baumgarten's coinage where philosophers talked about "the passions," and included within this sphere the whole gamut of sense impressions and emotional reactions that would later be parceled out into discrete enclaves of aesthetics, psychology, ethics, and so on.

The first fully sociological use of the term aesthetics likely appears in the work of Georg Simmel. His essay "Soziologische Aesthetik" of 1896 heralds an approach to the social that is attentive to the felt experience of social actors, attuned to the surface phenomena of culture (to be found in clothing and eating etiquette as much as, if not more than, in elite culture), and expressly concerned with new forms of social life (Simmel). Simmel's interest is in the formal aspects of culture, in the ways that social life is patterned. Simmel doesn't ignore an interest in beauty, rather our appreciation of certain formal shapes and arrangements is central to our ability to understand the world. Privileging symmetry and contrasts, for instance, would determine (and be detrimental to) our understanding of the web-like complexity of modern life. Part of the task of sociology, in its social aesthetic role, is to appreciate new and more complex patterns: "the more we learn to appreciate composite forms, the more readily we will extend aesthetic categories to forms of society as a whole" (Simmel [1968] 1896:74).

In recent years, the work of the French philosopher Jacques Rancière has given new impetus to an understanding of aesthetics that crosses between the sensual and affective orchestration of material life and the cultural forms we use to apprehend and manage material life. Rancière uses the phrase "the distribution of the sensible" (*le partage du sensible*) to describe this movement: the distribution of the sensible is

> the system of *a priori* forms determining what presents itself to sense experience. It is a delimitation of spaces and times, of the visible and the invisible, of speech and noise, that simultaneously determines the place and stakes of politics as a form of experience.
>
> *(Rancière 2004:13)*

Rancière's aesthetic thought is clearly political (what is and isn't perceivable matters socially), but it also transcends the distinction between an experience of sensorial life and the cultural forms (novels, films, diaries, and so on) that are used to explain and describe such experience. The "distribution of the sensible" would include within its orbit the parceling out of the social world undertaken by, for instance, a realist novel, a school building, and a dietary practice. In this way novels as much as herbs and spices "flavor" our world, arranging it in sensorial ways.

The political and sociological orientation of Rancière's aesthetics points to a major accomplishment of social aesthetics: the ability to overcome the separation of (human) subjects and (inhuman) objects because it purposefully privileges practices, processes, and interconnections. For Rancière, the social subject is constituted in a world patterned by arrangements of sensual and sensorial possibilities and impossibilities, and this arrangement is produced by human and non-human actions. Given that our societies (for all their differences) are structured unevenly (in terms of class, for instance, or gender), a radical social aesthetic perspective would see this structuring as a product of aesthetic arrangements rather than seeing aesthetic arrangements as a product of a structuring that might be explained by, for instance, economics. In this, social aesthetics doesn't attempt to demote the importance of the distribution of wealth, but to insist that economic factors always takes sensual, material forms and that these forms are aesthetic.

Such a short sketch of some of the roots and routes that the term aesthetics has taken cannot expect to do justice to the many nuanced arguments that have been conducted in its name. One thing, though, seems obvious: social aesthetics simply can't capitulate to the limitations imposed on aesthetics by those whose main task is to protect the sanctity of "art." This is not to say that art isn't important for social aesthetics – far from it – but rather than aesthetics signaling the autonomous value of art, the flag of social aesthetics is raised in order to insist on the deeply embedded connections between artworks and creaturely, material life. Indeed, it could be argued that social aesthetics places a higher value on art by seeing it as a generative agent in the orchestration of the sensorial. Social aesthetics has a promiscuous interest in all sorts of manifestations – artworks, travel guides, furniture showrooms, plumbing, legal documents, and on and on and on. What keeps it focused is its overriding interest in the "distribution of the sensible," the profoundly social and material work of patterning culture. But let me move away from these abstract discussions to offer some more concrete examples of the productivity, problems, and potential of social aesthetics.

Aesthetic attunements and modernization

Social thinkers following in the wake of Simmel have been increasingly attentive to what we can describe as the aesthetic aspect of the endless revolutionizing of daily life brought about by industrialization and its attendant social forms. In Simmel's day (the turn of the nineteenth to the twentieth century) important aesthetic changes might be recognized in the increase in motorized traffic in Berlin and the way that financial exchanges were becoming the predominant form of social communication. Since then, sociologically minded writers have drawn attention to shopping, cinema, fashion, music, and restaurants as crucial elements of a modern urban experience (see Charney and Schwartz 1996 for a set of examples). In a series of social and cultural historical books, the socio-cultural historian Wolfgang Schivelbusch represents the modern period (from the early eighteenth century onwards) as a particular set of aesthetic forces that works on our perceptions, our sensual environment, and our tastes, to perform what he calls the "industrialisation of the senses" (1977, 1988, 1993). Schivelbusch's historical work demonstrates how aesthetics does not have to refer to a value (beauty or sublimity, for instance) but can draw attention to our sensorial insertion in a world that is constantly altering what we see and hear, and how we see and hear it, as well as constantly orchestrating who it is that gets to be seen and heard.

Today we could name three arenas that are particularly important for those interested in social aesthetics: urban space, the home, and the digital, online world. Social aesthetics often goes by the name of "design" where urban space is concerned. The political and moral concerns of "good urban design" might include encouraging "beautiful forms," but it would be a particularly decadent administration if this were the sole intention of urban designers. More pertinently, then, urbanists have to think of how political and moral aims (for instance, equality of access, safe urban space, a fair distribution of resources) can find material-sensual forms in urban practices and policies (Tonkiss 2013). Urbanists are also attentive to the way that urban processes, particularly the uneven development of urban space demonstrated by the production of gentrified and ghettoized spaces, always have an aesthetic aspect and are articulated in such phenomena as variations in graffiti, distinctive eating establishments, and a hierarchical distribution of shopping outlets (Thompson 2015). Urban space (metropolitan and suburban) makes aesthetic work legible through the production, distribution, and consumption of cultural forms that shapes our experiences of race, gender and sexuality, and identity in general (Tongson 2011).

The home is a favorite site of analysis because it can rightly be seen as a privileged space of "ordinary aesthetics." We furnish our homes (within our means) with items we find attractive rather than ones we dislike. At home, we are constantly making aesthetic decisions: what to wear, what to watch, what to eat, and so on. And those aesthetic decisions are freighted with cultural meanings to do with the past, present, and future (Hurdley 2013). Home is the focus of an enormous amount of commercial energy that is clearly aesthetic in form: a large part of our media is dedicated to encouraging us to spend more and more money on our homes, so that we can acquire the accouterments for the "good life" (Allon 2008). Home is a space where ideas and practices around privacy, intimacy, gender, individuality, family, sex, age, and so forth have taken on particular sensual and material forms as they have been reconfigured over the decades (Highmore 2014).

Today, home can be a place for shopping, working, gambling, dating, trading, voting, and banking. At the same time, when we are out in public or traveling, we can be involved in exactly these same practices while taking elements of our "home" with us (photograph albums, music collections, media consumption, cookery books, and so on). Clearly the exponential growth of "online" life (and the ubiquity of this condition, for many in the industrial North, is making it more and more redundant to talk about it as a *particular* condition) is the latest installment in the endless revolutionizing of everyday life that has always fascinated social aestheticians. The world of digital communication and storage systems is radically altering a whole array of social values and behaviors, changing how we communicate, how we experience public and private space, and how we sustain our relationships. One way that social aesthetics has made a particularly valuable contribution to the study of digital mobile culture has been to treat it as a way of tuning and retuning the world around us, of seeing our digital devices as part of an ensemble of mood and emotion management tools (Bull 2007; Coyne 2010, 2016). Aesthetics, while it is often concerned with the micro scale of personal experience, can also be alert to much larger "distributions of the sensible."

Globalism in an aesthetic key

While some social and cultural theorists might see globalization as a recent phenomenon, it is at least as old as Columbus's voyage across the Atlantic in 1492. While there had been invasions and cultural appropriations prior to 1492, Columbus's voyage marked a new age of global power, one that has done much to constitute our contemporary world. We can glimpse the extent of this longer history of globalization by looking at the spread of languages: the global languages (primarily English, Spanish, and French, but also to a lesser degree Portuguese and Dutch) are the languages of the colonizers. If language is sensual and sensorial consciousness, then the oral and aural texture of the modern world has been indelibly stamped with the aesthetics of colonialism to a very basic degree.

The sensual landscapes of global modernity have been marked by the comings and goings of people and things. In the United Kingdom, for instance, every village, town, and city has a selection of Indian restaurants in its main street. The aesthetic registers of smell and taste within the UK have been shaped by Indian food, to the point where the unofficial English football anthem is named after the Goan dish Vindaloo. Following the sensual journey of this particularly spicy dish is to witness the aesthetic globalizing effects of colonialism and its neocolonial persistence. Vindaloo combines the Portuguese taste for pork (the Portuguese colonized this part of India) with the spicing practices of local Goans. Yet what characterizes this dish, and many of the most globally well-known Indian dishes, is its use of chillies. And it was the Portuguese that introduced chillies into India when they transported them from South America (Collingham 2005). Yet, once designed, vindaloo doesn't remain unchanged as it moves around the globe, but takes on new textures and flavors as it textures and flavors in turn. This is not to privilege the agency of the chilli over the practices of the cooks or the reception of eaters, but to claim that the experience of Vindaloo consumption in specific geographical and historical circumstances will always be a complex amalgam of sensual and symbolic social arrangements. Vindaloo cannot be adequately described or explained by recourse to socially symbolic values (for instance, its association with male, white "lad" culture in Britain) without also recognizing the intense sensual effects and affects of its consumption (see Highmore 2008).

If aesthetics is, after Baumgarten, sensual cognition, then the flavors, sounds, and smells of everyday life should be social aesthetics' first port of call. Academic work on food culture usually only explicitly employs aesthetics when it wants to make claims for the culinary excellence of a certain cuisine, or more often, of a highly select group of chefs. But social aesthetics should insist that elevating the ordinary to the level of "art" is a pointless game, and could instead respond by treating all sensual material as both worldly and singular. Social aesthetics is a form of close attention (to the specificity of things, to their phenomenal form) as well as a way of connecting specific things to lively worlds of other things and bodies. Elspeth Probyn's *Carnal Appetites* (2000) and her recent *Eating the Ocean* (2017) are exemplary instances of social aesthetics as they move between localized bodies eating specific foods and patterns of economic and social power. Here, eating is never a solitary act but materially connects to social and political realms. For social aesthetics the "food chain" (in all its human, animal, industrial, chemical, and geographical complexity) is a materializing instance of what it means to be embodied. For Probyn, Pierre Bourdieu's theorizing of the way that social practices are unnervingly regular even when they seem to be most spontaneous and improvised is a compelling intellectual resource. In her books the symbolic world of culture is made deeply physical and sensual through analytic descriptions that constantly move from actual sexed and gendered bodies savoring flavors or turning their noses up, to the material actuality of the larger patterns of food exchange and production (which also includes the production of ideas about food).

Philosophers and cultural critics frustrated at the limitations of traditional aesthetics to consider sensual formations that don't concentrate on the beautiful and the sublime suggest that we focus on more "minor" aesthetic forms. Sianne Ngai (2005, 2012), for instance, has suggested that privileging emotions like irritation and envy and cultural forms like the cute and the zany will provide a better understanding of our present times than maintaining a focus on strong feelings like anger and love, and formal values like ugliness and beauty. In this she draws upon the philosopher J.L. Austin, who sees ordinary life as providing wonderful opportunities for the study of language and suggests that it might also inspire the study of aesthetics "if only we could forget for a while about the beautiful and get down instead to the dainty and the dumpy" (Austin cited in Ngai 2012:53).

Globalizing culture is constantly being refashioned and reshaped, and in recent decades we have witnessed a trend manifesting from Japan, as well as from South Korea and East Asia more generally, that has been dubbed "globalized cute" (Dale et al. 2017). Cultural icons like Pokémon, Hello Kitty, Digimon, and Yu-Gi-Oh have spread across the globe via billions of trading cards, TV cartoons, computer games, brand identifiers, lunch boxes, stickers, toys, internet sites, clothing, bags, and so on. With bright, round eyes and fairytale landscapes, these figures offer an image of smiling lovability and easygoingness in a world organized around complex and rigid rules. Their amazing success has created a transnational Japan that both maintains aspects of national culture while also transforming it (there is a distinct lack of ethnic specificity in any of the brands). For social aesthetics, the emergence of "global cute" could be seen as both a softening of the phenomenal world and a hardening of its structuring abilities (for instance, the ability to instill "cute" docility as an aspect of girlhood). We recalibrate aesthetics by attending to different kinds of objects (traffic rather than theater, say), and we reorchestrate a sense of the world (albeit discursively) when we change our aesthetic categories (cute gives us a different orientation to the geographical world than beauty).

Conclusion and future possibilities

In 1928, Mikhail Bakhtin and Pavel Medvedev declared that "it is necessary to overcome once and for all the naïve apprehension that the qualitative uniqueness of, say, art, could suddenly turn out to be something other than sociological" (Bakhtin and Medvedev [1928] 1985:6). This suggests that socially orientated approaches to cultural objects like artworks need to be inoculated (from the start) against any transcendental understanding of aesthetics. This is the negative cargo of social aesthetics. The exploration of the cultural conditions of transcendental aesthetics is not without merit, though, and has produced some major contributions to sociological inquiry (for instance, Becker [1982] 2000). The less visible, positive challenge is for social aesthetics to apprehend the "qualitative uniqueness" of not just artworks but also cooking, gardening, media, furniture, business cultures, bureaucracies, and so on, *sociologically*. This means, I think, treating such cultural forms as agents of social life rather than mediated reflections of it; it means always asking how such forms distribute the sensible and what effects and affects such distribution has; it means looking at the feelings, moods, and modes that these forms generate. To give a concrete example, it means not simply recognizing that for a white racist, a plate of Bangladeshi food has a different meaning than it does for a Bangladeshi cook; it also means acknowledging that it will actually taste different – it will hit the taste buds differently, settle in the stomach in different ways, and so on. This is to recognize the sociality of our bodies and how our racial orientations are simultaneously ideational and embodied. It is at this concrete level of experience that the real potential of social aesthetics can be found, and its sociological power will not be guaranteed by treating food, for instance, as another marker of prestige or status but rather by generating sociological accounts of the qualitative uniqueness of food as a cultural phenomenon that circulates in phenomenologically different ways than furniture or films. At present, although there is a mass of sociological literature focused on aspects of sensual and sensorial life, there are few books that are aesthetically oriented to the social distribution of sensual and sensorial culture (examples like Probyn's work are a rarity).

Alongside providing analytic description, scholars of social aesthetics might consider their potential as cultural activists in producing new "distributions of the sensible." If aesthetics has always reflected on beauty, then the role of social aesthetics might necessitate involvement in the active transformation of beauty. If beauty can be seen as the materialization of pleasure, then the displeasure invoked by the "not-beautiful" is of huge social and political significance. For example, in an age where we are edging ever closer to environmental catastrophe, any aesthetic dispensation that automatically favors obsessive cleanliness and what is brand-spanking-new over what is worn, crumpled, and chipped will have serious long-term consequences. The social aesthetic challenge that climate change poses is to find new pleasures in the old, in refuse, and in the reused, and to find (perhaps more importantly) displeasure in the conspicuous waste of so much consumer culture (Hawkins 2006; Hawkins, Potter, and Race 2015).

But it would be a mistake to limit social aesthetics to a discourse of beauty (the central focus of traditional aesthetics), even if radically reconfigured. Social aesthetics must shape our understanding of worth and value more generally. One of the most important accomplishments of social movement activity over the past 60 years was to put inequalities (of race, class, gender, sexuality, etc.) at center stage, to call attention to the social, cultural, and economic forces, both structural and interpersonal, that sustained patriarchy, white privilege, and other forms of oppression. This required reconceptualizing the "value" of marginalized groups in order to redistribute power. Social aesthetics was fundamental to this effort, although it was never named as such.

References

Allon, Fiona. 2008. *Renovation Nation: Our Obsession with Home*. Sydney: New South.

Bakhtin, Mikhail, and Pavel Medvedev. [1928] 1985. *The Formal Method in Literary Scholarship: A Critical Introduction to Sociological Poetics*, trans. Albert J. Wehrle. Cambridge, MA: Harvard University Press.

Baumgarten, Alexander. [1750] 1998. "Prolegomena" [to *Aesthetica*]. Pp. 489–91 in *Art in Theory, 1648–1815: An Anthology of Changing Ideas*, edited by C. Harrison, P. Wood, and J. Gaiger. Blackwell: Oxford.

Becker, Howard S. [1982] 2008. *Art Worlds*. Berkeley: University of California Press.

Bull, Michael. 2007. *Sound Moves: iPod Culture and Urban Experience*. Abingdon: Routledge.

Charney, Leo, and Vanessa R. Schwartz, eds. 1996. *Cinema and the Invention of Modern Life Paperback*. Los Angeles: University of California Press.

Collingham, Lizzie. 2005. *Curry: A Biography*. London: Chatto and Windus.

Coyne, Richard. 2010. *The Tuning of Place: Sociable Spaces and Pervasive Digital Media*. Cambridge, MA: MIT Press.

———. 2016. *Mood and Mobility: Navigating the Emotional Spaces of Digital Social Networks*. Cambridge, MA: MIT Press.

Dale, Joshua Paul, Joyce Goggin, Julia Leyda, Anthony P. McIntyre, and Diane Negra, eds. 2017. *The Aesthetics and Affects of Cuteness*. London: Routledge.

Hammermeister, Kai. 2002. *The German Aesthetic Tradition*. Cambridge: Cambridge University Press.

Hawkins, Gay. 2006. *The Ethics of Waste: How We Relate to Rubbish*. Lanham, MD: Rowman & Littlefield.

Hawkins, Gay, Emily Potter, and Kane Race. 2015. *Plastic Water: The Social and Material Life of Bottled Water*. Cambridge, MA: MIT Press.

Highmore, Ben. 2008. "Alimentary Agents: Food, Cultural Theory, and Multiculturalism." *Journal of Intercultural Studies* 29(4):381–98.

———. 2014. *The Great Indoors: At Home in the Modern British House*. London: Profile.

Hurdley, Rachel. 2013. *Home, Materiality, Memory and Belonging: Keeping Culture*. Houndmills: Palgrave Macmillan.

James, William. 1884. "What is an Emotion?" *Mind* 9(34):188–205.

Marcus, Laura. 2007. *The Tenth Muse: Writing about Cinema in the Modernist Period*. Oxford: Oxford University Press.

Miller, Daniel. 2008. *The Comfort of Things*. Cambridge: Polity Press.

Ngai, Sianne. 2005. *Ugly Feelings*. Cambridge, MA: Harvard University Press.

———. 2012. *Our Aesthetic Categories: Zany, Cute, Interesting*. Cambridge, MA: Harvard University Press.

Probyn, Elspeth. 2000. *Carnal Appetites: FoodSexIdentities*. London: Routledge.

———. 2017. *Eating the Ocean*. Durham, NC: Duke University Press.

Rancière, Jacques. 2004. *The Politics of Aesthetics: The Distribution of the Sensible*, trans. Gabriel Rockhill. London: Continuum.

Schivelbusch, Wolfgang. 1977. *The Railway Journey: The Industrialization of Time and Space in the 19th Century*. New York: Berg.

———. 1988. *Disenchanted Night: The Industrialization of Light in the Nineteenth Century*, trans. Angela Davies. Berkeley: University of California Press.

———. 1993. *Tastes of Paradise: A Social History of Spices, Stimulants, and Intoxicants*, trans. David Jacobson. New York: Vintage Books.

Simmel, Georg. [1896] 1968. "Sociological Aesthetics." Pp. 68–85 in *The Conflict in Modern Culture and Other Essays*, trans. K. Peter Etzkorn. New York: Teachers College Press.

Thompson, Zoë. 2015. *Urban Constellations: Spaces of Cultural Regeneration in Post-Industrial Britain*. Farnham: Ashgate.

Tongson, Karen. 2011. *Relocations: Queer Suburban Imaginaries*. New York: New York University Press.

Tonkiss, Fran. 2013. *Cities by Design: The Social Life of Urban Form*. Cambridge: Polity Press.

17

From subtraction to multiplicity

New sociological narratives of morality under modernity

Mary Jo Neitz, Kevin McElmurry, and Daniel Winchester

Introduction

From its inception, sociology has been engaged with questions concerning the relationships between morality, religion, and the modern condition. These questions were central to Durkheim and Weber as well as prominent contemporary scholars like Robert Bellah, Peter Berger, Zygmunt Bauman, and Robert Putnam. Despite the diversity of ideas within this long tradition of theorizing modern moral and religious life, both classical and contemporary accounts have largely been organized within a narrative of moral decline. It is a narrative of crisis and loss, told, in various ways, by some of sociology's most eminent scholars. It is a story that goes something like this:

Once upon a time, in a social world far, far away, human beings lived under the yoke of moral orders. People lived short, hard lives working under the authority of various monarchs, feudal lords, and religious authorities. Literacy rates were low. Disease and morbidity rates were high. All social statuses were ascribed. Yet, despite all this, moral life flourished. People lived in close, well-integrated communities. They acted out of a sense of duty and obligation with regard to those around them. Steeped in a moral order based on rigid hierarchy and unwavering belief in a common religious culture, people knew where they stood in relation to what was good and valuable in life. There were no grand quests for meaning, no existential crises, no need for psychotherapists or guidance counselors. People lived their lives as characters in well-worn scripts. The good life was already spelled out; one only had to live out the script one's betters and one's gods had written.

But then modernity brought profound changes unsettling everything people knew about ethical and religious life. Capitalism replaced an agrarian economy with urban industry, alienating people from the land and the substantive value of their labor. Differentiation between church, state, home and market stretched and strained the well-woven social fabric, leading to more individual freedom but also breeding feelings of anomie, narcissism, and distrust. Science and rationality disenchanted the world and reduced belief in the gods to superstition. As people turned away from their gods and toward their own powers of reason, they gave up any sense of moral obligation beyond their own needs, wants, and desires.

Or so the story goes. Most readers will recognize the various threads of this narrative.

This narrative of moral and religious decline amounts to what Charles Taylor (2007) calls a "subtraction story" of modernity: as societies become modern, "traditional" elements like faith, virtue, morality, and substantive ethics are inevitably subtracted from the mix of cultural life. It has been a persuasive story, and while originally describing changes in Europe, it has influenced and directed sociological inquiry into ethical and religious life more generally for quite some time. But contemporary thinking and research in cultural sociology and beyond has demonstrated that the subtraction narrative – for all its coherence and elegance – has failed to tell the whole story. In fact, this research suggests that morality, ethics, and religiosity still matter a great deal in the late-modern world, in the Global North and in the Global South, but often in ways the subtraction narrative would not anticipate.

In the following portions of this chapter, we bring together some of this research. We argue that research on contemporary moral and religious life is developing a new story, one not of subtraction but of multiplicity.

This multiplicative narrative of modern moral life differs from the subtraction narrative in a number of important ways. First, as the numerical descriptor implies, a multiplicative narrative is a multivocal text; the story is not told from the position of a common moral culture (or lack thereof) but by a multiplicity of moral and religious voices in various degrees of harmony and conflict.

Second, a different theme characterizes a multiplicative story of modern moral and religious life. Whereas the subtraction story is characterized by tragedy, the multiplicative narrative is distinguished by suspense and sometimes mystery. In a multiplicative story, one does not always already know how the story will end. Indeed, the story could turn out to be tragic, but it could also be comedic, happy, violent, shocking, epic, mundane, and so forth. A multiplicative narrative is open-ended and unpredictable; one does not know how (or if) the story will take shape or end.

Third, being implicated in a multiplicative narrative of modern moral life places social actors (including sociologists) on different normative terrain. In many ways, the subtraction story of moral life lets its characters off the proverbial hook. One may lament the condition of a fallen, disenchanted world; one may critique and rail against its institutions. But, ultimately, there is not much one can do about it. The story itself has already been written. Modernity will prevail and morality, ethics, and the sacred will perish or be relegated to the periphery of life. A multiplicative story, however, demands that actors, situated as they are within the multiple moral and religious storylines that characterize contemporary life, make choices. Actors within a world characterized by moral multiplicity must exercise judgment, cultivate ethical sensibilities, confront, recognize, adopt, and disagree with different ways of being. Being a character in a multiplicative narrative means that one *can* act ethically in the modern world – even if doing so is complicated and even when a tragic outcome is always a distinct possibility.

Ultimately, we argue, telling a multiplicative story means moving away from grand narratives about a singular moral order and common religious culture (or lack thereof) and engaging in more grounded empirical work that examines how particular moral orders and identities are produced, negotiated, and put to use within and through specific sociocultural contexts. It also means attending to the ways that moral orders are produced outside the boundaries of institutional religion. It means, in short, telling a piece of the story, attending to a few of the many voices that make up contemporary moral and religious life, with theoretical sophistication and empirical rigor. In what follows, we highlight research on moral orders that we believe represents this kind of work, research that opens up space for asking and addressing new questions about moral multiplicity and complexity. To illustrate these issues we highlight studies on

(1) moral boundaries, (2) moral conflict, (3) hybridity, and (4) spirituality. Our examples point to general processes but show them at work among specific peoples and places, including Evangelicals in the United States, Pentecostals in Nigeria, Hindi Fundamentalists in India, and turtle rescuers in the United States.

Boundaries

Subtraction stories of moral decline might be understood from within their own contexts as reactions to a decline in the taken-for-granted universal authority of a moral ordering that developed in a particular time and place. In the United States that place was New England. As frontier settlements pushed farther westward throughout the nineteenth century, the image of the New England town square anchored at one end by a substantial Protestant church became further removed from the daily experiences of citizens. This was especially true for immigrant populations caught between the cross-pressures of collective identity and assimilation. For regions of the United States settled away from the eastern colonies, like the northwest, the Protestant vision of moral order may not have held sway over popular imagination (Silk 2005). Regional differences can serve as an interesting departure for rethinking the hegemony that many mourn through the narrative genre of decline and loss (Long 2008). Increasing urbanization in the east and (mid)west brought with it further growth within and contact among new populations, deepening the sense of loss of an overarching moral order. However, this was a sense of loss rooted largely in the experiences of white, middle-class members of historically mainline Protestant communities. The work of moral ordering can be examined in the creation and maintenance of these symbolic, social, and spatial boundaries.

The study of boundary work, long part of the social science tradition, has blossomed in recent scholarship on collective identities, inequalities, social organization, and spatial borders (see Lamont and Molnar 2002). Lamont (1992, 2000) provides a framework for understanding how moral boundary work serves as an important component of racial and class divisions by examining the criteria that people in France and the United States use to distinguish between others like and unlike themselves. She finds that the criteria used to distinguish "worthy persons" are rarely the same across social boundaries. For example, black and white working-class men evaluate their relationships to others like and not like themselves using largely incommensurable standards linked to social location (Lamont 2000). This focus on boundary-making activity emphasizes the negotiations that sustain multiple overlapping moral orders.

An assumption among observers of American culture has long been that religion is a constitutive carrier of moral order for society (Tocqueville [1992] 2000). This is true even in a period of relative diversity and ecumenicist impulse in a nation where religion often takes multiple forms. Edgell, Hartmann, and Gerteis (2006) and Edgell et al. (2016) have observed that positing a foundational link between religious belonging and American-style democracy, a focus on a Christian convergence around a common Judeo-Christian creed, and a corresponding emphasis on pluralism form three strands of a scholarly metanarrative of religious change in the twentieth-century US. They suggest that in this broadly construed formulation of "being religious" marks off wide spaces of inclusion while serving as a resource for personal and public identities. Edgell and her colleagues focus on the rejection of atheists (religions' "Other") to provide content to cultural membership, highlighting unacknowledged assumptions linking religious identity, citizenship, and moral worth in the US.

Contemporary trends among conservative evangelicals provide an instructive example of boundary work in the production of exclusivist moral orders under conditions of increasing pluralism. As mainline Protestantism has ceased to be the taken-for-granted religious form and denominational affiliation has become less central to individual religious identification, large independent and non-denominational churches have grown in size and public stature. These conservative congregations often collectively position themselves as a committed and contentious minority in a culture hostile to their vision of a good society (Smith 1998). Even their location on the edge of many towns and cities suggests this outsider stance (Wilford 2012). But rather than adopt the high boundary sectarian orientation of previous generations, many of these churches instead pursue their own "cultural other," sometimes imagined as an alienated non-believer, like the atheists described earlier, seeking moral direction.

River Chapel is one such conservative congregation, located in the Midwest with cultural and organizational roots in the Southern Baptist tradition (McElmurry 2009). Like many evangelical churches inspired by the success of the Chicago area Willow Creek megachurch, River Chapel was imagined by its founders as a church where the morally unanchored "seeker" would feel welcome. Theologically the church is committed to an exclusivist vision of truth and moral order. Yet in order to share their vision, its members are equally committed to eliminating outward distinctions between themselves and those they perceive as others. Like missionaries to a foreign country, the staff at River Chapel see themselves as engaging with an exotic and other postmodern culture on its own terrain and in its own language. In their efforts to create an environment where people can experience a moral order that hinges on feeling a personal connection between themselves and God, they stage elaborate weekly productions emulating popular music concerts with a "culturally relevant" biblical message.

Pursuit of the seeker renegotiates boundaries between sacred and secular culture, believers and non-believers. Conservative churches like River Chapel have rejected much of the distinctiveness of earlier, more sectarian fundamentalism in favor of relevance for and appeal to skeptical non-believers. In the congregational imagination, intended audience members are intimidated by the language and symbols of a tradition with which they are not familiar, and they are more likely to participate if many of the outward symbolic boundaries marking the religious community are downplayed or eliminated. To this end much of the traditional language and symbols of the faith is absent in the seeker church. In buildings that resemble light manufacturing plants, crosses, stained glass, and pictures are replaced by state of the art sound and video projection systems. Worship music is virtually indistinguishable from the adult-oriented rock radio format, and principles are illustrated through excerpts from popular television programs like *Friends* or *ER*. In the seeker church, the moral boundary is both widened (television programs and rock songs can symbolize God's love) and individualized (it is the profession of the faith that marks one as inside). In the seeker church, cultural content from outside is freely appropriated in the service of maintaining an exclusive identity (McElmurry 2009).

Conflict

In the previous example, negotiating the boundaries between postmodern culture and moral conservativism results in embracing "outside" cultural forms while maintaining a distinctive identity, and with little apparent conflict. However, our argument for a multiplicative story does not imply that all stories have equal weight or that the multiple stories always coexist in an atmosphere of harmony and mutual respect. Multiple groups with diverse perspectives do not automatically constitute pluralism or imply some level of mutual acceptance (Wuthnow 2004). In history, it is easy to find examples of religious groups' intolerance and even violent persecution of members of other groups. In the current era, we also find traditionally based religious moral orders positioning themselves against each other and modernity itself. Yet in one way or another, those who rely on tradition and condemn modernity are often marked by the modern context.

For example, fundamentalism, as we understand it, is a reaction to modernity and the cultural pluralism that came with it. The word was first used to describe a dispute within US Protestantism at the beginning of the twentieth century between those who followed the emerging critical scholars who read the Bible as a historical text and those Protestants who opposed modernist thought. The latter published a series of pamphlets between 1910 and 1915 called *The Fundamentals*, staking out their antimodern position (Marsden 1980). This was a battle among seminary elites, and within the mainline denominations the modernist position by and large won out. After the Scopes trial in 1925, fundamentalists withdrew from public debates. But by the 1970s, fundamentalists re-emerged with a strong institutional base from which to renew the fight against a society which violated their sense of moral order. In the United States, issues of sexuality, abortion, and gender roles were particularly salient, and in schools, concerns about teaching evolution and prayer continued to be important. What is interesting is that the reemergence of a public battle between fundamentalists and secular humanism in the United States coincided with the emergence of fundamentalist movements in most of the world religions and in places as diverse as Israel, Iran, Egypt, India, and Indonesia. Although there is disagreement as to whether these diverse movements can all be captured under the generic frame of fundamentalism, nonetheless, across the locales a defense of religion in response to secularism and modernity has emerged (Riesebrodt 2000). We can only understand the moral programs of fundamentalism by locating particular expressions in relation to the modern secularizing movements and moral orders that they accompany (Emerson and Hartman 2006). For example, the recent conflicts over the wearing of headscarves by female Muslim students is different in Turkey than in France, even though it occurs in both places. Each of these countries has had its own particular battles between secularizing states and religious authorities; however, in France wearing the headscarf also constitutes an assertion of Muslim identity by families who have moved from countries in which to be Muslim was to be in the majority to a place where they are a cultural minority.

The drawing of boundaries by sectarian organizations can promote not only challenges but also violent conflicts. In India today, competing movements combine ethnic, religious, and nationalist claims in their attempts to vie for cultural and political sovereignty. With the election of Narendra Modi as prime minister in 2014, Hindu nationalist claims are strengthened (Sharma 2016). The largest Hindu nationalist movement, the *Rashtriya Svayamsevak Sanngh*, and its women's wing, the *Samiti*, believe that Hindu culture and religion should be the basis for citizenship; for them, unassimilated Muslims constitute an unwelcome other. A study of Hindu nationalist paramilitary camps for women shows how middle-class women learn to think of themselves as potential victims of attack by Muslim males, reinscribing nationalist loyalties through intellectual, emotional, and embodied practices (Sehgal 2007). Physical training sessions occupy much of the time, with instruction in yoga, martial arts, fighting with wooden staves and daggers, marching, and games all serving as part of the regimen. The camps propagate the three Samiti discourses: female empowerment, constructing Hindu women as active and powerful citizen agents and mothers to the nation, and an underlying nationalist discourse of duty and self-sacrifice for the nation. However, Sehgal argues that the physical training brought to the surface women's generic fears of male violence, and portrayed that violence as occurring in public spaces and during riot-like circumstances: "Since these women had seldom directly encountered Muslim men in their daily lives, this depiction diverted their attention from harassment and violence in their homes and communities and focused it on a largely fictive threat" (Sehgal 2007:177). The training taught routines both that were more dancelike than defensive, and that failed to teach maneuvers actually of use to women in a confrontation. Yet through the use of political arguments, religious stories, and the embodied experience of imagining attackers, the women "internalized a bodily memory of a Muslim rapist against whom Hindu women needed to defend themselves" (Sehgal 2007:180). Although we characterize Samati as a right-wing fundamentalist organization, even on that point a close look shows modern elements layered with the old in the production of the boundary enforcing tradition of the moral Hindu woman.

Hybridity

In less antagonist circumstances, boundaries might be bridged rather than defended. In contrast with the preceding examples of cultural conflict, another response to cultural multiplicity is hybridity, a dynamic process of cultural change through incorporating elements of other cultures. One example is the diffusion of Pentecostalism in the non-Western world, especially South America and Africa. A religious movement originating in the United States at the beginning of the twentieth century among African American and white practitioners of Holiness sects, Pentecostalism got off the ground with the Azusa Street meetings in Los Angeles. Speaking in tongues, prophesy, and faith healing are among the religious practices that mark Pentecostal services. It is arguably the fastest growing religious movement in the world. A globalization frame might emphasize Pentecostalism as one more cultural export from the United States and assume that part of what is transmitted from the US institutional base is social and political conservatism. Yet the belief in following the "leadings of the spirit" that is central for Pentecostalism creates an opening for local responses. In addition to the activities of worldwide denominations such as the Assemblies of God across the Global South, Pentecostalism is growing through the emergence of local Pentecostal and charismatic churches. Although Christians in these places may take pains to distinguish their beliefs from indigenous ones, using a model of hybridity, we can ask how Pentecostalism differs from the North American model in these locations. For example, how do Pentecostals incorporate indigenous religious practices such as prophecy, trance, and healing? What about "reverse missions" in the African diaspora? (Adogame and Spickard 2010).

We may also need to rethink the assumption that Pentecostals in the Global South will be politically conservative (Miller 2007; cf. Steensland and Goff 2014). Research on a charismatic church in Nigeria shows the impact of charismatic evangelical movements on cultural models of women's sexuality (Pearce 2002, 2012). These charismatic groups tend to liberate women from limiting views that prevail in the previously established Christian evangelical churches and in the traditional culture. The charismatic groups encourage women to view sexuality as a sphere of pleasure and self-expression rather than merely a means of producing children. They encourage women to use contraception to limit and time their childbearing as a means of increasing the health and welfare of mothers and children. The charismatic churches also offer an alternative cultural definition of women who do not have children. Instead of seeing these women as "barren" and unfulfilled, these churches offer a number of alternative interpretations and avoid the devaluation of these women. In addition, the charismatic churches encourage women to consult physicians about issues of fertility, sexuality, and family planning. Finally, these churches support the strengthening of the nuclear family vis-à-vis the claims and demands of the extended family. Prophecy and other gifts of the spirit become tools in these Nigerian indigenous charismatic churches. Their complex message puts forth a new moral order that breaks the hold of the traditional society over the nuclear family and the sexuality of women, but at the same time offers clearly defined rules and practices that work for the women and men attracted to these churches.

As is evidenced in the preceding examples, we see moral orders under modernity as plural, existing in relation to one another and to modern secular culture. Even the most exclusive and fundamentalist sect is affected by the others around it. Although we lack the space to explore the question here, some researchers may ask why some groups consciously engage the other, some hybridize, and others choose conflict. In our examples, these categories are not exclusive and the boundaries, even for the most sectarian, are continually negotiated in reference to the moral "others."

Spirituality

Implicit in what we have presented so far is that we also see moral orders as constituted through embodied practices and feelings – the music at River Chapel or the physical training of young Hindu women – as much as through beliefs and values. Refocusing sociological thinking about moral orders on practices, and including what people are doing and feeling, become even more important when we begin to conceptualize moral orders outside of the boundaries of institutional religion. In this final section we consider "the nones," the increasing numbers of people in Europe and North America who claim no religious affiliation (Pew 2015a).

A very small proportion of these people are atheists: 23 percent of people in the United States now identify as nones, but only 3 percent call themselves atheists (Pew 2015b). Forty-seven percent of nonaffiliated respondents report a deep sense of wonder about the universe, and 40 percent say they feel "a deep sense of spiritual peace and well being" at least once a week (Pew 2015b). A study of sea turtle rescuers designed to explore the moral universe of non-religion and its everyday expression through world-repairing activities shows people with "no religion" committed to something they understand as spiritual (Beaman 2017). Many turtle rescuers have a framework more immanent than transcendent, respectful of each other and the turtles. Although individuals worked with others, their group ties were fluid – intense during the rescue season, less so at other times. They value cooperation and interdependence between species and see more similarities than differences across life forms (Beaman 2017).

Recent explorations of "lived religion" (Ammerman 2007; McGuire 2008) and contemporary spirituality (Bender 2010) give us insight into the many ways that people co-construct moral orders outside the bounds of institutionalized religion: through seeking to understand their own embodied experiences, interacting with others, attending workshops, and reading on their own, people still develop ways of exercising judgment and cultivating strong ethical sensibilities. Institutional religion continues to play a part in the story of modern moral life for many, but not for all.

Conclusion

Boundaries, conflicts, hybridity, diverse spiritual practices and subjectivities – such are the phenomena constitutive of a multiplicative moral and religious narrative. This plotline is one in which a diverse array of social actors are situated, including, we think it important to add, social scientists. We too are part of the story, even as we attempt to analyze and theorize its forms and contents.

Indeed, it has become increasingly apparent that a value-free social science is an impossible endeavor, that we cannot somehow extract ourselves from the moral orders that help constitute our social existence (see, for example, Haan et al. 1983; Harding 1986; Smith 2003). Like all social actors, social scientists are implicated in moral orders and bring to their inquiries moral values and sensibilities that cannot simply be left at the door. Given this, what is the ethical position of the sociologist of religious and moral life within a multiplicative narrative?

As Robert Orsi (2005) points out, the moral distinctions that scholars have so often made between "good" and "bad" religion are often not the result of a sustained and reflective practice of understanding others' moral and religious worlds – and all the good and ugliness associated with those worlds in particular times and places. Rather, they are the products of long-held biases crafted within the Western academy and the wider society over the course of historical time. To engage in moral inquiry does not require that we redeem or denounce religious and moral others, even and perhaps especially those that we initially find strange or even repugnant. It is also not to deny our moral perspectives. Rather, it is to subject our moral positions to scrutiny, to enter into moral conversation (which is not the same as conversion) with others, to allow them to subject our moral certainties to the same critical reflection as we often subject theirs.

The study of moral and religious life, then, requires engaging in a project of dialogue and understanding. Such a project is a "moral discipline in its commitment to examining the variety of human experience and to making contact across *boundaries* – cultural, psychological, spiritual, existential" (Orsi 2005:203, emphasis added). In a world characterized by moral multiplicity, by both conflict and cooperation, by both positive and tragic possibilities for human actors, this project of conversation and understanding is itself an ethical endeavor.

References

Adogame, A., and J. Spickard, eds. 2010. *Religion Crossing Boundaries: Transnational Religious Dynamics in Africa and the New African Diaspora.* Leiden, NL: Brill.

Ammerman, N., ed. 2007. *Everyday Religion: Observing Modern Religious Lives.* New York: Oxford University Press.

Beaman, L. 2017. "Living Well Together in a (non)Religious Future." *Sociology of Religion* 78(1):9–32.

Bender, C. 2010. *The New Metaphysicals: Spirituality and the American Religious Imagination.* Chicago: University of Chicago Press.

Edgell, P., D. Hartmann, and J. Gerteis. 2006. "Atheists as Cultural Other: Moral Boundaries and Cultural Membership in American Society." *American Sociological Review* 71(2): 211–34.

Edgell, P., D. Hartmann, E. Stewart, and J. Gerteis. 2016. "Atheists and Other Cultural Outsiders: Moral Boundaries and the Non-Religious in the United States." *Social Forces* 95(2):607–38.

Emerson, M., and D. Hartman. 2006. "The Rise of Religious Fundamentalism." *Annual Review of Sociology* 32:127–44.

Haan, N., R. Bellah, P. Rabinow, and W.S. Sullivan. 1983. *Social Science as Moral Inquiry.* New York: Columbia University Press.

Harding, S. 1986. *The Science Question in Feminism.* Ithaca, NY: Cornell University Press.

Lamont, M. 1992. *Money, Morals, and Manners: The Culture of the French and American Upper-Middle Class.* Chicago: University of Chicago Press.

———. 2000. *The Dignity of Working Men: Morality and the Boundaries of Race, Class, and Immigration.* Cambridge, MA: Harvard University Press.

Lamont, M., and V. Molnar. 2002. "The Study of Boundaries in the Social Sciences." *Annual Review of Sociology* 28:167–96.

Long, C. 2008. "New Orleans as an American City: Origins, Exchanges, Materialities, and Religion." Pp. 203–22 in *New Territories, New Perspectives: The Religious Impact of the Louisiana Purchase,* edited by R.J. Callahan Jr. Columbia: University of Missouri Press.

Marsden, G. 1980. *Fundamentalism in American Culture.* New York: Oxford University Press.

McElmurry, K. 2009. "Alone/Together: The production of Religious Culture in a Church for the Unchurched." PhD dissertation, Department of Sociology, University of Missouri, Columbia.

McGuire, M. 2008. *Lived Religion: Faith and Practice in Everyday Life.* New York: Oxford University Press.

Miller, D. 2007. "Progressive Pentecostals: The New Face of Christian Social Engagement." *Journal for the Scientific Study of Religion* 46(4):435–45.

Orsi, R. 2005. *Between Heaven and Earth: The Religious Worlds People Make and the Scholars Who Study Them.* Princeton, NJ: Princeton University Press.

Pearce, T.O. 2002. "Cultural Production and Reproductive Issues: The Significance of the Charismatic Movement in Nigeria." Pp. 21–50 in *Religion and Sexuality in Cross-cultural Perspective,* edited by S. Ellingson, and M. Christian Green. New York: Routledge.

————. 2012. "Reconstructing Sexuality in the Shadow of Neoliberal Globalization: Investigating the Approach of Charismatic Churches in Southwestern Nigeria." *Journal of Religion in Africa* 42(4):345–68.

Pew Research Center. 2015a. "The Future of World Religions: Population Growth Projections, 2010–2050." Retrieved October 17, 2017 (www.pewforum.org/2015/04/02/religious-projections-2010-2050/).

————. 2015b. "America's Changing Religious Landscape." Retrieved December 16, 2016 (www. pewforum.org/2015/05/12/americas-changing-religious-landscape/).

Riesebrodt, M. 2000. "Fundamentalism and the Resurgence of Religion." *Numen* 47(3):266–87.

Sehgal, M. 2007. "Manufacturing a Feminized Siege Mentality Hindu Nationalist Paramilitary Camps for Women in India." *Journal of Contemporary Ethnography* 36(2):165–83.

Sharma, M. 2016. "Narendra Modi and the New Education Policy: Retrospection, Reform and Reality." *Journal of Asian Public Policy* 9(2):140–53.

Silk, M. 2005. "Religion and Region in American Public Life." *Journal for the Scientific Study of Religion* 44(3):265–70.

Smith, C. 1998. *American Evangelicalism: Embattled and Thriving*. Chicago: University of Chicago Press.

————. 2003. *Moral Believing Animals: Human Personhood and Culture*. New York: Oxford University Press.

Steensland, B., and P. Goff, eds. 2014. *The New Evangelical Social Engagement*. New York: Oxford University Press.

Taylor, C. 2007. *A Secular Age*. Cambridge, MA: Belknap Press.

Tocqueville, Alexis de. [1992] 2000. *Democracy in America*. Chicago: University of Chicago Press.

Wilford, Justin. 2012. *Sacred Subdivisions: The Postsuburban Transformation of American Evangelicalism*. New York: New York University Press.

Wuthnow, R. 2004. "The Challenge of Diversity." *Journal for the Scientific Study of Religion* 43(2):159–70.

18

Demystifying authenticity in the sociology of culture

David Grazian

Introduction

The performance of authenticity pervades our popular culture and public life. In recent years "reality" television has proliferated not only because it is inexpensive to produce, but for its brazen attempts to capture "ordinary" people in unscripted moments of everyday life, warts and all (Grindstaff 2002). African American hip-hop music artists sell records on the basis of their ability to "keep it real" by remaining "true" to their neighborhood roots, even when they hail from middle-class suburbs (McLeod 1999). In American politics, wealthy candidates perform authenticity by emphasizing their humble roots or working-class tastes, especially when TV news cameras are around. During her 2016 US presidential campaign, former Secretary of State Hillary Clinton used her speeches as opportunities to emphasize her modest middle-class background rather than her degrees from Wellesley and Yale. As reported in the *Washington Post* during a 2015 campaign stop through Iowa:

> You may think of her as the wife of a president or as a globe-trotting diplomat, but Hillary Rodham Clinton wants voters here to see her as the granddaughter of an immigrant factory worker and the daughter of a small businessman who printed fabric for draperies and then went out and sold them. "A waste-not, want-not kind of a guy," she said, "and he provided a good living for us."
>
> *(Rucker and Gearan 2015)*

Meanwhile, Clinton's Republican opponent, self-described billionaire Donald J. Trump, tried to connect with blue-collar voters by posting on his Facebook, Instagram, and Twitter feeds images of himself feasting on McDonald's burgers and fries and a bucket of KFC fried chicken – all on his private jet (Parker 2016).

Authenticity can refer to a variety of desirable traits: credibility, originality, sincerity, naturalness, genuineness, innateness, purity, or realness. Since the nineteenth century, the search for authenticity has been a bourgeois reaction to the ravages of industrial society and monopoly capitalism, whether expressed by Marx's critique of alienated labor or Walt Whitman's and Henry David Thoreau's pastoral retreats. In our postindustrial age of high-tech frivolity as exemplified by the proliferation of Botox and filtered Instagram photos, Hollywood artifice and Auto-Tuned pop music, virtual reality and vampire chic, some consumers nostalgically seek out the authenticity suggested by symbols of agrarian simplicity (organic beets, raw honey) and old-fashioned folkways (handlebar mustaches, homemade taxidermy).

Like a badge of honor, authenticity connotes legitimacy and social value, but like honor itself, authenticity is also a social construct with moral overtones, rather than an objective and value-free appraisal. Given its socially constructed and thus elusive nature, authenticity itself can never be authentic, but must always be performed, staged, fabricated, crafted, or otherwise imagined (MacCannell 1976; Peterson 1997; Fine 2003; Grazian 2003). The performance of authenticity always requires a close conformity to the expectations set by the context in which it is situated. For instance, in American politics, authenticity is marked by straight talk, plain speech, and working-class cultural sensibilities, whereas food writers measure the authenticity of ethnic cuisine by its closeness to national, local, or regional sources of tradition (Lu and Fine 1995; Johnston and Baumann 2007; Gaytan 2008). Audiences may employ a range of ambiguous criteria when evaluating the symbolic efficacy of such authenticity performances, which can lead to controversy. Examples include the ongoing debate among musicians and critics concerning the authenticity of jazz performed in Japan (Atkins 2000) and the contestation surrounding Colombian and Cuban salsa dance styles displayed in London nightclubs (Urquia 2004).

Given the constructed nature of authenticity, sociologists of culture are uniquely positioned to critically demystify its performance in popular culture and public life. The social construction and attribution of authenticity occurs among culture-producing organizations, prestige-granting institutions, and other cultural authorities reliant on rhetorical and discursive strategies of classification, genre development, and reputation building (Bielby and Bielby 1994; Negus 1998; Fine 2003; Lena and Peterson 2008). Cultural producers from profit-seeking firms and entrepreneurs to individual artistic creators manufacture, stage, and promote authenticated artworks and entertainment within more extensive worlds of media and symbolic production (Peterson 1997; Grazian 2003). Lastly, authenticity performances represent elaborate strategies of impression management, social interaction, and emotional control well-suited for close dramaturgical analysis (Goffman 1959; Hochschild 1983).

In what follows I will take each of these strategies in turn – assigning authenticity through the production of discourse, staging authenticity as an integral part of the culture production process, and performing authenticity as an accomplishment of social interaction – in order to illustrate how the theoretical tools of cultural sociology can demystify the aura of authenticity surrounding the most hallowed of sacred cows and social myths. I conclude with a discussion of three emergent aesthetic practices – hybridity, irony, and transgression – that deconstruct or otherwise challenge the performance of authenticity as tradition-bound, pretentious, and essentialist.

Assigning authenticity

As a socially constructed myth, authenticity is produced through discourses that valorize certain qualities and assign or attribute them to cultural objects and symbols as a means of creating distinction, whether of status, prestige, or value; it is therefore ironic that authenticity is so often associated with hardship and disadvantage. Collectors assign legitimacy to the childlike artwork of uneducated, self-taught artists on the basis of its unmediated purity, its expression of the wild but innocent creativity of an unrefined mind (Becker 1982:258–69; Fine 2003). Music fans and ethnomusicologists romanticize the Delta blues melodies of poor sharecroppers as rural expressions of African American primitivism, and Anglo-Saxon folk ballads for their association with country living and working-class populism (Roy 2002). For similar reasons, international tourists and consumers seek out ethnic arts and crafts for purchase as exotic talismans of local authenticity, whether Mayan ceramics in Mexico, Lega masks in Zaire, or sacred Buddhist spirit houses in Thailand (Wherry 2006). In fair-trade stores like Ten Thousand Villages, consumers purchase handicrafts such as jewelry, embroidery, woodcarvings, and handwoven baskets made by indigenous artisans working in Guatemala, India, Bangladesh, Niger, and elsewhere throughout the Global South (Brown 2013).

While these examples illustrate how the attribution of authenticity can serve as an exercise in condescension, other cases reveal how authenticity claims can establish distinction through a more democratizing discourse. In gourmet food writing, culinary discourses validate ingredients, recipes, and dishes as authentic by associating them with a particular geographic region, whether Tuscan wild boar stew, Vietnamese beef wraps, Maryland crab cakes, or Nashville hot chicken. (The specificity of place serves as a marker of authenticity in discourses surrounding globally popular music as well, whether Punjabi bhangra or Jamaican reggae.) Other rhetorical strategies for legitimating foods as authentic include emphasizing the rustic quality of homegrown or organic produce – heirloom tomatoes, handpicked cilantro, shaved truffles – or else the modesty of handmade dishes such as black beans and rice, or mint cucumber salad (Johnston and Baumann 2007).

Whether generated out of self-interest or aesthetic convention, authenticity arguments are generally made by cultural authorities such as scholars, journalists, and critics, and commercial interests from local business entrepreneurs to city boosters. Given their invented quality, such claims must often be passionately defended, occasionally to ridiculous ends, if they are to masquerade as actual facts. Many locals insist that a truly authentic Philadelphia cheesesteak must be prepared with one of three kinds of cheese – American, provolone, or Cheez Whiz – even though the latter is perhaps the most artificial and synthetic of all foodstuffs, invented in a laboratory in 1952 (two decades after the introduction of the "original" Philly cheesesteak), and in Canada, no less. Food companies liberally draw on ideologies surrounding authenticity to euphemize the use of flavor additives and extracts as "natural" flavors and ingredients (Schlosser 2002). Meanwhile, national supermarket chains such as Whole Foods market their processed meals from frozen burritos and pizzas to TV dinners as "organic," as if such dishes were grown on small family farms rather than manufactured in industrial laboratories and packing plants (Pollan 2006).

Around the world, increased global flows of culture and capital generate new authenticity claims as local communities grow even more protective of their regional customs, collective identities, and territorial attachments (Appadurai 1990). In reaction to the modern unification of continental Europe, countries such as Italy, France, Spain, Greece, Portugal, and Germany have successfully applied to the EU to have more than 700 foodstuffs assigned protective status on the basis of national identity and cultural patrimony (DeSoucey 2010). For example, feta cheese and kalamata olives are both marked with a "Protected Designation of Origin" label that gives Greece the exclusive right to sell them in Europe, just as only certain regional Italian pork producers can refer to their cured ham as authentically "Prosciutto di Parma." (However, protected foods may be sold by foreign purveyors both in the US and elsewhere outside the EU, which is why one can buy cheese labeled "Bulgarian feta" in New York but not in Bulgaria.) DeSoucey refers to this labeling practice as an example of *gastronationalism*, in which "food is a contested medium of cultural politics that demarcates national boundaries and identities" in the context of globalization (2010:433).

Staging authenticity

Retail outlets and entertainment venues promote themselves on the basis of their staged authenticity and synthetic atmospherics. The Starbucks chain successfully transformed coffee into an upscale product by offering customers a thoroughly mediated experience steeped in the aesthetics of branded authenticity, as embodied in the wood-paneled décor of its stores, their soundtracks of folk, jazz, and indie rock, and a selection of fair-trade and shade-grown coffee from small local producers working in exotic locales from Kenya to Indonesia (Simon 2009). Their marketing materials sometimes include posters and brochures featuring "handsome, well-dressed peasants smiling and standing next to piles of beans" (Simon 2009:206). Starbucks (2013) promotes their Burundi Kayanza coffee by emphasizing its authentic origins:

> Juicy with herbal blackberry notes and tea-like flavors, this is a coffee unlike any African single-origin offering we've ever tasted. The microclimate of Burundi's rugged Kayanza Ridge is an ideal setting for farmers to grow this amazing coffee. Each farmer tends a small patch of just 50 to 250 coffee trees, making this a truly rare and special bean.

According to Goffman (1959), although our social lives are most successfully performed on front stages deliberately designed for the purpose of impressing others, we prepare for those performances in more private backstage regions. Professors write up their classroom notes in their messy and drafty offices, and deliver their pearls of knowledge in stately looking university lecture halls; young romantic lovers prepare for dates in their clothes-strewn bedrooms, but encounter one another on the whirling dance floors provided by glamorous nightclubs and cocktail lounges. Of course, the privatized nature of backstage areas can make them seem particularly intimate and alluring as regions of authenticity lacking in pretense and superficiality. For this reason, restaurants sometimes offer customers the opportunity to observe their chefs and cooking staffs working in normally concealed backstage zones. Although diners inevitably enjoy the privileged views afforded by coveted seats alongside the counters of sushi bars, exhibition-style kitchens, and even at expensive tables placed inside the kitchen itself, such experiences mask how these "backstage" spaces represent little more than disguised front stages themselves, with all workers in performance mode, and potentially embarrassing eyesores such as flypaper and mousetraps hidden safely out of view (Grazian 2004).

The backstage areas of the city itself – its skid rows, segregated ghettos, and corner taverns – offer similar thrills to the voyeuristically minded; this partially explains the fascination with local slaughterhouses, tobacco factories, morgues, and sewers shared among Parisian visitors and tour guides in 1900 (MacCannell 1976:57–76). A century later, jazz and blues bars in Chicago attract curious tourists and other spectators in search of the authenticity marked both by their simulated ramshackle appearance and by bar menus offering Mississippi and Louisiana favorites like crawfish tails, fried okra, and slabs of pork ribs (Grazian 2003). Other urban entertainment venues are similarly staged, even when designed to appear abandoned and atrophied. Cloaked in the symbolic indicators of authenticity and subcultural credibility, rock clubs are commonly dilapidated affairs with beer-stained floors and graffiti-marred bathrooms in varying states of filth and disrepair, even as their box office ticket sales bring in wildly enormous revenue sums. The dinginess of greasy-spoon eateries and dive bars located in affluent downtown neighborhoods can seem just as fabricated. According to a *New York Times* review of La Esquina, a latter-day speakeasy hidden behind an anonymous gray door in a downtown taco stand in Lower Manhattan:

> The décor, like the rabbit-hole descent, is so contrived as to feel uncontrived. . . . The rust on the wrought iron fence used decoratively throughout the restaurant was created by hydrochloric acid, not age. The brick walls were meticulously painted, scraped, and repainted to match the naturally decayed columns.

(Lee 2005)

Along with urban entertainment, the staging of authenticity is particularly pronounced in US politics, as noted in the introduction to this chapter. National electoral campaigns stage local "town hall" meetings as excessively orchestrated affairs that attempt to recall an idyllic American past, while presidential visits to public schools, factories, poor neighborhoods, and flooded cities often serve as little more than opportunities to be photographed in working-class settings with ordinary citizens.

Given that American consumers seem to value authentic experiences rooted in stereotypical images of reality rather than the messiness (and occasional unpleasantness) of everyday life as it is actually lived, the staging of authenticity can prove a risky balancing act. After all, few contemporary home buyers on the market for a "historically preserved" nineteenth-century Victorian carriage house are likely to desire one lacking indoor toilets. American diners at ethnic restaurants may crave exotic dishes from faraway lands, but not those foods so far removed from their customary palates as to be deemed inedible – such as Swiss horsemeat, or Malaysian webbed duck feet, or *bosintang*, a Korean soup prepared with dog meat. In fact, the representation of cultural authenticity in dining and other entertainment settings almost always relies on a somewhat imaginary and aesthetically pleasing simulation of reality. In mainstream Chinese restaurants in the US, dishes like Mongolian beef are prepared with lots of sugar to appeal to American tastes; soup is served as an appetizer course, rather than at the end of the meal (as it would be in China); and traditional Chinese dishes such as beef tripe, ox's tail, and pig's tongue are excluded from most menus (Lu and Fine 1995). Feigning authenticity, Mexican restaurants in the US serve tortilla chips before the meal, and burritos as a main course – not because traditional Mexican folkways demand it (they do not), but because Anglo customers do (Gaytan 2008:325–6).

Within the culture industries, the production of popular music relies on similarly strategic methods of representation. In the early era of country and western music, record companies portrayed their actual artists as authentic old-timers, hillbillies, and cowboys (Peterson 1997). Contemporary labels rely on racially charged stock characters to market their rap and hip-hop acts as gangbangers, street thugs, pimps, convicted felons, ex-cons, and drug users. (Meanwhile, female rap and pop stars from Nicki Minaj to Iggy Azalea to Lana Del Ray are regularly accused of being inauthentic – of not writing their own raps, of not being able to sing, of pretending to be "street"; of not keeping true to their roots.) Pop bands take their fashion cues from once-underground punk and skateboarding scenes in order to camouflage themselves in the symbolic authenticity of alienated youth and independent rock. Although blues club owners in Chicago often employ musicians of varying racial and ethnic backgrounds, in response to audience demand for the authenticity represented by black culture they almost exclusively hire African American bandleaders for profitable weekend gigs (Grazian 2003).

Performing authenticity

At an interactional level, authenticity performances represent elaborate strategies of impression management and emotional control. During interpersonal encounters, we usually associate authenticity with sincerity and self-transparency. In other words, we assume that people are who they say they are, and that they actually believe what they claim to be true. Although Goffman observes that to a certain extent all social interactions are performed, he also distinguishes between cynical masquerades in which the actor intends to deceive his audience, and more genuine acts in which the performer "can be sincerely convinced that the impression of reality which he stages is the real reality" (1959:17–18). Italian or Greek housewives who rely on traditional family recipes may sincerely believe in the authenticity of their cooking, just as folk and bluegrass songsters may genuinely embrace the authenticity attributed to Appalachian music. These examples illustrate how authenticity can be earnestly experienced as well as performed, even by the performers themselves. Indeed, comparative international research on prostitution in San Francisco, Stockholm, and Amsterdam reveals how sex workers sometimes perform "bounded authenticity" by providing genuine desire, affection, and erotic pleasure for their clients, at least within the temporal confines of a fleeting commercial sexual transaction (Bernstein 2007:103).

On the other hand, workers in a range of occupations (including sex work) regularly engage in cynical authenticity performances that rely on tactics of misrepresentation and guile. Police detectives break down their suspects through a variety of deceptive strategies during interrogation proceedings (including performances of good cop/bad cop). Service workers from flight attendants to cocktail waitresses perform emotional labor by responding with feigned laughter and sympathetic smiles to their customers' often unsavory come-ons and rude requests (Hochschild 1983). In a turn toward what the public relations industry refers to as "reality marketing," paid female publicists pose as ordinary customers in urban bars and nightclubs for the purposes of engineering the fun and excitement that paying patrons cannot be relied on to generate for themselves (Grazian 2008:86–90). More extreme examples of deceptive professionals include confidence artists, pool hustlers, double agents, fortune tellers, and used car salesmen. Of course, as sociologist Ned Polsky reminds us,

> Conning is only a matter of degree, in that all of us are concerned in many ways to manipulate others' impressions of us, and so one can, if one wishes, take the view that every man is at bottom a con man.
>
> *(1967:53)*

While feigning sincerity represents one kind of authenticity performance, other contexts invite participants to play roles commensurate with dominant stereotypes of authenticity based on gritty images of the urban poor. Black middle-class youth pose as hoodlums on New York City subways as well as in rap music videos. Affluent white suburban teenagers cloak themselves in street fashion from baggy jeans to torn clothing, even going so far as to beg for change in wealthy neighborhoods of nearby cities. In February 2008, Riverhead Books published *Love and Consequences*, a memoir of a half-white, half-Native American girl from South-Central Los Angeles who grew up in a foster home and eventually sold illegal drugs for the Bloods gang. Later that year the book was revealed to be pure fiction, written by a white woman raised by her biological family in the upscale Sherman Oaks neighborhood in the San Fernando Valley.

These last examples emphasize the conscious elaboration of racial or ethnic authenticity as an accomplishment of cultural performance and social interaction. Tabloid talk shows like Jerry Springer encourage working-class guests to overemphasize the performance of "trashy" stereotypes, and they oblige for the privilege of appearing on television (Grindstaff 2002), just as reality TV actors trade on clichéd stock characters (the effeminate gay man, the angry black woman, the sexy bimbo) for extra airtime. In Chicago blues clubs, African American musicians exaggerate the performance of blackness by appropriating racial caricatures reminiscent of antebellum black minstrelsy and more contemporary "blaxploitation" films – the country bumpkin, the cowboy, the sex machine, the dirty old-timer. In his club performances, one Mississippi blues singer "confesses" his passions for "blues, barbecue, watermelon, and pretty girls." Before his passing in 1998, James Ramsey, a popular Chicago blues figure dubbed the "Black Lone

Ranger," strolled around local blues bars in his minstrel regalia, replete with 10-gallon hat and black mask (Grazian 2003:54).

The demystification of authenticity as cultural practice

Sociologists have the necessary theoretical and analytical tools to demystify the fabrication of authenticity in everyday life, whether through the examination of discourse and the social construction of knowledge, organizational analysis and case studies of cultural production, or dramaturgy and symbolic interaction. But in addition, as they become more common in popular culture and public life, authenticity performances are increasingly challenged by alternative aesthetic practices that devalue, deconstruct, or otherwise problematize such performances as tradition-bound, pretentious, and essentialist.

First, the social status of authenticity is challenged by the celebration of *hybridity*, represented by attempts to meld together otherwise disparate cultures in a self-conscious manner in order to generate new possibilities for creative expression. In many ways the history of popular music in the twentieth century is marked by attempts at synthesis and fusion. Blues and jazz developed as a mélange of African and European musical traditions; similarly, early rock 'n' roll pioneers developed the genre by blending together urban blues and country music. Such experiments in hybridity are also evident in Bob Dylan's development of electric folk-rock (which signaled his supposed lack of authenticity among older folk music followers); Miles Davis's forays into free jazz, funk, and psychedelic rock on albums like *Bitches Brew* (1969) and *On the Corner* (1972); the appropriation of classical music techniques among 1970s and 1980s progressive rock and heavy metal artists like Rush, Deep Purple, Van Halen, Randy Rhoads, and Yngwie Malmsteen (Walser 1994); and the emergence of rap rock, an amalgam of punk, hard rock, and hip-hop music exemplified by 1990s acts such as Faith No More, the Beastie Boys, the Red Hot Chili Peppers, and Rage Against the Machine.

Moreover, the globalization of popular music privileges hybridity as performers around the world become more familiar with each other's work. Throughout the 1980s American and British rock artists drew on elements of African and Latin polyrhythmic pop music (and partnered with artists such as South Africa's Ladysmith Black Mambazo and Senegal's Youssou N'Dour) to produce some of the most critically heralded albums of the decade, including the Talking Heads' *Remain in Light* (1980) and *Stop Making Sense* (1984), Peter Gabriel's *Security* (1982) and *So* (1986), and Paul Simon's *Graceland* (1986) and *The Rhythm of the Saints* (1990). Today, black immigrants residing in low-income *banlieues* outside major cities in France perform politically charged hip-hop music that borrows from both American rap and African and Caribbean music traditions.

Like authenticity, adventures in cultural hybridity are also popular among culinary artists and foodies, as evidenced by the worldwide pervasiveness of global fusion cooking. In New York, San Francisco, Chicago, and even smaller cities such as Philadelphia, three- and four-star restaurants prepare fashionable exemplars of hybrid cuisine that combine French cooking with a mixture of ingredients from Japan, Italy, Mexico, and Morocco, among other regions. In local Philadelphia restaurants, gourmet fusion dishes include seared Kobe beef carpaccio, truffle-scented edamame ravioli, and chocolate mousse with fresh grated wasabi (Grazian 2003:233). In Los Angeles and other global cities, food truck vendors serve Korean-style tacos stuffed with kimchi and BBQ beef bulgogi; Vietnamese hoagies made with pork belly, daikon, and spicy mayo on *bánh mì* baguettes; and Indian burritos stuffed with chicken vindaloo and basmati rice. By evading the traditions common to regional cuisines, chefs and diners alike reject the social construction of authenticity in favor of global hybridity and multiculturalism.

If the pursuit of hybridity represents a challenge to cultural traditions, so do adventures in *irony*. We experience irony when we invert aesthetic and taste conventions to humorous effect, particularly when cultural creators and consumers playfully mock what they regard as the self-importance of authenticity displays. The self-consciously campy performances of gay drag queens call attention to the stylized artifice and theatricality of celebrity culture, as do pop music divas from Madonna to Lady Gaga and Katy Perry. The same can be said about the dead-on song parodies and music videos of Weird Al Yankovic, who has sold more than 12 million albums (more than any other comedy act ever) by sending up superstars such as Michael Jackson, Taylor Swift, Miley Cyrus, Pharrell Williams – and, yes, Madonna, Lady Gaga, and Katy Perry.

Finally, through practices of transgression, participants baldly reject what they take to be the essentialist qualities of authenticity, fabrication, and performance. As a reaction to typecasting in theater and film and normative role assignment in everyday life, since 1993 the Los Angeles Women's Shakespeare Company has performed plays from *Hamlet* to *Romeo and Juliet* to *Richard III* with all-female casts. (Of course, Shakespeare's plays were originally staged with men performing all roles.) In recent years white actors have similarly been cast in traditionally black roles: Patrick Stewart played the title lead (without the offensive blackface makeup) in a 1997 staging of Othello by Washington, DC's Shakespeare Theater. In *I'm Not There*, an experimental 2007 biopic of Bob Dylan and his multiple invented selves, the troubadour's many incarnations – each a riff off a different brand of authenticity and American myth – are performed by a cadre of actors varying in age, race, nationality, and gender, including Heath Ledger, Christian Bale, Marcus Carl Franklin, Richard Gere, and Cate Blanchett.

Conclusion

A central challenge among sociologists of culture remains the demystification of authenticity in entertainment, popular culture, politics, and public settings of everyday life. The construction of authenticity takes place in a context of collective involvement and social interaction, and requires the mobilization of a variety of interested actors, including reputational authorities, prestige-granting organizations, and mass communications outlets; media-producing firms, art worlds, and cultural entrepreneurs; and public performers, creative personnel, and naturally, their audiences. Along with the emergent aesthetic pursuits discussed earlier that deconstruct or otherwise challenge the performance of authenticity as tradition-bound, pretentious, and essentialist, the sociology of culture itself represents yet another critical practice designed to examine and debunk the dominant cultural myths of our time.

References

Appadurai, Arjun. 1990. "Disjuncture and Difference in the Global Cultural Economy." *Public Culture* 2(2):1–24.

Atkins, E. Taylor. 2000. "Can Japanese Sing the Blues?: 'Japanese Jazz' and the Problem of Authenticity." Pp. 27–59 in *Japan Pop! Inside the World of Japanese Popular Culture*, edited by T.J. Craig. Armonk, NY: M.E. Sharpe.

Becker, Howard S. 1982. *Art Worlds*. Berkeley: University of California Press.

Bernstein, Elizabeth. 2007. *Temporarily Yours: Intimacy, Authenticity, and the Commerce of Sex*. Chicago: University of Chicago Press.

Bielby, William T., and Denise D. Bielby. 1994. "'All Hits are Flukes': Institutional Decision-Making and the Rhetoric of Network Prime-Time Program Development." *American Journal of Sociology* 99(5):1287–313.

Brown, Keith R. 2013. *Buying Into Fair Trade: Culture, Morality, and Consumption*. New York: NYU Press.

DeSoucey, Michaela. 2010. "Gastronationalism: Food Traditions and Authenticity Politics in the European Union." *American Sociological Review* 75(3):432–55.

Fine, Gary Alan. 2003. "Crafting Authenticity: The Validation of Identity in Self-Taught Art." *Theory and Society* 32(2):153–80.

Gaytan, Marie Sarita. 2008. "From Sombreros to Sincronizadas: Authenticity, Ethnicity, and the Mexican Restaurant Industry." *Journal of Contemporary Sociology* 37(3):314–41.

Goffman, Erving. 1959. *The Presentation of Self in Everyday Life*. New York: Anchor.

Grazian, David. 2003. *Blue Chicago: The Search for Authenticity in Urban Blues Clubs*. Chicago: University of Chicago Press.

———. 2004. "The Production of Popular Music as a Confidence Game: The Case of the Chicago Blues." *Qualitative Sociology* 27(2):137–58.

———. 2008. *On the Make: The Hustle of Urban Nightlife*. Chicago: University of Chicago Press.

Grindstaff, Laura. 2002. *The Money Shot: Trash, Class, and the Making of TV Talk Shows*. Chicago: University of Chicago Press.

Hochschild, Arlie Russell. 1983. *The Managed Heart: Commercialization of Human Feeling*. Berkeley: University of California Press.

Johnston, Josee, and Shyon Baumann. 2007. "Democracy versus Distinction: A Study of Omnivorousness in Gourmet Food Writing." *American Journal of Sociology* 113(1):165–204.

Lee, Denny. 2005. "Remember, You Didn't Read About It Here." *New York Times*, July 31.

Lena, Jennifer C., and Richard A. Peterson. 2008. "Classification and Culture: Types and Trajectories of Music Genres." *American Sociological Review* 73(5):697–718.

Lu, Shun, and Gary Alan Fine. 1995. "The Presentation of Ethnic Authenticity: Chinese Food as a Social Accomplishment." *Sociological Quarterly* 36(3):535–53.

MacCannell, Dean. 1976. *The Tourist: A New Theory of the Leisure Class*. New York: Schocken.

McLeod, Kembrew. 1999. "Authenticity within Hip-Hop and Other Cultures Threatened with Assimilation." *Journal of Communication* 49(4):134–50.

Negus, Keith. 1998. "Cultural Production and the Corporation: Musical Genres and the Strategic Management of Creativity in the U.S. Recording Industry." *Media, Culture and Society* 20(3):359–79.

Parker, Ashley. 2016. "Donald Trump's Diet: He'll Have Fries with That." *New York Times*, August 8.

Peterson, Richard A. 1997. *Creating Country Music: Fabricating Authenticity*. Chicago: University of Chicago Press.

Pollan, Michael. 2006. *The Omnivore's Dilemma: A Natural History of Four Meals*. New York: Penguin.

Polsky, Ned. 1967. *Hustlers, Beats, and Others*. Garden City, NY: Anchor.

Roy, William G. 2002. "Aesthetic Identity, Race, and American Folk Music." *Qualitative Sociology* 25(3):459–69.

Rucker, Philip, and Anne Gearan. 2015. "Hillary Clinton Talks Middle-Class Roots in Pitch to Iowa Small Business Owners." *Washington Post*, April 15.

Schlosser, Eric. 2002. *Fast Food Nation: The Dark Side of the All-American Meal*. New York: Perennial.

Simon, Bryant. 2009. *Everything but the Coffee: Learning about America from Starbucks*. Berkeley: University of California Press.

Urquia, Norman. 2004. "'Doin' It Right': Contested Authenticity in London's Salsa Scene." Pp. 279–82 in *Music Scenes: Local, Translocal, and Virtual*, edited by A. Bennett and R.A. Peterson. Nashville, TN: Vanderbilt University Press.

Walser, Robert. 1994. "Highbrow, Lowbrow, Voodoo Aesthetics." Pp. 235–49 in *Microphone Fiends: Youth Music and Youth Culture*, edited by A. Ross and T. Rose. New York: Routledge.

Wherry, Frederick F. 2006. "The Social Sources of Authenticity in Global Handicraft Markets: Evidence from Northern Thailand." *Journal of Consumer Culture* 6(1):5–32.

19

Carnival culture

Karen Bettez Halnon and Harini Dilma Gunasekera

Introduction

Long the territory of literary scholars, historians, and anthropologists, the study of "carnival" is gaining visibility in cultural sociology because of the analytic purchase it yields on questions of aesthetics, performance, and power. *Carnelevare* (meaning literally "to lift up" or to say "farewell to the flesh") is a pre-Lenten meat-eating feast, dating back to about 965 CE (Kinser 1990). The years 1000 to 1300, the Christian Middle Ages, were known as the "cradle of carnival," and were followed by carnival's fullest European development from the 1300s to the 1500s. Subsequent diffusion occurred through colonization. Perhaps the world's most famous carnival, Carnevale, originated in Brazil in 1641. It is held in late February or early March, four days before Ash Wednesday, in Rio de Janeiro and Sao Paulo, as well as other cities such as Salvador, Porto Seguro, and Recife. Highlights today include over 100 *blocos* (block parades) around Rio and the lavish, high-profile competition between "sambo schools" that lasts the entire four nights of the festivities at the Sambodromo open stage. McGowan and Pessanha (1998) and Peronne and Crook (1997) provide historically contextualized and vividly ethnographic accounts of expressions of frivolity and sensuality on the beaches and in the streets, dance halls and clubs; these accounts convey carnival's roots in pre-Christian Greek and Roman celebrations and its arrival in Brazil as a "chaotic Portuguese entrudo" in which celebrants sling mud, dirt, flour balls, water, and other liquids at one another, often triggering riots (McGowan and Pessanha 1998:36; see also Peronne and Dunn 2002).

The most widely known contemporary rendition of carnival in the United States is Mardi Gras, a yearly public festival held in New Orleans, Louisiana, and Mobile, Alabama, with tracings to Caribbean roots (not French roots, as commonly supposed). This pre-Lenten Gulf Coast celebration lasts from 10 to 14 days and is held before Ash Wednesday (the number of days depending on the date of Easter). Like Carnevale, Mardi Gras involves the grandeur of street masking, costuming, dancing, drinking, feasting, chanting, cheering, bead tossing, and stripping amid parades of elaborate floats. Sexual repression is relaxed, and it is common to see bodies barely covered with paint, stripes, glitter, or feathers. The festivities climax (no pun intended) on Fat Tuesday with two parades: one at midday featuring the pseudo-monarchs and one in the early evening showcasing the two oldest secret societies – Mobile's Order of the Mystics and New Orleans's Krewe of Comus.

Latin American and/or Caribbean *carnavales*

Although less well-known, carnival culture extends throughout Latin American and the Caribbean, existing in diverse formulations. Before turning to analyses of carnival's social functions, we describe these formulations in some detail to give readers a sense of their international scope.

In Mexico, *carnaval* (as it is spelled in Spanish) begins the weekend before Lent, continuing for a full week. Clad in brightly hued costumes, dancers parade down the streets amid joyful live music, their costumes frequently connoting the area or the village in which the festivity is taking place. The King and Queen of Carnaval are presented as culminating features. Fair-like games and rides are also set up for the citizens to enjoy (Gagne 2011). Extending southeast to the city of Mazatenango, in Guatemala, carnaval has been a national holiday on July 9 since 1885 (Meneses 2013). Here, people come together en masse on dirt, cobblestone, and lava-paved roads to participate in parades featuring marching bands, costumed dancers, and picturesque floats. As in virtually all Latin American and/or Caribbean carnavales, the Queen of Carnaval, chosen by the city or town's designated group, marches in the parade. A signature feature of Guatemalan carnaval is the tradition of *cascarones* – eggs drained of their yolks and filled with effulgent confetti and small toys. Cascarones are typically cracked on another person's head as a mischievous gesture of celebration.

Costa Rican carnaval includes multiple festivals across different towns and cities within the country. Lougheed (2014) paints a vivid portrait of the four-day Costa Rican celebration in San José, Costa Rica's capital, and in the town of Oruro, where the celebration lasts a full week. The Oruro carnaval originated in 1789 after it was believed that the Virgin of Socavón fought and defeated the devil, thus liberating the town. The festival is a Catholic dramatization of good versus evil. It features a parade with dancers costumed as serpents, spiders, devils, and other creatures crawling on their hands and knees to invade the Sanctuary of the Virgin of Socavón; once inside, masks are removed a symbol of respect and the dancers pray and ask for blessings of good health, love, and prosperity. Also expressing Catholic folklore is the performance of *la Diablada*, the devil's dance, where performers in elaborate devil costumes spin down the street. The Sunday of the festival is known as the devil's biggest day – he is winning the battle – but the struggle continues and the following day he is vanquished, overcome by the forces of good. On the final day, families decorate their houses, sprinkle wine across different rooms, and light firecrackers to celebrate Pacha Mama (Mother Earth).

Panama City holds one of the largest carnaval celebrations in the Latin American world. Atypically, it is a state-sponsored event. It updates the tradition of *mojaderas* or *culecos* – getting drenched: during each day, the government provides big water trucks and hoses to cool off the crowd while individuals also use hoses, buckets of water, and water balloons to soak other celebrants. An additional feature of Panamanian carnaval is the Pollera Parade, which occurs on the Sunday prior to Ash Wednesday and features hundreds of women showing off their *polleras* – strikingly exquisite, voluminous, flowing skirts. Another common tradition is the rivalry between the uptown and downtown streets, each attempting to outdo the other with polleras, floats, dancers, music, and so forth. The festivities near conclusion on Ash Wednesday, during which time a mock ceremony is held, translated in English as the Burial of the Sardines (Soley 2009). People parade through the streets costumed as sardines in caskets, marking the end of carnaval and the start of Lent.

In Puerto Rico, carnaval is known as Carnaval de Ponce or Carnaval Ponceña. Dating back to the 1700s, it unfolds over the course of one week in the city of Ponce, concluding the day before Ash Wednesday. The parades feature terrifying and horrific characters, often sporting bulging eyes, long twisted horns, and fang-toothed grins; many of the costumes depict large, bat-like creatures with bat-shaped wings (Shafto 2009). Puerto Rican carnival is also known for its many brightly colored *vejigante* masks, which depict hollowed out eyes, horns, antlers, and the teeth and tongues of fish. Nearby in the Dominican Republic, carnaval is celebrated around the time of the country's Independence Day, February 27. Interestingly, Dominican carnaval expresses both its African and European origins. A key costumed character is the *diablo cojeulo*, representing a horned devil. *Las diablos cojeulos* lash out at spectators with rope reinforced by inflated cow bladders to purge the spectators of their sins. The costumes are intricately crafted of shells and jewels, frequently displaying amplified and distorted mouths such as thick lips or the jaws of a piranha. Another featured set of characters are the *Roba la Gallina*, who are cross-dressers. The character *Roba la Gallina* was inspired during the time of the Haitian occupation; women caught stealing chickens would be punished by having to walk in public plastered with chicken feathers (Perdomo 2014). There are also hundreds of wooden stalls, known as *casetas*, lining the street playing music and selling rum, beer, soda, snacks, and other sundry items (Foley, Jermyn, and Nevins 2016). Just to the west of the Dominican Republic, in Haiti, Kanaval is quite different, featuring the custom called *lamayoe*, in which young boys are dressed in costumes and whistle down viewers (NgCheong-Lum and Jermyn 2005). Passersby offer the whistlers a *lamayoe* – a box containing a lizard, mouse, or insect – in exchange for a few cents. In the past, people would traditionally burn their costumes on the last day of Kanaval, but today only the wealthy do this.

Farther south in the Afro-Caribbean is Trinidad's celebration of carnival. Here, carnival quite literally embodies the carnivalesque spirit of upturning the social-cultural-economic-political order. Traditionally, the festival was widely understood as a dramatic battleground pitting the anti-colonialist black and colored middle classes against British and French creole elites. Until fairly recently, mere participation was a form of rebellion against the elites because, as Green and Scher (2007:4) note, "the sexually suggestive and sometimes threatening styles of masquerade that dominated the Carnivals in the mid-1980s distressed the predominantly British Protestant middle-class that controlled the newspaper." At that time, the Afro-Trinidad middle class was the centerpiece of a national culture, and steel bands, with their dance-inspiring rhythmic beats, dominated the festivals. More recently, however, these bands have been replaced with recorded calypso and masquerade music. As oil revenue increased in the 1960s and early 1970s, the costumes and floats became much more lavish.

Finally, coming back eastward from the Caribbean to Europe, we find Notting Hill carnival. Founded in 1959, this carnival references the Windrush generation: hundreds of migrants on a ship by that name sailing from the Caribbean to Europe after World War II, known in part for their contributions to British swing music. The first carnival was organized in St. Pancras by communist and black activist Claudia Jones, after attacks on the West London black community. Notting Hill carnival represents traditions of Trinidadian costumes as well as calypso music (McKay 2015).

"Second life" and "second voice" in Bakhtin's medieval carnival

Deriving from the Latin *limins*, liminality means "a threshold passage betwixt and between two separate places," a "time filled with ambiguity" where there is "a confusion of all customary categories" (Carson 1997:3–4). For anthropologist Victor Turner (1995), liminality – where the individual is positioned marginally and ambiguously, irreducible to one thing or another – is a middle place, marked in relation to two other locations in an overall passage: separation (where the individual is detached from a prior state) and incorporation (where the individual re-enters the community in an altered state). Birth, death, marriage, puberty, and circumcision rituals are typical anthropological examples of liminality.

As conventionally applied to carnival, the concept of liminality clarifies it as a ritually organized and socially licensed time outside time that suspends, releases, and potentially changes those who pass through it. For Bakhtin ([1936] 1984), the foremost authority on medieval carnival, the "carnival spirit" offers a "chance to have a new outlook on the world, to realize the relative nature of all that exists, and to enter a completely new order of things" (Bakhtin [1936] 1984:89). An essential Bakhtinian understanding is that carnival is a festivity "giving birth" to a reality of its own, a second life, while being subject to its own utopian laws of freedom. Degradation and grotesque realism are central features that give voice to this second life. For Bakhtin, "to degrade is to bury, to sow, and to kill simultaneously. Grotesque realism . . . is the fruitful earth and the womb. It is always conceiving" ([1936] 1984:21). "Hence and to underline finally, through carnival's 'rebirth,' the 'world is destroyed so that it may be regenerated and renewed'" (Bakhtin [1936] 1984:48).

Bakhtin's studies, based on his reading of French author Rabelais, show that carnival peasant folk culture takes three distinct forms: (1) "ritual spectacles: carnival pageants, comic shows of the marketplace"; (2) "comic verbal compositions: parodies both oral and written"; and (3) "various genres of billingsgate: curses, oaths, popular blazons" (Bakhtin [1936] 1984:5). Bakhtin emphasized that, whatever its form, carnival only exists so long as spectatorship does not. Insisting as emphatically on this point as he did on carnival being a form of rebirth, he wrote, "Carnival is not a spectacle seen by the people; they live in it, and everyone participates because its very idea embraces all the people" (Bakhtin [1936] 1984:7). Hence, confusion and debate arise over whether certain writings, academic or mainstream, can be properly designated as "carnival." Although writing is performative (insofar as writers undertake the presentation of self for specific audiences) and participatory (at least insofar as there is engagement between authors and readers), it cannot be categorized as carnival unless it is performed publicly before an interactive crowd and located in a scene exhibiting carnival characteristics. Thus, in Bakhtin's conceptualization, contemporary comedic performances delivered via television, film, radio, or the internet – and specifically ones with carnival-grotesque dimensions that elicit laughter, shouting, revelry, and moral abandon – are better understood as *carnivalesque* than carnival per se.

In Bakhtin's description of public performances – notably, festive, pre-Lenten meat-eating feasts that bid "farewell to the flesh" – peasants let loose with dancing, parading, masking, drinking, hectoring, and sexual licentiousness. In such performances, the crowd becomes the "mass body." Rankings are obliterated, comically reversed, or inverted. Comic and grotesque "leaders" rule by consensus or by the immediate, fragile, and explicitly contingent will of the people. Barrier, boundary, and distance are replaced with absolute familiarity, with erotic and graphic exposure, with sensuous sweating, rubbing, and touching, and with equalizing farts and burps. Bakhtin's carnival rituals are centrally marked by the leveling, degrading, or "grotesque" exposure of what is otherwise hidden in or about the human body – genitals, breasts, orifices, fluids, and entrails. Bakhtinian carnival's symbol par excellence is the human body opened, exposed, and entirely unmitigated by repression or sublimation. The carnival body is distorted, deformed, degraded, decapitated, raped, sliced, mutilated, hacked, burned, desecrated, and so forth – all part and parcel of carnival's sundry and celebratory ludic violence. At the same time, however, the salivating, drooling, spitting, sneezing, defecating, urinating, bleeding, ejaculating, and violence that saturate Bakhtinian carnival are always consecrated with laughter.

However, it is not enough to upend officialdom, Bakhtin says, when seeking utopian freedom from the constraints of civility through festive rituals that trample temporarily over "official truth." Equally important is the suspension of conscience, judgment, superego, and the generalized other – what Bakhtin calls "the great interior censor." This latter process requires, for the entire duration of carnival, an exultant celebration of what in the first life of officialdom is typically repudiated as immoral, tasteless, deviant, or uncivilized.

The "positive" and "negative" functions of carnival

One of the basic tensions that cuts across studies of carnival cultures is the question of whether carnival's "second life" is conservative or transformative. Does it constitute a recuperative "safety valve" that releases pent-up steam only to ultimately preserve an oppressive status quo, or does it serve as a vehicle for challenging and potentially changing structural inequalities? Although Bakhtin regarded the opposition as a false one, subsequent scholars have nevertheless found it useful for analyzing contemporary instances of carnival culture, especially in the context of increasing commercialization, which inevitably shapes carnival's meanings and social effects.

The enduring applicability of Bakhtin's conceptualization of "second life" as "rebirth" is well-illustrated in Chris Humphrey's (2001) concept of "festive misrule," developed most fully in his essay "The Politics of Carnival: Festive Misrule in Medieval England." Humphrey argues against the notion that carnival is simply "a controlled release of pent-up steam" which serves to perpetuate the status quo (2001:6). But rather than applying Bakhtinian concepts directly, he employs the term "festive misrule," defined as any public and disruptive "custom" or "performance" that takes "place at a well-defined time of the year" and turns "upside down" or breaks "some established rules or norms in some way" (2001:40). His theorization of festive misrule relies on the broad concept of "symbolic inversion" (any transgression or inversion of meaning), which he elaborates in his own archival studies of festive practices in Norwich and Coventry such as mumming (festive cross-dressing), hocking (binding people of opposite sexes with ropes and charging money for release), feast of the boy-bishop, feast of fools, May Day, summer games, and Gladman's riding. These examples illustrates how symbolic inversion through festive misrule originated from a variety of sources and served a number of purposes, including complex and sometimes contradictory political and economic objectives.

In my own work, I (Karen) show how heavy metal music and its carnival culture express a dis-alienating politics of resistance (Halnon 2006). Drawing on extensive fieldwork at concerts and an analysis of music media (focusing on "high underground" bands such as Cradle of Filth, GWAR, and Insane Clown Posse), I apply Bakhtin's multifaceted conceptualization of the carnival-grotesque to argue that heavy metal music and heavy metal performances constitute a proto-utopian liminal alternative to the impersonal, conformist, superficial, unequal, and numbing realities of a society driven by commercialism and spectacle. In heavy metal carnival, the liminal second life is exemplified by grotesque bodies, inversion, experiences of collectivity and community, liberation from truth and order, liberation from interior censors, destructive humor, and rebirth. I argue, following Bakhtin, that liminal reality is reality – a creative medium for and by the people for imagining and living (at least for a few utopian hours) a radical difference from the everyday, oppressive status quo. I conclude that the elaboration and celebration of this radical difference reflects a desire to reclaim and recreate local culture according to a new sensibility; participants experience the dark side of heavy metal as "pregnant death, a death that gives birth" (Halnon 2006:46). At the same time, when "resistance" to the status quo goes mainstream and becomes commodified, the politics of alienation are transformed; the self-labeled "rejects," "freaks," and "trash" of transgressive artists and bands that claim to offer something "different" and "real" to fans in a society of the spectacle themselves become part of that spectacle. The commodification of alienated artists and their alienation experiences not only transforms alienation (at both points of production and consumption) into a source of profit, it may also forestall more conscious, directed, and pragmatic forms of rebellion (Halnon 2005).

Lucas's (1999) analysis of the rock band the Grateful Dead comes to a similar conclusion. He argues that much of the band's 25-year history exemplifies contemporary carnival (lyrics connecting the band to animals and the natural world, and cover art depicting fire-eaters, circus animals, and trapeze-swinging skeletons), but increasing commercialization led to the ultimate demise of this culture as the band incorporated and became Grateful Dead Productions – with a staggering multimillion-dollar upsurge in revenue, the result of soaring prices for concert tickets and branded merchandise in a context of manufactured scarcity. By contrast, Green (2002:283) criticizes what he calls "academic nostalgia," by which he means "the propensity of academics . . . to lament the supposed inauthenticity and commercialism that is said to accompany changes in Carnival." In his study of carnival in Trinidad and Tobago, Green suggests that academic nostalgia mirrors local critiques of carnival and is part of a larger recurring preoccupation with the supposed negative effects of commercialization on cultural life.

A more critical position toward the putatively progressive potential of carnival is taken by Samuel Kinser (1990:315), who argues that Mardi Gras rituals in the US conserve black-white barriers and are marked by "unregenerate elitism." In his words, "the social peace which reigns in Carnival is puzzling. Sexual and racial loves and hates, taboo the rest of the year, are lavishly displayed. In fact, Carnival is peaceful because it is explosive" (Kinser 1990:307). Phillip McGowan is similarly critical of carnival as egalitarian festive utopia. In "American Carnival: Seeing and Reading American Culture," McGowan suggests that carnivalesque forms may advance rather than eradicate inequality. Making comparisons between everyday conceptions of racialized "freaks" and their depiction in carnivalesque literary spaces, McGowan (2001:xi) argues that such spaces operate as "sanctioned territories in which the (white) spectator or tourist can witness carnivalized representations of Otherness." Departing from Bakhtin's temporal and spatial requisites for carnival, McGowan maintains that carnival is not limited in time and space. Rather, he sees it as a "symbiotic relationship of reinforcing belief systems . . . established between such overt locations as the side show, freak show, or World's Fair" and a "covert politics of seeing by which American society was categorized and interpreted" by a range of American literary figures including Nathaniel Hawthorne, Stephen Crane, Saul Bellow, William Faulkner, Lindsay Gresham, Walt Whitman, Ernest Hemingway, and Paul Auster (McGowan 2001:xi). In this conceptualization, carnivalesque forms (whether in literature or side shows) may be understood in fluid relation with the stratifying and objectifying mechanisms of everyday life. The particular point that McGowan stresses is that carnival's object is not an egalitarian eradication of inequality, but rather an inversion, reversal, or contestation of equalizing pressures. More specifically, his object is to show how equalities purported in "democracy's" "first life" are mitigated through the "second life" carnival form. This perspective resonates with that of Robert Bogdan, whose well-known *Freak Show* (1988) reveals in ethnographic detail the history of Barnum and Bailey, state fairs, and other traveling shows. Employing a symbolic-interactionist lens, Bogdan shows how "sideshow freaks" were constructed as spectacular human oddities for profit, and how carnival forms reconstruct and magnify the stigma associated with "deviance."

Other scholars approach the question of oppression versus transgression by arguing that the carnivalesque is both simultaneously. Gamson, for example, in his research on tabloid talk shows, calls attention to the "paradoxes of visibility that talk shows dramatize with such fury: democratization through exploitation, truths wrapped in lies, normalization through freak show" (1998:19). Gamson insists that there "is in fact no choice here between manipulative spectacle and democratic forum, only the puzzle of a situation in which one cannot exist without the other" (1998:19). Langman's (2008) study of body-adornment practices in "alternative" subcultures similarly calls attention to the double-edged nature of the carnivalesque. He argues that the "primitive" aesthetic exemplified by punk and heavy metal facilitates expressions of rage and protest, and that "porn chic" as a style implicitly critiques patriarchal codes of morality. At the same time, Langman (2008:657) argues that such phenomena can serve as "repressive desublimations that shunt discontent from the political economy to the culture and incorporate

potential dissidence." He reminds us that inequality for some (e.g., the asymmetric humiliation of women in pornography) can be a carnivalesque means of empowering others (e.g.,
relieving men of the everyday alienation they suffer under global capitalism). Langman's work
foregrounds the thesis developed by Mike Presdee (2000) that postmodern carnivalesque forms
tend to mask the pain of silenced or invisible subjects on whom the production of these forms
depends.

Although they too explore the safety valve function of the second life thesis, scholars Kevin
Fox Gotham, Chris Rojek, and Mike Presdee all analyze carnival in ways that do not fit neatly
within a "positive" and/or "negative" framing because of their emphasis on carnival's postmodern sensibilities. Gotham (2008:299) focuses on the worldwide cultural dispersion of Mardi
Gras, arguing that Mardi Gras has been simultaneously transformed by forces of modernity –
commodification and rationalization – and postmodernity – "the diversifying forces of difference and hybridity that constitute the postmodern condition." As a result, "local" features trace
to global industries, as exemplified by one of the most prominent icons of carnival, Mardi Gras
beads, which are produced by a handful of factories in China and reach gross annual worldwide sales approaching 500 billion. He suggests that in reconstructing local culture to fit the
demands of tourism, New Orleans is transformed into a contrived tourist destination and carnival becomes a "hyper-real" simulation of Mardi Gras, more real than the original (Gotham 2008;
see Peronne and Dunn 2002 for a similar account of the globalization of Brazilian carnival).
Taking a different tack, Rojek (2000) turns to postmodernism as the basis for theorizing his
carnival-like concept of "edgework" – activities and practices that invite temporary escape from
the dehumanizing conditions of everyday life. In elaborating this concept, Rojek (2000:186)
identifies three "abnormal" forms of leisure: "invasive," involving a lack of trust in or respect for
one's own self (such as excessive drinking or taking LSD); "mephitic," involving a lack of trust
in or respect for others (such as killing for recreation); and "wild," involving leisure practices that
"push limit-experiences momentarily over the edge for the purposes of personal gratification
and pleasure." Presdee (2000) takes a harder line, arguing against the recuperative function of
carnivalesque social formations in the postmodern context. For Presdee, unrelenting consumerism and the celebration of what he calls "the carnival of crime" precludes any possibility of
festival closure. His pessimistic diagnosis is that crime, violence, hatred, humiliation, and the
various pleasures they yield are the products of a largely deadened, hyper-rational, and shameless
social life that produces an unquenchable passion for destruction. We live in a world of endless
consumption, including the consumption of violence for fun, such that social integration is no
longer possible.

Future directions for carnival culture studies

The study of carnival culture is a relatively new topic for sociologists and therefore fertile
ground for future research. Studying carnival at a distance seems to undermine the whole notion
of carnival itself, as the philosophy of carnival emphasizes intimacy, dissolution of pretense, community, and commensality. Given that we live in a society where popular culture and consumer
culture are intimately intertwined, it will be necessary for future carnival studies to stretch the
traditional focus of ethnography and or ethnographic terrain into market relations while interrogating the slippery spaces of "utopia," "authenticity," and "dis-alienation."

Studies of specific carnival scenes may be guided by a number of fruitful topics of exploration and critique: the applicability and viability of traditional Bakhtinian carnival categories; the
carnivalesque as a pervasive feature of popular consumer culture; the implications of understanding carnival as a temporary or seasonal "second life" beyond the cultural dictates of everyday

life; carnivalesque consumption as an active response to alienation and/or dehumanization in a rationally organized and/or postmodern society; and the carnival production of "transgression" and "spectacle" as means of capitalizing on consumer desires for fun, escape, release, authenticity, difference, and enchantment (including the spiraling hegemonic effects of such production). Additional areas for exploration include the relationship between postmodernity, limit or "edgework" experiences, and the emotional consequences of rationally organized society; the various ways that commodified and commercialized renditions of the carnivalesque invert or reject efforts to achieve equalities of race, ethnicity, class, gender, sexuality, and religion (as well as the achievements resulting from such efforts); the dispersion of "Mardi Gras" and "Spring Break" festivities across numerous cities in the US and internationally; the meaning of carnival in specific traditions such as Halloween and the annual "Dracula's Ball" in Philadelphia; and the carnivalization of social protest.

Acknowledgments

It is with sadness that I note the passing of Karen Halnon on January 21, 2018. Karen was in the process of revising her chapter from the first edition, having taken on Ms. Gunesekera, an undergraduate student, as co-author, to assist with documenting the diverse manifestations of carnival throughout Latin America. The revision was incomplete upon her death, and so I undertook extensive editing and reorganizing, with Ms. Gunesekera's approval. The chapter presented here is thoroughly Karen's vision and largely the effort of the two co-authors. Karen made significant contributions to cultural sociology; she cared deeply about social injustice and devoted her life to researching the topic through a cultural lens.

—Laura Grindstaff, editor

References

Bakhtin, Mikhail. [1936] 1984. *Rabelais and His World*, trans. Helene Iswolksy. Bloomington: Indiana University Press.

Bogdan, Robert. 1988. *Freak Show: Presenting Human Oddities for Amusement and Profit*. Chicago: University of Chicago Press.

Carson, Timothy L. 1997. *Liminal Reality and Transformational Power*. Lanham, MD: University Press of America.

Foley, Erin, Leslie Jermyn, and Deborah Nevins. 2016. *Dominican Republic*. New York: Cavendish Square.

Gagne, Tammy. 2011. *We Visit Mexico*. Hockessin, DE: Mitchell Lane.

Gamson, Joshua. 1998. *Freaks Talk Back: Tabloid Shows and Sexual Nonconformity*. Chicago: University of Chicago Press.

Gotham, Kevin Fox. 2008. "Contrasts of Carnival: Mardi Gras between the Modern and Postmodern." Pp. 292–311 in *Illuminating Social Life: Classical and Contemporary Theory Revisited*. 4th ed., edited by P. Kivisto. Thousand Oaks, CA: Pine Forge Press.

Green, Garth L. 2002. "Marketing the Nation: Carnival and Tourism in Trinidad and Tobago." *Critique of Anthropology* 22(3):283–304.

Green, Garth L., and Philip W. Scher. 2007. *Trinidad Carnival: The Cultural Politics of a Transnational Festival*. Bloomington: Indiana University Press.

Halnon, Karen Bettez. 2005. "Alienation Incorporated: 'F★★★ the Mainstream Music' in the Mainstream." *Current Sociology* 53(4):441–64.

———. 2006. "Heavy Metal Carnival and Disalienation: The Politics of Grotesque Realism." *Symbolic Interaction: Special Issue on Popular Music in Everyday Life* 29(1):33–48.

Humphrey, Chris. 2001. *The Politics of Carnival: Festive Misrule in Medieval England*. Manchester: Manchester University Press.

Kinser, Samuel. 1990. *Carnival American Style: Mardi Gras at New Orleans and Mobile.* Chicago: University of Chicago Press.

Langman, Lauren. 2008. "Punk, Porn, and Resistance: Carnivalization and the Body in Popular Culture." *Current Sociology* 56(4):657–77.

Lougheed, Vivien. 2014. *Costa Rica's Caribbean Coast.* Edison, NJ: Hunter.

Lucas, Brad E. 1999. "Bakhtinian Carnival, Corporate Capital, and the Last Decade of the Dead." Pp. 79–88 in *Perspectives on the Grateful Dead: Critical Writings*, edited by R.G. Weiner. Westport, CT: Greenwood Press.

McGowan, Phillip. 2001. *American Carnival: Seeing and Reading American Culture.* Westport, CT: Greenwood Press.

McGowan, Chris, and Ricardo Pessanha. 1998. *The Brazilian Sound: Samba, Bossa Nova, and the Popular Music of Brazil.* Philadelphia, PA: Temple University Press.

McKay, George. 2015. *The Pop Festival: History, Music, Media, Culture.* New York: Bloomsbury Academic.

Meneses, Fernando. 2013. "Mazatenango's Carnaval." *Qué Pasa Magazine*, February 1. Retrieved May 25, 2017 (www.grupoquepasa.com/mazatenangos-carnaval/).

NgCheong-Lum, Roseline, and Leslie Jermyn. 2005. *Haiti.* New York: Cavendish Square Print.

Perdomo, Genesis. 2014. "Carnival Characters – #1 Roba la Gallina." *Casa de Campo Living*, February 11. Retrieved May 30, 2017 (http://casadecampoliving.com/carnival-characters-1-roba-la-gallina/).

Peronne, Charles, and Larry Crook. 1997. *Folk and Popular Music of Brazil.* Albuquerque, NM: Latin American Institute, University of New Mexico.

Peronne, Charles, and Christopher Dunn, eds. 2002. *Brazilian Popular Music and Globalization.* London: Routledge.

Presdee, Mike. 2000. *Cultural Criminology and the Carnival of Crime.* London: Routledge.

Rojek, Chris. 2000. *Leisure and Culture.* New York: Palgrave Macmillan.

Shafto, Daniel. 2009. *Carnival.* New York: Chelsea House.

Soley, La Verne M. 2009. *Culture and Customs of Panama.* Westport, CT: Greenwood.

Turner, Victor. 1995. *The Ritual Process: Structure and Anti-Structure.* Westport, CT: Greenwood Press.

Part IV
Culture and stratification

20

Status distinctions and boundaries

Murray Milner Jr.

Introduction

The thesis of this chapter is that both general theories and attention to cultural variations are needed to understand patterns of social behavior. Such patterned behavior in turn reproduces and changes the form and content of the culture. I will illustrate this thesis by focusing on the operation of status systems. After defining a few key terms and outlining a general theory of status relationships, I show how the processes and tendencies identified by the theory are accentuated or retarded by the content of the particular culture in which they operate. Proposing a general theory does not imply that culture is simply derived from or a reflection of structural relations, for structure is defined by cultural concepts, especially the concepts of social science.

What is status?

Although status has several meanings in social science (see Milner 2006), as used here it refers to the distinctions of rank or stature attributed to a person, group, idea, or object. Such distinctions are rooted in the accumulated expressions of approval and disapproval of other actors in a social environment. For individuals, these are typically the expressions of approval and disapproval by one's friends, family, and coworkers. But a person's status can also be affected by more indirect expressions of approval and disapproval, such as educational diplomas or criminal records. Organizations such as colleges, businesses, and voluntary associations can also have higher or lower levels of status. The same is true for cultural concepts and objects. Some are relatively abstract categories (e.g., occupation, ethnicity, and gender) or principles (e.g., values, norms, or rules). Others are more concrete physical objects (e.g., automobiles, paintings, buildings, or cities). Status is a form of power and, like economic and political power, can become a generalized social resource, which can be thought of as a form of capital. (I do not deal with the notions of social and cultural capital since they are considered elsewhere in this handbook.)

Having economic power or wealth can give one status, but this is not necessarily the case. People may admire a successful entrepreneur, but they do not generally praise successful burglars and embezzlers. Tyrants and those who have acquired great wealth by exploiting the vulnerable may receive deference, but they seldom have high approval ratings. The focus in this chapter is on status that is relatively independent of economic and political power. This is a kind of power in its own right. The ability of the pope, Martin Luther King Jr., or J.K. Rowling to influence people is not primarily because of their economic or political power. Hence, in addition to economic and political power, there is status power.

What are status systems?

Status is a relational concept: A person or thing has high or low status compared to someone or something else. Usually such relationships form a system, arena, or field. Each status system has its own specific status criteria. The attributes that give a chess player high status are different from the ones that give a boxer high status. Status systems vary in (1) how well defined their boundaries are, (2) how precisely they make status distinctions, and (3) how much these distinctions coincide with other forms of social inequality. In most modern professional armies, the boundaries of the organization are quite clear, positions are unambiguously ranked, and these ranks are highly correlated with pay and authority. On the other hand, for artists or public intellectuals, the system boundaries, individual rankings, and their correlation to income and authority are often ambiguous.

How do status systems work?

The theory of status relationships (Milner 2016:39–44) is aimed at explaining patterns of relationships that emerge when status is an important resource. There are two key assumptions. First, as stated earlier, status is not simply reducible to economic or political power. Second, for someone or something to have a social status, that person or thing must have some level of social visibility. *New York Times* columnists and conservative talk-radio hosts are well-known and have high status in relation to largely different segments of the US public; neither columnists nor hosts have visibility or social status in most Asian villages.

In addition to the assumption of social visibility, the theory has five elements. The first two elements focus on how status differs from other social resources.

Inalienability

Status is relatively inalienable. Although a person can give someone else their money, they cannot give away their status, nor can others simply appropriate it by force or purchase it with money. Hence, once a status – whether high or low – is acquired, it tends to be relatively stable. This is why the status of those with "old money" may last longer than their actual money.

None of this is to suggest that status is absolutely stable. The stability of status is affected by other factors, including the degrees of (1) institutionalization (i.e., being part of a long-organized, taken-for-granted pattern), and (2) insulation from economic or political rewards (e.g., politicians or preachers who become extravagantly rich lose their status and legitimacy).

Inexpansibility

Status is relatively inexpansible compared to wealth or political power. If everyone receives a Nobel Prize or is a member of the aristocracy, these are no longer bases of distinction. In contrast, the income of a person can triple and their objective circumstances change significantly, even though their relative status remains unchanged. This relative inexpansibility of status has two important implications. First, if someone moves up, someone else is likely to have to move down. Therefore, those with higher status tend to restrict upward mobility. If anyone could add their name to the Social Register or join the National Academies of Science, this would erode the status of all of the group's members. Second, one way of moving up is to put others down. This is the reason that teenage cliques, Indian upper castes, and country club members often disparage those below them. It is why "critique" – which, in part, is putdown by another name – is central to intellectual life and high culture.

The next two elements of the theory focus on the sources of status.

Conformity

A key source of status comes from conforming to the norms of a group – and it usually requires expressing the "right" values and beliefs and using the right symbols. Conformity to one set of norms and values may mean violating another set. The teenager who too enthusiastically follows official school norms usually violates the norms of his or her peers. A less obvious implication is that those who have high status often complicate the norms to make it difficult for others to conform. The elaborate manners and rituals of aristocracies are an obvious example. When it is relatively easy to copy high-status behaviors, high-status actors may change the norms frequently. This is why fashion is often important.

Association

Associating with higher-status individuals, groups, and objects raises one's status; associating with low-status people and things reduces one's status. Especially important are publicly visible, intimate, expressive relationships, as contrasted to instrumental relationships. Sharing food and sex are near-universal symbols of intimacy. Who you marry and who comes to your dinner parties has more effect on your status than which plumber you use. Teenagers are often preoccupied with who eats with whom in the lunchroom and who is "hooking up" with whom.

Pluralism

The theory also has implications for the sources of cultural pluralism. In a high school of 200, 10 percent, or 20 students, can constitute a very visible "popular crowd." In order for other students to improve their own status, they often copy the behavior of the popular crowd and adopt their style and symbols. Moreover, many students have direct interpersonal associations with members of this elite: they live in the same neighborhood, were friends in elementary school, or attend the same religious youth group. Such connections make the popular crowd less remote.

If, however, the school has 2,000 students, 10 percent comes to 200 individuals – far too many for them to be highly visible to everyone. The odds are much lower of having any direct contact with them, or becoming a member. Consequently, the excluded often create alternative crowds and cliques with different norms, values, beliefs, and symbols. The restrained tailored elegance of the preps is countered by the "in your face" eclectic exhibitionism of punks or hipsters.

If alternative subcultures grow strong, the result can be a near-complete rejection of the dominant subculture. In the case of teenagers, this can result in resentful, alienated students or school drop-outs. A parallel at the societal level involves 1960s protestors who became revolutionaries or emigrated to other countries. Strong subcultures can lead to conflict between groups. Conflicts between ethnic, religious, and language groups are common in schools, prisons, and whole societies. The existence of alternative cultures, however, can also foster a multicultural school or society in which individuals affirm being both Americans and Latino, or both French and

European. The key point is this: expanding the size of status systems produces structural pressures toward cultural differentiation and pluralism – but also conservative resistance to such changes.

Finally, pluralism is one of the ways in which the inexpansibility of status is qualified, but not eliminated. Multiple status systems may emerge as the result of pluralism, allowing different individuals to gain status in different systems. In pluralistic high schools, being in the popular crowd is not the only way for teenagers to receive respect and appreciation. However, different systems may themselves develop status relative to each other. Thus, great skill in playing dominos may create status among those who play dominos, but in the broader culture, grandmasters in chess have greater prestige than dominoes champions.

Boundaries

The notion of boundary suggests an especially strong distinction that includes and excludes. Clear boundaries reduce ambiguity. There are physical boundaries and symbolic boundaries, which are sometimes strongly correlated (e.g., Jewish ghetto walls) and sometimes not (e.g., the boundary lines between different cities or states in some metropolitan areas).

Status system boundaries vary greatly in their precision and rigidity. There tends to be little consensus about where to draw a clear line between smart and dumb, pretty and ugly, or moral and immoral. A coercive authority can impose such distinctions, but such categories have little legitimacy. That is to say, the status of such status boundaries would be low.

Intimate, expressive associations usually involve much stronger boundaries than instrumental ones. High-status executives may work closely with an array of lower-status assistants, but rarely are such subordinates invited home for dinner or to play golf. In racist societies, members of the dominant group may regularly interact with members of the subordinated group, but they do not intermarry. Stated another way, the manipulation of associations is a central mechanism of creating and maintaining social and cultural boundaries. As Michele Lamont (1992) has pointed out, the same culture may have different symbolic boundaries depending on whether the focus is on distinctions that are moral, socioeconomic, or cultural (in the sense of art, music, manners, etc.).

What are the effects of culture?

So far, I have focused on processes that shape the structure and operation of status systems in most, if not all, cultural contexts. Now let us turn to how the content of cultures affects these processes.

Ideologies of equality and hierarchy

A focus on certain ideologies like egalitarianism or hierarchy can affect a culture's status relations. Two polar examples are the US and traditional India. The US Declaration of Independence declares: "all men are created equal." Of course, it took many decades before American ideology made explicit that this included women, people of color; LGBTs have only recently (and incompletely) been included. Nonetheless, outside observers from Tocqueville on have noted that Americans are relatively egalitarian in their ideology and their interpersonal interactions. In contrast, throughout most of India's history, not only did the culture assume a hierarchy of castes, but a hierarchy of rulers existed, with the most powerful of kings seen as an incarnation of the god Vishnu. In contemporary India, egalitarian notions are incorporated in its constitution and articulated by politicians. Support for caste and hierarchical assumptions are articulated in relatively disguised form, but open expressions of suspicion and hostility toward non-Hindu minorities are not uncommon.

In the nineteenth and twentieth centuries, similar contrasts in ideology have been noted between the US and Europe (Lipset 1996). The key point is that although the structural tendencies outlined in the theory of status relations are operative in most societies, their intensity is modified by the extent to which the predominant culture legitimizes equality or hierarchy.

The status of status and its correlation with economic and political power

In societies and other social units, the relative importance (i.e., the status) of political power, economic power, and status power varies. Political power was central in the Soviet Union, whereas economic resources are the predominant form of power in most capitalist societies. In traditional India and Tibet, religious and ritual status were central forms of power in their own right; the power of Brahmins and Tibetan monks was not reducible to their economic and political power.

Closely related but logically distinct from the relative importance of a form of power is its correlation with, and convertibility to, other forms of power. In traditional India, wealth could not easily overcome the stigma of being born into a low caste. Brahmins were ritually superior to others, but only in a few regions were they the richest or most powerful caste. That is, caste status was an important form of power, but it was loosely correlated with wealth or political power. In contrast, in a number of aristocratic societies, status and political power were highly correlated (Geertz 1980; Elias 1983). Similarly, in the Soviet Union, political power was usually converted into status and economic privilege. Other forms of status, such as artistic accomplishment, might be converted into economic privilege, but were seldom the route to political power. In the US, new wealth can gain great respect relatively quickly, with Bill Gates, Warren Buffett, and George Soros being obvious examples.

Such variations in the relative importance of forms of power, and their convertibility, seem to be rooted in historical-cultural particularities. In India, caste status depended to a significant degree upon ritual purity and impurity (Dumont 1980; Milner 1994). In China, admission to the mandarin political bureaucracy was based on passing examinations on the Confucian classics. Differences in the levels of technology or wealth do not explain the centrality of caste in India or the centrality of the mandarin system in China. In each case, these key institutions were legitimized by particular ideological constructs, assumptions, and symbols that were both relatively unique and linchpins of their whole culture.

The content of culture

Many taken-for-granted notions are limited to a particular cultural context. Knowledge of Confucian classics was irrelevant in India, and Brahmin purification rituals would do nothing to improve one's status in China. Less apparent is the way that relatively specific cultural notions can shape the details of social interaction and relationships and patterns of social change. I will illustrate this with three examples. The first concerns the key symbols of intimacy, food, and sex.

Food, sex, and segregation

Racial segregation in the US was once frequently compared to the traditional Indian caste system (Cox 1948). Rigid hierarchies in principle allowed no mobility across race or caste lines. These lines were reinforced by notions of the purity of "superiors" and the impurity of "inferiors." In both cultures, intermarriage and eating together were barred. In India, however, notions of social and physical purity were closely linked (Marriott 1976). Impure foods changed the nature of one's physical substances, which in turn decreased one's purity and social standing. Consequently, who prepared the food was important because the impurities of the cook were transferred to the food, and in turn degraded the bodily substances (and status) of those who ate it. At events involving different castes, the cook was usually a Brahmin, so that no one would be contaminated. Unsurprisingly, such notions were emphasized more by upper castes than lower castes. In Swidler's (1986) terminology, an assumed link between social and physical purity was part of the general cultural toolkit, but upper castes used this tool more than lower castes.

In the pre-civil rights US, predominantly in the South, restaurants, water fountains, and restrooms were segregated. However, a clearer distinction was made between social purity and physical purity than in India – at least with respect to food. Black servants were frequently cooks, and upper-class whites sometimes competed to employ blacks noted for their culinary skills. Moreover, in the wake of the Civil Rights Movement of the 1950s and '60s, large numbers of African Americans more openly created a counterculture that had a higher status than the more repressed "Negro" subcultures of earlier years. This counterculture was symbolized by the phrase "black is beautiful." Many elements of culture became subject to revaluation. For example, what had been low status food – often the cheapest cuts of pork – became "soul food"; often it was considered a valued culinary specialty by whites as well as blacks.

For sex and procreation, physical purity did affect social purity. Although before the civil rights era, sex between white men and black women was common, whites had great concern about the status of the offspring of such liaisons. The result was the "one-drop" rule: anyone who had even "one drop of Negro blood" was considered black, and hence had low status. This was not simply a convention; it was incorporated in state laws. By contrast, in much of Latin America, although notions of pure and impure "blood lines" existed, there was not a "one-drop" rule even though people were often ranked on the basis of their color and ancestry.

These examples from traditional India, the pre- and post-civil rights US South, and Latin America illustrate that even though diverse groups share the tendencies outlined in the theory of status relations, important differences in patterns of behavior are often shaped by seemingly esoteric variations in relatively local cultural concepts.

The market, individualism, and the therapeutic society

Not only does the status of individuals, groups, and objects change over time, but fundamental cultural assumptions rise and fall in status. For example, the early acceptance of psychotherapeutic perspectives in the US was due to the therapy's compatibility with the core assumptions of liberal capitalism. Philip Reiff (1968) has noted and criticized what he calls "the triumph of the therapeutic" – a culture centered on personal fulfillment and thin notions of morality. Reiff (1968) and Lasch (1978) see this culture as having disturbing consequences – though others see the developments more positively (Marcuse 1974; Ziguras 2001; Woolfolk 2003; Hall, Neitz, and Battani 2003). My point is not to debate the consequences or merits of these developments, but rather to emphasize that they represent an enormous change in the status of alternative sets of core cultural norms and assumptions.

There have been moral ambiguities in every era, but certainly most Americans in the nineteenth century had a pretty strong sense that some things were "right" and some things were "wrong." Stated another way, it was relatively clear what would receive approval and disapproval, as were the moral boundaries that resulted. Thus, the shift from Victorian morality to a therapeutic morality was a fundamental shift in American cultural ideas and norms. Victorian cultural hallmarks such as Rudyard Kipling's "You'll be a man, my son," or Frank Buchman's "moral rearmament" implied radically different moral stances than such late twentieth-century maxims as "Go with the flow," "I'm OK, you're OK," "I am comfortable with that," or "Whatever." Compared to the resistance directed toward other major cultural innovations (e.g., Darwinism or legalizing abortion), criticism and resistance were modest given the scope and implications of the cultural change. The shift to a therapeutic culture seems to have been almost subliminal. How do we explain why there was so little resistance?

Freudian theory claims that mental illnesses result from the repression of painful experiences. Individuals so traumatized cannot act rationally because they live in a world of distorted information and reality – in the form of neuroses, obsessions, and even psychoses. Psychoanalysis enables people to recall the past deforming experiences and face up to the present situation that actually confronts them. The choices they face may involve unavoidable tragedy (e.g., becoming alienated from a domineering parent or spouse), but once healed, the patient can make such choices rationally. Other types of psychotherapy may attribute irrationality to other sources or propose other forms of therapy, but virtually all seek to help people overcome distorted ways of thinking or deforming emotions.

This is the same logic as that of the individual facing the market: rational choices depend upon both opportunities to choose alternatives and receiving accurate information about the cost and consequences of the alternatives. These options may not be appealing – sell now at a loss or sell later at a bigger loss – but the better the information and the more rational the actor, the better the decisions.

The preceding analysis suggests how existing cultural assumptions can shape the likelihood of new cultural innovations being accepted, that is, gaining a relatively high status. A more extensive test of the hypothesis would require not only much more detailed analysis of American society (e.g., Illouz 2007), but comparative analysis with other societies. There are existing studies of the reception of psychoanalysis and psychotherapies in India and Russia. Freud's ideas were enthusiastically accepted in the early years of the twentieth century in some intellectual circles in pre-revolutionary Russia. Even after the Russian Revolution, Freudianism was initially respected, though eventually banned. The Indian Psychoanalytic Society was officially recognized by the International Psychoanalytic Congress in 1922, before there was a recognized branch in France. But in both cases, Freudian thought ran up against both cultural assumptions that were antithetical to notions of the independent individual and the nuclear family, as well as other important cultural incompatibilities (Miller 1990; Hartnack 2001). As a consequence the overall impact of psychotherapy was quite limited in India and Russia.

My argument is that both classic liberal economic and political thought *and* psychotherapeutic perspectives promote the ideal of the rational individual making choices that are undistorted by false information or irrational emotions. In Weber's terms, there was an "elective affinity" between these two understandings of the optimal circumstances. Resistance to the therapeutic perspectives was so modest because "the Great Transformation" in the economic and political sectors, which had occurred in earlier centuries (Polanyi 1957), had already overcome cultural resistance to the notion of individuals making free, rational choices in the economic and political realms. The "triumph of the therapeutic" extended this conventional wisdom to the emotional and moral realm. In the terms of the theory of status relations, the therapeutic perspective conformed to norms and values that already had enormous status in other realms of the culture. My argument suggests how existing cultural assumptions shape the likelihood of cultural innovations being accepted, that is, gaining a relatively high status.

Pluralism, Brexit, and globalization

How might even structural changes hinge on cultural developments? Let us begin to address this question by identifying some structural tendencies characteristic of most status systems and cultures.

As noted earlier, pluralism usually increases as networks and social units become larger, in part because a higher percentage of the population tends to have little contact with the elite. The average individual is known to a smaller percentage of the enlarged population; because of the inexpansibility of status, most individuals tend to have less status. Hence, they often create or re-emphasize alternative subcultures. These subcultures are especially likely if the new broader economic and political structures benefit some much more than others. These structural factors suggested by the theory of status relations affect a wide variety of social units, from teen peer groups in high schools, to nation-states, to multinational organizations, to globalization. An additional structural factor is the age structure; young people are more likely to create new alternative subcultures; older people are more likely to hold on to or revive older identities based on ethnicity, language, religion, and so forth.

These structural factors contribute to an explanation of Brexit, the British vote in June 2016 to exit the European Union (EU). There are two related but separate questions. First, who in the British population supported the exit and who opposed it? In favor of leaving were (1) older people in rural counties, (2) people in the English midlands, which had declined both in prosperity and status, and (3) an array of others who felt threatened by the increasing number of immigrants. Support for the EU came from younger people, metropolitan London, and regions where many people long had felt dominated by England, that is, Northern Ireland, Scotland, and substantial parts of Wales.

But these structural factors have also affected other parts of Europe that remain committed to the EU. We must turn to historical and cultural factors to understand the difference between Britain and the rest of Europe. First, older British voters remember or have heard about the "glories" of the British Empire and have experienced Britain's decline as a world power. Second, the "special relationship" with the US and the British Commonwealth of Nations gives Britons a sense that there are other potential, largely English-speaking, non-European trading partners and political allies. Third, although England sustained enormous losses in both world wars, it was never invaded or occupied, as were the core units of the EU: France, Germany, Italy, and Belgium. Older Britons take pride in their victories in both world wars. In contrast, France, Germany, and Belgium are highly motivated to avoid the devastation of such wars through cross-national European cooperation and solidarity. That is to say, there are differences in the deep cultural assumptions of Britain and the rest of Europe.

With respect to the broader issue of globalization, the same structural features are relevant and they create tensions in a number of parts of the world. Because of the inalienability of status, it is usually easier to expand economic and political ties and boundaries than to change the significance of cultural boundaries. And the latter tend to be more fixed for older than younger people. It is not easy for the older British or French to demote the Union Jack or the Tricolor and be moved emotionally by the flag of the European Union. This reluctance to give up cultural boundaries and status symbols is seen in many parts of the world. The African Union has expanded economic and political ties, but certainly has not lessened internal struggles. As of this writing there are serious internal conflicts in the Democratic Republic of Congo, Gambia, Kenya, Libya, Nigeria, Somali, South Sudan, and Zimbabwe – to mention only some of the conflicts in Africa. In Asia serious internal divisions have emerged in Afghanistan, Bangladesh, Myanmar (Burma), Thailand, China, India, and Pakistan. These conflicts are often rooted in economic and political rivalries, but friends and enemies are typically defined by cultural and status boundaries such as differences in tribes, language, and religion. In short, it is easier to expand economic and political boundaries than the boundaries of shared culture, especially if this means undermining and sometimes demeaning established cultural symbols of solidarity. To a significant degree, the future of the UK, the EU, and globalization in general will be shaped as much by status and cultural concerns as by economic and political issues.

Conclusion

An adequate sociological analysis must conceptualize status as a distinct form of power, not reducible to economic or political power.

It is useful to consider not only the status of and the relationships between individuals and groups, but also the status and relationships between cultural objects – from particular commodities to core cultural assumptions.

Drawing on both general theories that focus on near-universal structural relationships and attending carefully to the details of particular cultures, including the history of their development, is the best strategy for understanding the nature of status relations in concrete historical settings.

References

Cox, O. 1948. *Caste, Class, and Race: A Study in Social Dynamics.* New York: Doubleday.

Dumont, L. 1980. *Homo Hierarchicus: The Caste System and its Implications.* Chicago: University of Chicago Press.

Elias, N. 1983. *The Court Society.* New York: Pantheon Books.

Geertz, C. 1980. *Negara:* The *Theatre State in Nineteenth-Century Bali.* Princeton, NJ: Princeton University Press.

Hall, J.R., M.J. Neitz, and M. Battani. 2003. *Sociology of Culture.* New York: Routledge.

Hartnack, Christiane. 2001. *Psychoanalysis in Colonial India.* New Delhi: Oxford University Press.

Illouz, E. 2007. *Cold Intimacies: The Making of Emotional Capitalism.* Cambridge: Polity Press.

Lamont, M. 1992. *Money, Morals, and Manners: The Culture of the French and American Upper-Middle Class.* Chicago: University of Chicago Press.

Lasch, Christopher. 1978. *The Culture of Narcissism: American life in an Age of Diminishing Expectations.* New York: Norton.

Lipset, S.M. 1996. *American Exceptionalism: A Double-Edged Sword.* New York: Norton.

Marcuse, Herbert. 1974. *Eros and Civilization: A Philosophical Inquiry into Freud*, with a new preface by the author. Boston: Beacon.

Marriott, M. 1976. "Hindu Transactions: Diversity Without Dualism." Pp. 109–42 in *Transaction and Meaning: Directions in the Anthropology of Exchange and Symbolic Behavior*, edited by B. Kapferer. Philadelphia, PA: Institute for the Study of Human Issues.

Miller, M.A. 1990. "The Reception of Psychoanalysis and the Problem of the Unconscious in Russia." *Social Research* 57(4):875–88.

Milner, M., Jr. 1994. *Status and Sacredness: A General Theory of Status Relations and an Analysis of Indian Culture.* New York: Oxford University Press.

———. 2006. "Status." Pp. 596–99 in *Encyclopedia of Social Theory*, edited by A. Harrington, B. Marshall, and H. Muller. London: Routledge.

———. 2016. *Freaks, Geeks, and Cool Kids: Teenagers in an Era of Consumerism, Standardized Tests, and Social Media.* 2nd ed. New York: Routledge.

Polanyi, K. 1957. *The Great Transformation: The Political and Economic Origin of Our Time.* Boston: Beacon Press.

Reiff, P. 1968. *The Triumph of the Therapeutic: The Uses of Faith after Freud.* New York: Harper and Row.

Swidler, A. 1986. "Culture in Action: Symbols and Strategies." *American Sociological Review* 51(2):273–86.

Woolfolk, Alan. 2003. "The Therapeutic Ideology of Moral Freedom." *Journal of Classical Sociology* 3(3):247–62.

Ziguras, Christopher. 2001. "Narcissism and Self-Care: Theorizing America's Obsession with Mundane Health Behavior." *Journal of Mundane Behavior* 2(2):260–77.

21

Culture and stratification

Omar Lizardo

Introduction

In contemporary sociology, the link between culture and stratification is a burgeoning area of research. Breaking with "materialist" forms of analysis in which culture is seen as epiphenomenal with respect to outcomes related to stratification and inequality, sociologists today are busy investigating the myriad ways in which seemingly inconsequential, and thus easy to miss, cultural processes operate to modulate access to social, material, and symbolic rewards (Savage, Warde, and Devine 2005; Lamont, Beljean, and Clair 2014). This work becomes more important as culture-infused arenas such as schools have come to acquire a predominant role in determining individual life chances across the world (Frank and Meyer 2007). A key insight here is that social institutions, especially educational institutions, are not culture-neutral but rather are saturated with the culture of the upper-middle classes, thus making it easier for upper-class individuals to successfully navigate them while making it harder for working-class individuals to do so (Stevens, Armstrong, and Arum 2008; Lareau 2011; Stephens et al. 2012; Armstrong and Hamilton 2013).

Status situations, class situations, and status cultures

The analytic foundations of modern culture and stratification research are rooted in the key distinction, first laid out by German sociologist Max Weber, between an individual's "status situation" and "class situation." Weber defines status situation as "every typical component of the fate of those individuals determined by means of a specific positive or negative social estimation" on the part of others (Weber 1994:113). The *class* situation, on the other hand, is best characterized by "opportunities to gain sustenance and income" (Weber 1946:301). Research in culture and stratification centers on specifying the ways in which an individual's status situation is affected by, and in turn affects, their class situation. Because status "expresses itself in the specifically stylized way of life to which all aspiring members [of the relevant group] are expected to adhere" (Weber 1994:114), the sociological analysis of status situations in culture and stratification research merges with the study of the origins and consequences of distinct *status cultures*.

In addition, because privileged status groups sustain and reproduce their position largely via the "monopolization of [access to] ideal and material goods" (Weber 1994:117), studies of culture and stratification are deeply tied to the sociology of cultural consumption and cultural taste (Peterson 2005; Khan 2011).

As a result, contemporary work on the link between culture and stratification conceives of the lifestyle characteristics of a status culture as being composed of a complex of elements, including values, skills, habits, and worldviews. Research thus endeavors to connect status-based cultural antecedents (e.g., an individual's current or previous status situation, as well as socialization into specific status cultures) to stratification outcomes further down the line. These outcomes are primarily trajectories of achievement or exclusion within the dominant institutional settings in charge of determining life chances and distributing stratification-relevant rewards (e.g., schools, labor markets, work organizations). This emphasis differentiates culture and stratification work from what sociologists usually refer to as "class analysis," which usually looks at the relationship between contemporary (or past) and future class situations (Savage et al. 2005).

The emergence of status cultures

We can divide contemporary research on the culture and stratification linkage into two broad strands. First is work seeking to examine how different status cultures emerge from specific interactional, institutional, and cultural processes, including material conditioning by the relevant class situation. This work, in turn, seeks to link distinct status cultures to other dominant institutions in society seen as relevant for stratification outcomes. The "linkage hypothesis" – that status cultures affect an individual's trajectory and rewards within society's major stratifying institutions – is thus central to contemporary culture and stratification research.

Socialization into status cultures

The work of Pierre Bourdieu (1984) has generated a major rethinking of both the "dynamic" (process) and "results" (outcomes) of the phenomenon of differential socialization across status groups. While retaining a focus on the origins of bounded class cultures in differentiated societies, Bourdieu differs from classical work on this subject (Collins 1975) in conceiving of socialization into status cultures as less driven by a reflective process of value or worldview inculcation (e.g., Kohn 1977) or a linguistically mediated process of transmission of class-specific "cultural codes" (e.g., Bernstein 1971) and more on an implicit, embodied, unconscious immersion in a holistic social, symbolic, and material environment.

This implicit immersion is driven by a child's exposure to parental practices keyed to instruction and socialization; her active, bodily interaction with material objects and built environments; and her exposure to specific experiences. The acquisition of such tacit competences leads to the development of an unconscious, undirected (but ultimately systematically organized) set of expectations, styles of appreciation, schemes of perception, and systems of practical action in the world – what Bourdieu called the "class habitus." The habitus is an enduring (but dynamic) cognitive structure that produces thoughts, reactions (aesthetic, cognitive, and moral) and choices (e.g., what to buy, what to major in, who to marry) that is in tune with (and attempts to recreate, within limits) the environment in which it developed (Bourdieu 1990). This explains why we can recurrently observe individuals socialized within distinct status environments "constructing class positions for themselves . . . without awareness that they . . . [are] engaged in doing so" (Bettie 2003:190).

Parental socialization into working- and middle-class status cultures

Annette Lareau's (2011) recent work on the emergence of specific orientations within working- and middle-class households largely tracks this conception of how status cultures emerge. She shows that by adopting a distinct, ideal-typical orientation toward child-rearing, middle-class parents are able to transmit distinct cultural advantages to their children. Middle-class parents rely on what Lareau calls the logic of "concerted cultivation," which involves constant participation in structured extracurricular educational, cultural, and athletic activities outside the home. Through these forms of social and cultural participation middle-class children come to be endowed with a set of habitual social skills – such as the ability to treat adults in position of authority as equals – allowing them to more readily navigate dominant institutions (such as schools) and more fully customize them for their needs.

Working-class parents adopt a different posture toward child-rearing: the logic of "natural growth." Here, the primary parental responsibility is to provide for the child's basic needs (e.g., food, shelter, safety). Because the natural growth approach sees children's talents as inherent in their person, following a logic of spontaneous maturation and expression rather than a logic of cultivation and learning, there is less perceived need for constant, competitive cultivation of special skills. This leads the child to spend more of her time among familiar same-age kin in unstructured domestic activities rather than developing the competencies needed to navigate established social institutions. When it comes to interacting with adults and professionals in positions of power in these institutions, working-class children are thus at a distinct interactional disadvantage because they cannot insist on a customized experience better suited to their individual needs. This is why schools come to be experienced by working-class children (across categories of race and gender) as impersonal and removed from everyday concerns; schools become sites of generic restraint rather than sites that facilitate personal growth.

Importantly, Lareau demonstrates that status cultures can be transmitted from parent to children in a largely implicit way. In fact, sometimes the status culture that is *actually* transmitted clashes with the culture that parents *believe* they are transmitting via their explicit instruction and guidance. For instance, Weininger and Lareau (2009) set out to test Kohn's (1977) proposal that middle-class parents emphasize an orientation toward "autonomy," "self-direction," and "freedom from control" in relation to established authorities and conventions whereas working-class parents emphasize an orientation toward "conformity," "obedience," and adaptation to extant rule structures. Their research, triangulating between interview-based and observational data, uncovers a paradox: the Kohn prediction seems to hold true *only* when it comes to adult self-reports of parenting style and socialization goals or in terms of what parents explicitly say to their kids. In these circumstances, middle-class parents do seem to emphasize a language of autonomy and independence (e.g., negotiation with children over rules, emphasizing choice behavior) and working-class parents do seem to emphasize a discourse of obedience (e.g., issuing directives without qualification, justifying decisions by reference to positional authority), especially when it came to intergenerational interactions within the household.

However, when it came to socialization processes linking the child to institutional realms outside of the household, middle-class parents spent countless hours attempting to shape their children's behavioral dispositions in a direction of conformity and adaptation to institutional environments populated by adults in authority, and maximizing the amount of "leisure" time spent in structured (rule-governed) activities under tight supervision and control. This type of enculturation occurred via both explicitly symbolized interaction (e.g., the issuing of verbal directives) and, most significantly, via the enmeshing of the child in organizational structures endowed with habitual routines attuned to the spatial and temporal rules of the institution, sometimes involving the direct manipulation of the body. On the other hand, working-class parents followed a practical rule of "autonomy" in which children spent the majority of their time in unstructured self- or peer-directed activities with very little in the way of intergenerational interaction. Here there was little to no exposure to practical enculturation dedicated to managing or navigating institutional environments controlled by adults in authority positions outside of the household.

In sum, while sometimes being hard to discern, systematically distinct class and status cultures continue to exist and reproduce themselves across generations. This reproduction does not need to be intentional or instrumental, as it can happen as a result of habitual dispositions. Socialization within these status cultures, in its turn, has important repercussions for the educational trajectories of youth.

The linkage between status cultures and dominant institutions

A primary warrant for studying the origins of status cultures for culture and stratification researchers has to do with the non-arbitrary links between status cultures and the trajectory of individuals in the social institutions most likely to affect stratification outcomes in contemporary society. One of Bourdieu's (1984, 1998) key contributions was to show how recognized and unrecognized linkages between status cultures and dominant institutional domains contribute to the stratification processes. His analysis combines Weber's emphasis on status situations as partially autonomous and capable of driving class situations, Marx's emphasis on power and cultural hegemony, and Durkheim's emphasis on the social origins of shared systems of thought and classification. For Bourdieu, status-based advantages produced within the family and in formal occupation-based class cultures come to be inscribed in the very classificatory framework of the institutions in charge of sorting persons into positions that monopolize the extraction of class-based advantages.

From this perspective, all of the major of institutions of market-based societies (e.g., education, science, art, the state) carry the "imprint" of the upper-middle-class status groups largely responsible for their emergence (Collins 1979; Stephens et al. 2012). It is thus impossible achieve a state of "universality" that is not grounded on some delimited, and usually privileged, status culture; what happens instead is that different status groups compete to for this claim to "universal" representation. Status group reproduction occurs when members of certain (privileged) status cultures transmit the habits, competencies, and dispositions most readily recognized and rewarded by social institutions, as discussed earlier. This provides senior members of dominant status cultures with a probabilistic advantage in terms of ensuring the success of their children within those institutional worlds, thus guaranteeing some form of intergenerational transmission of the symbolic means of institutional authority and control.

Cultural capital as linkage mechanism

The term "cultural capital" was introduced by Bourdieu and Passeron (1990) in order to better understand patterns of inequality – such as "educational inheritance" or the differential ability of the sons and daughters of educated parents to be judged as better students by their teachers – in educational outcomes in French schools. The concept of cultural capital has nevertheless enjoyed a much more flexible and generalized applicability, mainly due to the impact of Bourdieu's (1984) classic study *Distinction*, in which he used the concept to explain differential rates and styles of engagement in the (institutionally legitimated) arts. The book's key argument is that cultural elites display an "aesthetic disposition" (a valued way of acquiring and displaying knowledge) that functions as cultural capital because it is the most institutionally legitimated (e.g., through its reinforcement by educational institutions) way of appropriating aesthetic goods, although it is not the only one. Bourdieu concluded that it was this differential capacity to apply aestheticizing cognitive schemes to the different symbolic goods produced by the symbol-production fields of the more legitimate (and sometimes the popular) arts that served as the primary differentiating factor among arts consuming audiences in late-modern societies.

According to Bourdieu, any set of status-based dispositions embodied in habitus that produce advantage when deployed in a given institutional setting, counts as "capital." Thus, dispositions that facilitate the appropriation of collectively validated cultural goods at any historical point (e.g., the "fine arts") or the ability to master those forms of linguistic expression that are accorded most value in the larger society (e.g., "idiomatic" English; Bettie 2003; Carter 2005) — can be thought of as dominant cultural or linguistic capital when they provide the children of culturally advantaged class fractions with the ability to produce styles of self-presentation that are perceived (consciously or implicitly) by institutional gatekeepers as indicating the mark of a superior student, endowed with sophistication and intelligence.

In the Anglo-American literature, there are two primary conceptualizations of cultural capital informing contemporary theory and research on the culture and stratification linkage. One, partially based on Bourdieu's (1986) influential formulation, conceives of cultural capital as an *aptitude*, a *proficiency*, or a *skill* acquired in the combined realms of the upper-middle-class family and the school system. The other major conceptualization of cultural capital is concerned with addressing what are perceived to be ambiguities in this formulation. From an alternative perspective focused on *symbolic boundaries*, Lamont and Lareau (1988:164) define cultural capital as "the institutionalized repertoire of high status signals" useful for purposes of marking and drawing symbolic boundaries in a given social context. This definition attempts to forge a connection to a Weberian theory of status group closure: whatever counts as cultural capital are those symbolic resources that are actively mobilized by members of groups or class fractions to establish their difference from (and superiority over) other groups.

Carter (2005) shows how both of these definitions can be empirically relevant and put to illuminating theoretical use. In her studies of economically disadvantaged minority youth, she argues that what counts as cultural capital is context-specific and that *how* cultural capital is deployed determines its usefulness. Thus command of both dominant (institutionalized) cultural patterns (e.g., ability to speak in ways typical of the white majority) and familiarity with minority cultural patterns ("black" slang; taste for certain musical and sartorial styles associated with African American oppositional youth cultures) can serve as cultural capital. The former allows minority youth to navigate their way through established institutions (schools, the workplace, the law), while the latter can be used to claim "authentic" membership in their ethnic subculture. In this manner, cultural capital can be used not just a boundary-drawing resource, but also as a vehicle for claiming ownership of desirable ethnic and racial identities. More importantly, it is precisely those youth who develop the ability to "straddle" dominant and non-dominant forms of cultural capital who appear to reap the benefits of acceptance by both ethnic peers and representatives of conventional success.

In a related study, Warikoo (2011) shows that a similar model of multiple forms of cultural capital applies in a comparative context. In a study of first generation minority youth in London and New York City, Warikoo shows that fashion styles and musical tastes required to gain status among same-age peers, mostly derived from a now globally diffused hip-hop culture mainly produced by American black artists, are often interpreted by school authorities on both sides of the Atlantic as signifying "opposition" to school norms and link to "street" criminality. Yet, Warikoo finds little evidence that engagement with this sort of non-dominant cultural capital is associated with anti-school norms or less desire to do well academically. In this respect, the *meanings* immigrant minority youth give to certain forms of cultural engagement and styles of self-presentation can be systematically out of step with the meanings conveyed to adult authorities within and outside of the school context, with important consequences for the institutional trajectories of immigrant youth.

"Omnivorousness" and the new elite culture of "tolerant distinction"

A paradox besetting the sociological study of elite status cultures is the rise of what Ollivier (2008) once provocatively referred to as "conspicuous openness to diversity" and what most scholars, following Peterson and Kern (1996), refer to as "omnivorousness." This is the tendency on the part of contemporary cultural elites to claim a "multicultural" openness to a wide variety of aesthetic experiences involving a seemingly broad cross-section of cultural goods. Countless studies, across dozens of national settings using survey and interview methods to capture the stated preferences and associated motivational accounts of elites, find that high-status culture today seems to be characterized by an openness to cultural diversity and a refusal to reject specific cultural genres, forms, or objects (Lizardo and Skiles 2012).

In contrast, cultural analysts have observed that in spite of the ascendance of the language of multiculturalism – tolerance, respect for diversity, and non-comparability across forms of participation – elites continue to engage aesthetic objects in ways that seem to be both class-coded and linked to class-specific experiences (Khan 2011; Friedman and Kuipers 2013). When suitably prodded, the same elites betray an implicit preference for complexity, formal innovation, and a purposive authorial intention in cultural works even when engaging objects and experiences where these qualities are not to be expected (Holt 1998; Atkinson 2011). In other words, while the stated culture of contemporary elites is definitely attuned to the values of inclusion and cross-cultural expression, they continue to *engage* an ever-expanding set of cultural objects in inherently class-marked (i.e., exclusionary) ways (Johnston and Baumann 2014). This persists despite the fact that elites lack a coherent discourse marking their cultural engagement (or even themselves) as particularly distinct (Khan 2011). The gap between habit and discourse notwithstanding, it is clear that there has been a conservation of modes of cultural consumption distinctive to high-status groups such that the ways elites engage cultural goods can be understood as an extension of the set of exclusionary practices first developed in the traditional "fine arts" (Lizardo and Skiles 2012).

Consequently, forms of aesthetic appreciation and judgment linked to elite status cultures continue to be reliably fostered and transmitted in upper-middle-class households, and concomitantly predicted by the usual markers of privilege and advantage – without explicit exclusionary reference to alternative modes of engagement and without the transmission of an elaborate ideology anointing elite preferences as superior. As with the case of the transmission of paradoxical class cultures noted earlier (Weininger and Lareau 2009), the seeming paradox of high-status cultural consumption is important to assess critically because, left unexamined, it suggests that elite ways of *talking* about culture are synonymous with elite culture itself, with the corresponding (and problematic assumption) that status cultures do not make a difference for lifestyle practices (Atkinson 2011). One solution to this impasse is to recognize that elite cultural capital is a complex amalgam of both explicit discourses and non-explicit practices not necessarily liable to exhibit strong coherence and unity.

Moral repertoires of evaluations as constituents of status cultures

As we have seen, much research attempting to conceptualize the role of culture in marking divisions across status follows Weber and Bourdieu in keying in on the role of cultural aptitudes and lifestyle consumption patterns. Michèle Lamont's work (1992, 2000) has presented a creative and influential corrective to Bourdieu's emphasis on cultural aptitudes as the main "marker" of symbolic boundaries across status groups. (A related emphasis on moral dispositions as a distinct part of the class "habitus" has also been recently developed by Sayer [2005].)

In *Money, Morals and Manners*, an ambitious comparative analysis of the boundary-drawing discourses of members of the French and American upper-middle class, Lamont (1992) argues that upper-middle-class American men tend to draw boundaries between themselves and others on the basis of moral and economic criteria (e.g., hard work, economic achievement) whereas their French counterparts are more likely to rely on cultural criteria (e.g., aesthetic taste, abstract intellectualism). For upper-middle-class white men, then, boundary work – and even the operation of cultural capital more narrowly defined – is shaped by national context, reflecting national differences in the place/role accorded cultural concerns in the broader society as well as differences in how professional work is related to the market.

The importance of moral boundaries comes to full analytic fruition in *The Dignity of Working Men* (Lamont 2000), an equally ambitious comparative study of the French and American working class. Here, Lamont analyzes how nationally and ethnically specific "institutionalized cultural repertoires" (2000:243) come to regulate the boundary-drawing strategies of working-class men both when aiming "upwards" toward members of the upper-middle class or "laterally" toward perceived as undeserving members of excluded racial and ethnic groups. Lamont shows that it is impossible to understand these patterns of exclusion/inclusion and the role played by values such as "hard work" or "honesty" without getting a handle on the distinct, context-specific cultural models deployed by different fractions of the working class, both within a given national context (e.g., black versus white men in the US) or across national societies (e.g., the relatively higher emphasis of French working-class men on cross-racial solidarity based on trade unionism).

Conclusion: broadening and deepening the research agenda

As we have seen, contemporary analysts of the culture-stratification link are engaged in an active research agenda, seeking to understand the origins of status cultures and their consequences for individual trajectories in dominant institutions. A key focus has been on uncovering the cultural processes through which status-based advantage are transmitted across generations or produced and reproduced in concrete contexts (Lareau 2011; Stephens et al. 2012; Lamont et al. 2014).

Much of this work, even that taking a more comparative approach (e.g., Lamont 1992, 2000; Warikoo 2011), is centered on the Euro-American West, and is thus not as fully geographically and cross-culturally extensive as it could be. Although recent moves toward the study of "repertoires of evaluation" (Lamont 2012) promise to help expand the field, we have very limited knowledge of the relationship between status and class situations outside of the Euro-American context. We know especially little about how cultural repertoires deployed for the demarcation of symbolic boundaries operate in non-Western low-income or developing countries (but see Üstüner and Holt 2010).

Outside of sociology, there is a vibrant and growing literature on culture consumption and global media in anthropology and communication focusing on non-Western contexts, but few researchers in global media studies make use of fundamental sociological insights on the relationship between status-based stratification and lifestyle. An exception is the work of Joseph Straubhaar (2007), who has productively applied insights from Bourdieu's cultural capital framework to study the relative appeal of global versus local cultural products in Brazil. He finds that cultural and economic capital have a strong effect in inducing media choices for "cultural proximate" symbolic goods, with those culturally advantaged individuals gravitating toward "global" culture and those endowed with less cultural capital preferring regional and local fare. This work takes a good first step toward greater dialogue between globalization scholars and those studying culture and stratification.

Further progress in the field requires both a continuation of work looking at the processes that generate distinct status cultures and how membership in these cultures accrues status-based advantages for some groups and disadvantages for others (Lareau 2011; Stephens et al. 2012). It is critical to continue examining the increasingly complex linkages connecting status group membership to success within (for the privileged) and exclusion from (for the less privileged) dominant institutions (Armstrong and Hamilton 2013). It is also important to begin theorizing emergent institutional sites within which new forms of status-based exclusion are solidified (see for instance Illouz [2007] on the increasing importance of middle-class forms of "emotional capital" in contemporary workplaces), so that we may shed light on the sometimes surreptitious ways in which institutional logics based on particular class cultures come to acquire society-wide authority with consequences for social stratification.

In addition, we need more research that spotlights the fine-grained processes responsible for the transmission of cultural resources within and across generations and institutional sites. There remain gaps in our knowledge regarding the concrete realization and operation of the cultural and interactional mechanisms that generate status-based privilege and make possible the intergenerational transmission of cultural advantage, as well as their role in governing access to sites where material and symbolic rewards are allocated – such as hiring for prestigious jobs (Rivera 2012) or succeeding at elite schools (Khan 2011). It is only by having a clear handle on the micro-mechanisms and processes of status-based reproduction that we can understand the origins of the apparently "natural gifts" that allow members of privileged status groups to effectively navigate key institutional settings and acquire the social certification necessary for shaping the life chances of everyone in contemporary societies.

References

Armstrong, E.A., and L.T. Hamilton. 2013. *Paying for the Party*. Cambridge, MA: Harvard University Press.

Atkinson, W. 2011. "The Context and Genesis of Musical Tastes: Omnivorousness Debunked, Bourdieu Buttressed." *Poetics* 39(3):169–86.

Bernstein, B. 1971. *Class, Codes and Control*. Vol. 1, *Theoretical Studies Towards A Sociology of Language*. London: Routledge and Kegan Paul.

Bettie, J. 2003. *Women Without Class: Girls, Race, and Identity*. Berkeley: University of California Press.

Bourdieu, P. 1984. *Distinction: A Social Critique of the Judgement of Taste*. Cambridge, MA: Harvard University Press.

———. 1986. "The Forms of Capital." Pp. 241–58 in *Handbook of Theory and Research for the Sociology of Education*, edited by J. Richardson. New York: Greenwood Press.

———. 1990. *The Logic of Practice*. Stanford, CA: Stanford University Press.

———. 1998. *The State Nobility: Elite Schools in the Field of Power*. Stanford, CA: Stanford University Press.

Bourdieu, P., and J.C. Passeron. 1990. *Reproduction in Education, Society and Culture*. London: SAGE.

Carter, P.L. 2005. *Keepin' It Real: School Success Beyond Black and White*. Oxford: Oxford University Press.

Collins, R. 1975. *Conflict Sociology: Toward an Explanatory Science*. Cambridge, MA: Academic Press.

———. 1979. *The Credential Society: An Historical Sociology of Education and Stratification*. Cambridge, MA: Academic Press.

Frank, D.J., and J.W. Meyer. 2007. "University Expansion and the Knowledge Society." *Theory and Society* 36(4):287–311.

Friedman, S., and G. Kuipers. 2013. "The Divisive Power of Humour: Comedy, Taste and Symbolic Boundaries." *Cultural Sociology* 7(2):179–95.

Holt, D.B. 1998. "Does Cultural Capital Structure American Consumption?" *Journal of Consumer Research* 25(1):1–25.

Illouz, E. 2007. *Cold Intimacies: The Making of Emotional Capitalism*. Cambridge: Polity Press.

Johnston, J., and S. Baumann. 2014. *Foodies: Democracy and Distinction in the Gourmet Foodscape*. New York: Routledge.

Khan, S.R. 2011. *Privilege*. Princeton, NJ: Princeton University Press.

Kohn, M.L. 1977. *Class and Conformity: A Study in Values, with a Reassessment, 1977*. Chicago: University of Chicago Press.

Lamont, M. 1992. *Money, Morals, and Manners: The Culture of the French and the American Upper-Middle Class*. Chicago: University of Chicago Press.

———. 2000. *The Dignity of Working Men*. New York: Russell Sage Foundation.

———. 2012. "Toward a Comparative Sociology of Valuation and Evaluation." *Annual Review of Sociology* 38:201–21. https://doi.org/10.1146/annurev-soc-070308-120022

Lamont, M., S. Beljean, and M. Clair. 2014. "What Is Missing? Cultural Processes and Causal Pathways to Inequality." *Socio-Economic Review* 12(3):573–608.

Lamont, M., and A. Lareau. 1988. "Cultural Capital: Allusions, Gaps and Glissandos in Recent Theoretical Developments." *Sociological Theory* 6(2):153–68.

Lareau, A. 2011. *Unequal Childhoods: Class, Race, and Family Life*. Berkeley: University of California Press.

Lizardo, O., and S. Skiles. 2012. "Reconceptualizing and Theorizing 'Omnivorousness': Genetic and Relational Mechanisms." *Sociological Theory* 30(4):263–82.

Ollivier, M. 2008. "Modes of Openness to Cultural Diversity: Humanist, Populist, Practical, and Indifferent." *Poetics* 36(2–3):120–47.

Peterson, R.A. 2005. "Problems in Comparative Research: The Example of Omnivorousness." *Poetics* 33(5–6):257–82.

Peterson, R.A., and R.M. Kern. 1996. "Changing Highbrow Taste: From Snob to Omnivore." *American Sociological Review* 61(5):900–7.

Rivera, L.A. 2012. "Hiring as Cultural Matching: The Case of Elite Professional Service Firms." *American Sociological Review* 77(6):999–1022.

Savage, M., A. Warde, and F. Devine. 2005. "Capitals, Assets, and Resources: Some Critical Issues." *British Journal of Sociology* 56(1):31–47.

Sayer, A. 2005. *The Moral Significance of Class*. Cambridge: Cambridge University Press.

Stephens, N.M., S.A. Fryberg, H.R. Markus, C.S. Johnson, and R. Covarrubias. 2012. "Unseen Disadvantage: How American Universities' Focus on Independence Undermines the Academic Performance of First-generation College Students." *Journal of Personality and Social Psychology* 102(6): 1178–97.

Stevens, M.L., E.A. Armstrong, and R. Arum. 2008. "Sieve, Incubator, Temple, Hub: Empirical and Theoretical Advances in the Sociology of Higher Education." *Annual Review of Sociology* 34(1):127–51.

Straubhaar, J.D. 2007. *World Television: From Global to Local*. Thousand Oaks, CA: SAGE.

Üstüner, T., and D.B. Holt. 2010. "Toward a Theory of Status Consumption in Less Industrialized Countries." *Journal of Consumer Research* 37(1):37–56.

Warikoo, N.K. 2011. *Balancing Acts: Youth Culture in the Global City*. Berkeley: University of California Press.

Weber, M. 1946. "The Social Psychology of the World Religions." Pp 267–301 in *From Max Weber: Essays in Sociology*, edited by H.H. Gerth and C. Wright Mills. New York: Oxford University Press.

———. 1994. *Sociological Writings*, trans. W.V. Heydebrand. London: Continuum International.

Weininger, E.B., and A. Lareau. 2009. "Paradoxical Pathways: An Ethnographic Extension of Kohn's Findings on Class and Childrearing." *Journal of Marriage and Family Counseling* 71(3):680–95.

22

Cultural capital and tastes

The persistence of *Distinction*

David Wright

Introduction

Taste is variously invoked to describe a physical sensation, aesthetic sense, or moral sensibility, and it can be a characteristic of people or of things. It is a key concept in the sociology of culture, connecting accounts of the centrality of the choice and preference for goods in the struggle for status across the twentieth century with the various reflexive freedoms available for the construction of late-modern lifestyles. Foundational to this strand of study is *Distinction: A Social Critique of the Judgement of Taste* by the French sociologist Pierre Bourdieu, one of the most influential and controversial works of cultural sociology yet published. "Cultural capital" emerges from *Distinction* as the definitive Bourdieusian concept, and this chapter will concentrate on its changing role in processes of taste formation. It will argue for the continued centrality of Bourdieu's schema for understanding the role of cultural production and consumption in social stratification and reproduction, despite a range of transformations in both these processes themselves and in the ways in which they are researched and understood.

Although Bourdieu was not the first to reveal that an individual's taste is socially organized, the significant contribution of *Distinction* was to undermine the belief, stemming from Kant ([1790] 1987), that notions of aesthetic value are somehow ahistorical, reflecting a common sense of the beautiful. Bourdieu does more than reveal that tastes are socially constructed; he argues for a place for personal taste in struggles for social position – struggles ostensibly organized between class fractions. There are homologies for Bourdieu between hierarchies of "legitimate" and "popular" culture and the positions of those attracted to these forms in social and economic hierarchies. The appreciation of culture helps constitute class relations. Taste represents the lived experience of the social structure – a manifestation of an individual's stock of cultural capital, which can exist in three forms. First, cultural capital is *institutionalized*, meaning it emerges from forms of socially accredited institutions – nominally schools and universities, which bestow it in the form of qualifications as well as through the canonization of particular cultural texts, pieces of music, or works of art as worthy of study. Second, it is *objectified*, and is accrued by the ownership or knowledge of specific works of art, books, and pieces of music. Finally, it is *embodied*, revealed by the "correct" comportment of the body in dress or styles of speech. Different forms of cultural capital can be traded or accumulated in different arenas, or *fields*, of social life, but within the structuring, overarching field of power it is the possession of those forms which have been legitimized or consecrated by cultural elites which do most to cement one's social position.

Alongside this concern with the *consumption* of culture, Bourdieu makes a significant contribution to our understanding of the production of culture and, by extension, the production of *tastes*. In *Distinction*, tastes are produced by the consecration of legitimate culture by the education system and reproduced in the family via the class system, on the one hand, and by the operation of taste-makers or *cultural intermediaries* on the other. An emerging fraction of the middle class of 1960s France, cultural intermediaries are defined by Bourdieu as "all the occupations involving presentation and representation (sales, marketing, advertising, public relations, fashion, decoration and so forth) and in all the institutions providing symbolic goods and services" (Bourdieu 1984:359). If, as Bourdieu identifies, this was a group of increasing importance in the understanding of cultural life in 1960s France, their significance has grown rapidly since then in the societies of the Global North. In other work, Bourdieu (1993, 1996) argues that cultural capital is central to the *production* of cultural goods. Fields of cultural production, he suggests are variously organized according to the spread of cultural capital between two extremes or "poles." This spread maps onto the various commitments of producers and consumers as actors within fields to the concern with art for art's sake on the one hand (the "autonomous pole") and the concern with art for the sake of economic profit on the other ("the heteronomous pole"; Bourdieu 1996:124). The "game" of culture requires producers committed to the various positions in the field, with those richer in cultural capital tending toward the autonomous pole. It also requires consumers with similar commitments. Bourdieu describes the "universe of celebrants and believers" (Bourdieu 1996:169), rich in cultural capital and ready to accept the ideas of "canonical" or "classic" or avant-garde culture and to adhere to these labels in their judgments of taste (their own and others). The effect of the charismatic belief in culture, the *illusio* that cultural taste is outside of social struggles that Bourdieu lays bare, is the persistent preservation of good taste as the property of those in the cultural know, *naturalizing* relationships of class and power.

We might ask how an empirical study of the tastes of 1960s France can meaningfully engage us in other times and places. A model based upon apparently solid distinctions between legitimate and popular culture appears dated given the insights of new academic approaches to the complexity of popular culture, wrought, for example, by Cultural Studies. A model based upon the "rarity" and consecration of cultural activity and its policing by experts of various kinds fits uneasily into the contemporary experience of abundant culture, particularly that enabled by emerging media technologies which have multiplied and dispersed the means of cultural production and consumption. Such developments appear to allow the game of culture to be played out over wider and more accessible terrain than Bourdieu anticipated. Despite these qualifications, I argue that the relationship Bourdieu establishes between taste and power retains considerable explanatory power.

Cultural capital and taste since *Distinction*

In the 40 years since *Distinction* was written, and particularly in the 30 years since it was published in English, a number of researchers have engaged with Bourdieu's work, revealing important lacunae in the general relationships he uncovers. Such developments remind us that the relationship between cultural capital and taste is a methodological and empirical as well as a theoretical or conceptual one. Holt tellingly implies that, in the context of answering a survey – the basis of Bourdieu's work and the dominant instrument in subsequent studies – informants' responses "are best understood as ideological accounts constructed for rhetorical purposes of the survey situation" (Holt 1997:115). Similarly, Antoine Hennion, in a critical account of the dominant approaches to taste within the sociology of culture, suggests the assumed ability for a judgment of a like or a dislike to stand firmly for a social characteristic is consistent with a kind of determinism. In the real world, Hennion argues, such a relationship between taste and social characteristics "is rarely observed," at least away from the survey setting (Hennion 2007:101). Clearly the items which are asked in surveys of cultural activity and their relative importance, alongside the ways in which researchers categorize and construct the class structure of their specific social space and time will have an impact on the relationships such work can reveal. This emphasis on relationality is important for claiming the continued relevance of cultural capital. *Distinction* is an account of the process by which Bourdieu's respondents come to like things, based upon an assumption of their relative significance in relation to a vision of legitimate, consecrated, popular or mass culture, organized into a hierarchy which is assumed, for good empirical reasons, to be somehow settled and homologous with social hierarchies. The evidence of the 40 years since might suggest that both cultural and social forms of hierarchy can be constituted in different ways.

American sociology in particular has generated its own tradition of research into the relations between culture and class and reimagined the relationships that Bourdieu outlines, principally inspired by the empirical discovery of the cultural "omnivore" by Richard A. Peterson and colleagues (e.g., Peterson and Kern 1996). The figure of the omnivore, emerging from a developing research infrastructure of policy concerns to identify and measure cultural participation within national populations, seemed to challenge the homological relationships between cultural and social hierarchies. Specifically, research on "omnivorousness" discovered the selective incorporation of items of popular culture into the taste portfolios of the professional middle classes, suggesting a certain openness to the tastes of others among the professional classes and implying an end to crude forms of snobbishness. Efforts to find an omnivorous orientation, or some variant of it, have moved beyond the US and become something of a cottage industry within cultural sociology. In their review of the concept's methodological development, Kardamir Hazir and Warde (2016) identify 124 articles about the omnivore, some discussing the concept but most attempting to operationalize it through various empirical mechanisms. These contributions are spread across a range of countries. In his own review of the concept's career, Peterson (2005) identified 11 countries, primarily focused on North America and Europe, to which we can now add examples from Asia (Yoon, Kim, and Eom 2011), Africa (Snowball, Jamal, and Willis 2010), and Latin America (Torche 2010). It is clearly difficult to dismiss the weight of this empirical material and the persistent patterns that they identify between forms of cultural participation and social class or status. The meanings of these relationships, though, are less clear. If the early claims for the omnivore positioned it as a harbinger for new forms of tolerance (Erickson 1996), more recent reflections are as likely to imagine it as emblematic of new forms of distinction (Bennett et al. 2009; Atkinson 2011; Lizardo and Skiles 2012). If in the past one's cultural capital was displayed through disinterested contemplation, today it is just as often displayed through claims to eclecticism and tolerance. As Friedman et al. (2015) and Jarness (2015) explore in their work, the "what" of cultural capital (i.e., the particular objectified artifacts which can be deployed to demonstrate possession of cultural capital) has arguably become less important than the "how" of cultural capital – the strategic ways in which it is deployed and the confidence and competence that possession of it still implies for the incorporation or dismissal of cultural forms beyond Bourdieu's more restricted vision of "legitimate" culture.

This insight opens up some other of the apparent solidities of cultural capital as spelled out in *Distinction*. Recent interventions here emphasize that the aesthetic disposition, characterized (following Kant) as inherently detached and disinterested, is being replaced in the taste practices of the middle and upper classes with other attitudes. Savage and Prieur (2013) speculate about a decline in the level of respect afforded to traditional forms of high culture, which undermines the ability of high culture to confer social advantage. This declining respect does not necessarily entail the end of distinctions or the emergence of cultural democracy but it does suggest that the mechanisms through which cultural capital is produced and distributed are not fixed and eternal. The relationality inherent in Bourdieu's model implies as much. Hanquinet, Roose, and Savage (2014) put empirical flesh on these bones with their exploration of how aesthetic preferences are expressed by museum visitors in Belgium. Here, while oppositions between popular and legitimate remain, the content of legitimate aesthetics includes an assumption that art should be *about* something and engaged with ideas and concepts rather than just displaying beauty, harmony, or perfection of form. Far from being detached, museum visitors in this study expressed preference for work that narrated and reflected contemporary forms of experience and even aimed at generating reactions. For Hanquinet et al., this indicates a shift in the nature of aesthetics which reminds us that neither Kant's initial assertion about the pure, detached, aesthetic gaze, nor Bourdieu's rejection of it, can really be understood as ahistorical and eternal. If disinterestedness was part of the formation of the art world of the nineteenth century, in its twenty-first-century variant both producers and consumers now encourage and expect style *and* substance.

The geographical spread of the omnivore concept discussed earlier also highlights a second substantive criticism of *Distinction* which subsequent research has revealed; that Bourdieu's schema is not generalizable across space and time (Holt 1997). In particular, it is not applicable to the American context where, as the omnivore thesis initially implied, a more egalitarian or dynamic culture prevents the ossification of class and taste positions – though it does not prevent, as Lamont (1992) notably reveals, symbolic boundary-making along moral or racial lines. *Distinction* is resolutely French and therefore framed by the symbolic and cultural imaginaries of France. In light of processes of globalization, which often have questions of cultural practice and the role of the cultural industries at their heart, an avowedly national study is perhaps bound to feel anachronistic. Nevertheless, two recent developments in cultural capital research point toward the continuing significance of Bourdieu's conceptual template. First is the accumulation of more recent work which follows or attempts to update, critique, and develop the Bourdieusian framework, incorporating Bourdieu's conceptual or empirical approach in whole or in part and applying to other national spaces and/or historical moments – for example, twenty-first-century UK (Bennett et al. 2009), Denmark (Prieur, Rosenlund, and Skjott-Larsen 2008), or Finland (Kahma and Toikka 2012). The second is the emergence of comparative research that recognizes the limitations of the national character of *Distinction* and attempts to address this limitation through comparisons with other national and international studies (e.g., Katz-Gerro 2002; Kuipers 2015). This is itself a reflection of the challenges posed to sociology more generally by processes of globalization – especially if societies (sociology's de facto emphasis) are imagined as synonyms for nations. Such a position – reflecting what Chernilo (2006) describes as "methodological nationalism" – is perhaps increasingly unsustainable conceptually but is powerfully underpinned by the relations between the infrastructures of sociological research and their location in specific national spaces. The impetus to internationalize potentially undermines the principal arguments relating to taste and distinction through the application of comparative perspectives. Daloz (2010), for example, argues that comparison *between* nations inevitably loosens the grip of conceptual language derived from *within* nations. Comparison has the potential to open new frontiers of debate over the operation of cultural capital within and between national spaces, a move that poses a particular challenge for a theoretical model like Bourdieu's in which the nation is a container, even a synonym, for social spaces or fields, making the boundaries that constitute cultural capital in its various forms less legible. Bourdieu (1998) himself, in his reflections on the applicability of his approach to Japan, implies that the relationality of the model of capital, habitus, and field is transferrable but that the terms of the struggles for position – the items or preferences that might contribute to social advantage in a specific national space – might differ. As Purhonen and Wright (2013) explore in their comparison of the UK and Finland, the same preferences (e.g., liking English Premier League football) can express different meanings in different spaces and that attention to local (national) meanings remains an important corrective to superficial curiosity about different national taste cultures.

New rules in the game of culture

If the preceding examples reveal how scholars in the Bourdieusian tradition can adopt and adapt its methodological approaches and theoretical assumptions in reinvigorating the concept of cultural capital for different empirical times and places, in this section I consider two further contexts in which the explanatory power of the concept has been, and has the potential to be, productively applied.

First, and complementing the kind of comparative, international work described earlier, is research which makes links with debates about cosmopolitanism, the postnational form of subjectivity identified with varying degrees of optimism at the turn of the twenty-first century. Here, with an emphasis on the institutionalized forms of cultural capital associated with the market for education or the operation of international business, researchers have identified cosmopolitanism as a form of capital itself (Bühlmann et al. 2012) or as synonymous with cultural capital as it might be distributed across a global (rather than a national) social space and, therefore, contributing to new forms of distinction and division in that space (Weenink 2008; Kim 2011; Igarashi and Saito 2014). The ability of parents and students to access institutions which position themselves as significant in such a space (through, for example, the increasingly competitive modes of ranking and rating of colleges and universities operating in the market for international students) mean that the advantages of institutionalized forms of capital operate globally. As Igarashi and Saitao have it, "education systems operate as central institutional mechanisms that legitimate cosmopolitanism as a desirable attribute of the person living in a global world, while distributing this universally desirable attribute unequally within a population" (Igarashi and Saito 2014:223).

Still concerned with the rhetoric of cosmopolitanism but as it applies to questions of objectified cultural capital, Wright, Purhonen, and Heikillä (2013) focus on the UK and Finland, identifying distinctions, marked by age but also by educational experiences, between openness to and preferences for "the foreign" and "exotic" in food, film, music, or TV. Much as with claims for omnivorousness, the unevenness of these forms of disposition are significant. Preferences for exoticism become an indicator of comfort in a global and globalizing space, while rejections rhetorically imply stasis and intolerance – allowing attitudes to global culture to become one means of marking the uneven symbolic geographies of contemporary class positions (Skeggs 2004). Cvetačinin and Popescu's (2011) study of Serbia reveal the potential significance of these kinds of division: they contrast tastes for national, traditional forms of commercial culture with tastes for global forms, showing how taste distinctions map onto distinctions between the patriotic and the non-patriotic. In such instances, cultural capital is bound up with struggles over territory and belonging within national spaces and attitudes toward the globalizing world in ways that perhaps prefigure the symbolic distinctions between red and blue states in the US, or between latte-sipping "remainers" and "Brexiteers" in the UK so apparently central to the political traumas of 2016.

The influence of new technologies on the production and performance of taste is a second key area of potential research. A significant strength of Bourdieu's focus on social reproduction is its reluctance to fetishize novelty for its own sake. At the same time, the ways in which we come to produce, know, like, or dislike cultural items today are markedly different than they were when Bourdieu was researching the processes of cultural consumption in the 1960s, or when he was theorizing the shape of the field of cultural production in mid-nineteenth-century France. Many theoretical positions and empirical approaches in the social sciences are struggling to keep pace with technologically driven changes and continuities. In relation to cultural capital, the rarity of "legitimate" culture in the recent past allowed access to it to be policed by arbiters of taste such as artists, writers, academics, and critics of various kinds. In the contemporary context distinctions of cultural legitimacy are less tenable, as the quick circulation of culture enabled initially by television and now accelerated by digital technologies generates a greater volume of culture than even the most dedicated celebrant and believer can reasonably master. Simultaneously, technological innovations disperse the means of cultural production away from specialists based even within the commercial cultural industries and into the hands of enthusiastic amateurs able to produce and distribute culture outside of the traditional circuits of production and dissemination. This shift might represent both a broadening out of access to cultural production and a more intensive involvement of relatively privileged groups in society – notably well-educated young people – as access to technology and accompanying technological expertise are added to the constituent elements of contemporary cultural capital (Tepper 2008).

Moreover, the opposition between a "disinterested aesthetic" and commercial culture as site of the "choice of the necessary," as established in *Distinction*, is less coherent in societies characterized as "drenched" or saturated in culture. This *excess* of culture necessarily alters the position of the traditional high priests of taste and their ability to shape processes of taste formation. The cultural authority upon which pronouncements of taste rests does not disappear in this context, rather it is dispersed and fragmented between producers and consumers themselves who are able to range across digital and social networks in the pursuit of what is new, distinguishing, and "cool." One particularly intriguing development in this regard is the rise of social media profiles as sites where tastes are performed (Liu 2008), but also as sites where objectified forms of cultural capital are tacitly *measured* and displayed. Cultural capital is displayed when users draw on preferences for culture (film, television, music, books) as key means of producing their profiles, as well as through the imperative to share their cultural and leisure activities. Practices of this kind signal to others in a direct and immediate way the varieties of cultural activity one is participating in. In this sense, social media profiles become a kind of microcosm of a Bourdieusian social space in which users are able to judge their similarity to each other. Alongside this is the imperative toward measurement and the significance placed on "liking." As Van Dijk (2013) describes, one ambition of networks such as Facebook is to transform social norms so that the very meaning of "liking" and "sharing" are reoriented toward productive business models. This reorientation, and its centrality to the "like economy" (Gerlitz and Helmond 2013), has intriguing implications for how the value of cultural capital is maintained and circulated. The algorithmic sorting of the data produced by our liking and sharing enables the generation of advertising and recommendations for new products, providing a tacit hidden infrastructure through which items appear before us to be tasted. This involves new forms of expertise in which the cultural know-how of the high priests of culture – the kind of cultural intermediaries Bourdieu describes – is less immediately significant to the circulation of cultural capital than that of software engineers and marketers. Beer (2013:95) describes the implications: "if cultural encounters are shaped by culture finding us, then we might imagine that this will complicate any kind of reductive vision of how cultural capital might be accumulated."

Conclusion

Despite the methodological and theoretical changes that have occurred in the academic approaches to the study of culture since the publication of Bourdieu's influential work, the concept of cultural capital retains its purchase in examining processes of taste formation – even if it can no longer be easily attached either to particular modes of institutionalization linked to national spaces or to particular modes of objectification linked to established regimes of cultural value. Changes in the class dynamics of Western societies might also alter the strategies of distinction, but researchers taking a methodologically rounded approach to this question can reflect both the active processes of taste formation and the fluidity of cultural hierarchies. Inevitably these can only be partially "captured" in survey work alone. More work needs to be done on the influence of global flows, of both people and culture, in altering the terrain upon which hierarchies of taste and class might be built in the West, and in examining how relations of taste, class, and power might operate in non-Western countries as well as between national contexts in and outside the West. Even as this gap begins to be filled, a focus on the relations of cultural capital within nations perhaps misses the extent to which understanding relations of cultural capital between nations can help shed light on the continuing role of taste and culture in cementing forms of division and stratification with real and ongoing political consequences.

The dispersal of cultural authority away from the high priests of legitimate culture, and the reworking of cultural hierarchies by the various institutions and technologies engaged in the circulation of cultural value, also shift the foundations of cultural capital and power. The role of taste-makers (cultural intermediaries) as drivers of these changes and of the abundance of cultural goods and platforms merits reconsideration of the narratives of scarcity that underpin *Distinction*. Scholars must take account of these changed contexts in generalizing about social patterns of taste, nationally and globally. In the context of a quickened circulation of cultural value, and its algorithmic sorting, competing claims for cultural value may be made and recognized in a more variegated and diffuse field of power, but it is still one in which processes of consecration and legitimation are struggled over. The terms of refined taste may no longer hinge on aesthetic disinterestedness. They might now mark a distinction between a cosmopolitan, outward-looking mode of subjectivity and a locally, nationally oriented one, reimplicating cultural capital into narratives about the kinds of skills, knowledge, and tastes needed to thrive and be comfortable in the global space. In all these contexts, though, there retains an implicit distance, marked by cultural capital, between those who get to play the game of culture and those who watch from the sidelines.

References

Atkinson, W. 2011. "The Context and Genesis of Musical Taste: Omnivorousness Debunked, Bourdieu Buttressed." *Poetics* 39:169–86.

Beer, D. 2013. *Popular Culture and New Media: The Politics of Circulation*. Basingstoke: Palgrave Macmillan.

Bennett, T., M. Savage, E.B. Silva, A. Warde, M. Gayo-Cal, and D. Wright. 2009. *Culture, Class, Distinction*. London: Routledge.

Bourdieu, P. 1984. *Distinction: A Social Critique of the Judgment of Taste*. London: Routledge.

———. 1993. *The Field of Cultural Production*. Cambridge: Polity Press.

———. 1996. *The Rules of Art*. Cambridge: Polity Press.

———. 1998. *Practical Reason: On the Theory of Action*. Cambridge: Polity Press.

Bühlmann, F., Thomas, D. and Mach, A. 2012. "Cosmopolitan Capital and the Internationalization of the Field of Business Elites: Evidence from the Swiss Case." *Cultural Sociology* 7(2):211–29.

Chernilo, D. 2006. "Social Theory's Methodological Nationalism: Myth and Reality." *European Journal of Social Theory* 9(1):5–22.

David Wright

Cvetačinin, P. and Popescu, M. 2011. "The Art of Making Classes in Serbia: Another Particular Case of the Possible." *Poetics* 39:444–68.

Daloz, J. 2010. *The Sociology of Elite Distinction: From Theoretical to Comparative Perspectives.* Basingstoke: Palgrave Macmillan.

Erickson, B.H. 1996. "Culture, Class, and Connections." *American Journal of Sociology* 102(1):217–51.

Friedman, S., L. Hanquinet, A. Miles, and M. Savage. 2015. "Cultural Sociology and New Forms of Distinction." *Poetics* 53:1–8.

Gerlitz, C., and A. Helmond. 2013. "The Like Economy: Social Buttons and the Data Intensive Web." *New Media and Society* 15(8):1348–65.

Hanquinet, L., H. Roose, and M. Savage. 2014. "The Eyes of the Beholder: Aesthetic Preferences and the Remaking of Cultural Capital." *Sociology* 48(1):111–32.

Hennion, A. 2007. "Those Things that Hold Us Together: Taste and Sociology." *Cultural Sociology* 1(1):97–114.

Holt, D.B. 1997. "Distinction in America?: Recovering Bourdieu's theory of taste from its critics." *Poetics* 25:93–120.

Igarashi, H., and H. Saito. 2014. "Cosmopolitanism as Cultural Capital: Exploring the Intersection of Globalization, Education and Stratification." *Cultural Sociology* 8(3):222–39.

Jarness, V. 2015. "Modes of Consumption: From 'what' to 'how' in Cultural Stratification Research." *Poetics* 53:65–79.

Kahma, N., and A. Toikka. 2012. "Cultural Map of Finland 2007: Analysing Cultural Differences Using Multiple Correspondence Analysis." *Cultural Trends* 21(2):113–31.

Kant, I. [1790] 1987. *Critique of Judgement* trans. W.S. Pluhar. Indianapolis: Hackett.

Kardamir Hazir, I. and A. Warde A. 2016. "The Cultural Omnivore Thesis: Methodological Aspects of the Debate." Pp. 77–89 in *Routledge International Handbook of Sociology of Arts and Culture*, edited by L. Hanquinet and M. Savage. London: Routledge.

Katz-Gerro, T. 2002. "Highbrow Cultural Consumption and Class Distinction in Italy, Israel, West Germany, Sweden, and the United States." *Social Forces* 81(1):207–29.

Kim, J. 2011. "Aspiration for Global Cultural Capital in the Stratified Realm of Global Higher Education: Why Do Korean Students go to US Graduate Schools?" *British Journal of Sociology of Education* 32(1):109–26.

Kuipers, G. 2015. "Beauty and Distinction? The Evaluation of Appearance and Cultural Capital in Five European Countries." *Poetics* 53:38–51.

Lamont, M. 1992. *Money, Morals, and Manners: The Culture of the French and American Upper-Middle Class.* Chicago: University of Chicago Press.

Liu, H. 2008. "Social Network Profiles as Taste Performances." *Journal of Computer-Mediated Communication* 13(1):252–75.

Lizardo, O., and S. Skiles. 2012. "Reconceptualizing and Theorizing 'Omnivorousness': Genetic and Relational Mechanisms." *Sociological Theory* 30(4):263–82.

Peterson, R.A. 2005. "Problems in Comparative Research: The Example of Omnivorousness." *Poetics* 33:257–82.

Peterson, R. A., and R.M. Kern. 1996. "Changing Highbrow Taste: From Snob to Omnivore." *American Sociological Review* 61(5):900–7.

Prieur, A., L. Rosenlund, and J. Skjott-Larsen. 2008. "Cultural Capital Today: A Case Study from Denmark." *Poetics* 36:45–71.

Purhonen, S., and D. Wright. 2013. "Cultural Capital in the UK and Finland: Methodological Issues in National-Comparative Work on Tastes." *Cultural Sociology* 7(2):257–73.

Savage, M., and A. Prieur. 2013. "Emerging Forms of Cultural Capital." *European Societies* 15(2):246–67.

Skeggs, B. 2004. *Class, Self, Culture.* London: Routledge.

Snowball, J.D., M. Jamal, and K.G. Willis. 2010. "Cultural Consumption Patterns in South Africa: An Investigation of the Theory of Cultural Omnivores." *Social Indicators Research* 97(3):467–83.

Tepper, S.J. 2008. "The Next Great Transformation: Leveraging Policy and Research to Advance Cultural Vitality." Pp. 363–85 in *Engaging Art: The next great transformation of America's cultural life*, edited by S.J. Tepper and B. Ivey. New York: Routledge.

Torche, F. 2010. "Social Status and Public Cultural Consumption: Chile in Comparative Perspective." Pp. 109–38 in *Social Status and Cultural Consumption*, edited by T.W. Chan. Cambridge: Cambridge University Press.

Van Dijk, J. 2013. *The Culture of Connectivity: A Critical History of Social Media*. Oxford: Oxford University Press.

Weenink D. 2008. "Cosmopolitanism as a Form of Capital: Parents Preparing their Children for a Globalized World." *Sociology* 42(6):1089–106.

Wright, D., S. Purhonen, and R. Heikillä. 2013. "Comparing 'Cosmopolitanism': Taste, Nation and Global culture in Finland and the UK." *Comparative Sociology* 12(3):330–60.

Yoon, T.I., K.H. Kim, and H.J. Eom. 2011. "The Border-crossing of Habitus: Media Consumption, Motives, and Reading Strategies among Asian Immigrant Women in South Korea." *Poetics* 35(2–3):70–98.

23

The conundrum of race in sociological analyses of culture

Alford A. Young Jr.

The project for the cultural analysis of race

In what may very well be the most recognized statement in the history of social scientific inquiry on race, W.E.B. Du Bois ([1903] 1969) wrote in his classic book *The Souls of Black Folk* that the problem of the twentieth century is the problem of the color line. Race certainly became a central factor in social conflicts that emanated around the globe throughout that century. It also was a central factor in the formation and reformation of various nation-states, especially on the continent of Africa (McKee 1993; Rex 1986; Winant 2001). Indeed, the sociological investigation of race was initially rooted in a vision of race as a formidable structural force dividing social groups into hierarchies and affording them differential access to societal resources and rewards. A clear effect of this social dividing and positioning has been the production of cultural traits and properties (e.g., attitudes, worldviews, and practices) that are themselves racialized. Consequently, in the latter decades of the twentieth century cultural sociologists and other scholars of race began exploring how race operates as a dynamic cultural artifact as much as (if not more than) an element of the structural arrangements of society. They began intensive examination of the centrality of race in various patterns of action, meaning-making, and representation at both individual and collective levels, while also exploring how these patterns ultimately reshaped and reinforced the structural dimensions of society.

Cultural approaches to race attempt to explain how people consciously or inadvertently construct new meanings or interpretations about racial categories, how perceptions of self and of others as racial beings come to surface, how people perform and represent themselves as racial beings, and how people employ discursive and interactional strategies to downplay or diminish the significance of race in their understandings and interpretations of social reality. The research initiatives addressing these issues reveal the ways in which race shapes what people think and do, and that behavior (whether by choice, imposition, or some combination of the two) sometimes challenges and sometimes affirms the structural positions they occupy. This research also reveals the extent to which racial categories remain fluid despite the durability of race itself as a social construct.

In documenting cultural analyses of race in modern sociology, this chapter first will explore sociology's break from early understandings of race as a static dimension of social life and the move toward a logic based upon fluidity and dynamism. It will then consider how cultural analyses have addressed the transformation in racial categories and the meanings attached to them, and how cultural inquiry into racial identity, subjectivity, and representation has reshaped our understanding of everyday lived experience. I conclude by summarizing some of the key issues driving the cultural analysis of race both in the United States and worldwide.

Disturbing the rigidity of racial categories

Since its origins and through the first half of the twentieth century, sociologists committed to the study of race and race relations consistently employed classifications such as white, black, Asian, Hispanic, and Native American in ways that promoted the idea that such categories reflected natural and durable distinctions among people (Winant 2000, 2001). As racial categories were strongly associated with geographic regions (white with Europe and subsequently the Western Hemisphere, black with Africa, and Asian with Asia), they maintained fairly durable and consistent meanings because individuals were linked by their racial lineage to one of these regions. As sociology matured from a speculative and reflective field of inquiry into a more structured discipline with formalized research methods and analytical schemes, it was often taken for granted that peoples' identification or association with a geographic arena was central to the formation of their racial identity (Alba 1990; Glazer and Moynihan 1975; Jenkins 1997). Hence, much attention was given to analyzing how the degree of intensity of individuals' racial identification might be associated with social outcomes such as their desire for group boundary maintenance or their commitment to certain notions of collective socio-political outlook or ideology.

The strong turn toward cultural analysis in sociology over the past four decades has created opportunities to more fully inject, assess, and problematize the voices of those being studied. As a consequence, sociologists learned that people of color often maintained vastly different understandings of social reality compared to white majorities (i.e., those classified as white in the United States and Europe) or compared to whites with political power irrespective of numerical status (i.e., those classified as white in South Africa, and Latin and Central America). Furthermore, cultural inquiry has demonstrated the wide-ranging differences in how social reality in general, and identity in particular, is defined, interpreted, and made meaningful by people who share a racial classification – differences previously too often masked by research efforts that either falsely or minimally depicted the true diversity of lived experience (see Calhoun 1994; Lemert 2004, 2005). Both racial boundaries and racial categories are thus increasingly understood as porous and flexible. Consider the work of Michele Lamont (2000): in documenting the ways black and white working-class men draw conceptual boundaries between themselves and others, in both personal and collective terms, she demonstrates that cultural inquiry into race need not be restricted to studies of whether and how people think about race per se, but may focus instead on how people's racial classification informs their thinking about concepts such as dignity, respectability, and selfhood in a more general sense (see also Young 2004).

Consider, too, the growing body of critical sociological research that highlights the tremendous within-category racial diversity that exists in many communities. Research has documented that many individuals throughout the world who have been classified as black and who regard such classification as central to their self- and social consciousness may come to quite different personal understandings of the meaning of blackness (Frederickson 1995; Gilroy 2000; Winant 2001). For example, in his analysis of the 1994 genocide in Rwanda, Mahmood Mamdani (2001) argues that any notion of a collective racial consciousness was irrelevant in assessing why members of a black ethnic group, the Hutu, committed to killing so many members of another black ethnic group, the Tutsi. In effect, colonization by the Belgians created a logic of difference between the two factions – rooted in body type, facial features, and other demarcations, none of which had any demonstrable biological basis – that overrode any capacity for collective racial cohesiveness in Rwanda. This logic provided Belgian colonizers with a means of exerting social control without having to maintain an explicit presence in the region. In essence, those classified as Tutsi were put in a trustee status so that the social, political, and economic affairs of Rwanda would continue to benefit the colonizers. According to Mamdani, animosity between the two groups was so intense that, following the massacre in Rwanda, appeals by South African President Nelson Mandela for racial unity struck Rwandans of both ethnic groups as incomprehensible. Anthony Appiah (1992) similarly challenges the notion that collective racial consciousness is a predominant feature of social life in Africa. He criticizes what he calls the "Western fiction" of depicting Africans as uniform and homogenous regarding manners of cultural expression and socio-political perspective. This same one-dimensional vision of Africans is also explored in Mamdani's (1996) discussion of race-making in Africa.

Recent sociological attention to other regions largely populated by blacks underscores the complexity of racial meaning-making in modern life. Consider South Africa, where extreme social differences among black South Africans, often reflecting the numerous ethnic divisions within that racial group, drive patterns of social consciousness in which race plays a secondary or minimal role in how black South Africans think about social identity and cultural commonalities (Frederickson 1995). Brazil represents another nation-centered model of racial complexity, where a much larger scaffolding than the now common black-white-biracial troika (still to some measure alive and well in the United States) exists for documenting the variant forms of racial consciousness and identity in that country (Winant 2001).

Analyses of racial meaning-making outside the United States have driven the notion that blackness, as a racial category, not only has different meanings for people situated in vastly different places in the world and in different positions in social hierarchies, but also holds different degrees of relevance for forming interpretations of social reality. This insight applies equally well to the US context. Research on Afro-Caribbeans, for example, shows that many in this ethnic grouping do not read racial conflict or understand race relations in the ways that many African Americans do (Kasinitz, Mollenkopf, and Waters 2004; Waters 1999) because Afro-Caribbeans, like black Africans, lack extensive social experience living as racial minorities, and thus come to possess different kinds of subjective orientations about race in comparison to African Americans. As sociologist Mary Waters (1999) argues, Afro-Caribbeans experience relations with a white world through a lens viewed from their own history of colonization, which is based upon a much more socially distant relationship with whites given the independence that many Afro-Caribbean nations achieved in the early to mid-twentieth century. Thus, although race may play a salient and pervasive role in the social consciousness of the subcategory of black people labeled African Americans, it takes a wholly different form for many blacks in Africa and elsewhere, especially if they have not lived as racial minorities in their respective nation-states.

Beyond blackness in the cultural analysis of race

Clearly, cultural analyses that support rethinking the extent to which cohesion and consistency apply to the meanings attributed to racial categories have not been restricted to the study of black people. For instance, much of the early research in what has become known as "whiteness studies" suggests that a defining feature of whiteness is an engagement with racism and/or racial privilege (Mcintosh 1989; Frankenberg 1993). This research tradition explores the extent to which people classified as white embrace, reject, or work to transform their racial identity depending on the salience of race in their own lives (Hartigan 1999; Lewis 2003; Mcintosh

1989). Whiteness scholars also explore the complex variability of whiteness depending on its intersection with socioeconomic status and its connections to social power and societal resources (see Hartigan 1999; Wray 2006). For example, by demonstrating how certain privileged white Americans deem certain lower-income whites to be "white trash," and, therefore, not legitimately white, Matt Wray (2006) argues that class difference functions simultaneously to diversify white racial identity and reaffirm white racial superiority. More recently, Hughey (2012) has conducted comparative research on whites who do, on the one hand, and who do not, on the other, maintain a highly conscious sense of themselves as white, while Bush (2011) explores the quotidian behavior of people classified as white in a "post-racial" era. Over time, then, cultural analyses have tended to broaden our conceptualization of whiteness as defined primarily in relation to racism to a more complex and internally variegated identity.

In similar fashion, emerging cultural and culturally informed analyses of people labeled Asian and Asian American have broadened the template within which race is investigated and examined in cultural sociology. Kim (2008) and Prashad (2000, 2001) both highlight and critique the extent to which earlier scholarship placed Asians and Asian Americans at the midpoint of the black-white racial classification continuum. They provide a new perspective for exploring Asian and Asian American racialization that attends to historical and cultural specificity: racial identities are forged through varying degrees of attachment to particular ancestral homelands and by the different socio-political climates of the geographic regions through which people move; moreover, the construction of "Asian-ness" may not correspond in obvious ways to the construction of blackness, and this lack of correspondence challenges the often-implicit assumption that racial subordination in the US be read in relation to the African American experience – African Americans representing the paramount subordinate group (O'Brien 2008; Wu 2002).

Indeed, perhaps the most robust challenge to the notion of rigid racial categories has been provided by scholars studying the experiences of biracial and multiracial people. This research has shifted from efforts to determine how such people locate themselves along a linear continuum ranging from white to black identity (DaCosta 2007; Daniel 2002; Rockquemore and Brunsma 2008) toward a recognition of the continuum's irrelevance to many (and perhaps most) biracial and multiracial people. Some sociologists have explored the extent to which the very meanings attached to race by multiracial individuals may change radically throughout a given day. Their work has demonstrated that self-perception, social perception, and self-categorization are three distinct features of the biracial and/or multiracial experience (Harris and Sim 2002). The case of the colored in South Africa, who are biracial in the genealogical sense, further demonstrates the diversity of racial meaning-making. As a result of apartheid, the colored have cultivated a distinct ethnic and cultural sensibility that does not reflect the kind of contingencies to black or white racial categories that biracial citizens in the United States have often had to contemplate, reconcile, or explicitly reject (Frederickson 1995). Meanwhile, studies of biraciality and multiraciality in the United States have demonstrated that those with Asian or Latino ancestry are socially recognized as white to a much larger extent than biracial and multiracial people who have black ancestry (Lee and Bean 2012). Former US President Barack Obama is a good illustration. Despite being a black/white biracial man whose ancestry is one generation removed from Kenya, who has a half-sibling from Indonesia, and who did not explicitly articulate a racialized political agenda when he campaigned for office, Obama was repeatedly heralded in and outside the media as the country's first black president.

Performativity and intersectionality

Consistent with the general insight that racial boundaries and categories are porous and flexible is sociological scholarship that examines how racial identities and meanings – often in concert with class and gender – are "performed" in a dramaturgical sense. A key strand of this research focuses on youth in educational settings. Pamela Perry (2002), for example, explores how whiteness is performed differently by adolescents depending on the degree to which their educational context is racially and ethnically diverse: Caucasian students enrolled in racially diverse institutions are able to reflect on how they are "acting like white people," whereas Caucasian students in predominantly white schools remain unaware of how their racial identity might be guiding their actions and choices. Carter (2003, 2005) studied adolescents in school and indicated the wide-ranging ways in which blackness is read by whites as a problematic, if not dangerous, construct that threatens the effective functioning of the institution. Bettie's (2003) ethnographic analysis of young Latinas in high school documents the extent to which race-based styles of dress and behavior solidify for the girls an oppositional, class-conscious identity even while ensuring their continued exclusion from the avenues of social mobility afforded by schooling. This work complicates and extends the cultural-structural analysis of Paul Willis in his classic study *Learning to Labor* (1977), where "resistance" to the mandates of formal education on the part of low-income British boys helped secure their continued class marginalization. More recent scholarship on race and education challenges the widely held assumption that high-achieving students of color are "acting white" (Carbado and Gulati 2013; Harris 2011; Tyson 2011), notwithstanding the persistence of traditional arguments about the causal role of culture in perpetuating racial disadvantage (Patterson 2015). Beyond the realm of youth and schools, other recent work examines how upwardly mobile and professional class African Americans understand, identify with, and "perform" blackness in different organizational settings (Willie 2003) and in neighborhood contexts characterized by high degrees of racial and class diversity (Lacy 2007).

Much of the research focusing on the performative dimensions of racial identity is explicitly intersectional, exploring how other categories of difference such as gender, class, and sexuality work in concert with race to shape and inform individual and collective behavior. Intersectionality refuses an "additive" approach, instead insisting on the co-creation of meaning that results when multiple layers of difference are attended to simultaneously (Crenshaw 1989; Hill-Collins [1990] 2000).

De-emphasizing race and racial categories

Cultural studies of the transformation of meanings attached to racial categories have largely been centered on numerical minorities in various nations or black people in Africa and the Afro-Caribbean region (spaces marked as highly racialized). However, a growing body of work is now focusing on the discursive practices employed to deemphasize race as a significant feature of social reality. More specifically, some scholars are considering how whites in Europe and the US increasingly avoid talking about race altogether in public debates on socio-political issues – debates in which the very criteria for what constitutes a just or moral society (and how best to achieve it) reflect the interests of dominant racial groups.

Paul Gilroy (1987) early on pursued an analysis of this sort, arguing that the cultural politics of late twentieth-century Britain increasingly denied black Brits a voice in articulating a sense of nation, national identity, and national destiny. This conservative political project, best exemplified by the leadership of Margaret Thatcher in the 1980s, was characterized by a lack of explicitly racial language in civic discourse about what properly constitutes an English person, yet the result was the exclusion of people of color, especially blacks, from that constitution. The work of Paul Gilroy (1987, 1993a, 1993b, 2000), Stuart Hall (1988, 1997; Hall and du Gay 1996), and others involved with the Birmingham School of Cultural Studies played a crucial role in developing analyses of race as a dynamic, fluid, and ever-changing construct; they also paved the way for making sense of how racial inequality can be sustained in social life precisely through its omission in civic and public discourses concerning mobility, opportunity, and national identity.

Today, sociologists continue to investigate these practices, especially in the United States, where the cultural politics of race took a dramatic turn after the Civil Rights Movement. That turn left many black Americans and other people of color strongly cognizant of the social power and significance of race not only as a tool of oppression, but as a means of galvanizing social change (Carmichael and Hamilton 1967; Collins [1990] 2000; Cruse 1967, 1987; Dawson 1994, 2001), even while some white Americans became concerned, if not threatened, by the heightened emphasis on race promoted by people of color (Blauner 1989; Carson 1981; Hodgson 1976, 2004; Sitkoff 1981; Weisbrot 1990). Consequently, sociologists such as Michael Omi and Howard Winant (1994) argue that public discussion of race has been transformed since the 1960s, making it harder for formal organizations and groups to use race-specific arguments to encourage government intervention or redress for race-based inequalities. This argument has been more fully elucidated by Stephen Steinberg (1995), who suggests that a defining feature of contemporary socio-political thought concerning race is the absence of substantive public discussion on the matter.

A leading concept used to define the contemporary discourse in which race-based privileges are maintained – while race itself is rarely invoked – is "color-blind racism." Although there are seemingly as many definitions of color-blind racism as there are scholars who have explored the phenomenon, the language of Eduardo Bonilla-Silva (2003, 2010) captures it well. According to Bonilla-Silva, color-blind racism is constituted by four central frames: abstract liberalism (e.g., blanket claims that all people are equal, and thus preferential treatments of any sort are inherently racist); naturalization (e.g., explaining social segregation as the result of individuals' "natural" preference for homophily); cultural racism (e.g., privileging certain groups not on assumptions of inherent superiority but on assumptions of their more appropriate social functioning or adaptation); and the minimization of racism (e.g., claiming that acts of discrimination or prejudice are actually based upon some other factor or condition). Amanda Lewis's (2003) masterful summary of the relevant literature concludes that color-blind ideology asserts racial neutrality when such neutrality does not necessarily exist. Moreover, it often stigmatizes attempts to seek redress for racial inequality: those who raise objections are accused of "playing the race card" or of being committed to an outdated and disdained identity politics. All of this unfolds in the course of a robust denial of the salience of race in social interaction and other forms of social experience. So although racism is alive and well, it is not much talked about by those who benefit most from its persistence.

A more recent turn in the scholarly conversation about the diminished significance of race has been the utilization of "post-racial" as a descriptor of the contemporary American and (in some ways) global landscape. Upon the election of Barack Obama to the US presidency, some commentators began regarding the US as a post-racial society (for a critique, see Bonilla-Silva 2010; Dawson 2011; Goldberg 2015; Ikard 2013). In the early twenty-first century, many citizens of Brazil and other Latin American countries promoted the same kind of consideration (Emboaba Da Costa 2016; Lentin 2014). The argument put forth by those citizens was that ethno-racial policies threatened the achievement of nonracial belonging and citizenship. Ultimately, scholars argued that such post-racial ideologies served the purpose of rearticulating racial hierarchies, maintaining racial subordination, and delimiting the very social change that was presumably sought after in those nations (Emboaba Da Costa 2016).

Clearly, for many African Americans and other people of color, race has continued to be an extraordinarily salient feature of everyday life linked to structural opportunities for equality and social mobility (Dawson 2011; May 2001), making claims about post-raciality appear decidedly premature. Three recent developments testify to the continued significance of race and racial inequality. One is the rise of the Black Lives Matter movement in the US in response to the killing of black boys and men by police (Day 2015; Luibrand 2015; Miller 2016; Pew Research Center 2016; Ross 2015). The second is the presumption of racial threat that surged after 9/11 aimed primarily at Arab populations; the religious and cultural practices associated with Islam have been racialized and contrasted with notions of whiteness as a means of legitimating Islamophobia – a racializing strategy that, according to Meer (2013), parallels the experience of Jews with anti-Semitism. The third development is the election of US President Donald Trump in 2016. Trump's political agenda (particularly his proposed immigration policies) has not only intensified Islamophobia but also white nationalist sentiments within the country (see Hochschild 2016), sentiments that may not be new (see Hughey 2014) but are certainly newly energized.

Making meaning of race in the future: a cautionary word

Through studies of the flexibility, fluidity, and dynamism of racial categories, of the changing public and civic discourses pertaining to race, and of ways of thinking about, and enacting, racial difference, cultural sociology has significantly advanced our understanding of the social significance of race. The subfield has produced an impressive body of work that recognizes and explores the complexity and diversity of racial-formation processes among people who share the same racial classification and who, in the recent past, might have been thought to share a common identity and politics.

Although it is unwise to attempt to forecast the future, it appears evident that race will continue to play a significant and prominent role in social processes that underpin meaning-making and identity formation as well as more structural/institutional instantiations of racial inequality. It may also take unforeseen directions, which may require new nomenclatures for labeling racial categories or new ways of interpreting how race relates to individual and collective thought and action. Indeed, discussion of the extreme fluidity of race and racial classification is well-illustrated by the very public debate that took place in 2015 in response to media coverage of Rachel Dolezal, a white woman and former civil rights activist who was discovered to have allegedly been passing as African American while serving as an instructor of African American studies and the leader of a race-serving social service agency (Flaherty 2015). Hence, the fluidity of racial boundaries in the twenty-first century may be marked not solely by the continued politics of social classification, but also by the unique forms of agency engaged by people in order to fit themselves into whatever racial categories they desire irrespective of their genealogy or ancestry.

References

Alba, Richard D. 1990. *Ethnic Identity: The Transformation of White America.* New Haven, CT: Yale University Press.

Appiah, Kwame Anthony. 1992. *In My Father's House: Africa in the Philosophy of Culture.* New York: Oxford University Press.

Bettie, Julie. 2003. *Women without Class: Girls, Race, and Identity.* Berkeley: University of California Press.

Blauner, Robert. 1989. *Black Lives, White Lives: Three Decades of Race Relations in America.* Berkeley: University of California Press.

Bonilla-Silva, Eduardo. 2003. "New Racism, Color-Blind Racism, and the Future of Whiteness in America." Pp. 271–84 in *White Out: The Continued Significance of Racism,* edited by A. Doane and E. Bonilla-Silva. New York: Routledge.

———. 2010. *Racism without Racist*. 3rd ed. Lanham, MD: Rowman and Littlefield.

Bush, Melanie E.L. 2011. *Everyday Forms of Whiteness: Understanding Race in a "Post-Racial" World*. Lanham, MD: Rowman and Littlefield.

Calhoun, Craig. 1994. *Social Theory and the Politics of Identity*. Cambridge, MA: Blackwell.

Carbado, Devon, and Mitu Gulati. 2013. *Acting White?: Rethinking Race in "Post-Racial" America*. New York: Oxford University Press.

Carmichael, Stokely, and Charles V. Hamilton. 1967. *Black Power: The Politics of Liberation in America*. New York: Random House.

Carson, Clayborne. 1981. *In Struggle: SNCC and the Black Awakening of the 1960s*. Cambridge, MA: Harvard University Press.

Carter, Prudence L. 2003. "Black Cultural Capital, Status Positioning, and Schooling Conflicts for Low-Income African American Youth." *Social Problems* 50(1):136–55.

———. 2005. *Keepin' It Real: School Success Beyond Black and White*. Oxford: Oxford University Press.

Collins, Patricia Hill. [1990] 2000. *Black Feminist Thought: Knowledge, Consciousness, and the Politics of Empowerment*. Boston: Unwin Hyman.

Crenshaw, Kimberle. 1989. "Demarginalizing the Intersection of Race and Sex: A Black Feminist Critique of Antidiscrimination Doctrine, Feminist Theory, and Antiracist Politics." *Chicago Law Review* 1(8):139–67.

Cruse, Harold. 1967. *Crisis of the Negro Intellectual*. New York: William Morrow.

———. 1987. *Plural but Equal: A Critical Study of Blacks and Minorities and America's Plural Society*. New York: William Morrow.

DaCosta, Kimberly McClain. 2007. *Making Multiracials: State, Family, and Market in the Redrawing of the Color Line*. Stanford, CA: Stanford University Press.

Daniel, G. Reginald. 2002. *More than Black: Multiracial Identity and the New Racial Order*. Philadelphia, PA: Temple University Press.

Dawson, Michael. 1994. *Behind the Mule: Race and Class in African American Politics*. Princeton, NJ: Princeton University Press.

———. 2001. *Black Visions: The Roots of Contemporary African American Political Ideologies*. Chicago: University of Chicago Press.

———. 2011. *Not in Our Lifetimes: The Future of Black Politics*. Chicago: University of Chicago Press.

Day, Elizabeth. 2015. "#BlackLivesMatter: The Birth of a New Civil Rights Movement." *The Guardian*, July 19. Retrieved August 1, 2017.

Du Bois, W.E.B. [1903] 1969. *The Souls of Black Folk*. New York: New American Library.

Emboaba Da Costa, Alexandre. 2016. "Thinking 'Post-Racial' Ideology Transnationally: The Contemporary Politics of Race and Indigeneity in the Americas." *Critical Sociology* 42(4–5):475–90.

Flaherty, Colleen. 2015. "Passing in the Classroom: Academics Weigh In on the Curious Case." *Inside Higher Ed*, June 15. Retrieved November 26, 2016 (www.insidehighered.com/news/2015/06/15/academics-weigh-curious-case-rachel-dolezal?width=775&height=500&iframe=true).

Frankenberg, Ruth. 1993. *White Women, Race Matters: The Social Construction of Whiteness*. Minneapolis: University of Minnesota Press.

Frederickson, George. 1995. *Black Liberation: A Comparative History of Black Ideologies in the United States and South Africa*. Oxford: Oxford University Press.

Gilroy, Paul. 1987. *Ain't No Black in the Union Jack: The Cultural Politics of Race and Nation*. Chicago: University of Chicago Press.

———. 1993a. *The Black Atlantic: Modernity and Double Consciousness*. Cambridge, MA: Harvard University Press.

———. 1993b. *Small Acts: Thought on the Politics of Black Culture*. New York: Serpent's Tail.

———. 2000. *Against Race: Imagining Political Culture Beyond the Color Line*. Cambridge, MA: The Belknap Press of Harvard University Press.

Glazer, Nathan, and Daniel P. Moynihan, eds. 1975. *Ethnicity: Theory and Experience*. Cambridge, MA: Harvard University Press.

Goldberg, David. 2015. *Are We Post-Racial Yet?* London: Polity Press.

Hall, Stuart. 1988. *The Hard Road to Renewal: Thatcherism and the Crisis of the Left*. London: Verso.

————, ed. 1997. *Representation: Cultural Representations and Signifying Practices*. London: Sage.

Hall, Stuart, and Paul du Gay, eds. 1996. *Questions of Cultural Identity*. London: Sage.

Harris, Angel. 2011. *Kids Don't Want to Fail: Oppositional Culture and the Black-White Achievement Gap*. Cambridge, MA: Harvard University Press.

Harris, David R., and Jeremiah Joseph Sim. 2002. "Who Is Multiracial? Assessing the Complexity of Lived Race." *American Sociological Review* 67(4):614–27.

Hartigan, John, Jr. 1999. *Racial Situations: Class Predicaments of Whiteness in Detroit*. Princeton, NJ: Princeton University Press.

Hochschild, Arlie Russell 2016. *Strangers in Their Own Land: Anger and Mourning on the American Right*. New York: New Press.

Hodgson, Godfrey. 1976. *America in Our Time*. Garden City, NJ: Doubleday.

————. 2004. *More Equal Than Others: America From Nixon to the New Century*. Princeton, NJ: Princeton University Press.

Hughey, Matthew W. 2012. *White Bound: Nationalists, Antiracists, and the Shared Meanings of Race*. Stanford, CA: Stanford University Press.

————. 2014. "White Backlash in the 'post-racial' United States." *Ethnic And Racial Studies* 37(5):721–30.

Ikard, David H. 2013. *Blinded by the Whites: Why Race Still Matters in 21st-Century America*. Bloomington: Indiana University Press.

Jenkins, Richard. 1997. *Rethinking Ethnicity: Arguments and Explorations*. London: Sage.

Kasinitz, Phillip, John Mollenkopf, and Mary C. Waters, eds. 2004. *Becoming New Yorkers: Ethnographies of the 'New' Second Generation*. New York: Russell Sage Foundation.

Kim, Nadia. 2008. *Imperial Citizens: Koreans and Race from Seoul to LA*. Palo Alto, CA: Stanford University Press.

Lacy, Karyn. 2007. *Blue Chip Black: Race, Class, and Status in the New Black Middle Class*. Berkeley: University of California Press.

Lamont, Michele. 2000. *The Dignity of Working Men: Morality and the Boundaries of Race, Class, and Immigration*. New York: Russell Sage Foundation Press.

Lee, Jennifer, and Frank D. Bean. 2012. "A Postracial Society or a Diversity Paradox?" *Du Bois Review: Social Science Research on Race* 9(2):419–37.

Lemert, Charles C., ed. 2004. *Social Theory: the Multicultural and Classic Readings*. Oxford: Westview Press.

————. 2005. *Postmodernism Is Not What You Think: Why Globalization Threatens Modernity*. Boulder, CO: Paradigm.

Lentin, Alan. 2014. "Post-Race, Post Politics: The Paradoxical Rise of Culture after Multiculturalism." *Race and Ethnic Studies* 37(8):1268–85.

Lewis, Amanda E. 2003. *Race in the Schoolyard: Negotiating the Color Line in Classrooms and Communities*. New Brunswick, NJ: Rutgers University Press.

Luibrand, Shannon. 2015. "Black Lives Matter: How the Events in Ferguson Sparked a Movement in America." *CBS News*, August 7. Retrieved August 1, 2017 (www.cbsnews.com/news/how-the-black-lives-matter-movement-changed-america-one-year-later/).

Mamdani, Mahmood. 1996. *Citizen and Subject: Contemporary Africa and the Legacy of Late Colonialism*. Princeton, NJ: Princeton University Press.

————. 2001. *When Victims Become Killers: Colonialism, Nativism, and Genocide in Rwanda*. Princeton, NJ: Princeton University Press.

May, Reuben. 2001. *Talking at Trena's: Everyday Conversations at an African American Tavern*. New York: New York University Press.

Mcintosh, Peggy. 1989. "White Privilege: Unpacking the Invisible Knapsack." *Peace and Freedom* (July/August):10–12.

McKee, James B. 1993. *Sociology and the Race Problem: The Failure of a Perspective*. Urbana: University of Illinois Press.

Meer, Nasar. 2013. "Racialization and Religion: Race, Culture and Difference in the Study of Antisemitism and Islamophobia." *Race and Ethnic Studies* 36(3):385–98.

Miller, Ryan W. 2016. "Black Lives Matter: A Primer on What it is and What it Stands For." *USA Today*, July 12. Retrieved August 1, 2017 (www.usatoday.com/story/news/nation/2016/07/11/black-lives-matter-what-what-stands/86963292/).

O'Brien, Eileen. 2008. *The Racial Middle: Latinos and Asian Americans Living Beyond the Racial Divide*. New York: NYU Press.

Omi, Michael, and Howard Winant. 1994. *Racial Formation in the United States: From the 1960 to the 1990s*. 2nd ed. New York: Routledge.

Patterson, Orlando. 2015. *The Cultural Matrix: Understanding Black Youth*. Cambridge, MA: Harvard University Press.

Perry, Pamela. 2002. *Shades of White: White Kids and Racial Identities in High School*. Durham, NC: Duke University Press.

Pew Research Center. 2016. "On Views of Race and Inequality, Blacks and Whites Are Worlds Apart." Retrieved November 27, 2016 (www.pewsocialtrends.org/2016/06/27/on-views-of-race-and-inequality-blacks-and-whites-are-worlds-apart/).

Prashad, Vijay. 2000. *Karma of Brown Folk*. Minneapolis: University of Minnesota Press.

———. 2001. *Everybody Was Kung Fu Fighting: Afro-Asian Connections and the Myth of Cultural Purity*. Boston: Beacon Press.

Rex, John. 1986. *Race and Ethnicity*. Philadelphia, PA: Open University Press.

Rockquemore, Kerry Ann, and David Brunsma. 2008. *Beyond Black: Biracial Identity in America*. Lanham, MD: Rowman and Littlefield.

Ross, Janell. 2015. "How Black Lives Matter Moved from a Hashtag to a Real Political Force." *Washington Post*, August 19. Retrieved November 19, 2015 (www.washingtonpost.com/news/the-fix/wp/2015/08/19/how-black-lives-matter-moved-from-a-hashtag-to-a-real-political-force/?utm_term=.f4a955080ff1).

Sitkoff, Harvard. 1981. *The Struggle for Black Equality*. New York: Hill and Wang.

Steinberg, Stephen. 1995. *Turning Back: The Retreat from Racial Justice in American Thought and Policy*. Boston: Beacon Press.

Tyson, Karolyn. 2011. *Integration Interrupted: Tracking, Black Students, and Acting White After Brown*. New York: Oxford University Press.

Waters, Mary C. 1999. *Black Identities: West Indian Immigrant Dreams and American Realities*. New York: Russell Sage Foundation; Cambridge, MA: Harvard University Press.

Weisbrot, Robert. 1990. *Freedom Bound: A History of America's Civil Rights Movement*. New York: Norton.

Willie, Sarah Susannah. 2003. *Acting Black: College, Identity, and the Performance of Race*. London: Routledge.

Willis, Paul. 1977. *Learning to Labor: How Working Class Kids Get Working Class Jobs*. New York: Columbia University Press.

Winant, Howard. 2000. "Race and Race Theory." *Annual Review of Sociology* 26:169–85.

———. 2001. *The World is a Ghetto: Race and Democracy Since World War II*. New York: Basic Books.

Wray, Matt. 2006. *Not Quite White: White Trash and the Boundaries of Whiteness*. Durham, NC: Duke University Press.

Wu, Frank H. 2002. *Yellow: Race in America Beyond Black and White*. New York: Basic Books.

Young, Alford A., Jr. 2004. *The Minds of Marginalized Black Men: Making Sense of Mobility, Opportunity, and Future Life Chances*. Princeton, NJ: Princeton University Press.

24

Sexual meanings, placemaking, and the urban imaginary

Amin Ghaziani

Introduction

There is a well-developed literature on neighborhoods, as well as one on sexual identities and communities, but little research brings these two subfields together to explore the relationship between sexuality and the city. In this chapter, I suggest that urban sociology can meet the sociology of sexualities through culture. I use the reasons straight people provide for wanting to live in a gay district as an opportunity to reflect on how sexuality informs our imaginations of place. By examining residential logics, scholars can conceptualize "the city" as a culturally saturated site where neighbors negotiate the meanings and material significance of their sexuality alongside their sexual differences from others.

Culture and the city

What is the role of culture in urban sociology? Some scholars downplay culture because they see it as epiphenomenal, an aggregation of individual interests, while others consider culture outright irrelevant. Gans (2007:159) offers a strong position: "Culture *per se* is not a useful explanatory tool," he argues, because researchers overextend the concept to include values and beliefs, meanings and shared significance, art and expressive symbols, and identities and memories. All these are "worthy research topics," Gans (2007) hastens to add, but we cannot sweep them under the single term "culture." His concern, a conceptual one, resurrects an insight expressed earlier by Fine (1979:733), who described culture as "an amorphous, indescribable mist which swirls around society members." Hence, the concept "adds nothing," Gans concludes, and it "cannot lead to significant new insights" about the city (2007:160). If anything, it presents a paradox – and a particular problem of measurement, as I have shown in my work (Ghaziani 2009). By masquerading as everything, culture is uniquely nothing. The conundrum accounts for why some scholars use the concept to restate the "obvious" in "technical language" (Gans 2007:160). Gans (2007) also takes issue with cultural explanations for displaying "antipathy toward structural issues such as hierarchy, inequality, and power." He ultimately disavows culture as an "Uncaused Cause" (ibid.). Reflecting on his own study of urban villagers, Gans says that culture is a descriptive tool, and he advises scholars to examine "how urban cultures and practices *are shaped by* economic, political, and other power structures" (ibid., emphasis added). Apparently, culture cannot be strong (Alexander and Smith 2010) and independent.

Urbanists have responded to his polemic – culture "plays second fiddle" to economic and structural forces (Borer 2007:158) – by showing that people actively engage with meanings and symbols in nearly every aspect of city life. It is the cultures of cities (Zukin 1995) – from tall towers to toilets – that account for outcomes that range from individual happiness (Montgomery 2013) to abstract attitudes about gender (Molotch and Noren 2010). Culture explains why we sort into diverse social groups (Fischer 1975) or choose to live in ethnic enclaves (Abrahamson 2005). Culture is at work when we talk about neighborhood diversity (Deener 2012) and how that diversity provides a shared symbol of progressive politics (Berrey 2015), especially for young people as they seek places that will nurture a creative ethos (Florida 2002). Culture informs interpersonal interactions between building tenants and their doormen (Bearman 2005), tourists and their guides (Wynn 2011), and it influences how musicians and government leaders organize festivals (Wynn 2015), pride parades (Bruce 2016), and other expressions of the Warhol economies (Currid 2007) and neo-bohemias (Lloyd 2006) that transform cities into entertainment machines (Lloyd and Clark 2001) that are teeming with fashion shows (Mears 2011), nightclubs (Grazian 2008), and cocktail bars (Ocejo 2014). Together, these studies direct researchers to look at the authenticity and aesthetics of a place (Zukin 2010), its unique feel (Silver and Clark 2016), and its characterological distinctiveness (Molotch, Freudenburg, and Paulsen 2000).

Sexuality and the city

Culture has arguably been more foundational to sociological studies of sexuality, although here scholars have focused on identity, community, politics, and queer theoretic frameworks (Stein 1989; Taylor and Whittier 1992; Warner 1993; Stein and Plummer 1994; Gamson 1995; Seidman 2002; Ghaziani 2008, 2011). There is, however, a growing body of work that examines sexuality, culture, and placemaking. In my research on "gayborhoods" (Ghaziani 2014a, Ghaziani 2015), I argue that struggles over what a place means (its cultural character) and who belongs in it (its composition and symbolic boundaries) are indistinguishable from political factors like municipal governance and the growth machine coalition, as well as the economics of land, labor, and capital. Despite the influence of the Chicago School (Park 1925), this line of reasoning has deeper roots in anthropology (Newton 1993; Weston 1995), geography (Lauria and Knopp 1985; M. Brown 2014), and history (Heap 2003; Aldrich 2004) than it does in sociology.

A gay neighborhood has a distinct geographic focal point; people can point it out on a map, usually by singling out one or two specific streets (Keller 1968). The area has a concentration of residences (Gates and Ost 2004) and businesses (Murray 1996) that cater to LGBTQ people. These districts also stimulate extralocal attachments among nonresidents who make territorial claims (Greene 2014). Gayborhoods foster a quasi-ethnic (Murray 1979; Epstein 1987) culture; LGBTQ people "set the tone" (Chauncey 1994:228) of the place, which is why rainbow flags line the streets and ritual events like the pride parade are often staged there. The pursuit of sex and sociality in the safe, countercultural context of a gayborhood empowers "pleasure seekers" (Armstrong 2002) to create "sexy communities" (Orne 2017) that are removed from the straight gaze. Sexuality is an important part of life for all of us, but gayborhoods provide a crucible for the cultivation of a collective life that is visible and culturally queer.

Gay districts have a hand in nearly every aspect of modern life: from the municipal promotion of urban spaces to city planning and the shaping of real estate values, from the institutional development of LGBTQ communities to their civic engagements (Usher and Morrison 2010).

They promote policy discussions around sexuality and enable public health organizations to distribute critical resources (Carpiano et al. 2011). The presence of a gayborhood signals a city's commitment to diversity and tolerance, and research shows that officials can boost their local economy when they invest in them (Florida 2002). Gay districts facilitate the search for friendship, fellowship, sex and love for a group of people who are not corporeally marked (Laumann et al. 2004). Historically, LGBTQ people have used them as a base to organize as a voting bloc or social movement (Armstrong 2002). Because the personal is political, gayborhoods also represent a free space (Evans and Boyte 1986) that blunt the effects of heteronormativity (Wittman 1970). All these findings help us appreciate why LGBTQ people would want to live in these districts today, despite their past reputation as ghettos that exacerbated marginalization, exclusion, and inequality (Levine 1979; Castells 1983).

Straight to the gayborhood

A key lacuna in existing research is straight people. What is their relationship to the gayborhood? Why do they want to live there? Despite a surge of recent scholarly attention to heterosexuality (J. Katz 2007; Dean 2014; Ward 2015), few cultural or urban sociologists have addressed the question. In this section, I draw on my research to explain why straights seek to reside in gay districts. I use their rationales to reflect theoretically on how sexuality and culture jointly affect placemaking efforts in the gayborhood and the urban imaginary more broadly.

Safety

Castells (1983:161) characterized gay men and lesbians in the 1970s and 1980s as "moral refugees" who were seeking safe spaces. Four decades later, straights have appropriated similar claims and located them in gayborhoods once they realized that crime rates are lower than in other parts of the city (O'Sullivan 2005). Writing for the *New York Times*, one journalist remarked, "Predominantly gay neighborhoods have arisen in a dozen major cities over the last two decades, sometimes making tired neighborhoods safer and more attractive to heterosexuals" (De Witt 1994:A14). Florida (2002:xvii) offers a scholarly account for how claims to safety inform placemaking initiatives among heterosexuals: "I've had straight people, especially single women, tell me they *look* for cities with lots of gay people when they are hunting for a place to live and work." These accounts suggest a cultural reimagination of the gayborhood away from an area that provides a protective shield for gays to a place that promises lower crime rates for straights.

Child-friendliness

A headline from *SFGate* identified an emerging trend of young straight families who seek out gay neighborhoods:

> After 25 years at the heart of the gay movement, San Francisco's Castro district is going mainstream. Families and chain stores are moving in, and some are lamenting the loss of what has become an icon to gays and lesbians.
>
> *(Levy 1996)*

The baby stroller is a potent symbol in this conversation, as the *New York Times* notes: "The influx of baby strollers is perhaps the most blatant sign of change" (P. Brown 2007). The corresponding journalist interviewed a realtor who explained how the meaning of the area has changed as more straight people carve out a place for themselves in the gayborhood: "The Castro has gone from a gay-ghetto mentality to a family mentality" (P. Brown 2007). Another story from the same paper remarked on the cultural and institutional effects of straight in-migration: "In the Chicago area known as Boystown, business owners and residents say the influx of young heterosexual families has rendered the neighborhood's name an anachronism. The gay bookstore now sells more children's books than gay books" (Zernike 2003:A16).

Gays and lesbians also have children, of course, but it is the specific presence of straight families pushing strollers that has ignited the most controversy. "In just about any other place, the sight of a man and woman pushing a stroller would be welcomed as a sign of stability and safety," noted a journalist writing for the Associated Press (2007). But not necessarily in a gayborhood. "Gay leaders in the Castro and other gay neighborhoods around the country fear their enclaves are losing their distinct identities. These areas are slowly being altered by an influx of heterosexual couples" (Associated Press 2007). The overtime acceptance (Loftus 2001; Andersen and Fetner 2008) and normalization (Warner 1999) of gay and lesbian relations increases the perception among heterosexuals that gayborhoods are family-friendly areas. The greater number of straights that results on the streets is evidence that the symbolic boundaries of homosexuality are shifting away from signifying sickness and sin (stereotypes of gay men as child molesters) to safety and child-friendliness (gay bookstores that sell more children's books than LGBTQ books).

The cool quotient

In tandem with broad changes in public opinion, the state has also shifted its perception of gayborhoods away from a "regulatory problem" that required repression and containment in the 1970s and 1980s to a "marketing asset" in recent years (Rushbrook 2002:193). Redefining gayborhoods from red light to entertainment districts allows straights to "overcome their discomfort with being 'out of place' in gay space" (G. Brown 2006:133) and to feel at ease entering gayborhoods and other culturally queer spaces such as bars and community centers. This transforms gayborhoods into "the chic social and cultural centres of the city – the place to be seen . . . regardless of one's sexual preferences" (Collins 2004:1793). A writer for *Orbit* magazine reflected on evolving perceptions of the gayborhood:

> The rainbow flag that gays planted signaled to other assorted demographics – hipsters, liberal-leaning couples with young kids, actual artists, myself – that the neighborhood had been conquered, with flair. So we came, hungry for . . . a higher cool quotient.
>
> *(M. Katz 2010)*

These days, gayborhoods are less quasi-ethnic and more like tourist destinations for straights "on safari" (Orne 2017). The commodification of the gayborhood contributes to its "Disneyfication" (Zukin 1995:128), and it strips the area of its cultural and political significance.

Gentrification

In the late 2000s, the *New York Observer* published a headline that did not mince words: "Neighborhood Got Gays? No? Then You Don't Want To Live There" (Koblin 2007). What was "the first tip" that the journalist received from a realtor about "how to find the next hot neighborhood?" Three words: "Find the gays" (Koblin 2007). This sentiment embodies "gentrification," a word that Glass (1964) first coined to describe cycles of cultural, economic, and infrastructural renewal efforts in the city (see also Zukin 1987). Widespread urban revitalization in the United States proceeded in two stages. Federal interventions fueled the first, which was a response to white flight and inner-city decline in the 1960s (Wilson 1987). This stage involved isolated investments in "islands of renewal in seas of decay" (Berry 1985). Participants, many of whom were gay, thought of themselves as pioneers who were "taming the urban wilderness" as they searched for cheaper housing options (Brown-Saracino 2007). Gentrification resurged in the late 1990s in a second stage that corresponded with rising home prices. Changes in the financing system, privatization, realty speculation, and the dismantling of public housing incited the second surge. Although gays and lesbians built their gayborhoods in the first wave, the "super-gentrifiers" of the second wave are mostly straights who are transforming those same districts into "visible niche markets for retail commerce and realty speculation" (Hanhardt 2008:65). Second wave financers and straight newcomers prefer larger chain stores which threaten "the cultural icons of queer neighborhoods" (Doan and Higgins 2011:16). Once the culture changes, demographic transitions ensue as more straight residents replace gays and lesbians. These shifting spatial dynamics of the gayborhood give straights more power in their placemaking efforts.

Diversity

Young urbanites prize diversity (Jacobs 1961), even if this "powerful and plastic symbol" causes controversies among residents who share the same streets (Berrey 2005:143). One realtor in Chicago observed, "As far as attracting the straight community [to Boystown], young people today aren't bothered by diversity. They're used to it" (Sharoff 1997:E1). Consider as well an observation from Gulfport, Florida, where a local reporter remarked:

> What Gulfport has become is a place for everyone, a place where "diverse" is not a buzzword. During a stroll along the mostly commercial Beach Boulevard on a Saturday afternoon in early February, there were children playing in front of a worn duplex, 20-somethings shopping, traditional families with children, bikers, grandparents, great-grandparents, and gay couples... "We at the chamber call the community 'bohemian,'" said Greg Stemm, executive director of the Gulfport Chamber of Commerce.
>
> *(Daniel 2006:D8)*

Florida (2002:227) praises "places with a visible gay presence." He spoke with many young people who "oriented their location search to such places, even though they are not gay themselves." A young woman of Persian decent recounted to him:

> I was driving across the country with my sister and some friends. We were commenting on what makes a place the kind of place we want to go, or the kind of place we would live. We said: It has to be open. It has to be diverse. It has to have a visible gay community.
>
> *(Florida 2002:227)*

Florida explains this preference by citing the changing meanings of sexuality. "Homosexuality represents the last frontier of diversity in our society," he argues, "and thus a place that welcomes the gay community welcomes all kinds of people" (2002:255–56). Over the years, more frequent interactions between gays and straights have produced a greater tolerance for cultural differences (Gorman-Murray and Waitt 2009), which in turn has nurtured pro-equality sensibilities (Kanai and Kenttamaa-Squires 2015).

Conclusion

Three conclusions about culture emerge when we examine the gayborhood. First, culture has an autonomy (Alexander 1990), and it is not always reducible to the conventional variables that scholars use to explain urban change. Gans's critique of culture as an "uncaused cause" traps us into an infinitely circular search for analytic independence. There is no Garden of Eden for causality. Let us ask not whether culture is casual but instead how it makes a difference overall. A cultural sociology of the gayborhood illustrates the many ways in which sexuality informs our imaginations of place, contested efforts at placemaking on the ground, and the constitution of the urban imaginary.

Second, gayborhoods draw our attention to an understudied relationship between sexuality, space, and inequality (Brodyn and Ghaziani 2018). These districts first emerged following World War II as "a spatial response to a historically specific form of oppression" (Lauria and Knopp 1985:152). When the nature of oppression changes, so too should the spatial response. This hypothesis suggests that cultural explanations for the formation of gayborhoods and explanations for why they are changing today do not evince antipathy toward issues of inequality and power. The reduction of scholarship into binary propositions and analytical dualisms (Archer 1996) such as culture *or* structural inequality reduces the degrees of precision for our analysis, and it needlessly circumscribes how much of the variation of a phenomenon we can explain.

Finally, to ensure that a cultural sociology of the gayborhood remains rigorous and vibrant, future researchers should specify the "observable analytic units" (Ghaziani 2014b:375) of culture on which they focus. By bringing sexuality and the city into the cultural fold, I have hinted at several possibilities for how to study sexual meanings, placemaking, and the urban imaginary, including an examination of residential logics and extralocal attachments, intergroup interactions, the composition of businesses, the particular role of "anchor institutions" (ibid.) such as gay bookstores, contested symbols like strollers on the sidewalks or diversity discourse in conversations, community iconography like rainbow flags, ritual events such as Pride parades, and tourism campaigns. It seems to me that thinking about culture in terms of its observable analytic units can correct the "impossibly vague" (Sewell 1999:41) strategies of definitional and operational catholicity, and the propensity to see culture as "chameleon-like" (Binder et al. 2008:8). The problem is that chameleons "provide no particular angle or analytical purchase" (Sewell 1999:41) for the study of culture, especially as the concept is already plagued by an analytic mist (Fine 1979). The mandate for model specification should motivate us to place culture in the driver's seat. It is only by doing so that we can re-conceptualize the city as a culturally saturated site of meanings.

References

Abrahamson, Mark. 2005. *Urban Enclaves: Identity and Place in the World.* New York: Worth.

Aldrich, Robert. 2004. "Homosexuality and the City: An Historical Overview." *Urban Studies* 41(9): 1719–37.

Alexander, Jeffrey C. 1990. "Introduction: Understanding the 'Relative Autonomy' of Culture." Pp. 1–27 in *Culture and Society: Contemporary Debates*, edited by J.C. Alexander and S. Seidman. Cambridge: Cambridge University Press.

Alexander, Jeffrey C., and Philip Smith. 2010. "The Strong Program: Origins, Achievements and Prospects." Pp. 13–24 in *Handbook of Cultural Sociology*, edited by J.R. Hall, L. Grindstaff, and M. Lo. London: Routledge.

Andersen, Robert, and Tina Fetner. 2008. "Cohort Differences in Tolerance of Homosexuality: Attitudinal Change in Canada and the United States, 1981–2000." *Public Opinion Quarterly* 72(2):311–30.

Archer, Margaret S. 1996. *Culture and Agency*. New York: Cambridge University Press.

Armstrong, Elizabeth A. 2002. *Forging Gay Identities: Organizing Sexuality in San Francisco, 1950–1994*. Chicago: University of Chicago Press.

Associated Press. 2007. "Won't You Be My Gaybor? Gay Neighborhoods Worry about Losing their Distinct Identity." *Chicago Tribune*, March 13, p. 3.

Bearman, Peter. 2005. *Doormen*. Chicago: University of Chicago Press.

Berrey, Ellen. 2005. "Divided over Diversity: Political Discourse in a Chicago Neighborhood." *City and Community* 4(2):143–70.

———. 2015. *The Enigma of Diversity: The Language of Race and the Limits of Racial Justice*. Chicago: University of Chicago Press.

Berry, Brian J.L. 1985. "Islands of Renewal in Seas of Decay." Pp. 69–96 in *The New Urban Reality*, edited by P.E. Peterson. Washington, DC: Brookings Institution.

Binder, Amy, Mary Blair-Loy, John Evans, Kwai Ng and Michael Schudson. 2008. "The Diversity of Culture." *Annals of the American Academy of Political and Social Science* 619:6–14.

Borer, Michael Ian. 2007. "Culture Matters: A Reply to Gans." *City and Community* 6(2):157–59.

Brodyn, Adriana, and Amin Ghaziani. 2018. "Performative Progressiveness: Accounting for New Forms of Inequality in the Gayborhood." *City & Community* 17(2):307–29.

Brown, Gavin. 2006. "Cosmopolitan Camouflage: (Post-)Gay Space in Spitalfields, East London." Pp. 130–45 in *Cosmopolitan Urbanism*, edited by J. Binnie, J. Holloway, S. Millington, and C. Young. New York: Routledge.

Brown, Michael. 2014. "Gender and Sexuality II: There Goes the Gayborhood?" *Progress in Human Geography* 38(3):457–65.

Brown, Patricia Leigh. 2007. "Gay Enclaves Face Prospect of Being Passé." *New York Times*, October 30.

Brown-Saracino, Japonica. 2007. "Virtuous Marginality: Social Preservationists and the Selection of the Old-Timer." *Theory and Society* 36(5):437–68.

Bruce, Katherine McFarland. 2016. *Pride Parades: How a Parade Changed the World*. New York: NYU Press.

Carpiano, Richard M., Brian C. Kelly, Adam Easterbrook, and Jeffrey T. Parsons. 2011. "Community and Drug Use among Gay Men: The Role of Neighborhoods and Networks." *Journal of Health and Social Behavior* 52(1):74–90.

Castells, Manuel. 1983. *The City and the Grassroots: A Cross-Cultural Theory of Urban Social Movements*. Berkeley: University of California Press.

Chauncey, George. 1994. *Gay New York: Gender, Urban Culture, and the Making of the Gay Male World, 1890–1940*. New York: Basic Books.

Collins, Alan. 2004. "Sexual Dissidence, Enterprise and Assimilation: Bedfellows in Urban Regeneration." *Urban Studies* 41(9):1789–806.

Currid, Elizabeth. 2007. *The Warhol Economy: How Fashion, Art, and Music Drive New York City*. Princeton, NJ: Princeton University Press.

Daniel, Diane. 2006. "Where Diversity and Arts Shine." *Boston Globe*, February 15, p. D8.

De Witt, Karen. 1994. "Gay Presence Leads Revival of Declining Neighborhoods." *New York Times*, September 6, p. A14.

Dean, James Joseph. 2014. *Straights: Heterosexuality in a Post-Closeted Culture*. New York: New York University Press.

Deener, Andrew. 2012. *Venice: A Contested Bohemia in Los Angeles*. Chicago: University of Chicago Press.

Doan, Petra L. and Harrison Higgins. 2011. "The Demise of Queer Space? Resurgent Gentrification and the Assimilation of LGBT Neighborhoods." *Journal of Planning Education and Research* 31(1):6–25.

Epstein, Steven. 1987. "Gay Politics, Ethnic Identity: The Limits of Social Constructionism." *Socialist Review* 17(3–4):9–54.

Evans, Sara M., and Harry C. Boyte. 1986. *Free Spaces: The Sources of Democratic Change in America*. Chicago: University of Chicago Press.

Fine, Gary Alan. 1979. "Small Groups and Cultural Creation: The Idioculture of Little League Baseball Teams." *American Sociological Review* 44:733–45.

Fischer, Claude S. 1975. "Toward a Subcultural Theory of Urbanism." *American Journal of Sociology* 80(6):1319–41.

Florida, Richard. 2002. *The Rise of the Creative Class*. New York: Basic Books.

Gamson, Joshua. 1995. "Must Identity Movements Self-Destruct? A Queer Dilemma." *Social Problems* 42(3):390–407.

Gans, Herbert J. 2007. "But Culturalism Cannot Explain Power: A Reply to Borer." *City and Community* 6(2):159–60.

Gates, Gary J., and Jason Ost. 2004. *The Gay and Lesbian Atlas*. Washington, DC: Urban Institute.

Ghaziani, Amin. 2008. *The Dividends of Dissent: How Conflict and Culture Work in Lesbian and Gay Marches on Washington*. Chicago: University of Chicago Press.

———. 2009. "An 'Amorphous Mist'? The Problem of Measurement in the Study of Culture." *Theory and Society* 38(6):581–612.

———. 2011. "Post-Gay Collective Identity Construction." *Social Problems* 58(1):99–125.

———. 2014a. *There Goes the Gayborhood?* Princeton, NJ: Princeton University Press.

———. 2014b. "Measuring Urban Sexual Cultures." *Theory and Society* 43(3–4):371–93.

———. 2015. "'Gay Enclaves Face Prospect of Being Passé': How Assimilation Affects the Spatial Expressions of Sexuality in the United States." *International Journal of Urban and Regional Research* 39(4):756–71.

Glass, Ruth. 1964. *London: Aspects of Change*. London: Centre for Urban Studies.

Gorman-Murray, Andrew and Gordon Waitt. 2009. "Queer-Friendly Neighbourhoods: Interrogating Social Cohesion across Sexual Difference in Two Australian Neighbourhoods." *Environment and Planning A* 41(12):2855–73.

Grazian, David. 2008. *On the Make: The Hustle of Urban Nightlife*. Chicago: University of Chicago Press.

Greene, Theodore. 2014. "Gay Neighborhoods and the Rights of the Vicarious Citizen." *City and Community* 13(2):99–118.

Hanhardt, Christina B. 2008. "Butterflies, Whistles, and Fists: Gay Safe Street Patrols and the New Gay Ghetto, 1976–1981." *Radical History Review* (100):60–85.

Heap, Chad. 2003. "The City as a Sexual Laboratory: The Queer Heritage of the Chicago School." *Qualitative Sociology* 26(4):457–87.

Jacobs, Jane. 1961. *The Death and Life of Great American Cities*. New York: Vintage Books.

Kanai, Juan Miguel, and Kai Kenttamaa-Squires. 2015. "Remaking South Beach: Metropolitan Gayborhood Trajectories under Homonormative Entrepreneurialism." *Urban Geography* 36(3):385–402.

Katz, Jonathan Ned. 2007. *The Invention of Heterosexuality*. Chicago: University of Chicago Press.

Katz, Matt. 2010. "There Goes the Gayborhood." *Orbit Magazine*, April 2. (https://web.archive.org/web/20100409132653/http://www.obit-mag.com/articles/there-goes-the-gayborhood).

Keller, Suzanne. 1968. *The Urban Neighborhood: A Sociological Perspective*. New York: Random House.

Koblin, John. 2007. "Neighborhood Got Gays? No? Then You Don't Want To Live There." *New York Observer*, January 26. Retrieved September 30, 2010 (www.observer.com/node/35653).

Laumann, Edward O., Stephen Ellingson, Jenna Mahay, Anthony Paik, and Yoosik Youm, eds. 2004. *The Sexual Organization of the City*. Chicago: University of Chicago Press.

Lauria, Mickey, and Lawrence Knopp. 1985. "Toward an Analysis of the Role of Gay Communities in the Urban Renaissance." *Urban Geography* 6(2):152–69.

Levine, Martin P. 1979. "Gay Ghetto." Pp. 182–204 in *Gay Men: The Sociology of Male Homosexuality*, edited by M.P. Levine. New York: Harper and Row.

Levy, Dan. 1996. "There Goes the Neighborhood." *SFGate*, May 26. (www.sfgate.com/news/article/There-Goes-the-Neighborhood-After-25-years-at-3773959.php).

Lloyd, Richard. 2006. *Neo-Bohemia: Art and Commerce in the Postindustrial City*. New York: Routledge.

Lloyd, Richard, and Terry Nichols Clark. 2001. "The City as an Entertainment Machine." *Critical Perspectives on Urban Redevelopment* 6:357–78.

Loftus, Jeni. 2001. "America's Liberalization in Attitudes toward Homosexuality, 1973–1998." *American Sociological Review* 66(5):762–82.

Mears, Ashley. 2011. *Pricing Beauty: The Making of a Fashion Model*. Berkeley: University of California Press.

Molotch, Harvey, William Freudenburg, and Krista E. Paulsen. 2000. "History Repeats Itself, but How? City Character, Urban Tradition, and the Accomplishment of Place." *American Sociological Review* 65(6):791–823.

Molotch, Harvey, and Laura Noren, eds. 2010. *Toilet: Public Restrooms and the Politics of Sharing*. New York: NYU Press.

Montgomery, Charles. 2013. *Happy City: Transforming Our Lives through Urban Design*. Toronto, ON: Doubleday Canada.

Murray, Stephen O. 1979. "Institutional Elaboration of a Quasi-Ethnic Community." *International Review of Modern Sociology* 9(2):165–78.

———. 1996. *American Gay*. Chicago: University of Chicago Press.

Newton, Esther. 1993. *Cherry Grove, Fire Island: Sixty Years in America's First Gay and Lesbian Town*. Boston: Beacon Press.

Ocejo, Richard E. 2014. *Upscaling Downtown: From Bowery Saloons to Cocktail Bars in New York City*. Princeton, NJ: Princeton University Press.

O'Sullivan, Arthur. 2005. "Gentrification and Crime." *Journal of Urban Economics* 57(1):73–85.

Orne, Jason. 2017. *Boystown: Sex and Community in Chicago*. Chicago: University of Chicago Press.

Park, Robert E. 1925. "The City." Pp. 1–46 in *The City: Suggestions for Investigation of Human Behavior in the Urban Environment*, edited by R.E. Park and E.W. Burgess. Chicago: University of Chicago Press.

Rushbrook, Dereka. 2002. "Cities, Queer Space, and the Cosmopolitan Tourist." *GLQ: A Journal of Lesbian and Gay Studies* 8(1–2):183–206.

Seidman, Steven. 2002. *Beyond the Closet: The Transformation of Gay and Lesbian Life*. New York: Routledge.

Sewell, William H., Jr. 1999. "The Concept(S) of Culture." Pp. 35–61 in *Beyond the Cultural Turn: New Directions in the Study of Society and Culture*, edited by V.E. Bonnell and L. Hunt. Berkeley: University of California Press.

Sharoff, Robert. 1997. "Taking Sides on Neighborhood Pride." *Washington Post*, November 29, p. E1.

Silver, Daniel Aaron, and Terry Nichols Clark. 2016. *Scenescapes: How Qualities of Place Shape Social Life*. Chicago: University of Chicago Press.

Stein, Arlene. 1989. "Three Models of Sexuality: Drives, Identities and Practices." *Sociological Theory* 7(1):1–13.

Stein, Arlene, and Ken Plummer. 1994. "'I Can't Even Think Straight': 'Queer' Theory and the Missing Sexual Revolution in Sociology." *Sociological Theory* 12(2):178–87.

Taylor, Verta, and Nancy E. Whittier. 1992. "Collective Identity in Social Movement Communities." Pp. 104–29 in *Frontiers in Social Movement Theory*, edited by A.D. Morris and C. McClurg. New Haven, CT: Yale University Press.

Usher, Nikki, and Eleanor Morrison. 2010. "The Demise of the Gay Enclave, Communication Infrastructure Theory, and the Transformation of Gay Public Space." Pp. 271–87 in *LGBT Identity and Online New Media*, edited by C. Pullen and M. Cooper. New York: Routledge.

Ward, Jane. 2015. *Not Gay: Sex between Straight White Men*. New York: NYU Press.

Warner, Michael, ed. 1993. *Fear of a Queer Planet: Queer Politics and Social Theory*. Minneapolis: University of Minnesota Press.

———. 1999. *The Trouble with Normal: Sex, Politics, and the Ethnics of Queer Life*. New York: Free Press.

Weston, Kath. 1995. "Get Thee to a Big City: Sexual Imaginary and the Great Gay Migration." *GLQ: A Journal of Lesbian and Gay Studies* 2(3):253–77.

Wilson, William Julius. 1987. *The Truly Disadvantaged: The Inner City, the Underclass, and Public Policy*. Chicago: University of Chicago Press.

Wittman, Carl. 1970. *A Gay Manifesto*. New York: Red Butterfly.

Wynn, Jonathan R. 2011. *The Tour Guide: Walking and Talking New York*. Chicago: University of Chicago Press.

———. 2015. *Music/City: American Festivals and Placemaking in Austin, Nashville, and Newport*. Chicago: University of Chicago Press.

Zernike, Kate. 2003. "The New Couples Next Door, Gay and Straight." *New York Times*, August 24, p. A16.

Zukin, Sharon. 1987. "Gentrification: Culture and Capital in the Urban Core." *Annual Review of Sociology* 13:129–47.

———. 1995. *The Cultures of Cities*. Oxford: Blackwell.

———. 2010. *Naked City: The Death and Life of Authentic Urban Places*. New York: Oxford University Press.

25

Access to pleasure

Aesthetics, social inequality, and the structure of culture production

Ann Swidler

Introduction

Pierre Bourdieu's (1984) preoccupation with cultural capital as a resource to be deployed in the competition for advantage or "exchanged" for other forms of capital has obscured the ways that aesthetic pleasure matters for its own sake. *Distinction* (1984) analyzes how the exercise of socially shaped cultural taste – the "distinctions" people make, which in turn "distinguish" them – advantages or disadvantages people in the competition for social position, especially in the educational system. Cultural knowledge and taste become a kind of "capital" that can be exchanged at specific "ratios" for capital in other realms. Even *The Rules of Art* (Bourdieu 1992), which focuses on culture creators rather than cultural consumption, deploys vast erudition about Flaubert and his contemporaries to argue that culture creators are driven by concern about rivalries and sources of distinction in an existing artistic field, or by the aspiration to define a new artistic field in which they are supreme. Lost in Bourdieu's approach is the idea that a culture creator might be driven by the desire to create a certain aesthetic effect – to move, astound, delight, entertain, terrify, or simply *affect* an audience.

Here I explore a different but no less significant form of cultural stratification: the differential availability of aesthetic pleasures to those with differing social resources. I focus on the production of cultural objects, performances, and meanings; on the ways audiences are brought into relationship with cultural creators; and on the organizations and practices that frame aesthetic experience.

I start from the premise that aesthetic pleasure is one of the great goods of life. The view that people participate in playful aesthetic experience only as a poor substitute for something else – politics, class struggle, status, the pursuit of power – is inadequate, both as an ideal of how people ought to live and as a description of how they do live (Stromberg 2009).

I include under the broad category of "aesthetic pleasure" all forms of entertainment, from watching a wacky TV sitcom, to cruising YouTube for the latest political video, to the sometimes excruciating pleasures of serious drama, ballet, opera, or demanding music. Cultural expertise and the exercise of discriminating taste can serve to assert status, to intimidate others, and in some cases to gain access to material and other rewards (see, e.g., Rivera 2012). However, the Bourdieusian preoccupation with cultural distinction – both the amount of culture people "know" and the skills needed to decipher it – weakens cultural analysis by assuming that culture's major role is to reproduce inequality by either mystifying class hierarchy, legitimating inequality, or serving as opiate of the masses.

Taking the aesthetic function of culture seriously directs attention to the social-organizational factors that create differential access to aesthetic pleasure and to the social arrangements likely to produce such pleasure in greater or lesser measure. Social arrangements can stimulate or inhibit the creation of resonant cultural objects that appeal to particular sorts of audiences, and they can make the conditions for such enjoyment more and less available. Economic and educational inequalities matter partly because they deprive some groups of access to a full share of aesthetic pleasure – the pleasure of group expression and solidarity and the pleasure of intense, deep, rich, or thrilling cultural experience.

Meaning in social context

A sociologically useful approach to aesthetic pleasure focuses on "conventions" – the shared expectations that link culture creators and their audiences and allow them to communicate (Meyer 1956; Becker 1982; Griswold 1987; Olick 1999). As Becker argues, conventions help the producers of cultural works to coordinate their efforts, as when the conductor and members of an orchestra all know the conventions of musical notation or performance styles. But the deeper significance of conventions for aesthetic pleasure is that they structure aesthetic experience by shaping expectations – the recognition of that which is familiar, but also the frisson of excitement, the thrill, when something unexpected happens. As Leonard Meyer (1956) argued in explaining how music creates "emotion and meaning," shared conventions establish aesthetic expectations; violations of those expectations produce tension; and resolution of that tension creates aesthetic fulfillment.

When audiences and creators share conventions, creators can produce aesthetically powerful effects by playing off audience expectations. Variations on a melodic theme, puzzlement about "whodunit" in a murder mystery, or suspense about the outcome of a well-matched sporting event (Geertz 1973) produces just this sort of aesthetic tension and excitement for knowledgeable observers. Pleasurable anticipation, heightened attention, and absorbed involvement are the hallmarks of successful aesthetic engagement. For audiences that lack the relevant conventions, however, even a highly refined artistic product of an unfamiliar aesthetic tradition (Chinese opera for a Westerner unfamiliar with the genre, for example) may create no aesthetic pleasure.

The sociological question is: what allows some groups more than others (1) to develop a set of shared conventions and to refine or extend them so that variations on those conventions will be aesthetically meaningful, and (2) to support creators who will produce cultural objects or performances that respond to, develop, and continually renew those conventions? Since aesthetic pleasure depends both on shared expectations and on the creation of innovations that can surprise, unsettle, and delight, explaining differences in the availability and richness of aesthetic pleasure requires paying attention both to social forces that organize audiences and creators so that they share aesthetic conventions, and to social arrangements that stimulate extensions, refinements, and innovations that deepen or intensify cultural resonance.

If we examine class differences in aesthetic experience, we do not need to start from Bourdieu's (1984) essentializing claim that higher-class people, freed from material necessity, are inherently more likely to "aestheticize" experience (see Lizardo and Skiles 2012 for a strong defense of this position). The fanciful "styling" of the dress of poor teenagers, the working-class punks Hebdige (1979) described, who aestheticized ordinary material objects like torn clothes and safety pins, or the stylized aesthetics that Tom Wolfe (1965) found in varied American subcultures easily demonstrates the fallacy of such an argument. Instead we can ask how the resources different groups possess allow them to create and preserve cultural objects and practices that generate intense, meaningful, or thrilling aesthetic experience. Of course, such pleasure does not come from cultural objects or performances themselves, but from an interaction between an object and the educated skills, capacities, or interests of the appreciator (see Griswold 1986 on meaning as metaphor; Baxandall 1972 on the "period eye").

Revisiting the mass culture debate

The debate over "mass culture," which roiled intellectuals in the 1950s and '60s, has largely faded. In part this is the result of the important work of Paul DiMaggio (1982a; 1982b; see also Levine 1988), showing that the contemporary distinction between high and popular culture was socially constructed by particular groups in a specific historical era. The history of how, in the mid-nineteenth century, popular performances might mix Shakespearean orations, popular song, ribald humor, and classical music, while by the end of the nineteenth century classical music and high art were carefully segregated in museums and symphony halls, seemed to show that the distinction between "high" and "popular" culture is a purely artificial one. By this logic, high culture is any culture created and monopolized by social elites who want to preserve their exclusivity and assert their superiority. Museums, orchestras, and ballet and opera companies then simply police the (arbitrary, artificial) boundary between a valued elite culture and a devalued popular culture.

A focus on cultural enjoyment rather than cultural prestige, however, suggests the need to give attention to organizational and structural factors that shape opportunities for aesthetic pleasure. Groups differ in their access to satisfying cultural experiences due to systematic differences in the organization of cultural production and the structures that link potential audiences to culture creators.

Organizational bases for cultural pleasure

Two major, underappreciated texts – Paul DiMaggio's (1987) "Classification in Art" and Robert Escarpit's (1971) classic, *The Sociology of Literature* – provide a starting point for analyzing social variations in access to aesthetic pleasure. DiMaggio argues that distinctive cultural genres emerge from groups' needs to define or bound themselves. Cultural knowledge, including knowledge of specific cultural genres, he argues, operates not mainly to legitimate group claims to privilege, but to provide material for sociable interaction, for conversation, among those who want to enact or assert solidarity. This interpretation of cultural capital makes sense of the finding (one Bourdieu never explained satisfactorily) that social taste hierarchies are not exclusive. Higher-status and more educated people have taste for and participate in all sorts of culture, including classically high culture, whereas the less educated participate in a narrower range of less high-culture activities (on the "omnivore" pattern in higher-status groups, see Peterson and Kern 1996; Lizardo and Skiles 2012; for France, Coulangeon and Lemel 2007; for Denmark, Katz-Gerro and Jaeger 2013). This makes sense if, as DiMaggio argues, higher-status people want to be able to form sociable bonds with people like themselves by signaling familiarity with high culture, but also to benefit from friendly relationships with people from all social strata (Erickson 1996, 2007). Of course, familiarity with a diverse array of cultural forms can itself be a status marker (Peterson and Rossman 2007; Sullivan and Katz-Gerro 2007; Lizardo and Skiles 2012), but the proliferation of artistic genres (Lena and Peterson 2008) and group and individual engagement with aesthetic experience suggest that much more is going on than the assertion of status distinctions. People seek aesthetic pleasure in entertainments that they share with others, and all sorts of groups have an interest in developing and promoting cultural genres that represent, express, and reproduce their collective life.

DiMaggio's perspective complements the valuable insights of Robert Escarpit in *The Sociology of Literature* (1971). Escarpit distinguishes not high and popular culture, but two ways of organizing communication between culture creators and their audiences – the "Cultured Circuit" and the "Popular Circuit." Although these two organizational forms may be associated with high versus popular culture, folk cultures grounded in a cohesive community may have the structural features of the "cultured circuit," while certain elite cultural genres may lack them. The cultured circuit is characterized by extensive feedback from the consumers of cultural products to those who create them, usually via critics who both shape audience taste and transmit critical understandings back to creators or producers. Escarpit notes that in the cultured circuit, authors often receive active feedback on their work from likely audiences (these authors' friends tend to be the same sort of people as their readers) and from critics, who both respond to the work and organize and educate audiences. The "popular circuit" (mass market paperbacks or network television, for example), in contrast, lacks feedback except through the market: culture producers for the popular circuit know what to create only by observing what has sold in the recent past (see Hirsch 1972). Culture produced for the popular circuit thus tends to imitate successful formulas, or, like the "recombinant" TV shows that Todd Gitlin (1985) describes, to combine currently popular themes in slightly new ways.

The distinction between popular and cultured circuits can be used to analyze groups' varying access to culture that reinforces group solidarities, responds to distinctive tastes, and builds on shared tastes to innovate in ways that delight or entertain. This organizational distinction may not correspond to what we think of as high versus popular culture. Traditional high culture may stagnate – especially when those eager to maintain its boundaries rigidly patrol its content so that it does not evolve in response to the interests of its audiences. Some popular forms, such as jazz (especially in its formative period [Lopes 2002]), "indie" rock, or hip-hop, on the other hand, might bring culture creators face-to-face with knowledgeable, interested audiences who give direct feedback about what moves or excites them. Thus some popular genres are produced through structures resembling the "cultured circuit," and some high-culture genres may not have structures of production and distribution that generate vibrant cultural experience. In general, however, groups without wealth and leisure are also disadvantaged in the ability to create and control structures of cultural production that provide the greatest possibilities for aesthetic pleasure.

What circumstances are likely to promote the discrete, bounded genres that DiMaggio (1987) analyzes or the responsive feedback circuits that Escarpit describes? DiMaggio points out that however much those who create a new genre would like to keep it exclusive (as the youth cultures that generate new musical styles try to do [Hebdige 1979; Frith 1981]), commercial market interests seek to broaden audiences, thus diluting the symbolic exclusivity of a group's identification with a specific genre and weakening the link between culture producers and a specialized audience to whose sophisticated tastes they can respond. The commercial "massification" of any cultural genre is thus likely to make its cultural products more stereotyped, less innovative, and less exciting to the original fans, because now the genre also has to please less knowledgeable audiences, who are less experienced in the genre's particular conventions.

Diversity and innovation

Peterson and Berger's (1975) classic article, "Cycles in Symbol Production," analyzed sources of innovation and diversity in culture production. They distinguished periods of market concentration (in which a small number of producers control production and distribution of cultural products and inhibit innovation) from periods in which many producers compete, creating more diverse and innovative cultural products. Building on Peterson and Berger, Lopes (1992) distinguishes not only between different degrees of concentration among producers, but between more segmented versus massified markets. In a segmented market, culture is distributed through specialized channels, reaching more taste-homogeneous audiences. When, for example, radio diversified after television enticed away the mass audience, radio stations developed new formats geared toward small segments of the audience, creating specialized stations for jazz, soul, country, gospel, and rock (versus radio's pre-TV fare of variety shows, news, soap operas, dramas, and comedy). Diversified radio stations became specialized distribution channels for potential purchasers to hear recorded music, which in turn led to a flowering of varied genres of music and to the creation of dynamic new genres. Market segmentation allows specialized producers to thrive and makes it more likely that cultural producers will be able to find those who share their tastes and appreciate their aesthetic conventions, encouraging the rapid development of cultural products that speak to those tastes.

Culture produced for a mass market is likely to satisfy average tastes reasonably well, since producers have an incentive to maximize their appeal to the broadest group of consumers. But such culture is not likely to develop a deepened aesthetic vocabulary, innovative variations on existing conventions, or enhanced power to move audiences (including the power to thrill, shock, or delight): creators cannot presume an audience whose aesthetic vocabulary they know and share, and the mass market does not have rich feedback mechanisms through which a knowledgeable audience can communicate its responses and thus stimulate cumulative development of intensified meanings. Jazz in its early development had all the structural advantages of a segmented audience and a "cultured" feedback circuit: it was played by musicians for musicians in after-hours venues, so audiences consisted largely of other musicians, who could respond immediately and knowledgeably to what they heard (Lopes 2002). "Massified" culture, in contrast, is not directed to a particular audience's taste; its aesthetic power is limited if there are few shared conventions that allow creators to pursue cumulative innovation by working new changes on "educated" tastes (by "educated" I mean, for example, the knowledgeable tastes of teenagers who have played many video games and are looking for the next heightened thrill [Khanolkar and McLean 2012]; of movie-goers who have seen every horror film and are looking for a zombie-fest to top the last one; as well as of aesthetes who can appreciate the slightest movement of a ballerina's hand).

Structural sources of elite aesthetic advantage

If decidedly non-elite subcultures, like those of early punk rock (Hebdige 1979) or hip-hop, can produce vibrant, aesthetically powerful culture, then why as a general matter should those with greater wealth and privilege also have access to more aesthetic pleasure? The examples of punk music and hip-hop suggest one immediate reason: the subcultures that produce vibrant aesthetic experience have great difficulty maintaining control of their innovative cultural creations, which rapidly succumb to commercial pressures that dilute the culture's meanings and separate culture creators from knowledgeable audiences.

Maintaining specialized relations between creators and audiences

The aesthetic advantages of elites go beyond simple freedom from pressures to "massify" their favored cultural products. Escarpit (1971) points to some obvious ways in which those with greater material resources secure for themselves the advantages of more deeply embedded cultural production. The wealthy are more likely to be able to pay for specialized cultural outlets (like bookstores, fashion houses, specialized magazines, or book review journals) that bring together audiences that share similar tastes. Second, they are more likely to be able to support specialists in feedback, like literary critics, who let producers know what specific audiences like, and who tell those audiences where to find the best, or the newest, culture of a specific sort (Janice Radway [1984] described a bookstore owner who performed this function for women romance readers, but perhaps the fate of local bookstores makes the point about the disadvantages faced by non-elite culture consumers).

DiMaggio (1982a, 1982b) describes how the nineteenth-century Boston upper class created an organizational infrastructure that set high culture apart. He also describes powerful aesthetic advantages that accompanied the new structure. Enormous organizational effort and considerable financial resources were required to create the organizational basis for a distinctive high culture – in the case of the Boston Symphony Orchestra, a canon purged of popular music, specialized musicians who performed only classical work, and special venues (a symphony hall) where audiences and performers or creators could reliably meet.

Aesthetic advantages of control over space and time

DiMaggio (1982a, 1982b) describes new norms that elites imposed in such venues as museums and symphony halls – sacralization, a hushed reverence (in contrast to the cacophony of a London theater, or the sometimes rowdy behavior of audiences in the vaudeville or popular performance circuit). Although the reverent decorum of high-culture venues is contested in some contemporary art, it is worth noticing what these audience norms permit aesthetically. Creators who know that audiences will spend time and effort trying to fathom their work can create subtle effects that those who have to grab their audiences' attention cannot afford. Both music and theater can use silences as expressive devices. Where audiences commit themselves to attentive engagement, a story can start slowly and build gradually. If audiences accept conventions of reverent waiting, art can create ambiguity, because audiences will tolerate it, waiting until the "meaning" seeps through. Of course these conventions can also lead to sterile, pretentious, or vacuous works, with audiences squirming miserably in their seats as they try to seem engaged by some piece of abstruse high culture. But the bounded spaces for cultural reception that elites can create – and the reverent attitude they inculcate – can give creators aesthetic resources with which to produce a range of effects, from the dramatic sound that shatters a silence, to the complexity of poetic language, to the exquisite variation in a soprano's aria that only an opera lover can appreciate.

Art "versus" market

It is part of the institutional delineation of "high" versus "popular" art forms – the "classification" and "framing" described by DiMaggio (1982a, 1982b) – that high culture is insulated from commercial pressures. From the poorest art school student to the most eminent symphony conductor, the claim to be doing serious art has depended in part on (at least the pretense of) indifference to – or insulation from – market pressures. Indeed, the ideal of creators pursuing their autonomous aesthetic vision connotes indifference to or insulation from market forces. And the ideal of art as a purely aesthetic enterprise depends on the notion that someone somewhere – a wealthy patron, an endowed museum, an orchestra's wealthy board members – will protect the art from unmediated audience demands.

Why, however, should protection from market pressures be important for the creation of vibrant, aesthetically gratifying culture? After all, if people do not enjoy or appreciate a cultural form enough to pay for it, then it probably lacks the ability to move or excite them. For an answer to this question we have to return to DiMaggio's central point in "Classification in Art." The inability to buffer a genre against market pressures virtually guarantees that it will be diluted to satisfy a broader set of tastes than those of the group whose interests gave rise to it and brought initial success. It will then be less likely to have a rich set of conventions shared by a knowledgeable audience and to develop dynamic innovations and aesthetic intensification to delight a specialized group of skilled appreciators. At the same time, of course, culture that is so buffered from audience demands that it need move and excite no one at all – what is sometimes referred to as "academic" culture (Crane 1976) – can become sterile, providing very little aesthetic gratification. Nonetheless, the ability to buffer a genre against market pressures is not just a way of achieving the status of "art" (as Becker 1982 describes potters trying to do by slashing their ceramic bowls or making impossibly large or otherwise non-functional objects, to distinguish their "art" from "crafts"). Insulating one's genre against market pressures – as youth cultures from punks to "house" music aficionados try to do – is fundamental to being able to keep a genre dynamic and to preserving a direct relationship between culture creators and a specific audience that shares their conventions.

Collecting and preserving

The last critical element that has differentiated the high and popular arts is the ability to preserve and teach the history of the genre, adding what I would call cultural depth – a rich reservoir of potential associations – as an aesthetic resource that creators can draw upon. Artists who can visit museums – and who can take for granted that those who see their art have also visited museums and absorbed the history of the form – can make allusions, employ visual vocabularies, or challenge conventions that they know are shared.

Elites can afford to establish repositories for the history of their preferred genres, from the collections of antique batiks that wealthy Indonesian families preserve over centuries, to the collections of art museums, to the repertoires of theaters and orchestras. Elite institutions also maintain specialists who conserve and teach the inherited repertoire, analyzing it for new meanings and reproducing an educated audience of those who have studied "music appreciation" or "art history." Literature classes provide a background that those who write for educated readers can take for granted, even as universities and colleges revise and rearrange the canon that writers and educated readers share. Such "preservation" has typically been the way that new elites made claims for the value of "their" genre (as when new elites formed the Museum of Modern Art, and shortly after, the Whitney). It takes money to do this, and preservation – the attempt to raise the status of a genre by preserving its history and by having specialists catalog and analyze that history – is one of the fundamental acts that raises the stature, but also the shared aesthetic vocabulary, of a genre. The creation of the Academy of Motion Picture Arts and Sciences and the Academy of Television Arts and Sciences were attempts by cultural creators to raise the stature of their products. Film departments in universities perform such a critical and canon-defining function for movies. The recognition of jazz as a serious art form (Lopes 2002) depended in part on the emergence of critics, collectors, and eventually academics, who preserve and interpret its history.

These elements of "art-ness" – special places and moods (which bring audiences and creators together as well), protection from commercial pressures, preservation of the history of the genre – all permit richer meaning-making. These are advantages that the privileged are more likely to be able to create and maintain for the genres that they favor.

Technological change and aesthetic pleasures (Yelp!)

If cultural vitality and aesthetic pleasure derive from the structural features of systems of cultural production and distribution, rather than from the supposed qualities of elite versus less elite culture consumers, then technological changes can alter culture and the possibilities of aesthetic pleasure in fundamental ways. As the internet has made it possible for musicians to find and to produce music for tiny, geographically dispersed audiences – and as websites that critique and recommend music to those with shared musical tastes proliferate – there has been a revolution in the amount of musical creativity and the consequent possibilities for powerful aesthetic experience for both creators and audiences (see the examples in Tepper and Ivey 2007).

New technologies also make it possible for more genres to preserve their histories (movies and TV series from the entire history of the form available for streaming, for example) and thus for culture creators both to know more of that history and to presume a shared vocabulary of associations, references, and expectations in their audiences. With the web's discovery of "customer reviews," many more subcultures can share tastes with bevies of like-minded others who revel in good local barbecue reviewed on Yelp! or "swoon" (in Zagat's favorite terminology) at exquisitely subtle sushi. As craft beer aficionados gather to develop both the vocabulary and the palate that allows discriminating taste (Maciel and Wallendorf 2017) and skilled players of sophisticated massively multiplayer online games experience aesthetic exaltation that most artists could only dream of evoking in their audiences (Khanolkar and McLean 2012; see also Stromberg 2009), some elements of what was traditionally high-culture aesthetic pleasure become available to many groups of knowledgeable culture consumers. These sophisticated audiences in turn inspire creators of new aesthetic objects – craft beers and video games, among many others – to new heights of artistry. With the web to bring together groups of like-minded aficionados, almost any subculture can develop the shared conventions and the discriminating judgments that stimulate vibrant culture and intensified aesthetic pleasure. For members of many subcultures (like the tens of thousands of fans who attend Comic-Con conventions, achieving new pinnacles of wackiness in costumes they invent for themselves), the web has allowed a proliferation of new aesthetic arenas. Like high-culture genres, such commercially based cultures – from food and wine connoisseurship to fantasy sports – exercise pleasurable powers of discrimination, build solidarities, and heighten aesthetic appreciation, including the cultivation of specialized vocabularies and sensitized tastes. Nonetheless, even as new technologies widen the possibility of knowledgeable, cultivated taste and its concomitant aesthetic delights, these subcultures have aesthetic limitations. They do not nurture the deepened meaningfulness that emerges from cumulative historical experience of the form; serious devotees cannot exclude more casual, less knowledgeable participants (Khanolkar and McLean [2012] find that serious online gamers disdain players who find "cheap," less skill-intensive ways to win); few culture producers can make a full-time living from creative work in the field; and the apparatus of curating, criticism, and aesthetic codification is fragmentary and fleeting. Thus despite some important changes, elites are still more likely than others not only to control what can become *legitimate* culture, but to control the conditions for production of culture that are exquisitely adapted to produce intense, deep, or rich aesthetic pleasure in knowledgeable audiences.

To understand culture as a source of meaning and pleasure does not require that we ignore its important role in signaling group membership and enacting social hierarchy. But ignoring the social factors that shape possibilities for aesthetic enjoyment – and neglecting that enjoyment as one of the fundamental elements of a good life – also misses a major cost of social inequality.

References

Baxandall, Michael. 1972. *Painting and Experience in Fifteenth Century Italy*. Oxford: Oxford University Press.

Becker, Howard S. 1982. *Art Worlds*. Berkeley: University of California Press.

Bourdieu, Pierre. 1984. *Distinction: A Social Critique of the Judgement of Taste*. Cambridge, MA: Harvard University Press.

———. 1992. *The Rules of Art: Genesis and Structure of the Literary Field*. Stanford, CA: Stanford University Press.

Coulangeon, Philippe, and Yannick Lemel. 2007. "Is 'Distinction' Really Outdated? Questioning the Meaning of the Omnivorization of Musical Taste in Contemporary France." *Poetics* 35(2–3):93–111.

Crane, Diana. 1976. "Reward Systems in Art, Science and Religion." *American Behavioral Scientist* 19(6):719–34.

DiMaggio, Paul. 1982a. "Cultural Entrepreneurship in Nineteenth-Century Boston: The Creation of an Organizational Base for High Culture in America." *Media, Culture and Society* 4(1):33–50.

———. 1982b. "Cultural Entrepreneurship in Nineteenth-Century Boston, Part II: The Classification and Framing of American Art." *Media, Culture and Society* 4(4):303–22.

———. 1987. "Classification in Art." *American Sociological Review* 52(4):440–55.

Erickson, Bonnie H. 1996. "Culture, Class, and Connections." *American Journal of Sociology* 102(1):217–25.

———. 2007. "The Crisis in Culture and Inequality." Pp. 343–62 in *Engaging Art: The Next Great Transformation of America's Cultural Life*, edited by S.J. Tepper and B. Ivey. New York: Routledge.

Escarpit, Robert. 1971. *Sociology of Literature*, trans. Ernest Pick. London: Frank Cass.

Frith, Simon. 1981. *Sound Effects: Youth, Leisure, and the Politics of Rock 'n' Roll*. New York: Pantheon.

Geertz, Clifford. 1973. "Deep Play: Notes on the Balinese Cockfight." Pp. 412–53 in *The Interpretation of Cultures*. New York: Basic Books.

Gitlin, Todd. 1985. *Inside Prime Time*. New York: Pantheon Books.

Griswold, Wendy. 1986. *Renaissance Revivals: City Comedy and Revenge Tragedy in the London Theatre, 1576–1980*. Chicago: University of Chicago Press.

———. 1987. "A Methodological Framework for the Sociology of Culture." *Sociological Methodology* 17:1–35.

Hebdige, Dick. 1979. *Subculture: The Meaning of Style*. London: Methuen.

Hirsch, Paul. 1972. "Processing Fads and Fashions: An Organization-Set Analysis of Cultural Industry Systems." *American Journal of Sociology* 77(4):639–59.

Katz-Gerro, Tally, and Mads Meier Jaeger. 2013. "Top of the Pops, Ascend of the Omnivores, Defeat of the Couch Potatoes: Modeling Change in Cultural Consumption." *European Sociological Review* 29(2):243–60.

Khanolkar, Preeti R., and Paul D. McLean. 2012. "100-Percenting It: Videogame Play through the Eyes of Devoted Gamers." *Sociological Forum* 27(4):961–85.

Lena, Jennifer C., and Richard A. Peterson. 2008. "Classification as Culture: Types and Trajectories of Music Genres." *American Sociological Review* 73(5):697–718.

Levine, Lawrence W. 1988. *Highbrow/Lowbrow: The Emergence of Cultural Hierarchy in America*. Cambridge, MA: Harvard University Press.

Lizardo, Omar, and Sara Skiles. 2012. "Reconceptualizing and Theorizing 'Omnivorousness': Genetic and Relational Mechanisms." *Sociological Theory* 30(4):263–82.

Lopes, Paul D. 1992. "Innovation and Diversity in the Popular Music Industry, 1969 to 1990." *American Sociological Review* 57(1):56–71.

———. 2002. *The Rise of a Jazz Art World*. Cambridge: Cambridge University Press.

Maciel, Andre F., and Melanie Wallendorf. 2017. "Taste Engineering: An Extended Consumer Model of Cultural Competence Constitution." *Journal of Consumer Research* 43(5):726–46.

Meyer, Leonard B. 1956. *Emotion and Meaning in Music*. Chicago: University of Chicago Press.

Olick, Jeffrey K. 1999. "Genre Memories and Memory Genres: A Dialogical Analysis of May 8th, 1945 Commemorations in the Federal Republic of Germany." *American Sociological Review* 64(3):381–402.

Peterson, Richard A., and David G. Berger. 1975. "Cycles in Symbol Production: The Case of Popular Music." *American Sociological Review* 40(2):158–73.

Peterson, Richard A., and Roger M. Kern. 1996. "Changing Highbrow Taste: From Snob to Omnivore." *American Sociological Review* 61(5):900–7.

Peterson, Richard A., and Gabriel Rossman. 2007. "Changing Arts Audiences: Capitalizing on Omnivorousness." Pp. 307–42 in *Engaging Art: The Next Great Transformation of America's Cultural Life*, edited by S.J. Tepper and B. Ivey. New York: Routledge.

Radway, Janice A. 1984. *Reading the Romance: Women, Patriarchy, and Popular Literature*. Chapel Hill: University of North Carolina Press.

Rivera, Lauren A. 2012. "Hiring as Cultural Matching: The Case of Elite Professional Service Firms." *American Sociological Review* 77(6):999–1022.

Stromberg, Peter G. 2009. *Caught in Play: How Entertainment Works on You*. Stanford, CA: Stanford University Press.

Sullivan, Oriel, and Tally Katz-Gerro. 2007. "The Omnivore Thesis Revisited: Voracious Cultural Consumers." *European Sociological Review* 23(2):123–37.

Tepper, Steven J., and Bill Ivey, eds. 2007. *Engaging Art: The Next Great Transformation of America's Cultural Life*. New York: Routledge.

Wolfe, Tom. 1965. *The Kandy-Kolored Tangerine-Flake Streamline Baby*. New York: Farrar, Straus, and Giroux.

Part V
Groups, identities, and performances

26

Group cultures and subcultures

Gary Alan Fine

Introduction

Although it had once been conventional to treat culture as a "characteristic" or "feature" of societies, many cultural sociologists now emphasize the importance of examining cultures as actively constructed. Here, I explore the theoretical stakes of this shift to analyzing culture from a micro- or meso-level of analysis. Culture can be conceptualized as actions, material objects, performances, and forms of discourse used by groups. In this view, culture is a tool situated in local communities, shaping the contours of civic life (Fine 2012). As a result, culture is tied to shared pasts and prospective futures.

Although culture can be tied to large-scale social systems (macro-cultures), a "micro" or "meso" approach has value as well. Culture should be linked to interacting groups and to networked population segments, addressing the development of idiocultures, subcultures, and countercultures. This perspective, grounded in social psychology, suggests that the locus of culture need not only be society-based populations, but equally can manifest in social worlds and communication networks. Culture is a form of practice linked to local understandings and social relations.

On occasion, social scientists, as well as the larger public, facilely refer to characteristics of American culture, French culture, or Brazilian culture. Such analyses have value in providing strategies to understand how societies differ ("their exceptionalism"), differentiating a people or a nation from others. However, because of the diversity of a geographically bounded population, any analysis that assumes a national culture is necessarily imprecise. A national culture is in practice splintered in various ways, while holding to a belief in unity. In its totality, a national culture can be conceived as everywhere and nowhere, sensed but invisible.

Admittedly, nations and regions have elements of a "collective character" that reveal themselves in societal representations. However, the micro-sociological goal is to determine how these and other values and beliefs operate in group space and how multiple group cultures, similar to each other in their circulation of members, weak network ties, or common milieu, affect the belief in a national culture, given institutional support through media representation and collective commemoration. Place matters because people interact within groups, but also because they share imagination about larger systems.

Ultimately, cultural sensibilities are transmitted and displayed through action, a recognition that privileges examining locales in which culture is performed. The study of culture properly belongs to the analysis of groups – from primary groups (e.g., families), to interacting small groups (clubs, teams, cliques), to networked segments tied together through ongoing interaction, communication, spatial co-presence, or consumption (including populations based on age, race, gender, or region). I begin with the most molecular level of analysis – the domain of face-to-face groups and their linkage to group idiocultures – and then examine larger communities based upon socially differentiated networks that form subcultures and countercultures, the latter implying some level of resistance to hegemonic cultures.

Groups and their idiocultures

Every interaction scene, no matter how tiny and provisional, develops common, meaningful referents. These bits of communal understanding – collective memories – are established from the opening moments of group life. This finding was demonstrated in Fine's (1979) article on "Small Groups and Cultural Creation: The Idioculture of Little League Baseball" and subsequent studies that applied the "idioculture" model to other social domains, such as mental health organizations, congregations, workplaces, and social movements. The group-based analysis of culture takes as its presupposition the human desire to create tight communities with shared pasts and prospective futures. Culture is found in all kinds of groups. Some group cultures – for example, of policymakers (Janis 1982; Gibson 2012) and bureaucratic organizations (Herzfeld 1993) – have more external influence than others do. And despite the preponderance of US research, group cultures are worldwide phenomena, as is demonstrated by accounts of Israeli military units (Sion and Ben-Ari 2005), Middle Eastern terrorist cells (Sageman 2008), Argentinian opera lovers (Benzecry 2011), and Japanese motorcycle (*bosozuku*) tribes (Sato 1991) that depict powerful local norms and shared images. Wherever groups' participants see common problems and the likelihood of continued interaction, cultures are established. The micro-sociological approach, arguing for attention to the local conditions in which shared meaning is generated, suggests that the establishment of traditions, shared references, and customs is integral to identity and cohesion. Such creation depends upon ongoing performances that organize and routinize interaction, creating a group style (Eliasoph and Lichterman 2003). In turn, as Lawler, Thye, and Yoon (2008) have argued, different group structures may produce distinctive "micro social orders."

Any fully sociological understanding of the creation of group cultures must recognize extensive institutional influences that impact the local scene, providing the basis for shared action. The backgrounds (both demographic and habitus) of participants, coupled with the expectations that stem from group interaction, contribute to the expansion of a group's meaning system when there is a triggering event that sparks recognition of collective experience. This process incorporates external cultural themes within group discourse and action. Once established, cultural elements provide a mechanism by which members recognize their group as salient and create group cohesion. Every group can access the background culture (the known culture of the group), the moral standards of discourse (the usable culture), the instrumental goals that participants desire (the functional culture), and support for the status hierarchy (the appropriate culture). What eventually becomes recognized as characterizing group life is a result of immediate interactional demands (what becomes triggered).

The processes of this model of cultural development emphasize the pressing needs of ongoing micro-communities. The focus of a group-based approach is to understand the creation of culture through processes of interaction that depend upon recognition of shared pasts and planned futures, arguing for a *sociology of localism*. Cultural products cannot be divorced from social actors or essentialized by treating culture as timeless. Given that culture-creating processes are shaped by participants' knowledge, understandings, and goals, an integrated and thematic content-based culture reflects the past history, current desires, and imagined futures of members. Traditions unite groups, providing a cultural grounding for trust, affiliation, and cohesion that generates collective identity. This approach is evident in recent focus on the examination of *collaborative circles* in the arts (Farrell 2001), leisure (Corte 2013), and sciences (Parker and Hackett 2012). These studies demonstrate the stages through which creative groups develop and then dissipate, and how resources are mobilized to provide for ongoing group life and the reputation of participants. Tight-knit groups create culture, but in turn, culture facilitates the establishment of tight-knit groups (or occasionally disrupts them). As Perrin (2005) argues, civic organizations depend upon discussion based upon an understood political microculture that takes varying forms in distinct types of organizations.

Idiocultures are evident in small groups in all institutional domains, including dyadic relations. The examination of families, gangs, sociometric cliques, workgroups, sports teams, "cults," and fraternal organizations demonstrate how local cultures shape the content of social relations. The culture of the group provides a cognitive and emotional structure through which individuals recognize collective pasts and plan for shared futures (Katovich and Couch 1992; Harrington 2008). Inevitably, microcultures have a temporal dimension. By recognizing their small group culture, participants understand that they share traditions. These traditions can be invoked with the expectation that others will understand their significance. Thus they can address external challenges to the group.

This model of microcultures as structuring devices argues that social order is generated through the development of shared traditions and understandings. Following Collins (1981), collective attention constitutes a microfoundation for macrosociology. Groups build on each other, creating expansive structures through their network linkages. As Collins (2004:xiii) remarked, "The aggregate of situations can be regarded as a market for interaction rituals." Collins's approach is consistent with the process that James Scott refers to as mētis, emphasizing the knowledge from everyday, familiar experience. Scott writes, "Mētis resists simplification into deductive principles which can successfully be transmitted through book learning, because the environments in which it is exercised are so complex and nonrepeatable that formal procedures of rational decision making are impossible to apply" (1998:316). This is what Scott refers to as "the art of the locality."

To borrow from Jeffrey Goldfarb's resonant image, such a model of culture constitutes the sociology of small things, a perspective that captures the *place* of action. This metaphor recognizes that civic participation depends on joint action (Mische 2007; Lichterman and Eliasoph 2014; Fine 2014). Goldfarb starts by theorizing the kitchen table – a microcultural space. His point is not simply that small, mundane cultures must be theorized, but that the environment under which they are produced provides for allegiance and shared perspectives. Through their tight-knit culture, these domains motivate certain forms of action. The locale provides the basis for both social relations and the content of group life. Quoting Goldfarb, "When friends and relatives met in their kitchens, they presented themselves to each other in such a way that they defined the situation in terms of an independent frame rather than that of officialdom" (2006:15). Flowing from the hearth, a framework of meaning is established in light of the group's agentic responsibility. Communities can come to see their spaces, their microcultures, and their place in them in ways that are self-reflexive. The hearth becomes a central symbol in the resistance against Eastern European authoritarianism, but kitchens and porches are found throughout the globe as meeting points in which primary relations are strengthened and discourse responds to local challenges. Hearths are widely dispersed with individual microcultures that provide a remembered and referential past and encourage present talk. Similar locations of discussions include bookstores, salons, and clubs, as well as public meetings and gatherings (Habermas 1991; Emirbayer and Sheller 1998:732; Mische and White 1998:706). Scholars have come to examine small places in which participants assume that others share a history, emotional contours, and a sense of belonging (Parker and Hackett 2012; Gieryn and Oberlin 2015). Tiny publics (Fine 2012), small cultures of shared interest, provide the basis of a shared and robust public sphere and civil society.

Focusing on local cultures addresses several critical theoretical problems in the sociology of culture. This strategy addresses how innovation, socialization, affiliation, and change are manifested in action that, when successful, evokes an affiliative response. By understanding the dynamics of community and the creation of collective identities, an emphasis on local culture stands at the critical junction of the individual and the institutional, revealing forms of cohesion as well as disaffiliation. If participants in discussions are not explicitly part of a political project, they may respond to the political projects of others. The challenge for speakers in ongoing, unscripted interaction is to organize the unpredictable, interpreting it in light of beliefs of how society does and should operate, keeping interaction flowing, whether smoothly or with breaches and disruptions. The challenge they face is that events that shape collective life are readily understandable after the fact (reading backwards), but cannot be determined before they occur (looking forwards). Participants must shape their behavior, aligning ongoing interaction with established group standards, or they may choose to challenge those assumptions. Even if we cannot predict the moments of everyday life – the jokes, insults, errors, or queries found in conversation – participants see the interaction order as an ongoing project. Much sociology assumes the existence of a drive for harmony (Goffman 1974), but this commitment to stability is fragile and open to challenge.

Despite their fluidity and continual adjustment, conversations and collective action become routinized, grounded in shared practices, and embedded in group culture. Research within conversation analysis emphasizes this point, finding formal structures at the most granular level of talk (Schegloff 2007). Other scholars of conversation argue that practices of talk are responsive to external rules and pressures (Gibson 2008). Even when action sequences are substantially altered, people strive to persuade themselves that they remain much the same, evolving incrementally. However, despite the coordination of lines of action, breaks in coordination also serve valid social purposes, such as persuading participants to consider the moral grounding of their actions. Either smooth or rough interaction can build relations as long as the former does not create passivity and the latter long-term ruptures.

Ephemeral micropublics ("Goffman publics": White 1995; Ikegami 2000:997) pose a particular challenge in the creation of negotiated agreements to which participating social actors will adhere, but by means of establishing local cultures and practices, self-referential groups can overcome the problem through shared expectations and a commitment to ritual. As a result, a local sociology is related to, but distinct from, the Goffmanian approach to the interaction order (Goffman 1983). Despite a shared concern with interaction ritual, *dramatism*, examining free-floating, untethered interaction, is contrasted to *localism*, the claim that action is shaped by and responsive to the salience of the group. In contrast to a view that treats behavior as a response to the actions that have immediately proceeded it – seeing interaction as a form of continuous adjustments to an ever-changing and somewhat unpredictable stage, what Charles Tilly (1996) memorably refers to as the "invisible elbow" – localism emphasizes the stability of group life through norms, standards, and expectations. As a result, *practices*, actions understood by reference to local cultures, are central, in that such activity is linked to a bounded interactional domain, such as the kitchen table of Goldfarb's analysis. The response to situations as places in which social ties are displayed constitutes a grounded performance, shaped by actors and audiences within a continuing and self-referential public that is aware – albeit imperfectly – of norms, values, beliefs, and rituals. Treating groups as publics suggests that each ongoing group constitutes a local outpost of society. Even though actions extend beyond the interacting group, the boundary, as recognized by participants, establishes and consecrates the actions within. The local scene represents an instance of the larger culture, with its style, rules, and beliefs defining how social relations should be transacted (Eliasoph and Lichterman 2003).

Networks and their subcultures

Although I have emphasized the linkage of culture to interacting groups, a social psychological approach to culture is not limited to intense, face-to-face microsocieties but can be extended to larger social units by expanding the small-group model outside a narrowly defined interaction order. Relations extend outward from the group, linking a set of discrete social fields (Bourdieu 1985). Put another way, cultures, as they overlap, are based upon a network of social relations. This point could theoretically be broadened to encompass interpretation of national cultures established through the support of the mass (and, now, social) media and institutional support for widespread and mainstream cultural production and dissemination. Despite the potential for exploring national cultures, the examination of subsidiary social domains that lack formal institutional support will be particularly valuable because of the greater emphasis on creation of cultural forms within those networks that depend upon routine and ongoing interaction. Subcultures as exemplified in individual group cultures reveal that culture is not uniformly spread throughout a social system but is embedded in intimate clumps.

Social scientists have long recognized that culture operates not only on the level of the nation but is mapped on the basis of its subdivisions. These subdivisions can involve class, race, age, and gender, or any other demographic or cultural category that leads to a recognized common identity and a sense of belonging. Such domains include the truffle trade in Provence (De la Pradelle 2006:139–51), classical South Asian philosophy (Collins 1998:177–271), and poetry in Tokugawa Japan (Ikegami 2005:171–203). A micro-sociology of subcultural groups not only emphasizes the shared characteristics of the members as part of a social category, but also suggests how social characteristics shape the diffusion of cultural elements and the embedding of those traditions within a set of social relations based on common affiliation.

Group identity as a generator of cultural diffusion is crucial. Lines of communication are linked to social categories, such that boundaries direct interaction. As Tamotsu Shibutani (1955:566) famously remarked, "Culture areas are coterminous with communication channels." In this, Shibutani emphasized that subcultures do not depend only on physical co-presence. Rather, they depend upon lines of communication, as a network perspective suggests. Network nodes might consist of a set of gathering points – those "third places" that Ray Oldenburg (1989) describes – with continually changing attendees, or open nodes of dissemination, such as internet websites or social media. Such locations – physical or virtual – create spaces that draw in certain categories of individuals and, as a result, create knowledge boundaries in which some individuals are aware of cultural forms while others are not. Crucial is the intersection of interacting groups that share cultural traditions through media transmissions and other communications networks that link these nodes. Weaker bridging ties connect knots of strong ties, and as a result, a subculture can be conceived of as a network of group cultures. A common culture occurs through networks of small groups linked by media that target population segments or through other cross-group ties. A process of differential association links populations of actors to cultural forms. As a result, where and whether cultural forms will spread results from preferences and likelihoods of association within the segmental groups.

Although subcultures can include groups that are not hostile to the larger culture, such as ethnic subcultures, much subcultural theory has focused on groups that stand outside "mainstream culture," often deviant or rebellious groups that reject alignment with established norms and values. Although mainstream culture is itself internally differentiated and something of a fiction, many subcultural groups were treated as separate from socially accepted groups. The concept of subculture was, in effect, a means of establishing a cultural – and sometimes moral – boundary. As a consequence, researchers tended to focus on the more dramatic cultures of delinquency, cultures of poverty, or the Southern culture of violence. These analyses, popular in the middle decades of the twentieth century, were based upon the claim of an obdurate dialectic between categories of Us and Them. Subcultural theory typically depended on recognizing an Otherness coupled with a belief that those defined as Others conform to the norms, values, and rituals of their own social category. Even examinations of youth subculture emphasize the power of confrontational style (Hebdige 1981). Not every social segment is said to have a subculture; the operating assumption is that some segmental groups are fully embedded in civil society, whereas others stand apart. Of course, mainstream culture (however that diverse domain is defined) does not reflect the only set of choices possible.

The interactionist perspective on subculture (Fine and Kleinman 1979) emphasizes the importance of webs of contact in the creation, activation, and perpetuation of cultural traditions. This is aligned with the view that cultural systems constitute social worlds, a concept that derives from the work of Anselm Strauss (1978). David Unruh (1980:277) defines social worlds as "amorphous, diffuse constellations of actors, organizations, events, and practices which have coalesced into spheres of interest and involvement for participants [and in which] it is likely that a powerful centralized authority structure does not exist." Without relying on demographic categories, the social-world approach emphasizes the centrality of common interests and interpersonal contacts as the basis of community and the generation of culture. The existence of a subculture makes concrete the concerns of the group in absence of a clear authority structure, incorporating such elements as norms, values, beliefs, moral principles, and performances. Participants' recognition of shared standards leads to a collective identity.

This interactionist perspective locates culture within groups, but leaves open the question of explaining widespread understandings among population segments that are characterized by the lack of co-presence (Campos-Castillo and Hitlin 2013). Although a small group can be studied as a closed system, group members do not interact exclusively with one another. We must theorize how groups intersect and how culture is diffused within population segments. A small group is tied to numerous other groups through a system of *interlocks* or social connections. Such linkages take many forms, and can involve relations among individuals or small groups, but in each case the effect is to create a shared universe of discourse that serves as the referent for each local outpost of culture. The contents of subcultures emanating from group cultures subsequently shape other group cultures through diffusion. Although interlocks take many forms, I describe four: multiple group membership, weak ties, structural roles, and specialized media diffusion.

Multiple group membership

Few individuals participate only in a single group. More typically people are involved in several groups simultaneously, participating as each group is activated. As a result, cultural elements that are accepted in one group can easily be introduced into others through overlapping memberships. Consider the child who attends summer camp. Not only do camp cabins constitute groups with their own idiocultures and shared experiences, but each cabin serves as an agora – a trading zone – in which local knowledges are transmitted. When campers return home, these new cultures can be shared, expanding their range. The person who participates in two ongoing groups with only a few joint members has a crucial position that permits diffusion and cultural change. In that many groups have these linkages, ideas can pass through boundaries. The idea of a cultural "meme" emphasizes that certain elements are more transmittable (and more able to survive) and will have a wider range (Dawkins 2006).

Weak ties

No matter how intense and densely connected their core social relations, most individuals maintain acquaintanceship relations outside their stable, interacting groups. Networks based upon ongoing interacting groups are never fully bounded. Those external contacts or "weak ties" (Granovetter 1973) are crucial for disseminating information widely and rapidly. Studies of rumor, gossip, and news in times of crisis demonstrate that information spreads rapidly under favorable conditions – if the information is seen as significant and the relational structure is conducive to diffusion. In practice, weak ties in networks have boundaries – racial, class, age, geography, or gender – limiting these pools of knowledge from being easily accessible to all. Finding acquaintances across these boundaries is more unusual than establishing connections within the groups. It is certainly true that weak ties are more likely to cross boundaries than strong ties, but the boundaries are real. Further, different networks may transmit specialized cultural genres, based on the assumed interest of the target (e.g., off-color humor, health information, or celebrity gossip). Ultimately the creation of a network of relations depends upon the interests and social location of individual social actors.

Structural roles

Cultural information is also spread by those in favorable structural positions. Individuals who in their work or leisure roles interact with multiple groups, organizations, or communities can spread information outside tight networks. These include motivational speakers, itinerant preachers, and standup comics. Although their primary role obligation is not to diffuse culture from group to group, diffusion is an indirect result of their multigroup contact.

Media diffusion

The final interlock involves specialized media. Media reach numerous groups simultaneously, providing shared knowledge. Media productions (opera, rock fests) are not accessed by random audiences. To the contrary, awareness results from prior interest, as interest shapes the likelihood of exposure.

An important domain in the study of subcultures is that of countercultures, because, as noted, many subcultural groups are those that stand apart from the mainstream. However, in contrast to participants in subcultures, those within countercultural groups typically believe that they are oppositional or counter-hegemonic (Yinger 1982). As typically defined, countercultures politicize or define their cultural themes as social critique. More explicitly than subcultural participation in general, embracing a counterculture suggests an explicit identity that differentiates a person from the dominant class. Fortunately for social stability, such groups are typically limited in participation. A countercultural perspective is inevitably historically and geographically situated, and so, for example, countercultural movements were more prominent in the ferment of the late 1960s and early 1970s than they are currently, even though the distinctive styles of some youth groups (Goths, for instance) incorporate strong and visible countercultural elements. In societies with engaged youth movements, such as activist movements in Brazil (Mische 2007) or alienated youth in Japan (Sato 1991), such opposition networks can be quite robust.

Recently in the US, with the growth of the Occupy Wall Street and Black Lives Matter movements, and the election of Donald Trump, oppositional cultures have once again emerged in America. However, despite their activism and political critique, participants in these movements are rarely fully oppositional, instead typically seeing their political engagement as a means to broaden social participation. These groups typically embrace socially esteemed values to make their case for inclusion. Such movements straddle the line between subculture and counterculture, presenting an active and forceful critique of mainstream politics, while arguing that participation in the mainstream culture should be extended to groups and individuals that had once been excluded.

Conclusion

Just as the culture concept in sociology can be linked to macrosociological analysis, culture as a form of practice and as a negotiated order equally belongs to the micro- and meso-level. Culture ultimately comprises actions that are performed and viewed and objects that are manufactured and consumed. I began by describing culture as a behavioral domain that is constructed in and indigenous to small groups. Extending the analysis, I argued that society comprises a network of interlinked groups, which, when segmented into networks of groups, leads to the recognition of subcultures. Those subcultures that take an oppositional stance to the consensually recognized social order and in which identities support this rejection, permit some cultures – as in the case of countercultures – to be sites of resistance, not only in their ideas and their collective action, but also in the selves of actors.

References

Benzecry, Claudio. 2011. *The Opera Fanatic: Ethnography of an Obsession.* Chicago: University of Chicago Press.

Bourdieu, Pierre. 1985. "The Social Space and the Genesis of Groups." *Theory and Society* 14(6):723–44.

Campos-Castillo, Celeste, and Steven Hitlin. 2013. "Copresence: Revisiting a Building Block for Social Interaction Theories." *Sociological Theory* 31(2):168–92.

Collins, Randall. 1981. "On the Microfoundations of Macrosociology." *American Journal of Sociology* 86(5):984–1014.

———. 1998. *The Sociology of Philosophies: A Global Theory of Intellectual Change.* Cambridge, MA: Harvard University Press.

———. 2004. *Interaction Ritual Chains.* Princeton, NJ: Princeton University Press.

Corte, Ugo. 2013. "A Refinement of Collaborative Circles Theory: Resource Mobilization and Innovation in an Emerging Sport." *Social Psychology Quarterly* 76(1):25–51.

Dawkins, Richard. 2006. *The Selfish Gene.* 3rd ed. New York: Oxford University Press.

De la Pradelle, Michèle. 2006. *Market Day in Provence.* Chicago: University of Chicago Press.

Eliasoph, Nina, and Paul Lichterman. 2003. "Culture in Interaction." *American Journal of Sociology* 108(4):735–94.

Emirbayer, Mustafa, and Mimi Sheller. 1998. "Publics in History." *Theory and Society* 27(6):727–79.

Farrell, Michael. 2001. *Collaborative Dynamics: Friendship Circles and Creative Work.* Chicago: University of Chicago Press.

Fine, Gary Alan. 1979. "Small Groups and Culture Creation." *American Sociological Review* 44(5):733–45.

———. 2012. *Tiny Publics: A Theory of Group Action and Culture.* New York: Russell Sage Foundation.

———. 2014. "The Hinge: Civil Society, Group Culture, and the Interaction Order." *Social Psychology Quarterly* 77(1):5–26.

Fine, Gary Alan, and Sherryl Kleinman. 1979. "Rethinking Subculture: An Interactionist Analysis." *American Journal of Sociology* 85(1):1–20.

Gibson, David. 2008. "How the Outside Gets In: Modeling Conversation Permeation." *Annual Review of Sociology* 34:359–84.

———. 2012. *Talk at the Brink: Deliberation and Decision During the Cuban Missile Crisis*. Princeton, NJ: Princeton University Press.

Gieryn, Thomas, and Kathleen Oberlin. 2015. "Place and Culture-Making: Geographic Clumping in the Emergence of Artistic Schools." *Poetics* 50:20–43.

Goffman, Erving. 1974. *Frame Analysis: An Essay on the Organization of Experience*. Cambridge, MA: Harvard University Press.

———. 1983. "The Interaction Order." *American Sociological Review* 48(1):1–17.

Goldfarb, Jeffrey. 2006. *The Politics of Small Things: The Power of the Powerless in Dark Times*. Chicago: University of Chicago Press.

Granovetter, Mark. 1973. "The Strength of Weak Ties." *American Journal of Sociology* 78(6):1360–80.

Habermas, Jürgen. 1991. *The Structural Transformation of the Public Sphere*. Cambridge, MA: MIT Press.

Harrington, Brooke. 2008. *Pop Finance: Investment Clubs and the New Investor Populism*. Princeton, NJ: Princeton University Press.

Hebdige, Dick. 1981. *Subculture: The Meaning of Style*. London: Routledge.

Herzfeld, Michael. 1993. *The Social Production of Indifference*. Chicago: University of Chicago Press.

Ikegami, Eiko. 2000. "A Sociological Theory of Publics: Identity and Culture as Emergent Properties in Networks." *Social Research* 67(4):989–1029.

———. 2005. *Bonds of Civility: Aesthetic Networks and the Political Origins of Japanese Culture*. New York: Cambridge University Press.

Janis, Irving. 1982. *Groupthink: Psychological Studies of Policy Decisions and Fiascos*. Boston: Houghton Mifflin.

Katovich, Michael, and Carl Couch. 1992. "The Nature of Social Pasts and Their Use as Foundations for Situated Action." *Symbolic Interaction* 15(1):25–47.

Lawler, Edward, Shane Thye, and Jeongkoo Yoon. 2008. "Social Exchange and Micro Social Order." *American Sociological Review* 73(4):519–42.

Lichterman, Paul, and Nina Eliasoph. 2014. "Civic Action." *American Journal of Sociology* 120(3):798–863.

Mische, Ann. 2007. *Partisan Publics: Communication and Contention across Brazilian Youth Activist Networks*. Princeton, NJ: Princeton University Press.

Mische, Ann, and Harrison White. 1998. "Between Conversation and Situation: Public Switching Dynamics across Network Domains." *Social Research* 65(3):695–724.

Oldenburg, Ray. 1989. *The Great Good Place: Cafes, Coffee Shops, Bookstores, Bars, Hair Salons, and Other Hangouts at the Heart of a Community*. New York: Paragon House.

Parker, John, and Edward Hackett. 2012. "Hot Spots and Hot Moments in Scientific Collaborations and Social Movements." *American Sociological Review* 77(1):21–44.

Perrin, Andrew. 2005. "Political Microcultures: Linking Civic Life and Democratic Discourse." *Social Forces* 84(2):1049–82.

Sageman, Marc. 2008. *Leaderless Jihad: Terror Networks in the Twenty-First Century*. Philadelphia: University of Pennsylvania Press.

Sato, Ikuya. 1991. *Kamikaze Biker: Parody and Anomy in Affluent Japan*. Chicago: University of Chicago Press.

Schegloff, Emanuel. 2007. *Sequence Organization in Interaction: A Primer in Conversation Analysis*. Cambridge: Cambridge University Press.

Scott, James C. 1998. *Seeing Like a State: How Certain Schemes to Improve the Human Condition Have Failed*. New Haven, CT: Yale University Press.

Shibutani, Tamotsu. 1955. "Reference Groups as Perspectives." *American Journal of Sociology* 60(6):562–69.

Sion, Liora, and Eyal Ben-Ari. 2005. "Hungry, Weary and Horny: Joking and Jesting Among Israel's Combat Reserves." *Israel Affairs* 11(4):656–72.

Strauss, Anselm. 1978. *Negotiations*. San Francisco: Jossey-Bass.

Tilly, Charles. 1996. "Invisible Elbow." *Sociological Forum* 11(4):589–601.

Unruh, David. 1980. "The Nature of Social Worlds." *Pacific Sociological Review* 23(3):271–96.

White, Harrison. 1995. "Network Switchings and Bayesian Forks: Reconstructing the Social and Behavioral Sciences." *Social Research* 62(4):1035–63.

Yinger, J. Milton. 1982. *Countercultures: The Promise and the Peril of a World Turned Upside Down*. New York: Free Press.

27

Culture and micro-sociology

Iddo Tavory

Introduction

Meaning is always made somewhere, in a specific time and place, by specific actors who are facing specific circumstances (though, as Marx noted a while back, often not of their choosing). Even the most public of meaning structures is enacted in, if not emerges from, a micro-sociological context. While this point may not be overly controversial (cf. Jepperson and Meyer 2011), what it means for a sociology of culture is far from clear. This chapter outlines some of the ways in which micro-sociological traditions and kindred sociological researchers have sought to capture the relation between the construction of meaning in the situation and the enactment of patterned meaning structures.

Doing so, the gambit of this chapter is to think about the situational and the dispositional as the two poles between which we need to think about culture in action (see also Lahire 2011). In its cartoonish version, the difference is between meanings being fully formed before the interaction and then simply "activated" in concrete contexts, versus a protean world in which meanings always emerge in the specificities of the situation.

Of course, almost all theorizations of meaning in the social world have a way of connecting situations, mostly by noting that meaning is both layered across situations and leveraged within them. The second move I make in this chapter is therefore to argue that in addition to thinking of pragmatic actors and the history of situations, accounting for meaning in the micro-sociological tradition needs a more thorough rethinking – focusing not only on situations and their pasts, but also on what happens between situations; not only analyzing how situations "pile up" to form idiocultures or interaction ritual chains, but also about the rhythms that actors learn to anticipate, and the relationship between these different rhythms.[1]

Between situations and dispositions

Despite their wide divergences, the major micro-sociological traditions – from the interactionist (e.g., Blumer 1969) to the ethnomethodological (Garfinkel 1967) and the more embodied phenomenology (e.g., Katz 1999) – begin with the situation as their unit of analysis. The

Goffmanian (1967:3) call to study "moments and their men" already assumes that understanding the situation is paramount for the production of both selves and meanings.

However, with the exception of ethnomethodology, where larger action contexts were purposely bracketed, micro-interactional traditions did start off with some theory of the connecting tissue between situations. Indeed, without a theory of such connection, the patterns of everyday life would become quite mysterious. As Bourdieu (e.g., 1977:81) noted, the danger is one of falling into an "occasionalist illusion" in which people and meanings come into existence purely in the situation.

For early interactionists, the relation between situations was encapsulated in the pragmatist notion of habit – the sedimentation of knowledge, capacities, and problem-solving dispositions that makes both routine action and creativity possible (Dewey [1922] 2002; Joas 1996). But despite the constitutive place of habit in pragmatist thinking, the notion of habit fell out of vogue, given over to psychology as sociology secured its legitimacy (Camic 1986). Interactionists thus found themselves in a peculiar position – where habit both existed as a necessary constitutive assumption about the structuring of situations, but simultaneously accounted for in minimalist fashion, as actors' relatively uninteresting set of background capacities (e.g., Becker 1982).

In order to circle this square, some micro-sociologists looked for other ways to think of the emergence of meaningful patterns. Thus, one of the most compelling and "Simmelian" of interactionist research programs explained the patterning of social life by describing institutionalized situational constraints, and showing how actors' practical attempts to navigate such constraints give rise to typical meaningful solutions. Rather than relying on shared meaning or habit, it was the "stacking up" of the institutional deck that gave rise to predictable social patterns (see Rock 1979; for paradigmatic examples, see Becker et al. 1961; Davis 1959). Much like a line of ants can be understood by the situated pheromone exchange between each couple of ants walking up and down the line, what seemed to be explainable only by recourse to larger cultural patterns was simply an aggregation of situations.

Thus, despite the periodic reminders by leading interactionists that habit was still a crucial aspect of the patterning of situations (e.g., Fine 2011; Strauss 1993), interactionists remained suspicious of cultural explanations. Coupled with the ethnomethodological bracketing of wider cultural and structural considerations – which Garfinkel (1967) and later ethnomethodologists made in the effort to see how actors construct social order in their specific, and inherently indexical ways – micro-sociology seemed to stand in a tense relationship to the notion of culture.

Whereas the constitutive power of habit was minimized in much of micro-sociology, at the other end of the spectrum we can locate a sharply dispositional approach. This is perhaps most prominently visible in Pierre Bourdieu's theorization of the habitus – a deeply ingrained structure of dispositions and modes of being-in-the-world that is inculcated through specific life situations, and poised to reproduce these conditions.

Perhaps most telling in this regard is Bourdieu's (1977:80–1) early evocation of Leibniz's example of two clocks that seem to be moving "in perfect agreement" with each other. One possible reason for this happy coincidence, notes Bourdieu, is that they are somehow connected; another is that someone corrects them every time they fall out of step. Yet another, however, is that the clocks are made so well in advance that they only seem to affect each other or be otherwise connected. While the first of these is an interactionist approach, and the second is an approach that focuses on the explicit use of power, the third is the one Bourdieu espouses: where the reproduction of inequality occurs through the complicity of habitus and field.

Although Bourdieu writes that "The truth of the interaction is never entirely contained in the interaction" (1977:81), thus implying that there is at least a modicum of truth to it, the analysis of interactions in this kind of sociology is designed to show the activation of a preformed potential. Even when a seemingly surprising outcome emerges in a situation, the surprise is based on the creative activations of dispositions, or at most at the intertwining of different dispositions carried by diverse actors, rather than on the creative force of the interaction itself. Thus, although Bourdieu later seemed to see affinities between his approach and the pragmatist discussion of habit (Bourdieu and Wacquant 1992:122), he effectively closed off much of what made the relationship between habit and creativity so fertile for pragmatists – the unexpected and emergent possibilities of the situation.

Thinking about the poles of disposition vs. situational emergence, and through them about the relation between potential and activation, allows us to think about the place of "culture" in a way that doesn't fall back into a discussion of "micro vs. macro." A situational pole sees culture, to the degree that it sees it at all, as an uninteresting set of background assumptions that set up the "real action" within the situation; the dispositional pole sees culture – albeit in an embodied, sophisticated sense – as paramount (see also Alexander and Smith 1993). Situations, in this reading, are mere activations – or at best, minor refractions – of dispositions.

The layering and leveraging of meaning

However, as students of culture know well, the theoretical terrain was never really so stark. Between the situational and the dispositional poles lie many ways to string situations together that allow wider meaning systems to play a role in the actual situation. For the purposes of this chapter, it is useful to think about two clusters of strategies that sociologists have wielded in order to do so – *layering* and *leveraging*. The first way, layering, operates by tracing the ongoing sedimentation of meaning across situations. In that view, shared meanings get sedimented in the biographical patterns that actors – and groups more generally – move through. The second strategy, leveraging, is an attempt to think about the ways in which actors "wield" cultural knowledge and know-how in order to solve the situational problems that they face.

The first of these strategies takes the sedimentation, or "layering" of situations as a problem in its own right. Thus, throughout his career, and across different substantive topics, Fine (e.g., 1979, 2011) has been crafting a micro-sociology of culture. On this "idiocultural" scale, meaning emerges as actors within small groups encounter the world together, and as their ways of puzzling out the situations they encounter are sedimented into shared sets of meaning that are then evoked as the group moves forward in time. Although actors borrow from publicly available meanings rather than inventing the world from scratch (see also Eliasoph and Lichterman 2003), the focus of this program is on the layered emergence of meaning over time.

Using a different vocabulary and set of assumptions, such a layering narrative also structures Randal Collins's (2004) *interaction ritual chains*, one of the most ambitious programs to build up a macro-world of meaning from its micro-foundations. Based on a Goffmanian reading of Durkheim's notion of the emergence of collective effervescence in ritual, Collins argues that objects and meanings effectively serve as a battery that "stores" emotional energy. This, then, provides a moving picture of the social world in which interactions create and infuse (as well as diminish) shared symbols through a layering of rituals.

As against the layering of meaning, another influential way to think about situations and culture within the sociology of culture focuses on the ways in which meanings are *leveraged* in situations. Fueled by a pragmatist image of humans as constantly encountering problem situations and attempting to solve the problems they face, focusing on such leveraging brings together disparate theorizations, such as Goffman's dramaturgy, Swidler's repertoire theory, and Boltanski and Thévenot's neo-pragmatism.

First, in its by now classic formulation, Ann Swidler's (1986) metaphor of the "toolkit" provides a picture in which pragmatic actors use meanings and forms of practice as a way to solve ongoing problems. Thus, the movement from thinking about culture as "ends" to thinking primarily about meanings-as-means, turns "culture" from a relatively unified set of codes (e.g., Alexander and Smith 1993) into bundles of meaning that can be leveraged in specific situations. And, although the availability of these meanings is not equally distributed in the social world (thus hinting at a disposition-like logic), we never encounter a situation with only one way of "solving" it at hand. As Swidler later clarified (e.g., 2001; Tavory and Swidler 2009), such leveraging is not quite a free-for-all. Certain situations make demands on actors such that one set of meanings would be better suited than others to "solve" the ongoing dilemmas actors face. Still, even in this later formulation, meanings are not activated, but pragmatically leveraged.

A similar insight also forms an important, if little appreciated, part of Goffman's dramaturgical analysis. Although Goffman was much more attuned to the moral pressures of the interaction order, the interaction order he described is always sustained by actors' choices of "lines" of action (Goffman 1967). These "lines," in turn, are based on actors' stocks of knowledge, but they are not completely set in advance. Although people may be pressured to choose one line over another, the point that Goffman makes is more subtle: it is only once a line has been *chosen* that it comes to exert a moral pressure on interacting parties. In entering situations, people always have more than one possible line that they could take, which is precisely why Goffman is often read in an overly strategic manner.

A last example can be seen in the recent "sociology of worth" developed by Boltanski and Thévenot (2006). Like their American counterparts, they assume that there is always more than one "regime of worth" available to actors to draw from. Once an actor opts for one regime of worth (e.g., the artistic, or the industrial) over another, that regime exerts discursive pressures on what can or cannot make sense. Thus, more than Swidler or Goffman, Boltanski and Thévenot stress the kinds of repercussions that an initial choice of meaning-cluster entails. But, positing themselves directly against the dispositional sociology of Bourdieu, they argue that the choice of a regime of worth is not set in advance. Meanings are leveraged as contingent solutions to ongoing problems that actors face.

Thinking between situations

Although both the layering and leveraging of meaning capture important aspects of the relationship between situations and dispositions, studies of social time and temporality point toward the limitations of such approaches. Seen through the lenses of temporality, the relationship between dispositional and situational accounts is that of the difference between a past-based approach and one that is attuned to the immediate future of the project. A leveraging approach privileges the project-like immediate future of problem-solving that actors engage in; a layering approach explains local meaning-making mainly in terms of its past, which then serves an important collective resource for solving challenges that actors encounter together.

What this discussion neglects is that actors exist not only in situations but also between them. Actors exist in social time, that is, within "the system of rhythms and trajectories that humans create as they engage in interaction within social institutions" (Snyder 2016:11). In other words, a situation is always (or, almost always) a part of a rhythmically recurring set of similar situations. Although "to follow a rule" is never a straightforward application of a pre-existing construct (Garfinkel 1967; Wittgenstein 1953), we do encounter the world in similar, and recurring, ways. In much of our everyday life, we understand our actions as located in recurrences, rather than following the kind of linear directionality of the project that much work on action assumes. The meanings we make are located not only in relation to a past and future simple, but also in the ongoing beats of social time (see also LeFebvre 2004; Zerubavel 1985).

Thus, for example, Snyder's (2016) recent work traces the ways in which workers (and some unemployed) contend with the different rhythms of the new regime of "flexible" capitalism in the US. In one chapter, as Snyder follows long-haul truckers, he shows how they are located between the rhythms of a 14-hour shift, an 11-hour driving cap, their bodily rhythms, and the demands of the actual work – defined, in itself, by such rhythms as the waxing and waning of traffic, or the loading and unloading of goods. The ways in which both the truckers' projects and their embodied habits are experienced, as Snyder shows, are mediated by their attempt to work through these contending rhythms. At times, such contention produces exhilaration, but at other moments these rhythms clash such that truckers must juggle them by stretching the capacities of their bodies, sometimes to a breaking point.

While this emphasis on rhythms may seem to be tangential to the question of meaning, Snyder shows how the meanings that truckers gave their work arose precisely through the relationships among rhythms. Both the moments of elation and the frustrations with "this kind of work" were defined by these rhythms. Thus, Snyder's example, even in abbreviated form, allows us a glimpse into the importance of rhythms in the crafting of situational meanings. It thereby allows us to realize the analytical price paid by micro-sociologists of culture's neglect of the fact that the lives of the people they study always persist in the multiple rhythms of action they are enmeshed in and anticipate.

Moreover, and less visible in Snyder's work, the overlapping rhythms of social life also locate and infuse the local meanings people make. Thus, for example, in a study of Latino immigrants and leisure in Los Angeles, Trouille (2013; Trouille and Tavory 2016) shows that the meaning of violent episodes he experienced in the park could not be understood without understanding the ways in which violence worked in different situations. First seeing violence in the park as deeply worrisome, Trouille later encountered the ways that violence unfolded in other situations – in bars or in the neighborhoods they lived in – and he then realized just how "tame" and ritual-like the violence in the park was. Anonymous violence was far more troubling both for the ethnographer and for the men he studied (whether they were victims or sometimes perpetrators) than what transpired in the park. And, as Trouille shows, the men understood the meaning of violence in the park by comparing it to other situations.

In theoretical terms, these studies show how we make meaning, either implicitly or explicitly, in relation to other situations. To push the Saussurean picture of meaning as a structure of differences within social life, we have to account both for the fact that meanings are made differently in different situations – that is, that there are always different systems of differences at play (Tavory 2014; Trouille and Tavory 2016) – but also for the fact that people are aware of the ways in which one situation is located in relation to other situations. Accompanying the layered and leveraged enactment of meaning are the shadows of other situations, coloring situated meaning and allowing for moments of humor, metaphor, and transposition.[2]

Lastly, and perhaps even more important from the perspective of a micro-sociology of meaning, people undertake the rhythms of social time together. As they move through situations, it is not only actors' own anticipations that propel them and that shape how they make meaning within situations. As interactionists have stressed, a social world is crafted through a collective act.

The potential importance of thinking about meanings in terms of their rhythms and as co-produced in a collective act can be seen both in terms of the ways in which actors' situational meanings are elicited by others, as well as in how certain transpositions of meaning are blocked in interaction. To take one example, in an ethnography of an Orthodox social world, I show (Tavory 2016) that although Orthodox men and women often talked about *what* they did in their secular professions, they almost never talked about *who* they did it with except when talking about the challenges of the secular world. In the rare occasions in which people did make such transpositions, they were effectively blocked by other interactants in the Orthodox situation, who steered the conversations away from such profane matters.

If the dynamism of meaning often arises in the creative transpositions of semiotic structures among situations (Giddens 1984; Joas 1996; Sewell 1992), the collective act of vetting or blocking such transpositions in relation to the rhythms of a social world is crucial. In addition to accounting for the ways in which meaning become substantiated in action through layering and pragmatic leveraging, the degree of transpositional flexibility of meaning – or even the contours of its possibility – is defined through a collective act.

Situations, rhythms, and culture

The relation between micro-sociology and cultural sociology passes through the situation – the context of meaningful action with all of its subtleties. As discussed earlier, a tension structuring this relation had been between the situation as the site of the emergence of meaning, and the situation as the context of activation of preformed potentials.

As I argued in this chapter, sociologists of culture and micro-sociologists alike have attempted to mitigate this tension by thinking either of the sedimentation of meaning over time or about the ways in which actors leverage meaning from a given repertoire of sense-making strategies. Although both layering and leveraging provide important clues, they seem to accept the contours of the problem itself. The definition of the problem in terms of the situation – in the singular – has already loaded the theoretical dice.

To solve this problem, it is not enough to note that actors' dispositions are more complex and less unified than a dispositional account usually grants (Lahire 2011). Rather, my argument is that we need to think carefully about the assumptions that find their way to *the situation* as micro-sociology's unit of analysis.

People extend in time, constantly anticipating their futures, anticipating (whether explicitly or implicitly) the structure of the temporal landscapes and trajectories they are positioned upon (Tavory and Eliasoph 2013). The ways people extend in time, then, shapes the ways they understand their worlds. It is in this sense that thinking about rhythm provides a useful corrective to our usual ways of thinking about dispositions and situations. "A situation" does not only extend into the past through actors' dispositions but also into a rhythmic future. As Langer (1953:127 as cited in Snyder 2016:12) put it, "one can sense a beginning, intent, and consummation, and see in the last stage of one the condition and indeed the rise of another. Rhythm is the setting-up of new tensions by the resolution of former ones."

The situation may still remain the crucial unit of analysis for micro-sociology. But if micro-sociologists are to take on the challenge of culture – and if cultural sociologists are to take the local enactments of meanings seriously – they will need to understand situations as they extend in time. A micro-sociology of culture will need to think both of the rhythms (and probably syncopations) of social life, and of the ways in which actors' anticipations of such rhythms shape the way they make meaning together.

Notes

1   In doing so, the chapter zeroes in on a particular problem – that of explaining meaningful patterns of ongoing action in the world. This question needs to be analytically distinguished from that of studies (themselves coming out of different theoretical traditions) that attempt to explain the *historical transformation of meaning* through a series of situated actions and interactions. As such studies have demonstrated, one way of understanding historical processes is through the ongoing mobilization and enactment of meaning in multiple locations. In this view, meaningful action emerges from a complex choreography

of call and response, where actors' shaping of meaning in one moment and place affects not only their own, but also others' shaping of meaning later on. Meaning, in this view, "zigzags" across time and constituents, giving rise to proto-nationalist resistance (Kane 2011), mass suicide (Hall 2000), or scientific revolutions (Latour 1988). While the relation between the traditions I write about here and these explanations of historical processes are instructive – especially as both positions call for a complex view of temporality – such a dialogue goes beyond what this short chapter can hope to achieve.

2   One theorization that has been carefully attentive to the relationship between situations is that of Lahire (e.g., 2011). Positioning his work as an important amendment to Bourdieu's theory of habitus as a unified construct, Lahire theorizes a fragmented habitus, constructed out of multiple contexts of socialization. As Lahire argues, if we want to understand "sociology on the level of the individual," we need to construct a robust inter-situational variation. While this focus on a "plural actor" is important, Lahire's view is still heavily dispositional (if re-theorized as a complex and fragmented set of dispositions, activated in specific situations, instead of a unified one).

References

Alexander, Jeffrey. C., and Phillip Smith. 1993. "The Discourse of American Civil Society: A New Proposal for Cultural Studies." *Theory and Society* 22(2):151–207.

Becker, Howard S. 1982. "Culture: A Sociological View." *Yale Review* 71(4):513–28.

Becker, Howard S., Blanche Geer, Everett C. Hughes, and Anselm L. Strauss. 1961. *Boys in White: Student Culture in Medical School*. Chicago: University of Chicago Press.

Blumer, Herbert. 1969. *Symbolic Interactionism: Perspective and Method*. Englewood Cliffs, NJ: Prentice Hall.

Boltanski, Luc, and Laurent Thévenot. 2006. *On Justification: Economies of Worth*. Princeton, NJ: Princeton University Press.

Bourdieu, Pierre. 1977. *Outline of a Theory of Practice*. Cambridge: Cambridge University Press.

Bourdieu, Pierre, and Loic Wacquant. 1992. *An Invitation to Reflexive Sociology*. Chicago: University of Chicago Press.

Camic, Charles. 1986. "The Matter of Habit." *American Journal of Sociology* 91(5):1039–87.

Collins, Randal. 2004. *Interaction Ritual Chains*. Princeton, NJ: Princeton University Press.

Davis, Fred. 1959. "The Cab Driver and His Fare: Facets of a Fleeting Relationship." *American Journal of Sociology* 65(2):158–65.

Dewey, John. [1922] 2002. *Human Nature and Conduct*. New York: Dover.

Eliasoph, Nina, and Paul Lichterman. 2003. "Culture in Interaction." *American Journal of Sociology* 108(4):735–94.

Fine, Gary A. 1979. "Small Groups and Culture Creation: The Idioculture of Little League Baseball Teams." *American Sociological Review* 44(5):733–45.

Fine, Gary A. 2011. *Tiny Publics: A Theory of Group Action and Culture*. New York: Russell Sage Foundation.

Garfinkel, Harold. 1967. *Studies in Ethnomethodology*. Englewood Cliffs, NJ: Prentice Hall.

Giddens, Anthony. 1984. *The Constitution of Society: Outline of the Theory of Structuration*. Cambridge: Polity Press.

Goffman, Erving. 1967. *Interaction Ritual: Essays on Face-to-Face Behavior*. Garden City, NJ: Anchor.

Hall, John R. 2000. "The Apocalypse at Jonestown." Pp. 15–44 in *Apocalypse Observed: Religious Movements and Violence in North America, Europe and Japan*, edited by J. Hall, P.D. Schulyer, and S. Trinh. London: Routledge.

Jepperson, Ronald, and John W. Meyer. 2011. "Multiple Levels of Analysis and the Limits of Methodological Individualism." *Sociological Theory* 29(1):54–73.

Joas, Hans. 1996. *The Creativity of Action*. Chicago: University of Chicago Press.

Kane, Anne. 2011. *Constructing Irish National Identity: Discourse and Ritual during the Land War, 1879–1882*. New York: Palgrave Macmillan.

Katz, Jack. 1999. *How Emotions Work*. Chicago: University of Chicago Press.

Lahire, Bernard. 2011. *The Plural Actor*. Cambridge: Polity Press.

Langer, Susanne K. 1953. *Feeling and Form: A Theory of Art*. New York: Charles Scribner Sons.

Latour, Bruno. 1988. *The Pasteurization of France*. Cambridge, MA: Harvard University Press.

LeFebvre, Henri. 2004. *Rhythmanalysis: Space, Time and Everyday Life*. New York: Continuum.

Rock, Paul. 1979. *The Making of Symbolic Interactionism*. London: Macmillan.

Sewell, William H. Jr. 1992. "A Theory of Structure: Duality, Agency and Transformation." *American Journal of Sociology* 98(1):1–29.

Snyder, Benjamin. 2016. *The Disrupted Workplace: Time and the Moral Order of Flexible Capitalism*. Oxford: Oxford University Press.

Strauss, Anselm. 1993. *Continual Permutations of Action*. New York: Aldine.

Swidler, Ann. 1986. "Culture in Action: Symbols and Strategies." *American Sociological Review* 51(2):273–86.

———. 2001. *Talk of Love*. Chicago: University of Chicago Press.

Tavory, Iddo. 2014. "The Situations of Culture: Humor and the Limits of Measurability." *Theory and Society* 43(3–4):275–89.

———. 2016. *Summoned: Identification and Religious Life in a Jewish Neighborhood*. Chicago: University of Chicago Press.

Tavory, Iddo, and Nina Eliasoph. 2013. "Coordinating Futures: Towards a Theory of Anticipation." *American Journal of Sociology* 118(4):908–42.

Tavory, Iddo, and Ann Swidler. 2009. "Condom Semiotics: Meaning and Condom Use in Rural Malawi." *American Sociological Review* 74(2):171–89.

Trouille, David. 2013. "Jugadores del Parque: Immigrants, Play, and the Creation of Social Ties." PhD dissertation, Department of Sociology, University of California, Los Angeles.

Trouille, David, and Iddo Tavory. 2016. "Shadowing: Warrants for Intersituational Variation in Ethnography." *Sociological Methods and Research*. https://doi.org/10.1177/0049124115626171

Wittgenstein, Ludwig. 1953. *Philosophical Investigations*. New York: Macmillan.

Zerubavel, Eviatar. 1985. *Hidden Rhythms: Schedules and Calendars in Social Life*. Berkeley: University of California Press.

28

Culture and identity
A metatheoretical reformulation

Andreas Glaeser

Emic and etic entanglements

The modern concepts of "culture" and "identity" originated in early Romantic scholarly (i.e., analytic or, technically speaking, "etic") discourses. Yet today a wide variety of people commonly use these as everyday (or "emic") terms routinely deployed to perform social labor in a wide variety of ways – to claim rights, to assert privilege, to enforce conformity, to justify or explain difference, to exalt as superior and to denigrate as inferior, to normalize and to exoticize, and to include and to exclude, thereby drawing boundaries in both purely descriptive and in highly evaluative terms. Everyday use of "identity" and "culture" thus produces social and moral cartographies differentiating and linking individuals and collectivities by juxtaposing descriptively, aesthetically, and morally differentiated spaces of homogeneity. Their use generates pleasure in providing orientation and direction for everyday action, which makes these terms eminently suitable to mobilize people for political projects. The appropriation of these concepts for general use falls in line with the accelerating pluralization of Europeanoid lifeworlds during the last 200 years. Their eventual meaning takes shape in successive encounters with alterity near and far, resulting from the interaction of numerous historical processes that are usually grouped together under the heading of modernization.

The historicity and performativity of the terms culture and identity, as well as their deep implication in both making and locally reflecting on what happens in modern social life, make it difficult to distill from either the everyday or past scholarly uses adequate contemporary scholarly concepts that generate insights in actual analysis rather than gross anachronisms. Yet the prominence of these concepts, as well as the centrality of the kinds of social operations guided by them, makes it nearly impossible to avoid the development of them as scholarly concepts.

Not surprisingly, in view of the emic-etic entanglement of the concepts of culture and identity, there have been recurring efforts at crafting suitable scholarly definitions. Throughout much of the nineteenth century, predominant neo-Hegelian notions treated culture as the always latest momentary height of human achievement (e.g., Arnold [1869] 1993), and as a continuous force of human innovation caught up in a process of permanently outdoing itself (e.g., Burckhardt [1911] 1979). Culture in this sense carried two interconnected value accents. On the one hand, culture came to mark the extraordinary and creative as opposed to the ordinary and well-rehearsed. On the other hand, in conjunction with widely shared notions of a unitary path to progress, the term was deployed to mark the supposed more advanced from the less developed. These evaluative and directional notions of culture eventually gave way to neo-Herderian, more or less value-neutral definitions of culture as "all-that-can-differ" between social groups, regarded as an effect of human interaction rather than as a mere natural adaptive response (e.g., Tylor [1871] 1874; Boas 1901; Lévi-Strauss [1962] 1964). Subsequent takes on the cultural were more marked by quickly alternating approaches to the study of all-that-can-differ between comparable social units rather than any fundamental change in the most basic meaning of culture as "second nature." Thus, structuralist and structural-functionalist approaches soon came under competition from performative approaches, speech-act theory, phenomenology, ethnomethodology, and symbolic anthropology. Picking up the threads from older attention to non-conscious processes of habit formation, and combining them with class-theoretic analysis, practice theory swept in to critique all consciousness- and symbol-centric approaches, just to itself suddenly become subjected to unanticipated competition from neo-structuralist approaches of varied provenience, and so on.

Notably, the poststructuralist approaches developed since the late 1960s are – in view of the debunked partiality of their immediate predecessors (structuralism and structure-functionalism above all) – self-consciously and enthusiastically self-limiting: they only get to one or another dimension of what was previously subsumed under the heading of culture without taking recourse to either the term culture or identity. In fact, the proliferation of different approaches to studying culture and the awareness of the historical entanglements of scholarly and everyday concepts have reached a point since the 1980s that scholars, especially in anthropology, have drawn the academic use of concepts of culture and identity into question (e.g., Abu-Lughod 1991; Borneman 1992; Brightman 1995; Brubaker and Cooper 2000), thereby trying to launch a post-culturalist and post-identitarian agenda in social research. Indeed, it is possible to study linguistic structures, performances, meanings, practices, and speech acts (key successive concepts of the various approaches to the study of all-that-can-differ) quite well without making any reference to notions of culture and identity. And so the question becomes, why bother keeping them in play?

Rethinking culture and identity metatheoretically

Given the justified critique of emic/etic interlacing within a rich and useful landscape of conceptual innovations in the study of human variation, I here propose to approach the search for productive scholarly concepts of culture and identity from a different angle, namely, from a metatheory of social life. It is through metatheory that I will get to what I take to be a defensible notion of culture, and with it, one of identity. Elsewhere, I have argued that the best candidate for such a metatheoretical framework is an updated version of the original program of a social hermeneutics articulated by Vico ([1744] 1948) and Herder ([1772] 1987, [1784–91] 2002). Such a program offers possibilities for rethinking larger social wholes in a non-reductive manner while overcoming counterproductive analytic divisions organized around such misleading dichotomies as ideal-material, micro-macro, structure-culture, and structure-event. Such dichotomies can be transcended because social hermeneutics leads us to think dialectically about social life in terms of co-constitutive social processes (Glaeser 2014). Social hermeneutics also answers directly to the needs of our era because it was formulated precisely to consider the historical condition of pluralism in which the concepts of culture and identity ascended to prominence.

The revised program of social hermeneutics (which is, as will become apparent shortly, a form of institutionalism) proceeds from the simple assumption that the social world, in both its fluid as well as its more stable or structural components, exists in intricate webs of activity flows, such that most actions can be understood as creative reactions to a number of other people's temporally and spatially dispersed antecedent actions, in turn giving rise to a multitude of consequences. No action is complete: none of its meanings is final as long as others keep reacting to it. In order to differentiate this way of looking at interlacing activities from other concepts such as interaction, I term enchainments of activities "action-reaction effect sequences" (Glaeser 2015).

Action-reaction effect sequences or chains can create recursive loops. Indeed, where the flow of actions and reactions is repeated across time, institutions emerge. Seeing such institutions as existing in similarly replicated activity flows makes it easy to appreciate that they are embodied, emplaced, and temporal. It is easy enough to intuit how institutions emerge and exist in face-to-face networks of small communities, for example, constituting friendships or family rituals. However, to understand how "micro"-scale action-flows can constitute large or "macro"-scale institutions spanning generations and continents, it is important to recognize that action effects can be *projectively articulated* across time and space through socio-technological means of storage and recording, transportation, and communication.

Two questions emerge: First, how best to think about how the actions of others prompt, inspire, and motivate ego's actions? And second, how best to grasp how actions take their specific spatio-temporal, social, and experiential form? Following the hermeneutic tradition, I propose to employ a much expanded notion of *understanding* in order to answer these questions. Understanding is a partly conscious but mostly unconscious process of differentiating and integrating the world that provides orientation, direction, coordination, and justification for action. Understanding proceeds in three basic modes: discursively (symbolically), emotively, and sensorily. Each mode affords specific ways of analyzing and synthesizing the world.

The ordering effected in understanding is a process. If a given ordering (fleeting and spontaneous as it may be) becomes validated on a recurring basis, it can congeal into more objectified and thus memorable, transposable, and teachable forms, turning the ongoing activity of understand*ing* (grammatically a continuous) into *an* understanding (something more thing-like, grammatically a gerund) that is somehow validated. Analytically, it makes sense to distinguish three basic forms of validation. *Recognition* is the perceived direct or indirect evaluation of actions/ understandings by relevant authorities. *Corroboration* is the feedback derived from the consequences of actions other than recognition. And *resonance* is the perceived fit of one understanding with others previously validated. Precisely because understandings owe their existence as much to validation as to the ordering resulting from differentiation and integration, understandings are dependent on social, experiential, and mnemonic environments. That is, they are necessarily linked to a material, semiotic, and social world. Variations in the degree of validation create highly differentiated profiles of understandings with regard to their actionability. And precisely because validation issues from action environments (presence of authorities, context-specific possibilities for situational corroboration, mnemonic elements in the sensory environment, etc.), the question of which understandings are more or less actionable can change considerably with context. Accordingly, any given person can appear to be rather different under different circumstances, and people can hold rather contradictory understandings without difficulty.

Metaunderstandings are discursive, emotive, or sensory orderings that orient and direct the way in which first-order understandings are generated in practice. They offer methods to differentiate and integrate the world. Good examples for very basic metaunderstandings are the classical categories of thought (causality, quantity, quality etc.), sound scales, color charts, and hedonic tones. Metaunderstandings also govern what counts as validation, for example, who is an authority in a particular context; how consequences of acting are to be discerned and how feedback is to be drawn from them (e.g., by reading auspices or by applying the inductive method); and what it could possibly mean to fit in with other understandings (e.g., criteria of consistency, suitability). One could say that metaunderstandings provide a kind of grammar for primary understandings.

This model suggests that institutions can gain stability only by becoming articulated with other, already established institutions. Indeed, action-reaction chains can be stabilized only through already more crystallized understandings, and understandings can stabilize only through more regularized validations, which in turn can only issue from social, natural, and mnemonic environments that systematically generate particular validational effects. This process presupposes that such environments are institutionalized. Thus, processes of institution formation point to each other like signs in a sign-system. In analogy to Peirce's sign-system notion of semiosis as the interaction among object, sign, and interpretation, I call this process *institutiosis*. The social formations that we commonly call institutions, such as those concerned with governmental decision-making and enforcement, can be analyzed as complex assemblages of components held together by the effect flows of processes of institutiosis. Through these flows, the components are also integrated into a much wider social fabric, not least because many of them are shared with other institutions. Calendars, languages, laws, and work ethics are excellent examples of institutional arrangements readily appropriated in many other institutions. In this light, every institution is enabled by an already extant infrastructure of other institutional arrangements.

A poetic concept of culture

The hermeneutic and institutionalist model of social life just presented raises the question of whether, just as with other post-linguistic-turn efforts, the concept of culture has not been effectively replaced by a set of other notions, in this case, the couplet of understanding and validation. The answer is that the model presented here does indeed redirect attention to units of analysis much smaller than what is commonly understood as culture. Yet I would also urge close attention to how these more basic units come to hang together in the process of institutiosis to form larger relatively stable assemblages, that is, institutions of a higher order. I propose to differentiate analytically between two basic types of such assemblages – both of which are more or less bounded by the limited reach, the diminishing impact, and the recursivity of effect flows. The first, more encompassing kind of assemblage is constituted by the sum total of *all* effect flows purveyed through human action: I propose to call this kind *societal*. It includes everyone and everything connected by impactful and enduring action-effect flows.

The second kind of assemblage is constituted only by those effect flows that form, alter, or validate peoples' discursive, emotive, and sensory understandings (including metaunderstandings). I propose to designate these as cultural. Cultures are, in this sense, institutionalized complexes of understandings, people, and actual and possible validational experiences in material, socially organized, and mnemonic environments assembled by processes of institutiosis. The constitutive links across the different kinds of elements in cultural assemblages leading to institutiosis are what have often been overlooked in the analysis of cultures. Institutiosis takes the fundamental idea of a meaning-holism to an entirely new level, suggesting both that no kind of inventory-like method can get to the core of the cultural (cf. Biernacki 2012), and that semiotic- or practice-centric approaches are deficient in their own ways.

Nothing in this hermeneutic imaginary of cultural assemblages conjoined by institutiosis suggests that the understandings in play within it form something like a rational, contradiction-free, or otherwise aesthetically pleasing whole. Whether and how something like cognitive dissonance (Festinger 1957) occurs is merely a matter of institutional arrangements, as Weber ([1920]

1988) already persuasively argued. Also, by no means does everyone participating in a cultural assemblage have to share the same understandings. Anti-authorities, for example, are as much part of cultural assemblages as authorities; distinct subdomains may stand in a complementary relationship to each other; one form of expertise may depend on another for understandings within its domain. What matters in constituting a culture is significant hermeneutic relatedness in action-reaction effect flows, not sharing.

The point of distinguishing the societal from the cultural is not to reinstate the misleading distinction between hard structure and soft culture but to highlight a gap in the feedback dynamics of social life. This gap emerges because some action effects produce validational feedback while others simply do not and thus literally escape the attention of the actor. A friend may indeed complain about a certain behavior whereas somebody distantly affected may not even know who to complain to. These gaps between total effects and those with validational consequences are constitutive of the particular institutional form that social life takes. That is to say that some institutional arrangements endure only because feedback is not available or even disabled. However, such gaps can also contribute in major ways to the often tumultuous and violent dynamic of social life (see also Glaeser 2011, ch. 4). I propose to speak of these kinds of gaps as cultural (or hermeneutic) externalities. Cultural externalities are a common feature of social life on all levels of complexity. However, socio-technological means of projectively articulating action effects across time and space vastly expand the prevalence and possible import of cultural externalities, thus creating the potential for enormous surprises, misunderstandings, alienation, objectification, false consciousness, ideology, hegemony, and so forth. The classical example is Marx's ([1867] 1990) notion of commodity fetishism, which illuminates how capitalism not only produces cultural externalities on a massive scale by systematically abstracting the product from the social and material context of its production, but how its very operability is dependent on their systematic production because prices as relatively simple commensurating but also obfuscating indices are central to the functioning of markets. As a result, all participants in the process of production are systematically blinded to the consequence of their actions producing, selling, and buying products. The advent of the Anthropocene – which signals the conversion of major chunks of the natural environment into institutions jointly formed, maintained, and altered by both natural and social processes – has upped the ante on the importance of recognizing cultural externalities as a source of significant danger for social life.

The actual and possible incongruence between the societal and the cultural has given rise to extraordinary cultural innovation in two opposite directions. On the one hand, it has stimulated massive efforts of systematic forgetting, tabooing, sequestration, and studied inattention – all of which bear close resemblance to Freudian processes of repression. On the other hand, the awareness of cultural externalities has led both to efforts to bring the consequences of actions into view through new imaginaries, concepts, and methods of producing knowledge, as well as to efforts to draw up guidelines that make them manageable, that is, by orienting and directing actions toward improved outcomes for self and other. The great ethical, legal, and political knowledge frameworks – be they cast in what we now classify as concrete-mythological, abstract-philosophical, or later empirical-scientific form – are all in effect centrally concerned with closing the gap between the cultural and the societal in some important way.

This observation leads to two questions: first, how do cultural externalities manifest themselves as "problems" inducing culturally internalizing efforts? And second, what makes it possible for cultural formations to change in response to these problems? In response to the manifestation question, I must limit myself here to a single observation: it is no accident that internalizing ethical, legal, administrative, and political knowledge systems have emerged and were widely adopted in social contexts characterized by significant internal social differentiation and conflict and/or external expansion carried by expanded forms of projective articulation. To the degree that differentiated parts are implied in the intentional and organized formation of a given institution (say a reign, a state, a church) that becomes threatened by cultural externalities, the question of the "proper" relationship between these parts emerges as a problem of political knowledge. Imperial adoptions or restorations of Buddhism, Confucianism, Christianity, Roman law, and Islam, each increasing awareness of consequences and feedback, are cases in point.

Beyond the obvious possibility of catastrophic failures of institutional fabrics, the search for an answer to the readiness-for-change question draws attention to the character of metaunderstandings in play. I have shown elsewhere (Glaeser 2011:245–50) that there is a built-in conservatism that can be theoretically characterized as a drift toward self-amplification in validation processes. Innovation is only possible where this tendency is circumvented, because hermeneutic processes somehow become opened to possibilities of forgetting or disregarding time-honored understandings, or to possibilities that new authorities will contradict older ones, or that experiences will become opened to corroboration from novel action contexts without recourse to ad-hoc-ing. Metaunderstandings encouraging play, random encounters, and the plunging into new experiences open up cultures to innovation. These are not enough, however. Because new understandings have to be cultivated in collaboration with other human beings, there is a tendency to form new cultural assemblages (sects, schools, parties, etc.), which in turn are prone to create externalities all their own and which will eventually have to reopen themselves to the environments.

The traditional solutions to determining the boundary of cultural domains, namely, to identify them with the boundaries of corporate groups, has rightly drawn much criticism, not least because it is here that normative everyday uses of the term culture overlap with unreflexive scholarly uses. Once again, the idea of institutiosis helps to think through the question of boundaries of cultural domains and their relationship to each other, in this case, by complicating the issue on two different planes simultaneously. First, every action may participate in a number of institution-forming processes at the same time. An action thus may partake in partially distinct cultural domains. Second, every action is oriented toward and directed by the conjugation of a multiplicity of understandings in all three modes (discursive, emotive, and sensory). Actors thereupon call into play metaunderstandings both to help select and combine these primary understandings relative to a situation and to provide the methods by which the differentiating and integrating work of the primary understanding is done. Each of these understandings may be maintained in partially overlapping but also diverging processes of institutiosis. Sometimes these may stand in a nesting relationship to each other, sometimes they may be intersecting, and sometimes both – potentially on multiple levels at the same time.

Interpreted through the lens of hermeneutic institutionalism, actions are therefore collectors of a potentially diverse range of influences, thus unifying contexts and blurring boundaries. This said, actions, understandings, and validations are part and parcel of cultural assemblages, even if their relationship is not some simple two-dimensional topography of mutual exclusivity (as in a contemporary nation-state map of the world), but a hyperspace with intersecting planes whose boundaries may be more or less well defined, depending on how effect flows continue or are abruptly halted.

The objective of hermeneutic analysis is thus not so much the attempt to delineate cultures against each other, but much rather to understand the multifarious connections and social dynamics underlying cultural assemblages, and the processes that reproduce or change them in the course of time. Analysis is thus focused not on characterizing sets of people but on studying the institutional enablement or disablement of effect flows, including those that are partially steered in particular directions by claims of belonging or exclusion, patterns of attention and disregard, or assertions of rights to interfere or freedom from such interference in the name of culture and identity.

The poetics and politics of identities

From the perspective of hermeneutic institutionalism, in more complex social arrangements, the neat boundedness of cultural assemblages is an artifact of particular kinds of actions. It is most notably the effect of limited comparisons across contexts where lists of understandings are highlighted as definitive characteristics of a particular group in comparison with characteristics of other groups similarly conceived. Such limited comparisons of understandings are typically undertaken at the expense of many other possible ones that might have yielded a result of similarity rather than of difference. What is inevitably lost in such operations is the *specific* genetic and generative place of understandings in cultural assemblages. Such comparisons are very often undertaken to engage in the kind of social labor I pointed to at the beginning of this chapter. This is to say they are employed for political aims – among which the formation of identities is very prominent.

In emic (and similarly structured etic) uses, the notions of culture and identity are therefore closely associated with each other. Their relationship is almost logical in its dialectical insinuation of sameness and difference potentially playing out indexically across several levels of inclusion and exclusion. Both terms particularize through comparison with an alter, thus creating an identity. Moreover, they generalize these characteristics within the set, thus stipulating what is read as culture in this specific use. In other words, inclusion in the set (= enculturation) conveys identity vis-à-vis all actors outside of the set but not vis-à-vis insiders to the set, within which the play of particularization and generalization may proceed on less inclusive levels all the way to individual persons. A useful insight (most forcefully made by Brubaker et al. 2008) is that such comparative evocations of culture and identity in practice are not constants, pervading all interaction; instead, such conceptual deployment is undertaken only under certain circumstances in order to accomplish particular kinds of social and political work. For many of these uses, the point of claiming identities is to demand particular kinds of action from particular people and to provide guidance for how to do so properly. Persons who know who they or others "are," that is, persons who know their identities, are taken to stand a better chance of knowing how to act, or what actions to expect of others. For all this to work, the understandings making up an identity have to exhibit certain levels of certainty, stability, coherence, consistency, clarity, and boundedness. Not surprisingly, then, there has been a strong tendency to infuse claims of identity with a whole slew of normative expectations, that is, metaunderstandings that are hoped to play a stabilizing role in the process of institutiosis.

Seen through the lens of the social hermeneutics sketched earlier, what are often addressed in such comparative discourses as identities should be seen as institutionalized self-understandings of individuals or larger social formations. They can exist only in repeated acts of identification that differentiate the target from an environment by linking (integrating) it with characterizing features that particularize it vis-à-vis other possibilities. To become stable, these identifications need to be validated through recognition, corroboration, or resonance. In other words, they are the result of distributed experiences and social collaboration. Whether, how, and to what effect identity claims acquire normative force is open to empirical investigation by tracing these processes through layers of institutiosis. In modern contexts, more typically than not, such self-understandings are at most situationally unitary, but rather fragmentary and potentially contradictory across contexts (e.g., Goffman [1956] 1959; Bayart [1996] 2006).

In the previous section, for want of a better term, I made a case for the continued use of the term culture for hermeneutic assemblages on a larger scale. The rationale for a continuing use of the term identity in scholarly discourses is not as strong, but once more, it can be made for aesthetic reasons, as long as a scholar makes its meaning clear while remaining aware of the historically specific emic-etic entanglements of the term.

Conclusion

The terms culture and identity were crafted and came to be widely adopted from the eighteenth century onward because they proved descriptively and normatively useful in managing (for good or ill) rapidly diversifying and pluralizing Europeanoid lifeworlds. Imperialism and the subsequent proliferation of the nation-state form have effectively globalized them. And thus it has come to pass that we live in a time when people are now supposed to be part of particular cultures and where they are expected to have identities in order to count as proper members of modern societies, professions, clubs, and so forth. In other words, we now live in a global culture of cultures and identities. Organizations of all kinds now routinely define and celebrate what is distinctive about them in relationship to comparable alters, and people forming these organizations are supposed to carry these cultures as badges of their identity toward the outside world while developing distinct identities of their own that are not disruptive of organizational functioning on the inside.

Guided by the notions of culture and identity as metaunderstandings of celebratory differentiation and particularization, a whole slew of practices has emerged to generate and institutionalize cultures and identities as political projects of collective and individual self- and other-making. With collectivities as a target, these include such practices as the teaching of national cultures through "native" language classes, the writing and reading of novels making up a canon, and the publishing of histories of culture, ethnographies, and opinion polls. With the individualities of persons qua target institution, they include the posting of me-pages on social networks, the publication of memoirs, the writing of scholarly biographies, and similar projects.

Academic work, often without reflexive distance, has been deeply implicated in these political practices – crafting what it most of the time purports merely to describe. One of the advantages of the metatheoretical reformulation sketched in this chapter is to offer a language that enables the critical interrogation of such academic involvement in culture and identity projects because it induces us to search for both unsuspected or even denied constitutive relationships as well as historicizations of concepts of culture and identity as metaunderstandings in the formation of institutions. That reformulation also helps to avoid gross anachronisms and anatopisms in identifying the dynamics of institution-formation processes in distant times and places. Social hermeneutics as metatheory offers no panacea, but it is demanding enough in its call for processual detail to help us estrange ourselves from all too unreflexive uses of the terms culture and identity.

References

Abu-Lughod, Lila. 1991. "Writing Against Culture." Pp. 137–62 in *Recapturing Anthropology: Working in the Present*, edited by R. Fox. Santa Fe, NM: School of American Research Press.

Arnold, Matthew. [1869] 1993. "Culture and Anarchy." Pp. 53–211 in *Arnold: "Culture and Anarchy" and Other Writings*, edited by S. Collini. Cambridge: University of Cambridge Press.

Bayart, Jean-Francois. [1996] 2006. *The Illusion of Cultural Identity*. Chicago: University of Chicago Press.

Biernacki, Richard. 2012. *Reinventing Evidence in Social Inquiry: Decoding Facts and Variables*. New York: Palgrave Macmillan.

Boas, Franz. 1901. "The Mind of Primitive Man." *Science* 13(321):281–89.

Borneman, John. 1992. *Belonging in Two Berlins*. Cambridge: Cambridge University Press.

Brightman, Robert. 1995. "Forget Culture: Replacement, Transcendence, Relexification." *Cultural Anthropology* 10(4):509–46.

Brubaker, Rogers, and Frederick Cooper. 2000. "Beyond 'Identity.'" *Theory and Society* 29(1):1–47.

Brubaker, Rogers, Margit Feischmidt, Jon Fox, and Liana Grancea. 2008. *Nationalist Politics and Ethnic Identity in a Transylvanian Town*. Princeton, NJ: Princeton University Press.

Burckhardt, Jacob. [1911] 1979. *Reflections on History*. Indianapolis: Liberty Fund.

Festinger, Leon. 1957. *A Theory of Cognitive Dissonance*. Stanford, CA: Stanford University Press.

Glaeser, Andreas. 2011. *Political Epistemics: The Secret Police, the Opposition and the End of East German Socialism*. Chicago: University of Chicago Press.

———. 2014. "Hermeneutic Institutionalism: Towards a New Synthesis." *Qualitative Sociology* 37(2):207–41.

———. 2015. "Theorizing the Present Ethnographically." Pp. 65–103 in *Theory Can Be More than It Used to Be: Learning Anthropology's Method in a Time of Transition*, edited by D. Boyer, J.D. Faubion, and G.E. Marcus. Ithaca, NY: Cornell University Press.

Goffman, Erving. [1956] 1959. *The Presentation of Self in Everyday Life*. New York: Anchor Books.

Herder, Johann Gottfried. [1772] 1987. "Abhandlung über den Ursprung der Sprache." Pp. 251–400 in *Werke Volume II*, edited by W. Pross. Munich: Hanser.

———. [1784–91] 2002. "Ideen zu einer Philosophie der Geschichte der Menschheit." Pp. 7–832 in *Werke Volume III*, edited by W. Pross. Munich: Hanser.

Lévi-Strauss, Claude. [1962] 1964. *The Savage Mind*. Chicago: University of Chicago Press.

Marx, Karl. [1867] 1990. *Capital*. Vol. 1. London: Penguin.

Tylor, Edward Burnett. [1871] 1874. *Primitive Culture*. Vol. 1. Boston: Estes & Lauriat.

Vico, Giambattista. [1744] 1948. *The New Science*. Ithaca, NY: Cornell University Press.

Weber, Max. [1920] 1988. "Die Wirtschaftsethik der Weltreligionen." In *Gesammelte Aufsätze zur Religionssoziologie*.

29

Public multiculturalism and/or private multiculturality?

Rebecca Chiyoko King-O'Riain

Introduction

As people reflect on the presidency of Barack Obama, many appreciate the symbolic signifi-cance of the first mixed-race/black president as evidence of the success of US multiculturalism (Jolivette 2012). Others despair at the state of multicultural relationships in both the UK and the US, which seem to be crumbling from the weight of the ideologies behind Brexit and the Trump presidency. At their cores, both the Brexit and Trump campaigns were strongly sup-ported by the rhetoric of return to a patriarchal, "white" nation, focusing resentment on immi-grants, people of color, and Muslims (among others). Predictably, rhetorics of white nationalism have given rise to increasing expressions of hate against these populations. There has been a 41 percent rise in racially or religiously motivated hate crimes in the UK (Forster 2016).

In the US, federal data on hate crimes is not comprehensive, but FBI statistics from 2015 show an uptick in racial hate crimes by 6 percent. On the ground, with the rise of Donald Trump, expressions of racially and religiously motivated hate have become bold and unabashed, with swastikas and white supremacist language associated with pro-Trump graffiti appearing across the nation (Yan, Sgueglia, and Walker 2016). Clearly, with both the Brexit and Trump campaigns, awakened forces of fear and hate are increasingly expressed in violent forms. People of color, different cultures, languages, and religions continue to be regarded as forces against "whiteness" and the "nation" in both the UK and the US. Thus, issues of multiculturalism have never been more significant for democracy than they are today.

Multiculturalism basically involves appreciation of diverse cultures, races, and ethnicities. It is a social movement and an ideology advancing cultural ideas within legal, political, and national discourses. Multiculturalism in the United States is not an official government policy; it emerged out of the Civil Rights Movement and the racial/ethnic "power" movements that sought to gain equal representation and rights for people of color. Despite significant gains, however, the recent increased targeting of minority groups makes it difficult to envision the efficacy of multicultur-alism as ideal and policy.

In this chapter I briefly outline theories of multiculturalism in the US and use these theories to examine whether multiculturalism plays out similarly in other parts of the world, in countries with assimilationist (Japan), liberal (UK, Ireland), and cosmopolitan/social (France, Germany, and Sweden) models of multiculturalism.

I then proceed to analyze an example of mixed-race people and racial categorization in the US census to illustrate how the project of multiculturalism has failed in the US partly because it neglects the hybridity/transnationality of cultural identities and adopts a "top-down" approach to social diversity. I argue that multiculturalism should be reframed as an issue of "multiculturality" from the "bottom up" – built upon the everyday lived practices of groups of people with multiple allegiances and backgrounds living together – to influence state policies about rights and recognition. Multiculturality as a concept has been defined as denoting the lived experiences of cultural integration, which can be found in places such as Hawaii (Finney 1963) and Germany (Zank 1998). Multiculturality, when it occurs, challenges state notions of race and culture by allowing for multiplicity. In my use of the term, unlike multiculturalism, multiculturality posits a doubling and not a mutual exclusivity of multiple cultures. This concept then can be expanded from everyday cultural experiences to include cultural movements that challenge deeply embedded notions of culture in the state (e.g., census categories that treat racial identity as singular). The concept of multiculturality helps bring to light how ethnic and racial "communities" can become redefined through cultural interaction, how processes of identity formation operate at both individual and interactional levels, and how individuals' contacts across groups change both the form and content of those groups.

Perspectives on multiculturalism

Hartmann and Gerteis have outlined three perspectives on multiculturalism: cosmopolitanism, fragmented pluralism, and interactive pluralism. They describe *cosmopolitanism* as an approach that "recogniz[es] the social value of diversity, but is skeptical about the obligations[and con-straints that group membership and societal cohesion can place on individuals" (Hartmann and Gerteis 2005:228). In theories of cosmopolitan multiculturalism, the focus is on the "lack of cultural specificity and resulting vagueness of its external boundary; tolerance and individual choice rather than mutual obligations. Group differences may well be important, but group identities are not to be totalizing or the source of public rights or obligations" (Hartmann and Gerteis 2005:228). In turn, *fragmented pluralism*, they treat as focusing on

> the existence of a variety of distinctive and relatively self-contained mediating communities as a social reality, but also as a necessity and strength. Procedural norms rather than common moral bonds are important and a heavy emphasis is placed on the role of groups. This results in weaker macro-social boundaries but strong internal groups and boundaries.
>
> *(Hartmann and Gerteis 2005:229)*

The role of the state is important to manage rights claims, but these two perspectives both assume that the state is neutral. Finally, *interactive pluralism* "realizes the existence of distinct groups and cultures . . . it posits the need to cultivate common understanding across these differences through their mutual recognition and ongoing interaction" (Hartmann and Garteis 2005:231). Hartmann and Gerteis identify scholarship by Hollinger (1995) with multicultural cosmopolitanism, Portes and Rumbaut (2001) with fragmented multiculturalism and Taylor (1994) and Alexander (2001) with interactive pluralism. For Hartmann and Gerteis (2005), interactive pluralism seems a desirable outcome, but they posit as unanswered the question of whether, and how, interactive pluralism can be achieved.

The Hartmann-Gerteis typology is helpful for organizing theories of multiculturalism, but the theories are based primarily on the US context and do not account for several recent trends in non-US multicultural settings. Even given the date of its publication, Hartmann and Gerteis's typology can be faulted for its inability to account for the connections and obligations that social actors may feel toward more than one group or nation simultaneously (senses of transnationality, multiraciality, hybridity, etc.). This problem of multiple identifications has only become more pronounced as globalization has proceeded. The typology assumes homogeneity within groups/ nations when in fact many groups have transnational connections or multiple ethnic origins, thus yielding multiple allegiances. Intra-group heterogeneity has increased in the last 10 years, with a rise in the number of dual citizens, mass migrations of people across the globe, and increases in connections via digital technology.

The approaches presented by Hartmann and Gerteis also falsely counterpose a strong internal (racial/ethnic) group identity against a strong macro (national) identity. This understanding of multiculturalism fails to account for individuals and groups with *both* strong internal group identities *and* strong national identities, often facilitated by boundary-crossing dual allegiances, dual citizenship, or dual languages. Some global mixed-race people stand at exactly such a point of connection between multiple racial/cultural groups, multiple nations, and multiple allegiances (King-O'Riain et al. 2014).

In the next section, I compare how multiculturalism has played out differently abroad compared to the US to show what the US might learn from other parts of the world. In the post-culture war era of the 2010s, multiculturalism and its critiques are moving into Canada (Guo and Wong 2015), Australia (Ivison 2016), the United Kingdom (Lentin and Titley 2011), and to a lesser extent continental Europe and Asia. Examining different national and cultural contexts allows us to see how multiculturalism manifests in different ways and how they can be linked to the multicultural theories described by Hartmann and Gerteis.

Cultural assimilation (Japan)

Japan is an island nation long held to be historically racially and culturally homogenous, which can be seen as an example of a country moving toward cultural adaptation more than multiculturalism. Japan has a strong ideology of descent as linked to citizenship: traditionally one needed to have a Japanese family name to register children for school or to become a citizen. Burgess (2007) argues that while Japan has more immigrants and guest workers than ever before, it is now only beginning to recognize multicultural diversity. However, he argues that this recognition is often reluctant and driven by external pressure stemming from international relations rather than internal cultural appreciation. More recently, "Cool Japan" (Iwabuchi 2015) has sported a more international image with the selection of successive mixed-race "Miss Japan" beauty queens in 2015 and 2016. This development has triggered a media furor about beauty, what it means to be Japanese, and what it means to represent Japan on an international stage.

Weiner (2008) finds that even with growing minority groups in Japan, such as Koreans, Chinese, and Japanese Brazilians – clearly constituting a multiethnic society – there is still widespread denial about diversity. Keenly aware of the effects of being an island nation in a global economy, the Japanese state took measures to "recognize" its indigenous Ainu people through the Ainu Cultural Promotion Act in 1997, but only to protect Ainu culture, not Ainu people as a distinct people. The Japanese state, even as the country's population reaches 10 percent non-Japanese, continues to deny citizenship to immigrants in Japan. Tarumoto (2003) argues that the Japanese government made small changes to citizenship requirements but they did so based not on an "internal multicultural logic" in response to increasing cultural diversity, but rather on an "external logic" based on pressure brought by international relations with other countries (mainly in the West). Arudou (2015) argues that racism against "visible minorities" in Japan embeds racism into Japanese laws, which means that *interactive pluralism* is limited at best.

Liberal multiculturalism (United Kingdom and the Republic of Ireland)

In Europe, the multicultural question had increasingly intensified with the flow of refugees from Syria into the continent. The debate about migrants has driven other narratives of multiculturalism to take political form, for example, in relation to the Brexit vote in the UK.

There, immigrants typically come from former colonies and citizenship is based on residency and knowledge of British culture, not bloodlines. Panayi has argued that because of these historical factors and current political attitudes toward multiculturalism, immigrants and their descendants have "come to play a more important role in recent British history than their contemporaries in [countries such as] Germany, particularly if we examine their role in the political process and in popular culture" (2004:466).

In Ireland, there is no history of in-migration or of far-flung colonial subjects, and discussions of interculturalism and diversity were driven in large part by the "Celtic Tiger" economy (2001–2008), which brought rapid economic prosperity and significant and rapid increases in immigration. Today, many aspects of Irish society have been transformed by the presence of immigrants and increasing cultural, linguistic, and religious diversity, which are occurring without any formal policy regarding multiculturalism and with no formal approach to multicultural education. The rights of non-Irish workers and residents are protected under 1998 equality legislation and universal human rights laws. However, for the most part, multicultural understanding is shaped through everyday lived experience. Conway argues that Ireland is more "open" to embracing cultural diversity because of its colonial past (2006). While the country has no political far right or white supremacist groups, it has constituencies involved in groups like the non-governmental organization Immigration Control Platform, who believe there are too many immigrants and they should be controlled.

Boucher (2008) writes that the Irish government

> simply assumes that these newer groups of EU and non-EU immigrants will largely integrate into Irish society by themselves, through the neo-liberal modes of self-governance.... As such, the government does not need to abandon its present fragmented, cost-effective, de facto assimilationist and laissez-faire integration policy.
>
> *(Boucher 2008:23)*

There is no formal policy on the integration of immigrants into Irish society, although services are offered in multiple languages (mainly Mandarin, Polish, and French), and since 2006 there have been attempts to enumerate the changing demographics of the country through a new racial/ethnic question on the census.

Cosmopolitanism or social multiculturalism? (France, Sweden)

Despite the presence of different ethnic groups, multiculturalism in France is considered a "non-issue" as French citizens are integrated into "Frenchness" under the banner of "republican ideals" and through shared language and culture. However, the increase of violent terrorist acts by Islamic extremist groups in Europe in the last decade, particularly in France, Belgium, and Germany, has made issues of culture, religion, and race divisive and the vision of a multicultural Europe more and more illusory.

David Theo Goldberg takes this development as evidence that the "post-racial" era has not signaled the end of race, but instead "represents an emergent 'neo-raciality, racism's extension if not resurrection'" (quoted in Titley 2016:2269). Not all is calm in multicultural Europe. Research by Pap Ndiaye (2009) clearly shows that skin tone and identification as a "visible minority" in France is highly correlated with socioeconomic status, education, and occupation. In 2016, the ban on wearing burkinis in public in southern France, and its suspension by the highest administrative court, have ignited an ongoing debate about the usefulness of maintaining the republican ideal that "we are all French, regardless of skin color or culture." Jennings writes:

> Citizenship was grounded upon a set of democratic political institutions rather than upon recognition of cultural and/or ethnic diversity. Republicanism itself thus became a vehicle of both inclusion and exclusion. If, as can be argued, the existence of diverse cultural communities can be seen as a valuable element of a flourishing liberal society, republicanism needs to give a greater attention precisely to the claims of diversity, completing the move from recognition of the multi-ethnic nature of French society to the formulation of a multicultural conception of citizenship.
>
> *(Jennings 2000:597)*

Also in Europe, Sweden has a history of progressive immigration policies combined with a strong national identity, which together have produced a highly developed rhetoric about multiculturalism and strong state support for "integrating" immigrants and culturally diverse groups into Swedish life (Pred 2000). However, and despite the country's low levels of immigration following the enlargement of the EU in 2001, there is growing sense that "even in Sweden," racism is on the rise. Sweden, and other countries long considered socially progressive and tolerant of the multicultural agenda, are struggling with the "disjuncture between racist attitudes and behaviors and a widely held image of the self and the nation as altruistic and just" (Pred 2002:1). The growth of white supremacist and far-right groups in Sweden belie a deeper multicultural skepticism and hatred beneath the surface of a progressive society.

Lentin and Titley (2011) argue that the multicultural project identified with the US was a basic failure in practice and that this became transformed in Europe into a project of "diversity," which could more easily accommodate a wide range of "differences," including ones of disability, gender, and age. In their view, to deal with multiculturalism in Europe, Sweden, and some other countries are moving toward policies to embrace "diversity" and away from explicitly "multicultural" ideals per se.

The retreat from multiculturalism has enabled dominant groups to resist accepting difference based on minority group claims. Diversity, then, is one alternative to multiculturalism, which can also encompass private social interactions and may hold the promise of fostering *interactive pluralism* by making social boundaries more fluid and loyalties more complex.

Recognition and rights – institutionalizing diversity

If multiculturalism is on the wane, then why has the issue pierced the politics of so many nations so sharply? Goldberg argues that multiculturalism goes to the very essence of what it means to be a nation in our post-racial world (Goldberg 2015). The fundamental questions are: what or who gets celebrated at a national level in the US, and why? And can diversity as *interactive pluralism* be institutionalized?

To address these questions, I examine racial/ethnic categorization in the US census, including recent changes, as an example of *interactive pluralism* and a way to understand connections between private identities and public institutions such as the state. The census embeds "recognition" of cultural difference in the US state, thus offering a window on identity politics.

In 1977, the US Census Bureau adopted Directive 15, which provided standard classifications for recordkeeping based on racial categorization. Directive 15 then became a precursor basis for linking a certain understanding of "race" with "rights" (for more on the 2000 census, see Williams 2008). The result was the "racial pentagon" – American Indian/Alaskan Natives, Asian/Pacific Islanders, black, Hispanic, and white – the five categories of people recognized in the census. The directive encouraged a "fusing" of individual and collective identities around the construction of racial and ethnic categories as a basis for gaining "rights" – that is, one needed to be identified as a member of a protected group in order to make claims for equal rights in housing, employment, and voting. Because discrimination occurred along "racial" lines it therefore was to be "tracked" along those same lines. Recognition and rights became attached to the same racialized identities – today called Asian-Pacific American, African American, and the like. Before Directive 15 and the Asian Power movement in the 1970s, there was no term "Asian-Pacific American." Both the state, in order to conduct civil rights compliance, and the Asian American community via the Asian Power movement, pushed for "lumping" as a way to solve representational problems (King 2000). Such lumping inextricably linked individual identities along racial lines and simplified them so that the state (and some social movements) could utilize them.

In 2000, the census again changed the way it enumerated people based on race and ethnicity, allowing people to check multiple options. Opposition to changing racial/ethnic categorization in that census came most strongly from groups of color (the National Council de La Raza, the National Association for the Advancement of Colored People, etc.) – groups that feared allowing multiracial people to check more than one box would decrease the numbers of self-identified Latinos and African Americans (both categories with large numbers of multiracial people) and therefore resources. The move for "multiple checks" on the race question on the census thus garnered support not only from conservatives, but also from some liberals, who saw it as a recognition of multiraciality. The racial/ethnic category on the census was controversial not because of the categories or the people filling them out but because allocation of state resources was linked to the categories, yielding recognition and valorization that made some cultures "worth" more than others. Offering a multiple-response option allowed for the recognition of multiraciality, but in doing so, the census was regarded as "diluting" the salience of racial categories, thus making it harder for minority groups to retain distinctiveness. In the end, increasing numbers of people could argue that they were multiracial. Interestingly, there was less attention to the fact that the racial/ethnic question on the census was self-determined and could prompt cases of "racial fraud" on the part of individuals hoping to gain access to resources.

The US census is not unusual: an international study of 138 censuses from around the world found that 63 percent of them included some type of ethnicity question. About half of the censuses used the term "ethnicity," while others used terms such as "nationality" (in Eastern Europe) and "race" (most often in the Americas; Morning 2008:263). Most censuses that used the terms ethnicity and race did so in order to track, and in some cases, to try to offer reparations, for inequality.

Multiculturality through multiraciality

Multicultural policies and ideals embedded in the state through the census designed to institutionalize diversity are rare. Wimmer reminds us that multicultural philosophy "does not distinguish between what political leaders say about the relevance and pervasiveness of ethnicity on the one hand, and the everyday lived experience of members of an ethnic category on the other hand" (2008:257). Although there is genetic variety within racial and ethnic groups, and race is thus a social category rather than a biological one, still the categories have a very real effect on people who live their lives classified as belonging to one or another minority racial group. A program of *interactive pluralism* would depend on interaction between individuals and groups, and informal space would need to be provided for these interactions.

Early theories of multiculturalism did not have the capacity to conceptualize the lived reality of mixed-race or multicultural people, who often have multiple allegiances that cross-national boundaries and identities. An alternative approach, "multiculturality," moves from people's personal experience of mixed-race identities, to cultural experiences of multiraciality, and to the racialization of political institutions (in say the racial/ethnic categorization on the census), making it possible to track not only personal but also cultural and political boundaries. It also promotes groups' interactions, thereby hybridizing conceptions of cultural identity and the nation, yielding a form of lived *interactive pluralism*.

Kimberly McClain DaCosta (2007) has analyzed the multiracial movement and how it was successful at getting the 2000 US census changed, in large part due to the movement's family and community base. A certain form of organic multiculturality sprang up from the experiences of groups of multiracial people.

Advocates of multiculturalism – particularly in the media – have long used multiracial people as the "face of the future." But little scholarly attention is given to how multiracial families negotiate and honor cultural differences both within their families and in their larger community affiliations. Such processes can be brought to light by exploring one case. The Japanese American community, which faces low immigration, high interracial marriage rates, and an aging population, opened up the definition of who is Japanese American and welcomed white parents and other non-Japanese Americans into the community. Here can be found the microfoundation of a different kind of multiculturalism – what I understand to be "multiculturality" – the everyday lived experiences of people in multicultural interaction. For Japanese American millennials, there is recognition of both Japaneseness and whiteness, of dual ethnic group membership, and of porous boundaries of community that encompass rather than exclude (Omi, Nakano, and Yamashita forthcoming). The universality of the message is remarkable: the prior basis for collective identity was based on race and ethnicity; now, community membership is based on family, culture, and community, not just race. The criteria for community membership and collective self-identity have shifted. When constructions of race and ethnicity change, so too do the criteria for membership into the collective group known as "the community" (King-O'Riain 2006).

Conclusion

Multiracial lived experiences are essentially centered on the issue of where one group ends and another begins. Mixed-race people stand at the intersection of two groups, forming a shared zone between them. They live where *us* and *them* meet, and in being part of *both* groups, they create new definitions of community. Where two groups touch one another through shared members, conflicts over the meaning of race, ethnicity, and culture are thrown into clearest relief. Considering cases of mixed-race people also reveals the frequent operation of more fluid multicultural relations in micro-social interaction.

What can we take from the various examples of lived multiculturality by multiracial people and examples? First, that both community membership and solidarity may become redefined simultaneously through *interactive pluralism*; second, that multicultural processes operate at multiple levels of interactional and individual identities; and third, that contacts between groups change the form and content of the groups themselves, which in turn can affect even institutionalized realities such as race/ethnicity in censuses.

In the future, the power of census numbers to constitute communities seems likely to weaken, because definitions of communities and who are members of any given community are changing. Officially defined racial and ethnic groups will remain, but groups will be more porous than before and more open to claiming people once regarded as beyond their boundaries. What will this mean for society? It means that there will continue to be uniquely defined groups, but they will be less rigidly defined than in the past. It also means that the nature of intergroup conflicts will change as membership in the groups overlap in multiple ways.

Let us return to the concept of multiculturalism. Core to the politics of identity and recognition is the idea that people should be recognized for their unique identities. In the past, "uniqueness" was predicated on exclusive group membership: people chose one "ethnic option" or race over another even if they were "mixed" (Waters 1990). The public recognition of the "differentness" of identities and groups is a difficult issue for mixed-race people because the basis of their identity is the borderland. They are not confidently "founded" in one group/ethnicity/race, but instead primarily construct their identities in relation to being "between" groups. When they bring this private "borderlandness" to the collective public sphere shared with monoracial or monoethnic communities, they potentially redefine all racial and ethnic groups.

Lived experiences of multiplicity (or hybridity) combined with strong group identification may arise out of spaces for multicultural interaction. If a society embraces a goal of multicultural interactive pluralism, such spaces are crucial. Creating such spaces requires structural support, such as the racial integration of workplaces and schools. Social actors have agency to engage in multiculturality, but multiculturality is slow to spread socially because opportunities for meaningful social interaction between racial groups remain relatively rare. Reducing structural segregation based on race, culture, ethnicity, and class would be necessary to encourage lived multiculturality. Even if structural segregation were reduced, if resources were at stake, political conflicts over group loyalties would put newfound multicultural understandings to the test. Today, multiculturalism as a movement continues to mobilize people across racial, ethnic, cultural, gender, and class lines. Whether it will be a true multiculturality for all, and in what societies, remains an open question.

References

Alexander, Jeffrey C. 2001. "Theorizing the 'Modes of Incorporation': Assimilation, Hyphenation, and Multiculturalism as Varieties of Civil Participation." *Sociological Theory* 19(3):237–49.

Arudou, Debito. 2015 *Embedded Racism: Japan's Visible Minorities and Racial Discrimination*. Lanham, MD: Lexington Books.

Boucher, Gerry. 2008. "Ireland's Lack of a Coherent Integration Policy." *Translocations: The Irish Migration, Race and Social Transformation Review* 3(1). Retrieved November 2, 2017 (www.imrstr.dcu.ie/currentissue/Vol_3_Issue_1_Gerry_Boucher.htm).

Burgess, Chris. 2007. "Multicultural Japan? Discourse and the Myth of Homogeneity." *Japan Focus* 5(3). Retrieved November 2, 2017 (http://apjjf.org/-Chris-Burgess/2389/article.html).

Conway, Brian. 2006. "Who Do We Think We Are? Immigration and the Discursive Construction of National Identity in an Irish Daily Mainstream Newspaper, 1996–2004." *Translocations: The Irish Migration, Race and Social Transformation Review* 1(1). Retrieved November 2, 2017 (http://eprints.maynoothuniversity.ie/751/1/conway.pdf).

DaCosta, Kimberly McClain. 2007. *Making Multiracials: State, Family, and Market in the Redrawing of the Color Line*. Stanford, CA: Stanford University Press.

Finney, Joseph C. 1963. "Psychiatry and Multiculturality in Hawaii." *International Journal of Social Psychiatry* 9(5):5–11.

Forster, Katie. 2016. "Hate Crimes Soared by 41% after Brexit Vote, Official Figures Reveal." *Independent*, October 13. (www.independent.co.uk/news/uk/crime/brexit-hate-crimes-racism-eu-referendum-vote-attacks-increase-police-figures-official-a7358866.html).

Goldberg, David Theo. 2015. *Are We All Postracial Yet?* Hoboken, NJ: John Wiley and Sons.

Guo, Shibao, and Lloyd Wong. 2015. *Revisiting Multiculturalism in Canada: Theories, Policies and Debates.* Rotterdam, Netherlands: Sense.

Hartmann, Douglas, and Joseph Gerteis. 2005. "Dealing with Diversity: Mapping Multiculturalism in Sociological Terms." *Sociological Theory* 23(2):218–40.

Hollinger, David. 1995. *Post Ethnic America: Beyond Multiculturalism.* New York: Basic Books.

Ivison, Duncan. 2016. *The Ashgate Research Companion to Multiculturalism.* London: Routledge.

Iwabuchi, Koichi. 2015. *Resilient Borders and Cultural Diversity: Internationalism, Brand Nationality, and Multiculturalism.* Lanham, MD: Lexington Books.

Jennings, Jeremy. 2000. "Citizenship, Republicanism and Multiculturalism in Contemporary France." *British Journal of Political Science* 30(4):575–98.

Jolivette, Andrew J., ed. 2012. *Obama and the Biracial Factor: The Battle for a New American Majority.* Bristol, UK: Policy Press.

King, Rebecca Chiyoko. 2000. "Racialization, Recognition and Rights: Lumping and Splitting Multiracial Asian Americans and the 2000 Census." *Journal of Asian American Studies* 3(2):191–217.

King-O'Riain, Rebecca Chiyoko. 2006. *Pure Beauty: Judging Race in Japanese American Beauty Pageants.* Minneapolis: University of Minnesota Press.

King-O'Riain, Rebecca Chiyoko, Stephen Small, Minelle Mahtani, Miri Song, and Paul Spickard, eds. 2014. *Global Mixed Race.* New York: New York University Press.

Lentin, Alana, and Gavan Titley. 2011. *The Crisis of Multiculturalism: Racism in a Neo-Liberal Age.* London: Zed Books.

Morning, Ann. 2008. "Ethnic Classification in Global Perspective: A Cross National Survey of the 2000 Census Round." *Population Research and Policy Review* 27(2):239–72.

Ndiaye, Pap. 2009. "Skin Tone Stratification and Its Social Consequences in France." Presented at "Beyond the Black/White Binary" Colloquia, African American Studies, April 29, Northwestern University.

Omi, Michael, Dana Nakano, and Jeffrey Yamashita, eds. Forthcoming. *Japanese American Millennials.*

Panayi, Panikos. 2004. "The Evolution of Multiculturalism in Britain and Germany: An Historical Survey." *Journal of Multilingual and Multicultural Development* 25(5–6):466–80.

Portes, Alejandro, and Ruben Rumbaut. 2001. *Legacies: The Story of the Immigrant Second Generation.* Berkeley: University of California Press.

Pred, Alan. 2000. *Even in Sweden.* Berkeley: University of California Press.

———. 2002. "Somebody Else, Somewhere Else: Racisms, Racialized Spaces and the Popular Geographical Imagination in Sweden." *Antipode* 29(4):383–416.

Tarumoto, Hideki. 2003. "Multiculturalism in Japan: Citizenship Policy for Immigrants." *International Journal on Multicultural Societies* 5(1):88–103.

Taylor, Charles. 1994. *Multiculturalism: Examining the Politics of Recognition.* Princeton, NJ: Princeton University Press.

Titley, Gavan. 2016. "On *Are We All Postracial Yet?*" *Ethnic and Racial Studies* 39(13):2269–77.

Waters, Mary C. 1990. *Ethnic Options.* Berkeley: University of California Press.

Weiner, Michael. 2008. *The Illusion of Homogeneity.* London: Routledge.

Williams, Kim M. 2008. *Mark One or More: Civil Rights in Multiracial America.* Ann Arbor: University of Michigan Press.

Wimmer, Andreas. 2008. "The Left-Herderian Ontology of Multiculturalism." *Ethnicities* 8(2):254–60.

Yan, Holly, Kristina Sgueglia, and Kylie Walker. 2016. "'Make American White Again': Hate Speech and Crimes Post-Election." *CNN News*, December 22. (http://edition.cnn.com/2016/11/10/us/post-election-hate-crimes-and-fears-trnd/).

Zank, Wolfgang. 1998. *The German Melting Pot: Multiculturality in Historical Perspective.* New York: Palgrave Macmillan.

30

Bodies, beauty, and the cultural politics of appearance

Maxine Leeds Craig

Introduction

There was a time when sociologists studied people but not their bodies. With the publication of Bryan Turner's *The Body and Society* in 1984, Chris Shilling's *The Body and Social Theory* in 1993, the establishment of the journal *Body and Society* in 1995, the formation of the Body and Embodiment section of the American Sociological Association in 2009, and a steady flow of sociological articles, monographs, and reference works on the body, that has changed. The study of bodies and embodiment has been institutionalized into one of sociology's subfields.

The sociology of the body has developed with areas of emphasis and lacunae. In an earlier edition of this handbook (2010), I asked why the substantial sociological literature on physical appearance was rarely included as part of the sociology of the body, despite the importance of appearance to the embodied experience of gender and race. Girls are socialized to have heightened awareness of their appearance and to measure themselves against prevailing standards of beauty. Appearance is a powerful dimension of the experience of racialization. Racism has been described as a "visual centered ideology" (Mosse 1985:134). The significance of appearance in the embodied experience of gender and race was not reflected in the literature of the sociology of the body as it emerged in the 1980s and 1990s. Studies of beauty and fashion, many of which were keenly attuned to the intersecting dynamics of race, gender, and class, were more likely to be situated within the gender literature or, when they focused on people of color, treated as primarily about race. The limited place of studies of appearance in the early development of the sociology of the body signaled a broader problem. In the sociology of the body's first decades in Britain and the United States, the publications that came to define the subfield drew upon the work of Marcel Mauss, Norbert Elias, Michel Foucault, Anthony Giddens, and Pierre Bourdieu as theoretical foundations. In this subfield, gender and race were given limited attention.

The sociology of the body has shifted since then, and issues of physical appearance have gained a central place in its scholarship. The shift was driven by feminist scholars who, while still engaging with Bourdieu and Foucault, insisted on the importance of gender as it intersects with race and class for theorization of the body and embodiment. Their work has drawn the sociological scholarship on the body, gender, class, and race together. This chapter will consider the range of recent sociological scholarship on physical appearance to identify their common theoretical underpinnings, convergences, divergences, and areas that need additional attention. Clusters of scholarship have grown around four substantive areas related to physical appearance: debates regarding the relative weight of transnational versus local beauty standards, the uses of beauty in the projects of nations and other collectivities, the significance of appearance in employment, and the relationship between appearance norms and disabilities. While highlighting more recent scholarship, the chapter will include work by earlier scholars who led the way in bringing race and/or gender into the sociology of the body.

Theoretical underpinnings

A major stream of scholarship on appearance draws on Pierre Bourdieu's theorization of habitus and forms of embodied capital. The concept of habitus provides a bridge between macro-level structural forces and the nearness of living, breathing individuals. Class had a preeminent place in Bourdieu's work, overshadowing either gender or race as social forces. Nonetheless, a group of scholars, who may be called the feminist Bourdieusians, have used the concept of habitus to examine how class is lived through gender. Beverley Skeggs's theoretically rich ethnographic research analyzed how working-class British women used style and deportment to access both respect and pleasure (1997). Skeggs described working-class women's investment in their appearance as a defensive tactic through which a woman who is acutely aware of being the target of middle-class disdain "deflects classification and deters the flow of capital from the body" by minding her looks (1997:84). Skeggs, like Bourdieu (1984), situates working-class appearance as the negative reference point in contests for distinction, but not entirely or exclusively. Working-class women, especially when they are young, have fun, exhibit feminine competency, and by distancing themselves from dull, middle-class tastes, they express gendered class solidarity by wearing cosmetics and dressing up according to tastes shared by their friends (Skeggs 1997:104). Similarly, Merl Storr argues that working-class British women who buy luxury lingerie at home-shopping parties "reject more affluent forms of heterosexual femininity and embrace their own tastes and pleasures as more appreciative, more discriminating, quite simply as better than those of the middle and upper classes" (Storr 2002:34–5). In a high school where class and ethnicity were tightly connected, Julie Bettie (2003) found that Chicanas wore strikingly visible cosmetics to distinguish themselves from the white middle class, privileged and, from their perspective, undesirable girls they called "preps." The feminist Bourdieusians suggest that working-class tastes function as locally valued cultural capital, important and meaningful to girls and women even though they lack the social power to "convert their competencies into a form of authority, into symbolic capital" (Skeggs 1997:104).

A second stream of scholarship on appearance draws on Foucault's theorization of self-discipline and surveillance. The groundwork for this approach was laid by Sandra Lee Bartky in an essay in which she argued that "normative femininity is coming more and more to be centered on woman's body – not its duties and obligations or even its capacity to bear children, but its sexuality, more precisely its presumed heterosexuality and its appearance" (1990:80). The compulsively self-monitoring woman is a product of modern diffuse patriarchal power. Although this argument continues to be an important point of departure for much scholarship on beauty, recent work asks more precise questions about how, and by whom, beauty work and beauty norms are used, foregrounding race as it intersects with gender, nation, and class in studies of embodification. For example, Ginetta Candelario (2007) argues that in New York migrants from the Dominican Republic alter their hair texture to mark a boundary between a Hispanic identity and blackness. Intersectional studies have opened new avenues for theorizing racial embodification through analyses of how socially constructed race is lived through the body, and how individuals and communities use appearance and deportment to express and transform the meanings and boundaries of racial identities (Barber 2016; Cox 2015; Craig 2014).

Transnational circulation and contestation of beauty norms

Feminists brought beauty into the realm of politics by arguing that the social expectation that women will be beautiful burdens and devalues women and is linked to women's subordination. In the years since these arguments were first articulated, sociological and feminist debates on beauty have become significantly richer and more nuanced, taking account of the diversity of women's experiences, the pleasures associated with beauty culture, and the ways collective engagement with beauty culture may provide dominated groups vehicles for resistance. Instead of using Bartky's general category "woman," recent scholarship investigates how race, ethnicity, class, and sexuality combine to locate different women in distinct positions in relation to local and transnational beauty norms. Undoubtedly the reach of Hollywood into global markets and a fashion industry centered in the Global North transmit Eurocentric standards of beauty on a transnational scale. American and European model scouts travel the globe searching for faces and bodies that meet their judgments regarding the moment's ideal "look." Although a few women with dark skin or non-European features will be recruited to work in elite realms of the fashion industry, most of the women who are given work as models will conform to Eurocentric beauty standards. For example, scouts who travel to Brazil to find potential models generally go to Brazil's whiter south (Adelman and Ruggi 2008:562).

The faces chosen by the fashion industry will be visible in advertisements around the world and contribute to homogenizing standards of beauty on a global scale. Recent scholarship nonetheless demonstrates that even as images produced by mass media in the Global North circulate transnationally, beauty standards are experienced in, and informed by, local contexts. Multiple ways of seeing beauty circulate and compete, even in a single moment in any particular local setting. In a study of women in Mexico, Mónica Moreno Figueroa found that while on a national scale beauty standards were shaped by a "mestizaje logic" that favored light skin, women's sense of feeling beautiful was a fragile effect, generated as a response to being the object of transitory and inconsistent gazes (2013:138, 148). The Mexican women Moreno Figueroa studied were like the compulsively self-monitoring women described by Bartky, but the gazes that compelled their self-surveillance were not consistent. The women in Moreno Figueroa's study carried with them an uncertainty about their looks, and about the standards by which they would be judged, even as they were certain that appearance mattered.

Decentering whiteness

Prizing light and disparaging dark complexions is common in Mexico (Moreno Figueroa 2013) and in the United States – both within communities of color and in the judgments of whites (Hunter 2002; Keith 2009; Vaid 2009) – and drives the transnational market for skin lighteners (Glenn 2009; Rondilla 2009). Although an overall pattern of preference for lighter complexions could suggest the existence of a transnational hegemonic beauty norm, current scholarship argues that, on the contrary, people interpret beauty standards through local frames in which lighter and darker tones are given meaning in relation to local identities. That is to say, recent scholarship decenters the place of Euro/American whiteness in theorization of beauty ideals (Hoang 2014; Holliday and Elfving-Hwang 2012; Saraswati 2010; Vaid 2009). Scholars whose work is based in Asia and among Asian diasporic communities note that preferences for light skin may not be referencing Euro/American whiteness but instead expressing a mix of long-standing Asian aesthetics and more recently constituted local tastes (Vaid 2009:149). For example, addressing the widespread popularity of cosmetic surgery in South Korea for men and women, Ruth Holliday and Joanna Elfving-Hwang argue that local aesthetics and long-standing South Korean beliefs that facial features can determine a person's character and future are at least as important as a desire to obtain a white Western appearance (2012). In a study focused on sex work in Ho Chi Minh City, Kimberly Kay Hoang (2014) argues that sex workers who cater to Asian businessmen aspire to a look that can be characterized as "pan-Asian modernity." The arguments presented by these authors are critiques of simplistic models of cultural hegemony that disregard the force of locally generated tastes. That being said, local beauty standards are no less coercive and exclusionary than transnational ones.

The arguments emerging from recent scholarship on beauty standards in Asia echo to some degree earlier studies of beauty standards in African American communities and in Latin America. Both Rooks (1996) and Craig (2002) found that black women who straightened their hair understood the practice as a way to embody black respectability, not a desire to appear white. Casanova (2004) found that Ecuadorean girls were aware of transnational white Eurocentric beauty standards, but felt that they had no practical relevance for them. In everyday life, women model themselves and judge themselves in relation to women who look like them and live nearby. Without denying a larger context in which Eurocentric beauty standards prevail, these arguments displace white women as immediate reference points for local beauty standards including those circulating in US communities of color.

Beautiful women as political symbols

Groups that seek to establish their worth often turn to women deemed beautiful to do the work of embodying collective value. Collectivities of all sorts imagine and celebrate their genealogies, histories, and character via the bodies of beautiful women. These are political struggles through which nations and other collectivities stress certain genealogies and suppress others. For example, Megan Rivers-Moore found that Costa Ricans who boasted of the beauty of Costa Rican women explained that what distinguished them from their Central and Latin American neighbors was the absence of indigenous roots (2013:156). The politics of beauty are not separate from larger social movements. During times of heightened social movement activism, the discursive tools and practical techniques available for imagining and creating beauty will expand beyond existing conventions. Social movements can lead to innovations in beauty culture. In communities with long histories of anti-racist or anti-colonial struggle, expressed beauty preferences are likely to be articulated through a critical lens. Shirley Tate found that black Jamaicans inspired by Black Nationalist and Rastafarian movements rejected normative preferences for light skin and celebrated darker shades of brown. Situating her argument within a Butlerian frame, Tate described an iterative process of "beautying" that brings into being a counter-hegemonic sense of beauty (Tate 2013:225).

The beauty pageant is an institutional form that is well-suited to the process of defining and celebrating the distinctive worth of collectivities (Balogun 2012; Banet-Weiser 1999; King-O'Riain 2006; Roberts 2014; Tice 2012). Beauty pageants often incorporate political boundaries into their structures, as contestants frequently stand for cities, states, or nations. The aptness and adaptability of beauty pageants as vehicles for collective pride explains the endless proliferation of innovative pageants. Groups stage beauty pageants to crown their finest representatives and through that process engage in self-definition. Tension between sexualized displays, which are characteristic of beauty pageant conventions, and the quasi-sacred character of collective identities, is inherent in the beauty pageant form. This has been managed in beauty pageants by including, alongside judgments of appearance, contests of feminized forms of cultural competence. Oluwakemi Balogun studied two beauty pageants in Nigeria, one that that strives to represent Nigeria to the world and another that engages a Nigerian conversation regarding national identity. The first pageant aspires to cultivate Nigerian women who can win competitions when judged by standards centered in the Global North but deemed "universal." In the second pageant, contestants must be perceived as beautiful by local judges but also prepare a regional dish – a requirement that begins with a trip to an outdoor market to purchase the ingredients while adhering to a limited budget (Balogun 2012:365). This contest positions itself as the arbiter of authentic feminine national identity precisely through its distance from the pageants that groom women to compete internationally.

Aesthetic labor

Just as nations use beauty to represent themselves to local and national publics, so corporations create brands via the appearance of their workers. The global expansion of the service economy has led to an increase in the number of positions in which appearance is a factor in hiring decisions. Studies of service work reveal managers hiring, firing, rewarding, and penalizing workers on the basis of appearance (Avery and Crain 2007; Warhurst et al. 2000; Williams and Connell 2010). Many low-end service jobs explicitly require women to meet standards of attractiveness, which are delineated in "look policies." Christine Williams and Catherine Connell report that decisions regarding the right look are made at corporate headquarters of retail chains and put into practice at the store level by managers (2010); while looking for certain physical types they are also looking for an orientation toward consumption and dress, in a process Williams and Connell describe as hiring the habitus (2010:358).

Appearance norms communicated and enforced in workplaces reproduce race, class, ethnic, and gender inequalities. Although both men and women are held to standards of appearance in service occupations, women are more likely to have jobs in which appearance is treated as a qualification. When men and women are employed in the same occupations, women are generally held to more exacting standards of appearance. Among the rare occupations in which women typically earn more than men are three that involve display of the body: modeling, pornographic acting, and dancing in strip clubs. In a study of these occupations in which the usual gender wage gap is inverted, Ashley Mears and Catherine Connell argue that this anomalous corner of the labor market should not be interpreted as an indication of broad advantages available to women based on appearance. On the contrary, the inverted wage gap arises in part because men, not women, control the fashion, pornography, and strip club industries (Mears and Connell 2015:352). The most successful women models command great earnings, but they represent an extremely small percent of models. Like the majority of women who work as pornographic actors or strippers, models work in short-lived careers at temporary jobs for low pay with no benefits (Mears and Connell 2015:346). Furthermore, while the gender wage gap may be inverted in modeling, pornographic acting, and stripping, racial inequalities operate to limit opportunities for women of color in these fields just as they do in other occupations (Brooks 2010; Mears 2011:178–208). Despite the poorly paid reality of modeling work, the field has great appeal for young women for whom it appears to offer the promise of highly paid, glamourous employment. Girls' fascination with modeling produces an enormous pool of applicants who invest time and money in travel, assembling portfolios, and in creating what they believe will be the successful look in their attempts to enter a field in which the supply of aspirants is much larger than the opportunities available (Wissinger 2015:197).

Most of the sociological scholarship on beauty and aesthetic labor has focused on women in advanced capitalist societies and treated the social compulsion for women to be beautiful as unvarying. Scholars working in China have denaturalized the connection between women and consumption of beauty products in studies that document the recent intensification of social expectations for displays of femininity. The emergence of capitalism in China has demanded and cultivated new feminine subjectivities and embodiments (Otis 2012; Yang 2011). Maoist ideologies downplayed gender difference and celebrated women's contributions to the nation as agricultural and industrial laborers. Advertisements arising from the current market economy have heightened gender differences and promised women that their greatest fulfillment will come from their beauty (Yang 2011:335). The tremendous growth in the consumption of cosmetic products and services, including surgery, in China arises partly from intensified marketing and changing ideologies, but also from women's place in a new service economy (Otis 2012; Yang 2011:343–8). As in the West, the service economy ties production and consumption together. In order to obtain work in service occupations women must be consumers of the beauty products that create a feminized appearance deemed professional. In workplaces as different as luxury hotels owned by multinational corporations and small local beauty salons, women's employment in China's service economy depends upon a youthful appearance, conformity to norms of attractiveness, and the use of beauty products.

The linkages between processes of production and consumption, and of labor and leisure that are visible in studies of the service economy in China are found in all sites in which a cultivated appearance constitutes a workplace requirement, albeit with very different consequences for women of different classes. The importance of a cultivated appearance for service work means that the labor of preparing the body for work, often described as "aesthetic labor" (Warhurst et al. 2000), happens outside of the workplace at workers' expense. Unlike other forms of labor market preparation, such as the acquisition of educational credentials or occupational skills, investment in appearance will yield limited returns in a service economy that is only open to youthful workers.

Normalization of body modification and the pathologization of difference

At the beginning of the twentieth century in the United States, the use of visible facial cosmetics lost its stigmatized association with prostitution (Peiss 1998). It became ordinary for women to wear cosmetics and over time, cosmetics use became a social expectation for women. Indeed, many women who work in service occupations are required to wear cosmetics, even while cosmetics are forbidden for men employed in the same jobs (Avery and Crain 2007). In recent decades in the United States, Brazil, South Korea, Mexico, and Colombia, cosmetic surgery and the use of Botox, while not entirely escaping public criticism, is nonetheless becoming unexceptional (Berkowitz 2017; Gimlin 2010:57; Taussig 2012). Cosmetic surgeons promote aesthetic surgeries by framing them as the treatment of medical conditions (Merianos, Vidourek, and King 2013:11) or necessary for psychological health (Sanchez Taylor 2012:640). Indeed, in Brazil public and private subsidies reduce the cost of cosmetic surgery for poor women on the basis of its purported ability to alleviate psychological suffering (Edmonds 2007:367). In 2015 alone, 1,888,051 women worldwide had surgical procedures to increase the size of or lift their breasts, and 1,264,702 women underwent blepharoplasty, an eyelid surgery that creates a double eyelid (ISAPS 2016:2). In a study of British and American women who had undergone cosmetic surgery, Debra Gimlin shows how women and their doctors build legitimacy for the practice by distancing themselves from a "surgical other," that is to say, women perceived as having pursued the wrong kind of or excessive cosmetic surgery (2010:63–4). The anthropologist Michael Taussig called attention to the public's fascination with the death and disfigurement of cosmetic surgery patients in Colombia, a nation that is seventh overall in a worldwide ranking of number of facial and head cosmetic procedures performed (2012:ix; ISAPS 2016:4). Transformations of the body's appearance exist in unstable configurations of morality in which certain practices are treated as self-care, self-love, wise investment, and responsible body management, while others are deemed excessive, bizarre, in poor taste, or narcissistic.

When competence is judged by physical appearance and visible physical difference becomes the basis for exclusion, appearance norms contribute to the production of disability. As forms of body work and body modification become normative, the apparent refusal to submit to correction appears aberrant. Heather Laine Talley's research on facial disfigurement analyzes the ways in which, for those with faces defined as disfigured, the pressures to undergo body modification to achieve "unremarkability" are rarely challenged (2014). Critiques of the pathologization of difference build upon the work of feminist disability studies scholar Rosemarie Garland-Thomson (2005) and have been most developed within sociology in the scholarship on weight-based stigma (Kwan 2010; Murray 2009; Saguy 2013). These studies have found that fat individuals face a host of false and negative assumptions about their character and habits, and that fat women face more weight-based discrimination than fat men. Though diets generally fail and can lead to long-term weight gain, and though neither thinness nor fatness by itself is an accurate indicator of health, the belief that weight can and should be controlled increases the disparagement of those who are fat. Only recently have sociologists given sustained attention to beauty's opposite: ugliness. Engaging with theory coming from disability studies, scholars such as Talley and the group of sociologists writing on fatness question the norms underlying aesthetic judgments and the blurring of the distinctions between appearance and health: medical necessity and social norm. More studies are needed on the development and widespread acceptance of appearance-altering technologies. As such technologies become commonplace, they may be integrated into routine management of the body and become the basis for the production of new exclusions.

Physical appearance is the target of normalizing technologies, the object of celebration and disparagement, inclusion and exclusion, a vehicle for expressions of individual and collective identities, and a site of workplace regulation. Axes of race, gender, class, nation, sexuality, ability, and nation converge on the surface of bodies in each of these processes focused on appearance. Cultural sociologists must continue to study physical appearance. It is likely that appearance will matter more than ever as the service economy expands, appearance-altering technologies proliferate, and the line between politics and entertainment erodes.

References

Adelman, Miriam, and Lennita Ruggi. 2008. "The Beautiful and the Abject: Gender, Identity and Constructions of the Body in Contemporary Brazilian Culture." *Current Sociology* 56(4):555–86.

Avery, Dianne, and Marion Crain. 2007. "Branded: Corporate Image, Sexual Stereotyping and the New Face of Capitalism." *Duke Journal of Gender, Law and Policy* 14(1):13–123.

Balogun, Oluwakemi. 2012. "Cultural and Cosmopolitan: Idealized Femininity and Embodied Nationalism in Nigerian Beauty Pageants." *Gender & Society* 26(3):357–81.

Banet-Weiser, Sarah. 1999. *The Most Beautiful Girl in the World: Beauty Pageants and National Identity*. Berkeley: University of California Press.

Barber, Kristen. 2016. *Styling Masculinity: Gender, Class, and Inequality in the Men's Grooming Industry*. New Brunswick, NJ: Rutgers University Press.

Bartky, Sandra Lee. 1990. *Femininity and Domination: Studies in the Phenomenology of Oppression*. New York: Routledge.

Berkowitz, Dana. 2017. *Botox Nation: Changing the Face of America*. New York: New York University Press.

Bettie, Julie. 2003. *Women without Class: Girls, Race, and Identity*. Berkeley: University of California Press.

Bourdieu, Pierre. 1984. *Distinction: A Social Critique of the Judgement of Taste*. Cambridge, MA: Harvard University Press.

Brooks, Siobhan. 2010. *Unequal Desires: Race and Erotic Capital in the Stripping Industry*. Albany: SUNY Press.

Candelario, Ginetta E.B. 2007. *Black behind the Ears: Dominican Racial Identity from Museums to Beauty Shops*. Durham, NC: Duke University Press.

Casanova, Erynn Masi De. 2004. "'No Ugly Women': Concepts of Race and Beauty among Adolescent Women in Ecuador." *Gender & Society* 18(3):287–308.

Cox, Aimee Meredith. 2015. *Shapeshifters: Black Girls and the Choreography of Citizenship*. Durham, NC: Duke University Press.

Craig, Maxine Leeds. 2002. *Ain't I a Beauty Queen: Black Women, Beauty and the Politics of Race*. New York: Oxford University Press.

———. 2010. "Bodies, Beauty, and Fashion." Pp. 243–51 in *Handbook of Cultural Sociology*, edited by J.R. Hall, L. Grindstaff, and M. Lo. New York: Routledge.

———. 2014. *Sorry I Don't Dance: Why Men Refuse to Move*. New York: Oxford University Press.

Edmonds, Alexander. 2007. "'The Poor Have the Right to Be Beautiful': Cosmetic Surgery in Neoliberal Brazil." *Journal of the Royal Anthropological Institute* 13:363–81.

Garland-Thomson, Rosemarie. 2005. "Feminist Disability Studies." *Signs* 30(2):1557–87.

Gimlin, Debra. 2010. "Imagining the Other in Cosmetic Surgery." *Body & Society* 16(4):57–76.

Glenn, Evelyn Nakano. 2009. "Consuming Lightness." Pp. 166–87 in *Shades of Difference: Why Skin Color Matters*, edited by E.N. Glenn. Stanford, CA: Stanford University Press.

Hoang, Kimberly Kay. 2014. "Competing Technologies of Embodiment: Pan-Asian Modernity and Third World Dependency in Vietnam's Contemporary Sex Industry." *Gender & Society* 28(4):513–36.

Holliday, Ruth, and Joanna Elfving-Hwang. 2012. "Gender, Globalization and Aesthetic Surgery in South Korea." *Body & Society* 18(2):58–1.

Hunter, Margaret L. 2002. "'If You're Light You're Alright': Light Skin Color as Social Capital for Women of Color." *Gender & Society* 16(2):175–93.

International Society of Aesthetic Plastic Surgery. 2016. "International Survey on Aesthetic/Cosmetic Procedures Performed in 2015." Retrieved November 10, 2017 (www.isaps.org/news/isaps-global-statistics)

Keith, Verna. 2009 "A Colorstruck World: Skin Tone, Achievement, and Self Esteem among African American Women." Pp. 25–39 in *Shades of Difference: Why Skin Color Matters*, edited by E.N. Glenn. Stanford, CA: Stanford University Press.

King-O'Riain, Rebecca Chiyoko. 2006. *Pure Beauty: Judging Race in Japanese Beauty Pageants*. Minneapolis: University of Minnesota Press.

Kwan, Samantha. 2010. "Navigating Public Spaces: Gender, Race, and Body Privilege in Everyday Life." *Feminist Formations* 22(2):144–66.

Mears, Ashley. 2011. *Pricing Beauty: The Making of a Fashion Model*. Berkeley: University of California Press.

Mears, Ashley, and Catherine Connell. 2015. "Paradoxical Value in Deviant Cases: Toward a Gendered Theory of Display Work." *Signs* 41(2):333–59.

Merianos, Ashley L., Rebecca A. Vidourek, and Keith A. King. 2013. "Medicalization of Female Beauty: A Content Analysis of Cosmetic Procedures." *Qualitative Report* 18(46):1–14.

Moreno Figueroa, Monica G. 2013. "Displaced Looks: The Lived Experience of Beauty and Racism." *Feminist Theory* 14(2):137–51.

Mosse, George. L. 1985. *Nationalism and Sexuality*. Madison: University of Wisconsin Press.

Murray, Samantha. 2009. "'Banded Bodies': the Somatechnics of Gastric Banding." Pp. 153–67 in *Somatechnics: Queering the Technologisation of Bodies*, edited by N. Sullivan and S. Murray. Burlington, VT: Ashgate.

Otis, Eileen. 2012. *Markets and Bodies: Women, Service Work, and the Making of Inequality in China*. Stanford, CA: Stanford University Press.

Peiss, Kathy. 1998. *Hope in a Jar: The Making of America's Beauty Culture*. New York: Metropolitan Books.

Rivers-Moore, Megan. 2013. "Affective Sex: Beauty, Race and Nation in the Sex Industry." *Feminist Theory* 14(2):153–69.

Roberts, Blain. 2014. *Pageants, Parlors, and Pretty Women: Race and Beauty in the Twentieth Century South*. Chapel Hill: University of North Carolina Press.

Rondilla, Joanne L. 2009. "Filipinos and the Color Complex: Ideal Asian Beauty." Pp. 63–80 in *Shades of Difference: Why Skin Color Matters*, edited by E.N. Glenn. Stanford, CA: Stanford University Press.

Rooks, Noliwe. 1996. *Hair Raising: Beauty, Culture, and African American Women*. New Brunswick, NJ: Rutgers University Press.

Saguy, Abigail C. 2013. *What's Wrong with Fat?* New York: Oxford University Press.

Sanchez Taylor, Jacqueline. 2012. "Buying and Selling Breasts: Cosmetic Surgery, Beauty Treatments and Risk." *Sociological Review* 60(4):635–53.

Saraswati, L. Ayu. 2010. "Cosmopolitan Whiteness: The Effects and Affects of Skin-Whitening Advertisements in a Transnational Women's Magazine in Indonesia." *Meridians* 10(2):15–41.

Shilling, Chris. 1993. *The Body and Social Theory*. Thousand Oaks, CA: Sage.

Skeggs, Beverley. 1997. *Formations of Class & Gender*. Thousand Oaks, CA: Sage.

Storr, Merl. 2002. "Classy Lingerie." *Feminist Review* 71:18–36.

Talley, Heather Laine. 2014. *Saving Face: Disfigurement and the Politics of Appearance*. New York: New York University Press.

Tate, Shirley. 2013. "The Performativity of Black Beauty Shame in Jamaica and Its Diaspora: Problematising and Transforming Beauty Iconicities." *Feminist Theory* 14(2):219–35.

Taussig, Michael. 2012. *Beauty and the Beast*. Chicago: University of Chicago.

Tice, Karen W. 2012. *Queens of Academe: Beauty Pageantry, Student Bodies, and College Life*. New York: Oxford University Press.

Turner, Bryan S. 1984. *The Body and Society: Explorations in Social Theory*. New York: Oxford University Press.

Vaid, Jyotsna. 2009. "Fair Enough? Color and the Commodification of Self in Indian Matrimonials." Pp. 148–65 in *Shades of Difference: Why Skin Color Matters*, edited by E.N. Glenn. Stanford, CA: Stanford University Press.

Warhurst, Chris, Dennis Nickson, Ann Witz, and Anne Marie Cullen. 2000. "Aesthetic Labour in Interactive Service Work: Some Case Study Evidence from the 'New' Glasgow." *The Service Industries Journal* 20(3):1–18.

Williams, Christine, and Catherine Connell. 2010. "'Looking Good and Sounding Right': Aesthetic Labor and Social Inequality in the Retail Industry." *Work & Occupations* 37(3):349–77.

Wissinger, Elizabeth A. 2015. *This Year's Model: Fashion Media and the Making of Glamour*. New York: New York University Press.

Yang, Jie. 2011. "Nennu and Shunu: Gender, Body Politics, and the Beauty Economy in China." *Signs* 36(2):333–57.

31

Gender performance

Cheerleaders, drag kings, and the rest of us

Joshua Gamson and Laura Grindstaff

Introduction

Social theorists have long noted that people aren't simply male or female, rather they "do" gender. Gender is neither a fixed nor an essential property of the self but an outcome of ongoing performances in various interactional and institutional contexts. Gender, along with other axes of social difference, helps constitute the culture of everyday life and is central to the implicit codes that guide "normative" conduct (West and Zimmerman 1987; Butler 1990; West and Fenstermaker 1995). Sociologists have further noted that gender is a social structure, notably a patriarchal structure that men dominate and benefit from. People don't import gendered selves into neutral institutions; institutions themselves are gendered in the ways they organize and coordinate social life (Connell 1987; Acker 1990; Martin 1990; Lorber 1994; Messner 2002; Ridgeway 2011; Jenness and Fenstermaker 2014). Martin (2003) has usefully distinguished between "practicing gender" (the micro-level talk and action that signifies gender, often fleetingly and/or unintentionally) and "gendering practices" (the institutionalized ideas, structures, and behavioral repertoires that help to organize gender more systematically). The interplay between practicing gender and gendering practices is complex: each informs and shapes the other, the former reminding us of the possibilities of agency, creativity, and resistance; the latter reminding us of the macro structures that shape and constrain individual action.

This chapter works within and against these sociological traditions to explore the concept of "gender performance." On one level, gender is always performative: individuals repeatedly express and renew their taken-for-granted commitments to gender as they go about their daily lives. Goffman's (1959) theatrical metaphor – of the world as a stage peopled by actors, in roles, enacting scripts and so forth – suggests that individuals manage their own conduct in light of normative expectations on the part of real or imagined audiences about what it means to be male or female. Gender is thus always already a performance, and never entirely voluntary, even though it may feel "natural" and be largely unconscious.

But what about situations in which gender is not simply *accomplished* in everyday interaction but actively *displayed* in front of deliberately constructed audiences? What about situations in which gender scripts are not implicit but explicit – when the theatrical metaphor is no longer metaphorical? With some exceptions (see Alexander 2004), sociologists have had less to say about this more literal version of gender performance, largely because of the need to establish the point that gender performances are not the occasional endeavor of particular actors but something we all do all the time.

In fact, it is useful to conceptualize two quite different, if overlapping, sorts of gender performance. On one end of the spectrum is *performing gender*, in which the doing of gender is an implicit dimension of everyday action oriented toward some other purpose (as when women smile more often than their male counterparts in business meetings); at the other end is *gender performance*, in which the main purpose of interaction is the explicit dramatization of gender (as in a strip show). In the latter scenario, although participants are also performing gender in the interactive sense, the expression of gender is heightened, exaggerated, scripted, ritualized, and/or institutionalized in particular ways. Often there is a designated space for the performance, a collective organization of people to make it happen, a stage, costumes, props, and a clear distinction between performers and audience. These elements help construct a specific *culture* around and through which the gender performance unfolds.

We focus here primarily on explicit gender performance, using the concept to highlight the ongoing negotiations and tensions involved in doing gender in the broader sense. When gender performances are exaggerated and ritualized, they render the codes by which gendered norms and practices are constructed particularly visible, both to audiences and to participants themselves. Depending on the context, gender performances may either reinscribe traditional ways of doing gender or model new modes of gender enactment. Occasions for reflecting on – and critiquing – gender arise in either case, because exaggeration can foreground the power relations that tacit performances tend to obscure. Thus, far from merely calling attention to the gendered scripts at play in everyday life, gender performances do important cultural work of their own.

Of course, not all gender performances are alike, nor do they all do the same kind of cultural work. Certain cultural settings ritualize performance in ways that solidify the normal, taken-for-granted "rules" of gender, making these rules more apprehensible, thus encouraging their acceptance by both participants and audiences. We think of these as *inside-gender performances*. Inside-gender performances appear more natural because, in Alexander's (2004) terms, they "fuse" their cultural scripts with the background assumptions of audiences. Consider beauty pageants, which typically embody carefully scripted, normative ideologies about gender in concert with race and nation. As Banet-Weiser (1999:26) notes, the Miss America pageant has for most of its history actively constructed a national feminine identity based upon notions of "respectable" femininity, "typical" (white, Western) beauty, and a neoliberal "tolerance" for diversity that accommodates rather than highlights cultural, ethnic, and racial difference. A similar woman-as-nation trope, in which an "idealized" femininity and an "idealized" national ethnic identity mutually constitute one another, is observable in pageants for women of specific ethnic subgroups within the US – including Chinese Americans (Wu 1997), Japanese Americans (King-O'Riain 2006), and African Americans (Craig 2002) – as well as for pageants outside the West in countries such as India (Ahmed-Ghosh 2003), Guatemala (Schackt 2005), Nigeria (Balogun 2012), and Venezuela (Ochoa 2014). Although definitions of womanhood and nationhood vary by time and place, beauty contests generally represent, in distilled form, what it means to perform gender (here, femininity) "properly" on a given national or international stage. Other inside-gender sites such as proms (Best 2000), weddings (Nishimura 1996; Otnes and Pleck 2003; Ingraham [1999] 2008), debutante balls (Lynch 1999), and the "institutional core" of men's professional sport (Messner 2002), likewise articulate traditional gender scripts even as they may simultaneously afford opportunities for critique.

By contrast, some gender performances are organized in ways that primarily display, play with, challenge, and/or expose the very construction of gender itself. Here, the social rules of gender are not necessarily fused with background expectations; they may be displayed to an audience for the purpose of highlighting, subverting, or transforming their constructed nature. We think of these as *outside-gender performances*. Drag shows are a prime example. As Taylor, Rupp, and Gamson (2004:107) note, drag shows are arranged precisely to "call attention to the role of cultural markers and practices such as dress, bodily style, gesture, and voice, in constructing gender and sexual difference," thus "destabilizing institutionalized gender and sexological clas-sifications by making visible their social basis and by presenting hybrid and minority genders and sexualities" (see also Schacht 2002; Rupp, Taylor, and Shapiro 2010; Baker and Kelly 2016). Similarly, various musical performance traditions – glam rock (Auslander 2006), some elements of "conscious rap" and "feminist hip-hop" (Collins 2006; Rose 2008), disco (Gamson 2005), and alternative rock (Schippers 2002) – intentionally undercut or critique gender assumptions.

The same performance can simultaneously be "inside gender" in one sense and "outside gender" in another. For all the ways that beauty pageants normalize traditional gender differ-ence, their public nature also arguably invites critique of that difference. Non-Western pageants in particular call attention to widely varying notions of "ideal" womanhood/nationhood (see Cohen, Wilk, and Stoeltje 1996; Banet-Weiser 1999), as does the participation of transgender women in beauty pageants (see Ochoa 2014). Indeed, it is likely typical for gender performances to be both "inside" and "outside" to varying degrees. The institutional context may gener-ate an "inside" (gender-conformist) performance, while the performers' own conscious agency may add "outside" (gender-transgressive) elements; a performance intended as "outside" may be read by some audiences as "inside"; a performance may be "inside" in some of its ideological elements and "outside" in others. Understanding these inside-outside dynamics – the relative strengths of the traditional and transgressive aspects of the performance, and why the balance between them looks as it does – is our central analytic task. Through a detailed look at cheer-leading (a predominantly inside-gender genre) and drag shows (a predominantly outside-gender genre), we illustrate the utility of analyzing gender performances as sites of tension between conformity and nonconformity – ultimately, between accepting or challenging prevailing power arrangements.

Cheerleading: inside-gender performance

Cheerleading is ideally suited to analyzing the complexities of "inside-gender" performances. Of late nineteenth-century Ivy League origins, cheerleading was once an all-male, exclusively white activity designed to foster and discipline spectator involvement in American collegiate football; it became gradually "feminized" and by the 1960s had come to symbolize feminine attractiveness and popularity (Hanson 1995). The growth of "professional" cheerleading in the 1970s (e.g., the Dallas Cowboys Cheerleaders) served to solidify this image. "Doing gender" in the context of cheerleading meant enacting a feminine script that emphasizes supportiveness, enthusiasm, and sex appeal – what Connell (1987) calls "emphasized femininity." By definition this script also privileged heterosexuality and middle-class whiteness in a cultural if not strictly demographic sense. For much of the twentieth century "the cheerleader" stood as an idealized symbol of "typical" American girlhood; becoming a cheerleader meant adopting an inside-gender performance – as a woman on the sidelines supporting her man.

Although professional cheerleading has deviated little from this conventional script over the years, school-based cheerleading was reinvented in the wake of second-wave feminism, when notions of "ideal" girlhood began changing to incorporate the "masculine" qualities of com-petitiveness and athleticism. Today cheerleading is more popular than ever precisely because it adapted to this new ideal. In particular, the rise of competitive cheerleading (executing routines before judges in competitions against other squads), which school squads have embraced in addition to their sideline role, has fueled the growth of "all-star" cheerleading. All-star cheer occurs outside scholastic contexts altogether; participants join for-profit gyms for the sole purpose of competing with other all-star teams. The skills of cheerleading now include high-level tumbling, stunting, and pyramid-building, as well as cheering and dancing. Once an auxiliary to sport, cheerleading has become more sport-like itself: participants call themselves "cheer athletes," the term "team" is replacing the more traditional "squad," and some schools offer athletic scholarships to cheerleaders (Grindstaff and West 2006). In December 2016, cheerleading received provisional recognition from the International Olympic Committee, paving the way for its inclusion as an official Olympic sport (Ruiz 2016). The ruling no doubt reflects the global spread of cheerleading as well as its increased athleticism. Once an "all-American" activity, cheerleading now spans all five continents. The International Cheerleading Union, formed in 2004, currently boasts 110 national federation members and hosts the annual World Cheerleading Championships (http://cheerunion.org/home/).

Given the turn toward sport in cheerleading, it remains an inside-gender performance for women primarily because social institutions have accommodated historical changes in feminine ideals, such that assertiveness and physical toughness join the more traditional qualities of supportiveness and physical attractiveness. Indeed, the cultural "work" of cheerleading may well be to continually reconcile old and new versions of emphasized femininity, to transform outside-gender scripts into inside-gender performances. The athleticism required of women in contemporary competitive cheerleading is gender-appropriate (emphasizing grace, flexibility, and peppy enthusiasm as well as speed, strength, and competitiveness) and packaged in gender-specific ways (short skirt, makeup, hair ribbons, etc.). In effect, cheerleading allows young women to have their cake and eat it too, claiming the status of athlete but without anyone questioning their sexuality or feminine credentials (Adams and Bettis 2004; Grindstaff and West 2006). It allows girls and young women to perform sexy girlishness and disciplined physicality at the same time; in fact, it now *demands* this combination, because without athleticism the sexy girl risks being labeled a slut, and without sex appeal the athlete risks being labeled a dyke. For female cheerleaders, then, the majority of whom appear to be straight, white, and middle class, the "rules" of cheerleading and of normative femininity remain more or less aligned.

But although cheerleading might be an inside-gender performance for young women overall, "insider-ness" is also a matter of degree. Working-class white women and women of color typically have greater difficulty occupying the role of "authentic" cheerleader because the codes of femininity underpinning it have historically been associated with middle-class whiteness (Adams and Bettis 2003; Grindstaff and West 2010). Even for middle-class white women, the "fit" between performing gender in cheerleading and doing gender in everyday life is hardly seamless. Interviews with female cheerleaders reveal a more ambivalent relation to the activity than the uniformity of the outward performance might suggest, with some inhabiting the requisite feminine script more or less effortlessly and others expressing a more instrumental stance in which the feminine appearance and performance demands are tolerated for the sake of getting around to the "real" business of winning competitions (Grindstaff and West 2006; Grindstaff and West 2010).

For male cheerleaders on coed teams, the relations between "doing gender" and "gender performance," and between inside- and outside-gender performances, are more complex still. Since cheerleading is now generally perceived to be feminine territory, the participation of men can be understood as an outside-gender performance to the extent that male involvement challenges conventional notions of what "real" men should do. Thus, inside-gender performance for women is an outside-gender performance for men – as long as those men are presumed to be straight. For gay men, however, cheerleading might be classified as an "inside-gender" performance because of the cultural tendency to conflate gender with sexuality and assume that gay men, by virtue of their "wrong" sexuality, are also insufficiently masculine and gravitate "naturally" to feminine activities such as cheerleading. Indeed, male cheerleaders are often presumed to be gay simply because of their participation in cheerleading (Grindstaff and West 2006).

In reality, whether cheerleading signals an inside- or outside-gender performance for men depends not on sexual orientation but on the style of masculinity enacted. Cheer teams, whether scholastic or all-star, affiliate with established cheerleading organizations that train coaches, run summer camps, and host competitions, with different organizations promoting different performative styles through their regulations and judging criteria. Some teams enforce a rigid division of labor between female and male cheerleaders and a highly "masculine" mode of performance for the latter (no dancing, no "flying," no specialized jumps, and minimal emotion work), such that men deliver a traditionally masculine "inside-gender" performance within the overall "feminine" context of cheerleading. By contrast, other teams promote "outside-gender" performances to varying degrees by encouraging male cheerleaders – regardless of sexual orientation – to dance, execute jumps, smile, and enact spirited enthusiasm. Here, men "do gender" in ways conventionally aligned with women – not because of personal disposition or identity but because of how masculinity has been stylized and institutionalized (see Anderson 2005; Grindstaff and West 2006).

Cheerleading also illustrates how inside-gender performances can inspire outside-gender challenges. Precisely because its gender scripts are explicit and (for women) highly normative, cheerleading has proved fertile ground for parodying/critiquing conventional gender expectations. The "Spartan Cheerleaders" of *Saturday Night Live* is a familiar example. But consider, too, the lesser-known phenomenon of "radical cheerleaders" that emerged in the 1990s – an international network of third-wave feminists who appropriated cheerleading to engage in political protest. Sporting alternative "uniforms" of combat boots, striped leggings, and spiked hair, they energized crowds at political demonstrations with raucous, expletive-filled "cheers" about a host of gender-justice issues, from rape and reproductive health to transgender rights and equal pay (Ferrar and Warner 2006; personal interviews conducted by Grindstaff). Here, the fact that cheerleading seemingly epitomizes inside-gender femininity provides the basis for its feminist retooling.

Drag shows: outside-gender performance

Drag – on the streets or on a stage – is intentionally a show about gender, in which participants treat gender as a costume and gender roles as theatrical ones, building their performances around gender scripts. Drag comes in many forms, some that emphasize "passing" and others that reject that practice. The literature on drag performances reflects this diversity: some researchers conclude that "performances often draw on hegemonic gender norms and work to reinforce normative gender identities" while other researchers suggest that "drag queens pose a politicized challenge to beliefs about gender and sexuality in their performances" (Shapiro 2007:251; see also Dolan 1985; Schacht 2002; Rupp and Taylor 2003). And although there is overlap between the two cultures, drag queen shows do not necessarily do the same cultural work as drag king shows, which often eschew exaggeration for "the understatement of the male body" (Koenig 2002:150) and build on the lesbian-specific history of butch-femme roles, with its unique set of tensions surrounding "authenticity, performance quality, and transgression" and range of performances of female masculinity (Surkan 2002:168; see also Halberstam 1998; Baker and Kelly 2016). These different forms of drag testify to the diverse purposes to which gender performance can be put.

Historically, socially, and institutionally, however, drag shows are and have been primarily "outsider" performances, morphing from nineteenth-century female impersonation into central genres within marginalized sexual communities in the twentieth century, first at urban "balls" (Chauncey 1994) and later in gay male bars, only then becoming entertainment for straight audiences as well (Rupp and Taylor 2003). Drag kinging, with "female-bodied people performing masculinities," took hold in some American lesbian communities in the 1990s (Shapiro 2007; Baker and Kelly 2016). Drag typically aims to disrupt the gender-sexuality order by calling attention to the construction of gender. Indeed, even "impersonation" highlights the possibility that gender is an illusion. Drag performances have "a long history in same-sex communities as vehicles for the expression of gay identity and culture, the creation and maintenance of solidarity, and the staging of political resistance" (Taylor et al. 2004:107); some in the US might even be considered "counterpublic terrorism," highlighting "the nation's internal terrors around race, gender, and sexuality" (Muñoz 1999:100, 107; see also Bailey 2014).

The drag show is thus arguably the most outsider kind of gender performance, the mirror of cheerleading and beauty pageants. Taylor et al. (2004:113, 115–20) argue that the Key West drag shows they studied function as "protest episodes" and "oppositional performances" rather than "rituals of cultural affirmation." In the first place, these performances *contest* the gender status quo, rejecting or mocking traditional gender and sexuality, often appropriating dominant gender and sexual codes but using them to "construct a hybrid and more fluid model of gender and sexuality" (Taylor et al. 2004:117). Second, the drag queens *intend* to perform protest, consciously deploying sexuality to disturb gender and sexual categories, and making overt political points from the stage. Finally, the performances represent and enact collective identity for both performers and audiences, by expressing gay solidarity and challenging audiences to question, reach across, and expand gender and sexual identity classifications. Audience members often described a utopian sense of "the way it could be" (Taylor et al. 2004:128). Drag shows like these serve as transformative outside-gender performances for performers and audiences alike.

Yet even within drag we can see the tension between conformity and transgression. Although drag shows are outside-gender performances, they also contain "inside" elements. More significantly, outside-gender performances always, unavoidably, contain normative cultural assumptions about gender and sexuality – if sometimes only to counter them – and thus both articulate contradictory ideological components and leave room for a range of audience interpretations. For instance, drag performers "use the cultural equation of the penis with maleness to mix up gender categories" (Taylor et al. 2004:118), juxtaposing the "male" body (revealed through nudity or facial hair) to women's costume and persona in order to generate gender confusion. Yet this equation of genitals and gender is precisely one of the bedrock assumptions of the gender order (Lorber 1994). Similarly, the project of creating and expressing gay solidarity and collective identity often requires a sort of gender essentialism, an assertion that, as one performer put it to the audience, "We may look like women, but we're all homosexual men" (Taylor et al. 2004:125). For audience members, moreover, gender may not so much be radically destabilized or revealed as an ongoing performance, but instead become integrated into a liberal message of unity and tolerance across stable gender and sexual categories.

Outside-gender performances are often also in tension with the various other social identities to which gender and sexuality are inextricably linked. Observers of the reality television program *RuPaul's Drag Race* have noted, for instance, that drag performers often use racial and ethnic stereotypes to "strike comedic gold" (Strings and Bui 2013:829) and are rewarded for doing so (Zhang 2016). The stereotypical association of Asian men with femininity, for instance, allows gay Asian American drag queens "to better convince judges and audience members that they have achieved *realness*," such that they "trade the more stigmatized status of race with a less stigmatized status of queen using precisely the characteristics that lead to their stigmatization in the first place" (Han 2015:148). In this context of racialized gender expectations, an outside-gender performance becomes a stigma-management and status-elevating opportunity that emphasizes rather than undercuts conventional femininity (Han 2015).

In drag shows, we can again see how specific institutional locations impact gender performances and their reception. Drag performances often take place within recognizably "gay spaces," where outside-gender consciousness is accepted and even encouraged. But they may also occur in more commercial, "straight" venues, which neither support challenges to gender politics nor encourage audiences to connect their own everyday performances of gender to those onstage. Even here, however, political gender expression may enter under the cover of "just entertainment," as performers build politics into shows for audiences who might elsewhere be unreceptive (Taylor et al. 2004). Such covert politics can characterize a range of commercial settings, even hypermasculine ones like Mexican professional wrestling, known as *lucha libre*, which features *exoticos*, professional wrestlers who perform in drag as one means of offering audiences "a spectacular performance." The conventions of the genre as "a dramatic representation of machismo" position *exoticos* as figures of ridicule and contempt who are also serious wrestlers. These same conventions allow *exoticos*, through their appropriation of feminine signs, to "dominate and vacate the masculinity of 'real' men," and "problematize the idea of the ring as a masculine space" (Levi 1998:279, 282). Thus, specific venues structure gender performances in particular ways, reflecting differing degrees of fusion and defusion between scripts, performers, and audiences.

Shapiro (2007:256–7) reaches a similar conclusion in her study of a feminist drag king troupe, whose shows included both verbal and performed challenges to gender (cheerleading routines by "women" with facial hair, "men" in outfits revealing breasts, butch women, effeminate men, and so forth), and where members' gender identities were transformed through their participation. It was drag in its particular *organizational and ideological context* that challenged the gender order; drag's "disruptive power" was harnessed mainly because the troupe had given organizational form to an oppositional, collective feminist identity. Gender performances are structured – opportunities provided, limits set – by the synergy between performers' agency and the features of their institutional location.

Conclusion

We have argued for the sociological relevance of explicit gender performances, in which an institutionalized performance culture codifies, scripts, and heightens gender expressions – along a range from "inside gender" to "outside gender" events. Explicit performances, through their exaggeration, can make visible the ongoing dynamics of "doing gender" in everyday life: they spotlight the gender expectations to which we are routinely subject and the organizational and institutional mechanisms subtending these scripts. Along the way, they may model alternative ways of doing gender outside taken-for-granted routines. Gender performances are not, therefore, merely exaggerated versions of everyday modes of gender enactment. Foregrounding the difference between doing and performing, they facilitate a distinctive type of cultural work. This work is tied to questions of power: whereas the everyday doing of gender typically renders power relations as "natural" and invisible, explicit gender performances can help reveal power – sometimes only to reaffirm it (as in certain forms of cheerleading) and sometimes to create new paths for change (as in certain forms of drag). Significantly, gender performances usually do both simultaneously to varying degrees. This cultural work is shaped partly by the specific genres and institutional settings in which performances take place; generic conventions and institutional practices can encourage or discourage the affirmation or transgression of the gendered status quo. In this sense, the "gender code" and the "genre code" of a performance are related but not synonymous attributes. While the former channels particular ideas and practices related to gender scripts, the latter provides specific scaffolding within and upon which gender construction takes place.

Gender performances underscore the insight of queer theorist Judith Butler (1990) that gender is an iterative code predicated upon repetition and mimesis for its sense of solidity and consistency. To say that gender is a copy with no original does not deny its real presence and effects but instead insists that there is no fixed, objective ground from which to judge the relation between "normative" and "alternative" incarnations of gender. Masculinity presupposes, depends upon, and helps constitute femininity, and vice versa – whether or not these mutual interdependences are consciously acknowledged and understood. Gender repetition is necessary precisely because dependence on "the Other" puts "the Self" at perpetual risk of destabilization. The concept of gender performance can, and often does, foreground the possibility of destabilizing gender scripts, selves, and institutions.

References

Acker, Joan. 1990. "Hierarchies, Jobs, Bodies: A Theory of Gendered Organizations." *Gender & Society* 4(2):139–58.

Adams, Natalie, and Pamela Bettis. 2003. "Commanding the Room in Short Skirts: Cheering as the Embodiment of Ideal Girlhood." *Gender & Society* 17(1):73–91.

———. 2004. *Cheerleader!* New York: Macmillan.

Ahmed-Ghosh, H. 2003. "Writing the Nation on the Beauty Queen's Body: Implications for a 'Hindu' Nation." *Meridians: Feminism, Race, Transnationalism* 4(1):205–27.

Alexander, Jeffrey. 2004. "Cultural Pragmatics: Social Performance Between Ritual and Strategy." *Sociological Theory* 22(4):527–73.

Anderson, Eric. 2005. "Orthodox and Inclusive Masculinity." *Sociological Perspectives* 48(3):337–55.

Auslander, Philip. 2006. *Performing Glam Rock.* Ann Arbor: University of Michigan Press.

Bailey, Marlon. 2014. *Butch Queens Up in Pumps: Gender, Performance, and Ballroom Culture in Detroit.* Ann Arbor: University of Michigan Press.

Baker, Ashley, and Kimberly Kelly. 2016. "Live Like a King, Y'all: Gender Negotiation and the Performance of Masculinity among Southern Drag Kings." *Sexualities* 19(2):46–63.

Balogun, Oluwakemi M. 2012. "Cultural and Cosmopolitan Idealized Femininity and Embodied Nationalism in Nigerian Beauty Pageants." *Gender & Society* 26(3):357–81.

Banet-Weiser, Sarah. 1999. *The Most Beautiful Girl in the World: Beauty Pageants and National Identity.* Berkeley: University of California Press.

Best, Amy. 2000. *Prom Night.* New York: Routledge.

Butler, Judith. 1990. *Gender Trouble.* New York: Routledge.

Chauncey, George. 1994. *Gay New York.* New York: Basic Books.

Cohen, Colleen Ballerino, Richard Wilk, and Beverly Stoeltje, eds. 1996. *Beauty Queens on the Global Stage.* New York: Routledge.

Collins, Patricia Hill. 2006. *From Black Power to Hip Hop.* Philadelphia, PA: Temple University Press.

Connell, Robert W. 1987. *Gender and Power.* Stanford, CA: Stanford University Press.

Craig, Maxine. 2002. *Ain't I A Beauty Queen? Black Women, Beauty, and the Politics of Race.* New York: Oxford University Press.

Dolan, Jill. 1985. "Gender Impersonation Onstage: Destroying or Maintaining the Mirror of Gender Roles?" *Women and Performance* 2:5–11.

Ferrar, Margaret, and Jamie Warner. 2006. "Rah-Rah Radical: The Radical Cheerleaders' Challenge to the Public Sphere." *Politics & Gender* 2(3):281–302.

Gamson, Joshua. 2005. *The Fabulous Sylvester.* New York: Henry Holt.

Goffman, Erving. 1959. *The Presentation of Self in Everyday Life*. New York: Anchor Books.

Grindstaff, Laura, and Emily West. 2006. "Cheerleading and the Gendered Politics of Sport." *Social Problems* 53(4):500–18.

———. 2010. "Hands on Hips, Smiles on Lips! Gender, Race, and the Performance of 'Spirit' in Cheerleading." *Text & Performance Quarterly* 30(2):143–62.

Halberstam, J. 1998. *Female Masculinity*. Durham, NC: Duke University Press.

Han, C. Winter. 2015. *Geisha of a Different Kind: Race and Sexuality in Gaysian America*. New York: NYU Press.

Hanson, Mary Ellen. 1995. *Go! Fight! Win! Cheerleading in American Culture*. Bowling Green, OH: Bowling Green State University Popular Press.

Ingraham, Chrys. [1999] 2008. *White Weddings*, 2nd ed. New York: Routledge.

Jenness, Valerie, and Sarah Fenstermaker. 2014. "Agnes Goes to Prison: Gender Authenticity, Transgender Inmates in Prisons for Men, and the Pursuit of the 'Real Deal.'" *Gender & Society* 28(1):5–31.

King-O'Riain, Rebecca. 2006. *Pure Beauty: Judging Race in Japanese American Beauty Pageants*. Minneapolis: University of Minnesota Press.

Koenig, Sheila "Dragon Fly." 2002. "Walk Like a Man: Enactments and Embodiments of Masculinity and the Potential for Multiple Genders." *Journal of Homosexuality* 43(3/4):145–59.

Levi, Heather. 1998. "Lean Mean Fighting Queens: Drag in the World of Mexican Professional Wrestling." *Sexualities* 1(3):275–85.

Lorber, Judith. 1994. *Paradoxes of Gender*. New Haven, CT: Yale University Press.

Lynch, Annette. 1999. *Dress, Gender and Cultural Change: Asian American and African American Rites of Passage*. Oxford: Berg.

Martin, Patricia Yancey. 1990. "Rethinking Feminist Organizations." *Gender & Society* 4(2):182–206.

———. 2003. "'Said and Done' Versus 'Saying and Doing': Gendering Practices, Practicing Gender at Work." *Gender & Society* 17(3):342–66.

Messner, Michael. 2002. *Taking the Field*. Minneapolis: University of Minnesota Press.

Muñoz, José Esteban. 1999. *Disidentifications*. Minneapolis: University of Minnesota Press.

Nishimura, Yuko. 1996. "South Indian Wedding Rituals. A Comparison of Gender Hierarchy." *Anthropos* 91(4/6):411–23.

Ochoa, Marcia. 2014. *Queen For a Day: Transformistas, Beauty Queens, and the Performance of Femininity in Venezuela*. Durham, NC: Duke University Press.

Otnes, Cele, and Elizabeth Hafkin Pleck. 2003. *Cinderella Dreams*. Berkeley: University of California Press.

Ridgeway, Cecilia. 2011. *Framed by Gender: How Gender Inequality Persists in the Modern World*. New York: Oxford University Press.

Rose, Tricia. 2008. *The Hip-Hop Wars*. New York: Basic Civitas Books.

Rupp, Leila, and Verta Taylor. 2003. *Drag Queens at the 801 Cabaret*. Chicago: University of Chicago Press.

Rupp, Leila, Verta Taylor, and Eve Shapiro. 2010. "Drag Queens and Drag Kings: The Difference Gender Makes." *Sexualities* 13(3):275–94.

Ruiz, Rebecca. 2016. "Cheerleading and Muay Thai Given Provisional Olympic Status." *New York Times*, December 6. (www.nytimes.com/2016/12/06/sports/olympics/cheerleading-muay-thai-provisional-olympic-status.html).

Schacht, Steven P. 2002. "Turnabout: Gay Drag Queens and the Masculine Embodiment of the Feminine." Pp. 155–70 in *Revealing Male Bodies*, edited by N. Tuana, W. Cowling, M. Hamington, G. Johnson, and T. MacMullen. Bloomington: Indiana University Press.

Schackt, J. 2005. "Mayahood Through Beauty: Indian Beauty Pageants in Guatemala." *Bulletin of Latin American Research* 24(3):269–87.

Schippers, Mimi. 2002. *Rockin' Out of the Box*. New Brunswick, NJ: Rutgers University Press.

Shapiro, Eve. 2007. "Drag Kinging and the Transformation of Gender Identities." *Gender & Society* 21(2):250–71.

Strings, Sabrina, and Long T. Bui. 2013. "'She Is Not Acting, She Is': The Conflict between Gender and Racial Realness in *RuPaul's Drag Race*." *Feminist Media Studies* 14(5):822–36.

Surkan, Kim. 2002. "Drag Kings in the New Wave." *Journal of Homosexuality* 43(3/4):161–83.

Taylor, Verta, Leila Rupp, and Joshua Gamson. 2004. "Performing Protest: Drag Shows as Tactical Repertoire of the Gay and Lesbian Movement." Pp. 105–38 in *Research in Social Movements, Conflicts, and Change*. Vol. 25, *Authority in Contention*, edited by D.J. Myers and D.M. Cress. Bingley: Emerald Group.

West, Candace, and Sarah Fenstermaker. 1995. "Doing Difference." *Gender & Society* 9(1):8–37.

West, Candace, and Don Zimmerman. 1987. "Doing Gender." *Gender & Society* 1(2):125–51.

Wu, Judy Tzu-Chun. 1997. "Loveliest Daughter of Our Ancient Cathay! Representations of Ethnic and Gender Identity in the Miss Chinatown USA Beauty Pageant." *Journal of Social History* 31(1):5–31.

Zhang, Eric. 2016. "Memoirs of a GAY! Sha: Race and Gender Performance on *RuPauls' Drag Race*." *Studies in Costume & Performance* 1(1):59–75.

32

Rituals, repertoires, and performances in postmodernity

A cultural-sociological account

Ronald N. Jacobs

Introduction

In many respects, cultural sociology was established through the study of ritual. For Durkheim, ritual was the central social process that bonded the individual to society. At the same time, rituals served to reinforce core social values, through the division of the world into the two basic categories of sacred and profane. As a particular mode of action, ritual infuses culture with collective energy and affectivity, which increase its power and its ability to enact an identification of the individual with society.

In more recent times, however, scholars have criticized Durkheim's ritual theory for its functionalist assumptions. In the process, they have worked to rethink the connection between ritual and meaning in a way less mechanistic and more open to contingency, strategic action, and historical specificity. This chapter reviews these attempts through a critical examination of the work of Swidler, Bourdieu, Collins, and Alexander. Swidler and Bourdieu emphasize how ritual events facilitate strategic action as well as social integration. Collins and Alexander focus on the contingency of the ritual event, attempting to explain why some rituals are more successful than others. I illustrate the relative advantages that each approach offers by focusing on a single empirical case: the Olympic Games.

Durkheim on ritual

For Durkheim, rituals serve to integrate individuals into society through the production of social solidarity. Social attachment occurs through two related social processes. First, ritual functions by marking off and separating the sacred from the profane. This is a spatial, temporal, and cognitive division. Rituals serve to identify sacred places, sacred times, sacred events, and sacred symbols. Profane things are kept at a distance from the realm of the sacred, through a series of prohibitions that Durkheim ([1912] 1995:303–20) called "negative rites." These prohibitions make it easier to separate sacred things from the mundane world, providing a heightened affective environment where the social group can more easily reaffirm itself (Durkheim [1912] 1995:391). Ultimately – and this, for Durkheim, is the essential element of religion – the relationship between sacred things attains a systematic coherence, which is accepted and shared by all members of society. At this point, society becomes a collective reality acting upon individuals, inculcated within each individual as memories of the sacred.

In order for society to imprint itself in individuals, Durkheim insisted, these memories of the sacred need to be re-established and energized by a continuing cycle of ritual events. Rather than leaving the social bond as a purely cognitive entity, the cycle of rituals works to infuse social solidarity with emotion, affectivity, and collective effervescence. These events, which concentrate the public's attention on a common space and gather individuals into a shared communion of co-presence, are just as important for secular society as they are for more "religious" ones (Durkheim [1912] 1995:429). Durkheim believed that it was possible for the core integrative processes of religion to be transposed onto the more secular society of the modern nation-state. This shift would require a new cycle of celebrations, in which citizens take time out from their daily lives to join in a common communion, a celebration of a common past and a common future, and an affirmation of a common system of sacred symbols and meanings. Increasingly, as Dayan and Katz (1992) have argued persuasively, these moments of communion would be coordinated in and through media.

Dayan and Katz point to the Olympic Games as an example of a media event that performs the ritual functions that Durkheim identified. In the most recent Rio Olympics, 3.5 billion viewers – more than half of the world's population – tuned in to watch. In Brazil, more than 90 percent of the country's population watched at least part of the games. Similar concentrations of viewers could be found throughout South America and throughout the world.

There are a number of reasons why media events such as the Olympic Games are such powerful rituals, in a Durkheimian sense. First, they mark off sacred from mundane time through the interruption of normal broadcasting schedules. Furthermore, viewers tend to experience the Olympics as a form of communion, watching the events with other people, in shared time as well as shared space. Indeed, one of the distinguishing features of media *events*, as compared to ordinary media programming, is that audiences tend to gather in order to witness the event together, in the same social space, whether in a friend's family room, a hotel lounge, or a neighborhood bar. In the host city, in fact, viewers often gather by the thousands in designated parks and other common viewing areas to share in the collective energy and excitement of the ritual event. There is a fusion of society as people celebrate national triumphs and reaffirm the core values that the Olympics symbolize – achievement, sacrifice, cooperation, national greatness, and a specific kind of competitive international solidarity.

Although Durkheim's ritual theory clearly has a lot of descriptive and explanatory power, it also displays a number of weaknesses. Lukes (1975) argued forcefully that the integrative effects of civic ritual tend to be assumed rather than demonstrated empirically. In fact, Lukes argued, many people in modern society are either apathetic to ritual events or explicitly hostile to them. Lukes also argued, as did Tilly (1981), that Durkheim's ritual theory completely ignored power and conflict. For Lukes and Tilly, rituals are always organized by specific groups who have specific interests, and their meaning and authority is almost always challenged by competing groups. Indeed, this process was played out repeatedly throughout 2016 during the Olympic torch relay, as protesters used that ritual to challenge Brazil on a variety of issues, most notably its problems with corruption, unemployment, inequality, and police violence. As these events demonstrated, ritual is a site of struggle, with no guarantee of success.

The contingent and strategic basis of ritual was emphasized in a different way by Goffman (e.g., [1956] 1959, 1967), who focused on the work individuals need to do in order to manage their public image in interaction. He suggested a shift in orientation, away from the large public rituals that Durkheim emphasized and toward (1) the small, everyday rituals in which individuals negotiate their own presentation of selves, and (2) the small rituals of deference where they help others to create successful frontstage performances of self. Here, shared meanings and collective emotions of ritual are de-emphasized in favor of a focus on the strategic activities whereby individuals use ritual events to their own personal advantage. This emphasis encouraged a conceptual shift – from ritual to repertoire, and from rule to strategy.

From ritual to repertoire: Swidler and the cultural toolkit

Swidler's main contribution to ritual theory lay in a conceptual shift, to focus on how culture provides a common repertoire of habits, skills, and styles from which people can develop their own specific "strategies of action." Culture provides a pragmatic "toolkit," which "consists of symbols, stories, rituals, and worldviews, which people may use in varying configurations to solve different kinds of problems" (Swidler 1986:273). According to Swidler, the model of a unified, systematic, and coherent cultural system was mistaken; in its place, she suggested, theory should begin from the recognition that "real cultures" contain multiple and usually conflicting symbols and rituals, which actors draw upon in diverse ways in order to craft their own, context-specific guides to action (1986:277).

The second component of Swidler's theory derives from the distinction she made between "settled" and "unsettled" times. During settled times, there is a lower degree of commitment to the symbols and rituals that make up the common culture, and people can use the different elements of culture and ritual in more strategic ways, in a style that resembles what Goffman analyzed as impression management. On the other hand, during unsettled periods, culture acquires an added significance and power, as groups try to create new rituals that will reorganize the habits and modes of perception that individuals use to create their individual strategies of action. But these attempts are by no means guaranteed to succeed, because the fact that society is in flux means that competing groups will be deploying alternative rituals, designed to emphasize competing ideologies and cultural formations.

Returning to the Olympic Games and its cultural impact, Swidler's distinction between settled and unsettled times can help explain why different nation-states might have varying levels of effectiveness when they try to use the games to reproduce a strong sense of national unity. In nations that are in a "settled" period, the commitment to ritual should tend to be lower, as should the demand for cultural coherence. These conditions would create extra challenges for crafting a common cultural framework for a unified solidarity, because individuals would be likely to deploy the Olympics in a variety of ways, in order to advance specific strategies of action. Thus, many people watched streaming video of the games while sitting at their desks – not as a ritual of solidarity, but rather to avoid work. At home, they also may avoid the communion aspect of the ritual, recording the broadcast to watch it at their convenience, and so they can skip parts of the broadcast they find boring. In effect, they rely on the same habits and strategies of action that regulate their everyday lives. There is no reinforcement of shared values, no collective effervescence, and no social solidarity.

This is not to say that ritualistic dimensions of the viewing experience are wholly absent in more "stable" societies. Many viewers do, in fact, experience a heightened emotional and cultural connection when watching the games, just as a Durkheimian perspective would suggest. In other words, the putatively lower levels of cultural commitment that Swidler's theory suggests are not uniformly distributed across the population of a settled society. Nevertheless, the more deflated and strategic uses of the games create an additional integrative burden. Because viewers cannot always assume that others share their ritualistic involvement, they fear being ridiculed for their more pure and "naïve" experience of the events, and as a result they may limit their experience of the ritual to their own private spaces.

On the other hand, in "unsettled" countries, those experiencing more social change, the Olympics become a powerful and emotional battleground for competing ideologies. This was clearly the case for Brazil, where debates raged about the meaning of hosting the games. On one side, the official government position was that hosting the Olympics was a point of great national pride, showing that Brazil was a successful country of great beauty, excitement, and a distinctive culture. On the other side, the competing position, circulated on blogs by intellectuals and social activists, argued that the Olympics were a huge waste of money, that Brazil was not prepared to organize such a large event, and that the Olympics would end up being a national embarrassment. In this situation, the emotional involvement in the ritual was high. At issue was which cultural interpretation would prevail.

Although Swidler's distinction between settled and unsettled times can help to illuminate the general context in which strategies of action can be deployed through ritual, it has a more difficult time explaining how these different strategies of action are themselves structured. Instead, Swidler (2001) seems to adopt a pragmatist perspective, in which action is guided by the immediate problem confronting the individual. The difficulty is that this approach tends to overestimate agency, underestimate structure, and lead to the problem of the "randomness of ends" that Parsons ([1937] 1967) identified as a risk for theoretical programs based on an instrumental-action orientation, which fail to explain normative convergence. Even from an instrumentalist perspective, it is necessary to think about competing deployments of ritual.

From ritual to reproduction: Bourdieu, rituals, and distinction

Although Bourdieu shares Swidler's concern for strategies and repertoires of action, he has a much more structural understanding of strategic action and offers a stronger theory of ritual. For Bourdieu (1990:107–8), strategic deployments of cultural repertoires are connected to the agonistic processes of social reproduction and social advantage, where the ritualistic deployment of these repertoires will be shaped by the actor's "feel for the game."

Bourdieu argues that the repertoires of action an individual chooses are structured in significant ways by the *field* in which they are situated. Fields are "historically constituted areas of activity with their specific institutions and their own laws of functioning" (Bourdieu 1990:87). Fields tend to produce their "laws of functioning" by providing dominant principles of distinction and division, organized around debates concerning what constitutes good art, who is a real intellectual, what makes a great athletic performance, and so forth. The strategies of action available to an actor are shaped by that actor's position in the field, the distinctions she and her allies have deployed before, and the economic, social, and cultural capital she possesses.

There is also the possibility of employing socio-cultural distinctions that emerge from outside of the field, for example, relying on market principles to define artistic success. Indeed, much of the conflict that animates strategies of action within a given field is motivated by this distinction between "pure" criteria of success versus heterodox criteria that emerge from other social sources. The development of this form of binary distinction is one of the most important characteristics of modernity: aesthetic realms became differentiated from the social realm, new classes of artists and critics emerged, and pursuit of the pure aesthetic became a powerful new cultural repertoire, increasingly available as a social resource for certain types of people. Indeed, to borrow Swidler's language, conflict between aesthetic and heterodox principles of distinction gives most field-specific environments of action an "unsettled" character, which increases the power of ritual as well as the force of cultural coherence.

In fact, the distinction between autonomous and heterodox principles helps to illuminate certain aspects of ritual that typically go unexamined – specifically, the choice between a social and an aesthetic mode of engagement with ritual. Thus, to continue with considering the Olympics, social interpretations of the games – emphasizing national unity, shared values, or even competing ideologies – are all examples of heterodox criteria of distinction. To be sure, these are powerful modes of engaging ritual, and they provide the most obvious ways in which ritual is linked to power. After all, as Bourdieu (1996) argued, heterodox principles of distinction typically emerge from the field of power.

On the other hand, rituals in the games can also be approached using aesthetic criteria of distinction. Indeed, the professionals most involved with this sporting ritual – the athletes, the event organizers, and the broadcasters and journalists who cover the games for the public – are much more likely to make aesthetic interpretations than social ones. For the Olympics, aesthetic interpretations emphasize debates about what constitutes a great performance, as well as struggles to define the purity of sport itself. From this perspective, social interpretations – whether they are displays of political ideology or crass commercialism – are often seen as threats to the purity of the event and its ritual function.

In contemporary society, aesthetic interpretation is always available for discussing the significance of a ritual. This is true even for obviously political rituals, such as political inaugurations of new leaders, where the aesthetic features of the performance provide a ready source of discussion. Three groups are most likely to adopt the aesthetic mode of interpretation: (1) professionals in charge of organizing the ritual, (2) cultural critics who provide "legitimate" interpretations of public events, and (3) people possessing significant cultural capital who adopt the aesthetic mode as a form of detached irony, in order to distinguish themselves from putatively less sophisticated people.

By considering the structures that organize strategies of action, a Bourdieusian perspective clearly extends the analysis of repertoires and ritual. But a purely strategic approach to ritual has important limitations. To begin with, the understanding of ritual as a source of social solidarity has disappeared altogether. Emotional and intimate aspects of ritual are also obscured. For Durkheim, the structures that organize the co-presence of strategies of action and collective effervescence are central to ritual, because they provide an immediacy that serves to reduce social distance and replace it with a type of communion, which Victor Turner (1967) described as "communitas." The calculating agents that Swidler and Bourdieu describe seem to lack any interest in communion. Having no real commitment to ritual's symbolic environment and always scheming to figure out how they can turn ritual to their own advantage, these actors define themselves only by distance and detachment.

The strategic model of ritual has other, empirical blind spots. Perhaps the most important is its difficulty in addressing questions about why some rituals are more successful than others or what constitutes a successful ritual performance. In different ways, Randall Collins and Jeffrey Alexander have attempted to answer this important question: Collins through his micro-theory of interaction ritual chains, and Alexander through his macro-theory of cultural performance.

Emotional energy and interaction ritual chains

In many respects, Collins's theory of interaction ritual chains reprises concerns central to Durkheim that were largely abandoned by later theories. Identifying important points of commonality between Durkheim and Goffman, Collins (2004:7) defines a ritual as "a mechanism of mutually focused emotion and attention producing a momentary shared reality, which thereby generates solidarity and symbols of group membership." Central to this definition are the elements of *co-presence, mutuality* of focus, *emotion*, and *membership*. These elements all vary in their intensity, resulting in a complex array of contingencies that, taken together, help to explain the varieties of social life (Collins 2004:47). Included in these contingencies are diverse possibilities of failed rituals, which have their own distinctive consequences.

Collins argues that a successful ritual is one where a high level of mutual focus and emotional entrainment develops among participants in an interaction. When there is a low mutual focus and minimal emotional energy, the ritual is likely to fail. If an individual at an event only participates in "low intensity, perfunctory, or halting conversations," rather than being drawn into the mutual focus of the larger interaction ritual, she will not receive any emotional benefits from the interaction; in fact, if this style of interaction persists for too long, the individual is likely to find it tedious and emotionally draining (Collins 2004:52). On the other hand, where there are high levels of focus and emotional entrainment, ritual has powerful and durable cultural significance for the individual. Furthermore, because individuals tend to be drawn to situations where they receive the most emotional energy, their identities and associational life will be centrally shaped by their ability to find situations where they have regular access to successful rituals.

Collins's theory challenges the "strategies of action" approach in two important respects. First, it replaces Swidler's sweeping generalizations about "settled" and "unsettled" times with a focus on the contingencies and varying emotional intensities of specific situations. Collins suggests that low levels of symbolic commitment are less connected to macro-social dynamics than to the situation-specific failure of an interaction to produce a successful ritual. Second, Collins shifts the focus away from the calculating individual, emphasizing instead the *situation*,

> not as a cognitive construction but as a process by which shared emotions and intersubjective focus sweep individuals along by flooding their consciousness. It is not so much a matter of knowledgeable agents choosing from repertoires, as it is a situational propensity toward certain cultural symbols.
>
> *(2004:32)*

He goes on to argue that an analysis of interaction ritual chains can help predict when new cultural symbols will be created, when those new meanings will have a durable impact, versus when their influence will be more fleeting.

Although Collins would primarily seem to provide a micro-sociology of rituals, he also makes interesting macrosociological arguments about formal rituals and modernity. Of particular interest is his analysis of sporting ritual. Sporting events typically contain all the elements of successful ritual. There is a large crowd gathered together, all focused on the same thing, with high levels of emotional involvement. The results are a strong feeling of social solidarity and the reinforcement of a strong group identity. This is why people prefer watching a sporting event in person rather than on television. Even though the view on television is better, the mutuality of focus and the emotional entrainment tends to be weaker.

Collins's approach to the study of ritual redirects attention back toward emotion, mutuality of focus, and the contingency of particular situations. However, there remain important aspects in which it is less useful for cultural sociologists. First, and most problematic, Collins's theory of interaction rituals represents a movement away from meaning. Although he is surely correct to argue that the capacity of culture to have concrete causal force is connected to the emotional energy of interaction rituals, he does not have much to say about how rituals are shaped by culture. This critical point not only concerns the autonomous significance of culture. It also involves a historical argument about the way that cultural processes and formal rituals have come to be organized, since modernity, within a distinctively cultural arena that has taken over the creation, production, and legitimate interpretation of most public culture. In other words, a consideration of what makes many rituals today successful ritual must include examination of performers, critics, and audiences. This is the task that Alexander undertakes with his theory of cultural pragmatics.

Creating a successful ritual performance: Alexander and the theory of cultural pragmatics

In Alexander's (2004) theory of cultural pragmatics, the goal is to develop an understanding of culture and action that can incorporate the structural insights of ritual theory as well as arguments about repertoires and strategies of action that are emphasized more by contemporary practice theories. His theory involves a conceptual shift away from notions such as agency or practice and toward the concept of *performance*.

For Alexander, a ritual performance involves more than just the co-presence of individuals, or the simple enactment of a pre-existing cultural code. In fact, there are many "elements" of performance. One element consists of *systems of collective representation*, including background symbols and codes as well as the foregrounded "script." Another element comprises the *actors and performers* who are involved in the enactment of the ritual performance. There are also the performance's *audience*, the *means of symbolic production*, and the *mise-en-scène*, or general choreography, of the performance. Finally, there is *social power*, which involves (1) control over what kinds of texts are permitted, promoted, and encouraged; (2) what kinds of people are permitted to perform, and what kinds of people are permitted to attend, the performance; and (3) the extent to which the interpretation of the performance is controlled. The success of a ritual can be derailed by characteristics of any one of these elements of performance. Thus, Alexander's theory emphasizes the contingency of ritual, while paying attention to the structural sources that inform that contingency.

Like most of the contemporary theorists discussed earlier, Alexander favors a historical theory of ritual. For Alexander, the key transformation of ritual that has taken place in modern times is a general movement from fusion to defusion, as the primary way that audiences initially engage with ritual performances. In earlier, less differentiated societies – the ones most discussed in Durkheim's *Elementary Forms of the Religious Life* – rituals were characterized by fusion, in which there is no separation between actor and performance (Alexander 2004:537). In contrast, modernity brings an increasing social distance between the observers/audience and other elements of performance, creating a situation of institutionalized "de-fusion." Indeed, many elements of performance have become institutionalized in particular ways by complex professional organizations, with the precise intention of creating such social distance. Professional writers have largely taken over the production of scripts. Professional actors have taken over many of the performance roles, and where they have not, the actors often receive professional coaching. Professional critics have come to dominate interpretations of ritual performances. Social power is centralized in an increasingly bureaucratic state, often with its own ministry of culture. The means of symbolic production are largely controlled by the state or by the cultural industries. Under these circumstances, performances can seem artificial, contrived, and unconvincing (Alexander 2004:529).

Thus the challenge in modernity – the challenge of "re-fusion," of creating a successful ritual performance – requires both an emotional and a cultural connection. "The aim," Alexander (2004:547) argues, "is to create, via skillful and affecting performance, the emotional connection of audience with actor and text and thereby to create the conditions for projecting cultural meaning from performance to audience." Several tasks must be successfully completed for this connection to occur, and for the audience members to feel that they are witnessing an authentic performance. For writers and other creative personnel, the challenge is to fuse the foregrounded script and the background representations (i.e., the underlying cultural codes and narratives). For performers, the challenge is to create a fusion between actor and role, and for choreographers or directors it is to enact a successful fusion between script, action, and performative space. Those who control the means of symbolic production must be willing to provide technological and distributional support, while critics who control interpretations must accept the legitimacy, power, and aesthetic quality of the performance. If all of this happens, then there is a much higher likelihood for a successful fusion of audience and text to occur, and for the ritual performance to have a significant emotional and cultural impact.

Viewed from the perspective of Alexander's theory of cultural pragmatics, it becomes easy to see why the Olympics so frequently succeed as authentic and meaningful ritual performance. In addition, Alexander's theory points to specific ways that cultural fusion is likely to take place. One of the central features of the Olympics, as a contemporary ritual performance, is the fact that actor and role are already fused. Athletes spend their entire lives preparing. Their participation in the games is the crowning achievement in their athletic lives, and the opportunity to represent their country is their greatest source of collective attachment and pride. Thus, there is no need to manufacture an emotional commitment to the role. An easy fusion easily emerges between script and background representation. Each competition has heroic moments of triumph and tragic moments of disappointment, and some individuals have overcome great obstacles in their Olympic quests. Finally, those who control the means of symbolic production are active and willing participants in the organization and broadcast of the myriad events that make up the games. Even critics seem open to emphasizing the heroic and sacred character of the games – both in the spectacle of the opening ceremonies and the superhuman feats of athletic performance.

As a consequence of these elements of cultural performance, most viewers of the games are much more likely than usual to suspend their cynicism, to immerse themselves in the drama of the ritual, and to celebrate the scripts and the background representations that emerge. Importantly, the ritual performance of the Olympics provides two equally powerful and historically durable narratives for audience and script. On the one hand there are the narratives of national triumph and victory. When those particularistic narratives are unconvincing, however, there is a secondary set of more universalistic representations already inscribed in the official Olympic Charter – "to place sport at the service of the harmonious development of man, with a view to promoting a peaceful society concerned with the preservation of human dignity." Because performers, producers, official interpreters, audiences, the state, and the cultural industries are all working from this dual script, the likelihood of creating a successful ritual is increased immeasurably.

Conclusion

For a cultural sociology that is concerned to link meaning and action, the concept of ritual is one of the most useful conceptual resources. By providing a common horizon of meaning and attention, rituals bring actors together within a shared environment of action, enabling the production of social solidarity while encouraging a reproduction of common cultural codes and narratives.

However, most cultural sociologists are unwilling to accept the argument that rituals produce solidarity without conflict. They question how coordinated action can take place in the absence of strategic action. They pay close attention to the ways that rituals are connected to social power and to the reproduction of social advantage. These scholars reject the idea that all rituals are equally powerful, or even that rituals are destined to succeed. These challenges have produced a productive fragmentation in the cultural sociology of ritual, which has had the advantage of pointing to a number of important social processes and empirical questions. For those who are interested in the strategic elements of ritual processes, Swidler and Bourdieu provide useful resources. For those who are more interested in the contingent outcomes of ritual and the factors that explain the success of specific rituals, Alexander and Collins provide provocative conceptual vocabularies.

Still missing are empirical studies that make judgments and evaluations of these competing approaches. Indeed, many of the empirical claims about the Olympic Games that I have derived from these different approaches are in direct opposition to one another – for example, Collins versus Swidler on the degree of emotional entrainment likely to be found at a sporting event in a "settled" society, or Alexander versus Bourdieu on the proportion of aesthetic interpretations that critics make of the Olympics. There is also the question of group boundaries. Most theories privilege the nation as the default boundary, but there may be instances when subnational or transnational boundaries will be dominant. More studies are needed that can test these kinds of competing expectations.

References

Alexander, Jeffrey C. 2004. "Cultural Pragmatics: Social Performance Between Ritual and Strategy." *Sociological Theory* 22(4):527–73.

Bourdieu, Pierre. 1990. *In Other Words: Essays Towards a Reflexive Sociology*, trans. Matthew Adamson. Stanford, CA: Stanford University Press.

———. 1996. *The Rules of Art: Genesis and Structure of the Literary Field*. Stanford, CA: Stanford University Press.

Collins, Randall. 2004. *Interaction Ritual Chains*. Princeton, NJ: Princeton University Press.

Dayan, Daniel, and Elihu Katz. 1992. *Media Events: The Live Broadcasting of History*. Cambridge, MA: Harvard University Press.

Durkheim, Emile. [1912] 1995. *The Elementary Forms of the Religious Life*. New York: Free Press.

Goffman, Erving. [1956] 1959. *The Presentation of Self in Everyday Life*. New York: Doubleday.

———. 1967. *Interaction Ritual*. Chicago: Aldine.

Lukes, Steven. 1975. "Political Ritual and Social Integration." *Sociology* 9(2):289–308.

Parsons, Talcott. [1937] 1967. *The Structure of Social Action*. New York: Free Press.

Swidler, Ann. 1986. "Culture in Action: Symbols and Strategies." *American Sociological Review* 51(2):273–86.

———. 2001. *Talk of Love: How Culture Matters*. Chicago: University of Chicago Press.

Tilly, Charles. 1981. *As Sociology Meets History*. New York: Academic Press.

Turner, Victor. 1967. *The Ritual Process*. Chicago: Aldine.

Part VI
Making/using culture

33

Culture, social relations, and consumption

Frederick F. Wherry

Introduction

When people buy gifts, manage routine expenses, and talk about their reasons for spending or saving, they are engaged in cultural work. Culture is not a non-materialist concept but a set of meanings reflected in and modified through consumption. Rather than a biological necessity, consumption represents cultural intentions (Sahlins 1976), marking publicly how a group organizes interpersonal relationships, social hierarchies, and moral imperatives (Douglas and Isherwood 1979; Zelizer 1989, 2010). Social scientists have also approached consumption as a threat to culture or as a dynamic arena for creatively contesting it. Some marketers appear as manipulators of meaning, crafting iconic symbols, sacred concerns, moral understandings, and social divisions for the sake of economic profit. Other consumption practices and marketing efforts, by contrast, seem to be benign opportunities to negotiate the meanings of social life. Cultural sociologists have also noted that stage-like characters enacting roles populate the markets for consumption (Alexander 2004; Wherry 2012a), and their enactments become interventions in the social relationships to which the consumers are tied (Bandelj 2012; Bandelj, Wherry, and Zelizer 2017; Epp and Price 2008; Zelizer 2002).

At the level of micro-interactions, consumption depends on relational work. As Viviana Zelizer (2012) conceptualizes it, individuals use their consumption decisions to mark the types of relationships they are in, to initiate new relationships, and to contest, transform, or terminate a social tie. Therefore, consumption is not the work of isolated individuals actualizing idiosyncratic desires but rather the efforts of people interpreting and trying to maintain meaningful relationships. Consumption often happens in the presence of different audiences as the performance of a group style, as the affirmation of an authentic set of practices, or as a mechanism for binding a community together through the use of consumer goods (Arnould and Thompson 2005; Muñiz and O'Guinn 2001). Performing consumption, actors piece together culturally resonant scripts indicating who they are and with whom they are interacting. These performances have strategic goals as described by Goffman (1959), presenting a positive evaluation of the self in the presence of others, but that strategy relies on collective background representations that energize and constrain such social performances, as conceptualized by Alexander (2004).

Overarching meanings guide consumption performances, including deliberations over purchases. Here it is important not to adopt an overculturalized view of group behaviors (Wherry 2014; Zelizer 1988). The patterns of consumption that differentiate one group from another are not merely the aggregations of idiosyncratic preferences independently held by individuals, but nor are they dictated by rigid or pre-determined cultural scripts. Dramaturgically speaking, consumers accomplish their roles – for example, as mother/father, wife/husband, or playful child – through the acquisition and transfer of goods (Bandelj 2012, Wherry 2016, Zelizer 2012), and these roles exist independently of individuals' idiosyncrasies. While individuals can mix and match as they tailor role to situation, they are borrowing form pre-existing codes as they move closer to or further from widely known typifications. The rules governing these consumer transactions carry the weight of common sense (Bourdieu 1977), and those who defy the common may do so deliberately to contest the role they are playing or unconsciously as their audiences come to see them as the wrong type of actor for a particular script. Actors accomplish a match (or a mismatch) with a role through public consumption practices. And both actors and audiences implicitly reference a set of background representations to assess the match (Wherry 2016).

This chapter focuses on both the social performance of consumption (Alexander 2004) and the relational work these performances accomplish (Wherry 2012a). These performances happen explicitly in advertising campaigns and marketing strategies, but they also occur implicitly in the ways that individuals use and talk about branded commodities and services. There are the incessant negotiations over meanings and relationships as well as the remarkable intersubjective stability of these roles, scripts, and understandings. Typified consumption roles become crystal clear in advertisements and in marketing strategies. Indeed, advertisements narrate some meanings of consumption that their target audiences are likely to see as capturing reality, or at least capturing the aspirations that real people have.

The chapter unfolds in three sections: retail shopping as a public performance, household consumption decisions as relational work, and the role of rituals in consumer decision-making. The first section begins with retail shopping because consumption messages and the interactions between consumers, their loved ones, and meaningful objects become manifest in public spaces. Consumers can expect to have an audience that is physically co-present while contemplating one that is imagined. The second section flows from the first, leaving the public for the private sphere of household consumption where delicate negotiations unfold over the kinds of obligations parents have for children, kids have to their friends, and people in communities have with one another. The final section enters the world of rituals, reminding readers how sacred and profane distinctions and the traditions that communities hold dear can be enacted through branded goods and through commercialized festivals.

Retail shopping: public performances

Shopping malls and retail stores represent explicit stages of consumption where actors utilize scripts to engage consumers in the meanings of hoped for, accomplished, and despised purchases. The stages themselves are situated as landscapes, defined by Sharon Zukin as "an ensemble of material and social practices and their symbolic representations" (Zukin 1993:16). The scripts themselves anticipate emotions and pre-emptively manage them. These emotional responses come from consumers as well as the workers helping to guide consumers in expressing why a purchase feels imperative. Shopping spaces channel symbols, meanings, and emotional responses as systematically as factories assemble products along a conveyer belt (Ritzer 2010).

Historically, department stores were designed using templates from temples, cathedrals, and monuments to invite a sense of transcending everyday experience. Spatial arrangements alone, however, could not achieve this transcendence. Department store managers had to reritualize time, bringing in festivals and important holidays as central displays to focus the attention of shoppers on changes in merchandise and get shoppers to see merchandise as critical for achieving a cultural need, namely to participate in significant rituals. Today's consumers, for example, take for granted that the biggest parade on Thanksgiving Day is sponsored by Macy's and has carried the store's brand name since 1924.

It should come as no surprise that department stores tied themselves to national rituals given that these stores also functioned as cultural centers with free art exhibits, plays, lectures, anthropological displays, and even public library branches.

> Over time many Americans had come to consider the department store as an "eleemosynary institution maintained for purpose of serving the public without regard for profit." . . . As an English advertising manager from Harrods in London declared in 1919, "I do not know whether stores have created and fostered the demand for service which department stores recognized and met; but it certainly causes a tremendous amount of overhead expense, and it is a question if it has not been carried too far."
>
> *(Leach 1984:330)*

John Wannamaker himself declared in 1897 that his department store was "the people's store" (Leach 1984:331) that elevated cultural goals over financial ones. Wannamaker and others understood that department stores would not do well as mere sites where goods could be purchased based on calculations of price and quality. The social performances staged at the site of the transaction mattered.

The staging of performances relied on and reshaped shared societal understandings of childhood. Let's take the example of the biological and social stages of human development as it applied to children. How should department stores inscribe these meanings in their spatial layout? Daniel Thomas Cook investigates this question in his historical analysis of the commodification of childhood. He maps the spatial arrangement of retail stores, noting how it guides young children through areas targeting older children, inviting them to witness what would later be, quite literally, in store for them. In this way, retail spaces make concrete "the social divisions of childhood" (Cook 2004:97).

Even in today's retail shops, spatial layouts and the casting of workers into different roles sends signals about the proper "place" of different groups of people. In her study of large toy stores, Williams (2006) notes that those "cast" as stock-room workers looked different (in terms of gender and race) from those cast as cashiers. Likewise, the electronics section was typically stocked by Asians but gardening was not. In addition to observing the distribution of workers to different sections of the store, Williams showed how the color schemes and the types of toys allocated to different sections of the store reflected and reinforced taken for granted gender codes.

Not only the staging of retail spaces but the props used in those spaces affect how individuals deliberate over their consumption choices. Franck Cochoy (2008:17) argues that the shopping cart itself can help consumers switch how they understand value, with the cart "function[ing] as a scene or as a frame for collective 'calqulation' (from the French verb 'calquer,' i.e., adjusting one's standpoint to that of another, and vice versa)." Although Cochoy does not develop the concept of shopping as a scene of social performance, as a cultural sociologist might, he does show how the cart creates a "buffer zone" for storing items to be purchased (and not put back on the shelf) while protecting deliberations over their value from the idea of payment. This dissociation enables consumers to suspend immediate considerations of price and consider other criteria for making purchases. By taking a cart and filling it with "tokens," people demonstrate their understanding of the cart's function and their own role in the ritual. The calculative space afforded by the cart allows the "de-calculation" of price concerns (Callon, Millo, and Muniesa 2007) so that a more holistic social performance can unfold (Alexander 2011; Wherry 2012b).

Objects and spatial configurations influence how individuals negotiate retail spaces as they perform identity and acknowledge relationships, but the individuals themselves still engage in micro-strategies that can slightly alter, greatly disrupt, or (in some way) modify expected patterns. Anthropologist Jean Lave (1988) describes a grocery shopping scene with a 45-year-old woman and her 15-year-old daughter. A researcher is accompanying the mother-daughter pair to observe how families make sense of price and quality in the grocery store. She describes the mother improvising with a prop that the designers of the store did not anticipate, her eyeglasses. The mother can slow time down as she makes a calculation and can pretend not to see exactly what the prices are as she demonstrates her prowess at making price comparisons. The mother in this case wants to buy Heinz ketchup and thinks erroneously that she has a coupon that will allow her to do so at an advantageous price. "'Heinz has a special . . . I have a coupon in here for that.' The shopper discovers that her coupon, however, is for Kraft Sweet and Sour, not the [item] that's on the shelf" (Lave 1988:167). Upon discovering this, the mother reaches for her eyeglasses, changing the dynamics of the scene as she attempts to save face.

Household consumption: habitual performances and dynamic enactments

Sometimes household consumption resembles a habit, sometimes a dynamic virtuosic performance. Rather than spending a great deal of time focused on price and quality trade-offs, consumers can simply rely on the habits of their elders. Through a process of socialization in the household, they identify with and use whatever their parents, siblings, or neighbors used. What sustains these identifications and commitments, however, is the significance of the relationships and the incessant accomplishment of the scripts tying the relationships to the products. To see the results of socialization (habits) on consumer choices, consider the brand of laundry detergent that young women seem to prefer. They typically use the same brand that their own mothers used. Marketing scholars Elizabeth Moore, William Wilkie, and Richard Lutz (2002) identify how the intergenerational transfer of cultural practices identified by sociologists also apply to brand loyalty. They surveyed 102 mothers paired with 102 daughters about a range of products and brands. Key brands with high likelihood of intergenerational transfer included Tide laundry detergent, Maxwell House and Folgers coffee, Heinz ketchup, and Campbell's soup. The researchers then engaged in in-depth interviews with a focal sample of 25 young women so that they could talk to them by phone, meet with them in a grocery store, and then follow them home to conduct an audit of their pantries. They found considerable inertia as daughters discussed the influence their mothers had on them: "I buy Dawn just because – my mom always used Dawn . . . cleaning products, detergents, Downy softener, and the Downy ball – even when I'm here on my own I use those products. . . . So when I do my own shopping, I pick those products too" (Moore, Wilkie, and Lutz 2002:26). For many of these young women, branded products used by their mothers made their homes feel more homey. Mothers metaphorically pass their brand preferences along to their daughters like the torch handed off in the opening ceremonies of the Olympics.

Amber Epp and Linda Price (2008:50) remind us that families use branded products and consumption practices to answer a basic question: "Who are we as a family?" This is not merely a question of how collective resources will be allocated. There are bundles of relationships within a household that enable its inhabitants to consider individual, relational, and collective identities and the priorities associated with those different identity types. Families may see themselves as sharing common interests or activities (e.g., "We're a Carolina Panthers family" or "We are an outdoorsy type of family"). A number of consumer researchers focused too much on relational categories and assumed that there were static power dynamics in a heteronormative family hierarchy (Commuri and Gentry 2000). By contrast, Epp and Price (2008:51) argue:

> This completely misses the point that families countenance a range of possible identities (collective, relational, and individual) that affect their decisions. Consequently, firms might be better off considering products, services, and brands as resources for achieving relational and family identity goals.

Fathers interact differently with their children than do mothers (Lareau 2000) and children function as skilled social actors making sense of their lives through consumption (Cook and Kaiser 2004; DeVault 2003; Pugh 2009; Zelizer 2002).

Family, relational, and individual identities have to be enacted. Individuals accomplish these enactments through rituals, narratives, and social dramas. Within a ritual, family members engage in relational work, establishing, acknowledging, modifying, or rupturing different relationship types (Bandelj 2012; Zelizer 2012). Who gets invited into ritual participation, and what objects or activities are purchased, shared, or gifted to establish or reinforce relational boundaries? Concurrently, narratives help individuals offer accounts of their consumption practices and to act with tact in response to apparent inconsistencies.

Individuals can stage these narratives, crafting scripts and revising roles in their social performances (Alexander 2004). In doing so, they reference widely held narratives interpreted through a simplifying prism refracting those narratives as representations of the sacred versus the profane as well as the civil versus the non-civil. These performances allow cultural analysts to detect what the overarching understandings are that structure these scripts and the roles inhabiting them.

In households, individuals make connections with one another by virtue of the boundaries they establish between those who belong versus those who do not. More, members of the household mark the boundaries between the role of parent, child, and in-law as well as between older and younger members. They contest these roles as well through gifting practices that violate heteronormative gender norms. While individuals use their consumption practices to build a variety of household forms, they sometimes implicitly reference a nuclear family structure or use such typifications as an anti-reference point. These boundary-marking and boundary-busting practices constitute implicit social performances whereby spending practices, gifting, and routine consumption make those boundaries (and their violations) resonate as real (Zelizer 2005).

Household heads often help their children perform dignified and dignifying stories. Rather than only being concerned with status competition, households are also concerned with self-worth and having their dignity and the dignity of their children recognized by others. Allison Pugh (2009) describes this phenomenon as an "economy of dignity" in which children and their parents experience longing for a sense of community and a need to belong to the larger group. This sense of belonging is accomplished partly through consumption. Sociologist Bernadine Chee (2000) interviewed children aged 8 to 10 in Beijing and found that children would share their food at school to establish group boundaries. Children also identified important brands to affirm that in-group members shared the same tastes. Chee writes about a boy named Gao, who is asked by a classmate whether he has tried Wall's ice cream (a special brand). Gao says he has when he has not; he then insists that his father purchase Wall's without fully explaining to his father why, even though the ice cream is expensive and their household income limited. Chee's interview with the father reveals that he recognizes Gao's need to make good on his claim to have tried the ice cream because of its capacity to establish and maintain important social ties at school. Gao's father makes the purchase, exercising tact in allowing his son to complete his "frontstage" schoolyard performance by consuming the ice cream in the "backstage" of the household.

As the example of Gao illustrates, consumption performances may require others to play along. Whether and how this happens depends on the relationship between the actor performing the script and his or her relevant audiences and how closely aligned is the script with the broader set of themes available for actors to craft their lines, direct the narrative arc, and become identified with their role in the drama (Alexander 2011; Wherry 2012b). Although these macro-cultural concerns require abstraction away from the microdynamics of performances, they remain critical to their constitution.

Community consumption: enacting rituals and other collective scripts

When contemplating large-scale consumption rituals, Mardi Gras easily comes to mind. In New Orleans, Michelle Weinberger and Melanie Wallendorf (2012) have observed the gifting practices among people who are not intimately tied through households or through the intimacy that isolated communities foster. They take their investigations to the streets of the Mardi Gras festival, where the gifting practices follow the logic of a moral economy – "a system of transactions which are defined as socially desirable (i.e., moral), because through them social ties are recognized, and balanced social relationships are maintained" (Cheal 1988:15). Mardi Gras has been practiced in New Orleans since 1835 and its date depends on the Catholic liturgical calendar. After Hurricane Katrina led to devastation in Louisiana, the festival itself became a locus of consumption and community rebirth. Busy with merriment, the participants on the floats seem to disguise the role of money and corporate sponsorships in the parade. Yet as the participants engage in various commercial exchanges, they are able to "draw a boundary around the community in creating a sense of we-ness while also asserting acceptance of a hierarchical relation between different community members" (Weinberger and Wallendorf 2012:84).

Other types of community become manifest through consumer practices around a revered brand. Albert Muñiz and Thomas O'Guinn (2001) define a brand community as

> a specialized, non-geographically bound [group], based on a structured set of social relationships among admirers of a brand. . . . Like other communities, it is marked by a shared consciousness, rituals and traditions, and a sense of moral responsibility.
>
> *(Muñiz and O'Guinn 2001:412)*

They explain that people form a sense of community by using brands as totems of their tribe. Members of a brand community develop a shared consciousness by publicly marking their similarities with others like themselves who admire the brand and drawing boundaries against those with opposing values and traditions.

For example, in the 1990s and early 2000s a well-known split existed between "Mac people" and "IBM people": the former didn't vote for Reagan, didn't wear bland suits, and didn't aspire to work in a stodgy organization; the latter did (Muñiz and O'Guinn 2001:420). The Mac seemed to inhabit a realm of purity, impervious to computer viruses; the IBM remained polluted and polluting, infected with malware and eager to spread it around.

Jeep also proved to have a resilient brand community. Its members used storytelling to "creat[e] and maintain community" (Muñiz and O'Guinn 2001:423). Its most fervent advocates knew the history of the company and could tell stories about its founders and its founding principles. Core members of the Jeep brand community would band together to go on weekend pilgrimages into rugged terrain. These "Jeep Jamborees" required members to spend their own money and pay other fees to participate in the community. They also post on and respond to requests for advice (or help) online. Even those disinclined to engage in Jeep Jamborees may nonetheless flick their vehicle lights when encountering another Jeep on the road – perfect strangers brought into the community by virtue of the brand.

Consumerism works best when it follows tropes (icons, metaphors, allusions, etc.). What doesn't work is being literal – focusing exclusively on price. Take, for example, how buying a luxury car seems more attractive when the emphasis is not solely placed on quality and price but instead transcends market considerations; transcendence narratives invoke the religious process of being born – "born again" – becoming a new person through faithful practice and deep devotion to the religion's teachings. Metaphors of rebirth can be quite transparent: the production week for the new model of the BMW Mini, for example, unfolds through a highly ritualized process in which the branded commodity helps the consumer and the consumed experience a rebirth. Customers can name their cars, anticipate their arrival, and "create commemorative 'baby books' to document the new arrival[s]" (Schau, Muñiz, and Arnould 2009:36). These widely held tropes of birth and its religious counterpart of rebirth become accessible themes for the scripts crafted and enacted by the practicing script writers, scene setters, and members of the brand community who work hard to respect and protect it.

Finally, national communities increasingly find expression as brands. Nation branding represents an intentional performance of collective identity. The indicators of identity come in a variety of forms, including architecture, art, music, food, and landscape (Aronczyk 2013; Centeno, Bandelj, and Wherry 2011; Rivera 2008; Wherry 2007). These various elements come together to constitute a national identity that is distinct from other national identities and that is attractive for investors, tourists, and consumers purchasing goods made in the branded country. In *Branding the Nation*, Melissa Aronczyk brings her readers inside the world of image consultants, conferences, survey instruments, and focus groups where the national brand is forged. There stands field leader Wolff Olins, who declares:

> Interestingly, there is nothing particularly novel about the concept of branding the nation. Only the word "brand" is new. National image, national identity, national reputation are all words traditionally used in this arena and they don't seem to provoke the visceral hostility as the word "brand." Although the technologies are new and infinitely more powerful and pervasive than ever before, and the word "brand" is also new, the concepts which it encompasses are as old as the nation itself.
>
> *(Aronczyk 2013:68)*

Conclusion

This chapter has presented how consumption functions as a social performance, wherein individuals identify and work on their social ties, community norms and boundaries become manifest and challenged, and the meanings of social life are publicly staged and enacted. Consumption studies underscore the assertion of Jeffrey Alexander that consumers use their purchases and the exchange of goods to respond to and within an existing meaning system. Alexander (2011:477) writes:

> To believe in the possibility of a cultural sociology is to subscribe to the idea that every action, no matter how instrumental or coerced, is embedded in a horizon of affect and meaning. This internal environment imbeds action, presenting a culture structure in relation to which actors can never be fully reflexive.

Likewise, no matter how manipulated consumers may be by advertising and marketing professionals, they are also working on intimate relationships and co-constructing collective feelings of solidarity as they purchase and deploy branded goods in their daily lives.

References

Alexander, Jeffrey C. 2004. "Cultural Pragmatics: Social Performance between Ritual and Strategy." *Sociological Theory* 22(4):527–73.

———. 2011. "Market as Narrative and Character." *Journal of Cultural Economy* 4(4):477–88.

Arnould, Eric J., and Craig J. Thompson. 2005. "Consumer Culture Theory (CCT): Twenty Years of Research." *Journal of Consumer Research* 31:868–82.

Aronczyk, Melissa. 2013. *Branding the Nation: The Global Business of National Identity*. Oxford: Oxford University Press.

Bandelj, Nina. 2012. "Relational Work and Economic Sociology." *Politics & Society* 40(2):175–201.

Bandelj, Nina, Frederick F. Wherry, and Viviana A. Zelizer. 2017. "Advancing Money Talks." Pp. 1–24 in *Money Talks: Explaining How Money Really Works*, edited by N. Bandelj, F.F. Wherry, and V.A. Zelizer. Princeton, NJ: Princeton University Press.

Bourdieu, Pierre. 1977. *Outline of a Theory of Practice*. New York: Cambridge University Press.

Callon, Michel, Yuval Millo, and Fabian Muniesa. 2007. *Market Devices*. Malden, MA: Blackwell.

Centeno, Miguel A., Nina Bandelj, and Frederick F. Wherry. 2011. "The Political Economy of Cultural Wealth." Pp. 23–46 in *The Cultural Wealth of Nations*, edited by N. Bandelj and F.F. Wherry. Stanford, CA: Stanford University Press.

Cheal, David. 1988. "The Ritualization of Family Ties." *American Behavioral Scientist* 31(6):632.

Chee, Bernadine W.L. 2000. "Eating Snacks and Biting Pressure: Only Children in Beijing." Pp. 48–70 in *Feeding China's Little Emperors: Food, Children, and Social Change*, edited by J. Jing. Stanford, CA: Stanford University Press.

Cochoy, Franck. 2008. "Calculation, Qualculation, Calqulation: Shopping Cart Arithmetic, Equipped Cognition, and the Clustered Consumer." *Marketing Theory* 8(1):15–44.

Commuri, Suraj, and James W. Gentry. 2000. "Opportunities for Family Research in Marketing." *Academy of Marketing Science Review* 2000(8):1–34.

Cook, Daniel Thomas. 2004. *The Commodification of Childhood: The Children's Clothing Industry and the Rise of the Child Consumer*. Durham, NC: Duke University Press.

Cook, Daniel Thomas, and Susan B. Kaiser. 2004. "Betwixt and Be Tween Age Ambiguity and the Sexualization of the Female Consuming Subject." *Journal of Consumer Culture* 4(2):203–27.

DeVault, Marjorie L. 2003. "Families and Children Together, Apart." *American Behavioral Scientist* 46(10):1296–305.

Douglas, Mary, and Baron Isherwood. 1979. *The World of Goods*. New York: Norton.

Epp, Amber M., and Linda L. Price. 2008. "Family Identity: A Framework of Identity Interplay in Consumption Practices." *Journal of Consumer Research* 35(1):50–70.

Goffman, Erving. 1959. *The Presentation of Self in Everyday Life*. Garden City, NY: Doubleday.

Lareau, Annette. 2000. *Home Advantage: Social Class and Parental Intervention in Elementary Education*. Lanham, MD: Rowman & Littlefield.

Lave, Jean. 1988. *Cognition in Practice: Mind, Mathematics and Culture in Everyday Life*. New York: Cambridge University Press.

Leach, William. 1984. "Transformations in a Culture of Consumption: Women and Department Stores, 1890–1925." *Journal of American History* 71(2):319–42.

Moore, Elizabeth S., William L. Wilkie, and Richard J. Lutz. 2002. "Passing the Torch: Intergenerational Influences as a Source of Brand Equity." *Journal of Marketing* 66(2):17–37.

Muñiz, Albert M., and Thomas C. O'Guinn. 2001. "Brand Community." *Journal of Consumer Research* 27:412–32.

Pugh, Allison J. 2009. *Longing and Belonging: Parents, Children, and Consumer Culture*. Berkeley: University of California Press.

Ritzer, George. 2010. *Enchanting a Disenchanted World: Continuity and Change in the Cathedrals of Consumption*. Thousand Oaks, CA: Pine Forge Press.

Rivera, Lauren. 2008. "Managing 'Spoiled' National Identity: War, Tourism and Memory in Croatia." *American Sociological Review* 73(4):613–34.

Sahlins, Marshall. 1976. *Culture and Practical Reason*. Chicago: University of Chicago Press.

Schau, Hope Jensen, Albert M. Muñiz Jr., and Eric J. Arnould. 2009. "How Brand Community Practices Create Value." *Journal of Marketing* 73(5):30–51.

Weinberger, Michelle F., and Melanie Wallendorf. 2012. "Intracommunity Gifting at the Intersection of Contemporary Moral and Market Economies." *Journal of Consumer Research* 39(1):74–92.

Wherry, Frederick F. 2007. "Trading Impressions: Evidence from Costa Rica." *Annals of the American Academy of Political and Social Science* 610:217–31.

———. 2012a. "Performance Circuits in the Marketplace." *Politics & Society* 40(2):203–21.

———. 2012b. *The Culture of Markets*. Cambridge: Polity Press.

———. 2014. "Analyzing the Culture of Markets." *Theory and Society* 43(3–4):421–36.

———. 2016. "Relational Accounting: A Cultural Approach." *American Journal of Cultural Sociology* 4(2):131–56.

Williams, Christine L. 2006. *Inside Toyland: Working, Shopping, and Social Inequality*. Berkeley: University of California Press.

Zelizer, Viviana A. 1988. "Beyond the Polemics of the Market: Establishing a Theoretical and Empirical Agenda." *Sociological Forum* 3(4):614–34.

———. 1989. "The Social Meaning of Money: 'Special Monies.'" *American Journal of Sociology* 95(2):342–77.

———. 2002. "Kids and Commerce." *Childhood* 9(4):375–96.

———. 2005. *The Purchase of Intimacy*. Princeton, NJ: Princeton University Press.

———. 2010. *Economic Lives: How Culture Shapes the Economy*. Princeton, NJ: Princeton University Press.

———. 2012. "How I Became a Relational Economic Sociologist and What Does That Mean?" *Politics & Society* 40(2):145–74.

Zukin, Sharon. 1993. *Landscapes of Power: From Detroit to Disney World*. Berkeley: University of California Press.

34

The cultural life of objects

Claudio E. Benzecry and Fernando Domínguez Rubio

Introduction

What do people do with objects? And what do objects do to people? This chapter explores the dialectic between processes of objectification (how things become objects) and subjectification (how people become subjects) by rethinking typical assumptions about the passivity of the former and the agency of the latter. The chapter is divided into four parts, slowly building an argument about the weaker and stronger versions of the interrelation between objects and subjects. The first section explores both classic and recent approaches to how objects are imbued with special significance, as well as contemporary scholarship on attachment and affordances. Then we explore what objects allow us to do, the kinds of subjects they encourage us to be, and the kinds of activities they block or enable. Do they collaborate? Are they unruly or docile? The chapter concludes by offering some reflections about what this means for the study of meaning-making in particular and of culture at large.

Meaning *in* objects

A central line of inquiry within cultural sociology has been to analyze the long-term purchase of particular objects by establishing a one-to-one set equivalence between objects, individuals, and/or collectives, in which objects mean only one thing and there is a taken-for-granted link between meaning and emotion. One tradition, for instance, emphasizes the role of cultural structures, focusing on the collective effervescence produced by rituals that aim to produce fusion and catharsis between the object qua totem and the collective.

This tradition can be traced back to Emile Durkheim's *Elementary Forms of Religious Life* (1965) and has been continued and refined by subsequent scholars. Victor Turner (1967), for example, theorized concepts like social drama and "breach," in which change is an odd occurrence and continuity is achieved through rituals that restore the previous order. Mary Douglas (1966) looked at the role of objects in establishing binary boundaries, especially the assignation of "dirt" to those objects that do not fit neatly into the prevailing social order. Randall Collins's (2004) "interaction ritual chain" theory points to the highly contextualized ways in which an object becomes emotionally resonant with a collective. The work of Jeffrey

Alexander (2008) reveals the productive character of the distinction between sacred and pro-fane and the totemic role played by objects in producing "iconic consciousness," which in turn become vehicles for social action. Pierre Bourdieu (1984) explored how stable the meanings of objects are by emphasizing the role of homologies and dispositions in guaranteeing that objects (a) have only one available set of instructions and uses, (b) are closely related to particular posi-tions in the social structure, and (c) serve as boundaries that create distinctions between compet-ing groups (see also Lamont 1992). More recently Genevieve Zubrzycki (2011) has coined the idea of "national sensorium" to call attention to the multiplicity of media and sites – including soundtracks, advertising, food, and film – that concretize and bring to life relatively abstract and often emotion-laden ideas about the link between self and nation.

In an early departure from this tradition, Paul Willis (1978) proposed to study what cultural materials actually afford rather than assuming that meaning is arbitrarily attributed to them. Via the study of hippies and motor-bikers, he scrutinizes how objects lend themselves to expressing masculinity, authenticity, and spirituality. Willis shows how a group cannot just choose a random cultural item, and neither can a cultural item attach itself to just any group. Although the mean-ings are culturally constructed, the construction nevertheless derives from the "objective" given possibilities of the cultural items themselves.

Willis's early departure from Durkheimian and structuralist approaches opens up a new line of sociological inquiry. If objects offer more than a one-to-one physical replica of "culture," that is, if they are more than mere passive recipients of cultural schemes, then the relationship between sign and things is never purely arbitrary or self-evident since the object shapes the kind of relationship that can take place (Daston 2004). Our task then is to explore the particular kind of cultural work that objects perform in allowing (or disallowing) these relations of signification, and how, in so doing, they subtend or disrupt the kind of subjects we imagine ourselves to be.

What happens when the other is an object?

Thanks to object-centered sociologies we know that objects play a key role in shaping identity, social action, and subjectivity. We know, for example, that objects perform an important type of cultural work in what Molotch (2003) refers to as the "lashing-up" of cultural meaning, personal identities, and things. We also know that objects help human agents work toward particular states of being by providing patterns to which bodies can unconsciously latch onto (DeNora 2000, 2003), and that they are central in the long-term process of taste construction, where the actual material object (a musical piece, a pair of jeans, a soccer t-shirt) is both a result and a key co-producer of its own generation of meaning (Hennion 2007; Hennion and Fauquet 2001; Hennion and Gomart 1999).

This object-centered scholarship helps us see that the process of subjectification is not one-way, with subjects willfully imposing or co-opting objects to construct their identities, but rather a process that is more like a dance or choreography in which the object and the self co-produce each other through a delicate equilibrium of bodies, techniques, mediators, and situations. The exploration of this engagement of people with objects leads us to look at the role that objects play in how we present ourselves and craft our particular "moral careers." One of the practices in which this becomes evident are the accounts and claims about the self-actions that have in the literature been derided as inflated versions of culture. Objects often work as "plot devices" (Win-chester forthcoming) that make possible particular accounts of the self, and thus prompt agents to perform the cultural work of negotiating and accommodating narratives, attachments and self-identification to what the object affords, as well as to the work of sustaining these bonds as objects change (Benzecry 2011). One central example of this approach is the work of anthropologist

Sherry Turkle on intimacy and evocative devices (2007, 2008). Turkle writes about how objects connect us to the world, their capacity to serve as sieve, bridge, and boundary between self and external reality, and their use in our own self-cultivation. Her work brings back into the conversation two lines of inquiry that have fallen by the wayside in cultural sociology: first, the psychoanalytic approach of scholars such as Jacques Lacan, Sigmund Freud, and D.W. Winnicott, which theorized "objects" as a place for potential identifications as well as a key part of the process of subject development; second is Marx's work on commodity fetishism and what it says about our relationship to sensuous materials, which, under certain conditions, can assume life-like qualities.

Turkle focused her interest in Freud on the concept of the uncanny, but this prompts the question of how artifacts that are familiar to us become strange in the first place. Historical sociologist George Steinmetz (2008) mobilizes the Freudian distinction between melancholia and nostalgia to analyze the contrasting responses of white people in Detroit and Namibia, respectively, in making sense of the ruins of a more powerful past. Ruins work as evocative objects, and the memory regimes they invoke must take into account historical context, he argues. Detroit inhabitants engaged nostalgically with the industrial rubble of the automotive industry, whereas white Namibians oriented toward the leftovers of the German colonial past with melancholy, both acknowledging the end of the colonial relationship while longing for its restoration.

More recently, one of us (Claudio) reappropriated the Lacanian concept of partial object, or "object *a*," in order to explore how soccer and opera amateurs who have been attached to a cultural object for a long time seek out another object that will produce a similar emotional resonance (Benzecry 2015). I use the idea of partial object to explain how amateurs forge a connection to a second, similar object that, lashed together with the self, include some (but not all) of the technologies and practices of the self enabled by the "original" cultural object.

Although the Freudian concept of fetishism alludes to a substitution and the fixation of an object with the traces of a repressed history, Marx's classic discussion of the fetishism of commodities opens up another avenue of inquiry about the relationship between material and social life. Thanks to it we are able to think of two interrelated questions, one about the temporal arc under which objects are awoken or brought to life, and a second one that wonders under what conditions human laborers are made oblivious to recognizing their own work as inscribed in those objects. For Marx, it is as commodities – which deprive workers of seeing themselves in what they have made – that things come alive and adopt an extraordinary life of their own, as "if it were to begin dancing of its own free will" (Marx 1976:164).

The paradoxically alienated and detached version of the relationship between objects and subjects was elaborated in the realm of consumption by Simmel (1968), who argued that objects were able to sublimate and absorb the spiritual life of individuals, imprisoning life and rendering it unable to adapt to changing developments. Simmel saw a world in which object scarcity was not the problem but rather the hypertrophic production of constant novelty; he considered this the principle malaise of modern life ("the tragedy of culture") – a view revived by the British school of material culture studies (Hicks and Beaudry 2010) and, more particularly, by anthropologist Daniel Miller (1987, 2012). The authors in this tradition have pursued an object-centered analysis of consumption and waste which seeks to reveal how owning, keeping, and discarding objects have become increasingly central practices in the accelerated cycle of production and consumption through which contemporary identities are formed (Gabrys, Hawkins, and Michael 2013; Gregson 2007; Miller 2001). The literature on museums also demonstrates how these practices of keeping, ridding, and letting go of objects have played a fundamental role in the cultural work required to build collective identities and narratives (Macdonald 2006).

But the role that objects play is not restricted to providing material props through which we construct and display our individual and collective identities. They also play a much deeper role by shaping how we think, judge, and imagine. As recent developments in cognitive science argue, seemingly "internal" cognitive operations, like remembering, judging, or calculation should not be seen as a set of disembodied and internal operations taking place inside the mind but should be seen, instead, as a set of relations and operations embedded in the material world (Clark and Chalmers 1998; Hutchins 1995). Objects, in this sense, do not belong to some sort of "outside" but are actually *one* of the mediums through which cognitive operations are made possible in the specific way they do – much like an abacus is not simply an "external means" to represent mathematical operations, but the very medium through which a specific way of thinking mathematically becomes possible.

What are objects good for?

One of the key contributions of the study of objects in recent years has been to take seriously the fact that objects are not optional, but constitute obligatory passage points humans have to contend with in order to pursue their projects (Latour 1991). Objects are indispensable equipment for living (Luhmann 2000), which provide the particular kind of social glue (see Henderson 1999) that makes possible the taken-for-granted routines and tacit rules supporting the social bonds that hold us together (see Serres 1995). From this perspective, the attempt to create any analytical separation between "the social" (or "the cultural"), and the "the material" is pointless. As Latour famously put it, we are rarely, if ever, confronted with a pure "human interaction," since our lives always take place in situations that take the form of "H-NH-H-NH-NH-NH-H-H-H-H-NH (where H stands for a human-like actant and NH for a non-human)" (Latour 1991:110).

This line of thought has been foundational to the field of science and technology studies (STS), which has endeavored to show how objects should be seen as sui generis social agents, what Callon called "actants" (1984), endowed with a sui generis kind of social agency. Through a variety of empirical case studies, scholars have shown "the mangle of practice" (Pickering 1995) through which the social world is continually being co-produced (Jasanoff 2004) in the process of trying to "enroll" objects into our life projects and how they, in turn, resist these attempts and end up translating and changing plans and social relations (Latour 1999).

A parallel train of thought has emerged over the last decades in the field of cultural anthropology. Of particular importance here is the work of the late Alfred Gell in the anthropology of art. Building on the work of Charles Peirce and Marilyn Strathern, Gell (1998) developed a new anthropological approach to art in which objects are not seen as encoding the world symbolically but as social agents endowed with social efficacy, capable of acting upon other social agents in their vicinity. For this reason, Gell argues, art objects should be seen as "systems of actions" that participate in the creation of the network of social relations in which they are themselves embedded (1998).

The built environment offers another arena of research for exploring the nature of the social bond, and the role played by material infrastructure in creating silent linkages between action, choices, and judgments (Domínguez Rubio and Fogué 2015). Some scholars have studied how urban planning and architecture effectively hardwire moral and cultural categories into the built environment (Graham and MacFarlane 2015; Joyce 2003). Others focus on the role of the built environment in articulating different forms of participation and exclusion in the body politic (Marres and Lezaun 2011), while others analyze how contemporary processes of meaning-making or truth-making are mediated by the particular affordances offered by different media infrastructures and platforms (Gillespie, Boczkowski, and Foot 2014; Parks and Starosielski 2015). Chandra Mukerji (2009, 2012) has advanced this line of work in cultural sociology by showing how built environments such as the Canal du Midi or the Gardens of Versailles made possible different forms of cultural imagination.

Taken together, these approaches serve to show that "cultural" narratives and categories are not simply negotiated through beliefs, cognitive schemas, or bodily dispositions but are also silently negotiated through streets, buildings, walls, and media technologies. Such research is gaining a whole new salience as our lives become increasingly mediated through technologies and built environments designed to "make sense" of us, by registering and categorizing our actions, making inferences about future behaviors, and acting pre-emptively upon them (Greenfield 2013). Consider how we are nudged to buy certain products rather than others from the carefully designed aisles of the supermarket to casinos (Schüll 2012), how we are conditioned to make moral judgments or live healthier lives (Thaler and Sunstein 2008), or presented with data encouraging us to quantify, measure, and evaluate ourselves (Neff and Nafus 2016).

Repairing and maintaining "culture"

In the previous sections, we discussed those traditions that detail how objects provide the conditions for certain interpretations, social relations, and imaginaries. One of the limitations of these traditions is that they tend to start with a premise of the world as comprising objects already integrated or stabilized, with only isolated moments of destabilization in need of redress. This premise obscures the inherent tension between stasis and change that characterizes our relationship with objects and the work of stabilization and restabilization that is constantly required to keep these objects alive.

In considering things as simultaneously material and meaningful, we learn that matter constrains meaning and vice versa. On the one hand, this implies coming to terms with what sociologist Terry McDonnell (2016) – echoing Webb Keane (2003) and his idea of "bundling" – has recently dubbed "cultural entropy," which describes how the intended meanings and uses we assign to objects fracture over time, giving way to new meanings. On the other hand, we also need to attend to the arguments of the "new materialisms" when they claim that we are never dealing with inert matter (Barad 2007; Bennett 2010; Coole and Frost 2010; Domínguez Rubio 2016), and that, following the old Spinozian distinction, we should never see objects as *natura naturata*, that is, as the necessary but *passive* principle of creation, but as *natura naturans*, that is, as part of the active principle shaping and structuring the world.

Taking this fact seriously invites us to think about the material world not in terms of "objects," but in terms of the processes and conditions under which certain "things" come to be differentiated and identified as particular kinds of "objects" endowed with particular forms of meaning, value, and power. Adopting this view means accepting that we do not live in a world made of finite and discrete "objects" but in a world made of things that are always moving and changing and in which, consequently, cultural meanings, categories, and boundaries are always precariously achieved and have to be continually maintained over time

A key implication here is that "culture" *corrodes*. The things through which we construct meaning are always falling apart, wearing down, and malfunctioning and, as a result, they have to be constantly mended, repaired, retrofitted, or repurposed. Think, for example, of how those seemingly timeless monuments that enable collective narratives slowly crumble away, or how those artworks that help constitute our symbolic universes wane and perish. Or more simply, think about the wear and tear of all the mundane physical paraphernalia through which we erect the symbolic boundaries that make possible our cultural identities on a daily basis.

Interestingly, this kind of cultural work of maintenance and repair has remained largely understudied by cultural sociologists. Indeed, while we have paid plenty of attention to how we produce cultural objects (e.g., "cultural production paradigm") or how we interpret and consume them (e.g., "reception studies"), we have not paid much attention at all to the work devoted to repairing and maintaining them – which is actually quite strange when you think about it, since a great deal of our daily toil – and budgets! – consists, precisely, in trying to keep things legible as effective and meaningful cultural objects. This is why we are *constantly* mending and repairing stuff and, in so doing, why we are constantly engaged in the process of tweaking, changing, or stabilizing the physical fabric of meaning.

Only recently has this type of work of maintenance and repair begun to receive the attention it deserves, especially among STS scholars (e.g., Bellacasa 2011; Denis and Pontille 2014; Jackson 2014; Star and Ruhleder 1996), but also among geographers (DeSilvey and Edensor 2013), sociologists (Benzecry 2016; Dant 2010), and anthropologists (Lea and Pholeros 2010). One of the benefits of this new wave of studies is that they help us to move beyond traditional dichotomies of "working" versus "not-working" or "functioning" versus "malfunctioning" by showing how maintenance and repair are not exceptional practices emerging in those critical moments when the normal state of affairs is interrupted, but are indeed what makes any normal state of affairs possible in the first place.

Some concluding thoughts on materials and semiosis

In sociology, the study of semiosis, of how meaning is made, has been dominated over the last decades by a focus on how beliefs, values, or norms are linked to one another constituting a more or less coherent and autonomous system called "culture." One of the main shortcomings of this approach is that it relies on an unnecessary analytical distinction between "culture" and "material," "meaning" and "matter." This chapter, on the contrary, shows that objects are important because they are one of the sites of culture; they are one of the places where cultural distinctions are made, negotiated, maintained, and repaired. They are not an "external" material input that has to be "factored into" a cultural scheme. They do not belong to some sort of material outside but are one of the mediums through which practices, meaning, and cognitive processes are made possible and come into being in specific ways.

Cultural sociologists have explored objects as totems (Alexander 2008; Durkheim 1965), as the site for the imprinting of competing claims (Zubrzycki 2013), as fetishes that construct boundaries between groups (Bourdieu 1984), or as highly contextual stabilizations of interaction (Collins 2004). Taking stock of what we have learned from the sociologists and other scholars interested in cultural objects, our final entreaty is to understand all of these frameworks as gradients of cases, in which even in totem-like situations there is always the potential for more than one affordance – always the potential for the correspondence between affect, individual, and object to be other than a one-to-one homology – and in which we investigate and never take for granted the work of holding those correspondences together. In his path-breaking book on materiality, *Where Stuff Comes From*, Molotch (2003:10) wrote: "objects are social relationships made durable." The key, as we have tried to show here, is to specify when and how they are imprinted and made to last.

References

Alexander, Jeffrey. 2008. "Iconic consciousness: The Material Feeling of Meaning." *Environment and Planning D: Society and Space* 26(5):782–94.

Barad, Karen. 2007. *Meeting the Universe Halfway: Quantum Physics and the Entanglement of Matter and Meaning.* Durham, NC: Duke University Press.

Bellacasa, Maria Puig de la. 2011. "Matters of Care in Technoscience: Assembling Neglected Things." *Social Studies of Science* 41(1):85–106.

Bennett, Jane. 2010. *Vibrant Matter: A Political Ecology of Things.* Durham, NC: Duke University Press.

Benzecry, Claudio E. 2011. *The Opera Fanatic: Ethnography of an Obsession.* Chicago: University of Chicago Press.

———. 2015. "Restabilizing Attachment to Cultural Objects: Aesthetics, Emotions and Biography." *British Journal of Sociology* 66(4):779–800.

———. 2016. "Of Scales and Standards." *Perspectives* 38(2):10–15.

Bourdieu, Pierre. 1984. *Distinction: A Social Critique of the Judgement of Taste.* Cambridge, MA: Harvard University Press.

Callon, Michel. 1984. "Some Elements of a Sociology of Translation: Domestication of the Scallops and the Fishermen of St Brieuc Bay." Pp. 196–223 in *Power, Action, and Belief: A New Sociology of Knowledge?*, edited by J. Law. London: Routledge.

Clark, Andy, and D. Chalmers. 1998. "The Extended Mind." *Analysis* 58(1):7–19.

Collins, Randall. 2004. *Interaction Ritual Chains.* Princeton, NJ: Princeton University Press.

Coole, Diana H., and Samantha Frost. 2010. *New Materialisms: Ontology, Agency, and Politics.* Durham, NC: Duke University Press.

Dant, Tim. 2010. "The Work of Repair: Gesture, Emotion, and Sensual Knowledge." *Sociological Research Online* 15(3):7.

Daston, Lorraine, ed. 2004. *Things that Talk: Object Lessons from Art and Science.* Cambridge, MA: MIT Press.

Denis, Jérôme, and David Pontille. 2014. "Material Ordering and the Care of Things." *Science, Technology, & Human Values* 40(3):338–67.

DeNora, Tia. 2000. *Music in Everyday Life.* Cambridge: Cambridge University Press.

———. 2003. *After Adorno: Rethinking Music Sociology.* Cambridge: Cambridge University Press.

DeSilvey, C., and T. Edensor. 2013. "Reckoning with Ruins." *Progress in Human Geography* 37(4):465–85.

Domínguez Rubio, Fernando. 2016. "On the Discrepancy between Objects and Things: An Ecological Approach." *Journal of Material Culture* 21(1):59–86.

Domínguez Rubio, Fernando, and Uriel Fogué. 2015. "Unfolding the Political Capacities of Design." Pp. 143–60 in *What Is Cosmopolitical Design? Design, Nature and the Built Environment,* edited by A. Yaneva and A. Zaera Polo. London: Ashgate.

Douglas, Mary. 1966. *Purity and Danger; an Analysis of Concepts of Pollution and Taboo.* New York: Praeger.

Durkheim, Emile. 1965. *The Elementary Forms of Religious Life.* New York: Free Press.

Gabrys, Jennifer, Gay Hawkins, and Mike Michael. 2013. *Accumulation: The Material Politics of Plastic.* London: Routledge.

Gell, Alfred. 1998. *Art and Agency: An Anthropological Theory.* Oxford: Oxford University Press.

Gillespie, Tarleton, Pablo J Boczkowski, and Kirsten A Foot. 2014. *Media Technologies: Essays on Communication, Materiality, and Society.* Cambridge, MA: MIT Press.

Graham, Stephen, and Colin McFarlane. 2015. *Infrastructural Lives: Urban Infrastructure in Context.* London: Routledge.

Greenfield, Adam. 2013. *Against the Smart City.* New York: Do Projects.

Gregson, Nicky. 2007. *Living with Things: Ridding, Accommodation, Dwelling.* Wantage: Sean Kingston Pub.

Henderson, Kathryn. 1999. *On line and on Paper: Visual Representations, Visual Cultures, and Computer Graphics in Design Engineering.* Cambridge, MA: MIT Press.

Hennion, A. 2007. "The Things That Hold Us Together: Taste and Sociology." *Cultural Sociology* 1(1):97–114.

Hennion, A., and J.M. Fauquet. 2001. "Authority as Performance: The Love of Bach in Nineteenth-Century France." *Poetics* 29(1):75–88.

Hennion, A., and E. Gomart. 1999. "A Sociology of Attachment: Music Amateurs, Drug Users." Pp. 220–47 in *Actor Network Theory and After,* edited by J. Law and J. Hassard. Oxford: Blackwell.

Hicks, Dan, and Mary Carolyn Beaudry. 2010. *The Oxford Handbook of Material Culture Studies.* Oxford: Oxford University Press.

Hutchins, Edwin. 1995. *Cognition in the Wild.* Cambridge, MA: MIT Press.

Jackson, Steven. 2014. "Rethinking Repair." Pp. 221–40 in *Media Technologies: Essays on Communication, Materiality, and Society*, edited by T. Gillespie, P. Boczkowski, and K. Foot. Cambridge, MA: MIT Press.

Jasanoff, Sheila. 2004. *States of Knowledge: The Co-Production of Science and Social Order*. London: Routledge.

Joyce, Patrick. 2003. *The Rule of Freedom: Liberalism and the Modern City*. London: Verso.

Keane, Webb. 2003. "Semiotics and the Social Analysis of Material Things." *Language & Communication* 23(3–4):409–25.

Lamont, Michelle. 1992. *Money, Morals, and Manners: The Culture of the French and the American Upper-Middle Class*. Chicago: University of Chicago Press.

Latour, Bruno. 1991. "Technology Is Society Made Durable." *Sociological Review* 38(S1):103–31.

———. 1999. *Pandora's Hope: Essays on the Reality of Science Studies*. Cambridge, MA: Harvard University Press.

Lea, Tess, and Paul Pholeros. 2010. "This Is Not a Pipe: The Treacheries of Indigenous Housing." *Public Culture* 22(1):187–209.

Luhmann, N. 2000. *Art as a Social System*. Palo Alto, CA: Stanford University Press.

Macdonald, Sharon. 2006. *A Companion to Museum Studies*. West Sussex: Wiley-Blackwell.

Marres, Noortje, and Javier Lezaun. 2011. "Materials and Devices of the Public: An Introduction." *Economy and Society* 40(4):489–509.

Marx, Karl. 1976. *Capital: A Critique of Political Economy*. Vol. 1. London: Penguin Books.

McDonnell, Terence E. 2016. *Best Laid Plans*. Chicago: University of Chicago Press.

Miller, Daniel. 1987. *Material Culture and Mass Consumption*. Oxford: Blackwell.

———. ed. 2001. *Home Possessions: Material Culture Behind Closed Doors*. Oxford: Bloomsbury Academic.

———. 2012. *Consumption and Its Consequences*. Cambridge: Polity Press.

Molotch, Harvey. 2003. *Where Stuff Comes from: How Toasters, Toilets, Cars, Computers, and Many Others Things Come to Be as They Are*. New York: Routledge.

Mukerji, Chandra. 2009. *Impossible Engineering: Technology and Territoriality on the Canal Du Midi*. Princeton, NJ: Princeton University Press.

———. 2012. "Space and Political Pedagogy at the Gardens of Versailles." *Public Culture* 24(3 68):509–34.

Neff, Gina, and Dawn Nafus. 2016. *Self-Tracking*. Cambridge, MA: MIT Press.

Parks, Lisa, and Nicole Starosielski. 2015. *Signal Traffic Critical Studies of Media Infrastructures*. Urbana: University of Illinois Press.

Pickering, Andrew. 1995. *The Mangle of Practice: Time, Agency, and Science*. Chicago: University of Chicago Press.

Schüll, Natasha Dow. 2012. *Addiction by Design: Machine Gambling in Las Vegas*. Princeton, NJ: Princeton University Press.

Serres, Michel. 1995. *The Natural Contract*. Ann Arbor: University of Michigan Press.

Simmel, Georg. 1968. *The Conflict in Modern Culture and Other Essays*. New York: Teachers College Press.

Star, Susan Leigh, and Karen Ruhleder. 1996. "Steps Toward an Ecology of Infrastructure: Design and Access for Large Information Spaces." *Information Systems Research* 7(1):111–34.

Steinmetz, George. 2008. "Harrowed Landscapes: White Ruingazers in Namibia and Detroit and the Cultivation of Memory." *Visual Studies* 23(3):211–37.

Thaler, Richard, and Cass Sunstein. 2008. *Nudge: Improving Decisions about Health, Wealth, and Happiness*. New Haven, CT: Yale University Press.

Turkle, Sherry, ed. 2007. *Evocative Objects: Things We Think With*. Cambridge, MA: MIT Press.

———. ed. 2008. *The Inner History of Devices*. Cambridge, MA: MIT Press.

Turner, Victor. 1967. *The Forest of Symbols: Aspects of Ndembu Ritual*. Ithaca, NY: Cornell University Press.

Willis, Paul. 1978. *Profane Culture*. London: Routledge.

Winchester, Daniel. Forthcoming. "'A Part of Who I Am': Material Objects as 'Plot Devices' in the Formation of Religious Selves." *Journal for the Scientific Study of Religion*.

Zubrzycki, Geneviève. 2011. "History and the National Sensorium: Making Sense of Polish Mythology." *Qualitative Sociology* 34(1):21–57.

———. 2013. "Aesthetic Revolt and the Remaking of National Identity in Quebec, 1960–1969." *Theory and Society* 42(5):423–75.

35

Pop culture

From production to socio-technical moments

Marshall Battani

Introduction

In the US, the study of popular culture developed into a legitimate sociological specialty as sociologists of culture harnessed conceptual toolkits already developed for the study of organizations and occupations to focus on the systemic institutionalized nature of the creation, distribution, and valuation of pop culture. The production of culture perspective is the foundation of this orientation and it has had a tremendous influence on sociological work on culture (Peterson and Anand 2004). Although the production perspective arguably emphasizes a complex duality of mutually constructed cultural and social structures, it is often considered, even by its practitioners, to be more narrowly focused on institutional constraints on cultural objects (see Santoro 2008). This narrow focus on institutions is problematic in light of the more recent recognition that popular culture is now sometimes created outside of institutions and exists fleetingly in what some describe as "socio-technical moments" (Gomez Cruz and Meyer 2012; Koliska and Roberts 2015; Villi 2015). This chapter examines the field of production studies in relation to other contemporaneous approaches to culture (especially cultural studies, associated with Birmingham School in the UK, and the work of French anthropologist Michel de Certeau) to suggest that the production of culture approach is still a useful tool to the extent that it can be agnostic regarding the boundaries between institutions and their environments.

The production of culture: institutions and their environs

The production perspective emerged from a perceived impasse as grand functionalist and Marxist theorists had failed to recognize their potential shared interest in empirical studies of culture (Battani and Hall 2000). The production perspective is typically unconcerned with distinctions between popular culture and high culture and quintessential production studies include subjects ranging from art (White and White 1965; Becker 1982; Crane 1989) to music (Dowd 2004) and fashion (Crane and Bovone 2006; Crane 2012). The production perspective tends to explain culture as an outcome of the social structures within which it is created. Early studies of news production, for example, illustrate how the organization of news-gathering into "beats," in combination with the conventions of a given news medium (column inches, server space, live feeds, deadlines, news cycles, etc.) creates a "news-net" (Tuchman 1978) that will capture only a very particular and narrow vision of the world. News-making studies of this sort have been one of the most active areas of inquiry in popular culture institutions (see Altheide 1974; Altheide and Rasmussen 1976; Tuchman 1978; Gitlin 1980; Schudson 1981, 1982, 1989; Miladi 2003), especially since digital and social media technologies have transformed how and by whom news is created and disseminated (Alasuutari, Qadir, and Creutz 2013; Usher 2013; C.W. Anderson 2013, 2014; Lewis and Usher 2013, 2014; San Cornelio and Gomez Cruz 2014; Schlesinger and Doyle 2015; Klein-Avraham and Reich 2016).

Much like news content, the narrow range of content in television programming before and after the proliferation of cable channels and the advent of narrowcasting is explained by focusing attention on the constraints imposed on production by the everyday and routine organization of work (Gitlin 1983; Bielby and Bielby 1994; Scott 2004; Wei 2012), by the narrowly defined target audience (Villarejo 2016), and by the demands of a highly integrated multiplatform digital environment constituting what some refer to as television's third golden age (cf. Wayne 2016). Productive interactions become normalized, institutionalized, and routinized over time and, as a result, particular conventions of style and meaning emerge, predominate, and become normalized and institutionalized. In the current era, when televisual consumption practices have shifted dramatically, the production perspective is still a viable tool for understanding both the social construction of audiences and the content generating practices emerging in response to new audience habits (Serazio 2013; Stein 2015).

The production perspective has been employed to explain the style and content of Hollywood movies (Baker and Faulkner 1991; Baumann 2001), Bollywood movies (Desai 2004; Bandyopadhyay 2008; Shankar 2008; Thussu 2008; Dudrah 2012; Ganti 2012; Balaji and Hughson 2014), the form, content, and distribution of magazines (Haveman 2004; Moeran 2006; L. Davidson, McNeill, and Ferguson 2007), photographic meanings in the US (Rosenblum 1978a, 1978b; Battani 1999) and Japan (Edwards and Hart 2004), as well as industry emergence and contemporary music production in Korea (Han et al. 2013; Jin 2016). Studies of music abound, and they range in locale from India (Booth 2015), Turkey (Bates 2016), Israel and Palestine (Brinner 2009), Beirut (Burkhalter 2013), the UK (Frith, Cloonan, and Williamson 2009; Pettinger 2015; Cloonan 2016), Zimbabwe (Mhiripiri 2010), France (Briggs 2015), and the US (Peterson and Berger 1971; Peterson 1997; Santoro 2015; Wynn 2015).

Ideological critique

Sociological analysis of pop culture at its most critical (and least subtle) generally investigates the substance of popular culture (mostly the content of news, advertising, and television, but sometimes cultural or subcultural practices as well) to reveal the powers working to perpetuate the appearance of social solidarity that is, in reality, an ideologically and materially self-interested effort to maintain the status quo. Drawing (often implicitly) on Frankfurt School concepts of affirmative culture, this work tends to focus on the political economy of mass media and their biases (Chomsky and Herman 2002; Mullen 2010; Bagdikian 2014) as well as on advertising and public relations (Ewen 1996, 1999, 2008a, 2008b; Leiss et al. 2005; Auerbach 2015). The critical theoretical distinction between authentic culture (emergent, fulfilling, open to human agency) and popular culture (rigidly structured, empty, reifies structures) informs work ranging from the analyses of the commodification of music (Seiler 2000; Dowd 2002; Taylor 2007; Larsen 2008) to the intimate connections between bookstores, shopping malls, amusement parks, and cities (Fjellman 1992; Miller 1999, 2006; Gottdiener, Collins, and Dickens 2000; Gottdiener 2001; Bryman 2004; Hannigan 2005; Ritzer 2011). The role of pop culture in spreading neoliberalism across the planet is examined in a wide range of settings from the global (Berdayes and Berdayes 2016; McGuigan 2016), to specific foci on the US (G. Williams 2002), Latin America (G. Williams 2002), New Zealand (Falcous and Newman 2016), India (Roy 2016), and Islam (van Nieuwkerk, LeVine, and Stokes 2016).

A significant body of critical work has been inspired by the Centre for Contemporary Cultural Studies at the University of Birmingham (also known as the "Birmingham School") in the UK, whose main focus was the interplay between hegemonic power and the potential for ideological resistance. Although the Birmingham School arose contemporaneously with the production of culture approach, its incorporation into American sociology came later, largely spurred by the institutionalization of cultural studies into the American academy. The classic examples include Gilroy (1987), Hall and Jefferson (1993), Hebdige (1979), and Willis (1977). More recent studies in this tradition often delineate the creation and management of ambivalent identities within particular institutional settings. Grindstaff (2002) and Gamson (1998) have studied television talk shows and illustrate how practices in the institutional field of TV talk intersect and overlap with US traditions of the public sphere. The resulting interactions in the production and airing of TV talk shows give voice to stigmatized members of society while at the same time recreating and reinforcing status structures of sexuality, class, and ethnicity. Amy Best's ethnographic studies of US teenagers' emergent identities in relation to the high school prom (Best 2000) and car subcultures (Best 2006) illustrate this ambivalence as well. In her studies one sees teens constructing identities for themselves that embrace *and* resist social structures of gender, sexuality, class, and ethnicity at play in the popular institutions central to their lives (see also Shankar 2008; Gray 2009; Ito et al. 2009; Garot 2010; Davidson 2011; Gartman 2012; Kawamura 2013).

The skateboarder and documentary filmmaker Stacy Peralta takes an approach similar to Best's in his *Dog Town and Z-Boys* (Peralta 2001), as he chronicles the transformation of skateboarding from a Southern California fad into a subculture that, in turn, became institutionalized as a multibillion-dollar global industry in the late 1970s via the marketing of the identities of a small group of skaters from Santa Monica, California. The skaters were transformed as well, some leaving behind their working-class lives to become celebrities, others embracing their working-class identity in a fatalistic rebellion much like the English "lads" described by Paul Willis in his work explaining institutionalized class and gender reproduction in British schools (Willis 1977). The conclusions of such studies often depict a mutually reinforcing relationship between emerging and established cultural institutions and social structures.

Meanings and active audiences

Santoro argues that we would be wise to conceptualize the everyday cultural practices (like the rebelliousness of California skaters or English lads) as one more form of production amenable to analysis via the production of culture perspective and that the production of culture perspective is in fact well-suited for studying "the informal processes of production of culture in everyday life" (2008:14). But while production of culture studies at their best treat the meaningful activity of audiences as endogenous to the production process, it is really the scholarship on fandom inspired by Michel de Certeau's *The Practice of Everyday Life* (1984) that breaks down the binary opposition of production and consumption. In Certeau's argument, readers actively "poach" texts, disregarding cultural authority to create their own meanings, while making tactical moves in a struggle to carve out both psychological and physical space within and around dominant cultural institutions.

With Certeau as their inspiration, sociologically informed analyses of consumers, audiences, and fans look carefully and critically at how people collectively make aesthetic judgments and create meaning (Jenkins 1992; Press 1994). The women in Janice Radway's (1984) classic study of romance novel readers, for example, construct from the novels empowering gendered meanings and edifying reading practices that qualify and even contradict the patriarchal dynamics assumed by literary elites. Elites and romance readers employ very different aesthetic standards and it is a mistake to presuppose the predominance of one over another. Audiences, it would seem, just don't always interpret things in ways wholly predicted by social structures. JoEllen Shively's (1992) study of the Hollywood western genre, for example, found that Native American audience members identified more closely with cowboy characters than they did with Native American characters. In this case the qualities of "good vs. bad" were more salient than race or ethnicity. Similarly, there is growing research on the social characteristics of online gamers and the imaginative variety of roles they play in creating a gaming experience (Harper 2014; Chee and Kim 2015; Cote 2015; Kirkpatrick 2015; Massanari 2015; A. Williams 2015; Huntemann and Aslinger 2016).

Likewise with global media, audiences are active interpreters of meaning and do not simply absorb and assimilate meaning determined elsewhere. See Liebes and Katz (1990) and Ang (1991) on the worldwide popularity of the US soap opera *Dallas*, Hafez and Paletz (2001) on mass media, globalization, and patterns of political and social change in the Middle East, and Denise Bielby and C. Lee Harrington's (2004) explanation of how the concept of genre facilitates cross-cultural interpretations of television shows on the global market. Avihu Shoshana (2016) has studied ethno-class distinctions in relation to the reception of the reality show *Big Brother* in Israel and as various forms of reality television have become staples of production around the globe their audiences' practices, actions, and interpretations are increasingly studied (Sender 2012; Skeggs and Wood 2012; Allen and Mendick 2013) and research ranges widely in subject matter from hip-hop (Gibson 2014), to Hooters restaurants (Newton-Francis and Young 2015), to Chinese youth watching American television (Gao 2016) and ironic television consumption (McCoy and Scarborough 2014).

Pop culture production in socio-technical moments

For Gomez Cruz and Meyer (2012) the pervasive use of iPhone cameras is a new moment in which the relationship between institutionalized production of images on the one hand and consumption or reception on the other all but disappears. Photographic images, they argue, are created in socio-technical moments when "a set of technologies, meanings, uses, and practices align" (Gomez Cruz and Meyer 2012:204). The amateur photographer, for the first time, has (nearly) complete control over the creation, processing, and distribution of photographic images. All of these processes have now been collapsed into one moment. The consequences of this control are evident in the wide variety of ways that camera phone images have been created and distributed across institutional contexts – as in the Black Lives Matter movement, for instance, where images of black boys and men being beaten or killed by police helped counter official narratives of policing and galvanize resistance. A more recent example is the 2017 "Unite the Right" rally in Charlottesville, Virginia. Terrifying amateur images of the moment when counter protester Heather Heyer was murdered appeared on personal Facebook feeds, appeared on cable news platforms, and provided raw material for the creation of memes expressing political and ideological views. Live amateur Facebook streams during the confrontation also later provide video for news broadcasts. Both amateur and professional images (appearing on social media and on news outlets) have been used by counter protesters to document crimes as well as to identify and publicly expose racists to their families, communities, and workplaces. In these ways camera phone images cut across institutional boundaries (journalism, photojournalism, law enforcement, social movement organizations).

The productive power of people with smartphones in the US, Europe, and parts of Asia (especially South Korea) has given rise to whole new genres of popular culture in which production and consumption are diffused across massive networks. Selfies, the ubiquitous new genre of our digital lives, have redefined some of the social boundaries between public and private (Walsh and Baker 2016), and have inspired studies of identity, the presentation of self (Frosh 2015; Wargo 2015), and branding (Eagar, Dann, and Schroeder 2016). Wiggins and Bowers (2015) have defined the internet meme as a pop culture genre, others have created typologies and studied the network structures of memes (Segev et al. 2015) as well as memes' role in producing collective identity (Gal, Shifman, and Kampf 2015), resistance to authority (Bayerl and Stoynov 2016), and political satire in Iran (Rahimi 2015). Soha and McDowell (2016) show how the meme phenomenon challenges ideas about authorship and the uses of copyright in contradictory ways. YouTube has monetized memes and grown to market dominance by first using aspects of copyright law to protect itself from the liabilities of hosting user-generated content that violated copyright law and then, once dominant, used copyright law again but this time to force content creators and copyright holders into YouTube's own licensing practices and payment schemes.

Conclusion

Memes and selfies would not have become what they are today without the infrastructure and networks of digital social media, and so production and reception of pop culture is not completely independent of institutions. But now, rather than being organized around the different modes of production on the one hand and reception or consumption by audiences and fans on the other, digital networks create a stage to facilitate varieties of text-based and visual social interaction. That stage is, of course, why institutions still matter for understanding pop culture. The presence and power of a social media organization like Facebook becomes clear when changes to its user experience raise issues of privacy, of creative control, and of copyright (Stutzman, Gross, and Acquisti 2012; Wilson, Gosling, and Graham 2012; Milazzo 2013). Institutionalized power and authority also emerge when enacted on behalf of users and their reasonable expectations that social media sites work to reduce or prevent trolling, abuse, and cyber-bullying (Phillips 2015; Coles and West 2016; Dynel 2016). When user-generated content (UGC in industry circles) takes center stage and upwards of 300 hours of video are uploaded to YouTube every minute, the idea of institutionally defined producers on the one hand and (even "active") consumers on the other is theoretically clumsy. Production is accomplished now by users as much as consumers or producers. The production of culture perspective will continue to be useful for analyses of pop culture to the extent that it can put users center stage and appreciate how user activity produces content and meaning across and within multiple institutional contexts.

References

Alasuutari, P., A. Qadir, and K. Creutz. 2013. "The Domestication of Foreign News: News Stories Related to the 2011 Egyptian Revolution in British, Finnish and Pakistani Newspapers." *Media, Culture and Society* 35(6):692–707.

Allen, K., and H. Mendick. 2013. "Keeping it Real? Social Class, Young People and 'Authenticity' in Reality TV." *Sociology* 47(3):460–76.

Altheide, D.L. 1974. *Creating Reality: How TV News Distorts Events*. Beverly Hills, CA: Sage.

Altheide, D.L., and P.K. Rasmussen. 1976. "Becoming News: A Study of Two Newsrooms." *Work and Occupations* 3(2):223–46.

Anderson, C.W. 2013. "Towards a Sociology of Computational and Algorithmic Journalism." *New Media and Society* 15(7):1005–21.

———. 2014. "The Sociology of the Professions and the Problem of Journalism Education." *Radical Teacher* (99):62–8. https://doi.org/10.5195/rt.2014.108

Ang, I. 1991. *Desperately Seeking the Audience*. London: Routledge.

Auerbach, J. 2015. *Weapons of Democracy: Propaganda, Progressivism, and American Public Opinion*. Baltimore, MD: Johns Hopkins University Press.

Bagdikian, B.H. 2014. *The New Media Monopoly: A Completely Revised and Updated Edition with Seven New Chapters*. Boston, MA: Beacon Press.

Baker, W.E., and R.R. Faulkner. 1991. "Role as Resource in the Hollywood Film Industry." *American Journal of Sociology* 97(2):279–309.

Balaji, M., and K. Hughson. 2014. "(Re)producing Borders and Bodies: Masculinity and Nationalism in Indian Cultural Texts." *Asian Journal of Communication* 24(3):207–21.

Bandyopadhyay, R. 2008. "Nostalgia, Identity and Tourism: Bollywood in the Indian Diaspora." *Journal of Tourism and Cultural Change* 6(2):79–100.

Bates, E. 2016. *Digital Tradition: Arrangement and Labor in Istanbul's Recording Studio Culture*. Oxford: Oxford University Press.

Battani, M. 1999. "Organizational Fields, Cultural Fields and Art Worlds: The Early Effort to Make Photographs and Make Photographers in the 19th-century United States of America." *Media, Culture and Society* 21(5):601–26.

Battani, M., and J.R. Hall. 2000. "Richard Peterson and Cultural Theory: From Genetic, to Integrated, and Synthetic Approaches." *Poetics* 28(2):137–56.

Baumann, S. 2001. "Intellectualization and Art World Development: Film in the United States." *American Sociological Review* 66(3):404–26.

Bayerl, P.S., and L. Stoynov. 2016. "Revenge by Photoshop: Memefying Police Acts in the Public Dialogue about Injustice." *New Media and Society* 18(6):1006–26.

Becker, H.S. 1982. *Art Worlds*. Berkeley: University of California Press.

Berdayes, V., and L. Berdayes. 2016. "Slicing Up Societies: Commercial Media and the Destruction of Social Environments." Pp. 71–86 in *Neoliberalism, Economic Radicalism, and the Normalization of Violence*, edited by V. Berdayes and J.W. Murphy. Cham, Switzerland: Springer International.

Best, A.L. 2000. *Prom Night: Youth, Schools, and Popular Culture*. New York: Routledge.

———. 2006. *Fast Cars, Cool Rides: The Accelerating World of Youth and Their Cars*. New York: NYU Press.

Bielby, W.T., and D.D. Bielby. 1994. "'All Hits Are Flukes': Institutionalized Decision Making and the Rhetoric of Network Prime-Time Program Development." *American Journal of Sociology* 99(5):1287–313.

Bielby, D.D., and C.L. Harrington. 2004. "Managing Culture Matters: Genre, Aesthetic Elements, and the International Market for Exported Television." *Poetics* 32(1):73–98.

Booth, G. 2015. "Copyright Law and the Changing Economic Value of Popular Music in India." *Ethnomusicology* 59(2):262–87.

Briggs, J. 2015. *Sounds French: Globalization, Cultural Communities and Pop Music, 1958–1980*. New York: Oxford University Press.

Brinner, B. 2009. *Playing across a divide: Israeli-Palestinian musical encounters*. New York: Oxford University Press.

Bryman, A. 2004. *The Disneyization of Society*. London: Sage.

Burkhalter, T. 2013. *Local Music Scenes and Globalization: Transnational Platforms in Beirut*. New York: Routledge.

Chee, F., and S. Kim. 2015. "Transformative Mobile Game Culture: A Sociocultural Analysis of Korean Mobile Gaming in the Era of Smartphones." *International Journal of Cultural Studies* 18(4):413–29.

Chomsky, N., and E. Herman. 2002. "A Propaganda Model." Pp. 1–35 in *Manufacturing Consent: The Political Economy of the Mass Media*. 2nd ed. New York: Pantheon Books.

Cloonan, M. 2016. *Popular Music and the State in the UK: Culture, Trade or Industry?* Abingdon: Routledge.

Coles, B.A., and M. West. 2016. "Trolling the Trolls: Online Forum Users Constructions of the Nature and Properties of Trolling." *Computers in Human Behavior* 60:233–44.

Cote, A.C. 2015. "'I Can Defend Myself': Women's Strategies for Coping With Harassment While Gaming Online." *Games and Culture* 12(2):136–55. https://doi.org/10.1177/1555412015587603

Crane, D. 1989. *The Transformation of the Avant-Garde: The New York Art World, 1940–1985*. Chicago: University of Chicago Press.

———. 2012. *Fashion and its Social Agendas: Class, Gender, and Identity in Clothing*. Chicago: University of Chicago Press.

Crane, D., and L. Bovone. 2006. "Approaches to Material Culture: The Sociology of Fashion and Clothing." *Poetics* 34(6):319–33.

Davidson, E. 2011. *The Burdens of Aspiration: Schools, Youth, and Success in the Divided Social Worlds of Silicon Valley*. New York: NYU Press.

Davidson, L., L. McNeill, and S. Ferguson. 2007. "Magazine Communities: Brand Community Formation in Magazine Consumption." *International Journal of Sociology and Social Policy* 27(5/6):208–20.

de Certeau, M. 1984. *The Practice of Everyday Life*. Berkeley: University of California Press.

Desai, J. 2004. *Beyond Bollywood: The Cultural Politics of South Asian Diasporic Film*. New York: Routledge.

Dowd, T.J. 2002. "Culture and Commodifictation: Technology and Structural Power in the Early US Recording Industry." *International Journal of Sociology and Social Policy* 22(1/2/3):106–40.

———. 2004. "Production Perspectives in the Sociology of Music." *Poetics* 32(3):235–46.

Dudrah, R. 2012. *Bollywood Travels: Culture, diaspora and border crossings in popular Hindi cinema*. New York: Routledge.

Dynel, M. 2016. "'Trolling is not stupid': Internet Trolling as the Art of Deception Serving Entertainment." *Intercultural Pragmatics* 13(3):353–81.

Eagar, T., S. Dann, and J. Schroeder. 2016. "Classifying the Narrated #selfie: Genre Typing Human-branding Activity." *European Journal of Marketing* 50(9/10):1835–57.

Edwards, E., and J. Hart, eds. 2004. *Photographs Objects Histories: On the Materiality of Images*. New York: Routledge.

Ewen, S. 1996. *A Social History of Spin*. New York: Basic Books.

———. 1999. *All Consuming Images: The Politics of Style in Contemporary Culture*. New York: Basic Books.

———. 2008a. *Captains of Consciousness: Advertising and the Social Roots of the Consumer Culture*. New York: Basic Books.

———. 2008b. *PR!: A Social History of Spin*. New York: Basic Books.

Falcous, M., and J.L. Newman. 2016. "Sporting Mythscapes, Neoliberal Histories, and Post-colonial Amnesia in Aotearoa/New Zealand." *International Review for the Sociology of Sport* 51(1):61–77.

Fjellman, S.M. 1992. *Vinyl Leaves: Walt Disney World and America*. Boulder, CO: Westview Press.

Frith, S., M. Cloonan, and J. Williamson. 2009. "On Music as a Creative Industry." Pp. 74–89 in *Creativity, Innovation and the Cultural Economy*, edited by A.C. Pratt and P. Jeffcutt. Abingdon, UK: Routledge.

Frosh, P. 2015. "The Gestural Image: The Selfie, Photography Theory, and Kinesthetic Sociability." *International Journal of Communication* 9:1608–28.

Gal, N., L. Shifman, and Z. Kampf. 2015. "'It Gets Better': Internet Memes and the Construction of Collective Identity." *New Media and Society* 18(8):1698–714. https://doi.org/10.1177/1461444814568784

Gamson, J. 1998. *Freaks Talk Back: Tabloid Talk Shows and Sexual Nonconformity*. Chicago: University of Chicago Press.

Ganti, T. 2012. *Producing Bollywood: Inside the Contemporary Hindi Film Industry*. Durham, NC: Duke University Press.

Gao, Y. 2016. "Fiction as Reality: Chinese Youths Watching American Television." *Poetics* 54:1–13.

Garot, R. 2010. *Who You Claim: Performing Gang Identity in School and on the Streets*. New York: NYU Press.

Gartman, D. 2012. "Bourdieu and Adorno: Converging Theories of Culture and Inequality." *Theory and society* 41(1):41–72.

Gibson, M. 2014. "'That's hip-hop to me!': Race, Space, and Temporal Logics of Authenticity in Independent Cultural Production." *Poetics* 46:38–55.

Gilroy, P. 1987. *There Ain't No Black in the Union Jack*. Chicago: University of Chicago Press.

Gitlin, T. 1980. *The Whole World is Watching: Mass Media in the Making and Unmaking of the New Left*. Berkeley: University of California Press.

———. 1983. *Inside Prime Time*. New York: Pantheon.

Gomez Cruz, E. and E.T. Meyer. 2012. "Creation and Control in the Photographic Process: iPhones and the Emerging Fifth Moment of Photography." *Photographies* 5(2):203–21. https://doi.org/10.1080/17 540763.2012.702123

Gottdiener, M. 2001. *The Theming of America: Dreams, Media Fantasies, and Themed Environments*. Boulder, CO: Westview Press.

Gottdiener, M., C. Collins, and D.R. Dickens. 2000. *Las Vegas: The Social Production of an All-American City*. Malden, MA: Wiley-Blackwell.

Gray, M.L. 2009. *Out in the Country: Youth, Media, and Queer Visibility in Rural America*. New York: NYU Press.

Grindstaff, L. 2002. *The Money Shot: Trash, Class, and the Making of TV Talk Shows*. Chicago: University of Chicago Press.

Hafez, K., and D. Paletz. 2001. *Mass Media, Politics, and Society in the Middle East*. New York: Hampton Press.

Hall, S., and T. Jefferson. 1993. *Resistance through Rituals: Youth Subcultures in Post-war Britain*. Abingdon, UK: Psychology Press.

Han, J., S.K. Han, E.J. Zhang, and D.H. Kwon. 2013. "The Formation and Differentiation of Modern Korean Music World." *Korean Social Sciences Review* 3(1):107–31.

Hannigan, J. 2005. *Fantasy City: Pleasure and Profit in the Postmodern Metropolis*. New York: Routledge.

Harper, T. 2014. *The Culture of Digital Fighting Games: Performance and Practice*. New York: Routledge.

Haveman, H.A. 2004. "Antebellum Literary Culture and the Evolution of American Magazines." *Poetics* 32(1):5–28.

Hebdige, D. 1979. *Subculture: The Meaning of Style*. London: Routledge.

Huntemann, N., and B. Aslinger, eds. 2016. *Gaming Globally: Production, Play, and Place*. New York: Springer.

Ito, M., S. Baumer, M. Bittanti, D. Boyd, R. Cody, B.H. Stephenson, H.A. Horst, P.G. Lange, D. Mahendran, K.Z. Martínez, et al. 2009. *Hanging Out, Messing Around, and Geeking Out: Kids Living and Learning with New Media*. Cambridge, MA: MIT Press.

Jin, D.Y. 2016. "K-pop: Popular Music, Cultural Amnesia, and Economic Innovation in South Korea." *Pacific Affairs* 89(1):200–2.

Jenkins, H. 1992. *Textual Poachers: Television Fans and Participatory Culture*. New York: Routledge.

Kawamura, Y. 2013. *Fashioning Japanese Subcultures*. London: Bloomsbury Academic.

Kirkpatrick, G. 2015. "Game Addicted Freaks." Pp. 73–100 in *The Formation of Gaming Culture: UK Gaming Magazines, 1981–1995*. London: Palgrave Macmillan.

Klein-Avraham, I., and Z. Reich. 2016. "Out of the Frame: A Longitudinal Perspective on Digitization and Professional Photojournalism." *New Media and Society* 18(3):429–46.

Koliska, M., and J. Roberts. 2015. "Selfies: Witnessing and Participatory Journalism with a Point of View." *International Journal of Communication* 9:1672–85.

Larsen, A.E. 2008. "Selling (Out) the Local Scene: Grunge and Globalization." MFA Thesis, Department of Media Studies, State University of New York, Buffalo.

Leiss, W., S. Kline, S. Jhally, and J. Botterill. 2005. *Social Communication in Advertising: Consumption in the Mediated Marketplace*. 3rd ed. New York: Routledge Taylor & Francis Group.

Lewis, S.C., and N. Usher. 2013. "Open Source and Journalism: Toward New Frameworks for Imagining News Innovation." *Media, Culture and Society* 35(5):602–19.

———. 2014. "Code, Collaboration, and the Future of Journalism: A Case Study of the Hacks/Hackers Global Network." *Digital Journalism* 2(3):383–93.

Liebes, T., and E. Katz. 1990. *The Export of Meaning: Cross-Cultural Readings of Dallas*. Cambridge: Polity Press.

Massanari, A.L. 2015. "Gaming at the Edge: Sexuality and Gender at the Margins of Gamer Culture." *American Journal of Play* 8(1):139–42.

McCoy, C.A., and R.C. Scarborough. 2014. "Watching 'bad' Television: Ironic Consumption, Camp, and Guilty Pleasures." *Poetics* 47:41–59.

McGuigan, J. 2016. *Neoliberal Culture*. London: Palgrave Macmillan.

Mhiripiri, N.A. 2010. "The Production of Stardom and the Survival Dynamics of the Zimbabwean Music Industry in the post-2000 Crisis Period." *Journal of African Media Studies* 2(2):209–23.

Miladi, N. 2003. "Mapping the Al-Jazeera Phenomenon." Pp. 149–60 in *War and the Media: Reporting Conflict 24/7*, edited by D. Kishan Thussu and D. Freedman. London: SAGE.

Milazzo, M.J. 2013. "Facebook, Privacy, and Reasonable Notice: The Public Policy Problems with Facebook's Current Sign-up Process and How to Remedy the Legal Issues." *Cornell Journal of Law and Public Policy* 23(3):661.

Miller, L.J. 1999. "Shopping for Community: The Transformation of the Bookstore into a Vital Community Institution." *Media, Culture and Society* 21(3):385–407.

———. 2006. *Reluctant Capitalists: Bookselling and the Culture of Consumption.* Vol. 3. Chicago: University of Chicago Press.

Moeran, B. 2006. "More Than Just a Fashion Magazine." *Current Sociology* 54(5): 725–44.

Mullen, A. 2010. "Twenty Years On: The Second-order Prediction of the Herman-Chomsky Propaganda Model." *Media, Culture and Society* 32(4):1–18.

Newton-Francis, M., and G. Young. 2015. "Not Winging it at Hooters: Conventions for Producing a Cultural Object of Sexual Fantasy." *Poetics* 52:1–17.

Peralta, S. 2001. *Dogtown and Z-boys.* [DVD] New York: Sony Pictures Classic.

Peterson, R.A. 1997. *Creating Country Music: Fabricating Authenticity.* Chicago: University of Chicago Press.

Peterson, R.A., and D. Anand. 2004. "The Production of Culture Perspective." *Annual Review of Sociology* 30:311–34.

Peterson, R.A., and D.G. Berger. 1971. "Entrepreneurship in Organizations: Evidence from the Popular Music Industry." *Administrative Science Quarterly* 16(1):97–108.

Pettinger, L. 2015. "Embodied Labour in Music Work." *British Journal of Sociology* 66(2):282–300.

Phillips, Whitney. 2015. *This is Why We Can't Have Nice Things: Mapping the Relationship Between Online Trolling and Mainstream Culture.* Cambridge, MA: MIT Press.

Press, A. 1994. "The Sociology of Cultural Reception: Notes Toward an Emerging Paradigm." Pp. 221–45 in *The Sociology of Culture*, edited by D. Crane. Cambridge, MA: Blackwell.

Radway, J. 1984. *Reading the Romance: Women, Patriarchy, and Popular Literature.* Chapel Hill: University of North Carolina Press.

Rahimi, B. 2015. "Satirical Cultures of Media Publics in Iran." *International Communication Gazette* 77(3):267–81.

Ritzer, G. 2011. *The McDonaldization of Society 6.* Newbury Park, CA: Pine Forge Press.

Rosenblum, B. 1978a. *Photographers at Work: A Sociology of Photographic Styles.* New York: Holmes and Meier.

———. 1978b. "Style as Social Process." *American Sociological Review* 43(3):422–38.

Roy, S. 2016. "Slumdog Millionaire: Capitalism, a Love Story." *Journal of Popular Culture* 49(1):155–73.

San Cornelio, G., and E. Gomez Cruz. 2014. "Co-creation and Participation as a Means of Innovation in New Media: An Analysis of Creativity in the Photographic Field." *International Journal of Communication* 8:1–20.

Santoro, M. 2008. "Culture As (And After) Production." *Cultural Sociology* 2(1):7–31.

———. 2015. "Production Perspectives." Pp. 127–39 in *The Routledge Reader on the Sociology of Music*, edited by J. Shepherd and K. Devine. New York: Routledge.

Schlesinger, P., and G. Doyle. 2015. "From Organizational Crisis to Multi-platform Salvation? Creative Destruction and the Recomposition of News Media." *Journalism* 16(3):305–23.

Schudson, M. 1981. *Discovering the News: A Social History of American Newspapers.* New York: Basic Books.

———. 1982. *The Power of News.* Cambridge, MA: Harvard University Press.

———. 1989. "The Sociology of News Production." *Media, Culture and Society* 11(3):263–82.

Scott, A.J. 2004. "The Other Hollywood: The Organizational and Geographic Bases of Television-Program Production." *Media, Culture and Society* 26(2):183–205.

Segev, E., A. Nissenbaum, N. Stolero, and L. Shifman. 2015. "Families and Networks of Internet Memes: The Relationship between Cohesiveness, Uniqueness, and Quiddity Concreteness." *Journal of Computer-Mediated Communication* 20(4):417–33.

Seiler, C. 2000. "The Commodification of Rebellion: Rock Culture and Consumer Capitalism." Pp. 203–26 in *New Forms of Consumption: Consumers, Culture, and Commodification*, edited by M. Gottdiener. Lanham, MD: Rowman & Littlefield.

Sender, K. 2012. *The Makeover: Reality Television and Reflexive Audiences.* New York: NYU Press.

Serazio, M. 2013. "Selling (Digital) Millennials: The Social Construction and Technological Bias of a Consumer Generation." *Television and New Media* 16(7):599–615. https://doi.org/10.1177/1527476413491015

Shankar, S. 2008. *Desi Land: Teen Culture, Class, and Success in Silicon Valley.* Durham, NC: Duke University Press.

Shively, J. 1992. "Cowboys and Indians: Perceptions of Western Films Among American Indians and Anglos." *American Sociological Review* 57(6):625–734.

Shoshana, A. 2016. "Ethno-Class Distinctions and Reality (TV)." *Sociological Forum* 31(1): 53–71.

Skeggs, B., and H. Wood. 2012. *Reacting to Reality Television: Performance, Audience and Value.* Abingdon, UK: Routledge.

Soha, M., and Z.J. McDowell. 2016. "Monetizing a Meme: YouTube, Content ID, and the Harlem Shake." *Social Media + Society* 2(1): 1–12.

Stein, L.E. 2015. *Millennial Fandom: Television Audiences in the Transmedia Age.* Iowa City: University of Iowa Press.

Stutzman, F., R. Gross, and A. Acquisti. 2012. "Silent Listeners: The Evolution of Privacy and Disclosure on Facebook." *Journal of Privacy and Confidentiality* 4(2):7–41.

Taylor, T.D. 2007. "The Commodification of Music at the Dawn of the Era of Mechanical Music." *Ethnomusicology* 51(2):281–305.

Thussu, D.K. 2008. "The Globalization of 'Bollywood.'" Pp. 97–113 in *Global Bollywood*, edited by A.P. Kavoori and A. Punathambekar. New York: NYU Press.

Tuchman, G. 1978. *Making News: A Study in the Social Construction of Reality.* New York: Free Press.

Usher, N. 2013. "Al Jazeera English Online: Understanding Web Metrics and News Production When a Quantified Audience is Not a Commodified Audience." *Digital Journalism* 1(3):335–51.

van Nieuwkerk, K., M. LeVine, and M. Stokes. 2016. *Islam and Popular Culture.* Austin: University of Texas Press.

Villarejo, A. 2016. "Adorno by the Pool; or, Television Then and Now." *Social Text* 34(2 127):71–87.

Villi, M. (2015). "'Hey, I'm here Right Now': Camera Phone Photographs and Mediated Presence." *Photographies* 8(1):3–22.

Walsh, M.J., and S.A. Baker. 2016. "The Selfie and the Transformation of the Public–Private Distinction." *Information, Communication and Society* 20(8):1185–203.

Wargo, J.M. 2015. "'Every selfie tells a story . . .': LGBTQ Youth Lifestreams and New Media Narratives as Connective Identity Texts." *New Media and Society* 19(4):560–78. https://doi.org/10.1177/1461444815612447

Wayne, M.L. 2016. "Cultural Class Analysis and Audience Reception in American Television's 'third golden age.'" *Interactions: Studies in Communication and Culture* 7(1):41–57.

Wei, J. 2012. "Dealing with Reality: Market Demands, Artistic Integrity, and Identity Work in Reality Television Production." *Poetics* 40(5):444–66.

White, H.C., and C.A. White. 1965. *Canvases and Careers: Institutional Change in the French Painting World.* Chicago: University of Chicago Press.

Wiggins, B.E., and G.B. Bowers. 2015. "Memes as Genre: A Structurational Analysis of the Memescape." *New Media and Society* 17(11):1886–906.

Williams, A. 2015. "Race, Gender, and Deviance in Xbox live: Theoretical Perspectives from the Virtual Margins." *New Media and Society* 17(10):1754–55.

Williams, G. 2002. *The Other Side of the Popular: Neoliberalism and subalternity in Latin America.* Durham, NC: Duke University Press.

Willis, P.E. 1977. *Learning to Labor: How Working Class Kids Get Working Class Jobs.* New York: Columbia University Press.

Wilson, R.E., S.D. Gosling, and L.T. Graham. 2012. "A Review of Facebook Research in the Social Sciences." *Perspectives on Psychological Science* 7(3):203–20.

Wynn, J.R. 2015. *Music/City: American Festivals and Placemaking in Austin, Nashville, and Newport.* Chicago: University of Chicago Press.

36

New amateurs revisited

Popular music, digital technology, and the fate of cultural production

Nick Prior

Amateurs: idiots or lovers?

What does the term "amateur" mean to you? Passion for an object or activity, perhaps, dependent on serious investments of time, money, and energy? In other words, an effervescent overflow of enthusiasm carried by love, but which goes unpaid? Or something more pejorative, such as lack of talent, knowledge, or skill that ends up in failure to reach standards set by professionals? *Amateurish* is still a synonym for a shoddy job, after all. That the term drifts between these meanings tells us a lot about how social change impacts and is shaped by the terms of reference we use to describe various forms of activity. What is at stake in the definition of the amateur are evaluative standards that classify and name certain roles as credible or not. But these standards are not immutable: they are subject to shifting boundaries around knowledge and power and the mechanisms (including techniques and technologies) by which people make and shape things. No wonder, then, that in the so-called digital age the figure of the amateur has become central to debates about the transformation of cultural production. On the quantitative axis, a radical upsurge in the amount of digital cultural production that gets done – from blogs, wikis, and podcasts to citizen science, image boards, and fan forums – opens up questions around the spread of digital technology as a condition for the democratization of cultural production. On the qualitative axis, debate hinges on whether all this amounts to anything more than a huge proliferation of low-grade dross. More and more is less and less, goes this argument, because quality-control mechanisms that once characterized professional infrastructures, such as gatekeeping, have eroded. Instead, what Keen calls the "dictatorship of idiots" (Keen 2007:35) ends up flattening cultural hierarchies, replacing the seriousness of connoisseurship with the frivolities of the part-timer. And yet for Anderson (2008), it is precisely this flattening that undergirds a shift from a production logic based on scarcity (few to many) to a logic of superabundance (many to many), giving rise not just to an outpouring of latent and repressed niche tastes, but to a blurring of outmoded boundaries between producer and consumer, author and reader, expert and non-expert.

This chapter focuses on one domain where these debates play out most acutely, that of popular music. It interposes the figure of the "new amateur" as a motif for the transformation of ordinary capabilities among a widening segment of technologically enabled groups and individuals whose engagements are having dramatic effects on the nature of music cultures, industries, and practices. If the "old" amateur was positioned as modern professionalism's "other," as lacking in skill or knowledge, new amateurs are changing the very auspices under which these terms play out. Their increasing centrality parallels the transformation of cultural landscapes associated with digital processes that invite critical interrogation by sociologists of everyday creative agency among widening and networked populations.

Digital transformations of popular music

Indeed, the digital lies at the center of claims regarding root-and-branch changes in the way culture is produced, disseminated, and consumed. Sometimes lauded as a revolutionary new set of creative practices, sometimes denigrated as a technological beast responsible for destroying music, the digital has become a technocultural leitmotif for the twenty-first century (Orton-Johnson and Prior 2013). The globalized circulation of music in ones and zeros is implicated in a radical overhaul of the music industry. In the early to mid-2000s, for instance, the practice of digital downloading via peer-to-peer networks and file-sharing programs seemed, initially at least, to point to a dissolution of the hegemony of major entertainment conglomerates, replacing product-based economies of scale and control with gift-like networks of dematerialized exchange (Leyshon 2003). Ultimately, the industry retrieved the situation through a series of takeovers and adaptations, such as the introduction of online subscription services like Apple Music and Spotify (Prior 2015). And yet the threat to mainstream channels of distribution raised the possibility that user-based networks of creation could undermine chains of production based upon rights and ownership.

Meeting these undercurrents of "disintermediation," mainstream musicians are seemingly taking their cue from bottom-up developments in digital consumption. In the early to mid-2000s, high-profile acts like Prince, Nine Inch Nails, and Jay-Z distributed content direct to consumers via the internet, through newspapers, or in constituent digital parts that allowed fans to re-version tracks. More recently, music instrument companies like Native Instruments have embraced the open, multitrack audio format known as "stems" – a set of four separate tracks comprising drums, bass, melody, and vocals that allows producers to remix pre-existing materials with ease. On the distribution side, the 2007 release of Radiohead's album *In Rainbows* was (initially at least) not only an all-digital affair, but an invitation to fans to download the album at whatever price they thought fair, including for free. Meanwhile, consumers (and industry bodies) are increasingly invested in loops of feedback, commentary, and customization in the digital spaces of new music media (Savage 2013). They are making use of digital infrastructures to pool knowledge with other music fans – annotating, filtering, and linking content and creating their own dissemination channels, as well as maintaining and supporting the digital ecologies of their favorite artists. As Baym (2015) notes, social media are integral to the work of sustaining musical careers, but much of this work is now in the hands of fans, some of whom invest their technical and emotional labor to build and maintain the connective circuits that define the online presence of musicians.

The implication is clear: if the classic model of the 1950s and 1960s involved a few firms and various independent labels controlling the flow of production to sale, the contemporary model is much more diffuse and multiplicitous. The power that once resided in record companies to control the infrastructure and techniques needed to produce, promote, and disseminate commercial products is less universal and, in the view of many commentators, has hemorrhaged (Ryan and Hughes 2006). In its wake has emerged a decentralized system of postindustrial cells – individually insignificant, but collectively powerful in providing alternatives to the mainstream commercial industry. In short, of all the identifiable trends that might be significant harbingers of systematic change in music over the last 30 years, from the rise of hip-hop and sampling to portable tape machines and CDs, the most vivid and far-reaching are processes and practices associated with digitalization.

This means that our understanding of the structure and culture of popular music needs to change if we are to analyze post-1980s developments in fast-paced, highly technologized societies. Diagnosing change always has its perils, of course, and this is particularly apparent with new technologies, where the idea of transformation (namely, digital "revolution") is often overplayed, as if digitalization is a new "year zero" in popular music's history. Clearly, older industry structures of rights, contracts, and high-value capital remain intact, albeit in adaptive form. Moreover, an infrastructure of bedrooms, clubs, gigs, studios, festivals, garages, rehearsal rooms, and record companies continues to be significant in the cultural life of any music scene, virtual or not. To assume nothing has changed, however, is exactly the mistake made by centralized firms in the music industry, shocked and overtaken by less than superficial changes in consumer practices.

The rise of the new amateurs

For all the attention heaped upon Napster and music piracy, there is a less obvious but by no means unimportant shift in the way music is created and circulated – a quieter, more subtle evolutionary process at work, threaded through these developments. It is a shift that brings into question the very separation between production and consumption as well as traditional boundaries around cultural expertise. If the "direct access relationship" between musicians and fans fulfilled an ideal of unmediated contact between the two constituencies, another ideal is being serviced by digital technologies, that of the self-sufficient "amateur" producer. Digital technologies and corresponding practices undoubtedly have twisted, stretched, and radicalized older tendencies in modern culture, but they have also extended the very notion of production into realms previously remote from academic and cultural analysis.

When *Time* magazine made "you" the person of the year in 2006, it bucked the popular trend of identifying "great men" as sole influential agents of history, instead placing ordinary people at the center of an upsurge of productivity and innovation. "You" were the passionate producers in a range of cultural forms and media, from home videos to personal blogs, bedroom songs to podcasts. Harbingers of a "digital democracy," ordinary people were making culture with an energy and in quantities never seen before, *Time* suggested. The dizzying proliferation of digital folk culture is nowhere more apparent than on the new digital repositories of demotic creativity – YouTube (for videos), Tumblr and Twitter (for blog-related content), and Flickr (for photos). There, content is dominated by non-specialists at a range of levels and in a range of forms, circulating through rapidly expanding global networks of communication. Beyond the hype of "web 2.0" and the fact that leisure time, technical capital, and access to a computer are still fundamental passports to this form of creativity, the underlying point is incontrovertible. Huge swathes of the population are making, filtering, editing, and distributing digital culture, creating micro-organizational worlds with systematic, macrological effects.

This point should not be lost on cultural sociologists, not least because it has implications for how we see production, expertise, and modes of creativity. If those who were previously considered non-specialists are actively producing websites, online photography galleries, how-to guides, radio broadcasts, and the like, not only are they failing to fit models of passive consumers suggested by the Frankfurt School and "hypodermic syringe" models of consumption (media and technology studies scholars have known about this poor fit for a long time), but they are undermining the very boundaries between professional and amateur, expert and non-expert, so central to modern social configurations. The welling up of small-scale, specialized, and partici-patory projects is, in other words, meeting top-heavy delivery of content head-on, potentially chipping at the surety bestowed upon modern credentialism and the status of the modern professional.

In historical terms, this valorization is actually a return. Just over a century ago, the amateur was lauded as the epitome of virtue, respectability, and grace. In eighteenth- and nineteenth-century Britain, the evaluative standards of the aristocratic amateur were central to the devel-opment of "polite culture." By dint of their supposed disinterestedness and their adherence to neo-platonic truths – both, ideological products of a privileged structural location – amateurs were exclusively qualified to act as arbiters of taste, shaping the contours of public virtue and the ideals of civic heroism. Processes of modern professionalization and commercialization eventu-ally inverted this status hierarchy, consigning the amateur to the status of dabblers whose exper-tise was weakened both by lack of time for their pursuits and by lack of institutional affiliation, training, and certification. Thus, for most of the twentieth century, the amateur was a fringe fig-ure, propping up hierarchies of quality in a normative system dominated by professional groups.

In the last two decades or so, the status and position of the amateur has been redeemed: a new, less aristocratic, breed of amateur has emerged. Technologically literate, seriously engaged, and committed practitioners are now working to professional standards but often without the infrastructural support or conventional credentials accorded to professionals. Disproportionately though not exclusively drawn from the educated middle classes, they deploy their cultural capi-tal in projects and self-organized cultural milieus (Bourdieu 1990; Battani 1999; Leadbeater and Miller 2004). They are unlikely to earn much of their total income from their activities, but their sense of identity is firmly attached to the pursuit of "serious leisure" (Stebbins 2007).

If the twentieth-century professional was defined partly by a monopoly over a specialized field of knowledge, objects, and esoteric skills, such monopolies are mutable and under erosion. This development has partly to do with material and technological processes: the objects and tools that once separated amateur and professional now travel between them more readily. The complex machines and spaces that once imposed financial barriers to production are no longer the prerequisites for quality. And boundaries around technical expertise are more permeable with the rise of mass higher education and dispersed digital technologies of communication. It is nowadays a fairly straightforward exercise to find out how to make your own movie, add expressive filters to your photos, or publish your own newsletter. If only three decades ago we regarded computers as esoteric business machines and word processors, we now think of them as cultural devices for generating images, editing movies, and mixing tracks. The smartphone has, in many respects, miniaturized these processes, lodging powerful computers in the pockets of globally networked populations (Miller and Matviyenko 2014).

Convergence and the fate of "DIY" music production

In the domain of music, the idea of the "amateur" has received little attention. Indeed, with the exception of Ruth Finnegan's (1989) now classic ethnography of music-making in a small English town and Hennion's (2007) neo-phenomenological take on amateurs as bona fide lovers of music, very few studies have tackled the amateur in any detail. Finnegan herself notes how musi-cological analysis has gravitated to the "best" or "highest" forms of music-making. In popular music studies, this has skewed attention to the highly commodified and spectacular domains of the large-scale subfield (Bourdieu 1993). A careful stock-taking of music-related activity, how-ever, reveals a diverse set of amateur networks, practices, and creative forms outside the com-mercial domain, from choirs and brass bands to family gatherings and karaoke. In the UK, one music-participation survey suggests that around 9 percent of the population play instruments, 2 percent play to audiences, and 5 percent sing to audiences at least once a year (Leadbeater and Miller 2004), while a more recent survey finds that 79 percent of young people "know how to play" an instrument (ABRSM 2014). Indeed, many of the musical organizations noted in Finnegan's 1989 study still exist, including formal music-making communities and choirs.

Electronic and digital technologies have expanded these networks, not just by bringing like-minded musicians together, but by establishing alternative modes of creativity through non-institutional means. In an initial phase of distribution in the 1980s and 1990s, the development of affordable technology for music production significantly lowered thresholds for making professional-sounding music. As the prices of four-track recording devices, drum machines, effects boxes, and synthesizers dropped, they migrated from high-end studios to the bedrooms of non-professional producers. Associated techniques like multitracking, once the preserve of experimental producers and super-studios like Abbey Road, became relatively normalized practices outside the studio (Théberge 2012).

In a subsequent phase, an expanding global market for domestic personal computers and music-authoring software (in some cases, as with Apple's GarageBand, shipped free with the computer) has transferred a colossal bulk of recording equipment onto the desktops and laptops of ordinary musicians (Tavana 2015). All-in-one software studios like Cubase, Logic, Acid, Ableton Live, and Reason combine the functions of a range of separate hardware devices such as mixers, compressors, sequencers, and samplers into a single virtual unit. Whole orchestras – indeed music's whole sonic palette – can be conjured up in these digital spaces, giving rise to new stylistic combinations and borrowings not just in electronic dance music and hip-hop, but in pop and rock generally (Brøvig-Hanssen and Danielson 2016). What a state-of-the-art recording studio once contained as its top-end equipment is now commonly used, in simulated form, by non-professionals, many of whom have never set foot in a "real" studio – or, indeed, had a music lesson.

On the distribution side, the new amateurs are taking advantage of music promotion and dissemination sites like Soundcloud to reach audiences directly, bypassing the mediating chains populated by older gatekeepers, marketers, A&R men, and label bosses. In effect, the internet has become the stage for a continuous performance and audition, a space for hopeful musicians to arrange gigs or try out songs. But it is only one of a multitude of stages. No longer dependent on live performances, musicians are taking advantage of file-swapping, streaming and CD-burning capabilities to create their own demos for distribution among local communities, friends, and fans, potentially turning their homes and laptops into production plants. These possibilities were unthinkable just over a decade ago, when the music business had a monopoly over factory production, the pressing of vinyl, and CDs.

Such developments are convergent in nature. After all, what is distinctive about the computer, and increasingly the smartphone, is that they are a meta-devices – the first devices in the history of popular music to converge production, distribution, and reception. Operations and techniques that were once separate have been unified in the digital spaces of sequencing software and Digital Audio Workstations, making it possible (and in some respects expected) for musicians to write, record, mix, master, upload, distribute, promote, download, and listen to music using a single unit. Convergence is also, by implication, an occupational folding. Distinctions between tasks that were discretely allocated in earlier modes of production have collapsed, giving new amateurs the opportunity to become specialists in a range of professional occupations.

Kealy (1979) provides a benchmark for comparison. He sketched the occupational transformation of the sound mixer from craftsman to artist in the United States during the 1950s and 1960s, as this group became professionalized and unionized. This shift was dependent upon protectionist strategies and boundary work designed to stave off the encroachments of other emerging audio professions. Nowadays, however, sound mixing is just one of a range of practices undertaken by self-producers whose amateur curricula vitae are boasting expertise in all phases of production – from composition and sound engineering to promotion and distribution. They are learning their multiple trades in formal educational establishments and through informal networks of friends, online databases, consumer magazines, and discussion forums.

All this makes for a denser cultural life, where pluralized expressions of creativity are bubbling up among a diversifying body of creators. With cultural gatekeepers less allied to centralized bodies, musicians are getting closer to fulfilling the "do-it-yourself" ideologies of punk and hip-hop, reinstating practices of homemade art that existed long before the rise of transnational media conglomerates and mass distribution. And they are making a difference, not just in the dark corners of the internet but much more widely. For, although non-professionals and independent producers have always been active producers of music, they rarely matched the success of those sponsored by the established culture industries. Today, they still suffer structural disadvantages, not least in advertising, promotion, and marketing. But they are making up some ground.

Hatsune Miku: the crowdsourced virtual singer

Here's a case in point. Hatsune Miku is a Japanese virtual idol who dances, performs, and sings "live" in concert. She began life in 2007 as an advertising image for a piece of music-making software called Vocaloid, which allowed amateur musicians to input synthetic vocal phrases into their songs without having to use a "real" singer. But Miku's popularity soon outstripped the conventional limits of marketing: fans started to make their own designs and fan art. Fairly quickly, something like a million "derivative works" (*niji sousaku*) had been produced. These included videos, illustrations, 3D models, plastic figures, anime, and manga stories. Crypton Future Media, the Japanese corporation behind Miku, recognized that fans had become the sustaining force behind her image and put her under the Japanese equivalent of a Creative Commons license. This meant that any amateur producers who wrote music using the Vocaloid software and did not benefit commercially from the music were Hatsune Miku producers. And they did produce, in their droves, to the sum of over 100,000 songs in a variety of genres – from J-pop and rock ballads to doom metal and glitch electronica. As the world's first crowdsourced singer, Miku is constituted by millions of networked interactions among amateur producers in a community of shared interests and activity: there is no "Hatsune Miku" songwriter or foundational presence behind the image. She is the product of networked participatory culture and the creative chains that gesture toward new ways of organizing music production, collaboratively and non-hierarchically, from bottom up, with very little intervention of the big industry players (Zaborowski 2016). In other words, Miku opens up a space for massively crowdsourced innovation based on amateur and fan practices, rather than a neoliberal system of profit, accumulation, and value. It is DIY fandom at its most energetic.

Amateur musicians have always sought ways to "make do" in the sense implied by De Certeau (1984). In many respects, they are the consummate "creative consumers," improvising resourcefully with whatever materials and channels are available to them. In the past, this has meant sourcing equipment from unusual places, financing the recording, designing the sleeve, pressing and distributing the record, or even setting up a micro label. In other words, this DIY system has long been a viable option.

The difference today is one of global reach, speed, ease of use, and absolute scale. I would suggest that the DIY ethic so cherished by punk rockers is no longer an activist ideology, but a systematic, structural condition of the production of music itself. And not just in the developed West, for although the digital divide between rich and poor countries undoubtedly exists in a climate where "ethnic sounds" are sampled and fetishized by Western musicians for their "exotic" quality, impoverished musicians in places like Peru and the Dominican Republic are managing to find access to digital recording facilities in order to record and press CDs on very tight budgets (Hernandez 2004). Meanwhile, digitalization has accompanied a creative cross-pollination of styles from around the world in a context of intensified migration, displacement, and mobility. Contemporary bhangra, for instance, remixes Punjabi folk dance with Western popular music – rock, hip-hop, rap, and house music, in particular – in an articulation of the hybrid identities of Asian migrants and their descendants in British and North American cities (Maira 2002). Here, the evolving complexity of diasporic identities is a product not only of urban or national settings but also of global soundscapes embedded within increasingly tangled webs of mass-mediated, transnational communication systems, including the internet (Connell and Gibson 2003).

Add the material affordances of smartphones and wireless-capable laptop computers, and these global hybridities and DIY processes are infinitely flexible and geographically mobile. Musicians are making music on the move with others, in the spatial and temporal interstices of life, on a little-and-often basis. They are untethering cultural production from fixed locations and sending music into a fluid network of exchanges (Prior 2008). As broadband communication infrastructures become more widespread, they are collaborating remotely with other musicians – via email, virtual worlds, teleconferencing, or streaming audio technologies – displacing the need to be physically co-present with collaborators. Finally, they are finding new spaces in which to play and consume music, in the interactive media domains such as smartphone apps and video games, where mainstream music-making overlaps with music simulations, virtual gigs, and gamified media forms (Miller 2012). Production has truly evolved into "prosumption."

Conclusion: why 1983?

Stock histories of popular music often gravitate to a "golden age" of rock, usually located in the late 1950s or early 1960s – a period of rapid socioeconomic change that begot a pantheon of rockers, from Elvis Presley to the Beatles. In an article titled "Why 1955? Explaining the Advent of Rock Music," Richard A. Peterson (1990) pointed to that as the year consolidating legal, technological, and organizational developments conducive to the birth of rock music in the United States. These included the development of a "dual structure" industry of small firms and oligopolies, the spread of network radio programming, and the development of 45 rpm vinyl records (Peterson 1990). Even if there is a whiff of nostalgia in this analysis, the point is sound: a unique confluence of occupational, technological, and cultural elements in the mid-1950s instituted a system of production geared to the total transformation of the popular music industry.

What, then, of the last 35 years? If popular music is a moving object, how much has it moved during this time, how significant has this era been in transforming the auspices of pop, and what role have digital technologies played in catalyzing these developments? It is clearly perilous to assume that free-floating technologies in themselves have revolutionized music. New technologies do not create music worlds from scratch. But they have facilitated or afforded new possibilities.

The years 1982 to 1983 were particularly propitious for pop. First, two of the most influential musical works of recent times were produced and disseminated. One, Michael Jackson's album, *Thriller* remains the biggest selling album in history and turned Jackson into a global superstar. The other, New Order's *Blue Monday*, is widely perceived to be the biggest selling UK 12-inch record of all time and presaged a shift to dance-based pop of the 1980s. Second, in production terms, 1983 saw the invention of several influential musical devices and processes – their presence emblematic of a fundamental shift in the global structure of the electronics industry toward East and Southeast Asia. Such devices included the first commercially successful digital synthesizer – the Yamaha DX7, affordable drum machines, commercial audio software packages, and the first desktop computers with monitors and graphic user interfaces. The year 1983 also witnessed the invention of MIDI, or "Musical Instrument Digital Interface," an industry-standard protocol set up by Japanese electronics corporations to enable different instruments to communicate streams of algorithmic data with one another. Like the spread of other universal languages and technical standards, MIDI unified what could have potentially become a fragmented landscape, in this case, of musical instruments, "locking in" subsequent technological developments around a new paradigmatic frame of recording and performing. Third, CDs and CD players were introduced to the mass market in late 1982 – another step in a long line of format shifts in the history of music that have changed how we listened to music. Finally, 1983 was the year that ARPANET (the first manifestation of internet technologies) was switched over to the TCP/IP protocol, establishing networking capabilities across different and hitherto incompatible computers. Today, the internet is largely based upon TCP/IP software that connects different networks of computers.

None of these four developments was independently responsible for creating the momentum necessary for wholesale changes in popular music. In many respects, they replicated and attended to an already emergent series of global processes that ushered in advanced, high-tech, networked societies favoring a reordering of modes of cultural production. In other words, they articulated with contemporary social, economic, and political practices to emplace key struts of a reconfigured system of cultural production and consumption – one that has blurred this very separation. The digital is many things – a rhetoric, a claim, a set of technologies. But it is also a shorthand, a formation, and a condition that opens up creative agency, unhooks it from place, and feeds into flows of global information. What we hear, where we hear it, how we listen to new music, who produces it: these have all traveled. Musical styles have diversified and novel ways of making music have emerged. But in many ways, these are no more than the latest twists in popular music's history in the *longue durée*, a cat-and-mouse story of conservation, innovation, and subversion, a reconfiguration rather than a revolution. There is no last word to be had on these changes, not just because disagreements abound over their character and extent, but also because the pace of change leaves analysis invariably trailing behind. What is certain is that the struggle between technology, use, and control over protean networks and colonizing organizations will continue. As will the music.

References

ABRSM (Associated Board of the Royal Schools of Music). 2014. "Making Music: Teaching, Leaning, and Playing in the UK." Retrieved March 2, 2017 (http://gb.abrsm.org/en/making-music/).

Anderson, Chris. 2008. *The Long Tail: Why the Future of Business is Selling Less of More.* New York: Hyperion.

Battani, Marshall. 1999. "Organisational Fields, Cultural Fields, and Art Worlds." *Media, Culture and Society* 21(5):601–26.

Baym, Nancy. 2015. "Connect With Your Audience! The Relational Labor of Connection." *The Communication Review* 18(1):14–22.

Bourdieu, Pierre. 1990. *Photography: A Middle-brow Art.* Stanford, CA: Stanford University Press.

———. 1993. *The Field of Cultural Production.* Cambridge: Polity Press.

Brøvig-Hanssen, Ragnhild, and Anne Danielson. 2016. *Digital Signatures: The Impact of Digitization on Popular Music Sound.* Cambridge, MA: MIT Press.

Certeau, Michel de. 1984. *The Practice of Everyday Life*. Berkeley: University of California Press.

Connell, John, and Chris Gibson. 2003. *Sound Tracks: Popular Music, Identity and Place*. London: Routledge.

Finnegan, Ruth. 1989. *The Hidden Musicians: Music-Making in an English Town*. Middletown, CT: Wesleyan University Press.

Hennion, Antoine. 2007. "Those Things That Hold Us Together: Taste and Sociology." *Cultural Sociology* 1(1):97–114.

Hernandez, Deborah Pacini. 2004. "Building Bridges across the Digital Divide: An Interview with Giovanni Savino." *Journal of Popular Music* 16(1):99–108.

Kealy, Edward R. 1979. "From Craft to Art: The Case of Sound Mixers and Popular Music." *Sociology of Work and Occupations* 6(1):3–29.

Keen, Andrew. 2007. *The Cult of the Amateur*. London: Nicholas Brealey.

Leadbeater, Charles, and Paul Miller. 2004. *The Pro-Am Revolution: How Enthusiasts are Changing our Economy and Society*. London: Demos.

Leyshon, Andrew. 2003. "Scary Monsters? Software Formats, Peer-to-Peer Networks, and the Spectre of the Gift." *Environment and Planning D: Society and Space* 21(5):533–58.

Maira, Sunaina Marr. 2002. *Desis in the House: Indian American Youth Culture in New York City*. Philadelphia, PA: Temple University Press.

Miller, Kiri. 2012. *Playing Along: Digital Games, YouTube, and Virtual Performance*. Oxford: Oxford University Press.

Miller, Paul D., and Svitlana Matviyenko. 2014. *The Imaginary App*. Cambridge, MA: MIT Press.

Orton-Johnson, Kate, and Nick Prior, eds. 2013. *Digital Sociology: Critical Perspectives*. Basingstoke: Palgrave Macmillan.

Peterson, Richard A. 1990. "Why 1955? Explaining the Advent of Rock Music." *Popular Music* 9(1):97–116.

Prior, Nick. 2008. "OK Computer: Mobility, Software and the Laptop Musician." *Information, Communication and Society* 11(7):912–32.

———. 2015. "Beyond Napster: Popular Music and the Normal Internet." Pp. 493–508 in *The Sage Handbook of Popular Music*, edited by A. Bennett and S. Waksman. London: Sage.

Ryan, John, and Michael Hughes. 2006. "Breaking the Decision Chain: The Fate of Creativity in the Age of Self-Production." Pp. 239–53 in *Cybersounds: Essays on Virtual Music Culture*, edited by M.D. Ayers. New York: Peter Lang.

Savage, Steve. 2013. *Bytes and Backbeats: Repurposing Music in the Digital Age*. Ann Arbor: University of Michigan Press.

Stebbins, Robert. 2007. *Serious Leisure: A Perspective for our Time*. Edison, NJ: Transaction.

Tavana, Art. 2015. "Democracy of Sound: Is GarageBand Good for Music?" *Pitchfork*, September 30. Retrieved January 5, 2017 (http://pitchfork.com/features/article/9728-democracy-of-sound-is-garageband-good-for-music).

Théberge, Paul. 2012. "The End of the World as we Know it." Pp. 77–90 in *The Art of Record Production*, edited by S. Frith and S. Zagorski-Thomas. Aldershot: Ashgate.

Zaborowski, Rafal. 2016. "Hatsune Miku and Japanese Virtual Idols." Pp. 111–28 in *The Oxford Handbook of Music and Virtuality*, edited by S. Whiteley and S. Rambarran. Oxford: Oxford University Press.

37

The fall of cyberspace and the rise of data

Martin Hand

Introduction

The term "cyberspace" has been a key metaphor in both academic analyses of cultural change and wider popular discourse for around three decades. The coupling of Norbert Weiner's cybernetics with a notion of space has provided the most pervasive representation of "where" electronic data are and what our relations with them are. Its etymology of "steering" or "navigating" translated into "surfing" and "mapping" has shaped research agendas and precipitated new ways of thinking about what "culture" is (Hand and Sandywell 2002). Here, I want to trace the fate of cyberspace as a metaphor for conceptualizing the relations between digital media technologies and culture in its broadest sense. Rather than debating the various merits and pitfalls of internet-related research, I will point to how the term cyberspace itself has morphed and what this can tell us about theorizing the relations that constitute the internet, social media, and associated technologies. There have been substantial changes in digital media alongside shifting epistemological and methodological problems of digital research. In the cultural imaginary, cyberspace has to some extent been seamlessly replaced with "the cloud" (Hu 2015). In other ways, it has been dismantled altogether in favor of ubiquitous social media interactions that dominate everyday experience (Turkle 2015). To review the entire spectrum of digitally related cultural sociology would be a Herculean task, as digitization has affected all dimensions of culture and its analysis albeit in different ways. Here, I have condensed diverse developments into what I see as three largely heuristic variants, each of which has been periodically dominant, cyberspace as: an immaterial cultural autonomy, a central myth of Western culture, and material, data-centric everyday practices.

Cyberspatial autonomies

During the late 1980s and early 1990s the metaphor of cyberspace most commonly referred to an autonomous cultural environment. This autonomy, for some, was and perhaps still is intensely theological. In an explicit form, cyberspace transcends the materialities and spatiotemporal constraints of bounded cultures. Thus, Apolito observed, "The Web . . . has no need for the presence of a real world beyond, because it replaces it with its own world beyond, that is, with its own virtual world" (2005:16). In discourses of transcendence, the "space" element of cyberspace was conceptualized as a non-physical environment (Bolter and Grusin 1999:181). The ability to evade the markers of physical embodiment suggested transcendence of "the bloody mess of organic matter" (Wertheim 2000:19). The important implication was that the ethnic, gendered, embodied nature of sociocultural life might therefore also be transcended and deconstructed. Popular-science magazines such as *Wired* and some cyberpunk fiction similarly articulated cyberspace through a specific rejection of embodiment (Flichy 2007).

Virtual community and identity

More sociologically, those who debated the kinds of interaction (or "life") emerging within cyberspace as environment looked toward concepts of "community" and "identity" in trying to situate novel forms of interaction and representation. In the context of late-modern "disembedded" society, communities are not simply temporally reproducible expressions of mutual reliance and shared cultural values, but can emerge in a strong form through fleeting "moments" when "enough people carry on those public discussions long enough, with sufficient human feeling, to form webs of personal relationships in cyberspace" (Rheingold 1993:5). Although mostly about discussion forums on the internet ("the Net"), this idea also characterized "virtual reality" environments, role-playing games such as the "virtual worlds" of MMORPGs (massively multiplayer online role-playing games) and MUDs (multi-user dungeons), all of which involve participants who never meet outside of the screen and are, in this sense, unrelated to place. Ironically, such a conception of autonomous virtual culture was reproduced through its initial critique when Sardar (1996) and Jones (1997) argued that transient mutual interest rather than mutual obligation or proximity makes such arenas simulations of community.

If community was disembedded, then identity was disembodied. It has been argued that "self-identity" is an endeavor that is continuously worked at and reflexively reconstructed, particularly as it is increasingly tied to patterns of consumption (Featherstone 2007). As performed in cyberspace, virtual identity allows for an anonymous identity choice to be made, thereby positioning users as "authors." Such participants do not simply enact their given identities but rewrite them in a "post-social" world (Hayles 1999). Indeed, Turkle argued early on that MUDs offered the opportunity for players not only to create the text (or graphics) of the game but also to construct "new selves though social interaction" (1997:12). Our interactions with networked machines encourage performances of multiple selves, which are further enhanced when we recognize the possibilities of nonlinear identities and a "distributed presence" (Turkle 1997:12–13).

Indeterminacy and virtuality

Commentators drawing explicitly upon poststructuralist theory and/or analyses of postmodernity conceptualized the technologies of cyberspace as decidedly indeterminate (Lash 2002; Manovich 2001). Mark Poster (2001) argued that we simply misunderstand the internet unless we appreciate its nonrepresentational character, where the "flow of signifiers" disrupts the fixed categories associated with earlier oral and written cultures. The mistake of modern theorizing is to think exclusively in terms of either digitization's emancipatory effects upon pre-existent identities or the irrevocable "loss" of the human subject to all-encompassing convergent media/technology (Taylor and Harris 2005). The sheer contingency of cyberspatial interaction inaugurates a democratization of communication where "The magic of the Internet is that it is a technology which puts cultural acts, symbolizations in all forms, in the hands of its participants" (Poster 2001:184).

In a broad sense "culture" is thus simultaneously received, mediated, and manipulated. The flows of information are always open to reconfiguration, because they are never concretized in specific time-spaces (unlike, say, print objects). Web pages are always in process, always deferred, as new links are created and followed, old links disappear, and endless ways of navigating beyond seem possible. Moreover, where the subject is constituted and reconstituted within electronic databases, it is both disembodied and disembedded from the traditional anchorage of social and cultural institutions and territories. Exploration of the resulting possibilities of "e-topia" has not been limited to cultural theory. Cyberspace also has been embraced by Western governments, transnational agencies, non-governmental organizations, and so forth, as a sphere within which political arrangements could be redrawn and a "citizen-based" democratization of communication might be fostered. But the significance of theorizing cyberspace as a zone of cultural autonomy has been its impact upon how we think about digital technology and culture as "less material" or even immaterial as a "cloud" (Hu 2015).

Mythologies of cyberspace

Theorizing cyberspace can be pursued in dialectical terms when the promise of transcendence is met with the threat of colonization. The imagined outcomes of postmodern information machines appeared a little celebratory because the possibilities of subjectivity were limited to individual, disembodied self-exploration. A series of interventions that became dominant from the mid- to late 1990s – including the political economy of communication, ethnographic explorations of internet-related activity, and the integration of the web in social network analyses – all had the effect of disaggregating cyberspace as a distinctive cultural formation.

Production of cyberspace

Post-Marxist analyses of "cyberculture" have been concerned with the digital divides laundered by the more celebratory accounts of community and identity formation, but they have also operated as a means of critiquing postmodern and poststructuralist conceptions of culture in light of web commercialization. If cyberspatial autonomy privileges cultural discontinuity, from this perspective it is clear that "Continuity is painfully apparent in everything" (Robins and Webster 1999:234). The "culture industry" is endlessly extending through cyberspace. The sheer production of cyberspace as proliferating new markets – and the accompanying efforts to regulate and monitor internet traffic, and to enforce laws of intellectual property – represents a perfected alignment between technology, capital, and culture (Taylor and Harris 2005; Fuchs 2014). The central concern of productionist analyses was thus to introduce modern conceptions of capitalist power into the study of cyberspace.

Research in the productionist vein has directed our critical attention to the longer military and commercial history of information processing and the rhetorics of novelty at work in cyberspatial narratives, especially as wielded by government departments, corporate bodies, and the computing industries. From this perspective, cyberspace as cultural autonomy amounts to spectacle and commodity (Mosco 2004, 2014; Fuchs 2014). The apparent immaterialism of cyberspace and the cloud, alongside the assumption of a kind of cultural separatism, are revealed as ongoing mythologies of digital capitalism. For Hu (2015:X11): "by producing a seemingly instant, unmediated relationship between user and website, our imagination of a virtual 'cloud' displaces the infrastructure of labor within digital networks."

Integrative practices

The political economy of electronic communication dismantled the speculative assumptions about cybercultures at the level of state and corporation, and remains important for developing critiques of the largely indistinguishable rhetorics of "the cloud" and "big data" in the context of multinational social media companies. A second trajectory of analysis has dismantled cyberspace from the ground up. The idea that cyberspatial practices are divorced from the dynamics of everyday life came under sustained critique from anthropological perspectives. In the most influential example, concepts of "cyberspace" or "virtuality" are bracketed in favor of exploring how the practices of everyday life integrate (or not) elements of internet technology into the rhythms of everyday practice (Miller and Slater 2000). The internet, dissolved into its multifarious components, may or may not be assembled into "cyberspace" by individuals in daily life. A significant element to Miller and Slater's ethnographic work was its location in Trinidad, which exposed the ways in which Euro-American assumptions about individualized computer use, alienation, and postmodern identity politics had structured previous Manichean models of cyberspace. Their research convincingly showed that people incorporate elements of media into existing material-symbolic arrangements and, in this case, counterintuitively use the internet to "make concrete" rather than virtualize national identities. The current uses of social media to articulate various forms of nationalism appear to confirm this point.

The attempts to "contextualize cyberspace" through detailed ethnographic exploration have yielded a complex arena for debate (Hine 2015) because of the shifting ground of where access to cyberspace takes place (from the "static" home, library, and cybercafé to the "mobile" smartphone) and the proliferating range of uses related to ever-evolving technologies and techniques (multiplying social media platforms; texting, gaming, education, shopping, photography). Moreover, efforts to understand the "contexts" of cyberspatial activity reveal their inseparable interrelation with cyberspace and the ongoing reconfiguration of both, now pursued through the multifaceted approaches of "digital ethnography" (Pink et al. 2015).

The debates about cyberspace and community revolved around utopian transcendence or dystopian simulation, both of which maintained the autonomy of cyberspace as a cultural space in its own right. In contrast, like those doing ethnography, those concerned with social-network analysis have consistently argued that such a distinction is deeply problematic, as in reality the so-called online world is an extension and often an enhancement of pre-existing social relations, which themselves have become increasingly orientated through "networks" rather than spaces or places (Rainie and Wellman 2012). The metaphor of autonomous "space" was thus challenged by a model in which internet activity was enveloped in wider practices of network formation and maintenance. In accounting for the material bases of power, the texture of everyday life, and the integration of networked communication practices, all these rather different approaches questioned the conception of "cyberspace" as a useful, accurate or generative way of researching cultural forms and practices.

The fall of cyberspace and the rise of data

The Manichean dialogue about cyberspace has been transcended by theoretical and technical developments. For some time, analysts have recognized that the distinction between "online" and "offline" cultures is highly problematic on conceptual and methodological grounds, reifying technology or culture and making little sense experientially or phenomenologically (Miller 2011; Couldry and Hepp 2017). Over the last 10 years the technologies of digital communication have altered somewhat dramatically. Changes in the quantity, range, and character of consumer-level devices coupled with burgeoning social media platforms has enabled different practices to emerge. Although people still spend time in "virtual worlds," the ways in which these compound technologies and systems now facilitate *continual* "interfacing," connected presence, and the "mediation of everything" (Livingstone 2009) facilitate a rethinking of "culture" in terms of *data circulations*. Next, I highlight three current challenges to earlier conceptions of cyberspace that extend and problematize the critiques discussed so far.

Materially mediated life

The idea of "cyberspace" (online) on the one hand and "users" (offline) on the other has been subject to serious critique. But further, the work of Latour (2005) and others in the "sociology of associations" shifted the agenda in cultural sociology by asking us to rethink people's relations with things per se. Latour wants to extend the capacities and dynamism of things themselves in a "relational materialism" (2005). He argues:

> Objects are never assembled together to form some other realm anyhow, and even if it were the case they would be neither strong nor weak – simply "reflecting" social values or being there as mere decorum. Their action is no doubt much more varied, their influence more ubiquitous, their effect much more ambiguous, their presence much more distributed than these narrow repertoires.
>
> *(Latour 2005:85)*

The issue here is one of recognizing that the social is technical, that "action" is the outcome of socio-technical associations, and that we should take a route beyond the semiotics of technologies and their content that treats them as simply "reflective" of cultural meanings or "projectors" of hegemonic interests. The significance, then, concerns the dynamics of mutual interdependence.

There are three dimensions of current importance here, related to the ways in which smartphones and other "things" now mediate almost all everyday activities. First, such devices co-evolve with the dynamics of systems of which they are part. The characteristics and agency of specific technologies – such as smartphones, platforms, algorithms, and databases – shift alongside changes in the computer industries, the socioeconomic ebbs and flows of the capitalist marketplace, the patterns of demand in each market, and so on. Second, technical characteristics evolve in tandem with shifting conventions and practices of use (Oudshoorn and Pinch 2002; Couldry 2012). For example, many social media applications (e.g., Twitter, Facebook, Tumblr) have recently developed their image uploading and sharing capacities, becoming solidly image-based media. Third, whole "suites of technology" (Shove, Watson, Hand, and Ingram 2007) are emerging because increasingly, discrete technologies are designed to "sync" with others, creating systems or networks of interdependence (e.g., between smartphones, Instagram, calendars, and "smart" domestic appliances) that mediate reality. Given this complexity, the dynamics of uses will have different kinds of impacts upon trajectories of both production and consumption. Moreover, smart mobile devices as mediators are designed to facilitate multiple interpretations and uses. In other words, digital technologies are "inscribed" with open-ended ambivalence in symbolic, practical, and material ways. Current digital technologies are mobile, additive, and adaptable, designed to be active. The what, when, where, and how of cultural activity is changing in relation to *continuous mediation*, whether we are considering activities of listening, looking, reading, writing, or photography.

Visualization and datafication

The rethinking of what "things" are and how they are relationally defined is augmented by the new technicality of compound devices that appear to be explicitly performative. Indeed, one of the most striking aspects of contemporary culture is the sheer number of digital devices through which data is said to flow. From laptops to smartphones, image capture machines, self-tracking devices, "smart" watches, toys, fabrics, and the like, a proliferating materialization, visualization, and datafication of culture emerges via the mobility of bodies (e.g., Lupton 2016).

Accounts of an "internet of things" and of the "automatic production of space" (Thrift 2005) suggest that these devices are also increasingly interactive and constitutive of everyday life in the form of interoperable mobile environments. As Couldry and Hepp (2017:2, original emphasis) argue, media "comprise platforms which, for many humans, literally *are* the spaces where, through communication, they *enact* the social." This development has, in turn, yielded two important phenomena. First, as social media platforms connected to smartphones have become the prominent means through which cultural production, distribution, and consumption occur, much of our daily interaction becomes primarily *visual* (Hand 2012; Rose 2016). People routinely use still and moving images in ordinary communication, access the majority of news visually in social media, and coexist with their personal screens (e.g., smartphones) as they go about their daily activities (think of how people "see" events they are "present" at through their screens). This shift positions users as "interfacing" rather than "using" or "entering." The emerging practices of continual visual presencing and archiving that these technical devices make possible – and are themselves enfolded within – are quite different from earlier kinds of "virtual life" discussed earlier.

Second, as mobile digital devices are woven into multiple cultural practices – from shopping to sport, eating to parenting – the visual, textual, transactional, and locational detail of those practices becomes available for examination by a variety of institutional and individual agents (Bowker 2013; Ruppert 2013). We might think of this interfacing as "datafication" through which everyday practices are subject to monitoring, data collection, and analysis. For some scholars, this development is presenting an unprecedented opportunity to analyze culture (e.g., Manovich's 2001 "cultural analytics"; Bail 2014; Mohr and Rawlings, this volume). Digital traces of cultural activity, particularly those visible in social media, are exponentially increasing in volume and have several novel qualities, including potential for unlimited algorithmic classification, malleability, transience, and persistence over space and time (Chun 2011). Such "private" information (thought, personal information, images, tastes), placed in the "public" domain, encourages a radical reversal of the relation between "public" and "private" life that characterized the modern archive (Gane and Beer 2008). It is also increasingly non-anonymous and recursive: individuals encounter and reflect on their own and others' data on a daily basis.

In these ways, it is not that "we" access cyberspace or the cloud, but that digital interfaces have come to intervene and mediate nearly all aspects of everyday life, whether we know it or not. We live among data that is produced through ordinary practice and, in turn, is shaping the possibilities of practice. This is what Couldry and Hepp (2017) call "deep mediatization" and others have termed a "culture of connectivity" (Van Dijck 2013). Instead of "going online," we are both presented with and increasingly filtering our preferences through complex algorithmic processes that are largely obscured from our view (Dourish 2016; Gillespie 2010). We now live in an "algorithmic culture" (Striphas 2015). We are always, in effect, online, whether in person or not.

Translocalities

If the computer screen through which people once "entered" cyberspace is now a mobile "interface" where the data finds us, then what happened to the territorial notions of space and network? To some extent, the spatial imaginary of cyberspace has been replaced with that of the cloud. The material infrastructures (e.g., vast data servers) and cultural rhetorics (e.g., autonomy versus surveillance) of both are similar (Hu 2015). A key difference perhaps is that the cloud is where we imagine "our data" lives, rather than a place we "go." On the other hand, there is renewed significance in "localities," which are now interpenetrated with data. Smartphones are "locative media" (Frith 2015) through which "physical" space is experienced in new ways. Most media use is "translocal" in the sense that it pulls together meaning and experience from many locations. Instead of existing as an externality (cyberspace, clouds) or extensions (networks, data flows), varieties of large and small data now restructure actual geographic territories (city, neighborhood) through automated classification systems such as neighborhood profiling, Google Maps, GPS systems, loyalty cards, public Wi-Fi, and so on (Burrows and Gane 2006). Data produced through ordinary practice (made visible as "consumer data") are algorithmically classified and databased as "big data." With some similarity to earlier rhetorics of cyberspace, and more empirical accounts of the "network society" (Castells 1996) or the "new social operating system" (Rainie and Wellman 2012), enthusiasts for big data often conjure a world now *made of data* – "a universe comprised essentially of information" (Mayer-Schonberger and Cukier 2013:96).

Aside from hyperbole, what we see here are (1) often invisible processes of structuring and restructuring due to the proliferation and recursivity of data, as it becomes materialized in more devices, and (2) given that the data produced does not "represent" but *performs* judgment in Latour's sense, the increasing significance of spatial classification. One of the key criticisms of cyber-theory in its most technophilic variant centered on the hidden, rather stark stratified inequality of access – locally, regionally, nationally, and globally. This inequality remains a significant issue, but such a "digital divide" has been overlaid with many other divides. The general concern about enabling equitable access to, and use of, information machines now has to incorporate a third layer of divisions performed by the algorithms that determine what people are able to "see" (e.g., news, preferences) based on their locational data. Such algorithmic sorting is of course a form of "social sorting" (Lyon 2003).

If the space of cyberspace was once thought a "place" to enter, live, and construct democratized culture, or simply the latest spectacle produced by digital capitalism, it has now become the hidden technical apparatus of Euro-American societies, producing an "automated spatiality" (Kitchin 2014). The collection and classification of data increasingly organizes the flows of people and things. It is often becoming the means through which contemporary cultural practices are articulated, understood, and valued.

Conclusion

I have not provided an exhaustive review of cyberspace scholarship; far from it. Rather, the modest task here has been to document some dominant conceptions of cyberspace over the last 30 years and comment on changes in the character and theorization of "technological culture" more generally. Conceptions of cyberspace as a specific cultural realm certainly have not disappeared (think here of current efforts to reintroduce "virtual reality"). Neither is the political economy of information technology (the reshaping of the cultural economy by Google, Facebook, Instagram, and Apple) no longer relevant for cultural sociology. Each of these phenomena has become even more pervasive precisely because what was previously visible as the hardware of technoculture and information culture is now increasingly the invisible infrastructure of contemporary culture. Culture, in terms of shared symbolic and material resources and relations, increasingly circulates as visual, transactional, and locational data in social media in ways that transcend many previous spatiotemporal boundaries. Such data is no longer confined to the realm of cyberspace. In that sense it does not have external spatial qualities, despite new metaphors of "clouds" and "dataverses." The consequences of continual mediation are being variously theorized as producing new modes of isolation in tandem with connection (Turkle 2015), as intensifying existing tendencies in capitalism (Wajcman 2015), and radically reconfiguring what we think of as the social world (Couldry and Hepp 2017).

Most analyses of cyberspace have been consistently skewed toward Euro-American cultures. There have been historically good reasons for this. Most obviously, the sites of technological development have been primarily located in the Global North as have the dominant users of such technologies. This may now be subject to considerable shifts in interesting and important ways. First, although I have argued that the Global North has undergone the fall of cyberspace and the rise of data, this is not necessarily the case elsewhere. Although in advanced market economies across Asia there are similar increases in the mobility of internet use (Minges 2005), notions of linear development in relation to internet infrastructure and the cultural embeddedness of uses are highly problematic. This is most clear in relation to the largely market-driven governmental idea of Africa "leapfrogging into Modernity" via cyberspace – an idea that simultaneously resurrects cyberspace as virtuality, ignores material-structural inequities between North and South (Alden 2003), and pays little attention to the dynamics of consumption and production. In other words, transition in the Global North is historically, technologically, and culturally specific.

Second, arguably, much of the invisibility occurring when cyberspace becomes infrastructural is related to some elements of the material production and laboring of that infrastructure shifting to the Global South. For example, much of the material work (manufacturing, service industries, data collection, and storage) enabling ubiquitous computing and mobile communication to occur in the North is conducted in the new data processing centers of India and Latin America. The experience of seamless digitization and convergence in the North often rests upon the specific concentration of its materiality elsewhere (Sassen 2006). Third, the automatic production of cultural-spatial classifications previously discussed in terms of "big data" has serious implications for how people in non-Western regions are categorized, and what the implications are for the increased movement of peoples, allocation of capital, and the circulation of culture.

Finally, the understandings of cyberspace here, and all that is suggested by them, are "in play" in contemporary cultures. It is the relations between them that raise so many more important issues. Indeed, one of the most pressing issues of our time will be how the application of specific material law now predicated on the notion of territorial "cyberspace" comes to terms with the cultural dynamics of ubiquity, flow, visibility, and invisibility inaugurated by the datafication of culture. This challenge is perhaps most apparent in current debates about hacking, "fake news," and the degree to which the meaning of data can ever be "contextualized."

The shifting relations between materiality and immateriality raise important research questions around the significance of past and present cyberspatial activity as it will be understood in the future. When the internet as cyberspace was positioned as autonomous, anonymous, and "immaterial," it was thought that digital texts, objects, and images left no memory traces. The turn to data materiality, both in theory and in practice, is producing some rather different trajectories. It is becoming clear that the materiality of digital traces is partly one of an impossibility of erasure (e.g., Twitter) and the increasing possibility of resurrection because of routine archiving.

In terms of what and how societies remember, as more cultural life is enacted through social media, individuals and cultural institutions are presented with dilemmas of how to store, manage, and preserve the vastness of "cyberspatial" activity. In contrast to the dialectic of liberation and domination implied in earlier accounts, if cyberspace has been transformed into the infrastructure of ordinary cultural practice, then it is also the archive of everyday life.

References

Alden, C. 2003. "Let them Eat Cyberspace: Africa, the G8 and the Digital Divide." *Millennium: Journal of International Studies* 32(3):457–76.

Apolito, P. 2005. *The Internet and the Madonna: Religious Visionary Experience on the Web*. Chicago: University of Chicago Press.

Bail, C.A. 2014. "The Cultural Environment: Measuring Culture with Big Data." *Theory and Society* 43(3):465–82.

Bolter, J.D., and R. Grusin. 1999. *Remediation: Understanding New Media*. Cambridge, MA: MIT Press.

Bowker, G. 2013. "Data Flakes: An Afterword to Raw Data is an Oxymoron." Pp. 167–71 in *Raw Data is an Oxymoron*, edited by L. Gitelman. Cambridge, MA: MIT Press.

Burrows, R., and N. Gane. 2006. "Geodemographics, Software and Class." *Sociology* 40(5):793–812.

Castells, M. 1996. *The Rise of the Network Society*. Oxford: Blackwell.

Chun, W.H.K. 2011. *Programmed Vision: Software and Memory*. Cambridge, MA: MIT Press.

Couldry, N. 2012. *Media, Society, World*. Cambridge: Polity Press.

Couldry, N., and A. Hepp. 2017. *The Mediated Construction of Reality*. Cambridge: Polity Press.

Dourish, P. 2016. "Algorithms and Their Others: Algorithmic Culture in Context." *Big Data & Society* 3(2):1–11.

Featherstone, M. 2007. *Consumer Culture and Postmodernism*. London: Sage.

Flichy, P. 2007. *The Internet Imaginaire*. Cambridge, MA: MIT Press.

Frith, J. 2015. *Smartphones as Locative Media*. Cambridge: Polity Press.

Fuchs, C. 2014. *Social Media: A Critical Introduction*. London: Sage.

Gane, N., and D. Beer. 2008. *New Media: The Key Concepts*. Oxford: Berg.

Gillespie, T. 2010. "The Politics of 'Platforms.'" *New Media & Society* 12(3):347–64.

Hand, M. 2012. *Ubiquitous Photography*. Cambridge: Polity Press.

Hand, M., and B. Sandywell. 2002. "E-Topia as Cosmopolis or Citadel." *Theory, Culture & Society* 19(1–2):197–225.

Hayles, N.K. 1999. *How We Became Posthuman*. Chicago: CUP.

Hine, C. 2015. *Ethnography for the Internet: Embedded, Embodied and Everyday*. London: Bloomsbury.

Hu, Tung-Hui. 2015. *A Prehistory of the Cloud*. Cambridge, MA: MIT Press.

Jones, S., ed. 1997. *Virtual Culture*. London: Sage.

Kitchin, R. 2014. *The Data Revolution*. London: Sage.

Lash, S. 2002. *Critique of Information*. London: Sage.

Latour, B. 2005. *Reassembling the Social: An Introduction to Actor-Network Theory*. Oxford: Oxford University Press.

Livingstone, S. 2009. "On the Mediation of Everything." *Journal of Communication* 59(1):1–18.

Lupton, D. 2016. *The Quantified Self: A Sociology of Self-Tracking*. Cambridge: Polity Press.

Lyon, D. 2003. *Surveillance as Social Sorting*. London: Routledge.

Manovich, L. 2001. *The Language of New Media*. Cambridge, MA: MIT Press.

Mayer-Schonberger, V., and K. Cukier. 2013. *Big Data: A Revolution that will Change How We Live, Work and Think*. London: John Murray.

Miller, D. 2011. *Tales from Facebook*. Cambridge: Polity Press.

Miller, D., and D. Slater. 2000. *The Internet: An Ethnographic Approach*. Oxford: Berg.

Minges, M. 2005. "Is the Internet Mobile? Measurements from the Asia-Pacific Region." *Telecommunications Policy* 29(2):113–25.

Mosco, V. 2004. *The Digital Sublime: Myth, Power, and Cyberspace*. Cambridge, MA: MIT Press.

Mosco, V. 2014. *To the Cloud*. Boulder, CO: Paradigm.

Oudshoorn, N., and T. Pinch, eds. 2002. *How Users Matter*. Cambridge, MA: MIT Press.

Pink, S., H. Horst, J. Postill, L. Hjorth, T. Lewis, and J. Tacchi. 2015. *Digital Ethnography*. London: Sage.

Poster, M. 2001. *What's the Matter with the Internet?* Minneapolis: University of Minnesota Press.

Rainie, L., and B. Wellman. 2012. *Networked*. Cambridge, MA: MIT Press.

Rheingold, H. 1993. *The Virtual Community*. Reading, MA: Addison-Wesley.

Robins, K., and F. Webster. 1999. *Times of the Technoculture*. London: Routledge.

Rose, G. 2016. *Visual Methodologies*, 4th ed. London: Sage.

Ruppert, E. 2013. "Rethinking Empirical Social Sciences." *Dialogues in Human Geography* 3(3):268–73.

Sardar, Z. 1996. "Cyberspace as the Darker Side of the West." Pp. 14–41 in *Cyberfutures*, edited by Z. Sardar and J. Ravetz. London: Pluto Press.

Sassen, S. 2006. *Territory, Authority, Rights*. Princeton, NJ: Princeton University Press.

Shove, E. Watson, M. Hand, and M. Ingram, J. 2007. *The Design of Everyday Life*. Oxford: Berg.

Striphas, T. 2015. "Algorithmic Culture." *European Journal of Cultural Studies* 18(4–5):395–412.

Taylor, P., and J. Harris. 2005. *Digital Matters: The Theory and Culture of the Matrix*. London: Routledge.

Thrift, N. 2005. *Knowing Capitalism*. London: Sage.

Turkle, S. 1997. *Life on the Screen: Identity in the Age of the Internet*. New York: Simon and Schuster.

———. 2015. *Reclaiming Conversation*. New York: Penguin.

Van Dijck, J. 2013. *The Culture of Connectivity: A Critical History of Social Media*. Oxford: OUP.

Wajcman, J. 2015. *Pressed for Time*. Chicago: University of Chicago Press.

Wertheim, M. 2000. *The Pearly Gates of Cyberspace*. New York: W.W. Norton.

38

Culture and the built environment

Between meaning and money

David Gartman

Introduction

The environment that humans construct for habitation has always been more than mere utility. From the beginning, groups have invested their domiciles and cities with meanings, making their built structures symbolic of their beliefs and values (Bourdieu 1990:271–83; Mukerji 1997). It is only with the rise of modern capitalist societies, however, that the artifacts of the built environment take on another status beyond either utility or symbol – that of a commodity. In capitalism the utility and symbolism of building are confounded with and eventually dominated by its status as a commodity to be sold on the market for profit. In capitalist societies, then, the built environment has a hybrid character, shaped by both money-making and meaning-making. To be built, a building must be not only aesthetically pleasing and meaningful in the culture, but also profitable enough to attract capital.

Once having recognized these two distinct and potentially contradictory social forces shaping the built environment in most modern societies, sociologists – especially cultural sociologists – must specify their interaction. Is one more powerful than the other? Are their effects on the environment independent or interactive? And at what level are these effects generated and experienced – macro, micro, meso? Current scholarship on the built environment answers these questions in different ways, some of which are more productive than others.

Built environment as capitalist commodity

The most powerful argument for the built environment as a commodity shaped by the market imperative for profit is John Logan and Harvey Molotch's *Urban Fortunes: The Political Economy of Place* (1987). The authors argue that real estate in market societies simultaneously has exchange value (generating rent for owners) and use value (providing accommodations for residents), and that these two functions conflict. Those interested in land as commodity unite into a "growth machine," a group of interlocking pro-growth associations and agencies that seek to increase the exchange value of real estate through growth. Those interested in land as use value often organize to fight growth, which drives up rents and displaces residents. But even though houses and neighborhoods provide to residents not merely utilities like physical shelter but also cultural meanings like "home" and "security," Logan and Molotch's economic model provides no place for the influence of cultural factors on the built environment.

The work of Marxist geographer David Harvey (1985a, 1985b) also offers a conception of the built environment as commodity, but one that pays more attention to the cultural dimension. Like Logan and Molotch, Harvey sees the landscape in capitalist societies as a social product molded by the contradiction between space as a means of exchange and space as a place of human community and consumption. The two capitalist imperatives – to move commodities rapidly over the landscape for exchange and to make land itself a commodity of exchange – both tend to level and homogenize space, destroying its differentiated meanings valued by human occupants. Thus, capitalism generates struggles not merely in the workplace but also in the landscape, as people resist homogenization of the built environment and seek to build distinctive communities. Unlike Logan and Molotch, however, Harvey (1985a:53–5) argues that cultural needs beyond mere shelter shape consumers' demands on the built environment: consumers want homes and communities that, through images of an unspoiled, pastoral nature, provide an escape and respite from the alienation of the factory. Capitalists are driven to meet these cultural needs in the built environment not just to sell real estate, but also to make workers happy and docile for their production work. So the landscape is shaped by both economic and ideological needs. And the fulfillment of both needs requires responding, at least superficially, to the cultural demands of consumers.

Despite these insights on culture, however, Harvey's conception of the built environment is, like Logan and Molotch's, driven mainly by an overwhelming macroeconomic logic in which capitalists manipulate the built environment for their economic interests. So, for example, he suggests that the American state's massive subsidy for suburban housing after World War II was undertaken as a Keynesian solution to the underconsumption problem of an economy of Fordist mass production (Harvey 1985b:203–11). The importance of the culture in stimulating consumer demand for suburban housing goes largely unexplored.

Cultural Marxism and the space of postmodernism

However, not all Marxists have been blind to the independent role of culture in the built environment, as demonstrated by the critical discourse around the topic of postmodernism. The tradition of cultural Marxism, pioneered by Georg Lukács and the Frankfurt School, transcends the deterministic base-superstructure model offered in Harvey and others, and thereby assigns culture a more autonomous role in society. Thinkers in this tradition hold that the main influence of the economy on culture is found in its unconscious forms rather than its conscious content. So they examine culture not for overt legitimations of the economy and its dominant class, but for its forms of expression, which they see as unconsciously reflecting the contradictions of economy and class. Thus, Fredric Jameson (1971, 1981), an important contemporary exponent of cultural Marxism, argues that every mode of production generates social contradictions that shape human experience. Cultural producers grapple with these contradictions, seeking to resolve them in artistic forms. Their productions offer social legitimations because these solutions are unconsciously limited by the artists' class interests. So for cultural Marxists, the meanings of the built environment are not directly dictated by the economic interests of bourgeois producers. They are unconsciously molded by the attempts of bourgeois artists, especially architects, to symbolically solve the social contradictions of the day, especially the contradictory experiences of space and time in a class society.

Perhaps the most influential application of cultural Marxism to the built environment is Jameson's analysis of postmodern architecture as a symbolic response to the contradictions of late capitalism (Jameson 1991, 1994). The postmodern aesthetic, he argues, is an attempt to resolve aesthetically the problems created by the new post-Fordist capitalism that emerged in the mid-1970s to replace the Fordist economy of mass production and mass consumption. Fordism had produced a modernist built environment that resolved the contradictions of its day. The rapid introduction of new technologies like the assembly line and the automobile undermined any sense of permanence by accelerating and objectifying time and generating the shock of the new. However, the constant improvement of mass-produced goods created within these rapid changes a unifying direction of technological progress. Modern architects reflected this ideology of progress in a functionalist, rectilinear aesthetic that promised to increase both the efficiency and order of the built environment. Fordist innovation also compressed and objectified space, turning once separated, heterogeneous places into simultaneous, homogeneous units of real estate. But rural and peripheral landscapes of difference still existed to relieve leveling, and architects accentuated these spatial differences with an organic aesthetic compensating for the machine aesthetic of urban areas. By formally addressing the temporal and spatial contradictions of their times, modern architects unconsciously produced a landscape that culturally furthered bourgeois interests.

Jameson argues, however, that the aesthetic resolutions of the modernist built environment were unraveled by the rise of post-Fordist capitalism, characterized by the disintegration of mass markets and the rise of global systems of flexible production producing a variety of ever-changing products. This new economy produced new experiences of time and space that demanded new aesthetic resolutions. On the dimension of time, the changes in diversified goods became so rapid and arbitrary that any sense of unified technological progress was lost. On the dimension of space, the spread of the homogenizing market into rural areas and underdeveloped countries caused the landscape to lose its differentiated use value. Postmodern architecture arose to resolve these problems. When people could no longer believe in progress, they turned to the past for meaning, so architects created an eclectic mix of historical styles to give them a reassuring place in time. And to compensate for a world losing its spatial differences to globalization, postmodern architects superficially differentiated spaces for diverse cultures and markets, often drawing on popular culture.

Jameson's analysis is non-reductionist in its treatment of the form of the built environment as an unconscious cultural response to the experiential contradictions created by the economy. But he only vaguely ties these responses to concrete classes and their interests. Although he states that the postmodern built environment ideologically corresponds to the new professional-managerial class (Jameson 1991:407), he does not detail what its interests are. And Jameson remains exceedingly vague about how economic forces are translated into cultural changes in the built environment. He implies that economic shifts change individual artists' psychological experiences of time and space, which motivates them to create new aesthetic solutions. But this short-circuited link between macroeconomics and micropsychology leaves out important mediating relations at the meso or institutional level. As sociologists have shown, artists are not isolated individuals responding separately to macro forces but social actors in a profession whose structure mediates their responses to the larger society. Both the extent of competition in a field of art and its autonomy from outside social forces affect how and whether they respond to macro changes. And these responses are not uniform: they vary by artists' positions in the profession, which are often related to the class divisions of the larger society. Only by examining the professional structure of the art form most important to the built environment – architecture – can we give a full accounting of its changing aesthetics.

David Gartman

Institutional analysis of the built environment

Several sociologists focus on the institutional level of the architectural profession to specify more concretely how economic and political macro trends impact the aesthetics of the built environment. Their general argument is that architecture is a partially autonomous profession that affects aesthetics through its internal structure and struggles. But the larger society impacts this structure by determining both the supply of qualified practitioners and the demand for architectural services. In this vein, Mauro Guillén (2006) has argued that modern architecture's aesthetic of technological efficiency and rationality was not merely a reflection of the industrialization of the larger economy. Modernism was strong only where engineers and their scientific management movement substantially influenced the profession of architecture. The modernist aesthetic thus emerged in countries where architects were trained in engineering schools, not art schools, and thus based their claims of professional expertise on technological knowledge, not aesthetics. So even though the United States and Britain were far more advanced economically than Germany, only the latter was an important breeding ground for modernism because of the influence of engineering and scientific management on architecture.

David Brain's (1989) institutional analysis helps to explain why engineering was not influential on architecture in the US. He argues that by the mid-1800s American architects were losing control over aesthetics to clients from the emerging commercial and financial elite, whose demand for ornamental excess to display their wealth resulted in stylistic chaos. In 1857 architects seized control back from clients and achieved autonomy by establishing the American Institute of Architects, which institutionalized the Beaux-Arts aesthetic. Thus, architecture and its claims to expertise were already professionalized around a particular aesthetic by the time, later in the century, that engineers and scientific management rose to prominence.

In treating aesthetics as a tool in struggles for professional control, however, both Guillén and Brain largely ignore the demand for architecture in the larger society, on which cultural Marxists focus. This problem is addressed by Magali Sarfatti Larson (1993) in her institutional analysis of the rise of postmodern architecture in the American built environment. Although she similarly focuses on the internal dynamics of the architectural profession, she recognizes that the external demand of a changing economy also shapes internal aesthetic struggles. Larson argues that an opportunity to challenge the dominance of modern architects, who had risen to power in the post-war profession, was created by post-Fordist capitalism, which economically devastated many urban areas through deindustrialization. Many cities responded by seeking to attract middle-class consumers back downtown with new consumption venues such as convention centers, shopping malls, and upscale housing in historic neighborhoods. But the competition between cities for consumer dollars forced each to differentiate its "urban product" from those of others. This demand in turn pressured architects to produce eye-catching buildings while simultaneously holding down costs, thus favoring an aesthetic of superficial, often historical, ornamentation that became known as postmodernism.

Postmodern architecture was produced, Larson argues, by the confluence of this external demand with the internal dynamics of the profession. In the late 1960s and early 1970s, young architects inspired by the broader youth movement began to challenge the complicity of the modernist establishment in creating a divided and unequal built environment. Their challenge was strengthened by a mismatch in the profession between supply and demand. In the 1970s a flood of young architects trained in an expanded system of higher education poured into a profession suffering from declining demand due to recession. To compete in this crowded field required heightened aesthetic innovation, which was steered by market demand into superficial decoration (Larson 1993:243–50).

Larson's model, however, seems to suffer from unexplained contingency. Although she incorporates the preferences of both producers and consumers of architecture, Larson does not explain whose preferences matter more, and under what circumstances. Her analysis seems to subscribe to the general rule of the production-of-culture perspective (DiMaggio 1977), that the more competition there is between producers, the more important consumer demand is in shaping products. Yet, neither she nor the other institutionalists really have addressed what either producers or consumers desire aesthetically. Just about any exclusive body of technical or aesthetic knowledge, whether modernist, Beaux Arts, or postmodern, would seem to suffice for the purpose of monopolizing professional expertise. What factors select one over the others? Competition encourages innovation, but where do new aesthetics come from? Do larger class interests play a role, as the cultural Marxists postulate? If so, how do these interact with producers' professional interests? These questions can only be answered by a perspective which simultaneously takes into account the cultural demands of both producers and consumers, how these are affected by the larger economic organization of society, and how all of these factors are filtered through the institutional structure of professions. To my knowledge, the only theory of culture that does all this is Pierre Bourdieu's.

A Bourdieu model for the built environment

Pierre Bourdieu (1984) offers a powerful theory that helps to explain the effects of both money-making and meaning-making on the built environment. First, his explanation of cultural preferences is grounded in the economy and its class structure. Individuals growing up in different classes are exposed to different material conditions that ingrain different sets of unconscious preferences, which Bourdieu calls habitus. The abundant resources of the upper-class condition its members to be unconcerned with the material necessities of life, and thus to privilege form or aesthetics over material function. In the built environment such a habitus determines a taste for accommodations formally designed in classical styles that are sedately indulgent. Conversely, the meager resources of those in the working class condition them to be constantly concerned with material necessities, and thus to privilege function over form. In the built environment such a habitus manifests itself as a taste for accommodations that are comfortable and convenient, but also incorporate a kitschy prettiness. Because society as a whole validates the superiority of the tastes of the dominant class, this class's cultural consumption makes its members seem personally superior, thereby justifying their superior resources.

Thus, class habitus shapes consumer demand in built environment, which in turn helps determine what producers like architects and developers build. But do producers simply give the largest group of consumers what they demand in order to maximize profits? Or do their own cultural preferences, which might differ from those of consumers, also mold their productions? For Bourdieu (1993, 1996), the answer depends on the producers' locations in the cultural field. The cultural field is divided into two subfields that are distinguished by the degree of producer autonomy from the economic market. In the subfield of large-scale or mass production, producers possess more economic capital (money) than cultural capital (education and knowledge), and thus seek to maximize economic profits by catering to the cultural preferences of consumers in the market. Markets within this subfield are usually stratified, with some producers filling the demand of high-class consumers, and others producing for petty-bourgeois or working-class tastes.

The subfield of small scale or restricted production is composed of the high arts, and is autonomous from the market. Having more cultural capital than economic capital, producers here seek not money but recognition from other cultural producers on the basis of aesthetic standards. They thus cater to what Bourdieu calls the dominated fraction of the dominant class or the intellectual bourgeoisie, whose members have a taste for "aristocratic asceticism," that is, goods that deny indulgence in the name of cerebral appropriation. There are two factors, Bourdieu states, that determine the cerebral standards on which these autonomous producers base their productions – the habitus of producers and the dynamics of the field. Producers often originate from different class backgrounds, which give them different habitus that determine preferences for different styles of art (Bourdieu 1996). These habitus initially distribute producers between the competing stylistic positions in a field. But competitive dynamics also influence aesthetic standards. When competition is high, often as a result of new entrants, producers are more likely to pioneer new styles of art, creating niches that distinguish them from competitors and thus bring recognition or symbolic profits. Ultimately, however, the new styles must also find consumers among other cultural producers whose habitus are predisposed to them.

Bourdieu's model clearly recognizes that the economic and cultural dimensions of the built environment interact at the macro, meso, and micro levels. The macroeconomic structure not only produces specific cultural tastes in individual consumers and producers, but also determines the impact of these tastes on culture by affecting the autonomy of professional fields.

Applying Bourdieu's model to modern architecture

I will demonstrate the power of Bourdieu's model by applying it to the differential development of modern architecture in the United States and Europe. Mauro Guillén (2006) seeks to explain the differential development of modernism in the built environment with an institutional model that focuses on the influence of engineering and scientific management on the professionalization of architects. But his model cannot account for the fact that while American engineers pioneered and applied scientific management in industry, they were not influential on architecture. In Europe, by contrast, engineers and scientific management were largely uninfluential in industry, but did influence architecture toward modernism. This disjuncture between economic and cultural influence can be explained, however, if we examine the autonomy of the profession from the market and the cultural preferences of consumers themselves.

I argue that the modern movement in architecture reflected the culture of not merely engineers but the larger professional-managerial class, whose positions depended more on cultural capital than economic capital (Gartman 2000, 2009). The stark, rectilinear, unadorned aesthetic of modernism was a form of "aristocratic asceticism," which Bourdieu argues is characteristic of this intellectual bourgeoisie. Modern architecture arose mainly in Europe, not the US, because the position of this class was different there. Around the turn of the twentieth century, the professional-managerial class in both regions gave rise to a technocratic movement glorifying knowledge over wealth, of which modern architecture was a part. In the US, two architects who were attached to this movement, Frank Lloyd Wright and Louis Sullivan, pioneered the style of the Chicago School, a protomodern architecture characterized by relatively functional and unadorned forms. Both architects had habitus and tastes conditioned by middle-class intellectual backgrounds and technical training, which distinguished them from the upper-class backgrounds and Beaux-Arts training of the architects dominating the American profession more widely. The habitus of Wright, Sullivan, and other American protomodernists placed them at the periphery of the architectural field, where they struggled to displace the established Beaux-Arts elite. The latter architects were motivated by money-making to supply members of the industrial and commercial bourgeoisie of the day with sedate but decorative historical forms that revealed their wealth but hid its industrial origins. Wright and Sullivan, by contrast, often found clients among the emerging professional-managerial class, whose members sought to assert through functional forms the preeminence of their efficiency and rationality over the money of industrialists.

In America, however, the technocratic movement of this new class was cut short, depriving the Chicago School of supporting clients. Early in the century modernizing capitalists integrated knowledge professionals, including designers and architects, into mass-production corporations in order to increase profits and contain conflict. Once integrated into these economic organizations, such professionals lost autonomy, moving from the cultural subfield of restricted production into the subfield of large-scale production. There, their creations were subjected to the market demand of the working masses, who rejected ascetic functionalism in favor of their own characteristic aesthetic of kitschy decoration. This demand affected urban architecture because most workers lived in cities and visually consumed the aesthetics of buildings like movie theaters, department stores, and corporate headquarters. To cater to this mass market, American architects created an expressive, decorative aesthetic known as Art Deco, which replaced the protomodernism of the Chicago School.

In interwar Europe, however, the technocratic movement of the professional-managerial class was stronger. This class's incorporation into industry was blocked by a capitalist class reluctant to modernize due to its alliance with the Old Regime. So educated professionals mounted an autonomous technocratic movement to rationalize industry, and modern architecture was an important part of it. The pioneers of modernism argued that architects and designers should cooperate with industrial engineers to design housing and other products that were compatible with mass production. These products, they argued, would help placate restless workers and forestall revolution. Finding no support for their program among industrialists, the intellectual bourgeoisie turned to social-democratic governments, which launched programs to encourage industrial rationalization. One such state program funded the building of mass-produced public housing designed by modern architects such as Ernst May and Bruno Taut. This state support meant that architecture remained in the subfield of restricted production, subject to the tastes not of the masses but of architects and others in the intellectual bourgeoisie. In contrast to the US during this period, where the built environment was shaped by the market and subject to mass demand, in Europe workers were forced to accept the modern aesthetic favored by the habitus of the educated elite.

The depressionary rise of America's compromised modernism

The fortunes of modern architecture in America improved, however, during the 1930s, when the Great Depression loosened the grip of the capitalist market on building. The private market for new construction collapsed, leaving the New Deal government of Franklin Delano Roosevelt as the main client for architecture. To stimulate the construction industry and create jobs, the federal government undertook the largest public construction project in the nation's history. Under the auspices of numerous government agencies and programs, FDR's New Deal undertook to put people to work by putting a roof over the heads of displaced and underhoused Americans. Because these projects were not subject to the market demand of consumers, government-employed architects were free to design in styles of their own choosing. Many modernist architects were able to realize their preferred style for the first time in government housing projects. Since decent, low-cost housing was scarce for the lower classes during the Depression, people could not be choosy about the style of government-built and government-subsidized housing. But government architects also understood that they could not totally disregard the tastes of the masses, to whom they owed their jobs. So they tempered their preferred modernism with elements of popular taste. The aesthetics of these construction projects unconsciously testified to the New Deal political coalition by combining the modernist asceticism of the professional-managerial class with the popular and historical styles preferred by the working masses.

David Gartman

This tense aesthetic compromise was visible in Greenbelt, Maryland, the first of three new suburban communities constructed by the Resettlement Administration. Modeled on Ebenezer Howard's (1898) garden-city concept, these greenbelt towns sought to decentralize the crowded, overbuilt working-class neighborhoods of industrial cities, which were thought to create the dangerous contagion of class consciousness. Greenbelt was built on undeveloped land on the outskirts of Washington, DC. The town took its name from the barrier of undeveloped land that surrounded the community and protected it from the evils of urban overdevelopment. One of its innovations was the separation of foot traffic from the streets, where working-class children traditionally played and class-conscious adults assembled to communicate and organize (US Government Resettlement Administration 1936).

Not only the layout of Greenbelt but also the architectural aesthetics of its apartment blocks and public buildings unconsciously symbolized New Deal politics. American modernists R.J. Wadsworth and Roland Wank were hired to design housing at Greenbelt. But given the chance to realize a pure modernism, they demurred and compromised with more popular and historical styles. They thus unconsciously expressed in their bifurcated designs the New Deal coalition of the popular classes with the professional-managerial class. Greenbelt did contain flat-roofed, ribbon-windowed white cubes of modernist apartments that would have been right at home in the Berlin housing estates of the 1920s. But even these were compromises with more popular and historic styles. The architects broke up the long windows with short stretches of rustic clapboard siding reminiscent of rural cabins. And some of the apartment blocks incorporated elements of the Georgian style of the early republic, with pitched slate roofs, flat facades, and walls of brick. In the commercial buildings of the town center, like the movie theater, drugstore, and barber shop, architects incorporated the smooth curves of the streamline moderne style, which was popular in the Depression as a metaphor for slipping effortlessly through turbulent times (Anonymous 1936).

Even in TVA (Tennessee Valley Authority) dams, the high-tech constructions of the Depression, there were concessions to more popular and decorative styles and motifs, notably in visitor centers built to promote the technological marvels that the professional-managerial class was providing for the masses. At Norris Dam, for example, the modernist émigré architect Roland Wank was not content to give public visitors merely acres of unadorned concrete to view. In public areas, like the powerhouse and visitors' center, Wank made the cold, homogeneous, machine-made material look handmade by lining the pouring forms with thin strips of rough-cut lumber that alternated from horizontal to vertical in adjacent blocks. When removed, these forms had imprinted on this cold industrial material the warm look of hand-loomed cloth (Tennessee Valley Authority 1940:150–1).

Conclusion

Bourdieu's model holds out the possibility of incorporating both cultural and economic determinants into explanations of the built environment. Unlike those who see the landscape merely as an economic commodity, he reveals that it also has cultural meanings, which are conditioned by the economic positions of both producers and consumers. And unlike the cultural Marxists, who postulate short-circuited connections between economic interest and cultural meaning, Bourdieu shows these connections are mediated by the structure of potentially autonomous fields that organize the work of cultural producers like architects. But the model has its limitations, as critics have suggested. I have argued (Gartman 2002) that Bourdieu's theory of culture as class distinction is valid mainly in more unequal societies, whereas in more equal ones, distinctive class cultures become leveled and hybridized. For example, the more equal distribution of both economic and cultural capital in post-World War II Western societies seems to have undermined elite modernism and given rise to a postmodern architecture that combined elite and popular culture. Keynesian economic programs not only gave the lower classes more money to buy cultural goods but also more education to appreciate high culture. Upwardly mobile individuals developed a hybrid habitus that combined a childhood taste for mass culture with an acquired knowledge of high arts. Such a habitus inclined both architectural producers and consumers toward the combination of high and low symbols that became known as postmodernism.

The applicability of Bourdieu's model may be limited to Western societies, but it is difficult to know due to the paucity of research on the built environment in non-Western societies. And the little research that exists is distorted by the battles within the Western architecture field. For example, from their research on Lagos, Nigeria, and China's Pearl River Delta, Rem Koolhaas and his students in the Harvard Design School Project on the City (2000) have concluded that a new urbanism of contingency and difference is emerging in the developing world that cannot be understood by Western models. But the unqualified praise they sing to real estate speculation in China and proliferating squatter villages in Lagos leaves the impression that these Western architects view the undeveloped world through the struggles of the architectural field of the developed one. Koolhaas became an architectural star in the 1980s by denouncing modernism's rational planning in favor of postmodernism's difference and contingency. By viewing the built environment of the developing world through this polemical position within Western architecture, he mistook the poverty and overcrowding of Lagos for vitality and diversity. In the years to come, we can determine the applicability of Bourdieu's model to places outside the Western world only by viewing them through their own social structures and institutions, not through the struggles of Western ones.

References

Anonymous. 1936. "Comparative Architectural Details in the Greenbelt Housing." *American Architect and Architecture* 149:20–36.

Bourdieu, P. 1984. *Distinction: A Critique of the Social Judgement of Taste*. Cambridge, MA: Harvard University Press.

———. 1990. *The Logic of Practice*. Stanford, CA: Stanford University Press.

———. 1993. *The Field of Cultural Production*. New York: Columbia University Press.

———. 1996. *The Rules of Art*. Stanford, CA: Stanford University Press.

Brain, D. 1989. "Discipline and Style: The Ecole des Beaux-Arts and the Social Production of an American Architecture." *Theory and Society* 18(6):807–68.

DiMaggio, P. 1977. "Market Structure, the Creative Process, and Popular Culture: Toward an Organizational Reinterpretation of Mass-culture Theory." *Journal of Popular Culture* 11(2):436–52.

Gartman, D. 2000. "Why Modern Architecture Emerged in Europe, not America: The New Class and the Aesthetics of Technocracy." *Theory, Culture and Society* 17(5):75–96.

———. 2002. "Bourdieu's Theory of Cultural Change: Explication, Application, Critique." *Sociological Theory* 20(2):255–77.

———. 2009. *From Autos to Architecture: Fordism and Architectural Aesthetics in the Twentieth Century*. New York: Princeton Architectural Press.

Guillén, M. 2006. *The Taylorized Beauty of the Mechanical: Scientific Management and the Rise of Modernist Architecture*. Princeton, NJ: Princeton University Press.

Harvey, D. 1985a. *Consciousness and the Urban Experience: Studies in the History and Theory of Capitalist Urbanization*. Baltimore, MD: Johns Hopkins University Press.

———. 1985b. *The Urbanization of Capital*. Oxford: Basil Blackwell.

Howard, E. 1898. *To-morrow: A Peaceful Path to Real Reform*. Cambridge: Cambridge University Press.

Jameson, F. 1971. *Marxism and Form*. Princeton, NJ: Princeton University Press.

————. 1981. *The Political Unconscious*. Ithaca, NY: Cornell University Press.

————. 1991. *Postmodernism, or, the Cultural Logic of Late Capitalism*. London: Verso.

————. 1994. *The Seeds of Time*. New York: Columbia University Press.

Koolhaas, R., S. Boeri, S. Kwinter, N. Tazi, and H. Ulrich Obrist. 2000. *Mutations*. Barcelona: Actar.

Larson, M.S. 1993. *Behind the Postmodern Façade*. Berkeley: University of California Press.

Logan, J., and H. Molotch. 1987. *Urban Fortunes: The Political Economy of Place*. Berkeley: University of California Press.

Mukerji, C. 1997. *Territorial Ambitions and the Gardens of Versailles*. Cambridge: Cambridge University Press.

Tennessee Valley Authority. 1940. *The Norris Project: A Comprehensive Report on the Planning, Design, Construction, and Initial Operations of the Tennessee Valley Authority's First Water Control Project*. Washington, DC: US Government Printing Office.

US Government Resettlement Administration. 1936. *Greenbelt Towns: A Demonstration in Suburban Planning*. Washington, DC: Resettlement Administration.

39

Public institutions of "high" culture

Victoria D. Alexander

Introduction

This chapter focuses on institutions that distribute "high" culture via public or quasi-public mechanisms. High culture includes (Western) fine arts, such as classical and contemporary visual arts, opera, classical music, and ballet. I discuss art museums, symphony orchestras, and opera, drama, and dance companies, organizations constituting what is known as the "supported arts sector" because they are reliant to some degree on public (governmental) funding for their continued operation. After noting some difficulties with the concept of high culture, I outline the organizational forms used to distribute high culture, which include nonprofit and non-governmental organizations and government agencies. Then I look at the public funding of fine arts institutions and consider several issues facing these institutions, including the conflict among missions and the effects of various external pressures. The chapter concludes with a discussion of topics that may be fruitful in the continuing study of public institutions of high culture.

"High" culture as a problematic term

"High" culture tends to refer to those art forms traditionally associated with the upper social classes; in contrast, "low" culture includes the popular arts produced by cultural industries for large audiences, and the folk arts, made by people in local settings. (Scare quotes often accompany such terms to highlight the problematic, and usually elitist, assumptions inherent in them.) "High" culture is defined (favorably) against other types of culture (cast as inferior), which enables connoisseurs to claim status honor, or "distinction" (Bourdieu 1984).

The creation of institutions of "high" culture took active work on the part of social elites (DiMaggio 1982a, 1982b, 1991a, 1992), who elevated certain types of art over others. Levine (1988) discusses this "sacralization" as it happened in America toward the end of the nineteenth century and similar processes occurred around this time in Europe (Prior 2002; Weber 2008; Wolff and Seed 1988). "High" culture is, therefore, a historically situated, Western concept, thoroughly enmeshed with power.

The "high culture model"

In the United States, most institutions of high culture are nonprofit organizations. They are legally incorporated as 501(c)(3) organizations, which means that they are exempt from some kinds of taxes and can receive charitable contributions that attract tax relief for the donor. Nonprofit organizations are, in fact, private forms, but their nonprofit charters require that they operate in the public interest, and they are often publicly funded (see below). As central actors in the distribution of high culture in the US and other countries, nonprofits must be included when considering of public institutions of high culture.

DiMaggio (1992) describes the nonprofit organizational form as central to the "high culture model" of producing and/or distributing the arts. (The nonprofit, of course, has other functions in other sectors.) DiMaggio (1982a, 1982b) shows how elites in Boston – known as the Boston Brahmins – established the Museum of Fine Arts and the Boston Symphony Orchestra in 1870 and 1881, respectively, as a way of claiming cultural capital and status for themselves. Prior to this time, the demarcation between what we now consider the high and low arts had not been clearly drawn. By establishing charitable institutions to house and showcase only the fine arts, changing the ways fine arts were received, and "educating" the populace in the superiority of these forms, the Boston Brahmins were "cultural entrepreneurs" who worked to draw symbolic boundaries between cultural forms of different social classes. Such boundary work is a crucial part of the high culture model.

According to DiMaggio (1992), museums and symphony orchestras were established as nonprofit enterprises throughout the United States in the late nineteenth and early twentieth century. Nonprofit theaters, dance companies, and opera houses were founded subsequently, in the early half of the twentieth century. During the founding process, champions of each art form needed to create a boundary between high-status versions of the art and its more popular and commercial relatives, and to protect high-status art from commercial pressures of the marketplace. The marketplace works against distinctions in culture, as it "drives entrepreneurs to elide aesthetic distinctions in order to create larger audiences" (DiMaggio 1992:43–4).

Santoro (2010) shows how, in Milan at the turn of the twentieth century, cultural entrepreneurs at *La Scala* embraced a version of the "high culture model" by drawing boundaries between serious opera and related forms (comic opera, operetta) and adopting a nonprofit form, the "autonomous body" (*ente autonomo*). However, in Italy, opera remained a popular as well as an elite taste, and the institutionalization of the artistic field also included a political process whereby the state exerted control, suggesting that the high culture model may vary from country to country.

In other nations, public institutions of high culture may be governmental organizations, or they may be quasi-non-governmental organizations (QUANGOs). In the United Kingdom, for instance, the national museums are non-departmental public bodies, governed by a board of trustees; as charitable organizations, they can receive covenanted gifts that are tax sheltered (Alexander and Rueschemeyer 2005). Other British arts organizations exist in nonprofit forms, such as registered charities or corporations limited by guarantee. In contrast, most French institutions of high culture, including the major museums and the state theater sector, are both owned and run by central or local government, although since the 1980s the *management* of many of these institutions has been delegated to private, nonprofit groups (Toepler and Zimmer 2002).

Public funding of fine arts institutions

A key element in the public nature of fine arts institutions is the fact that they receive, in one form or another, government support. The Arts Council of Great Britain was chartered in 1946, and worked at arm's length from government, meaning it made funding decisions based on a panel of art world experts outside the influence of political parties. Today, public funding of arts institutions in the United Kingdom is channeled through the Department for Digital, Culture, Media and Sport (DCMS). The UK government funds the DCMS, which in turn provides grants-in-aid to the National Museums and to Arts Council England. (Culture is a devolved policy area and is funded by the Scottish Parliament, the National Assembly for Wales, and the Northern Ireland Assembly in these countries, each of which has an arts council.) The DCMS has a say on who is appointed to the boards of museums. Government grants-in-aid do not cover all costs associated with running museums and galleries, however, so these organizations are required to fundraise from other sources (Alexander 2007, 2008; Gray 2000.)

In the United States, the federal government supports the Smithsonian museums and funds the National Endowment for the Arts (NEA), which, in turn, provides arts funding to nonprofit organizations, schools, and state and local governments. The NEA was established in 1965 as an arm's-length body, but after the "culture wars" of the 1990s, in which religious and political conservatives castigated the arts on moral grounds, Congress constrained the remit of the NEA and cut its funding (Alexander and Rueschemeyer 2005; Dubin 1992). Private initiative plays an important role, even in what remains of NEA funding, as grants must be matched by funding from other sources. A notable feature of American public funding of the arts is that a large portion of it is indirect, through tax relief (Schuster 1986). The American tax system, along with a strong philanthropic tradition, encourages individual and corporate patronage of the arts.

Toepler and Zimmer (2002) contrast this "Anglo-Saxon" model of public funding with the "Continental European" model and the "Nordic" model. The Continental model, as typified by France, is a centralized, top-down, bureaucratic system in which the state plays a central role in the provision of culture, especially high culture. Relatively high levels of public funds are committed to culture, which is seen as an important element of national identity. Private funding of culture "remains undeveloped" due to "the traditional antimarket and antibusiness attitudes of policy makers" (Toepler and Zimmer 2002:36). The Nordic model, as typified by Sweden, is a decentralized, corporatist approach in which national government takes responsibility for financing the arts and culture, but devolves decision-making to regional and local institutions. Like France, Sweden does not rely on private funding of the arts, and in contrast to France, Swedish funding includes a broad array of "popular and grass-roots cultural activities" as well as high culture (Toepler and Zimmer 2002:39).

Issues in public institutions of high culture

A crucial issue in public institutions of high culture involves what Zolberg (1986) calls "tensions of missions." Zolberg describes the conflict within art museums between elitist and curatorial goals on the one hand, and populist and educational goals on the other. This conflict has been inherent in art museums since their inception: they were founded to conserve and display works of art and have been run by curators with scholarly goals; at the same time, they were founded as educational institutions that operated for the benefit of the public. DiMaggio (1991a) discusses the increasing ascendancy of curatorial goals at the expense of educational goals in American museums of the 1920s. In the United Kingdom, the Arts Council of Great Britain was established (in 1946) with similar tensions, summed up by the phrase "raise or spread" (Minihan 1977). The debate was whether public taste should be raised to the highest standards with only excellent (often London-based) art supported, or whether art should be made available to a wide audience across the geographic spread of the nation.

These tensions continue to exist for most institutions of high culture, although in recent years the emphasis has been to move the balance more toward the popular, inclusive role of arts institutions and away from their curatorial and scholarly functions. Ballé (2002), for instance, discusses the "democratization" of French art museums. She traces the roots of this process back to the French Revolution, which "codified the democratic concept of the museum as a public institution, encompassing the state's responsibility for its heritage and the museum's obligation toward the citizens" (Ballé 2002:134). While the pressure for democratization has deep roots, more recent, and complex, events (since the 1980s in Europe, earlier in the United States) have pressed cultural institutions toward even more inclusive policies.

In addition to the problem of balancing excellence and access, art museums and other public institutions of culture have been increasingly subject to other pressures, most notably an emphasis on management issues (Alexander 1996a, 1996b, 2018; Hewison 1995). Glynn (2000) describes symphony orchestras as "dual identity" organizations in which the business side stands in contrast to the musical/artistic side and often conflicts with it. Increasing managerialism has many roots, including the introduction of new types of personnel, pressures from funders (both governmental and corporate) for accountability, and general societal trends and neoliberal political tastes that favor the application of managerial styles drawn from the business world to charitable, nonprofit, and governmental organizations. The arts face chronic budget shortages, and managerial approaches are seen as a path to "sustainable" futures.

A crucial issue for cultural institutions relates to difficult funding climates. In 1966, Baumol and Bowen identified the problem of "cost disease" in performing arts organizations. They argued that these organizations face inherent financial issues because their chief costs are for personnel. A Shakespeare play has exactly the number of characters specified by the script today as in Elizabethan times. A symphony orchestra needs roughly 100 musicians to play the classical repertoire, and a quartet is always four. These facts mean that there will always be intrinsic cost pressures in performing arts organizations, as personnel costs inexorably rise.

Baumol and Bowen's discussion underpins a "market failure" argument for public support of performing arts organizations: because the market will produce a financial shortfall over time, the state should step in. But Baumol and Bowen wrote in a period of increasing government support for the arts; in recent decades, states have increasingly stepped away from public funding of the arts, pushing the supported arts sector back toward the market. In the 1990s when the US Congress slashed funding for the arts (which had a particularly negative impact on the visual and performing arts) private funding, or earned income, had to fill the gaps. In the United Kingdom, Margaret Thatcher dramatically reduced funding for the arts in the 1980s with the express purpose of encouraging cultural organizations to find alternative funding. The recent coalition and Conservative governments in the UK also cut funding and explicitly encouraged private philanthropy through what they called their "Big Society" manifesto.

As the case of the UK suggests, the American system of "plural funding" or "mixed economy support" for high culture institutions has come to be seen by other national governments as the correct direction in which to take cultural funding. "Privatization" has become a keyword for fine arts institutions across Europe. Regardless of the previous level of state support for the fine arts, most European countries have cut back public funds, requiring arts institutions to seek more earned income and private sponsorship, and many have instituted other reforms to reduce the influence of the state, including transferring management functions from the state to nonprofit entities (Boorsma, van Hemel, van der Wielen 1998).

Future directions

There are many unanswered questions about public institutions of high culture. Here, I suggest five areas of promising future study.

First, *what happens to institutions of "high" culture as boundaries between different genres of art weaken*, both in the wider society and within fine arts institutions themselves? Many institutions of high art have offered more popular programming, as the marketization of arts institutions and increasing commercial pressures encourage performances or exhibitions that have the potential to attract larger audiences (Alexander 1996a; DiMaggio 1991b). So-called warhorse programming (the most popular and familiar works from the traditional repertoire) attracts audiences, but may conflict with the urge to present other works (new and old) for the sake of innovation per se or to provide variety and challenge to musicians, actors, or dancers (McCarthy et al. 2001). Contemporary audience members have broadened their cultural repertoires to become high-status "cultural omnivores" with eclectic tastes (Peterson and Kern 1996). DiMaggio and Mukhtar (2004) show changes in US arts participation consistent with the omnivore model: cultural participation has declined overall, but increased in certain areas such as art museums and jazz concerts. As they note, the arts remain central to the acquisition of cultural capital but there are changes in *the composition of artistic cultural capital* in response to the rise of multiculturalism and efforts toward greater social inclusivity. "In so far as the attendance rates are indicators, the big losers among the high-culture arts are two art forms whose repertoires remain rooted in nineteenth-century Europe: classical music and ballet" (DiMaggio and Mukhtar 2004:190). High-culture institutions will change as the cultural objects at their heart change in status and as their audience base shifts.

Second, *to what extent are high-culture institutions affected by where the money comes from?* This question relates to state sponsorship and private philanthropy, both individual and corporate. How do arts organizations respond as governments attempt to shape their artistic policy (e.g., by requiring institutions to foster social inclusiveness) or management structure (e.g., by requiring institutions to prepare strategic plans, by appointing directors or boards, or by shifting governance structures from public to private entities)? What influence do business corporations have on cultural institutions in countries where corporate philanthropy is common?

Government funding of the arts is consequential. Feder and Katz-Gerro (2015) show how, in Israel, government priorities in cultural funding reflect wider social hierarchies. Israeli cultural policy reinforces existing privilege, for instance, by providing more funding to cultural organizations representing privileged ethnic groups than to those representing the disadvantaged even while acting as a democratizing force as the disparity between funding for arts organizations in the center versus the periphery declines. In the UK, Tony Blair's government (1997–2007) focused on instrumental outcomes in cultural policy (Belfiore 2012), a focus rooted in neoliberalism which has profound effects (Alexander 2018).

Cultural organizations that rely on funding from non-governmental sources find they must accede to funders' desires in some ways. Wu (2002) and Philips and Whannel (2013), among others, draw attention to the influence of corporate sponsors on the arts. In the past, in the museum field, corporate funders may have changed programming *indirectly* by providing funds for certain types of popular and "blockbuster" shows, thereby increasing the number and proportion of such exhibitions, but they did not actually request changes to individual exhibitions (Alexander 1996b). However, British museums have recently been accused of acceding to direct demands from a corporate sponsor to include particular works of art in an exhibition and to provide information on union membership among museum employees (Macalister 2016).

Third, *what happens to artistic production, especially in terms of innovation and artistic autonomy*, as governments provide less insulation from the marketplace and public institutions of high culture become embedded in more market-based systems? Large organizations may be best positioned to present high culture in marketized systems, as they can capture income and audiences that are not available to smaller organizations (Hewison 1987; McCarthy et al. 2001). Since 2006, for example, the Metropolitan Opera has simulcast high-definition transmissions of live performances to hundreds of cinemas in many countries, affording the Met a revenue stream not readily available to smaller, less prestigious companies.

McCarthy et al. (2001) hypothesize that commercial pressures may lead to the demise of medium-sized cultural institutions. They suggest that, in the future, cultural organizations will be divided into two groups: a small number of large, nonprofit organizations in major cities and a much larger number of small, nonprofit organizations aimed toward local, specialized markets. Small organizations will be able to survive because their costs are relatively low. The large organizations, particularly, will adopt business strategies from the profit-seeking sector, relying on advertising and marketing campaigns promoting celebrity performers and traditional materials designed to attract the broadest share of relatively stable markets that can pay premium ticket prices (McCarthy et al. 2001). If large organizations favor the popular, well-established, unproblematic traditional repertoires, will smaller organizations be able to continue offering innovative or controversial work?

Fourth, *what effect do the internet and other platforms and technologies have on public institutions of high culture?* DiMaggio and Mukhtar (2004) point out new technologies provide various types of competition for leisure time and may therefore reduce live audiences for exhibitions and performances. Conversely, new technologies may provide new markets. For instance, live transmission of theater performances in movie cinemas expand the audience base. Most museums and galleries have digitized collections, and performing arts organizations produce trailers of coming attractions. Google's Art Project provides "360-degree" tours of more than 60 museums from across the world, using an indoor version of their Street View technology. The ramifications of such initiatives are woefully understudied. Walmsley's (2016) mixed-methods research on digital engagement with dance suggests that digital tools can be effective with audiences, sparking the interest and developing the confidence of people who rarely, if ever, attend live dance performances. However, Walmsley also found it was easy for audience members to disengage from the digital platform, leaving it unclear whether deep connections to cultural organizations can be forged through digital means, at least for now. Since technology changes rapidly, it is likely to outpace research into its impacts, which may be substantial, on public institutions of high culture.

Fifth, *how do the concepts of high culture and institutions dedicated to high culture translate or travel from the West to other regions of the world?* Many Western art forms (e.g., classical music) have become firmly rooted in non-Western nations, as have some institutions for the display of cultural artifacts (e.g., the museum). Whereas in the past it was colonial officials who exported cultural ideas (arguably as part of their colonial mission), Tomooka, Kanno, and Kobayashi (2002) show that, in the late nineteenth century after the Meiji Restoration of 1868, leaders in Japan looked to the West as a "reference point" for its own culture: Japan imported such concepts as culture, visual arts, and fine arts, and reconceptualized some of its own cultural forms in these terms, specifically to increase the prestige of Japan abroad. (Of course, while contemporary Japanese high culture may have been influenced by Western ideas during the Meiji period, its origins are not Western but deeply embedded in Japanese history; see Ikegami 2005.) In today's postcolonial world, what factors play into the creation of high arts institutions in non-Western societies? For instance, in December 2007, China opened its National Center for the Performing Arts in Beijing. The building, colloquially called "the Egg," includes three venues, each with a large seating capacity to display both Western and Chinese performing arts. In November 2008, Qatar opened its Museum of Islamic Art in a building designed by I.M. Pei. These prestige venues, with impressive and distinctive architecture (created by so-called starchitects), are clearly designed to generate esteem for the increasingly successful nation-states they represent. They also draw on ideas, institutionalized in Western settings, on how to display culture, and draw on Western notions of high culture as prestigious. But why have non-Western nations adopted these institutions, and do the institutions function differently depending on national context?

Let me close with one final example which draws together several of the themes mentioned earlier. Abu Dhabi is currently building a cultural district on Saadiyat Island. In addition to a concert hall and a performing arts center, the island will feature a Guggenheim Museum (designed by Frank Gehry) and a Louvre Museum (designed by Jean Novel). After significant delays, the Louvre Abu Dhabi opened on November 8, 2017, but there is currently no scheduled opening date for the Guggenheim Abu Dhabi. The Guggenheim has built several "branch" museums since the 1990s, and the licensing of the Guggenheim name to this new museum has not been particularly controversial (although the museum has been caught up in controversy due to perceived human rights abuses of construction workers). In contrast, many French observers saw the "desert Louvre" as a shocking departure from French norms against commercial exploitation of the nation's patrimony. The French government has licensed the Louvre "brand" – which includes 30 years' use of the Louvre name, curatorial expertise, and the leasing of a selection of its art treasures – for USD 1.3 billion (Riding 2007). Critics believe that the French government has sold the soul of the Louvre through this transaction and abandoned its historic commitment to protecting French culture from market pressures. If France accedes to the commercial logic of global capitalism in the cultural sphere, what hope is there for public institutions of high culture in other nations with weaker anti-capitalist traditions?

Conclusion

Public institutions of high culture take different organizational forms in different countries. Government policies also vary nation by nation. Nevertheless, these institutions share a broad definition, formulated relatively recently in the West, of what "high" culture is (status-enhancing fine arts) and how it should be displayed (in museums or performing arts venues where audiences consume culture "seriously"). In recent years, public institutions of high culture in many nations confront common challenges, particularly decreased government funding and pressure to attract audiences through more popular fare. They find themselves operating with more managerial and business world strategies in increasingly marketized and commercialized settings. And although the concepts of high culture were institutionalized in the West, non-Western nations play an increasing role in the production and display of high culture in our globalizing world.

References

Alexander, Victoria D. 1996a. "Pictures at an Exhibition: Conflicting Pressures in Museums and the Display of Art." *American Journal of Sociology* 101(4):797–839.

———. 1996b. "From Philanthropy to Funding: The Effects of Corporate and Public Support on American Art Museums." *Poetics* 24(2–4):89–131.

———. 2007. "State Support of Artists: the Case of the UK in a New Labour Environment and Beyond." *Journal of Arts Management, Law and Society* 37(3):185–200.

———. 2008. "Cultural Organizations and the State: Art and State Support in Contemporary Britain." *Sociology Compass* 2(5):1416–30.

———. 2018. "Heteronomy in the Arts Field: State Funding and British Arts Organizations." *British Journal of Sociology* 69(1):23–43.

Alexander, Victoria D., and Marilyn Rueschemeyer. 2005. *Art and the State: The Visual Arts in Comparative Perspective*, St Antony's Series. London: Palgrave Macmillan.

Ballé, Catherine. 2002. "Democratization and Institutional Change: A Challenge for Modern Museums." Pp. 132–45 in *Global Culture: Media, Arts, Policy, and Globalization*, edited by D. Crane, N. Kawashima, and K. Kawasaki. London: Routledge.

Baumol, William J., and William G. Bowen. 1966. *Performing Arts: The Economic Dilemma*. New York: Twentieth Century Fund.

Belfiore, Eleonora. 2012. "'Defensive Instrumentalism' and the Legacy of New Labour's Cultural Policies." *Cultural Trends* 21(2):103–11.

Boorsma, Peter B., Annemoon van Hemel, and Niki van der Wielen, eds. 1998. *Privatization and Culture: Experiences in the Arts, Heritage and Cultural Industries in Europe*. London: Kluwer.

Bourdieu, Pierre. 1984. *Distinction: A Social Critique of the Judgement of Taste*. Cambridge, MA: Harvard University Press.

DiMaggio, Paul. 1982a. "Cultural Entrepreneurship in Nineteenth-Century Boston: The Creation of an Organizational Base for High Culture in America." *Media, Culture and Society* 4(1):33–50.

———. 1982b. "Cultural Entrepreneurship in Nineteenth-Century Boston, Part II: The Classification and Framing of American Art." *Media, Culture and Society* 4(4):303–22.

———. 1991a. "Constructing an Organizational Field as a Professional Project: U.S. Art Museums, 1920–1940." Pp. 267–92 in *The New Institutionalism in Organizational Analysis*, edited by W.W. Powell and P.J. DiMaggio. Chicago: University of Chicago Press.

———. 1991b. "Social Structure, Institutions and Cultural Goods: The Case of the United States." Pp. 133–55 in *Social Theory for a Changing Society*, edited by P. Bourdieu and J.S. Coleman. Boulder, CO: Westview Press.

———. 1992. "Cultural Boundaries and Structural Change: The Extension of the High Culture Model to Theater, Opera and the Dance, 1900–1940." Pp. 21–57 in *Cultivating Differences: Symbolic Boundaries and the Making on Inequality*, edited by M. Lamont and M. Fournier. Chicago: University of Chicago Press.

DiMaggio, Paul, and Toqir Mukhtar. 2004. "Arts Participation as Cultural Capital in the United States, 1982–2002: Signs of Decline?" *Poetics* 32:169–94.

Dubin, Steven C. 1992. *Arresting Images: Impolitic Art and Uncivil Actions*. New York: Routledge.

Feder, Tal, and Tally Katz-Gerro. 2015. "The Cultural Hierarchy in Funding: Government Funding of the Performing Arts Based on Ethnic and Geographic Distinctions." *Poetics* 49:76–95.

Glynn, Mary Ann. 2000. "When Cymbals become Symbols: Conflict over Organizational Identity within a Symphony Orchestra." *Organization Science* 11(3):285–98.

Gray, Clive. 2000. *The Politics of the Arts in Britain*. London: Macmillan.

Hewison, Robert. 1987. *The Heritage Industry: Britain in a Climate of Decline*. London: Methuen.

———. 1995. *Culture and Consensus: England, Art and Politics since 1940*. London: Methuen.

Ikegami, Eiko. 2005. *Bonds of Civility: Aesthetic Networks and the Political Origins of Japanese Culture*. New York: Cambridge University Press.

Levine, Lawrence W. 1988. *Highbrow, Lowbrow: The Emergence of a Cultural Hierarchy in America*. Cambridge, MA: Harvard University Press.

Macalister, Terry. 2016. "Museums Face Ethics Investigation Over Influence of Sponsor BP." *Guardian*, April 29.

McCarthy, Kevin F., Arthur Brooks, Julia Lowell, and Laura Zakaras. 2001. *The Performing Arts in a New Era*. Arlington, VA: Rand.

Minihan, Janet. 1977. *The Nationalization of Culture: The Development of State Subsidies to the Arts in Great Britain*. New York: New York University Press.

Peterson, Richard A., and Roger M. Kern. 1996. "Changing Highbrow Taste: From Snob to Omnivore." *American Sociological Review* 61(5):900–7.

Philips, Deborah and Whannel, Garry (2013) *The Trojan Horse: The Growth of Commercial Sponsorship*. London: Bloomsbury Academic.

Prior, Nick. 2002. *Museums and Modernity: Art Galleries and the Making of Modern Culture*. London: Berg.

Riding, Alan. 2007. "The Louvre's Art: Priceless. The Louvre's Name: Expensive." *New York Times*, March 7. Retrieved January 28, 2017 (www.nytimes.com/2007/03/07/arts/design/07louv.html).

Santoro, Marco. 2010. "Constructing an Artistic Field as a Political Project: Lessons from *La Scala*." *Poetics* 38:534–54.

Schuster, J. Mark Davidson. 1986. "Tax Incentives as Arts Policy in Western Europe." Pp. 320–60 in *Nonprofit Enterprise in the Arts: Studies in Mission and Constraint*, edited by P. DiMaggio. New York: Oxford University Press.

Toepler, Stefan and Annette Zimmer. 2002. "Subsidizing the Arts: Government and the Arts in Western Europe and the United States." Pp. 29–48 in *Global Culture: Media, Arts, Policy, and Globalization*, edited by D. Crane, N. Kawashima, and K. Kawasaki. London: Routledge.

Tomooka, Kuniyuki, Sachiko Kanno, and Mari Kobayashi. 2002. "Building National Prestige: Japanese Cultural Policy and the Influence of Western Institutions." Pp. 49–62 in *Global Culture: Media, Arts, Policy, and Globalization*, edited by D. Crane, N. Kawashima, and K. Kawasaki. London: Routledge.

Walmsley, Ben. 2016. "From Arts Marketing to Audience Enrichment: How Digital Engagement Can Deepen and Democratize Artistic Exchange with Audiences." *Poetics* 58:66–78.

Weber, William. 2008. *The Great Transformation of Musical Taste: Concert Programming from Haydn to Brahms*. New York: Cambridge University Press.

Wolff, Janet, and John Seed, eds. 1988. *The Culture of Capital: Art, Power and the Nineteenth-Century Middle Class*. Manchester: Manchester University Press.

Wu, Chin-tao. 2002. *Privatising Culture: Corporate Art Intervention since the 1980s*. London: Verso.

Zolberg, Vera L. 1986. "Tensions of Mission in American Art Museums." Pp. 184–98 in *Nonprofit Enterprise in the Arts: Studies in Mission and Constraint*, edited by P. DiMaggio. New York: Oxford University Press.

40

Cultural policy

Steven J. Tepper and Alexandre Frenette

What is cultural policy?

How can sociological research, theories, and methodologies inform cultural policy and broaden our understanding of the diverse ways in which arts and culture gets produced, distributed, and consumed by individuals and communities?

In the US, cultural policy work primarily focuses on public funding for the arts, including the activities of the National Endowment for the Arts (NEA), state, and local arts agencies. Scholars and arts leaders interested in cultural policy typically limit discussion to nonprofit arts: museums, orchestras, dance, and theatre. Employing a broader frame, though, we can define cultural policy as comprising those decisions that influence the production, distribution, and consumption of arts and culture, including live performing arts, recorded media, visual art, design, fashion, crafts, literature, and nonfiction. These decisions can be made by governments through regulation and codes, subsidy, trade agreements, and legislation; by private businesses and trade associations (e.g., film studio, record label, streaming service, Google) and nonprofits (museums, theaters, orchestras) through contracts, licensing, hiring, and capital investments; and by unions, foundations, and other private philanthropy, and education institutions – from K-12 schools to universities.

Discussions of cultural policy and research often conflate advocacy with policy. For example, the most significant type of research commissioned in the arts sector has been economic impact studies showing that the arts constitute a large sector of the economy and that every dollar invested in the arts results in multiple dollars of economic return through expenditures on materials, labor, food, hotels, and increased tax revenue. In spite of significant flaws in methods and underlying assumptions (see Seaman 1987), arts leaders continue to commission and use economic impact studies because they are effective in making the case to legislators (at every level of government) to maintain or increase public investment. However, policy requires prioritization of resources; rather than simply arguing for more funding for the arts, true policy requires us to make hard decisions among competing interests – for example, which investments should we make and what laws should we enact to support which types of culture toward what aims? To understand how culture works and, importantly, how culture can work better, we need the help of sociologists.

The value of a sociological lens

A sociological lens is critical for getting beyond advocacy and case-making. Sociologists do not begin their inquiry with the intention of advancing a specific policy outcome (e.g., "how do we get more money for this thing we like?"). Rather, sociologists are interested in the interconnections between different elements of our cultural life. For example, Wendy Griswold's (2012) "cultural diamond" is a useful heuristic for thinking about the different interacting components of culture: the artist, the artwork, the audience, and society. Such a framework can identify where the biography (personality, experience, motivation) of a particular creative individual intersects with history (the economic, social, and cultural forces at work at any particular time and place); it can help us understand the gatekeepers that stand between an artist and her/his audience; it can help us think about how tastes are shaped by larger social forces. Howard Becker's (1982) discussion of art worlds provides another useful framework for understanding the day-to-day conditions of cultural production. Becker identifies a complex web of collaborators – from the core creative artist to a range of support personnel including editors and producers, venue managers, suppliers, engineers, technicians, marketers, designers, dealers, agents, managers, funders, and so forth. A key insight from Becker's work is that not all of the collaborators are aligned in terms of their own professional interests; as a result, creativity is constantly negotiated and never the natural result of a single artistic vision. Without a fuller understanding of the complex systems of constraints, interaction, and behavior surrounding cultural production and consumption, policymakers are flying blind when trying to advance desired cultural outcomes. Policies of all kinds will have unintended consequences and will yield suboptimal results if we do not take into account the structures (institutional patterns) and culture (norms, values, beliefs) that influence how artists behave, how organizations work, and how people deploy and use culture in everyday life. In addition to the complex web of interactions and motivations, sociologists also address other critical questions related to culture and the arts. For example, how does art reproduce inequality and existing power structures? (Bourdieu 1984). How can art challenge power and drive social change? (Eyerman and Jamison 1998; Roy 2010). How does art help individuals and groups forge unique identities and how does it serve to erect or reinforce barriers or boundaries between groups? (Bryson 1996; Lamont and Fournier 1992). Are there invisible biases that influence what gets counted as culturally important or valuable? (Baumann 2007; Negus 1999). In sum, the questions that sociologists ask about culture and the arts force policy leaders to consider not only what might be in the best interest of "art," but more importantly what is in the best interest of people and communities who are connected by and through art, with a particular emphasis on issues of fairness, equity, and inclusion.

Cultural policy from a sociological lens: five questions

Next we consider five questions that illustrate sociology's potential contributions to cultural policy. Although not exhaustive of all cultural policy areas, the following questions address some key avenues for supporting a vibrant arts and culture ecosystem, including how to inform efforts to support and sustain (1) arts participation, (2) artists' careers, (3) freedom of expression, (4) diverse cultural institutions, and (5) robust markets for exchange.

How do we encourage more citizens to participate in arts and culture?

Since the 1970s, cultural leaders and policymakers have been interested in the size and composition of arts audiences, primarily in an attempt to understand trends that might impact attendance (and ticket sales) at the benchmark arts: museums, classical music, theater, ballet, and jazz. The National Endowment for the Arts has sponsored the national Survey of Public Participation in the Arts (SPPA) that has been administered regularly since 1982, with dozens of reports that show the demographic makeup of arts audiences, trends over time, geographic predictors of attendance, and changes in modes of participation (live, broadcast, internet).

Key theoretical insights from sociology can inform policies around increasing participation. First, Max Weber (2009) argued that people's behavior is influenced not only by their desire to improve their economic position (class) but also by their desire to achieve social prestige (status). Participating in the arts has been shown to be a pathway for increasing status, especially consuming elite forms of European art such as opera, classical music, and ballet (see Bourdieu 1984; DiMaggio and Useem 1978; Levine 1988). Nonprofit arts organizations in the US were originally established to help legitimate the tastes and the status of the upper classes. These institutions were organized around the social prestige of their patrons, creating exclusive boards, hosting black-tie fundraisers, and choosing a repertoire and a style of presentation that was less accessible to non-elites. But status symbols and the dynamics of prestige change over time. Sociologists have pointed out that perhaps consuming elite culture today provides less status than being an omnivore – a global consumer of many different types of culture (Peterson and Kern 1996). Milner (2010) argues that celebrity is a new form of status; as people spend more time online, he argues, the ability to get noticed and draw the attention of friends, acquaintances, and strangers is a powerful form of status. Thus, we see the rise of "life catching" – the idea that an event is not worth participating in unless we can photograph ourselves at the event and post it to our social network sites. Many cultural events today are staged to provide multiple opportunities for audience members to "capture" themselves in highly visible ways (e.g., pop-up backdrops throughout venues designed for quick fan photo shoots and selfies). What other forms of status might be emerging that will influence how people engage and participate in arts and culture? With the democratization of the means of production (home studios, editing software, high-quality cameras embedded in our mobile devices, the capacity to publish and broadcast free online, and the availability of pervasive online arts instruction), there has been a rise in personal arts practice – everyone is making, creating, posting, presenting, and performing (Tepper and Ivey 2008). What are the status payouts for personal creative practice? Do people who post and share their own creative projects (visual art, films, recorded music, poetry, photography) generate new forms of status and prestige? Without understanding contemporary markers of status and prestige, policymakers will fail to understand key drivers and motivations of arts participation in the twenty-first century.

In addition to issues of status, sociological analysis helps us see cultural participation less in terms of a "special occasion" or event and more in terms of its relevance in everyday life. Tia DeNora (2000), for example, shows how people use culture to manage their identities and emotions over the course of a day or week – as they interact with different types of people (using culture to express different identities and roles depending on context) and attempt to achieve and manage different emotional states (sadness, anger, joy). Janice Radway (1984) shows how certain women read romance novels as a means of daily compensation affording themselves time and pleasure apart from the demands of their children and husbands. One lesson from this work for cultural policy is that art must be customizable, portable, accessible on multiple platforms and easily manipulated, reused, and deployed in ways that help people "use" culture to manage their personal and social lives.

How do we ensure that professional artists have sustainable careers?

Cultural leaders have long been concerned with the working conditions facing those who pursue professional pathways as artists. Studies have pointed out high unemployment rates of artists, decreased wages, lack of affordable housing and work space, lack of insurance, and the loss of opportunities for aging artists (Alper and Wassall 2006; Ennis and Bonin 1983; Horowitz 1993; Thomson and Cook 2013).

Policy approaches, especially among grantmakers, have historically focused on increasing funding for individual artists through grants and fellowships (for a review, see Guay 2012). However, importantly, this approach of subsidizing or improving the living and working conditions of individual artists ignores fundamental economic and sociological analysis that explains the distinctive characteristics of the artistic labor force. Pierre-Michel Menger (1999) points out that artistic work is driven by symbolic rewards – the possibility of achieving widespread fame, gaining prestige among a subculture of peers, the promise of autonomy and the benefits of doing work you love, and strong occupational identity ("I was meant to be an artist"). Aspiring artists also overrate their chances of success by paying attention to the many highly successful and visible cases, rather than taking into account the many artists who remain largely invisible. The symbolic rewards of being an artist combined with the chronic overestimation of career success creates an oversupply of aspirants which, in any normal labor market, increases unemployment and drives down wages. If funders and policymakers attempt to improve the conditions (salary, benefits, job prospects) of individual artists, they will simply encourage more aspirants and thereby perpetuate the fundamental conditions that result in poor job outcomes for artists.

Scholars have also demonstrated that artistic labor markets tend to reward a small number of artists with high wages and abundant opportunity while leaving the majority to struggle to make ends meet. This "superstar" effect has been well documented across many artistic fields and results, in part, from the inability to predict success for new creative projects such as films, paintings, songs (see Bielby and Bielby 1994; Caves 2000). Thus, consumers and gatekeepers tend to choose those artists that have had previous success – returning to what feels like a sure and familiar winner rather than take a chance on an emerging and unknown artist. Finally, policymakers who care about the working conditions of artists should consider the work of Richard Lloyd (2006), who documents how the idea of bohemia (the grit, glamor, and authenticity of the starving artist who repudiates economic success) animates the lifestyle choices of artists – "poverty by choice." The culture of bohemia further reinforces the oversupply of artists because it justifies the idea of waiting tables or working in low-level service jobs, especially for otherwise well-educated middle-class professionals in the pursuit of a likely mythical artistic career. In summary, without a complex understanding of the culture and the motivations that lead individuals to pursue careers in the arts, policymakers may find themselves unintentionally encouraging the very conditions they are trying to ameliorate. Rather than focus on subsidizing more professional artists, perhaps policymakers should invest in helping aspiring or retiring artists transition to other careers, deploying their creativity in many other fields. Here, the work of Lindemann, Tepper, and Talley (2017) on creative identity is illuminating. The authors hypothesize that some artists develop the capacity to see themselves as creative across multiple contexts and roles, while others can only see themselves as creative when working as full-time artists. For policymakers interested in supporting more robust creative identities, they might need to support a change in the culture of arts schools so that students are not socialized into very narrow definitions of success and instead come to understand that there are many ways to be an artist in the world.

How do we ensure that artists have autonomy and freedom to express themselves and to challenge the status quo?

Over the past 150 years in the US, arts leaders have battled with censors and would-be censors over the rights of artists to freely express themselves. Art dealers fought with Anthony Comstock in the late nineteenth century over the right to exhibit nude paintings and drawings and to send postcards or catalogues of exhibitions featuring such images through the mail (Beisel 1998). Fredric Wertham (1954) attacked the comic book industry in the 1940s and 1950s, fearing that violent or sexual cartoons were corrupting the minds of youth. And the 1980s and 1990s saw repeated clashes between religious and civic leaders and artists over rap and heavy metal music (see Bryson 1996), films, books, public art, exhibitions, and theater (Dubin 1992; Tepper 2011). Policymakers and leaders of cultural institutions responded to these challenges through three arguments: (1) artists must be free and autonomous from social norms if they are to serve as social critics and truth tellers; (2) curators and managers of cultural institutions are professionals (like lawyers, doctors, and engineers) and must be trusted to make decisions in the public interest, free from public opinion and the interference of "know nothings"; and (3) any attack on cultural expression is an attack on the First Amendment – therefore attempts to alter or remove a book, painting, play, or song leads us down a slippery slope ending in despotism and a loss of freedom. These three arguments tend to produce "silencing tactics" – discrediting critics, erecting barriers to honest conversation, and choosing legal recourse as a first response to any challenge or concern.

Importantly, work by Tepper (2011) and Dubin (1992) show that conflicts over art and culture are rooted in complex social dynamics that go far beyond knee-jerk responses to offensive material. Instead, conflicts are reactions to social change, as members of a community seek to assert their values, voice, and lifestyle in the face of dramatic demographic and economic changes. When we see arts controversies as democratic attempts to negotiate social change and to assert feelings of belonging, then the three "silencing tactics" described earlier may be counterproductive. Therefore, rather than see conflicts over art as threats that we must aggressively police, arts leaders might welcome them as signs of relevancy. Art that is important enough for people to fight over is art that is playing a role in helping communities work through important differences and accommodate social change.

How do we ensure that arts institutions are representative of the creative diversity of our country?

While the cultural sector is perceived as being relatively progressive and egalitarian in its orientation and values, it contends with the same structural inequities found in society at large. Consequently, concerns about diversity, equity, and representation frequently emerge within cultural policy debates as related to classification (what is validated as "art"), audiences (who has access to arts and culture), and the sector's workforce. These interrelated issues converge in *Fusing Arts, Culture and Social Change*, a seminal report by Holly Sidford (2011) on the state of equitable grantmaking in the arts. In the report, Sidford documents a rich ecology of over 100,000 nonprofit arts and cultural organizations in the United States, many of which represent diverse artistic traditions; however she finds that organizations with budgets over USD 5 million per year – which make up slightly less than 2 percent of the country's nonprofit arts universe – received 55 percent of the sector's revenue in 2009 (in grants, gifts, and contributions). None of those institutions is primarily dedicated to underrepresented (non-European) artistic traditions, nor were they founded (or run) by members of racial minority groups. Attendees at the benchmark arts events (opera, ballet, etc.) run by these organizations are predominantly white and from upper-income levels (Sidford 2011; Silber and Triplett 2015). The report spurred national conversation among funders about inclusion and equity in the arts, particularly as related to racial/ethnic and class-related biases.

While there is no silver bullet for addressing long-standing patterns of inequity, sociological research could inform policies aimed at building a more diverse arts ecology, notably by teasing out contradictions between the sector's stated goals and its deep-seated systemic issues. Even though funders like the Ford Foundation, the Kresge Foundation, and others have made conscious efforts to adopt an equity lens in their support of arts and culture organizations, since its inception the US nonprofit arts infrastructure has been predicated on classification (high vs. low culture) and exclusion (DiMaggio 1982). In the latter half of the nineteenth century, urban elites built "high-culture" nonprofit organizations that existed mostly outside of market pressures, depending instead on boards consisting of wealthy patrons. In her study of boards at elite museums and opera companies, Francie Ostrower (2002) found that in the twenty-first-century context of growing market competition, fluctuating government funding, and shifting demographics, high-culture nonprofits try to appeal to wider segments of the population – often by advancing community-oriented programming – while its trustees nonetheless aim to further their own class and status interests. Importantly, elites are ultimately more likely to support institutions promoting art forms consistent with their tastes and values (in the traditional Western European canon), and are less likely to support community-based or popular arts, which reach a more diverse audience (Ostrower 2002). McDonnell and Tepper (2014) also argue that the ideology of exclusion is baked into the high-culture nonprofit's organizational form, and is mostly obscured by rhetoric about serving the public, but this ideology becomes evident at times of crisis. In their analysis of the metaphors arts advocates use when high-culture nonprofits face financial turmoil, McDonnell and Tepper (2014) find that such advocates forgo habitual public claims to broader community support in an effort to secure an elite donor (a "white knight"). Supporters of high-culture nonprofits therefore seek to weather financial storms by signaling their fragility, distinction, and inherently special status at the expense of more egalitarian claims. Such research suggests that the arts ecology will hardly become more inclusive without fundamentally changing the structure of how it gets supported, and protected, by elite stakeholders (donors, boards, etc.).

In addition, recent attempts to address "pipeline issues" within the nonprofit arts sector by introducing internships and other relatively informal training opportunities should consider sociological research which shows how these programs are rife with ambiguity and often reproduce social inequalities (Frenette 2013). Research on arts and design graduates finds that paid internships are far more effective than unpaid ones in leading to professional success, but graduates with more financial means hold a disproportionate number of paid internships while groups at a historical economic disadvantage (women, black, and Hispanic/Latino graduates) tend to do less-valued, unpaid internships (Frenette et al. 2015). These findings are consistent with other sociological research showing how the use of vague (and class-coded) criteria such as "talent" and "merit" by potential employers may systematically bias applicants from different backgrounds, who might not appear to have the "right stuff" (Kanter 1977; Rivera 2015).

How do we support robust markets for exchange and innovation so that consumers and audiences have access to diverse and innovative art?

The Federal Communications Commission (FCC) and the Federal Trade Commission (FTC) have a mandate from Congress to ensure that cultural markets are fair and competitive. Over the past 30 years we have witnessed considerable market concentration in media and entertainment industries. In his book *The Media Monopoly*, published in 1983, Ben Bagdikian revealed the alarming fact that 50 corporations owned 90 percent of the media. Today, more than 90 percent of the media is owned by just six companies (Lutz 2012). While governments are mainly worried about price and access for consumers, cultural critics and cultural leaders are concerned about whether consolidation reduces cultural variety and innovation and if it limits freedom of expression. Here again, sociologists have provided important insights. Peterson and Berger's (1975) work on cycles in symbolic production provides evidence that consolidation leads to homogeneity in cultural offerings and market competition leads to diversity. Importantly, their work shows that the structure of markets often precedes and perhaps causes innovation in culture – new styles of music, new types of lyrics, new artists, and new songs emerge after periods of heavy industry concentration when smaller labels begin to gain a foothold in the market. Others have challenged Peterson and Berger by showing the corporate strategies for production and development that are more open and less routinized have more to do with innovation and diversity than the size of the company or the degree of consolidation (Lopes 1992). And, most recently, Gabriel Rossman's work (2012) has shown that consolidated media companies tend to support those artists and "hit songs" that conform to certain identifiable genres and categories, thereby limiting diversity over the airwaves.

Conclusion

Cultural policy is ultimately concerned with creating a vibrant cultural life where every citizen has access to diverse cultural expression, where artists find ample opportunities to connect to audiences, where artistic innovation is frequent and pervasive, and where art and culture serve to advance a more just and inclusive society. Historically, policymakers and arts leaders have advocated for more public funding of the arts as a means to achieve a vibrant cultural life. They have also focused on regulations and laws that promote unfettered markets for cultural exchange and that protect some forms of culture (traditional "high arts") from commercial markets altogether. Such approaches are based on notions that artistic forms are stable, that artworks are easily categorized into genres and styles, that the commercial and nonprofit art sectors are distinctive and serve different purposes, and that there are clear hierarchies between high and low art – with different claims to public resources and critical attention. Importantly, cultural policy tends to focus on institutions as the key sites for intervening in arts and culture. Cultural sociologists, as expected, challenge many of these assumptions. They focus on movement of art across boundaries, the impermanence of cultural categories and the ways in which such categories (such as genres, or notions of artistic success, or ideas about property) may temporarily constrain how we produce and consume culture. An awareness of these constraints will help policymakers better understand the behaviors of artists and their audiences as well as provide insight into how different language and labels might enable greater expressive possibilities. Sociologists also show us that culture is bound up with notions of status and prestige, and that decisions to consume or make art are organized as much around symbolic rewards as economic rewards. And, sociologists show us that culture is part of everyday life. It is not sequestered in cathedrals of consumption – theaters, symphony halls, museums – where we go on special occasions to experience something extraordinary. Instead, the arts are part of how people connect to one another, express their identities, manage their emotions, build their communities, and, for some, make their careers. Ultimately, cultural policy will succeed or fail based on how well it takes into account the complex social and human dynamics that shape how culture moves through the world as well as how people move through the world with culture.

References

Alper, Neil O., and Gregory H. Wassall. 2006. "Artists' Careers and Their Labor Markets." *Handbook of the Economics of Art and Culture* 1:813–64.

Bagdikian, Ben H. 1983. *The Media Monopoly*. Boston: Beacon Press.

Baumann, Shyon. 2007. *Hollywood Highbrow: From Entertainment to Art*. Princeton, NJ: Princeton University Press.

Becker, Howard S. 1982. *Art Worlds*. Berkeley: University of California Press.

Beisel, Nicola Kay. 1998. *Imperiled Innocents: Anthony Comstock and Family Reproduction in Victorian America*. Princeton, NJ: Princeton University Press.

Bielby, William T., and Denise D. Bielby. 1994. "'All Hits Are Flukes': Institutionalized Decision Making and the Rhetoric of Network Prime-time Program Development." *American Journal of Sociology* 99(5):1287–313.

Bourdieu, Pierre. 1984. *Distinction: A Social Critique of the Judgement of Taste*. London: Routledge.

Bryson, Bethany. 1996. "'Anything but Heavy Metal': Symbolic Exclusion and Musical Dislikes." *American Sociological Review* 61(5):884–99.

Caves, Richard E. 2000. *Creative Industries: Contracts between Art and Commerce*. Cambridge, MA: Harvard University Press.

DeNora, Tia. 2000. *Music in Everyday Life*. New York: Cambridge University Press.

DiMaggio, Paul. 1982. "Cultural Entrepreneurship in Nineteenth-century Boston: The Creation of an Organizational Base for High Culture in America." *Media, Culture & Society* 4(1):33–50.

DiMaggio, Paul, and Michael Useem. 1978. "Social Class and Arts Consumption." *Theory and Society* 5(2):141–61.

Dubin, Steven C. 1992. *Arresting Images: Impolitic Art and Uncivil Actions*. New York: Routledge.

Ennis, Philip H., and John Bonin. 1983. *Understanding the Employment of Actors*. (Research Division Report #3). Washington, DC: National Endowment for the Arts.

Eyerman, Ron, and Andrew Jamison. 1998. *Music and Social Movements: Mobilizing Traditions in the Twentieth Century*. New York: Cambridge University Press.

Frenette, Alexandre. 2013. "Making the Intern Economy: Role and Career Challenges of the Music Industry Intern." *Work and Occupations* 40(4): 364–97.

Frenette, Alexandre, Amber D. Dumford, Angie L. Miller, and Steven J. Tepper. 2015. *The Internship Divide: The Promise and Challenges of Internships in the Arts*. Bloomington, IN: Indiana University and Arizona State University, Strategic National Arts Alumni Project.

Griswold, Wendy. 2012. *Cultures and Societies in a Changing World*. 4th ed. Thousand Oaks, CA: SAGE.

Guay, Abigail. 2012. "In Support of Individual Artists." *Grantmakers in the Arts Reader* 23(1).

Horowitz, Harold. 1993. "The Status of Artists in the USA." *Journal of Cultural Economics* 17(1):29–47.

Kanter, Rosabeth M. 1977. *Men and Women of the Corporation*. New York: Basic Books.

Lamont, Michèle, and Marcel Fournier. 1992. *Cultivating Differences: Symbolic Boundaries and the Making of Inequality*. Chicago: University of Chicago Press.

Levine, Lawrence W. 1988. *Highbrow/lowbrow: The Emergence of Cultural Hierarchy in America*. Cambridge, MA: Harvard University Press.

Lindemann, Danielle J., Steven J. Tepper, and Heather Laine Talley. 2017. "'I Don't Take my Tuba to Work at Microsoft:' Arts Graduates and the Portability of Creative Identity." *American Behavioral Scientist*. https://doi.org/10.1177/0002764217734276

Lloyd, Richard. 2006. *Neo-bohemia: Art and Commerce in the Postindustrial City*. New York: Routledge.

Lopes, Paul D. 1992. "Innovation and Diversity in the Popular Music Industry, 1969 to 1990." *American Sociological Review* 57(1):56–71.

Lutz, Ashley. 2012. "These 6 Corporations Control 90% of the Media in America." *Business Insider*, June 14. Retrieved January 4, 2017 (www.businessinsider.com/these-6-corporations-control-90-of-the-media-in-america-2012-6).

McDonnell, Terence E., and Steven J. Tepper. 2014. "Culture in Crisis: Deploying Metaphor in Defense of Art." *Poetics* 43:20–42.

Menger, Pierre-Michel. 1999. "Artistic Labor Markets and Careers." *Annual Review of Sociology* 25:541–74.

Milner Jr., Murray. 2010. "Is Celebrity a New Kind of Status System?" *Society* 47(5):379–87.

Negus, Keith. 1999. *Music Genres and Corporate Cultures*. New York: Routledge.

Ostrower, Francie. 2002. *Trustees of Culture: Power, Wealth, and Status on Elite Arts Boards.* Chicago: University of Chicago Press.

Peterson, Richard A., and David G. Berger. 1975. "Cycles in Symbol Production: The Case of Popular Music." *American Sociological Review* 40(2):158–73.

Peterson, Richard A., and Roger M. Kern. 1996. "Changing Highbrow Taste: From Snob to Omnivore." *American Sociological Review* 61(5):900–7.

Radway, Janice A. 1984. *Reading the Romance: Women, Patriarchy, and Popular Literature.* Chapel Hill: University of North Carolina Press.

Rivera, Lauren A. 2015. *Pedigree: How Elite Students Get Elite Jobs.* Princeton, NJ: Princeton University Press.

Rossman, Gabriel. 2012. *Climbing the Charts: What Radio Airplay Tells Us about the Diffusion of Innovation.* Princeton, NJ: Princeton University Press.

Roy, William. 2010. *Red, Whites, and Blues: Social Movements, Folk Music, and Race in the United States.* Princeton, NJ: Princeton University Press.

Seaman, Bruce A. 1987. "Arts Impact Studies: A Fashionable Excess." *Economic Impact of the Arts: A Sourcebook.* Washington, DC: National Conference of State Legislatures.

Sidford, Holly. 2011. *Fusing Arts, Culture and Social Change: High Impact Strategies for Philanthropy.* Washington, DC: National Committee for Responsive Philanthropy.

Silber, Bohne G., and Tim Triplett. 2015. *A Decade of Arts Engagement: Findings from the Survey of Public Participation in the Arts, 2002–2012.* (Research Report #58). Washington, DC: National Endowment for the Arts.

Tepper, Steven J. 2011. *Not Here, Not Now, Not That! Protest over Art and Culture in America.* Chicago: University of Chicago Press.

Tepper, Steven J., and Bill Ivey, eds. 2008. *Engaging Art: The Next Great Transformation of America's Cultural Life.* New York: Routledge.

Thomson, Kristin, and Jean Cook. 2013. *Taking the Pulse of the Artist Community: Artists + Health Insurance: Online Survey Results.* Future of Music Coalition and Artists' Health Resource Center. Washington, DC: Future of Music Coalition. Retrieved January 10, 2017 (http://futureofmusic.org/sites/default/files/Artistsandhealthinsurancereport1013.pdf).

Weber, Max. 2009. *From Max Weber: Essays in Sociology.* New York: Routledge.

Wertham, Fredric. 1954. *Seduction of the Innocent.* New York: Rinehart.

41

Rethinking the sociology of media ownership

Rodney Benson

Introduction

The problem with most media ownership research, according to the noted media law scholar C. Edwin Baker (1994:12), is that its focus on commercial media makes it "too narrow": it leaves to the side "whether other ownership forms," such as nonprofit or public ownership, would be more oriented toward democratic values. As new nonprofit, public, and hybrid models proliferate, a revived media and cultural sociology (Brienza and Revers 2016) will need to pay close attention to ownership's multiple forms.

Indeed, prominent sociologists such as Manuell Castells and Jeffrey Alexander have increasingly focused on news media, but their analyses are anemic and overly optimistic precisely because of their failure to theorize ownership variation. For example, in an article assessing the future of journalism, Van Der Haak, Parks, and Castells (2012) identify "new tools and practices" of digital journalism that are contributing to the "adequate performance of a democratic society": networked journalism; crowdsourcing and user-generated content; data mining, data analysis, data visualization, and mapping; visual journalism; point-of-view journalism; automated journalism; and global journalism. Van Der Haak et al. attribute their findings to the "open, networked structure of the Internet" (2012:2934), but even a casual glance at their listing of exemplary news organizations reveals an overrepresentation of public service broadcasters (BBC, NOS, Arte), state broadcasters (Al Jazeera), government agencies (National Film Board of Canada), elite broadsheet newspapers shielded by formal or informal "trust" ownership forms (*Guardian, New York Times*), foundation-supported nonprofits, and small-donor supported media, compared to large privately held or stock market traded commercial companies. Lacking a sophisticated understanding of media ownership models, these "network society" analysts only tell us what "can" happen with digital media, but offer no way of sorting out when a particular outcome is more or less likely to occur.

In similar fashion, Jeffrey Alexander insists that the "cultural power" of professional ethics and norms has successfully averted a significant crisis in journalistic quality despite widespread observations to the contrary (Alexander, Butler Breese, and Luengo 2016). This Pollyannaish "Strong Program" of cultural sociology ignores ownership, and thus has no way of explaining why some quality news organizations have thrived or revived (*New York Times, Washington Post,* ProPublica), while others have declined or disappeared.

The purpose of this chapter is to show how and why sociology must reincorporate owner-ship into our understanding of contemporary media.

Four institutional logics of media ownership

Society is composed of differentiated, semi-autonomous fields (Bourdieu 2005; Fligstein and McAdam 2012). Journalism is a field, with its own distinctive logic of practice. But its prac-tices exist in the shadow of externally imposed forms of ownership: journalists rarely own the organizations they work for. Ownership, thus, can be categorized according to the originating field outside of journalism.

Most owners in Western industrialized democracies are linked to the economic field, selling news to generate profits. There can be many ways to distinguish such commercial owners (e.g., whether or not they are only in the media business or also derive profits from non-media busi-nesses). One important dividing line, however, is between media *companies that are traded on the stock market* and *those that are privately held*, often by wealthy individuals or families. The latter are somewhat insulated from stock market demands for profit maximization.

In Western Europe, *the state (or a quasi-state agency)* is also an important owner of media: public service broadcasters such as the BBC in the UK, SVT in Sweden, and ZDF in Germany are rep-resentative of this ownership form, in which funding is also generally derived from a dedicated license fee or other tax revenues. In this ownership form, commercial pressures are obviously less although not always completely absent (as in cases where there is partial dependence on advertising).

Civil society (churches and other religious groups, labor unions, political parties, arts societies, and other types of associations) constitutes a final form of ownership that is really a constella-tion of forms. A religious organization may have different practices, values, and rules than a labor union, suggesting that they operate according to distinct "institutional logics" (Thornton, Oca-sio, and Lounsbury 2012). At the same time, civil society ownership, across its many subtypes, is likely to share with public ownership a certain distance from commercial pressures.

Four modes of ownership power

If media ownership exerts power, what kind of power is this? At the broadest level, this power can be either "allocative" or "operational" (Napoli 1997; Ohlsson 2012). Owners' allocative power – to establish goals and priorities and determine the overall level of resources available – is generally acknowledged. Operational control refers to the specific implementation of policies already determined, which is likely delegated to top editors; even so, owners may intervene at this level as well, making their views known directly (Chomsky 2006) or indirectly.

Ownership power can also, however, be categorized according to its effects on news con-tent. Amid a diversity of particular strategies and practices, such as decisions of who to hire, promote, or fire; budgeting; management styles and organizational policies; and overt or covert attempts to shape news content or editorials (Breed 1955; Bowers 1967; Chomsky 1999, 2006; Brüggemann, Esser, and Humprecht 2012), modes of ownership power affecting news content ultimately tend to group into four broad categories: political instrumentalism, economic instru-mentalism, audience adjustment, and public service (orientation/commitment).[1]

Political instrumentalism (Hallin and Mancini 2004; Hardy 2008:97–133) refers to overt or covert attempts to use a media outlet to promote or attack politicians, social movements and/or issues of special concern to the owners. In *Personal History*, Katharine Graham (1998) relates several instances when her husband and predecessor as publisher of the *Washington Post* acted as a political kingmaker. He was the key negotiator in assuring Lyndon Johnson the vice presidential spot on the Kennedy ticket in 1960; he also used the newspaper's news and editorial pages to promote political causes he cared about. In retrospect, Graham (1998:186) viewed this kind of political instrumentalism as a violation of contemporary standards of journalistic ethics and professionalism. Yet clearly such practices have not disappeared. Political instrumentalism is a frequent accusation leveled at Rupert Murdoch's media properties, as when Fox News prematurely (and for evident political strategic reasons) called the election for George W. Bush over Al Gore in 2000 (Morris 2005; see also Benson 2012); political instrumentalism is also evident at the Huffington Post, MSNBC, and various other progressive media outlets.

Economic instrumentalism is manifest through publicizing (or failing to publicize) events or topics related to one's own business concerns or those of one's competitors, in order to gain a competitive advantage. Bagdikian (2004) provides examples of vertically concentrated media behemoths cross-promoting their products across all possible mediums, genres, and outlets (see also Noam 2017).

Audience adjustment is the strategic effort to increase revenues or profits by identifying a target audience and responding to perceptions of this audience's interests or preferences. Such audience adjustment is similar to what Bourdieu (1984) refers to as the "homologous" circuits of production and reception, but differs from Bourdieu in emphasizing the managerial agency that has to go into creating such homologies. Owners adjust their news content and design in order to maximize their reach to a designated targeted audience, or alternatively deploy sales and marketing staff to locate the audience best attuned to what they have to offer (Andersson and Wiik 2013).

Public service *orientation* is manifested in an ongoing investment in reporting and commentary that serves normative ideals of accountability, diversity, public participation, and comprehensiveness; public service *commitment* is evident in decisions to "stick one's neck out" and publish news or views with a potentially high economic or political downside for the organization. Public service has a long tradition in the United States: for most magazine founders during the early nineteenth century, serving societal and community needs was a far stronger motivation than financial self-interest (Haveman 2015:133). To the extent that public service resource investments are consistent with economic goals, they can also be linked to audience adjustment (Socolow 2010); for all but a handful of elite news outlets, however, responding to audience demand tends to go hand in hand with a decline in public service journalism (O'Shea 2011). Public service commitment is most strongly indicated when owners make choices that have no clear economic upside and may even entail a potentially dangerous downside (e.g., loss of audiences or advertisers, costs of defending against a lawsuit). It entails not only day-to-day resource allocation but also rare moments of courageous decision-making (as with Watergate and the *Pentagon Papers*) to publish items that go against prevailing elite or public opinion (Baker 1994:14).

A focused reading of the literature in sociology of news can help reveal the various ways in which ownership forms are linked to these four modes of ownership power.

Linking ownership forms with modes of ownership power

Public media

Content analysis studies have consistently shown that public service broadcasters offer more public affairs and international news, more in-depth news, a greater diversity of speakers and viewpoints, and more critical news than commercial broadcasters (Aalberg and Curran 2011;

Cushion 2012; Humprecht and Esser 2017); similar findings hold for subsidized newspapers in Sweden, Norway, and France (Benson 2011). Acknowledging that many public media mix tax-payer and advertising support, research has further specified that public service-oriented news content increases in tandem with the proportion of taxpayer funding (de Vreese, Esser, and Hop-mann 2016). Created and funded in ways designed to create firewalls against excessive market or political pressures, public service media thus offer the clearest proof that the form of media ownership matters and can crucially shape the kind of news that is produced.

Political instrumentalism is likely to be greater at those public service media systems in which nonpublic funds (individual donations, foundations, and business sponsorships) make up more than half of all revenues, as is the case in the US: indeed, US public media have sometimes had to return funds from major donors with controversial political agendas (Benson, Powers, and Neff 2017). US public media have been charged with economic instrumentalism when they create corporate- or foundation-sponsored programs that promote the interests of their sponsors (Sirota 2014), not an uncommon occurrence. Faced with increasing competition, public media around the world are also becoming more concerned with audience adjustment, although not as much as commercial media (Andersson and Wiik 2013).

Stock market traded and privately held commercial media

While both stock market traded[2] and privately held companies may be large corporations (e.g., Hearst is privately held), the stock market traded company emphasizes maximization of share-holder value over every other non-market consideration. By the 1970s, many leading US news-papers had become part of stock market traded companies. In theory, trading on the stock market provides the company with more resources to invest; it also encourages financial disci-pline to make the company less wasteful and more efficient (Picard and van Weezel 2008). In practice, stock market traded companies often achieve higher profits by cutting costs and sacri-ficing editorial quality (Klinenberg 2007).

Studies comparing "independent" (often family-owned) and "chain-owned" (a rough proxy for stock market traded) newspapers have generally shown that the latter place a higher emphasis on profits over professional or community goals and have smaller news staffs (Edmonds 2004); Rohlinger and Proffitt (2016) show that "independently owned newspapers cover controversial ideas more often" than their corporate chain-owned counterparts. Coulson and Hansen (1995) found that after the stock market traded Gannett Corporation purchased the independently owned *Louisville Courier-Journal*, article word length shortened, the proportion of "hard news" decreased, and the proportion of wire-service to staff-written articles increased. In a study of political campaign news coverage, Dunaway (2008) found that stock market traded corporate ownership was associated with lower substantive issue coverage than privately held ownership both for newspapers and television news.

One variant of public stock ownership is the "dual-stock" structure established by the found-ing families at the *New York Times* (Sulzbergers), *Washington Post* (Grahams), and *Wall Street Jour-nal* (Bancrofts). Of the three, only the *Times* still has this structure, in which the family controls voting shares, while non-voting shares are sold to the public. Sulzberger family control is widely credited for providing the resources and support necessary to maintain high-quality journalism at the *New York Times* (Tifft and Jones 2000).

On the other hand, family control does not guarantee how a publisher will react to mount-ing financial pressures to sustain profitability. In contrast to the *New York Times'* expansionist approach, the *Washington Post* under the leadership of Katharine Weymouth, niece of Katharine Graham, chose a cautious strategy of retrenchment. Since selling to Amazon founder Jeff Bezos in 2012, the *Post*, now entirely privately held and with no need to answer even partially to Wall Street demands, is pursuing a long-term strategy of online growth with a special emphasis on national political news (Meyer 2014). It must also be acknowledged that there are many cases of family-owned newspapers (either entirely privately held or with dual stock structures) whose public service records are not clearly superior to those of their stock market traded counterparts (Cranberg, Bezanson, and Soloski 2001).

Economic instrumentalism of various types is likely to be high, relative to non-commercial media, at both stock market traded and privately held news companies. News outlets in large, vertically integrated companies, such as Fox and Time Warner, have been shown to exhibit bias (either in scores or selection) in their reviews of movies produced by affiliated studios (Della Vigna and Kennedy 2011). In relation to audience adjustment, to the extent that privately held companies have the ability to set their own level of profitability rather than succumb to Wall Street pressure, they may selectively choose to ignore audience demands (thus, perhaps offering slightly more public affairs content or investigative reporting than audiences would prefer if given the choice).

Political instrumentalism is usually assumed to be higher at privately held than at stock market traded companies (Noam 2017), though the evidence for this claim is mixed. If private companies or stock market traded companies with a dominant shareholder forgo maximum profits, they thereby gain increased flexibility to support pet political or community causes. Economist Riccardo Puglisi (2011) analyzed *New York Times* election coverage from 1964 to 1997 and found that the *Times* gave "more emphasis to issues over which the (Republican) incumbent is weak" in ways that cannot be accounted for by audience demand, thus suggesting political instrumentalism at work. Similarly, Daniel Chomsky's (1999, 2006) archival excavation of correspondence between *New York Times* publisher Arthur Hays Sulzberger and editor Taylor Catledge documents a clear intent (and frequent success) of the publisher of a family-controlled newspaper to influence both opinion and news content. Wagner and Collins (2014) compared the *Wall Street Journal*'s opinion pages before and after Rupert Murdoch's News Corporation bought out the newspaper from the Bancroft family. They found that the change made the already conservative opinion pages even more conservative: "far less supportive of government intervention in the economy, much more negative to Democrats, and much more positive to Republicans" (Wagner and Collins 2014:758). In this case, a determined dominant family share-holder changed the type and intensity of political instrumentalism expressed by the news outlet under a previous dominant shareholder.

These studies demonstrate the existence of political instrumentalism at family-controlled, stock market traded news media, but they do not prove that political instrumentalism is always lower at "pure" stock market traded media without a dominant shareholder. Indeed, as audiences fragment in the digital environment, partisanship becomes less about the non-financial "amenity potential" of media ownership (Napoli 1997:211) and more of a direct strategy to increase audiences and profits: this helps explain, for instance, CNN's more pronounced liberal stance to differentiate itself from Fox, even though CNN is owned by a large stock market traded company without an overt partisan agenda. For some news organizations, like Fox and popular right-wing radio shows and online sites, both political instrumentalist and audience adjustment modes may be at work (Berry and Sobieraj 2014).

Civil society/nonprofit media

Nonprofit and other civil society-based media represent a "hybrid" space in the middle between commercial and public service media; as noted, they also encompass a range of ownership forms linked to distinct organizational fields: religious, secular associations, academic, trade unions, and employee ownership (Levy and Picard 2011). In principle, one might expect a variety of distinctive news practices within the overarching category of civil society/nonprofit, linked to these diverse organizational fields. Research to date, however, has not explored such a fine-tuned question.

Because they forgo profits, nonprofit media generally spend a relatively higher proportion of their revenues on reporting. A study by the Knight Foundation (Patel and Maness 2013) of 18 nonprofits representing local, regional, and national investigative organizations found that they devoted from 34 percent to 85 percent of their budgets to editorial, compared to an average for commercial news operations of 12 percent to 16 percent (Doctor 2013). In a comprehensive survey of 172 nonprofit news organizations founded since 1987, the Pew Research Center (2013:6) showed that more than half focus on investigative reporting, government, or public and foreign affairs. In the United States, it is certainly the case that some of the largest, most prominent investigative news organizations are now nonprofit news organizations primarily funded by large foundations: ProPublica, the Center for Investigative Reporting, and the Center for Public Integrity (Benson 2017).

Recent studies suggest that nonprofits, similar to taxpayer-supported public media, provide more public affairs and investigative reporting than commercial media (Benson 2013; Cagé 2016; Konieczna 2018). Carpenter, Boehmer, and Fico (2016) found that nonprofit journalists were more likely than their for-profit counterparts to include "interpretation" in their articles. The overall public service impact of nonprofit news outlets, however, may be limited given their generally small (and elite) audience reach and precarious financing (Benson 2017).

One Pew study of nonprofit news websites covering state and local news found that 44 percent were openly partisan (Pew Research Center 2011). Although overt partisanship is generally not encouraged by the major foundations, some degree of political instrumentalism is fostered by foundation donors' tendencies to prefer project-based over long-term operational funding; economic instrumentalism, likewise, may be on the rise as philanthropic funders urge nonprofits to diversify their funding sources and increase corporate sponsorships (Benson 2017). Nonprofit media are closely attuned to demand, although the demand in question is not the general audience but that of funders. The metric is not only eyeballs but also public policy or social "impact," as measured by foundations.

Conclusion

In sum, how does media ownership matter? Powerful organizations and individuals pursue strategies with some degree of discretion and maneuver. Opportunities may or may not be seized to fit the product to a market niche or to surreptitiously promote economic self-interests. Risks to invest in public service may or may not be taken. Political causes may or may not be embraced or effectively promoted. Far from being entirely random, however, it seems likely that these strategies take shape within institutional structures that tend to favor some types of action over others.

Certainly, the program for media ownership research described in this chapter is far from complete. Future research on media ownership should also closely examine variations in systems of funding, which may or may not correlate with particular ownership forms. For instance, in France, *Le Monde Diplomatique* and Médiapart are both technically privately held commercial companies, but their subscription-only funding models and commitment to reinvesting all profits back into the business lead them to behave more like nonprofits (Alfon 2017). Konieczna (2018) finds differences in news styles between US national nonprofits that are able to generate long-term foundation funding and local nonprofits that rely on more project-based funding from a diverse array of local businesses, foundations, and individual donors.

Cross-national research is also needed in order to place the power of media ownership in national context, which may highlight the ways in which a dominant national logic can lessen the degree of differentiation between media outlets with different ownership forms. For instance, in my research (Benson 2013) on French and US news treatment of immigration, I found that market logics tended to be relatively stronger across the US journalistic field (regardless of ownership type), whereas civic logics tended to be stronger throughout the French journalistic field (see also Powers and Vera Zambrano 2016). Confirming the influence of the national field of power, one recent comparative study of 48 news sites in six countries found that "online news attains the highest level of [content] diversity in national environments with strong public service media" (Humprecht and Esser 2017).

Serious attention must also be paid to variation within institutional forms of ownership. Picard and van Weezel (2008:29) emphasize such variation when they write: "Ownership form itself is not a necessary and sufficient condition for good performance in the public interest, and both good and poor performance can result under all forms." This perspective emphasizes the complex contingencies of history, place, and other circumstances that make every individual news organization distinct.

More research needs to go beyond the usual suspects in North America and Western Europe, building on studies by Stetka (2012), Hallin and Mancini (2012), Noam (2016), and others. We also need to know more about the institutional logics at work in new forms of ownership, such as the private equity investment company (Abernathy 2016), "portfolio diversification" by institutional investors (Noam 2016:11), or the merging of public and nonprofit news organizations (Ferrucci et al. 2017). We should also explore the effects on news content of increasing news-sharing agreements between nonprofits and commercial media (Graves and Konieczna 2015) and the ways in which new technological platforms create opportunities for the private ownership form to challenge dominant national field logics (Usher 2017). Finally, the question of ownership is important not only for news but also for the full range of cultural production upon which we rely for aesthetic as well as civic public goods. For instance, production of culture scholars could explore the institutional and organizational logics that have facilitated the resurgence of high-quality television series by HBO, Netflix, and other online and legacy media companies.

Notes

1 This list is based on close readings of the secondary literature as well as publisher memoirs and biographies and more than 60 in-depth interviews conducted from 2011 to 2017 with publishers, business managers, editors, and reporters at a range of commercial, civil society/nonprofit, and public news organizations in the US, France, and Sweden. I conducted this research in collaboration with Julie Sedel (University of Strasbourg), Mattias Hessérus (Ax:son Johnson Foundation), and Tim Neff (New York University), as part of a larger study.

2 Throughout this chapter, I use the label "stock market traded" rather than "publicly traded" to avoid any confusion with public (government-supported) media.

References

Aalberg, Toril, and James Curran, eds. 2011. *How Media Inform Democracy: A Comparative Approach.* London: Routledge.

Abernathy, Penelope Muse. 2016. *The Rise of a New Media Baron and the Emerging Threat of News Deserts.* Chapel Hill, NC: Center for Innovation and Sustainability in Local Media, UNC School of Media and Journalism (http://newspaperownership.com/newspaper-ownership-report/).

Alexander, Jeffrey, Elizabeth Butler Breese, and Maria Luengo. 2016. *The Crisis of Journalism Reconsidered*. Cambridge: Cambridge University Press.

Alfon, Dov. 2017. *Mediapart: A Viable Model?* Stigler Case No. 1, March 13. University of Chicago Stigler Center for the Study of the Economy and the State. Chicago: Stigler Center. (https://research.chicago-booth.edu/~/media/9F86BCAEF28941B2A55663969C34929B.pdf).

Andersson, Ulrika, and Jenny Wiik. 2013. "Journalism Meets Management: Changing Leadership in Swedish News organizations." *Journalism Practice* 7(6):705–19.

Bagdikian, Ben. 2004. *The Media Monopoly*. Boston: Beacon.

Baker, C. Edwin. 1994. *Ownership of Newspapers: The View from Positivist Social Science*. Research Paper R-12. The Joan Shorenstein Center for Press, Politics, and Public Policy, Harvard Kennedy School. Cambridge, MA: Shorenstein Center.

Benson, Rodney. 2011. "Public Funding and Journalistic Independence: What Does Research Tell Us?" Pp. 314–19 in *Will the Last Journalist Please Turn Out the Lights?* edited by R. McChesney and V. Pickard. New York: New Press.

———. 2012. "Murdoch in the United States? Kingmaker or Ringmaster?" *Global Media and Communication* 8(1):4–7.

———. 2013. *Shaping Immigration News: A French-American Comparison*. Cambridge: Cambridge University Press.

———. 2017. "Can Foundations Solve the Journalism Crisis?" *Journalism*: 1–19. https://doi.org/10.1177/1464884917724612

Benson Rodney, Matthew Powers, and Timothy Neff. 2017. "Public Media Autonomy and Accountability: Best and Worst Policy Practices in 12 Leading Democracies." *International Journal of Communication* 11:1–22.

Berry, Jeffrey M., and Sarah Sobieraj. 2014. *The Outrage Industry*. Oxford: Oxford University Press.

Bourdieu, Pierre. 1984. *Distinction*. Cambridge, MA: Harvard University Press.

———. 2005. "The Political Field, the Social Science Field, and the Journalistic Field." Pp. 29–47 in *Bourdieu and the Journalistic Field*, edited by R. Benson and E. Neveu. Cambridge: Polity Press.

Bowers, David R. 1967. "A Report on Activity by Publishers in Directing Newsroom Decisions." *Journalism & Mass Communication Quarterly* 44:43–52.

Breed, Warren. 1955. "Social Control in the Newsroom: A Functional Analysis." *Social Forces* 33(4):326–35.

Brienza, Casey, and Matthias Revers. 2016. "The Field of American Media Sociology: Origins, Resurrection, and Consolidation." *Sociology Compass* 10(7):539–52.

Brüggemann, Michael, Frank Esser, and Edda Humprecht. 2012. "The Strategic Repertoire of Publishers in the Media Crisis." *Journalism Studies* 13(5):742–52.

Cagé, Julia. 2016. *Saving the Media*. Cambridge, MA: Harvard University Press.

Carpenter, Serena, Jan Boehmer, and Frederick Fico. 2016. "The Measurement of Journalistic Role Enactments: A Study of Organizational Constraints and Support in For-Profit and Nonprofit Journalism." *Journalism & Mass Communication Quarterly* 93(3):587–608.

Chomsky, Daniel. 1999. "The Mechanisms of Management Control at the *New York Times*." *Media, Culture & Society* 21:579–99.

———. 2006. "'An Interested Reader': Measuring Ownership Control at the *New York Times*." *Critical Studies in Media Communication* 23(1):1–18.

Coulson, David C., and Anne Hansen. 1995. "The Louisville Courier-Journal's News Content After Purchase by Gannett." *Journalism & Mass Communication Quarterly* 72(1):205–15.

Cranberg, Gilbert, Randall Bezanson, and John Soloski. 2001. *Taking Stock: Journalism and the Publicly Traded Newspaper Company*. Ames: Iowa State University Press.

Cushion, Stephen. 2012. *The Democratic Value of News: Why Public Service Media Matter*. London: Palgrave Macmillan.

Della Vigna, Stefano, and Alec Kennedy. 2011. "Does Media Concentration Lead to Biased Coverage? Evidence from Movie Reviews." Unpublished Working Paper.

de Vreese, Claes H., Frank Esser, and David Hopmann. 2016. *Comparing Political Journalism*. London: Routledge.

Doctor, Ken. 2013. "The Newsonomics of Pulitzers, Paywalls, and Investing in the Newsroom." *Nieman Journalism Lab*, April 18. Retrieved October 15, 2017 (www.niemanlab.org/2013/04/the-newsonomics-of-pulitzers-paywalls-and investing-in-the-newsroom/).

Dunaway, Johanna. 2008. "Markets, Ownership, and the Quality of Campaign News Coverage." *Journal of Politics* 70(4):1193–202.

Edmonds, Rick. 2004. "News Staffing, News Budgets and News Capacity." *Newspaper Research Journal* 25(1):98–109.

Ferrucci, Patrick, Frank Michael Russell, Heesook Choi, Margaret Duffy, and Esther Thorson. 2017. "'Times are a Changin': How a Merger Affects the Construction of News Processes." *Journalism Studies* 18(3):247–64.

Fligstein, Neil, and Doug McAdam. 2012. *A Theory of Fields*. Oxford: Oxford University Press.

Graham, Katharine. 1998. *Personal History*. New York: Vintage.

Graves, Lucas, and Magda Konieczna. 2015. "Sharing the News: Journalistic Collaboration as Field Repair." *International Journal of Communication* 9:1966–84.

Hallin, Daniel C., and Paolo Mancini. 2004. *Comparing Media Systems*. Cambridge: Cambridge University Press.

———, eds. 2012. *Comparing Media Systems Beyond the Western World*. Cambridge: Cambridge University Press.

Hardy, Jonathan. 2008. *Western Media Systems*. London: Routledge.

Haveman, Heather. 2015. *Magazines and the Making of America: Modernization, Community, and Print Culture, 1741–1860*. Princeton, NJ: Princeton University Press.

Humprecht, Edda, and Frank Esser. 2017. "Diversity in Online News: On the Importance of Ownership Types and Media System Types." *Journalism Studies*: 1–23. https://doi.org/10.1080/1461670 X.2017.1308229

Klinenberg, Eric. 2007. *Fighting for Air*. New York: Metropolitan Books.

Konieczna, Magda. 2018. *Journalism without Profit*. Oxford: Oxford University Press.

Levy, David A.L., and Robert G. Picard, eds. 2011. *Is There a Better Structure for News Providers? The Potential in Charitable and Trust Ownership*. Oxford: Reuters Institute for the Study of Journalism.

Meyer, Michael. 2014. "Brick by Brick: After Years of Shrinking Ambition, Jeff Bezos has the *Washington Post* Thinking Global Domination." *Columbia Journalism Review* (July/August):26–33.

Morris, Jonathan S. 2005. "The Fox News Factor." *International Journal of Press/Politics* 10:56–79.

Napoli, Philip M. 1997. "A Principal-Agent Approach to the Study of Media Organizations: Toward a Theory of the Media Firm." *Political Communication* 14:207–19.

Noam, Eli. 2016. *Who Owns the World's Media: Media Concentration and Ownership Around the World*. New York: Oxford University Press.

———. 2017. "Beyond the Mogul: From Media Conglomerates to Portfolio Media." *Journalism*. https://doi.org/10.1177/1464884917725941

Ohlsson, Jonas. 2012. "The Practice of Newspaper Ownership: Fifty Years of Control and Influence in the Swedish Local Press." PhD dissertation, Department of Journalism, Media and Communications, University of Gothenburg, Sweden.

O'Shea, James. 2011. *The Deal from Hell: How Moguls and Wall Street Plundered Great American Newspapers*. New York: Public Affairs.

Patel, Mayur, and Michael Maness. 2013. *Finding a Foothold: How Nonprofit News Ventures Seek Sustainability*. Miami, FL: Knight Foundation. Retrieved October 15, 2017 (www.knightfoundation.org/publications/finding-foothold).

Pew Research Center. 2011. *Non-Profit News: Assessing a New Landscape in Journalism*. Washington, DC: Pew Research Center. Retrieved November 26, 2017 (www.journalism.org/2011/07/18/non-profit-news/#assessing-a-new-landscape-in-journalism).

———. 2013. *Non-Profit Journalism: A Growing but Fragile Part of the U.S. News System*. Washington, DC: Pew Research Center. Retrieved October 15, 2017 (www.journalism.org/2013/06/10/nonprofit-journalism/).

Picard, Robert, and Aldo van Weezel. 2008. "Capital and Control: Consequences of Different Forms of Newspaper Ownership." *The International Journal on Media Management* 10:22–31.

Powers, Matthew, and Sandra Vera Zambrano. 2016. "Explaining the Formation of Online News Startups in France and the United States: A Field Analysis." *Journal of Communication* 66(5):857–77.

Puglisi, Riccardo. 2011. "Being the *New York Times*: the Political Behaviour of a Newspaper." *The B.E. Journal of Economic Analysis & Policy* 11(1):1–32.

Rohlinger, Deana, and Jennifer M. Proffitt. 2016. "How Much Does Ownership Matter? Deliberative Discourse in Local Media Coverage of the Terri Schiavo Case." *Journalism*:1–18. https://doi.org/10.1177/1464884916665404

Sirota, David. 2014. "The Wolf of Sesame Street: Revealing the Secret Corruption Inside PBS's News Division." *Pando Daily*, February 12. Retrieved (https://pando.com/2014/02/12/the-wolf-of-sesame-street-revealing-the-secret-corruption-inside-pbss-news-division/).

Socolow, Michael J. 2010. "A Profitable Public Sphere: The Creation of the *New York Times* Op-Ed Page." *Journalism & Mass Communication Quarterly* 87(2):281–96.

Stetka, Vaclav. 2012. "From Multinationals to Business Tycoons: Media Ownership and Journalistic Autonomy in Eastern and Central Europe." *International Journal of Press/Politics* 17(4):433–56.

Thornton, Patricia H., William Ocasio, and Michael Lounsbury. 2012. *The Institutional Logics Perspective*. New York: Oxford University Press.

Tifft, Susan E., and Alex S. Jones. 2000. *The Trust: The Private and Powerful Family Behind the New York Times*. Boston, MA: Back Bay Books.

Usher, Nikki. 2017. "Venture-backed News Startups and the Field of Journalism." *Digital Journalism*. https://doi.org/10.1080/21670811.2016.1272064

Van Der Haak, Bregtje, Michael Parks, and Manuel Castells. 2012. "The Future of Journalism: Networked Journalism." *International Journal of Communication* 6:2923–38.

Wagner, Michael W., and Timothy P. Collins. 2014. "Does Ownership Matter? The Case of Rupert Murdoch's Purchase of the *Wall Street Journal*." *Journalism Practice*:1–14. https://doi.org/10.1080/17512786.2014.882063

Part VII
Cultures of work and professions

42

Work cultures

Robin Leidner

Introduction

Frameworks of meaning shape work experiences as surely as do organizational structures, technology, and patterns of ownership. Motivation, effort, discipline, group identifications and boundaries, and self-understanding all depend on work cultures. These factors are molded in obvious ways by structural and material factors both within and beyond the workplace, yet work cultures do more than express and embody differences in power, authority, interests, and advantage. They have their own effects on how work is done, how organizations operate, how people understand themselves, and to whom they feel loyal. While drawing on elements of the broader culture that order solidarities and identities, whether based on nation, gender, or other social distinctions, cultures of work can also affect surrounding cultural milieus.

Work cultures, broadly defined, are sets of values, beliefs, norms, and sentiments about work activities and the symbols and rituals that express them. Sociological and historical research demonstrates the significance of work cultures that operate at a variety of levels, from specific workplaces and occupations to organizations to nations and supranational systems. These cultures are neither static nor uncontested. They can provide the impetus and resources for struggles over control of work, inclusion and exclusion, goals and rewards.

This chapter emphasizes the continual interplay between culture and economic conditions, structures, and practices. It first argues that cultural frameworks always guide economic activity, even as changes in the structures and practices of work shape consciousness, identities, and ideologies. The discussion then moves from large-scale cultural shifts to the operation of culture within more sharply delineated structures of work, noting change over time in the significance of occupational cultures, workplace cultures, and organizational cultures. At all of these levels, workers aim to maintain control over their tasks and their environment, sometimes offering resistance to efforts by others, especially bosses, to interfere with the norms of their work culture. Yet solidarity among those who share an occupation or a workplace may be weakened by cultural distinctions imported from beyond the workplace. The chapter concludes with a discussion of how changing conditions of work – currently driven by globalization – transform elements of culture at all levels, providing ongoing challenges to sociologists seeking to understand the complex interplay of economic structures, everyday work experiences, and surrounding cultures.

Robin Leidner

Culture and economics

Weber called attention to the ways that pre-existing cultures shape orientations to new kinds of work, noting, for example, that efforts to motivate peasants to work longer hours at harvest time by increasing wage rates had the opposite effect because they did not see material gain as a route to a better life. *The Protestant Ethic and the Spirit of Capitalism* (Weber [1904–05] 1958) points to the rise of a novel cultural framework, a system of religious beliefs, as a necessary part of the causal chain leading to the development of capitalism. Weber's approach complicates the Marxist view of culture as part of the superstructure that derives from the material, economic base.

The nature of the relation between cultural frameworks and economic developments remains open to debate, but historical and sociological research, especially cross-cultural studies, demonstrates that these realms cannot be separated. Social structures stimulate and limit aspirations and ideas about how to fulfill them, but the mixture of motivation and compulsion employers use to control their workers depends in part on the workers' cultural frameworks. In addition, cultural settings help shape workplace practices; economic relations help determine individual and group identities; and structures of work affect the surrounding cultures.

Economists and organizational theorists often treat individualistic rationality and efficiency as primary and unproblematic principles of action. The aggressive spread of bureaucracies around the world may seem to be the result of inherent efficiencies, but rationality and efficiency take form only within particular ideological traditions and social contexts. Neither timeless values nor constants of human behavior can explain the variable workings of the economy in general or of particular organizations. In reality, cultural frameworks with their own histories always guide economic activity. Neoinstitutional theorists explain the nearly ubiquitous reach of bureaucracies as the result of a kind of cultural imperialism, the creation of a world culture dominated by Western ideas (Meyer et al. 1997, cited in Morrill 2008:26) consonant with the bureaucratic organization of work.

Still, even in the same bureaucratized industry, work cultures may vary across nations. In a detailed historical account, Biernacki (1995) demonstrates that disparate understandings of labor as a commodity developed in Germany and Britain in the nineteenth-century textile industry, apparently as the result of differential timing in the emergence of wage labor. He argues that culture is an autonomous force, but that in each country cultural assumptions came to be embedded in work practices, which in turn conveyed and reproduced the logic upon which they were based. These nationally distinctive principles, he writes, produced distinctive patterns of industrial relations.

Once such cultural assumptions are built into social structures and practices – the length of the working day, how pay is calculated – they are reproduced by the practices of everyday life, shaping the consciousness, the taken for granted, the common sense of all involved. Whenever and wherever the labor market moves people into the unfamiliar world of industrial or bureaucratic work and they prove recalcitrant to its demands, owners and managers try to reform them, and they generally succeed. Populations of newly industrializing countries, immigrant workers, rural people drawn into industrial work, former welfare recipients, people from neighborhoods lacking models of steady employment, and former housewives all must give up familiar notions about who is entitled to organize their time, determine their effort, and decide the best ways to do things. Showing up for work every day, on time, dressed appropriately, with a proper willingness to accommodate oneself to workplace regulations and norms does not come naturally to people who previously regarded work as properly regulated by tradition, family members, the dictates of the weather and hours of daylight, their own needs and standards, or community scrutiny.

Methods of acculturating workers have become more sophisticated with time but the essential program has not changed. When the International Harvester Corporation hired immigrant Polish laborers in the United States a century ago, it set about teaching them how to live by the demands of the industrial order. Lesson One included a text that provided guidance for the workday: "The whistle blows at five minutes of starting time. I get ready to go to work. I work until the whistle blows to quit" (Gutman 1977:6). Ultimately, these Poles learned to abandon their old ways and conform to the new order of highly rationalized work. Contemporary firms making use of new pools of labor now do the same kind of things in a great variety of cultural settings all around the planet.

Occupational and workplace cultures

Historically, *occupational* groups have been central in defining cultural expectations for many workers. Occupations, including professions, typically develop specific sets of norms that are passed on to novices both during training and on the job. Some have extensive periods of training and socialization during which initiates' sense of themselves and their status relative to others is remade. They learn and internalize not only knowledge and skills, but also the occupation's ideology, ethos, traditions, and norms, including criteria for judgment, craft pride, and rules for interacting among themselves and with various others. Strong occupational cultures delineate social boundaries, affect patterns of interaction, and generally intensify struggles over status and autonomy vis-à-vis coworkers, workplace superiors, customers and clients, occupational groups that have related mandates, and the general public (Hughes [1971] 1984a).

Much of what Hughes ([1971] 1984b) called "the social drama of work" derives from efforts by the members of an occupation to act on their values in order to maintain their prerogatives and their dignity rather than comply with others' standards. Jazz musicians who resent squares' attempts to influence the performance (Becker 1951), male firefighters who refuse to abandon sexist practices to make women feel welcome (Chetkovich 1997), and professionals who consider some kinds of work beneath them are all defending occupational self-determination.

However, those who share an occupation do not necessarily share a culture. *Workplaces* often have their own distinctive cultures – what industrial sociologists once called shop-floor cultures – that can alter occupational values or override occupational barriers. Researchers have found that cultural fit can influence hiring decisions (Rivera 2012) and individual occupational attainment (Goldberg et al. 2016). Moreover, within and across occupational boundaries, differences based on race and ethnicity, gender, sexuality, language, nationality, and citizenship status may be imported into the workplace or developed there, their significance magnified or downplayed in part by how they map onto job placement, organizational hierarchy, and seniority. Such features of everyday work life as dress, patterns of interaction, and topics of conversation depend on workers' cultural background and their incorporation into workplace groups. For example, the radically different workplace cultures of elementary school teachers and coal miners can be explained in large part by the distinct demands of the work, but the gender order beyond the workplace has a significant impact as well.

Both occupational and workplace cultures often reproduce patterns of exclusion. Although some workers are relatively accepting of cultural differences, sexism, racism, and ethnocentrism flourish in many occupations and at many work sites. Barriers to entry into an occupation have often had disparate effects, intentionally or not. Within the workplace, traditional forms of cultural expression can be used to pursue disputes with competing groups. A dispute may be limited to a struggle for control over expression, as when Latino athletes want to hear salsa music in the locker room and African Americans want to hear rap, but the dispute may also carry forward battles about material interests. Hostile joking, obscenity, religious rituals or proselytization, and political symbols and slogans all can be used by one group to make the workplace uncomfortable for potential newcomers, thus to preserve control over jobs.

As in many other circumstances, the degree of solidarity among members of an occupation or among coworkers at a particular workplace is influenced by the salience of boundaries between in-group and out-group members and of struggles over access to resources. When outsiders, be they customers, bosses, members of other departments, or those in allied jobs, act in ways that threaten workers' autonomy, convenience, or self-regard, we can expect to see relative solidarity among those who are similarly situated. Divisions among coworkers and members of occupations are most likely to surface when access to jobs, promotions, and preferred tasks is threatened from within or when newcomers challenge existing elements of workplace culture.

Organizational culture

Traditionally, decisions about how to carry out daily tasks came from occupational groups, but organizational forms such as guilds and craft unions that formerly upheld occupational cultures have disappeared or declined in their relevance. Professional associations still flourish, but professionals are far less likely to set up in practices for themselves than they once were and are therefore less autonomous. Most work now takes place in organizations, which have sharply undercut the strength of occupational cultures by taking over control of work and distributing it with scant regard for traditional divisions of labor, and also by trying to impose *organizational* cultures that reorder solidarities and values.

Some aspects of *occupational* cultures, including hostile attitudes between different kinds of workers, can be useful to management insofar as they undermine worker solidarity. In general, however, when organizations bring together workers with a strong occupational ethos, owners and managers seek to override group norms so that they can exercise control over the distribution of tasks, workers' level of effort, work standards, pace, and technique. Braverman (1974) argued that the indispensability of workers' knowledge, experience, and skill was dramatically diminished by managements' successful imposition of work systems that deskilled the work. Reallocation of the right and ability to control work processes undercuts not only workers' power and wages but also their occupational identities and cultures. But managerial control measures do not typically eliminate struggle over the conduct and rewards of work. Rather, the weakening of occupational bonds can strengthen class solidarity within and across organizations, such that the work site remains contested terrain (Edwards 1979).

Occupational subcultures do often survive within organizations as sources of norms and values that contrast with those of management (Trice 1993). They can serve as bases of struggle over status and workplace control and provide communities of resistance to managerial dictates. Although professionals increasingly work in bureaucracies, they do not altogether abandon their formally prescribed ethics and standards or their carefully cultivated worldviews when subjected to organizational discipline. Similarly, distinctive elements of gender or ethnic cultures can uphold priorities and solidarities that challenge managements' cultural impositions.

Morrill (2008) describes how managerial attention to culture as a means of improving production and winning workers' commitment surged and ebbed throughout the twentieth century, intermittently countering or complicating more straightforward emphasis on hierarchy and bureaucratic efficiency. Some firms took a paternalistic stance toward employees, aiming to foster identification with the organization by promoting a familistic culture and providing programs and facilities that strengthened workers' commitment to and dependence on the company. The Hawthorne experiments of the 1920s demonstrated that simply paying attention to a specific work group could increase its productivity, forming the basis of the human-relations approach to management that emphasized consideration of workers' emotional well-being as part of the organization's strategy for building loyalty and increasing output. Edwards (1979) argues that elaborate bureaucratic systems of job ladders fostered not only identification with the company but also an individualistic culture in which workers focused on their own mobility opportunities. All of these approaches often led workers to identify with the organization as a whole rather than form class-based or occupation-based identifications.

In the last decades of the twentieth century, several significant trends made culture an even more central managerial concern in the US. Foremost among them was competition from abroad, in particular from Japan, where corporate cultures and production processes differed markedly from those in the US in emphasizing employee participation and responsibility, team-work across barriers of rank, and activities aimed at building solidarity. Many US corporations experimented with similar practices, while among management consultants "corporate culture" became a buzzword. Acknowledging that companies varied greatly in ethos, the consultants urged corporate executives to make culture an explicit focus of leadership. Top-down cultural strategies might center on customer satisfaction, on continual innovation, or on a given company's tradition of quality, but the shared goal was creating a positive, unifying ethos that motivated workers and contributed to corporate success.

The expansion of high-tech and service industries also prompted renewed attention to business culture. High-tech companies dependent on the creative work of young technical workers developed famously informal yet intense work cultures that promoted long hours of self-driven labor. Companies whose success requires attracting and pleasing customers strove to create cultures of service that called on workers to reshape their orientations and self-presentations. As Hochschild (1983) argues, service workers are frequently required to perform "emotional labor" in order to produce a desired feeling state in those on the receiving end of services. Such labor is shaped in large part by norms of gender and class. Since customers are necessarily involved in this sort of work, often as participants as well as evaluators, the practices of service businesses both draw on and exert influence over the surrounding culture.

Organizational efforts to manage work cultures do not go unchallenged. Workers often consider such efforts manipulative and see them as potentially lessening their dignity, their independence, and their class or other loyalties. Class-based resentment and a pervasive suspicion of managerial intentions can generate resistance to such attempts, but resistance also can arise in defense of informal workplace practices. Oppositional stances do not necessarily undermine managerial aims, however, as has been demonstrated in a range of workplaces from manufacturing to engineering. Cultures of resistance may take forms that subtly elicit acquiescence to exploitation (Burawoy 1979) or that support ironic distancing rather than creative engagement (Kunda 1992). Women's work cultures and their associated rituals may uphold alternative values and justify a degree of autonomy, but employers can also draw on codes of femininity to manipulate workers (Salzinger 2003).

Managerial emphasis on controlling organizational culture varies by setting and fluctuates over time for a variety of reasons. The costs of creating and imposing a culture, the relative effectiveness of other kinds of controls, including material incentives, the difficulty of attracting and keeping desirable employees, and management fads are all significant factors. Recent structural changes in the corporate economy have, on the whole, made organizational cultures a less important managerial strategy. In general, under pressure of international competition, rapid technological change, and market uncertainty, companies increasingly limit their commitment to employees. When companies lay off large numbers of employees, outsource work, hire workers on short-term contracts, or otherwise match skill and labor precisely to demand at a given moment, the resulting instability of careers within particular organizations means that management is less apt to rely on a unified culture to spur motivation and to create long-term loyalties. Corporate mergers, increasingly frequent late in the century, have also had an effect because of the difficulties of meshing contrasting cultures. Besides, mergers almost always entail uncertainty and layoffs, which produce a workplace culture marked by cynicism and disaffection. Dubious that workers' loyalty to the company yields significant benefits, some managers have taken to cultivating an employee ethos of competitive individualism, readiness to redefine oneself, and personal entrepreneurship (van Maanen and Kunda 1989). Vallas and Cummins (2015) show that popular business literature similarly urges people to think of themselves as brands to be marketed and that many people are persuaded by such advice.

Thus changing contexts of work have eroded some of the conditions that support organizational cultures, as well as occupational and workplace ones – conditions that previously could be taken for granted. The physical isolation of telecommuting workers, the brief communities created by short-term contracts, the individualism promoted by the replacement of fixed employment with independent contracting, as well as the movement of work across national borders all undercut the kinds of face-to-face interaction and the awareness of a community of fate that promote workplace and occupational cultures and that can attach workers to an organization's culture.

Yet surprisingly powerful work cultures can be maintained under unlikely circumstances. Actors and other theater personnel form tight communities for strictly limited time periods and preserve professional traditions regardless of employment; direct selling organizations create intense cultures that bind together independent contractors (Biggart 1989); even temporary production workers can identify strongly with an organizational culture (Smith 2001). In none of these cases, however, is the occupational culture a significant source of resistance to managerial power. Moreover, the growth of service work, which often incorporates non-employees into the labor process, encourages employers to take control of workers' attitudes and presentation of self in dramatically more thoroughgoing ways (Leidner 1993).

Work cultures in an era of globalization

In the contemporary world, the increasingly swift movement of capital, organizational processes, technology, and cultural products has wrought many changes in the culture of work and in the relevant elements of the surrounding culture. The power of the globalizing economy to effect great changes in work cultures is notable throughout the world, even where there has been highly organized resistance to market economics. In the formerly socialist nations and in China, globalization, which has exposed workers to market forces once unimaginable, has provided vivid evidence of how rapidly work cultures shift when state regimes change. Lee's collection of ethnographies of work in contemporary China (2007) documents how employment insecurity and new demands for attracting and keeping customers undermine familiar cultural suppositions, disorienting workers who must play by new rules. Otis (2012) describes how the self-presentations of young Chinese women new to employment are shaped by markets, the vestiges of Communist-era social programs, and their own efforts to maintain their dignity. The lack of preparation of those who emigrate from rural areas in search of work replicates the disorienting experiences of agricultural and small-town people in other parts of the world in the earlier stages of industrialization and capitalist development.

Globalization and advanced rationalization are modifying and perhaps transforming not only work cultures but local and national cultures as well. However, the consequences are quite variable and difficult to predict. Two examples illustrate this indeterminacy: the effects of globalization on women's identities and the cultural consequences of service corporations' worldwide expansion. Sociological research on the ways that women workers employed by transnational corporations express their gender identities amply demonstrates the variability of globalization's cultural effects. Even as companies are pursuing their own ends, women employed by foreign-owned firms reshape their identities as women while participating actively in creating work cultures that draw on the surrounding culture, affect their home culture, and make use of the norms and resources of their employers. Radhakrishnan (2011), for example, describes women employed in information technology in India who understand themselves to be participating in a global business culture yet take pride in asserting their "Indianness" in ways that shake expectations about what traditional Indian women are like. Salzinger (2003) shows that transnational manufacturing firms moved factories to Mexico to make use of the "productive femininity" of subservient women assembly workers they believed would be found there. Yet her fieldwork reveals that, rather than drawing on pre-existing character types, each of four assembly plants produces a distinctive "gendered subject," ranging from docile to combative (Salzinger 2003). Freeman (2000) finds that data-entry workers employed by foreign companies in Barbados collectively generated a new style of femininity that asserts a status superior to other workers and that flaunts their womanliness and creativity. The complex and elusive cultural effects of outsourcing and similar transfers of jobs out of highly industrialized nations form an especially promising subject for further research.

The cultural effects of service companies such as McDonald's that have spread around the world are also more complicated than might be assumed. They export not only products but also physical settings and styles of interaction that have numerous cultural effects. They do not simply superimpose the organizational culture onto the receiving culture, however. Cultural imperialism is too gross a concept to capture the interplay of myriad influences on either the culture of the workplace or the surrounding culture. Watson's edited volume on McDonald's outlets in East Asian countries (1997) shows that customers in various countries make use of the facilities in ways that fit their own cultural patterns, sometimes forcing the owners to adapt to their preferences. Similarly, although the business model of McDonald's and other fast-food companies grew out of a legal environment that offers workers virtually no voice and few rights, their efforts to impose their workplace cultures in countries in which workers have more power often run into both legal and informal resistance (Royle and Towers 2002).

Conclusion

The uncertainty about the interplay of nearly incessant economic change and culture presents sociologists with a challenging and perhaps daunting research agenda. The task facing sociologists of work and culture is to understand this interplay in a global economy with massive and sometimes apparently overpowering international transfers of capital, technology, personnel, and organizational and occupational cultures. The research agenda includes specifying the effects when societies experience the arrival of large numbers of workers from unfamiliar cultures or when significant sectors of the economy come under the control of foreign corporations or when new technologies disrupt occupational traditions.

Outcomes are likely to be quite variable, with national differences in responses to economic restructuring providing evidence of the enabling and constraining powers of long-standing cultural and structural patterns. But in all societies, the changing character of work raises many questions about culture. On the one hand, existing cultures variably shape people's capacity to cope with the fluidity of work arrangements. On the other, changes in the structures of work and career can give rise to cultural innovation. They also may lead to changes in beliefs about what workers are owed, about who is to blame for individual occupational failure, and about who should bear the costs of change.

Cultural resources undoubtedly shape individuals' capacity to cope with fluidity in work arrangements. In turn, changes in the structures of work and career can be expected to give rise to cultural innovation. If, for large numbers of workers, work no longer takes place in relatively stable groups and large numbers of people switch occupations during the course of their working lives, work and occupational cultures may decline in importance as significant bases of personal identity. What will replace them? Societal notions of the place of work in individual lives, the proper orientation toward work, and the kinds of qualities assumed to be required for success at work will still be important, but their content may shift markedly, as is happening in China.

The study of work cultures draws together sociological studies of work and economic life and studies of culture. Understanding the reciprocal impact of structural economic change, everyday experiences of work, and the surrounding culture is the major task facing students of work culture.

Acknowledgments

Thanks to Annette Lareau for her encouragement and suggestions, to Sam Kaplan for his extensive contributions, and to the editors for their helpful comments.

References

Becker, Howard S. 1951. "The Professional Dance Musician and His Audience." *American Journal of Sociology* 57(2):136–44.

Biernacki, Richard. 1995. *The Fabrication of Labor: Germany and Britain, 1640–1914*. Berkeley: University of California Press.

Biggart, Nicole W. 1989. *Charismatic Capitalism: Direct Selling Organizations in America*. Chicago: University of Chicago Press.

Braverman, Harry. 1974. *Labor and Monopoly Capital: The Degradation of Work in the Twentieth Century*. New York: Monthly Review Press.

Burawoy, Michael. 1979. *Manufacturing Consent: Changes in the Labor Market under Monopoly Capitalism*. Chicago: University of Chicago Press.

Chetkovich, Carol A. 1997. *Real Heat: Gender and Race in the Urban Fire Service*. New Brunswick, NJ: Rutgers University Press.

Edwards, Richard. 1979. *Contested Terrain: The Transformation of the Workplace in the Twentieth Century*. New York: Basic Books.

Freeman, Caroline. 2000. *High Tech and High Heels in the Global Economy: Women, Work, and Pink-Collar Identities in the Caribbean*. Durham, NC: Duke University Press.

Goldberg, Amir, Sameer B. Srivastava, V. Govind Manian, William Monroe, and Christopher Potts. 2016. "Fitting In or Standing Out? The Tradeoffs of Structural and Cultural Embeddedness." *American Sociological Review* 81(6):1190–22.

Gutman, Herbert G. 1977. *Work, Culture, and Society in Industrializing America: Essays in American Working-Class and Social History*. New York: Vintage Books.

Hochschild, Arlie. 1983. *The Managed Heart: Commercialization of Human Feeling*. Berkeley: University of California Press.

Hughes, Everett C. [1971] 1984a. "The Study of Occupations." Pp. 283–97 in *The Sociological Eye: Selected Papers*. New Brunswick, NJ: Transaction Books.

———. [1971] 1984b. "Work and Self." Pp. 338–47 in *The Sociological Eye: Selected Papers*. New Brunswick, NJ: Transaction Books.

Kunda, Gideon. 1992 *Engineering Culture: Control and Commitment in a High-Tech Corporation*. Philadelphia, PA: Temple University Press.

Lee, Ching Kwan, ed. 2007. *Working in China: Ethnographies of Labor and Workplace Transformation*. New York: Routledge.

Leidner, Robin. 1993. *Fast Food, Fast Talk: Service Work and the Routinization of Everyday Life*. Berkeley: University of California Press.

Meyer, John W., John Boli, George M. Thomas, and Francisco Ramirez. 1997. "World Society and the Nation-State." *American Journal of Sociology* 103(1):144–81.

Morrill, Calvin. 2008. "Culture and Organization Theory." *Annals of the American Academy of Political and Social Science* 619(1):15–40.

Otis, Eileen M. 2012. *Markets and Bodies: Women, Service Work, and the Making of Inequality in China*. Stanford, CA: Stanford University Press.

Radhakrishnan, Smitha. 2011. *Appropriately Indian: Gender and Culture in a New Transnational Class*. Durham, NC: Duke University Press.

Rivera, Lauren. 2012. "Hiring as Cultural Matching: The Case of Elite Professional Service Firms." *American Sociological Review* 77(6):999–1022.

Royle, Tony, and Brian Towers, eds. 2002. *Labour Relations in the Global Fast-Food Industry*. London: Routledge.

Salzinger, Leslie. 2003. *Genders in Production: Making Workers in Mexico's Global Factories*. Berkeley: University of California Press.

Smith, Vicki. 2001. *Crossing the Great Divide: Worker Risk and Opportunity in the New Economy*. Ithaca, NY: ILR Press.

Trice, Harrison M. 1993. *Occupational Subcultures in the Workplace*. Ithaca, NY: ILR Press.

Vallas, Steven P., and Emily R. Cummins. 2015. "Personal Branding and Identity Norms in the Popular Business Press: Enterprise Culture in an Age of Precarity." *Organization Studies* 36(3):293–319.

Van Maanen, John, and Gideon Kunda. 1989 "'Real Feelings': Emotional Expression and Organizational Culture." Pp. 43–103 in *Research in Organizational Behavior*, edited by L.L. Cummings and B.M. Staw. Greenwich, CT: JAI Press.

Watson, James L., ed. 1997. *Golden Arches East: McDonald's in East Asia*. Stanford, CA: Stanford University Press.

Weber, Max. [1904–05] 1958. *The Protestant Ethic and the Spirit of Capitalism*. New York: Charles Scribner's Sons.

43

Everywhere and nowhere

Reconceiving service work as culture

Eileen M. Otis

Introduction

In 2007 the service sector replaced manufacturing as the largest employer worldwide (International Labour Organization 2007). This remarkable shift in the structure of the world economy has yet to receive adequate attention by scholars. Specifically, scholars know little of the organization and enactment of service labor outside of the Anglo-American context. Services are an employment mainstay not only in advanced economies but also in many developing countries around the globe. Despite the regional and international proliferation, cultural and geographical diversity has thus far largely been neglected in the analysis of service labor. The expansion of service across regions and cultural domains, as well as their export from Western nations, reveals a seemingly obvious yet frequently overlooked fact: service labor, which pivots on social interaction, requires workers to exhibit cultural competence. In other words, service workers are always culture workers. Culture is the substance of service work, yet this basic fact is overlooked in sociological analyses. Culture, in other words, is everywhere and nowhere.

In this chapter I first assess the utility and limits of existing frameworks for the study of interactive service work across diverse cultural settings. These approaches illuminate organizational dynamics but without regard for the ways interaction and interactive norms may vary across space and time. I then explore associated concepts that promise to extend our analytic reach to new domains of culture. Then I reflect upon the question: once we open the Pandora's box of culture and find potentially endless variety, are we left to merely inventory the myriad cultural practices observed in service labor? To begin to chip away at this problem, I suggest that we use culture to think about how power relations are created and naturalized in the dynamics of service labor processes.

Labor studies of service work

Studies of labor that center on interaction with customers and clients has largely focused on Anglo-American contexts, where services became a dominant sector of employment rather early on, in the 1970's. The service sector is a broad category that includes handsomely paid professionals like lawyers, doctors, financiers, and engineers as well as those workers who are modestly and poorly compensated, like teachers, day-care workers, nannies, and anyone who is paid to interact with customers, including retail, restaurant, and hotel workers. Today in both the US and England, the service sector employs more workers than ever, with most relegated to the lower range of the service-sector labor market in poorly paid, insecure work. US and European firms export brand-name services abroad, with the global development of national hotels, fast-food, and retail chains (for example, see Watson 1997). Advanced economies have become "service societies," as manufacturing moved to export-production platforms in the global south.

The shifts occurring in the employment landscape begged for new theories and new concepts, and sociologists gradually began to examine service-sector labor processes. But unpacking the basic competencies of interactive service labor proved a daunting task because the product is immaterial and ephemeral. Unlike the manufacturing and agriculture sectors that produce items of material substance, much of the product generated by the service sector is not tangible. Indeed, service labor is defined as much by what it is not as by what it is. Service commonly refers to an act of assistance for pay that does not revolve around production of a physical object. At its core is human interaction, whether in real time or virtual. This interaction involves an exchange of information and sentiment, and may be part of the purveyance of a material object, as in retail services in which clerks and cashiers assist customers select and purchase goods or in restaurants in which food servers assist customers by delivering food, along with a smile. Service also describes the labor of professionals who convey to clients valued or scarce information, like lawyers, therapists, or financial advisors. Some services primarily treat the customers' body, but the process requires that the professional – whether she be a brain surgeon, a manicurist, or a barber – elicit cues from the customer about their feelings and the state of their body (Barber 2016; Kang 2010). Although the affective product contains value to be exchanged on a market, it is quite literally immaterial, a point emphasized by the Italian Autonomists (Lazzarato 1996). Paradoxically, service "products" cannot be separated from the bodies that render them; services involve direct and embodied interaction between the producer and the consumer. A working definition of service labor, then, is the paid effort of interacting with another human being in order to produce a combination of material, cognitive, and affective outcomes.

Thus, much service labor unfolds in the fleeting realm of human sentiment, sensibility, and culture. To varying extents, all service workers are paid to produce a range of affect for customer consumption: a sense of security, happiness, calm, delight, excitement, and sometimes even titillation. Even surgeons must convey information to patients in a calming and clear manner. The centrality of affect and its content may vary between, say, lawyers, teachers, therapists, and nannies. But all varieties of service worker must manage their own and their customers' affects. However, due to the immateriality of service labor, its conditions, production, and outcomes often elude empirical analysis. For this reason, ethnography is the method of choice for examining service work (although an important exception is Wharton 1993). As an "embodied" methodology that engages the researcher's multiple senses, ethnography requires immersion in the work setting. The ethnographer ventures close to experiencing firsthand how workers "do interaction" and navigate social relationships with customers and managers. In-depth interviewing allows ethnographers to explore how workers themselves understand the process of producing a range of affect in their work. With such studies, scholars have developed a variegated repertory of concepts for analyzing the labor dynamics of the service sector.

Arlie Hochschild's *The Managed Heart* (1983) altered labor scholars' perception of service work. She cast light on the mental-emotional proficiency required of service workers who interact with customers, terming the emotional adjustments that service workers perform on their own moods "emotion work." The concept illuminated a set of competencies that had previously been invisible. Service workers labor on the self, argued Hochschild, exercising a profound degree of control over their feeling states with the objective of producing affective responses in customers. Hochschild compared the American flight attendants she studied to method actors who perform intense emotional labor by summoning sentiment-laden memories to induce the forms of expression that they seek to portray in their characters. Through similar methods of emotional laboring, she argued, workers replace their own learned emotional responses with the affective imperatives of the firm. To accomplish this, workers draw from the emotional well-spring of the private realm of household, transferring it to the world of commercial interchange (by, for example, likening customers to children or guests in their home). Hochschild argued that such deep work on the self, enacted in the interest of profit, threatens the authentic selfhood of workers. The research was conducted among American service workers, yet the conclusions drawn were, at least implicitly, applied to all interactive labor, regardless of place.

US scholars responded to the theory of emotion work by developing productive organizational analyses, using investigations of the labor of security guards, secretaries, paralegals, waitresses, fast-food workers, hotel workers, beauticians, and retail salespeople to reflect upon and assess emotion work. One major adjustment in Hochschild's original framework emerged from a study of fast-food workers at the American chain, McDonald's. In this research, Leidner (1993) argued that the use of pre-formulated scripts, which some firms require workers to recite, may not compromise a deeply felt sense of authenticity as much as Hochschild's study suggests. Instead, workers may use scripts as a shield to protect their private senses of self. Scripts provide interactive armor against the endless stream of customers with whom workers contend, by allowing employees to control and process service interactions efficiently, avoiding both lengthy conversations in which patrons may "overshare" details of their lives and experiences, as well as additional and burdensome requests that increase the worker's labor load. This important work questioned the desirability of bringing authenticity to the workplace. But it did not interrogate the status of authenticity, its desirability and content, across cultural divides. Research from China suggests that more central to the service interaction is an economy of "face-giving" and "face-protecting." Workers strive to preserve their own status and dignity not by expressing their individuality in relationships with customers or by using employer-provided scripts but rather by keeping interaction decidedly off the terrain of the personal and engaging ritual-like enactments of status giving that function to a certain extent like scripts (Otis 2016).

Another insight into the organizational structure of service work complicated dualistic worker-manager models of the labor process derived from industrial employment. In particular, Leidner recognized the central role of the customer in the disciplinary dynamics of labor. Service workers are formally subject to the authority of managers. However, customers are often empowered to direct the labor of service workers. Leidner's analysis thus reveals the triangles of potential conflict and cooperation between consumers, managers, and workers, as these actors forge situationally strategic two-way alliances to gain an advantage over the third party. To optimize control over this three-way labor interaction, management attempts to recruit customers into the labor process to control workers. Employers do so by enlisting customers to discipline and reward workers (Fuller and Smith 1991), using tipping systems that incentivize workers to offer especially friendly and ingratiating service (Sallaz 2002), employing secret shoppers who pose as customers but inform management about employees who do not conform to standards of performance (Ott 2016), and distributing customer satisfaction surveys that invite patrons to evaluate the service provided by workers (Fuller and Smith 1991). Employers also use service workers to control customers by routinizing and scripting interactions to reduce the scope of interaction and direct customers to whatever task is at hand (Leidner 1993) and transforming the identities and bodies of workers to influence customer behaviors (Leidner 1993; Macdonald and Sirianni 1996).

These studies advance our understanding of service-sector labor processes, but they overlook the potentially vast variation in cultural norms of service across communities of interaction. In Hochschild's original emotion work frame, culture was everywhere and nowhere. There was some gesturing to (American) middle-class culture. For example, she asserted that airline "recruiters screened for outgoing middle class sociability" (Hochschild 1983:97). Also, some semblance of a cultural analysis can be found within the brief recognition of brand differen- tiation among service providers who cater to different consumer markets. These brand types include "upper class," "comfortable," and "down home." And while the analysis recognizes, in principle, that the cultural organization of emotional expression will vary from place to place, the question of culture never extends to the possibility that alternative mechanisms or labor processes might produce the social and bodily expression required by service firms, and these processes might be rooted in different cultural legacies and dispositions (Otis 2011).

A more challenging limitation would arise in any effort to transpose Hochschild's analysis to settings outside the US, given its conceptual and empirical grounding in Western institutional and normative traditions. Hochschild bases her central critique of the performance of emotion work for a wage on a notion of separate spheres – a non-commercial, domestic, private sphere, on the one hand, and a second commercial, public sphere. She argues that service work enters and defiles a sanctum of human authenticity otherwise protected in the private sphere, which is presumed to be non-commercial. Yet the domestic sphere is a preeminent site of the consump- tion of commercial products and a place where money entwines with and enables intimate rela- tions (Zelizer 2007). The ideology and institutional practice of separate spheres emerged in the process of Western industrialization. The extent to which society is divided into two opposing spheres, or even idealized as such, should not be assumed when investigating service labor across national boundaries.

Another impediment to using Hochschild's analysis across cultural settings is a definitional reliance of the core concept of emotion work on Konstantin Stanislavski's performance theory, popularly known as method acting. Emotion work is defined as the labor of displaying an emo- tion so as to elicit an intended feeling in a customer. Hochschild draws an analogy between method acting and emotion work to illuminate the latter's basic psychological mechanics. Sim- ply put, the method involves conjuring a memory with emotional resonance to prompt the expression of a desired emotion, which in turn allows the actor to create naturalistic displays of feeling. Actors can induce the most natural display of emotions, it is assumed, by drawing upon deeply affective memories. The theory reflects a strongly individualist disposition in that it focuses solely on the personal interior as the wellspring of emotions and affective displays.

We should be attentive to the relevance of the analogy between service labor and acting for different types of workplaces and varieties of cultural settings. Furthermore, scholars gain leverage on understanding the labor of service work by recognizing the differences as well as the similarities between acting (for an audience) and interacting (with a paying customer). Although the preeminent sociologist Erving Goffman likened all interaction to acting, there are limits to his metaphor. Actors take on roles in relationship to other roles as structured by a script. They relate simultaneously to a fellow actor playing out a role *and* the audience. The role played is to entertain the audience through scripted interaction with another character. While the act- ing analogy might resonate with interaction writ large, the relation to the service work, with its structured power relation between customer and worker may conceal important dimensions specific to the paid labor of interaction. Unlike service workers, actors usually do not directly anticipate or respond to the idiosyncratic needs of paying patrons. Actors are not required to do the bidding of customers. On the contrary, actors are more likely to exercise control and influence over the audience through their arts. Actors create a world apart for their audience, a world that the audience enters. Indeed, actors have been deemed "elite emotion managers" (Orzechowicz 2008). Workers, on the other hand, are more likely to enter into and navigate the class and cultural worlds created to appeal to their customers. These service environments are more likely to reflect the habits and aesthetics of the customers than the employees. A play, on the other hand, may amuse, disturb, or prompt further reflection, by introducing the audience to unfamiliar worlds or revealing some unfamiliar angle on a seemingly familiar context. The actors generally do not play roles that adapt to the idiosyncratic habits and practices of the audience. On the contrary, they are more likely to create characters that surprise and bring novel experiences and perspectives to the audience. Both offer spectacle to varying degrees but the service worker must attend to, and submit to, the individual whereas the actor creates entertainment for a collective audience. Although the theater analogy has been useful for highlighting certain elements of interactive service work, it presents limits for the study of service by diverting attention away from the power dynamics specific to the emotional and interactive content of service interactions. These power dynamics are shaped by cultural contexts in which workers labor.

The neglect of culture is in part a by-product of disciplinary practice: sociology's geographical focus is primarily domestic contexts, and practitioners often generalize (often implicitly) about other settings based on observations derived solely from the US, and other advanced economies. Carrying out studies of service beyond the Anglo-American context, including following service firms as they travel across national boundaries, can address these shortcomings. By recognizing service work as a performance or embodiment of cultures, we can better understand the relationship between the substance of the affect produced in the workplace and the labor processes involved in its production.

Bringing culture in

Culture is often taken as a mode of control in the sociology of labor, as firms endeavor to manipulate symbols, practices, and interactions in order to channel desirable workplace behaviors (Kunda 2006). Aside from the creative industries, like film and marketing, culture is rarely understood as a dimension of work, something that workers *do*. This is because participants in the workplace (employees, managers, customers, and clients) often share assumptions about what is normative, and therefore appropriate, behavior.

Since few sociological analyses of service work venture beyond US borders or explore the cultural presuppositions of service interactions, they tend to take for granted regionally and historically specific norms of civility and etiquette (exceptions include Gottfried 2003; Hanser 2006; Poster 2007). Given that interactive service work revolves around both subtle and overt communication that is the substance of human relationships, it rests on long-standing cultural practices, including rules of etiquette, norms regarding how and when to express feelings, and guidelines for maintaining appropriate social boundaries. In other words, the bodily display of affect through gestures like smiling, nodding the head, grimacing, and so forth is subject to norms and rules that vary from place to place and from time to time. To enact service labor successfully, the worker must have expertise in shared understandings of, for example, what is considered pleasant, appropriate, and respectful behavior by locals. They must have cultural competence. In the arena of service labor, where work tasks require interaction and, more specifically, induce an affect in a customer, cultural ideas about what is appropriate, satisfying, and aesthetically desirable interaction are particularly central to producing relationships with customers that prompt the behavior desired by the firm. Service workers must be skilled in local bodily and interactive codes that convey the sentiments desired by employers.

Aesthetic labor, a relatively new framework for the study of service work, imports Pierre Bourdieu's (1984) concern with culture as a site of struggle for class distinction and recognition into the examination of service work, opening potential channels for grasping multiple codes, signals, and symbols that are part of class cultures. For Bourdieu, class inequality is generated not only through stratified distributions of wealth, income, and occupational positions, but also via access to non-monetary resources like education (and certain ordained forms of knowledge), modes of consumption, social networks, and symbols that conceal the relationship between status and money, thereby naturalizing status as linked to talent, rather than material investment. For Bourdieu, then, status distinction is linked to class cultures. The *culture* of the higher classes gains recognition in schools and allow class elites to reproduce and naturalize their status. Ways of speaking, gesturing, bodily deportment, knowledge of classical music, adoption of appropriate clothing, and so forth are rewarded in schools by teachers who tend to take upper-class culture as a proxy for educational distinction. Class actors' use of consumption to distinguish themselves from other "less desirable" classes directly implicates service workers in retail, food service, and other arenas of consumption used to cultivate distinction. Service workers are purveyors of consumption who thereby facilitate distinction struggles.

Scholars who adopt Bourdieu's frame in the study of service work regard the central activity of service as a labor of aesthetics, and they describe the ways in which workers' manner of dress, style, grooming, and speech must meet the expectations of a posh or hip clientele. The adoption of the term "aesthetic" is a rather direct acknowledgment of the centrality of cultural performance in the world of service work. For Bourdieu aesthetics are a cultural site and weaponry of struggle between classes, with the working class possessing a taste for necessity and the higher classes deploying modes of cultural consumption for status distinction.

Aesthetic labor focuses on the materiality of the service worker's body and its alteration by employers for a profit. The advantage of this framing is that it views the core activity of service work as labor that is shaped by historically specific class expectations and ambitions of customers to whom firms appeal in the interest of profit. One problem is that this recent body of literature has yet to fully grasp a labor process involved in aesthetic labor; researchers suggest that laborers are hired for already well learned class manners, for "looking good and sounding right" and that these manners may be extended in the workplace but they are not learned there (Warhurst and Nickson 2009; Williams and Connell 2010). Although employers hire workers for the class capital they exude, research so far offers little in the way of comprehending how workers learn to enact cultural protocols related to the services they provide. Much like Bourdieu's sociology, the acquisition of cultural protocols thus is relegated to the black box of early childhood socialization in the family. Employers seek to hire workers whose socialization reflects the class cultures (or the cultural aspirations) of their customers. More importantly, existing research tends to focus on Western contexts – England and the US in particular – offering little consideration for the modes of legitimate expression of class distinction struggles, the implicit rules of engagement, and the credible as well as discrediting symbols that provide the resources for such struggles across cultural boundaries. This also raises questions about interactions between class, race, and gender inequalities, as well as the extent of and effects of tolerance for inequality across various cultural settings on the service-work relation itself.

Moreover, existing studies are limited to retailers who market services to the upper-middle class. Many working-class people labor in service jobs in which they are asked to adopt new cultural rules and scripts. One question that is absolutely critical is the effect of consumer service work on working-class individuals who must abandon the manufacturing sector in the era of industrial decline due to automation and globalization. When working class people take up jobs as baristas, retail greeters, and cashier, they often must adapt their modes of interaction, dress, and behavior. How does this aesthetic shift alter the terrain of class inequality? Do working-class laborers continue, as Bourdieu asserts, to have a "taste for necessity," that is, an orientation to consume things for their practical over aesthetic value? If people of the working class, who once labored "with their hands," now adopt the manners of the middle classes, how does this affect their sense of class as well as race and gender identity? And does this transformation affect the distinction strategies of the middle classes, whose performances of class are mirrored by the working classes in the service sector?

Overlooked by both the aesthetic-labor and emotion-work schools is the cultural effort workers make to learn new ways of expressing emotions, novel styles of presenting themselves, and unfamiliar modes of interacting when their customers originate from different nations, classes, and cultures. To remedy these limitations and generate a fuller understanding of cultural processes and their role in sustaining power asymmetries involved in service, I have followed the path of one of the largest hoteliers in the world, a US chain, to Beijing, China. I conducted an ethnography of an outlet of this hotel chain, interviewing workers and managers. In this hotel, managers hire and train young women who are native to Beijing to enact what I term "bridge-work" – the acquisition of body and feeling rules dominant among customers whose national and cultural origins diverge from workers. Customers at the hotel were mostly white, male, and upper class, and they traveled from the US and other places in the Global North to engage in various business ventures while lodging at the Beijing Transluxury (a pseudonym). The hotel's interactive workers, local women, were required to speak English, adopt English names, and comport themselves in a manner reflective of an American middle-class femininity. Managers spent countless hours training these young women workers to adopt the emotional expressions, modes of interaction, and manner of comportment expected by their customers. Managers showed them how and when to smile, and when not to smile. Workers were taught how to greet customers using the appropriate titles and making eye contact. They were even taught how to walk. Consistent with American middle class notions of femininity, they were not allowed to lift tables or heavy trays, and they wore uniforms that limited their range of motion, preventing even occasional heavy labor. Managers sought to create a staff of young women workers who would appeal to the heterosexual and middle class sensibilities of their clientele. These workers served as a bridge that allowed American customers to navigate China with ease. But there was a constant tug-of-war between workers' long-held sense of appropriate behavior and the new practices workers were required to enact. A few workers resisted some of the practices; a more common response was to reinterpret the new standards of behavior to conform to workers' previous sense of etiquette and ethics.

Combined with the availability of familiar foods, beverages, and surroundings, the hotel created a space in which customers feel comfortable, competent, and knowledgeable, even while traveling to destinations far from home. Such ease of traversing national and cultural boundaries facilitated by bridging labor creates a kind of cosmopolitan capital. To put it more simply, workers' adoption of the cultural practices of customers relieves those customers of the effort required to engage in and understand new cultural practices when they travel across borders, allowing them to traverse the globe with few cultural obstacles. The dynamic reproduces and extends the advantages – and power – of the largely white, male, upper-class clientele of the hotels and organizations like it.

In sum, while research has found that service workers must "look good and act right," to use the phrase that has come to define aesthetic labor. I find that they must *look familiar and sound understandable*, which is taken for granted when workers and customers share cultural traditions, languages, symbols, and expectations for comportment and interaction. The concept of bridge-work pinpoints the efforts required by wage workers to manage these differences; its partner concept, cosmopolitan capital, suggests that customers benefit from these efforts in their ability to crisscross national and cultural boundaries without the burden of learning regional languages and practices. They retain a sense of competence in interaction, and thus status and dignity, even while traveling to distant locales. The labor of bridgework that enables customers' accumulation of cosmopolitan capital illuminates a power relation structured by global political-economic hierarchies.

Other sociologists are using case studies from cultural contexts outside the US to understand contemporary shifts in service work as well as the specific cultural underpinnings of service in diverse places. Of particular note is Winifred Poster's (2007) research on call centers in India, where managers subject workers to immersion in American cultural practices, in what she terms "national identity management." Hanser (2006) examines the impact of socialist organization on a department store in China. Gottfried (2003) uses the concept of aesthetic labor to describe service labor in Japan, a term that leaves open the possibility of inquiring about the cultural and historic specificity of service labor. Collectively, these are promising points of departure, first, for reaching beyond Anglo-American boundaries and addressing some of the culturally bound assumptions that have been part of studies of service work, and, second, for specifying how and under what conditions the more generic properties of the labor process occur, as well as how they combine with local forms of culture and organization. The task remains, though, to build these studies into comparative frameworks that can explain how cultural practices are reshaped by and reshape service labor in diverse times and places.

Conclusion

The sociology of service labor is a relatively new scholarly field, one that has struggled in the shadow of industrial labor, long thought to embody the most progressive forces of social change. The key feature of service work, its immateriality, renders it particularly challenging to research. Whether it is the labor of a doctor, lawyer, therapist, teacher, retail cashier, or food server, service labor centers on human interactions that are ephemeral and difficult to study directly without fundamentally altering their character. Scholars have begun to face these challenges by conceptualizing various dimensions of service work, including its emotional, aesthetic, and interactive facets, its triangles and bridges. This chapter insists that the study of service now ought to acknowledge the rich bedrock of culture that sustains and contours the substance of this labor. The cultural foundation of service becomes most apparent when scholars move between cultural boundaries as they study service-labor processes. Notions of service that prioritize aesthetic presentation of the body also help to point us in the direction of culture (Nickson and Baum 2017). But the absence of studies that focus on cultural variation in the form and content of service labor limits our understanding of the fundamental role of culture in its performance. My own research suggests the ways that service professionals straddle cultures by reaching beyond their primary body and feeling rules to learn to perform habits and norms familiar to their customers. Such work sustains global power relations by preserving travelers' (in this case mostly Western, male elites') sense of cultural competence across international boundaries, even as workers enact new cultural competencies involved in engagement with their patrons' body and feeling rules.

References

Barber, Kristen. 2016. *Styling Masculinity: Gender, Class, and Inequality in the Men's Grooming Industry.* New Brunswick, NJ: Rutgers University Press.

Bourdieu, Pierre. 1984. *Distinction: A Social Critique of the Judgment of Taste*. London: Routledge and Kegan Paul.

Fuller, Linda, and Vicki Smith. 1991. "Consumers' Reports: Management by Customers in a Changing Economy." *Work, Employment and Society* 5(1):1–16.

Gottfried, Heidi. 2003. "Temp(t)ing Bodies: Shaping Gender at Work in Japan." *Sociology: Journal of the British Sociological Association* 37(2):257–76.

Hanser, Amy. 2006. "A Tale of Two Sales Floors: Changing Service-Work Regimes in China." Pp. 77–98 in *Working in China: Ethnographies of Labor and Workplace Transformation*, edited by C.K. Lee. London: Routledge.

Hochschild, Arlie Russell. 1983. *The Managed Heart: Commercialization of Human Feeling*. Berkeley: University of California Press.

International Labour Organization. 2007. *Key Indicators of the Labor Market*. Geneva: International Labour Organization.

Kang, Miliann. 2010. *The Managed Hand: Race, Gender, and the Body in Beauty Service Work*. Berkeley: University of California Press.

Kunda, Gideon. 2006. *Engineering Culture: Control and Commitment in a High-Tech Corporation*. Philadelphia, PA: Temple University Press.

Lazzarato, M. 1996. "Immaterial Labor." Pp. 133–47 in *Radical Thought in Italy: A Potential Politics*, edited by P. Colilli, E. Emery, M. Hardt, and P. Virno. London: University of Minnesota Press.

Leidner, Robin. 1993. *Fast Food, Fast Talk*. Berkeley: University of California Press.

Macdonald, Cameron Lynne, and Carmen Sirianni. 1996. *Working in the Service Society*. Philadelphia, PA: Temple University Press.

Nickson, Dennis, and Tom Baum. 2017. "Young at Heart but What about My Body? Age and Aesthetic Labour in the Hospitality and Retail Industries." Pp. 539–59 in *The Palgrave Handbook of Age Diversity and Work*, edited by E. Parry and J. McCarthy. London: Palgrave Macmillan.

Orzechowicz, David. 2008. "Privileged Emotion Managers: The Case of Actors." *Social Psychology Quarterly* 71(2): 143–56.

Otis, Eileen. 2011. Markets and Bodies: Women, Service Work and the Making of Inequality in China. Palo Alto: Stanford University Press.

Otis, Eileen M. 2016. "Bridgework: Globalization, Gender, and Service Labor at a Luxury Hotel." *Gender & Society* 30(6):912–34.

Ott, Brian. 2016. "The Limits of Control in Service Work: Interactive Routines and Interactional Competence." Pp. 155–83 in *Research in the Sociology of Work*. Vol. 29, edited by S. Vallas. Bingley: Emerald Group.

Poster, Winifred. 2007. "Who's on the Line: Indian Call Center Agents Pose as Americans for U.S.-Outsourced Firms." *Industrial Relations* 46(3):271–304.

Sallaz, J.J. 2002. "The House Rules: Autonomy and Interests among Service Workers in the Contemporary Casino Industry." *Work and Occupations* 29(4):394–427.

Warhurst, Chris, and Dennis Nickson. 2009. "'Who's Got the Look?' Emotional, Aesthetic and Sexualized Labour in Interactive Services." *Gender, Work and Organizations* 16(3):385–404.

Watson, James L. 1997. *Golden Arches East: McDonald's in East Asia*. Stanford, CA: Stanford University Press.

Wharton, Amy. 1993. "The Affective Consequences of Service Work: Managing Emotions on the Job." *Work and Occupations* 20(2):205–32.

Williams, Christine, and Catherine Connell. 2010. "'Looking Good and Sounding Right': Aesthetic Labor and Social Inequality in the Retail Industry." *Work and Occupations* 37(3):349–77.

Zelizer, Viviana. 2007. *The Purchase of Intimacy*. Princeton, NJ: Princeton University Press.

44

Carework
Cultural frameworks and global circuits

Pei-Chia Lan

Introduction

Carework refers to the work of caring for others, including unpaid care for family members and friends, and paid care for wards and clients. As a form of reproductive labor, carework is necessary to the maintenance of individuals, families, and communities. It includes emotional and nursing care for children, elders, the sick, and the disabled, as well as domestic work such as cooking and cleaning (Misra 2007). By deploying the term "carework," scholars and advocates emphasize that care is hard work – physically and emotionally – the value of which is nevertheless overrated and underpaid.

This chapter considers how culture constitutes the ways we understand and conduct carework. "Culture" designates two meanings here. First, the cultures of carework refer to the ideologies, values, norms, customs, and common senses about how care should be organized and done. They provide "toolkits" of cultural resources (Swidler 1986) from which individuals and families develop strategies of actions. Second, the scripts and practices of carework vary and travel across socio-cultural contexts. Here culture designates worldviews and lifestyles shared within particular ethnic groups, religious communities, or nation-states.

Privatization is a dominant cultural framework that shapes how we think about, arrange, and make sense of care. It also creates a paradox between the moralization of unpaid care and the devaluation of paid carework. The employment of migrant women as helpers, nannies, and caregivers has grown around the globe. However, the ethnic boundary and cultural distance between care providers and care recipients pose challenges to the performance of such intimate labor. Various societies, with distinct combinations of care regime and migration regime, develop different institutional solutions to this conundrum. People located in various segments of what I call "global care circuits" manage to negotiate the cultural meaning of care at the intersection of the public-private, paid-unpaid, and love-money dichotomies.

Privatization of care

The public-private divide has greatly influenced the ways people think about care, but what constitutes "private" and "public" is developing over time across various historical and social

417

contexts (Armstrong and Armstrong 2005). I identify four different ways in which people refer to the privatization of care; these discursive frameworks are analytically distinct and yet intertwined in reality.

First, care is viewed as a family responsibility that is preferably conducted in private homes. Here the "private" refers to the domestic realm as opposed to space outside it. The doctrine of "separate spheres," which became influential in nineteenth-century Europe and the US under the impact of industrial capitalism, placed a moral value on the domestic sphere in contrast to the commercial world. The home was defined as a haven from the uncertainties and calculation of commercial life and also as "the locus of social and personal morality" (Laslett and Brenner 1989:387).

Second, carework is viewed as women's natural endowment and social calling, either at home or in the labor market. The "cult of domesticity" as a Victorian cultural legacy made housekeeping women's vocation and associated carework with maternal love and feminine virtues (Cott 1977). Although much reproductive labor that used to be done at home has been outsourced to the market, what is consistent across forms is that reproductive labor is constructed as feminine as opposed to masculine as "public" (Nakano Glenn 1992).

The doctrine of domestic intimacy assumes a particular model of family that consists of two heterosexual parents, including a male breadwinner. The nuclear family is nevertheless a recent social organization that is mostly limited to white, Protestant, bourgeoisie in Northwest Europe and North America; it is also a class-specific, highly gendered, ideological construct that echoes the cultural belief in individualism and connotes self-sufficiency and personal freedom (Dalley 1988). This hegemonic ideology overlooks family variations along social divides such as race, class, and marital status (Smith 1993); it also disguises the fact that even privileged, middle-class Euro-American families rely on networks of care and interdependency (Hansen 2005).

Third, carework is considered a "labor of love," an emotional labor or intimate labor "tending to the intimate needs of an individual inside and outside their home" (Boris and Parrenas 2010:5). Here the public-private binary distinguishes intimacy and sentiments from economic rationality and market transactions. Neoliberal economists, along with lay observers, assume that care workers, whether paid or unpaid, have altruistic motivations and receive moral rewards from their caregiving; this "prisoners of love" argument explains the low wage and devaluation of carework (England 2005).

Finally, the privatization of care also refers to the marketization or commodification of care. The public-private distinction is conflated with the divide between state administration and market economy. Marketization of care describes the processes that replace public services and welfare provisions with care services bought and sold in the market. This trend is particularly salient in Europe in recent decades. Facing the critique that public services are too costly and lead to care dependence, politicians introduced the market principle as a neoliberal solution to the restructuring of welfare states (Knijn 2000).

Paying for care often raises concerns about possible corruption and disruption regarding the informal relations of intimacy. Viviana Zelizer (2004) argues that this conception of "hostile worlds" treats economic activities and intimate relations as distinct arenas, the mixing of which will result in inevitable disorder. On the one hand, market compensation would contaminate and undermine moral obligation. On the other hand, emotional ties may complicate and even undermine business-like service relations.

The cultural scripts of privatizing care orient people's preferences about the arrangement of care; they also shape policy debate about how to distribute care services and responsibilities among the state, market, family, and voluntary sector. The meanings and practices of carework are nevertheless subject to transformation, especially in the contexts of transnational migration.

Global care chains

Well-to-do households around the globe are hiring women of ethnic minorities or immigrant status to be maids, nannies, or caregivers. Arlie Hochschild (2000:131) uses the term "global care chains" to refer to "a series of personal links between people across the globe based on the paid and unpaid work of caring." The concept rephrases what Rhacel Parrenas (2001) describes as the "international division of reproductive labor" or "transnational transfer of caretaking": migrant women from poor countries work overseas to pick up the carework transferred from middle-class women in rich countries, while leaving their children back home to be cared by local domestic workers from even poorer households.

The global care chains present a paradox between the moral elevation of unpaid caring labor and the monetary devaluation of paid carework. On the one hand, the ideological value of childcare has become greater than ever in the receiving countries. Sharon Hays (1996) coined the term "intensive mothering" to observe that child-rearing is viewed as child-centered, expert-guided, emotionally absorbing, and financially expensive. On the other hand, childcare as an occupation remains underpaid, deskilled, low status, and thus not preferred by local workers. How do we explain such a paradox? How do people reconcile intensive mothering with the reality of marketization and racialization of carework?

The expanding recruitment of migrant domestic workers is a result of the privatization of care. When care is considered a family duty and women's responsibility, the facilities of social care remain in shortage and husbands' share of labor is limited. Women thus seek market surrogates to be their "shadow laborers" (Macdonald 1998); they rely on the labor of other women to achieve their duties as wife, mother, and daughter-in-law. Besides, women prefer hiring live-in helpers because they consider in-home care a better arrangement that approximates the ideal of care provided by stay-at-home mothers and family members.

Market outsourcing of care nevertheless stirs a sense of guilt, jealousy, or deprivation among women. Anxious mothers try to maintain a hierarchical division of labor by distinguishing the "menial" and "spiritual" aspects of carework. This split enables middle-class women to magnify the significance of mothers at home and to minimize the presence of nannies (Macdonald 1998). As mothers they can transfer part of carework to colored or working-class women without disturbing the norm of female domesticity or the moral meaning of home (Roberts 1997).

Viewing caring labor as women's familial duty weakens the labor position of hired caregivers. A female employer tends to treat the worker as "an extension of the more menial part of herself rather than an autonomous employee" (Rollins 1985:183). She transfers to the surrogate not only the work but also the social expectations placed upon women associated with unpaid carework. Thus, she often makes requests that are unreasonable by the standards stipulated in employment contracts, and she ignores that a worker's labor performance is not bound by moral norms tied to emotional commitment or family responsibility.

Hochschild (2003) applies Marx's notion of surplus labor to conceptualize the transfer of emotion and affect from "Third World" mothers to "First World" children as subtracting "emotional surplus value." The exploitation of emotional labor along global care chains is analogous to the "global commodity chains" found in manufacturing (Yeates 2005). Conceptually thinking in terms of global care chains has attracted criticism: First, it treats emotion as a fixed, stable commodity and fails to account for the production of multiple affections and the shifting networks of emotion that arise during migrations and transnational encounters (Brown 2015). Second, it assumes a linear model of transferring and extracting care labor as one-way traffic without explicating how the care of migrant mothers for their own children changes and continues in a new, transnational mode (Yeates 2005).

Third, the concept of global care chains is criticized for reinforcing geographic and ideological binaries such as the Global North/Global South and First World/Third World (Kofman and Raghuram 2012). Finally, the portrait focuses on the links of transnational care transfer between a series of nuclear families (Yeates 2005), privileging the experiences of heterosexual women with children and overlooking the participation of single women and gay men in the global care chain (Manalansan 2006).

The remainder of the chapter addresses these lacunas by looking into the institutional configurations of carework and the microdynamics of outsourcing care. The intersection of care regime and migration regime explains institutional differentiation across countries, even among East Asian countries sharing a similar tradition of familism. Focusing on the case of Taiwan, I examine how adult children negotiate the meanings of care and divide caring labor with their market agents in the global care circuits.

Care regime and migration regime

Feminist scholars have proposed the concept *care regime* to describe a specific policy logic that divides care between the state, market, family, and the voluntary sector (Daly and Lewis 2000) by association with particular scripts of "care culture," that is, dominant national and local cultural discourses on what constitute appropriate care and who should provide it (Williams 2012). For example, Diane Sainsbury (1999) identifies three different kinds of care regimes: the male-breadwinner regime (carework is privatized, unpaid), the separate-gender-roles regime (women receive state benefits for caring responsibilities in the family), and the individual-earner-care regime (care in and outside of the family is subsidized by the state).

Another institutional factor that shapes the employment of migration care workers is *migration regime*, which concerns a multitude of state regulations that promote or discourage the entry and employment of migrants (Lutz 2016). It involves national norms and practices that constitute ethnonational boundaries and govern relationships between the ethnic majority and minority groups (Williams 2012).

The various ways of interweaving care regimes and migration regimes result in distinct policy patterns. Due to limited welfare benefits, southern European countries (Spain, Italy, Greece) develop a "migrant-in-the-family" pattern in which households rely on live-in migrant caregivers to sustain the cultural tradition of familism (Bettio, Simonazzi, and Villa 2006). By contrast, Germany, the Netherlands, and the Nordic states have hardly acknowledged the need for such labor migration, leaving migrant care workers to live and work illegally (Lutz 2016).

Although the familistic model of care has widely existed in East Asia, their policies regarding recruitment of migrant care workers differ. Ito Peng (2016) offers a typology to map various approaches to care and the uses of foreign care workers in East Asia. Taiwan, Hong Kong, and Singapore adopt a *liberal market-oriented* approach in which much care is commodified through the purchase of care services in the private market, often by hiring foreign workers, whereas Japan and Korea share a *regulated institutional* approach to the outsourcing of care: long-term care insurance schemes collectivize and socialize the purchase of services in which cultural preference is given to the employment of native or co-ethnic workers, limiting the use of foreign workers.

The case of Japan demonstrates the adaptability and resilience of care culture. Although a substantial amount of elder care is still borne by family members, Japan implemented long-term care insurance (LTCI) in 2000, transforming elderly care "from a needs based care provision model to a rights-based universal social insurance scheme" (Peng 2002:430). The rapid expansion of social care for the elderly has created a demand for qualified care workers that could not be met by existing labor pools, but the government has been hesitant to recruit foreign workers. Japan's migration regime opts for the employment of skilled migrants instead of guest workers and prefers ethnic affinity to ethnic difference when hiring foreigners.

Only recently did Japan's government start to recruit migrant care workers under careful regulation. Since 2008 Japan has accepted registered nurse and certified care workers based on the Economic Partnership Agreements (EPAs) with Indonesia, the Philippines, and Vietnam. Although this new policy indicates a relaxation of Japan's migration regime, it affirms Japan's care culture of institutional professionalism. The EPA program recruits only skilled foreigners who are expected to take the national exams for certification after a training period, and their workplaces are limited to care facilities and hospitals. Japan's emphasis on the cultural significance of care – ideal care is strongly associated with familiarity with local language and culture – reinforces its distrust of foreign workers. The training curriculum aims to bridge cultural distance and tame the otherness of migrants so that they can perform professional care as a localized cultural practice (Lan 2016).

Subcontracting filial piety

Despite facing problems of population aging and care deficit similar to those of Japan, Taiwan has adopted a different approach – recruiting live-in migrant care workers as temporary "guest" labor. The ethnic difference of migrant caregivers is considered a means to rationalize their inferior status at the employer's home and their social exclusion in the receiving country. I coined the term "subcontracting filial piety" to describe how Taiwanese adult children transfer the filial duty of caring for their aging parents to non-family employees (Lan 2002, 2006). By incorporating migrant workers as surrogate family, employers can maintain the traditional family form of three-generation cohabitation as well as the cultural ideal of filial piety.

Instead of viewing market service and domestic intimacy as "hostile worlds," I follow Zelizer's (2005) approach of "connected lives" to explore how moral obligations can be confirmed and assured by market transactions. In this view, paying for quality care provided by non-family caregivers is itself an act of care and an expression of love. Joan Tronto offers a way to identify various components of care: caring about (recognizing the necessity of care), taking care of (assuming some responsibility for the identified need and determining how to respond to it), care-giving (the direct meeting of needs for care), and care-receiving (the object of care responds to the care it receives). The market transfer of care divides these components and assigns them between agents across social divides: "Caring about, and taking care of, are the duties of the powerful. Care-giving and care-receiving are left to the less powerful" (Tronto 1993:114).

In Han Chinese societies, *taking care of* aging parents is traditionally considered the duty of sons, although the actual work of *caregiving* is mostly borne by the sons' wives. The traditional idea of caregiving is associated with the hierarchical concept of "serving" rather than the more egalitarian notion of "caring" (Liu 1998). Hiring a migrant caregiver becomes a bargaining strategy for Taiwanese daughters-in-law to avert subordination to patrilineal family authority. In other words, there is a "transfer chain of filial care" consisting of two linkages: first, *gender transfer* of the filial duty from the son to the daughter-in-law; and second, *market transfer* of carework from the daughter-in-law to non-family employees, who are still predominantly women.

The metaphor of "subcontracting filial piety" may seem to suggest that adult children outsource most of the physical and emotional labor to migrant women. Yet in fact, most adult children I interviewed are still in charge: they carry out a substantial amount of carework, including managing medical and physical care, supervising care workers, and comforting both the elderly and migrant workers who have to deal with seniors with stubborn personalities or emotional difficulties. Their filial duty and care labor are not simply outsourced, as a linear model of transfer chain implies; rather, they are transformed and reconstituted in the transnational division of carework.

The adult children develop a stratified division of labor with migrant care workers and form a network of horizontal cooperation between kin and fictive-kin caregivers. These arrangements could improve rather than diminish the quality of care. In some cases, aging parents feel less embarrassed to receive hands-on care, such as helping with toileting or bathing, from migrant women than from their own children. Outsourcing certain parts of care labor may help to maintain the dignity of care recipients. In addition, some aging parents prefer to hire migrant workers to unburden their children from hands-on care and also to help their children with housework and childcare. In these cases, paying for care does not disrupt but facilitates intimate ties and reciprocal exchanges across generations.

Many Taiwanese elders develop strong emotional ties with their migrant helpers, moving their contract relations into the terrain of moral economy. Migrant care workers shared with me narratives similar to this one: "*A-ma* ('Grandma' in Taiwanese dialect) calls me daughter. She does not treat me like a worker or maid. She treats me like her daughter." At the time when migrant workers are leaving for vacation or at the end of a contract, the seniors often burst into tears and migrant workers also feel emotionally torn. The elderly and migrant home caregivers, both socially vulnerable, may develop relationships of reciprocity and solidarity.

Market-based interpersonal relationships can produce new forms of intimacy and affect that are not regulated by filial piety or constrained by existing cultural norms. Affective display to children, especially through verbal communication and body language such as kisses or hugs, was not common among earlier generations of Taiwanese parents. When observing the interaction between migrant caregivers and their clients, I was often surprised at the changing behaviors of Taiwanese elders. While the caregivers softly kissed their cheeks or tightly hugged them saying "I love you," the elders, who probably never verbally expressed affection to their children in an explicit way, replied in broken English, with a naughty smile: "I love you, too!"

Global care circuits

Replacing a linear model of "global care chains" or "filial care chains," the concept of "global care circuits" describes relations of interdependence, mutual exchange, and reciprocal influence in the performance of reproductive labor between different actors and across generations, sectors, and locales. The idea of *circuit* refers to networks that connect multiple actors situated in different geographic and social locales and that consist of dynamic, meaningful, incessantly negotiated interactions (Zelizer 2004). The exchanges of labor, emotions, and resources via global care circuits are not one-way traffic of "care drain" but take place in multiple directions and with interchangeable forms.

The notion of global care circuits echoes what Loretta Baldassar and Laura Merla (2014) describe as "care circulation" within the extended networks of transnational families: informal care is given and returned at different times and to varying degrees across the life course between migrant and non-migrant kin. Similarly, the previous section has shown reciprocal, yet asymmetrical, interchange between migrant caregivers and Taiwanese elders, as well as new ways of care circulation between adult children and aging parents.

The global care circuits also encompass care circulation across paid and unpaid sectors. Migrant women are often involved in multiple forms of reproductive labor in their intersecting routes of labor and marriage migration (Kofman 2012; Lan 2008). Migrant women may seek marriage as a strategy to escape the deskilling status of domestic work and a means to gain residency and citizenship in receiving countries (McKay 2003). Some even marry their employers, who are usually middle-aged divorced or windowed men, and continue caring for their frail or ill parents; their foreign husbands see them as marriageable precisely because their experience of paid carework (Lan 2006). Many marriage migrants choose the occupation of carework as a socially respectable position; for example, Filipina entertainers who marry Japanese men become local care workers to escape sexualized stigmas associated with their previous job (Suzuki 2007). At different stages of the life cycle, migrant women partake in multiple forms of migration and carework to improve their life chances in relation to racialized constraints and feminized niches in the global care circuits.

Global care circuits also link the carework conducted by migrant workers in receiving countries with their unpaid care labor for their own families back home. Much research has examined migrant workers' practice of "transnational motherhood" (Hondagneu-Sotelo and Avila 1997; Parrenas 2001); despite their physical absence, migrant mothers use the flows of remittance, gifts, and telephone calls and messages to maintain their virtual presence in their children's lives. Research has yet to explore the topic of "transnational daughterhood," that is, how migrant daughters' care for their own parents continues and changes in a transnational mode.

Some single daughters grab the opportunity of working overseas to escape parental control at home, especially the pressure for getting married (Lan 2006). Yet, some migrant daughters struggle emotionally because overseas posts deprive them of the physical proximity needed to take care of their own parents. Many migrant daughters compensate their physical absence by sending remittances and gifts back home. The ways of "paying back" for their parents also include the purchase of land or building or renovating the family house, and helping out brothers and other siblings with educational expenses or economic investments such as buying a means of transportation or opening a small business like a grocery store or an internet café.

While working overseas to take care of others' parents, migrant women are often critical about the decline of filial tradition in Taiwan. For instance, Jenny, from Indonesia, was taking care of a paralyzed elderly Taiwanese man. She pitied the client for receiving inadequate care and weak affection from his son and daughter-in-law: "My employer [the eldest son] comes here maybe five times a year. The daughter-in-law just comes here bringing the food, and they don't care if he eats or not." And she firmly said: "I will not leave my parents to a stranger."

Migrant workers like Jenny disapprove of the outsourcing of elderly care. Instead, they claim a more authentic version of familism in their own country with its sustained tradition of filial care and strong emotional bonds among extended family members. The care culture in sending countries may also influence how migrant workers understand and conduct their paid jobs overseas. In sum, global care circuits do not "extract" or "exploit" the filial care of migrant daughters but can strengthen their cultural belief in familism and sustain the kinship ties through various means of transnational links.

Conclusion

The cultures of carework are parts of toolkits from which social agents construct interpersonal relations in care service as well as policy logics of welfare regimes. Despite facing similar problems of care deficits and labor shortages, various countries develop distinct policy solutions depending on the intersecting formation of migration regime and care regime. The privatization of care is a dominant cultural script that locates ideal care in the private sphere of nuclear families as the moral duty of female kin. The outsourcing of care, however, does not necessarily interrupt domestic intimacy or lower the quality of care, but it can become a means for the family to sustain kin networks and moral obligations through cooperation with market agents.

My concept "global care circuits" can be used to examine the multidirectional exchanges of care, emotions, and labor between different actors and across generations, sectors, and locales. The concept decenters the nuclear family and incorporates local and transnational networks of kin and fictive kin; instead of focusing on the exploitative effect of commodification, it looks into the moral economy of carework. It thereby opens up a series of possibilities for future researchers to explore how people negotiate the intertwined meanings of care and reconfigure power relations in the uneven terrain of social inequalities under conditions of migration and globalization.

References

Armstrong, Pat, and Hugh Armstrong. 2005. "Public and Private: Implications for Care Work." *Sociological Review* 53(2):167–87.

Baldassar, Loretta, and Laura Merla. 2014. "Locating Transnational Care Circulation in Migration and Family Studies." Pp. 25–58 in *Transnational Families, Migration and the Circulation of Care: Understanding Mobility and Absence in Family Life*, edited by L. Baldassar and L. Merla. New York: Routledge.

Bettio, Francesca, Annamaria Simonazzi, and Paola Villa. 2006. "Change in Care Regimes and Female Migration: The 'Care Drain' in the Mediterranean." *Journal of European Social Policy* 16(3):271–85.

Boris, Eileen, and Rhacel Salazar Parrenas. 2010. *Intimate Labors: Cultures, Technologies, and the Politics of Care*. Stanford, CA: Stanford University Press.

Brown, Rachel H. 2015. "Re-examining the Transnational Nanny: Migrant Carework Beyond the Chain." *International Feminist Journal of Politics* 18(2):210–29.

Cott, Nancy F. 1977. *The Bonds of Womanhood: "Woman's Sphere" In New England*. New Haven, CT: Yale University Press.

Dalley, Gillian. 1988. *Ideologies of Caring: Rethinking Community and Collectivism*. Basingstoke, Hampshire: Macmillan Education.

Daly, Mary, and Jane Lewis. 2000. "The Concept of Social Care and the Analysis of Contemporary Welfare States." *British Journal of Sociology* 51(2):281–98.

England, Paula. 2005. "Emerging Theories of Care Work." *Annual Review of Sociology* 31:381–99.

Hansen, Karen V. 2005. *Not-So-Nuclear Families: Class, Gender, and Networks of Care*. New Brunswick, NJ: Rutgers University Press.

Hays, Sharon. 1996. *The Cultural Contradictions of Motherhood*. New Haven, CT: Yale University Press.

Hochschild, Arlie R. 2000. "Global Care Chains and Emotional Surplus Value." Pp. 130–46 in *On the Edge: Globalization and the New Millennium*, edited by T. Giddens and W. Hutton. London: Sage.

———. 2003. *The Commercialization of Intimate Life: Notes from Home and Work*. Berkeley: University of California Press.

Hondagneu-Sotelo, Pierrette, and Ernestine Avila. 1997. "'I'm Here, But I'm There': The Meanings of Latina Transnational Motherhood." *Gender and Society* 11(5):548–71.

Knijn, Trudie. 2000. "Marketization and the Struggling Logics of (Home) Care in the Netherlands." Pp. 232–48 in *Care Work: Gender, Class, and the Welfare State*, edited by M.H. Meyer. New York: Routledge.

Kofman, Eleonore. 2012. "Rethinking Care Through Social Reproduction: Articulating Circuits of Migration." *Social Politics* 19(1):142–62.

Kofman, Eleonore and Parvati Raghuram. 2012. "Women, Migration, and Care: Explorations of Diversity and Dynamism in the Global South." *Social Politics* 19(3):408–32.

Lan, Pei-Chia. 2002. "Subcontracting Filial Piety: Elder Care in Ethnic Chinese Immigrant Households in California." *Journal of Family Issues* 23(7):812–35.

———. 2006. *Global Cinderellas: Migrant Domestics and Newly Rich Employers in Taiwan*. Durham, NC: Duke University Press.

———. 2008. "New Global Politics of Reproductive Labor: Gendered Labor and Marriage Migration." *Sociology Compass* 2(6):1801–15.

———. 2016. "Deferential Surrogates and Professional Others: Recruitment and Training of Migrant Care Workers in Taiwan and Japan." *Positions: Asia Critique* 24(1):253–79.

Laslett, Barbara, and Johanna Brenner. 1989. "Gender and Social Reproduction: Historical Perspectives." *Annual Review of Sociology* 15:381–404.

Liu, Zhong-Dong. 1998. *Women's Medical Sociology*. Taipei: Feminist Bookstore.

Lutz, Helma. 2016. "Introduction: Migrant Domestic Worker in Europe." Pp. 1–10 in *Migration and Domestic Work: A European Perspective on A Global Theme*, edited by H. Lutz. New York: Routledge.

Manalansan, Martin F. 2006. "Queer Intersections: Sexuality and Gender in Migration Studies." *International Migration Review* 40(1):224–49.

Macdonald, Cameron. 1998. "Manufacturing Motherhood: The Shadow Work of Nannies and Au Pair." *Qualitative Sociology* 21(1):25–53.

McKay, Deirdre. 2003. "Filipinas in Canada – De-skilling as a Push Toward Marriage." Pp. 23–52 in *Wife or Worker?: Asian Women and Migration*, edited by N. Piper and M. Roces. Lanham, MD: Rowman and Littlefield.

Misra, Joya. 2007. "Carework." Pp. 402–4 in *Blackwell Encyclopedia of Sociology*, edited by G. Ritzer. Malden, MA: Blackwell.

Nakano Glenn, Evelyn. 1992. "From Servitude to Service Work: Historical Continuities in the Racial Division of Paid Reproductive Labor." *Signs* 18(1):27–69.

Parrenas, Rhacel. 2001. *Servants of Globalization: Women, Migration and Domestic Work*. Stanford, CA: Stanford University Press.

Peng, Ito. 2002. "Social Care in Crisis: Gender, Democracy, and Welfare Restructuring in Japan." *Social Politics* 9(3):411–43.

———. 2016. "Shaping and Reshaping Care and Migration in East and Southeast Asia." Paper presented at Im/mobilities and Care Work: Social Reproduction and Migrant Families Workshop, August 8, University of Toronto.

Roberts, Dorothy. 1997. "Spiritual and Menial Housework." *Yale Journal of Law and Feminism* 9(1):49–80.

Rollins, Judith. 1985. *Between Women: Domestics and their Employers*. Philadelphia, PA: Temple University Press.

Sainsbury, Diane. 1999. "Gender and Social-Democratic Welfare States." Pp. 47–74 in *Gender and Welfare State Regimes*, edited by D. Sainsbury. New York: Oxford University Press.

Smith, Dorothy E. 1993. "The Standard North American Family: SNAF as an Ideological Code." *Journal of Family Issues* 14(1):50–65.

Suzuki, Nobue. 2007. "Carework and Migration: Japanese Perspectives on the Japan-Philippines Economic Partnership Agreement." *Asian and Pacific Migration Journal* 16(3):357–81.

Swidler, Ann. 1986. "Culture in Action: Symbols and Strategies." *American Sociological Review* 51(2):273–86.

Tronto, Joan C. 1993. *Moral Boundaries: A Political Argument for an Ethic of Care*. New York: Routledge.

Williams, Fiona. 2012. "Converging Variations in Migrant Care Work in Europe." *Journal of European Social Policy* 22(4):363–76.

Yeates, Nicola. 2005. "A Global Political Economy of Care." *Social Policy and Society* 4(2):227–34.

Zelizer, Viviana A. 2004. "Circuits of commerce." Pp. 122–44 in *Self, Social Structure, and Beliefs: Explorations in Sociology*, edited by J. Alexander, G. Marx, and C. Williams. Berkeley: University of California Press.

———. 2005. *The Purchase of Intimacy*. Princeton, NJ: Princeton University Press.

45

Legal culture and cultures of legality

Susan S. Silbey

Introduction

Culture is a hotly debated and contested construct, evidenced by the existence and content of this handbook. Understandably, the importation of this term into legal scholarship is thus fraught with unfortunate confusion. Some of it derives from intermingling two meanings of culture: one meaning names a particular world of beliefs and practices associated with a specific group; the second meaning is analytic rather than empirical, referring to the outcome of social analysis – an abstracted *system* of symbols and meanings, both the product and context of social action. In the former use, referring to the distinctive customs, opinions, and practices of a particular group or society, the term is often used in the plural, as in the legal cultures of Japan and China, or in reference to African or Latin cultures. In the latter analytic sense, the word is used in the singular, as in legal culture, or the culture of academia.

Since the cultural turn of the 1980s, use of the word "culture" has proliferated so much that the historic confusion has infested scholarship in almost every field of inquiry where it is invoked. In addition to the thousands of journal articles, one can find hundreds of books with law and culture or legal culture in the title. Some of these call for cultural study of law, as if it had not been going on for decades; others title collections of diverse essays under a general rubric of law and culture; yet others treat culture as a serious theoretical concept (e.g., Benton 2002; Bracey 2006; Rosen 2006). The unprecedented and rapidly proliferating use of the concept has unfortunately exacerbated the traditionally unruly discourse. In this chapter, I hope to offer helpful clarification, distinguish alternative uses, and provide a short lexicon to some of the concept of legal culture's progeny in legal scholarship – legal ideology, legal consciousness, legality, and cultures of legality.

A concise conceptualization

Contemporary cultural analyses have moved beyond conceptions of culture as either everything humanly produced or as only what calls itself culture (e.g., arts, music, theater, fashion, literature, religion, media, and education). In its most effective and theoretically plausible uses, the concept of culture names an analytically identified system of symbols and meanings and their associated social practices. It is invoked (1) to recognize signs and performances, meanings and actions as inseparable; (2) yet, "*to disentangle, for the purpose of analysis* [only], the semiotic influences on action from the other sorts of influences – demographic, geographical, biological, technological, economic, and so on – that they are necessarily mixed with in any concrete sequence of behavior" (Sewell 2005:160, emphasis added). (3) Although formal organizational attributes and human interactions share symbolic and cognitive resources, many cultural resources are discrete, local, and intended for specific purposes. Nonetheless, (4) it is possible to observe general patterns so that we are able to speak of a culture, or cultural system at specified scales and levels of social organization. "System and practice are complementary concepts: each presupposes the other" (Sewell 2005:164), although the constituent practices are neither uniform, logical, static, nor autonomous. (5) As a collection of semiotic resources deployed in interactions, "culture is not a power, something to which social events, behaviors, institutions, or processes can be causally attributed; it is a context, something within which [events, behaviors, institutions, and processes] can be intelligibly – that is, thickly – described" (Geertz 1973:14). (6) Variation and conflict concerning the meaning and use of these symbols and resources are likely and expected because at its core culture "is an intricate system of claims about how to understand the world and act on it" (Perin 2005:xii).

Genesis of the term "legal culture"

Despite often abstruse debate, many scholars find the concept of culture particularly useful when they want to focus on aspects of legal action that are not confined to official legal texts, roles, performances, or offices. Friedman (1975) is credited with introducing the concept to emphasize the fact that law is best understood and described as a product of social forces and itself a conduit of those same forces. Friedman was a founding father of American law-and-society (or socio-legal) scholarship, and as such he was intent on making explicit the unofficial, and what otherwise would have been thought of non-legal, behaviors as nonetheless important for shaping what is more conventionally understood as legal. Although law can be defined as "a set of rules or norms, written or unwritten, about right and wrong behavior, duties, and rights" (Friedman 1975:2), according to Friedman, this conventional notion attributed too much independence and efficacy to the law on the books and acknowledged too little the power and predictability of what is often called the law in action. To advance a social scientific study of law in action, Friedman adopted the model of a system – a set of structures that process inputs (demands and resources) from an environment to which it sends its outputs (functions) in an ongoing recursive feedback loop. He identified three central components of the legal system: (1) the social and legal forces that, in some way, press in and make "the law," the *inputs*; (2) the law itself – structures and rules that *process* inputs; and (3) the impact of law on behavior in the outside world, the *outputs or functions* of the system. "Where the law comes from and what it accomplishes – the first and third terms – are essentially the *social* study of law," he wrote (Friedman 1975:3, emphasis added).

Friedman chose the phrase legal culture to name the subject of this social study of law, the "social forces . . . constantly at work on the law," "those parts of general culture – customs, opinions, ways of doing and thinking – *that bend social forces toward or away from the law*" (1975:15, emphasis added). As an analytic term, legal culture emphasized the role of taken-for-granted and tacit actions that operate on and within the interactions of the legal system and its environment. As a descriptive term, it identified a number of related phenomena: public knowledge of and attitudes toward the legal system, as well as patterns of citizen behavior with respect to the legal system. These included judgments about the law's fairness, legitimacy, and utility.

To the extent that patterns of attitudes and behaviors are discernible within a population and vary from one group or state to another, it was possible, Friedman wrote, to speak of the legal culture(s) of groups, organizations, or states (1975:194). As the "ideas, values, expectations, and attitudes toward law and legal institutions, which some public or some part of the public holds," legal culture was meant to name a range of phenomena that would be, in principle, measurable (Friedman 1997:34). Although Friedman never fully elaborated the concept of legal culture and reformulated it several times in different texts, he remained convinced that it offered a useful way of "lining up a range of phenomena into one very general category" (1997:33).

Confusions and debates

Following its introduction, researchers began using the concept in a range of empirical projects including studies of children's knowledge of and attitudes to law (Tapp and Levine 1974), rights consciousness among Americans (Scheingold 1974), the practices of criminal courts (Nardulli, Eisenstein, and Flemming 1988; Kritzer and Zemans 1993), and comparative analysis of different groups and nation-states (Kidder and Hostetler 1990; Tanase 1990; Bierbrauer 1994; Barzilai 1997; Gibson and Caldeira 1997; Gibson and Gouws 1997; French 1998; Chanock 2001). For those who attempt to measure variations in legal cultures, the indicators include such diverse phenomena as litigation rates and institutional infrastructures (Blankenburg 1994, 1997) or crime rates (Kawashima 1963).

Predictably, given the historic confusion surrounding legal culture as a term, debates have arisen among researchers who have attempted to use the concept in empirical projects (Nelken 1997). The most persistent divide and heated dispute seems to align with the two uses named earlier: culture as an analytic concept within a more developed theory of social relations and legal culture as concrete, measurable phenomena. Those who attempted to use the concept as a focus for comparative research moved quickly toward measurement and a more limited concept. Some researchers insist that legal culture is that which is produced and studied most effectively among professional legal actors, while others insist that such a narrow definition belies the theoretical utility of the concept of legal culture as a way of mapping the connections between law and everyday life – just the analytically conceived feedback loop that Friedman posited in his notion of a legal system.

For some of these researchers, when the concept of legal culture is used with insufficient specificity, the distinction between all of culture and legal culture is unclear, and what constitutes the legal seems unspecified (Blankenburg 1994, 1997). Cotterrell insists that "everything about law's institutions and conceptual character needs to be understood in relation to the social conditions which have given rise to it. In this sense law is indeed an expression of culture" ([1984] 1992:26). Nonetheless, Cotterrell is unwilling to accept a concept of legal culture if it is indistinguishable from other forms of social control or normative ordering. Somewhere between a "thoroughgoing legal pluralism" ([1984] 1992:42) in which "law can be distinguished from other social norms only in vague terms" (ibid.) and a too narrow, too simple conception of state law, Cotterrell seeks a middle ground that recognizes the cultural influences on and from law but yet retains a recognition of the distinctiveness of legal forms and doctrines.

To some extent, these socio-legal debates reproduce controversies plaguing the concept of culture generally. The most important issues are less empirical than theoretical. The measurement problems decried by those studying national legal cultures derive from the theoretical arguments: how is legal culture evident and measurable and yet diffuse and abstract? What is the relative importance of causal explanation as against description and interpretive understanding?

How central is formal legal doctrine in understanding participation in, support for, and consequences of law?

Constitutive theories of legal culture

The cultural turn that swept across the humanities and social sciences in the 1980s brought some clarification to the analytic concept, if not entirely for those seeking precise quantifiable measurement. In the interdisciplinary community of law and society scholars, psychologists, anthropologists, sociologists, historians, geographers, and law professors spoke across traditional divides, even if they often spoke from and retreated back to their disciplines. They worked in the crosshairs of different disciplinary lenses, tacking back and forth and producing – I think much before it happened in most of the disciplines – a new set of theories and methods, exemplifying some of the most important insights that would eventually emerge in most social science fields. What was that insight? The "site" of social action matters to the meaning and organization of that action, whether that site is legal, scientific, or organizational. Moving away from large-scale theory development and abstract modeling to more situated, contextualized analyses of sites of social action, researchers found ways to bridge the epistemological and theoretical paradigms that had both fueled their knowledge production and simultaneously created deep chasms between and within disciplines. The emergence of cultural analysis signaled an effort to synthesize behavioral and structural as well as micro and macro perspectives.

In socio-legal scholarship the cultural turn had three components. First, it abandoned a "law-first" paradigm of research (Sarat and Kearns 1993). Rather than begin with legal rules and materials to trace how policies or purposes are achieved or not, scholars turned to ordinary daily life to find, if there were, the traces of law within. They were as interested in the absences where law could have been and was not, as much as they were interested in the explicit signs of formal law. Law and society had already moved beyond what Friedman (1985:29) had identified as lawyer's law ("of interest to legal practitioners and theorists") to legal acts ("the processes of administrative governance, police behavior") and legal behavior ("the unofficial work of legal professionals"). Cultural analysis added a new focus on the unofficial, non-professional actors – citizens, legal laymen – as they take account of, anticipate, imagine, or fail to imagine legal acts and ideas, seeking the "rule of law" in the everyday lifeworlds of ordinary people.

Second, it abandoned the predominant focus on measurable behavior that preoccupied those comparing national legal cultures. Analyses turned to Weberian conceptions of social action, tracing meanings and interpretive communication within social transactions. From this perspective, law is not merely an instrument or tool working on social relations, as Friedman suggested, but also a set of conceptual categories and schema that help construct, compose, and interpret social relations.

Third, and perhaps most fundamentally, the turn to everyday life and the cultural meanings of social action required a willingness to shift from the native categories of actors as the object of study (e.g., the rules of the state, the formal institutions of law, and the attitudes and opinions of actors) to the researcher's definition of the subject as an analytically conceptualized unit of analysis: legal culture. By studying law with insufficiently theorized concepts and by using the subject's native language as the tools for analysis, conceptual muddles characterized deployment of the word culture. New theoretical materials and research methods were necessary (cf. Gordon 1984; Munger and Seron 1984). To construct better accounts of how law works, and show how legality is an ongoing structure of social action (Ewick and Silbey 1998:33–56), attention shifted to the venerable traditions of European social theory. In particular, scholars writing about legal culture began to address questions of collective consciousness, ideology, and hegemony in efforts to understand how systems of domination persist, are tolerated, and also embraced by subordinate populations.

What became known as the constitutive perspective, or cultural turn, recaptured some of the critical tradition of law-and-society research that had been waning after decades of path-breaking scholarship. Focused on the everyday life of citizens, scholars also began to interrogate the ideals and principles that legal institutions announce. Even if they fail to consistently implement them, might these policy efforts and abstract principles nonetheless play important roles in everyday life and be a part of how legal institutions create their power and authority? The ideals of law – such as open and accessible processes, rule governed decision-making, or similar cases being decided similarly (despite being incomplete as descriptions of how law works) – might be part of the popularly shared understandings of what law is. They might serve as aspirations that would help shape and mobilize support for legal institutions. They might also be part of what allowed the system to be appear to be what Hannah Arendt (1972:178) labeled a headless tyrant. In this way, researchers reconceived the relations between legal texts and actions and the commonplace events and interpretations through which, they theorized, legality circulates.

From the mid-1980s to the present, a steady stream of empirical literature has described the mediating processes through which local practices are aggregated and condensed into systematic institutionalized power (Silbey 1992, 1998, 2005a, 2005b). Unfortunately, multiple uses of similar terms recreated anew the conceptual confusion that had achieved, for a while, quiescence through constitutive/cultural theories. Within the more general discourse on legal culture, however, one can find four strong threads.

Legal ideology

Without necessarily using the term legal culture, research on legal ideology explores "the power at work in and through law. Studies of law and ideology also suggest that the power associated with signs and symbols is being exercised unjustly" (Silbey 1998: 273). Thus, in studies of legal culture, "adopting and deploying the term ideology is a form of social criticism" (Silbey 1998: 273; cf. Ewick 2006).

Legal consciousness

One can also find studies of legal consciousness, defined as participation in the construction of legality, where legality refers to the meanings, sources of authority, and cultural practices that are commonly recognized as legal, regardless of who employs them or for what ends (Ewick and Silbey 1998:22). As with legal culture, however, we can also find many and confusing uses of the term "legality," which is an English language term meaning that which is within the specifications and boundaries of formal law. Many law review articles use the term this way, specifically distinguishing culture and legality as two independent social phenomena, exactly what constitutive theories of legal culture try to combine. Constitutive socio-legal theories treat legal culture and/or legality as a set of schema or narratives circulating in popular discourse, sustaining legal hegemony, and creating, or failing to create, opportunities for resistance. Such research is not limited to the US (see Cowan 2004; Cooper 1995; Pelisse 2004; Halliday and Morgan 2013), although work focused on the discourses of law and legality in colonial and postcolonial "theatres" more often refers to the "cultures of legality . . . constitutive of colonial society" (Comaroff 2001; Maurer 2004).

Legalities, cultures of legality, and counter-law

Some work invokes the phrase cultures of legality to identify and highlight the fetishization of popular constructions – such as legality or rule of law – that are actively and broadly mobilized for diverse political (national and international) projects. In discussions of corporate capitalism, financial transparency, globalization, and state-building, as well as analyses of resistance movements, law is invoked for legitimation not simply of itself but for the specific interests or institutions being promoted. Comaroff and Comaroff (2004, 2006) ask why the discourse of law and disorder are so often conjoined, especially in postcolonial situations. Why is law posed as the alternative of disorder? Do legal procedures and discourses offer mechanisms of commensuration (Espeland and Stevens 1998), real or otherwise, to manage what seems disordered among globally diverse norms, structures, and processes? Does legality suggest the universal availability of historically successful, although limited, transactional channels and mechanisms – so much so that legality's myriad forms and cultural instantiations can be both buried and fetishized under the rubric of a universal rule of law? Some authors talk about the cultures of legality through the term "counter-law," emphasizing the illiberal use of law (Ericson 2007; Levi 2009). By using the phrase "cultures of legality," authors call attention to the excess meanings that are being deployed for often disguised purposes and interests not limited to law or legality.

The unruly slippage in language may derive as much from authors' normative commitments (wanting to both relativize and normatively support, both valorize different cultures yet identify common ground) as from professional interests in carving scholarly networks through terminological variation. Some of the linguistic variation may also indicate an attempt to differentiate studies of legal culture from research on legal attitudes and opinions that fail to theorize the aggregation (i.e., cultural system) in which persons are participating (see Silbey 2005a).

The structure of legality

Finally, Ewick and Silbey (1998) describe a general pattern in legality, what they refer to as the structure of legality; elsewhere they suggest that the narrative and normative plurality characteristic of legality is apparent in other institutions and social structures as well (Ewick and Silbey 2002). Legal culture, or the schematic structure of legality, is a dialectic composed of general normative aspirations and particular grounded understandings of social relations. A general, ahistorical, truth (the objective rational organization of legal thought; disinterested decision-making in rule-ordered roles) is constructed alongside, but as essentially incomparable to, particular and local practices (unequal quality of legal representation; the inaccessibility of bureaucratic agents; the violence of police). The apparent incomparability of the general and the particular conceals the social organization linking the ideals of due process to diverse, uneven material practices, including unequal access and the mediating role of lawyers. Thus, legality becomes a place where processes are fair, decisions are reasoned, and the rules are known beforehand, at the same time as it is a place where justice is only partially achieved, if at all, where public defenders don't show up, sick old women cannot get disability benefits, judges act irrationally and with prejudice, and the haves come out ahead (Ewick and Silbey 1999).

Any singular account of legality, or the rule of law and the spread of its rationality globally, conceals the social organization of law by effacing the connections between the concrete particular and the transcendent general. Because legality has this complexity, among and within its several schema, legality can be a hegemonic structure of society, embracing the range of conventional experiences of law. Any particular experience or account can fit within the diversity of the whole. Rather than simply an idealized set of ambitions and hopes, in the face of human variation, agency, and interest, legality is observed as both an ideal as well as a space of practical action. As a consequence, power and privilege can be preserved through what appears to be the irreconcilability of the particular and the general. Thus, this analysis of legal culture argues that instead of resting with one account, legality or legal culture should be understood in its plaited heterogeneity.

Empirical research exploring what has been identified as "legal cynicism" provides additional support for this concept of a plaited, dialectical conception of culture. Legal cynicism refers to "a cultural orientation in which law and the agents of enforcement, such as police and courts, are viewed as illegitimate, unresponsive, and ill equipped to ensure public safety" (Kirk and Papachristos 2011:1191). More subtle, nuanced accounts identify not subcultures of oppositional antagonism to the rule of law, for example, as expressed by radical environmental activists (Fritsvold 2009; Halliday and Morgan 2013) or as resistance (Ewick and Silbey 2003), but expressions of what some scholars call attenuated norms (Carr, Napolitano, and Keating 2007), orientations, or interpretative frames. "While individuals may believe in the substance of law, antagonism toward and mistrust of the agents of law may propel some individuals toward violence simply because they feel they cannot rely upon the police to help them resolve grievances" (Kirk and Papachristos 2011:1191). Violence becomes a form of self-help when the law is experienced as unreliable (cf. Black 1983), with residents of high-crime neighborhoods regularly telling ethnographers that they are equally afraid of the police as they are of the perpetrators of crime (Carr, Napolitano, and Keating 2007). Thus, while "most residents of socially disadvantaged neighborhoods believe in the substance of the law and express little tolerance for violence and crime (Sampson and Bartusch 1998), . . . many still engage in violations of the law despite these beliefs" (Kirk and Papachristos 2011:1191).

Further study of legal culture

Although conceptual muddles have accompanied the widespread use of the concept of legal culture, carefully designed research might help untangle some of the theoretical knots. For example, data collection using a standard conversational protocol across national sites might map cultures of legality, resolve inconsistencies in the current literature, and advance theory on the spread, support, or resistance to the rule of law. By adopting sampling strategies used in large comparative projects but deploying close observation, in-depth interviewing, and discursive analysis, comparative projects might produce important theoretical as well as empirical advances.

Second, Maurer (2004) suggests that some advance might be achieved by adopting a conceptual innovation from the social studies of science. He worries that social studies of science may have come up against theoretical exhaustion, discovering more and more sociality in science just as law and society scholars discovered that "the law is all over" (Sarat 1990). However, science studies have a unique insight that legal scholars are now only beginning to pick up (Valverde 2008). Social studies of science push against both theoretical exhaustion and anthropocentric accounts of scientific culture by tracing the "network of human and nonhuman agents that, *together*, push back against the 'social' and in the process make their own moral [as well as material] claims known" (Maurer 2004: 848, my insert). Studies of legal culture need to do the same (Latour 2004).

Third, and finally, Ewick and Silbey (2002) suggest that cultural analyses might provide avenues for studying long-term institutional and social change – a central question in sociology. If we observe cultural heterogeneity and contradiction in a variety of social institutions, is it possible that competing and contradictory accounts sustain those institutions as structures of social action? Is it possible that the alternative narratives not only create a protective covering that inures institutions against more systemic challenge, but that structures actually rely upon the articulation and polyvocality of each distinct narrative in order to exist? As a corollary, might the absence of that polyvocality – or what we might call significant imbalances in the narrative constitution of social structures – create vulnerability and increase the likelihood of structural transformation? If cultural analyses show that social structures rely on the contradictory rendering of experience for both legitimation and durability over time, it should be possible to trace the cultural ascendance of institutions and social structures such as law to the degree of contradiction they encompass. By taking a broad historical view, we should be able to trace the rise and fall of institutions to the sorts of stories people tell, or are enabled to tell, by the availability of diverse and sometimes contradictory discursive referents or schemas.

References

Arendt, H. 1972. *Crisis of the Republic*. New York: Harcourt Brace Jovanovich.

Barzilai, G. 1997. "Between the Rule of Law and the Laws of the Ruler: The Supreme Court in Israeli Legal Culture." *International Social Science Journal* 49(152):143–50.

Benton, L. 2002. *Law and Colonial Cultures*. Cambridge: Cambridge University Press.

Bierbrauer, G. 1994. "Toward an Understanding of Legal Culture: Variations in Individualism and Collectivism Between Kurds, Lebanese, and Germans." *Law and Society Review* 28(2):243–64.

Black, D. 1983. "Crime as Social Control." *American Sociological Review* 48(1):34–45.

Blankenburg, E. 1994. "The Infrastructure of Legal Culture in Holland and West Germany." *Law and Society Review* 28(4):789–809.

———. 1997. "Civil Litigation Rates as Indicators for Legal Cultures." Pp. 41–68 in *Comparing Legal Cultures*, edited by D. Nelken. Brookfield, VT: Dartmouth.

Bracey, J.H. 2006. *Exploring Law and Culture*. Long Grove, IL: Waveland Press.

Carr P.J., L. Napolitano, and J. Keating. 2007. "'We Never Call the Cops and Here is Why': A Qualitative Examination of Legal Cynicism in Three Philadelphia Neighborhoods." *Criminology* 45(2):445–80.

Chanock, M. 2001. *The Making of South African Legal Culture 1902–1936: Fear, Favour and Prejudice*. Cambridge: Cambridge University Press.

Comaroff, John. 2001. "Colonialism, Culture, and the Law: A Foreword." *Law and Social Inquiry* 26(2):305–14.

Comaroff, John, and Jean Comaroff. 2004. "Policing Culture, Cultural Policing: Law and Social Order in Postcolonial South Africa." *Law & Social Inquiry* 29(3):513–45.

———. eds. 2006. *Law and Disorder in the Postcolony*. Chicago: University of Chicago Press.

Cooper, D. 1995. "Local Government Legal Consciousness in the Shadow of Juridification." *Journal of Law and Society* 22(4):506–26.

Cotterrell, R. [1984] 1992. *The Sociology of Law: An Introduction*. 2nd ed. London: Butterworth.

Cowan, D. 2004. "Legal Consciousness: Some Observations." *The Modern Law Review* 67(6):928–58.

Ericson, R. 2007. *Crime in an Insecure World*. Cambridge: Polity Press.

Espeland, W., and M. Stevens. 1998. "Commensuration as a Social Process." *Annual Review of Sociology* 24:313–43.

Ewick, P. 2006. *Consciousness and Ideology*. Aldershot, UK: Ashgate.

Ewick, P., and S. Silbey. 1998. *The Common Place of Law: Stories From Everyday Life*. Chicago: University of Chicago Press.

———. 1999. "Common Knowledge and Ideological Critique: The Importance of Knowing Why the 'Haves' Come Out Ahead." *Law & Society Review* 33(4):1025–42.

———. 2002. "The Structure of Legality: The Cultural Contradictions of Social Institutions." Pp. 149–65 in *Legality and Community: On the Intellectual Legacy of Philip Selznick*, edited by R.A. Kagan, M. Krygier, and K. Winston. Berkeley: University of California Press.

———. 2003. "Narrating Social Structure: Stories of Resistance to Legal Authority." *American Journal of Sociology* 108(6):1328–72.

French, J.D. 1998. "Drowning in Laws but Starving (for Justice?): Brazilian Labor Law and the Workers' Quest to Realize the Imaginary." *Political Power and Social Theory* 12:181–218.

Friedman, L.M. 1975. *The Legal System: A Social Science Perspective.* New York: Russell Sage Foundation.

———. 1985. *Total Justice.* Boston: Beacon Press.

———. 1997. "The Concept of Legal Culture: A Reply." Pp. 33–40 in *Comparing Legal Cultures*, edited by D. Nelken. Brookfield, VT: Dartmouth.

Fritsvold, E.D. 2009. "Under the Law: Legal Consciousness and Radical Environmental Activism." *Law & Social Inquiry* 34(4):799–824.

Geertz, C. 1973 *The Interpretation of Cultures.* New York: Basic.

Gibson, J.L., and G.A. Caldeira. 1997. "The Legal Cultures of Europe." *Law and Society Review* 30(1):55–85.

Gibson, J.L., and A. Gouws. 1997. "Support for the Rule of Law in the Emerging South African Democracy." *International Social Science Journal* 49(152):173–91.

Gordon, R.W. 1984. "Critical Legal Histories." *Stanford Law Review* 36(57):57–125.

Halliday, S., and B. Morgan. 2013. "I Fought the Law and the Law Won? Legal Consciousness and the Critical Imagination." *Current Legal Problems* 66:1–32.

Kawashima, T. 1963. "Dispute Resolution in Contemporary Japan." Pp. 41–72 in *Law in Japan*, edited by A. von Mehren. Cambridge, MA: Harvard University Press.

Kidder, R.L., and J.A. Hostetler. 1990. "Managing Ideologies: Harmony as Ideology in Amish and Japanese Societies." *Law and Society Review* 24(4):895–922.

Kirk, D.S., and A.V. Papachristos. 2011. "Cultural Mechanisms and the Persistence of Neighborhood Violence." *American Journal of Sociology* 116(4):1190–233.

Kritzer, H.M., and F.K. Zemans. 1993. "Local Legal Culture and the Control of Litigation." *Law and Society Review* 27(3):535–57.

Latour, B. 2004. *La fabrique du droit: Une ethnographie du Conseil d'Etat.* Paris: Editions Decouverte.

Levi, R. 2009. "Making Counter-Law: On Having No Apparent Purpose in Chicago." *British Journal of Criminology* 49(2):131–49.

Maurer, B. 2004. "The Cultural Power of Law? Conjunctive Readings." *Law and Society Review* 38(4):843–50.

Munger, F., and C. Seron. 1984. "Critical Legal Theory Versus Critical Legal Method: A Comment on Method." *Law and Policy* 6(3):257–99.

Nardulli, P.F., J. Eisenstein, R.B. Flemming. 1988. *The Tenor of Justice: Criminal Courts and the Guilty Plea Process.* Urbana: University of Illinois Press.

Nelken, D. 1997. *Comparing Legal Cultures.* Brookfield, VT: Dartmouth.

Pelisse, J. 2004. "From Negotiation to Implementation: A Study of the Reduction of Working Time in France (1998–2000)." *Time & Society* 13(2/3):221–44.

Perin, C. 2005. *Shouldering Risks: The Culture of Control in the Nuclear Power Industry.* Princeton, NJ: Princeton University Press.

Rosen, L. 2006. *Law As Culture.* Princeton, NJ: Princeton University Press.

Sampson, R., and D.J. Bartusch. 1998. "Legal Cynicism and (Subcultural?) Tolerance of Deviance: The Neighborhood Context of Racial Differences." *Law and Society Review* 32(4):777–804.

Sarat, A. 1990. "'. . . The Law is All Over': Power, Resistance, and the Legal Consciousness of the Welfare Poor." *Yale Journal of Law and Humanities* 2(2):343–79.

Sarat, A., and T. Kearns. 1993. "Beyond the Great Divide." Pp. 21–61 in *Law in Everyday Life*, edited by A. Sarat and T. Kearns. Ann Arbor: University of Michigan Press.

Scheingold, S.A. 1974. *The Politics of Rights: Lawyers, Public Policy, and Political Change.* New Haven, CT: Yale University Press.

Sewell, W.H. 2005. *Logics of History.* Chicago: University of Chicago Press.

Silbey, S.S. 1992. "Making A Place for Cultural Analyses of Law." *Law and Social Inquiry* 17(1):39–48.

———. 1998. "Ideology, Justice, and Power." Pp. 272–308 in *Justice and Power in Law and Society Research*, edited by B. Garth and A. Sarat. Evanston, IL: Northwestern University Press.

———. 2005a. "After Legal Consciousness." *Annual Review of Law and Social Science* 1:323–68.

———. 2005b. "Everyday Life and the Constitution of Legality." Pp. 332–45 in *The Blackwell Companion to the Sociology of Culture*, edited by M. Jacobs and N. Hanrahan. Oxford: Blackwell.

Tanase, T. 1990. "The Management of Disputes: Automobile Accident Compensation in Japan." *Law and Society Review* 24(3):651–91.

Tapp, J.L., and F.L. Levine. 1974. "Legal Socialization: Strategies for an Ethical Legality." *Stanford Law Review* 27(1):1–72

Valverde, M. 2008. "The Ethic of Diversity: Local Law and the Negotiation of Urban Norms." *Law & Social Inquiry* 33(4):895–923.

46

Medical cultures

Mary-Jo DelVecchio Good and Seth Hannah

Introduction

The social sciences have a long and robust tradition analyzing the myriad ways that medical knowledge, training, and care are deeply embedded in social relations and imbued with profound and often soteriological cultural meanings (B. Good 1994). Our chapter addresses cultural studies of biomedicine, distinguishing between studies of the culture *of* medicine and studies of culture *in* medicine.

Medical cultures are socially constructed worlds of illness and healing that vary across contexts. They stem from the dynamic relationship between the local and global worlds of the production of knowledge, technologies, markets, and clinical standards. Modern biomedicine, often popularly conceptualized as "Western medicine," is frequently regarded as a universalized domain of science and technology largely devoid of cultural variations at its bioscience core. Contemporary biomedicine or "cosmopolitan medicine" has become an integral part of scientific as well as popular cultures worldwide. And although biomedicine is fostered through an international political economy of biotechnology and by the investment in medical knowledge by an international community of medical educators, academic physicians, clinical investigators, and bioscientists, medicine is taught, practiced, organized, and consumed in local contexts (M. Good et al. 1999).

Cultural approaches to the study of contemporary biomedicine are rooted in the work of mid-twentieth-century anthropologists and sociologists who began to examine the social construction of health and illness and the institutional and cultural foundations of healing systems around the world. In the 1960s, involvement in public health projects led anthropologists to investigate how biomedical knowledge is received and understood. They argued that individuals are not "empty vessels" waiting to be filled and that medical "habits and beliefs" constitute elements in elaborate "cultural systems." In the 1970s, social scientists engaged a comparative agenda, studying medical systems across a variety of cultural settings from small preliterate villages to the great traditions of practice in Ayurvedic/Indian and Chinese classical and folk medicine. The comparative agenda challenged assumptions that medical cultures are closed systems that develop autonomously. Rather, it was shown that medical traditions evolve from transnational flows of knowledge and practices that are integrated into local cultures, and that "cosmopolitan medicine" was a parallel system to the classical traditions.

Cultures *in* and *of* medicine

Social scientists popularized culture as an analytic lens to understand the worlds of biomedicine, often in comparison with other contemporary medical systems. Sociologists enthusiastically built upon the work of Talcott Parsons (1951) and Renee Fox (1979) with many of the leading scholars engaging in studies of medical work, biomedical research and clinical practice, patient experience, and the culture of contemporary medicine (Bosk 1979; Glaser and Strauss 1968; Zola 1966). In anthropology, cultural studies of biomedicine flourished as did new journals, including *Culture, Medicine, and Psychiatry: A Journal of Cross-cultural and Comparative Research* (B. Good 1994; M. Good 1995a, 1995b; Hahn and Gaines 1984; Kleinman 1980).

Social scientists writing on the culture of medicine also influenced how the concept of culture is used in and for medicine to enhance relations between the worlds of medicine and the lifeworlds of patients, to promote health policies, and define the modernist projects of biomedicine. A key development was the move to understand patients' "explanatory models" (Kleinman, Eisenberg, and B. Good 1978) and to explore how clinicians could better incorporate these into treatment regimens. Currently, we are witnessing a robust effort through medical institutions to shape the meaning of culture *in* medicine for political and marketing purposes and to respond to the needs of increasingly diverse patient populations. This effort is taking multiple forms: (1) defining new "cultural" diagnoses, particularly in mental health; (2) setting standards for "cultural competence" in response to civil rights and identity politics agendas; and (3) developing politically generated health-policy agendas, including the Surgeon General's Report *Mental Health: Culture, Race and Ethnicity* (US Department of Health and Human Services 2001), which emphasized "culture counts" and the Institute of Medicine's *Unequal Treatment* on racial and ethnic disparities in healthcare (M. Good et al. 2002–03; Kirmayer 2012; Lewis-Fernandez et al. 2015; Smedley, Stith, and Nelson 2002–03). Cultural experts advocate for changes in clinical medicine to increase access to care at national, state, and local levels (Betancourt, Green, and Ananeh-Firempong 2003). Olafsdottir and Pescosolido (2009) identify a new turn toward culture in medical sociology; yet, they too recognize in citations a long tradition of scholarship on the "culture" of medicine and the "culture" of patients in medicine and psychiatry.

The culture of medicine

Classics in mid-twentieth-century medical sociology include Fox and Merton's work in *The Student Physician* (1957), Becker et al.'s *Boys in White* (1961), Hafferty's *Into the Valley: Death and the Socialization of Medical Students* (1991), and Bosk's *Forgive and Remember* (1979). These works explore the process of acculturation in medical education and training whereby medical students are transformed into doctors. Building upon this work, Byron Good's (1994) cultural analyses of late twentieth-century medical education documents historical depth and continuity in the culture of medicine. Students come to embody a medical gaze and persona during their initial training. Developing a professional way of seeing and speaking is essential to entering the clinical world. Students visually learn "biology's natural hierarchical order" via "modern imaging techniques [that] give a powerful sense of the authority of biological reality" (B. Good 1994:65–75). In clinical training, speaking and writing practices through case presentations and medical records teach students how to "construct" the patient through medically relevant narratives. Such practices authorize students' clinical interactions with patients, even as they legitimize an "editing out" of putatively medically irrelevant data. Through experiences such as these, students are socialized into contemporary clinical biomedicine. The cultural core of medical education persists despite a sea change in the gender, race, and ethnicity profiles of medical students, the extraordinary transitions in disease burdens, morbidity, and mortality rates, the revolutionary innovations in biotechnologies, and the major reorganization and financing of healthcare. Within this rapidly changing environment, clinical trainees actively develop a new subjectivity; they make choices, resist subjugation, accommodate power differentials, and actively craft themselves internally throughout the process of becoming a new kind of professional (Holmes, Jenks, and Stonington 2011). This production of subjectivity calls attention to what one of us has called "the inner life of medicine" (M. Good 2011).

Variations in "transnational" cultures of medicine arise through local practices, for example, in the culture of responsibility and obligation within professional hierarchies. Notable crises in coverage, teaching, and oversight have occurred, for example, in Kenya's national teaching hospitals and to a lesser extent in Indonesia's leading medical schools. These crises highlight different cultures of obligation and expectations about availability and responsibility that are common or idealized in most American academic medical settings. Variations in standards of clinical practice and obligations to patients, along with errors in practice and compromises in quality of clinical care, are common difficulties that also vary by locality within societies as well as among societies. Moral and ethical dilemmas in medicine range from the mundane to the spectacular and include problems ranging from the dilemma of disclosing AIDS diagnoses to spouses to the challenge of halting the commoditization of body parts for the international organ trade.

Policy contests over use of financial resources, organizational cultures of healthcare systems, and programs to promote equitable healthcare coverage are related to the degree to which societies tolerate inequalities. Even among specialty practices following national practice guidelines, significant differences occur in rates of various procedures. In the US, breast-conserving surgery and radiation, for example, are conducted more frequently than mastectomies in the northeastern states than the western states (M. Good 1995b). Invasive and expensive medical tests are performed much more often in one Texas town than in surrounding towns (Gawande 2009). Such stories are legion, and they remind us of the salience of local medical cultures in determining how treatment is delivered.

Local and cosmopolitan worlds of biomedicine

When we write about contemporary biomedicine, cosmopolitan medicine, or Western medicine, the realities of local contexts compel us to ask what is culturally, politically, and economically specific as well as what is truly cosmopolitan. Indeed, the brute facts of local practice often overwhelm even the best that biomedicine can offer. For example, when professional prestige among US academic physicians is measured by the skillful use of experimental high-technology therapeutics, and at times "salvage therapies"; when a British-trained Kenyan oncologist knows how to cure most children on his pediatric oncology ward such as those with Burkitt's lymphoma but does not have the wherewithal to access to the necessary chemotherapies; or when East African doctors face wards so full of patients suffering HIV and multiple-drug-resistant tuberculosis (MDR-TB) that they become "overwhelmed by disease entity" even though they have some access to the latest antiretrovirals – in cases such as these, the brute facts of local practice and political economies defy any reified analysis of a singular category of "biomedicine" (M. Good 1995a).

The antiretroviral therapy (ART) stories underscore how local cultures of medical practice are influenced by biotechnological innovation as well as by transnational systems of patents, World Trade Organization policies, laws governing the production of generics, and the policies of the World Health Organization (WHO). The "3 × 5" agenda designed by anthropologist/physician Jim Yong Kim for WHO urged governments to work toward enrolling three million

HIV patients in ART by 2005 (Kim and Farmer 2006). This agenda had a profound influence on the global cultures of medical care: treatments became increasingly deliverable and effective even in societies where existing healthcare systems were limited. Antiretroviral therapies and other "technically sweet" innovations from the biosciences have recast local medical cultures even as they have introduced new moral and ethical dilemmas, challenging ultimate questions of who "should" receive medications and care.

At this writing, the global economy is recovering from a severe recession, with many countries enduring deep financial austerity, which poses the question: will the public and private global funds that poured into HIV treatment over the past decade be reduced? Some in the AIDS research community are working to develop vaccines and efficient technologies of delivery such as nano-techniques for longer acting and more compact medication doses, however many goals are as yet unrealized. Local meanings are overlaid by global standards and technologies in nearly all aspects of biomedicine, as in the HIV examples. This is especially true for analyses of global humanitarian medicine, especially provided in zones of war and conflict. These interventions are culturally imbued with notions of official neutrality that view the clinic as a protected space apart from local politics. Recent ethnographies have ruptured this perception of neutrality, revealing that although many clinicians and combatants aspire to maintain impartiality and safety in the midst of war, these spaces are often politicized and shaped by the very conflicts from which they seek immunity and protection (Benton and Atshan 2016). This was vividly illustrated by the recent bombing of a Médecins sans Frontières (MSF) trauma hospital in Kunduz, Afghanistan, and the efforts of the White Helmets in Syria who risk their lives to save civilians in the midst of a brutal civil war.

Theoretical approaches to this connectedness resonate with Marcus's (1995:3) and Fischer's (1991) notions of "multiple regimes of truth" in which they urge multisited ethnographies. Works in this vein include Marcus's edited collection *Technoscientific Imaginaries* (1995), Rabinow's ethnography of a biotechnology firm and the "making of PCR" (polymerase chain reaction; 1996), Dumit's analysis of positron emission tomography (PET) and how new medical imaging technologies relate to wider cultural imaginaries (2004), and a vast body of research on organ donation. Many studies document locally specific medical practices that disregard the legal and ethical stances of American and European organ transplantation standards, which conceive of organs as gifts from "donors" rather than as commodities procured from prisoners or the poor (Fox and Swazey 1992). In the arena of genetics, Heath and Rabinow were among those who first turned anthropological attention to the culture of the human genome project and related genetic technologies (1993). An astonishing twenty-first-century global revolution in technological capacities has made possible rapid and relatively inexpensive mapping of individual genomes, thereby profoundly influencing genetic medical research.

Comparative perspectives and interpretive concepts

A comparative perspective encourages several questions: How do local and international political economies of medical research and biotechnology shape medicine's scientific imaginary, its cultural, moral, and ethical worlds, and the distribution of medicine's material and cultural products? How do local and international ideologies about population health and individuals' rights to healthcare influence professional and institutional responses to specific needs of particular societies – from the HIV epidemic to post-conflict trauma to extreme scarcity of resources? What form does "the political economy of hope" take in contexts of great wealth and in contexts of extreme poverty? Questions such as these led to four interrelated interpretive concepts to guide explorations of how the culture of medicine "lives" in respective societies. These are

(1) the medical imaginary, (2) the political economy of hope, (3) the biotechnical embrace, and (4) the clinical narrative. These concepts are intended to be dynamic and responsive to new empirical studies (M. Good et al. 1990; M. Good 1995a, 2001, 2007).

Ethnographic studies of high-technology medicine suggest ways that the affective and imaginative dimensions of biotechnology envelop physicians, patients, and the public in a "biotechnical embrace." The medical imaginary, that which energizes medicine and makes it a fun and intriguing enterprise, circulates through professional and popular culture, creating the potential to "embrace" and to "be embraced by" medicine. Clinicians and their patients are subject to "constantly emerging regimes of truth" in medical science, and those who suffer serious illness become particularly susceptible to the hope generated by the medical imaginary. The connection between bioscience and patient populations can be measured in part by the degree of support for disease-specific philanthropies, the power of political health-action groups (for AIDS, breast cancer), and taxpayer support for government financing of the National Institutes of Health. Americans clearly invest in the medical imaginary – the "many possibilities" enterprise – culturally, emotionally, and financially. Enthusiasm for medicine's possibilities arises not only from products of therapeutic efficacy but also through the production of ideas about potential but as yet unrealized therapeutic usefulness (such as an HIV vaccine, designer anti-cancer therapies, or stem cell-generated treatments for debilitating diseases). As an officer in one of the most successful biotechnology firms in the US told us, biotechnology firms are in the business of producing ideas about potential therapeutics.

The circulation of knowledge and products of the medical imaginary is uneven, and the robustness of local scientific and medical communities influences how people use globalized medical knowledge. Videos of Tanzanian teenagers acting in popular community theatrical performances designed to teach about the biology of the HIV virus and how antiretroviral therapies combat the virus illustrate the global appeal of the twenty-first century's medical imaginary (Earls and Carlson 2009). Recent studies on HIV in Brazil (Biehl 2008), French cutting-edge science (Rabinow 1999), and the elevation of community health workers into twenty-first-century deliverers of high-technology therapeutics (Kim and Farmer 2006) attest to the cultural power of medicine. Medical errors, fraud, and failures are also a part of the medical imaginary, yet these negative components are often hidden by the larger narrative of hope that energizes modern medicine.

The "biotechnical embrace" brings into relief the subjective experiences of clinicians and their patients, and it pays particular attention to the affective dimension of clinical relationships. "Embracing" and "being embraced by" science and medicine fundamentally links high-technology bioscience to the wider society, just as it links clinicians to patients in their care. Whether new reproductive technologies, therapies for infectious disease, innovative organ transplantation procedures, progress in gene manipulation, or breakthroughs in cancer and heart disease research, the medical imagination drives the political economy of hope as well as our society's investment in medical adventures and, occasionally, misadventures. The "biotechnical embrace" reaches even beyond the clinic and the research bench into popular fascination with DNA-based genealogy missions and re-emerging debates about the biological basis for human "racial" difference and the use of "race" for targeted therapies (Nelson 2016).

Clinical narratives capture the dynamics of clinical interactions between physicians and their patients. Narrative analysis and literary concepts – plot, emplotment, and narrative time – introduce new ways of making sense of everyday clinical life and the plotting of a therapeutic intervention and course. Narrative analysis also illuminates how affect and desire play out in clinical narratives through which evidence-based medicine is incorporated into clinical culture, seducing patients and clinicians into a world of the medical imagination and therapeutic action. Although physicians drive the clinical story for patients and utilize a variety of narrative strategies to convey meaning and hope, patients also shape clinical narratives as they read their own bodies and disease process in light of narratives of treatment. Narrative analysis also highlights specialty power by incorporating findings from the latest research and from clinical trials to justify choices among treatment options. In radiation and medical oncology in particular, the aesthetics of statistics – how clinicians convey odds and chances of treatment actions – are central in clinical narratives, addressing the immediacy of therapeutic activities, even as ultimate questions of death are avoided. In the US culture of oncology, when cancer is resistant to standard therapies, patients expect their physicians to invite them to enter the world of experimental therapeutics. Through these invitations to salvage therapies, such as autologous stem cell treatments, clinical narratives wed the experimental to the therapeutic, directing the meaning of technological interventions and inscribing treatment experiences on patients' psyche and soma (M. Good 1995a, 2007).

Culture *in* medicine: addressing healthcare disparities

In 2001, the Institute of Medicine requested a background paper for *Unequal Treatment* on the culture of medicine and how it might produce disparities in medical care. As one of us (M. Good et al. 2002–03) argued, the culture of medicine taught physicians to embody the "medical gaze" and to focus on medically relevant data. Patients who physicians considered social "train wrecks," who might "derail the smooth workings of the medical machine," threaten time and efficiency, which is highly prized, thus illness narratives are minimized. Physicians interviewed hypothesized that patients who resist being patients or are distrustful of clinicians and institutions of care may indeed receive less than equal treatment. When asked who these patients might be, "no shows" and "drug users and abusers" were most often mentioned rather than any particular cultural group or social identity. Especially evident in these discussions, "culture" was a salient category for many physicians and for the institutions where they work. Culturally tailored services and language translation were policy mechanisms designed to attract potential patient populations in the clinics' catchment areas. In *Shattering Culture: American Medicine Responds to Cultural Diversity* (M. Good et al. 2011), we investigated the ways that "culture" is used within medicine in response to increasingly diverse patient populations. We found that culture remained relevant within the institutions we studied, but physicians were beginning to recognize the limits of culturally specific treatment models, given the increasing relevance of different forms of diversity (social class, immigration status, and nationality in addition to race and ethnicity) and changes in the political economy of care, which stripped their professional autonomy and prioritized efficiency and accountability.

Cultural responses as correctives to disparities in care

The US Surgeon General's *Mental Health: Culture, Race, and Ethnicity* (US Department of Health and Human Services 2001), followed by the Institute of Medicine's *Unequal Treatment* (Smedley et al. 2002–2003), built political cases to redress disparities in mental health services and quality medical care for ethnic minorities. "Culture" became equated with social identities – most often race and ethnicity. Institutions of medical care and training were mandated by local and national governments to address disparities and to respond to increased diversity of patient populations. These political mandates reenergized attention to patients' culture which had long been a mainstay of cultural psychiatry. Cultural differences between patients and providers have been debated as one source of possible disparities and inequalities in care, with language differences identified as the ultimate barrier to a therapeutic alliance (Willen 2011). Burdens of difference have been attributed to "ethnic" cultural beliefs, behaviors, and fears of stigma (Guarnaccia and Rodriguez 1996; Lewis-Fernandez and Diaz 2004).

Attending to ethnicity and culture has a long tradition in American medicine, exemplified by the ethnic community health clinics established in the 1960s. In the past decade, aggressive marketing and packaging of "culture" has led to "cultural competence" and "diversity" training for hospital staff. The recent politicization of "culture" as in "Culture Counts" in mental health care and "race and ethnicity count" in *Unequal Treatment*'s documentation of disparities in healthcare has led to reexamining standards of practice and clinical norms. Newly revised culturally based educational programs and culturally specific services have been introduced by physician leaders in medicine's efforts to shape the meaning and appropriate uses of "culture" (Betancourt et al. 2003; Hinton and Good 2009). Hospitals routinely track the racial and ethnic composition of their patient populations, and during the past decade many adopted the goal of providing high quality and equitable care for all racial, ethnic, and cultural groups.

These efforts by medical institutions rely on the existence of group-bounded cultural characteristics in order to offer culturally tailored services (Kirmayer and Sartorius 2007). However, it is unclear to what extent cohesive group identities are among the most salient social categories in today's America, and to what extent such social categories are clinically relevant (Idler 2007). More recent innovations in cultural-competence training and research have incorporated these critiques and are much more sensitive to the individualism of patients and the internal diversity within populations (Gone 2015; Kirmayer 2012).

Our recent research explores the cultures of medicine in highly diverse settings where the cultural identities of patient populations are often fluid and ambiguous (M. Good et al. 2011; Good and Hannah 2015; Hannah 2011). We found that some clinics provided rich layers of cultural and linguistic services as essential to the core mission of the practice. Others attended minimally to cultural matters, yet cared for highly diverse patient populations and staff. Clinicians and support staff at both types of clinics were often culturally attuned to racial and ethnic groups, cultural traditions, and languages. In these complex social environments, broad identity categories such as African American, Hispanic, West Indian, Russian-Jewish, or Asian failed to capture the most salient cultural characteristics of individual patients. Often there were greater cultural differences among individuals within ethnic or racial groups than between them.

We developed a theoretical concept to illustrate these findings, referring to the preceding treatment settings as "cultural environments of hyperdiversity" (Hannah 2011). Five scenarios illustrated how the use of culture to address disparities in care was challenged by the complex interaction of culture and identity: (1) *multiplicity*, where the sheer number of different racial-ethnic groups makes organizing services based on identity impractical; (2) *ambiguity*, where racial-ethnic group membership is not easily labeled or understood; (3) *simultaneity*, where labeling is difficult because individuals simultaneously occupy multiple racial/ethnic categories; (4) *misidentification*, where a patient is mistakenly labeled a member of a particular racial/ethnic group; and (5) *misapplication*, where an individual's racial-ethnic group membership is correctly identified but the individual fails to share significant cultural characteristics with others from that group.

These scenarios suggest that culturally specific services based on census racial or ethnic categories were difficult to design due to ever-shrinking degrees of cultural similarity and increasingly blurred boundaries. In the cultural environments of hyperdiversity that we observed, clinicians and staff often eschewed the use of racial/ethnic categories as proxies for cultural characteristics in the treatment of immigrant and minority patients. Instead, they were more likely to regard language, need, disadvantaged class status, nativity, illness, or individual behaviors such as drug use of greater relevance to their clinical tasks than race or ethnicity.

Conclusion

There is a central tension between universalism and particularism inherent in the culture *of* medicine and how culture is used *in* medicine. A psychiatrist colleague devised ways to bring "culture" into the diagnostic process in psychiatry through his commitment to revising the cultural components of the *Diagnostic and Statistical Manual* (DSM-5). For him, "culture" has become a political trope, a way to argue for public support for adequate and culturally sensitive mental care for Hispanic populations in need. At a professional meeting, he discussed the tension in much of contemporary medicine and psychiatry, between universalism and cultural specificity. Arguing for greater clinical attention to the uniqueness of *ataques de nervios*, the psychiatrist resolved, "I am not anti-universalism in psychiatry, but for a *more informed universalism*" (Personal correspondence between Lewis-Fernandez and M. Good 2009). It is this tension that we observe in the way "culture" is used in medicine today.

From the perspective of clinicians, universalism is the heart of the culture of medicine. Yet we see from cross-national variation the influence that particular cultural traditions have in shaping the way medicine is practiced in local contexts. It is these local practices that reshape the universal culture of medicine itself – creating an evolving, more informed cosmopolitan standard. In the US, these trends were strongly supported when the Patient Protection and Affordable Care Act (ACA) was passed by President Barack Obama in 2010. The ACA dramatically expanded access to private and public health insurance and included large investments in community health centers at the front lines of the battle to provide healthcare for the poor and reduce racial and ethnic disparities in care. Much of the recent work to attend to "culture" and "hyperdiversity" in medicine was enabled by the ACA and the political work done during the Clinton and Bush administrations to expand research and health interventions targeted at diverse populations. New government agencies such as the National Institute on Minority Health and Health Disparities raised the profile of these efforts and directed large new initiatives to improve the health of poor and minority. We fear, however, that political trends are reversing, as a new era of budget cuts threatens these vital institutions and the ACA is vulnerable to being eroded in the wake of the 2016 election. This has the potential to undermine the cultural authority of medicine to work on behalf of greater equality.

References

Becker, H., B. Geern, E.C. Hughes, and A. Strauss. 1961. *Boys in White: Student Culture in Medical School.* Chicago: University of Chicago Press.

Benton, A., and S. Atshan, eds. 2016. "The Clinic in Crisis: Medicine and Politics in the Context of Social Upheaval." *Culture, Medicine and Psychiatry, Special Issue* 40(2).

Betancourt, J.A., J.E. Green, and O. Ananeh-Firempong. 2003. "Defining Cultural Competence." *Public Health Reports* 118(4):293–302.

Biehl, J. 2008. *Will to Live: AIDS Therapies and the Politics of Survival.* Princeton, NJ: Princeton University Press.

Bosk, Charles. 1979. *Forgive and Remember.* Chicago: University of Chicago Press.

Dumit, J. 2004. *Picturing Personhood Brain Scans and Biomedical Identity.* Princeton, NJ: Princeton University Press.

Earls, F., and M. Carlson. 2009. "Working with Children Affected by HIV/AIDS in Tanzania." Lecture presented to HST 934: Introduction to Global Medicine, Harvard Medical School, Spring Semester, Boston, MA.

Fischer, M.J. 1991. "Anthropology as Cultural Critique: Inserts for the 1990s Cultural Studies of Science, Visual-Virtual Realities, and Post-Trauma Policies." *Cultural Anthropology* 6(4):525–37.

Fox, R.C. 1957. "Training for Uncertainty." Pp. 207–42 in *The Student Physician: Introductory Studies in the Sociology of Medical Education*, edited by R.K. Merton, G.G. Reader, and P.L. Kendall. Cambridge, MA: Harvard University Press.

Fox, R.C. 1979. *Essays in Medical Sociology: Journeys into the Field*. New York: Wiley.

Fox, R., and J. Swazey. 1992. *Spare Parts: Organ Replacement in American Society*. New York: Oxford University Press.

Gawande, A. 2009. "The Cost Conundrum: What a Texas Town Can Teach us about Health Care." *New Yorker*, June 2009, pp. 36–44.

Glaser, B., and A. Strauss. 1968. *A Time for Dying*. Chicago: Aldine.

Gone, J.P., ed. 2015. "Evidence-Based Practice and Cultural Competence." *Transcultural Psychiatry, Special Issue* 52(2).

Good, B.J. 1994. *Medicine, Rationality, and Experience: An Anthropological Perspective*. Cambridge: Cambridge University Press.

Good, M.D. 1995a. *American Medicine: The Quest for Competence*. Berkeley: University of California Press.

———. 1995b. "Cultural Studies of Biomedicine: An Agenda for Research." *Social Science & Medicine* 41(4):461–73.

———. 2001. "The Biotechnical Embrace." *Culture, Medicine and Psychiatry* 25(4):395–410.

———. 2007. "The Medical Imaginary and the Biotechnical Embrace." Pp. 362–80 in *Subjectivity*, edited by J. Biehl, B.J. Good, and A. Kleinman. Berkeley: University of California Press.

———. 2011. "The Inner Life of Medicine." *Culture, Medicine and Psychiatry* 35(2):312–27.

Good, M.D., B.J. Good, C. Schaffer, and S.E. Lind. 1990. "American Oncology and the Discourse on Hope." *Culture, Medicine and Psychiatry* 14(1):59–79.

Good, M.D., and S.D. Hannah. 2015. "'Shattering Culture': Perspectives on Cultural Competence and Evidence-based Practice in Mental Health Services." *Transcultural Psychiatry* 52(2):198–221.

Good, M.D., C. James, B.J. Good, and A.E. Becker. 2002–2003. "The Culture of Medicine and Racial, Ethnic, and Class Disparities in Healthcare." Pp. 594–625 in *Unequal Treatment: Confronting Racial and Ethnic Disparities in Health Care*, edited by B.D. Smedley, A.Y. Stith, and A.R. Nelson. Washington, DC: National Academy Press.

Good, M.D., E. Mwaikambo, E. Amayo, and J.M. Machoki. 1999. "Clinical Realities and Moral Dilemmas: Contrasting Perspectives from Academic Medicine in Kenya, Tanzania, and America." *Daedalus* 128(4):167–96.

Good, M.D., S.S. Willen, S.D. Hannah, K. Vickery, and L.T. Park, eds. 2011. *Shattering Culture: American Medicine Responds to Cultural Diversity*. New York: Russell Sage Foundation.

Guarnaccia, P., and O. Rodriguez. 1996. "Concepts of Culture and Their Role in the Development of Culturally Competent Mental Health Services." *Hispanic Journal of Behavioral Sciences* 18(4):419–43.

Hafferty, F. 1991. *Into the Valley: Death and the Socialization of medical Students*. New Haven, CT: Yale University Press.

Hahn, R., and A. Gaines, eds. 1984. *Physicians of Western Medicine: Anthropological Approaches to Theory and Practice*. Dordrecht: D. Reidel.

Hannah, S. 2011. "Clinical Care in Environments of Hyperdiversity." Pp. 35–69 in *Shattering Culture: American Medicine Responds to Cultural Diversity*, edited by M. Good, S. Willen, S. Hannah, K. Vickery, and L. Park. New York: Russell Sage Foundation.

Heath, D., and P. Rabinow, eds. 1993. "Bio-Politics: the Anthropology of the New Genetics and Immunology." *Culture, Medicine and Psychiatry, Special Issue* 17(1).

Holmes, S.M., A.C. Jenks, and S. Stonington. 2011. "Clinical Subjectivication: Anthropologies of Contemporary Biomedical Training." *Culture, Medicine and Psychiatry* 35(2):105–12.

Hinton, D., and B. Good, eds. 2009. *Culture and Panic Disorder*. Palo Alto, CA: Stanford University Press.

Idler, J.E. 2007. *Officially Hispanic*. Lanham, MD: Lexington Books.

Kim, J.Y., and P. Farmer. 2006. "AIDS in 2006 – Moving toward One World, One Hope?" *New England Journal of Medicine* 355(7):645–47.

Kirmayer, L.J., ed. 2012. "Rethinking cultural competence." *Transcultural Psychiatry, Special Issue* 49(2).

Kirmayer, L., and N. Sartorius. 2007. "Cultural Models and Somatic Syndromes." *Psychosomatic Medicine* 69(9):832–40.

Kleinman, A. 1980. *Patients and Healers in the Context of Culture*. Berkeley: University of California Press.

Kleinman, A., L. Eisenberg, and B.J. Good. 1978. "Culture, Illness, and Care: Clinical Lessons From Anthropologic and Cross-Cultural Research." *Annals of Internal Medicine* 88(2):251–58.

Lewis-Fernandez, R.F., N.K. Aggarwal, L. Hinton, D.E. Hinton, and L.J. Kirmayer, eds. 2015. *DSM-5® Handbook on the Cultural Formulation Interview.* Washington, DC: American Psychiatric.

Lewis-Fernandez, R.F., and N. Diaz. 2004. "The Cultural Formulation: A Method for Assessing Cultural Factors Affecting the Clinical Encounter." *Psychiatric Services* 73(4):271–95.

Marcus, G. 1995. *Technoscientific Imaginaries: Conversations, Profiles and Memoirs.* Chicago: University of Chicago Press.

Merton, R.K., G.G. Reader, and P.L. Kendall. 1957. *The Student Physician; Introductory Studies in the Sociology of Medical Education.* Cambridge, MA: Harvard University Press.

Nelson, A. 2016. *The Social Life of DNA: Race, Reparations, and Biological Determinism in the Genetic and Genomic Era.* Boston, MA: Beacon Press.

Olafsdottir, S., and B. Pescosolido. 2009. "Drawing the Line: The Cultural Cartography of Utilization Recommendations for Mental Health." *Journal of Health and Social Behavior* 50(2):228–44.

Parsons, T. 1951. *The Social System.* Glencoe, IL: The Free Press.

Rabinow, P. 1996. *Making PCR: A Story of Biotechnology.* Chicago: University of Chicago Press.

———. 1999. *French DNA.* Chicago: University of Chicago Press.

Smedley, B.D., A.Y. Stith, and A.R. Nelson, eds. 2002–2003. *Unequal Treatment: Confronting Racial and Ethnic Disparities in Health Care.* Washington, DC: National Academy Press.

US Department of Health and Human Services. 2001. *Mental Health: Culture, Race, and Ethnicity – A Supplement to Mental Health: A Report of the Surgeon General.* Rockville, MD: US Department of Health and Human Services, Substance Abuse and Mental Health Services Administration, Center for Mental Health Services.

Willen, S.S. 2011. "Pas de Trois: Medical Interpreters, Clinical Dilemmas, and the Patient-Provider-Interpreter Triad." Pp. 70–93 in *Shattering Culture: American Medicine Responds to Cultural Diversity*, edited by M. Good, S. Willen, S. Hannah, K. Vickery, and L. Park. New York: Russell Sage Foundation.

Zola, I.K. 1966. "Culture and Symptoms: An Analysis of Patient's Presenting Complaints." *American Sociological Review* 31(5):615–30.

47

Science cultures

Francesca Bray

Introduction

To cheer viewers in troubled times and reassure them that the world was steadily getting better, US newsreels and TV programs of the mid-twentieth century regularly included shorts of the nation's scientists at work (Kinolibrary 2014). They show calm, intent figures in white lab coats carrying out complex experiments with precision. The commentators reverently intone the scientific creed: disciplined and supremely rational, objectively observing, systematically recording, impartially testing and logically analyzing, scientists follow where nature leads, toward new frontiers of knowledge. They work toward a grand collective goal: advancing human understanding and control of nature, thus improving the human condition and bringing glory to the nation. The old film clips portray an idealized vision of what science is and how it is done that persists today: although scientists are humans, the scientific vocation requires them to set human frailty aside in the disinterested pursuit of truth.

In her path-breaking study of communities of high-energy physicists, Sharon Traweek (1988:162) characterized modern science as the "culture of no culture," that is, an "extreme culture of objectivity ... which longs passionately for a world without loose ends, without temperament, gender, nationalism or other sources of disorder – for a world outside human space and time." It is this culture of no culture – the politics of the apolitical, the contingencies and limitations of the universal, the embodiment or rhetoric of abstract reasoning – that social scientists and cultural critics seek to unpack in what is broadly termed science studies (Franklin 1995).

Demystifying science

In Europe, investigations of science as a human and therefore necessarily cultural, social, and political activity date back to the 1930s. The Soviet philosopher Hessen (1931) electrified left-wing scientists in the UK when he presented a Marxist analysis of the economic and social factors shaping Newton's *Principia*, viewed hitherto as a pure product of reason. The Polish biologist Fleck ([1935] 1979) proposed the concept of the "thought collective" to explain resistance to innovation in science. The medically trained French philosopher Canguilhem ([1943] 1991) demonstrated that definitions of normal or pathological changed through history. Science studies took off in the US a little later. The sociologist Merton's functionalist analyses ([1942] 1973) showed scientists as social groups stabilized by shared norms and values. Like Fleck, the historian Kuhn (1962) denied that intellectual advances in science were a matter of pure logic, with better explanations smoothly and inevitably displacing inferior predecessors. Rather, ingrained intellectual habits inclined scientists to accept minor adjustments to "normal science" but to resist radically new evidence or theories that required a complete "paradigm shift."

Critiques of scientific knowledge as an instrument of power gathered momentum in the 1960s and '70s. They ranged from Foucault's inquiries into problematization (1967) – tracing historically how regimes of truth and concepts of normality or deviance emerge – to the Strong Programme of the Edinburgh Science Studies Unit, which insisted that it is just as important to provide a sociological explanation for why "true" science succeeds as for why "false" theories fail (Bloor 1976; Shapin 1994).

Feminist theory, gathering momentum in the 1970s, sought to explain not only gender distinctions but all social hierarchies and regimes of subordination. It stimulated new critiques of science as power, beginning with feminist analyses of how scientific thought, past and present, translated gender stereotypes and physical and mental hierarchies into theory and practice. This work included tracing the processes through which science became identified as the special aptitude of white men, with women, servants, or non-white populations treated as objects, not producers, of scientific enquiry (Haraway 1985; Harding 1986; Schiebinger 1993; Shapin 1994; Milam and Nye 2015), and exploring the entangled hierarchies of gender, race, and knowledge that shaped colonial and imperialist science, with legacies in the contemporary world (Harding 1998; Stoler 2002; Carney 2009). Feminism and Foucauldian research converged in a growing fascination with the body and "biopower," asking what bodily norms different sciences or scientific styles produce, and how states mobilize bioscience to exercise power over people's intimate lives and civic identities (see below; also Foucault 1973; Farmer 1993; Martin 1994; Mol 2002; Petryna 2009).

Anthropologists too began examining the cultural dimensions of science, studying scientists ethnographically as tribes or lineages, investigating their rituals, bonding games, and practices of inclusion and exclusion, and analyzing the moral and aesthetic values that underpin the criteria of truth in particular scientific fields (Traweek 1988; Nader 1996; Gusterson 1998). They went on to study the phenomenological, embodied nature of scientific work in different fields and its impact on epistemological styles (see below; also Turkle and Papert 1990; Knorr-Cetina 1999).

Another angle on science as culture comes from approaches of semiotics, linguistics, and literary criticism. Themes for critical study include the metaphors that science shares with vernacular speech (e.g., biomedical imagery of the body as a fortress [see below], or invocations of competition as a force for progress in capitalist economic and evolutionary theory), and the rhetorical or literary art with which supposedly transparent scientific arguments are made (Beer 1983; Haraway 1989; Martin 1991, 1994; Nelkin and Lindee 1995). Treating science as a complete fiction – or as an act of purely social or cultural creation apparently independent of the constraints of the "real" world and its natural laws – is, however, contentious and potentially ridiculous, as the science wars of the 1990s showed. How to negotiate the tricky boundaries of "constructivism" has been another important concern for analysts of science cultures (Hacking 1999; Jasanoff 2000; Stavrianakis 2012).

Perhaps the most notorious and intriguing approach to scientific culture is actor-network theory (ANT), which challenges the "genius" approach to scientific innovation through the principle of *generalized symmetry*, according equal weight to all actors, both human and non-human (artifacts, lab rats, institutions). The actors are not predefined but co-create each other. The "natural objects" of scientific investigation (microbes, soil types) only come into being through the interest of scientists; likewise scientific identities and practices depend on the extent to which the non-human partners can or will cooperate. Both playfully and seriously, ANT attributes agency to scallops and ethics to seat belts, tracing processes of *translation*, in which networks of actors are persuaded to agree that a new system is worth building and defending, and work together to construct it (Callon 1984; Latour 1988, 1993).

Science in society

These fields of enquiry not only illuminate scientific cultures within communities of practicing scientists or technocrats. They also help us to understand the wider public culture within which such worldviews are embedded and with which they interact. What do people think science is and does? How should it be developed and applied? Should it be controlled or allowed to run free, and why? What dreams, fears, and desires does science promise to fulfill?

In the last quarter century, science studies and STS[1] have flourished and diversified worldwide. Journals in which science cultures feature as the core theme include *Science and Society*; *Science, Technology and Human Values*; *Science in Context*; *Science as Culture*; *Technology and Culture*; *Configurations: A Journal of Literature, Science and Technology*; and *Cultural Studies of Science Education*. Here I list three key, crosscutting themes of recent science studies.

The risk society, "second modernity," and the demands of deliberative democracy

Until the 1960s, Ulrich Beck (1992) argued, we lived in a "first modernity" characterized by public trust in science. A succession of nuclear accidents and other unpredicted disasters, and growing awareness of the dangers of products like DDT or thalidomide (which scientists had initially declared perfectly safe), eroded public confidence in technocratic expertise. We now live, Beck contended, in a society full of manufactured risks, where individuals as well as institutions are continually called upon to "decide about the undecidable." For Beck, this recognition of risk bears democratic promise.

First, public consultation can be built into risk governance so that decisions are taken more democratically, and expertise can be shared between recognized authorities (e.g., scientists), "lay experts," and indeed all "stakeholders" (i.e., those likely to be affected). An excellent example is the expert knowledge that Welsh sheep farmers were able to contribute, when they were eventually consulted, to managing nuclear pollution and the consequent regulation of safety standards in UK farming in the aftermath of Chernobyl (Wynne 1992). Another involves the public consultations built into US and UK government policy on regulating nanotechnology (Pidgeon et al. 2009). But extending recognition and/or authority to "lay experts" requires a significant adjustment in the culture of professional scientists and technocrats. More typically, they prefer to dissuade dissent by beefing up campaigns of top-down science communication (Fortun 2004).

Second, globalization distributes risks but also offers new possibilities for *risk-sharing*, Beck noted. People may link local issues to global impact and their own bodies to others' dangers, and forge coalitions to promote the common, global good. Global coalitions opposing the commercialization of genetically modified (GM) crops, or today's environmental-justice movements, are good examples (Bray 2003; Schlosberg 2004).

Consumers, users, citizens

Since the end of the Cold War, academic theory has reflected everyday life in treating consumption as a primary form of agency rather than a by-product of production. Foucault argued that medical science is one means through which regimes of power are *inscribed* upon and *discipline* the body. STS theorists extended this insight into a semiotic reading of technology, arguing that the design of technological artifacts incorporates *user scripts* that *configure* the social identity of the user (Oudshoorn and Pinch 2003:8). This passive representation of users of technology was countered first by the argument that user-consumers make choices between competing technologies, thus influencing production decisions (Mackenzie and Wajcman 1985; Cowan 1987). Having acquired the technological gizmo of their choice, users do not tamely submit to the instruction sheet but actively adapt it to their own purposes: they *appropriate* or *domesticate* it, thus building a reciprocal relationship of *co-production* between experts-designers-producers and public-consumers (Oudshoorn and Pinch 2003).

The relation between scientists, government, and public can similarly be envisaged as one of active engagement and mutual influence rather than a simple one-way transmission of objective truth. But when is this a marriage of convenience (Biagioli 1993), when a corruption of scientific objectivity and integrity (Lexchin et al. 2003), and when a democratization of technocracy within the risk society? (Pidgeon et al. 2009).

Foucault proposed the concept of *biopower* to analyze how modern states regulate their subjects through "an explosion of numerous and diverse techniques for achieving the subjugations of bodies and the control of populations" (1978:1). The terms *biosociality* and *biocitizenship* suggest a more active role, a more conscious science culture, on the part of subjects in the global era. Disasters like Bhopal, Chernobyl, and Fukushima; global epidemics like AIDS; or everyday contacts with industrial contaminants all etch horrendous marks upon individuals and communities. Advances in medical research or genetics promise potential cures for terrifying diseases like cancer or multiple sclerosis. Whose entitlement to special support is recognized – by the state, the scientific establishment, society at-large, or the global community? Which groups of sufferers succeed in persuading governments or corporations to fund scientific research, to approve treatments, or subsidize drugs, and whose needs are ignored, who are treated as experimental guinea pigs? (Farmer 1993; Petryna 2004, 2009). What do answers to these questions tell us about adjustments in scientific culture and the understanding of whom science should serve? Do biocitizens operate in an economy of hope, or of despair? (Rose and Novas 2005; Brekke and Sirnes 2011).

Globalization, transnationalism and decentering

Another important new theme is the *globalization* of flows of finance, ideas, people, commodities, materials, and images. One focus is *global assemblages*. In social science terms, an assemblage is a historical construct, a contingent local convergence of networks or flows that is inherently continually shifting but may be stabilized by various means. Thus a city can be viewed as an assemblage of flows of people, capital, materials, energy, and vehicles temporarily stabilized by its urban institutions and its material infrastructure, and the international AIDS industry, viewed as an assemblage cobbled together out of "global flows of organisms, drugs, discourses, and technologies of all kinds" (Nguyen 2005:125).

In terms of science cultures, the assemblage approach draws attention, among other things, to the production of such stabilizing devices as datasets, reports, funding proposals, or even organizational charts – skilled activities that are fundamental to scientific success, but that are typically rendered invisible in accounts both of how science is done and how it achieves authority and influence (Latour and Woolgar 1979; Rabinow 1996; Riles 2000).

A somewhat different approach to science cultures in global perspective is found in transnational histories of science and technology. Here the emphasis is on a world in which nation-states have constructed significant boundaries to the unimpeded flow of knowledge, people, and resources. There are substantial power differentials between nations, and thus major obstacles to the free circulation of scientists or their access to data, employment, and funding. These hierarchies and barriers are largely invisible to the scientist-citizens of nations such as the US or UK, who take their privilege for granted. They loom large, however, in the life histories, strategizing, and networking of scientists from less favored nations. Furthermore, specific sciences or scientific ideas and applications will be valued differently in different national contexts. Transnational studies of science endeavor to map these uneven topographies of scientific practice and culture (Krige in press).

Quite closely related are recent efforts to decenter not only science but also science studies. Following from feminist and postcolonial challenges, and typically taking the view from the "periphery," contributors to the debate ask not only whether and how science differs when produced or applied in different contexts, but also whether the theories of science studies and their frameworks of interpretation travel (Anderson 2009; Tilley 2010). The journal *EASTS* (*East Asian Science, Technology and Society: An International Journal*) is a key player here, providing a forum for discussing the benefits and pitfalls of thinking from outside the Western metropolis, and asking questions that arise from the specifics of the East Asian historical experience, the articulations of regional colonial configurations and legacies (with Japan, not the US, as colonial power and cultural hegemon) – in other words, thinking with regions (Fu 2007; Fan 2012; Moore 2014; Lin and Law 2015).

Case studies

After a necessarily concise summary, let me illustrate the potential of science studies to illuminate science cultures with two sets of examples, inevitably selective and a reflection of my personal predilections.

Epistemic or epistemological cultures

A feminist physicist who pioneered several fields in cultural studies of science, Evelyn Fox Keller is a leader in this field. Her early study of the Nobel Prize-winning cytogeneticist Barbara McClintock shows that McClintock thought quite differently from her colleagues, with empathy, one might say, about her experimental organisms. This empathy imbued her with the passion to persevere with her research despite the prevailing misogyny within the scientific establishment and despite the fact that the radically new concepts she derived from her research fell largely on deaf ears, coming at a time when a revolution in molecular biology was taking the world of genetics by storm (Keller 1983:xviii). Keller (e.g., 2009) has since turned her attention to the importance of metaphors in shaping scientific understanding.

Whereas Keller has looked principally at the power of metaphor within the scientific community, others have pointed to its power to enroll the public. In her study of AIDS patients and their treatment at the Johns Hopkins University Hospital in Baltimore, Emily Martin highlights the prevalence of military metaphors in immunology: the healthy body is a fortress, weak bodies are attacked, defenses must be mobilized, enemy cells invade and must be destroyed (1994). This military view of disease encourages therapeutic choices that can be more drastic in their effects than simple neglect (Mukherjee 2010). So are military metaphors helpful for persons with AIDS and their careers, or even for doctors and researchers? Do they accurately reflect the lived experience of the disorder or its evolution? US AIDS activists propose various alternatives; however, since metaphors are culture-bound, they might not travel to other AIDS communities.

Returning to epistemologies within the laboratory, Karin Knorr-Cetina compares how knowledge is made and validated in two phenomenologically contrasting scientific cultures, high-energy physics and molecular biology, fields which she studies as cultures of knowing (Knorr-Cetina 1999). High-energy physics is a cerebral and visual mode of inquiry; the scientists are concerned mostly with the manipulation of signs and symbols. Molecular biologists have a "rich material culture" focused on "object-oriented processing" requiring skilled manual labor. Objects in experimental work are "subject to almost any imaginable intrusion and usurpation": smashed into fragments, evaporated into gasses, dissolved in acids, reduced to extractions, mixed, purified, washed, centrifuged, inhibited, precipitated, exposed to high voltage, heated, frozen, and reconstituted. The biologists grow cells on lawns of bacteria, raise, feed, mate, kill, and dissect animals – this is a five-senses, hands-on science where colleagues judge the quality of research results based on the experimenter's tidiness as well as dexterity (Knorr-Cetina 1999:85–6). Contrasting the two cultures of knowledge production, we see that scientific standards and the scientific method are far from universal.

Annemarie Mol also looks at practice and knowledge-making. She observes a poorly understood chronic disease, atherosclerosis, in which it seems that no two cases are alike. Interviewing doctors and patients, observing consultations, examinations, and operations, Mol shows how a shared understanding of disparate experiences as a single condition is brought about: "the disease is made to cohere through a range of tactics including transporting forms and files, making images, holding case conferences, and conducting doctor-patient conversations," leading Mol to reflect upon the "multiplicity of reality in practice" (2002:back cover).

Science cultures in China

As examples of decentering both science and the analysis of science cultures, let me present some cases from China. Grace Shen's (2014) investigation of the relationship between geological science and nationalism in Republican China (1911–1949) is a valuable contribution to the history of the emotions in science. Chinese geologists were of course taught within and indebted to the international discipline of geology. But in a newly fledged Chinese republic struggling to establish itself as a modern nation after decades of colonialist disdain, the eager young geologists' cosmopolitan training was infused with patriotism and a love of China and its land in all its variations. Shen depicts the transformative experience of fieldwork: venturing far from the normal habitat of intellectuals, the cities, into the hinterlands, "the belly of the country," which was at that time under continual threat of foreign claims, the young scientists had to overcome mandarin ideals of intellectual strength lodged in a physically delicate and fastidious body, attuning themselves instead to rough physical labor. For many this experience was an exhilarating self-discovery, consolidating their patriotic commitment. It is not surprising that so many eminent geologists chose to remain in the People's Republic of China after 1949, rather than fleeing to Taiwan or emigrating to the United States.

There is a wealth of science studies on such themes as intellectual property or bioethics in China, many of which echo Shen's study in suggesting that patriotic imperatives or responsibility to society frequently trump individual rights in research protocols and in governance. Is this communitarianism, a legacy of the socialist science ethic of the Maoist period? (Wei and Brock 2013; Schmalzer 2016). Or does it reflect more blatant national ambitions to rise to world dominance? The ethical mismatch with supposedly universal conventions hampers China's integration into the global scientific community (Salter 2011; Sleeboom-Faulkner 2013). It also suggests that analysts of science cultures should look more critically at the prioritization of individual rights in international research ethics and intellectual property law emanating from Western nations.

The individual does also figure in Chinese science cultures, but enmeshed in society in distinctive ways. Take one peculiarly Chinese expression of biocitizenship, the spread of *yangsheng* (literally "nourishing life") in the PRC. *Yangsheng* refers to a spectrum of regimens of self-care, typically including diet, exercise, breathing, and so forth, widely practiced by retired Chinese to prolong active and healthy life. Over time, as China's population ages and public provision of healthcare dwindles and private healthcare increases in cost, *yangsheng* practices have exploded, supporting a booming industry of books, tonics, and other health aids. Here, citizens self-identified as elderly and vulnerable are not demanding recognition from the state, as in the case of Chernobyl victims (Petryna 2004): they accept that public support is lacking and compensate by undertaking self-care. The spending power thus unleashed has built the *yangsheng* industry into "the fifth biggest sector in China's economy, following real estate, IT, automobiles and tourism" (Sun 2015:286).

Is *yangsheng* then a classic example of neoliberal biocitizenship, in which individuals exercise biological agency and claims in their own interest, independently of the state, within an "economy of hope"? (Rose and Novas 2005). Is it rather, perhaps, an honorable complicity with the developmental state, a political commitment to pursuing solutions that will not undermine the social order? Might the Western concept of biocitizenship not underestimate the real emotional as well as bodily rewards of self-discipline in pursuit both of improved personal health and longevity, and of the common good? (Farquhar and Zhang 2012).

Science studies in action

In highlighting the social and cultural factors that shape scientific projects, practices, and institutions, the goal of science studies is not to challenge the factual truth of specific scientific findings but rather to draw attention to the politics, the tacit assumptions, and value systems that underpin scientific activities and professional as well as public cultures of science. In the contemporary world the knowledge produced by science carries unique authority. Science studies offer an essential critique, demonstrating that despite its claims to universal objectivity, science, like any other human activity, is never socially or politically neutral. As a critique of one of contemporary society's most powerful institutions, exposing the play of power relations and advocating for the integration of the perceptions, experiences, and rights of subordinated or unacknowledged groups, science studies is thus an inherently emancipatory project. It is also recognized as a useful discipline: exploring how science is done and how it might be done better, experts in science studies are often called upon as consultants or mediators by governments, research bodies, industry, and non-governmental organizations.

As a critique, beyond exposing the power structures and cultural assumptions embedded in science itself, science studies – like anthropology or cultural sociology – take us an essential step further, inciting us to question the universality of the very categories that constitute our objects of observation and frameworks of analysis. As the Chinese cases just cited indicate, such concepts as intellectual property rights, biocitizenship, the boundaries and constitution of body and self, or the sense of scientific vocation all merit re-evaluation as historical (and typically Western) products. In this sense science studies is a philosophical project, a comparative investigation of ontologies, ethics, and phenomenology.

The ultimate charm of science studies, in my opinion, is that it enriches our vision of science. By challenging the inevitability of scientific questions and practices, by insisting upon the beliefs, rituals, and sacrifices, the rhetoric and the craft, the personal dealings, emotions, and sensations that go into doing science, science studies rehumanizes and re-enchants this magical domain of seeking the secrets of the world in which we live and die.

Note

1 An acronym sometimes spelled out as "science, technology, and society," sometimes as "science and technology studies." The former reading is supposedly more political, the latter more cultural.

References

Anderson, Warwick. 2009. "From Subjugated Knowledge to Subjugated Subjects: Science and Globalization, or Postcolonial Studies of Science?" *Postcolonial Studies* 12(4):389–400.

Beck, Ulrich. 1992. *Risk Society: Towards a New Modernity*. London: Sage.

Beer, Gillian. 1983. *Darwin's Plots: Evolutionary Narrative in Darwin, George Eliot and Nineteenth-century Fiction*. London: Routledge & Kegan Paul.

Biagioli, Mario. 1993. *Galileo, Courtier: The Practice of Science in the Culture of Absolutism*. Chicago: University of Chicago Press.

Bloor, David. 1976. *Knowledge and Social Imagery*. London: Routledge & Kegan Paul.

Bray, Francesca. 2003. "Genetically Modified Foods: Shared Risk and Global Action." Pp. 185–207 in *Revising Risk: Health Inequalities and Shifting Perceptions of Danger and Blame*, edited by B. Herr Harthorn and L. Oaks. Westport, CT: Praeger.

Brekke, Ole Andreas, and Thorvald Sirnes. 2011. "Biosociality, Biocitizenship and the New Regime of Hope and Despair." *New Genetics and Society* 30(4):347–74.

Callon, Michel. 1984. "Some Elements of a Sociology of Translation: Domestication of the Scallops and the Fishermen of St. Brieuc Bay." *Sociological Review* 32:196–233.

Canguilhem, Georges. [1943] 1991. *The Normal and the Pathological*, trans. Carolyn R. Fawcett. New York: Zone Books.

Carney, Judith Ann. 2009. *Black Rice: the African Origins of Rice Cultivation in the Americas*. Cambridge, MA: Harvard University Press.

Cowan, Ruth Schwartz. 1987. "The Consumption Junction: a Proposal for Research Strategies in the Sociology of Technology." Pp. 261–80 in *The Social Construction of Technological Systems*, edited by W. Bijker, T. Hughes, and T. Pinch. Cambridge, MA: MIT Press.

Fan, Fa-ti. 2012. "Doing East Asian STS is Like Feeling an Elephant, and That is a Good Thing." *EASTS* 6(4):487–91.

Farmer, Paul. 1993. *AIDS and Accusation: Haiti and the Geography of Blame*. Berkeley: University of California Press.

Farquhar, Judith, and Qicheng Zhang. 2012. *Ten Thousand Things: Nurturing Life in Contemporary Beijing*. New York: Zone Books.

Fleck, Ludwik. [1935] 1979. *The Genesis and Development of a Scientific Fact*, trans. Fred Bradley and Thaddeus J. Trenn and edited by T.J. Trenn and R.K. Merton. Chicago: University of Chicago Press.

Foucault, Michel. 1967. *Madness and Civilization: A History of Insanity in the Age of Reason*. London: Tavistock.

———. 1973. *The Birth of the Clinic*. London: Tavistock.

———. 1978. *The Will to Knowledge: The History of Sexuality*. Vol. 1. London: Penguin.

Fortun, Kim. 2004. "From Bhopal to the Informating of Environmentalism: Risk Communication in Historical Perspective." *Osiris* 19:283–96.

Franklin, Sarah. 1995. "Science as Culture, Cultures of Science." *Annual Review of Anthropology* 24(11):163–84.

Fu, Daiwie. 2007. "How Far Can East Asian STS Go? A Position Paper." *EASTS* 1(1):1–14.

Gusterson, Hugh. 1998. *Nuclear Rites: A Weapons Laboratory at the End of the Cold War*. Berkeley: University of California Press.

Hacking, Ian. 1999. *The Social Construction of What?* Cambridge, MA: Harvard University Press.

Haraway, Donna. 1985. "A Cyborg Manifesto: Science, Technology, and Socialist-feminism in the Late Twentieth Century." *Socialist Review* 80:65–108.

———. 1989. *Primate Visions: Gender, Race, and Nature in the World of Modern Science*. New York: Routledge.

Harding, Sandra. 1986. *The Science Question in Feminism*. Ithaca, NY: Cornell University Press.

———. 1998. *Is Science Multicultural? Postcolonialisms, Feminisms, and Epistemologies.* Bloomington: Indiana University Press.

Hessen, Boris. 1931. "The Social and Economic Roots of Newton's Principia." Pp. 151–212 in *Science at the Crossroads*, edited by N. Bukharin. London.

Jasanoff, Sheila. 2000. "The 'Science Wars' and American Politics." Pp. 27–40 in *Between Understanding and Trust: the Public, Science and Technology*, edited by M. Dierkes and C. von Grote. London: Routledge.

Keller, Evelyn Fox. 1983. *A Feeling for the Organism: The Life and Work of Barbara McClintock.* San Francisco, CA: W.H. Freeman.

———. 2009. *Making Sense of Life: Explaining Biological Development With Models, Metaphors, and Machines.* Cambridge, MA: Harvard University Press.

Kinolibrary. 2014. "Archival Laboratory Science, Scientists, Experiments, 1930s–1960s." Retrieved October 23, 2016 (www.youtube.com/watch?v=y1A0_sPiaL8).

Knorr-Cetina, Karin. 1999. *Epistemic Cultures: How the Sciences Make Knowledge.* Cambridge, MA: Harvard University Press.

Krige, John. In press. "Introduction." In *Writing the Transnational History of Science and Technology*, edited by John Krige. Chicago: University of Chicago Press.

Kuhn, Thomas S. 1962. *The Structure of Scientific Revolutions.* Chicago: University of Chicago Press.

Latour, Bruno. 1988. *The Pasteurization of France.* Cambridge, MA: Harvard University Press.

———. 1993. *We Have Never Been Modern.* Cambridge, MA: Harvard University Press.

Latour, Bruno, and Steve Woolgar. 1979. *Laboratory Life: The Social Construction of Scientific Facts.* Beverly Hills, CA: Sage.

Lexchin, Joel, Lisa A. Bero, Benjamin Djulbegovic, and Otavio Clark. 2003. "Pharmaceutical Industry Sponsorship and Research Outcome and Quality: Systematic Review." *BMJ* 326(7400):1167.

Lin, Wen-yuan, and John Law. 2015. "We Have Never Been Latecomers!? Making Knowledge Spaces for East Asian Technosocial Practices." *EASTS* 9(2):117–26.

MacKenzie, Donald, and Judy Wajcman. 1985. *The Social Shaping of Technology: How the Refrigerator Got Its Hum.* Milton Keynes, UK: Open University Press.

Martin, Emily. 1991. "The Egg and the Sperm: How Science has Constructed a Romance Based on Stereotypical Male-Female Roles." *Signs* 16(3):485–501.

———. 1994. *Flexible Bodies: Tracking Immunity in American Culture from the Days of Polio to the Age of AIDS.* Boston: Beacon Press.

Merton, Robert K. [1942] 1973. "The Normative Structure of Science." Pp. 267–80 in *The Sociology of Science: Theoretical and Empirical Investigations*, edited by N.W. Storer. Chicago: University of Chicago Press.

Milam, Erika, and Robert Nye, eds. 2015. *Osiris.* Vol. 30, *Scientific Masculinities.* Chicago: University of Chicago Press.

Mol, Annemarie. 2002. *The Body Multiple: Ontology in Medical Practice.* Raleigh, NC: Duke University Press.

Moore, Aaron Stephen. 2014. "Japanese Development Consultancies and Postcolonial Power in Southeast Asia: The Case of Burma's Balu Chaung Hydropower Project." *EASTS* 8(2):297–322.

Mukherjee, Siddhartha. 2010. *The Emperor of All Maladies: A Biography of Cancer.* New York: Simon and Schuster.

Nader, Laura, ed. 1996. *Naked Science: Anthropological Inquiry into Boundaries, Power, and Knowledge.* London: Routledge.

Nelkin, Dorothy, and M. Susan Lindee. 1995. *The DNA Mystique: The Gene as a Cultural Icon.* New York: Freeman.

Nguyen, Vinh-Kim. 2005. "Antiretroviral Globalism, Biopolitics, and Therapeutic Citizenship." Pp. 124–44 in *Global Assemblages: Technology, Politics, and Ethics as Anthropological Problems*, edited by A. Ong and S. Collier. New York: Blackwell.

Oudshoorn, Nelly, and Trevor Pinch. 2003. *How Users Matter: the Co-Construction of Users and Technology.* Boston: MIT Press.

Petryna, Adriana. 2004. "Biological Citizenship: the Science and Politics of Chernobyl-Exposed Populations." *Osiris* 19:250–65.

———. 2009. *When Experiments Travel: Clinical Trials and the Global Search for Human Subjects*. Princeton, NJ: Princeton University Press.

Pidgeon, Nick, Barbara Herr Harthorn, Karl Bryant, and Tee Rogers-Hayden. 2009. "Deliberating the Risks of Nanotechnologies for Energy and Health Applications in the United States and United Kingdom." *Nature Nanotechnology* 4(2):95–98.

Rabinow, Paul. 1996. *Making PCR: A Story of Biotechnology*. Chicago: University of Chicago Press.

Riles, Annelise. 2000. *The Network Inside Out*. Ann Arbor: University of Michigan Press.

Rose, Nikolas, and Carlos Novas. 2005. "Biological citizenship." Pp. 439–63 in *Global Assemblages: Technology, Politics, and Ethics as Anthropological Problems*, edited by A. Ong and S.J. Collier. New York: Blackwell.

Salter, Brian. 2011. "Biomedical Innovation and the Geopolitics of Patenting: China and the Struggle for Future Territory." *EASTS* 5(3):341–57.

Schiebinger, Londa L. 1993. *Nature's Body: Gender in the Making of Modern Science*. Boston: Beacon Press.

Schlosberg, David. 2004. "Reconceiving Environmental Justice: Global Movements and Political Theories." *Environmental Politics* 13(3):517–40.

Schmalzer, Sigrid. 2016. *Red Revolution, Green Revolution: Scientific Farming in Socialist China*. Chicago: University of Chicago Press.

Shapin, Steven. 1994. *A Social History of Truth: Civility and Science in Seventeenth-Century England*. Chicago: University of Chicago Press.

Shen, Grace Yen. 2014. *Unearthing the Nation: Modern Geology and Nationalism in Republican China*. Chicago: University of Chicago Press.

Sleeboom-Faulkner, Margaret. 2013. "Competitive Adaptation: Biobanking and Bioethical Governance in China Medical City." *EASTS* 7(1):125–43.

Stavrianakis, Anthony. 2012. "Are there Modes of Veridiction in Science Studies?" Retrieved May 15, 2016 (http://anthropos-lab.net/bpc/2012/03/are-there-modes-of-veridiction-in-science-studies).

Stoler, Ann Laura. 2002. *Carnal Knowledge and Imperial Power: Race and the Intimate in Colonial Rule*. Berkeley: University of California Press.

Sun, Wanning. 2015. "Cultivating Self-Health Subjects: *Yangsheng* and Biocitizenship in Urban China." *Citizenship Studies* 19(3–4):285–98.

Tilley, Helen. 2010. "Global histories, Vernacular Science, and African Genealogies; or, Is the History of Science Ready for the World?" *Isis* 101(1):110–19.

Traweek, Sharon. 1988. *Beamtimes and Lifetimes: The World of High Energy Physicists*. Cambridge, MA: Harvard University Press.

Turkle, Sherry, and Seymour Papert. 1990. "Epistemological Pluralism: Styles and Voices within the Computer Culture." *Signs* 16(1):128–57.

Wei, Nancy Chunjuan, and Darryl E. Brock, eds. 2013. *Mr. Science and Chairman Mao's Cultural Revolution: Science and Technology in Modern China*. New York: Lexington Books.

Wynne, Brian. 1992. "Misunderstood Misunderstanding: Social Identities and Public Uptake of Science." *Public Understanding of Science* 1(3):281–304.

Part VIII
Political cultures

48

Inventing the social, managing the subject

Governing mentalities

Jackie Orr

Introduction

> [T]he ethos offered by "governmentality" was fashioned in relation to specific inter-
> locutors and in a singular . . . political environment. Foucault was not first of all
> developing a set of tools for empirical social science research . . . but taking a kind of
> action or rather, a set of loosely related actions, in a multiply conditioned domestic
> and international political situation. The challenge for us . . . [is] not to ossify this
> perspective into a permanent and unchanging set of instruments of analysis but to
> adopt its ethos. Our present is different from Foucault's.
>
> *(Dean 2010:7)*

Governmentality, writes Michel Foucault, is an "ugly word" ([2004] 2007:115) for articulating
the political rationality, or the practices and reason of rule, that constitute the field of operations
for political power. Sifting the archives from early modern Europe through twentieth-century
post-war economic thought, Foucault identifies the "birth of a new art" (2000a:217) for exercising power in the name and the vital interests of "society," bringing the heterogeneous life of
populations and an ever-widening range of individual actions into the realm of explicit political
calculation (2000a, [2004] 2007, [2004] 2008). As an "experiment of method" (Foucault [2004]
2007:358), a genealogy of contemporary power, a challenge to Left political culture, *governmentality* marks an extraordinarily generative conceptual space launched by Foucault in 1978 in his
annual series of public lectures at the Collège de France. In the face of the "failure of the major
political theories nowadays," Foucault turns "not to a nonpolitical way of thinking but rather to
an investigation of what has been our political way of thinking during this century" (1988a:161).
Governmentality, then, like so much of Foucault's intellectual project, offers a history of the
present aimed at countering a form of power that not only rules our actions and perceptions,
but produces them:

> My project is . . . to bring it about, together with many others, that certain phrases can
> no longer be spoken so lightly, certain acts no longer . . . so unhesitatingly, performed; to

contribute to changing certain things in peoples' ways of perceiving and doing things. . . . I hardly feel capable of attempting much more than that.

(Foucault 1991:83)

My task here is to trace the enormously influential notion of governmentality as it is theorized by Foucault in the late 1970s, and elaborated by an early group of affiliated scholars who inter-rogate how neoliberal governmentality reconfigures contemporary political, social, and market relations. Next, I turn to more recent work on neoliberal governmentalities, including analytics of governance focused beyond Euro-North American circuits and work focused on resistance within neoliberal forms of rule. Then, taking up the limits of Foucault's original conception, I look at notions of colonial and transnational governmentality that critically reorient the con-cept to address histories of colonial and postcolonial power, and current practices of govern-ance complexly networked across state and national boundaries. Throughout, I foreground the implications of governmentality for the politics of knowledge-production itself, and I end with questions we might want to ask ourselves, as cultural sociologists, in the face of contemporary assemblages of power – including the "authoritarian governmentalities" (Dean 2010) – that are animating and producing "us" today.

Power's double itinerary: policing and pastoral care

At the heart of Foucault's analysis of the emergence of a new governmental reason is an image of *the social* as a new surface, a previously unintelligible and not yet politicized space of relation-ships, across which techniques of governance can extend their reach and geography of effects. If governmentality is entangled with the constitution of the modern state as a general technology of power "at once internal and external to the state" (Foucault 2000a:221), then the constitu-tion of society becomes a "necessary correlate" to the governmentalizing state (Foucault [2004] 2007:350). The state works to reveal "a new reality with its own rationality": that reality is civil society, materializing for the first time as "a possible domain of analysis, knowledge, and intervention" for which the state has responsibility (Foucault [2004]2007:348–50). Here, in the defamiliarizing gesture of an effective history of the present,

> it is the social that suddenly looms as a strange abstraction . . . [so that] perhaps the most sur-prising thing is the status that "the social" has thus won in our heads as something we take for granted. A strange aquarium that has become . . . the reality principle of our societies.
>
> *(Donzelet [1977]1979:xxvi)*

Tracking the reality principle of the social back to its historic invention, Foucault identi-fies the seventeenth and eighteenth century "science of police" as an experimental site for producing a newly governable real (Foucault [2004] 2007:311–54). Policing (predecessor not only to today's police but to "policy" and public administration as well) attempts to deploy a vast, detailed regulatory apparatus across proliferating domains of social activity: the circulation of people, goods, wealth; the surveillance of the birth, death, value, health, and productivity of individual citizens and aggregate populations; and the administration of the security, competi-tiveness, and expansion of state and non-state institutions. Dismantled and redistributed over the next century into the discrete governing practices embedded in population management; in political economy and market analyses; in law and the regulation of freedom; and in a police apparatus as we know it today (Foucault [2004]2007:354), policing establishes *population* as a key target of governmental reason (see Foucault 1988a; Pasquino 1991). Population becomes the scene of a newly "real" social body in its calculable and statistically communicable, policy-oriented and evermore policed form.

Even as eighteenth-century liberal thought secures the well-being of "the social" – measured via the happiness and prosperity of the population – as the central problematic of modern governmentality (Foucault 1997), Foucault continues to trace the double itinerary of a power that moves *between* managing aggregate social relations and governing individual conduct. As a strategy for regulating civil society and population, *and* as a "political technology of individuals," governmentality is historically entwined with that "strangest form of power, the form of power that is most typical of the West" – Christian pastoral power (Foucault [2004]2007:130). An "individualizing" power at its core, pastoral power demands a knowledge of the "truth" of one's self in exchange for the spiritual guidance and protection of a pastoral figure. The role of pastoral power, buried deep in the logic of today's political rationality, is "to constantly ensure, sustain, and improve the lives of each and every one" (Foucault 1988b:67).

Here, at the intersection of a science of administering society *in its totality*, and the pastoral task of perpetual care for the flock through an *individualizing* knowledge of each member, the paradoxical power of governmental technologies operating "in whole, and in detail" takes shape (Foucault 1988b:62). The simultaneously totalizing and individualizing effects of governmental power are, for Foucault, precisely the source of its peculiar efficacy and its particular violence: at the same time that the Christian West has produced "the most creative, the most conquering, the most arrogant, and doubtless the most bloody" of societies, the individual has also "learned to see himself as a sheep in a flock" ([2004]2007:130). How to address the "political double bind" of this "individualization and totalization of modern power structures" (Foucault 2000b:336), and the consequent "coexistence in political structures of large destructive mechanisms and institutions oriented toward the care of individual life" (Foucault 1988a:147), become profoundly troubled questions for contemporary social struggles, as well as for those individualized, historically situated effects of governmentalized agencies: our selves.

A neoliberal turn

The multiple provocations of governmentality become evident more than a decade before Foucault's 1978–1979 lectures begin to circulate in English translation in 2008. *The Foucault Effect: Studies in Governmentality* (1991), edited by Graham Burchell, Colin Gordon, and Peter Miller, assembles a collection of essays, many of them originally written in the 1970s, announcing the early preoccupations of "governmentality studies": the social management and rationalization of everyday life via insurance and new technologies of risk; the governmentalizing aims and effects of expert knowledges such as criminology and statistics; and the constitution of new forms of political and social identity as the target and medium of liberal governance (see Burchell, Gordon, and Miller 1991).

Threaded through several of these essays is a critical concern with neoliberalism as a twentieth-century mutation in political rationality, shifting the terrain of contemporary subjectivity, culture, and economies. Foucault ([2004] 2008) devoted the bulk of his public lectures in 1979 to an analysis of post-World War II neoliberal thought in Germany and the United States, and the notion of "neoliberal governmentality" has become one of the most influential trajectories of governmentality studies today (see Barry, Osborne, and Rose 1996; Rose 1999; Ferguson and Gupta 2005; Nadesan 2008; Raffnsoe et al. 2009; Cotoi 2011; Brown 2015). Through a relentless extension of market values and logics into non-economic realms, neoliberalism practices a kind of "economic administration of the social" (Donzelet 1991:278) in which governance and entrepreneurial models of cultural and political activity become inextricably linked. With neoliberal reason, the "promotion of an 'enterprise culture' as a new model for social and economic citizenship," paves the way for a social reality in which "individual citizens should be the entrepreneurs of themselves and their lives" (Gordon 1987:315). Governed by our freedom to choose, regulated by the responsibility to optimize our own value as "human capital," neoliberal subject-citizens incorporate an expansive social demand for self-development and self-investment.

The cultural politics that accompany this neoliberal blend of entrepreneurial pastoralism with a macropolitics of market expansion and a selective state withdrawal from welfare-based practices, include new technologies of care for the affective and physical well-being of individuals and populations. Today, therapeutic cultures popularize an aggressive "will to health" amplified by consumer advertising and marketing, where the maximization of well-being (mental, emotional, physical, sexual, economic) becomes the responsibility of individual customer-patients (Rose 2001:17–18). Neoliberal well-being is managed not only through population-level measures of aggregate risk for depression, diabetes, anxiety disorders, breast cancer, and so on (coupled with disease prevention campaigns aimed at risk-stratified populations and individual behaviors), but self-governance is also increasingly coordinated at "pre-individual" or "molecular" levels of genetic function and affective matter (Deleuze 1991; Clough 2007). Blurring the boundaries between consent and coercion, desire and control, neoliberal technologies of care operate as a form of political subjection all the more seductive for appearing as a quest for our own efficacy and freedom.

In the move toward economization – the installation of market logics and rationales of (self-)governance at the heart of neoliberal cultures – previously heterogeneous social fields and identities are assembled together in new forms of equivalence and value. Wendy Brown writes of neoliberal reason:

> All market actors are rendered as little capitals (rather than as owners, workers, and consumers) competing with, rather than exchanging with each other. Human capital's constant and ubiquitous aim, whether studying, interning, working, planning retirement, or reinventing itself in a new life, is to entrepreneurialize its endeavors, appreciate its value, and increase its rating or ranking. In this, it mirrors the mandate for contemporary firms, countries, academic departments or journals, universities, media or websites.... [A]s neoliberal rationality disseminates market value and metrics to new spheres, this does not always take a monetary form: rather, fields, persons, and practices are economized in ways that vastly exceed literal wealth generation.
>
> *(Brown 2015:36–7)*

In Michelle Murphy's (2017) analysis of the "economization of life" in postcolonial Bangladesh, neoliberal techniques of governance introduced via family planning campaigns in the 1970s did not aim solely at wealth accumulation. Rather, the racialized and sexualized experiments in population control promoted an "NGOization of governmentality," and the building of new infrastructures across uneven domains of knowledge and expertise, local and transnational organizations, everyday cultures, and individual women's "choice" (Murphy 2017:87–9). The value of such infrastructural assemblages included the political capacity to approach aggregate life itself as a "recomposable" domain: open to experimental intervention, subject to calculated regulation (Murphy 2017:80). Poverty and precarity for millions of Bangladeshi households were not erased by neoliberal interventions into "population"; they were redistributed and reinvested through an economization of life that saturated embodied, everyday worlds far beyond the economic.

Rethinking resistance

If politics, as Foucault offers, is "no more or less than that which is born with resistance to governmentality, the first uprising, the first confrontation" ([2004] 2007:390), then how are the politics of resistance addressed in governmentality studies? How to think about resistance to neoliberal governmentalities' regulated well-being (for some) and redistributed precarity (for others)? A wide body of recent scholarship looks at how rights-based identity movements have been incorporated into neoliberal governing mentalities, where social inclusion and cultural citizenship become tactics to administer, not contest, power-charged histories of exclusion. Focusing on US education policy vis-à-vis disability activism, Shelley Tremain argues that the social gains associated with access and inclusion are cut through with governmentalizing effects; here, students with disabilities can find themselves "included" in a governmentalization of education driven by a neoliberal dream of "act[ing] upon a totality of individuals who all exercise freedom *in the same way*" (2005:221). Inderpal Grewal analyzes the marketization of feminist and multicultural social movements whereby "lifestyles of empowerment" are made available through consumer market segmentation, with consumer "choice" operating as a strategy for individual and collective identity-making (2005:16). In her ethnographic study of campaigns to end sex trafficking, Elizabeth Bernstein (2018) identifies an emergent "carceral feminism" that couples women's "empowerment" with technologies of globalizing neoliberal governance, as previous struggles for gender and sexual justice are forged together with the policing arm of the state. As both a political and cultural project, carceral feminism "meld[s] new techniques of governance with particular imaginations of gendered freedom," blurring distinctions "between the 'progressive' and the 'conservative' as well as between 'the civil,' 'the economic,' and 'the political'" (Bernstein 2018: 21).

Soo Ah Kwon's study of youth of color organizing in Oakland, California, also highlights the entanglement of social justice movements with neoliberal governance strategies. A combination of youth experts, private philanthropic foundations, nonprofit organizations, and state initiatives deploy the "empowerment" of urban youth of color as a strategy of self- and community-governance, without "oppos[ing] the relations of power that made them powerless" (Kwon 2013:11). But Kwon's ethnography also finds that youth of color activism can directly address the contradictions between oppositional politics and professionalized nonprofit or state "support" – developing innovative coalitions that confront neoliberal democratic cultures as a part of the problem, not the solution.

Youth of color activists can be situated within what Tazzioli (2015:xii) names a "strugglefield of governmentality," where movements and subjects challenge the governmentalization of lived worlds, contesting for other political relations and practices of freedom. Tazzioli reminds us that Foucault's "diagnostic of the present" was intended as transformative work, including his genealogies of governmentality. While scholars by no means agree on how – or whether – an analytics of governmentality can effectively open spaces of resistance, it is worth remembering that Foucault once wrote: "Liberation can only come from attacking . . . political rationality's very roots" (1988b:85). It is perhaps this attack that Moten and Harney (2011) perform in "Blackness and Governance." Wary of politics, of the grassroots, of the community, of the "smirk of governmentality by all" – they ask, "Will we be in on the joke that we all know governmentality so well? We can all read it like a book" (Moten and Harney 2011:356). Instead, they conjure blackness as an outside to governance, an underside that refuses to participate, an inside flight toward a "utopian sensuality" and its unmanageable claim on "a now unfathomable debt of wealth" (Moten and Harney 2011:355, 357) – the debt owed by governance? A refusal aimed at the very roots of governmentalizing power?

Colonial and postcolonial governmentalities

> The view that illiberal practices are an exception to a liberal norm rather than a measure woven into the way liberal democracy and liberal empire has functioned throughout modernity becomes less tenable the more that we understand the normalcy of illiberal practices within colonial rule.
>
> *(Walters 2015:15)*

In response to Foucault's conspicuous silence regarding modes of governmentality operating outside the geographies of Europe and the US, scholars from a range of disciplinary and inter-disciplinary sites have challenged the historical and conceptual limitations of his thought (Stoler 1995, 2002; Scott 1999; Chatterjee 2004; Inda 2005; Kalpagam 2014). Their work elaborates ethnographically and theoretically rich notions of colonial, imperial, or transnational governmentalities that use elements of Foucault's analytics to understand histories of colonial rule and the dynamic complexities of a postcolonial present. Colonial governmentality gives name to those political rationalities that – often machined together with violent logics of military conquest and enslaved or indentured labor – were exercised "in relation to new targets, new forms of knowledge, and new technologies, and . . . [the] production of new effects of order and subjectivity" (Scott 1999:51). Practices of affective investment, racialized cultural regulation, and the creation of intimate desires characterized colonial remakings of the social as a strategic space for enacting forms of collective and individual subjection (Stoler 1995). How to theorize a specifically modern "imperial" governmentality that utilizes governing mechanisms that Foucault largely ignores? Refusing Foucault's presumption of the state as a discrete analytic space, how to think about transnational governmentality, and its recombinant technologies of state and non-state practices, in relation to shifting geographies of power and authority? (Ferguson and Gupta 2005). How, in short, to make governmentality speak in the language of colonial histories, and postcolonial or transnational circuits of power?

Recent scholarship in sociology narrates the role of the social sciences in imperial and colonial governance (Connell 2007; Go 2013). "Epistemological conquest" accompanied and enabled other, more visible, forms of colonial power through the constitution of categories of thought, systems of classification, and new statistical objects that could be acted upon (Kalpagam 2014:4). The archives of postcolonial governance show traces of such epistemological in(ter) ventions, while also conveying the nuance and hybridity of knowledge systems forged in intimate contact between neoliberal reason, indigenous practice, global expertise, colonial legacies, everyday "life strategies," and state policies – as seen, for example, in the biopolitics of HIV/ AIDS in post-apartheid South Africa (Decoteau 2013).

A burgeoning literature on the Middle East and North Africa draws on governmentality as theoretical method to analyze US military occupation, and the Arab Spring and its aftermath, including recent migrant and refugee movements out of North Africa (Tagma, Kalaycioglu, and Akcali 2013; Tazzioli 2015; Akcali 2016; Dag 2016). The accumulated effects of a top-down imposition of neoliberalism in the region, partnered directly with authoritarian regimes and largely benefitting select local clienteles along with the US, the World Bank, and the International Monetary Fund (IMF), has been succeeded by the promotion of a "bottom-up" neoliberal governmentality by the EU after the Arab revolts in 2011 (Tagma et al. 2013:376–7). Aimed at refashioning individual-level subjectivities (particularly youth), and building "capacity" at the level of civil society and non-state actors, the EU's investments in the governmentalization of democratic cultures ignores that it was precisely *the failure* of neoliberalizing reforms that contributed to popular revolts in Egypt and elsewhere (Tagma et al. 2013:387). In Iraq, the US also attempted an imposition, through military occupation and political conquest, of a top-down framework of neoliberal governmentality; indigenous resistance has repeatedly guaranteed the failure of that framework, while alternative formations of state and civil society remain stalled (Dag 2016).

If scholars of North Africa and the Middle East are cautious about the limits of neoliberal governmentality in understanding contemporary postcolonial political cultures, they are likely far more aware than many North American scholars of Foucault's intimate engagements with the Iranian revolution in 1978, and student revolts in Tunisia a decade earlier (see Ghamari-Tabrizi 2016). Foucault's time in Tunisia and Iran, and his passionate involvement with Islamist revolutionary politics, in no way spares governmentality from prolific critique as a flawed Euro-centric concept, born out of a selective history of political liberalism seemingly voided of its colonial violence. But we are reminded, with the epigraph to this chapter, that the promise of governmentality today is its ethos of active intervention in a singular domestic and international political situation, enormously different from Foucault's. Paul Amar's *The Security Archipelago* (2013) exemplifies precisely this ethos, with an analysis of emergent techniques of postcolonial governance generated, in part, out of a "Global South-centered approach" that recognizes the political vibrancy and dynamism of what used to be called the "semiperiphery" (30). Focusing on the globalizing megacities of Cairo and Rio de Janeiro, Amar identifies a new form of "human-security governance" that assembles together the end of neoliberalism (except in Global North scholarship!) with elements of local and transnational security/policing regimes, progressive social movements and queer resistances, sexualized biopolitics, and humanitarian policies – producing new, unlikely postcolonial subjects of both coercion and potential emancipation.

In-conclusions: governing cultural sociology?

My last point will be this: The emergence of social science cannot . . . be isolated from the rise of this new political rationality and from this new political technology.
(Foucault 1988a:162)

The measure of genealogy's success is its disruption of conventional accounts of ourselves – our sentiments, bodies, origins, futures. It tells a story that disturbs our habits of self-recognition, posing an "us" that is foreign.
(Brown 2001:106)

Foucault's genealogy of governmentality carries with it a demand to dis-locate our selves – as subjects of governmentality, and as sociologists whose disciplining is deeply implicated in the emergence of a political rationality that depends on knowledge practices that come to be known as the social sciences. As governmentality invents the social as a new field for generating power effects, it also provokes a field of new knowledges to help administer a "real" which governmental reason both rules and produces. Foucault's work suggests that the first strategic practitioner of a cultural politics may have been a governmentalizing state, as rationalities of rule began to reach further into domains of cultural practice and individual conduct.

As an analytic, governmentality contributes, along with several decades of cultural studies scholarship, to the undoing of foundational dualisms structuring many older grammars of cultural theory: domination/freedom, economy/culture, coercion/consent, private/public, society/market. But today the most potent promise of a governmentality approach may be to help us intervene in forms of contemporary political reason and rule for which we do not have adequate language or collective political response. The return, with a vengeance and with a difference, of right-wing populisms, racist nationalisms, neofascist politics, and white supremacist violence, to national political cultures across a wide swath of the Global North (though not only), presents a singular domestic and international situation animated by immediate dangers. "Authoritarian governmentality" offers one analytic grid for grasping how elements of sovereign power and biopolitical violence can intersect with the freedom-domination nexus of liberal governmentality (Dean 2002, 2010). A recent history of scholarship exists that is attuned to the necropolitical zones where powers of detention, deportation, incarceration, and social death *have always already been selectively folded in* to liberal and neoliberal configurations of governance (see Wacquant 2009; Clough and Willse 2011; Fassin 2011; Bernstein 2018).

What form of cultural analysis can interrupt global and national reorderings of governance that threaten, in old and acutely new ways, to destroy populations, mobilities, and collective imaginaries of refuge, of radical elsewheres? How might a history of governing mentalities, bound to a story of political power's search for new methods of extension and intensification, give us – an "us" now made somewhat foreign to our selves – other sensations of what's possible? Other signposts toward different methods for making up and remaking, again, what's real?

References

Akcali, E. 2016. "Introduction." In *Neoliberal Governmentality and the Future of the State in the Middle East and North Africa*, edited by E. Akcali. New York: Palgrave Macmillan.

Amar, P. 2013. *The Security Archipelago: Human-Security States, Sexuality Politics, and the End of Neoliberalism*. Durham, NC: Duke University Press.

Barry, A., T. Osborne, and N. Rose, eds. 1996. *Foucault and Political Reason: Liberalism, Neo-liberalism, and Rationalities of Government*. Chicago: University of Chicago Press.

Bernstein, E. 2018. *Brokered Subjects: Sex, Trafficking, and the Politics of Freedom*. Chicago: University of Chicago Press.

Brown, W. 2001. *Politics Out of History*. Princeton, NJ: Princeton University Press.

———. 2015. *Undoing the Demos: Neoliberalism's Stealth Revolution*. Cambridge, MA: The MIT Press.

Burchell, G., C. Gordon, and P. Miller, eds. 1991. *The Foucault Effect: Studies in Governmentality*. Chicago: University of Chicago Press.

Chatterjee, P. 2004. *The Politics of the Governed: Reflections on Popular Politics in Most of the World*. New York: Columbia University Press.

Clough, P. 2007. "Introduction." Pp. 1–33 in *The Affective Turn: Theorizing the Social*, edited by P. Clough. Durham, NC: Duke University Press.

Clough, P., and C. Willse. 2011. "Human Security/National Security: Gender Branding and Population Racism." Pp. 46–64 in *Beyond Biopolitics: Essays on the Governance of Life and Death*, edited by P. Clough and C. Willse. Durham, NC: Duke University Press.

Connell, R. 2007. "Empire and the Creation of a Social Science." Ch. 1 in *Southern Theory: The Global Dynamics of Knowledge in Social Science*. Cambridge: Polity Press.

Cotoi, C. 2011. "Neoliberalism: A Foucauldian Perspective." *International Review of Social Research* 1(2):109–24.

Dag, R. 2016. "The Failure of the State (Re)Building Process in Iraq." Pp. 31–43 in *Neoliberal Governmentality and the Future of the State in the Middle East and North Africa*, edited by E. Akcali. New York: Palgrave Macmillan.

Dean, M. 2002. "Liberal Government and Authoritarianism." *Economy and Society* 31(1):37–91.

———. 2010. *Governmentality: Power and Rule in Modern Society*. 2nd ed. Los Angeles: Sage.

Decoteau, C.L. 2013. *Ancestors and Antiretrovirals: The Biopolitics of HIV/AIDS in Post-Apartheid South Africa*. Chicago: University of Chicago Press.

Deleuze, G. 1991. "Postscript on the Societies of Control." *October* 59:3–7.

Donzelet, J. [1977] 1979. *The Policing of Families*, trans. R. Hurley. New York: Pantheon Books.

———. 1991. "Pleasure in Work." Pp. 251–80 in *The Foucault Effect: Studies in Governmentality*, edited by G. Burchell C. Gordon, and P. Miller. Chicago: University of Chicago Press.

Fassin, D. 2011. "Policing Borders, Producing Boundaries: The Governmentality of Immigration in Dark Times." *Annual Review of Anthropology* 40:213–26.

Ferguson, J., and A. Gupta. 2005. "Spatializing States: Toward an Ethnography of Neoliberal Governmentality." Pp. 105–31 in *Anthropologies of Modernity: Foucault, Governmentality, and Life Politics*, edited by J.X. Inda. Malden, MA: Blackwell.

Foucault, M. 1988a. "The Political Technology of Individuals." Pp. 145–62 in *Technologies of the Self: A Seminar with Michel Foucault*, edited by L. Martin, H. Gutman, and P.H. Hutton. Amherst: University of Massachusetts Press.

———. 1988b. "Politics and Reason." Pp. 57–85 in *Michel Foucault: Politics, Philosophy, Culture*, edited by L.D. Kritzman, trans. Alan Sheridan and others. New York: Routledge.

———. 1991. "Questions of Method." Pp. 73–86 in *The Foucault Effect: Studies in Governmentality*, edited by G. Burchell, C. Gordon, and P. Miller. Chicago: University of Chicago Press.

———. 1997. "The Birth of Biopolitics." Pp. 73–9 in *Michel Foucault: Ethics*. Vol. 1, edited by P. Rabinow, trans. R. Hurley and others. New York: New Press.

———. 2000a. "Governmentality." Pp. 201–22 in *Michel Foucault: Power*. Vol. 3, edited by J.D. Faubion. New York: New Press.

———. 2000b. "The Subject and Power." Pp. 326–48 in *Michel Foucault: Power*. Vol. 3, edited by J.D. Faubion. New York: New Press.

———. [2004] 2007. *Security, Territory, Population: Lectures at the Collège de France, 1977–78*, trans. G. Burchell. New York: Palgrave Macmillan.

———. [2004] 2008. *The Birth of Biopolitics: Lectures at the Collège de France, 1978–79*, trans. G. Burchell. New York: Palgrave Macmillan.

Ghamari-Tabrizi, B. 2016. *Foucault in Iran: Islamic Revolution after the Enlightenment*. Minneapolis: University of Minnesota Press.

Go, J. 2013. "Sociology's Imperial Unconscious: The Emergence of American Sociology in the Context of Empire." Pp. 83–105 in *Sociology & Empire: The Imperial Entanglements of a Discipline*, edited by G. Steinmetz. Durham, NC: Duke University Press.

Gordon, C. 1987. "The Soul of the Citizen: Max Weber and Michel Foucault on Rationality and Government." Pp. 293–316 in *Max Weber, Rationality and Modernity*, edited by S. Lash and S. Whimster. London: Allen & Unwin.

Grewal, I. 2005. *Transnational America: Feminisms, Diasporas, Neoliberalisms*. Durham, NC: Duke University Press.

Inda, J.X. 2005. "Analytics of the Modern: An Introduction." Pp. 1–20 in *Anthropologies of Modernity: Foucault, Governmentality, and Life Politics*, edited by J.X. Inda. Malden, MA: Blackwell.

Kalpagam, U. 2014. *Rule by Numbers: Governmentality in Colonial India*. London: Lexington Books.

Kwon, S.A. 2013. *Uncivil Youth: Race, Activism, and Affirmative Governmentality*. Durham, NC: Duke University Press.

Moten, F., and S. Harney. 2011. "Blackness and Governance." Pp. 351–61 in *Beyond Biopolitics: Essays on the Governance of Life and Death*, edited by P. Clough and C. Willse. Durham, NC: Duke University Press.

Murphy, M. 2017. *The Economization of Life*. Durham, NC: Duke University Press.

Nadesan, M.H. 2008. *Governmentality, Biopower, and Everyday Life*. New York: Routledge.

Pasquino, P. 1991. "Theatrum Politicum: The Genealogy of Capital – Police and the State of Prosperity." Pp. 105–18 in *The Foucault Effect: Studies in Governmentality*, edited by G. Burchell, C. Gordon, and P. Miller. Chicago: University of Chicago Press.

Raffnsoe, S., A. Rosenberg, A. Beaulieu, S. Binkley, S. Opitz, J.E. Kristensen, M. Rabinowitz, and D. Vilstrup Holm, eds. 2009. "Neoliberal Governmentality." Special issue of *Foucault Studies* 6:1–4.

Rose, N. 1999. *Powers of Freedom: Reframing Political Thought*. Cambridge: Cambridge University Press.

———. 2001. "The Politics of Life Itself." *Theory, Culture & Society* 18(6):1–30.

Scott, D. 1999. "Colonial Governmentality." Pp. 23–52 in *Refashioning Futures: Criticism after Postcoloniality*. Princeton, NJ: Princeton University Press.

Stoler, A. 1995. *Race and the Education of Desire: Foucault's History of Sexuality and the Colonial Order of Things*. Durham, NC: Duke University Press.

———. 2002. *Carnal Knowledge and Imperial Power: Race and the Intimate in Colonial Rule*. Berkeley: University of California Press.

Tagma, H. M., E. Kalaycioglu, and E. Akcali. 2013. "'Taming' Arab Social Movements: Exporting Neoliberal Governmentality." *Security Dialogue* 44(5–6):375–92.

Tazzioli, M. 2015. *Spaces of Governmentality: Autonomous Migration and the Arab Uprisings*. London: Rowman & Littlefield International.

Tremain, S. 2005. "Foucault, Governmentality, and Critical Disability Theory." Pp. 1–24 in *Foucault and the Government of Disability*, edited by S. Tremain. Ann Arbor: University of Michigan Press.

Wacquant, L. 2009. *Punishing the Poor: The Neoliberal Government of Social Insecurity*. Durham, NC: Duke University Press.

Walters, W. 2015. "Reflections on Migration and Governmentality." *Movements* 1(1):1–25.

49

Making things political

Nina Eliasoph and Paul Lichterman

Introduction

In this chapter we focus on the everyday situations in which people politicize or depoliticize issues. By "politicizing" we mean action, collective or individual, that makes issues or identities into topics of public deliberation or contestation. Depoliticizing means making once-salient issues or identities inaccessible to deliberation or contestation.

Until recently, political scientists and sociologists examining political culture have focused either on society-wide traditions or on consciousness. Research on society-wide traditions has emphasized the role of shared values or widespread discourses of the good citizen or good society (Almond and Verba 1963; Bellah et al. 1985). Studies of consciousness have emphasized propaganda, agenda-setting, or subtle media effects (see Gramsci 1971; Lukes 1974; Hall 1977; Gaventa 1980). Both approaches, at bottom, have assumed the conventional definition of power as A's ability to make B do something against B's will, or to prevent B from even thinking of alternatives.

Rather than conjuring up a society's culture in general, our definition of "political culture" focuses on situated communication. Rather than making individuals the subjects of politics, we focus on relationships and speech genres in settings that actors usually can recognize and "typify" already (Cicourel 1981), using their own understandings. While we could not possibly deny the horrific power of the media to convince people of half-truths or outright fabrications, neither do we reduce political culture to ideological domination. Our research shows that people can express and think thoughts in one situation that they cannot easily express or even think in another. Similarly, we do not deny that a relatively few political and moral discourses may circulate widely in a society, but people in complex, diverse societies use them in too many different ways, in different settings, for the notion of shared traditions to facilitate research unless we specify and elaborate further. The differences between two societies may very well be in how they distribute situations, how people learn what is possible to say and do in a union versus a political party versus a charity group, or even in different kinds of political parties (Faucher-King 2005). Focusing on how people in various societies learn the proper etiquette for a political party versus a religious charity is different from asking how different societies create a certain kind of taken-for-granted consciousness in people. On this point our view differs also from some uses of Foucault's work which equate power with the creation of subjectivities that people in a society share, without talking about how the creation, maintenance, and transformation of identities varies from one situation to another.

Rather than assuming that some issues or groups are inherently more political than others, we call for examining how and where, if at all, people acting in concert make things political. We argue that before asking "who is wielding power over whom," researchers have to take a prior step, to ask how people, groups, or institutions politicize and depoliticize issues or people. Rather than reading off amounts of power from people's race, class, gender, or other social positions in the same way wherever the people go, we investigate how and where, if at all, inequalities *materialize* differently in different everyday situations. That is why our approach to cultures of politics focuses on interaction, whether in institutions, formal organizations, or informal settings.

With our focus on interaction, we say that cultures of politics are shared methods of politicizing or depoliticizing. Like other cultural sociologists, we maintain a "strong" sense of culture as a relatively autonomous force in social life — symbolic patterns that cannot be explained away by relations of domination and subordination. We agree with cultural sociologists who say that symbols exert their own enabling and constraining influence on action. We depart from some cultural sociologists, however, when we follow culture's effects, and sources, all the way down to the level of everyday interaction.

Shared methods of politicizing: elements of a cultural analysis

Following Durkheim (Alexander 1988; Durkheim [1915] 1995), we focus on a society's "collective representations," though we do not suppose all members of a society share or affirm collective representations uniformly. By collective representations we mean conventional vocabularies or moral narratives that shape people's motives, by putting them into words that others easily can apprehend. In interviews, pamphlets, and position statements, or in moments of conflict, Americans might tell each other that it is good to be active in community life because "I am doing God's work," or "we are giving back to the community," or "it feels good to help other people," or because "the people united will never be defeated." These are structured vocabularies of motive, moral languages we use to make our acts meaningful and compelling to ourselves and others, as sociologists such as Robert Wuthnow would point out (1992). To understand such collective representations, we look to Geertz (1973), Ricoeur (1991), or Frye (1957) for models of culture's durably patterned qualities. Though we start with shared symbols, we do not end with them, because symbols sometimes absorb radically different meanings from the contexts in which people invoke them. The differences, however, are not simply random (Burke 1945).

Discourses or representations become meaningful in specific scenes, in relation to the style of action that people share in the scene. In Goffman's terms ([1974] 1986) a scene is a sequence of action guided by participants' rough sense of "what we are doing here." *Scene style* is participants' routine way of coordinating action and implicitly defining the meaning of acting together in a scene (Eliasoph and Lichterman 2003; Lichterman and Eliasoph 2014). Scene styles are enduring, often structure-like cultural forms, not momentary improvisations. A society's political life hosts a finite number of scene styles. Different scene styles create different textures of "group," even within one organization.

To discover scene style, a researcher can notice several dimensions. First, participants imagine themselves on a wider social map; those maps show members how their group is related to a world that they may imagine as full of conflict or harmony, highly structured, or vague. Second, participants sustain *bonds* that define a set of good members' obligations to each other. These may vary according to the category of person — a man's obligations versus a woman's, for example, or a volunteer's versus a paid staff member's. Third, participants observe speech norms that define the meaning of speech itself differently in different situations within the overall organization – confession, or testimony, or flirting, or serious debate, for example. Finally, words, gestures, or images are not the only bearers of meaning. People interact using material, physical affordances as well – furniture, buildings, and space, for example (Glaeser 2001; Thévenot 2006). The ways that people interact based on their relationships to these material affordances is also part of style.

The concept of "scene style" implies that participation, even in informal groups, cannot be reduced to an unpredictable flow of emergent definitions of the situation, as some symbolic inter-actionists (e.g., Blumer 1969) might argue. Rather, people quickly have to recognize what kind of meaning-making situation they have entered, or else everyone would be learning every time from scratch how to act differently at school versus in a courtroom versus in a volunteer group.

In this chapter we will focus much more on style than collective representations since style inflects representations in everyday interaction, and our concept of style makes our approach quite different from other approaches to political culture. Readers interested in fuller treatments of our approach can consult other works (Eliasoph and Lichterman 2003; Lichterman 2005; Eliasoph 2011; Lichterman and Eliasoph 2014; Eliasoph 2016). Here we use ethnographic illustrations from our studies of church-based community service groups (Lichterman 2005) and youth civic engagement projects (Eliasoph 2011) – both in a mid-sized, midwestern US urban area.

Politicizing is more than "sounding political"

Many studies have used the concept of "framing" to investigate the uses of political culture in social movements and other public places (Snow et al. 1986). The term originates in Erving Goffman's work, where it described the implicit assumptions about speech that operate in a particular setting. In scholarship on "framing," in contrast, the concept refers to the ideological theme or worldview that is supposed to motivate some instance of communication. The scene style concept departs from this latter use of Goffman. It helps us explain the successes or frustrations of politicizing in ways that scholarship on framing would not. The concept of scene style also keeps us from assuming that "political"-sounding language must signify that only politicization and not also depoliticization is happening.

One example is the case of the Justice Task Force, a local group of liberal church representatives in a midwestern US city who wanted to publicize the dangers of welfare policy reform in the 1990s. Members of the task force shared a vocabulary of social criticism familiar to many US grassroots progressives: they criticized corporate capitalism. Yet the way they communicated about corporate interests often scared away people who did not share their style, *even people who likely agreed with their viewpoints*. The Justice Task Force's communication style encouraged members to talk angrily whenever possible (speech norms), reject people who did not have the same intense commitment to left ideology (group bonds), and think of the group as lonely prophets poised against corporate power, complacent state officials, and false images circulated by the mass media (group boundaries). Members enacted what we have called the "social critic" style.

The Justice Task Force put together educational workshops intended to teach churchgoers that welfare reform benefited the rich and the corporations at the expense of the poor. At one meeting, 12 members listened as one member delivered an hour-long critique of corporate neoliberalism. The host of a radical radio talk show came to the meeting, sat silently for a long time, and finally told us in a rising voice that he represented "a race [African American] that doesn't live as long . . . There are lots of Blacks who don't care a lot about ideology." He thought the group should be able to "act on our faith underpinnings." And at last he blurted out, "We know who the number-one activist is, the one who risked everything – Jesus!" There was an awkward silence. No one else spoke up for Jesus. The radio announcer did not come back to another meeting. The Justice Task Force thought any association that was serious about welfare policy should be bound together by leftist solidarity, not faith in Jesus. They did not consider whether or not some African Americans would be more accustomed to and comfortable with a different *style* of group, with more religious bonds, in order to voice the same criticisms of welfare policy, and their response to the radio announcer in effect depoliticized racial identity. The Justice Task Force remained small, marginal, and socially homogenous, unable to talk even with people who would agree with much of its collective representations of welfare reform "on paper." Their method of politicizing disempowered the message.

Another example, from the Youth Civic Engagement Projects (YEP) in the same city, shows that how people do or do not politicize their actions can diverge remarkably from the image one would get if one only analyzed the frames in their public statements. For a handful of organizers, part of these projects' agenda was to make a connection between volunteering and political activism. Organizers spoke about not just feeding the hungry, for example, but of encouraging young people to ask, "Why is there hunger in such a wealthy country?" From the organizations' written statements, and from organizers' discussions, it would look like these projects were "politicizing" young people by framing issues in terms that would link social change with individual caring. Moral vocabularies of compassion and social justice lived together on paper and in organizers' discussions among themselves.

However, youth participants never actually did talk about why there was hunger in the US. One of the extremely rare moments of political controversy arose when a girl tried to flirt with a boy but got the scene style wrong (and also failed at flirting): her gambit was to get his attention by vehemently telling him that she was anti-abortion and pro-capital punishment. Acting as a typical member of the organization, the boy politely tried to avoid saying that he disagreed with her positions. Talking politics had to be out of place in this organization if it was to be welcoming to all. Although nearly all the organizers were vaguely liberal, they did not consider it fair to impose their ideas on young people, because they did not want to exclude any participants – even the anti-abortion, pro-capital punishment girl – and organizers assumed that disagreement would scare participants away. In group sessions with the youth, one of the main scene styles was that of "club-style volunteering," which called for smoothing out political disagreements in the name of inclusive and harmonious group bonds, vague and conflict-free maps, and polite, upbeat speech.

Organizers encouraged their program members to attend county board hearings to testify that their programs deserved money. This may look like an unequivocal example of "politicizing," because youth participants were putting pressure on the state. But from our perspective, what is most interesting is the how – how this seemingly political activity came to appear to youth as uncontroversial and apolitical. Every year the youth members who went to the county board meeting saw that if they won, youth programs would get money, while other programs, such as those for old people or disabled babies, would not. Every year, youth mused over whether there would be any way for everyone to get what they needed, and every year, adult organizers neglected to address this question. It could only be answered by widening the map that the group imagined on its social horizon, and by addressing conflict. Every year the question quickly died, and a potentially political set of hearings became depoliticized when the bigger picture vanished.

Depoliticizing is more than social-structural domination

The adult organizers and funders of YEP hoped that volunteer work would bring diverse youth together, make them better citizens, and make them feel more like equals who could help usher in a more egalitarian society. Though participants did not live as equals in the rest of their lives, organizers hoped they could leave their unequal pasts behind when they joined together as volunteers. They often said that doing the work together, walking the walk, would set participants on equal footing in a volunteer group. So talking directly about members' inequality was taboo in the regional YEP's monthly meetings and in the service projects that members planned and attended.

Although participants could not talk about this inequality in most scenes, they had to know about it, just in order to make sense of interaction. There were two very distinct groups of participants. Disadvantaged youth of color came to the YEP's evening meetings from their after-school "prevention programs" for "at-risk youth." The organizers of the programs drove them in a big group. On the other hand, the non-poor volunteers, nearly all of them white, arrived in their own cars or were driven by their parents. Standards for success differed for the two groups: for the first, organizers said to each other that just the fact of their being at the meeting instead of committing crimes or taking drugs was a triumph. For the second, doing something active was required, to show that their motives went beyond pumping up their curricula vitae for college admission. Creating a haven from inequality meant learning how to ignore these differences, even though everyone had to know about them, just to decipher action.

Organizers had to talk about youth participants as members of categories when communicating with each other and with important outsiders – their government and nonprofit funders. The YEP got funding partly because it served the needy. Diversity and inequality helped justify these projects' existence, and, indeed, they were much more diverse than typical voluntary associations usually are, since those are usually very socially homogeneous (Verba, Lehman Schlozman, and Brady 1995; Popielarz and Miller McPherson 1995). Typical voluntary associations create one kind of social inequality; the civic projects created another (Eliasoph 2016).

A purely social-structural analysis might ask if YEP projects "reproduced" inequality or cultivated "resistance" to oppression. However, the sum of all these differences was not a simple reproduction of pre-existing inequality. YEP projects created a *specific* kind of inequality in everyday interaction, one that materializes in scenes in which participants are expected to speak as if they are equals when they know they are not. Youth of color knew where they stood partly because they had heard statistics about people like them, for example, from organizers who had to chase funding by documenting that their programs helped disadvantaged youth of color defy the odds, statistically speaking, for crime, teen pregnancy, and drug abuse. Organizers had to make sure that that this achievement was visible, literally, so it was important in public events to put obviously non-white youth on the podium, while equally poor, rural white youths' presence was not as urgent.

This practice created certain kinds of inequality and certain grounds for politicization. For example, youth participants inevitably overheard organizers' ways of documenting diversity, and sometimes repeated it. When a black 13-year-old boy who was asked to speak from personal experience instead recited statistics about the drop-out rates for black males in town and described how it felt to be treated like someone who would fulfill that prediction, was this a case of politicization? Statistics can politicize or not, depending on who is using them, and for what ends – to denounce structural racism, as other black speakers did, or to document for fundraising purposes, as organizers did, or to describe the feeling of being treated as a failure waiting to happen, as the black boy did, for example. All of these offer different possibilities for politicization.

The point here is that while class and racial inequality mattered in YEP projects and structured the experiences of participants, scene styles generated and politicized or depoliticized inequality in patterned ways that could not simply be read off from the class and race positions of YEP organizers and volunteers. So, we cannot assume social inequality offers a complete guide to power relations.

Another usual tack that social researchers take would assume that differences between ordinary citizens and state agencies translate reliably into a story of power and domination. However, a focus on "cultures of politics" can show that elements of scene style – in this case, the map that orients a scene – can have unintended depoliticizing consequences even apart from what external, state entities force groups to do or avoid doing.

Two other church-based community service alliances will illustrate this point. In the first case, members of the Humane Response Alliance (HRA) *assumed* from the beginning that their association was an adjunct to the state and would work inside the categories of state policy. As one of HRA's leaders said, the group needed to find a role within policies "set by the local government." No one pressed the issue further.

Of course, churchgoers could not simply offer their own social services and usurp government authority without consequences. Yet they did not necessarily have to map themselves in terms of the state's own categories, especially in the US context, in which people assume that citizens are free to organize civic efforts apart from state mandates. They did not have to propose doing the state welfare service's job in order to come up with some other role beyond that "set by the local government."

Paradoxically, for someone who expected the state to dominate the volunteers, it was a *state* employee who came up with just such a role. He suggested that the HRA organize forums in which people newly cut off from financial assistance describe their troubles directly to state agents. In our terms, the state employee was suggesting that HRA help people *politicize* welfare reform in new ways, while HRA leaders already had *depoliticized* welfare reform – removing it as a potential object of deliberation or contention. To find power working inside the HRA's own style, its own maps and bonds, offers a more nuanced, useful story of power relations than to say, as some critical observers might (McKnight 1995), that "the state dominated the HRA."

In the other example – an evangelical-sponsored support program for former welfare-receiving families – many volunteers considered the program nonpolitical, even though the director conceived it as a church-based complement to welfare reform. It would be easy for a researcher to assume the volunteers enlisted in this "Adopt-a-Family" program because they were ideologically or politically invested in cutting welfare. Other researchers would assume that their job is to show how ideologically manipulated these volunteers were.

Both approaches would impute silent motives to people by fiat, and neither would attend to the volunteers' own ways of distinguishing "political" from "not political." Neither could offer much help, then, in understanding how ordinary citizens make sense of policy agendas. Many of the volunteers were strikingly indifferent to the various political ideologies surrounding welfare policy. Welfare reform as a political fact was not very salient to them. They articulated their motives much more in terms of an evangelical Protestant-inflected version of compassion. They said that volunteering for this program was a way to perform "Christ-like care." They enacted Christ-like care in a distinct style. While volunteering in the program, they tried to imagine themselves on an unchanging map that highlighted not groups, communities, or institutions but one fundamental boundary between Christ and individuals worldwide who need Christ. They saw Adopt-a-Family as simply one Christ-like service opportunity among others, and not an opportunity to step into history and take a stance on an enormous institutional change, as many social scientists would view welfare reform. Attributing ideological or political motives to these volunteers would have produced a very distorted picture of their participation. The volunteers' own ways of politicizing or depoliticizing welfare reform became clear only from following their own communication and their own relationship-building in the program.

Cultures of politics in global perspective

Given our attention to how people draw lines between political and nonpolitical, our approach is especially useful for understanding "politics" in places where an already sedimented political culture does not define some relationships and forms of speech as "politics" a priori. In Albania, for example (Sampson 1996), or Uzbekistan (Makarova 1998), figuring out what to count as "politics" is not easy for the analyst, much less the actors. Would an Islamic gathering place in Uzbekistan – a *mahalla* that plans funerals, doles out something that looks to a Westerner like social welfare, and builds schools – be a "political" entity, making political decisions? Asserting that it is or is not "political" is not as interesting as saying *how* it becomes political, how issues or identities become topics of public deliberation or silencing, and how the process of politicizing creates and recreates the typical *mahalla* in Uzbekistan. When squatters in India siphon water from the city's water mains without paying, is it more "political" if they do it visibly to make a public statement, or if they make under-the-table deals with local politicians, or if they simply take what they consider to be rightfully theirs? (Chatterjee 2004). Some activists in Brazilian youth organizations value harmony and others value loud disagreement, and others just want to accomplish practical projects (Mische 2007). As Mische's work shows, newcomers can recognize the scene style in play by observing how members push some feelings, ideas, and relationships off the horizon here, but spotlight them there. But which style is more "political"? Along with "postcolonial studies" scholars, we argue that they might all be "political" in different ways that highlight different dilemmas, shape different arguments, and, eventually, different outcomes.

Conclusion: qualities of political engagement in everyday interaction

Our interaction-centered approach to cultures of politics differs from prominent alternatives of the past 25 years. Older approaches have ignored differences in setting and reduced political culture to dominant ideology that social elites use consciously to manipulate subordinates (Ewen 1976; Lasch 1979). A more nuanced version of this argument holds that people carry dominant ideologies ambivalently, and sometimes contest domination. In Stuart Hall's example, a working-class person who is watching the national news on TV hears "the national interest" but decodes that message as "the interest of the ruling elite," but also may identify partially with the ruling elite's interest because it seems so commonsensical. In contrast, a member of the ruling elite assumes what the newscaster assumed when writing the piece, which is that the national interest is the same as his or her own interest. Hall's approach improves greatly on the "dominant ideology" approach, but still ignores settings and assumes that the listener's social background is all we need to know. Political culture is, for these analysts, a process of either accepting or resisting dominant ideology, albeit ambivalently, a lot of the time.

Pierre Bourdieu (1984) advances a step by not reducing political culture to class in the Marxist sense. He says that different groups compete to politicize or depoliticize issues. For him, a political language becomes prestigious and persuasive simply because prestigious and powerful groups use it. In his approach, then, interaction serves largely to reproduce inequalities between actors competing in grossly slanted fields.

The concept of "field" seems, at first glance, to resemble our notion of scene. Bourdieu writes that he treats fields as games, within which different moves have different meanings: what is deemed worthy for fine museum art, for example, is not considered worthy for cool, graffiti-inspired art. But in most of his work, hierarchical power struggles appear in the end to be the only really important game; after his earlier ethnographic studies (Bourdieu 1990), he rarely got close enough to the ground to see how people create fields and make moves in them, in everyday interaction, so for him, styles reduce to hierarchical positions.

Our examples show, in contrast to these two approaches, that it is difficult to describe actual instances of politicizing and depoliticizing completely in terms of domination, resistance, or group position. Methods of politicizing and depoliticizing are more situation-specific, more a product of scene style, than these other approaches presume. Instead of being certain about which inequalities matter where, or which side will win, a focus on cultures of politics asks how people create situations that politicize or depoliticize issues. We do not argue that people all have the same chances to politicize issues. Rather, we ask how and when people decide they are doing something "political," instead of defining individuals, organizations or issues as political, powerful, or not powerful by scholarly fiat.

References

Alexander, Jeffrey. 1988. *Durkheimian Sociology: Cultural Studies*. Berkeley: University of California Press.

Almond, G.A., and S. Verba. 1963. *The Civic Culture: Political Attitudes and Democracy in Five Nations*. Princeton, NJ: Princeton University Press.

Bellah, Robert N., Richard Madsen, William M. Sullivan, Ann Swidler, and Steven M. Tipton. 1985. *Habits of the Heart: Individualism and Commitment in American Life*. Berkeley: University of California Press.

Blumer, Herbert. 1969. *Symbolic Interactionism: Perspective and Method*. Englewood Cliffs, NJ: Prentice-Hall.

Burke, Kenneth. 1945. *A Grammar of Motives*. New York: Prentice Hall.

Bourdieu, Pierre. 1984. *Distinction*, trans. Richard Nice. Cambridge, MA: Harvard University Press.

———. 1990. *The Logic of Practice*, trans. Richard Nice. Palo Alto, CA: Stanford University Press.

Chatterjee, Partha. 2004. *The Politics of the Governed: Reflections on Popular Politics in Most of the World*. New York: Columbia University Press.

Cicourel, Aaron. 1981. "Notes on the Integration of Micro- and Macro-Levels of Analysis." Pp. 51–80 in *Advances in Social Theory: Toward an Integration of Micro- and Macro-Sociologies*, edited by K. Knorr-Cetina and A. Cicourel. Boston: Routledge & Kegan Paul.

Durkheim, Emile. [1915] 1995. *The Elementary Forms of Religious Life*, trans. K.E. Fields. New York: Free Press.

Eliasoph, Nina. 2011. *Making Volunteers*. Princeton, NJ: Princeton University Press.

———. 2016. "The Mantra of Empowerment Talk." *Journal of Civil Society* 12(3):247–65.

Eliasoph, Nina, and Paul Lichterman. 2003. "Culture in Interaction." *American Journal of Sociology* 108(4):735–94.

Ewen, Stuart. 1976. *Captains of Consciousness: Advertising and the Social Roots of Consumer Culture*. New York: McGraw-Hill.

Faucher-King, Florence. 2005. *Changing Parties: an Anthropology of British Political Party Conferences*. New York: Palgrave Macmillan.

Frye, Northrop. 1957. *Anatomy of Criticism: Four Essays*. Princeton, NJ: Princeton University Press.

Gaventa, John. 1980. *Power and Powerlessness: Quiescence and Rebellion in an Appalachian Valley*. Chicago: University of Chicago Press.

Geertz, Clifford. 1973. *The Interpretation of Cultures: Selected Essays*. New York: Basic Books.

Glaeser, Andreas. 2001. *Divided in Unity: Identity, Germany and the Berlin Police*. Chicago: University of Chicago Press.

Goffman, Erving. [1974] 1986. *Frame Analysis: An Essay on the Organization of Experience*. Boston: Northeastern University Press.

Gramsci, Antonio. 1971. *Selections from the Prison Notebooks*, trans. Q. Hoare and G. Smith. New York: International.

Hall, Stuart. 1977. "Culture, the Media and the Ideological Effect." Pp. 70–94 in *Mass Communication and Society*, edited by J. Curran, M. Gurevitch, and J. Woollacott. London: Edward Arnold.

Lasch, Christopher. 1979. *The Culture of Narcissism*. New York: W.W. Norton and Co.

Lichterman, Paul. 2005. *Elusive Togetherness: Church Groups Trying to Bridge America's Divisions*. Princeton, NJ: Princeton University Press.

Lichterman, Paul, and Nina Eliasoph. 2014. "Civic Action." *American Journal of Sociology* 120(3):798–863.

Lukes, Steven. 1974. *Power: A Radical View*. London: Macmillan.

Makarova, Ekatarina. 1998. "The Mahalla, Civil Society and the Domestication of the State in Uzbekistan." Paper presented at the annual conference of the Association for the Study of Nationalities, April 1998, New York.

McKnight, John. 1995. *Careless Society: Community and its Counterfeits*. New York: Basic Books.

Mische, Ann. 2007. *Partisan Publics: Communication and Contention across Brazilian Youth Activist Networks*. Princeton, NJ: Princeton University Press.

Popielarz, P.A., and J. Miller McPherson. 1995. "On the Edge or in between: Niche Position, Niche Overlap, and the Duration of Voluntary Association Memberships." *American Journal of Sociology* 101(3):698–720.

Ricœur, Paul. 1991. "Life: A Story in Search of a Narrator." Pp. 425–40 in *Reflection and Imagination: A Paul Ricœur Reader*, edited by M.J. Valdés. Toronto: University of Toronto Press.

Sampson, Steven. 1996. "The Social Life of Projects: Importing Civil Society to Albania." Pp. 127–42 in *Civil Society: Challenging Western Models*, edited by C. Hann and E. Dunn. New York: Routledge.

Snow, David A., E. Burke Rochford Jr., Steven K. Worden, and Robert D. Benford. 1986. "Frame Alignment Processes, Micromobilization, and Movement Participation." *American Sociological Review* 51(4):464–81.

Thévenot, Laurent. 2006. *L'action au Pluriel: Sociologie des Régimes d'Engagement*. Paris: La Découverte.

Verba, Sidney, Kay Lehman Schlozman, and Henry Brady. 1995. *Voice and Equality: Civic Voluntarism in American Politics*. Cambridge, MA: Harvard University Press.

Wuthnow, Robert, ed. 1992. *Vocabularies of Public Life: Empirical Essays in Symbolic Structure*. New York: Routledge.

50

Narratives, networks, and publics

Ann Mische and Matthew J. Chandler

Introduction

How do people learn to talk across differences in experiences, interests, and status positions? How do they build (or fail to build) the capacity to engage with others in spaces "in between" their more segmented day-to-day lives? This is the core challenge that people face in constructing publics, and one that raises analytic challenges for cultural sociology. In this chapter, we expand existing theoretical conceptions of publics by drawing on recent work on narratives and networks in order to explore relational and performative challenges to the constitution and durability of publics. We argue that the construction of publics hinges not just on the joint expression of shared identities, but also on the joint *suppression* of diverging ones. Thus publics are often fraught, precarious, and in need of continual renewal and repair.

The public sphere is generally understood as a realm of communicative interaction in which people from diverse backgrounds debate their understandings of and proposals for their community and/or the broader world. Publics are plural, contested, and structured by the multiple networks and power differentials of modern society. Nevertheless they are also sites where people gain the capacity to "act in concert," as Arendt (1998) famously said, to exercise their freedom and autonomy, and to develop new relationships and solidarities. As Gutman and Goldfarb (this volume) note, "publics form as people meet as equals in their differences." And yet as Lo (this volume) notes, this process is often messy and contested, as "social groups struggle to make sense of the tensions between the multiple social positions that their participants simultaneously occupy." Here, we propose an analytical framework and practical strategies for understanding how publics are formed (and unformed) in the face of these tensions, contradictions, and challenges.

Why publics are hard

While publics can be normatively and politically valuable, they are difficult to build and sustain. This difficulty is a product of their strength. By definition, publics are sites positioned "in between" more segmented networks marked by homophily, hierarchy, and specialization. In publics people can build common ground and joint projects with others who may have very different positions, perspectives, and interests. Without publics bridging the highly differenti-ated (yet partially intersecting) networks of contemporary life, we would spin off into separate milieus or experience schizophrenic jolts in switching from one interaction site to the next (White 1995; Mische and White 1998). Publics are thus essential and ubiquitous in modern life – occurring not only in sites of high-minded normative debate about the public good, but wherever participants from segmented groups seek to build commonality in order to coordinate ideas and action. A public could, for example, consist of an interagency planning session, a social movement coalition meeting, a student leadership summit, or a mediation session between feuding groups. Publics vary in their styles of communication; some may be more oriented toward cooperation or competition, or toward the production of ideas or action. They may shift over time in whether they understand themselves as exploratory or pragmatic, ideologi-cally grounded or tactically defined (Mische 2008; Lichterman and Eliasoph 2014). Such styles develop as they respond to the *relational challenges* posed by the complex intersections from which they are composed.

The theory of publics has a long history, moving from the foundational work of Jürgen Habermas (1989) and Hannah Arendt (1998) through recent critical rearticulations concern-ing marginalized or excluded groups, emotion and embodiment, and political contention (e.g., Calhoun 1992; Benhabib 1996; Young 2000; Gutmann and Thompson 2004; Pateman 2012). Here, we dig underneath these debates by focusing on the discursive and relational mechanics by which publics are constituted. Publics bridge across more segmented and particularistic net-works, and they can contribute to shared narratives, mutual learning, and innovation (Emirbayer and Sheller 1998; Lo, this volume). But if they are to serve as buffering zones for conflicting identities and interests (and associated power differentials), they require *selective representation and performance* of the multiple identities and relations that are "carried in" by individual participants. Publics are hard to constitute precisely because they require this *selectivity*.

People bring to any public interaction many more potential identities and ties than can be activated or expressed if meaningful communication and coordination is to occur. Publics are only "public" in relation to other arenas. But these include not only the "private sphere" of fam-ily, friendship, or personal market transactions, but also other segmented milieus that a particular public bridges – some of them, other publics. So, for example, the black student publics that Mis-che (2008) studied in 1990s Brazil brought together student leaders from different regions of the country; different political parties and factions; different academic and professional specializa-tions; and other kinds of civic, student, and religious venues not centrally organized around race. Moreover, constituting a public around the unifying identity of race meant coming to an inter-actionally negotiated and enforced understanding about which of these *other* affiliations could or could not be expressed. This was needed in order to define the public as focused centrally on issues of racial exclusion. Ideologically differentiating partisan narratives stemming from factional affiliations on the left – in which they often opposed each other in the power disputes and status hierarchies of student politics – had to be actively and self-consciously suppressed when they met "as black students." This suppression could provisionally equalize relations of specialization, conflict, and hierarchy predominant in other settings, thus facilitating pragmatic and ideological work toward building a counter-hegemonic presence within the academy and broader student movement, where they often felt invisible and unwelcome.

This example reminds us that the identities and narratives around which publics are com-posed cannot be taken for granted. These student leaders participated in other publics (student, partisan, civic, religious) in which their blackness was, relatively speaking, invisible – in part because their racial identities were not understood to be a salient footing for sharing ideas and coordinating action in those publics. They did not form a "black public" because they were black. Even though all of the participants considered themselves "non-white," they all went through a personal process of coming to understand themselves as "black activists." Publics are hard because they require relational work to determine, enforce, and sometimes contest which subset of myriad *possible* participant identities will constitute a particular public.

Text, context, and interaction

Given the work required to constitute publics, studying them requires us to theorize the links between narratives, networks, and interaction. Communication in publics comprises two intertwined elements: the world-constituting *narratives* by which participants situate themselves in time and space (text), and the *networks* of relations that participants build with each other as they move through those worlds and co-constitute them through word and action (context). Narratives orient participants toward publics through joint storytelling about ongoing social dramas, while mapping collective action backward and forward in time (Somers 1994; Polletta 2006; Hall 2009; Kane 2011). In any public convergence, multiple possible narratives may come into play, sometimes conflicting with or talking past one other. Communication in publics is only possible when participants can understand one another through some shared language for interpreting and generating text. Something like a "group style" (Eliasoph and Lichterman 2003) may emerge, including context-specific linguistic norms that are not defined by the lexicon and grammar of any particular natural language. Overall, interaction is more efficient when participants become fluent in a special language of public discourse, but the interstitial character of publics often undercuts institutionalization of textual conventions.

Styles of communication in publics emerge from the cultural dynamics of complex, intersecting networks. Sociometry has tended to treat social ties as static relations, independent of transmission processes. However, conceiving of networks only as substrata for culture truncates the temporality of network formation, ignoring the processes that define and establish social ties in the first place. Harrison White (1992, 2008) made this point in *Identity and Control*, inspiring other sociologists to explore the link between narratives and social relations (see Emirbayer and Goodwin 1994; Mohr 1998; Fuhse 2009; Pachucki and Breiger 2010; Mische 2011; Erikson 2013). Building on this work, we understand networks as dramaturgically enacted within interaction settings in which particular subsets and dimensions of ties are performatively highlighted or suppressed. Networks are constituted through continual processes of collective storytelling that spin those ties backward and forward in time.

From this cultural and interactionist understanding of network ties, we find our way to publics via Simmel, Goffman, White, and Bakhtin. Our approach tunnels under classical understandings of the public sphere in normative political theory by understanding publics as situated, fragile, performatively constructed social entities. These entities are composed of, and also serve as sites of intervention in, both text (narratives) and context (networks). From Simmel (1955; cf. Breiger 1974), we take a focus on intersecting social circles, as well as the tensions and possibilities generated by movement within and across groups. With Goffman (1959, 1963, 1974, 1981), we focus on public dramaturgy in the representation of both the self and the self-in-relation (McLean 2007) and on the performance of categorical boundaries and identities (Stryker, Owens, and White 2000; Tilly 2005; Reger, Myers, and Einwohner 2008). We also draw from Goffman's account of the stylized and reduced character of interaction in public spaces, and note how contextualized talk frames the "footing" or style of group interaction (Eliasoph and Lichterman 2003).

Harrison White (1995, 2008) takes inspiration from both Goffman and Simmel in characterizing publics as interstitial buffer zones or "bubbles" that momentarily suspend participants from ongoing specialized sets of involvements in "network-domains." This suspension allows for the provisional suspension of status hierarchies and power relations; everyone in a public is fully connected during the public encounter, even if those connections are tenuous and ritualized. In fact, the thinner the ties among individuals, the stronger the need for ritualization of public identity. The tipping of the hat in the public square (Goffman 1963) as a limiting example can be extended to other kinds of publics, in which internal difference and dissension are masked by veneers of civic unity and egalitarianism.

Publics also enable relational mixing and "switching" into new sites, linguistic forms, and patterns of social involvement (Mische and White 1998; Godart and White 2010; Fontdevila, Opazo, and White 2011). Like White, we build upon Bakhtin's (1986) dialogic conception of intersecting discursive streams or "speech genres," composed of the interplay of text, context, and audience. Multivocal appropriations and "interanimations" of these genres inform talk in contentious political settings and sites of collective action (Ansell 1997; Steinberg 1999; Mische and Pattison 2000). The intersecting discourses that circulate can foster creativity and innovation (Clemens and Cook 1999; Padgett and Powell 2012), but also relational tensions and disruption.

In synthesizing these approaches, we define publics as *performatively constructed spaces in which actors temporarily suspend at least some aspects of their identities and involvements in order to generate the possibility of provisionally equalized and synchronized relationships* (Mische 2008). This definition underscores the dynamic and relational character of publics, as well as the uneasy and at times troubled terms of their constitution. In what follows, we unpack this definition and show its empirical applicability.

A temporal template for studying publics

If publics are hard to compose from the point of view of participants, they are also hard to study. This is because they are both more and less than they appear. Many more *possible* relations and narratives have the *potential* to be expressed in a setting than are in fact actively represented or performed. However, the non-expressed identities and ties may still hover around publics in a state of potentiality, generating tension, bridging and/or monitoring efforts, and the risk of disruption. The study of publics must therefore adopt a strategy for making these dynamics – along their sources in and repercussions through broader networks – visible to the analyst. This requires a temporally differentiated approach that attends to network embeddings, narrative engagement, and interactional contingencies as these play out over time *before*, *during*, and *after* people convene in publics.

Before

Analysis of the phase before public interaction is guided by a simple question: what do participants bring to publics? We can distinguish between properties tied to individual participants and to the social groups they represent. At the individual level, properties include knowledge and skill sets cultivated in previous kinds of "civic action" – that is, coordinated action understood as contributing to the "common good" within a larger imagined collectivity (Lichterman and Eliasoph 2014) – as well as in their more particularistic networks of interpersonal ties and group affiliations. At the group level, properties include each group's history of public interactions and coordinated action with other groups, as well as organizational repertoires and positions within broader social fields (Fligstein and McAdam 2012; cf. Lo, this volume). Cutting across both levels, this phase of analysis maps the proximities and differences that condition subsequent public interactions.

Researchers can systematically examine the distinct constituents of text and context that participants carry into public interactions. A research project would need to focus on a subset of these, keeping others on the horizon. For example, to analyze the relational *context* of publics, researchers can examine *formal associational affiliations*, such as participation or membership in neighborhood, professional, or activist organizations. These formal affiliations may intersect with *informal or categorical sources of identity affiliation*, such as community, region, or nation of origin; family lineages; ethnic, racial, religious, gender, or sexual identifications; and generational or class-based subcultures. Alternatively, researchers can examine how public talk is influenced by *direct ties between individuals or organizations*, including positive relations of collaboration, trust and respect; negative relations of opposition, distrust, or disdain; and power relations grounded in asymmetrical exchanges of material and symbolic resources.

To understand the *textual* constitution of publics, researchers can examine how interactions in various segmented networks and interaction sites structure *narratives, projects, and temporal landscapes* (Tavory and Eliasoph 2013), including those associated with collective memory and imagined communities, with individual trajectories and aspirations, and with the social change projects of collective actors (Blee 2012). Finally, researchers can compare *communication skills and practices*, such as specialized jargon, procedures for running meetings, or mechanisms for making decisions and mediating disputes (Fligstein 2001) that are learned and routinized within more segmented sites. These skills are carried into publics, where they may be more or less appropriate to the norms of communication in that setting.

During

Once researchers know what people bring into publics, they can focus on how the elements of text and context are activated or performed within public interactions. A number of scholars have emphasized the dramaturgy of publics, highlighting, for example, story structure (McFarland 2004) and performativity (Alexander 2010). Publics are indeed rife with drama, because they compel participants to engage in matters of import deliberately and passionately, even while managing the complexities of their own identities and their relations with other participants. Every scene is a tapestry of crisscrossing storylines that inform relations-in-progress, between individual participants and among the groups they represent.

Study of public interaction begins by observing who is and is not present and how they present themselves at the outset. As participants converge in a public setting, they simultaneously generate and scan the immediate relational network, gathering information about the needs for identity activation and suppression. Since participants often downplay aspects of their identities that they perceive to be incompatible with the setting, the researcher must use information gathered *before* (or in some cases, *after*) the event to gauge which actors are displaying which aspects of their identities. Our theorization of publics anticipates that performances of inclusivity will be pervasive, albeit selective. A common indication is the use of identity qualifiers (Mische 2003), such as "I speak as a representative of ___ but I am open to hearing other perspectives." Speakers may also employ other kinds of ambiguous or multivocal bridging talk, including hypotheticals, subjunctive modalities, or polysemous metaphors. Figures of speech and symbolic codes may be used to mediate multiple and divergent processes of meaning-making – for example, metonymy (Polletta 2006) and multivalent symbolic actions (Ansell 1997). Importantly, participants' attempts to key into the operative linguistic conventions of a public may falter due to lack of practice or the giving off of contradictory non-verbal signals (Goffman 1974, 1981). Researchers therefore should be attentive to *switches* in the communication styles of participants, within a particular public in relation to their patterns of talk in other settings.

As talk in a public proceeds, investigators should note who initiates dialogue, how agendas are set, and how participants claim and alternate speaking turns. Relational centrality and vocalized initiative are markers of power and status asymmetries (Bourdieu 1992; Gibson 2005), and these may persist even in publics that understand themselves in egalitarian terms. Although publics often cut across established hierarchies and allow for provisional, even novel, forms of communicative equalization, they do not eliminate structures of authority altogether (Ikegami 2005). Some kinds of formal authority (facilitation, chairing, podium space) may derive from the institutional scaffoldings of publics, while informal authority may emerge in the form of differential recognition and respect. Even so, attempts by some participants to dominate the discussion, to vocalize "intrusive" narratives, or to dramatize identities in ways that others deem inappropriate to the public's self-understanding will often spark contestation. Such pushbacks may be gentle at first. However, if a vocal minority continues to steamroll the conversation, the majority can view it as undermining the foundations of the public and respond by shifting the agenda to a reflexive mode (i.e., discussion of rules of order, requests to appoint facilitators, or questioning the "standing" or implicit status positions of participants). If contestations escalate, then researchers should expect a breakdown of the performances that typify public engagement. Identity qualifiers may be stripped away, phrasing may shift from subjunctive to declarative and imperative, and relations may polarize or factionalize. However, typically, most participants will persist in their public orientation and adopt procedures to constrain domineering actors and prevent conflict escalation. Sometimes these responses will have an overcorrecting effect, leading to a shrinking or homogenization of discourse. In other cases, publics will embrace the productive tension among their divergent constituent elements.

So long as interaction remains public, there will always be tensions over power relations, communicative styles, and the substantive issues at stake. Researchers should not expect to see harmonious conclusions to public interactions. The inexhaustible potential for conflict in publics is also a wellspring of opportunity for creative problem-solving and cross-boundary collaboration. Thus, researchers should be on the lookout for new narratives and relations that emerge.

After

After a given public interaction draws to a close, participants return to their respective milieus. They may carry information to pass on to others, proposals for action steps, additional observations and insights, and changes in attitude or orientation that affect their personal identities and relations. Any such changes become updated context for future public interaction, and the cycle repeats.

Researchers can identify several markers of change that result from public interaction. First, they may see changes in *memberships and trajectories*. Participants may join or leave groups as a result of their movement through publics, and their functional roles or leadership careers within organizations can change as well. Second, they may see shifts in *identity saliences*. Provisional identity suppression may change how some participants prioritize and display identities in other contexts; public constraints on identity expression may lead others to compensate by re-emphasizing suppressed identities later on. For example, after participating in caucuses of black students within broader student congresses, some Brazilian youth leaders shifted toward a less partisan, more racially oriented self-understanding and political praxis "as black activists" (Mische 2008). Third, *interpersonal and organizational networks* may become restructured: new alliances, partnerships, and collaborations may form as a result of co-participation in publics, or conversely, contestation in publics may lead to weakened or severed ties. Fourth, researchers may observe shifts in *organizational projects, narratives, and activities*: the articulation of bridging narratives within publics and deliberation over joint projects can alter the approaches that organizations take to their own programs and activities. Finally, actors can acquire *skills for navigating publics*, allowing them to better manage interactional tensions and contingencies and enhance their leadership and visibility in future publics.

Empirical applications and challenges

We have proposed a conception of publics that focuses on their relational, narrative, and performative constitution. Publics are communicatively constructed spaces located between more segmented settings, informed both by the cultural texts that circulate through them and by the relational contexts in which they are embedded. They work by simplifying the array of possible narratives and networks in play, which does not eliminate internal diversity and disagreement, but helps to manage and channel these. Although publics are sustained by different kinds of institutional scaffoldings and develop distinct styles of communication, they are vulnerable to disruption and fragmentation. Suppressed or backgrounded identities – and associated alliances and power relations – can always resurface and challenge the public's communicative footing. Publics exist through dynamic processes of interaction, wherein participants listen, learn, rearticulate ideas, and take home changed perspectives and relationships.

Our approach offers a flexible and non-idealized framework for studying publics, attuned to their dynamism, internal complexity, and performative challenges. Among many possible applications, we will sketch three exemplary types. First, this approach is useful for studying *coalition building*, in which previously segmented (and often "strange bedfellow") groups create provisional alliances in moments of threat or opportunity (Bandy and Smith 2004; Van Dyke and McCammon 2010). These alliances – often fragile and short-lived – are articulated in publics in which diverging identities and narratives are quite purposefully suppressed, even as leaders blend their discourses and cultivate new relationships. Second, the dynamics we have described are visible in *stakeholder consultations* in which diverse and contending groups are invited to give input into public policy decisions (Fung and Wright 2003; Lee, McQuarrie, and Walker 2015). Although such publics can facilitate civic consensus-building and creative problem-solving, they may also clamp down on dissenting voices, paper over power imbalances, and privilege some stories and relations over others. Third, our approach can be brought to bear on sites of *conflict mediation*, which require delicate processes of public construction (Burton 1996; Fisher and Ury 2011). In the practice of negotiation, mediators stress the need to suppress identity positionality in order to focus on core interests; they often invest tremendous energy into creating an environment where parties can communicate via a provisional language of compatible needs and mutual benefit.

The empirical study of publics poses a number of methodological challenges. Identifying and comparing the elements of publics can be tricky, since their functionality and drama often result from what is *not* said (or made visible), which gains meaning from its (sometimes obscured or misrecognized) relation to public representations and performances. By comparing what happens *within* publics to what happens *before* and *after* they convene, a researcher can specify participants' shifts, omissions, and obfuscations. More generally, our framework suggests a dialogue between multiple analytical lenses: some methods can reveal aspects of text, context, or interaction that are largely hidden in others. Researchers can use ethnographic, interview, and discourse methods to understand the interpretive and performative dynamics of publics, and use network analysis, formal modeling, or automated text analysis to elucidate structures of interpersonal or discursive relations. For example, Mische (2008) compared findings from activist surveys and network mappings to multisite observations of meetings, allowing her to track which affiliations they highlighted or backgrounded across diverse publics. Likewise, interviews helped her compare activists' reflective analysis of events to what they publicly said and did, providing insight into public meaning-making as well as the strategic representation of networks and identities.

Another important challenge is to extend research to bigger arenas, including virtual publics constituted in social media platforms and other technological and institutional scaffoldings that broaden publics in space and time (cf. Varnelis 2008). We believe that many of the dynamics of public construction outlined earlier apply to larger, technologically mediated publics, although there will be important differences due to the increased speed, scale, heterogeneity, and relative anonymity of such publics. Still, "old-fashioned" face-to-face publics of diverse sorts will remain ubiquitous and consequential in contemporary life, and thus in need of continued theorization and empirical study. Our framework allows researchers to probe beneath dominant normative understandings to understand the relational and discursive challenges – and real life troubles and possibilities – of their joint construction.

References

Alexander, Jeffrey C. 2010. *The Performance of Politics*. New York: Cambridge University Press.

Ansell, Christopher K. 1997. "Symbolic Networks: The Realignment of the French Working Class, 1887–1894." *American Journal of Sociology* 103(2):359–90.

Arendt, Hannah. 1998. *The Human Condition*. 2nd ed. Chicago: University of Chicago Press.

Bakhtin, Mikhail M. 1986. *Speech Genres and Other Late Essays*, edited by C. Emerson and M. Holquist, trans. Vern W. McGee. Austin: University of Texas Press.

Bandy, Joe, and Jackie Smith, eds. 2004. *Coalitions Across Borders: Negotiating Difference and Unity in Transnational Coalitions Against Neoliberalism*. Boulder, CO: Rowman and Littlefield.

Benhabib, Seyla. 1996. *Democracy and Difference: Contesting the Boundaries of the Political*. Princeton, NJ: Princeton University Press.

Blee, Kathleen M. 2012. *Democracy in the Making: How Activist Groups Form*. Oxford: Oxford University Press.

Bourdieu, Pierre. 1992. *Language and Symbolic Power*, edited by J.B. Thompson, trans. Gino Raymond and Matthew Adamson. Cambridge: Polity Press.

Breiger, Ronald L. 1974. "The Duality of Persons and Groups." *Social Forces* 53(2):181–90.

Burton, John W. 1996. *Conflict Resolution: Its Language and Processes*. Lanham, MD: Scarecrow Press.

Calhoun, Craig. 1992. *Habermas and the Public Sphere*. Cambridge, MA: MIT Press.

Clemens, Elisabeth, and James Cook. 1999. "Politics and Institutionalism: Explaining Durability and Change." *Annual Review of Sociology* 25:441–66.

Eliasoph, Nina, and Paul Lichterman. 2003. "Culture in Interaction." *American Journal of Sociology* 108(4):735–94.

Emirbayer, Mustafa, and Jeff Goodwin. 1994. "Network Analysis, Culture, and the Problem of Agency." *American Journal of Sociology* 99(6):1411–54.

Emirbayer, Mustafa, and Mimi Sheller. 1998. "Publics in History." *Theory and Society* 28(1):145–97.

Erikson, Emily. 2013. "Formalist and Relationalist Theory in Social Network Analysis." *Sociological Theory* 31(3):219–42.

Fisher, Roger, and William L. Ury. 2011. *Getting to Yes: Negotiating Agreement without Giving In*, edited by B. Patton. Revised ed. New York: Penguin Books.

Fligstein, Neil. 2001. "Social Skill and the Theory of Fields." *Sociological Theory* 19(2):105–25.

Fligstein, Neil, and Doug McAdam. 2012. *A Theory of Fields*. Oxford: Oxford University Press.

Fontdevila, Jorge, M. Pilar Opazo, and Harrison C. White. 2011. "Order at the Edge of Chaos: Meanings from Netdom Switchings Across Functional Systems." *Sociological Theory* 29(3):178–98.

Fuhse, Jan A. 2009. "The Meaning Structure of Networks." *Sociological Theory* 27(1):51–73.

Fung, Archon, and Eric Olin Wright, eds. 2003. *The Real Utopias Project*. Vol. 4, *Deepening Democracy: Institutional Innovations in Empowered Participatory Governance*. New York: Verso.

Gibson, David R. 2005. "Taking Turns and Talking Ties: Network Structure and Conversational Sequences." *American Journal of Sociology* 110(6):1561–97.

Godart, Frederic C., and Harrison C. White. 2010. "Switchings under Uncertainty: The Coming and Becoming of Meanings." *Poetics* 38(6):567–86.

Goffman, Erving. 1959. *The Presentation of Self in Everyday Life*. New York: Anchor Books.

———. 1963. *Behavior in Public Places*. Glencoe, IL: Free Press.

———. 1974. *Frame Analysis*. New York: Harper and Row.

———. 1981. *Forms of Talk*. Philadelphia: University of Pennsylvania Press.

Gutmann, Amy, and Dennis Thompson. 2004. *Why Deliberative Democracy?* Princeton, NJ: Princeton University Press.

Habermas, Jürgen. 1989. *The Structural Transformation of the Public Sphere: An Inquiry into a Category of Bourgeois Society*, trans. Thomas McCarthy. Cambridge, MA: MIT Press.

Hall, John R. 2009. *Apocalypse: From Antiquity to the Empire of Modernity*. New York: Polity Press.

Ikegami, Eiko. 2005. *Bonds of Civility: Aesthetic Publics and the Political Origins of Japanese Publics*. Cambridge: Cambridge University Press.

Kane, Anne. 2011. *Constructing Irish National Identity: Discourse and Ritual during the Land War, 1879–1882*. New York: Palgrave Macmillan.

Lee, Caroline W., Michael McQuarrie, and Edward T. Walker. 2015. *Democratizing Inequalities: Dilemmas of the New Public Participation*. New York: New York University Press.

Lichterman, Paul, and Nina Eliasoph. 2014. "Civic Action." *American Journal of Sociology* 120(3):798–863.

McFarland, Daniel A. 2004. "Resistance as a Social Drama: A Study of Change-Oriented Encounters." *American Journal of Sociology* 109(6):1249–318.

McLean, Paul D. 2007. *The Art of the Network: Strategic Interaction and Patronage in Renaissance Florence*. Durham, NC: Duke University Press.

Mische, Ann. 2003. "Cross-talk in Movements: Rethinking the Culture-Network Link." Pp. 258–80 in *Social Movements and Networks: Relational Approaches to Collective Action*, edited by M. Diani and D. McAdam. Oxford: Oxford University Press.

———. 2008. *Partisan Publics: Communication and Contention Across Brazilian Youth Activist Networks*. Princeton, NJ: Princeton University Press.

———. 2011. "Relational Sociology, Culture, and Agency." Pp. 80–97 in *The SAGE Handbook of Social Network Analysis*, edited by J. Scott and P.J. Carrington. Los Angeles: SAGE.

Mische, Ann, and Philippa Pattison. 2000. "Composing a Civic Arena: Publics, Projects, and Social Settings." *Poetics* 27(2–3):163–94.

Mische, Ann, and Harrison White. 1998. "Between Conversation and Situation: Public Switching Dynamics Across Network-Domains." *Social Research* 65(3):695–724.

Mohr, John. 1998. "Measuring Meaning Structures." *Annual Review of Sociology* 24:345–70.

Pachucki, Mark A., and R.L. Breiger. 2010. "Cultural Holes: Beyond Relationality in Social Networks and Culture." *Annual Review of Sociology* 36:205–44.

Padgett, John F., and Walter W. Powell. 2012. *The Emergence of Organizations and Markets*. Princeton, NJ: Princeton University Press.

Pateman, Carole. 2012. "Participatory Democracy Revisited." *Perspectives on Politics* 10(1):7–19.

Polletta, Francesca. 2006. *It Was Like a Fever: Storytelling in Protest and Politics*. Chicago: University of Chicago Press.

Reger, Jo, Daniel J. Myers, and Rachel L. Einwohner, eds. 2008. *Identity Work in Social Movements*. Minneapolis: University of Minnesota Press.

Simmel, Georg. 1955. *Conflict and The Web of Group Affiliations*, trans. Kurt H. Wolff and Reinhard Bendix. New York: Free Press.

Somers, Margaret R. 1994. "The Narrative Constitution of Identity: A Relational and Network Approach." *Theory and Society* 23(5):605–49.

Steinberg, Marc W. 1999. "The Talk and Back Talk of Collective Action: A Dialogic Analysis of Repertoires of Discourse among Nineteenth-Century English Cotton Spinners." *American Journal of Sociology* 105(3):736–80.

Stryker, Sheldon, Timothy J. Owens, and Robert W. White, eds. 2000. *Self, Identity, and Social Movements*. Minneapolis: University of Minnesota Press.

Tavory, Iddo, and Nina Eliasoph. 2013. "Coordinating Futures: Toward a Theory of Anticipation." *American Journal of Sociology* 118(4):908–42.

Tilly, Charles. 2005. *Identities, Boundaries, and Social Ties*. Boulder, CO: Paradigm Press.

Van Dyke, Nella, and Holly J. McCammon, eds. 2010. *Strategic Alliances: Coalition Building and Social Movements*. Minneapolis: University of Minnesota Press.

Varnelis, Kazys, ed. 2008. *Networked Publics*. Cambridge, MA: MIT Press.

White, Harrison. 1992. *Identity and Control: A Structural Theory of Social Action*. Princeton, NJ: Princeton University Press.

———. 1995. "Network Switchings and Bayesian Forks: Reconstructing the Social and Behavioral Sciences." *Social Research* 62(4):1035–63.

———. 2008. *Identity and Control: How Social Formations Emerge*. 2nd ed. Princeton, NJ: Princeton University Press.

Young, Iris. 2000. *Inclusion and Democracy*. Oxford: Oxford University Press.

51

The cultural constitution of publics

Yifat Gutman and Jeffrey C. Goldfarb

Introduction

The public sphere, or as we prefer, the sphere of publics (Calhoun 1997:100), appears as a structure of a particular place and time. As a fundamental support in the making of democracy, both historically and in contemporary polities, it has spread and developed, and has become multiple and global. To understand these propositions, we must remember that publics appear metaphorically as structures. They are given their structural appearance through regularized patterns of social interaction. They are culturally constituted in human interaction. Publics form as people meet as equals in their differences, and develop together a capacity to act among themselves and with other publics. Democracy is created in the interactive life of publics.

To substantiate this position, we will review the changing history of publics and the different theoretical approaches to the public. We will analyze the cultural constitution of publics. *We will move from the analysis of the structural transformation of the public sphere toward the analysis of the making of publics and spheres of publics.* We will also move from a consideration of the public as a specific site for rational deliberation, toward the analysis of other key cultural forms of public action – appearance, display, embodiment, contestation, competition, and other forms of political participation. As we proceed, the normative dimension of publics and their study will be addressed.

Habermas's public sphere

The starting point in contemporary discussions of publics is Jürgen Habermas's *The Structural Transformation of the Public Sphere* (1989). Habermas identified a distinctively modern development, the emergence of the autonomous public sphere in discursive gatherings and communication via the print media of bourgeois men in the late seventeenth- and eighteenth-century Europe. He saw that this sphere was one of the central structures of the modern order, along with the modern economy (capitalism) and the modern state. The participants in this sphere, according to Habermas, read, wrote, and discussed matters of state and economy in coffee shops and salons, separated from the public institutions of the state (1989:23, 25, 27, 106). Engaged in rational communicative action, suspending their individual interests, these men were able to reach consensual understandings about the common good (Habermas 1984:328–30). Their free (from the state as well as self-interest) rational debate led them to knowledge that balanced and limited state power (Habermas 1989:54–6).

Habermas's approach to this public sphere contains a radical change from the classical Greek notion of the public sphere. In the Greek polis, freedom was public – the realm of autonomous citizens which is free from the necessity that characterizes the private household. In the public sphere, Habermas observes, individuals become capable of public action in their homes, and freedom is found in the private realm, or at least the unofficial space, separated from the state and protected from its authority (Calhoun1993:6–7; Habermas 1989:50–2). Habermas's public sphere "appropriates" the classical concept of participation in the polis and applies it to complex modern societies with differentiated spheres of the economy, the law, family, culture, and politics. Seyla Benhabib, developing the implications of Habermas's approach, has mapped out the substantial consequences, not fully specified by Habermas. In modern societies, according to Benhabib, participation is widened to other spheres of life, and is made possible by the formation of a discursive will. Participation, for Habermas, emphasizes the practical debate among those who are affected by general norms and decisions. Emphasizing practical debate allows or even assumes various publics and debates, even as many publics as there are debates (Benhabib 1993:86–7). Considering multiple publics, then, grows out of Habermas's approach.

Arendt's public domain

Hannah Arendt, most extensively in her *The Human Condition* ([1958] 1998), presents a different, but related, way of considering the problem of the public domain in modern societies in light of ancient Greek experience. Her position explicitly opens up the analysis to publics (in the plural) and to cultural activities beyond rational discourse, although not as directly recognizing the special modern circumstance and structure of modern public life. Using the Athenian polis as the definitive public space, she describes the public as the space of appearances. In the public domain, people meet as equals, according to Arendt, in their differences. In public, they see, hear, and talk to others and in the process initiate action, bringing something new into the world. In this way, they form their individual identities and realize the power of the public, the power of people acting in concert, political power, as the opposite of coercion (Arendt [1958] 1998:57).

Arendt's approach opens the analysis of public life to a broad array of cultural actions and representations. How we appear, how arguments are embodied, visual grace and power, and much more are all part of public life and are central to the primary political ideal of freedom. Unlike Habermas, Arendt insists upon the Greek connection between freedom and the public sphere, asserting that individuals interacting in public are free from the necessity of the private home. The realm of necessity includes the family and economy. They reach informed opinion, not truth, by viewing a matter from the many different perspectives of individuals in different social positions (Arendt [1958] 1998:57). Such communicative and discursive acts in public are for Arendt synonymous with the political – the ongoing activity of citizens coming together so as to exercise their capacity for action, to conduct their lives together by means of free speech (broadly understood, beyond rational discourse), appearance, and persuasion (Benhabib 1993:78; 1996:26, 179). Publics are the very center of politics and its primary ideal. Arendt's distinctive political theory suggests a complementary normative approach to that of Habermas, something that he recognized (Habermas 1977). Social theorists and historians have been exploring such complementarity in their critiques of Habermas's seminal approach.

The bourgeois public sphere: theoretical and historical revisions

As Habermas has pushed his argument for the rational-critical nature of the discursive interaction in the public sphere in his later work on communicative action and the "ideal speech situation" (1990), he has received critical responses from scholars who searched for a broader notion of public debate. While he has worked for a more philosophically sound basis for public life as rational discourse, many critics suggest moving in a different direction, pointing toward a new and more culturally inflected approach to the study of publics that accords with Arendt's position.

They start from the position that rational judgment as the single model for discursive interaction in the public sphere is problematic. Centrally, this model underplays the importance of other forms of communicative action such as rhetoric and play, and by so doing limits public participation and debate. By prioritizing rational-critical debate, Habermas problematically creates a binary opposition between information/informed publics and entertainment/uninformed publics, which excludes many people from participation. However, realistically, a democratic public life includes a broad array of persuasion, for better and for worse.

Moreover, Habermas's conception of the public sphere does not do justice to much that is most interesting and significant about publics, notably, social movements operating in ways that challenge the codes of social orders. Movements, once they appear, publicly and culturally enact alternative commitments through their very appearance on the public stage (as Arendt would emphasize) and in their performances (Melucci 1989; Touraine 1981). This is true especially for movements that reveal the normative hierarchies hidden behind the "rational." For such movements – which are often discriminated against by the "neutral" and commonsensical, by what appears to be the rational – the overrationalized public sphere is a principle example of the problematic social relations that they fight to change and disrupt (Warner 2005:54).

The consensual mutual understanding that is the goal of Habermas's critical-rational public debate is confronted by the notion of counterpublics – publics that are defined by conflict and tension with the larger or dominant public (Warner 2005:56). It is also confronted by competing public spheres, such as the paths constructed by North American women in the nineteenth century as contemporaries of the bourgeois public sphere (Eley 1993:330–1; Ryan 1993:272–3)

Ironically, the very universal rationality that is supposed to keep the public sphere accessible to all humans, suspending hierarchies of status, class, and gender, has been deployed as a strategy of exclusion (Fraser 1993:115). This rationality was part of an ethos and practice that marked the distinction of the bourgeois class from other, competing, classes and publics (Eley 1993:297–306; Fraser 1993:114; Landes 1998:89; Ryan 1993:272–3). This suggests the existence, from the start, of a sphere of competing publics, sometimes in conflict, with different degrees of power. The very idea of a single public sphere has been criticized for excluding, or at least limiting, the participation of marginal groups, and thus opposing the ideal of full participatory equality. According to Fraser, this is due first to the impossibility of isolating the public sphere from its social context of inequalities, and second to the tendency of the deliberative process to benefit a dominant group, whose cultural expression of ethos and rhetoric are central to it even in the absence of formal exclusions (Fraser 1993:122–8).

How should we revisit the bourgeois public sphere today in light of these critiques? The bourgeois public sphere can be viewed as a moment in an extended "chain" of partial or "damaged" but real discursive public spheres (Warner 2005:50–1). Another moment with even greater potential is the current one of modern social movements. These movements can be seen as operating in the same "public sphere environment" that Habermas drew or even emerging from that context, while they make right the faults of the bourgeois public sphere (Lee 1993:407; Warner 2005:50–1, 56).

Furthermore, publics and counterpublics demonstrate that the sphere of publics is not just a stage for representation and discussion of the interests of group members, but also an important space for the formation, shaping, and reinforcement of identities, which can reopen Habermas's division between public and private (Benhabib 1993:89–90; Calhoun 1997:82, 86; Warner 2005:57).

Social interaction and the formation of publics

Habermas's critics help establish publics as plural and culturally constituted, yet attention should also be paid to the formation and actions of publics. To investigate this requires the sort of philosophical and macrosociological approaches reviewed earlier, but it also requires looking more closely at the details of social interaction and its cultural fabric. Erving Goffman has studied this dimension of publics and their constitution.

Goffman's sociology is focused phenomenologically on the life of the public as Arendt understands it. Appearance, meeting and speaking to each other, significant gestures, and the like are common concerns of these thinkers, though they address these concerns from radically different intellectual traditions. In Goffman's work, the social texture of what people do when they meet and act in each other's presence is sociologically analyzed. People perform and constitute their selves and their situations. They communicate with one another not only through speech acts, but through gestures, and engage in interaction rituals (Goffman 1967:77; 1971:x). This process enacts the social order, since even large institutions are made of interacting individuals, but it can also yield an alternative order of social institutions, the under-life of the social order. Usually these individuals conform to social rules and norms, but not always. In studies of prisons and asylums, Goffman illuminates acts of resisting and breaking the rules (1967:48–9). From our point of view, this analysis points in the direction of the creation of alternative public spaces, not only in independent frameworks of regularized interaction (i.e., alternative institutions and movements), but also beyond the reach of command in formal institutions. The attention of Habermas and Arendt was focused on official public space, but in fact social movements and the under-life of social institutions are no less important for ongoing publics. This becomes apparent through an interactionist perspective.

Goffman researched the under-life of social institutions in the most peculiar of circumstances, total institutions. But the very peculiarity stands as compelling evidence that it is a general aspect of organizational life. In Goffman's analysis of total institutions, he recognizes the complexity of the politics of public interaction, in a way that is implicit in much of his work, but never fully developed. He in this way presents central insights into the cultural constitution of publics.

Total institutions are places that radically disrupt a definitive characteristic of modern societies, social differentiation. In the modern order, people in different social positions do different things, at different times, with different people. How we present ourselves to others changes when we are at home, at work, at church, in a political institution, and so forth. We interactively give definition to each of these situations, as we present and define ourselves in them, and keep these social definitions of self and situation separate. Total institutions, from boarding schools to prisons, break the separation. They process unified definitions of self that break down modern complexities. But Goffman, in the conclusion of his study, highlights interesting limits to this process, illuminating what we might call the sociological setting of public-making capacity:

> Without something to belong to, we have no stable self, and yet total commitment and attachment to any social unit implies a kind of selflessness. Our sense of being a person can come from being drawn into a wider social unit; our sense of selfhood can arise through

the little ways in which we resist the pull. Our status is backed by the solid buildings of the world, while our sense of personal identity often resides in the cracks.

(Goffman 1961:320)

In these cracks, publics are born. Alternative presentations and definitions of self and situation are developed. Public interaction of the sort that Arendt had in mind is built into the modern institutional structure. This has been especially true in the formation of publics associated with modern social movements.

Social movements are directed against some aspect of the institutional order, often emerging from the cracks in the order, but they are places where people meet and discuss, appear and reveal who they are and how they can act together. This is characteristic of new social movements generally, the feminist movement, the civil-rights movement, the antiwar movement, and most recently, the waves of mass protest around the globe. Each is about specific ends, but just as important, each is about exploring in the emerging publics who the participants are as individuals and as groups (Melucci 1989). There are patterns of deference and demeanor that define what it means to be a woman (Goffman 1956), but emerging from those patterns, women define themselves not only within institutionalized patterns but also against them. As women do so together, an alternative public is formed, supporting alternative politics, emerging in everyday interaction, developing in social movements (see DuPlessis and Snitow 1998). And as the publics form, as the movements' members speak and act in each other's presence, committed to their freedom and their autonomous action (Arendt's definition of public freedom), they develop a capacity to act in concert (Arendt's definition of political power). They then address not only each other, but also those outside their immediate circle (i.e., other publics and a more general sphere of publics). In this way, interacting individuals develop publics and political power, as John Dewey outlined in his opening pages of *The Public and Its Problems* (1954). This is still relevant today, when social media and digital technologies shape people's interaction.

Media and the cultural constitution of publics and the sphere of publics

Central to social interaction in general, media plays an important role in the analysis of the question of publics and deliberative democracy. One's approach to media leads to a specific evaluation of publics and their problems. This is most evident in Habermas's seminal 1989 study, in which the development of media forms – from public life centered on the spoken word to one that is centered on the interaction between the spoken and the written – is a key part of the analysis. But when it comes to listening and watching through the electronic media, Habermas sees a determined decline. Rationality is not possible. Commodity exchange prevails over intellectual exchange. Years later, he revised this determinist position, but that he made it is indicative of not systematically considering the relationship between media and publics (Habermas 1982).

In the place of face-to-face interaction, electronic and digital media usually facilitate virtual or no interaction, and instead offer visibility and virality (Dayan 2005; Nahon and Hemsley 2013). If print media operate along a linear timeline – writing, reading, and talking are lined up in time – electronic media operates in space, in that all the information is displayed immediately and simultaneously, often visually. These inverted features influence the capacity of media to facilitate publics and public debate. Electronic media bring people together for discussion as print media have done in the past, but they also offer types of interaction and appearance that were not available before. This has a significant effect on the constitution of publics.

Two views prevail. There is the view that Habermas assumes in his master work and revised later on: the electronic media give an illusion of democracy but in fact reproduce a social system of inequalities (the state, the capitalist market). TV "amuses us to death" (Postman 1986), "manufacturing consent" (Chomsky 1989) and a society of spectacles and simulations (Baudrillard 1988; Debord 1994). These critiques highlight how the present media regime substitutes entertainment for enlightenment, or at least confuses the two, owned as it is by the corporate elite, serving its interests, distancing people from their immediate circumstances, making illusions seem more real, or at least as real, as perceptions and human experiences. On the other hand, electronic media continue to make publics and to constitute alternative ones. In Marshall McLuhan's seminal 1964 work *The Medium Is the Message* ([1964] 1994), media are viewed first and foremost as transformative forces that not only extend our senses and knowledge, but also introduce new scale and pace that bring new patterns of social relations. Already in 1936, Walter Benjamin revealed the political potential that underlies media technologies in *The Work of Art in the Age of Mechanical Reproduction* ([1936] 1998). He described media technologies as enabling people to gain a more realistic understanding of their social life and introducing a new scope of collective action (Benjamin [1936] 1998:237–8). This was an expansion of the political potential found in appearance as Arendt studied the matter.

Although spectacle and the eclipse of the public are certainly on one side of the electronic media coin, the other side involves new forms of participation. John Dewey (1954) highlighted the critical point: "Vision is a spectator. Hearing is a participator." He insisted that even if the press (and radio, television, and social media, we should add), provides partial information, this is not the basis of democracy. The conversation of local publics and communities is what gives public opinion its reality (Dewey 1954:219). The message of the media is defined by the interactive communities that live with them. Elihu Katz and Daniel Dayan beautifully develop this point in *Media Events* (1992), showing how the centered publics of nation-states engage in rituals of public confirmation through a certain type of media presentation. Breaking the rhythms of television presentation, the same sorts of rituals associated with transfers of power, celebration of collective values, and political authority that existed before television now are enacted through television. This is the case not only in the central publics associated with national television, but also in the formation and development of multiple publics, counterpublics, as is strikingly the case through the internet.

Enabling publics to communicate for the first time without face-to-face interaction, the internet accommodates types of debates and publics that were previously not possible. Witness the events surrounding the recent global waves of mass mobilization, in which similar protest practices were used to express parallel types of claims in different social and political contexts. These protests – from the Arab Spring, Israeli Summer, and Occupy Wall Street to the demonstrations in Ukraine and protests in Turkey and other places (for comparative analysis, see Glasius and Pleyers 2013) – and their organization and direction via social media helped spawn the birth of new publics within local spheres of publics. Enhanced by the use of digital and social media, the subsequent global visibility of these new publics inspired the creation of local publics in other places around the globe.

However, although social media often gave voice to alternative definitions of the situation and political claims, it was the interplay of social media and mainstream media that determined the scope of their dissemination and mobilization for collective action (Brown and Hoskins 2010; Nahon 2016). This was soon understood and cleverly exploited by governments. For example, in 2016, when the initiators of a coup d'état attempt in Turkey occupied the national television and radio studios, President Recep Tayyip Erdoğan reinstated his regime via live video call from his personal mobile phone while it was being held by a news anchorwoman (Nahon 2016).

The decentralized character of virtual publics – in opposition to the centered publics of televised media events – is another obstacle for collective action. As multiple publics and counterpublics form at exponential rates in the age of social media, their lack of connection, their atomization, renders the task of establishing the common grounds for an understanding of the facts ever more difficult. This scenario favors manipulation and promotes new forms of authoritarianism.

In sum, the media have facilitated the creation of new publics more that they have undermined them, and these publics, on the left and on the right, have expressed strong oppositional claims, with positive and negative results for democratic practice.

Conclusion

The political potential of digital media to facilitate public debates and mediate publics brings us back to the central argument of this chapter. Arendt's political realm of appearance extends and complements Habermas's notion of the deliberative public sphere. In the midst of the digitally mediated new sphere of publics are performance, visibility, and interaction. These practices of publics maintain the potential of a deliberative public sphere, as Habermas first described, in an age of new media and global circulation of powers, people, and ideas. However, the decentralized character of publics and counterpublics that form every day using digital media also poses a significant threat to this ideal – the loss of a center that assures agreement on basic facts in the face of rising populism around the world.

Our central argument is grounded in empirical reality and new media forms. It also and crucially has a normative side. Publics have a normative edge and practical political consequences. Believe that the norms of public life are the ones that Habermas identifies and your politics will be of one sort. Believe that they are more like the norms identified by his critics and you will engage in politics in a different, though related way. Believe that Arendt has it right, and your political judgment and action will be yet of another related but different variety. The place of expert knowledge, rationality, images, identity politics, social media, and the mass media will be differently evaluated and acted upon according to the different conceptualizations.

Therefore, we base our argument that publics are culturally constituted on more than theoretical and empirical grounds. They are social phenomena and people constitute them. Publics are not simply structures or discursive orders. They are formed through human interaction in everyday life and in formal occasions, in more and less official public spaces and online, in social movements and in the under-life of total institutions and regimes. In the context of modern power relations and social control, such interaction has two aspects: *empirically*, people are unequal and they appear in their differences in public, express their different views in each other's presence; *normatively*, they can develop a capacity to act as equals. Not all publics are equal, nor do all publics view equality as desired, but they form and operate against one another within a sphere of publics that they cannot transcend. This makes media doubly important, as they not only facilitate the formation and interaction of public. They also may amplify or diminish the cultural capacities of publics.

In this view, those who see decline in the sphere of publics could be said to have a narrow view of culture. On the other hand, from our point of view, in acknowledging the distance from the Habermasian ideal there is not distortion or a loss, but the gain of recognizing the cultural complexity of public life today. We believe we have not only demonstrated empirical qualities of modern publics, but also staked out a normative position that opens public life to new kinds of participation, of different publics and counterpublics. We have also pointed out some of the challenges that spheres of publics face from new forms of authoritarianism.

Conflict and competition, play and display, embodiment and appearance, aesthetics and belief are all parts of the life of publics, as these publics look inward at themselves and outward at other publics through a variety of different media and cultural forms. This sociological lens to publics, different from philosophical or political theories that make a claim to universality, studies publics as a social problem. It is, in fact, one of the fundamental social problems of modernity, which began in a specific place and time and spread all over the world, carrying with it not just new empirical realities, but also a range of normative positions, with practical political consequences regarding the modern democratic project. From Arendt to Goffman to Benjamin, we have traced a cultural richness that has developed together with new media forms and opened up new democratic possibilities that are not available through a strictly rational, exclusive, and universal debate on public life.

References

Arendt, Hannah. [1958] 1998. *The Human Condition*. Chicago: University of Chicago Press.

Baudrillard, Jean. 1988. Pp. 166–84 in *Selected Writings*, edited by M. Poster. Stanford, CA: Stanford University Press.

Benhabib, Seyla. 1993. "Models of Public Space: Hannah Arendt, the Liberal Tradition, and Jürgen Habermas." Pp. 73–98 in *Habermas and the Public Sphere*, edited by C. Calhoun. Cambridge, MA: MIT Press.

———. 1996. "Toward a Deliberative Model of Democratic Legitimacy." Pp. 67–94 in *Democracy and Difference: Contesting the Boundaries of the Political*, edited by S. Benhabib. Chichester, UK: Princeton University Press.

Benjamin, Walter. [1936] 1998. "The Work of Art in the Age of Mechanical Reproduction." In *Illuminations: Essays and Reflections*, edited by H. Arendt, trans. Harry Zohn. New York: Schocken Books.

Brown, S.D., and A. Hoskins. 2010. "Terrorism in the New Memory Ecology: Mediating and Remembering the 2005 London Bombings." *Behavioral Sciences of Terrorism and Political Aggression* 2(2):87–107.

Calhoun, Craig. 1993. "Introduction." Pp. 6–8 in *Habermas and the Public Sphere*, edited by C. Calhoun. Cambridge, MA: MIT Press.

———. 1997. "Nationalism and the Public Sphere." Pp. 75–102 in *Public and Private in Thought and Practice: Perspectives on a Grand Dichotomy*, edited by J. Weintraub and K. Kumar. Chicago: University of Chicago Press.

Chomsky, Noam. 1989. *Necessary Illusions: Thought Control in Democratic Societies*. Boston, MA: South End Press.

Dayan, Daniel. 2005. "On Mothers, Midwives and Abortionists: The Genealogy and Obstetrics of Audiences and Publics." Pp. 43–76 in *Audiences and Publics: When Cultural Engagement Matters for the Public Sphere*, edited by S. Livingstone. Portland, OR: Intellect Books.

Dayan, Daniel, and Elihu Katz. 1992. *Media Events: The Live Broadcasting of History*. Cambridge, MA: Harvard University Press.

Debord, Guy. 1994. *The Society of the Spectacle*. New York: Zone Books.

Dewey, John. 1954. *The Public and its Problems*. Chicago: Swallow Press.

DuPlessis, Rachel Blau, and Ann Snitow. 1998. *The Feminist Memoir Project: Voices from Women's Liberation*. New York: Three Rivers Press.

Eley, Geoff. 1993. "Nations, Publics, and Political Cultures: Placing Habermas in the Nineteenth Century." Pp. 289–339 in *Habermas and the Public Sphere*, edited by C. Calhoun. Cambridge, MA: MIT Press.

Fraser, Nancy. 1993. "Rethinking the Public Sphere: A Contribution to the Critique of Actually Existing Democracy." Pp. 109–42 in *Habermas and the Public Sphere*, edited by C. Calhoun. Cambridge, MA: MIT Press.

Glasius, M., and G. Pleyers. 2013. "The Moment of 2011: Democracy, Social Justice and Dignity." *Development and Change* 44(3):547–67.

Goffman, Erving. 1956. "The Nature of Deference and Demeanor." *American Anthropologist* 58(3):473–502.

———. 1961. *Asylums*. New York: Knopf.

———. 1967. *Interaction Rituals*. Garden City, NY: Anchor Books.

———. 1971. *Relations in Public: Microstudies of the Public Order*. New York: Basic Books.

Habermas, Jürgen. 1977. "Hannah Arendt's Communications Concept of Power." *Social Research* 44:3–24.

———. 1982. "A Reply to My Critics." Pp. 219–317 in *Habermas: Critical Debate*, edited by J.B. Thompson and D. Held. London: Macmillan.

———. 1984. *The Theory of Communicative Action*. Vol. 1. Boston: Beacon Press.

———. 1989. *The Structural Transformation of the Public Sphere*, trans. Thomas Burger. Cambridge, MA: MIT Press.

———. 1990. *Moral Consciousness and Communicative Action*. Cambridge, MA: MIT Press.

Landes, Joan. 1998. *Women and the Public Sphere in the Age of the French Revolution*. Ithaca, NY: Cornell University Press.

Lee, Benjamin. 1993. "Textuality, Mediation, and Public Discourse." Pp. 402–20 in *Habermas and the Public Sphere*, edited by C. Calhoun. Cambridge, MA: MIT Press.

McLuhan, Marshall. [1964] 1994. *Understanding Media: The Extensions of Man*. Cambridge, MA: MIT Press.

Melucci, Alberto. 1989. *Nomads of the Present: Social Movements and Individual Needs in Contemporary Society*. Philadelphia, PA: Temple University Press.

Nahon, Karin. 2016. "The Coup in Turkey against Traditional Networks and Social Networks." *Gatekeeper*, July 17. Retrieved November 14, 2016 (https://ekarine.org/heb/turkeycoup/) [Hebrew].

Nahon, Karin, and Jeff Hemsley. 2013. *Going Viral*. Malden, MA: Polity Press.

Postman, Neil. 1986. *Amusing Ourselves to Death: Public Discourse in the Age of Show Business*. New York: Penguin Books.

Ryan, Mary P. 1993. "Gender and Public Access: Women's Politics in 19th Century America." Pp. 259–88 in *Habermas and the Public Sphere*, edited by C. Calhoun. Cambridge, MA: MIT Press.

Touraine, Alain. 1981. *The Voice and the Eye: An Analysis of Social Movements*. New York: Cambridge University Press.

Warner, Michael. 2005. *Publics and Counterpublics*. New York: Zone Books.

52

Cultures of democracy

A civil society approach

Ming-Cheng M. Lo

Introduction

After Donald J. Trump's election to the US presidency in 2016, two Harvard political scientists asked in a *New York Times* opinion piece, "Is Donald Trump a threat to democracy?" (Levitsky and Ziblatt 2016). That such a question would be relevant for a well-established democracy, such as the US, begs the question of why its institutional checks and balances would be considered insufficient to safeguard against the then president-elect or, for that matter, *any* president-elect. The answer, explain the authors, is that democratic institutions "must be reinforced by strong informal norms. Like a pickup basketball game without a referee, democracies work best when unwritten rules of the game, known and respected by all players, ensure a minimum of civility and cooperation" (Levitsky and Ziblatt 2016). In other words, the consolidation of democratic culture is key to the proper functioning of a society's democratic institutions. What, then, are the conditions or mechanisms that facilitate democratic cultural consolidation, especially in the face of serious social divisions?

Scholars in the US have long considered this question to be more relevant for young, fragile democracies in postcolonial Asia and Africa than for their own society. Indeed, few of these countries have achieved stable, multicultural civil societies; many have experienced outbreaks of civil war, tribalism, or regression into authoritarian rule (Moore 2001; Magnusson and Clark 2005). Faced with the challenge of building a coherent society after decades of colonialism, dictatorship, and anti-colonial struggles, most postcolonial democracies are stretched between addressing legacies of profound anger and inequality and establishing civil communities capable of communication and cooperation across deep racial and political divides (Monga 1995). Overall, these societies have followed, sometimes in combination, three paths: "to separate along the lines of their differences, to repress their differences, or to constitute their unity through discourse across the lines of their differences" (Calhoun 1995:268–9). Although the "third option" is no doubt the most desirable, its realization is also the most difficult. Now, this challenge – establishing and sustaining cultural norms to enable meaningful conversations across deep social divides – seems just as relevant for America, after all. In this chapter, I discuss how to think about this cultural challenge, in both Western and non-Western contexts, proceeding from a civil society framework.

Ming-Cheng M. Lo

Toward the possibility of civic solidarity

"Civil society" can be conceptualized as (1) located in a social sphere of associations or informal networks that is autonomous from the state and the family, and (2) sharing a ubiquitous culture of civility that informs individuals' participation in this social sphere (Hall 1995; Bryant 1995; see Alexander 2006 for a detailed discussion of the concept). While most contemporary students of civil society trace the concept's origin to Scottish Enlightenment thinkers, scholars continue to debate its proper definition, notably concerning whether the notion of an autonomous sphere of association should include or exclude the economy and religion, whether legacies of rational individualism are the *definition* of the culture of civility or merely one of its numerous possible empirical manifestations, and how well the concept of civil society can travel outside of its Western birthplace. Detailing these discussions is beyond the scope of this chapter. What is important, for the discussion at hand, is that diverse approaches generally agree on the importance of civic solidarity – a sense of "we-ness" that sustains a healthy tension between differences and social integration, either as a defining cultural feature or a desired goal of civil society.

Largely inspired by Habermas ([1962] 1989), discussion of civic solidarity challenges any assumption that "the public" or "the people" is a natural set available to be released in political expression. Instead, these debates establish the premise that a public has to constitute its own identity as both the subject and the object of democratic representation. In other words, people have to debate and negotiate about exactly who is or isn't part of a given public (e.g., "should undocumented immigrants be considered part of the public?") as well as deliberate over public positions (e.g., "should we provide healthcare for undocumented immigrants and why?"). The articulation of civic identities entails the process of delineating a symbolic, collective community, a sense of "we-ness" as Alexander (1992) describes it. Yet, in a democratic community, this sense of we-ness must also capture its internal divisions. Cultural practices in civil society are expected to sustain a sense of integration while facilitating meaningful engagement about internal differences.

The tension between integration and differences has been invoked to challenge Habermas's formulation of a unitary public sphere and, subsequently, stimulated competing theorizations. Habermas's concept of the ideal speech community was itself an attempt to address this tension. In his view, all people, across cultural, racial, and gender lines, hold the capacity for rational-critical thinking. As long as democratic rules and procedures protect every citizen's right to speak up, participants in the public sphere have the rational capacity to evaluate an argument based on its merits rather than the status of the speaker. Habermas argued that the foundation of this public sphere is universal because it is communicative. As Rabinovitch (2001:347) has commented, "Any individuals or groups may argue for continued incorporation into the decision-making process simply by demonstrating their ability to reason and to express their point of view." Habermas considered this potential for inclusiveness as the self-transforming quality of the bourgeois public sphere. For him, only communicative action can achieve the social integration necessary for a democratic public sphere without suppressing social and cultural differences.

Scholars subsequently have questioned Habermas's faith in communicative action. Historical studies show that different social groups are more likely to form separate publics than to join the dominant public (Eley 1992; Ryan 1992), thereby cultivating unequal and relatively separate symbolic systems in which actual rational-critical discourses are embedded. Thus, even when a civil society is formally open and inclusive to all, its dominant cultural vocabulary can become an informal mechanism of exclusion, because it is composed of styles of speech and discursive codes that have been shaped by legacies of power inequality. Fraser (1992) argued that recognizing the cultural hegemony of public discourses is part of how "true" (or, in her words, "radical") democracy works. She proposed the concept of "subaltern counter-publics" to describe marginalized discursive arenas where subordinated social groups invent and circulate counter-discourses to "formulate oppositional interpretations of their identities, interests, and needs" (Fraser 1992:123). For her, the relationships between subaltern counterpublics and hegemonic publics are posited to be hierarchical and conflictual; their cultural difference remains largely irreconcilable through communicative action.

For his part, Alexander attempted to explain "exactly that which both Habermas and Fraser omitted: how it is that people successfully argue that they are in fact members of the symbolic community of 'common humanity' without losing sight of their distinct cultural identities" (Rabinovitch 2001:351). Alexander shifted the basis of integration from Habermas's universal rationality to shared discursive binaries. He argued that the binary normative code of sacred and profane provides the fundamental cultural language for articulating democratic ideals. To make sense of social events, the public resorts to characteristics associated with the sacred/civil and the profane/uncivil in their shared cultural repertoire. Rather than seeing marginal groups as enjoying a fair hearing in Habermas's ideal speech community or only able to find their voice in Fraser's counterpublics, Alexander (2006) contended that they are often unfairly coded with stigmatized/uncivil categories within a shared system of meaning, or what he called the code of liberty. In a multicultural civil society, marginal groups can potentially succeed at gaining the freedom and resources to argue in the dominant public that their stigmatized qualities are in fact a valid, if different, manifestation of characteristics of the sacred/civil. Such counter-hegemonic struggle, he argued, involves a process of multicultural incorporation rather than separatism, because the opposing groups actually operate with shared binary systems. Empirically, at least in the case of the United States, struggle is often carried out through social movements – a form of "civic repair" in Alexander's terms. If successful, women, racial minorities, or other previously marginalized groups are eventually recognized as possessing specific cultural qualities that manifest broad democratic ideals (e.g., rationality, justice, altruism). Through an ongoing process of "particularizing the universal," cultures of civil society become broader and richer while core civic values are simultaneously reinforced across social groups.

Civic associations, group styles, and collective narratives

However, even in societies with relatively strong legacies of the liberty code, broad civic ideals alone do not dictate *how* cultures of civil society will develop. Although the liberty code may provide the underlying "grammar" of civil society discourses, it is when social groups use the code to structure narratives and arguments that concrete patterns of democratic cultural practices take shape. Group-level ties, styles, and narratives can be seen as key mechanisms for the formation and transformation of civil society cultures.

As much as individual autonomy is valued by advocates for democracy, an atomized society threatens to weaken the very social fabric of democracy. As Putnam (2000) and other neo-Tocquevillian scholars have warned, cynicism, apathy, and other forms of political disengagement by citizens signal a decline in civility and foreshadow collective democratic non-participation. This insight has inspired much research focusing on measuring the density of group ties in the associational sphere. Although critics complain that this approach tends to quantify civic ties at the expense of their meanings, the emphasis on civic ties is useful in establishing the premise that practices of group-level association nurture a sense of social connectedness, which in turn is foundational to political engagement. More broadly speaking, horizontal group ties can become social mechanisms against state monopoly of power in non-democratic settings (Ryan 2001). Thus, Ikegami (2005) argues that Japanese "aesthetic publics," or loose cultural circles devoted to tea ceremonies, poetry, music, and other arts that developed during the Tokugawa period, constituted realms of sociability that brought together strangers from drastically different social backgrounds. These horizontal networks not only eroded the Tokugawa hierarchical social order but nurtured social capital later mobilized in democratization movements, after the collapse of the Tokugawa shogunate.

Beyond their direct significance for polities, social groups and associations facilitate citizens' expressions of agency and creativity. Indeed, civil society is both an arena for expressing fairly established identities and also a realm of sociability where identities develop, transform, and are articulated creatively (Calhoun 1995; Mische and Chandler, this volume). Social groups produce songs, symbols, narratives, and so forth, as the means both to think through and to express their identities. For example, the "submerged networks" (Melucci 1989) or "free spaces" (Evans and Boyte 1986) in social movements can serve as cultural laboratories where groups experiment with new identities. Sometimes, in these spaces, social groups struggle to make sense of the tensions between the multiple social positions that their participants simultaneously occupy, for example, as both African Americans *and* women (Robnett 1997), as both colonial subjects *and* high-status professionals (Lo 2002), or as both members of the middle class *and* a racialized minority (Agius Vallejo 2012), producing narratives and ideas not reducible to social structures but rather registering their creative responses to intersecting boundaries.

However, even in a civil society with a large number of robust associations, there is no guarantee that these groups will deeply engage with intergroup differences. The question remains: why are certain groups better at encouraging reflexive consideration of differences than others? Lichterman and Eliasoph's research provides some answers. They argue that a group's "scene styles," or informal, group-specific styles of interaction and conversations, nurture or limit the group's capacity for social reflexivity (Lichterman 2008; Lichterman and Eliasoph 2014). Scene style can be understood in terms of several analytical dimensions, including participants' vision for where they exist on a wider social map, their shared understandings for how they sustain internal bonds, and the group's informal "speech norms" that define the meaning of speech itself – which topics are appropriate, how differences are supposed to be handled, and what activism, social justice, and other ideals mean (Lichterman and Eliasoph 2014; Eliasoph and Lichterman, this volume). Scene styles inform how group members position themselves in relation to other social groups, as well as what they recognize – or fail to recognize – as legitimate assumptions in group conversations. Along similar lines, Mische (2008) develops a typology of four modes of communication (Habermasian, Gramscian, Deweyian, and Machiavellian), arguing that it is important to analyze social actors' skills for flexible "discursive switching" across institutional settings rather than to regard one communicative action as inherently more virtuous than another.

It is also useful to consider how groups' narratives contribute to larger social narratives beyond their own group boundaries, for example, in shaping the commonly shared narratives of national trauma, honor, or tragedy. To be sure, collective narratives are never singular or static; they often undergo hegemonic contestation. But even when a more or less settled collective position emerges about certain events in a society (e.g., slavery is inhuman; apartheid is uncivil; Hiroshima is a reminder of the cruelty of war), diverse group narratives may continue to encourage and enrich reflexive understandings of national events. When various groups and multiple publics reflect upon shared histories, they do so within the matrix of social relationships where they are situated, thereby developing explanatory stories that connect, highlight, suppress, and rearrange chronological events in different ways (Somers and Gibson 1994). The 1992 Rodney King beating offers a telling example: mainstream media and black newspapers reported events in drastically different ways. Both sides shared a critical stand against police brutality and a commitment to racial equality, but – and this is key – they offered two very different stories of who the heroes and villains were and what the romance/tragedy of civic repair was about (Jacobs 1996). Similarly, the attempt to archive black women's pictorial and written testimony in a "Memory Cloths" program in South Africa represented a crucial step toward fleshing out marginalized aspects in the collective memory of apartheid. The representations of the past by black women were not only important for black women themselves, but also for the national narrative about past wrongs (McEwen 2003). In both examples, the multiple and diverse accounts of "storied life" added layers of meaning to larger social narratives about shared histories and consolidated political positions. To enhance their democratic potential, big national narratives are best structured in multistranded and multilayered ways, as their discursive richness renders them more inclusive and flexible, better able to accommodate future reinterpretations and revisions without an immediate threat of cultural fragmentation.

The recent discussions about scene styles and broad social narratives show that civil society is better positioned for success if it has in stock a cultural "toolkit" for engagement with – rather than passive tolerance of – inter-group and intra-group differences. In one telling example, Eliasoph and Lichterman (this volume) describe how, without such a toolkit, a progressive church group inadvertently alienated and disempowered non-members who held similar ideals but came from different backgrounds. The authors observe that the church group lacked a cultural style that easily could be used to question its own assumptions, in this case the assumption that social activists "should be bound together by leftist solidarity, not faith in Jesus." Having experienced similar limitations, other faith-based community coalitions have begun to actively cultivate "bridging cultural practices," such as prayers with which different faith groups might connect, as bases for relationship-building across racial and socioeconomic divides (Braunstein, Fulton, and Wood 2014). Though not without controversy and criticisms, Hochschild's (2016) powerful ethnography of Tea Party supporters in Louisiana challenges activists and social scientists to consider why their narratives of social justice have failed to "break down the empathy wall" and speak to the white working class.

Beyond the codes of liberty

Thus far, the research I have discussed shows that the liberty code provides a broad cultural vocabulary for civil society discourses, and that group ties, styles, and narratives provide the meso-level mechanisms of mediation therein. An important question remains unaddressed: must the same cultural properties be reproduced in non-Western societies that aspire for democratic consolidation? With the expansion of Western imperialist powers, many societies in other parts of the world acquired "a skeleton of institutions similar to those . . . [in] the West," even if the West's culture of rational individualism "has not become the dream of these societies" (Mardin 1995:295). Therein lies the question, both academic and political, of whether and how such societies might develop their own cultures of civil society. Many scholars are skeptical, not so much because they are convinced of Western cultural superiority, but because they view civil society as intrinsically tied to rational individualism. But can there exist a culture of civility that differs in origin and content from rational individualism, yet is functionally similar and thus recognizable as one of its variants?

Such functional comparability, to recall Alexander's conceptualization, refers to the capacity of a cultural system to treat differences as legitimate by constructing them as variations on the theme of common humanity. This is only possible if "the particular is viewed . . . as a concrete manifestation of the universal" (Alexander 2006:259). Gellner (1994) does not see other cultural systems – which he famously describes as "cousin-ridden" – as possessing this crucial feature.

Similarly, Alexander ponders, if an alternative ethics such as caring "bases itself on such ties as love . . . then there is no theoretical room for compelling commitment to abstract social rules . . . Such an ethic is well and good for the intimate sphere, but can it actually be extended to the civil one?" (Alexander 2006:261).

However, beyond Gellner and Alexander, *relationality* can and does exist as an abstract principle that is detached from concrete *relational ties*, informing abstract, universalistic civil society ethics (Lo and Bettinger 2001). This is made possible when cultural systems undergo the historical process of what Gellner (1994) terms "modularization." In Gellner's insightful but Western-centered observation, modularization refers to a process of the ascendance and subsequent collapse of a strong cultural center. Historically, the cultural system we know as rational individualism is a product of the fragmentation of the Roman Catholic Church. The collapse of the Church as a cultural center liberated individuals from institutionalized ideological control, while the remnants of this shared cultural legacy provided them with a flexible cultural motif. In other words, strangers found it easy to form associational ties because they more or less shared the same abstract cultural values, but they became free to enter these relationships or exit from them voluntarily – free from the supervision of the Church. What is important for the discussion at hand, however, is that parallel examples have been documented in other parts of the world.

As a corrective to Gellner's ethnocentrism, I and a colleague have shown that the family state in pre-war Japan also represented a political and cultural center that subsequently underwent a similar process of fragmentation. A familial culture became a shared legacy that was detached from a totalizing center, and was afforded voluntary and flexible application in the associational sphere in post-war Japan (Lo and Bettinger 2001). Having become modularized, familial civility developed into a culturally specific ethic of relationality, which required *not* that individuals pledge loyalty to the familial state or remain attached to specific family members, but that they honor the obligations, cultures, and well-being of the groups which they voluntarily chose to join in the civic sphere. Familialism may or may not continue to regulate relationships in the private sphere, but today another form of familialism, a "generalized particularism," operates generally and broadly in post-war Japan as a civic ethics, beyond the confines of primordial relationships. Just as rationality is not inherently public even if it was historically regarded as the cultural logic of the public sphere, relationality should not be regarded as an inherently private culture despite past histories or cultural biases. Certainly, not all cultures of relationality become modularized and develop into a *civic* ethics. But in a reasonable effort to provincialize Europe, it is important to recognize that rational individualism is not the only cultural foundation for civic ethics.

To further substantiate our understandings of the diverse cultural origins and historical trajectories of civic ethics, future research documenting histories of cultural modularization in non-Western contexts would be needed. However, instead of assuming diverse civil ethics to always develop in isolation from one another, it is perhaps more fruitful to consider when and how different cultures of civil society may interact across porous, fluid national boundaries. For example, in their pursuits of democratization, social groups in emergent civil societies often import and appropriate the code of liberty for their own use. Sometimes, we witness competition or mutual displacement between democratic and authoritarian codes, raising challenges as to whether and how a civil ethics will indeed take root (Ku 2001). In other cases, social groups mix and match multiple cultural codes that have become available to them. Scholars have yet to engage in systematic studies of the patterns and conditions of hybridized civic ethics. But a few compelling cases suggest that sometimes social actors find it challenging to sustain the inclusive potential of civil society discourses solely through the code of liberty (e.g., in the face of severe social polarization or unspeakable past wrongs). When full application of the principles of justice and rationality would lead to daunting consequences, sometimes social groups temper these principles by developing alternative visions (e.g., of forgiveness, reconciliation, caring, or a shared future). For example, social groups in Taiwan and Hong Kong have both been shown to operate with an imported code of liberty in their civil society discourses. Yet when struggles for democratization brew deep political polarization or profound cynicism, democratic ideals are invoked almost entirely to determine who is uncivil and deserves exclusion from society. To remedy this lopsided discourse of democracy, some social groups have turned to the ethics of caring and relationality as they contemplate how political opponents may still recognize each other's common humanity (Lo and Fan 2010). In the case of post-apartheid South Africa, the exclusion of all past perpetrators would be tantamount to producing a mass exodus from the nation; instead, the civic repair processes have proceeded through the vision of a deep moral transformation (as, for example, in the Truth and Reconciliation Commission). The hybridization of the liberal ethics of justice and truth and the religious virtues of reconciliation and grace makes it possible to talk about a coherent vision of nation-rebuilding. But the delicate tension between responsibility and vilification, reconciliation and denial, also remains a difficult challenge and unsettling force in South African cultures of democracy (Nagy 2004).

Conclusion

With its focus on the tension between difference and integration, the civil society approach offers a conceptual tool for analyzing the cultural processes of democratic consolidation. Alexander theorizes that the ethic of civic solidarity, concretely manifested in the American case as the code of liberty, offers a universalistic cultural vocabulary through which hegemonic struggles are carried out without leading to social fragmentation. The works of Putnam, Lichterman, Eliasoph, and others further specify key meso-level mechanisms that shape how the code of liberty is concretely deployed: acts of associating provide a foundation for political engagement in civil society; social movement networks facilitate resistance, self-empowerment, and creative cultural expression; customs and styles shape a civic group's capacity for social reflexivity and self-restraint. At an intergroup level, such discourses of resistance and reflexivity can help promote nuanced and flexible social narratives about national pride or trauma. Recently, studies of non-Western cases further suggest that the code of liberty does not define the only civic ethics. Historically, cultural vocabularies that share similar functions but differ in content have developed elsewhere, through the process of modularization. Recognizing this process opens up questions about code competition and hybridization. Of particular interest are questions about how hybridized cultural discourses may facilitate, limit, or otherwise shape processes of democratic consolidation in fledgling civil societies.

Looking forward, research can benefit from more systematic comparisons. We need more empirical work comparing civil society discourses inspired by the liberty code and alternative civic ethics in order to better understand their alternative potentials and limitations. Such empirical studies will illustrate concretely the historical construction of universalistic ideals, as paradoxical as that notion might seem. In addition, we need to recognize that research on how meso-level cultural mechanisms work in non-Western contexts to balance between empowerment and reflexivity, or resistance and cooperation, has been relatively underdeveloped, perhaps because such tasks – the desired but difficult "third option," to recall Calhoun's phrasing – are particularly challenging in young democracies. But precisely for this reason, the topic is all the more relevant. Finally, with the insights learned from Asian and African cases, we may ask if participants in civil society in the West also resort to non-liberty ethics in their "civic repairs." If so, under what conditions, and with what consequences? Issues of code hybridization, for example, between religious values and democratic ones, between the ethics of caring and empathy and that of liberty and justice, are likely to inspire new research questions about cultural practices in established democracies. These questions may be especially relevant during a time when even many established democracies are experiencing uncertainty and anxiety about their existing cultural underpinnings. The cross-fertilization of insights from Western and non-Western contexts, one hopes, will move us toward new, more rigorous, and more actionable understandings about cultures of democracy.

References

Agius Vallejo, J. 2012. "Socially Mobile Mexican Americans and the Minority Culture of Mobility." *American Behavioral Scientist* 56(5):666–81.

Alexander, Jeffrey C. 1992. "Citizen and Enemy as Symbolic Classification: On the Polarizing Discourse of Civil Society." Pp. 289–308 in *Where Culture Talks: Exclusion and the Making of Society*, edited by M. Fournier and M. Lamont. Chicago: University of Chicago Press.

———. 2006. *The Civil Sphere*. New York: Oxford University Press.

Braunstein, Ruth, Brad Fulton, and Richard L. Wood. 2014. "The Role of Bridging Cultural Practices in Racially and Socioeconomically Diverse Civic Organizations." *American Sociological Review* 79(4):705–25.

Bryant, Christopher G.A. 1995. "Civic Nation, Civil Society, Civil Religion." Pp. 136–58 in *Civil Society: Theory, History, Comparison*, edited by J.A. Hall. Cambridge: Polity Press.

Calhoun, Craig. 1995. "Nationalism and Difference: The Politics of Identity Writ Large." Pp. 231–82 in *Critical Social Theory*, edited by C. Calhoun. Cambridge, MA: Blackwell.

Eley, Goeff. 1992. "Nations, Publics, and Political Cultures: Placing Habermas in the Nineteenth Century." Pp. 289–339 in *Habermas and the Public Sphere*, edited by C. Calhoun. Cambridge: MIT Press.

Evans, Sara M., and Harry C. Boyte. 1986. *Free Spaces: The Sources of Democratic Change in America*. New York: Harper and Row.

Fraser, Nancy. 1992. "Rethinking the Public Sphere: A Contribution to the Critique of Actually Existing Democracy." Pp. 109–42 in *Habermas and the Public Sphere*, edited by C. Calhoun. Cambridge: MIT Press.

Gellner, Ernest. 1994. *Conditions of Liberty: Civil Society and Its Rivals*. London: Hamish Hamilton.

Habermas, Jürgen. [1962] 1989. *The Structural Transformation of the Public Sphere*, trans. Thomas Burger with the assistance of Frederick Lawrence. Cambridge: MIT Press.

Hall, John A. 1995. "In Search of Civil Society." Pp. 1–31 in *Civil Society: Theory, History, Comparison*, edited by J.A. Hall. Cambridge: Polity Press.

Hochschild, Arlie Russell. 2016. *Strangers in Their Own Land: Anger and Mourning on the American Right*. New York: New Press.

Ikegami, Eiko. 2005. *Bonds of Civility: Aesthetic Networks and the Political Origins of Japanese Culture*. New York: Cambridge University Press.

Jacobs, Ronald N. 1996. "Civil Society and Crisis: Culture, Discourse, and the Rodney King Beating." *American Journal of Sociology* 101(5):1238–72.

Ku, Agnes S. 2001. "The 'Public' Up Against the State – Credibility Crisis and Narrative Cracks in Postcolonial Hong Kong." *Theory, Culture and Society* 18(1):121–44.

Levitsky, Steven, and Daniel Ziblatt. 2016. "Is Donald Trump a Threat to Democracy?" *New York Times*, December 16. Retrieved October 27, 2017 (www.nytimes.com/2016/12/16/opinion/sunday/is-donald-trump-a-threat-to-democracy.html).

Lichterman, Paul. 2008. "Religion and the Construction of Civic Identity." *American Sociological Review* 73(1):83–104.

Lichterman, Paul, and Nina Eliasoph. 2014. "Civic Action." *American Journal of Sociology* 120(3):798–863.

Lo, Ming-Cheng M. 2002. *Doctors within Borders: Profession, Ethnicity, and Modernity in Colonial Taiwan*. Berkeley: University of California Press.

Lo, Ming-Cheng M., and Christopher P. Bettinger. 2001. "The Historical Emergence of a 'Familial Society' in Japan." *Theory and Society* 30(2):237–79.

Lo, Ming-Cheng M., and Yun Fan. 2010. "Hybrid Cultural Codes in Non-Western Civil Society: Images of Women in Taiwan and Hong Kong." *Sociological Theory* 28(2):167–92.

Magnusson, Bruce A., and John F. Clark. 2005. "Understanding Democratic Survival and Democratic Failure in Africa: Insights from Divergent Democratic Experiments in Benin and Congo (Brazzaville)." *Comparative Studies in Society and History* 47(3):552–82.

Mardin, Şerif. 1995. "Civil Society and Islam." Pp. 278–300 in *Civil Society: Theory, History, Comparison*, edited by J.A. Hall. Cambridge: Polity Press.

McEwan, Cheryl. 2003. "Building a Postcolonial Archive? Gender, Collective Memory and Citizenship in Post-Apartheid South Africa." *Journal of Southern African Studies* 29(3):739–57.

Melucci, Alberto. 1989. *Normads of the Present*. London: Hutchinson Radius.

Mische, Ann. 2008. *Partisan Politics: Communication and Contention across Brazilian Youth Activist Networks*. Princeton, NJ: Princeton University Press.

Monga, Celestin. 1995. "Civil Society and Democratisation in Francophone Africa." *Journal of Modern African Studies* 33(3):359–79.

Moore, David. 2001. "Neoliberal Globalisation and the Triple Crisis of 'Modernisation' in Africa: Zimbabwe, the Democratic Republic of the Congo and South Africa." *Third World Quarterly* 22(6):909–29.

Nagy, Rosemary. 2004. "The Ambiguities of Reconciliation and Responsibility in South Africa." *Politic Studies* 52(4):709–27.

Putnam, Robert D. 2000. *Bowling Alone: The Collapse and Revival of American Community*. New York: Simon & Schuster.

Rabinovitch, Eyal. 2001. "Gender and the Public Sphere: Alternative Forms of Integration in Nineteenth-Century America." *Sociological Theory* 19(3):344–70.

Robnett, Belinda. 1997. *How Long? How Long? African-American Women in the Struggle for Civil Rights*. New York: Oxford University Press.

Ryan, Mary. 1992. "Gender and Public Access: Women's Politics in Nineteenth-Century America." Pp. 259–88 in *Habermas and the Public Sphere*, edited by C. Calhoun. Cambridge: MIT Press.

———. 2001. "Civil Society as Democratic Practice: North American Cities During the Nineteenth Century." Pp. 221–46 in *Patterns of Social Capital: Stability and Change in Historical Perspective*, edited by R. Rotberg. New York: Cambridge University Press.

Somers, Margaret R., and Gloria D. Gibson. 1994. "Reclaiming the Epistemological 'Other': Narrative and the Social Constitution of Identity." Pp. 37–99 in *Social Theory and the Politics of Identity*, edited by C. Calhoun. Cambridge, MA: Blackwell.

53

National culture, national identity, and the culture(s) of the nation

Geneviève Zubrzycki

Introduction

Until relatively recently, scholars of nationalism primarily used *culture* to stand for language, ethnicity, and broadly defined traditions. Culture was that stuff out of which nations were built and which nationalists sought to protect and perfect under the aegis of the modern nation-state. Alternatively, culture was regarded as a "thing" requiring invention in order for people to care about, and fight for, in the establishment of nation-states. By embracing the so-called cultural turn, a new generation of scholars changed both the lens and the focus of the field: the object of study shifted from an emphasis on nationalism to one on national identity. From this new vantage point, the nation is not a reified object but a symbol that social actors compete over, nationalism is a field of debates about the symbol of the nation, and national identity is a relational process enacted in social dramas and "events" as well as in everyday practices.

This chapter analyzes the various ways in which culture has been conceptualized in the scholarship on nations and nationalism. It then discusses the import of the "cultural turn" on the field, with a specific focus on recent contributions and new directions afforded by another turn – that to materiality. Visualizing those turns, however, presupposes some knowledge of the road and the maps by which we navigated before. To that end, I begin with a brief consideration of the pre-history of "national culture."

Archeology of the field: esprit, character, civilization

Long before the advent of nationalism – and even longer before it became a topic of scholarly interest – philosophers reflected on what differentiated one people from another. That "nations" had distinctive "spirits," "souls," "genius," or "characters" was widely taken for granted; what remained to be explained was their source. For Hobbes (1588–1679), Kant (1724–1804), Herder (1744–1803), Montesquieu (1689–1755), and Rousseau (1712–1778), to name only the most prominent thinkers on the issue, it was the idiosyncratic configuration of a variety of factors that produced moral traits specific to a people, the unique *Geist* of a given nation. Those factors ranged from the physical characteristics of the inhabitants and the geophysical properties of the soil, landscape, and climate to the language, folk traditions, and art of the population; the form of political institutions and laws; and religious beliefs, mores, and rituals. Montesquieu, for instance, saw climate as especially significant in shaping a nation's *esprit*. As he argued in *The Spirit of the Laws*, it influenced personality, social dynamics, and political systems, so that people in very warm regions tended to be "hot-tempered" and politically unstable, whereas those living in northern parts of the world were overly stiff and passive. France's temperate climate thus explained the unusual qualities of the French people.

If some thinkers were concerned about the origins of specific national cultures, others considered their impact on political life and international relations. Rousseau, for example, argued that a well-defined, coherent "national character" was a necessary condition for national self-awareness and patriotism, and in turn a key step toward political sovereignty. Since national character played such a crucial role in the establishment of sovereignty and free government, he insisted, it would have to be created in places where it did not already exist – presciently anticipating the arduous work of cultural imagination and institutional invention that nation-builders all over the world applied throughout the nineteenth and the early part of the twentieth centuries.

Whereas Rousseau understood national character as the result of a dynamic interplay between culture and politics and in terms of the role it played in fostering national consciousness and the general will, the notion of national character later evolved into a static and often stereotypically descriptive and normative category. The reified fusion of individual moral traits and national culture was then used as an alleged predictor of political behavior. For example, influenced by Freudian theory, the "culture and personality school" in the US of the 1930s to 1950s took as its point the departure the view that, through their culturally determined child-rearing practices, different societies tend to foster specific personality types. National character studies, primarily associated with the work of Ruth Benedict and Margaret Mead, took this argument even further. They claimed that these personality types, taken as an aggregate, constituted distinct national characters that would shape political organizations and influence, for example, military versus more pacific propensities.

The psycho-cultural approach has since been discredited for its impressionistic tone, selective use of evidence, and looseness in empirical demonstration. Still, some scholars have tried to salvage the idea that different nations have specific attitudes and values that constitute distinct "national characters." This agenda has been carried forward most prominently by political scientist Alex Inkeles (1997), who sought to demonstrate the empirical existence of national characters through innovative survey instruments and sophisticated quantitative analysis. Although that approach had lost much traction by the 1990s, the notion of national character persisted, albeit in a new incarnation, in Huntington's (1996) thesis of the "clash of civilizations." That controversial theory of global conflict rested on the idea that culture – and more specifically religion – drives how people see themselves and understand their place in the world. "Civilizational" fault lines, according to Huntington, draw the battle lines of the future.

This reification of culture and the division of the world into different and conflicting civilizations is reminiscent of the distinction made in the aftermath of World War II by the early theorist of nationalism, Hans Kohn (1946), who distinguished between what he termed "Western" and "Eastern" types of nationalism. For Kohn, nationalism in the West was the product of the Age of Reason and its ideas of liberty, equality, and fraternity, and was closely related to individualism, liberalism, constitutionalism, and democracy more generally. As nationalism spread eastward and developed in closed, authoritarian societies, however, it morphed into a collectivist ideology that rejected the ideas of the Enlightenment and embraced xenophobia instead. For Kohn, nationalism was a force promoting liberal ideals through political institutions in the West, while in the East it found expression in the concept of the *Volk* and its "authentic" culture.

In this lineage, national culture is seen as an enduring, relatively impermeable *substance* defining the nation and its identity – a substance predating political projects and therefore a valued resource for building and legitimizing them. This "substance" idea of national culture is what nationalists later on sought to define, protect, and elevate under the aegis of national states. In contemporary scholarship on nations and nationalism, this last argument has been made most forcefully and often over the last three decades by Anthony D. Smith (1986), who locates the origins of modern nations in premodern cultures (what he calls *ethnies*). Ethnies constitute the basis for, and provide the original cells from which, the modern nation and its defining ally, the nation-state, were allegedly hatched.

The recent "turn" in the study of national culture began as an angling off from the lineage described earlier. But what direction did scholars turn *to*? They turned toward the idea that national cultures, far from being ancient and coherent wholes that shaped national identity and built nation-states, had to be somehow created in the first place.

Culture as construction tool: inventing national culture and promoting a culture of the national

Ernest Gellner's theory of nationalism, initially articulated in a chapter of *Thought and Change* in 1964, rigorously questioned the putative causal power of a pre-existing culture in the formation of nations and nationalism. In what is now a famous reversal of commonsensical understandings of the relationship between culture and nationalism, he insisted that it is not "the nation" – a bounded national culture – that creates nationalism, but the other way around. Nationalism, he argued, was the process *through which* homogeneous high cultures were created in modernity. In fact, Gellner explained, nationalism came into being in the modern era in order to fulfill that specific function. With industrialization and the erosion of traditional social structures, a common "high culture" – defined as a unified language and literacy – became increasingly important to facilitate communications and economic exchanges, as well as to shape social relationships. Achieving these goals required a standardized education system. Such a system, Gellner argued, could only be created and sustained in a modern nation-state – a political unit larger than local-regional political organizations but smaller than imperial structures. Nationalism, then, was the pragmatic push toward such political entities, and toward their ideological justification in the claim that political and cultural units should be congruent.

Although Gellner's theory of nationalism was wedded to modernization theory and suffered from many problems commonly attributed to functionalism, it nevertheless offered a novel way to think about the relationship between culture and nationalism. Instead of taking national culture for granted, as a "pre-existing condition" reified as something that elites manipulated in the service of nationalism, or as something that they evoked to mobilize support for nationalism because it needed to be saved, protected, or promoted, Gellner showed that nationalism actually came into being for national culture's very creation.

Eric J. Hobsbawm took up the issue of national culture's creation in his canonical *The Invention of Tradition* (Hobsbawm and Ranger1983), where he carefully documented that process and explained the various motivations behind it. He convincingly showed that most of what people consider part of their national culture was invented in a specific historic period (1870–1914) by self-interested actors. Government agencies applied themselves to create traditions, myths, and symbols that would foster affective horizontal bonds at a moment of social and political unrest, and vertical allegiance to newly created nation-states and their political elites. The establishment of public collective celebrations such as national holidays and memorial days honoring those who died for the nation, the creation of public spaces and construction of monuments, and the designing of national symbols such as flags and national anthems all contributed to that broader project.

The intensity with which a national culture had to be forged depended, according to Hobsbawm, on the strength of the initial national project. In the case of France, the "Revolution had established the fact, nature and the boundaries of the French nation and its patriotism" (Hobsbawm and Ranger 1983:278). Therefore the need for extensive symbols and traditions was relatively small. In the German case, however, at the time the national project began, the national definition was still vague, the unity shaky, and the identification with the Second Empire less precise, and as a result there was a greater need to establish the "national fact" (1983:278). Karen Cerulo (1995), who studied the syntactic structure of national symbols, also found that "younger," or less established nations often show an expansiveness in content in their national symbols, and that the more intense the cognitive focus of the target (as in post-1789 France), the less elaborate the accompanying symbolic structure.

The creation of national identity through the production of a homogeneous national culture and a master narrative of the nation comes at a price: it necessarily implies the repression of alternative memories, identities, and loyalties (local or religious, for example). As historian of China Prasenjit Duara rightly pointed out, "the attention devoted to the process whereby national identities are formed has neglected to see that it is the same process whereby other identifications and nation-views are repressed and obscured" (1995:164). This hegemonization of national culture through its homogenization is not merely discursive, but "pictorial" as well. In *Siam Mapped*, Tongchai Winichakul (1994) showed that Western, modern conceptions of space, geography, and territoriality led to "national" map-making, and that the creation of such "geo-bodies" represented on paper and thereby reified de facto created nations where they previously did not exist.

It is therefore vital to recognize the dual constructive and destructive processes involved in the creation of national culture. If mandatory primary education, commemorations, public monuments, museums, and maps were critical in forging a uniform national culture and creating a unified national identity, they also participated in the annihilation of other (local) cultures, memories, traditions, geographies, and identities. Eugen Weber (1976), to take one prominent example, showed how public primary schools simultaneously imposed a particular version of the French language and (often violently) repressed *patois*, local dialects. The investigation of forgotten, silenced, or repressed stories is crucial not only to restore the voices that allow a fuller understanding of local histories, but also because these investigations expose an ineluctable aspect of nation formation, namely, its annihilative power.

National culture as discourse and structure of meaning

Whereas the works of Gellner and Hobsbawm were determinative in establishing social constructivist approaches to the study of nations and nationalism as the new orthodoxies in the field, Benedict Anderson's *Imagined Communities* (1991) must be flagged as especially significant concerning the role of culture. Here is where the most dramatic turn was made. *Imagined Communities* moved the center of the discussion on nationalism from Europe to the so-called periphery and it more strongly centered the field on cultural analysis. The advent of nations and nationalism in modernity, Anderson argued, had been possible because of epochal cultural transformations on the one hand, and because of daily practices on the other. His intervention stimulated new approaches that remained sociologically grounded but that henceforth paid attention to the *discursive* formation of the nation and the production of meaning.

Just as the paradigm shift from primordialism to social constructivism in the 1980s had entailed a shift from the study of nationalist movements and conflicts to that of the nation and its making, the discursive turn inaugurated by Anderson initiated the redefinition of the very object of study, from the nation to national *identity*. In the wake of *Imagined Communities*, scholars moved even further away from "objectivist" stances and toward "subjectivist" ones. Duara, for example, sees national identity as a "subject position produced by representations in relation to other representations," the national self being constituted "within a network of changing and often conflicting representations" (1995:7). In that context, nationalism is neither a unified ideology nor a movement, but rather a discursive field where different views of the nation compete and negotiate with each other. The ultimate outcome of these discursive struggles – which are embedded in social and political structures and backed by institutional power – is the creation of the nation as a compelling symbolic configuration. Though the process may therefore be regarded as "productive," one should not overlook the fact that it also necessarily entails the use of power, including the discrediting, dislocation, repression, and even destruction of alternative visions, and the marginalization of social actors representing them. Understanding the nation as a symbol competed over by different groups maneuvering to monopolize its definition and enjoy its legitimating effects, scholars of nationalism must identify the global, societal, and institutional contexts in which different groups fight for the exclusive capacity to define the nation and to what ends (Verdery 1993:39; cf. Bourdieu 1991). The focus on the conflict *within* the nation over the nation's meaning and identity, its project, and destiny is where some of the most interesting discussions may now be found.

In my own work on post-communist Poland (Zubrzycki 2006, 2011), I have shown that national identity is constituted through specific social dramas and events in which the meaning of the nation is contested and potentially transformed. As Poles injected communism into a series of narratives of conquest, occupation, and oppression by powerful neighbors, and of their own historical struggle for independence, the long decade between the fall of communism in 1989 and Poland's accession to the EU in 2004 was emplotted as the latest chapter in the epic of Poland's fight for independence. The post-communist transition was therefore first and foremost understood by Poles as a *national* one; it was a period not merely characterized by democratization and marketization, but primarily by the construction of a national state. Given this project, the issue of what exactly constitutes "Polishness" has been a recurring theme in public discourse for the past 25 years and in those debates, Polish national identity's "traditional" association with Catholicism has been seriously questioned. One point here is that without considering the *meaning* of the post-communist transition, much of the public debates that have punctuated the decade following the fall of communism, as well as the *type* and *pace* of institutional reforms that took place then, remain incomprehensible. But the point is also that meaning is constituted through perduring narratives of the nation that have been ossified into a national culture – canonized in history books and maps, inscribed onto the landscape, allegorized in poetry, folktales, popular sayings, and music, visualized in paintings, monuments, and popular art, materialized investments, jewelry, and other embodied practices, and memorialized in family photographs and memoirs. These multiple sites and forms not only establish a canonical national culture in the traditional sense of the term, but also constitute a specific culture of the nation, a prism through which national subjects see institutions, understand political transformations, and *feel* themselves to be related to historical events – what I call the national sensorium (Zubrzycki 2011).

In the end, nationalism is the result of perceptions of history and their aesthetic representation in material symbols and performance in rituals that succeed in taking hold as a "thinly coherent" national culture, to borrow William H. Sewell Jr.'s (1999) apposite phrase. Paying attention to this process is important because it is through symbols and the narratives they carry that people become emotionally invested in the nation and, potentially, mobilized or recruited into nationalist action. As a coveted symbol constructed out of subsymbols, events, and narratives – that is, a thinly coherent national culture – the nation is constituted through the intersection of diverse discourses and practices, with political and cultural actors struggling to determine the direction of advance. Instead of the nation as a "thing" or as a historical and sociological fact, we have the nation as a constant work-in-progress constituted through debates about what comprises "its" culture, its key symbolic representations.

The continual process of nation-making, I observed earlier, is far from harmonious. It is instead characterized by conflictual debates as to what defines the national "self," as well as by "othering" practices. If the exclusion of "others" can be expressed through institutional-legal channels and even sometimes through violent means, it can also be enacted through more "subtle" discursive practices and symbolic violence (Bourdieu 1991). In Poland, for example, Catholicism is used by certain groups to define the symbolic boundaries of the "Polish nation": one is said to "truly" belong depending on one's commitment to the religion and to a very specific – and narrow – vision of Polishness that is symbiotically fused with Catholicism. Jewishness, in that discourse, is configured as the polar opposite of "true Polishness" through its association with secularism and civic nationalism. Through a complex chain of associations and double entendres, then, a "Jew" is anyone who does not adhere to a strictly exclusive ethno-Catholic vision of Poland. From this perspective, "true" Poles believe Poland to be ruled by "Jews," by *symbolic* Jews. Hence, we witness the strange phenomenon of anti-Semitism in a country virtually without Jews, but also its mirror image, *philo*-Semitism. Indeed, the recent emergence and increasing popularity of Jewish festivals, the opening of Jewish restaurants, and the popularization of Klezmer music in Poland index not merely the folklorization of Jews and things Jewish in that country but also the attempt to reclaim a past that had been eradicated with the Holocaust and ideologically erased and suppressed by the socialist state. Although tourism and other economic considerations certainly play an important role in the ongoing "Jewish turn," a key objective of the cultural entrepreneurs engaged in Jewish-centered cultural production is actually to create a *plural* Polish national culture. For, if "Jews," for the ethno-religious Right, symbolize a pernicious civic vision of the nation that destroys national culture, for the secular Left, "Jews" serve as the symbol of an *emancipating* civic vision defined by "post-national" national culture (Zubrzycki 2016a).

New lines of research: everyday practices, material culture, and the senses

Hobsbawm rightfully insisted that nations and their associated phenomena, although "constructed essentially from above, . . . cannot be understood unless also analyzed from below, that is in terms of the assumptions, hopes, needs, longings, and interests of ordinary people" (1990:10). This is, of course, easier said than done.

The daunting empirical challenge of analyzing "everyday nationalism" has been taken up by Rogers Brubaker and his colleagues, who investigated the daily, routine construction of national identity and the nation by "ordinary" people in the Transylvanian town of Cluj, Romania (2006). Cluj is an interesting place to study how subjects are "nationed" in political discourses and by institutions on the one hand, and through everyday practices on the other, as the city is populated by a majority of Romanian speakers and a significant Hungarian minority. The question Brubaker and his colleagues pose is whether, when, how, and why (ethno)national culture and (ethno)national identifications matter for "ordinary people" in a place that is construed as the respective cultural "core" of neighboring nations. They therefore analyze the processes through which ethno-nationality becomes a significant modality of experience for individuals, situating "nation-ness" in the broader social worlds that its subjects inhabit – from the schools they go to, the churches they attend, the newspapers they read, and the stores they patronize to the partners they marry and the languages they speak at home, at work, and in the street. By showing how and when ethnicity matters for ordinary people in a "mixed" setting, the authors offer an incisive and novel way to think about national culture and provide a methodological guide to research on other cases.

Another area where the challenge of studying "everyday" constructions of the national self is being taken up is in relation to material and visual culture, aesthetics, and consumption (e.g., Zubrzycki 2017). If the discursive turn pressed scholars to consider national identities as partially shared ways of speaking and reading, the more recent material turn invites reflection on the ways national cultures are made and maintained through a broader sensory range of images, sounds, textures, smells, and even tastes. Visual culture, to take only one example, provides an interesting point of entry into national identity and its transformation because images have a special capacity to mediate imaginary, linguistic, intellectual, and material domains (Morgan 1998:8). By grabbing our attention and serving as concrete substitutes for abstract discourse (Agulhon 1981), images become agents of socialization. Because of their immense rhetorical power, they can also influence thought and behavior, which is why images play such an important role in marketing and propaganda (Bonnell 1997). Deciphering the various components of what French historian Maurice Agulhon (1981) has called "pictorial discourses" set forth by institutions and social actors is therefore another way to learn how subjects are nationalized and how they become emotionally invested in the abstract idea of "the nation." The analysis of pictorial discourses, iconomachy, and iconoclasm is also useful to track and explain conflicts about, and changes in, national visions, as I show in my research on the redefinition of national identity in 1960s Quebec (Zubrzycki 2016b).

Because practices that engage all the senses seem especially important in reifying national culture, they become specific foci of scholarly analysis. Kristin Surak (2013) studied the Japanese tea ceremony as such a sensory site that facilitates a concentrated experience of Japanese culture. She analyzed how the spaces, objects, and practices of the tea ceremony are similar to, yet fundamentally distinguished from, mundane counterparts in everyday life. This disjuncture demands a disciplined attentiveness that sustains what many practitioners call a "Japanese experience." Her analysis shows that cultural practices can become sites of total experience for sensing, enacting, and even embodying the nation. The recent attention to the visual and material aspects of national culture thus significantly allows a better understanding of the phenomenology of national identity.

The focus on material culture and consumption is another fruitful development in the sociology of nationalism. Virág Molnár (2017), for example, explores the intersections between national culture and new forms of nationalism in contemporary Hungary by looking at the manufacturing, sale, and consumption of commodities like T-shirts. She argues that the increasing right-wing radicalization of Hungarian politics has been fueled by an expanding industry that effectively commodifies these radical sentiments by banalizing them through benign, folkloric representations of the nation. Here, mainstream national culture is used to "pacify" radical nationalist ideologies.

The question of producing and reproducing the senses of national identities has been pushed forward in part by the issue of spatial dislocation. Whether under the rubric of diaspora, the transnational, or the global, the question of how non-territorial national affiliations are maintained and transformed over time is, while not new as such, a growing area of contemporary research. Satellite television and the internet allow consumers to consume aspects of national identity from thousands of miles away from the homeland. Music is similarly mobile. However, other material features of national culture – say, agricultural techniques or the choreography of large-scale ritual events – are less transmissible. This means that long-distance or diasporic national cultures may take on quite different material forms and performative qualities from territorially based national cultures. As multiple versions of "the same" national culture emerge, they present new lines of fracture and change, and these require close attention.

Consider, for example, the Black Caribs of the Caribbean, also known as the Garifuna. The group is descended from both Africans and Amerindians, speaks an indigenous tongue, and has members residing in at least five different states – Honduras, Belize, Guatemala, Nicaragua, and the US. Thus the Garifuna possess multiple plausible national affiliations and multiple historical horizons available for activation. As Paul Christopher Johnson (2007) has shown, as a third of the group migrated from the Caribbean basin to US urban centers in the last half century, many adopted an heretofore mostly unknown "African diasporic" identity. In part this occurred because they came to be read as simply "black" within strictures of American racial codes, and in part due to their adoption of a diasporic self-understanding as cultural resistance to that racial reduction. This case shows the malleability of what constitutes national culture but also the limits of that malleability, for although selectively remembering the past and the "homeland" (Central America or Africa?) can create new opportunities for social and political alliances among those who emigrated, these new identifications and affiliations fashioned "in diaspora" may become sources of social conflict when remitted to country of origins and juxtaposed with local practices, resulting in distinct "indigenous" versus "cosmopolitan" forms of even an allegedly single nation.

Another important issue related to globalization that tends to be overlooked is the impact that process has on national culture itself. In *Branding the Nation: The Global Business of National Identity*, Melissa Aronczyk (2013) convincingly shows that national culture, far from being eroded by globalization forces, can in fact be reasserted as the result of nations' desire to brand themselves in order to be competitive in the global market. She emphasizes, however, that this national branding comes at a cost, because it brings about a certain "flattening" of national culture, wherein plural cultural voices are effaced in the making of a strong, unified national "brand."

Conclusion

Research on nationalism and national identity since the 1980s has left behind the old notions of culture as a static "thing." Instead, national culture is now approached as a set of meaningful discursive and ritual practices shared by individuals, but only shared sufficiently to allow for contest and debate. National cultures, moreover, do not exist outside of history, but rather "are" only as a series of interventions and enactments – in social dramas and "events" as well as everyday practices. National cultures are therefore neither reified "things" nor rarified abstractions. Rather, they are created and are instantiated in material objects and symbols, located in everyday practices, and rendered meaningful in specific social worlds. The space where the ideal/discursive and the material/practical meet is where, I believe, our continued efforts to understand national identity and its relationship to national culture should focus. Important works discussed in this chapter have already laid the flagstones of that path.

References

Agulhon, Maurice. 1981. *Marianne into Battle: Republican Imagery and Symbolism in France, 1789–1880*. Cambridge: Cambridge University Press.

Anderson, Benedict. 1991. *Imagined Communities: Reflections on the Origins and Spread of Nationalism*. London: Verso.

Aronczyk, Melissa. 2013. *Branding the Nation: The Global Business of National Identity*. New York: Oxford University Press.

Bonnell, Victoria. 1997. *Iconography of Power: Soviet Political Posters under Lenin and Stalin*. Berkeley: University of California Press.

Bourdieu, Pierre. 1991. *Language and Symbolic Power*. Cambridge: Harvard University Press.

Brubaker, Rogers, Margit Feischmidt, Jon Fox, and Liana Grancea. 2006. *Nationalist Politics and Everyday Ethnicity in a Transylvanian Town*. Princeton, NJ: Princeton University Press.

Cerulo, Karen A. 1995. *Identity Designs: The Sights and Sounds of a Nation*. New Brunswick, NJ: Rutgers University Press.

Duara, Prasenjit. 1995. *Rescuing History from the Nation: Questioning Narratives of Modern China*. Chicago: University of Chicago Press.

Gellner, Ernest. 1964. "Nationalism." Pp. 147–78 in *Thought and Change*. Chicago: University of Chicago Press.

Hobsbawm, E.J. 1990. *Nations and Nationalism since 1780: Programme, Myth, Reality*. Wiles Lectures. Cambridge: Cambridge University Press.

Hobsbawm, Eric J., and Terrence Ranger, eds. 1983. *The Invention of Traditions*. London: Verso.

Huntington, Samuel P. 1996. *The Clash of Civilizations and the Remaking of World Order*. New York: Touchstone.

Inkeles, Alex. 1997. *National Character: A Psycho-Social Perspective*. New York: Transaction.

Johnson, Paul Christopher. 2007. *Diasporic Conversions: Black Carib Religion and the Recovery of Africa*. Berkeley: University of California Press.

Kohn, Hans. 1946. *The Idea of Nationalism: A Study in Its Origins and Background*. New York: Macmillan.

Molnár, Virág. 2017. "The Mythical Power of Everyday Objects: The Material Culture of Radical Nationalism in Postsocialist Hungary." Pp. 147–72 in *National Matters: Materiality, Culture and Nationalism*, edited by G. Zubrzycki. Palo Alto, CA: Stanford University Press.

Morgan, David. 1998. *Visual Piety: A History and Theory of Popular Religious Images*. Berkeley: University of California Press.

Sewell, William H. Jr. 1999. "The Concept(s) of Culture." Pp. 35–61 in *Beyond the Cultural Turn*, edited by V.E. Bonnell and L. Hunt. Berkeley: University of California Press.

Smith, Anthony D. 1986. *The Ethnic Origins of Nations*. New York: Blackwell.

Surak, Kristin. 2013. *Making Tea, Making Japan: Cultural Nationalism in Practice*. Palo Alto, CA: Stanford University Press.

Verdery, Katherine. 1993. "Whither 'Nation' and 'Nationalism'?" *Daedalus* 122(3):37–46.

Weber, Eugen. 1976. *Peasants into Frenchmen: The Modernization of Rural France, 1870–1914*. Stanford, CA: Stanford University Press.

Winichakul, Thongchai. 1994. *Siam Mapped: A History of the Geo-Body if a Nation*. Honolulu: University of Hawaii Press.

Zubrzycki, Geneviève. 2006. *The Crosses of Auschwitz: Nationalism and Religion in Post-Communist Poland*. Chicago: University of Chicago Press.

———. 2011. "History and the National Sensorium: Making Sense of Polish Mythology." *Qualitative Sociology* 34(1):21–57.

———. 2016a. "Nationalism, 'Philosemitism' and Symbolic Boundary-Making in Contemporary Poland." *Comparative Studies in Society and History* 58(1):66–98.

———. 2016b. *Beheading the Saint: Nationalism, Religion and Secularism in Quebec*. Chicago: University of Chicago Press.

———. ed. 2017. *National Matters: Materiality, Culture and Nationalism*. Palo Alto, CA: Stanford University Press.

54

The cultural of the political

Toward a cultural sociology of state formation

Xiaohong Xu and Philip Gorski

Introduction

In the human sciences, the study of culture and the study of the state have often been separate enterprises. The state is assigned to political science and diplomatic history, while culture is placed in care of anthropology and cultural sociology. This division of labor is underwritten by aligning the state/culture opposition with various other binaries: state and nation, self-interest and solidarity, institutions and culture, power and language, and so on. These oppositions are quite stable – and quite old: their genealogy can be traced back through the history of Western political philosophy to Christian ethics.

This order of things naturally has come under challenge again in recent decades. The challenge arose from multiple conjunctures and can be observed across multiple fronts. The historical turn within anthropology (Comaroff and Comaroff 1991) and the cultural turn within sociology both generated a number of "culturalist" studies of the state (Steinmetz 1999). The Foucauldian impact within the humanities led some literary scholars to roam into politics. Among early modern historians, meanwhile, the "confessionalization paradigm" generated considerable interest in the relationship between state-building and religious reformations.

Certainly, there are plenty of countertrends. These days, the buzz in history is about "political economy" and empire, not culture and the state. In political science, quantitative methods and experiments are the order of the day and a mention of "Foucault" or "culture" is likely to elicit a befuddled grin. In sociology, the once busy intersection of cultural and historical work generated impressive works but – thus far – no general research program. Meanwhile, cultural sociology has always been somewhat presentist and Americanist in orientation.

Is state formation just a bridge too far for cultural sociology? Not in principle. Many of the binaries that sustain the divisions between state and culture have been challenged (Sparrow, Novak, and Sawyer 2015; Morgan and Orloff 2017). Culturalist approaches have yielded considerable insight on other, seemingly unpromising topics, such as money and scientific institutions (e.g., Zelizer 1994; Vaughan 1996). Moreover, as contemporary state-building has now attracted more attention both from the public and the US government (e.g., Fukuyama 2004), there is also a practical reason to give a cultural account of the historical formation of modern state to counter both the naïvely universalistic policy of exporting regime change and its nationalist-isolationist antithesis.

In this chapter, we will first review the theoretical threads in sociological lineages that can inspire the cultural approaches to state formation; second, examine the state of affairs and the problematics in current literature on state and culture; and, last, tease out four subject areas in which a cultural sociology of state formation may bear fruits.

Cultural approaches to the state in sociological lineages

Karl Marx

Though cultural Marxists have been mainly concerned with the cultural barriers to, and pre-conditions for, proletarian revolution – in a word, with the problem of "hegemony" and "ideology" (e.g., Gramsci 1971; Althusser 1971), it is in fact possible to do a cultural sociology of state formation in Marxist terms, as demonstrated by Philip Corrigan and Derek Sayer's classical work, *The Great Arch* (1985). While linking English state formation back into the process of the "long making of bourgeois civilization" and of the embourgeoisement of English society, they also showed how the changing cultural dynamics in the objectification of social relations and human personality shaped the English state. Into this line of inquiries of culture, class formation, and state formation also falls Jürgen Habermas's early work, *The Structural Transformation of the Public Sphere* ([1965] 1989), which tracked the emergence – and decline – of a "bourgeois public sphere" in early capitalist societies.

Max Weber

Strangely enough, the best starting point for a Weberian theory of culture and the state is not his political sociology but his sociology of religion. Consider two of Weber's most famous metaphors: the "switchman" and "elective affinity." The "switchman" metaphor arises out of Weber's attempt to grasp the long-term impacts that subtle differences in religious doctrine have on economic conduct, but a similar mode of analysis has been employed in thinking about the impact of culture and/or religion on *political* conduct, the *locus classicus* being Michael Walzer's (1965) analysis of Puritanism, selfhood, and revolution in seventeenth-century England. There, Walzer argues that the Puritan movement forged a disciplined self, capable of extraordinary feats of world transformation.

The second metaphor of "elective affinity" is an attempt to grapple with the same problem. In this case, however, the relationship is between two cultural constructs: the "spirit of capitalism" and the "Protestant ethic," that is, between two ethics of conduct each of which melds interests and ideas already, and whose combination has a catalytic effect on economic development. This mode of analysis can also be applied to the relationship between culture and the state, if we focus on potential affinities between religio-cultural and political ethics or spirits (Gorski 2003).

Two other Weberian constructs that are potentially useful for a cultural theory of the state are value spheres and carrier groups. In his version of differentiation theory, Weber makes "ultimate values" the gravitational force around which the various spheres take shape. These values are transmitted and elaborated by "carrier groups" that have material and ideal interests in the preservation and influence of these values. The value spheres concept allows us to pose questions about cultural boundaries – between the political and the religious, say, or the political and the aesthetic. It also instructs us to conceive of such boundaries as the result of ongoing struggles between carrier groups, seeking to expand the reach of their cultural authority. This line of analysis is developed further in Bourdieu's theory of "fields" and "classification struggles."

Weber famously defined the state as an organization that claims a "monopoly of legitimate violence" within a particular territory or community. Norbert Elias (1994) has spelled out the underlying cultural significance of this definition. It involved a "civilizing process" that transformed the dispositions first of the ruler, then of the ruled. And as Ikegami has shown, the civilizing process is not a purely Western phenomenon (Ikegami 1995).

Emile Durkheim

Durkheim is often charged with ignoring power and politics. But Durkheimian political sociology is not an oxymoron. Rationalist approaches to politics generate a series of vexing problems: "principal-agent problems," "collective action problems," and "equilibrium problems." A Durkheimian approach suggests that we should attend to how these "problems" are solved in practice: by means of collective rituals, collective emotions, and collective identity. The fruitfulness of this neo-Durkheimian political sociology is evident in works on court ritual, political festivals (Ozouf 1988), "political religion" (Gentile 1996; Falasca-Zamponi 1997), and "civil religion" (Bellah 1975; Gorski 2017).

Durkheim's analysis of law suggests a second approach. Historical criminologists of a neo-Durkheimian bent – and that includes Foucault – have effectively shown how changing practices of punishment can be used to track changes in the character and efficacy of state power (Foucault 1995; Smith 2003; Garland 2006).

A third possible starting point for a neo-Durkheimian political sociology is a pair of lesser-known works: *Moral Education* (Durkheim 1961) and *Professional Ethics and Civic Morals* (Durkheim 1958). These writings anticipate themes that are now drawing increasing attention. One is the relationship between state formation and subjectivity. While the standard trope suggests that the growth of state power is associated with a devaluation of the individual, Durkheim counters that the growth of the state is in fact accompanied by a higher degree of individuation and often with respect for, and protection of, human rights (Joas 2013). If Durkheim is right, then, a cultural analysis of state formation must be complemented by studies of individualistic ideologies (Koselleck 1988), as the formulation of autonomous political judgments has become both an important right and duty of the modern, democratic citizen (Schneewind 1998).

Michel Foucault

Few contemporary social theorists have had a greater impact on state theory than Michel Foucault. Contrary to the commonplace understanding of state power as top-down, centralized, coercive, legal, and ideological, Foucault asserts that power is diffuse and productive. Real state power, he argues, operates at the micro-level, not the macro-level (capillary power). It works on the body, not the mind, and it does so through the organization of space rather than the promulgation of laws (disciplinary power). It is more concerned with bringing the lost sheep back into the fold (pastoral power) than with building fences (Locke). It works not through the prohibition of sex, but through the shaping of sexuality. Foucault does not give much attention to religion. But his theories of "disciplinary power" and "governmentality" can be adapted and applied to religious movements and to the pre-Enlightenment era (Gorski 2003).

Pierre Bourdieu

Insofar as Bourdieu's work represents a synthesis of the classical traditions, it is a fitting way to conclude our survey. In his theory of "classification struggles," the stakes are not simply power relations between already existing classes, but the very reality of competing bases of group formation, what Bourdieu calls "principles of vision and di-vision" (2000). The outcome of such struggles, he argues, is determined, not solely by material conditions, but also by symbolic struggles. If this outcome influences the state, the reverse is also true. Bourdieu refers to the state as the "central bank of symbolic credit" (Bourdieu 1996:376; see also Bourdieu 2015). Simply put, the state is often the final arbiter of classificatory systems, through its authority over language and the law.

Like Weber, Bourdieu traces the emergence of the state field mainly to intra-elite conflicts, first within royal households, and then between religious and secular intellectuals and administrators. He also links the formation of the state to the differentiation of various species of capital (Bourdieu 2004). The separation of the political rule, first from economic production, and then ideological production (i.e., religion), is accompanied by the primitive accumulation of three species of capital: symbolic, economic, and cultural.

Research agendas

A "cultural sociology of state formation" could be many different things, depending on how one defines "culture" and "the state," and on the direction of the causal arrow that conjoins them. Next we outline a few of the main questions and approaches. The first concerns the ontology of culture – what culture *is*. We may distinguish three basic approaches. The first conceives of culture as a kind of grammar, as the "code" that underlies and structures language and ritual. The key task of the cultural sociologist is to discover the rules and crack the codes. The second conceives of culture as "values." From this perspective, the main task is to identify the central values of a culture and specify their relationship to social imaginaries. There is also an intermediate view, which understands culture as a "map" or a "script," which people use to orient themselves. Here, the key task is to identify the various types of cultural performances.

The second major question concerns the relationship between culture and action. In the first tradition, action simply manifests and reproduces culture. Culture is *enacted*. In the second tradition, culture provides one set of ends, material interests another, and action arises out of the clash between them. Culture exerts a force *on* action. In the third tradition, culture provides scripts for performing a role or maps for traveling to a destination.

A third and final area of difference concerns the relationship between culture and social structure. On a broadly Durkheimian view, the relationship is homologous and unitary. Social boundaries are cultural boundaries. On a broadly Marxist view, the relationship is homologous but stratified. Class boundaries are also cultural boundaries, but the dominant class dominates the culture. On a more Weberian view, finally, the relationship is fractured and stratified. Societies are divided into autonomous and antagonistic value spheres, and the value spheres are dominated by a class of "virtuosos."

We can distinguish three broad categories in theories of the state as well: neo-Marxian, neo-Weberian, and neo-Smithian. Neo-Marxian approaches conceptualize the state as an instrument of class domination. They therefore focus on state-society relations and state policies. There is little attention to institutional structures or interstate relations. These are precisely the principal concerns of many neo-Weberians, for whom state formation is synonymous with state organization and geopolitical conflict is the key causal mechanism. In the neo-Smithian approach, finally, the state is conceptualized as a hierarchy of self-interested principals (i.e., rulers) and agents (officials) engaged in various forms of predation and deception. Most work on the state is focused on conflict between self-interested actors, collective and individual. The dominant approach to the state within contemporary sociology is undoubtedly the neo-Weberian one, sometimes alloyed with a bit of class analysis, sometimes with a bit of rational-choice theory. Insofar as culture figures at all in comparative historical work on the state, it is mainly as a "dependent variable." Thus states build nations, construct ethnicities, legitimate professions, but not the other way around.

What would be the most fruitful direction for a new cultural sociology of the state? Surveying the terrain, we suggest the following four subject areas: (1) state ideas, (2) state boundaries, (3) state rituals, and (4) state classifications.

State ideas

A cultural sociology of state formation needs to address the cultural constructions of the state idea. Cultural sociologists should see the formation of state ideas itself as part and parcel of "real" state formation. A paradigmatic example in this vein is Bourdieu's explication of the role that the *noblesse de robe* and their republican inheritors have played in constructing the centrality of the state idea in France's political life. Historical analyses of the revival of Roman law (P. Anderson 1974:26–9; Berman 1983) and the emergence of "reason of state" (Viroli 1992; Oestreich 1982; Skinner 1989) were "carried" by jurists and bureaucrats, respectively. Both developments helped augment the symbolic power of the central authority and transform the "king's house" into an impersonal state. Meanwhile, the symbolic power of the state also encountered its organizational delimitation with the emergence and autonomization of other spheres. State formation involved a great deal of boundary work.

State boundaries

This boundary work is both internal and external. Territorial states must differentiate themselves from internal social formations, such as kinship networks or religious communities. The idea of "sovereignty" was integral to this process, and jurists played a particularly important part in its articulation (Spruyt 1994). With the subsequent "rise of the West," the territorial nation-state became *the* legitimate model of political organization (Meyer 1999). Once a territorial state has been consolidated, a new problem of internal boundary formation emerges: the boundary between state and society (Mitchell 1999). Externally, nations must be bounded off, not only from other states but also from imperial subjects. The making of colonial states went hand in hand with the construction of "native" societies (Steinmetz 2007; Wilson 2011).

State-society boundaries were also historically and culturally constructed. In early modern Europe, this process was above all marked by the emergence of the pre- or non-political public space, often denoted as "civil society" or the "public sphere" (Habermas [1965] 1989). This sphere was by a formal equality between contracting agents or conversational partners and tacit rejection of the traditional hierarchy that characterized dynasties, corporations, and other quasi-familial structures (Ikegami 2005; Knights 2005). The autonomy of "society" sets limits to state power, even as state power shapes debates and alliances within society (E. Anderson 2013; Sparrow et al. 2015; Mayrl and Quinn 2016).

The boundary between state and economy has also been contested and variable. As Foucault (1991) reminds us, "economy" was originally private or household economy and only gradually came to be redefined in impersonal terms that legitimated state involvement ("governmentality"). However, we should not imagine that the boundaries of state power are always expanding. The upshot of the eighteenth-century debate between mercantilist and laissez-faire theories of political economy was to contract the boundaries of the state and free the economy from political control. And the neoliberal ideologies of the present era simply repeat this strategy.

Similarly, the boundaries between state and religion can also be problematized in cultural-sociological terms. How shall we explain the historical relationship between the emergence of the modern state and the separation of church and state in the context of confessional strife in early modern Europe? To what extent can we compare the Western experience with those of other parts of the world? These questions have still received too little attention from sociologists. The church/state relationship has also not been as simple as modernist narratives would lead us to believe.

State rituals

In comparison to the study of state boundaries, this is a relatively developed field of inquiry, having been cultivated by cultural sociologists, cultural historians, and sociologists of religion, as well as political scientists. Well-known among them are, for instance, Ernst Kantorowicz's study (1957) of the funereal rituals designed to contain the contradiction between the immortality of kingship and the mortality of kings with the (to us) peculiar doctrine of "the king's two bodies"; Mona Ozouf's monograph on "French revolutionary festivals" (1988), which staged the revolutionary break and connected the new regime to transcendent purposes by means of elaborate processions and liturgies; Emilio Gentile's fine-grained analyses (1996) of Mussolini's use of ritual to legitimate his new regime, and Falasca-Zamponi's (1997) and Berezin's (1997) retheorizations; and finally Robert Bellah (1975) and Philip Gorski's (2017) analyses of "American civil religion." Much of this work has been focused on social stability and reproduction. That ritual analysis can also be used to understand processes of historical rupture and transformation has been shown by William Sewell Jr.'s (1996) study of the cultural improvisation and invention that occurred during the storming of the Bastille and the subsequent influence of these events and their construction on the Revolution as a whole. Historically speaking, the scale of state ritual only expands with the growth of state power and the development of communication. The crowd participating in a coronation ritual of the sixteenth century only numbered a few thousands in contrast to millions of people taking in today's presidential inaugurations.

Contemporary cultural sociology has offered two major strands of thought, both neo-Durkheimian, that may bear fruits in studying state rituals. Jeffrey Alexander's social-performance theory (2004) can be employed to analyze how state actors (symbolic persons such as figureheads, diplomats, etc.) succeed or fail in "re-fusing" the elements of successful social performance in front of their audiences. Even in stable democracies, the maintenance of state power cannot dispense with the façade of these "stately" performances. Randall Collins's interaction ritual theory (2004), which focuses on collective, rather than individual, performances, could also be applied to political life. While Alexander and Collins both emphasize the "higher rituals" of the state, its "lower rituals" (e.g., bureaucratic rituals) can also be studied in light of Goffman's work.

State classifications

In the works of Durkheim and Mauss, the theory of ritual was closely associated with a theory of classification. Strangely, the latter subject has received relatively little attention. One important exception is Chandra Mukerji's work (1997). In seventeenth-century France and other early modern states, she shows, the building of states went hand in hand with a reshaping of the "natural" environment. While conventional accounts might be more apt to portray the Garden of Versailles as a symbol of fiscal irresponsibility, Mukerji suggests that such projects were symbols of something else – the centralization and territorialization of political power. Murkeji shows that group boundaries were themselves "planted" in the material environment.

The limits of such construction projects are ably demonstrated by James Scott (1998). By the nineteenth century, rulers were looking to reshape landscapes and cityscapes so as to increase their efficiency and output for economic and fiscal reasons. State-owned forests were reconfigured to maximize timber harvests. State-managed housing developments were constructed to maximize labor productivity. Alas, the hyper-rationalist models of "high modernist" aesthetics failed to capture many aspects of natural and social ecologies – aspects that turned out to be crucial to their long-term vitality. That such utopian schemes were ever implemented had mostly to do with their "elective affinity" with the ethos and interests of managerial elites on the one hand, and the weakness of civil society on the other.

Of course, one of the most important forms of state classifications is individual identification and the issuance of corresponding documents. John Torpey (2000) uses the history of the passport to track the state's gradual monopolization of control over movement across borders and its use of civil registration as a means of public mobilization (e.g., in mass conscription). However, such projects can also fail, as Mara Loveman (2007) shows in her study of popular opposition to civil registration in Brazil's "war of the wasps." And with far-reaching consequences: absent such basic information about the populace, the Brazilian state was unable to establish a "modern" army and therefore had to rely on semi-feudal systems of military recruitment. Here again, symbolic power proved all too "real."

Conclusion

The "third wave" of comparative historical sociology arose out of a powerful confluence of transdisciplinary currents during the late 1980s, when the "second wave" of neo-Marxian and left-Weberian work intersected with cultural sociology, cultural history, Geertzian anthropology, and historicist forms of literary scholarship. The result was a dramatic upsurge in culturally inflected, historical analysis. But many of these currents have now weakened. This is not to say that the sands have not shifted in their wake. Historians now routinely do comparative work. Comparative methods are de rigueur in such diverse areas as urban ethnography and international relations. Historical anthropology is a stable subfield.

Today, a new wave of cultural work on state formation, and cultural analysis of politics more generally, would probably have to draw its energy from other sources. Which ones? Surveying the horizon, we see three or four possibilities. One, of course, is cultural sociology itself, a field that has been remarkably Amero-centric and presentist in its orientations, but where transnational scholarly networks have become denser and cross-national comparison is increasingly common (Lamont and Thévenot 2000). Another is political theory, where old-school exegesis of classical texts has been increasingly supplanted by empirically informed (if methodologically unsystematic) philosophical reflection on citizenship, cosmopolitanism, toleration, minority rights, the public/private distinction, and other subjects closely related to the research program sketched earlier (Kymlicka and Norman 2000; Benhabib 2002). The last is historical work by literary scholars, which increasingly engages topics such as publicity, secularism, civil religion, state subjectivity, and so on (Warner 2002; Visconsi 2008).

In a sense, promoting a cultural sociology of state formation not only means engaging substantive questions about the state and its historical formation as a way to reclaim the analytical territories that sociologists have surrendered to other disciplines, but also to reinvent sociology itself in the process.

References

Alexander, Jeffrey C. 2004. "Cultural Pragmatics: Social Performance between Ritual and Strategy." *Sociological Theory* 22(4):527–73.

Althusser, Louis. 1971. "Ideology and Ideological State Apparatuses." Pp. 127–86 in *Lenin and Philosophy and Other Essays*. Trans. Ben Brewster. New York: Monthly Review Press.

Anderson, Elisabeth. 2013. "Ideas in Action: The Politics of Prussian Child Labor Reform, 1817–1839." *Theory and Society* 42(1):81–119.

Anderson, Perry. 1974. *Lineages of the Absolutist State*. London: N.L.B.

Bellah, Robert N. 1975. *The Broken Covenant: American Civil Religion in Time of Trial*. New York: Seabury Press.

Benhabib, Seyla. 2002. *The Claims of Culture: Equality and Diversity in the Global Era*. Princeton, NJ: Princeton University Press.

Berezin, Mabel. 1997. *Making the Fascist Self: The Political Culture of Interwar Italy*. Ithaca, NY: Cornell University Press.

Berman, Harold J. 1983. *Law and Revolution: The Formation of the Western Legal Tradition*. Cambridge, MA: Harvard University Press.

Bourdieu, Pierre. 1996. *The State Nobility: Elite Schools in the Field of Power*. Trans. Lauretta C. Clough. Oxford: Polity Press.

———. 2000. *Pascalian Meditations*. Trans. Richard Nice. Cambridge: Polity Press.

———. 2004. "From the King's House to the Reason of State: A Model of the Genesis of the Bureaucratic Field." *Constellations* 11(1):16–36.

———. 2015. *On the State*. Cambridge: Polity Press.

Collins, Randall. 2004. *Interaction Ritual Chains*. Princeton, NJ: Princeton University Press.

Comaroff, Jean, and John L. Comaroff. 1991. *Of Revelation and Revolution*. Vol. 1. Chicago: University of Chicago Press.

Corrigan, Philip Richard D., and Derek. Sayer. 1985. *The Great Arch: English State Formation as Cultural Revolution*. Oxford: Blackwell.

Durkheim, Emile. 1958. *Professional Ethics and Civic Morals*. Trans. Cornelia Brookfield. Glencoe, IL: The Free Press.

———. 1961. *Moral Education: A Study in the Theory and Application of the Sociology of Education*. Trans. Everett K. Wilson and Herman Schnurer. Ed. Everett K. Wilson. New York: Free Press.

Elias, Norbert. 1994. *The Civilizing Process: Sociogenetic and Psychogenetic Investigations*. Trans. Edmund Jephcott. Oxford and Malden, MA: Blackwell.

Falasca-Zamponi, Simonetta. 1997. *Fascist Spectacle: The Aesthetics of Power in Mussolini's Italy*. Berkeley: University of California Press.

Foucault, Michel. 1991. "Governmentality." Pp. 87–104 in *The Foucault Effect: Studies in Governmentality*, edited by G. Burchell, C. Gordon, and P. Miller. Trans. Rosi Braidotti and revised by Colin Gordon. London: Harvester Wheatsheaf.

———. 1995. *Discipline and Punish: The Birth of the Prison*. Trans. Alan Sheridan. New York: Vintage Books.

Fukuyama, Francis. 2004. *State-building: Governance and World Order in the 21st Century*. Ithaca, NY: Cornell University Press.

Garland, David. 2006. "Concepts of Culture in the Sociology of Punishment." *Theoretical Criminology* 10(4):419–47.

Gentile, Emilio. 1996. *The Sacralization of Politics in Fascist Italy*. Trans. Keith Botsford. Cambridge, MA: Harvard University Press.

Gorski, Philip. 2003. *Disciplinary Revolution: Calvinism and the Rise of the State in Early Modern Europe*. Chicago: University of Chicago Press.

———. 2017. *American Covenant: A History of Civil Religion from the Puritans to the Present*. Princeton, NJ: Princeton University Press.

Gramsci, Antonio. 1971. *Selections from the Prison Notebooks of Antonio Gramsci*. Edited and trans. Quintin Hoare and Geoffrey Nowell Smith. New York: International.

Habermas, Jürgen. [1965] 1989. *The Structural Transformation of the Public Sphere: An Inquiry into a Category of Bourgeois Society*. Trans. Thomas Burger and Frederick Lawrence. Cambridge, MA: MIT Press.

Ikegami, Eiko. 1995. *The Taming of the Samurai: Honorific Individualism and the Making of Modern Japan*. Cambridge, MA: Harvard University Press.

———. 2005. *Bonds of Civility: Aesthetic Networks and the Political Origins of Japanese Culture*. Cambridge: Cambridge University Press.

Joas, Hans. 2013. *The Sacredness of the Person: A New Genealogy of Human Rights*. Washington, DC: Georgetown University Press.

Kantorowicz, Ernst H. 1957. *The King's Two Bodies: A Study in Medieval Political Theology*. Princeton, NJ: Princeton University Press.

Knights, Mark. 2005. *Representation and Misrepresentation in Later Stuart Britain: Partisanship and Political Language*. Oxford: Oxford University Press.

Koselleck, Reinhart. 1988. *Critique and Crisis: Enlightenment and the Pathogenesis of Modern Society*. Oxford; New York: Berg.

Kymlicka, Will, and Wayne Norman, eds. 2000. *Citizenship in Diverse Societies*. Oxford: Oxford University Press.

Lamont, Michèle, and Laurent Thévenot, eds. 2000. *Rethinking Comparative Cultural Sociology: Repertoires of Evaluation in France and the United States*. Cambridge: Cambridge University Press.

Loveman, Mara. 2007. "Blinded Like a State: The Revolt against Civil Registration in Nineteenth-Century Brazil." *Comparative Studies in Society and History* 49(1):5–39.

Mayrl, Damon, and Sarah Quinn. 2016. "Defining the State from within: Boundaries, Schemas, and Associational Policymaking." *Sociological Theory* 34(1):1–26.

Meyer, John W. 1999. "The Changing Cultural Content of the Nation-State: A World Society Perspective." Pp. 123–43 in *State/Culture: State Formation after the Cultural Turn*, edited by G. Steinmetz. Ithaca, NY: Cornell University Press.

Mitchell, Timothy. 1999. "Society, Economy, and the State Effect." Pp. 76–97 in *State/Culture: State Formation after the Cultural Turn*, edited by G. Steinmetz. Ithaca, NY: Cornell University Press.

Morgan, Kimberly, and Ann Shola Orloff, eds. 2017. *The Many Hands of the State: Theorizing Political Authority and Social Control*. New York: Cambridge University Press.

Mukerji, Chandra. 1997. *Territorial Ambitions and the Gardens of Versailles*. Cambridge: Cambridge University Press.

Oestreich, Gerhard. 1982. *Neostoicism and the Early Modern State*. Edited by B. Oestreich and H.G. Koenigsberger, trans. David McLintock. Cambridge: Cambridge University Press.

Ozouf, Mona. 1988. *Festivals and the French Revolution*. Trans. Alan Sheridan. Cambridge, MA: Harvard University Press.

Schneewind, Jerome. 1998. *The Invention of Autonomy: A History of Modern Moral Philosophy*. Cambridge: Cambridge University Press.

Scott, James C. 1998. *Seeing like a State: How Certain Schemes to Improve the Human Condition Have Failed*. New Haven, CT: Yale University Press.

Sewell, William Jr. 1996. "Political Events as Structural Transformations: Inventing the Revolution at the Bastille." *Theory and Society* 25(6):841–81.

Skinner, Quentin. 1989. "The State." Pp. 90–131 in *Political Innovation and Conceptual Change*, edited by T. Ball, J. Farr, and R.L. Hanson. Cambridge: Cambridge University Press.

Smith, Philip. 2003. "Narrating the Guillotine: Punishment Technology as Myth and Symbol." *Theory, Culture and Society* 20(5):27–51.

Sparrow, James T., William J. Novak, and Stephen W. Sawyer, eds. 2015. *Boundaries of the State in US History*. Chicago: University of Chicago Press.

Spruyt, Hendrik. 1994. *The Sovereign State and Its Competitors*. Princeton, NJ: Princeton University Press.

Steinmetz, George, ed. 1999. *State/Culture: State Formation after the Cultural Turn*. Ithaca, NY: Cornell University Press.

———. 2007. *The Devil's Handwriting: Precoloniality and the German Colonial State in Qingdao, Samoa, and Southwest Africa*. Chicago: University of Chicago Press.

Torpey, John. 2000. *The Invention of the Passport: Surveillance, Citizenship, and the State*. Cambridge: Cambridge University Press.

Vaughan, Diane. 1996. *The Challenger Launch Decision: Risky Technology, Culture, and Deviance at NASA*. Chicago: University of Chicago Press.

Viroli, Maurizio. 1992. *From Politics to Reason of State: The Acquisition and Transformation of the Language of Politics, 1250–1600*. Cambridge: Cambridge University Press.

Visconsi, Elliott. 2008. *Lines of Equity: Literature and the Origins of Law in Later Stuart England*. Ithaca, NY: Cornell University Press.

Walzer, Michael. 1965. *The Revolution of the Saints: A Study in the Origins of Radical Politics*. Cambridge, MA: Harvard University Press.

Warner, Michael. 2002. *Publics and Counterpublics*. New York: Zone Books.

Wilson, Nicholas Hoover. 2011. "From Reflection to Refraction: State Administration in British India, circa 1770–1855." *American Journal of Sociology* 116(5):1437–77.

Zelizer, Viviana. 1994. *The Social Meaning of Money*. New York: Basic Books.

55

Postcolonial nation-building and identity contestations

Daniel P. S. Goh

Introduction

Since its grounding in Barrington Moore's *Social Origins of Dictatorship and Democracy* (1966), comparative historical sociology has been focused on the political-economic vectors of modernization of nation-states. By virtue of its global scope, *longue durée* timeframe, comparative approach, and topical focus, comparative historical sociology is an important genre in American sociology that attracts an international field of scholars. For many students from and of the Global South obtaining their doctoral training in the United States, comparative historical sociology has offered the promise of illuminating the developmental conditions and prospects of their country and region. There is but one problem. The nation, which is a primary basis of identity and substantive issue for many postcolonial scholars, remains something of a blind spot in the field.

My own biography may be emblematic. Beguiled by stories of older generations who lived under three flags – the Union Jack, the federation flag of Malaysia, and the national flag of the Republic of Singapore – and sang three anthems, I long sought to understand my own identity as a postcolonial Singaporean with cosmopolitan sensibilities. I grew up in the era after Singapore became independent in 1965 by fiat, separating from Malaysia after political disagreements led to fatal racial riots between the Chinese and Malays. Under a pragmatic but autocratic one-party state, Singapore prospered as one of the four East Asian newly industrializing economies. Unlike Taiwan and South Korea, Singapore has resisted democratization despite the modernization of society. A postcolonial person, I am also, among other things, an English-speaking ethnic Chinese residing in the discomforting hybrid space between Southeast Asia, East Asia, and the West (Goh 2012).

More than a decade ago, I enrolled in the University of Michigan for doctoral studies with the aim of studying the political economy of Southeast Asian countries that had experienced different developmental trajectories. I soon concluded that although the state had become a central category of analysis in comparative historical sociology, the nation was a theoretical black box that acted as the unconscious in the field, structuring both the analytical frame as well as the terms of analysis. I found, as I elaborated my research question, that I had to return to the colonial origins of state formation and nation-building to understand the postcolonial politics and the decisions of nationalist leaders. It was then I turned to engage the sociology of empire and the cultural sociology of the state. Culture and empire were at the beginning of my intellectual journey.

In the following section I outline the unconscious of the nation in comparative historical sociology and discuss the cultural turn in comparative historical sociology that subsequently has proven so fruitful for the study of empire and state formation. These developments have led to a minimalist definition of nationalism that is crucial for comparative analysis but deeply unsatisfactory for the study of postcolonial nationalisms. A second section examines postcolonial theory and the critical questioning of Eurocentric theories in mainstream sociology. I argue that even this belated incorporation of postcolonial theory into sociology is not adequate for the purposes of understanding the nation and its cultural complexions.

Finally, I consider emerging bodies of decolonizing scholarship on and from Asia, Africa, and Latin America. By focusing on inter-referencing and intersecting identities, decolonizing scholarship shows that the sociology of nationalism needs to go beyond comparative methods. We should treat our knowledge production as a form of political practice, so as to create deeper layers of shared histories and social theories that would make those of the West less central to identity formations in Asia and elsewhere, in order to truly internationalize academic knowledge.

The unconscious of the nation in sociology

There have been three significant meta-theoretical shifts in comparative historical sociology. Through these shifts, the nation as an analytical category has gradually taken shape, unconsciously at first, subsumed in the concepts of the state and culture, and then appearing, quite paradoxically and more consciously but still vaguely minimalist, in the concept of the empire.

The first shift was toward analysis of the state itself. Rather than take the state as outcomes of social compacts and conflicts, scholars focused on state formation (Skocpol 1979; Tilly 1985). This approach emphasized Weberian processes of institutionalization, focusing on the contingency of actions framed by different rationalities and the relative autonomy of the state vis-à-vis social classes. The second shift has been referenced as the cultural turn. In part, this shift also has been driven by the elaboration of Weberian concepts. The various ideal types of rationality, legitimacy, and authority lend themselves to the analysis of cultural contestations implicated in state formation. Concepts derived from emerging historical, anthropological, and literary scholarship also began to influence sociological studies of states.

George Steinmetz's edited volume, *State/Culture*, captured the essence of the double turn. In his introduction, Steinmetz (1999:17) observed that the neo-Weberian state-centered scholarship had located culture in society, posited as separate from the legal-rational field of the autonomous state, thus marginalizing culture from analysis of states. There were exceptions, invariably found in non-Western states, the relative autonomy of which was seen as compromised by social forces and cultural traditions. This unsatisfactory Eurocentric treatment of culture in state theory had led a new generation of scholars to rethink the relationship between the state and culture.

However, despite the cultural turn, the "nation" remains an unconscious term in the pairing, "nation-state," and that concept has continued to be the fundamental unit of analysis for comparative historical sociology. In *State/Culture*, four invocations of the "nation" do much of the taken-for-granted cultural work, drawing from theoretical work on nationalism in Western scholarship during the 1980s. First, John Meyer's (1999) argument that modern nation-states are recognizably similar actors operating with the same global cultural model follows Ernest Gellner's (1983) location of nationalism in the industrial social system of mass literacy and universal education. Second, Steven Pincus's (1999) case of English nationalism born out of the Glorious

Revolution closely corresponds to Benedict Anderson's ([1983] 1991) imagined communities born out of print capitalism. Third, drawing from Eric Hobsbawm's (1983) work on the invention of traditions to legitimize nations, Andrew Apter (1999) discusses the continued subvention of the colonial durbar in Nigeria to legitimize the oil-rich postcolonial state. Finally, Bob Jessop (1999) argues that the reorganization of the Keynesian welfare state would lead to the denationalization of the state and the growth of translocal regimes, echoing Eric Hobsbawm's ([1990] 1992) conclusion in his survey of nationalism since 1780.

In all these studies, the nation is the evocative term in *State/Culture*, performing the boundary work that both separates and connects the state and culture. This situation threatens to turn Steinmetz's critique on itself, by preserving the state as a rational field of action and locating culture as the irrational force permeating into the rational field through the nation as an unconscious category. Nevertheless, the cultural turn did alert us to the hyphen, that the nation is the unconscious in theoretical work on the state.

The third and most recent shift is the turn to empire. In his study of the new American imperialism, Michael Mann (2003) found that the US would use its military might to bully small states to extract economic benefits. However, the US did not leave any lasting political and social institutions because it failed to insist upon the very democratic ideals it supposedly embraced. This ambivalence of American empire toward democracy has fueled a recurrent tension between empire and the nation as forms of political order and identity formation. As case studies by sociologists, anthropologists, and historians in *Lessons of Empire* (Calhoun, Cooper, and Moore 2006) show, during an era of crucial global expansion of the capitalist system in the last few centuries, the nation-state and empire co-existed and oftentimes alternated (see also Kumar 2013).

The burgeoning corpus of fine-grained analysis of colonial state formations is inching toward a delineation of nationalism as influenced by the vicissitudes of colonialism. In his study of the influence of ethnographic racial discourses on German colonialism in Qingdao, Samoa, and Southwest Africa, George Steinmetz (2007) sees colonial afterlives that live on as forms of material culture, such as German trains and beer becoming symbols of Chinese nationalist modernity. In her study of the close relationship between the great family patriarchs and the rise and fall of the Dutch Empire, Julia Adams (2005) illuminates the patrimonial aspects of colonialism, and thus nationalism, whereby elite men and their familial networks play a crucial part in consolidating postcolonial rule. Julian Go (2008) shows that the American colonizers adopted a cultural program to school the Hispanic elites of the Philippines and Puerto Rico in American-style democracy, which the elites then hybridized into their own nationalist discourse to enhance their political power as the rising ruling classes. These and similar studies suggest that the sociology of empire is complex not only because of the complicated histories of imperialism, colonialism, and nationalism, but also because the nation is bound up with the enduring unequal categories of race and ethnicity, gender, and class through colonial state formation.

However, how nations were formed and came to be bound up with the complexities of race, gender, and class are not yet explicit questions in the sociology of empire; the current scholarship focused on the colonial state implies them. Although empires and colonial states have become more theoretically determinate in comparative historical sociology, the risk is that by default, the nation becomes what does not appear to be like an empire or a colonial state. The nation remains an unconscious category, or in Lyn Spillman and Russell Faeges's (2005) view, theoretically underdetermined, leading to the proliferation of meanings of nationalism.

Spillman and Faeges offer a working definition that they assert unites the dimension of political mobilization with cultural dimensions of the nation as "a discursive field generated in the orientation of political action to claims-making about legitimate political authority, claims-making about shared features of the putatively relevant population, and distinguishing that population from others" (2005:435). Yet this minimalist definition is based on studies of the nationalisms of Western Europe, with added insight from Spillman's own comparative study of the United States and Australia, complicated as they all are by empire. I believe the time is ripe to consider the *decolonizing* scholarship on and from Asia, Africa, and Latin America in order to offer an alternative global version of this definition.

Postcolonial theory: the question of difference

In his introduction to the edited volume *Decolonization*, Prasenjit Duara (2004:13–15) lists four factors that affected the nations of the Global South after the Second World War: (1) modern colonial states marshaling all resources through territorial sovereignty; (2) the problem of ethnicity produced by the native policies of colonial states in territories marked by pluralism; (3) the discourse of national rights emanating from the Americas and the French Revolution; and (4) the international system of states institutionalized in the United Nations and framed by the Cold War. Significantly, Duara's volume included the writings of influential nationalists – Sun Yat-sen, Ho Chi Minh, Jawaharlal Nehru, Frantz Fanon, Jalal Al-i Ahmad and Kwame Nkrumah – focusing not on their polemics but on their social theory. One emphasis that stands out is Sun and Nehru's point that the modern nation is at its heart cosmopolitan and open to the world, and that non-Western nations must take a different trajectory in pursuing cosmopolitanism – by justice instead of force.

Other than Fanon, nationalist thinkers have largely been ignored in the study of nationalism and nation-building. This circumstance is reflected in *Decolonization* itself, as the ideas contained in the front chapters by nationalist thinkers are ignored in the chapters by Western historians, who express skepticism about the viability and prospects of the postcolonial nation. Ironically, this skepticism is one of the key contributions to Western social theory by the South Asian scholars known as the Subaltern Studies Collective, whose works are nominally grouped under postcolonial theory.

Among the collective, Partha Chatterjee has been most influential for the study of postcolonial nationalism. Chatterjee's (1986) first critical response to Ernest Gellner and Benedict Anderson blames Western theory for treating nationalism in reified terms as a homogeneous culture established in Europe before imperialism and spreading in modular fashion to the rest of the world through colonialism. Chatterjee proposed that anti-colonial nationalisms in India were distinctly different and varied. He expanded and elaborated this proposition in *The Nation and Its Fragments* (Chatterjee 1993). The common thread of the varied nationalisms expounded by social thinkers in India is that they all split culture into spiritual and material domains. The nationalists surrendered the latter to the colonial state while, in order to lay claim to national sovereignty, they worked on redefining the spiritual domain as represented by religion, caste, the family, and the peasantry. More than just ideological work, their redefinitions of the spiritual sphere empowered the nationalists to reorganize and mobilize the groups represented in the spiritual domain for anti-colonial contestations.

Yet despite these thinkers' creative imaginings of nationalisms, nationalism became singular and modular in the end. Gellner and Anderson are not wrong, but the twist for Chatterjee is that the nationalists' surrendering of the material domain would return to subvert their own hegemony. The inheritance of the colonial state with all its technologies of social reproduction and techniques of governmentality disciplined and molded myriad nationalisms into the familiar nationalism that pits one collective identity against another rather than producing membership in an inclusive cosmopolitan fraternity. Following Foucault, Chatterjee (1993:18–19) argued that the "rule of colonial difference" of the modern state prescribes both the mutually constitutive rationalization of government and the racialization of domination. Thus, British colonial state formation led to the deadly Partition and the enduring conflict between Indian and Pakistan.

It is unfortunate that Chatterjee's argument rested on the critique of the first edition of Anderson's *Imagined Communities*, published in 1983. By the time Chatterjee completed *The Nation and Its Fragments*, Anderson had published a revised second edition of *Imagined Communities* that recognized its "Eurocentric provincialism" (Anderson 1991:xiii) and added two appendices to correct theoretical flaws. One of the appendices is a fresh chapter on "Census, Map, Museum," inspired by Thongchai Winichakul's *Siam Mapped* (1994), which discussed the three cultural forms used by colonial states in Southeast Asia to frame the objects and subjects of its rule, ironically in turn shaping the nationalism that would rise and conquer it. In this indictment of the colonial state as the main culprit forcing a modular nationalism onto diverse imaginations, between South Asia and Southeast Asia at least, there is much convergence between Anderson's and Chatterjee's histories.

Nevertheless, Chatterjee's central contribution is not in insisting on the existence of post-colonial difference between Western and Asian nationalisms, but in theorizing the dialectical relationship between the inherited elite spaces of the state, civil society, and the nation in relation to persistent spaces of communities. Chatterjee would find the succinct expression of the latter in Rabindranath Tagore's concept of the *samāj*, a distinct social organization of Hindu civilization that could only be rendered against the nation and the state being imposed on India, "not the nation, but *samāj* . . . . not the political unity of the state, but the social harmony of the *samāj*" (Chatterjee 2011:103). Evolving cultural logics of subaltern communities defy the universal rationality of the nation-state, even as modern institutions and elite rulers depend on the subaltern cultures in order to exercise and realize their power.

The main weakness in postcolonial theories of the nation is their failure to deal with what Anderson (1998) rather aptly called "the specter of comparisons" afflicting nationalist idealizations in their self-conscious confrontations with the world. The specter of comparisons refers to the dizzying experience of looking at a familiar object through an inverted telescope of the Other who places the object in a different register of meanings. The once-familiar object thereby loses its matter-of-fact immediacy, instead seen through a doubled vision as both near and far. Anderson (1998:2) cites his own experience of interpreting a scene in José Rizal's nationalist *Noli Me Tangere* of the *mestizo* hero returning from Europe to Manila and seeing the botanical gardens in a different light haunted by the sister gardens in Europe, an experience which Rizal names as "the demon of comparisons."

For Anderson (1998), the stupendously diverse Southeast Asia, caught between migratory streams from the Indian and Pacific Oceans, is filled with such hauntings. Nationalism here is always ambivalent, caught up in alternations between the universal plurals of nationalists, workers, socialists, and so on, versus finite categories such as ethnicity (Anderson 1998:29). Postcolonial theory, obsessed with historical difference and stuck in the specific localisms of India, has not been capable of theorizing how inter-local relationships and imaginations, and not just the rule of colonial difference between metropole and colony, affect nationalisms and national identities.

Decolonizing the nation: inter-referencing and intersecting identities

One scholarly movement that has strongly influenced Asian studies is the Inter-Asia Cultural Studies collective. Having taken shape in the 1990s, the collective publishes the eponymous journal and brings together hundreds of academics from South, Southeast, and Northeast Asia for biannual conferences, rotating between cities across the region. The intellectual thrust of the group is captured in the term "Inter-Asia," which simultaneously adopts and disavows the conceptual reality of Asia, thus drawing attention to the Western construction that is Asia and the intersecting identities that go into making Asia as a lived reality for Asians.

Kuan-Hsing Chen, a key founder, published *Asia as Method* in 2010 as a manifesto of sorts for the collective. Writing first from his experience in Taiwan during the time when its nationalist discourse shifted from the Chiang's Sinocentric chauvinism to an appropriation of the nativist identity combined with a "southward advance" toward closer relationship with Southeast Asia, Chen detected the imperialist eye in the reworking of the nation at the end of the Cold War. He and his colleagues in the collective sought to enact self-conscious networked practices of knowledge production around the *Inter-Asia Cultural Studies: Movements* journal project, oriented toward the entangled tasks of decolonization, deimperialization, and deconstruction of the Cold War. The result is Chen's (2010:212) theorization of the method of using the very colonial, imperialist, and Cold War idea of Asia as "an imaginary anchoring point" for Asian societies to become "each other's points of reference" to rebuild subjectivities and provide alternative identities beyond the nation for political mobilization.

Citing the inspirational moment when he translated and listened to Partha Chatterjee when he visited Taiwan, Chen (2010:224–5) wrote about the flashes of recognition he experienced that linked the stories of subaltern struggles of squatter communities in India and in Taiwan. But as an intellectual on the bend of political agency, Chen was not just haunted by the specter of comparisons. He seized the opportunity to reference Chatterjee's concept of political society to the concept of *minjiān* used by radical activists in Taiwan. Inter-Asia referencing, or "Asia as method," is more than just a matter of adopting comparative approaches to study mutually constitutive social fields: it positions academic knowledge production as a form of political practice in order to create deeper layers of shared histories that would make the West less central to identity formation in Asia. Chen's method is a necessary recognition that scholarship on the nation cannot be politically neutral but is inescapably ensnared in the politics of knowledge production, and that moving sideways to a regional network instead of looking to the metropolitan center might be a way to weaken imperial and colonial power.

A remarkably similar conceptual disassembly of the nation has been developed for Latin America, resulting in intellectual affinities with postcolonial theory and Inter-Asian studies. In fact, Latin American scholars would claim that their subaltern modernities began much earlier and following a longer trajectory – from the sixteenth century to contemporary globalization, with the alien nation-state form taking almost magical hold against the backdrop of genocidal slavery and verdant forests (Coronil 1997). The birth of new nations in the revolutionary wars of the early nineteenth century pushed the question of the popular will and the inclusion of large but marginalized indigenous communities into the forefront. Like Chatterjee, Walter Mignolo (2000:11) keenly advocated the recovery of local histories so as to produce "border gnosis" at the interior borders (class conflicts, hegemonic culture) and exterior borders (colonization and decolonization) of the "modern/colonial world system." But Mignolo has been wary of the subalternization of knowledge, which has resulted in postcolonial theory's insular localism. Deploying Black Atlantic concepts such as "double consciousness" and "transculturation," he (2000:326) has sought new transnational languages that would bring the deconstruction of Western theories into a complementary relationship with decolonization. Here, there is convergence with Chen's deimperialization stance in relation to the nation-state and academic knowledge production.

More than convergence, a unique feature of Mignolo's work is that it is far more expansive and circulatory than the works of the Asians, whose questions of colonial difference and specters of comparisons have been limited to travels within metropole-postcolony or inter-Asian circuits. Mignolo has been traveling across the Pacific to Hong Kong, Singapore, and elsewhere in Asia to engage Asian scholars and witness different national formations for himself. He has thus been able to peer into the production of global futures and theorize the trajectories offered by knowledge production beyond the nation and the state in different regions.

In *The Darker Side of Western Modernity* (2011), Mignolo discusses five trajectories: dewesternization in East and Southeast Asia, rewesternization of the West, reorientation of the Left in the West, decolonial options in the Global South and also developed North, and spiritual options complementary to decolonial options. The key differentiation is that the last two options take on a stance of "objectivity in parentheses," privileging intersubjective experiences and open dialogues over "objectivity without parentheses," which asserts the sovereignty of the author-observer and the external legitimacy of objects observed to validate truths (Mignolo 2011:71).

Mignolo sees the bifurcation of dewesternization into the open, "in parentheses" and closed, "without parentheses" routes. Dewesternization involves the pursuit of material modernization for a national domain and for the middle classes, while repudiating Western political projects such as the democratization of the public sphere, a repudiation most apparent in East Asia. The difference between "in parentheses" and "without parentheses" dewesternization is that the latter also rejects Western cultural framings and seeks to produce new subjectivities based on more communitarian values. In turn, the main difference between dewesternization and decolonization is that the latter seeks the same material quality of life for the entire planet as well while rejecting any essential definition of modernity in terms of material technologies such as electricity, telecommunications, and so on.

But there is one crucial gap in Mignolo's worlding survey of decolonial options: where are the African options? In this regard, the work of Achille Mbembe (2001) on the perverse banality and libidinal violence of power as reproduced in the artificially constructed and imposed states of Africa is very instructive. Drawing on the psychoanalytic and bodily registers of Frantz Fanon's work on colonial and anti-colonial violence, Mbembe has rejected the nation as a fetish produced by banal power and located the postcolony as an ultimately meaningless place where the reduction of humanity to animality and the exploitation and oppression of bodies subvert all symbolic frames. What we are left with, then, are not the fragments of nationalisms, traditions, or local histories to rebuild our collective identity, but, echoing Giorgio Agamben's (1999) ethics of bare life, bodily remnants to witness and reimagine our shared humanity.

Conclusion

Where does all this critical work deconstructing and decolonizing the nation leave postcolonial sociology? Returning to Spillman and Faeges's minimalist working definition of the nation, I would modify it to cover the study of nationalisms in the Global South as follows:

> A discursive field inherited and generated through the modern state's framing of political contestation about legitimate political authority, contestation about comparative differences and similarities of peoples that involve the use of local histories, inter-referencing knowledge, inter-subjective experiences, and biopolitical violence.

This definition is no longer minimalist. Instead, it represents an effort to cover the range of postcolonial critiques of the nation discussed in this chapter. Formally, the role of the sociologist is to witness, in person (doing research) and in writing (publishing texts) the postcolonial contestations around and beyond the nation. But as the postcolonial critics have argued, the very questions of difference and history, approaches of inter-reference and intersecting identities and biopolitical realities of the colonial state, all involve the contestation of ideas and concepts, from which no scholar can escape.

This contestation is especially relevant for scholars embedded in the local universities of Asia, Africa, and Latin America. I opened this chapter in a critically reflexive manner precisely to emphasize this point. I have been fortunate to be based at the National University of Singapore, a globalizing university that has greeted a steady stream of visiting scholars crossing from West to East and North to South, giving me firsthand experiences of inter-referencing knowledge production and intersecting identities. It has enabled me to link up to the Inter-Asia Cultural Studies network and I have been playing my part, at the margins of the movement, thinking through the nation and the Inter-Asia project itself, while forging intersecting identities with fellow postcolonial critics across Asia.

In the conclusion to the collection of essays I co-edited with Chih-ming Wang from Academia Sinica – *Precarious Belongings: Affect and Nationalism in Asia* (Goh 2017) – I reflect on the rising hating-and-loving nationalisms that the contributors document. The nation has become a lightning rod attracting the passions of a post-Cold War generation caught up in the crisis of capitalism and searching for transcendental meanings in belonging to a larger community. We no longer witness the specter of comparisons, as Anderson did, but lurking behind each of the shrill or subtle nationalisms is the rising specter of imperialistic China looming over the region. I feel increasingly discomforted as an ethnic Chinese in Chinese-majority Singapore championing a cosmopolitan Singaporean identity. Our work begins anew.

References

Adams, Julia. 2005. *The Familial State: Ruling Families and Merchant Capitalism in Early Modern Empire*. Ithaca, NY: Cornell University Press.

Agamben, Giorgio. 1999. *The Remnants of Auschwitz: The Witness and the Archive*, trans. Daniel Heller-Roazen. New York: Zone Books.

Anderson, Benedict. [1983] 1991. *Imagined Communities: Reflections on the Origin and Spread of Nationalism*. Revised ed. London: Verso.

———. 1998. *The Spectre of Comparisons: Nationalism, Southeast Asia and the World*. London: Verso.

Apter, Andrew. 1999. "The Subvention of Tradition: A Genealogy of the Nigerian Durbar." Pp. 213–52 in *State/Culture: State Formation after the Cultural Turn*, edited by G. Steinmetz. Ithaca, NY: Cornell University Press.

Calhoun, Craig, Frederick Cooper, and Kevin W. Moore, eds. 2006. *Lessons of Empire: Imperial Histories and American Power*. New York: New Press.

Chatterjee, Partha. 1986. *Nationalist Thought and the Colonial World: A Derivative Discourse?* London: Zed Books.

———. 1993. *The Nation and Its Fragments: Colonial and Postcolonial Histories*. Princeton, NJ: Princeton University Press.

———. 2011. *Lineages of Political Society: Studies in Postcolonial Democracy*. New York: Columbia University Press.

Chen, Kuan-Hsing. 2010. *Asia as Method: Toward Deimperialization*. Durham, NC: Duke University Press.

Coronil, Fernando. 1997. *The Magical State: Nature, Money and Modernity in Venezuela*. Chicago: University of Chicago Press.

Duara, Prasenjit. 2004. "Introduction: The Decolonization of Asia and Africa in the Twentieth Century." Pp. 1–18 in *Decolonization: Perspectives from Now and Then*, edited by P. Duara. London: Routledge.

Gellner, Ernest. 1983. *Nations and Nationalism*. Ithaca, NY: Cornell University Press.

Go, Julian. 2008. *American Empire and the Politics of Meaning: Elite Political Cultures in the Philippines and Puerto Rico during U.S. Colonialism*. Durham, NC: Duke University Press.

Goh, Daniel P.S. 2012. "Oriental Purity: Postcolonial Discomfort and Asian Values." *Positions: East Asia Cultures Critique* 20(4):1041–66.

———. 2017. "Conclusion: The Geopolitical Unconscious of Inter-Asia." Pp. 219–24 in *Precarious Belongings: Affect and Nationalism in Asia*, edited by C. Wang and D. Goh. London: Rowman and Littlefield.

Hobsbawm, Eric J. 1983. "Introduction: Inventing Traditions." Pp. 1–14 in *The Invention of Tradition*, edited by E. Hobsbawm and T. Ranger. Cambridge: Cambridge University Press.

———. [1990] 1992. *Nations and Nationalism Since 1780: Programme, Myth, Reality*. 2nd ed. Cambridge: Cambridge University Press.

Jessop, Bob. 1999. "Narrating the Future of the National Economy and the National State: Remarks on Remapping Regulation and Reinventing Governance." Pp. 378–405 in *State/Culture: State Formation after the Cultural*, edited by G. Steinmetz. Ithaca, NY: Cornell University Press.

Kumar, Krishan. 2013. "Empires and Nations: Convergence or Divergence?" Pp. 279–99 in *Sociology and Empires: The Imperial Entanglements of a Discipline*, edited by G. Steinmetz. Durham, NC: Duke University Press.

Mann, Michael. 2003. *Incoherent Empire*. London: Verso.

Mbembe, Achille. 2001. *On the Postcolony*. Berkeley: University of California Press.

Meyer, John W. 1999. "The Changing Cultural Content of the Nation-State: A World Society Perspective." Pp. 123–43 in *State/Culture: State Formation after the Cultural*, edited by G. Steinmetz. Ithaca, NY: Cornell University Press.

Mignolo, Walter. 2000. *Local Histories/Global Designs: Coloniality, Subaltern Knowledges, and Border Thinking*. Princeton, NJ: Princeton University Press.

———. 2011. *The Darker Side of Western Modernity: Global Futures, Decolonial Options*. Durham, NC: Duke University Press.

Moore, Barrington. 1966. *Social Origins of Dictatorship and Democracy: Lord and Peasant in the Making of the Modern World*. Boston: Beacon Press.

Pincus, Steven. 1999. "Nationalism, Universal Monarchy, and the Glorious Revolution." Pp. 182–210 in *State/Culture: State Formation after the Cultural*, edited by G. Steinmetz. Ithaca, NY: Cornell University Press.

Skocpol, Theda. 1979. *States and Social Revolutions*. New York: Cambridge University Press.

Spillman, Lyn, and Russell Faeges. 2005. "Nations." Pp. 409–37 in *Remaking Modernity: Politics, History, and Sociology*, edited by J. Adams, E.S. Clemens, and A. Shola Orloff. Durham, NC: Duke University Press.

Steinmetz, George. 1999. "Introduction: Culture and the State." Pp. 1–49 in *State/Culture: State Formation after the Cultural*, edited by G. Steinmetz. Ithaca, NY: Cornell University Press.

———. 2007. *The Devil's Handwriting: Precoloniality and the German Colonial State in Qingdao, Samoa, and Southwest Africa*. Chicago: University of Chicago Press.

Tilly, Charles. 1985. "War Making and State Making as Organized Crime." Pp. 167–91 in *Bringing the State Back In*, edited by D. Rueschemeyer, P.B. Evans, and T. Skocpol. New York: Cambridge University Press.

Winichakul, Thongchai. 1994. *Siam Mapped: A History of the Geo-Body of the Nation*. Honolulu: University of Hawaii Press.

Part IX
Global cultures, global processes

56

Consumerism and self-representation in an era of global capitalism

Gary G. Hamilton and Donald Fels

Introduction

"What a difference a century makes," observed the distinguished anthropologist, G. William Skinner (1999:56). A century ago cities in China looked Chinese. Buildings had a distinctively Chinese architecture. The cities were laid out with a distinctively Chinese sense of space and propriety. The shops lining the streets sold distinctively Chinese products that were to be consumed in distinctively Chinese ways. And the people walking up and down the street looked distinctively Chinese, dressed in characteristic clothes and shoes, and talked in an array of local dialects. A century later, the outer appearance of things is no longer uniquely Chinese.

Today, in Chinese cities, high-rise buildings, urban space, and public propriety seem completely at home with culture found in newly constructed cities throughout the world. The ubiquitous shopping malls are filled with products that could be bought most anywhere; the people in the stores and on the street wear the same clothes worn by stylish and not-so-stylish people throughout the world; and although people still speak Chinese, they most likely use Mandarin in their daily life, which has become the standardized form of communication throughout the Chinese-speaking world. Skinner's point is well taken: in the past century, China has been transformed.

The same set of observations could be made for most countries. A century ago, the way of life in cities everywhere resonated with local culture. A century later, there is considerable uniformity in the look and feel of most major cities around the world. Today, urbanites dress and act in similar ways – shopping in malls and supermarkets and online, buying more or less the same standardized products that are consumed in similar ways. The use of local dialects is declining everywhere in favor of official languages, and English is rapidly becoming the standardized form of communication on the internet, in meetings, and international conferences.

The easy conclusion is that we are witnessing a global cultural convergence. Indeed, in many spheres of their lives, people around the world have embraced a common vision of what it means to be modern, and they have adopted an increasingly similar range of ideal and material goods to signify that modernity. And this modernity is fundamentally, if not exclusively, Western – based overwhelmingly on patterns of American consumerism – or as George Ritzer (2008 [1993], 2004–7) would say, "McDonaldization" – resulting in the "globalization of nothing." This conclusion is indeed easy, but in fact, it is incorrect.

Theories of cultural convergence are deceptive, as we will show. Nevertheless, the observations on which such theories are based beg for our attention: the last half century has been a period of profound and ongoing global transformations in the culture of everyday life. It may be easy to describe these transformations as a convergence toward Western consumerism. Yet examining the actual changes should make us a lot less confident that a global convergence is underway. Instead, these transformations reflect crucial changes in the organization of global capitalism, changes that lay a new foundation for an increasingly sophisticated articulation of social and cultural differences.

The theories of cultural convergence

Various different theories of global cultural convergence all make the same basic assumption: the forces of globalization are so powerful and pervasive that local cultures necessarily have to bend, if not to break, to accommodate Western patterns of consumption. Theorists are often so confident in making this assumption that they confine their analyses to the irresistible forces causing the change and largely ignore the consequences of those same forces, not only in non-Western societies but in Western societies as well.

One of the best known theories of convergence is George Ritzer's thesis on "the McDonaldization of society." In a series of books and articles dating from the 1980s, Ritzer argues that modern societies are becoming increasingly rationalized, a process that he identifies as being similar to that used by McDonald's, the fast-food chain. Citing Weber's theory of rationalization as his inspiration, Ritzer ([1993] 2008) submits that McDonaldization is a process in which efficiency, calculability, predictability, and centralized control pervade the organization of all kinds of activity, ranging from the production of food to education, the delivery of healthcare, and family life.

Ritzer's concept plays on a clever analogy. McDonald's is a worldwide success, and the McDonald's model of fast-food delivery has been widely imitated. At the core of this model, however, is the logic that Fredrick Taylor (1911) called "scientific management" and that factory owners have widely applied to the production of whatever they make. This logic of using a division of labor to achieve an efficient system of mass production was first outlined in Adam Smith's example of organized production in a pin factory (1976). McDonald's merely, but very successfully, applied this logic to an area in which it had not previously been employed – the efficient production and delivery of hamburgers. To apply this logic, McDonald's created upstream supply lines to obtain the necessary components (beef, potatoes, and the other accouterments) to make the products that they sell in their small, widely dispersed, but highly efficient factories. What Ritzer brings to this discussion is a certain shock value that comes in using McDonaldization as the analogy for global convergence.

Ritzer's use of this analogy is similar to Karl Marx's attempt to argue that factory production is inherently better – that is, more efficient and profitable, and therefore more likely to survive – than any previous system of production. Marx's concept, which he called "capitalism," included a factory system of production very much like the one Smith described. Unlike Smith, Marx believed that this system depended on the exploitation of labor. But like Smith, Marx believed that capitalist factories produced products that were obviously superior and cheaper than handicrafts made by artisans. However, neither Marx nor Ritzer attempts to understand "factorization" from the viewpoint of those buying the products. Instead they simply assume the factory system to be a force producing irresistibly priced goods. As Marx (1959:11) put it,

> Cheap commodity prices are the heavy artillery with which (the bourgeoisie) batters down all Chinese walls and forces the barbarians' obstinate hatred of foreigners to capitulate . . . It compels them to introduce what it calls civilization in their midst, i.e., to become bourgeoisie themselves.

To paraphrase Marx, Ritzer is arguing that McDonaldization produces goods for the Chinese that introduce Western civilization in their midst, that is, so that they become Western consumers themselves.

A subtler account of globalization is found in the theories of global institutional convergence developed by John Meyer and his colleagues (Meyer and Hannan 1979; Drori, Meyer, and Hwang 2006). According to these theories, countries around the world are converging on certain institutional ideals emanating from the West. The range of institutionalized organizational spheres, such as the nation-state or the US system of higher education, creates normative ideals that other countries are drawn into emulating. They emulate these ideals because of coercive pressures from international agencies (i.e., the United Nations) or because, in conditions of uncertainty, they want to imitate the best practices of leading nations and leading universities. This process of isomorphism generates an irreversible global, cultural, and institutional convergence leading to the most profound type of Westernization – a transformation in the meaning of modernity.

Like McDonaldization, however, this concept maps global "normalization" as a one-way street, where all forces of globalization come from one direction on their way to all other locations, with uniform and irresistible consequences. Normalization involves a process of conforming to forms and ideas that happen to come from the West and particularly from the United States. And they are "consumed" by people who find them irresistible because they symbolize and therefore represent the very essence of modernity. Western organizational forms are the heavy artillery that batter down all non-Western walls and force non-Western Others to introduce civilization in their midst (i.e., to become Westerners themselves).

The obvious problem with these and other similar theories of global convergence is that they do not consider the perspectives of those who buy or who otherwise take hold of the ideal and material goods that are introduced from the outside. In economic terms, they offer supply-side interpretations of globalization with no corresponding theories of demand. These theories do not take consumers into account; they merely assume uniformity in consumption without conceptualizing consumers as agents in their own right. Our point is the opposite: the processes of globalization are better viewed as "demand driven" than as "supply driven."

The retail chain: the link between suppliers and buyers

To conceptualize demand-driven processes, let us first examine one of its most important organizational manifestations – the rise of global retailing and brand-name merchandising. We will then widen our scope of analysis.

Global retailing increasingly uses point-of-sales data to organize business "backwards" from the consumer to the manufacturer. Retailers are the intermediaries and the most important players in this process. On one side of their businesses, they create, maintain, and attempt to stabilize *consumer markets* for their products. They locate their stores and their websites so that consumers will find them easily; they select, display, and price their goods so that consumers will find it easy to buy what they offer. The sellers seek out and tantalize consumers through promotions and advertising, and reassure them by offering money-back guarantees, easy returns, and warranties on the goods they sell. Consumers are the target.

On the other side, sellers create *supplier markets* in order to acquire the goods they sell. They need to find purchasing agents and manufacturing firms that can supply them with the products that they wish to sell. They are the "big buyers" (Gereffi 1994) who negotiate with manufacturers or their agents a price and level of quality that allows them to earn a profit at the point of sales. They need to find shippers, truckers, and other logistic suppliers to deliver goods efficiently to consumers. With point-of-sale information, they can instantly track which goods are selling and which are not, adjusting their orders and their supply chains accordingly.

Retail stores were not always able to operate like this. Before the 1960s, retailers were, by today's standards, small, locally or regionally based, and privately owned stores. With a few exceptions, such as Sears, Roebuck and J.C. Penney, these retail stores lacked much influence on either consumer or supplier markets. In the last half century, however, a "retail revolution" has changed the global economy, including retailing. The main elements of the retail revolution are straightforward (Feenstra and Hamilton 2006; Hamilton and Kao 2018). Starting in the 1960s, retailers began substantially to reorganize the way they did business. This process of reorganization began first with retailers in the US, but soon retailers in Europe and Japan followed suit.

At the core of this phenomenon in the US was a rapid commercial building boom, especially in less expensive outlying areas, fed by supportive tax reform. In a relatively short time, the number of shopping malls in the US jumped from about 500 small malls in 1954 to 7,600 in 1964, of which nearly 400 were very large regional shopping malls, accounting for about 30 percent of all retail sales in the US. While this building boom occurred, the interstate highway system was constructed and widespread suburbanization began. Less than 40 years later, in 2002, there were over 50,000 shopping malls in the US. In the same interval, tens of thousands more shopping malls were built around the world, some even larger than the largest malls in the US.

A main component of these shopping centers is the chain store. The same stores began to pop-up in malls all across the US and now are seen all across the world. Downtown department stores such as Macy's, J.C. Penney, and Sears were common retail chains before malls became widespread. They were among the first stores to "anchor" the large new shopping centers, but they were soon joined by several new types of stores. First came Walmart, Kmart, Kohl's, and Target, which all started general discount retailing in the same year, 1962. Then came the specialty retailers, chain stores like The Limited (founded in 1963), The Gap (1969), TJX (1977), and Best Buy (1983). In the 20-year span between 1975 and 1995, every major retail segment consolidated into large chains – hardware by Home Depot (1978); drugs by CVS (1963), Rite Aid (1968), and Walgreen's; consumer electronics by Circuit City (1968) and Best Buy (1983); toys by Toys 'R' Us (1978); books by Barnes and Noble and Borders (1971); office supplies by Staples (1986) and Office Depot (1986); and warehouse stores by Costco (1983). In the US, by 2000, the two or three chains in each segment, together with the general discounters that sell across all product lines (e.g., Walmart), accounted for nearly 90 percent of all sales in these retail segments.

In the 1970s, when chains began to expand rapidly, they needed to locate or otherwise establish large and reliable suppliers to stock their shelves. Many retail chains were eager to stock their shelves with brand-name products, which they could sell at a discount. This eagerness promoted the creation and rapid growth of brand-name merchandisers without factories, such as Ralph Lauren (1967), Anne Klein (1968), and Nike (1972), as well as the rapid growth of existing brands, some of which were initially manufacturers, such as Levi's, Schwinn, Eddie Bauer, Sony, and Panasonic. Other retail chains, such as The Limited, The Gap, and even Macy's and J.C. Penney, needed suppliers for in-house or private-label brands. General discounters such as Walmart and specialty retailers such as Home Depot needed huge quantities of a considerable range of branded and non-branded goods. To obtain these goods, brand-name merchandisers and retailers became big buyers.

Starting in the late 1960s and rapidly increasing in the 1970s, big buyers began to source both brand-name and private-label goods from factories in Asia. Most of these buyers established offices in Asia that specialized in locating and, at times, creating suppliers. They worked closely with Asian manufacturers, transferring technology, lending capital, and providing large orders. In the 1970s and 1980s, most of the goods produced under these arrangements came from factories located in Taiwan, South Korea, Hong Kong, and Japan. Economies in these countries became *demand-responsive*. Thus great portions of their entire economies were organized around export production based on big buyers' orders for goods. In the 1980s, manufacturers in these core Asian countries began to move portions of their production to other Asian countries. In the 1990s, Southeast Asia and especially China began to grow very rapidly in response to the intra-Asian movement of capital, expertise, and big buyer orders (Feenstra and Hamilton 2006; Hamilton and Kao 2018).

One of the key factors is the 1990s restructuring of Asian economies was the spread of lean retailing (Abernathy et al. 1999). In the 1970s, Uniform Product Codes (UPC) had been established, bar codes and scanners invented, and computerization began in earnest. By the 1980s, most large chains had established computerized inventory systems and transfer stations instead of large warehouses. These changes allowed reorganization to make them more responsive to point-of-sale information. These changes were facilitated by the simultaneous creation of a global logistics system, which included widespread containerization, container terminals, and trucking companies – all of which facilitated the integration of Asian factories into the big buyers' organizations for selling products (Bonacich and Wilson 2008). With all the pieces in place, supply chains, instead of distribution channels, became the standard methodology of organizing the global economy. At the core of this methodology is the "retail chain" – the feedback loop between retailers and customers – in which the consumer serves both as the final purchaser of goods and also as the initiator of the next round of decisions about what to sell in the future.

The expansion of global retailing

For the global economy, the 1990s was when the tail began to wag the dog. In the early days of capitalism, when consumers could buy any color of car as long as it was black, or watch any television show as long as it was *I Love Lucy*, there was a very large gap between manufacturers' production and consumers' demand. Factory owners always had to guess what final demand for any product would be, and consumers had limited, if any, influence over what goods were available to buy. When producers overshot the mark, they had fire sales, and when they undershot, they lost out on business. It was usually one or the other. Lean retailing closed that gap considerably, but in so doing it decisively shifted the balance of power away from manufacturers and toward retailers. With that shift, the consumer plays a larger and larger role in determining which products are actually offered for sale.

In 1990, having built large, reliable, and flexible supply chains, retailers consolidated consumer markets in their home territories and expanded their consumer markets internationally. With modest-sized home markets, European retailers were the first movers. The largest retailers in France (Carrefour), England (Tesco), and Germany (Metro, Aldi) all expanded beyond the home country and beyond Europe to establish international operations. Walmart soon followed suit, as did other US retailers such as Costco and Home Depot. The main driver of this global expansion was food retailing. Before 1990, most people around the world, especially outside the US, Europe, and Japan, bought food products from local markets and small sundry stores. Starting in the 1990s, however, supermarket chains began to penetrate and then to dominate food retailing in most countries. Reardon, Henson, and Berdegue (2007) show that the diffusion of supermarkets has completely revamped the organization of suppliers of food products, creating rationalized supply chains and larger and more reliable suppliers, with small farmers losing and large agribusinesses winning places in the chain. Many supermarkets now also sell a range of other goods beside food, making them more like general discounters than simply grocery stores.

At first glance, it seems that the world's largest retailers, stores like Walmart and Carrefour, would grow at the expense of other retailers. Although these firms expanded exponentially in the years before 2007, by presenting a model and building the infrastructure they also have created new consumer markets for goods that other, smaller retailers are now providing. McDonald's may have been among the first fast-food firms to establish itself globally, but now it has competitors everywhere. The same is true for Walmart and Carrefour. Even the threat of Walmart's entry into a new location has spurred mergers between, and a comprehensive reorganization of, local firms to use lean retailing techniques to create and to respond to local demand. Most importantly, all these brick-and-mortar stores now face fierce competition from online retailers. The largest of these online retailers, Amazon and Alibaba, are even more driven by consumer demand and organize far larger groups of suppliers than conventional stores. Huge numbers of smaller online retailers have joined Amazon and Alibaba, suggesting that the retail revolution will continue for some time.

Stratification, demand-driven lifestyles, and the art of self-representation

The rapid growth and global presence of all types of retailers and their contract manufacturers signal a fundamental transformation in global capitalism. It is now "demand led." Sellers of ideal and material goods rely on consumer choice for their profits. Consumers, however, are not just "out there" waiting to make their choices. Instead, the new capitalists actively seek to create new consumer markets throughout the world not simply by offering cheaper prices, for that is usually not the case, but rather by promising a new way of life for people who come to see themselves in a new light.

Social scientists have long known that people consume as a means of conveying to others a sense of who they are as individuals. Thorstein Veblen, in *The Theory of the Leisure Class* ([1899] 1953), was the first social scientist to develop a demand-driven theory of the economy. He showed that the logic of consumption was to convey a sense of self-worth to others by means of making invidious distinctions. People who regard themselves as privileged in one way or another will use status-marking objects and actions to establish their distinctiveness. For Veblen ([1899] 1953), writing in the Gilded Age, distinctiveness was based on class identity: to establish oneself in the upper class was to create an image of non-utilitarian consumption of goods and time, in what Veblen called "conspicuous consumption" and "conspicuous leisure."

A long line of sociological research has substantiated Veblen's insights: consumption and stratification go hand in hand. But more recent sociologists have also qualified this insight by showing that class stratification is not what it used to be. When asked, most people in the US of any means identify as middle class. Although the actual objects and practices of consumption vary greatly from person to person, the invidiousness attached to them cannot be easily ranked by class position. Instead of class, they increasingly attach to lifestyles, which are only indirectly associated with class and income. Today, lifestyles, not class, are the vehicles of self-representation, and of stratification too (Holt 1997).

The key to understanding this phenomenon is to see that capitalists today, in whatever business, have entered into virtual, and sometimes actual, conversations with their customers. Customers discover who they are by exploring what is being offered to them, and once those identities form and once those identities signify a lifestyle filled with ideal and material goods, then businesses strive to supply those goods, and in so doing expand the lifestyle. Demand-driven marketing responds to buying. What is bought gets made, and what is made gets bought, establishing the feedback loop.

What only the very rich could afford to do in Veblen's time has now become available to people of a wide range of incomes. Instead of being synonymous with class, lifestyles are stratified according to levels of income. Eating foie gras in France and bird's nest soup in Hong Kong, playing golf at Pebble Beach and doing yoga at Borobudur, climbing the Matterhorn and snorkeling off the Great Barrier Reef – all these are conspicuous activities that people can do today even with modest incomes. And the very rich may not even have the most fun anymore. Only the very poor and dispossessed get left out, and the knowledge of their exclusion makes their plight all the more unbearable. For everyone else, an array of lifestyles is there for choosing. Select the lifestyle that suits you, refine that lifestyle through reachable goals, Google those goals on the web, and, presto! There they are: travel agents to help you arrange your trip, retailers to give you a price and a delivery date for the objects you want to buy, clubs to join to help you become sophisticated consumers of a given activity, even friends and potential friends with whom to enjoy your way of life.

This is not Veblen's world, but it is the world we live in today, a variegated and expanding world of diverse lifestyles and identities that go with them. This diversity is particularly striking when we consider demand-driven internet and cable television competition for viewers. Online users, on sites such as Facebook and Snapchat, and on cable channels such as Fox News and MSNBC, learn who they are by the choices they make. And consumer demand for those choices encourages these competitors to continue to deliver distinctive brands of experience based on ratings. In this sense, lifestyles potentially become all encompassing, worlds unto themselves, demand-driven realities. Whatever their sources, however anachronistic, these lifestyles, identities, and realities are necessarily contemporary ones. They are up to date precisely because capitalist purveyors provide the necessary accouterments to mirror a contemporary way of life. Without these purveyors, a particular lifestyle might be difficult if not impossible to establish – difficult to find the right stuff, difficult to find others to associate with, difficult even to know about. Demand-driven capitalism helps define and fill out lifestyles that would not necessarily or strongly exist otherwise.

It is also clear that, around the world, the feedback loop between capitalists and new consumers has helped to create new identities out of the apparent convergences that so many people have observed, between music, movies, the internet, technology hardware and software, vacations and tourism, strategic English, standardized national languages, houses that call for interior decoration, cuisines that require specialized kitchenware, occupations that require a standardized education, and politics that require a specific set of "truths" – the list goes on. But what this listing obscures is the fact that these are not the vessels of cultural convergence; they are the media of differentiation.

Demand-driven capitalism allows consumers to create distinct worlds out of standardized points of entry. Youth everywhere use smartphones to text to their friends and create their own rap songs; in turn, media relay to the audience what it means to be young and in a particular place. Bollywood helps Indians to understand who they are or might be, a fact that can be shared with moviegoers around the world, who in turn can understand who they are not. Google and other internet search engines are, strictly speaking, demand driven; they rely on information fed by its users. They adapt to each locale, and they help to differentiate among locales. The increasing divides in modern societies that have become so apparent today are heavily driven by differentiation, ironically based on common points of entry.

The standardization of entry points encourages cultural differentiation, and encourages the formation of new worlds filled with new identities to explore. Mathews and Lui (2001) show that shopping in Hong Kong has become a way of life – not a Western way of life, but a new Hong Konger way of life. Chua (2003), in *Life Is Not Complete without Shopping*, makes the same argument for Singapore. In both locations, a unique consumer culture now includes styles of clothing, home décor, movies, and food. Mona Abaza (2001) similarly shows that shopping malls in Cairo offer a new space for Egyptians, not as Westerns, but as Egyptians forging new identities to fit the times, for women who are finding a space away from Islamic restrictions, for couples who can look into each other's eyes longingly and without shame. And in *Golden Arches East: McDonald's in East Asia*, James Watson and colleagues (2006) make it clear that there is nothing uniform in the diffusion of McDonald's in Asia. Like everything else, McDonaldization is a source of differentiation, the globalization of differentiation.

Examining only the objects of diffusion, it is easy to jump to the conclusion that a global convergence is underway, for indeed carriers of identity are becoming standardized around the world. Ready-made apparel, accessories and shoes, cuisines, cultural media (television, movies, DVDs, and the internet), communication systems (cell phones and the internet), and even languages – all become vehicles that people use to establish identities and at the same time distinguish themselves from others. These standardized media vehicles greatly expand the range of choices individuals are able to make about how to represent themselves in relation to others, both the real ones close by and the imagined ones further away. The range of accessible choices encourages individuals everywhere to develop an awareness – of a personal identity rooted in a locale, of a political "reality" that one selects, or perhaps even of what Kuah-Pearce (2006) calls a "transnational self." Whatever choices people make, their awareness of making choices about their lives also encourages them to develop some "artfulness" to their self-representation, some distinctive touch that differentiates one individual from another, one group from another.

The awareness of the necessity to make choices about one's life and the lives of others nearby is producing something equivalent to an existential crisis in societies around the world today. Rather than simply living a traditional life because no other options are known or available, offered an array choices, people now have to opt in if they are to embrace traditionalist and fundamentalist ways of living. The necessity of choosing one's way of life transforms such taken-for-granted routines into lifestyle choices, which capitalists can then target with specialized products, with everything from videos, music, and books having religious and political themes to armaments to fortify and defend a way of life.

The art of representation is essential and integral to the feedback loop that modern capitalism establishes. By listening closely to customers, global capitalists turn customers into consumers, people who use ideal and material goods to establish who they are in a modern world. This is a world of both convergence and differentiation, and these processes are intimately connected with each other.

References

Abaza, Mona. 2001. "Shopping Malls, Consumer Culture and the Reshaping of Public Space in Egypt." *Theory, Culture, and Society* 18(5):97–122.

Abernathy, Frederick H., John T. Dunlop, Janice H. Hammond, and David Weil. 1999. *A Stitch in Time: Lean Retailing and the Transformation of Manufacturing – Lessons from the Apparel and Textile Industries*. New York: Oxford University Press.

Bonacich, Edna, and Jake B. Wilson. 2008. *Getting the Goods: Ports, Labor, and the Logistics Revolution*. Ithaca, NY: Cornell University Press.

Chua, Beng Huat. 2003. *Life Is Not Complete without Shopping: Consumption Culture in Singapore*. Singapore: Singapore University Press.

Drori, Gili S., John W. Meyer, and Hokyu Hwang, eds. 2006. *Globalization and Organization: World Society and Organizational Change*. New York: Oxford University Press.

Feenstra, Robert C., and Gary G. Hamilton. 2006. *Emergent Economies, Divergent Paths: Economic Organization and International Trade in South Korea and Taiwan*. Cambridge: Cambridge University Press.

Gereffi, Gary. 1994. "The Organization of Buyer-Driven Global Commodity Chains: How U.S. Retail Networks Shape Overseas Production Networks." Pp. 95–122 in *Commodity Chains and Global Capitalism*, edited by G. Gereffi and M. Korzeniewicz. Westport, CT: Greenwood Press.

Hamilton, Gary G., and Cheng-shu Kao. 2018. *Making Money: How Taiwanese Industrialists Embraced the Global Economy*. Stanford, CA: Stanford University Press.

Holt, Douglas B. 1997. "Poststructuralist Lifestyle Analysis: Conceptualizing the Social Patterning of Consumption in Postmodernity." *Journal of Consumer Research* 23(4):326–50.

Kuah-Pearce, Khun Eng. 2006. "Transnational Self in Chinese Diaspora: A Conceptual Framework." *Asian Studies Review* 30(3):223–40.

Marx, Karl. 1959. *Basic Writings on Politics and Philosophy*. New York: Anchor Books.

Mathews, Gordon, and Tai-lok Lui. 2001. *Consuming Hong Kong*. Hong Kong: Hong Kong University Press.

Meyer, John W., and Michael T. Hannan. 1979. *National Development and the World System: Educational, Economic, and Political Change 1950–1970*. Chicago: University of Chicago Press.

Reardon, Thomas, Spencer Henson, and Julio Berdegue. 2007. "'Proactive Fast-Tracking' Diffusion of Supermarkets in Developing Countries: Implications for Market Institutions and Trade." *Journal of Economic Geography* 7:399–431.

Ritzer, George. 2004–7. *The Globalization of Nothing*. 1st and 2nd ed. Thousand Oaks, CA: Sage.

———. 2008 [1993]. *The McDonaldization of Society*. 8th ed. Thousand Oaks, CA: Pine Forge Press.

Skinner, G. William. 1999. "Chinese Cities: The Difference a Century Makes." Pp. 56–69 in *Cosmopolitan Capitalists: Hong Kong and the Chinese Diaspora at the End of the Twentieth Century*, edited by G.G. Hamilton. Seattle: University of Washington Press.

Taylor, Frederick. 1911. *The Principles of Scientific Management*. New York: Harper and Brothers.

Veblen, Thorstein. [1899] 1953. *The Theory of the Leisure Class*. New York: Mentor Books.

Watson, James, ed. 2006. *Golden Arches East: McDonald's in East Asia*. Stanford, CA: Stanford University Press.

57

Culture and globalization

Victoria Reyes

Introduction

In the past three decades, "globalization" has become a buzzword in popular culture, news, and academia. Yet interconnections between different groups of people, places, and things are not new. Globalization has occurred for hundreds of years and has taken multiple forms – from colonial conquests to trade routes like the Manila-Acapulco galleon route, the Atlantic slave trade, and the Silk Road. What characterizes the current epoch of globalization is the increasing speed and intensity of these dynamics, not their very existence.

What are these global dynamics? Some scholars refer to "separate spheres" of globalization, such as cultural, political, or economic globalization. In this perspective, cultural globalization encompasses cultural goods, products, and symbols that are distinct from political and economic flows between nation-states (Held et al. 1999; Held and McGrew 2000). Yet, we know that culture is not limited to artifacts or the diffusion of symbols. Rather, it consists of discourses, logics, practices, styles, habits, tastes, skills, and meanings, as well as material items (DiMaggio 1997; Lamont and Molnar 2002), and has become part of sociologists' "toolkits" (Swidler 1986) in analyzing most arenas of social life because of its central role in (re)producing inequality (Bourdieu 1984; DiMaggio 1987, 1997).

To understand the relationship between culture and globalization, in this chapter I show how four common scholarly models of culture and globalization that are traditionally seen as aligning with the separate-spheres view of globalization actually begin to break down these walls. By juxtaposing these models with three emerging perspectives that more explicitly focus on the mutually constitutive relationship between culture, politics, and economics, I argue that the study of globalization is the study of culture, and vice versa. This is because the global and the local interact, influence, and shape one another in everyday life.

By interrogating the concepts "culture" and "globalization," this analysis shifts scholarly focus from viewing culture as separate from other processes of globalization to exploring how cultural routines, practices, and interactions among people, places, and things around the world are constitutive of globalization. The study of culture and globalization is not limited to recent globalization efforts like free-trade agreements or the proliferation of McDonald's around the world, nor is it confined to conceptions of a "global sociology" as something that occurs only when US researchers study non-US locations. Rather, to study globalization or culture is to necessarily study the other, and both shape daily life on the ground.

Culture as a separate sphere of globalization?

In 1993, Samuel Huntington put forth a provocative claim: conflict in the post-Cold War era was being defined by a "clash of civilizations." That is, geopolitics was no longer based on rival superpowers or a homogenizing diffusion of Western ideals, but was now defined by multiple civilizations – broad cultural identities defined at the level of the nation-state and beyond. He called these civilizations "the West and the Rest" (Huntington 1996), and claimed that world conflicts would be defined by differences between civilizations, rather than differences within civilizations (e.g., related to socioeconomic status and ethnicity). Later, Huntington held these clashes to be critical in understanding the post-9/11 world (2003, 2007, 2013), and contemporary Latino/a migration to the US (2004a, 2004b).

Yet, although Huntington's perspective on culture and globalization rests on an assumption that civilizations involve deeply held cultural commonalities that supersede internal variation, he acknowledges that although "civilizations endure, they also evolve" (Huntington 1996:44). In these terms, "culture" is *relatively* static and divisive. If culture is the root of conflict, then "globalization" is the water of conflict – the increasing interconnection between people, places, and things around the world that drives conflict to erupt.

Other scholars see "culture" and "globalization" as hegemonic tools of the West. For example, Edward Said (1993) connects political processes of oppression and imperialism to everyday cultural forms. In understanding culture in this way, he argues that Western imperialism is fundamentally tied to cultural ways of knowing and delineating the "West" from the "East." Culture and conquest are entwined. American race scholars similarly see race – and increasingly other social identities that intersect with race, such as gender and nationality, among others – as a socially constructed category, which necessarily entails culture and power structures (Omi and Winant [1986] 2015; Bonilla-Silva 2015; Collins 2015).

Similarly, world-systems theory relies on the precept that "all of the economic, political, social, and cultural relations among the people of the earth" are interconnected (Chase-Dunn and Grimes 1995:389). Although these scholars tend to focus on economic, political, or military factors and pay less attention to the role of culture in the reproduction of global inequality, Wallerstein suggests that culture takes two forms – one that focuses on between-group differences, the other, on within-group variation. In Wallerstein's view, the former is not relevant for in-depth historical analyses, while the latter is "an ideological cover to justify the interests of some persons . . . within any given 'group' . . . against the interests of other persons within this same group" (1990:34). Thus, culture is an "idea-system" that is the outcome and justification of socio-political events and broad inequalities (Wallerstein 1990:38). Here, we see similarities to both Said (1993) and Huntington (1993, 1996), as culture becomes "the key ideological battleground" within a world-system (Wallerstein 1990:39).

Likewise, McDonaldization – "the process by which the principles of the fast-food restaurant are coming to dominate more and more sectors of American society as well as the rest of the world" (Ritzer 2010:4) – also treats the relationship between "culture" and "globalization" as based on hegemony, power, and inequality. The proliferation of the McDonald's fast-food chain exemplifies the spread of rationalization and bureaucracy (namely efficiency and calculability) around the world, as anticipated by Weber (1978). Despite its name, McDonaldization is not limited to the titular chain. It also unfolds through the spread of organizations and institutions, including English education (Wilkinson 2006), the US criminal justice system (Shichor

1997; Robinson 2010), and sex industries (Hausbeck and Brents 2010). Here, culture is diffused through practices and values associated with organizations, which are sometimes seen as promoting the spread of cultural imperialism or the spread of US or other Western "values" to less developing countries. The globalization of culture tends to flow from the West to "the Rest."

Whereas critical, world-systems, and McDonaldization scholarship examines conflict, power, and the causes and consequences of inequality, researchers using a world-polity perspective or world-society theory focus on the diffusion of institutional processes and models across countries. Scholars using this lens emphasize organizational and/or policy-based similarities, rather than differences, among nation-states (Meyer et al.1997), including education (Ramirez and Boli 1987), women's rights (Ramirez, Soysal, and Shanahan 1997), population policies (Robinson 2015), the number of applications from asylum seekers (Yoo and Koo 2014), abortion policies (Boyle, Longhofer, and Kim 2015), science (Schofer 2003), world heritage (Elliot and Schmutz 2012), and fair trade (Shorette 2014).

Yet foregoing analyses of difference does not imply that scholars envision a homogenous adaptation of world institutions. For example, there is often a decoupling between adapting policies and the ability to implement them (Meyer et al. 1997), and the adoption of said institutions can be coercive or normative (Robinson 2015; see also DiMaggio and Powell 1983). Diffusions of policies also do not occur evenly across countries (Boyle, Longhofer, and Kim 2015), and the structure of the world polity itself is fragmented (Beckfield 2003, 2010). Despite scholars' questions regarding whether observed similarities are due to the world polity or other factors (Marshall 2015; see also the exchange between Li and Hicks 2016 and Wimmer and Feinstein 2016), the world-polity approach has substantial influence on sociological research on culture and globalization. In this perspective, culture is shorthand for institutions that are common around the world, while globalization is the means by which these are diffused and enforced.

Another common scholarly model of culture and globalization focuses on cultural hybridity, or "glocalization" – the incorporation of the local into global processes (Robertson 1995). The hybridity model rejects viewing the relationship between "culture" and "globalization" as a homogenizing force related to cultural imposition by external actors, and emphasizes local adaptations of the global. We see this general process in adaptations of food (Matejowsky 2007), laws (Randeria 2003), sports (Giulianotti and Robertson 2004, 2006, 2007; Jijon 2013), religion (Roudometof 2013), television shows (Bielby and Harrington 2004; Derne 2005), and advertising (Kobayashi 2012). In hybrid processes, "culture" encompasses more than just material items and globalization entails local adaptation of foreign culture. The approach took hold in the late 1990s and early 2000s. Although there continues to be some engagement with it, many authors who similarly examine local adaptations of global practices and meanings (e.g., safer sex practices such as condom use; Tavory and Swidler 2009) tend to frame the negotiations they describe in relation to broader social conversations about the role of culture in social life.

To this point, I've described theoretical models that are often seen as relegating culture to a "separate sphere" from politics or economics, whether through a lens of civilizations, hegemony, diffusion, or hybridization. And yet, these three spheres cannot be so easily separated. So-called clashes of civilization and cultural hegemony necessarily entail political economies, whereas diffusion-of-culture and hybridization models involve economic and political organizations and instruments.

Culture, politics, and economics as constitutive of globalization

Exciting new theoretical developments in the past few decades explicitly treat culture, politics, and economics as constitutive of one another. Here culture is considered to be dynamic, shifting, and used strategically, albeit inconsistently (DiMaggio 1997; Lamont and Molnar 2002), and global flows are seen as relational processes that inform both everyday life and broader social structures. Here, I highlight three of these scholarly developments to consider how the study of culture, politics, and economics necessarily entails the study of globalization.

First, the cultural wealth of nations is a relatively new perspective in the field of economic sociology that focuses on how places' myths, reputations, images, and narratives shape economic activity within them (Bandelj and Wherry 2011; Reyes 2015a). A play on words on Adam Smith's *Wealth of Nations*, this perspective unites Bourdieu's (1984) concept of distinction with recent advances in economic sociology that treat culture as constitutive of economic life (Zelizer 2005, 2011). Research in this vein has examined how indigenous participation in markets is shaped by countries' historical and contemporary narratives (Colloredo-Mansfeld 2002; Wherry 2007) and how actors purposefully reimagine or recreate countries' marketing or images to increase tourism (Rivera 2008; Gaggio 2011). For example, artisans and government officials in Thailand draw on their indigeneity when marketing their products, whereas Costa Rican artisans are constrained in their ability to sell their products because officials emphasize Western similarities at the expense of an indigenous past (Wherry 2008).

However, not all countries are able to rewrite their histories. Officials are still constrained because cultural claims must also be externally validated (Reyes 2014). For example, many sites nominated to the UNESCO World Heritage list are rejected because they do not meet the criteria of possessing "outstanding universal value" (Elliot and Schmutz 2012). In a related vein, the *Mundo Maya* tourism project between the Mexican, Guatemalan, Belizean, Honduran, and El Salvadorian governments failed precisely because it did not highlight particularities of the Mayan people but rather, emphasized a homogenous historical narrative across different landscapes (Bair 2011). In doing so, project officials' claims to a particular version of a shared history were unsuccessful precisely because they did not coincide with internal claims of heritage.

Although research on countries' images has an extensive history in the fields of marketing and tourism, what is exciting about the new development is its theoretical link between culture, economy, and globalization. The theoretical ties to symbolic resources and economic activity on a macro scale situate the cultural wealth of nations perspective as something of interest to a general audience and mainstream sociology. Here, culture is seen as something that is adaptive, strategic, and entwined with economic life, while globalization is seen as not only involving the overt diffusion or direct presence of foreign corporations but also occurring through the indirect influences that other countries have on domestic relations and the ways in which the foreign and local are entwined.

In another stream of research, scholars debate the causes and consequences of global inequality. Much of this work centers on questions of measurement and tries to tease out differences in between- and within-country inequality (e.g., Korzeniewicz and Moran 2009). Here, scholars show how relationships among countries remain unequal vis-à-vis trade, ties among world city networks or international organizations, and currency used, among other features (Snyder and Kick 1979; Smith and Timberlake 2001; Mahutga 2006; Clark and Beckfield 2009; Taylor et al. 2009; Centeno and Cohen 2010:69–71). In these network analyses, the primary focus is on structural positions of countries and their ties to one another (Wasserman and Faust 2009; Barabasi 2014).

However, research on global flows of inequality also incorporates the role of culture and its constitutive relationship with the economy. For example, Bandelj (2002, 2008, 2009) shows how foreign direct investment in post-socialist countries is not the result of the collapse of communism and a one-way progression defined by capitalism fulfilling the void; rather, it is a relational and social process between post-socialist countries and the countries that invest in them. Drawing and extending on Bandelj, I have examined the structure of globalized travel to show how the effects of globalization are neither universal nor consistent, but are relational; they depend upon the identities of countries involved and their relationships with one another (Reyes 2013).

Here we see how even when culture is something adaptive and changing, it continues to reproduce inequality and shape socioeconomic and political relations not just on the micro scale but also at the nation-state and global levels. Culture plays a role in globalization, but not one that is static and fundamentally divisive because of "deep" cultural differences. Nor is it inherently the imposition of other countries' policies and practices. Rather, culture is fundamental to globalization precisely because it is a fundamental part of social life, and hence the increasing interconnectedness among nation-states.

A third exciting development related to the study of culture and globalization involves research on empire and colonialism. According to Steinmetz (2014:79), empires are "expansive, militarized, and multiethnic political organizations that significantly limit the sovereignty of the peoples and polities they conquer," and imperialism "is a strategy of political control over foreign lands that does not necessarily involve conquest, occupation, and durable rule by outside invaders." Colonialism, on the other hand, is "the conquest of a foreign people followed by the creation of an organization controlled by members of the conquering polity and suited to rule over the conquered territory's indigenous population" (Steinmetz 2014:79–80) and this conquest is based on a "rule of difference" (Chatterjee 1993:221). Although colonialism necessarily entails empire and imperialism, these are distinct concepts.

Research has highlighted the multifaceted role that culture plays in colonialism and the reproduction of inequality from the perspective of varied colonialized and colonizer actors. For example, in his work on the German overseas empire, Steinmetz (2008) details the important role that ethnographic capital – knowledge and experience in a colony – played in colonizers' formulation of colonial policies, while Go (2008) emphasizes both how US colonial overlords used culture as a "tool of rule" and how Philippine and Puerto Rican colonial elite subjects creatively and selectively engaged and adapted these tools. On a related dimension, Adams (2005) uses a cultural analysis of the Dutch empire to argue that patrimonial rule is gendered and based on interrelations among elite families and the mercantile class, and Cooper (2014) shows the evolution of competing claims and meanings of citizenship and colonial subjects in French Africa and France. Stoler's (2002, 2006) work shifts focus to how intimate relations and meanings of race, gender, and intermixing are regulated and negotiated as part of colonial projects.

This scholarship uniting agentic, flexible, and adaptive cultural analyses to the political projects of empire represents an exciting direction. It shifts focus from a purely political or economic analysis of colonialism either from the "bottom up" or the "top down" to an empirically driven understanding of the varied ways of knowing, meanings, and complex social relations that occur within empire and how these have shaped empires' legacies.

Conclusion

What does the study of culture and globalization tell us? That the study of one necessarily entails the study of the other. I've shown how theoretical models that tend to be seen as classifying culture as difference, hegemony, diffusion, and mobility do not necessarily relegate politics and economics to "separate spheres." Rather, the underlying relationship among them is not explicit and therefore, often gets lost. Additionally, recent advances in the fields of economic sociology, global inequality, and colonialism represent exciting avenues of research precisely because they take a more explicit view of culture as agentic, adaptive, and strategically used, and globalization as occurring not only in relations among nation-states but also in everyday life.

Yet the work I have covered here only provides a beginning foundation. Scholars need to pay more attention to the explicit links between global processes and cultural meanings, and the ways in which they are entwined for different sets of actors. One way to do this is to further the research in the aforementioned fields of economic sociology, global inequality, and colonialism, and explicitly engage in the questions that scholars pursuing such research have raised. Another way to study the co-constitutive relationship is to treat culture and globalization as analytic lenses, that is, as ways to view the world. As I have detailed elsewhere (Reyes 2015b), using culture and globalization as ways to view the world and being explicit about our analytic strategies in doing so allows us to unite seemingly disparate topics and units of analysis under a broader theoretical umbrella and thereby push forward our theoretical and empirical knowledge about how culture and globalization work. Some may critique this view by saying if everything is cultural and globalization, then nothing is. However, arguing about whether something is "cultural" or "global" is focusing on the wrong question. Instead, we should ask to what extent, under what circumstances, how, why, and when culture and global processes interact. This approach allows us to understand the complexity of social life and how seemingly different entities interrelate. In doing so, we can move toward a globally focused cultural sociology that pays close attention to how the global and local interact, influence, and shape one another in everyday life around the world.

References

Adams, Julia. 2005. *The Familial State: Ruling Families and Merchant Capitalism in Early Modern Europe*. Ithaca, NY: Cornell University Press.

Bair, Jennifer. 2011. "Constructing Scarcity, Creating Value: Marketing the *Mundo Maya*." Pp. 177–96 in *The Cultural Wealth of Nations*, edited by N. Bandelj and F.F. Wherry. Stanford, CA: Stanford University Press.

Bandelj, Nina. 2002. "Embedded Economies: Social Relations as Determinants of Foreign Direct Investment in Core and Eastern Europe." *Social Forces* 81(2):411–44.

———. 2008. *From Communists to Foreign Capitalists: The Social Foundations of Foreign Direct Investment in Postsocialist Europe*. Princeton, NJ: Princeton University Press.

———. 2009. "The Global Economy as Instituted Process: The Case of Central and Eastern Europe." *American Sociological Review* 74(1):128–49.

Bandelj, Nina, and Frederick F. Wherry, eds. 2011. *The Cultural Wealth of Nations*. Stanford, CA: Stanford University Press.

Barabasi Albert-Laszlo. 2014. *Linked: How Everything is Connected to Everything Else and What it Means for Business, Science and Everyday Life*. New York: Basic Books.

Beckfield, Jason. 2003. "Inequality in the World Polity: The Structure of International Organization." *American Sociological Review* 68(3):401–24.

———. 2010. "The Social Structure of the World Polity." *American Journal of Sociology* 115(4):1018–68.

Bielby, Denise D., and C. Lee Harrington. 2004. "Managing Culture Matters: Genre, Aesthetic Elements and the International Market for Exported Television." *Poetics* 32:73–98.

Bonilla-Silva, Eduardo. 2015. "The Structure of Racism in Color-Blind, 'Post-Racial' America." *American Behavioral Scientist* 59(11):1358–76.

Bourdieu, Pierre. 1984. *Distinction: A Social Critique of the Judgement of Taste*. Cambridge, MA: Harvard University Press.

Boyle, Elizabeth H., Wesley Longhofer, and Minzee Kim. 2015. "Abortion Liberalization in World Society, 1960–2009." *American Journal of Sociology* 121(3):882–913.

Centeno, Miguel A., and Joseph N. Cohen. 2010. *Global Capitalism: A Sociological Perspective*. Cambridge: Polity Press.

Chase-Dunn, Christopher, and Peter Grimes. 1995. "World-Systems Analysis." *Annual Review of Sociology* 21:387–417.

Chatterjee, Partha. 1993. *The Nation and its Fragments: Colonial and Postcolonial Histories*. Princeton, NJ: Princeton University Press.

Clark, Rob, and Jason Beckfield. 2009. "A New Trichotomous Measure of World-system Position Using the International Trade Network." *International Journal of Comparative Sociology* 50(1):5–38.

Collins, Patricia Hill. 2015. "Intersectionality's Definitional Dilemmas." *Annual Review of Sociology* 41:1–20.

Colloredo-Mansfeld, Rudi. 2002. "An Ethnography of Neoliberalism: Understanding Competition in Artisan Economies." *Current Anthropology* 43(1):113–37.

Cooper, Frederick. 2014. *Citizenship between Empire and Nation: Remaking France and French Africa, 1945–1960*. Princeton, NJ: Princeton University Press.

Derne, Steve. 2005. "The (Limited) Effect of Cultural Globalization in India: Implications for Culture Theory." *Poetics* 33:33–47.

DiMaggio, Paul. 1987. "Classification in Art." *American Sociological Review* 52(4):440–55.

———. 1997. "Culture and Cognition." *Annual Review of Sociology* 23:263–86.

DiMaggio, Paul, and Walter W. Powell. 1983. "The Iron Cage Revisited: Institutional Isomorphism and Collective Rationality in Organizational Fields." *American Sociological Review* 48(2):147–60.

Elliott, Michael A., and Vaughn Schmutz. 2012. "World Heritage: Constructing a Universal Cultural Order." *Poetics* 40(3):256–77.

Gaggio, Dario. 2011. "Selling Beauty: Tuscany's Rural Landscape since 1945." Pp. 90–113 in *The Cultural Wealth of Nations*, edited by N. Bandelj and F.F. Wherry. Stanford, CA: Stanford University Press.

Giulianotti, Richard, and Roland Robertson. 2004. "The Globalization of Football: A Study in the Glocalization of the 'Serious Life.'" *British Journal of Sociology* 55(4):545–68.

———. 2006. "Glocalization, Globalization, and Migration: The Case of Scottish Football Supporters in North America." *International Sociology* 21(2):171–98.

———. 2007. "Forms of Glocalization: Globalization and the Migration Strategies of Scottish Football Fans in North America." *Sociology* 41(1):133–52.

Go, Julian. 2008. *American Empire and the Politics of Meaning: Elite Political Cultures in the Philippines and Puerto Rico During U.S. Colonialism*. Durham, NC: Duke University Press.

Hausbeck, Kathryn, and Barbara G. Brents. 2010. "McDonaldization of the Sex Industries? The Business of Sex." Pp. 102–18 in *McDonaldization: The Reader*, edited by G. Ritzer. Thousand Oaks, CA: Pine Forge Press.

Held, David, and Anthony McGrew. 2000. *The Global Transformations Reader*. Cambridge: Polity Press.

Held, David, Anthony McGrew, David Goldblatt, and Jonathan Perraton. 1999. *Global Transformations: Politics, Economics, and Culture*. Stanford, CA: Stanford University Press.

Huntington, Samuel P. 1993. "The Clash of Civilizations?" *Foreign Affairs* 72(3):22–49.

———. 1996. *The Clash of Civilizations and the Remaking of World Order*. New York: Simon & Schuster.

———. 2003. "America in the World." *Hedgehog Review* 5(1):7.

———. 2004a. "The Hispanic Challenge." *Foreign Policy* 141:30–45.

———. 2004b. "One Nation, Out of Many: Why 'Americanization' of Newcomers is Still Important." *American Enterprise* 15(6):20–5.

———. 2007. "The Clash of Civilizations Revisited." *New Perspectives Quarterly* 24(1):53–9.

———. 2013. "The Clash of Civilizations Revisited." *New Perspectives Quarterly* 30(4):46–54.

Jijon, Isabel. 2013. "The Glocalization of Time and Space: Soccer and Meaning in Chota Valley, Ecuador." *International Sociology* 28(4):373–90.

Kobayashi, Koji. 2012. "Corporate Nationalism and Glocalization of Nike Advertising in 'Asia': Production and Representation Practices of Cultural Intermediaries." *Sociology of Sport Journal* 29(1):42–61.

Korzeniewicz, Roberto Patricio, and Timothy Moran. 2009. *Unveiling Inequality: A World-Historical Perspective*. New York: Russell Sage Foundation.

Lamont, Michele, and Virág Molnár. 2002. "The Study of Boundaries in the Social Sciences." *Annual Review of Sociology* 28:167–95.

Li, Xue, and Alexander Hicks. 2016. "World Polity Matters: Another Look at the Rise of the Nation-State Across the World, 1816 to 2001." *American Sociological Review* 81(3):596–607.

Mahutga, Matthew C. 2006. "The Persistence of Structural Inequality? A Network Analysis of International Trade, 1965–2000." *Social Forces* 84(4):1863–89.

Marshall, Emily A. 2015. "When do States Respond to Low Fertility?: Contexts of State Concern in Wealthier Countries, 1976–2011." *Social Forces* 93(4): 1541–66.

Matejowsky, Ty. 2007. "SPAM and Fast-Food 'Glocalization' in the Philippines." *Food, Culture & Society* 10(1):24–41.

Meyer, John W., John Boli, George M. Thomas, and Francisco Ramirez. 1997. "World Society and the Nation-State." *American Journal of Sociology* 103(1):144–81.

Omi, Michael, and Howard Winant. [1986] 2015. *Racial Formation in the United States*. 3rd ed. New York: Routledge.

Ramirez, Francisco O., and John Boli. 1987. "The Political Construction of Mass Schooling: European Origins and Worldwide Institutions." *Sociology of Education* 60(1):2–17.

Ramirez, Francisco O., Yasemin Soysal, and Suzanne Shanahan. 1997. "The Changing Logic of Political Citizenship: Cross-National Acquisition of Women's Suffrage Rights, 1890 to 1990." *American Sociological Review* 62(5):735–45.

Randeria, Shalini. 2003. "Glocalization of Law: Environmental Justice, World Bank, NGOs, and the Cunning State in India." *Current Sociology* 51(3/4):305–28.

Reyes, Victoria. 2013. "The Structure of Globalized Travel: A Relational Country-Pair Analysis." *International Journal of Comparative Sociology* 54(2):144–70.

———. 2014. "The Production of Cultural and Natural Wealth: An Examination of World Heritage Sites." *Poetics* 44:42–63.

———. 2015a. "Cultural Wealth of Nations." Pp. 527–30 in *The SAGE Encyclopedia of Economics and Society*, edited by F.F. Wherry and J. Schor. Thousand Oaks, CA: SAGE.

———. 2015b. "Investigating Globalizing Cultures: Its Creation, Structure, and Meanings." Pp. 21–38 in *Globalizing Cultures: Theories and Paradigms Revisited*, edited by V. Mele and M. Vujnovic. Leiden, Netherlands: Brill Academic.

Ritzer, George. 2010. "An Introduction to McDonaldization." Pp. 3–24 in *McDonaldization: The Reader*. 3rd ed., edited by G. Ritzer. Thousand Oaks, CA: Pine Forge Press.

Rivera, Lauren. 2008. "Managing 'Spoiled' National Identity: War, Tourism, and Memory in Croatia." *American Sociological Review* 73(4):613–34.

Robertson, Roland. 1995. "Glocalization: Time-Space and Homogeneity-Heterogeneity." Pp. 25–44 in *Global Modernities*, edited by M. Featherstone, S. Lash, and R. Roberton. London: Sage.

Robinson, Matthew B. 2010. "McDonaldization of America's Police, Courts, and Corrections." Pp. 85–100 in *McDonaldization: The Reader*. 3rd ed., edited by G. Ritzer. Thousand Oaks, CA: Pine Forge Press.

Robinson, Rachel Sullivan. 2015. "Population Policy in Sub-Saharan Africa: A Case of Both Normative and Coercive Ties to the World Polity." *Population Research and Policy Review* 34(2):201–21.

Roudometof, Victor. 2013. "The Glocalizations of Eastern Orthodox Christianity." *European Journal of Social Theory* 16(2):226–45.

Said, Edward. 1993. *Culture and Imperialism*. New York: Vintage Books.

Schofer, Evan. 2003. "The Global Institutionalization of Geological Science, 1800 to 1990." *American Sociological Review* 68(5):730–59.

Shichor, David. 1997. "Three Strikes as a Public Policy: The Convergence of the New Penology and the McDonaldization of Punishment." *Crime & Delinquency* 43(4):470–92.

Shorette, Kristen. 2014. "Nongovernmental Regulation and Construction of Value in Global Markets: The Rise of Fair Trade, 1961–2006." *Sociological Perspectives* 57(4):526–47.

Smith, David A., and Michael F. Timberlake. 2001. "World City Networks and Hierarchies, 1977–1997: An Empirical Analysis of Global Air Travel Links." *American Behavioral Scientist* 44(10):1656–78.

Snyder, David, and Edward L Kick. 1979. "Structural Position in the World System and Economic Growth, 1955–1970: A Multiple Network Analysis of Transnational Interactions." *American Journal of Sociology* 84(5):1096–126.

Steinmetz, George. 2008. "The Colonial State as a Social Field: Ethnographic Capital and Native Policy in the German Overseas Empire before 1914." *American Sociological Review* 73(4):589–612.

———. 2014. "The Sociology of Empires, Colonies, and Postcolonialism." *Annual Review of Sociology* 40:77–103.

Stoler, Ann Laura. 2002. *Carnal Knowledge and Imperial Power: Race and the Intimate in Colonial Rule.* Berkeley: University of California Press.

———. 2006. *Haunted by Empire: Geographies of Intimacy in North American History.* Durham, NC: Duke University Press.

Swidler, Ann. 1986. "Culture in Action: Symbols and Strategies." *American Sociological Review* 51(2):273–86.

Tavory, Iddo, and Ann Swidler. 2009. "Condom Semiotics: Meaning and Condom Use in Rural Malawi." *American Sociological Review* 74(2):171–89.

Taylor, Peter J., Ben Derudder, Cándida Gago García, and Frank Witlox. 2009. "From North-South to 'Global' South? An Investigation of a Changing 'South' Using Airline Flows between Cities, 1970–2005." *Geography Compass* 3(2): 836–55.

Wallerstein, Immanuel. 1990. "Culture as the Ideological Battleground of the Modern World-System." *Theory, Culture and Society* 7(2):31–55.

Wasserman, Stanley, and Katherine Faust. 2009. *Social Network Analysis: Methods and Applications.* Cambridge: Cambridge University Press.

Weber, Max. 1978. *Economy and Society: An Outline of Interpretive Sociology*, edited by G. Roth and C. Wittich. Berkeley: University of California Press.

Wherry, Frederick F. 2007. "Trading Impressions: Evidence from Costa Rica." *ANNALS American Academy of Political and Social Science* 610:217–31.

———. 2008. *Global Markets and Local Crafts: Thailand and Costa Rica Compared.* Baltimore, MD: Johns Hopkins University Press.

Wilkinson, Gary. 2006. "McSchools for McWorld? Mediating Global Pressures with a McDonaldizing Education Policy Response." *Cambridge Journal of Education* 36(1):81–98.

Wimmer, Andreas, and Yuval Feinstein. 2016. "Still No Robust Evidence for World Polity Theory." *American Sociological Review* 81(3):608–15.

Yoo, Eunhye, and Jeong-Woo Koo. 2014. "Love Thy Neighbor: Explaining Asylum Seeking and Hosting, 1982–2008." *International Journal of Comparative Sociology* 55(1):45–72.

Zelizer, Viviana. 2005. *The Purchase of Intimacy.* Princeton, NJ: Princeton University Press.

———. 2011. *Economic Lives: How Culture Shapes the Economy.* Princeton, NJ: Princeton University Press.

58

Cultures, transnationalism, and migration

Michel Wieviorka

Introduction

In popular conceptions of culture relevant to migration, there are two polar opposite approaches. At one pole, culture seems like an essence: it is bequeathed to individuals; they receive it as a legacy; it is reproduced. Culture here comes close to another conceptually vexed term – identity. In the most extreme cases, culture is naturalized. It becomes a fact of nature foundational to both some racist ideologies as well as wider conceptions of ethnicity. People in a host society who perceive migrants from the viewpoint of their own presumed and more or less naturalized cultural identity usually also invoke the dominant culture of their own host society, which is also essentialized.

However, as we will see, migrants – although they may hold on to certain cultural habits and traditions – are also very capable of breaking away to participate in a new life, with novel cultural dimensions. At the other pole, culture thus is regarded as unfolding, a ceaselessly changing mixture, produced, not reproduced. In relation to migration, it mirrors in symbolic terms biological processes of creolization and the mixing of "races." Here, the dominant group in a host society may embrace much more open perceptions of migrants and a generally democratic and progressive conception of culture. For their parts, migrants, because they are increasingly well educated, not surprisingly often engage cultural life as a matter of innovation and creativity, rather than simply one of tradition. Nevertheless, difficult economic conditions, racism, and processes of exclusion and ghettoization may encourage migrants and their descendants to incorporate traditions, even if they are reinvented ones, resulting in what Claude Lévi-Strauss called "bricolage."

Thus, popular ideologies about immigrants and culture (and to some extent, scholarly descriptions of them) counterpose identity, reproduction, traditions, and essence versus race-mixing, production, invention, change. In any actual historical instance, there may be elements that belong to one pole or to the other, and intermediate variants. For research, in contrast to popular ideologies of culture and although these two extremes have some shared theoretical sources, it is not a question of affirming one conception of culture as opposed to another, but of recognizing a considerable diversity of concrete possibilities that may combine within a population, group, or individual. Even a single member of a host society may valorize the culture of certain migrants, regarding it as a source of dynamism for the wider society, and still be concerned, for racist reasons, about the presence of other migrant groups.

The basic terms of debates about culture were shaped, in many respects, in the nineteenth century, but the same is not true for migration, which became an object of serious intellectual focus only in the twentieth century. And since the 1990s, profound changes have been taking place in relation to migration, which is better considered a "notion" rather than an ontological "concept": the same could be applied to culture.

Two classical traditions and what unites them

In the humanities and social sciences, two major traditions have dominated scholarship on migratory phenomena, which were mainly considered from the viewpoint of a receiving society. The issue was therefore one of immigration rather than emigration.

Prior to the 1990s, in the English-speaking world, driven by the Chicago School in the early twentieth century, immigrants were studied in ecological terms and recognized as having specific cultural habits and traditions. But there was also the thesis of the "melting pot," whereby cultural specificities were expected to merge. Although researchers acknowledged cultural specificities of different groups, usually defined by national origin, the main questions concerned whether and how immigrants framed their relationships to American society and adapted to its ethos, while retaining some cultural and religious attributes linked to their origins. In these approaches, it was possible to take an active interest not only in American culture, but also in that of bonds to the country of origin. Thus, in their classical study, *The Polish Peasant in Europe and in America*, published between 1918 and 1920, William I. Thomas and Florian Znaniecki considered assimilation to be desirable. Their sociology is hardly an early forerunner of multiculturalism.

In France, only in the 1980s did research belonging to a second major tradition, which can be called Durkheimian, began to develop. The social sciences in France had long largely ignored migrants because it was presumed that migrants coming in waves from Central Europe and Italy from the end of the nineteenth century, then later from Spain and Portugal, would completely disappear into the nation and society of the French Republic, becoming, in Maurice Chevalier's well-known song lyrics, "excellent French citizens." The canonical French Republican model only recognized French citizens. As a consequence, no cultural or religious specificity could be accepted in the public sphere. There was thus little basis for research on migrants' culture. The priority was to promote assimilation, the capacity of the system to facilitate the dissolution of differences and the absorption of immigrants, to the benefit of the economy and law and order within the Republic and the nation. When research did begin, in the first instance by historians like Gérard Noiriel (1988), it mainly demonstrated that the successive waves of immigrants had until then succeeded in integrating, thanks to the Catholic Church, the trade unions, and some political parties, notably the French Communist Party. This narrative was not very open to the recognition of cultural specificities and research did not focus on migrants themselves, their society of origin, or what the move from one country to another meant for them.

Despite the differences between these two scientific and political traditions – American and French – they were both framed in the host society. To be sure, the Chicago School and more recently theories of segmented assimilation (Portes and Zhou 1993; Waters et al. 2010) demonstrated some interest in cultural hybridization and, to a lesser degree, the subjectivity of the "marginal man" who straddles two cultures, and they did occasionally consider not only the host society but also the society of origin. However, research on immigration in both traditions was dominated by questions of assimilation or integration of migrants, and it was largely undertaken within the framework of what Ulrich Beck (2007) called "methodological nationalism," sometimes supplemented by an interest in international relations. Considering migration almost completely from the viewpoint of the host society, researchers focused on the conditions enabling immigrants to become citizens, with their integration through employment ensuring that sooner or later their specificities would be dissolved in a "melting pot," even if, depending on the political culture of the society in question, differences in language, diet, clothing, and so forth might persist. Such persistences might even extend to accepting the making of minorities into more or less visible social groups, the members of which would have a full role to play in social, civil, and political life, and in the nation and the state.

Some studies, of course, lay outside the mainstream. For example, Philip Mayer (1962) pursued the theme of transnationalism. But most research nevertheless approached migration from the viewpoint of the host country. Very little research started with the migrants themselves, their subjectivity, their itineraries, their hopes, or their desires (Sayad 1991). And there was scant attention to the point of departure, much less the space and time that separate departure from arrival. Migratory flows were reduced to one-way arrivals of workers.

The watershed of the 1990s

Beginning in the 1990s, research agendas fundamentally changed. At the same time, it became obvious that the central public questions about migration had shifted from those of even the recent past. This is not to suggest that there was a direct, immediate, and automatic relation between social and political change and changes in social science research. Nevertheless, whereas before, researchers focused mainly on *immigration* and *immigrants*, more and more researchers began considering *migrations* and *migrants*. An extensive body of literature developed, to a certain extent breaking with previous paradigms.

With the end of the Cold War, in the midst of the "postcolonial" era and globalization, new social scientific orientations emerged. Scholars began to prefer to analyze migratory phenomena holistically, addressing them at an international, even global level, in a way paralleling contemporaneous approaches to economic questions, and occasionally cultural and religious issues. Such an approach – "thinking globally" – means going beyond the traditional framework of the nation-state and international relations. As Ulrich Beck (2016) insists in a posthumous book, it is a question of the "cosmopolitanization" of the world. Even apparently very local questions are now increasingly perceived as also connected to issues such as global risks, terrorism, climate change, and natural disasters, external to a given society.

Given that the weakening of states, institutions, and political systems (whether real or imagined) has widely been regarded as a consequence of globalization, one (only apparently paradoxical) result has been a shift in focus – to the elements that either withstand or confront globalization directly, notably, the individual person or the subject. The result for research is a difficult "balancing act" (Wieviorka 2008): the emergent theoretical framework encompasses a vast space extending from the most intimate, individual processes of subjectivation, desubjectivation, and resubjectivation to the most general and most global processes. As a consequence of this conceptual spanning, research increasingly has given culture its rightful place as a subjective, inventive choice – of both migrants and their descendants, as well as members of a host society.

New categories of thinking about migratory phenomena have therefore moved beyond more traditional approaches, which themselves have changed. At the same time, the study of migration has begun to constitute a field in which the top specialists sometimes feel slightly marginal in relation to the rest of the social sciences (Castles 2010), as if they were not integrated in more general debates. Nevertheless, there has been a considerable increase in empirical knowledge, exemplified by atlases that display varied and complex processes of migrations at the global level (e.g., Wihtol de Wenden and Benoit-Guyaud 2012). Such publications enable us to avoid preconceptions and ethnocentrism. Furthermore, migratory phenomena are increasingly addressed with the aid of ways of thinking in which the cultural dimensions of the experience of migration are widely presented. This is for instance the case in numerous museums and art exhibitions all over the world.

Present-day migration dynamics can best be understood in the context of an overarching "migratory system" (Massey 2003). This approach reveals a paradoxical characteristic of present migratory flows. Migrants usually move in restricted spaces, as is also shown by case studies on the Mediterranean region (Schmoll, Thiollet, and Wihtol de Wenden 2015). Such regionalization is all the more marked as a result of their globalization (Massey 2003).

The current debate on transnationalism

Transnationalism has been gaining attention as a conceptualization since the pioneering work of Basch, Glick-Schiller, Szanton-Blanc (1992), and others, which thematized the intellectual ferment at the time. Research has given a new and broader meaning to the concept of diaspora, while the diasporas themselves have seemed to multiply, constituting, to quote Arjun Appadurai (1996), "imagined communities" that no longer function just at a national level, as Benedict Anderson (1983) showed, but at global level. Stéphane Dufoix's (2012) excellent book demonstrates the many uses of the word diaspora. Gradually it has become clear that migrants have not only a country of departure with which they maintain relations, but also transnational networks, diasporic connections, and "imagined communities" – all linked by shared culture, as clearly stated by Levitt and Schiller (2004), whose notion of a transnational social field has been quite influential in research. Simultaneously, other developments emerged. On one hand, there are initiatives by the migrants and their descendants to create functioning transnational cultural and economic spaces. On the other, a number of host societies have experienced the exacerbation of a differentialist cultural racism coupled with demands for strong national borders.

Functional transnationalism and cultural difference seem to operate at a global level: there are people who feel threatened by them and who can only lay claim to a national identity. The array of developments is complex, and it calls for new directions in research. Increasingly, migrants are analyzed as individuals and as groups and not only as an issue for host societies. They have their own subjectivities, both individual and collective, and their own economic and political agendas beyond the borders of any given country. They transfer funds – for instance, the *remesas* of the Latin Americans living in the United States and Canada; they create associations; and they communicate via networks in order to stay up to date on public and private issues of concern to them. They create small businesses. They facilitate marriages – sometimes "arranged." The Brazilians of Japanese origin who chose to "return" to Japan in the 1970s and 1980s love the samba and football, and they are often more "Brazilian" than people born in Brazil (Perroud 2008). Indians of the diaspora follow the production of Bollywood films. Rap and hip-hop culture in the *banlieues* in France, basically imported from the US, took hold among young people, especially those of North African immigrant origin. Countless migrants and their children participate in cultural activities that are largely mixed, whether in music, dance, the plastic arts, or the theater. This is why it is important to distinguish various types of acculturation, and to discuss the issue of assimilation (Waters et al. 2010). In particular, the concept of "segmented assimilation," which describes various possible outcomes in the process of adaptation of migrants, is today quite relevant.

Migration is an experience that changes people – those who observe it firsthand or in the media, but it is also true for the migrants themselves. In the various countries involved, migration also affects collective realities – culture, the economy, political life, forms of shared commitment, the media, and social networks. And it brings into question rationales about change, both of social life and of the individual.

Cultures in host societies, like cultures in the societies that migrants leave behind and the societies through which they transit, are all subject to change. The diasporas and quasi-diasporas that are developing – Turkish, Chinese, or Moroccan, for example – are not simple agents of reproduction of identities: they are in many respects more like inventions of identity. An extreme case is given by those that have no historical and cultural depth other than that of the recent history of transplanted populations, who have invented a new culture, in particular, a musical one. This is the case of the *Black Atlantic* described by Paul Gilroy in 1993, which is primarily cultural and functions mainly between the United States and the United Kingdom with at its center the English-speaking Caribbean (Jamaica).

Connections forged through migration are hardly new. Migrants in host societies have long been able to support political movements in their countries of origin, while, for their parts, some sending countries have used their migrants for diplomatic purposes. Thus, we have to distinguish between "transnationality" and "transnationalism": it is rather like making a distinction between multicultural realities, and proposals for addressing those realities politically, which are invoked as "multiculturalism." The present interest in a transnational standpoint can enhance our understanding of migratory phenomena not only of today, but also for the past.

Contemporary analyses of migration also address whole sets of nation-states involved and their borders, rather than focusing only on the problems that arise once migrants have arrived in a host society. They also consider the ways in which concepts like those of subject and of subjectivation and desubjectivation bring to light an essential feature of migration: certainly today, and perhaps in the past, people migrate not necessarily to survive but to construct themselves anew as the subjects of their own existence. Some scholars also emphasize the capacity that migrants have to network with each other and with other actors. Thus Dana Diminescu (2012) has studied the ways that "logged in" migrants use their mobile phones and the internet. Here, migrants are once again sources of innovation. They know how to take advantage of new technologies: they use them for empowerment and action against discrimination and racism, or in setting up networks for information, mutual assistance, and solidarity.

Analyzing migration in relation to transnationalism focuses on the links that migrants sustain and even construct toward their countries of origin. It no longer sets the state at the center of analysis, which had tended to deemphasize interstate relations and agreements concerning immigration (Waldinger 2015). Conceptualized in transnational terms, migratory phenomena can involve several countries, suggesting the existence of a transnational civil society, breaking with the classical image of civil society encased within the nation-state. Nevertheless, as Roger Waldinger has strongly insisted since the early 2000s, states intervene, implement public policies on social welfare, employment, and integration, and maintain relations with each other that establish the broad framework for migratory phenomena. At the extreme are the declarations of President Donald Trump concerning the wall that, he asserts, must be built to separate Mexico from the US.

For many migrants, however, orientations are quite different. In relation to their country of origin, the important point of reference is to a village, a region, or a minority culture, and not necessarily to the nation-state. Equally, when they settle in a host society, they often define themselves in local terms, of a district or town. Here, then, is a further invitation to break with any framework privileging the nation-state in defining migrants' points of departure and arrival. In origin, transit, and host societies, we should not underestimate the importance of municipalities and other local entities, especially in relation to reception of migrants, but also for daily life – in employment, consumer behavior, visibility in public space, and so on.

Once the question of migration is no longer restricted to one of integration or assimilation of migrants, the image that emerges is one of a tremendous diversity of cultures. However, today, in many host countries, public discussion becomes a forum for the expression of fears and anxieties, which, on the contrary, evoke standardized, homogeneous images of immigration that then become associated with a posited threat to the cultural unity of the nation, along with its economic efficiency and security.

The diversity of migrations

Migration should not be reduced to any single model. To begin with, it is important to recognize that migrants in any given country do not necessarily want to live there. They may be in transit, and the transit may involve relatively long periods of waiting in a third country. Recent experience in France illustrates this issue. France discovered, to its utter surprise, and perhaps also as a blow to its national ego, that sizeable numbers of migrants from the Middle East did not want to settle there at all: they were seeking to reach the United Kingdom or Scandinavia. Hence the bottleneck in the Pas de Calais region and the subsequent crisis in the small town of Sangatte, near the entrance to the Eurotunnel to the UK: beginning in 1999, migrants found themselves marooned there. France thus began to realize that it is not solely a destination for immigration. Moreover, many French citizens migrate abroad. Approximately 150,000 French citizens are known to the French consulates in Germany and many more in the United Kingdom. This does not include older people who retire in sunnier climes in Morocco or Tunisia. Furthermore, although they may come from North Africa, primarily for reasons of trade, people whom Alain Tarrius (2002) provocatively calls "worker ants" circulate in the thousands across territory that includes France, but can extend from the Maghreb to the Levant or sub-Saharan Africa. These "worker ants" invent their own culture, which is nomadic, with its own codes, its iconic figures, its modes of communication and relations, its ways of life, and its routes, stopovers, and ports of call.

In some situations, the circulation is not of the migrant who crosses the border, but of the border that cuts through the migrant, as Yvon Le Bot (2009) puts it, describing those Mexicans continuously moving back and forth between Mexico and the United States. Here again, there are specific cultural forms: the Spanish language, artistic expressions, creativity, and a capacity for collective action, the latter of which was expressed in significant political demonstrations in the US in February 2006.

Often, for example, in Asia and the Middle East, migrants are recruited for employment. For example, tens of thousands of women from the Philippines work as "Cinderellas" or home helpers in Hong Kong. In some countries in Europe, and in North America, immigrants can no longer be stereotyped as workers recruited on a temporary basis in agriculture, as was the case with the "Braceros" program for Mexican agricultural workers in the United States (1942–1964) or in the 1950s and 1960s with agricultural and factory "immigrant workers" (*travailleurs immigrés*) in France and "guest workers" (*Gastarbeiter*) in Germany. Men who, until then, had been considered uniquely as a source of labor began to settle with their wives and children. They were then perceived in the host society as having become a permanent resident population with their own cultural and religious specificities – one of which in Western Europe is Islam. Broadly speaking, this development is perceived as dangerous by those who make no distinction between Islam as a religion and radical Islamism and terrorism. More generally, as there is now frequently considerable diversity among the migrants settled in a host country, governments are beginning to consider introducing multiculturalist policies, which typically become sources of controversy.

Today, the profile of typical migrants has also changed. They are not only men but also women and children. Their educational level is often high, as Hervé Le Bras (2017) has demonstrated. It is no longer simply a question of peasants who have left the land. Frequently the underlying reasons for migration are multiple and multidirectional – for example, combining the search for a job, studying, and tourism. Migrants typically want to develop their skills and they are capable of cultural innovation. Sometimes migrants are able to move easily from place to place, for example, in Europe if they come from nation-states in the Schengen Common Travel Area. For others, it is much more difficult.

Migrants originating in Central America who wish to enter the US have long known the dangers of the journey and the risks involved in crossing the border between the US and Mexico. We only have to look at the wall running for several miles alongside the road from the airport to the town of Tijuana. Every few yards there is a cross and the name of someone who died trying to get to the US side. More recently, Europe has discovered these possibilities of danger and death. The problem is already very visible in the Mediterranean, with its *pateras* (small flat-bottom boats) and other means of crossing the sea, along with other natural or artificial obstacles – the barbed wire and walls in Ceuta and Melilla, for example. And the situation has become much more complex with the confusion and problems arising from the crises in the Middle East that have resulted in the more or less forced departure of millions of people as a result of war, violence, and insecurity. The Mediterranean is a cemetery: there are said to have been some 300,000 attempts to cross in 15 years, and thousands of deaths every year, estimated at 29,000 between 2000 and 2015. In addition, many emigrants die in the desert as victims of criminals, people smugglers, bandits, and militias. As the social anthropologist Michel Agier (2011) shows, there are walls and obstacles all over the world today and they are becoming increasingly numerous. Migrants live – or die – in camps and in dangerous conditions of transit, and they may end up stranded in detention centers, transit camps, or shantytowns.

Questions about migration have become inseparable from the immense suffering experienced by many refugees, asylum seekers, and exiles. The interconnected but separate developments have become consolidated in public opinion in both the US and Europe as overarching crises in which the classical features of migration combine with terrible human dramas, with intense political consequences, specifically, a division of public opinion, with one side veering to the right, while the other side invokes humanitarian, ethical, and moral values. Thus, even in Germany, despite the firm position of Angela Merkel, there has been an increase in calls for closures of borders and reasserting national sovereignty at the expense of solidarity and humanism. And we should bear in mind that the impact of the migrations associated with the dramas in the Middle East is much less in Europe than in countries in the region itself, especially Lebanon, Jordan, and Turkey.

Although migrants are perceived as a danger by those in receiving societies who resist welcoming them, this danger is only partly considered to be an economic threat to the employment of nationals. It is also and often primarily expressed in cultural and religious terms. European opponents of migration often hold that migrants bring with them cultures and values incompatible with those of the continent's societies and that this incompatibility is absolute.

Culture and migration: a new basis for the research agenda

Migratory phenomena are sufficiently varied to suggest the need for a corresponding variety of public policies, as well as proactive efforts to encourage political discussion. Political stances and policies are produced by actors within their own national frameworks, backed, to various degrees, by populations holding similar opinions. As a result, paradoxically, policies bring the migratory question, which is global, back to the context of the nation-state. The politics yields a revenge of "policy nationalism" akin to Beck's "methodological nationalism," and indeed, the statistical data produced by research is often financed by states. The result is a tension between the social science project of thinking "globally" and distancing itself from methodological nationalism, and, on the other hand, the very national reality of the debates triggered by the research. Thus, Janine Dahinden (2016:2211), who critically exposes "the alliance between scientific research and the state migration apparatus," wonders whether it may be necessary to stop studying "migrations" in order to break with the categories that in effect are imposed by states and their systems of knowledge production. For Dahinden, it would be preferable to employ concepts other than commonsense categories about "migration," for example, by utilizing the conceptualization of mobility suggested by the late John Urry. Thus a concept of "mobile worker" rather than "migrant" can be used to describe a person who has moved within his or her country, or from one country to another, in order to work. Instead of treating borders as obstacles that migrants cross with various degrees of difficulty, should we not consider the way in which borders are produced through the processes which make them symbolic, or material, enabling inclusion or exclusion? Tens of thousands of miles of borders have been transformed all over the world in the past 20 years, by the addition of walls, barbed wire, electronic sensors, and other barriers, increasingly supplemented by all sorts of filters – refusal of entry, imprisonment, prevention of movement of migrants, and camps and other types of detention centers.

Migratory phenomena must henceforth be addressed with the broader tools of the social sciences. For example, here we have discussed culture, globalization, and thinking globally, subjectivation, the difficult balancing act of research, and cosmopolitanization. There is a general tendency in the social sciences to fragment and form thematic subfields, which end up having little communication with one another. As a result, the categories on which specialized knowledge is based are insufficiently critiqued. This tendency is sustained by researchers who are not necessarily interested in participating in general discussions or ones distant from their own expertise. We must refuse both these tendencies, as well as their opposite, merely folding the object of research, "migrations," into the social sciences in general. The more we grapple with migratory phenomena in their diversity and their complexity, the greater the number of new perspectives for specialized research. However, this does not mean that migratory phenomena will be marginalized or dissociated from more general theoretical considerations.

In conclusion

The diversity of migratory phenomena is not only economic, political, or spatial; it is also profoundly cultural. Beyond the countless definitions of culture – a "conceptual jungle" in the words of Kroeber and Kluckhohn (1952), the social sciences clearly have moved far from any form of essentialism and, more generally, from any idea of pure cultural reproduction. The preference has been to analyze the processes through which culture is transformed, produced, and mixed, sketching an image primarily of rationales of *métissage* or creolization. This general approach holds true for migrants. Not only are they increasingly well educated and likely to participate in the cultural innovations and changes that concern them; they are also likely to participate in the societies in which they live or through which they transit. Furthermore, they are always likely to play a part in the important transformation processes ongoing in their countries of origin, or even in their community or village. They send money back, for example the "*remesas*" in Latin America, but they also promote ways of life and elements of modernity, one instance being modern relations between men and women. As a result of the internet and new communication technologies, they are often in ongoing contact with each other, within a diaspora, for example, as they are with their community or with the groups they come from. These days, migratory phenomena are both products of cultural change and producers of cultural change.

References

Agier, Michel. 2011. *Le couloir des exiles. Etre étranger dans un monde commun.* Vulaines sur Seine: Éditions du Croquant.

Anderson, Benedict. 1983. *Imagined Communities: Reflections on the Origin and Spread of Nationalism.* London: Verso.

Appadurai, Arjun. 1996. *Modernity at Large: Cultural Dimensions of Globalization.* Minneapolis: University of Minnesota Press.

Basch, Linda, Nina Glick-Schiller, and Cristina Szanton-Blanc. 1992. *Towards a Transnational Perspective on Migration: Race, Ethnicity, and Nationalism Reconsidered.* New York: Academy of Sciences.

Beck, Ulrich. 2007. "La condition cosmopolite et le piège du nationalisme méthodologique." Pp. 223–36 in *Les Sciences sociales en mutation,* edited by M. Wieviorka. Auxerre, France: Éditions Sciences Humaines.

———. 2016. *The Metamorphosis of the World.* London: Polity Press.

Castles, Stephen. 2010. "Understanding Global Migration: A Social Transformation Perspective." *Journal of Ethnic and Migration Studies* 36(10):1565–86.

Dahinden, Janine. 2016. "A plea for 'de-migranticization' of research on migration and integration." *Ethnic and Racial Studies* 39(13):2207–25.

Diminescu, Dana. 2012. *e-Diasporas Atlas.* Paris: Éditions MSH.

Dufoix, Stéphane. 2012. *La Dispersion. Une histoire des usages du mot diaspora.* Paris: Éditions Amsterdam.

Gilroy, Paul. 1993. *The Black Atlantic: Modernity and Double Consciousness.* Cambridge, MA: Harvard University Press.

Kroeber, Alfred L., and Clyde Kluckhohn. 1952. *Culture, A Critical Review of concepts and Definitions.* New York: Vintage Books.

Le Bot, Yvon. 2009. *La grande révolte indienne.* Paris: Éditions Robert Laffont.

Le Bras, Hervé. 2017. *L'âge des migrations.* Paris: Éditions Autrement.

Levitt, Peggy, and Nina Glick Schiller. 2004. "Conceptualizing Simultaneity: A Transnational Social Field Perspective on Society." *International Migration Review* 38(3): 1002–39.

Massey, Douglas. 2003. "A Synthetic Theory of International Migration." Pp. 143–53 in *Scientific Series: International Migration of Population: Russia and the Contemporary World.* Vol. 10, *World in the Mirror of International Migration,* edited by V. Iontsev. Moscow: Max Press.

Mayer, Philip. 1962. "Migrancy and the Study of African Towns." *American Anthropologist* 64(3):576–92.

Noiriel, Gérard. 1988. *Le creuset français. Histoire de l'immigration (XIXème-XXème siècle).* Paris: Éditions du Seuil.

Perroud, Melanie. 2008. "Retour au Japon: Migrations des Brésiliens d'origine japonaise et invention identitaire." Thèse de Doctorat en Sociologie, EHESS, Paris.

Portes, Alejandro, and Min Zhou. 1993. "The New Second Generation: Segmented Assimilation and its Variants." *Annals of the American Academy of Political and Social Science* 530(1):74–96. https://doi.org/10.1177/0002716293530001006

Sayad, Abdelmalek. 1991. *La double absence. Des illusions de l'émigré aux souffrances de l'immigré.* Paris: Éditions du Seuil.

Schmoll, C., H. Thiollet, and C. Wihtol de Wenden. 2015. *Migrations en Méditerranée.* Paris: CNRS Editions.

Tarrius, Alain. 2002. *La Mondialisation par le bas.* Paris: Éditions Balland.

Waldinger, Roger. 2015. *The Cross-border Connection: Immigrants, Emigrants, and their Homelands.* Cambridge, MA: Harvard University Press.

Waters, Mary C., Van C. Tran, Philip Kasinitz, and John H. Mollenkopf. 2010. "Segmented Assimilation Revisited: Types of Acculturation and Socioeconomic Mobility in Young Adulthood." *Ethnic and Racial Studies* 33(7):1168–93. https://doi.org/10.1080/01419871003624076

Wieviorka, Michel. 2008. *Neuf leçons de sociologie.* Paris: Éditions Robert Laffont.

Wihtol de Wenden, Catherine, and Madeleine Benoit-Guyaud. 2012. *Atlas des migrations: Un équilibre mondial à inventer.* Paris: Éditions Autrement.

59

Migration and cultures

Yến Lê Espiritu

Introduction

US immigration studies have been greatly influenced by the historical production of immigrants as bearers of cultural difference. The dominant theories in the field – theories of assimilation (including segmented assimilation), amalgamation, the "melting pot," and cultural pluralism (or multiculturalism) – all conceptualize the immigrants' "original" culture as fundamentally opposed to white "American" culture. Though describing different outcomes, these immigration theories focus on the degrees of transformations of ethnic consciousness, that is, how much individuals or communities assimilate into American life or retain their community-of-origin ties. The present chapter argues that this conceptualization of cultural identity – as bipolar and linear – promotes a discourse of race in which "cultural difference," defined as innate and abstracted from unresolved histories of racial inequality, is used to explain or explain away historically produced social inequalities. Here, I challenge the very authority and authenticity of the term "cultural identity," asserting instead that culture – or more precisely, culture-making – is a social, historical, and transnational process that exposes multiple and interrelated forms of power relations and that articulates new forms of immigrant subjectivity, collectivity, and practice.

In the American sociology of race relations, Robert Park and the Chicago School of Sociology more generally have been most influential in extending a project of racial knowledge. This project, inaugurated by the science of man and twentieth-century anthropology, explicates the "immigrant problem" as a signifier of cultural difference. Allied with such intellectuals as anthropologist Franz Boas, the Chicago sociologists advocated a cultural rather than a biological definition of race. However, as Henry Yu points out, although University of Chicago sociologists claimed to eliminate biology as a consideration, they merely shifted the importance of the physical body into another realm (2001:46). Because of their strong interest in the massive immigration in the nineteenth and early twentieth centuries, Chicago theorists such as Robert Park linked "cultural differences" with the foreign origins of certain human bodies: where a person came from became an important source of one's cultural consciousness (Yu 2001:47). This mapping of race reinscribes "the 'others of Europe'" as "absolutely different" – and the cultures and geographies from which they come as fundamentally opposed to modern American society (Silva 2007:153; see also Lowe 1996:5). In other words, when Park appropriates the "stranger" as a spatial metaphor to describe "the problem of race relations," he advances a project of knowledge that is "predicated on a definition of the exotic, of what is absolutely foreign and different about one place and another" (Yu 2001:6). This approach effectively incarcerates the immigrants in culture, locking them in bounded, timeless, and unchanging "traditions."

Park's early twentieth-century rewriting of racial difference as a signifier of cultural difference is key here: by linking cultural consciousness not with the physical body but with the body's origins in physical space, Park and his associates literally mapped where "cultural" groups existed in space, fixing their places in the world, vis-à-vis white America (Yu 2001:47). Thus, the perceived origins of one's biological ancestors mattered: "the marginalization of the non-European immigrant is concomitant to the marginalization of the world he or she comes from – a country and culture viewed as alien, backward, poor, and unhappy" (Vassanji 1996:112). To take an example, in the US, Asia and America are viewed as mutually exclusive binaries – based in a primitive and stagnant East versus a modern and mobile West. The Orientalist construction of Asian cultures and geographies as fundamentally antipathetic to modern US society racializes Asian Americans as "perpetual foreigners" – as less American than their White counterparts, even when born in the US (Devos and Ma 2008). In a similar vein, anti-immigrant groups have consistently charged that the influx of unwanted immigrants will transform the United States into a third world nation. This reference to the "third world" must be seen as a strategic marker that "metaphorically alludes to social evolution and the threat of immigration leading to a de-evolution of 'American civilization'" (Chavez 1997:67). It was this tenet of Chicago-school sociology – which posited the intimate connections between race, culture, and space – that profoundly marked many scholars' understanding of the process of immigrant adaptation and incorporation, informing the logic of both the assimilationist and pluralist perspectives.

Park's Americanization cycle – which theorized that two groups coming into contact always undergo a series of social interactions, beginning with competition and ending with assimilation – established an expectation that immigrants would assimilate and integrate into the dominant culture by shedding their "original" culture. Although this interaction cycle described the trajectory of many European immigrants, it could not explain the experiences of people with origins in subjugated "races and cultures," who simultaneously confronted the political pressure to assimilate and the cultural racism that prevented assimilation. By the 1960s, in light of the new social movements that exposed the material histories of racialization, segregation, and economic discrimination, the prescription of assimilation was revised into "multiculturalism," a new liberal vision that publicly affirmed and celebrated the kaleidoscope of cultures in American society. Scholarly research accordingly shifted from documenting assimilation toward explaining the persistence of ethnic cultures, mainly focusing on the continuing importance of ethnicity among white ethnics of European origin (Novak 1973; Cohen 1977). In an influential article on this topic, Herbert Gans (1979) argued that for the middle-class descendants of European immigrants, "symbolic ethnicity" was all that was left. These later-generation white ethnics, Gans argued, abstracted ethnic symbols from the older "original" culture and looked for easy and intermittent ways to express their ethnic identities – ways that did not require rigorous practice of ethnic culture or active participation in ethnic organizations. But the influx of the largely non-European immigrants, precipitated by world upheavals and changes in US immigration law in 1965, raised an important research question: how much can we generalize from the experiences of white European ethnic groups to the experiences of racialized immigrant populations?

The new social movements of the 1960s transformed the academy, ushering in new critical social knowledges. Contesting the depoliticization of culture, critical scholarship rejected assimilation theory but also critiqued multiculturalism theory's aim to treat differences, in the words of Lisa Lowe, as "*cultural* equivalents abstracted from the histories of racial inequality"

(1996:30). According to Lowe, the characterization of the United States as a "polyvocal symphony of cultures" leveled important differences and contradictions within and among racial and ethnic groups, deploying the liberal promise of inclusion to mask the history of exclusion. Providing an instance of this process, Leah Perry has argued that the rise of Latina/o pop culture in the 1990s – heralded as an example of America's commitment to multicultural inclusion and diversity – has the effect of "overlooking and looking over race and gender" (2016:178). In other Western societies, where multiculturalism has been widely endorsed, however incompletely, public discourses similarly define the problem of immigrant integration as a cultural one, thus exempting the dominant society from any responsibility toward the "immigrant problem" (Ossman and Terrio 2006; Roggeband and Verloo 2007). Thus, the multiculturalism model, even as it challenges the inevitability and desirability of assimilation, constitutes ethnic cultures as temporally and geographically distant, much like the assimilation model propagated by Robert Park.

As Vijay Mishra (2012) has pointed out, many advocates of multiculturalism, while endorsing cultural diversity, cast culture as primordial, fixed, and homogeneous, thereby ascribing certain immutable traits to the peoples within these presumed cultural groupings. This conception of culture essentializes difference by assuming that "the link between race and culture is organic, rather than contingent and historical" (Mishra 2012:427). For example, in a case study of Vietnamese American students in New Orleans, Min Zhou and Carl Bankston (1998) argued that the youths' achievement is rooted in their "core cultural values" – a strong work ethic, high regard for education, and family values – that is, in their "difference." Other scholars have critiqued this essentialization of culture – the idea that it is a bounded and internally consensual system into which one is born and integrated – and warned that the exclusive focus on cultural difference obscures the connections between the cultural and the material (Roggeband and Verloo 2007). In a study of the riots waged by frustrated and disenfranchised suburban immigrant youths in France in 2005, Ossman and Terrio (2006) denounced the discourse of cultural essentialism that undergirded public reaction to the rioting youths. They reported that key French institutions – legal, political, social scientific, and media – linked the causes of "immigrant delinquency" to what they identified as the culture of poverty of immigrant neighborhood enclaves. Noting the influence of the Chicago school's cultural-ecology model on this public framing of the riots, Ossman and Terrio (2006) show how Parisian jurists and juvenile judges criminalized the cultural origin of the overwhelmingly poor children and families of non-European ancestry by linking their purported "delinquent" actions to "aberrant cultural norms and dangerous social milieus" (Ossman and Terrio 2006:12). Paris officials thus attributed the "immigrant problem" to the hegemony of people's culture of origin rather than to political and economic forces within the "new country." Ossman and Terrio (2006) argue that by reifying and criminalizing what was perceived to be the culture of these immigrant youth, culturalist policies set the stage for the deportation of immigrants as a new tool for defending the nation from external threats (Ossman and Terrio 2006:14).

Some advocates of multiculturalism also produce gendered discourses and policies that construct patriarchy as particular to immigrant culture. In line with the global crusade for women's rights, ratified by the 1979 Convention on the Elimination of All Forms of Discrimination against Women (CEDAW), scholars and the larger public became preoccupied with "harmful traditions" that allegedly legitimate abuse of women in minority immigrant communities (Silva 2004). In the post-9/11 period, much Western discourse on Islam has represented the "Muslim woman" largely "as a victim of her patriarchal religion" (Ruby 2013:134). For example, in the Netherlands, gender-equality policies have shifted to an almost exclusive focus on migrant Muslim women; and "minority policies" have moved more and more toward gender relations. As Roggeband and Verloo (2007) observe, Dutch official and popular discourses construct patriarchy as a signifier of migrant Muslim culture, which shifts the responsibility for Muslim "failure" to fully integrate in Dutch society to Muslim migrants, and away from the dominant culture and society. Anti-immigration agendas in Britain have also become entangled with public initiatives to protect migrant women. Targeting the Muslim migrant community, the media have focused on four "cultural" issues affecting women: forced marriage, honor killing, female genital cutting, and women's Islamic dress. Dustin and Phillips (2008) contend that media treatment of these issues has been problematic, producing discourses that misrepresent Muslim cultural groups as monolithic and naturally oppressive entities. Thus, efforts that purport to address abuses of migrant women simultaneously promote cultural stereotypes, setting women's rights in false opposition to multiculturalism.

Academic writings on immigrant family and gender relations have also emphasized "an ethnically specific patriarchal culture" that freezes immigrant men as subjects who oppress women (Kang 2002:43–4). For example, literary studies scholars (and the larger public) are fascinated with narratives about young immigrant girls coming to the US and finding liberation. In her assessment of the critical work produced in response to Julia Alvarez's novel *How the Garcia Girls Lost Their Accent*, Sarika Chandra (2008) argues that the book is read almost exclusively so as to emphasize the girls' identity formation and self-assertion against the perceived overbearing and overprotective patriarchal old-world traditions of the Dominican Republic. Chandra argues that the near-exclusive focus on gender politics obscures the novel's engagement with the role that US interventions in the Dominican Republic played in inducing the Garcias and other Dominicans to flee the island in the first place. By conceptualizing intergenerational strain as a product of "cultural clash" between "traditional" immigrant parents and their more "modernized" children born or raised in the US, rather than as a social, historical, and transnational affair, scholars represent the United States as self-evidently less sexist than the "old country" and they thus fail to expose the multiple and interrelated forms of power relations connecting the origin and destination countries. In the same way, in a study on Europe's immigrants and gender egalitarianism, Antje Röder and Peter Mühlau assert that gender attitudes constitute "the main dividing line between Western countries and other world regions" and conclude that as immigrants acculturate, they shed their supposed inegalitarian beliefs and adopt the more egalitarian gender values of their European residency country (2014:899). Relatedly, in a provocative analysis of the cultural politics of US immigration from the 1980s and early 1990s, Leah Perry (2016) concludes that "multicultural" immigrants, even when they were embraced, were simultaneously disciplined through gendered discourses of respectability.

A more dynamic approach to culture conceptualizes cultural identities not as an essence but as a *positioning*: "the names we give to the different ways we are positioned by, and position ourselves within, the narratives of the past" (Hall 1990:225). Employing this approach, I have argued that Filipino immigrants' cultural claims – that Filipino culture is more family oriented and thus morally superior to white American culture – constitute a strategy of resistance against the colonial racial denigration of their culture, community, and women (Espiritu 2003:215). Instead of assuming that these cultural claims perfectly correspond to a bounded and static set of practices imported from the home country into the host society, I underscore the immigrants' ability to maneuver and manipulate meanings within the domain of culture in an effort to counter the alternative assumption of inevitable white American superiority. In the same way, Purkayastha (2005) explains young South Asian women's invocation of their homeland culture – specifically the closeness and sense of mutual obligation of their extended family relationships – as an effort to combat their cultural marginalization in the United States, which is based on cultural stereotypes about arranged marriages and other presumed patriarchal South Asian practices. By stressing what they perceive to be positive South Asian cultural values, these young women manage "to compare their families to that of their peers in ways that *their* families become the norm and those of their peers 'flawed'" (Purkayastha 2005:67). It is true that the immigrants' gendered discourse of moral superiority often leads to patriarchal calls for cultural "authenticity," which locates family honor and national integrity in its female members and renders them emblematic of the community's cultural survival (Espiritu 2003). However, this critique of patriarchal practices differs from the (multi)culturalist stereotyping of immigrant culture in that it positions culture in the shifting terrain of histories, economics, and politics. As this line of research shows, the multiculturalist approach to gender is problematic because it misrepresents "patriarchal culture" as indigenous to immigrant communities, rather than as a constantly negotiated strategy deployed by racialized immigrants to claim through gender the power denied them by racism.

In a related process, as numerous case studies of immigrant cultures demonstrate, many immigrants themselves appear to have internalized a definition of culture that is tied to homeland traditions and represented by a fixed profile of shared traits such as language, ethnic food, and folk songs. However, a more critical examination of these cultural claims indicates that the immigrants' seemingly reified comments about their own culture in fact refer to cultural practices that have been reconstituted and transformed in the host society. If we conceptualize culture not as a series of depoliticized and fixed attributes but as a set of evolving practices constituted within webs of power relations, then the immigrants' cultural claims are less about cultural authenticity and more about strategic self-representation, especially in the context of a hostile host society. For example, Nobue Suzuki (2002) reports that Filipina "mail-order brides" in Japan respond to their dehumanization and eroticization by eagerly showcasing various aspects of "Filipino lifestyles and culture" at local schools and community events, including giving talks on their history, performing arts, and crafts, and displaying their ethnic cuisine and dresses. By showing "the height of their culture," the women strategically tap into the Japanese gendered ideal of housewife and mother, in the hope that the Japanese audience will recognize the "elegance of the Filipinas" and accordingly "reformulate classificatory categories more analogous to their own subjective conceptualizations" (Suzuki 2002:197). In another example, Sunaina Maira reports that in the post-9/11 racial climate of intensified hostility and scrutiny, South Asian Muslim teens in New England dealt with their liminal positions by fashioning everyday identifications with India or Pakistan through the consumption of popular culture found in Bollywood films, South Asian television programs, and Hindi music websites (Maira 2008:708–09). Such longing to be more "authentically" tied to the "original" culture continues to be very powerful for immigrant youth because it is directed, in Frantz Fanon's words, "by the secret hope of discovering beyond the misery of today, beyond self-contempt, resignation and abjuration, some very beautiful and splendid era whose existence rehabilitates us both in regard to ourselves and in regard to others" (Fanon 1963:170). Although these examples appear to confirm a fixed concept of culture, they in fact demonstrate how immigrants deliberately and strategically memorialize and represent the "original" culture as a strategy of resistance to situations and practices in the host country that are patently anti-immigrant.

In the last 25 years, the globalization of labor and capital, the restructuring of world politics, and the expansion of new technologies of communication and transportation all have driven the movement of people and products across the globe at a dizzying pace, thus further invalidating the notion of culture as spatially bounded. Recent writings on the "transnational sociocultural system," "the transnational community," "transmigrants," the "deterritorialized nation-state," and "transnational grassroots politics" have challenged previously conventional notions of *place*, reminding us to think about places not only as specific geographic and physical sites but also as circuits and networks. These writings have contradicted localized and bounded social science conceptualizations of community and culture, calling attention instead to the transnational relations and linkages among overseas communities, and between them and their homeland (Basch, Glick Schiller, and Szanton Blanc 1994; Levitt 2001; Smith 2006). Living between the old and the new, between homes, between languages, and between cultural repertoires, immigrants do not merely insert or incorporate themselves into existing spaces in a given host society; they also transform these spaces and create new ones, for example, the "space between" (Small 1997:193). Transnationalism is thus a valuable concept that can be used to highlight the range and depth of migrants' lived experiences in multinational social fields, thus disrupting the narrow emphasis on cultural assimilation or cultural diversity characteristic of much of the published work in US immigration studies.

A critical transnational perspective also provokes us to be attentive to the global relations that set the context for immigration and immigrant life. As a rhetorical trope, multiculturalism, with its focus on culturalist identity politics, obscures the role of the US and other receiving countries in producing phenomena of immigration. Because the framework of multiculturalism is "subordinated to and divorced from the historical and socioeconomic conditions of (im)migration" (Chandra 2008:847), it cannot take into account the way that a long and continuing history of US imperialism shapes processes of migration, racialization, and marginality. Consider as a case in point the relationship of the Philippines and the United States, the origins of which lie in a history of conquest, occupation, and exploitation. A study of Filipino immigrant culture must begin with this history, and not with US domestic multicultural identity issues. Coming from a former US colony, Filipinos have long been exposed to US lifestyles, cultural practices, and consumption patterns, so much so that before "the Filipino . . . sets foot on the U.S. continent – she, her body, and sensibility – has been prepared by the thoroughly Americanized culture of the homeland" (San Juan 1991:118). With the imposition of English as the language of education in the Philippines came a flood that reached all Filipinos of US printed materials and mass media – textbooks, novels, news services, magazines, music, and especially movies. These cultural products infected Filipinos with American norms, standards, ideals, values, and viewpoints (Espiritu 2003:72–3). Thus, in a critically acclaimed 1990 novel, *Dogeaters*, Jessica Hagedorn portrays neocolonial Manila, from about 1956 to 1985, as a world in which American popular culture and local Filipino tradition mix flamboyantly. In other words, Filipino culture is always already transnational, thus eliding easy localization.

By the opposite token, Amy Kaplan (1993) reminds us that US imperialism contributes not only to the cultural Americanization of the colonized "other" but also to the consolidation of a dominant imperial culture at home. George Lipsitz has made a similar point: US armed conflicts against "enemies" in Asia "functioned culturally to solidify and reinforce a unified U.S. national identity based in part on antagonism toward Asia and Asians" (1998:70–2). These studies suggest that we need to examine migration and cultures not only for what they tell us about the integration of immigrants but more so for what they say about the racialized economic, cultural, and political foundations of the US. In other words, migrant cultures and US national culture(s) are mutually constituted. By situating US national culture within a globalist framework, scholars call attention to the deep entanglement of the domestic and the foreign, and thus to how both US national and immigrant cultures are shaping and being shaped by intersecting social and historical relationships. This scholarship suggests that a critical transnational perspective is not just a methodological approach; it is fundamentally a theoretical orientation. That is, a critical transnational perspective is not necessarily or only about doing multisited projects; it is more about linking the study of culture and immigration inextricably to the study of empire, even when the research focus is on the domestic front.

In an influential work on Asian American cultural politics, Lisa Lowe (1996) urges her readers to consider the role that critical cultural works play in exposing the racialized foundations of the nation. Calling attention to the importance of critical remembering, Lowe has argued a position also articulated by others, that "culture is a . . . mediation of history, the site through which the past returns and is remembered, however fragmented, imperfect, or disavowed" (1996:x). For participants in racialized immigrant communities who have had to struggle for access to means of representation, she notes, "the question of aesthetic representation is always also a debate about political representation" (Lowe 1996:4). As Elaine Kim (2003) suggests, many Asian American artists are committed to a cultural politics that challenges, resists, and hopes to transform US nationalized memory and culture. For instance, in recent years, Vietnamese American artists have begun to grapple with the war's disastrous consequences for Vietnam and its people, giving rise to oft-haunting artistic and cultural representations imagining, remembering, and tracing the complex genealogies of war and forced displacements that preceded and shaped Vietnamese resettlement in the United States (Espiritu 2010).

For the most part, migration to the United States "has been the product of specific economic, colonial, political, military, and/or ideological ties between the United States and other countries . . . as well as of war" (Ngai 2004:10). And yet, much of the published work in the field of immigration studies has not situated US immigration history within a transnational or global framework, opting instead to focus on the immigrants' integration into the nation. The latter framework, focused on "modes of incorporation," assesses the assimilability of immigrants but leaves uninterrogated the racialized and gendered foundations of the US. In this chapter, I have argued that the scholarly focus on immigrants' integration – and the concomitant failure to connect US foreign interventions with US-bound migration – stems from the historical production of the immigrants as bearers of cultural difference. Today, many immigration studies scholars continue to invoke "cultural difference" to individualize and explain (away) immigrants' perceived "lacks," thereby eliding the role that "U.S. world power has played in the global structures of migration" (Ngai 2004:11). In other words, the essentializing and liberal tendencies of multiculturalism obscure the continuation of racial violence, both physical and symbolic, in the United States and globally. At this moment of reinvigorated US imperialism and soaring immigration to the US, it is imperative that immigration studies scholars recognize and analyze the intimate connection between US foreign interventions and migration to the United States, in order to be mindful of what Amy Kaplan (2003) calls the "entanglement of the domestic and the foreign." To do so, we first need to link culture to history, economics, and politics in order to better scrutinize the United States as a historical entity with policies that play a key role in producing (im)migration.

References

Basch, Linda, Nina Glick Schiller, and Cristina Szanton Blanc. 1994. *Nations Unbound: Transnational Projects, Postcolonial Predicaments, and Deterritorialized Nation-States*. Langhorn, PA: Gordon and Breach.

Chandra, Sarika. 2008. "Re-Producing a Nationalist Literature in the Age of Globalization: Reading (Im)migration in Julia Alvarez's *How the Garcia Girls Lost Their Accents*." *American Quarterly* 60(3):829–50.

Chavez, Leo R. 1997. "Immigration Reform and Nativism: The Nationalist Response to the Transnational Challenge." Pp. 61–77 in *Immigrants Out! The New Nativism and the Anti-Immigrant Impulse in the United States*, edited by J.F. Perea. New York: New York University Press.

Cohen, Steven M. 1977. "Socioeconomic Determinants of Intraethnic Marriage and Friendship." *Social Forces* 55(4):997–1010.

Devos, Thierry, and Debbie S. Ma. 2008. "Is Kate Winslet More American Than Lucy Liu? The Impact of Construal Processes on the Implicit Ascription of a National Identity." *British Journal of Social Psychology* 47(2):191–215.

Espiritu, Yen Le. 2003. *Home Bound: Filipino American Lives across Cultures, Communities, and Countries*. Berkeley: University of California Press.

———. 2010. "Negotiating Memories of War: Arts in Vietnamese American Communities." Pp. 316–42 in *Art in the Lives of Immigrant Communities in the U.S.*, edited by P. DiMaggio and P. Fernandez-Kelly. New York: Rutgers University Press.

Dustin, Moira, and Anne Phillips. 2008. "Whose Agenda Is It?: Abuses of Women and Abuses of 'Culture' in Britain." *Ethnicities* 8(3):405–24.

Fanon, Frantz. 1963. *The Wretched of the Earth.* New York: Grove Press.

Gans, Herbert. 1979. "Symbolic Ethnicity: The Future of Ethnic Groups and Cultures in America." *Ethnic and Racial Studies* 2(1):1–20.

Hagedorn, Jessica. 1990. *Dogeaters.* New York: Penguin.

Hall, Stuart. 1990. "Cultural Identity and Diaspora." Pp. 222–37 in *Identity, Community, Culture, Difference*, edited by J. Rutherford. London: Lawrence and Wishart.

Kang, Laura Hyun Yi. 2002. *Compositional Subjects: Enfiguring Asian/American Women.* Durham, NC: Duke University Press.

Kaplan, Amy. 1993. "'Left Alone with America': The Absence of Empire in the Study of American Culture." Pp. 3–21 in *Cultures of United States Imperialism*, edited by A. Kaplan and D.E. Pease. Durham, NC: Duke University Press.

———. 2003. *The Anarchy of Empire in the Making of U.S. Culture.* Cambridge, MA: Harvard University Press.

Kim, Elaine H. 2003. "Introduction: Interstitial Subjects – Asian American Visual Art as a Site for New Cultural Conversations." Pp. 1–50 in *Fresh Talk, Daring Gazes: Conversations on Asian American Art*, edited by E. Kim, M. Machida, and S. Mizota. Berkeley: University of California Press.

Levitt, Peggy. 2001. *The Transnational Villagers.* Berkeley: University of California Press.

Lipsitz, George. 1998. *The Possessive Investment in Whiteness: How White People Profit from Identity Politics.* Philadelphia, PA: Temple University Press.

Lowe, Lisa. 1996. *Immigrant Acts: On Asian American Cultural Politics.* Durham, NC: Duke University Press.

Maira, Sunaina. 2008. "Flexible Citizenship/Flexible Empire: South Asian Muslim Youth in Post-9/11 America." *American Quarterly* 60(3):697–720.

Mishra, Vijay. 2012. *What Was Multiculturalism?: A Critical Retrospective.* Carlton, VIC: Melbourne University Press.

Ngai, Mae. 2004. *Impossible Subjects: Illegal Aliens and the Making of Modern America.* Princeton, NJ: Princeton University Press.

Novak, Michael. 1973. *The Rise of Unmeltable Ethnics: Politics and Culture in the Seventies.* New York: Macmillan Co.

Ossman, Susan, and Susan Terrio. 2006. "The French Riots: Questioning Spaces of Surveillance and Sovereignty." *International Migration* 44(2):5–19.

Perry, Leah. 2016. *The Cultural Politics of U.S. Immigration: Gender, Race, and Media.* New York: New York University Press.

Purkayastha, Bandana. 2005. *Negotiating Ethnicity: Second-Generation South Asian Americans Traverse a Transnational World.* New Brunswick, NJ: Rutgers University Press.

Röder, Antje, and Peter Mühlau. 2014. "Are They Acculturating?: Europe's Immigrants and Gender Egalitarianism." *Social Forces* 92(3):899–928.

Roggeband, Conny, and Mieke Verloo. 2007. "Dutch Women Are Liberated, Migrant Women Are a Problem: The Evolution of Policy Frames on Gender and Migration in the Netherlands, 1995–2005." *Social Policy & Administration* 41(3):271–88.

Ruby, Tabassum Fahim. 2013. "The Question of Muslim Women's Rights and the Ontario Shari'ah Tribunals: Examining Liberal Claims." *Frontiers: A Journal of Women Studies* 34(2):134–54.

San Juan, E. Jr. 1991. "Mapping the Boundaries: The Filipino Writer in the U.S." *Journal of Ethnic Studies* 19(1):117–31.

Silva, Denise Ferreira da. 2004. "Mapping Territories of Legality: An Exploratory Cartography of Black Female Subjects." Pp. 203–22 in *Critical Beings: Race, Nation, and the Global Subject* edited by P. Truitt and P. Fitzpatrick. Aldershot, UK: Ashgate.

———. 2007. *Toward a Global Idea of Race.* Minneapolis: University of Minnesota Press.

Small, Cathy. 1997. *Voyages: From Tongan Villages to American Suburbs*. Ithaca, NY: Cornell University Press.

Smith, Robert Courtney. 2006. *Mexican New York: Transnational Lives of New Immigrants*. Berkeley: University of California Press.

Suzuki, Nobue. 2002. "Women Imagined, Women Imaging: Re/presentation of Filipinas in Japan since the 1980s." Pp. 176–206 in *Filipinos in Global Migrations: At Home in the World?*, edited by F. V. Aguilar Jr. Quezon City: Philippine Migration Research Network and Philippine Social Science Council.

Vassanji, M.G. 1996. "Life at the Margins: In the Thick of Multiplicity." Pp. 111–20 in *Between the Lines: South Asians and Postcoloniality*, edited by D. Bahri and M. Vasudeva. Philadelphia, PA: Temple University Press.

Yu, Henry. 2001. *Thinking Orientals*. New York: Oxford University Press.

Zhou, Min, and Carl K. Bankston III. 1998. *Growing Up American: How Vietnamese Children Adapt to Life in the United States*. New York: Russell Sage.

60

Globalization and cultural production

Denise D. Bielby

Introduction

Among the many transformations in the world economy during the last quarter century is the expanded trans-nationalization of cultural production. In 2015, the United States earned USD 31,529 billion in revenue from filmed entertainment (Statista 2016), and as a singular measure this figure is but one small indicator of how the robust production and distribution of cultural products that include film, radio, television, books, music, and other forms of media now constitute an overwhelmingly vibrant global economic sector. Although world markets are not new, what has changed is the rapid acceleration of the globalizing world economy, and, in particular, the organizational arrangements that underlie it. As organizations have become increasingly transnational in scope, industrial arrangements of production and distribution have become more complex. Social theorists (Weber [1921] 1978) recognized that globalization of industrial forms would be the end point of modernity, itself the outgrowth of scientific technology and industrial production that has yielded a world of economic markets, legal settings, and political organizations in which social institutions operate under rational organization principles. In the study of these arrangements, however, organization scholars found that when firms expand into less familiar cultural locales, they are often confronted with ambiguous marketplaces and no clear route to success – requiring firms to reconceptualize how their market is structured along lines of, for example, competitive strategies (Fligstein 1996), labor relations (Dobbin et al. 1993), and organization boundaries (Davis, Diekmann, and Tinsley 1994) in order to augment familiar institutional strategies for action. Strategic corporate leaders play a pivotal role in the process (Fligstein 2001), as do trust and reputation (Kollock 1994).

According to neo-institutionalists, the global spread of organizational forms leads to growing interdependencies among countries, with social institutions eventually resembling one another through worldwide adoption of shared cultural understandings of economic and legal systems. These claims pertain to some extent to the production of cultural products in a global context, but their applicability is less straightforward. As global theorists have observed, incorporating the concept of culture, "the signifying system through which necessarily (among other means) a social order is communicated, reproduced, experienced, and explored" (Williams 1981:13), into understanding societal, national, or organizational levels of development is complicated by the many ways in which culture itself is understood as a focus of study. Britain's 2016 Brexit referendum to exit the European Union notwithstanding, concepts such as national identity and national culture, for example, are no longer regarded as unitary, and likely never could be. Despite the fact that cultural products are circulated by powerful corporations, the symbolic creativity they organize, produce, and distribute is not immune from the inequalities of class, gender, and ethnicity present in the industries of contemporary capitalist societies; in addition, cultural products are increasingly significant sources of wealth and employment in many economies.

Because cultural production as an industrial system encompasses "outputs [that] are marked by high levels of aesthetic and semiotic content in relation to their purely practical uses" (Scott 2000:2), and symbolic content plays an increasingly important role in how countries, nations, regions, and cultures interconnect on organizational levels, this chapter addresses what sociologists understand about globalization and cultural production, that is, the transnational institutional arrangements that are associated with creation or execution, reproduction, circulation, and exhibition of cultural products. I focus especially on meso-level analyses of cultural production because of their ability to reveal the mechanisms by which culture shapes and is shaped by structural forces and local action.

Studying globalization and cultural production

The political-economic perspective is perhaps the best known scholarly approach to understanding how global cultural production is embedded in economic systems that are interrelated with political, social, and cultural life. Insights by scholars who assume an overtly critical stance about the consequences of these interconnections have tended to dominate this approach to the field, especially in the study of media. A perhaps unintended consequence of an overtly critical perspective is that it can encumber empirical approaches to the study of cultural production at the global level (Scott 2005). This is because, as Hesmondhalgh and Saha (2013:188) note,

> some versions fail to recognize the ambivalence and complexity of popular culture and are little interested in a historical understanding of the development of cultural production . . . or in the highly varied forms that cultural production might take in different societies and among different cultures within those societies.

Scholarship focused on national industries, especially in the US, Europe, Canada, Latin America, and Australia, tends to avoid these pitfalls, offering keen insights about the organizations and markets associated with cultural industries and about the creative labor of art worlds contributing to cultural production at the global level. Yet this approach raises problems, too; in aiming to contextualize the contribution of creative workers adequately, it obscures the ways in which the work of cultural industries intersects with issues of power and structure, including matters of race and ethnicity. Taking these varied considerations into account, at this juncture the field of globalization and cultural production can be characterized as a composite of scholarship that on the one hand consists of grounded empirical work, usually at the national level but increasingly transnational in scope, whose implications for understanding the political-economic contexts of globalization and cultural production are undertheorized, and on the other hand relies upon top-heavy conceptual perspectives that overtheorize the hegemony of cultural industries in a world economy (see Guillen 2001).

Alternatively, scholars in the US, Australia, and Europe, especially those who study the television, film, and music industries, have been calling for middle-range theoretical approaches

(Merton 1949) that bridge this divide by targeting meso-level conceptualization, evidence, and analysis (Bielby and Moloney 2008). This intermediate approach emphasizes the importance of grounded analysis of institutional logics – the cultural determinants of organizational decisions (Douglas 1986), alongside production logics – the social contexts and historical contingencies that shape markets and mediate the effect of concentration and competition on product homogeneity (Blyler and Dowd 2002). Analysis of institutional logics focuses on, for example, which organizational issues and problems stakeholders attend to in order to survive, or what answers and solutions are available or deemed appropriate (Thornton 2004), such as governance regimes that delineate legal obligations and prerogatives (Christopherson 2008), while examination of production logics considers, for example, how new technologies transform markets and how successful strategies toward technology (rather than the technologies themselves) are what prompt market changes (Dowd 2002). An obvious recent case is how the television format revolution (Chalaby 2012) and emergence of over-the-top distribution systems (Steemers 2014) have transformed the global television industry.

Although studying institutional and production logics of markets as such is important, it is also necessary to bring evidence of organizational, institutional, or economic issues into cultural explanations to better understand the mechanisms by which such logics operate. Scholars seeking a middle ground, where matters such as technological development are placed alongside aspects of the political economy rather than subordinated to it, have begun incorporating cultural concerns into traditional organizational and institutional analysis (Friedland and Mohr 2004). Granovetter's (1985) seminal insight, that market action is influenced by its embeddedness in a web of networked social roles and relations, was important to launching this line of thinking. Biggart and Beamish (2003) extended Granovetter's insights, arguing that it is also necessary for the study of market arrangements to focus on how institutional and organizational structures, practices, customs, and modes of operation in market contexts are themselves socially and culturally constructed – an approach that redirects attention to the agency of institutional actors in marketplaces and the factors that account for their actions. Scholarship on the sociology of markets and the sociology of consumption that examines exchange relationships between buyers and sellers attends to the types of products appropriate for exchange, the cultural meaning behind products, the relative power of actors over the supply and demand of what is being exchanged and their relative dependence on it, and the ever-important matter of trust (Dauter and Fligstein 2007). In sum, a shift to a middle-range theoretical approach to global cultural production invites a different set of questions, ones that advance an empirically grounded understanding of the mechanisms and dynamics as well as the structures that constitute the vibrant economic sector of global cultural production.

Culture industries

More than four decades ago, organizational sociologist Paul Hirsch ([1972] 1991) identified the distinctive characteristics of the organizations that make up cultural-products industries. Today, understanding the social organization and dynamics of the creative worlds in which cultural production takes place is crucial to achieving a more nuanced and empirically informed approach to the study of global cultural production. Cultural products are shared significance embodied in form (Griswold 2013), meaning that they are expressive in nature and may be transcendent in effect. Hirsch himself described them as embodying live, one-of-a-kind performances and/or containing a unique set of ideas (Hirsch [1972] 1991). Such products originate from art worlds (Becker 1982), which are themselves organized around shared understandings among artists and their associates about materials, performance, expertise, criteria for evaluation, quality of production, and so forth. Thus, the properties of cultural products, unlike those for strictly utilitarian use, encompass aesthetic or expressive functions. Consequently, cultural products flow in and out of fashion due to changing tastes, preferences, and patronage of consumers, creating unpredictable cycles of demand and tremendous business uncertainty. Although Hirsch's particular focus at the time was national-level industries, his insights are just as relevant to those at the level of global cultural production.

As symbolic forms that connote, suggest, or imply expressive elements that may be appropriated for the creation of social meanings, cultural products not only face demand uncertainty, their innovation can be uncertain as well. This added dynamic has implications for understanding cultural production at the level of the organization, whether it occurs at the global or the local level: the oversight of artistic origination, creation, and production is difficult to regulate bureaucratically because it relies upon intangible expertise – a situation akin to craft administration (Stinchcombe 1959), where the quality of the work cannot be unambiguously evaluated based on technical and measurable features of the finished product. Instead, the quality of the work and the competence of its creator are evaluated post hoc based on the acceptance and success of the work within the marketplace – an arrangement that significantly complicates the implementation of the rational bureaucratic organizational form and its control over the creative labor of employees.

The production-of-culture perspective, which is the prevailing conceptual approach to studying contexts of production (Peterson and Anand 2004), points to the importance of the effect of market structure (Dowd 2004a), embeddedness of organizations (Dowd 2004b), industry transformation (Jones and Thornton 2005), and classification of cultural industries (Janssen, Kuipers, and Verboord 2008) as central determinants of product range and diversity. Although this perspective has been widely adopted for the study of national industries and contexts, it has yet to be extensively applied to analyses of cultural production at the global level even as there is increased recognition of its existence (Wasko and Erickson 2008). In particular, there is a need to study the cultural spaces of creative labor, especially how access to collaborative arrangements is formulated and interacts with the conduct of day-to-day work practices (McRobbie 2004; Baker and Hesmondhalgh 2011).

In describing just how uncertain the demand for cultural products is, Hirsch ([1972] 1991) highlights the complexity of organizational control over the process of distribution. Manufacturers overproduce and from that abundance selectively sponsor large-scale promotion of new items in order to surmount the uncertainty of the market, an aspect of culture industry systems that necessitates specialized, labor-intensive approaches to product dissemination. Other scholars expand on this insight in specifically cultural ways. Because cultural products are symbolic and expressive, and their complex aesthetic properties resonate differently in different contexts, their marketing is based upon establishing meaningful social relationships that utilize personalized or charismatic strategies (Biggart 1989), which are more effective at revealing the potential personal utility (i.e., the pleasure, transcendence, or resonance) of such products (Hirschman 1983). However, as particularistic transactions, they introduce vast interorganizational complexities into the mix. They go beyond mere interconnections and interdependences among firms and individuals in key roles and the actions they take at the "input" and "output" boundaries of organizations (Hirsch 2000).

Observing such interorganizational dependencies associated with distribution of cultural products, especially at the global level, can be a challenge because they may include activity that is not readily visible to outside observers. This might encompass, for example, intra-organizational product modification following manufacturing – which can fundamentally transform a product from its original form to another for use in other locales (Bielby and Harrington 2008) – or complicated co-production agreements between firms from different countries. Such arrangements are intended to reduce uncertainty by anticipating the tastes of consumers in different nations, but they still can fail miserably (see Hubka 2002). Conglomerates may modify product repertoires for different locales, but ever shifting tastes may overtake the market, circumventing well-developed corporate strategies altogether. In short, although enterprising producers and distributors of cultural products can come to dominate a nation, global region, or even the global market itself, cultural production and dissemination do not occur in an unfettered way. Although these complexities in cultural production were not directly anticipated in Hirsch's seminal contribution, his work continues to make possible keen insights about the organization of cultural industries.

Consideration of further constraints to cultural production adds yet another layer to the conceptual and empirical complexities that a middle-range theoretical approach can bring to the field. Peterson (1982) pointed out that cultural production at the national level is constrained by at least five factors: law, technology, market, organizational structure, and occupational careers. By identifying these hurdles, Peterson explicitly intended to problematize the production-of-culture perspective, organizational analysis, and institutional or economic perspectives, which do not always recognize such limits or constraints as central to the analysis of production in cultural industries. Important work by others adds factors to Peterson's list, a pivotal one being cultural policy per se (Crane 2002). As the location where social power writ large is brought into the mix of global cultural production, cultural policy is the site where national interests are developed and enacted as formal instruments to facilitate cultural standing and to protect cultural authority within and across national borders or regions. In arguing for its inclusion when studying globalization and cultural production, Crane (2002) identifies three observable strategies or lines of action available to national governments, urban governments, and cultural organizations for preserving, protecting, and enhancing their cultural resources on the international level – protecting the country's culture, creating and maintaining images, and developing and protecting international markets and venues.

Crane's suggestions are important when considering the study of globalization and cultural production because nations vary in the degree to which they subscribe to a cultural policy – if one even exists. The US, for example, offers minimal oversight of forms of high culture, whereas other nations such as France are vigorous in protecting encroachment upon their national cultural identity. Several international policy agencies predominate in the cultural production arena, each with its own membership and agenda: the European Union (EU), North American Free Trade Association (NAFTA), Mercado Commun del Sur (MERCOSUR), Association of Southeast Asian Nations (ASEAN), General Agreement on Tariffs and Trade (GATT), World Trade Organization (WTO), and General Agreement on Trade in Services (GATS). All were created to encourage free (or freer) trade between member countries but also in some instances to set quotas on export of content to forestall overwhelming one nation or a set of nations. How such associations foster trade that creates advantages for wealthier nation-members is an empirical question (Baker 2016). These organizations notwithstanding, there are other less formal but equally concerted strategies within nations that are intended to manage cultural products at the local level. These, according to Crane (2002), include the process of culturally "reframing" aspects of specific national urban and historic sites so that they are more (or less) accessible to non-locals. Such strategies can blunt national efforts to maintain a balance between local and global exposure (Tinic 2006).

Commodity chains and regionalism

Work by cultural geographers holds promise for advancing middle-range sociological approaches to globalization and cultural production. To some, global production occurs through seemingly straightforward ties between manufacture and distribution – so-called commodity chains, which are the networks of labor, production, trade, and service activities that yield commodities (Hopkins and Wallerstein 1986:159). Transnational chains array components of the production process across the world economy by relying upon key nodes of operation in different locations in the production process (Gereffi 1992:94). Within the chain structure, business transactions and intra-firm transfers contribute or "add" the value that moves production along to conclusion.

Although the metaphor of a chain structure is useful for conceptualizing how elements of cultural production flow across borders, it is really just a starting point because of the vastly more complicated nature of cultural products with complex aesthetic properties. Especially for geographers whose focus is the industries of television and film, basic concepts such as commodity chains are supplanted by the importance of geographic regions to sustaining synergies among workers with the creative skills necessary for the creation, production, and distribution activities that make up cultural industries. As sites of economic activity, geographic regions shape how development (the process of building and rearranging economic resources in the interest of enhanced productivity) and growth (the expression of that enhancement in terms of increments to gross product) actually occur (Scott 2002). Because of the interconnections among creative workers in art worlds, regional economies exhibit "efficiency promoting properties" among transactions at the local level, and particularly successful regions can effectively "push" national development and growth because of their strong network structure of production, technology systems, local labor markets, and regional business culture (Storper 1997). Hollywood is a particularly successful example of regional agglomeration, as is France's film industry, Latin America's telenovela production, and India's Bollywood. The concept of agglomeration – the concentration of capital and labor comprising modern production systems – is crucial here. According to Scott, the synergy of agglomeration – coupled with strong industry marketing and distribution capabilities sustained by the influx of capital and labor to magnet-like metropolises such as Milan, Vancouver, Paris, Miami, or Hong Kong – is what accounts for a region's unshakable competitive advantage despite an increasingly dispersed, polycentric global media commodity chain and strong national and regional industries elsewhere around the globe (Scott 2004). In short, the concept of regional agglomerations of cultural production offers considerable explanatory power for understanding globalization and cultural production in the absence of a culture industry's ability to bureaucratically mange creative labor or control the conventions that organize and sustain art worlds where creative production takes place.

At the same time, there is evidence of a counterbalancing effect of cultural and political policies upon local, regional, and national economies. Scott acknowledges these factors as relevant but secondary to his emphasis on the concept of agglomeration as a fundamental explanation for the strength of regional production centers. The work of Michael Curtin (2005) speaks to this unresolved matter. Curtin (2005) studied how the institutional logics of politics, market, and cultural production and distribution in China thwarted Rupert Murdoch's attempt to completely penetrate that country with his STAR satellite system of television distribution. In spite of Hong Kong's unquestionable influence as a regional center of cultural production – a robustness that is due to its unique position at the periphery of China and its strong links to the West, primarily Europe – China's openness to Hong Kong's influence did not extend to an acceptance of STAR's organizational mechanisms (its business strategy for growth, expansion, and development), which were fundamentally disrupted by China's culturally distinct expectation that the market be subordinate to political institutions and ideologies. In this instance, Western conventions about the interconnections between the market and corporate growth were not shared because the cultural assumptions underlying transnational co-orientation were absent, miscommunicated, out of reach, unknown, or unattainable. In short, the business plan could not proceed as Murdoch intended because it ran counter to China's practice of subordinating the business of its economy to government interests. Another example that involves STAR's presence in South Asia entails – unlike in China – its successful entry into the vast television market of India (McMillan 2003). Ironically, here the *absence* of strict government oversight of violations to television production regulations unexpectedly enabled local private television companies and cable operators to grow and consolidate into strong regional networks that successfully compete with and, to some extent, displace the STAR's penetration. Further work that systematically examines the conditions under which cultural and political policies counterbalance or undermine altogether the synergies of agglomeration is clearly necessary.

Conclusion

The study of globalization and cultural production is ready for a focused theoretical integration. Such a project will necessarily bring evidence of organizational, institutional, or economic issues into cultural explanations, consistent with the "cultural turn" in sociology. Studies of organizations and institutions ably document the forms and structure of conglomerates and consolidation, but it is those who study the structure of markets and the cultural specificities that affect them who often come closest to conceptually engaging what is pertinent to theoretical integration – particularly when they go beyond strictly national-level interests. Such efforts frequently entail reading across disciplinary boundaries. Although media scholars may be inclined to focus on topics such as industry concentration in the context of globalization and cultural production, they often overlook the importance of markets and institutional organization.

Empirical study of the impact of cultural policy on globalization and cultural production is crucial to advancing theoretical integration, but it remains to be seen how useful the valorization of the local-global dichotomy and attention to top-down effects of media institutions can be in moving the field forward. Moreover, in order to more effectively address the connections between globalization, cultural production, and political economy, scholars will need to reconsider Western assumptions that saturate thinking about modern organizational forms in light of challenges by ideological nationalism, differences in business relationships – such as Asian expectations that they be based on personal networks and relations of mutual obligation (*guanxi*) – and political cultures that foreground policy over institutional mandates (Appelbaum, Felstiner, and Gessner 2001).

With a revised agenda in mind, Hesmondhalgh (2013:64–117) offers several useful questions to guide our thinking as the field of globalization and cultural production develops. To what extent, he asks, have the cultural industries become increasingly important in national economies and local business? What are the implications of the further commodification of culture? What are the effects of the growth in size and power of cultural industry corporations on both cultural production and the wider society? To what extent have the dynamics of cultural production's distinctive organizational form – a combination of loose control of creative input and tighter control of reproduction and circulation – changed since the foundational work on creative labor conducted in the 1970s? Has the cultural labor market – especially its working conditions and systems of reward for cultural workers – improved or deteriorated since then, given the broader post-Fordist trends toward economic insecurity and precarity? To what extent does the increasingly global reach of the largest firms mean an exclusion of voices from cultural markets or an increase in opportunities to gain access to new global networks of cultural production? In what ways have digitalization and the internet transformed cultural production and consumption, and the barriers between them? Finally, what can be said about the quality of cultural texts, and to what extent are the texts produced by the cultural industries growing more or less diverse?

Denise D. Bielby

References

Appelbaum, Richard, William Felstiner, and Volkmar Gessner. 2001. "Introduction: The Legal Culture of Global Business Transactions." Pp. 1–36 in *Rules and Networks: The Legal Culture of Global Business Transactions*, edited by R. Appelbaum, W. Felstiner, and V. Gessner. Oxford: Hart.

Baker, Dean. 2016. *Rigged: How Globalization and the Rules of the Modern Economy Were Structured to Make the Rich Richer*. Washington, DC: Center for Economic and Policy Research.

Baker, Sarah, and David Hesmondhalgh. 2011. *Creative Labor: Media Work in Three Cultural Industries*. London: Routledge.

Beamish, Thomas, and Nicole Biggart. 2003. "The Economic Sociology of Conventions: Habit, Custom, Practice, and Routine." *Annual Review of Sociology* 29:443–64.

Becker, Howard. 1982. *Art Worlds*. Chicago: University of Chicago Press.

Bielby, Denise, and C. Lee Harrington. 2008. *Global TV: Exporting Television and Culture in the World Market*. New York: NYU Press.

Bielby, Denise, and Molly Moloney. 2008. "Considering Global Media: Sociological Contributions." Pp. 269–300 in *Media Ownership: Research and Regulation*, edited by R. Rice. Cresskill, NJ: Hampton Press.

Biggart, Nicole. 1989. *Charismatic Capitalism: Direct Selling Organizations in America*. Chicago: University of Chicago Press.

Blyler, Maureen, and Timothy Dowd. 2002. "Charting Race: The Success of Black Performers in the Mainstream Recording Market, 1940 to 1990." *Poetics* 30(1–2):87–110.

Chalaby, Jean K. 2012. "Producing TV Content in a Globalized Intellectual Property Market: The Emergence of the International Production Model." *Journal of Media Business Studies* 9(3):19–39.

Christopherson, Susan. 2008. "Behind the Scenes: How Transnational Firms Are Constructing a New International Division of Labor in Media Work." Pp. 41–84 in *Cross-border Cultural Production: Economic Runaway or Globalization?*, edited by J. Wasko and M. Erickson. Amherst, NY: Cambria Press.

Crane, Diana. 2002. "Culture and Globalization: Theoretical Models and Emerging Trends." Pp. 1–25 in *Global Cultures: Media, Arts, Policy, and Globalization*, edited by D. Crane, N. Kawashima, and K. Kawasaki. New York: Routledge.

Curtin, Michael. 2005. "Murdoch's Dilemma, or 'What's the Price of TV in China?'" *Media, Culture, & Society* 27(2):155–75.

Dauter, Luke, and Neil Fligstein. 2007. "The Sociology of Markets." *Annual Review of Sociology* 33:105–28.

Davis, G.F., K.A. Diekmann, and C.H. Tinsley. 1994. "The Decline and Fall of the Conglomerate Firm in the 1980s." *American Sociological Review* 59(4):547–70.

Dobbin, Frank, John Sutton, John Meyer, and Richard Scott. 1993. "Equal Opportunity Law and the Construction of Internal Labor Markets." *American Journal of Sociology* 99(2):396–427.

Douglas, Mary. 1986. *How Institutions Think*. Syracuse, NY: Syracuse University Press.

Dowd, Timothy. 2002. "Culture and Commodification: Technology and Structural Power in the Early U.S. Recording Industry." *International Journal of Sociology and Social Policy* 22(1/2/3):106–40.

———. 2004a. "Concentration and Diversity Revisited: Production Logics and the U.S. Mainstream Recording Industry, 1940–90." *Social Forces* 82(4):1411–55.

———. 2004b. "Introduction: The Embeddedness of Cultural Industries." *Poetics* 32(1):1–3.

Fligstein, Neil. 1996. "Markets as Politics: A Political-Cultural Approach to Market Institutions." *American Sociological Review* 61(4):656–73.

———. 2001. "Social Skill and the Theory of Fields." *Sociological Theory* 19(2):105–25.

Friedland, Roger, and John Mohr. 2004. "The Cultural Turn in American Sociology." Pp. 1–68 in *Matters of Culture: Cultural Sociology in Practice*, edited by R. Friedland and J. Mohr. Cambridge: Cambridge University Press.

Gereffi, Gary. 1992. "New Realities of Industrial Development in East Asia and Latin America: Global, Regional, and National Trends." Pp. 85–112 in *States and Development in the Asian Pacific Rim*, edited by R. Appelbaum and J. Henderson. Newbury Park, CA: Sage.

Granovetter, Mark. 1985. "Economic Action and Social Structure." *American Journal of Sociology* 91(3):481–510.

Griswold, Wendy. 2013. *Cultures and Societies in a Changing World*. Los Angeles: Sage.

Guillen, Mauro F. 2001. "Is Globalization Civilizing, Destructive, or Feeble? A Critique of Five Key Debates in the Social Science Literature." *Annual Review of Sociology* 27:235–305.

Hesmondhalgh, David. 2013. *The Cultural Industries*. 3rd ed. London: Sage.

Hesmondhalgh, David, and Anamik Saha. 2013. "Race, Ethnicity, and Cultural Production." *Popular Communication* 11(3):179–95.

Hirsch, Paul M. [1972] 1991. "Processing Fads and Fashions: An Organization-Set Analysis of Cultural Industry Systems." Pp. 313–34 in *Rethinking Popular Culture*, edited by C. Mukerji and M. Schudson. Berkeley: University of California Press.

———. 2000. "Cultural Industries Revisited." *Organization Science* 11(3):356–61.

Hirschman, Elizabeth C. 1983. "Aesthetics, Ideologies and the Limits of the Marketing Concept." *Journal of Marketing* 47(3):45–55.

Hopkins, Terence K., and Immanuel Wallerstein. 1986. "Commodity Chains in the World-Economy Prior to 1800." *Review* 10(1):157–70.

Hubka, David. 2002. "Globalization and Cultural Production." Pp. 233–55 in *Global Cultures: Media, Arts, Policy, and Globalization*, edited by D. Crane, K. Kawasaki, and N. Kawashima. New York: Routledge.

Janssen, Susanne, Giselinde Kuipers, and Marc Verboord. 2008. "Cultural Globalization and Arts Journalism: The International Orientation of Arts and Cultural Coverage in Dutch, French, German, and U.S. Newspapers, 1955–2005." *American Sociological Review* 73(5):719–40.

Jones, Candace, and Patricia Thornton. 2005. "Transformation in Cultural Industries: Introduction." Pp. xi–xxi in *Research in the Sociology of Organizations*. Vol. 23, *Transformations in Cultural Industries*, edited by C. Jones and P. Thornton. Greenwich, CT: JAI Press.

Kollock, Peter. 1994. "The Emergence of Exchange Structures: An Experimental Study of Uncertainty, Commitment, and Trust." *American Journal of Sociology* 100(2):313–45.

McMillan, Divya C. 2003. "Marriages Are Made On Heaven: Globalization and National Identity in India." Pp. 341–59 in *Planet TV: A Global Television Reader*, edited by S. Kumar and L. Parks. New York: New York University Press.

McRobbie, Angela. 2004. "Making a Living in London's Small-Scale Creative Sector." Pp. 130–43 in *Cultural Industries and the Production of Culture*, edited by D. Power and A.J. Scott. New York: Routledge.

Merton, Robert. 1949. *Social Theory and Social Structure*. Glencoe, IL: Free Press.

Peterson, Richard A. 1982. "Five Constraints on the Production of Culture: Law, Technology, Market, Organizational Structure and Occupational Careers." *Journal of Popular Culture* 16(2):143–53.

Peterson, Richard A., and N. Anand. 2004. "The Production of Culture Perspective." *Annual Review of Sociology* 30:311–34.

Scott, Allen J. 2000. "French Cinema: Economy, Policy and Place in the Making of a Cultural-Products Industry." *Theory, Culture & Society* 17(1):1–38.

———. 2002. "A New Map of Hollywood: The Production and Distribution of American Motion Pictures." *Regional Studies* 36(9):957–75.

———. 2004. "The Other Hollywood: The Organizational and Geographic Bases of Television-Program Production." *Media, Culture & Society* 26(2):183–205.

———. 2005. *On Hollywood*. Princeton, NJ: Princeton University Press.

Statista. 2016. "Filmed Entertainment Revenue in Selected Countries Worldwide in 2015 (in Million U.S. Dollars)." Retrieved November 9, 2016 (www.statista.com/statistics/296431/filmed-entertainment-revenue-worldwide-by-country/).

Steemers, Jeanette. 2014. "Selling Television: Addressing Transformations in the International Distribution of Television Content." *Media Industries Journal* 1(1):1–10.

Stinchcombe, Arthur. 1959. "Bureaucratic and Craft Administration of Production." *Administrative Science Quarterly* 4(2):168–87.

Storper, Michael. 1997. *The Regional World: Territorial Development in a Global Economy*. New York: Guildford Press.

Denise D. Bielby

Thornton, Patricia H. 2004. *Markets from Culture: Institutional Logics and Organizational Decisions in Higher Education Publishing.* Stanford, CA: Stanford University Press.

Tinic, Serra. 2006. "Global Vistas and Local Reflections: Negotiating Place and Identity in Vancouver Television." *Television & New Media* 7(2):154–83.

Wasko, Janet, and Mary Erickson. 2008. "Introduction." Pp. 1–9 in *Cross-border Cultural Production: Economic Runaway or Globalization?*, edited by M. Erickson and J. Wasko. Amherst, NY: Cambria Press.

Weber, Max. [1921] 1978. *Economy and Society: An Outline of Interpretative Sociology.* Berkeley: University of California Press.

Williams, Raymond. 1981. *Culture.* London: Fontana.

61

Media technologies, cultural mobility, and the nation-state

Scott McQuire

Introduction

On August 27, 2015, social media behemoth Facebook announced that, for the first time ever, more than one billion people logged on to the site in a single day (Zuckerberg 2015). This statistic condenses a number of the trajectories that characterize the contemporary mediascape. First, Facebook's "numbers" are mind-boggling for a company a little more than a decade old. Its audience far outreaches that achieved by single companies using older media platforms such as radio or television. Second, Facebook's popularity is not entirely predicated on providing specific "content" to attract its audience. Rather, in the manner of web 2.0 services, Facebook provides a *platform* that can be populated with a broad range of content, including highly individuated, user-generated media.

The dispersed nature of the Facebook audience underpins a third point. Like most web 2.0 platforms, Facebook is notionally "free" to use. At first glance, this bears some resemblance to the prior model of "free-to-air" broadcasting. However, attention on Facebook is monetized not by being aggregated into the mass "audience-commodity" that Dallas Smythe (1981) attributed to television, but by joining the minutely differentiated "long tail" of digital marketing (Anderson 2006). The capacity of Facebook (and other digital platforms) to exploit this long tail ultimately depends on their ability to deliver targeted advertising, which underlines the importance of user data and metadata to platform operators – information about who is using a service, the person's location, the time and type of device, his/her networks of relations, and information about choices, values, opinions, and behaviors, all of which can be harvested from posts and activities on the site.

Finally, we might note that, as a born-digital service, Facebook does not have a long prior history as a nationally based platform that subsequently became global. Rather, it achieved significant global reach very early on. Of course, the fact that one billion users logged in on August 27, 2015, means that more than 80 percent of the world's population *didn't* use the service that day. Although claims about global reach cannot be equated with universal access, the fact that we are even beginning to talk about media platforms operating on a *planetary* scale is significant.

I have begun this chapter with Facebook because social media platforms exemplify key dynamics that are altering the relation between media technologies, cultural experiences, and national territories. In what follows, I argue that modern media, led by broadcasting, played a major role in constituting the nation-state as the dominant social and cultural frame in the twentieth century. Although this model was always subject to conflict and instability, the extension of global digital networks has accentuated tensions in the alignment of territory, culture, and sovereignty. In short, media which once served to define and promote the nation-state as the primary container for social life are increasingly implicated in the production of new patterns of cultural affiliation and belonging, many of which are yet to be solidified into formal institutions or stable alignments.

Media and the social shaping of space-time

Media technologies have long contributed to the transformation of the social relations of space and time. To conceptualize space and time as *social relations* is, first of all, to insist that they are neither "natural" systems, nor "objective" and unchanging values. Rather, it is to suggest that understandings of space and time emerge from complex interactions involving technologies, institutions, material infrastructures, forms of knowledge and imagination, and embodied experience – all the tangled practices, objects, and relations that make up the social.

The period of "modernity" can itself be characterized by distinctive shifts in the social relations of time and space. Karl Marx, the most influential political economist of the nineteenth century, identified the expansion of markets and the acceleration of capital circulation as central to the dynamic of industrial capitalism. For Marx (1973:539),

> the more developed the capital . . . the more extensive the market over which it circulates, which forms the spatial orbit of its circulation, the more does it strive simultaneously for an even greater extension of the market and for greater annihilation of space with time.

New transport technologies such as railways and steamships played a key role in linking the world as a global entity. However, as I shall describe, new forms of media also play a critical role in sustaining the information flows needed for the coordination of more extended and more mobile social forms.

Increased mobility as a characteristic of modernity not only powered the expansion of industrial capitalism but also altered the patterns of human habitation. At a national level, migration from the country to city became the dominant demographic trend, providing the conditions for the rapid urbanization of social life. At a transnational level, new forms of technological mobility underpinned the colonization of much of the globe by the West, and ushered in the "age of migration" characterized by the flow of Europeans to "settler societies" such as the US, Canada, and Australia. Both trajectories produced significant collisions in space-time patterns, as the slower, cyclical rhythms of rural existence and the supposedly "backward" condition of indigenous populations were increasingly measured against the emerging norms of uniform linear time and urban speed (McQuire 1998).

If the emergence of modern media technologies, including mass newspapers, photography, and cinema played a strategic role in the conquest of territory and the management of empire from the second half of the nineteenth century, such trajectories have vastly intensified in the present. Sociologists such as David Harvey (1990) have placed the experience of "space-time compression" at the heart of contemporary life. Harvey (1990:240) argues that new capacities to bridge distance at high speed "so revolutionizes the objective qualities of space and time that we are forced to alter, sometimes in quite radical ways, how we represent the world to ourselves." Similarly, Anthony Giddens (1991:21) figured contemporary global society "as expressing fundamental aspects of time-space distanciation." Giddens argues that "globalisation concerns the intersection of presence and absence, the interlacing of social events and social relations 'at distance' with local contextualities" (21). For Giddens, space-time distanciation is not simply about the heightened capacity for distant events to intrude into everyday consciousness via avenues such as news media, but also concerns the way in which intimate exchanges with family and friends are now routinely mediated across vast distances.

Clearly, it would be reductive to regard media technologies such as the internet as the cause of contemporary space-time compression or time-space distanciation. As I have indicated earlier, the key is the articulation of media with other processes such as urbanization, migration, and the systemic integration of industrial capitalism into a more tightly linked global market. Media technologies play a significant role in conditioning the current global order. Media form a primary source of information about both "home" and "foreign" territories, thus helping to orchestrate complex psycho-social processes of identification and belonging; media flows also offer visible demonstrations of the impact of global processes on national sovereignty. If the global reach of digital platforms such as Facebook is one prominent example, another is the difficulty that national regulatory regimes experience in the face of contemporary media, leading to intense and as yet unsettled debates about piracy, privacy, and security.

Print media and the formation of the nation-state

Toward the end of his career, Canadian economic historian Harold Innis examined the way in which different modes of human communication influenced the entire fabric of social existence, including forms of economic life, politics, religion, education, and culture. Innis (1951) proposed that different media were "biased" according to whether they favored distribution in space or time, and further argued that changes from one medium to another were a significant factor in explaining major shifts in social organization. Media such as stone and clay tablets were what he called *time-biased*: durable, but heavy, bulky, and difficult to transport. Paper, in contrast, was *space-biased*: light and easily transportable, but also fragile and susceptible to the depredations of time. Whereas time-biased media such as imprinted clay tablets "helped sustain centralised religious forms of tradition . . . Transportable media favoured the growth of administrative relations across space, thereby facilitating the decentralised growth of secular and political authority" (Innis 1951:116). In his account, the invention of paper, and its spread from China and the Middle East to the West, were central factors in the decline of oral culture and the subsequent emergence of spatially extensive forms of political authority such as the Roman Empire.

Innis influenced another Canadian scholar, literary professor Marshall McLuhan, who shot to fame in the 1960s on the back of his provocative argument concerning the transformative effects of television. McLuhan has often been criticized, notably by Raymond Williams (1990), for espousing a form of technological determinism that treats technology as an autonomous cause of social change. Williams rightly insisted that new technologies, and their patterns of use, were not simply "invented," but depended upon the interplay of specific conditions, from short-term corporate power to determine patterns of investment to longer-term issues, such as the need for increasingly mobile workforces that supported the development of market capitalism. McLuhan pays scant attention to these questions of social context and power. Nevertheless, his work offers important insights into modern media. Prior to McLuhan, the dominant paradigm of communication studies tended to treat the medium as "neutral" and debate was largely limited to questions of "content." In contrast, McLuhan ([1964] 1974:27) insisted that "the effects of technology do not occur at the level of opinions or concepts, but alter sense ratios or patterns of perception." In his early writings, McLuhan followed Innis in extolling the importance of print media – the so-called Gutenberg Galaxy – in underpinning the growth of modern rationality and individualism as well as supporting the growth of national cultures. For McLuhan ([1964] 1974:158), the newspaper culture which spread rapidly in the nineteenth century was the "architect of nationalism."

A similar thesis was advanced in far more historical detail by both critical theorist Jürgen Habermas (1989) and sociologist Benedict Anderson (1983). For Anderson, the rise of print culture in Europe was the structural condition which enabled "vernacular languages" to undermine the dominance of Latin and the authority of the church. By creating larger-scale zones of unified communication and exchange, print became the joint vehicle that carried both the emerging national economy and novel forms of national consciousness, resulting in the spread of what Anderson aptly dubs "print capitalism." In Anderson's account, the expanded circulation of printed information is fundamental to the construction of the "imagined community" that characterizes the modern nation-state. The modern national community is "imagined" because it comprises a large-scale mass of citizens who will never actually meet face-to-face, but who nevertheless develop forms of affective attachment and political solidarity mediated by print forms such as the newspaper and the book.

Jürgen Habermas (1989) also stresses the role of print culture in the expansion of markets for goods and for news/information. News circuits functioned to "nationalize" more limited town-based economies and discursive practices, thereby constituting a foundation of the modern nation-state. In his influential account of the formation of the "public sphere," Habermas locates its emergence in the transition from feudal to proto-democratic systems of political authority. The public sphere is the arena in which the bourgeoisie find a political voice, as part of the process by which the legitimacy of noble birth waned in favor of authority based on the will of "the people." "Public opinion," a term that first entered the Oxford Dictionary in 1781, comes to be allied with a new conception of the press as the "Fourth Estate." For Habermas, the press becomes the key instrument through which private citizens engage in rational public discourse to comment on "society" as a public affair. Of course, this ideal formulation has a troubled existence in reality. Habermas himself argued that the increasing commercialization of the press, which helped to secure its independence from state control, also created the conditions for what he terms a "re-feudalization" of the public sphere: instead of articulating a broader *public* interest, public opinion as manifest in the commercial press comes to be dominated by coalitions of private interest.

The debates generated by Habermas remain relevant in the present. The key issue in this context is the role of print media in establishing the nation-state as the primary frame for modern culture and social life. Spatially extended and temporally compressed communication circuits such as those established by mass daily newspapers help to create the conditions in which more locally based forms of identity ceded ground to identification of citizens as *national* subjects. The formation of the modern nation-state involved what Anthony Giddens characterized as the "disembedding" of traditional, locally based social systems, and a "stretching" of social relations, so that local markers of time and space such as places and seasons give way to more abstracted forms of knowledge such as news cycles and railway timetables. Like McLuhan and Anderson, Giddens (1991:25–6) recognizes the mosaic form of the newspaper page as a key index of the way that the social relations of the modern space-time nexus combine both fragmentation *and* continuity. Disparate events are routinely juxtaposed on the same page of the newspaper, unified only by the time of their occurrence; a single "present" that now extends over an entire territory by virtue of the novel speed and reach of the newspaper as a communication form.

Electronic media and national space

McLuhan soon moved on from print culture. His astounding popularity and influence in the 1960s was predicated on his bold extension of Innis's thesis concerning spatial and temporal "bias" to electronic media. The "big flip" that McLuhan identifies in relation to the spread of electronic media such as television involves the displacement of the individualized culture and private detachment fostered by print in favor of a "global village" in which everyone is profoundly "involved" with everyone else. If McLuhan's analysis remains contentious in its tendency toward determinism, it does serve to highlight the profound ambiguity of electronic broadcasting in relation to the space of the nation-state. As John Thomson (1995) points out, although late nineteenth-century newspapers were able to gain mass distribution via rail and also to draw on dispersed sources of information about distant events via the telegraph, the logistics of physical distribution meant that their primary audience remained restricted to a single city or region. Electronic broadcasting was far less bound by such limits. The capacity of radio waves to cross-national borders with impunity was a key reason for the urgency with which different national governments moved to assert control over radio in the early twentieth century. Moreover, following the launch of the first geostationary satellites in 1962, broadcasting could both relay "live" events from locations across the world and develop networks which bore no necessary relationship to the physical bounds of the nation-state.

Yet despite growing technical capacity to travel across borders, radio and television remained decisively national industries and institutions into the 1980s. Individual nation-states asserted control over radio and television services within their territories through a combination of licensing, regulation, and provision of funding for public service or state-run broadcasters. This led to a system in which the media space of most nation-states was dominated by relatively few broadcasters, especially for television – an arrangement that proved remarkably stable even across the major geopolitical divides of the period. Unified national television programming arguably became a key means by which Anderson's "imagined community" was *enacted* in the second half of the twentieth century.

The political function of broadcasting in defining a national polity situates the major debates concerning "media imperialism" (Schiller 1969) which emerged in the 1960s and 1970s. These debates, which reflect concern over the exportation of US television programming but soon extended to Western dominance over communication infrastructure and the call for a "new world information and communication order" (NWICO), began to change in the 1980s as new technologies opened up gaps in the fit between national territory and media regulation. Fiber optics allowed cables to carry more channels, while satellite distribution enabled cable operators to cover much larger territories. The launch of HBO as a national cable network in the US in 1975 was followed by the establishment of "global" channels such as CNN (1980) and MTV (1981). In Europe, expansion in the number of channels coincided with growing privatization of television services and the formation of new policy settings, including the "Television without Frontiers" Directive (1989), which advocated greater cross-border media circulation within the European Union. Direct satellite broadcasting became the vehicle chosen by Rupert Murdoch's News Corporation to advance its ambitions to operate a global television network (ultimately frustrated by inability to secure a foothold in China). Satellite television also enabled the launch of non-Western services, and operators such as Mumbai-based ZEE TV (1992) and Doha-based Al Jazeera (1996) soon gained traction as global players. The growing complexity of transnational flows in the broadcasting sector was itself increasingly outflanked by the rapid expansion of the internet, as user numbers began to grow exponentially in the 1990s.

Digital networks and postnational space

The increasing influence of the internet led those such as urban sociologist Manual Castells (1989:6) to posit "the emergence of a *space of flows* which dominates the historically constructed space of places." In his influential essay "The Overexposed City," French social theorist Paul Virilio (1991:13) argued that pervasive networked media were dissolving traditional spatial dimensions in favor of instantaneous interactions. As the dotcom boom gained momentum in the late 1990s, economists such as Frances Cairncross (1997) announced the "death of distance" while the "Magna Carta for the Knowledge Age" written by Dyson et al. (1994:26) proclaimed "The central event of the 20th century is the overthrow of matter." Borders, distance, and material features not only seemed less constraining, but irrelevant, as national territory seemed poised to be entirely overtaken by global processes.

Yet subsequent history reveals a far more complex picture. Instead of the wholesale disappearance of physical space that Virilio, Cairncross, and others prophesied, digital networks retain a distinct geography. It is no accident that the "fattest pipes" enabling the fastest data exchange in the 1990s were those linking North America and Western Europe. In her pioneering work on the global city as the command and control center of contemporary global capitalism, sociologist Saskia Sassen (1991) observed the heavy dependence of "global cities" on digital infrastructure. Sassen argued that digital networks enabled simultaneous processes of concentration *and* dispersion. Cities required digital infrastructure to attract tech-dependent industries such as financial services, stock exchanges, banking, and legal and management services, while advanced digital capabilities enabled these industries to link across multiple locations. Sassen later theorized that digital networks facilitated a partial disaggregation of national space in favor of the emergence of new subnational (global cities) and supranational (global markets) configurations. Although this does not entail the wholesale dismantling of the nation-state, it presents a new set of challenges to the logic of the national (Sassen 2006).

Dependency on network infrastructure is only one dimension of the paradoxical fit between media platforms and national territories in the present. On the one hand, we can observe that media technology now spans the earth more rapidly and routinely than ever before. Performing a simple activity such as a web search using Google is estimated to activate anywhere between 1,000 and 20,000 servers situated in different sites around the world (something that has significant implications for internet energy consumption). Contemporary digital platforms, from social media and search engines to personal video calls, enjoy transnational reach with little or no additional cost or effort to users. This context of expanded global connectivity ensures that networked digital media remain powerful machines for intensifying the space – time trajectories shaping social organization and cultural flows that were first analyzed by Innis and McLuhan. On the other hand, digital media have become increasingly personalized and in this respect they have greater capacity to orient toward local situations and interactions than broadcast platforms. Paradoxically, then, as much as digital networks enable emancipation from place and national space, they have also become a key modality for operationalizing new forms of placemaking and "local" social organization.

Following the widespread processes of public protest and activism associated with the Arab Spring and the Occupy movements in 2011, Sassen advanced the concept of the "global street" as a means of conceptualizing this emergent nexus between digital networks and distinct urban materialities and cultures. She (Sassen 2011:578) argues that the different logics of networks and cities are now intertwined in particular situations, according to "the capacity of collective action in the city to *inscribe* a technology"; networks are never simply technical but "deliver their utility through complex ecologies that include (a) non-technological variables (the social, the subjective, the political, material topographies), and (b) the particular cultures of use of different actors."

Sassen's analysis is useful for conceptualizing the new patterns and potentials that characterize contemporary media flows. It does not repeat superficial assertions that the Arab Spring was a "Facebook revolution," but rather recognizes that low-cost, distributed digital communication platforms have altered one of the fundamental constraints on public assembly. Where rapid mobilization was once restricted to extremely hierarchical organizations such as the military and the police, digital networks open this possibility to a much broader range of actors. Second, actions initiated in particular localities can now receive publicity and amplification along different avenues, as social media attention can be leveraged into mainstream media attention. Of course, traditional media gatekeeping structures still exert significant power: it is worth remembering that the events in Tunisia went largely unreported in the West until the president fled. Mainstream media silence forced activists to adopt novel strategies – such as their appeal to celebrity Stephen Fry to leverage his million-plus Twitter "followers" in support of their cause. Nevertheless, there is greater potential for local protests to find global audiences. Importantly, such events are no longer "reported on" only by mainstream media. As Kluitenberg notes of the Arab Spring:

> The predominant image of the protests is no longer that of the distanced media professional, or even of the artist, who is after all still a professional of sorts. It is not even clearly the perspective of the "activist," as most of the protesters do not regard themselves as activists. They are much rather ordinary citizens longing for some form of meaningful social and political change, and new modes of expression and self-determination to recapture their sovereignty as political subjects.
>
> *(Kluitenberg 2011:47)*

These different currents underline the complexity of the relation between media and national space in the present. The new global platforms dependent on the internet remain susceptible to strong forms of national regulation and influence. One dramatic example was the Egyptian government shutting off all internet access to the country shortly after 10 p.m. on January 28, 2011, in an unsuccessful attempt to quell the protest movement there. More persistent examples include China's "Great firewall," and the operations of the US National Security Agency (NSA) revealed by Edward Snowden in 2012. At the same time, these current forms of monitoring and control on a national and even global scale advance hand in hand with the potential for low-cost, citizen-initiated, transnational exchanges and collaboration.

Convergent digital platforms have clearly contributed to a new media geography and global information order. This order is by no means equal, and the "digital divide" remains a major issue both nationally and internationally. Nevertheless, the last decade has seen significant shifts in use of the internet. Where more than 80 percent of internet users were native English speakers in 1996, by 2010 this number had fallen to 27.3 percent. More strikingly, while 2000–2010 saw an overall trebling of the number of English-speaking internet users, the growth in China and the Arab world was both greater in volume and far faster (Zuckerman 2013). As internet theorist Geert Lovink (2008:xi) noted a decade ago, "the majority of internet traffic these days is in Spanish, Mandarin, and Japanese, but little of this seems to flow into the dominant Anglo-Western understanding of Internet culture."

The cultural implications of these shifts are significant. The emergence of China as the world's second biggest economy is epitomized by its rapidly expanding media sector. Today, it is notable that the dominant digital platforms including Apple, Facebook, Google, Microsoft, Amazon, and eBay, which are all headquartered in the US, now find themselves with few real rivals other than Chinese-based companies: Baidu in search, and the suite of social media and ecommerce operations run by companies such as Shenzhen-based TenCent (WeChat, QQ) and Alibaba (Tmall, Tabao, Alibaba.com), founded in Hangzhou. New partnerships with Hollywood-based content producers are only the visible tip of the growing Chinese ambition for global media expansion.

Digital platforms play an important role in servicing the needs of diasporic communities, as well as many other dispersed "communities of interest." These audiences, considered too small to interest national broadcasters, once relied on the physical exchange of media such as tapes and DVDs but this changed with the establishment of specialist cable and satellite channels in the 1990s and 2000s, followed by the proliferation of communication networks that reach across national borders using internet telephony, video conferencing, blogs, and social networking websites. The increased availability of such circuits consolidates new modes of cultural belonging, in which place of residence is no longer the threshold condition for participation in one's "home" culture.

Many ordinary social interactions now involve complex technological mediations, which means media have become integral to enacting social ties. As Scott Lash (2002:15) expressed it, "because my forms of social life are so normally and chronically at-a-distance, I cannot navigate these distances, I cannot achieve sociality apart from my machine interface." "At-a-distance" is not only about contacting those who are faraway, but also about the reconfiguration of local practices and relations of proximity. The fact that these different scales and trajectories are now dependent on the same communication systems – a dependency highlighted when supposedly "private" messages go "viral" on social media – indicates a growing instability in the coordinates of "public" and "private."

Homi Bhabha (1994) pointed out long ago that one legacy of colonialism and mass migration, intended or not, was the *internal* fracturing of the colonizing national homeland. New, more turbulent patterns of migration and movement of people (Papastergiadis 2000) and the rise of what Ong (1999) calls "flexible citizenship" demand that we consider the increased significance of transnational exchanges. Harald Kleinschmidt (2006) argues that the default paradigm of what he terms "residentialism" is increasingly problematic – instead of treating mobility primarily in terms of the *threat* it poses to national borders and state sovereignty, he suggests we recognize the long history of regional and transnational mobility, along with the agency of migrants in creating transnational social spaces of varying scales, durations, and structures. Networked media technologies support this *migratory effect*, accentuating the sense in which "home" is no longer necessarily bound to a particular place, or synonymous with a single language, homogeneous people, or unified culture. In this respect, the mediatization of contemporary social life forms a significant part of the condition which led Urry (2007) to call for sociology to address new mobilities.

In the present context, in which neither the internal nor the external borders of the nation as "home" remain secure, new possibilities for breaking away from fixed and exclusionary stereotypes are emerging. Instead of identity being circumscribed by place of origin, identity might be redefined to include the overlapping, interpenetrating spaces and contradictory affiliations we inhabit in the present. The development of a global and cosmopolitan public sphere seems fundamental to supporting the complex communication processes needed to deal with entrenched global problems, including poverty, resource depletion, and climate change. However, a more genuinely *transnational* public sphere can no longer afford the old universalisms that so often masked the imperialism of powerful nations. Instead, it requires the nurturing of lateral, horizontal exchanges that emphasize both cultural locatedness and cultural interconnectedness as dynamic forms of translation and creativity.

References

Anderson, B. 1983. *Imagined Communities: Reflections on the Origin and Spread of Nationalism*. London: Verso.

Anderson, C. 2006. *The Long Tail: Why the Future of Business is Selling Less of More*. New York: Hyperion.

Bhabha, H. 1994. *The Location of Culture*. London: Routledge.

Cairncross, F. 1997. *The Death of Distance: How the Communications Revolution Will Change Our Lives*. Boston, MA: Harvard Business School Press.

Castells, M. 1989. *The Informational City: Information Technology, Economic Restructuring, and the Urban-Regional Process*. Oxford: Blackwell.

Dyson, E., G. Gilder, G. Keyworth, and A. Toffler. 1994. "A Magna Carta For The Knowledge Age." *New Perspectives Quarterly* 11(4):26–37.

Giddens, A. 1991. *Modernity and Self-Identity: Self and Society in the Late Modern Age*. Stanford, CA: Stanford University Press.

Habermas, J. 1989. *Structural Transformation of the Public Sphere: An Inquiry into a Category of Bourgeois Society*, trans. T. Burger. Cambridge, MA: MIT Press.

Harvey, D. 1990. *Condition of Postmodernity: An Enquiry into the Origins of Cultural Change*. Oxford: Blackwell.

Innis, H. 1951. *The Bias of Communication*. Toronto: University of Toronto Press.

Kleinschmidt, H. 2006. "Migration and the Making of Transnational Social Spaces." Paper presented at the "Mobility, Culture and Communication" Symposium, June 11, University of Melbourne. Retrieved (www.researchgate.net/publication/37643091_Migration_and_the_Making_of_Transnational_ Social_Spaces).

Kluitenberg, E. 2011. *Legacies of Tactical Media: The Tactics of Occupation: From Tompkins Square to Tahrir*. Amsterdam: Institute of Network cultures.

Lash, S. 2002. *Critique of Information*. London: Sage.

Lovink, G. 2008. *Zero Comments: Blogging and Critical Internet Culture*. London: Routledge.

Marx, K. 1973. *Grundrisse: Foundations of the Critique of Political Economy*, trans. M. Nicolaus. London: Allen Lane/NLR.

McLuhan, M. [1964] 1974. *Understanding Media: The Extensions of Man*. London: Abacus.

McQuire, S. 1998. *Visions of Modernity: Representation, Memory, Time and Space in the Age of the Camera*. London: Sage.

Ong, A. 1999. *Flexible Citizenship: The Cultural Logics of Transnationality*. Durham, NC: Duke University Press.

Papastergiadis, N. 2000. *The Turbulence of Migration: Globalization, Deterritorialization, and Hybridity*. Malden, MA: Polity Press.

Sassen, S. 1991. *The Global City: New York, London, Tokyo*. Princeton, NJ: Princeton University Press.

———. 2006. *Territory, Authority, Rights: From Medieval to Global Assemblages*. Princeton, NJ: Princeton University Press.

———. 2011. "The Global Street: Making the Political." *Globalizations* 8(5):573–79.

Schiller, H. 1969. *Mass Communications and American Empire*. New York: A.M. Kelley.

Smythe, D. 1981. *Dependency Road*. Norwood, NJ: Ablex.

Thomson, J. 1995. *The Media and Modernity: A Social Theory of the Media*. Cambridge: Polity Press.

Urry, J. 2007. *Mobilities*. Cambridge: Polity Press.

Virilio P. 1991. *The Lost Dimension*, trans. D. Moshenberg. New York: Semiotext(e).

Williams, R. 1990. *Television, Technology and Cultural Form*. 2nd ed. London: Routledge.

Zuckerberg, M. 2015. Retrieved November 24, 2015 (www.facebook.com/zuck/posts/1010232 9188394581).

Zuckerman, E. 2013. *Rewire: Digital Cosmopolitans in the Age of Connection*. New York: W.W. Norton.

62

Tourism and culture

Kevin Fox Gotham

Introduction

Over the decades, scholars have sought to understand and explain the changing institutional, political, and socioeconomic linkages between culture and tourism. Much scholarship has investigated the ways in which local cultural practices and identities shape the production and organization of tourism on a grassroots level. In conventional accounts, tourism is a set of discrete economic activities, a mode of consumption, or a spatially bounded locality or "destination" of reiterated performative acts (e.g., sanctifying a locality, admiring a site, commemorating an event). By contrast, recent research conceptualizes tourism as a highly complex set of institutions and social relations that involve capitalist markets, state policy, and flows of commodities, technology, cultural forms, and people. Here, tourism is embedded within broader patterns of societal transformation as well as local networks and cultural practices.

Both "tourism" and "culture" are multidimensional, heterogeneous, and fluid categories that attain their significance in relationship with each other. Moreover, the boundaries between tourism and culture are porous and ever changing as these categories become both sites and objects of consumption, entertainment, and spectacle (Hoffman, Fainstein, and Judd 2003; Rath 2007). John Urry's famous "tourist gaze" refers to tourists viewing or gazing upon particular sites and sights because "there is an anticipation, especially through day-dreaming and fantasy, of intense pleasures, either on a different scale or involving different sense from those customarily encountered" (1990:132). Influenced by Michel Foucault, Urry argues that a variety of non-tourist practices, such as film, newspapers, TV, magazines, records, and videos construct tourist experiences and circulate the signs and symbols by which consumers are coached to view tourist attractions and understand their experiences as tourists. In *Tourism Mobilities: Places to Play, Places in Play*, Mimi Sheller and John Urry (2006) use a mobilities approach to show how places to play are also places in play – made and remade by the mobilities and performances of tourists and workers, images and heritage, the latest fashions, and the newest diseases. The burgeoning interest in tourism points to a broader concern with the changing nature of consumption and media, the repackaging of neighborhoods and cities as sites of tourist consumption (Gotham 2005b), and the ways in which local festivals become key motivators for tourism investment in cities (Gotham 2002, 2005a, 2005c, 2011b, 2011c).

My scholarship examines the ways in which tourism affects culture (both positively and negatively), how culture structures the development of tourism in a particular locale, and how tourism and culture transform each other as different actors and organized interests compete over access to and control over political and economic resources. In my past work, I have developed and applied the concept of "touristic culture" as a heuristic device to illustrate the ways in which culture and tourism increasingly share similar themes, symbols, discourses, and interpretive systems. Whereas a "culture of tourism" is premised on showcasing local culture to attract tourists, a "touristic culture" refers to the blurring of boundaries between tourism and other major institutions and cultural practices. Specifically, touristic culture is a process by which tourist modes of staging, visualization, and experience increasingly frame meanings and assertions of local culture, identity, authenticity, and collective memory. The concept of touristic culture can provide novel insights into several areas of scholarship including the relationship between tourism and ethnicity/race, the rise of niche tourism, and constructions of authenticity in tourism.

Ethnicity and race

The concept of touristic culture draws attention to the role tourism discourses and practices play in constructing and reproducing ethnic identities and ethnic relations, a concern shared by other scholars. For Dean MacCannell (1973; 1992:168), tourism systematically purveys a "reconstructed" ethnicity, and thereby a rhetorical and symbolic expression of cultural difference that is packaged and sold to tourists. Robert E. Wood's (1998) analysis of ethnic groups in Asia and the Pacific Rim, Jane Desmond's (1999) examination of tourism in Hawaii, and Diane Barthel-Bouchier's (2001) study of the Amana Colonies in southeastern Iowa suggest that ethnicity can be constructed and strategically deployed by different groups for instrumental purposes, including confronting the values, categories, and practices of the dominant culture, challenging the dominant culture's perception of a minority group, and contesting public policy within the political arena. Today, ethnic group interaction with tourism is an integral part of the construction and reproduction of ethnic identity. Local meanings of ethnicity shape and are shaped by tourism advertising and promotional strategies. In this way, tourism creates new bases of struggle and conflict over meanings of ethnicity.

In the repertoire of tourism marketing and advertising, terms such as "diversity," "culture," and "ethnicity" have considerable symbolic value and utility for cities. Their use does not rule out any particular group, and they can refer to almost any artistic or entertaining activity associated with tourism. More important, "culture" and "ethnicity" are not actively resisted by consumers and tourists in part because they do not carry the negative connotation that "race" has for many people (Gotham 2011a). For tourism boosters and promoters, "race" signifies inequality, oppression, domination, and subordination. To neutralize this signification, place marketers deploy the terms "diversity," "ethnicity," and "culture" to create the impression that cities are both non-hierarchical and egalitarian. What the tourism industry seeks to promote is a simulated or ersatz culture and ethnicity of no offense. Tourism discourses highlight ethnic differences and diversity while ignoring social divisions, conflicts, and struggles. Thus, whether ethnic and cultural differences are real or false is irrelevant, for tourism marketing seeks to efface social categories and identities of all meaning except the signification of pleasure (Gotham 2007a).

Today, ethnicity is taking on an expanded role in urban economies and is increasingly becoming a fundamental theme which distinguishes tourist destinations and entertainment-enhanced developments. In my work on New Orleans, I have found that assertions and constructions of ethnicity reflect a dual process of globalization and localization (Gotham 2007a, 2007e, 2011a). That is, tourism is a force for globalizing ethnicity (e.g., delocalizing and disembedding ethnicity from place) and a force for localizing ethnicity (e.g., producing and reinforcing ethnic distinctiveness in place through indigenous networks and place-bound social bonds). In short, the notion of touristic culture suggests that tourism is a major structuring element of ethnic culture and identity and not something that is external, a priori, or outside of these social categories (see also Crang 2004; Hannam 2006; Canavan 2016).

Niche tourism

In recent years, scholars have devoted increasing attention to theorizing and examining the rise of niche tourism in which various marketers and promoters tailor the tourism product to meet the desires and needs of a particular audience/market segment. Niche marketing refers to the development of new forms of cultural fragmentation, differentiation, and specialization that split consumers and markets into ever smaller segments or niches. Consumer demand driven perspectives view niche tourism as a behavioral phenomenon, a product of tourist preferences and desires to see the exotic and extraordinary. By contrast, attraction-supply driven perspectives of niche tourism emphasize the importance of tourism suppliers in creating the niche tourism sights and sites that allow consumers to satisfy and fulfill their desires. In this conception, consumer desires and niche markets reflect the production of commodity-images as ruled by profiteering motives and the logic and dictates of commodified media culture. Thus, consumer demands and preferences do not necessarily translate into the actual production of specific niche tourism sights or sites. Rather, consumer demands can be activated and exploited by particular advertising strategies to persuade potential tourists to visit particular locales to consume culture, entertainment, history, environment, and so on.

Disaster tourism and "voluntourism"

The example of post-Katrina New Orleans provides an empirical case to study the linkages between consumer demand and attraction-supply explanations of niche tourism (Gotham 2007f). In the years after the disaster, tourism promoters capitalized on the damage and destruction to create a new industry of "disaster tourism" that involves the circulation of people to flooded neighborhoods in a guided tour bus (Gotham 2007b). For several years, Gray Line New Orleans Bus Tours offered its "Hurricane Katrina: America's Worst Catastrophe!" tour through devastated neighborhoods. The bus tour presented flooded neighborhoods as spectacular and entertaining sites to visit (Gotham 2007b, 2007d; Gotham and Lewis 2015). What is important is that the constitution of flooded neighborhoods as tourist sites intimates local culture as a spectacle to the extent that local history, residential life, and neighborhoods are (re)presented in such a way to emphasize the dramatic, spectacular, and the unusual. Disaster tourism depends on the commodification of leisure and the transformation of tragic events as objects of entertainment and fascination where otherwise ordinary places are constructed as exotic attractions that can deliver extraordinary experiences, a process that is occurring around the world (Gotham and Greenberg 2014).

Another example of niche tourism is "voluntourism," which refers to the integration of voluntary service experiences with entertainment-based tourist activities to attract people to assist with post-disaster recovery and rebuilding efforts. While the combination of volunteerism and tourism has a long history, over the last decade or so, tourism organizations and nonprofits have used voluntourism as a major strategy to attract volunteer labor to help in the post-Katrina rebuilding effort. In addition, the niches that comprise voluntourism are growing rapidly and can include charity tourism, moral or religious tourism, and eco-tourism. In the 1980s, the success of international initiatives, such as the global exposure of Band Aid/Live Aid, provided a new promotional outlet for the voluntary and charity sectors with established icons of society popularizing charitable contributions. Since then, Brad Pitt's Make It Right (MIR) Foundation to rebuild disaster-damaged housing in New Orleans and other cities, Angelina Jolie's campaigns for UN Refugee Agency, and Bono's launch of Product (Red) in 2006 have garnered media and scholarly attention on the impact and influence of celebrities in raising public awareness about particular issues (Gotham 2012). Suffice, the growing attention to goodwill activities by celebrities has prompted charities to exploit new opportunities available to them to promote their cause and link volunteerism with tourism promotion (Callanan and Thomas 2005).

Niche tourism activities such as voluntourism can have both positive and negative consequences. On the one hand, volunteering can allow the tourist to donate time and labor to help a needy group or locale while offering the opportunity to enjoy some leisure time and learn about a new culture. Ethnographic research by Palacios (2010) on an Australian program that organizes short-term group placements for university students in Vietnam, Mexico, and Fiji found that voluntourism projects can enhance students' global engagement, career development, and inter-cultural competence.

On the other hand, research on "AIDs Orphan Tourism" in South Africa and elsewhere has found that "orphan tourism" – in which visitors volunteer as caregivers for children whose parents have died or otherwise can't support them – has become so popular that critics accuse orphanages of operating more like for-profit businesses than humanitarian charities. Research by Richter and Norman (2010) suggests that some orphanages misrepresent the status of the children and intentionally subject children to poor conditions in order to entice unsuspecting volunteers to donate more resources. In addition, the constant arrivals and departures of volunteers is linked to attachment disorders in children. That is, short-term attachments formed between children in group residential care and volunteers may worsen known impacts of institutional care.

Medical/health tourism and sex tourism

Medical and health tourism, where people travel overseas for medical and health-care, is a significant area of growth in the export of medical, health, and tourism services, especially for developing countries. The recent trend is for people to travel from developed countries to third-world countries for medical treatment because of cost considerations and access to treatment that may not be legal in the home country, such as some fertility procedures. Many countries including China, Cuba, Hungary, India, Thailand, Malaysia, and Singapore actively compete to attract medical and health tourists. These countries also provide niche private services such as cosmetic and dental surgery, transplants, and infertility treatments (Rachel 2013). Chen and Wilson (2013:1752) suggest that "individuals who receive medical care abroad are a vulnerable, sentinel population, who sample the local environment and can carry home unusual and resistant infections." Medical tourists are at risk for hospital-associated and procedure-related infections as well as for locally endemic infections. The high demand and large informal flow of patients from countries neighboring South Africa has prompted the South African government to formalize arrangements for medical travel to its public hospitals and clinics through inter-country agreements in order to recover the cost of treating nonresidents. According to Crush and Chikanda (2015:31), the danger, for nonresidents who fall outside these agreements is that the healthcare system may deny and exclude treatment. Thus, much scrutiny and debate surrounds the field of medical tourism particularly over concerns related to different cross-national cultures of healthcare, socio-legal regulations, ethics, and broader health issues.

Recent years have witnessed the growth of a burgeoning literature on sex tourism and its impacts on both tourists and destinations. "Sex tourism" often refers to commodified cash-for-sex exchanges between tourists and locals (Rivers-Moore 2016; Kibicho 2016). Many studies focus on less developed countries where affluent male tourists search for sexual experiences unobtainable in the West. Other scholarly analyses situate and highlight sex tourism in the context of the exploitation of developing countries (for an overview, see Bandyopadhyay 2013). A major component of sex tourism involves men of various racial and ethnic backgrounds interacting with poor women of color. Here, as scholars have pointed out, issues of race and ethnicity interlock with conceptions of gender and sexuality to influence how people conceptualize, organize, and experience tourism (Sheller 2003; Cabezas 2004).

Sex tourism is a contested concept and researchers increasingly debate the similarities and differences among sex tourism and romance tourism. Romance tourism is used by scholars to highlight the romantic, emotional, and intimate connections cultivated between foreign tourists and local men and women in tourist destinations. The distinction between romance tourism and sex tourism is often split along gendered lines. Sexual/romantic encounters between tourist women and local men are more likely to be referred to as romance tourism, while similar encounters between tourist men and local women are often referred to as "sex tourism." Some researchers have emphasized that because female tourists are more likely than their male counterparts to seek emotional intimacy as well as physical intimacy in their sexual relationships with locals, their situation is better described as "romance tourism" than "sex tourism" (Sanchez Taylor 2015). Some studies focus on women's agency in the construction of international sexual relationships and the impact of sex tourism on gendered identities (for an overview, see Sanchez Taylor 2015). Less attention has been paid to the wider structural factors that constrain actors and shape sexual encounters. Gregory (2014) explores the ways in which sexualized racisms and global structures of inequality influence the options, motivations, and desires of local men and tourist women in tourist settings. Despite its liberating potential for some tourist women, however, Smith (2015:382) concludes that sex tourism "[relies] upon and reinforce[s] historically entrenched national and cultural demarcations that tend to marginalize people (partners, families, communities) of targeted destinations in the developing world."

Authenticity in tourism

One long-standing debate in the study of tourism and culture relates to the quest for authenticity in the tourist experience and the construction of authenticity to attract tourists to cities. The cultural invention model of tourism contends that tourism provides a set of symbols, imagery, and discourses that local people can (re)interpret and use/deploy to produce new expressions of local culture. In this conception, tourism can accentuate local particularity by making possible unique appropriations of culture and heritage, thus encouraging the proliferation of difference and diversity. As a positive force for communities, tourism can help build and sustain important cultural linkages, institutional connections, and global-local networks that can bring a wealth of new products, ideas, and economic opportunities to local people and visitors.

Early, Dean MacCannell (1973) developed the concept of "staged authenticity" to refer to the manufacturing of local culture to create an impression of authenticity for a tourist audience. MacCannell conceived of culture as primordial and viewed tourists as alienated consumers who strive to experience an authentic encounter with authentic sites, objects, or events. Writing more than 20 years later, Ritzer and Liska (1997) disagree, arguing that people prefer inauthentic and simulated tourist experiences because these can be highly predictable and efficient vehicles for delivering fun and entertainment. Ritzer (2006) even refers to tourism as the global production of "nothing," meaning a social form "centrally conceived, controlled, and comparatively devoid of distinctive content." Other scholars have used the concept of "Disneyification" to examine the spread of Disney theme-park characteristics to cities and urban culture. This city-as-theme-park explanation suggests that urban cultural spaces are being refashioned to attract visitors and enhance entertainment experiences through the production of fake histories and phony cultures that masquerade as "authentic" (Sorkin 1992; Bryman 1999; Reichl 1999; Eeckhout 2001).

At the same time, the "staged authenticity" model has been assailed as theoretically misleading and factually incorrect. Terms like "staged," "fabricated," or "simulated" authenticity assume that processes of commodification and rationalization are imposed from above onto passively accepting people (Gotham 2007c). Simon Coleman and Mike Crang's (2003) discussion of tourism as "between place and performance" casts tourism as a set of localized practices that frame meanings of local culture and help constitute place identities and authenticity. Erik Cohen's (1988) notion of "emergent authenticity" suggests that authenticity is a mutable and negotiated category whose meaning varies by time and context. Going further, Cohen argues that local people may initially view certain tourism products and images as contrived and artificial but over time redefine them as authentic representations of local culture and heritage. The larger point is that not all tourism is oriented toward communicating authenticity nor does the deliberate staging of local culture amount to a massive deception that dupes local people or visitors (Shepherd 2002; Varley, Taylor, and Johnson 2013).

In my published work, I have elaborated on the concept of touristic culture to examine the actions of local elites in using tourism practices, images, symbols, and other representations to build a New Orleans community identity during the first half of the twentieth century (Gotham 2007c). It is important to note that the terms "culture," "authenticity," "community," or "identity" are not created by abstract collectives but are fashioned in the struggles of factions and groups to create and control material resources and the content of collective representations. The social construction of culture, community, authenticity, and related urban representations is always a conflictual and contested process. As I point out, powerful groups and organized interests often deploy symbols and imagery in an attempt to unite local citizens and build a supportive constituency for tourism development. As a political strategy, the symbol of "community" contains a multiplicity of meanings that provide social actors with a strategic vocabulary but one that leaves the specifics artificially ambiguous. In this sense, we can view terms like "authenticity," "community," and "identity" as a form of cultural capital that elite groups wield more or less self-consciously in their social and political struggles to influence local meanings of authenticity and shape urban culture.

Overall, I have found that tourism practices can support and invigorate existing modes of authenticity, help reconstruct old forms of authenticity, and promote the creation of new meanings of authenticity and local culture. Rather than viewing authenticity as immutable and primordial, I examine the process of authentication, focusing on how and under what conditions people make claims for authenticity and the interests that such claims serve. A major concern is to show how pre-existing social structures – including values, norms, beliefs, interpretive systems, and formal and informal organizations – can shape and constrain the symbols and themes available to people in their efforts to construct placed-based meanings, including definitions of authenticity. In short, social-structural forces shape and frame assertions of authenticity in the production of culture and tourism. As my work on New Orleans shows, authenticity is an adaptable and hybrid category that is constantly being created anew as social movement participants, cultural authorities, and other groups struggle to legitimate selective and idealized perceptions of local culture as fixed and immutable. My overall conclusion is that tourism discourses and practices can mobilize people to create new authenticities, reinvent culture, and foster new identities of place.

References

Bandyopadhyay, R. 2013. "A Paradigm Shift in Sex Tourism Research." *Tourism Management Perspectives* 6:1–2.

Barthel-Bouchier, Diane. 2001. "Authenticity and Identity: Theme-Parking the Amanas." *International Sociology* 16(2):221–39.

Bryman, Alan. 1999. "Disneyization of Society." *Sociological Review* 47(1):25–47.

Cabezas, Amalia. 2004. "Between Love and Money: Sex, Tourism, and Citizenship in Cuba and the Dominican Republic." *Signs: Journal of Women in Culture and Society* 29(4):987–1015.

Callanan, M., and S. Thomas. 2005. "Volunteer Tourism: Deconstructing Volunteer Activities Within a Dynamic Environment." Pp. 183–200 in *Niche Tourism*, edited by M. Novelli. New York: Routledge.

Canavan, B. 2016. "Tourism Culture: Nexus, Characteristics, Context and Sustainability." *Tourism Management* 53:229–43.

Chen, L.H., and M.E. Wilson. 2013. "The Globalization of Healthcare: Implications of Medical Tourism for the Infectious Disease Clinician." *Clinical Infectious Diseases* 57(12):1752–59.

Cohen, Erik. 1988. "Authenticity and Commodification in Tourism." *Annals of Tourism Research* 15(3):371–86.

Coleman, Simon, and Mike Crang, eds. 2003. *Tourism: Between Place and Performance*. London: Berghahn Books.

Crang, Michael. 2004. "Cultural Geographies of Tourism." Pp. 74–84 in *A Companion to Tourism*, edited by A. Lew, M.C. Hall, and A. Williams. New York: Blackwell.

Crush, J., and A. Chikanda. 2015. "South – South Medical Tourism and the Quest for Health in Southern Africa." *Social Science & Medicine* 124:313–20.

Desmond, Jane C. 1999. *Staging Tourism: Bodies on Display from Waikiki to Sea World*. Chicago: University of Chicago Press.

Eeckhout, Bart. 2001. "The 'Disneyification' of Times Square: Back to the Future?" Pp. 379–428 in *Critical Perspectives on Urban Redevelopment*, edited by K.F. Gotham. New York: Elsevier Press.

Gotham, K.F. 2002. "Marketing Mardi Gras: Commodification, Spectacle, and the Political Economy of Tourism in New Orleans." *Urban Studies* 39(10):1735–56.

———. 2005a. "Tourism From Above and Below: Globalization, Localization, and New Orleans's Mardi Gras." *International Journal of Urban and Regional Research* 29(2):309–26.

———. 2005b. "Tourism Gentrification: The Case of New Orleans's Vieux Carre (French Quarter)." *Urban Studies* 42(7):1099–121.

———. 2005c. "Theorizing Urban Spectacles: Festivals, Tourism, and the Transformation of Urban Space." *City: Analysis of Urban Trends, Culture, Theory, Policy, Action* 9(2):225–46.

———. 2007a. *Authentic New Orleans: Race, Culture, and Tourism in the Big Easy*. New York: New York University Press.

———. 2007b. "Critical Theory and Katrina: Disaster, Spectacle, and Immanent Critique." *City: Analysis of Urban Trends, Culture, Theory, Policy, Action* 11(1):81–99.

———. 2007c. "Destination New Orleans: Commodification, Rationalization, and the Rise of Urban Tourism." *Journal of Consumer Culture* 7(3):305–34.

———. 2007d. "Fast Spectacle: Reflections on Hurricane Katrina and the Contradictions of Spectacle." *Fast Capitalism* 2(2). Retrieved (www.fastcapitalism.com/).

———. 2007e. "Ethnic Heritage Tourism and Global-Local Connections in New Orleans." Pp. 125–42 in *Tourism, Ethnic Diversity and the City*, edited by J. Rath. New York: Routledge.

———. 2007f. "(Re)branding the Big Easy: tourism rebuilding in post-Katrina New Orleans." *Urban Affairs Review* 42(6):823–50.

————. 2011a. "Reconstructing the Big Easy: Racial Heritage Tourism in New Orleans." *Journal of Policy Research in Tourism, Leisure and Events* 3(2):109–20.

————. 2011b. "Resisting Urban Spectacle: The 1984 Louisiana Exposition and the Contradictions of Mega Events." *Urban Studies* 48(1):197–214.

————. 2011c. "Theorizing Carnival: Mardi Gras as Perceived, Conceived, and Lived Space." Pp. 93–118 in *Alienation and the Carnivalization of Society*, edited by J. Braun, and L. Langman. New York: Routledge.

————. 2012. "'Make it Right?' Brad Pitt, post-Katrina Rebuilding, and the Spectacularization of Disaster." Pp. 97–113 in *Commodity Activism: Cultural Resistance in Neoliberal Times*, edited by S. Banet-Weiser, and R. Mukherjee. New York: New York University Press.

Gotham, K.F., and M. Greenberg. 2014. *Crisis Cities: Disaster and Redevelopment in New York and New Orleans.* New York: Oxford University Press.

Gotham, K.F., and J. Lewis. 2015. "Green Tourism and the Ambiguities of Sustainability Discourse: The Case of New Orleans's Lower Ninth Ward." *International Journal of Social Ecology and Sustainable Development* 6(2):60–77.

Gregory, S. 2014. *The Devil Behind The Mirror: Globalization And Politics In The Dominican Republic.* Berkeley: University of California Press.

Hannam, Kevin. 2006. "Tourism and Development III: Performances, Performativities, and Mobilities." *Progress in Development Studies* 6(3):243–49.

Hoffman, Lily K., Susan S. Fainstein., and Dennis R. Judd, eds. 2003. *Cities and Visitors: Regulating People, Markets, and City Space.* New York: Blackwell.

Kibicho, W. 2016. *Sex Tourism in Africa: Kenya's Booming Industry.* New York: Routledge.

MacCannell, Dean. 1973. "Staged Authenticity: Arrangements of Social Space in Tourist Settings." *American Journal of Sociology* 79(3):589–603.

————. 1992. *Empty Meeting Grounds: The Tourist Papers.* New York: Routledge.

Palacios, C.M. 2010. "Volunteer Tourism, Development and Education in a Postcolonial World: Conceiving Global Connections Beyond Aid." *Journal of Sustainable Tourism* 18(7):861–78.

Rachel, Michal. 2013. *Extractions: An Ethnography of Reproductive Tourism.* Nahman, Hampshire: Palgrave Macmillan.

Rath, Jan, ed. 2007. *Tourism, Ethnic Diversity, and the City.* New York: Routledge.

Reichl, Alexander J. 1999. *Reconstructing Times Square: Politics and Culture in Urban Development.* Lawrence: University Press of Kansas.

Richter, L.M., and A. Norman. 2010. "AIDS Orphan Tourism: A Threat to Young Children in Residential Care." *Vulnerable Children and Youth Studies* 5(3):217–29.

Ritzer, George. 2006. *The Globalization of Nothing.* 2nd ed. Thousand Oaks, CA: Pine Forge Press.

Ritzer, George, and Allan Liska. 1997. "'McDisneyization' and 'Post-Tourism': Contemporary Perspectives on Contemporary Tourism." Pp. 96–112 in *Touring Cultures: Transformations in Travel and Leisure*, edited by Chris Rojek and John Urry. London: Routledge.

Rivers-Moore, M. 2016. *Gringo Gulch: Sex, Tourism, and Social Mobility in Costa Rica.* Chicago: University of Chicago Press.

Sanchez Taylor, Jacqueline. 2015. "Sex Tourism (Female)." Pp. 1115–1354 in *The International Encyclopedia of Human Sexuality*, edited by P. Whelehan, and A. Bolin. New York: Wiley-Blackwell.

Sheller, Mimi. 2003. *Consuming the Caribbean: From Arawaks to Zombies.* London: Routledge.

Sheller, Mimi, and John Urry. 2006. *Tourism Mobilities: Places to Play, Places in Play.* New York: Routledge.

Shepherd, Robert. 2002. "Commodification, Culture, and Tourism." *Tourist Studies* 2(2):183–201.

Smith, B. 2015. "Privileges and Problems of Female Sex Tourism: Exploring Intersections of Culture." Pp. 123–48 in *Handbook of Research on Global Hospitality and Tourism Management*, edited by Angelo A. Camillo. New York: Wiley-Blackwell.

Sorkin, Michael, ed. 1992. *Variations on a Theme Park: The New American City and End of Public Space.* New York: Hill and Wang.

Urry, John. 1990. *The Tourist Gaze.* Thousand Oaks, CA: Sage.

Varley, P., S. Taylor, and T. Johnson. 2013. *Adventure Tourism: Meaning, Experience and Learning.* New York: Routledge.

Wood, Robert E. 1998. "Touristic Ethnicity: A Brief Itinerary." *Ethnic and Racial Studies* 21(2):218–41.

Part X

Movements, memory, and change

63

Movement cultures

Francesca Polletta

Introduction

Many social movements seek to enact in their own operation the society they hope to bring into being. Their members may make decisions by consensus and rotate leadership. They may trade conventional gender roles, swap sexual partners, sign over their paychecks to the group, or refuse to eat animal products. Sometimes, movement groups succeed in creating enduring communities that are nonviolent, egalitarian, self-sustaining, and/or sexually liberated. Often, they collapse, imploding amid mutual recriminations and charges of bad faith. And occasionally, whether or not they endure, they pioneer organizational forms, interactional styles, and cultural objects that make their way into the mainstream. Food co-ops, blue jeans as a young person's fashion statement, *Ms.* magazine, participatory democratic decision-making, organic food, folk music, and alternative media all began in movements, but each one outlasted the movement and era in which it was born.

It is tempting to see movement cultures as idealistic and expressive, as experiments in alternative living that offer activists a respite from, or alternative to, the more instrumental tasks of engaging opponents, mobilizing support, and negotiating with allies. In recent years, however, scholars have drawn attention instead to the political and instrumental dimensions of movement cultures. Holding hands and singing Kumbaya can serve practical functions. By the same token, a self-consciously hard-nosed and instrumental orientation may produce its own kinds of inefficiencies.

While not downplaying the experimental character of how movements operate internally, scholars also have recognized that movement cultures are rarely created de novo. They have therefore probed the institutional *sources* of activists' ideas about how to operate in a feminist or democratic or traditional way. This research, in turn, has shed light on a practical difficulty activists have faced in enacting their countercultural ideals – namely, the limited repertoire of behavioral models that activists have had to draw upon in practicing those ideals.

Not only expressive, experimental but not created out of whole cloth, movement cultures are also less ephemeral than we tend to think. They have impact beyond the movements in which they are forged. Surprisingly, there has been relatively little scholarship on this third theme. I raise it nevertheless because, like the other two themes, it has implications for cultural processes outside movements as well as within them. In short, studying the conditions in which elements of movement cultures diffuse can shed light on dynamics of cultural change more broadly.

Before I go any further, let me define a few terms. I define a movement as an organized effort to produce institutional or cultural change through the use of non-institutionalized means. Movements are often composed of organizations (such as NOW [National Organization for Women] and NARAL [National Abortion Rights Action League] for the American women's movement), but they are also composed of more informal networks and transient groupings. I define culture as shared beliefs, values, ideas, and practices. I emphasize practices, since when we talk about movement cultures colloquially, we are usually referring to styles of action and, especially, interaction that distinguish participation in the movement from participation in institutions outside it. If you went to a meeting of Occupy Wall Street activists, you learned rather quickly – or should have learned quickly – that wearing a suit or flashing your copy of *Robert's Rules of Order* would elicit suspicion. To be sure, particular movement organizations have norms that are more or less extensive and more or less exigent. Compare, for example, the culture of NOW with that of some radical feminist groups that have required their members to live together, renounce intimate relationships with men, and follow strict procedures for ensuring equality. I will argue later that scholars have erred in studying the latter kinds of movement cultures at the expense of the former. For now, though, I simply want to note that when I refer to cultural practices, I do not imply that those practices are equally constraining.

Occasionally in the following, I will treat as *cultural* certain practices that many scholars treat as *non-cultural*, for example, tactics like sit-ins and organizational forms such as bureaucracy. I do so because I want to show that ostensibly brass-tacks, hard-nosed, non-ideological practices, just as much as ideologically laden ones, are also cultural insofar as they are animated by shared beliefs (see Hart 2001 for a similar point).

Movement cultures as political and instrumental

When activists in the 1960s sought to make of their organizations experiments in radical egalitarianism and freedom, sociologists tended to treat them as acting on the basis of a youthful repudiation of authority that was at odds with the demands of effective political reform. Participatory democratic organizations in the New Left and women's movement were conceptualized as "expressive" or "redemptive" in contrast to their "instrumental" and "adversary" bureaucratic counterparts (for reviews, see Breines 1989; Polletta 2002).

Wini Breines's (1989) account of the 1960's American New Left offered a provocative challenge to that conceptualization. Experiments with egalitarian and cooperative decision-making were a kind of politics; just not the politics of parliamentary maneuver and bureaucratic manipulation. By "prefiguring" within the current practices of the movement the values of freedom, equality, and community that activists wanted on a grand scale, they were helping bring those values into existence.

The notion of prefiguration was valuable in restoring political purpose to understandings of activists' efforts to live countercultural ideals. Still, Breines treated activists' prefigurative purposes as in inevitable tension with their strategic ones. The tendency to see movement cultures as, by definition, at odds with effective action continued in analyses of the movement cultures of 1960s anti-Vietnam War activism, 1970s feminism, and 1980s antinuclear activism. It was increasingly challenged, however, by movement scholars interested not only in activists' purposes in creating unconventional structures and relationships, but also in the contribution of such efforts to familiar movement tasks such as sustaining members' commitment, developing innovative strategies, managing resources, and delegitimizing opponents.

For example, through a comparison of feminist organizations, Suzanne Staggenborg (1995) showed that decentralized and informal organizational structures generated innovative tactics by encouraging group input. Francesca Polletta (2002) argued that collectivist decision-making in the US civil rights movement was a practical way to train activists who had had little prior experience of politics. In an analysis of the National Women's Party – a militant feminist group that remained active after the passage of suffrage legislation – Verta Taylor (1989) demonstrated how the rich affective bonds that developed among a cadre of committed women helped to sustain feminism during a period of political inhospitability. American anti-nuclear Plowshares activists were more successful in retaining members than were their European and Australian counterparts because of their deep and extensive movement culture, Sharon Nepstad argues (2008). Retreats, rituals, intense Bible study, and a discourse of Catholic suffering sustained American members' commitment and faith, even through long prison sentences. In the anti-AIDS direct action group, ACT UP, the erotically charged character of meetings both kept people participating in what were otherwise tedious deliberations and was itself direct action. At a time when the societal response to AIDS was to encourage sexual puritanism, flirting and cruising in meetings was a radical affirmation of sex (Gould 2009).

To recognize the instrumental benefits of cultures prized more for their emotional and ideological substance has not meant ignoring their instrumental liabilities. On the contrary, relinquishing the assumption that organizations built on countercultural values are doomed to fail has allowed researchers to probe more carefully the obstacles facing such organizations. Certainly, some of the steepest obstacles have come from outside movements. Funders often require explicit job descriptions, assessment criteria, and conventional boards of directors (Matthews 1994). The US Internal Revenue Service's complex standards for retaining tax-exempt status led organizations to hire legal and financial experts (McCarthy, Britt, and Wolfson 1991). These and similar challenges push movements toward the mainstream.

But scholars have also drawn attention to dynamics operating within movements that have made it difficult for groups to enact their countercultural commitments. Critically, these dynamics often result less from a group's formal operating procedures than from its informal ways of doing things. Movement and organizational cultures shape a group's ability to act democratically, effectively, and efficiently. Comparative studies are particularly illuminating in this regard. For example, contrary to the common claim that consensus-based decision-making is impossibly time-consuming, some of the German collectivist groups that Darcy Leach (2016) studied made even difficult and contentious decisions quickly and efficiently, without silencing members or removing decisions from group control. Other collectivist groups were not efficient, but what distinguished the efficient collectives was neither their small size nor their reliance on paid staff. Instead, their members tended to be steeped in a consensus-oriented culture: they might live in a squat, shop at a food cooperative, volunteer for community projects run as collectives, and eat meals in a dining collective. Together these experiences reaffirmed members' commitment to consensus at the same time as it gave them practice in its use.

Another example: in the European Social Forum, meetings that involved national groups speaking different languages were experienced by participants as more inclusive than meetings within a single national group (Doerr 2012). The difference was that the multilingual meetings relied on simultaneous translation. Again, it was not the formal procedure of translation that was important, but rather a *culture* of translation, which helped to valorize difference and protect easily marginalized speakers. Half a century earlier, folk music was used both by US communists and the 1960s civil rights movement activists: indeed, they often sang the same songs. But where communists performed music to a passive audience, civil rights activists drew on the tradition of the Black church, where music was co-created by performer and audience.

As a result, activists were able to use music not only to entertain audiences but also to mobilize them (Roy 2010).

In each of these cases, the cultures in which participants were embedded made the difference between decision-making that was efficient or inefficient and inclusive or exclusive and between movements that were more or less mobilizing. Movement cultures supplied norms of interaction, but also the skills to enact those norms effectively. Again, this does not mean that strong movement cultures and deep affective bonds do not come with liabilities. In the alternative health center studied by Sherryl Kleinman (1996), a focus on interpersonal relations both kept people from leaving a group in which they were underpaid, and at the same time, frustratingly redefined structural inequities as interpersonal problems. Jeff Goodwin (1997) describes a "libidinal economy" of movements, in which members' affective and erotic attachments to people outside the movement compete with their attachment to the group. And James M. Jasper (2004) describes the "Dilemma of Reaching In and Reaching Out" faced by many groups, in which appealing to people outside the group jeopardizes the tight intimacy that members enjoy.

However, there is another important point. Recent scholarship has shown not only that what often passes as expressive action has instrumental benefits, but also that what counts as instrumental action has expressive benefits. In an important sense, instrumental rationality is *performed*. This means that practices prized for their cool-headed practicality may also come with practical liabilities. For example, in her study of fledgling movement groups, Kathleen Blee (2012) found that participants almost always resisted talking about the character of interpersonal relations in the group. They were uninterested in time-consuming quasi-therapeutic talk, they said. They wanted to engage in practical action. Even when relations within the group had frayed to the point of jeopardizing the group's survival, participants' response was to launch more actions. But participating in joint actions neither solved the interpersonal problems that had prompted them, nor kept people from drifting away from the group. The anti-Gulf War activists observed by Stephen Hart (2001) similarly relied on a pragmatic, nuts-and-bolts style in their internal discussions, effectively ruling out of order discussions of participants' personal commitments or broad ideological visions. But that "constrained" discursive style served them less effectively than did the "expansive" discourse characteristic of faith-based organizing groups, in which participants' ethical commitments threaded through all discussions. A discourse valued for its pragmatism, ironically, proved less effective than one valued for its moral depth.

One more example: the animal rights activists whom Julian Groves (2001) studied discouraged women from serving in leadership positions because they believed that women were seen by the public as prone to the kind of emotionalism that would cost the movement credibility. Activists spent little time discussing whether women were in fact prone to emotionalism, however, or whether emotional accounts were more or less effective than rational arguments. Their strategic calculations were based on a thoroughly gendered schema of reason.

My point is not to deny that movement groups face objective practical challenges. Such challenges are often rooted in material realities such as the scarcity of resources, the existence of a field of competitors and opponents, the difficulty of sustaining trust in large networks, and so on. Cultural norms within the group help to handle those challenges (Hall 1988), however. They do so in part by defining what even counts as a resource and what trust means and entails.

Movement cultures as inherited and emergent

So far, I have treated movement cultures as self-consciously created by their members. They are that, but they are never created out of whole cloth. A number of scholars in recent years have probed the sources of movement cultures. One source of ideas about how a movement group should operate are the networks of activism that predate the group. Movement cultures, like strategies and tactics, are preserved in the "abeyance structures" (Taylor 1989) or "halfway houses" (Morris 1984) that subsist between periods of mass mobilization.

The diffusion of cultural forms and practices from one movement to another can take place much more quickly, of course. Sit-ins, boycotts, the construction of mock shantytowns characteristic of South African apartheid, consensus-oriented decision-making, and the use of big puppets in marches have all been adopted by groups and movements far removed from the progenitors of these strategies (Tarrow 2013). The proven effectiveness of a strategy, tactic, or style is by no means a precondition for its spread. Rather, the stature of the initiator movement, perceived similarities between diffusing and adopting groups (Soule 2004), the resonance of the new form with ideas already circulating within movement groups (Tarrow 2013), and a group's ability to experiment with new forms (Wood 2012) seem to matter more.

A second source of ideas about how movements should operate are *nonpolitical* structures and relationships. Activists adapt ways of interacting from relationships with which they are familiar, turning those relationships into reference points for abstract concepts like equality, solidarity, care, and authority. For example, in her study of participatory democracy in movements in the 1960s, Polletta (2002) found that although there were older activists on the scene who might have schooled younger ones in Quaker practices of consensus-based decision-making, by and large that did not happen. Instead, student activists invented participatory democracy as they went along – or so they thought. For, in fact, they drew interactional norms from relationships that were already familiar to them: relationships of religious fellowship, tutelage, and, especially, friendship. Treating each other as friends made collective decision-making easy and efficient. It also created problems, however, when newcomers joined the group and felt excluded by a core of insiders.

Familiar relationships have also shaped the culture of racist hate groups (Blee 2002). Such groups delineated a role for women that extended their stereotypically maternal roles. Women's activism was defined as an expression of their nurturing capacities. In this respect, they were not unlike groups on the other end of the political spectrum, as Marian Mollin (2006) has documented in her study of gender in the ostensibly egalitarian pacifist movement, and Jocelyn Viterna (2013) has done in her study of the Salvadoran guerrilla war. Not gender, but *class* may shape movement cultures – in a way that creates difficulties for movement groups. In the progressive groups studied by Betsy Leondar-Wright (2014), working-class members were not bothered by middle-class members' tendency to use abstract language, as much as they preferred concrete talk with vivid examples. What did bother them was middle-class activists' reluctance to exercise leadership. Their no-leaders ethos was off-putting to people who put great store in the trustworthiness of their leaders. Middle-class activists, for their part, were frustrated by working-class activists' tendency to evaluate a group by how much they trusted its leader. Norms of interaction came from the different class cultures in which members had grown up.

In his study of the anti-vice, abolitionist, and temperance movements of the 1830s US, Michael Young (2006) detailed the process by which norms of interaction migrated from a nonpolitical sphere to a political one. At the same time that Protestant churches were creating a vast network of benevolent societies aimed at eradicating national sins like Sabbath-breaking and drinking, upstart Methodist sects were popularizing a revivalist style that focused on public confession. Schemas of sin and confession joined to produce what Young calls a confessional mode of protest, in which activists fused bids for self- and social transformation.

Today, digital media may be contributing to a new mode of protest. The fact that much of protest is online has meant that movement organizations have declined in importance. Protests are often organized by small groups, "lone wolves," or participants who never even meet each other (Earl and Kimport 2011). But offline protest has also changed in the digital era. People are recruited to participate in public protests and occupations less by long-standing organizations than by the tweets, blog entries, and Facebook posts of people already participating who share their experiences under broad but personalizable themes like "we are the 99 percent" (Bennett and Segerberg 2013). This was the case, say scholars, in the 2011 Arab Spring protests, the Occupy Wall Street movement, the 15M movement in Spain, and anti-austerity protests in Greece and Brazil. Even before these movements, argues Jeffrey Juris (2008), global justice activists organized themselves on the model of the internet, with multiple nodes of decision-making in a loose network. Coalitions were deliberately temporary, and autonomy was prized over unity.

The internet has served as a model for the movement culture of the American right as well as the left. "This is an Open-Source movement," an organizer said of the Tea Party movement, referring to the software that encourages modifications by its users. "The movement as a whole is smart" (Rauch 2010:29). In China, the internet has produced a style of protest that is more prosaic, satirical, and carnivalesque than the earlier epic style, in which protesters expressed noble aspirations and death-defying resoluteness (Yang 2009).

None of the works I have described maintains that movement cultures, once given, are fixed for all time. Each one recognizes that cultures are emergent. But teasing out their roots sheds light on an important obstacle in realizing countercultural ideals. The very *materials* that activists rely on to enact their countercultural ideas – materials such as the interactional norms of familiar relationships, class cultures, and popular role definitions – may operate in ways that reproduce rather than challenge existing structures of power and inequality.

Movement cultures as evanescent and enduring

"Consciousness-raising," a cultural practice that gained fame in the radical women's movement, has become a familiar political strategy. By contrast, the feminist practice of allocating tasks within the group by lot never really took off. Why? What accounts for why some aspects of movement cultures endure and others fall into disuse?

One might speculate that the movement practices most prone to institutionalization are those that can be detached from their originating movement context in a way that preserves their tone of political idealism without actually encouraging protest. So, for example, participatory democracy as a form of decision-making oriented to consensus has been touted in a variety of mainstream institutions, including for-profit businesses. However, participatory democracy as new leftists meant it – a polity in which ordinary people participated in the decisions that affected them – has dropped out of our political idiom. Current understandings of consciousness-raising, some feminists complain, mistake it for group therapy rather than as preparation for collective action. If it is true that practices and styles that can be detached from their political purposes are prone to institutionalization, then movement objects that can be commercially marketed are even more likely to go mainstream. Blue jeans, peace signs, and rainbow flags fit this category.

Against this analysis, though, one might point out that even today participatory democracy provides tools for naming and challenging inegalitarian practices in organizations. Muslim women's practice of wearing headscarves has been interpreted, at different times and places, as a sign of religious belief or as a political challenge. The political associations of a depoliticized cultural style can be recuperated in a way that gives the style a contentious edge. The term "male chauvinist" was first used by Communist Party members in the 1930s, then disappeared before it was picked up again by women's liberationists in the late 1960s. By the 1990s, it had become a popular epithet: 63 percent of women in a national survey reported having used it, and 58 percent of women who did not identify as feminist reported using it (Mansbridge and Flaster 2007).

Yet another twist is suggested by the changing cultural status of the folk song "Kumbaya." The old spiritual was popularized by Pete Seeger in 1958 and Joan Baez in 1962, and it became closely associated with the civil rights movement. Today, however, the song is most often invoked sarcastically, to refer to naïve romantics who think the world's problems can be solved by "holding hands and singing 'Kumbaya,'" in a common phrasing. What accounts for the devaluing of the song? Probably the fact that its association with the civil rights movement led it to be adopted by a range of mainstream groups, including the Boy Scouts, the YMCA, countless summer camps, and Catholic Church folk masses. Thus mainstreamed, the song's movement credentials eroded.

In the absence of empirical research, these possibilities remain speculative. Along with the dearth of research on movement cultures in mainstream and conservative groups, our failure to analyze the impacts of movement cultures on practices outside the movement constitutes a significant gap in scholarship.

Conclusion

What can we learn about culture by studying its enactment within movements? One lesson is about the obstacles to putting countercultural ideals into practice. Those obstacles are in part structural. For example, US Internal Revenue Service codes require a formal organizational hierarchy even in organizations committed to equality. But the obstacles to practicing countercultural values lie also in the very ways in which we make sense of abstract ideals such as freedom or sisterhood. Relying on the norms associated with familiar roles and relationships makes it easier to enact those values, since they let us know what kinds of behaviors are expected. It would be hard to figure out just what equality meant in every interaction without those expectations. But norms derived from familiar roles and relationships also militate against creating new kinds of relationships. They risk promoting intimacy at the expense of inclusivity, responsibility at the expense of innovation, respect at the expense of an openness to dissent.

A second lesson is how important culture is to strategic action. This lesson is missed when we rely on an expressive-instrumental binary, with emotions, rituals, and beliefs on one side, and cognition, rules, and rationality on the other. Scholars have shown that at the individual level, emotions can sharpen rational cognition. This is true at the group level too. Instrumental tasks of mobilizing people to participate, sustaining their commitment, and making and implementing effective strategies all depend on the habits that come from strong movement cultures. At the same time, of course, such cultures may discourage efforts to recruit diverse members, and familiar cultural habits may unwittingly reproduce the values the movement is trying to challenge. This is true, however, even when the cultural habits activists rely on are associated with a cool-headed and practical orientation.

The third thing we can learn about culture from movements is that familiar notions of instrumental rationality have powerful force. Movements are illuminating in this regard because they have a stake in adopting mainstream ideas about what is strategic when it serves them and ignoring such ideas when it does not. The fact that activists sometimes embrace a narrow definition of what counts as strategic even when it hurts their prospects points to the truly constraining character of our common sense about strategy.

There is more to be learned about culture from movements. Scholars have just begun to study culture in movement groups that are right-wing, and few have studied culture in movement groups that are pragmatic, moderate, and mainstream. How is instrumental rationality performed in the National Organization for Women or the Sierra Club? What feeling rules (Hochschild 1979) govern interactions in the professionalized, Washington-based organizations that dominate the movement field? Scholars have tended to study "hot" emotions such as anger, love, anxiety, and pride rather than "cool" emotions such as boredom, condescension, and calm. Professionalized movement organizations offer valuable sites in which to investigate the political functions of cool emotions.

Finally, although I have referred to studies of movement cultures in Europe, Latin America, the Middle East, and China, the majority of my examples have come from US movements. This reflects the fact that dominant models of social movements have been based on US cases. Where scholars have turned to non-US movements, however, they have found reason to modify the models. This suggests that, should we look outside the United States, we may find very different answers to the questions I have posed about the sources of movement culture and the obstacles to realizing countercultural values.

There is another reason for studying movement cultures around the world. Scholars of culture have been rightly wary of efforts to delineate national and regional cultures since they seem to imply that such cultures are unitary, along the lines of a Dutch or American or South African "character." However, the coalition work that has become central to transnational protest – coalition work that is often made difficult by so-called cultural differences (Juris 2008) – provides a vital opportunity to see how national and regional cultures are performed and experienced.

References

Bennett, W.L., and A. Segerberg. 2013. *The Logic of Connective Action: Digital Media and the Personalization of Contentious Politics.* New York: Cambridge University Press.

Blee, K.M. 2002. *Inside Organized Racism: Women in the Hate Movement.* Berkeley: University of California Press.

———. 2012. *Democracy in the Making: How Activist Groups Form.* New York: Oxford University Press.

Breines, W. 1989. *Community and Organization in the New Left, 1962–1968: The Great Refusal.* New Brunswick, NJ: Rutgers University Press.

Doerr, N. 2012. "Translating Democracy: How Activists in the European Social Forum Practice Multilingual Deliberation." *European Political Science Review* 4(3):361–84.

Earl, J., and K. Kimport. 2011. *Digitally Enabled Social Change: Activism in the Internet Age.* Cambridge, MA: MIT Press.

Goodwin, J. 1997. "The Libidinal Constitution of a High-Risk Social Movement: Affectual Ties and Solidarity in the Huk Rebellion, 1946 to 1954." *American Sociological Review* 62(1):53–69

Gould, D.B. 2009. *Moving Politics: Emotion in ACT-UP.* Chicago: University of Chicago Press.

Groves, J. 2001. "Animal Rights and the Politics of Emotion: Folk Constructions of Emotion in the Animal Rights Movement." Pp. 212–29 in *Passionate Politics: Emotions and Social Movements*, edited by J. Goodwin, J.M. Jasper, and F. Polletta. Chicago: University of Chicago Press.

Hall, J.R. 1988. "Social Organization and Pathways of Commitment: Types of Communal Groups, Rational Choice Theory, and the Kanter Thesis." *American Sociological Review* 53(5):679–92.

Hart, S. 2001. *Cultural Dilemmas of Progressive Politics: Styles of Engagement among Grassroots Activists.* Chicago: University of Chicago Press.

Hochschild, A. 1979. "Emotion Work, Feeling Rules, and Social Structure." *American Journal of Sociology* 85(3):551–75.

Jasper, J. 2004. "A Strategic Approach to Collective Action." *Mobilization* 9(1):1–16.

Juris, J.S. 2008. *Networking Futures: The Movements against Corporate Globalization.* Durham, NC: Duke University Press.

Kleinman, S. 1996. *Opposing Ambitions: Gender and Identity in an Alternative Organization.* Chicago: University of Chicago Press.

Leach, D.K. 2016. "When Freedom Is Not an Endless Meeting: A New Look at Efficiency in Consensus-Based Decision Making." *Sociological Quarterly* 57(1): 36–70.

Leondar-Wright, B. 2014. *Missing Class*. Ithaca, NY: Cornell University Press.

Mansbridge, J., and K. Flaster. 2007. "The Cultural Politics of Everyday Discourse: The Case of 'Male Chauvinist.'" *Critical Sociology* 33(4):627–60.

Matthews, N. 1994. *Confronting Rape: The Feminist Anti-Rape Movement and the State*. New York: Routledge.

McCarthy, J.D., D.W. Britt, and M. Wolfson. 1991. "The Institutional Channeling of Social Movements by the State in the United States." *Research in Social Movements, Conflicts, and Change* 13:45–76.

Mollin, M. 2006. *Radical Pacifism in Modern America: Egalitarianism and Protest*. Philadelphia: University of Pennsylvania Press.

Morris, A.D. 1984. *The Origins of the Civil Rights Movement: Black Communities Organizing for Change*. New York: Free Press.

Nepstad, S.E. 2008. *Religion and War Resistance in the Plowshares Movement*. New York: Cambridge University Press.

Polletta, F. 2002. *Freedom Is an Endless Meeting: Democracy in American Social Movements*. Chicago: University of Chicago Press.

Rauch, J. 2010. "How the Tea Party Organizes without Leaders." *National Journal Magazine*, 11 September, p. 29.

Roy, W.G. 2010. *Reds, Whites, and Blues: Social Movements, Folk Music, and Race in the United States*. Princeton, NJ: Princeton University Press.

Soule, S. 2004. "Diffusion Processes within and across Movements." Pp. 294–310 in *The Blackwell Companion to Social Movements*, edited by D. Snow, S.A. Soule, and H. Kriesi. Malden, MA: Blackwell.

Staggenborg, S. 1995. "Can Feminist Organizations Be Effective?" Pp. 339–55 in *Feminist Organizations*, edited by M.M. Ferree and P.Y. Martin. Philadelphia, PA: Temple University Press.

Tarrow, S. 2013. *The Language of Contention: Revolutions in Words, 1688–2012*. Cambridge: Cambridge University Press.

Taylor, V. 1989. "Social Movement Continuity: The Women's Movement in Abeyance." *American Sociological Review* 54(5):761–75.

Viterna, J. 2013. *Women in War: the Micro-Processes of Mobilization in El Salvador*. New York: Oxford University Press.

Wood, L.J. 2012. *Direct Action, Deliberation, and Diffusion: Collective Action after the WTO Protests in Seattle*. New York: Cambridge University Press.

Yang, G. 2009. *The Power of the Internet in China: Citizen Activism Online*. New York: Columbia University Press.

Young, M. 2006. *Bearing Witness against Sin: The Evangelical Birth of the American Social Movement*. Chicago: University of Chicago Press.

64

Cultural movements

Elizabeth Cherry

Introduction

Until the "cultural turn," social movement scholars largely neglected culture, much less cultural movements. When they did consider culture in their analyses, they tended to view it in opposition to social structures, and as an arena free of constraints and full of agency. Now, sociologists view culture as a structuring force in itself, and scholars understand that movements may seek to change cultural structures not only through traditional political organizing, but also by enacting changes in people's lifestyles, identities, consumption practices, and much more.

"Cultural movements" is a phrase used to describe diffusely organized efforts to promote individual changes in lifestyle and consumption practices as a way to effect broader social changes. To improve understanding of cultural movements, this chapter first explores the different definitions of "culture" that social movement scholars have used in relation to state-oriented social movements and diffuse cultural movements. Then, I will show how contemporary understandings of cultural and lifestyle movements emerged from these early conceptions. The following section explores the everyday work of movements – how people are mobilized into cultural movements and how cultural movements intertwine their goals and means. I then consider how cultural movements face a paradox: they must be culturally challenging, but at the same time, they must work within a given culture to be viewed as culturally legitimate. This chapter ends with suggestions for future research on cultural movements.

Several contemporary movements could be considered cultural movements. To illustrate the issues, I explore as examples three cultural movements that focus on lifestyle and consumption patterns – veganism, straight edge, and green living. Vegans are strict vegetarians who, for ethical and animal rights reasons, avoid all animal products in their food, clothing, and other products. Straight edge is a movement that emerged from the punk rock subculture and that encourages clean living, especially avoiding drugs and alcohol. Green living describes people who have modified their houses, lifestyles, and consumption patterns to be as environmentally friendly as possible. Additional cultural movements include communal living and other intentional communities (Aguilar 2013); freegans, locavores, and other food-based movements (Barnard 2016); and anarchists and other movements at the nexus of political and personal practices (Portwood-Stacer 2013).

Culture and social movement studies

Cultural movements have long existed, for example, in ancient religious practices oriented toward self-discipline. Sociologists' understanding of cultural movements, though, grew out of social movement scholars' understanding of the relationship between culture and social movements. Around the same time that Douglas McAdam (1994) described the "structural bias" of social movement studies, most expressly its neglect of culture, sociologists began paying more attention to culture in social movements.

Early attempts to incorporate culture into social movement studies looked at movement cultures. Scholars studying movement cultures examined the movements' values, objects, stories, gatherings, roles, and the identities of participants (Lofland 1995). They wondered about the distinctiveness of movement values, and to what extent movement values resembled or differed from those in the larger society (Luker 1984). Analyzing movement culture alone did not address the "structural bias," as scholars still did not understand how movements might affect culture, or how activists might use culture as a tool. Scholars of cultural movements have taken on these issues and more, but in order for this analytic shift to occur, social movement studies had to first develop an understanding of activists' uses of culture.

Scholars began to understand how culture might be a useful tool for activists when they began to study "frame alignment processes" (Snow et al. 1986). In framing, activists attempt to align their movement's beliefs with those of their targets. If a target is religious, then activists might use a religious argument to help that target understand the problem that the movement is seeking to solve, the solution the movement proposes to that problem, and/or the motivation to participate in the movement. In these practices, cultural beliefs and values are tools that activists can deploy to encourage the mobilization of new participants. However, viewing culture as primarily a tool to be deployed gives the sense that culture is purely agentic and that culture does not itself provide constraints or opportunities to activists.

With this initial consideration of culture in social movement studies that conventionally regarded social movements as primarily operating in political arenas, culture came to be treated as an agentic tool used to challenge political and social structures. However, as I will show, in cultural movements, culture is a constraining force as well as an enabling one. Thus scholars' ability to conceptualize cultural movements adequately necessitated rethinking the relationship between culture, structure, and agency.

The study of cultural movements draws upon newer sociological perspectives of culture as a structuring force in itself. Following the work of foundational cultural theorists (Bourdieu 1977; Giddens 1984; Sewell 1992), social movement scholars have taken up the argument that culture acts as a restricting, yet empowering structure. Sharon Hays (1994) argued that sociologists need to be more specific when using the terms "structure" and "agency." Since the term "structure" is often contrasted with agency and with culture, culture often becomes synonymous with agency (Hays 1994; Polletta 2004). For scholars of cultural movements, this lack of clarity means the way in which culture constrains or shapes action becomes obscured.

To adequately understand the role of culture in social movement studies, scholars should follow Sharon Hays's argument that culture should also be thought of as a social structure. The idea of culture as a social structure contrasts with functionalist sociological definitions of structure and culture, and is more aligned with anthropological definitions, where the term "structure" normally refers to culture. Hays (1994:65) defined culture as simultaneously material and ideal, constraining and enabling, and as a social structure in itself.

Although the work of Francesca Polletta (2004) focuses on the cultural aspects of political structures, she helped pave the way for scholars of cultural movements to use the concept of culture effectively as describing a social structure. Polletta treats culture as the symbolic dimension of all structures, institutions, and practices, and she argues scholars should look at structures as cultural, although not solely cultural. To Polletta, culture is not simply a dimension that enables people to act agentically. Culture is patterned and patterning, enabling and constraining. And it is observable nearly everywhere – in linguistic practices, institutional rules, and social rituals. Many of the areas that Polletta describes – language, rituals, and everyday actions – are precisely what actors in cultural movements seek to change.

Understanding culture as a structure helps scholars to better understand the ways in which activists in conventional social as well as cultural movements might target cultural values, practices, and beliefs as part of their work. In this understanding, culture is both a means and an end, both a goal and a tactic.

Douglas McAdam (1994) discussed several cultural consequences of social movements. Movements do not only change political and social structures; movements also change culture. McAdam (1994) argued that social movements have created revolutionary ideologies, master frames, new identities, new forms of protest, new forms of material and non-material culture (e.g., dress, hairstyles, language), and they have changed how mainstream cultural institutions, such as churches, have functioned. Although McAdam was describing the cultural consequences of traditional, state-oriented social movements, his argument perfectly describes the targets, goals, and outcomes of cultural movements. Using this view of culture as a constraining and enabling entity, social movement scholars were able to better understand cultural movements, as this chapter shall detail.

Definitions of cultural movements

The emergent perspectives on culture as structure helped scholars better understand diffuse social movements whose participants seek to change their own or others' cultural beliefs, values, and practices. Cultural movements take a variety of forms, and they include phenomena sometimes described as lifestyle movements (Haenfler, Johnson, and Jones 2012) and new social movements (Melucci 1988). Both types of movements can be subsumed under the broader category of "cultural movements," defined as diffusely organized efforts to promote individual changes in lifestyle and consumption practices as a way to effect broader social changes. Activists in cultural movements seek to change culture, and they use existing culture to achieve their goals.

If both lifestyle movements and new social movements more broadly can be called "cultural movements," we must clarify how they resemble and differ from one another. Cultural movements, lifestyle movements, and new social movements are not necessarily empirically different types of movements. Rather, we need different theoretical and conceptual models to fully understand the range of cultural movements and their growth, goals, and tactics. On the one hand, vegans, green living, and anarchist movements all include professional social movement organizations that target the state, and they also encourage members to make their own everyday lifestyle changes. In this sense, they may resemble new social movements that include collective identity as an important component of movement participation alongside state-centered actions. On the other hand, vast numbers of people practice veganism, green living, and anarchism without becoming members of movement organizations; hence the need for social movement scholars to develop approaches to better understand participants who are not constituents or adherents of these traditional social movement organizations. To better understand these differences and the conceptual models scholars have developed to understand them, I shall outline the similarities and differences between new social movements, lifestyle movements, and the broader term of cultural movements.

The term "new social movements" describes the move from class-based movements to more cultural movements, or from "citizenship movements" to "post-citizenship movements" (Jasper 1997). Post-citizenship movements typically involve the participation of people already integrated into society who are seeking cultural changes, to establish new identities, or to seek wider recognition of previously devalued identities or lifestyles. The "new" in "new social movements" is a bit of a misnomer, since these foci have existed in older movements. Melucci (1988) and other scholars used the term as a way to distinguish between long-established forms of class conflict and newer, developing forms of collective action.

Activists in new social movements seek to change "cultural codes" (Melucci 1984), such that the entire form of the movement is a challenge to dominant patterns. One of the primary ways that movement participants operate is by developing and sustaining collective identities. In this process, a group of people comes to see themselves, and are seen by others, as explicitly seeking social change. Activists forge this shared sense of collective identity by creating a "we," which means that they agree upon their goals, their means, and their field of action (i.e., culture, lifestyle, discourse; Melucci 1988). This process of collective identity formation also requires active social networks and emotional investment.

Collective identity projects and other cultural challenges arising in new social movements are not only means or tactics; they are also goals in themselves. Activists' tactics serve as symbolic challenges to society. Activists engage in prefigurative politics (Breines 1982), practicing in the here-and-now the changes that they seek to establish more widely in the future.

Despite the inclusion of prefigurative politics and broader cultural challenges in research on new social movements, much of this research centers on internal processes related to collective identity. Scholars of cultural movements called "lifestyle movements" have helped broaden the focus of cultural movements to other activists' cultural goals and tactics. Lifestyle movements shift the focus to people's everyday lifestyles and consumption choices. According to Haenfler et al. (2012), although they overlap with new social movements in a number of significant ways, they also have important differences: new social movements tend to be centered in social movement organizations, whereas lifestyle movements more often involve individual activists and individual action. New social movements tend to target the state, whereas lifestyle movements tend to target cultural codes and individual cultural practices. New social movements tend to focus on collective identity, whereas lifestyle movements tend to focus on personal identity. Thus, conceptualizing cultural movements focuses on both identity politics and consumption patterns in a way that bridges the gaps between theorizations of new social movements and lifestyle movements.

How might we best understand cultural movements theoretically and empirically? One way is to consider their origins. Some cultural movements grow out of subcultures, whereas other cultural movements emerge from traditional social movements. Straight edge, voluntary simplicity, and freeganism all grew out of subcultures that incorporated lifestyle politics as part of their discourses and practices. Veganism, green living, and anarchism all emerged from traditional social movements that encouraged members to change aspects of their everyday lives, in addition to challenging state laws, policies, and practices. Each of these lifestyle movements grew out of a preliminary stage as an element of another subculture or social movement into a relatively autonomous cultural movement that gained adherents on its own.

Thus to understand cultural movements, researchers need to use diverse theoretical perspectives. We need to understand culture as a structuring element of everyday life, to consider how culture might influence mobilization into movements, and to view changing culture as both a goal and a means to achieve that goal.

Mobilization, goals, and means of cultural movements

How do people join cultural movements? Mobilization into cultural movements differs significantly from mobilization into conventional social movement organizations. Haenfler (2004a) noted that cultural movements are diffuse, meaning that there is no central organization for people to join as "members." Instead, cultural movement participants primarily learn about a movement and become interested in it through informal social networks. These can include in-person gathering spaces such as concerts and food co-ops or virtual spaces such as social media (Haenfler et al. 2012). Because participation in these organizations requires a changing of one's lifestyle and identity, initial participation in a cultural movement can be slow and gradual. Green living advocates gradually changed their lifestyle and consumption practices, and they viewed their participation as a lifelong project of learning and refining their habits (Lorenzen 2012). Vegans, in contrast, often described "catalytic experiences" that quickly and clearly motivated a dramatic change in lifestyle (McDonald 2000).

How do participants in cultural movements create change? The goals and the means of a given movement are interchangeable, and purposefully so. As Haenfler et al. (2012) note, prefigurative politics closely aligns with this type of movement. In her generative study of the New Left's organizing principles, Breines described prefigurative politics as tactics that must be consistent or compatible with a movement's goal: "to create and sustain within the lived practice of the movement relationships and political forms that 'prefigured' and embodied the desired society" (1982:6). Many activists and scholars reference Mahatma Gandhi's "truth force" (Nepstad 2015) or Martin Luther King Jr.'s "beloved community" (Williams 2002) as early examples of prefiguration. They were creating, in the present day, and through their actions, the type of world they were fighting to create in the future. Thus, "the methods advance the goal, even before the end goal is fully attained" (Nepstad 2015:13). Cultural movements use prefigurative politics, but they do not necessarily target the state – more often, they target cultural beliefs and practices.

Activists in cultural movements engage prefigurative politics in order to change some aspect of cultural structures and to create that change in the here-and-now. Cultural movements encourage people to make changes in their lifestyles, identities, consumption practices, and even ways of speaking about the world. Haenfler et al.'s (2012:5) delineation of lifestyle movements helps us to understand the range of cultural movement practices: lifestyle movements encourage individual, private, ongoing actions, which participants see as part of their personal identity, and which they view as working toward larger social change. New social movement theories help scholars understand how these meaningful personal identities may fit into larger collective identities, but they are less useful for understanding some of the practice-based and consumption elements of cultural movements. To better understand these interlocking goals and means of cultural movements, this chapter focuses on three different types of cultural movements: veganism, straight edge, and green living. All three rely on changing significant elements of one's daily life and consumption practices. Thus, scholars have looked to identity and social networks as ways of helping cultural movement participants maintain these practices.

Culture structures our eating habits in such a way that it is considered "normal" to eat animals and animal products, as well as to use animals for other purposes, such as for clothing, testing cosmetics, or entertainment. Veganism is a lifestyle movement that aims to end such uses of animals. Ethical vegans avoid consuming animal products or products tested on animals for animal rights purposes. The ultimate goal for vegans is cultural: they seek a world without animal exploitation. Therefore, the means they use to accomplish this goal are also cultural: they avoid animal exploitation in the here-and-now, through their consumption and lifestyle practices. They follow a plant-based diet, eating whole grains, vegetables, and legumes, while avoiding meat, poultry, fish, dairy products, eggs, and other animal by-products such as gelatin. Vegans purchase personal grooming and household products that are not tested on animals, and they avoid clothing items made from leather and fur. They also avoid entertainment that exploits animals, such as Sea World or circuses with animal performers.

Culture also contributes to mobilization of vegans, as many people learn about veganism through participation in subcultures such as punk rock, and "vegan" becomes a salient aspect of their identity. Greenebaum (2012) argued that embracing a vegan identity means publicly declaring one's morals and lifestyle, and that it is important, for vegans' personal fulfillment as well as for their role serving as the face of a cultural movement, for them to construct a meaningful, authentic identity as a vegan. Although identity is important, it alone is insufficient to maintain a vegan lifestyle, for another study has found that more people identify as vegan than practice a strictly vegan lifestyle; as with new social movements, supportive social networks help vegans maintain the practices that align with that identity (Cherry 2006).

The culture of the punk rock subculture created the straight edge movement. Straight edge is a cultural movement that originated in the punk subculture as a countermovement to the drugs and alcohol that permeated a certain nihilistic segment of the scene. The straight edge movement encouraged participants to avoid drugs and alcohol as a way to resist these self-destructive behaviors, and to keep their minds clear in order to create a better world. Culture also aided in mobilization for straight edge as a cultural movement, as straight edge participants learned about the movement through participation in the punk subculture, and their identity as straight edge was reinforced and maintained through such participation.

It is difficult to discern one specific goal that unites the diffuse cultural movement of straight edge, although Haenfler (2004a:790) notes that bands "sang about the virtues of a clean life, resisting mainstream society, supporting one's friends, staying positive, and a variety of social issues including racism, sexism, and environmentalism." In a cultural movement, straight edge youth put these goals into practice in their everyday lives, by living out all of these diverse goals. Maintaining and displaying an identity as straight edge is also important: straight edge youth would proudly "X up" before shows, drawing large X's on their hands before attending a concert as a way to demonstrate that they were not interested in drinking at the show. Many straight edge youth also have straight edge tattoos to declare their identity publicly. Although collective identity largely held straight edge participants to the same "essential" behaviors, Haenfler (2004b) still found there to be a difference between what participants viewed as "secondary" or "peripheral" behaviors.

The cultural movement of green living offers another example. After World War II, the US moved from a wartime culture of thrift and recycling to a "throwaway" lifestyle characterized by single-use items, plastic products, and increased consumption more generally (Cohen 2003). Green living emerged as a cultural response to this consumer culture. Green living is a term used to describe people who have changed aspects of their lifestyle and consumption practices for environmental purposes. If the ultimate goal of green living is for people to reduce their carbon footprint and minimize their effect on the earth, green living advocates practice this goal in the present through their lifestyle choices.

Lorenzen (2012) found three main types of groups involved in green living – voluntary simplifiers who sought to limit their overall consumption, religious environmentalists who saw environmental protection as part of their religious duty, and green homeowners who sought to make their homes as efficient as possible in terms of energy, water, and building materials.

They all also often engaged in everyday lifestyle practices such as recycling, water and energy conservation, vegetarianism and veganism, and eating locally. Green living advocates go out of their way, beyond typical conservation practices, to live their lives in the most environmentally friendly way possible. For green living, supportive social networks help participants maintain these practices (Kennedy 2011).

In each of these cases, participants in cultural movements seek to change a particular element of culture through changing people's everyday lifestyle and consumption practices. But to effectively promote these changes, each movement has to work within the broader culture in which they exist. Although cultural movements seek to push people to change various elements of their lives, they must also work to be seen as legitimate, as movements deserving serious consideration, and not as easily dismissed "fringe" elements.

The paradox of cultural movements

In that culture is both constraining and enabling (Hays 1994), it provides both opportunities and roadblocks for cultural movements. Cultural structures can constrain activists by preventing them from seeing opportunities for action or by preventing the broader public from hearing, much less understanding, certain discourses (Emirbayer and Goodwin 1994). Conversely, cultural structures can enable activists by giving them a shared worldview and by helping construct their identities (Emirbayer and Goodwin 1994).

Given these structured elements of culture, cultural changes can create new cultural opportunities, which can signal shifts in the symbols, ideologies, and arguments available to cultural movements. These shifts open up new meanings, creating new opportunities for social movements to put forth culturally resonant arguments. Cultural resonance "is a contingent process based on an alignment of legitimate cultural expressions, dominant ideological formations in society, and the cultural resources used by movement actors" (Williams and Kubal 1999:234). The concept of cultural resonance highlights a persistent dilemma for cultural movements focused on cultural change: how to package demands in a way that resonates in the culture in which they operate, especially when the demands are themselves culturally challenging (d'Anjou and Van Male 1998, Williams 2002). Cultural resonance can explain why the Civil Rights Movement in the United States drew so successfully upon Christianity, since Christianity is regarded as a legitimate aspect of the US culture. It also explains why Raelians are less successful in promoting their movement, because intelligent design by extraterrestrials is not considered to be an accepted element of US culture.

Cultural shifts may create opportunities, but they can also create new challenges. A lack of cultural change may also anchor existing cultural constraints. These divergent potential outcomes reflect the duality of culture as well as the duality of social structures. Jasper (2006) critiques the traditional concept of structures, preferring to see structures as barriers created by opponents strategically attempting to block actors' moves. In the case of cultural movements, Jasper's definition of structures seems more likely to apply if opponents mobilize a specific cultural argument in order to block the resonance of activists' arguments. Sometimes, however, such cultural arguments exist in everyday discourse and reflect the status quo, in which case they may be considered elements of the broader cultural field rather than as elements of opponents' strategic moves.

Conclusions and future research

Cultural movements represent an important divergence from and companion to traditionally organized, state-oriented social movements. The diffuse nature of cultural movements as well as their focus on everyday lifestyle and consumption practices allows for potentially much more widespread participation than in organizationally centered social movements. Nevertheless, people's ability to customize their participation at their own comfort levels may undermine significant, sweeping changes. As with other social movements, in cultural movements, identity and social networks are important for maintaining challenging lifestyle and consumption practices.

Although cultural movements have existed for centuries, research on cultural movements is relatively new. There are many areas for such research to expand in the future. Scholars should conduct more research about the outcomes of cultural movements. Scholars have already studied some of the cultural outcomes of conventional state-oriented social movements (McAdam 1994). But what are the effects of cultural movements directed at changing people's everyday lifestyle and consumption practices? Scholars have studied the effects of boycotts and buycotts (Willis and Schor 2012), and continuing these lines of research will better help sociologists to understand whether cultural movements have the wide-ranging outcomes that their practitioners hope they will have.

Much of the recent research on cultural and lifestyle movements has focused on individual-oriented cultural movements in one cultural context in the United States. Future research should expand this focus globally, and it should include comparative studies of different cultural movements, as well as of the same movement in different cultural contexts. Studying cultural movements in cross-national comparative perspective will help researchers understand the variations in cultural movements. Comparative research will help scholars tease out the important variables in terms of recruitment, retention, and outcomes of cultural movements.

References

Aguilar, Jade. 2013. "Situational Sexual Behaviors: The Ideological Work of Moving Toward Polyamory in Communal Living Groups." *Journal of Contemporary Ethnography* 42(1):62–87.

Barnard, Alex V. 2016. *Freegans: Diving into the Wealth of Food Waste in America*. Minneapolis: University of Minnesota Press.

Bourdieu, Pierre. 1977. *Outline of a Theory of Practice*. Cambridge: Cambridge University Press.

Breines, Wini. 1982. *Community and Organization in the New Left: 1962–1968*. New York: Praeger.

Cherry, Elizabeth. 2006. "Veganism as a Cultural Movement: A Relational Approach." *Social Movement Studies* 5(2):155–70.

Cohen, Lizabeth. 2003. *A Consumer's Republic: The Politics of Mass Consumption in Postwar America*. New York: Alfred A. Knopf.

d'Anjou, Leo, and John Van Male. 1998. "Between Old and New: Social Movements and Cultural Change." *Mobilization* 3(2):141–61.

Emirbayer, Mustafa, and Jeff Goodwin. 1994. "Network Analysis, Culture, and the Problem of Agency." *American Journal of Sociology* 99(6):1411–54.

Giddens, Anthony. 1984. *The Constitution of Society: Outline of the Theory of Structuration*. Berkeley: University of California Press.

Greenebaum, Jessica. 2012. "Veganism, Identity and the Quest for Authenticity." *Food, Culture & Society: An International Journal of Multidisciplinary Research* 15(1):129–44.

Haenfler, Ross. 2004a. "Collective Identity in the Straight Edge Movement: How Diffuse Movements Foster Commitment, Encourage Individualized Participation, and Promote Cultural Change." *Sociological Quarterly* 45(4):785–805.

———. 2004b. "Rethinking Subcultural Resistance: Core Values of the Straight Edge Movement." *Journal of Contemporary Ethnography* 33(4):406–36.

Haenfler, Ross, Brett Johnson, and Ellis Jones. 2012. "Lifestyle Movements: Exploring the Intersection of Lifestyle and Social Movements." *Social Movement Studies* 11(1):1–20.

Hays, Sharon. 1994. "Culture and Agency and the Sticky Problem of Culture." *Sociological Theory* 12(1):57–72.

Jasper, James. 1997. *The Art of Moral Protest: Culture, Biography, and Creativity in Social Movements*. Chicago: University of Chicago Press.

———. 2006. *Getting Your Way: Strategic Dilemmas in the Real World*. Chicago: University of Chicago Press.

Kennedy, Emily Huddart. 2011. "Rethinking Ecological Citizenship: The Role of Neighborhood Networks in Cultural Change." *Environmental Politics* 20(6):843–60.

Lofland, John. 1995. "Charting Degrees of Movement Culture: Tasks of the Cultural Cartographer." Pp. 188–216 in *Social Movements and Culture*, edited by H. Johnston and B. Klandermans. Minneapolis: University of Minnesota Press.

Lorenzen, Janet A. 2012. "Going Green: The Process of Lifestyle Change." *Sociological Forum* 27(1):94–116.

Luker, Kristin. 1984. *Abortion and the Politics of Motherhood*. Berkeley: University of California Press.

McAdam, Doug. 1994. "Culture and Social Movements." Pp. 36–57 in *New Social Movements: From Ideology to Identity*, edited by E. Laraña, H. Johnston, and J.R. Gusfield. Philadelphia, PA: Temple University Press.

McDonald, Barbara. 2000. "'Once You Know Something, You Can't Not Know It': An Empirical Look at Becoming Vegan." *Society & Animals* 8(1):1–23.

Melucci, Alberto. 1984. "An End to Social Movements?" *Social Science Information* 23:819–35.

———. 1988. "Getting Involved: Identity and Mobilization in Social Movements." Pp. 329–48 in *International Social Movement Research*. Vol. 1, edited by B. Klandermans, H. Kriesi, and S. Tarrow. Greenwich, CT: JAI Press.

Nepstad, Sharon Erickson. 2015. *Nonviolent Struggle: Theories, Strategies, and Dynamics*. New York: Oxford University Press.

Polletta, Francesca. 2004. "Culture is Not Just in Your Head." Pp. 97–110 in *Rethinking Social Movements: Structure, Meaning, and Emotion*, edited by J. Goodwin and J. Jasper. Lanham, MD: Rowman and Littlefield.

Portwood-Stacer, Laura. 2013. *Lifestyle Politics and Radical Activism*. New York: Bloomsbury.

Sewell, William. 1992. "A Theory of Structure: Duality, Agency, and Transformation." *American Journal of Sociology* 98(1):1–29.

Snow, David, Burke Rochford, Steven Worden, and Robert Benford. 1986. "Frame Alignment Processes, Micromobilization, and Movement Participation." *American Sociological Review* 51(4):464–81.

Williams, Rhys. 2002. "From the 'Beloved Community' to 'Family Values': Religious Language, Symbolic Repertoires, and Democratic Culture." Pp. 247–65 in *Social Movements: Identity, Culture, and the State*, edited by D. Meyer, N. Whittier, and B. Robnett. Oxford: Oxford University Press.

Williams, Rhys H., and Timothy J. Kubal. 1999. "Movement Frames and the Cultural Environment: Resonance, Failure, and the Boundaries of the Legitimate." *Research in Social Movements, Conflicts, and Change* 21:225–48.

Willis, Margaret, and Juliet B. Schor. 2012. "Does Changing a Light Bulb Lead to Changing the World? Political Action and the Conscious Consumer." *Annals of the American Academy of Political and Social Science* 644(1):160–90.

65
Cultural diffusion

Elihu Katz

I

Long before there were media of mass communication, ideas and practices found ways to traverse vast distances. One would think that broadcasting and the internet would have superseded the interpersonal networks that are implicit here, but they have not; the media, new and old, have a share in the flow of influence, but they are only part of the process, even today. Diffusion research seeks to follow innovations as they spread, within and between social structures, over time and space. Focused on the flow of influence, diffusion research unravels the mix of formal advocacy, informal persuasion, identification, imitation, contagion, resistance, withdrawal, and the like. Thus, the study of diffusion amounts to observing the microdynamics – the "retailing," so to speak – of this more or less voluntary form of social and cultural change that is based on communication – in contrast, say, to simultaneous invention, evolutionary change, or change imposed by fiat or by force.

Interest in how ideas and things travel, and how they aggregate, is integral to most of the social sciences and the humanities, and to some of the natural sciences as well. Early anthropology and cultural history, for example, tried to trace the progress of civilization (monotheism, alphabet, etc.) from its supposed origin in the "fertile crescent." Anthropologists and geographers found interest in the spatial distribution of certain "traits" and in the direction of their movement. Rural sociologists have had a long-standing interest in the diffusion and adoption of new farm practices, and in the role of agricultural extension agencies in their promotion; for a while, they joined with anthropologists in fostering "modernization" overseas. Historians of religion have been fascinated by the rapid diffusion of Christianity and Islam in the old days, and nowadays in the spread of Mormonism and new-age doctrines. Linguists are interested in the geography of speech. Students of fashion, folklore, literature, art, and archeology have investigated the diffusion of style, while social scientists have tracked the diffusion of technical change, and lately of social movements. Social psychologists have long nurtured a passion for ostensibly unstructured forms of "collective behavior" that include news, rumor, gossip, crowds, moral panics, audiences, and public opinion. And, of course, epidemiologists of the flu or of HIV and other infectious diseases are continually occupied with the dynamics of their spread, and with the success of attempts to combat them. Meaning much the same thing, marketing researchers now speak of computer-driven word of mouth as "viral marketing." Even terrorist organizations seem to imitate each other's changing tactics.

Several of the classics of sociology have tried to generalize across these domains. Gabriel Tarde ([1890] 1969) went farthest, perhaps, in his *Laws of Imitation*, arguing (against his contemporary, Emile Durkheim), that sociology could ill afford to overlook invention and influence as the pathways of social change. In the same spirit, Georg Simmel ([1904] 1957) saw emulation as the engine of change whereby the symbolic striving for upward mobility led each social class to emulate the class above, thus constraining the upper classes to seek ever new ways to differentiate themselves. Thorstein Veblen's (1899) "conspicuous consumption" is obviously related. In rebuttal, Harvard sociologist Pitirim Sorokin (1941) rejected the idea of "trickle down" diffusion in favor of a theory of exchange whereby the lower classes export "raw materials" such as cotton or folk songs to be processed and re-exported by the upper classes. Sorokin dwelled on the agents of diffusion such as missionaries, troubadours, traveling salesmen, and the like, on the routes they charted, and on their salesmanship, so to speak, all as part of his larger interest in social and cultural mobility. Along the same lines, Darnton (1982) cites the bookseller, and Erikson and Bearman (2006) credit the captains of British ships to India for the beginnings of global trade. Innis (1951) studied the tension between media of space (papyrus, printing) and media of time (pyramids, canonic texts) and between custodians of existing knowledge and their challengers. Multiple editions of Everett Rogers's *Diffusion of Innovations* ([1962] 1994) over a 40-year period catalog the increase in diffusion studies, as if to illustrate the "S-curve" that has come to characterize the trajectory of innovations that "take off." Gladwell's (2000) *The Tipping Point* has popularized the field, as have "small world" studies such as Milgram's (Travers and Milgram 1969), and even earlier, Pool and Gurevitch (Gurevitch 1961). These classics, it should be noted, are flawed by an overemphasis on "successful" innovations to the neglect of innovations that fail (cf. Mosse 1975; Strang and Soule 1998).

In spite of the seeming centrality of these concerns, it comes as a surprise that serious sociological studies of diffusion have been so sparse and so sporadic. While anthropologists, archeologists, and linguists may have continued uninterruptedly, sociologists, geographers, and others seem to have abandoned the subject between the 1940s and the 1970s of the past century. This may be because Durkheim's macrosociological emphasis prevailed over Tarde's, or more likely because the prospect of media influence prevailed over the interpersonal. A still better explanation, however, is that the post-war surge of empirical sociology had not yet forged the tools to cope with the social networks that channel the flow of interpersonal influence. For example, it took some 20 years for Paul Lazarsfeld's Bureau of Applied Social Research at Columbia University to progress from rediscovery of the mediating role of interpersonal influence in the mass communications of change (Lazarsfeld, Berelson, and Gaudet 1944) to the incorporation of full-blown social networks in the design of its research (Coleman, Katz, and Menzel 1966). Methodologically, this amounted to a wedding of sociometry and survey research, made possible by the ever-increasing capacity of the high-speed computer to track the person-to-person transmission of information and influence. Diffusion research is now riding high on the coattails of the explosion of computational research in the social sciences (Watts 2003). For example, the "virality" of message content and form (Berger and Milkman 2012) can be measured by selectivity of exposure, and by extent of "sharing" (John 2016); so-called big data (see Papacharissi 2015) can be mined for the geographic flow of an epidemic, the weather, or of public opinion; one can observe networks of social relations in action (or in construction) by following the so-called memes that they manufacture (Shifman 2014). The latter recalls Tarde's (Katz, Ali, and Kim 2014: 13) definition of "conversation" as "any dialogue without direct and immediate utility in which one talks for pleasure, as a game, or out of politeness."

II

Given the resurgence of interest, it is all the more surprising that the several domains of diffusion research have shown so little recognition of each other, and of the underlying "accounting scheme" that they share (Katz, Levin, and Hamilton 1963). Yet, it is evident that, whatever the domain, the study of cultural diffusion may be characterized as (1) the reception, or adoption, (2) of some idea or innovation, (3) over time, (4) by units of adoption – individuals, groups, organizations, nations, linked by (5) channels of communication, internal and external, (6) social structures, and (7) systems of norms and values.

Ostensibly, these components vary so widely from domain to domain that their comparability may be obscured. Who would think that the diffusion of hybrid corn seed among farmers in Iowa (Ryan and Gross 1942) might parallel the diffusion of a new antibiotic among physicians in four Midwestern towns? (E. Katz 1971). Yet they parallel each other very closely. Both studies aim to show how an innovation was introduced into a professional community, the "reception" it received, and the extent of its saturation. Both aimed to describe the role of the formal media and the extent to which interpersonal influence was active. Both wished to identify the parts played by exogenous influences, the early and late adopters, and the inside influentials, and the rate at which the innovation spread. As if following the shared "accounting scheme," both studies were able to date first use of each adopter (date of first prescription for MDs, season of first planting for farmers), to identify the socioeconomic status of each and his/her sociometric location in the web of community relations, and to reconstruct the cognitive and communicative steps in the process of decision-making. In their conclusions, both studies found advertising and salespeople to be harbingers of the innovation, while later stages in the decision-making process were increasingly dependent on professional media and collegial talk. Both studies found evidence of interpersonal influence at work and a positive correlation between social status and time of adoption. However, this correlation is likely limited to innovations that are "compatible" with community norms, implying that innovations that are alien will follow a different trajectory (Menzel 1960).

A study of the diffusion of "nouvelle cuisine" among French restaurants makes similar points (Rao, Monin, and Durand 2003). In spite of its ostensible departure from tradition, the innovation was deemed compatible both with the egalitarian turn in the larger French culture and with the professional self-image of the most-highly rated chefs. Thus the path of acceptance proceeded from the highest-starred establishments in the *Guide Michelin* to the lesser-ranking ones, rather than following a revolutionary path. By contrast, the diffusion of jazz in the United States climbed the social ladder from the bottom up (Lopes 2002), while today's fashions, no longer dictated from Paris, have, according to Diana Crane (1999), altogether lost their sense of direction.

Broadly, two interlocking principles are operative here. The first is the principle of *compatibility*, and the second is *social integration*. For an innovation to gain acceptance, it must be seen to be compatible with community and personal norms. It must be proposed by trustworthy sources and delivered in culturally acceptable circumstances. It must be capable of operation by the social unit to which it is addressed. If it "takes a village," the village is the unit to address, just as the kibbutz (in the old days) insisted that members take their tea and coffee only in the communal dining hall (Spiro 1956). Reflecting the same principle, Christianity – with its patrilineal symbolism – fared better in patrilineal tribes than in matrilineal ones (Hawley 1946) and, similarly, the expressiveness of Italian culture contributed to the flourishing of early opera in Italy (R. Katz 1986).

When an innovation is perceived to defy group norms, the most marginal members of the group will be early to adopt, if at all. Individuals who are linked to more than one group may often serve as innovators and influentials, however weak their ties (Granovetter 1973; Burt 1999a). Altogether, social location – the boss's secretary, for example – may account for greater influentiality than gregariousness or interest in a particular domain. As a rule, influence is more likely to be exchanged among persons who share the same demographic characteristics (Weimann 1994). However, inasmuch as influentials, or "opinion leaders," require followers, the flow of influence may be asymmetrical. Thus, younger women are more likely than equally interested older women to be sought out for fashion advice. The reverse holds for grocery shopping, where the opinion leadership of older women is more likely to be sought, both by their age-peers and by younger women (Katz and Lazarsfeld [1955] 2006). Sometimes, "epidemics" originate in certain segments of the population, as when children at school spread the flu virus, or when children serve as agents for linguistic change (Labov 2007).

Extending the channels of influence implicit in social location and social cohesion, relatively newer research has called attention to the imitative influence implicit in "structural equivalence" (Burt 1999b). The idea is that persons or groups situated in similar positions – connected to the same or similar constituencies – will keep abreast of each other as far as innovativeness is concerned. One will do what the other does, as noble courts of the seventeenth and eighteenth centuries began to introduce the new medium of opera. This process began with the competitive appointment of resident composers, usually Italian, just as opera was making its way from its "origin" in Florence to other Italian cities (R. Katz 1986). In a similar manner, universities were popping up all over Europe, followed, much later, by football teams (Hobsbawm 1983). The same process is on view today in the parade of self-respecting cities that are clearing their slums to make space for "avenues of the arts." And sociologists are investigating the roles of diffusion and equivalence in the "isomorphism" of organizational structures (Dimaggio and Powell 1983).

Thus, the study of diffusion is well served by the aforementioned "accounting scheme," which contains both a checklist of relevant observations and a set of implicit hypotheses that connect them. Let us consider each of these elements in turn:

1   Reception must be parsed as to whether the potential adopter is aware of the item, is interested in it, has considered its adoption, has tried it, has continued use after trial, and so forth. The student of diffusion must settle on one of these definitions of acceptance or adoption – for instance, whether an individual has tried to stop smoking, or has actually stopped, or restarted. There is considerable interest in the question of which media are effective at each stage of the decision to adopt (Van den Bulte and Lilien 2004). These "levels" of internalization correspond to those theories of behavior change that posit stages in decision-making and to theories in which change is thought to entail a disconnect from an earlier norm or practice – such as cigarette smoking – before proceeding to another.

2   The attributes of the diffusing item must be scrutinized from the subjective points of view of potential adopters. For example, how "complex" is it (in the sense of how much else has to change if one adopts an innovation such as, say, homosexual "outing," or religious conversion, or vegetarianism)? Is the item packaged as part of a "pattern" or system, or is it technical and relatively self-contained? Is the proposed change functional or primarily symbolic? Is it aimed to dislodge a competing item? Will it enhance an occupational role? Does it save time or money? Is it easy to operate? Can it be tried in "installments"? Has it found acceptance in positive or negative reference groups? (Berger 2007). Note that the item itself may change its image during the course it of its spread; it may become more or less risky, for example, or more or less popular, or be found to serve unanticipated needs. Innovations often also undergo "reframing," as did "organic food" in its early appeal to environmentalism and later appeal to "health." Adopters may also alter the function of an innovation,

as when the telegraph and, later, the radio, were transformed from interactive media to broadcast media, thus also changing the orbits of their diffusion (Blondheim 1994). Certain innovations do not succeed in diffusing until they are stripped of unnecessary or unattractive "adhesions" that confound their essence (Mead 1955). In a word, innovations and even the arcs of their diffusion are hard to hold still. The "meme" falls at an amusing extreme, because it invites recipients to introduce their own changes before "sharing."

3   Diffusion takes time. The simultaneity of response assumed by advertisers is alien to diffusion research. Obtaining information on time of adoption is often the most daunting problem of the researcher. While it is now possible to monitor consumer response to any type of computerized message or appeal, the problem of dating – measuring time of adoption – continues to challenge other areas of diffusion research. Archeology employs systems of dating and measurements of distance that make it possible to infer how far an artifact has traveled from its point of origin and how long it took (e.g., Speier 1921). Social science sometimes finds appropriate statistics on time of adoption, as when pharmacists could be asked to date physicians' first prescriptions for a new medication, or municipalities to date their adoption (or rejection) of fluoridation, or producers of music or of automobiles to keep track of how many of each model were sold in a succession of seasons. Bibliometrics were devised to follow the flow of published ideas (Borgman 1990).

4   Unit. Not all adopters are individuals. The item itself may dictate the appropriate unit; "it takes two to tango," for example, or to telephone. In the diffusion of fluoridation of water in the United States, which its opponents defamed as "socialized medicine," the unit of adoption was the municipality (Crain, Katz, and Rosenthal 1969). Of course, when the adopter is not an individual, there may also be a division of labor in the decision-making process (Dimaggio and Powell 1983). Even ostensibly individual adopters may make joint decisions with others, as when a parent decides for whom the family should vote, or what movie to see.

5   The channels of communication must be accounted for, first of all by distinguishing among the rapidly proliferating media of communication, and the formal and informal modes of interpersonal communication. These channels may then be associated with the different phases of decision-making, and with different types of items. For example, it was once thought that the relative privacy and precision of print, at least in literate societies, was more appropriate and more effective than television for advertising contraceptive practice. The key question, however, is how news of an innovation, and of its attractiveness, reaches a community or network from "outside," and how it circulates "inside" (Stark 1996; Mendels 1999). A missionary, or a salesman, or a magazine may make contact from outside, but there is ample research to show that such intervention, even from friendly sources, is almost never enough to explain non-trivial change or even to ignite interpersonal consideration of a proposed change, without the active initiative and participation of group members.

6   A map of the social structure of a community and the place of potential adopters within it is a key to analyzing diffusion. Such measures range from the density of a community, to the patterns of interaction at different times of the day. Sensational news, for example, may spread interpersonally during the daytime but not at night (DeFleur 1987). Emulation may work in a class-stratified society but not in one based on caste. Social integration will work, positively or negatively, depending on the compatibility of the proposed innovation with the norms of the group. "Structural equivalence," as already noted, may substitute for direct influence. Social, ethnic, and geographic boundaries often block the flow of influence (Hagerstrand 1967). Variations in the structure of such relationships – even between conqueror and conquered peoples, for example – have been associated with different kinds of

borrowings, and in both directions (Spicer 1954). Individuals with even weak ties to more than one group may be a source of innovation; consider the role of ship captains in establishing trade between Britain and the East Indies (Erikson and Bearman 2006). Of course, weak ties and low status may also breed dissidence and "reformist" social movements.

7   Culture. The appropriateness of invoking the concept of compatibility is obvious in any discussion of culture change, but that does not make it easy to apply. It involves analysis of the "fit" between potential adopter and diffusing item. It is easy to argue that the music of the Beatles somehow fit the youth culture of the 1960s, but it is very difficult to prove (and even harder to predict). Is there a method that will allow us to confirm Gitlin's (1983) suggestion that the most popular television programs in a given year somehow "fit" the values of the incumbent president? Can it be established that "suicide bombing" will diffuse mostly in cultures that offer a glorious afterlife to their martyrs?

III

It seems fair to say that the cultural sciences, and some of the natural sciences, share an interest in the origin of ideas and practices, and in how they spread. Yet, as has been noted, the several disciplines do not seem to have paid much attention to each other, and there have been only a few now-outdated (but still worthwhile) attempts to generalize across domains. This segmentation must surely result from the academic appeal, to different kinds of scholars, of the telephone, or Marxism, or "impressionism," or the measles. Scholars such as Tarde, Innis, or Sorokin did not overlook their similarities, nor, more recently, do Rogers ([1962] 1994), Brown (1981), or Strang and Soule (1998).

Recently, there appears to be renewed attention to the dynamics of diffusion within the several domains and even across domains. This may be related to the diffusion of interdisciplinarity, or more likely, to the near-universal diffusion of the computer, and with it, the relative ease of tracking change across time and space and social networks. For example, anthropologists are studying the diffusion of AIDS (Watkins 2004), sociologists are comparing the diffusion of radical changes of style with the diffusion of contentious politics (Rao et al. 2003), and linguists are comparing language change with fashions in children's names (Labov 2007; Lieberson 2000).

It follows that processes of diffusion ought to have a larger share in studies of change – past and present – and that diffusion research must draw its data from a large variety of domains. It is important to overcome the temptation to treat the diffusion of each new item as its very own story. Indeed, items should be compared in terms of the curves of their diffusion. Communications research, in particular, should forgo the specializations that tend to separate media studies from interpersonal communication, rather than to explore the dynamics of their interaction. Students of diffusion must strive to develop a content-analytic scheme to characterize diffusing items (innovations) from the subjective point of view of potential adopters and to stay abreast of how the perception of an item undergoes change even while it is diffusing. The content scheme should be expanded to explore the compatibility of an item with the social, cultural, and communicative contexts in which the potential adopter is embedded.

Diffusion research can contribute to the conceptualization of many different problems. Consider one. We think we know a lot about how opinions are formed, and how they are represented in polls of public opinion. But individual opinions are not "private" property. Circumstances conspire with the media to make an issue salient, and preliminary responses may arise, if they do, from predisposition, thought, and social interaction. But public opinion is not the sum total of individual opinions, as reported in polls. How, we should ask, did a myriad of fuzzy individual inclinations become salient, how did they condense into two opinions – pro-life and pro-choice, for example? Was this the form in which they spread among their constituencies? The aggregation of public opinion is a problem of diffusion, in which the media, social networks, and individuals have a share, as Gabriel Tarde ([1898] 1969) tried to show.

In sum, diffusion research seeks to formalize the role of communications in the study of social and cultural change, past, present, and future, in the spirit of Paul Lazarsfeld's (1964) essay on "The Obligations of the 1950 Pollster to the 1984 Historian." But whereas Lazarsfeld called for periodic portraits of the climate of opinion, diffusion research calls for weather maps of change in action.

References

Berger, J. 2007. "Where Consumers Diverge from Others: Identity Signaling and Product Domains." *Journal of Consumer Research* 34(2):121–33.

Berger, J., and K.L. Milkman. 2012. What Makes Online Content Viral? *Journal of Marketing Research* 49(2):192–205.

Blondheim, M. 1994. *News Over the Wire*. Cambridge, MA: Harvard University Press.

Borgman, C.L., ed. 1990. *Scholarly Communication and Bibliometrics*. Newbury Park, CA: Sage.

Brown, L.A. 1981. *Innovation Diffusion: A New Perspective*. London: Routledge.

Burt, R.S. 1999a. "The Social Capital of Opinion Leaders." *Annals of the American Academy of Political and Social Science* 566(1):37–54.

———. 1999b. "Social Contagion and Innovation: Cohesion vs. Structural Equivalence." *American Journal of Sociology* 92(6):1287–335.

Coleman, J., E. Katz, and H. Menzel. 1966. *Medical Innovation*. Indianapolis, IN: Bobbs Merrill.

Crain, R., E. Katz, and D. Rosenthal. 1969. *The Politics of Community Conflict: The Fluoridation Decision*. Indianapolis, IN: Bobbs Merrill.

Crane, D. 1999. "Diffusion Models and Fashion: A Reassessment." *Annals of the American Academy of Political and Social Science* 566(1):13–24.

Darnton, R. 1982. What is the history of books? *Daedalus* 111(3):65–83.

DeFleur, M.L. 1987. "The Growth and Decline of Research on the Diffusion of News." *Communication Review* 14(1):109–30.

Dimaggio, P.J., and W.W. Powell. 1983. "The Iron Cage Revisited: Institutional Isomorphism and Collective Rationality in Organizational Fields." *American Sociological Review* 48(2):147–60.

Erikson, E., and P. Bearman. 2006. Malfeasance and the Foundations for Global Trade: The Structure of English Trade in the East Indies, 1601–1831. *American Journal of Sociology* 112(1):195–230.

Gitlin, T. 1983. *Inside Prime Time*. New York: Pantheon.

Gladwell, M. 2000. *The Tipping Point*. Boston: Little, Brown.

Granovetter, M.S. 1973. "The Strength of Weak Ties." *American Journal of Sociology* 78(6):1360–80.

Gurevitch, M. 1961. "The Social Structure of Acquaintanceship Networks." PhD dissertation, Department of Economics, Political Science Division, Massachusetts Institute of Technology.

Hagerstrand, T. 1967. *Innovation Diffusion as a Spatial Process*. Chicago: University of Chicago Press.

Hawley, F. 1946. "The Role of Pueblo Social Organization in the Dissemination of Catholicism." *American Anthropologist* 48(3):407–15.

Hobsbawm, E. 1983. "Mass-Producing: Europe, 1870–1914." Pp. 263–307 in *The Invention of Tradition*, edited by E. Hobsbawm and T. Rangers. Cambridge: Cambridge University Press.

Innis, H. 1951. *The Bias of Communication*. Toronto: University of Toronto Press.

John, N. 2016. *The Age of Sharing*. Cambridge: Polity Press.

Katz, E. 1971. "The Social Itinerary of Technical Change." Pp. 761–97 in *Process and Effects of Mass Communication*, edited by W. Schramm and D. Roberts. Urbana: University of Illinois Press.

Katz, E., and P.F. Lazarsfeld. [1955] 2006. *Personal Influence: The Part Played by People in the Flow of Mass Communication*. Glencoe, IL: Free Press.

Katz, E., M.L. Levin, and H.H. Hamilton. 1963. "Traditions of Research in the Diffusion of Innovation." *American Sociological Review* 28(2):237–53.

Katz, E., C. Ali, and J. Kim. 2014. *Echoes of Gabriel Tarde: What We Know Better or Different 100 Years Later.* Los Angeles: USC-Annenberg Press.

Katz, R. 1986. *Divining The Powers of Music.* New York: Pendragon.

Labov, W. 2007. "Transmission and Diffusion." *Language* 83(2):350–59.

Lazarsfeld, P.F. 1964. "The Obligations of the 1950 Pollster to the 1984 Historian." *Public Opinion Quarterly* 14:618–38.

Lazarsfeld, P.F., B. Berelson, and H. Gaudet. l944. *The People's Choice: How People Make up Their Minds in an Electoral Campaign.* New York: Columbia University Press.

Lieberson, S. 2000. *A Matter of Taste: New Names, Fashions, and Culture Change.* New Haven, CT: Yale University Press.

Lopes, P. 2002. *The Rise of a Jazz World.* Cambridge: Cambridge University Press.

Mead, M. 1955. *Cultural Patterns and Social Change.* Paris: World Federation for Mental Health, UNESCO.

Mendels, D. 1999. *The Media Revolution of Early Christianity.* Grand Rapids, MI: Eerdmans.

Menzel, H. 1960. "Innovation, Integration, and Marginality: A Survey of Physicians." *American Sociological Review* 25(5):704–13.

Mosse, G.L. 1975. *Nationalization of the Masses.* New York: H. Fertig.

Papacharissi, Z. 2015. *Affective Publics: Sentiment, Technology, and Politics.* Oxford: Oxford University Press.

Rao, H., P. Monin, and R. Durand. 2003. "Institutional Change in Toque Ville: Nouvelle Cuisine as an Identity Movement in French Gastronomy." *American Journal of Sociology* l08(4):1211–48.

Rogers, E. [1962] 1994. *Diffusion of Innovation.* 5th ed. New York: Free Press.

Ryan, B., and N. Gross. 1942. "The Diffusion of Hybrid Seed Corn in Two Iowa Communities." *Rural Sociology* 8(1):15–24.

Shifman, L. 2014. *Memes in Digital Culture.* Cambridge, MA: MIT Press.

Simmel, G. [1904] 1957. "Fashion." *American Journal of Sociology* 62(6):541–58.

Sorokin, P. 1941. *Social and Cultural Mobility.* Glencoe, IL: Free Press.

Speier, L. 1921. "The Sundance of the Plains Indians: Its Development and Diffusion." *Anthropological Papers of the American Museum of Natural History* 16:451–527.

Spicer, E.H. 1954. "Spanish-Indian Acculturation in the Southwest." *American Anthropologist* 56:663–78.

Spiro, M. 1956. *Kibbutz: Venture in Utopia.* Cambridge, MA: Harvard University Press.

Stark, R. 1996. *The Rise of Christianity: How the Obscure, Marginal Jesus Movement Became the Dominant Religious Force in the Western World in a Few Centuries.* Princeton, NJ: Princeton University Press.

Strang, D., and S.A. Soule. 1998. "Diffusion in Organizations and Social Movements: From Hybrid Corn to Poison Pills." *Annual Review of Sociology* 24(1):265–90.

Tarde, G. [1890] 1969. *The Laws of Imitation.* New York: Holt.

———. [1898] 1969. "Opinion and Conversation." Pp. 297–318 in *Gabriel Tarde on Communication and Social Influence*, edited by T. Clark. Chicago: University of Chicago Press.

Travers, J., and S. Milgram. 1969. "An Experimental Study of the Small World Problem." *Sociometry* 32(4):425–43.

Van den Bulte, C., and G.L. Lilien. 2004. "Two-stage Partial Observability Models of Innovation Adoption." Working paper, The Wharton School, University of Pennsylvania.

Veblen, T. 1899. *The Theory of the Leisure Class.* New York: Macmillan.

Watkins, S.C. 2004. "Navigating the AIDS Epidemic in Rural Malawi." *Population and Development Review* 30(4):693–705.

Watts, Duncan. 2003. *Six Degrees: The Science of a Connected Age.* New York: W.W. Norton.

Weimann, G. 1994. *The Influentials.* Albany: State University of New York Press.

66
Medium theory and cultural transformations

Joshua Meyrowitz

Introduction

We often distinguish ourselves from other animals by pointing to the complex manner in which humans communicate. Yet, most scholars of culture have been hesitant to explore the ways in which *changes* in the forms of communication may encourage new patterns of social organization and undermine old ones.

Even in the field of media studies, the primary focus has been on the safer and simpler view of media as relatively passive conduits that deliver "messages." Most media research has focused on topics such as how audiences perceive and respond to media content or how political and economic forces shape dominant media messages. Such content-focused research has led to many significant findings, but it has ignored larger questions about the ways in which changes in media, apart from specific messages, may alter the texture and forms of social life.

At the same time, a scattering of scholars from a variety of fields – including history, anthropology, literary studies, the classics, political economy, and legal studies – have tackled these more complex questions about the influence of different media of communication. I have called their approach "medium theory" (Meyrowitz 1985:16, 2009), using the singular "medium" to highlight their focus on the distinct characteristics of each medium (or of each *type* of media) and how those characteristics may encourage or constrain forms of interaction and social organization.

Medium theory can be divided into microlevel and macrolevel issues. Microlevel medium theory explores the consequences of the choice of one medium over another in a particular situation, such as in initiating or ending a personal relationship, applying for a job, commanding troops, or interacting with one's children. Macrolevel medium theory explores broader questions about the ways in which changes in media have influenced modes of thinking, patterns of social organization, status differences, value systems, collective memory, and even the physical layout of the built environment.

This chapter provides a brief overview of the work of medium theorists, outlines four major communication/cultural phases as conceived of by macrolevel medium theory, and describes a few key limits of the medium-theory perspective.

Joshua Meyrowitz

The medium theorists

The study of media in themselves gained prominence in the mid-1960s with the publication of Marshall McLuhan's *Understanding Media* ([1964] 1994). McLuhan's provocative puns and aphorisms helped to make him a media celebrity, with both passionate adherents and savage critics.

The history of medium theory, however, is much deeper and broader than McLuhan's work. The Ten Commandments, for example, distinguish between acceptable and unacceptable media in which to portray God. Socrates (469–399 BC) detailed ways in which written communications were profoundly different from spoken ones. Johannes Gutenberg (ca. 1398–1468), the inventor of printing based on movable type, expressed awareness of how printing bypassed scribal writing and thus could threaten the religious information monopoly of the Catholic Church. Martin Luther (1483–1546) and his followers enacted Gutenberg's vision by consciously employing the new communication technology to circulate the Bible and other religious texts in the "lowly" languages of the people, thereby orchestrating the first mass-media public-relations campaign and splitting the Church through the Protestant Reformation. In the nineteenth century, an implicit medium-theory perspective underlay the birth of the field of sociology, whose founders understood that the influences of machines of mass production (the "media") could not be reduced to an inventory of the manufactured products (the "content"). The new means of production, they argued, had to be measured in terms of new forms of social relations, such as urbanization and bureaucratization. In the 1930s, film enthusiast Rudolf Arnheim defended the motion picture as an art form against critics who said that film was merely a mechanical reproduction of reality. In what he termed *Materialtheorie*, Arnheim argued that "artistic and scientific descriptions of reality are cast in molds that derive not so much from the subject matter itself as from the properties of the medium – or *Material* – employed" (1957: 2).

In the 1930s, Canadian political economist Harold Adams Innis (1950, 1951) began to explore how his research on the fur trade and on the pathways and waterways that shaped the flow of staples could be extended into an exploration of the flow of information through different media. Innis's interest in economic monopolies led him to theorize that the characteristics of some media (such as very complex writing systems) supported hierarchal control over information, whereas other media forms encouraged more egalitarian communication systems.

Innis's theories of media were among the influences that led literary scholar Marshall McLuhan to turn away from his analyses of advertising content to the study of media themselves. McLuhan downplayed Innis's concerns with political power and monopolies, emphasizing instead how different media altered the balance of the senses and changed patterns of perception and thought. Writing and printing, argued McLuhan, gave tribal peoples an "eye for an ear," amplifying the lineality of visual perspective over simultaneous, multisensory experience. Although McLuhan personally cherished literature, his dispassionate scholarly assessment was that electronic media were making print culture "obsolescent." He did not anticipate the end of literacy, but argued that electronic patterns undermined the once dominant "Gutenberg galaxy" of print-inspired forms, including linear thinking, nationalism, standardization, fixed identity and narrowly defined "jobs," assembly line mass-production and mass-education, simple cause-and-effect thinking, and fragmentation of knowledge into distinct disciplines. With his often-misunderstood pun, "the *medium* is the message," McLuhan chided media researchers for being too focused on media content and paying insufficient attention to the influences of each form of media, including the "change of scale or pace or pattern that it introduces into human affairs" ([1964] 1994:8). McLuhan claimed, for example, that electronic media were "retribalizing" people and encouraging humans everywhere to become emotionally involved in distant affairs in the electronically facilitated "global village."

Innis and McLuhan are unique in terms of the boldness and breadth of their analyses. Yet other scholars have offered more focused explorations of aspects of media evolution and cultural change, such as the shift from orality to literacy (e.g., J.C. Carothers 1959; Jack Goody and Ian Watt 1963) and the shift from script literacy to print literacy (e.g., Elizabeth Eisenstein 1979).

The spread of electronic media has led to a surge of interest in medium theory. Building on his careful analyses of earlier communication shifts, Walter Ong (1967) argues that electronic media create a "secondary orality" that retrieves some aspects of the "primary orality" of preliterate societies, while also being distinct from all earlier forms of communication. Historian Daniel Boorstin (1973) compares and contrasts technological revolutions with political revolutions. He describes how electronic media level time and space and reshape conceptions of history, nationality, and progress by "mass-producing the moment" and creating "repeatable" experiences. In my role-system version of medium theory (Meyrowitz 1985), I argue that electronic media tend to reshape everyday behaviors associated with group identity, socialization, and hierarchy by undermining print-era patterns of what different types of people know about each other and relative to each other. Electronic media, I claim, foster changes in roles by providing more shared access to social information, blurring distinctions between our public and private spheres, and weakening the age-old connection between physical location and experience. Ethan Katsh (1989) details how electronic data storage and processing undermine print-era forms of legal precedent and monopoly over knowledge of law. Digital media, according to Manuel Castells (1996), facilitate the global dominance of "the network," an ancient form of connection that once could exist only on a small scale. In a medium-theory approach to changes in international relations, Ronald Deibert (1997) reviews millennia of history to show how the "chance fitness" between the characteristics of a new medium and particular pre-existing social forces helped to bring those newly "media-favored" processes from the margins of society to the center. Deibert then demonstrates how the era of hypermediation is similarly facilitating major shifts in world order toward "de-territorialized communities, fragmented identities, transnational corporations, and cyberspatial flows of finance" (1997:ix). In *Here Comes Everybody* (2008), Clay Shirky examines the implications of digital media providing the tools for people to collaborate without the structure of traditional organizations. Nicholas Carr (2010) emphasizes how even traditional forms of textual content (such as in an e-book) are processed differently because of the inherent structure of the internet (with such elements as hyperlinks) resulting in a "shallowing" of thought and a rewiring of our brains. Sherry Turkle's writings (e.g., 2011) document how engagement with digital media facilitates new forms of experimentation with identity, but also leads to expecting more from technology and less from each other. Paul Levinson's (2012) analyses of "new new media" detail how blogging, Wikipedia, YouTube, Facebook, and similar media in which consumers are also producers are altering the texture of social and political life. In *Pax Technica* (2015), Philip Howard argues that the "internet of things" – comprised of everyday objects that are increasingly equipped with sensors and internet addresses, often as a means of surveillance and control – creates the potential for a new form of global political life.

In recent years, the concept of "mediatization" (cf. Couldry and Hepp 2017) has been used to grapple with the pervasiveness of technologically sophisticated media in contemporary societies and with the dialectical process through which changes in communication are interwoven with processes of cultural transformation.

Although the preceding theorists and others doing similar work might not consider themselves to be members of a common intellectual tradition, their theories, when reformulated into a single narrative, present a surprisingly coherent and consistent view of how the use of various media of communication may contribute to large-scale cultural changes. The next section provides an outline of four communication/cultural phases as conceived of within medium theory.

I have space to present only broad sketches of each phase, stripped of nuance and qualification. Yet, this exercise offers a preliminary sense of the promises – and challenges – of this perspective.

Cultural phases à la medium theory

Traditional oral cultures

In oral societies, sound and speech are the dominant forms of interaction. The culture's history, philosophy, and customs must be stored in memory and conveyed orally, supported by embodied action, song, dance, and ritual. This living storage system and biological delivery process tie members closely to each other. To facilitate memorization and transmission, cultural content is often put in the form of rhythmic poetry and mythic narratives that consist of familiar stories with formulaic actions and stock phrases. Because oral communication requires physical co-presence, oral cultures have few (if any) means of interacting with the experience or thinking of those who do not share the same time/space arena.

Such societies are "conservative" in the sense of working hard to conserve what they already know and are. People from other places are perceived as profoundly "strange." Moreover, the modern notion of the "individual" as the prime social unit has relatively little chance of developing. Members of each society tend to have very similar cultural experiences and knowledge. Novel ideas and complex original arguments can gain little traction because such concepts are difficult to remember (even by the people who develop them) and almost impossible to pass on to many others, given the lack of means other than memory through which to retain them. Indeed, extreme individual creativity would be potentially destructive of the social cohesion based on a shared stock of knowledge, custom, and belief.

Because human beings naturally develop the abilities to understand and utter speech, oral societies have relatively few status distinctions, which are typically based on different sets of social information and experience. Nomadic oral societies are particularly egalitarian, since they have limited opportunities to separate people of different ages, genders, and other categories into different information systems based on physical segregation. In oral agricultural societies, however, ties to location make distinctions in status more feasible, since rudimentary separations of physical spheres allow for some segregation of male/female, child/adult, and leader/follower experiences and roles. Yet, even settled oral cultures find it difficult to isolate members into many different spheres. Children as a group can be partially separated from adults as a group, but year-by-year age distinctions are difficult to support.

In oral societies, words are not objects to be viewed or held, but time-bound *events*, much like thunder or a scream. It is more difficult to escape spoken words and other sounds than it is to look away from visual objects. (Humans have eyelids but not earlids, and sounds come from all directions, not just from in front of us.) The shapes of the built environment in oral societies tend to mimic these circular contours of sound and hearing. In oral societies, both dwellings and villages are usually round. Oral peoples are always at the center of their communication world, with few opportunities or perceptual tools to stand back from it and analyze it.

The transitional scribal phase

The development of writing begins to change the structure of oral societies. Since writing is not a "natural" human ability, writing systems segregate those who can read and write from those who cannot. Different stages of mastery of writing and reading foster different levels of authority. Moreover, different *types* of writing systems have different influences. Writing systems with many complex symbols support greater distinctions in status, whereas simpler writing systems encourage more egalitarian social roles. Additionally, pictographic writing systems (in which each object or idea has its own "meaningful" symbol) sustain concrete thinking, whereas phonetic systems (in which meaningless symbols represent each sound) tend to promote more abstract thinking.

At first, writing is used to record what was previously only spoken (poetry, dialogue, formulaic myths, etc.). In the long run, however, phonetic writing in particular tends to break down the tribal cohesion of oral societies because it offers a relatively simple way to preserve prose and construct extended strings of connected abstract thought that would be almost impossible for oral peoples to develop, memorize, or transmit to others.

Writing splinters and unites people in new ways. As writing spreads, people living in the same places begin to know and experience very different things, while those who read the same material begin to feel connected to each other regardless of their respective locations. Yet, the complexity of learning to read and write, combined with the initial scarcity of written materials, means that fledgling literate modes of social organization compete with powerful and enduring oral modes and have limited impact until the development of movable type and the printing press. Indeed, readers of early written texts have difficulty reading without speaking the words aloud.

Modern print culture

Although the Chinese develop the art of printing long before Gutenberg's fifteenth-century invention in Germany, the Chinese ideographic writing system, with thousands of different characters needed even for basic literacy, impedes the impact of printing in that culture. In the phonetically alphabetized West, however, the growing availability of printed materials helps to reorganize social structures based on new patterns of shared and unshared communication. Conceptions of "them" versus "us" change. Literate readers and writers engage with ideas that their illiterate neighbors (and their own young children) cannot hear, speak, or remember. And different readers and writers develop different individual "perspectives." By allowing easy access to social information apart from face-to-face interaction, printing encourages retreat from the surrounding oral community and from extended kinship ties and fosters greater isolation of the nuclear family. Yet, printing also bypasses the local community in the opposite direction with the development of larger intellectual, political, and religious units. The Protestant Reformation is facilitated by making the Bible (as well as religious commentary and critique) widely available in the vernacular, thereby ending the Catholic Church's monopoly over direct access to the word of God and to the paths to eternal salvation. The new patterns of sharing and not sharing religious *texts* stimulate new patterns of religious unity across vast distances and eras, along with growing disunity among those in the same places at the same time. "Strangers" are increasingly present in one's locale.

Printing in the vernacular also permits readers to *see* on a printed page the larger "reality" of what was once expressed only in local voices. Readers feel an abstract unity with all those who share the same language, wherever they may be, rather than feeling connections only to those who share the same concrete local space. This encourages the development of nationalism. Connections based on face-to-face loyalties – such as feudal ties based on oral oaths – yield over time to nation-states based on printed constitutions and other political, social, and legal documents that literally "constitute" the shared conceptions, customs, language, and laws of the nation.

Unlike the verbal *events* of oral societies, printed texts encourage the experience of words as *objects*, spatially fixed on a page. In oral interaction, even a few seconds of delay in responding can seem rude or inappropriate. With print, in contrast, a reader can stare at words, read them at his or her own pace, turn away from them, and reread them. Most significantly, a reader can think about words before forming a reaction to them. And formal written responses can be revised multiple times before being shared publicly. Utterances, in contrast, cannot be taken back or erased. These characteristics of reading and writing facilitate the growth of internal dialogue, introspection, and individualistic thinking. Moreover, literate persons' physical, social, and mental positions are no longer exclusively at the center of oral events; they can stand away from the communications of others and develop a more distant, refined, reflective, and individualized "point of view."

Print encourages modes of thinking and social organization that mimic its physical forms. "Rationality," highly valued in a print culture, is structured like the letters of type: step-by-step abstract reasoning along a continuous line of argument and analysis. In a print culture, the simultaneous, overlapping events and expressions of oral interaction must compete with a one-thing-at-a-time and one-thing-after-another world of linear thought. In place of "outmoded" views of human life as involving repeating cycles of nature, society comes to be seen as striving for constant linear development, improvement, and "progress." "Circular reasoning" is dismissed as deficient. Visual and linear metaphors pervade a print society's modes of discourse: Do you *see* my *point?* I *follow* your *line* of thinking.

As the quantity of information explodes in a print culture, features exclusive to print are used to manage the overload – page numbers, alphabetized indexes, cross-referenced category systems. Print's emphasis on sequence and on segregation of one thing from another encourages the separation of topics and approaches into different disciplines, along with the ranking of material within each discipline in terms of degrees of difficulty and stages of mastery. Distinctions in "levels" of reading are seen as tied to natural differences in social identity and status. Modern conceptions of "childhood" and "adulthood" are invented in sixteenth-century Europe, and their intensification follows the spread of literate schooling. Schools increasingly segregate children into year-by-year groupings associated with different stages of reading skill and step-by-step access to adult information. Distinct literatures for each sex foster greater distinctions in gender roles. Leadership in print societies is based on distance and inaccessibility, delegated authority, and tight control over public image. Roles in businesses are structured via printed organizational charts with narrowly defined job descriptions in rectangular boxes connected by fixed "lines of authority."

New patterns of perception and thought are echoed in the built environment. Habitats evolve from round dwellings in round villages with winding paths to right-angle structures with straight streets in grid-like cities. Outdoor marketplaces with nonlinear arrangements evolve into stores with straight rows and labeled sections. Production of goods moves from holistic crafting to fragmented steps on assembly *lines*. Print-era classrooms are constructed with chairs bolted to the floors in rows that resemble the evenly spaced letters and words fixed on a printed page. Such arrangements of classrooms, offices, and other spaces tend to discourage informal oral interactions, even among those in the same space.

Social passages – such as birth, aging, mental decline, and death – are increasingly denaturalized and removed from the center of community and family life and placed in isolated institutions. The physical and social membranes around such institutions thicken and harden as print culture matures. The school, hospital, prison, military barracks, and factory become highly distinct settings with restricted access to them and distinct rules and roles inside them. The people within a single chamber of a single institution (fifth graders, assembly line workers, bank tellers, etc.) are increasingly viewed as standardized interchangeable parts. At the same time, those people in one institution (or in one subdivision of an institution) and those in another institution (or in another subdivision of the same institution) are increasingly perceived as very different from each other. The world comes to be seen as naturally layered and segmented, with a distinct place for every thing and for every body, and with each thing and body in its designated place.

Postmodern global electronic culture

As with earlier communication shifts, electronic media take time to spread and saturate societies before having significant and visible influences on social forms. Indeed, the harbingers of a new media era – the telegraph and telephone – come into use as print culture is reaching its full power, with the push for universal literacy and the dominance of print-encouraged forms of thought and social organization.

In the long run, however, electronic media such as radio, television, computer, the internet, and mobile devices undermine many features of print culture. They therefore have their most dramatic influences in the West, where the patterns of print culture have become so pervasive. Electronic media retrieve some key aspects of oral societies, including the dominance of sensory experiences and the near simultaneity of action, perception, and reaction. On radio and TV, the word returns as an event, rather than as an object. Unlike print media, which fostered new means of sharing knowledge, electronic media tend to facilitate new forms of shared *experience*. Yet the secondary orality of the electronic era differs from preliterate oral communication in multiple ways. Electronic interactions are not subject to prior limits of time or space. Electronic communications can travel almost instantaneously across great distances, and they can be preserved beyond the lifetimes of the communicators.

Electronic media also bypass the stages and filters of literacy that supported age, gender, and status distinctions. A child does not need to watch television shows or surf the internet in a particular order in the way that children typically need to read simple books before reading complex books. As a result, children are now routinely exposed to topics that adults spent several centuries trying to hide from children. Even those women who remain largely isolated at home are able to observe closely the "male realms" of culture – business, war, sports, politics – that they have, until recently, been told are off-limits to them. Articulate, street-smart members of a studio audience (or radio listeners who call in) are often able to run verbal circles around a talk-show guest with a PhD or high political status.

Electronic experiences thrust all of us among people with whom we have not shared the same literatures, territories, or even languages. As electronic patterns of interaction and experience diverge from the neat lines of print-supported sequences of ranks and hierarchies, there is a decline in the influence of political parties, unions, gender- and age-specific activities, organizational charts, and government and school bureaucracies. Digital media facilitate seemingly random patterns of collaborative and quickly shifting neo-feudal ties irrespective of territorial borders and traditional social groupings. "Wiki" formations, based on the power of open peer collaborations, change the notion of "authoritative" knowledge. And with processes such as cloud computing, the "tools" and "materials" that people employ and manipulate are increasingly not those kept in particular locations.

Unlike written and printed words, which emphasize ideas, many electronic media highlight feeling, appearance, and mood. Political and other figures in the public realm are increasingly judged by "dating criteria," in addition to "résumé criteria." That is, rather than primarily asking "What has he accomplished?" or "How well educated is she?," the public is also very concerned with the questions "What's he like?" and "Do I like her?" Even analyses of statements in televised political debates, now tend to deemphasize print-era questions such as "Is it true or is it false?" with increasing attention to electronic-era questions such as "What impression does it make?" and "How does it feel?"

Along with the enhanced focus on feeling and emotion and other criteria of evaluation that require no special training, information implosion leads to the blurring of disciplinary boundaries, an appreciation for generalism, and the growing sense that everyone has the right to his or her opinion (whether "informed" or not!). The extended single "story line" yields to less linear forms in jokes, literature, drama, and political rhetoric. And those who claim to be able to tap into "right-brain holistic thinking" are now often praised as "advanced," rather than being dismissed as unsophisticated.

As with earlier changes in media, the shape of the built environment evolves to mimic the forms of electronic information flow. Classroom desks are unbolted from the floor and often set in circles, and there is more mixing of the ages. Office walls are torn down and replaced with semi-open cubicles that let in sound from all directions. Management consultants suggest "quality circles" to improve productivity. Many once-marginalized populations are "mainstreamed." The fanciest stores, abandoning grid-like rows of the print era, are arranged more like unpredictable pathways in oral villages. The membranes around institutions become more permeable. Birth and death are brought back into many homes, while many birthing and hospice facilities welcome the whole family into spaces that are decorated to look like home bedrooms. Even those places that remain unchanged in appearance change in function. If a child's room is connected to other people and places through radio, television, mobile phone, and computer, banishment to his or her room no longer serves as a punishment based on excommunication from social interaction. Similar changes in the relationship between physical place and social "place" occur for prisoners, minorities, the poor, and others in once informationally remote locations. There are more similarities between people in different locations and institutions, just as there is an acceptance of greater diversity and idiosyncrasy within the same places and institutions. Greater sharing of information and communication options increases demands for (and often tensions over) more equal roles and opportunities in the local, national, and global arenas.

Even in an electronic age, however, some boundaries are blurred while others are reinforced; many institutions become more porous, yet others become more defended. And previously marginalized populations are mainstreamed unevenly and incompletely.

Medium theory in perspective

The grand scope of macrolevel medium theory, as just outlined, makes the theory difficult to test using typical "social scientific" methods. This perspective is also susceptible to criticism for relative lack of attention to exceptions and variations within cultures, from culture to culture, and from one era to another. Most medium theory, for example, has focused too narrowly on changes among the middle and upper classes in Western societies.

The unevenness of change, and variations in it, may be the result of many factors, including enduring historical, cultural, and religious differences. Additionally, the coexistence of multiple forms of communication within a culture obscures the distinctions among media. People in literate societies continue to speak, and those in electronic cultures still read, write, and use print. Technological convergence similarly complicates medium-theory work. Mobile phones, as one example, are now also typewriters, mail systems, news sources, voice and music recorders and players, alarm clocks, calendars, calculators, photo/video cameras and viewers, global positioning and navigation systems, broadcasting systems (via tweets and live video streaming), and many other devices. A great deal more medium-theory work could certainly add needed detail and texture.

Moreover, in pointing to largely neglected dimensions of media experience, medium theory often suffers from its own limits: it gives insufficient consideration to the influence of media content and media production variables and to the political, social, and economic forces that stimulate the development of new media, constrain the uses of existing media, and shape the "stories" that are told through most media (Meyrowitz 1998, 2006, 2008).

Jack Goody and Ian Watt (1963) argue that oral societies can easily modify their histories because they do not need to be faithful to earlier written records. Yet even literate and post-literate cultures have manifested amazing feats of amnesia. Consider, as just one of many possible examples, how the stories in the corporate-owned American news media about the threats posed to the United States by the theocratic government of Iran rarely mention the CIA's role in overthrowing a democratic secular government in Iran in 1953, the US backing of the dictatorial Shah of Iran and his savage secret police for the next 26 years, or the US's encouragement and military support for Saddam Hussein's bloody invasion of Iran after the popular Iranian revolt against the Shah in 1979. Similarly, many Americans' narrative of the origins of the American nation includes only fuzzy and incomplete images of how much the country's Founding Fathers relied on African slave labor in support of their lifestyles and their revolution in the name of "liberty," and how the subsequent dominance over a continent from "sea to shining sea" entailed the slaughter and cultural suppression of millions of Native Americans.

The promising potential of digital media to facilitate new forms of collaborative creativity and equality is being challenged by multinational communication conglomerates that are fighting against "net neutrality" in order to establish elite, high-speed pay channels and that threaten those who try to access and remix "proprietary" material. Even supposedly "non-profit" educational conglomerates essentially steal intellectual work from unpaid or low-paid academic authors and then hide the published work behind steep pay walls that limit students' and scholars' access to knowledge. Moreover, the permeability of boundaries that digital media facilitate in many positive ways (including enhancing political engagement and accountability) also leads to pervasive digital surveillance and data mining – by corporations, governments, and individuals – as means of marketing, abuse, exploitation, and control (such as to intimidate and undermine investigative journalists and political activists). The more that digital technologies hold medical and financial and other records, operate electrical grids and other utilities, guide transportation systems, and so on, the more susceptible we all become to major forms of disruption through glitches, hacks, and malicious attacks.

Medium theorists wisely explore the understudied role of media as distinct social environments and information systems. This perspective is essential to understanding one of the variables that influence the evolution of cultural forms. Yet medium theory is best used to supplement, rather than displace, other explorations of media, including critical analyses of the role of media as "disinformation systems" and as tools of both collective memory and collective amnesia.

References

Arnheim, Rudolf. 1957. *Film as Art*. Berkeley: University of California Press.

Boorstin, Daniel J. 1973. *The Americans: The Democratic Experience*. New York: Random House.

Carothers, J.C. 1959. "Culture, Psychiatry, and the Written Word." *Psychiatry* 22(4):307–20.

Carr, Nicholas. 2010. *The Shallows: What the Internet Is Doing to Our Brains*. New York: W.W. Norton.

Castells, Manuel. 1996. *The Rise of the Network Society*. Oxford: Blackwell.

Couldry, Nick, and Andreas Hepp. 2017. *The Mediated Construction of Reality*. Cambridge: Polity Press.

Deibert, Ronald J. 1997. *Parchment, Printing, and Hypermedia: Communication in World Order Transformation*. New York: Columbia University Press.

Eisenstein, Elizabeth. 1979. *The Printing Press as an Agent of Change: Communications and Cultural Transformations in Early-Modern Europe*, 2 vols. Cambridge: Cambridge University Press.

Joshua Meyrowitz

Goody, Jack and Ian Watt. 1963. "The Consequences of Literacy." *Comparative Studies in Society and History* 5(3):304–45.

Howard, Philip. 2015. *Pax Technica: How the Internet of Things May Set Us Free or Lock Us Up*. New Haven, CT: Yale University Press.

Innis, Harold Adams. 1950. *Empire and Communications*. London: Oxford University Press.

———. 1951. *The Bias of Communication*. Toronto: University of Toronto Press.

Katsh, M. Ethan. 1989. *The Electronic Media and the Transformation of Law*. New York: Oxford University Press.

Levinson, Paul. 2012. *New New Media*. 2nd ed. Boston: Penguin/Allyn & Bacon.

McLuhan, Marshall. [1964] 1994. *Understanding Media: The Extensions of Man*. Cambridge, MA: MIT Press.

Meyrowitz, Joshua. 1985. *No Sense of Place: The Impact of Electronic Media on Social Behavior*. New York: Oxford University Press.

———. 1998. "Multiple Media Literacies." *Journal of Communication* 48(1):96–108.

———. 2006. "American Homogenization and Fragmentation: The Influence of New Information Systems and Disinformation Systems." Pp. 153–86 in *Media Cultures*, edited by W. Uricchio and S. Kinnebrock. Heidelberg: Universitätsverlag.

———. 2008. "Power, Pleasure, Patterns: Intersecting Narratives of Media Influence." *Journal of Communication* 58(4):641–63.

———. 2009. "Medium Theory: An Alternative to the Dominant Paradigm of Media Effects." Pp. 517–30 in *The Sage Handbook of Media Processes and Effects*, edited by R.L. Nabi and M.B. Oliver. Thousand Oaks, CA: Sage.

Ong, Walter J. 1967. *The Presence of the Word: Some Prolegomena for Cultural and Religious History*. New Haven, CT: Yale University Press.

Shirky, Clay. 2008. *Here Comes Everybody: The Power of Organizing Without Organizations*. New York: Penguin Press.

Turkle, Sherry. 2011. *Alone Together: Why We Expect More from Technology and Less from Each Other*. New York: Basic Books.

67

Culture and collective memory

Comparative perspectives

Barry Schwartz

Introduction

When South Korean university students were recently asked to name the three events in their nation's history that aroused in them "a sense of dishonor, disgrace, shame, and/or remorse," they listed, in order of frequency, Japanese colonial rule, an International Monetary Fund loan, the Korean War, wrongdoings of former presidents, and collapse of the Sung Soo Bridge and Sam Poong Department store. One of the investigators, an American, found the Korean response bizarre. Why should occupation by a foreign power and acceptance of a loan to support a troubled economy be shameful? Why should approximately equal proportions of respondents consider the crimes of individual politicians, the Korean War, which preserved the existence of their country, and the collapse of a bridge and department store, as instances of national disgrace?

That the field of collective memory contains too few surprises like these is a sign of its provincialism. In the Western stockpile of collective memory concepts, nothing makes these findings comprehensible, let alone generalizable. For the past quarter century, it is true, many scholars around the world have labored over the sources and consequences of national memory, but efforts to build a collective memory discipline have been confined to the West. The present chapter addresses this imbalance, pressing non-Western cultures and their memories to the service of widening existing concepts. Doing so, it moves collective memory scholarship intellectually (not just topically) into a global field.

I

Culture is conceived here as "an *historically* transmitted pattern of meanings embodied in symbols, a system of *inherited* conceptions expressed in symbolic forms by means of which men communicate, perpetuate, and develop their knowledge about and attitudes toward life" (Geertz 1973:89, emphases added). Collective memory, in turn, is a means for the preservation of cultural forms, for it enables us to engage the past in at least two ways. First, collective memory is a model *of* society – a reflection of its present problems and mentalities. Second, collective memory is a model *for* society – a program that prescribes appropriate behavior and feeling, articulates moral values, and defines the meaning of its members' experience.

However, the adjective "collective" does not mean that everyone perceives the past in the same way. Collective memory, an analogue of public opinion, refers to the distribution of individual beliefs, feelings, and moral judgments about the past, whether it be that of a family, community, or nation.

In modern societies, collective memory draws from commemoration as well as the written word. Historical narratives are products of research and appear in analytic monographs, textbooks, and encyclopedia entries. Commemoration lifts from those narratives the events that express a society's most cherished and despised values, then it highlights them through eulogy and ritual oratory, monuments, shrines, relics, statues, paintings, and ritual observances.

History and commemoration perform different functions. History enlightens by revealing the causes and consequences of events. Commemoration designates those events' moral significance. History and commemoration, however, are interdependent: just as history dramatizes the values that commemoration sustains, commemoration is rooted in historical knowledge. History and commemoration are essential sources of collective memory.

II

In the twentieth century's early decades, many scholars touched on the social contexts of history, commemoration, and memory, but Maurice Halbwachs's work was the most profound. His influence since then, however, has been sporadic. Between 1945 – the year of his death in the Buchenwald concentration camp – and the early 1980s, American sociologists ignored him. After Mary Douglas (1980) introduced the English version of his essays in 1950, Halbwachs was cited time and again, even though his two major books, *The Social Frames of Memory* and *The Legendary Topography of the Gospels in the Holy Land*, had not been translated into English. (Lewis Coser's selected translations from Halbwachs's collected works did not appear until 1992.) Halbwachs was therefore dragged into a program of research of which he was not the only source.

Two perspectives on collective memory, the *presentist* and *traditionalist*, organize this late twentieth-century groundswell. These perspectives are neither verifiable nor falsifiable; they are analytic fictions in terms of which observations of experience and memory can be compared. In the presentist perspective, inferred from constructionist and postmodern models of memory, different elements of the past become more or less relevant as circumstances change. "Presentistism" focuses on changing social situations as the basis of the past's changing perception and representation. In this perspective, memory is always in transition, always precarious. Memory refers to communities' forging a past compatible with their shifting concerns and predicaments (see, e.g., Bodnar 1992).

The second, traditionalist, perspective refers to models for society, namely, standards and frames for the present. Assuming the historical record to be *essentially* authentic, such models construe collective memory as a source of inspiration, knowledge, and moral direction. Memory's effects, however, are irregular: in one time and place their influence is strong; in other times and other places, weak. At all times and places its influence is real. Because traditionalism places so much weight on the reality of the past, collective memory appears, in its light, to be inherited rather than self-created. History and tradition, on this view, constantly revise themselves, but they are modifying the essence of existing ideas rather than creating new ones (Shils 1981).

Traditionalist theory is sensitive to differences *within* cultures but finds most significance in differences *between* cultures. The latter contrasts – and there is no way to overemphasize the point – consist of tendencies governed by a binary "axial principle" under which analyses are performed. Cultures of self-denial, for example, distinguish themselves from cultures of self-fulfillment; Apollonian cultures from Dionysian; inner- from other- and tradition-directed cultures; communitarian from individualist. Traditionalism asserts a discontinuity in kind among cultures, distinguishing itself from theories that reduce culturally autonomous beliefs and values to politically motivated texts, narrative inventiveness, metaphoric constructions, arbitrary classifications and boundary-making (Alexander 2003; Wertsch 2002; Zerubavel 2003), none of which are inherited but supposedly rooted in the structure of present experience.

III

Arising in the West to systemize post-World War I disillusionment and doubt, presentism shaped early collective memory scholarship, including Halbwachs's, and dominates the field today. Almost 20 years after that war ended, Louis Wirth (1936:xxv) observed:

> At a time in human history like our own, when all over the world people are not only merely ill at ease, but are questioning the bases of social existence, the validity of their truths, and the tenability of their norms, it should become clear that there is no value apart from interest and no objectivity apart from agreement. Under such circumstances it is difficult to hold tenaciously to what one believes to be the truth.

For the first time, ordinary people and intellectuals alike began to believe there were no longer absolutes of time and space, of good and evil, or even of knowledge.

"Demystifying" knowledge was central to social science in the 1920s and 1930s, and its implications were broad. The "unmasking turn of mind," which refutes ideas by revealing their functions, inevitably challenges the authority of the past, for once one sees interests concealed by an idea, that idea loses its efficacy (Mannheim [1928] 1952:140). The cynical science of memory construction, with its emphasis on transparent and disputable pasts, prospers in a world of reciprocal distrust and cynicism.

By the late 1960s, the past became more meaningless to more people. The young not only thought about it differently; they thought about it less, remembered less, and felt less strongly about what they remembered. The past's reality and relevance diminished together as identification with tradition weakened (Nora 1996). Underlying this erosion was the discrediting of grand narratives – the legends, myths (Lyotard [1979] 1984), and historical realities that once inspired and consoled nations (Warner 1958). What distinguishes the West, then, is not new or revised historical narratives but an unprecedented sense that all such narratives are irrelevant.

IV

By the 1980s and 1990s, a great wave of research linked collective memory to power relations, identity politics, and the "production" of culture. Conceiving the past as a mask for the interests and hegemony of the privileged led to great excesses. Memory became something "invented," "fabricated," "created," and "remade." Its favorite topics included misdeeds, victims, unpopular wars, and other malevolent happenings. Holocaust and slavery topics abounded. This pattern accompanied the late twentieth-century rise of multiculturalism, recognition of minorities' entitlements, diversity, and erosion of social boundaries that once separated racial, religious, and ethnic groups.

Three recent developments, however, limit the presentist bias. First, the obduracy of history has been convincingly reaffirmed by demonstration rather than assertion. Michael Schudson's (1992) and Barry Schwartz's (2015) analyses of the past's resistance to distortion and Gary Fine's treatments of "cautious naturalism" (2001) and of historical events as "action templates" (Fine and McDonnell 2007) all react against models that reduce collective memory to pragmatic construction. What is known about the past, as it essentially was, limits its interpretive malleability.

Second, collective memory scholarship need no longer infer individual beliefs from historical texts and commemorative objects. Many scholars, most prominently Howard Schuman and his students (Schuman and Scott 1989; Schwartz and Schuman 2005; Corning and Schuman 2015), have moved the field forward by developing national surveys that directly assess individual beliefs, feelings, and judgments of historical events in the context of the locations they occupy in society.

Application of the dialogical perspective, which defines collective memory in terms of both cause and consequence, is the third new development. Individuals holding beliefs about the past are not passive end-links on some chain of social causation; they reinforce and modify the oral messages, texts, and symbols that they consume. If "culture creation" and "culture-reception" are inseparable, then collective memory, an aspect of culture, must be a context for and against which historians and commemorative agents react. In this sense, memory is *path-dependent*: earlier representations of the past affect the availability and resources required for present reinterpretations. Collective memory can be seen as an ongoing process of meaning-making (Olick 1999).

Different research settings direct theoretical trends in different ways. Consider the movement from Western to Eastern cultures.

V

"Western" and "Asian" are shorthand for two clusters of nations, each having a definite core but indefinite boundaries. Western nations are exemplified by central and Western Europe, Great Britain and its four major settler societies – the United States, Canada, New Zealand, and Australia. Northeast Asia is exemplified by three nations – China, Japan, and South Korea. Homogeneity cannot be claimed for these nations, but the differences *among* them – in religion, philosophy, literature, the visual arts, architecture, music, moral values, worldviews, histories, and memories – are small compared to differences *between* them and the nations of the West. This "East-West" divide is not to be dismissed as a product of Eurocentric history and interests: it is palpable and consequential. (For convenience, the term *Asia* will henceforth be abbreviated *Northeast Asia*.)

In recent years, Asian memory has been studied within a presentist framework applied directly or indirectly to World War II (Fujitani, White, and Yoneyama 2001; Jager and Mitter 2007). But to say that World War II memories are constructed, then manipulated to strengthen the state and flatter or console the public, ignores important questions. Why do elites choose a 75-year-old war as their hegemonic tool? Are any parts of this war remembered but not used for the purpose of manipulation? Moving from one nation to another, which parts of the war justify indignation; which require expressions of regret? In the West, the "politics of regret," a subfield of collective memory, now grows rapidly (Olick 2007), but it assumes a conception of guilt only partially felt by most Asians, including those who, from a Western standpoint, have most to be guilty about.

Memory runs deeply and vitally through Asia, whose elites have developed a concept, "the history problem," to describe it. Ordinary citizens recognize and feel this problem in their personal lives, while in public life the tone and texture of the history problem is nowhere more evident than in Asia's "textbook incidents." When, in 1982, the Japanese Ministry of Education demanded that an author revise his textbook to show that Japan "advanced" into rather than "invaded" Chinese cities, the Chinese and Korean governments reacted explosively: they withdrew ambassadors, condemned the Ministry's action, and declared that bilateral relations would never be the same. In the streets, Chinese and Korean students demonstrated their indignation. Japan's chief cabinet secretary issued a statement assuring that the error would be corrected. Later, in November 1982, the Ministry adopted a "Neighboring Country Clause" to make history textbooks consistent with international harmony. The concession was inconsequential. Because the Neighboring Country Clause was only a symptom of the history problem, textbook crises continued to inhibit transformative politics, slowed the pace of national and regional growth, and obscured the importance of relations with the widening world community. Such inhibition is still magnified by the multitude of fabrications, omissions, and distortions in Korean and Chinese as well as Japanese textbooks.

No comparable "history problem" exists in the West. Westerners remember their own nations' noble and shameful pasts, but in every sphere of international relations – technology, popular culture, politics, trade – the past is a second thought, not the first. Because America's relations with former enemies are free of recrimination, international business proceeds without reference to the conduct of earlier generations.

The history problem, by contrast, concerns the ways that Asians invoke the past, play the history card in their relations with one another, and conceive and symbolize the historical dimensions of events. For example, national surveys commissioned by two competing Japanese newspapers (*Asahi Shimbun* and *Yomiuri Shimbun*) asked national samples about Japan's "history issues." If a question about "history issues" were asked in the United States concerning relations with other countries, no one would understand it. Japanese respondents, no less than Chinese and Korean, were very familiar with the matter. In 1999 a national sample was asked "What should Japan do to better relations with China?" Sixty-six percent mentioned "respect Chinese culture and history" (*Yomiuri Shimbun*, September 30, 1999:14). In 2001 and 2005, another newspaper asked "Do you think the history issues are important for Japan's relations with China and South Korea?" Sixty-seven percent and 75 percent, respectively, replied "important" (*Asahi Shimbun*, December 25, 2001:9; April 27, 2005:8). In 2002, Japanese were asked "What do you think both China and Japan should do in order to improve the relationship between the two countries?" The most frequent of 10 categories of response (37 percent) was "Solve history issues between Japan and China" (*Yomiuri Shimbun*, September 11, 2002:1, 34). A full 60 percent answered negatively when asked "Do you think that the history issue of Japan's compensation to the former victims in the era of colonization has been solved?" (*Asahi Shimbun*, April 27, 2005:8). The same percentage answered "No" to the question of whether "the issue of Japan's history issue with neighboring countries such as China and South Korea has been solved" (*Asahi Shimbun*, June 28, 2005). The content of these history issues includes material compensation, but they turn on the question of cultural as well as monetary values. The *history* problem is a *memory* problem so far as it centers on moral judgments of the past.

Recognition of history issues does little to increase the Japanese, Chinese, and Korean people's affection for one another. Recent international surveys demonstrate Japanese contempt for Chinese and Koreans being reciprocated by the Chinese and Korean people's hatred of the Japanese. This emotional triangle shows up in the tangled political and military relations among the three parties. When Chinese president Xi Jinping addressed a 2015 UN meeting on Syria and ISIS, he framed his words with China's grievances against Japan (Fish 2015). South Koreans, for their part, remember China's 1950 invasion and resent its present support for their North Korean enemy. Yet, Korea's continued hostility toward Japan, whose military ambitions they fear far more than China's, subverted the United States' call for strategic cooperation between South

Korea and Japan in order to contain China's regional designs. Korea's wariness of Japan persists despite their common enmity against North Korea (Pew Research Center 2014, 2015).

Internal resentments over history and memory remain. Korea's biographical encyclopedia of collaborators during the Japanese occupation (Kim and Fine 2013), not to mention Japan's angrily withdrawing its envoy in response to the erection of a Comfort Woman statue outside its Busan consulate, reminds all that the history problem is still relevant. Meanwhile, Japan's ideologically driven debate over the deaths resulting from the Nanking Massacre (which ranges from 300,000 on the political left [the same number China claims] to 10,000 on the right) incites more resentment than remorse. That the actual victim count probably ranged from 50,000 to 70,000 (Schwartz 2012) is an atrocity by any standard, but it nevertheless sustains many Japanese perceptions of their neighbors' exaggerations and hostility. (For a comprehensive account of Japan's history problem, see Akiko Hashimoto [2015].)

VI

Unlike Western traditions rooted in "cultures of dignity," Asian traditions are historically rooted in "cultures of honor." Dignity and honor cultures require different kinds of memory. Peter Berger has explained:

> It is through the performance of institutional roles that the individual participates in history, not only the history of the particular institution but that of his society as a whole. It is precisely for this reason that modern consciousness, in its conception of the self, tends toward a curious ahistoricity. In a world of honor, identity is firmly linked to the past through the reiterated performance of prototypical acts. In a world of dignity, history is the succession of mystifications from which the individual must free himself to attain "authenticity."
>
> *(Berger 1973:91)*

Honor is significantly outdated in the West (Berger 1973) and attenuated in Asia, but if we take honor and dignity as analytic tools rather than descriptions of reality, we can differentiate societies more precisely. Japan, Korea, and China are centralized, modern societies, but contrary to the otherwise excellent observations of Charles Stewart (2015) on honor and shame, distinct remnants of feudal honor distinguish them from most of the West (Schwartz and Kim 2002).

"Honor cultures" maintain order by inducing both guilt and shame, but shame does most of morality's heavy lifting. Shame, unlike guilt, requires an audience. It is a reaction to one's perception of others' criticism of oneself. Thus, when Americans are asked to name the historical events which promote in them a sense of pride, they are most likely to refer to the American founding and World War II, and they do this casually, with little concern for the impressions these events make on other peoples. When Koreans are asked the same question, they most often mention the 1988 Olympic Games, which brought them world attention. In China, too, the 2008 Olympic Games swelled national pride and efforts to impress the world. Japanese survey respondents designate victory in international sports and economic and technological development in almost identical numbers (Schwartz and Kim 2002; Schwartz, Fukuoka, and Takita-Ishi 2005). Honor rests on achievements that other people notice.

It must be emphasized that the relevance of honor as a standard for thought, action, and feeling is probably fading at a faster rate in Asia than in the West, where it is already approaching its plateau. That every person possesses a right to autonomy, respect, and protection from arbitrary power is a conviction stemming from the human rights movement, which has advanced more rapidly in some Asian countries than in others, but the direction of change is everywhere certain and seemingly relentless. On the other hand, there is a floor, East and West, below which honor cannot descend. This limit cannot level cultural differences overnight. Before the deep roots of Asian honor are completely Westernized, then, many decades, perhaps centuries, must pass.

Because honor and shame play a more important role in Asia than in the West (Wallbott and Scherer 1995), new perspectives are required to understand Asian memory. Japan illustrates these requirements not through the detail of World War II atrocities but the spectacle of its officials minimizing them and attributing exculpatory motives to those having committed them. These same limits are manifest in the staunch refusal of Chinese and Koreans to accept sincere declarations of regret, to demand in every gesture of apology a level of incontestable "sincerity" – in short, proof of the unprovable.

Many reasons are advanced to explain why Asia's memory problem became so pronounced during the last decades of the twentieth century. These include new international discourse on justice and human rights, victim nations' rising economic power, nationalism, and growing political and economic interdependence coupled with muted approval among governing elites of public indignation against former oppressors. Yet, these conditions cannot explain why *historical* events are the primary objects of Asian conflict. One is left to wonder why the *past* resonates so powerfully in the Asian mind.

VII

World War II was a watershed of Western history and memory. Emerging from the experience of this war's atrocities was the ideal of a common humanity, universal rights and dignity. No one can dispute World War II's salience to European memory, but it is absolutely central to Asian memory. Japanese atrocities of the 1930s and early 1940s are not only sources of humiliation to post-war generations of Chinese and Koreans; they preserve memories of still earlier aggression.

Japan's war against Asia began with Europe's mid-nineteenth-century colonial conquests. Reactions to colonialism varied. Japan adapted to it and became a world power; China, once the object of unbounded reverence, sank in dignity, wealth, and influence; Korea vanished into what proved to be the beginning of a Japanese empire. Meiji elites adopted an attitude of stern superiority toward the rest of Asia. Japan thus chose not to resist the Western powers but to become one of them, and the rest of Asia knew it. China, after millennia of dominance, lost the most. Its "century of humiliation" lasted from the time it submitted to the 1842 Nanjing Treaty imposed by Great Britain to the 1980s economic expansion under Deng Xiaoping.

During the first several decades after World War II, Japan remained Asia's dominant economic and political power. Japan's neighbors, however, remembered their long disgrace. Japanese officials knew that only the clearest expressions of regret could begin to mitigate their neighbors' resentment, and one prime minister after another extended apologies. However, China and Korea, under the influence of Confucian ritual formalities, remained too aware of the telltale signs of inauthentic remorse. But how does any official of any nation act "authentically"? Does not the very deliberativeness of expressing a feeling subvert the impression of its sincerity? Here lays a deep perceptual dilemma augmenting the memory problem.

Neither in the existing archive of official Japanese apologies nor in public reactions to survey questions about Japanese regret do we find the slightest recognition of lost honor, which is most important to the Chinese and Korean people. Japan's apologies acknowledge physical suffering but not the humiliation of conquest and subordination. There is no mention of humiliation because there is no vocabulary of apology for the wounding of a foreigner's honor.

In dignity cultures (Taylor 1994), such matters are less urgent. Jewish survivors of the Holocaust, for example, do not condemn Germany for humiliating them. Many captured American and British soldiers died in Japanese prisoner-of-war camps, but the survivors feel no dishonor. Like Holocaust survivors, they condemn their tormentors for murdering their friends and ruining their lives. Violation of rights and dignity, not honor, is at stake.

VIII

Asian memory is at once presentist and traditionalist, but presentism and traditionalism do not tell us what makes an event memorable or what makes people disagree about it in the first place. Without this knowledge we are at a loss to know why commemoration tells us what it does, for its job, as we recall, is to designate the historical significance of events by lifting them from the historical record and marking their memory through rituals and symbols.

The advent of the history problem reflects both a malleable past, because its salience is linked to the changing realities of Asian countries, and an obdurate past, because it formulates tradition, which includes traumas that cannot be forgotten by victims or perpetrators. But the history problem tells something more, namely, the power of culture to make memory resonate, to get under people's skin, to make them take notice when history is represented in the "wrong" way.

For almost 40 years, the volume of collective memory scholarship has grown, but the intellectual payoff is leveling. Presentists can only say so much about the way interests distort historical perception; traditionalists, the way memory endures. Presentist and traditionalist perspectives continue to be elaborated and qualified, but we are reaching the limit of what they can tell us. To grasp the uniqueness of the Asian memory problem, the concepts of honor and shame are necessary, for they remain significant aspects of Asian culture and bring to life past experience.

Culture's role in collective memory may now be summarized. The memory problem is so embedded in Asia's current economic and political issues because honor and shame bind individuals to their nation in a way that dignity and guilt cannot. No memory problem afflicts Western societies because their cultural values protect their members from stern historical and communal demands, demands that Asians cannot ignore. Bringing Asia into the field of collective memory studies, not as a site for the testing of Western concepts but as a mine of new concepts and new propositions, thus widens the existing state of the field.

References

Alexander, Jeffrey. 2003. *The Meanings of Social Life: A Cultural Sociology.* New York: Oxford University Press.

Berger, Peter. 1973. "On the Obsolescence of the Concept of Honor." Pp. 83–96 in *The Homeless Mind: Modernization and Consciousness,* edited by P. Berger, B. Berger, and H. Kellner. New York: Vintage.

Bodnar, John. 1992. *Remaking America: Public Memory, Commemoration, and Patriotism in the Twentieth Century.* Princeton, NJ: Princeton University Press.

Corning, Amy, and Howard Schuman. 2015. *Generations and Collective Memory.* Chicago: University of Chicago Press.

Coser, Lewis A., ed. 1992. *Maurice Halbwachs on Collective Memory.* Chicago: University of Chicago Press.

Douglas, Mary, ed. [1950] 1980. *The Collective Memory.* New York: Harper.

Fine, Gary Alan. 2001. *Difficult Reputations: Collective Memories of the Evil, Inept, and Controversial.* Chicago: University of Chicago Press.

Fine, Gary Alan, and Terence McDonnell. 2007. "Erasing the Brown Scare: Referential Afterlife and the Power of Memory Templates." *Social Problems* 54(2):170–87.

Fish, Isaac S. 2015. "In U.N. speech, Xi focuses on Japan." Retrieved September 28, 2015 (www.foreignpolicy.com/2015/09/28/).

Fujitani, Takashi, Geoffrey M. White, and Lisa Yoneyama, eds. 2001. *Perilous Memories: The Asia-Pacific War.* Durham, NC: Duke University Press.

Geertz, Clifford. 1973. *Interpretation of Cultures*. New York: Basic Books.

Hashimoto, Akiko. 2015. *The Long Defeat: Cultural Trauma, Memory, and Identity in Japan*. New York: Oxford University Press.

Jager, Sheila Miyoshi, and Rana Mitter, eds. 2007. *Ruptured Histories: War, Memory, and the Post-Cold War in Asia*. Cambridge, MA: Harvard University Press.

Kim, Jeong-Chul, and Gary Fine. 2013. "Collaborators and National Memory: The Creation of Pro-Japanese Collaborators in Korea." *Memory Studies* 6(2):130–45.

Lyotard, Jean-Francois. [1979] 1984. *The Postmodern Condition*. Minneapolis: University of Minnesota Press.

Mannheim, Karl. [1928] 1952. "The Problem of Generations." Pp. 276–320 in *Essays on the Sociology of Knowledge*, edited by P. Keckemeti. London: Routledge & Kegan Paul.

Nora, Pierre. 1996. *Realms of Memory: Rethinking the French Past*. Vol. 1. New York: Columbia University Press.

Olick, Jeffrey K. 1999. "Genre Memories and Memory Genres: A Dialogical Analysis of May 8th, 1945 Commemorations in the Federal Republic of Germany." *American Sociological Review* 64(3):381–402.

———. 2007. *The Politics of Regret: On Collective Memory and Historical Responsibility*. New York: Routledge.

Pew Research Center. 2014. "Global Attitudes and Trends." Retrieved November 2, 2015 (www.pewglobal.org/2014/07/14/ chapter-4-how-asians-view-each-other/).

———. 2015. "Global Attitudes and Trends." Retrieved November 2, 2015 (www.pewglobal.org/09/02/15/ how-Asia-Pacific-publics-see-each-other-and-their-national-leaders/).

Schudson, Michael. 1992. *Watergate in American Memory*. New York: Basic Books.

Schuman, Howard, and Jacqueline Scott. 1989. "Generations and Collective Memories." *American Sociological Review* 54(3):359–81.

Schwartz, Barry. 2012. "Rethinking Conflict and Collective Memory: The Case of Nanking." Pp. 529–63 in *The Oxford Handbook of Cultural Sociology*, edited by J.C. Alexander, R.S. Jacobs, and P. Smith. New York: Oxford University Press.

———. 2015. "Rethinking the Concept of Collective Memory." Pp. 9–21 in *Routledge International Handbook of Memory Studies*, edited by A.L. Tota and T. Hagen. London: Routledge.

Schwartz, Barry, Kazuya Fukuoka, and Sachiko Takita-Ishi. 2005. "Collective Memory: Why Culture Matters." Pp. 253–71 in *The Blackwell Companion to the Sociology of Culture*, edited by M.D. Jacobs and N. Weiss Hanrahan. Oxford: Blackwell.

Schwartz, Barry, and Mikyoung Kim. 2002. "Honor, Dignity, and Collective Memory: Judging the Past in Korea and the United States." Pp. 209–26 in *Culture in Mind: Toward a Sociology of Culture and Cognition*, edited by K. Cerulo. New Brunswick, NJ: Rutgers University Press.

Schwartz, Barry, and Howard Schuman. 2005. "History, Commemoration, and Belief: Abraham Lincoln in American Memory, 1945–2001." *American Sociological Review* 70(2):183–203.

Shils, Edward A. 1981. *Tradition*. Chicago: University of Chicago Press.

Stewart, Charles. 2015. "Honor and Shame." Pp. 181–84 in *International Encyclopedia of the Social and Behavioral Sciences*. 2nd ed. Vol. 11, edited by J.D. Wright. Oxford: United Kingdom.

Taylor, Charles. 1994. "The Politics of Recognition." Pp. 25–73 in *Multiculturalism*, edited by A. Gutman. Princeton, NJ: Princeton University Press.

Wallbott, Harald G., and Klaus R. Scherer. 1995. "Cultural Determinants in Experiencing Shame and Guilt." Pp. 465–87 in *Self-Conscious Emotions: The Psychology of Shame, Guilt, Embarrassment, and Pride*, edited by J. Price Tangney and K.W. Fischer. New York: Guilford Press.

Warner, Lloyd W. 1958. *The Living and the Dead*. New Haven, CT: Yale University Press.

Wertsch, James V. 2002. *Voices of Collective Remembering*. Cambridge: Cambridge University Press.

Wirth, Louis. 1936. "Preface." Pp. x–xxx in Karl Mannheim's *Ideology and Utopia*, trans. Louis Wirth and Edward Shils. New York: Harcourt, Brace and World.

Zerubavel, Eviatar. 2003. *Time Maps: Collective Memory and the Social Shape of the Past*. Chicago: University of Chicago Press.

68

The changing culture and politics of commemoration

Hiro Saito

Introduction

To have "memory" of an event, people have to experience it themselves. Learning of an event secondhand, individuals acquire knowledge, but not memory. Yet, when sociologists speak of "collective memory," they routinely include as agents of memory those who do not have first-hand experience of a past event. This inclusion originates from Maurice Halbwachs's (1992) pioneering work that examined the relationship between collective memory and commemoration in terms of group solidarity and identity: collective memory emerges when those without firsthand experience of an event identify with those who have such experience, establishing both sets of actors as sharing membership in the same social group. The creation of this affect-laden, first-person orientation to a past event is at the crux of *commemoration* – simply put, a ritual that transforms "historical knowledge" into "collective memory," consisting of mnemonic schemas and objects that define meaning of a past event as a locus of group identity. According to Halbwachs's formulation, commemoration is a vehicle of collective memory.

However, it is crucial for sociologists to distinguish commemoration from collective memory and clearly specify the relationship between the two. This is so because more than a small number of researchers have used "collective memory" metaphorically as a category of analysis, obscuring its underlying causal mechanisms and reifying it as a stable and homogeneous entity (Bell 2003). Nevertheless, it is unwise to abandon the concept of collective memory, for it has proved to be a powerful heuristic and produced many important studies. To retain and refine collective memory as a category of analysis, I submit that sociologists should turn to the concept of commemoration, foregrounding a *process* of remembering and focusing on participants, settings, and interactional dynamics. Such a conceptual move can help sociologists not only combat against the "substantialist" view of collective memory (Olick 2003), but also probe into causal mechanisms through which collective memory is constructed, contested, and transformed over time.

In this chapter, I first elaborate on the Halbwachsian concept of commemoration in light of the cultural sociology of ritual and performance, clarifying the causal mechanisms through which commemoration generates collective memory as a basis of group solidarity and identity. At the same time, it is important to recognize that commemoration can also lead to intergroup conflict because different groups remember a past event differently and compete for power to legitimate their own commemoration. To illustrate this contentious aspect of commemoration, I introduce recent research that has drawn on field theory and social movement studies to examine political struggles over the past. This research also shows that the politics of commemoration has expanded beyond national borders in recent decades because of the globalization of human rights discourse and media networks. Specifically, the politics of commemoration now involves cosmopolitanism as a new logic, creating an institutional contradiction with nationalism as a focal point of political struggles. In short, a crucial challenge in sociological research on commemoration today is to illuminate the dual nature of commemoration – as a source of both group solidarity and intergroup conflict – against the backdrop of the changing culture and politics of the increasingly global world.

Commemoration as ritual

Human social life is marked and made meaningful by an array of commemorative practices. Various anniversaries mark our collective calendar – Independence Day, Martin Luther King Jr. Day, and 9/11, to name only a few American examples. When people commemorate – whatever the scale of commemoration may be – they always do so as members of a social group, be it a family, a school, a city, or a nation. Their membership in these groups does not simply pre-exist this process, but is actually constituted *through* commemoration. By providing actors with objects and performances that narrate a past event as part of a shared group identity, commemoration constitutes social groups. Furthermore, as autobiographical memory is crucial to generating and maintaining personal identity, commemoration provides people with autobiographical narratives of their purportedly shared past as a group and induces them to feel and accept such narratives as authentic.

This felt authentication of a collective autobiography is made possible by the ritual nature of commemoration. As Randall Collins (2004:42) argued, rituals are "occasions that combine a high degree of mutual focus of attention, that is, a high degree of intersubjectivity, together with a high degree of emotional entrainment . . . [which] result[s] in feelings of membership that are attached to cognitive symbols." The collective effervescence that commemoration generates by virtue of its ritual nature helps participants feel authentic about autobiographical narratives of their purportedly shared past. As Jeffrey Alexander (2004:527) further unpacked the nature of rituals,

> episodes of repeated and simplified cultural communication in which the direct partners to a social interaction, and those observing it, share a mutual belief in the descriptive and prescriptive validity of the communication's symbolic contents and accept the authenticity of one another's intentions.

Commemorations capitalize on this affective power of rituals to prompt participants to generate mutual identifications as members of a social group. Thus Collins's and Alexander's theories of ritual corroborate Halbwachs's formulation: commemoration is an "alchemy" that transforms historical knowledge into collective memory, making emotionally charged interpretation of past events integral to people's social identities as they shift from a subject position of audience/observer to actor/participant.

Imaginary identification with participants of a past event is most intense and visible in cases of traumatic events (LaCapra 2001), but sociologists have considered such identification a defining feature of "collective memory" in general. The sociological concept of collective memory is meant to capture the misrecognition of secondhand knowledge as living memory by virtue of identifications on the part of participants in commemoration. When commemorative rituals succeed in providing people with vicarious experiences of a past event, secondhand knowledge begins to be felt as living memory among those who lack firsthand experience. In symbolic-interactionist terms, participants of commemorative rituals take attitudes of those who have firsthand experience (Fine and Beim 2007). Commemorative rituals typically force such symbolic interactions by positioning those who have firsthand experience at the center of the rituals. This set up tends to lead those who lack firsthand experience to fix their attention on those with firsthand experience and induce the former to experience a past event vicariously from the imaginary first-person perspective of the latter. The emotional intensity of commemorative rituals, exemplified by moments of collective effervescence, promotes such misrecognition and imagination of secondhand knowledge as shared living memory.

For commemorative practices to constitute a social group, however, not all members have to be present in the same physical space. As is the case with national anniversaries, mutual awareness that other members of the nation in other places are marking the same occasion helps to produce feelings of group membership and solidarity among individuals. Print capitalism facilitated the formation of national communities (Anderson 1991) partly because it enabled commemorative rituals – such as Independence Day celebrations – to extend beyond face-to-face interactions: increasingly distant people were able to imagine their shared participation in commemorative rituals as members of the same social group. In such processes, mass media play a decisive role in generating collective memories at the national level (Dayan and Katz 1992). Whether and how an event is represented in mass media thus constitutes an important subject for the sociological analysis of commemoration.

Moreover, as implied by Alexander's formulation, "symbolic objects" play significant roles in commemorative rituals. Not only do such objects provide focal points for participants' attention, but the contents of symbolic objects shape mnemonic schemas and patterns of thinking and feeling about the purportedly shared past. Symbolic objects in the context of commemorative rituals thus constitute built environments that operate as gigantic mnemonics, enveloping participants. In this light, Pierre Nora (1989) spoke of the disappearance of "milieux de mémoire" as the result of the rapid and radical transformation of built environments within modernity: technological, economic, and demographic changes ushered in by industrialization and urbanization uprooted people from the built environments that had previously served as mnemonics of their past. Creatively rethinking the phrase "out of sight, out of mind" as "out of site, out of mind" nicely captures the constitutive role of built environments in human memory. When the built environments that people inhabit change, what they remember and how they remember it also change – mnemonic schemas are always mediated by mnemonic objects (see Mukerji, this volume). From this perspective, "collective memory" is best understood as being "distributed" partly in human actors themselves, and partly in the world of mnemonics (Wertsch 2002). Thus elaborated, the Halbwachsian concept of commemoration helps clear up confusions surrounding "collective memory" as an "under-theorized and yet grossly over-employed" category of analysis (Bell 2003:74) because it specifies how collective memory is causally produced by rituals that distribute and enforce shared mnemonic schemas and objects.

However, although people come together and affirm their group solidarity and identity through commemorative rituals, heterogeneous versions of a past event always exist because people with different socioeconomic statuses, political orientations, life trajectories, and ethnic and racial identities remember the same event differently (Halbwachs 1992; Schuman and Scott 1989). Importantly, heterogeneous groups do not commemorate a past event in isolation from one another: they are likely to interact and, as the result, notice disjunctions in how they commemorate the past event. These disjunctive commemorations can then become sources of controversy and even conflict between individuals and groups, precisely because the foundations of their collective identities are at stake.

The politics of commemoration

Conflict between different groups vis-à-vis their commemorations comes to the fore in cases of "difficult pasts" – namely, morally ambiguous events that generate more controversy than solidarity. Sociological research on such commemorative contention was pioneered by Robin Wagner-Pacifici and Barry Schwartz (1991), who examined the Vietnam War as a difficult past for Americans: various groups of actors, from veterans to peace activists, not only failed to share a unified mnemonic schema for interpreting the event, but also continued to contest the meaning of key mnemonic objects meant to commemorate it. Similarly, Vera Zolberg's (1998) study of controversies surrounding the 1996 Smithsonian exhibit on the atomic bombing of Hiroshima and Vered Vinitzky-Seroussi's (2002) study of efforts to commemorate the legacy of Yitzhak Rabin showed the strong political dynamics that can be involved in commemoration. These studies highlight how different groups mobilize to promote their particular versions of commemoration, thus advancing their own political interests and symbolic legitimacy. Commemorations of difficult pasts are particularly contentious because they often involve psychologically and morally traumatic events. However, intergroup conflicts and political struggles are part and parcel of all commemorations.

To systematically investigate the politics of commemoration, a small but growing number of sociologists have begun to draw on two theoretical traditions. First, Jeffrey Olick (2007:ch. 5) imported Pierre Bourdieu's field theory into collective-memory studies, emphasizing the heterogeneous and dynamic nature of commemoration. According to Olick, construction of collective memory involves multiple fields – artistic, social, political, and so on. Each field has distinct rules of engagement, and actors compete to legitimate their own commemorative positions by deploying different strategies and mobilizing different amounts of resources at their disposal. Although different fields produce different collective memories, they are also interdependent: dynamics and trajectories of fields are shaped not only internally but also externally. Moreover, relations among fields are structured hierarchically: the political field tends to dominate other fields because struggles in it center on the government that has the power to define an official commemoration as a parameter for struggles in other fields. To put it in Bourdieu's words, the government is able to "exercise power over the different fields" because it "establishes and inculcates ... social frameworks of perceptions, of understanding or of memory" among citizens (Bourdieu 1999:58, 68). The political field is therefore "a sort of metafield" in relation to other fields of collective memory (Olick 2007:93).

Olick is right that Bourdieu's field theory can help sociologists map how political struggles over a legitimate version of the past unfold over time in terms of power relations among relevant actors and fields. Nevertheless, as Neil Fligstein and Doug McAdam (2011:20) have pointed out, "[t]he Bourdieusian conception of field thus focuses mostly on individuals gaining position and power not on collective actors who work to build and then hold their groups together in the face of struggle in a broader field." Such a focus on individuals can create problems for studying the politics of commemoration because organizational actors, such as non-governmental organizations (NGOs), political parties, and government agencies, tend to play more important roles than individual actors. To be sure, individual heroes and victims can publicly narrate their past experiences, but when they do, they almost always act as representatives of one or another group. In light of Fligstein and McAdam's critical observation, then, it seems advisable to map a given field of commemoration in terms of political struggles among organizational, as well as individual, actors.

In this light, field theory can be fruitfully combined with the second theoretical tradition that sociologists of collective memory increasingly draw on – namely, social movement studies that focus on organizations and their collective actions (Armstrong and Crage 2006; Ghoshal 2013; Saito 2016). Typically, sociologists of collective memory borrow three major concepts from social movement studies: mobilizing structures, political opportunities, and framing processes. In the context of political struggles over commemoration, mobilizing structures refer to organizations and their networks that provide human and financial resources for mobilizing collective actions to promote certain commemorative positions. Importantly, these organizational vehicles are not static: some organizations exit the field, whereas others enter, and networks of organizations change over time. Mobilizing structures alone, however, are not sufficient for a commemorative position to gain legitimacy; organizations also need the "right" political opportunities in order to influence the structure of a given field of commemoration, especially when they are challenging the government, the actor in the field with the power to define official commemoration. But, ultimately, the effects of both mobilizing structures and political opportunities are always mediated by framing processes, which structure interpretations of actions and events. An NGO, for example, works to expand its support base by constructing a certain frame or "slogan" capable of generating emotional resonance that can turn bystanders into new recruits. NGOs also seek to frame political opportunities in such a way that their supporters are compelled to believe that they have a good chance to change the official commemoration by joining rallies, signature collection campaigns, and other collective actions.

Thus, field theory and social movement studies can help systematically investigate how different groups engage in political struggles over a legitimate commemoration. Field theory, on the one hand, enables sociologists to conceptualize the politics of commemoration in terms of a field consisting of relevant actors and their interactions. Social movement studies, on the other hand, provide more specific analytical tools for examining the causal processes and mechanisms underlying political struggles within fields. Field theory and social movement studies therefore allow sociologists to illuminate a conflictive aspect of commemoration, even when commemoration is fundamentally generative of group solidarity and identity. Indeed, the politics of commemoration simultaneously divides and unites relevant actors: although political struggles may lead one group of actors to dominate others, it may also lead previously disparate groups to form a coalition that will expand the scope of solidarity and identity.

To fully understand the political dynamics of commemoration, however, it is also crucial to pay attention to the changing culture of commemoration in the contemporary world – specifically, to the emergence of cosmopolitanism and its articulation with nationalism as the previously dominant logic of commemoration. Put another way, the politics of commemoration is constituted not only by interactions among relevant actors in a given field, but also by the institutional environment in which these actors are embedded and supplied with interpretive schemas for organizing their commemorative practices.

Cosmopolitanism as a new logic

Over the past two centuries, nationalism, a political doctrine and cultural idiom that defines the world as divided into discrete nations, has been institutionalized as a dominant organizing principle for a variety of economic, political, social, and cultural practices, including commemoration.

In turn, commemoration has served as an important vehicle of nationalism, allowing people to construct a shared autobiographical narrative and imagine a nation. When people commemorate the past according to the logic of nationalism, they focus on what happened to their co-nationals without sufficient regard for foreign others. This exclusive focus on co-nationals manifests most clearly in nationalist commemoration of an armed conflict that often elevates fallen soldiers to immortal heroes of the nation while disregarding what these soldiers might have done to foreign others. In such commemorations, one's own nation becomes sacred above all else. Nationalism excludes foreign others from commemoration in another way: the principle of national sovereignty prohibits foreign others from participating in the process that shapes the content of commemoration. When a government plans a memorial ceremony for war dead at a national cemetery, for example, it typically does not allow foreign governments to influence the content of the ceremony. History education is another situation in which national sovereignty over commemoration continues to be asserted, when only historians who are citizens of a given country are authorized to write "national history." Indeed, nationalism has been such a dominant logic of commemoration to the extent that much of the sociological research on collective memory has assumed the nation as a unit of analysis.

However, nationalism is no longer the only logic of commemoration available. As Ulrich Beck (2005) argued, cosmopolitanism, an orientation of openness to foreign others, is increasingly institutionalized in a variety of human practices in the contemporary world, due to the globalization of human rights discourse and growing sociocultural interactions across national borders. It presents a new logic of feeling, thinking, and acting that takes humanity, rather than nationality, as a primary frame of reference. By drawing on the logic of cosmopolitanism, people can doubly include foreign others in commemoration: they remember what happened to foreign others as members of humanity, but they also invite those others to contribute to shaping the content of commemoration. As Beck (2005:43) put it, cosmopolitan commemoration involves

> acknowledging the history (and the memories) of the "other" and integrating them into one's own history ... where the national monologues of victimization that are celebrated as national memory are systematically replaced by transnational forms and forums of memory and dialogue, which also enable the innermost aspects of the national realm – the founding of myths – to be opened up to and for one another.

Cosmopolitan commemoration thus allows people to extend identification beyond national borders and engage in transformative dialogues with foreign others in ways that critically reflect on the nationalist biases in their own nationalist versions of history.

According to Daniel Levy and Natan Sznaider (2006), cosmopolitanism manifests most clearly in the commemoration of the Holocaust. This is because representations of the Holocaust were circulated worldwide through musical and film adaptations of *The Diary of a Young Girl* in the 1950s, the news coverage of the 1961 Eichmann trial, the 1978 American television miniseries *Holocaust*, and the 1993 film *Schindler's List*, among many other cultural productions. Specifically, these media representations served as focal points for those who did not experience the Holocaust firsthand to identify with victims and remember the event vicariously. This identification was further reinforced by the globalization of human rights discourse that defined humanity as a primary frame of reference: after all, the United Nations Declaration of Human Rights was inspired by the Holocaust. Levy and Sznaider (2006:5) thus argued that the commemoration of the Holocaust became cosmopolitan as it was "dislocated from space and time, resulting in its inscription into other acts of injustice and other traumatic national memories across the globe."

Globalization of human rights discourse, coupled with the transnational circulation of media representations of the Holocaust, undoubtedly contributed to "cosmopolitanization" of the Holocaust remembrance, but this is only part of the story. In fact, sociologists have yet to systematically investigate the causal mechanisms through which globalization differentially impacts commemorative practices in different parts of the world (Inglis 2016). Take, for example, the so-called history problem in East Asia, where Japan is embroiled in intense controversies with South Korea and China over how to commemorate the Asia-Pacific War that ended more than 70 years ago. To name but a few, points of contention include interpretations of the Tokyo War Crimes Trial, apologies and compensation for foreign victims of Japan's past aggression, prime ministers' visits to the Yasukuni Shrine, and history textbooks. This history problem in East Asia intensified in the 1990s, precisely when the human rights discourse, associated with cosmopolitanism, came to be increasingly institutionalized around the world (Saito 2016). The East Asian case thus shows that cosmopolitanization of collective memory is not teleologically determined by globalization.

Indeed, cosmopolitanism does not replace nationalism in a zero-sum manner. Rather, the relationship between the two logics is open-ended because nationalism continues to operate as a central organizing principle in the contemporary world. As Beck and Sznaider (2006:20) put it, "cosmopolitanism does not only negate nationalism but also presupposes it." Although UN organizations promote human rights policies, national governments are still responsible for implementing them in education systems and other societal institutions. Similarly, even though membership in humanity is emphasized, national citizenship continues to structure access to socioeconomic resources and political rights. Since both nationalism and cosmopolitanism are legitimated, this creates an "institutional contradiction," wherein opposed but equally legitimate logics clash with each other (Friedland and Alford 1991). This institutional contradiction serves as a focal point of political struggles for a legitimate commemoration, and such struggles are likely to be intense and protracted because all sides, subscribing to nationalism and cosmopolitanism differently, have plausible claims to legitimacy. Although some extreme groups in a given field might subscribe exclusively either to the nationalist or cosmopolitan logic of commemoration, most groups probably combine the two logics in different ways. As a result, a typical outcome of political struggles is likely to compromise nationalism and cosmopolitanism.

But compromise can become a source of further political contention because it is always characterized by what Luc Boltanski and Laurent Thévenot (2006:226) called "the monstrosity of composite setups," where "the coexistence of objects of different natures makes several groupings equally possible and creates uncertainty about the nature of the test under way." That is, the compromise of nationalism and cosmopolitanism tends to trigger more controversy because respective proponents of the competing logics can always contest the compromise by criticizing it for failing to conform adequately to one logic or another. Such compromise is likely to be the norm rather than the exception in an increasingly global world, where nationalism continues to enjoy its legitimacy alongside with cosmopolitanism. Thus, for sociologists of collective memory, the new culture of commemoration – the coexistence of nationalism and cosmopolitanism – reinforces the importance of engaging with field theory and social movement studies to understand how the politics of commemoration is evolving in the contemporary world.

Conclusion

In this brief chapter, I have elaborated Halbwachs's formulation in light of recent studies of ritual and performance in cultural sociology and used it as a point of departure for exploring the frontiers of sociological research on commemoration. Simply put, commemoration generates collective memory as a basis of group solidarity and identity: commemoration is a ritual that emotionally induces people to experience a past event vicariously and thereby imagine their secondhand knowledge of it as living memory that they possess as members of a social group. This Halbwachsian concept of commemoration allows sociologists to investigate the causal mechanisms and processes through which certain mnemonic schemas and objects, constitutive of collective memory, are constructed and disseminated among people.

However, commemoration also functions as a focal point of political struggles because different groups remember a past event differently and compete for power to legitimate their commemorative positions. Commemoration is generative of both group solidarity and intergroup conflict. In fact, the politics of commemoration has become potentially more contentious in recent decades. This is not only because many commemorative practices are now increasingly transnational and involving a greater number of participants from different countries and regions, but also because the two logics of commemoration – nationalism and cosmopolitanism – create an institutional contradiction as a source of intergroup conflicts that are not easy to resolve. For sociologists of collective memory to keep pace with this changing culture and politics of commemoration in the increasingly global world, they must continue to refine their analytical tools by drawing on field theory, social movement studies, and other relevant theoretical traditions in sociology.

References

Alexander, Jeffrey C. 2004. "Cultural Pragmatics: Social Performance Between Ritual and Strategy." *Sociological Theory* 22(4):527–73.

Anderson, Benedict. 1991. *Imagined Communities: Reflections on the Origin and Spread of Nationalism.* London: Verso.

Armstrong, Elizabeth A., and Suzanna M. Crage. 2006. "Movements and Memory: the Making of the Stonewall Myth." *American Sociological Review* 71(5):724–51.

Beck, Ulrich. 2005. *Power in the Global Age: A New Global Political Economy.* Cambridge: Polity Press.

Beck, Ulrich, and Natan Sznaider. 2006. "Unpacking Cosmopolitanism for the Social Sciences: A Research Agenda." *British Journal of Sociology* 57(1):1–23.

Bell, Duncan. 2003. "Mythscapes: Memory, Mythology, and National Identity." *British Journal of Sociology* 54(1):63–81.

Boltanski, Luc, and Laurent Thévenot. 2006. *On Justification: Economics of Worth.* Princeton, NJ: Princeton University Press.

Bourdieu, Pierre. 1999. "Rethinking the State: Genesis and Structure of the Bureaucratic Field." Pp. 53–75 in *State/Culture: State Formation After the Cultural Turn*, edited by G. Steinmetz. Ithaca, NY: Cornell University Press.

Collins, Randall. 2004. *Interaction Ritual Chains.* Princeton, NJ: Princeton University Press.

Dayan, Daniel, and Elihu Katz. 1992. *Media Events: The Live Broadcasting of History.* Cambridge, MA: Harvard University Press.

Fine, Gary Alan, and Aaron Beim. 2007. "Introduction: Interactionist Approaches to Collective Memory." *Symbolic Interaction* 30(1):1–5.

Fligstein, Neil, and Doug McAdam. 2011. "Toward a General Theory of Strategic Action Fields." *Sociological Theory* 29(1):1–26.

Friedland, Roger, and Robert R. Alford. 1991. "Bringing Society Back in: Symbols, Practices, and Institutional Contradictions." Pp. 232–63 in *The New Institutionalism in Organizational Analysis*, edited by W.W. Powell and P.J. DiMaggio. Chicago: University of Chicago Press.

Ghoshal, Raj Andrew. 2013. "Transforming Collective Memory: Mnemonic Opportunity Structures and the Outcomes of Racial Violence Memory Movements." *Theory and Society* 42(4):329–50.

Halbwachs, Maurice. 1992. *On Collective Memory.* Chicago: University of Chicago Press.

Inglis, David. 2016. "Globalization and/of Memory: On the Complexification and Contestation of Memory Cultures and Practices." Pp. 143–57 in *Routledge International Handbook of Memory Studies*, edited by A.L. Tota and T. Hagen. New York: Routledge.

LaCapra, Dominik. 2001. *Writing History, Writing Trauma*. Baltimore, MD: Johns Hopkins University Press.

Levy, Daniel, and Natan Sznaider. 2006. *The Holocaust and Memory in the Global Age*. Philadelphia, PA: Temple University Press.

Nora, Pierre. 1989. "Between Memory and History: Les Lieux de Mémoire." *Representations* 26:7–24.

Olick, Jeffrey K. 2003. "Introduction." Pp. 1–15 in *States of Memory: Continuities, Conflicts, and Transformations in National Retrospection*, edited by J.K. Olick. Durham, NC: Duke University Press.

———. 2007. *The Politics of Regret: On Collective Memory and Historical Responsibility*. New York: Routledge.

Saito, Hiro. 2016. *The History Problem: The Politics of War Commemoration in East Asia*. Honolulu: University of Hawaii Press.

Schuman, Howard, and Jacqueline Scott. 1989. "Generations and Collective Memories." *American Sociological Review* 54(3):359–81.

Vinitzky-Seroussi, Vera. 2002. "Commemorating a Difficult Past: Yitzhak Rabin's Memorials." *American Sociological Review* 67(1):30–52.

Wagner-Pacifici, Robin, and Barry Schwartz. 1991. "The Vietnam Veterans Memorial: Commemorating a Difficult Past." *American Journal of Sociology* 97(2):376–420.

Wertsch, James V. 2002. *Voices of Collective Remembering*. Cambridge: Cambridge University Press.

Zolberg, Vera. 1998. "Contested Remembrance: The Hiroshima Exhibit Controversy." *Theory and Society* 27(4):565–90.

69

Culture and cosmopolis . . . liquid-modern adventures of an idea

Zygmunt Bauman

Introduction

How have the implications of culture changed in the twenty-first century? That is the question that must haunt us. Artistic offers, Pierre Bourdieu memorably insisted just a few decades ago, are all class-addressed and class-selected; the triple effect of the separation of classes, class-assignment, and signification of class membership is their main raison d'être, the most seminal of social functions, and perhaps their latent, even if not their manifest, purpose.

In Bourdieu's view, objets d'art meant for aesthetic consumption indexed, signaled, and protected class divisions, legibly marking and fortifying the borders that kept classes apart. To sign the borders unambiguously and to guard them effectively, all or most objets d'art had to be assigned to mutually exclusive sets – sets that could neither be mixed nor appreciated and/or possessed conjointly. What counted was not so much their substance and intrinsic virtues, or lack thereof, as the prohibition against mixing them – misrepresented as their inherent resistance to gelling with each other. There was a highbrow, middlebrow, and lowbrow artistic taste, and they could be jumbled together no more than fire and water.

From Bourdieu's *Distinction* (1984), culture emerged chiefly as a contraption – used, and possibly also meant, to signify the differences between classes and to keep them different. This was a technology to be deployed in building and protecting class difference, separation, and *hierarchy*. It emerged much as it had been situated almost a century earlier by Oscar Wilde: "Those who find beautiful meanings in beautiful things are the cultivated. . . . They are the elect to whom beautiful things mean only Beauty" ([1891] 1992:3).

To put it in a nutshell, culture (the set of culturally prompted and "culturally relevant" choices) was a *socially conservative* force. And to acquit itself properly of that function, it needed to apply two apparently opposite expedients: it needed to be as strict and uncompromising about *exclusion* as it was about *inclusion*.

When Bourdieu's *Distinction* was published in the late 1970s, it turned upside down the original, Enlightenment-born and bequeathed idea of "culture." The cultural practice that Bourdieu discovered, revealed, and put on record was a far cry from the earlier model of "culture" construed at the time when the concept was coined and ushered into public vocabulary in the third quarter of the eighteenth century, almost simultaneously with the English concept of "refinement," and the German, of *Bildung*.

At its birth, the idea of "culture" was intended to stand for an instrument of the (power-assisted) progress toward a universal human condition. "Culture" denoted a *proselytizing* mission, intended to be undertaken and adumbrated in the form of a resolute and sustained effort of *universal* cultivation and enlightenment, social amelioration and spiritual uplifting, and the promotion of the "lowly" to the level of those "on top." Or, in Matthew Arnold's inspired and widely echoed 1869 phrase from *Culture and Anarchy* ([1869] 1994), culture "seeks *to do away with classes*; to make the best that has been thought and known in the world current everywhere; to make all men live in an atmosphere of sweetness and light."

"Culture," then, entered the modern vocabulary as a declaration of *intent* – as a name of an intended *mission* yet to be undertaken. It stood for the planned and hoped for compact between those in the know (and above all confident of being in the know) and the ignorant (or people defined as ignorant by those confident of being knowledgeable) – a compact signed unilaterally and put into operation by the emergent "knowledge class" seeking for its calling-the-tune role to be duly respected in the emergent new order about to be built on the ruins of the ancien régime. The declared intent was to educate, enlighten, improve, and ennoble *le peuple*, freshly recast as *les citoyens* of the newly established *état-nation*: the marriage of the emergent nation self-elevating into a sovereign state, with the emergent state claiming the role of the nation's guardian. The "project of Enlightenment" allocated to culture (understood as the *labor of cultivation*) the status of a principal tool of nation, state, and nation-state *building*. Simultaneously, it appointed the knowledge class as that tool's principal operator. In its travels from political ambition to philosophical ruminations and back, the two-pronged objective of the Enlightenment venture (whether explicitly proclaimed or tacitly presumed) had promptly crystallized as the discipline of *state-subjects* and the solidarity of *nationals*.

The emergent nation-state felt emboldened by the fast swelling numbers of "the people," since the rising number of potential workers/soldiers was believed to raise its power differential. The nation-building efforts, conjointly with economic progress, sedimented growing numbers of "redundant" individuals (indeed, entire categories of population that urgently needed to be disposed of, lest the sought-after order fail to emerge, or its growth be severely disturbed; see Bauman 2005). In turn, the newly established nation-state was also soon pressed to start looking for spaces outside its borders fit to accommodate the excess of products and people it could not absorb itself. The resulting empire-building and colonizing efforts gave a powerful boost to the Enlightenment-born idea of "culture" – and an altogether new dimension to the proselytizing mission that it implied. In the likeness of the "enlightening the people" vision emerged the concepts of the "white man's burden" and "lifting the savages out of their savagery." "Developed societies" became the global center with a missionary role toward the rest of humanity. The future role of that center was conceived to replicate the function of the knowledge elite in its relation with "the people" inside the colonial metropole.

Bourdieu carried out his study at a time when the Enlightenment work of culture by and large had been completed – at least in the "center" where the maps of the world and its anticipated/postulated futures were drawn, though not in its imperial extensions, from which the expeditionary forces of the "center" were forced into retreat well before bringing the realities on the ground up to its cultural standards. Inside the center, however, the intended product ("the people" reincarnated as "citizens") was in place, and the position of knowledge classes in the new order was, or at least was believed to be, secure. Rather than as a bold, iconoclastic crusade and mission, culture looked like a homeostatic contraption, a sort of gyroscope rendering the established nation-state resistant to cross-winds and keeping it on steady course (or, in Talcott

Parsons's systems-theory phrase influential in the 1950s, "self-equilibrating"). Precisely in this historical moment (a brief and transient moment, as it was soon to become clear) "culture" was caught – immobilized and frozen snapshot-style, explored, and recorded – in Bourdieu's *Distinction*. But culture in this function was already on its way to imminent redundancy.

That redundancy was the outcome of several processes contributing to the passage from the "solid" to the "liquid" form of modernity – the presently prevailing state of the modern condition that other authors have variously termed "postmodernity," "late modernity," "second modernity," or "hypermodernity." What makes modernity "liquid" is the unstoppably accelerating "modernization" through which – just like other liquids – no forms of social life are able to retain their shapes for long. "Melting of solids," an endemic and defining feature of *all* modern forms of life, continues, but melted solids are no longer intended, as before, to be replaced by "new and improved," "more solid" solids, no longer hoped to be immune to further melting.

The realities about to be "dissolved in the darkness" at the time when Bourdieu's study was published were those viewed and described through the prism of the "self-equilibrating system" – the ideal model that the nation-states of the "solid" phase of the modern era repeatedly declared to be their intention to attain, and a condition that they time and again, with keen help of their learned panegyrists, pretended to have reached. As long (but only as long) as ambitions to construe a self-equilibrating system stayed alive, the homeostatic vision of culture did not need to fear serious contestation. But the ambitions started to fade and eventually, reluctantly at first but later willingly, had to be abandoned under the pressure of globalization and, more recently, a range of liquid counter-globalizations. Dissipation of ambitions gradually exposed the vulnerable and increasingly fictional nature of system boundaries and in the end drew into question territorial sovereignty – and so also self-sustained and self-equilibrating systems.

Many people still believe in "progress," but we now have to view its blessings as mixed with curses, with the curses growing steadily in volume while blessings are getting ever fewer and further between. Even the most recent generations before us still believed the future to be the safest and most promising location for hopes. But now we tend to locate manifold fears, anxieties, and apprehensions in the future: of growing scarcity of jobs, of falling incomes (and so also of our and our children's life chances), of yet greater frailty of our social positions and temporality of our life achievements, of unstoppably widening gaps between tools, resources, and skills at our disposal in the face of the immensity of life challenges, and, all in all, of control over our lives slipping from our hands even as we are degraded to the status of pawns relegated to the margins of a chessboard by the unknown players indifferent to our needs and dreams, if not all too ready to sacrifice them in pursuit of their own objectives. What the thought of the future, not so long ago associated with more comfort and convenience, nowadays brings to mind for many is the growing menace of being identified and classified as inept and socially unfit, denied value and dignity, marginalized, excluded, and outcast. A great and rising majority of people has by now learned from experience to discredit the uneven, capricious, unpredictable, and notoriously disappointing future as the location for investment of hopes.[1]

In short, past and future are in the course of exchanging positions. It is now the future, whose time seems to have arrived to be pillorized, decried for its untrustworthiness and unmanageability, that is booked on the debit side. And it is now the past's turn to be booked on the side of credit – as a site of still free choice and investment of as yet undiscredited hope.

In other words, the 2016 Brexit episode, the US election of Donald Trump, as well as other contemporary populist movements are manifestations of a "retrotopian tendency" (Bauman 2017). They index the collapse of trust in the capability of the territorially sovereign state's political establishment to deliver desired change (or indeed any promised change). Given voters' frustration with the extant political elite and their refusal to invest trust in any one of its parts, the Brexit referendum provided a unique occasion to match polling choices with sentiments struggling for expression. How unlike was that unique occasion to routine parliamentary elections! In the latter, you may express your frustration, your anger against the most recent in a long line of power-holders and promise-givers, but the price you pay for this emotional relief is inviting to ministerial offices the opposition, as inseparable a part of the "political establishment" as the government that it replaces in the endless musical chairs game; you come nowhere near expressing the *total*, comprehensive nature of your dissent. The Brexit referendum was completely different: you could use your single vote for "leave" to release your frustration and anger against all the establishment in one go.

As for Trump's election, public opinion – inspired, nudged, and abetted as usual by the media chorus – all but agreed (just as with the Brexit vote) that votes for Trump were a massive, indeed fully and truly *popular* protest against the political establishment and political elite of the US *as a whole*, with which a large and continually growing part of the population in recent years grew frustrated for failing, systematically and routinely, to deliver on its promises. Not being part of that elite, never having occupied any elected office, coming from outside of the political establishment, and staying stubbornly at loggerheads even with the party of which he was formally a member, Trump offered the first credible, indeed unique, occasion for wholesale condemnation of the entire political system.[2]

Trump gained the presidency on the anti-establishment card. Presenting himself as a strong man with his hands untied by selfish partisan interest, and for that reason able to set off a new beginning or a return to the glorious past, capable of playing down and sweeping aside the establishment's sacrosanct principles of political/legal correctness and its double sin of impotence to act effectively and indifference to what needs to be done. Trump prevailed because *his voters* dreamed all along of a strong leader, hands untied, and for that reason able to set off a new beginning or a return to the glorious past.

What we are currently witnessing, not just in the US but in considerable and rapidly expanding sectors of the EU, is a thorough rehashing of allegedly untouchable, indeed defining principles of "democracy." I do not think that the term itself will be abandoned as the name of the political ideal: as a *signifiant*, as Claude Lévi-Strauss would have branded it, "democracy" has been absorbing and is still capable of parenting many and different *signifiées*. Nevertheless, there is a distinct possibility that the traditional safeguards (like Montesquieu's division of power into three autonomous sectors – legislative, executive, and judiciary – or English "checks and balances") will fall out of public favor and become stripped of significance, replaced explicitly or in fact by consolidation of power in an authoritarian or even dictatorial model.[3] Symptoms multiply of a tendency to pull power down from the nebulous, unreachable, and impenetrable elitist heights into a quasi-direct communication between the strong leader at the top and the pulverized and eminently fluid and fissiparous aggregate of supporters/subjects, equipped with "social websites" serving as apparently wide open and widely accessible gates to the public arena and to new media forms of indoctrination.

Political elites' consensual neoliberal embrace of globalization was perhaps the crucial policy that fueled their rejection. The seminal impacts of globalization – especially the divorce of power from politics, and in its consequence, the progressive surrender of its traditional functions by states that were weakening, and the ensuing exemption of those functions from political control – by now have been thoroughly investigated and described in great detail. Here, I will focus on one aspect of globalization that is too seldom considered in connection with the study of culture – changing patterns of global migration that have been crucially driven by counter-globalization.

There were three different phases in the history of modern-era migration. The first wave of migration followed the logic of the tri-partite syndrome: Territoriality of sovereignty, "Rooted" identity, Gardening posture (TRG). This involved the emigration from the "modernized" center (read: the home of order-building and of economic progress – the two main industries turning out and off the growing numbers of "wasted humans"), about 60 million people altogether, to "empty" lands (read: lands whose native population could be struck off from most calculations and accounts, literally "uncounted" and "unaccounted for"), founding new and hopefully perfected replicas of England, Scotland, or Wales, and London, Berlin, Amsterdam, or Warsaw. Whatever had remained of the indigenous population after a spate of wholesale murders and similarly massive epidemics has been cast as another edition of "the people" awaiting "acculturation" – dealt with under the rubric of the "white man's mission."

The second wave of migration can be best modeled as the "Empire emigrating back." With the dismantling of colonial empires, a number of colonized people in various stages of "enlightenment" and "cultural advancement" followed their colonial superiors to the metropolis. Upon arrival, they were cast in the only worldview-strategic mold available: one construed earlier, in the nation-building era, to deal with the categories earmarked for "assimilation," a process aimed at annihilation of cultural difference and casting the "minorities" at the receiving end of crusades, *Kulturkämpfe*, and proselytizing missions (currently renamed, following the rules of political correctness, as "citizenship education" aimed at "integration"). This story is not yet finished: just as with the first, TRG, phase of migration, however, efforts to squeeze the drama of the "empire migrating back" into the frame of the "white man's burden" syndrome are in vain.

The third wave of modern migration, now in full force and still gathering momentum under dialectical processes of globalization and counter-globalization, leads into the age of *diasporas* – creating a worldwide archipelago of ethnic/religious/linguistic settlements oblivious to the trails blazed and paved by the imperialist-colonial episode and following instead the globalization-induced logic of survival under the planetary redistribution of life resources and political power. Contemporary diasporas are scattered and diffuse. They extend over many nominally sovereign territories, ignore territorial claims to supremacy (and preferably exclusivity) of local populations, and are locked in the double bind of "dual (or multiple) nationalities" and dual (or multiple) loyalties. Present-day migrations differ from the two previous phases by moving both ways (virtually no countries are nowadays exclusively "immigrant" or "emigrant"), and privileging no routes (imperial/colonial links of the past are no longer determinative). They explode the old TRG syndrome and replace it with Extraterritoriality, "Anchors" that displace "roots" as primary tools of identification, and a Hunting strategy (EAH).

The most striking difference distinguishing the present "refugee crisis" from the shape of the influx of foreigners immediately preceding it is that it cannot be administered, monitored, and controlled by means that were until relatively recently assumed to be effective. It is precisely such inadequacy and inefficacy of controlling migration that raised the anxiety concerning inflows of strangers to the level of "panic." What the latest tides laid wide open is the ongoing transformation of geopolitical conditions under which the movement of populations takes place. The concept "diasporisation" suggests a crucial trait of contemporary migrations – that they are much more subject to grassroots processes and influences than subject to top-down regulation.

The new migrations cast a question mark upon the bond between identity and citizenship, individual and place, and neighborhood and belonging. As the acute and insightful observer of the fast changing frames of human togetherness, Jonathan Rutherford (2007:59–60), notes, the residents of the London street on which he lives form a neighborhood of different communities, some with networks extending only to the next street, others that stretch across the world. The neighborhood has porous boundaries that make it difficult to identify who belongs and who is an outsider. What is it we belong to in this locality? What is it that each of us calls home, and when we think back and remember how we arrived here, what stories do we share?

Living in a diaspora among diasporas for the first time forces onto the agenda the issue of "living with *multiple* differences" – which now appear on the agenda only because the differences are no longer seen as merely temporary, and so now, unlike in the past, urgently require arts, skills, teaching, and learning, if a retreat into militant intolerance is to be countered. The idea of "human rights," promoted in the EAH setting to replace/complement the TRG institution of territorially determined citizenship, translates today as *the right to remain different*. By fits and starts, that new rendition of the human-rights idea sediments, at best, *tolerance*; it has as yet to start in earnest to sediment *solidarity*. And a moot question remains as to whether it is fitting to conceive of group solidarity in any other form than that of the fickle and fray, predominantly virtual "networks," galvanized, and continually remodeled by the interplay of individual connecting and disconnecting, calling and messaging initiatives, and their termination.

The new rendition of the human-rights idea also disassembles hierarchies and tears apart the imagery of upward ("progressive") evolution. Forms of life float, meet, clash, crash, catch hold of each other, merge, and hive off with (to paraphrase Simmel) equal specific gravity. Steady and stolid hierarchies and evolutionary lines are replaced with interminable and endemically inconclusive battles of recognition – at the utmost, with eminently renegotiable pecking orders. We would tell who is to assimilate to whom, whose dissimilarity/idiosyncrasy is destined for a chop and whose is to emerge on top, were we only given a hierarchy of cultures. Well, we are not given it, and are unlikely to get one anytime soon.

Indeed, in the part of the world where pleas on behalf of culture are composed and voiced, avidly read and hotly debated, the arts have lost (or at any rate are fast losing) their function as the handmaiden of social hierarchy struggling to reproduce itself. One by one, all such tasks have either lost their application and topicality or come to be performed by other means and using different instruments. Most recently, for example, social media have simultaneously collapsed and intensified difference.

The "us" versus "them" dialectic is an anthropological *constant* of the human condition. That dialectic entails, however, also historical, time-bound *variation* as the game of self-identification and separation (or, more to the point, the game of separation *because* of self-identification and the game of self-identification *through* separation) encounters new issues and challenges precipitated by changing techniques of domination and technologies of social actions that serve them.

One such new challenge has been the need to design a replica/equivalent/simile, or an updated version of the orthodox, territorial variety of separation inside the online cyberspace of informatics so notorious for allowing freedom to bypass border-posts and ignore borders. This challenge has been met: contrary to many a hopeful prognosis, the near-universal and 24/7 online availability of instant communication independently of geographical distance facilitated the job of mental separation and non-communication to a degree unattainable in the offline part of the universe we inhabit. As shown by research on practices deployed by a great majority of internet users, the DIY "comfort zones," "echo chambers," or "halls of mirrors" are much more effective at creating and sustaining separation than the most refined technologies of "gated communities" or state-installed frontier walls, barbed wires, ingenuous passport-and-visas arrangements, and heavily armed border patrols.

Emancipated from the missionary – and later the homeostatic – functions of the labors imposed on their culture-creators and culture-operators, the arts (which in the era of intense individualization and widening sphere of "life politics" came to include the art of life) are free to serve the individual concerns with self-identification and self-assertion, and these shift the issue of "belonging" from the "before" to the "after" of individually made choices. We may say that culture (and most conspicuously, though not at all uniquely, its artistic branch) is in its liquid-modern phase made to the measure of (willingly pursued, or endured as obligatory) *individual* freedom of choice (enacted, to be sure, on the grids of consumer choices and social media applications). And that it is *meant* to service such freedom. And that it is meant to insure that the choice remains *unavoidable*: a life necessity, and a duty. And that responsibility, the inalienable companion of free choice, stays where the liquid-modern condition forced it – on the shoulders of the *individual*, now appointed the sole manager of "life politics."

This is not a mere paradigm *shift*. We could and should speak instead of a "paradigm *earthquake*." One might say that, in the liquid-modern setting, the term "paradigm" has joined the fast-growing family of the (as Ulrich Beck would have said) "zombie concepts" or (as Jacques Derrida would have preferred) concepts that need to be used *sous rature* – or better yet, not used at all. Liquid modernity is a permanent war of attrition waged against any and all paradigms – and indeed any other homeostatic, conformity-and-routine-promoting contraptions meant to sustain monotony and repetitiveness of events. That condition frames the paradigmatic (bequeathed by solid modernity) *concept* of culture as much as it does the *culture* itself (the sum total of human-made, intentional artifices), which that concept intended to grasp and render intelligible.

Today culture consists of *offers*, not *norms*. As already noted by Bourdieu, culture lives by seduction, not normative regulation; PR, not policing; creating new needs/desires/wants, not coercion. Ours is a society of consumers, and just like the world as-seen-and-lived by consumers, culture turns into a warehouse of meant-for-consumption products – each vying for the shifting/drifting attention of prospective consumers in the hope of attracting it and holding for a bit longer than a fleeting moment, or just a click. Abandoning stiff standards, indulging indiscrimination, serving all tastes while privileging none, encouraging fitfulness and "flexibility" (the politically correct name of spinelessness), and romanticizing unsteadiness and inconsistency are therefore the proper (the only reasonable?) strategies to follow (fastidiousness, raising brows, stiffening upper lips are not recommended). These are commendable and indeed seemly qualities in a society in which networks replace structures, where the attachment/detachment game and an unending procession of connections and disconnections replace "determining" and "fixing."

The current phase of the graduated transformation of the idea of "culture" from its original Enlightenment-inspired form to its liquid-modern reincarnation is prompted and operated by the same neoliberal forces that promote emancipation of the markets from any remaining constraints of a non-economic nature – social, political, and ethical constraints among them. In pursuing its own emancipation, liquid-modern consumer-focused economy relies on the excess of offers, their accelerated aging, and quick dissipation of their seductive power – which, by the way, makes it an economy of profligacy and waste. Since there is little knowing in advance which of the offers may prove tempting enough to stimulate consuming desire, the best way to find out leads through trials and costly errors. A continuous supply of new offers and a constantly growing volume of goods on offer are also necessary to keep the circulation of goods rapid and the desire to replace them with "new and improved" goods constantly refreshed – as well as to prevent consumer dissatisfaction with individual products from condensing into general disaffection with the consumerist mode of life as such.

Liquid-modern culture has no "people" to "cultivate." It has instead clients to seduce. And unlike its "solid modern" predecessor, it no longer wishes to work itself, eventually but the sooner the better, out of a job. Its job is now to render its own survival permanent – through temporalizing all aspects of the lives of its former wards, now reborn as clients.

In the face of such developments, so many voices currently ask, do we need a new humanism for the twenty-first century? What we need in my view, and urgently, is the closing or at least considerable narrowing of the "cultural lag" stretching between the novel condition of the world and increasingly outdated consciousness of its population (particularly its opinion-making elite). The late Ulrich Beck (2006), a most acute master of vivisecting our world's weaknesses and inanities, argued convincingly that in our globalized world of universal interdependence, we are all already cast in a "cosmopolitan *situation*" but we haven't as yet embarked in earnest on the long and wobbly road leading to the acquisition of its necessary complement, cosmopolitan *awareness* – worldview, mindset, and attitude. And no wonder: those prospective "us," embracing this time – for the first time in human history – the *whole* of humanity, would need to acquire such consciousness with no help from our enemy, a *shared* enemy, legitimizing and demanding for that reason the solidarity of all of "us." Is this however, at all possible, indeed, conceivable? The next leap in the history of expanding integration – if it ever happens – will have to do *without* the crutch of a shared enemy – of new divisions, new separations, and new walls needed to accommodate (indeed, to give meaning) to the unity of the expanded "us." To become a realistic proposition, this process would require nothing less than an uphill struggle to renegotiate and replace the thousands-years-old, deeply ingrained human mode of being-in-the-world.

Alas, Beck was hardly heard. On a planet tightly crisscrossed by trade routes and information highways, we (including our political elites) guide our thought and actions by precepts inherited from the era of territorial sovereignties – moats, drawn bridges, stockades, barbed wires, ad-hoc coalitions, and walls. Following the cosmopolitan program doesn't seem in the cards in the foreseeable future. On the contrary: most of the current symptoms, which I attempted to list in my study of "retrotopia" (2017), point to the ardent search for "them" – preferably the old-fashioned, unmistakable, and incurably alien, hostile, and pugnacious them, fit for the job of identity-reinforcement, boundary-drawing, and wall-building. The reactions of a rising number of powers-that-be to the progressive erosion of their territorial sovereignty tends to be an effort to loosen their suprastate commitments and retreat from previous agreements to join resources and coordinate policies – that is, moving yet farther away from complementing their objectively cosmopolitan plight with programs and undertakings at a similar level. Such a state of affairs only adds to the disarray that underpins the gradual yet relentless disablement of the extant global institutions of political power. The prime winners are extraterritorial finances, investment funds, and commodity trading in all shades of semi-legality, whereas economic and social equality and principles of intra- and inter-state justice are the losers, together with a large part, possibly a growing majority, of the world population.

Instead of an earnest, consistent, and coordinated long-term effort to uproot the resulting existential fears, governments all around the globe have jumped at the chance of filling the vacuum of legitimation left behind by shrinking social provisions and abandoned post-World War II efforts to lay foundations under a "family of nations," embarking on a powerful push toward a so-to-speak "securitization" of social problems and, in consequence, also a securitization of political thought and action. Popular fears – aided and abetted by an intimate, truly buddy-buddy alliance of political elite and mass-information and entertainment media and spurred yet further by the rising hegemony of "strong man" (and woman) demagoguery – are for all intents and purposes welcome as a most precious ore fit for continuous smelting of fresh political capital coveted by increasingly unleashed commercial powers and their political lobbies.

Acknowledgments

Zygmunt Bauman, born in 1925, died on January 9, 2017, before completing revisions to his chapter published in the first edition of the *Handbook of Cultural Sociology*. In the previous year,

Professor Bauman and I had been in correspondence about his contribution, and on December 8, 2016, I provided him with a first draft of his chapter that he and I had agreed I would undertake. In response to my queries of December 8 about his views on recent social developments (immigration, Brexit, and the election of Donald Trump to the US presidency), he sent along newly drafted writings ("three pieces I have scribbled") and asked me to update the chapter by incorporating these writings as I saw fit. On December 19, I emailed him a revised draft. He acknowledged receiving it but by then was no longer able to comment concerning its substance. Subsequently, I determined that slightly different versions of two of the "scribblings" have been published (Bauman 2016a, 2016b); in the present chapter, the places of brief parallel quotations are indicated by notes. His final efforts on his chapter for the present handbook, as well as the two recent publications, demonstrate that Zygmunt Bauman maintained a strong intellectual engagement with contemporary events up to the very end of his life. I hope that the chapter here does justice to his vision.

—John R. Hall, editor

Notes

1   A slightly different version of this and the following paragraph appears in Bauman (2016b).
2   A slightly different version of this sentence appears in Bauman (2016a).
3   A slightly different version of the first three sentences in this paragraph appears in Bauman (2016a).

References

Arnold, Matthew. 1994 [1869]. *Culture and Anarchy*. New Haven, CT: Yale University Press.
Bauman, Zygmunt. 2005. *Wasted Lives*. Cambridge: Polity Press.
———. 2016a. "Trump: A Quick Fix for Existential Anxiety." *Social Europe*. Retrieved February 6, 2017 (www.socialeurope.eu/2016/11/46978/).
———. 2016b. "Living towards the Past: Zygmunt Bauman Talks Retrotopia and Humanity's Disillusionment with the Future." *Spiked Review*. Retrieved February 6, 2017 (www.spiked-online.com/spiked-review/article/living-towards-the-past/).
———. 2017. *Retrotopia*. Cambridge: Polity Press.
Beck, Ulrich. 2006 [2004]. *Cosmopolitan Vision*. Cambridge: Polity Press.
Bourdieu, Pierre. 1984 [1979]. *Distinction*. Cambridge, MA: Harvard University Press.
Rutherford, Jonathan. 2007. *After Identity*. London: Lawrence & Wishart.
Wilde, Oscar. 1992 [1891]. *The Picture of Dorian Gray*. Ware, Hertfordshire: Wordsworth Editions.

70

Cosmopolitanism and the clash of civilizations

Bryan S. Turner

Introduction: alterity, ancient and modern

Inter-civilizational contact invariably creates a sense of the otherness or alterity of different societies and cultures. Any society with a more or less coherent cultural boundary or civilizational identity, acting as an inclusionary social force, tends to have an exclusionary notion of membership and hence otherness; the more inclusive the feeling of ethnicity and national membership, the more intense the notion of an outside. Thus, a paradoxical relationship exists between the growing cultural hybridity, interconnectedness, and interdependency of the globe – indeed, the modernization of societies – and the notion of alterity in politics, philosophy, and culture.

We should be careful to distinguish between a number of separate meanings of the other, otherness, and alterity. The concept of the other has been important in phenomenology and psychoanalysis, where the self as a subject presupposes the existence of a non-self or other. And in existentialism the other often assumes an antagonistic relationship with the self. Because the individual resides in a world of other subjectivities, there exists a mode of existence that is properly referred to as "being-for-others." Thus, for Emmanuel Levinas (1998), the face of the other challenges us to take responsibility for the other, and hence otherness creates the conditions that make ethics possible. Jacques Derrida (2000), playing on the etymological connections between "stranger" and "host" (*hostis* and *hospes*), neatly summarized the issue by saying that ethics is hospitality.

This philosophical analysis of the role of the other in modern ethical discourse has an important relationship to nationalism, ethnic cleansing, and globalization. Following the collapse of the Soviet Union beginning in 1989, there has been a resurgence of ethnic identity as the basis of political communities, and ethnic violence has largely replaced class conflict as the major arena of political confrontation. The disintegration of Yugoslavia that began in 1991 and the 1992 crisis in Bosnia were tragic illustrations of the importance of ethnicity in international conflicts. Following the 1979 Iranian Revolution came global conflicts between Sunni and Shi'ite Muslims, often between hitherto harmonious communities (Nasr 2006), and a series of proxy wars between Saudi Arabia and Iran culminating in the bloody conflict over Syria. Where globalization weakens the nation-state and promotes identity politics, alterity can drive violence in ethnic conflict.

Modern ethnic conflicts are removed from once successful patterns of social cooperation between Muslims, Jews, and Christians. Medieval Spain is a well-known example (Menocal 2002). More recently, in France, Jews and Muslims, having similar experiences of displacement and marginalization, enjoyed a history of peace and mutuality before the conflicts in Algeria and Palestine soured their peaceful relationship with the host community (Mandel 2014). And in Germany, Muslim communities have had been relatively successful in terms of upward mobility into the middle class, and German converts to Islam are not uncommon (Özyürek 2015).

By connecting alterity with twentieth-century globalization, we must not ignore the historical roots of the sense of otherness. Fear of the other was fundamental to Greek politics, because endless wars against "barbarians" always involved the threat of capture and enslavement. Alterity arose out of the growth of international trade and warfare, and it was expressed powerfully in the anthropological writings of Herodotus. With the collapse of the ancient world, the question of alterity became closely associated with the Abrahamic religions of Judaism, Christianity, and Islam. Because Yahweh was a jealous god, there was a sacred covenant between God and the tribes of Israel, which excluded those who worshiped idols and false gods. In Christianity, Paul's letters to the Galatians and Romans expressed a universalistic orientation that rejected circumcision as a condition of salvation. Because the uncircumcised (non-Jews) could be among the righteous, the message of Jesus had, at least in Pauline theology, a global significance (Badiou 2003). Because Christianity and Islam developed as evangelical faiths that stressed human equality, they in a sense denied the problem of alterity. However, the persistence of slavery in both Christendom and Islam raised a stubborn problem about the nature and depth of universalism and egalitarianism in both religions (Segal 2001).

The struggle to end slavery thus played a large part in the uneven growth of universal humanitarianism. In *The Origins of Global Humanitarianism*, Peter Stamatov (2013) showed how in the early sixteenth century, Catholic missionaries in Latin America – notably Bartolome de Las Casas (1484–1566) – campaigned against the enslavement of human beings, especially if they had been converted to Christianity. Jesuits spoke out against the mistreatment of indigenous peoples and criticized the greed of landlords and imperial powers. Later Protestant sects such as the Quakers developed "long-distance advocacy" to connect London and Philadelphia in an abolitionist network.

The construction of the other is never a simple binary between an inside and an outside. Christian attitudes toward Muslims are an important illustration of this complexity. The Christian West, at least from the late eleventh century onwards, developed a hostile view of Islam. Because Christian theology treated Islam as a false religion, many in the West imagined Islam as an irrational, stagnant, and licentious sect, thus promoting what Edward Said (1978) described as "Orientalism."

Important exceptions need to be kept in mind, however. Consider John Locke and Thomas Jefferson. Locke's letter on tolerance (1955) is often regarded as a foundational document of modern liberalism. Though with obvious limits in its scope, Locke's letter argued that tolerance extended not just to other kinds of Christians, but to "Turks" and "Jews." His arguments had a profound impact on Jefferson in the construction of the US Declaration of Independence and the Constitution's First Amendment. To be sure, there were contradictions. Jefferson owned 187 slaves and hence the rights of property could be said to trump those relating to freedom of religion. Nevertheless, although in the 1770s Jefferson had never met a Muslim, embracing the idea that the state had no basis to interfere with private conscience, he proposed tolerance not only for dissenters but also for Turks and Jews. Thus, contending threads of alterity and tolerance trace through the long arc of Western history.

Bryan S. Turner

The Huntington thesis

Today, for over two decades, Samuel Huntington's (1993) article on "the clash of civilizations" has defined much of the academic debate about inter-cultural understanding and misunderstanding. The Huntington thesis follows Carl Schmitt's *The Concept of the Political* (1996) in treating history as a struggle between friend and foe. In retrospect, Said's criticisms of Orientalism and especially his *Representations of the Intellectual* (1996) offered some prospect that intellectuals could forge a cross-cultural pathway toward mutual respect and understanding. But after 9/11, in the era of the "war on terror," Huntington's bleak analysis of the development of micro-fault line conflicts and macro-core state conflicts has more successfully captured the mood of foreign policy in the West. Huntington believed that the world's major civilizational division is between the Christian and Muslim worlds. Subsequently, he more openly wrote about the widespread Muslim grievance and hostility toward the United States (Huntington 2003), such that any attempt to engage with Islamic civilization is now seen in some quarters as a "war for Muslim minds" (Kepel 2004).

Opposing the Huntington thesis is not easy, particularly because it is in many respects a self-fulfilling prophecy. The more scholars have talked about it, the more it appeared to shape American foreign policy. Much of the criticism of Huntington has been couched at an empirical level, for example, showing that conflicts within Christianity (e.g., in Northern Ireland) and within Islam (between Sunni and Shi'ite) are at least as important as conflicts between religions. In addition, Huntington is said to have no real explanation for the conflict, because his thesis is "an ethnocentric blind to avoid having to discuss the things that Muslim opponents of the US actually care about" (Mann 2003:169).

Although it is important to question the Huntington thesis empirically, his argument opens up the opportunity to engage in a normative and epistemological debate about the moral grounds for respecting other cultures. I shall call this normative stance "cosmopolitan virtue," by which I mean the ethical imperative for respect, mutual dialogue, recognition, and care (Turner 2008a).

This normative discussion is both necessary and important: we should not underestimate the problems facing cosmopolitan virtue in the contemporary global crisis, which includes violence between Muslims and Buddhists in Myanmar, the destruction of Christian communities in Iraq and Syria, conflicts between Muslims and Copts in Egypt, the destruction of heritage sites in Syria by ISIS, and the refugee crisis in Europe, which is to a large extent the legacy of the American invasion of Iraq, European support for the fall of President Gaddafi, and the failure of the West to confront President Assad's regime effectively. These conflicts, rightly or wrongly, are defined in terms of a "clash of civilizations" that has engendered a widespread "Islamophobia."

One starting point for considering cosmopolitan virtue is the early German Enlightenment, especially the work of the philosopher Wilhelm Gottfried Leibniz (1646–1716). In the twentieth century, especially after the attack by the critical theory of Horkheimer and Adorno (1947), the Enlightenment became a target of critical inspection, precisely because its vision of universal reason was said to be blind to cultural differences. Reading Leibniz on China shows how misguided this interpretation has often been. Leibniz lived in a period when European trade with the outside world, including Asia, was expanding rapidly. Alongside this emerging capitalist world trade, Leibniz advocated a "commerce of light," namely a trade of mutual enlightenment. Against Spinoza's view that there is only one substance, Leibniz argued that the world is characterized by its infinite diversity and richness. According to Leibniz (1991) in his *Discourse on Metaphysics*, God has created the best of all possible worlds (a theodicy) which is "the simplest in hypotheses and the richest in phenomena."

Recognition of the diversity of cultures and civilizations leads to an embrace of the inherent value of difference. Leibniz, like Spinoza, advocated a tolerance of diverse views, but went beyond the philosophers of his day to establish a moral imperative to learn from cultural diversity. Applying this ethic to himself and committing much of his life to studying China from the reports of missionaries and merchants, Leibniz went about establishing a philosophical platform for cosmopolitanism. Differences between entities or "monads" require exchange, but they also establish a commonality of culture.

Leibniz was not, in modern terms, a cultural relativist: if all cultures are equal (in value), why bother to learn from any one of them? Although all knowledge of the outside world is relativistic, Leibniz argued that there are enough innate ideas to make an exchange of enlightenment possible. From the doctrine of interacting monads, he developed a hermeneutics of generosity and hospitality that treated inter-cultural understanding as an ethical imperative. Leibniz's implicit cosmopolitan virtue is a rational and moral antidote to Huntington that offers a guide for advancing a cosmopolitan ethos in our own times, especially a "commerce of light" between the West and Islam.

Despite Leibniz's cosmopolitan openness to other cultures, the Enlightenment has often been treated as the origin of modern universalism, which ironically functions as the basis for cultural domination and exclusion. The Enlightenment set in motion a series of binary oppositions between the universalistic world of bourgeois civility and citizenship versus local practices and customs that were considered antithetical to the march of progressive world history. The result was to create a world of others who were seen to be in need of education, reform, modernization, and regeneration, leading wherever possible to an eventual assimilation.

There is of course much more to this story. In 1793 in *Religion within the Boundaries of Mere Reason* (1998), Immanuel Kant thematized a modernist division between the moral impulse of Protestant rationalism and the "cultic religions" that promised to give health and prosperity to ordinary people, provided they surrendered themselves to the gods through the magical powers of the shaman, the wizard, and the witch. He created, at least implicitly, a comparative view of a division between the popular religions of the uncivilized world and the ascetic this-worldly religions of modernity – a contrast that more than a century later formed the basis for Max Weber's (1966) comparative sociology of the economic ethics of world religions. It was not only a Kantian view of world development.

G.W.F. Hegel, in a series of lectures between 1821 and 1831, developed the idea of Christianity as the religion in which the evolution of the spirit or *Geist* of history found its contemporary "consummation" (Hodgson 1985). For Kant and Hegel, Judaism did not belong to this world of rational consummate religions. It was on the basis of such reasoning that the revolutionary republican call of Napoleon Bonaparte summoned the Jewish community to assimilate under a banner of rationalist secularism. Progressive secular Jews would leave their ancestral allegiances and throw off their ancient customs to become French or German citizens.

The issue of Jewishness is inevitably connected with Karl Marx's critique of bourgeois capitalist society in his 1843 "On the Jewish Question" (Marx and Engels 1975). Marx used the debate about Jewishness to criticize bourgeois liberalism as a shallow political doctrine in which social emancipation was necessary to give political emancipation any substantial content. Genuine citizenship was not possible in capitalism because abstract Man was an alienated creature in which political life had become detached from the real conditions of existence. This discussion in many respects became the fatal starting point of the long history of the separation of universal rights of Man from the social transformation of class society by revolutionary action.

We cannot escape modernity, thus, we cannot escape the identity conflicts that result in civil disturbance, and we cannot easily guard against the threat of communal violence. Cleaning up the language of discrimination partly legitimated by Enlightenment thought is not going to significantly change the politics of ethnic violence. The current crisis of liberal secularism involves a struggle over claims to identity – a struggle that can no longer be housed within the legacy of the Treaty of Westphalia, in which it was assumed that religion could be simply a matter of private consciousness. The Treaty of 1648 came at the end of the Wars of Religion. Separating church and state, it made religion a matter of personal belief rather than public practice and allowed princes to decide which version of Christianity would be hegemonic within their principalities. However, these arrangements are breaking down, partly because, although they may have been relevant to Christian conflicts in the seventeenth century, they are less relevant in the modern period, when "public religions" have reasserted themselves – in Poland, Latin America, the US, and Iran (Casanova 1994). Although public religions sometimes had progressive consequences in the late twentieth century, it is difficult to be optimistic about future prospects. The Arab Spring and associated social movements appear to have failed, and Tunisia (arguably the cradle of such developments) now faces a desperate struggle with terrorist intrusions from Libya. Is there no alternative to this growth of ethnic conflict, especially in societies where the state appears to take sides with the majority against minorities, for instance, in Thailand between a majority Buddhist culture and Muslim minority one, or in Malaysia where a policy of Islamization of law and education weighs against Buddhists, Hindus, and Christians? (McCargo 2007). Perhaps the most extreme example has been President Assad's Syria: drawing support from Shia and Alawites, recent reports suggest, the regime has murdered thousands of Syrians who have opposed his rule. What models or metaphors of cosmopolitanism could one appeal to against such state violence?

One possibility of cosmopolitan inspiration is illustrated by a story told by Abul Kalam Azad, who confronted a flock of sparrows invading his prison cell during his incarceration by the British in Western India during World War II. After some fruitless confrontation and after many tentative steps of negotiation and persuasion, Azad eventually fed the birds, and through this "conference of birds" an ethics of coexistence emerged. (This little story is in fact based on a twelfth-century Sufi allegory by the Persian poet Fariduddin Attar.) Writing about South Asia, Aamir Mufti (2007:171–2) concludes that such allegorical narratives "reveal the utter human poverty of the politics of separatism and communalism" and that they "contain the elements of a critique of the implicit majoritarianism of 'secular' nationalism itself and its failure ultimately to produce a convincing ethico-political practice of coexistence in an undivided India." His attempt "to unravel the assumption of inevitability" that has become attached to the endless cycle of ethnic violence in modern societies represents a major contribution to the ethics of hospitality in a world deeply divided between hosts, guests, and strangers. Although cosmopolitanism is seriously challenged by the eruption of global violence, it is difficult to identify any other candidate as the basis of an ethical response to violence.

Cosmopolitan virtue

We can usefully distinguish between negative and positive alterity. Negative alterity exclusively defines the other as dangerous, inferior, and antithetical to the subject's own culture; Orientalism is the classical form of negative otherness. By contrast, positive alterity recognizes the other, embracing the ethical opportunities afforded by global diversity. In contemporary social theory, a variety of authors have defended recognition ethics, multiculturalism, and diversity as positive aspects of globalization. Although successful democracies may require safe, if porous, borders, patriotism can be usefully distinguished from nationalism. Cosmopolitan virtue – celebrating difference, and promoting the care of the other – is an ethical consequence of globalization and an obligation that complements human rights.

Contemporary philosophical debates about the other have their origins in Hegel's theory of recognition (Williams 1997). The master–slave dialectic suggests that neither slave nor master can achieve authentic recognition, and hence, without some degree of social equality, no ethical community – a system of rights and obligations – can function. Rights presuppose relatively free, autonomous, and self-conscious agents capable of rational choice. Recognition is required if people are to be mutually acceptable as moral agents, but life is unequal. Economic scarcity undercuts the roots of solidarity (community), without which conscious, rational agency is compromised. A variety of modern writers, notably Charles Taylor (1992), have appealed to recognition ethics as the baseline for the enjoyment of rights in multicultural societies. Without recognition of minority rights, no liberal-democratic society can function. The growth of human rights is a major index of the growth of juridical globalization, and recognition of the rights of others is an ethical precondition for global governance. Cosmopolitanism now appears as the most articulate alternative to a bleak set of assumptions about the clash of civilizations.

It is important to note that cosmopolitanism is neither new nor Western. We need to recognize the long history of Sanskrit cosmopolitanism as well as Buddhist cosmopolitanism. More recently various writers have drawn attention to Islamic cosmopolitanism (Marsden 2008). This openness to the alternative versions of cosmopolitanism could be developed as a more general platform for communication between religions and for recognizing opportunities for mutuality that are present in other traditions (Seligman 2004). The search for religious roots of cosmopolitanism can offer a useful counterpoint to the dominant view that cosmopolitanism is an essentially secular quest. Religious notions about human vulnerability can be deployed to support the view that human rights are not simply part of a Western juridical tradition (Turner 2006).

Religious roots of cosmopolitanism notwithstanding, in the twentieth century much of the burden of cosmopolitan hope was borne on the shoulders of human-rights initiatives, and even here the question of the universality of culture became a deeply problematic issue. To counter arguments that humanity is divided by race, early cultural anthropologists sometimes affirmed the commonality of culture, especially the capacity for language, in the definition of humanity. The great champion of culture as a category and of cosmopolitanism as a moral and political platform was Franz Boas. In *Race and Democratic Society* (Boas 1945) and *Anthropology and Modern Life* (Boas 1962), he condemned racism, imperialism, and colonialism as factors that prevented people from openness to the full spectrum of human culture, and he attacked nation and nationalism as artificial and inappropriate receptacles of human cultural production. In almost Kantian terms, Boas embraced a philosophy of cosmopolitanism and international peace as necessary consequences of the integrating power of human culture. It is ironic that contemporary anthropology (e.g., Abu-Lughod 1991; Kahn 1989), having had a transfusion of poststructuralism and postmodernism, now deconstructs the Boasian concept of culture, which is considered too essential, bounded, and rigid to cope with the idea of culture as process. But without a notion of culture, does anthropology still exist? (Turner 2008b). This ironic question takes us back to Leibniz and the problems of cultural relativism. Whereas Boas tried to use "culture" in his campaign against nationalism and racism, much of the relativism that fueled the postmodern critique of Enlightenment came from anthropological ethnographic research. However, with the assault on culture there is little common ground for defending some idea of social justice, human dignity, or human rights (Bauman and Briggs 2003).

Terror and jihad

In the aftermath of the attacks on the United States in 2001, the social tensions between the West and Islam have intensified. Political Islam, in the post-Cold War period, has now replaced communism as the enemy of liberal capitalism. As a result, the Huntington thesis of a "clash of civilizations" is compelling, and optimism about our political future is in short supply. In this chapter I have explored the case for recognition ethics and cosmopolitan virtue. However, the defense of these normative positions is problematic in the light of civil wars in Iraq and Syria, and military conflicts in Afghanistan, Thailand, Chechnya, and the Sudan. The Huntington thesis has plausibility because in all of these conflicts Islam has been prominent.

Of course there is a compelling argument that orthodox Islam does not condone or counsel violence, offering instead the prospect of religious pluralism and mutual respect (Sachedina 2001). In one interpretation, Islamic radicalism has involved the reinterpretation of "jihad" in response to Western colonialism. Originally a personal struggle against evil, it became under Sayyid Qutb a doctrine of struggle against foreigners to protect the faith and under Ali Shariati a revolutionary doctrine against state oppression and foreign intervention (Rahnema 1998). By contrast, Olivier Roy (2004:41) counsels us that all attempts to sort out the "correct" theological interpretation of jihad are largely sterile, since the term is highly contested within Islam itself and it is not the role of sociology to adjudicate between different theological claims. Rather, our task is more properly to understand the social forces that sustain different interpretations. If there is to be an open dialogue between civilizations, it will not be intellectually adequate to pretend that radical Islam is deeply democratic. Recognition cannot begin with artificial characterization of difference. Cosmopolitanism must begin with a recognition of cultural differences. With respect to jihad, Western observers will also have to recognize the parallel role of the notions of crusade and just war in the West.

Much of the intellectual equipment that would be valuable in criticizing the Huntington thesis – such as the idea of a common human culture or a Leibnizian commitment to dialogue – has been compromised or at least brought into question by intellectual movements such as postmodernism and poststructuralism. Academics who retain a commitment to ideas about universalism, recognition ethics, and cosmopolitanism will need to defend some version of human rights as a transnational movement, some notion of human dignity, and some explication of our common vulnerability if a "commerce of light" is to survive.

Conclusion: the populist challenge to cosmopolitanism

Since the first edition of this volume was published in 2009, the grounds for optimism over cosmopolitanism have been eroded by the growth of right-wing populism, the referendum to take the United Kingdom out of the European Union, the resurgence of nationalist movements across Europe, genocide in the Middle East, the rise of strong-man politics in China, Russia, and the Philippines, and the strategies of President Donald Trump to "make America great again" by embracing protectionism, promising to build a wall along the Mexico-US border, and withdrawing from international trade agreements such as the Trans-Pacific Partnership.

It has been widely suggested that the rise of right-wing populism is a response of the "left behind" (such as unemployed men in the blue-collar sector of the labor market) and that the plight of marginalized communities is associated with the globalization of the economy. Popular anger directed at elites has been driven in part by the erosion of job security, by the decline in real wages, and by the increase in income inequality. The proletariat is now described as a "precariat" and there is a general sentiment in the West that citizens are merely denizens (Turner

2016). Resentment is now widespread in the United States, and not simply among the "left behind" but among the middle class, whose position in society has also been weakened. If the Tea Party was a protest of mainly white seniors fearful of their pensions and healthcare entitlements, then Occupy Wall Street was mainly a protest among white, educated, young, white-collar workers.

What are the communal bonds that might hold Americans (and other national communities) together? Historically religion (including civil religions) have been such a bond, but in the contemporary political conflict, religion has helped drive divisions over gay marriage, abortion, and national identity. Islamophobia is an important element in populist rhetoric. Religion (or more specifically Christianity) has emerged in populist opposition to Islam insofar as Muslim migrants are widely regarded as actual or potential jihadists (Marzouki, McDonnell, and Roy 2016).

Although the mixing of politics and religion may seem like a new development, in the United States, especially since the rise of the Moral Majority in the late 1970s, religion has never been far removed from politics. It is explicitly present in the conflict over the legal decision (*Roe v. Wade*) that sanctioned legal abortion. It is also implicit in the references to the criminality of illegal Latin American (primarily Mexican) migrants to the US. In the period after the 2016 election of Donald Trump as president, religious issues and identities have become more prominent. Trump drew support for his anti-abortion stand (from both Catholics and evangelical Protestants), for his pro-Israeli stance (from orthodox Jews), and from "Tender Warriors" (evangelical Protestants embracing masculinity and conventional gender roles). He has basked in the benediction of televangelist Paula White, who affirmed that Trump has a "hunger for God." And at the National Prayer Breakfast on February 2, 2017, Trump promised to "destroy" the Johnson Amendment that separated politics and pulpit for religious organizations classified as tax-exempt. It appears that religion is extending Trump's base, increasingly as a dimension of American populism.

Internationally, political developments have exposed a major division within the Roman Catholic Church. Pope Francis has emerged as a major figure in the defense of the universal message of the Christian gospel in his welcome to migrants and refugees fleeing persecution in the Middle East and North Africa. His message, alongside the stance of Angela Merkel, is a shining example of cosmopolitan virtue grounded in Catholic notions of justice and human dignity. But this cosmopolitanism has divided the Church between conservatives such as the US cardinal Raymond Burke and Catholic liberals who defend the pope's embrace of outsiders. The conservative position of Burke has received support from Trump's chief strategist, Stephen K. Bannon, who regards the pope as closer to socialism than to Christianity (Horowitz 2017). Burke and Bannon agree on the view that the West is dangerously weakened by European societies that have departed from the Christian foundations of the West and that the political elite is remote from and indifferent to the crisis of Western civilization.

The pope's pastoral entreaty to extend charity to Catholics who have divorced and to homosexuals has also exacerbated tensions within the Church. Conservative cardinals are reluctant to openly challenge the authority of the pope, whose message is a major underpinning of religious cosmopolitanism. Nevertheless, posters appeared in Rome in February 2017 critical of his inclusive agenda.

The other underpinning of cosmopolitanism has been the law. One can interpret laws relating to hate speech, gender equality, just treatment of minorities, and freedom of religion as a significant juridical wall against prejudice, discrimination, inter-communal violence, and injustice. Broadly speaking, the rule of law is a major guardian of social justice, the protection of the individual, and a conduit of shared values. However, especially during the presidency of Barack Obama, the law also became deeply politicized. In the US, conservatives have argued that the law has replaced democratic processes in decision-making and liberals fear the appointment of conservative judges to the Supreme Court. This battle around the Supreme Court was manifest in the career of Justice Antonin Scalia – an ardent Catholic and a defender of "originalism" – the legal philosophy that rulings concerning the constitution must abide by the clear wording and intentions of the men who created it and that an evolutionary approach to the interpretation of the constitution to suit modern values has to be challenged (Calabresi 2007). Inevitably this position undergirds conservative interpretations that would reject laws supporting recognition of abortion, same-sex marriage, and homosexuality. Although Scalia objected that his Catholicism did not influence his decisions as a lawyer, critics have suggested that the "textualism" of originalist methodology is a form of Catholic epistemology (Biskupic 2009).

Values of universalism and hospitality, the rule of law, and democratic procedures can serve as a defense of cosmopolitan virtue against narrow prejudice against outsiders. These conditions can serve in defense of the recognition of "common necessity" in international law, including protection of the environment, open sea-lanes, regulation of nuclear power, and human rights respect for the dignity of the individual. It would however be a fateful delusion to believe that we are safe from nuclear conflict, communal violence, authoritarian rule, and the persecution of minorities. Cosmopolitanism as a transcendent cultural value, if it survives at all, will require constant vigilance in law, politics, and religion.

References

Abu-Lughod, Lila. 1991. "Writing against Culture." Pp. 137–62 in *Recapturing Anthropology: Working in the Present*, edited by R.G. Fox. Santa Fe: School of American Research Press.

Badiou, Alain. 2003. *Saint Paul: The Foundation of Universalism*. Stanford, CA: Stanford University Press.

Bauman, Richard, and Charles L. Briggs. 2003. *Voices of Modernity: Language Ideologies and the Politics of Inequality*. Cambridge: Cambridge University Press.

Biskupic, Joan. 2009. *American Original: The Life and Constitution of Supreme Court Justice Antonin Scalia*. New York: Farrar, Straus and Giroux.

Boas, Franz. 1945. *Race and Democratic Society*. New York: J.J. Augustin.

———. 1962. *Anthropology and Modern Life*. New York: W.W. Norton.

Calabresi, Steven G., ed. 2007. *Originalism: A Quarter-century Debate*. Washington, DC: Regnery.

Casanova, Jose. 1994. *Public Religions in the Modern World*. Chicago: University of Chicago Press.

Derrida, Jacques. 2000. *Of Hospitality*. Stanford, CA: Stanford University Press.

Hodgson, Peter C., ed. 1985. *Hegel Lectures on the Philosophy of Religion*. Berkeley: University of California Press.

Horkheimer, Max, and Theodor W. Adorno. 1947. *Dialectic of Enlightenment*. London: Allen Lane.

Horowitz, Jason. 2017. "Steve Bannon Carries Battle to Another Influential Hub: The Vatican." *New York Times*, February 7.

Huntington, Samuel P. 1993. "The Clash of Civilizations." *Foreign Affairs* 72(3):22–48.

———. 2003. "America in the World." *The Hedgehog Review* 5(1):7–18.

Kahn, J. 1989. "Culture: Demise or Resurrection?" *Critique of Anthropology* 9(2):5–25.

Kant, Immanuel. 1998. *Religion within the Boundaries of Mere Reason*. Cambridge: Cambridge University Press.

Kepel, Giles. 2004. *The War for Muslim Minds: Islam and the West*. Cambridge: Belknap Press.

Leibniz, G.W. 1991. "Discourse of Metaphysics." Pp. 303–30 in *Philosophical Papers and Letters*, edited by L.E. Loemker. Dordrecht: Kluwer Academic.

Levinas, Emmanuel. 1998. *Entre Nous: On Thinking-of-the-other*. London: The Athlone Press.

Locke, John. 1955. *Letter Concerning Toleration*. Indianapolis: Bobbs-Merrill.

Mandel, Maud S. 2014. *Muslims and Jews in France: History of a Conflict*. Princeton, NJ: Princeton University Press.

Mann, Michael. 2003. *Incoherent Empire*. London: Verso.

Marsden, Magnus. 2008. "Muslim Cosmopolitans? Transnational Life in Northern Pakistan." *Journal of Asian Studies* 67(1):213–47.

Marx, Karl, and Friedrich Engels. 1975. *Collected Works*. Vol. 3. London: Lawrence & Wishart.

Marzouki, Nadia, Duncan McDonnell, and Olivier Roy, eds. 2016. *Saving the People: How Populists Hijack Religion*. Oxford: Oxford University Press.

McCargo, Duncan, ed. 2007. *Rethinking Thailand's Southern Violence*. Singapore: NUS Press.

Menocal, Maria Rosa. 2002. *Ornament of the World: How Muslim, Jews and Christians created a Culture of Tolerance in Medieval Spain*. Boston: Little, Brown.

Mufti, Aamir R. 2007. *Enlightenment in the Colony: The Jewish Question and the Crisis of Postcolonial Culture*. Princeton, NJ: Princeton University Press.

Nasr, Vali. 2006. *The Shia Revival. How Conflicts within Islam Will Shape the Future*. New York: W.W. Norton.

Özyürek, Esra. 2015. *Being German, Becoming Muslim: Race, Religion, and Conversion in the New Europe*. Princeton, NJ: Princeton University Press.

Rahnema, Ali. 1998. *An Islamic Utopian: A Political Biography of Ali Shariati*. London: I.B. Taurus.

Roy, Olivier. 2004. *Globalised Islam: The Search for a New Ummah*. London: Hurst.

Sachedina, A. 2001. *The Islamic Roots of Democratic Pluralism*. Oxford: University of Oxford Press.

Said, Edward W. 1978. *Orientalism*. New York: Pantheon.

———. 1996. *Representations of the Intellectual*. New York: Vintage.

Schmitt, Carl. 1996. *The Concept of the Political*. Chicago: University of Chicago Press.

Segal, Ronald. 2001. *Islam's Black Slaves: The History of Africa's other Black Diaspora*. London: Atlantic Books.

Seligman, Adam. 2004. *Modest Claims: Dialogues and Essays on Tolerance and Tradition*. Notre Dame, IN: University of Notre Dame Press.

Stamatov, Peter. 2013. *The Origins of Global Humanitarianism. Religion, Empires and Advocacy*. Cambridge: Cambridge University Press.

Taylor, Charles. 1992. *Multiculturalism and the Politics of Recognition*. Princeton, NJ: Princeton University Press.

Turner, Bryan S. 2006. *Vulnerability and Human Rights*. University Park: Pennsylvania State University Press.

———. 2008a. *Rights and Virtues*. Oxford: The Bardwell Press.

———. 2008b. "Does Anthropology Still Exist? Towards a Theory of Cultural Survival." *Society* 45(3):260–66.

———. 2016 "We Are all Denizens Now: On the Erosion of Citizenship" *Citizenship Studies* 20(6–7):679–92.

Weber, Max. 1966. *The Sociology of Religion*. London: Methuen.

Williams, Robert R. 1997. *Hegel's Ethics of Recognition*. Berkeley: University of California Press.

Index

Index

Index

Printed in the United States
by Baker & Taylor Publisher Services